# A PEOPLE & A NATION
## A History of the United States

### Eighth Edition

**Mary Beth Norton**
*Cornell University*

**Carol Sheriff**
*College of William and Mary*

**David M. Katzman**
*University of Kansas*

**David W. Blight**
*Yale University*

**Howard P. Chudacoff**
*Brown University*

**Fredrik Logevall**
*Cornell University*

**Beth Bailey**
*Temple University*

**HOUGHTON MIFFLIN COMPANY**     Boston     New York

Publisher: *Suzanne Jeans*
Senior Sponsoring Editor: *Ann West*
Marketing Manager: *Katherine Bates*
Senior Developmental Editor: *Jeffrey Greene*
Senior Project Editor: *Jane Lee*
Art and Design Manager: *Jill Haber*
Cover Design Director: *Tony Saizon*
Senior Photo Editor: *Jennifer Meyer Dare*
Composition Buyer: *Chuck Dutton*
New Title Project Manager: *James Lonergan*
Editorial Associate: *Adrienne Zicht*
Marketing Assistant: *Lauren Bussard*
Editorial Assistant: *Carrie Parker/Anne Finly*

Cover image: *Julianita* by Robert Henri, ca. 1917. Private Collection, courtesy Gerald Peters Gallery, New York and John G. Hagan.

Chapter opener montage (pp. 3, 33, 61, 91, 119, 145, 169, 197, 221, 249, 283, 311, 337, 367, 395, 435, 467, 497, 529, 563, 591, 621, 647, 677, 707, 739, 766, 795, 825, 857, 889, 921, 951): American Indian, far left: Northwestern University Library, Edward S. Curtis's *The North American Indian: Photographic Images, 2001;* second from left: *Women of Protest: Photographs from the Records of the National Woman's Party*, Manuscript Division, Library of Congress, Washington, DC; center, second from right, and far right: Courtesy of the Library of Congress, Washington, DC.

Printed in the U.S.A.

Library of Congress Catalog Number: 2007936065

ISBN 13: 978-0-618-951314
ISBN 10: 0-618-951318

2 3 4 5 6 7 8 9-WEB-11 10 09 08

# Brief Contents

# Contents

# 1 Three Old Worlds Create a New, 1492–1600    2

# 2 Europeans Colonize North America, 1600–1650    32

# 3 North America in the Atlantic World, 1650–1720    60

# 4 American Society Transformed, 1720–1770    **90**

# 5 Severing the Bonds of Empire, 1754–1774    **118**

# 6 A Revolution, Indeed, 1774–1783    **144**

# 7 Forging a National Republic, 1776–1789    **168**

# 8 The Early Republic: Conflicts at Home and Abroad, 1789–1800    **196**

# 9 Defining the Nation, 1801–1823    **220**

# 10 The Rise of the South, 1815–1860                                    248

# 11 The Modernizing North, 1815–1860                                    282

# 12 Reform and Politics in the Age of Jackson, 1824–1845                310

# 13 The Contested West, 1815–1860                                       336

## 21 The Progressive Era, 1895–1920    590

## 22 The Quest for Empire, 1865–1914    620

## 23 Americans in the Great War, 1914–1920    646

# 24 The New Era, 1920–1929    676

# 25 The Great Depression and the New Deal, 1929–1941    706

# 26 The United States in a Troubled World, 1920–1941    738

# 27 The Second World War at Home and Abroad, 1941–1945    766

# Special Features

## MAPS

# FIGURES

## TABLES

## LINKS TO THE WORLD

## LEGACY FOR A PEOPLE AND A NATION

# Preface

In this eighth edition, *A People and a Nation* has undergone both reorganization and revision, while still retaining the narrative strength and focus that have made it so popular with students and teachers alike. In the years since the publication of the seventh edition, new materials have been uncovered, new interpretations advanced, and new themes have come to the forefront of American historical scholarship. All the authors—joined by one new member, Carol Sheriff—have worked diligently to incorporate those findings into this text.

Like other teachers and students, we are always recreating our past, restructuring our memory, and rediscovering the personalities and events that have influenced us, injured us, and bedeviled us. This book represents our continuing rediscovery of America's history—its diverse people and the nation they created and have nurtured. As this book demonstrates, there are many different Americans and many different memories. We have sought to present as many of them as possible, in both triumph and tragedy, in both division and unity.

## About *A People and A Nation*

*A People and a Nation*, first published in 1982, was the first major textbook in the United States to fully integrate social and political history. From the outset, the authors have been determined to tell the story of *all* the people of the United States. This book's hallmark has been its melding of social and political history, its movement beyond history's common focus on public figures and events to examine the daily life of America's people. All editions of the book have stressed the interaction of public policy and personal experience, the relationship between domestic concerns and foreign affairs, the various manifestations of popular culture, and the multiple origins of America and Americans. We have consistently built our narrative on a firm foundation in primary sources—on both well-known and obscure letters, diaries, public documents, oral histories, and artifacts of material culture. We have long challenged readers to think about the meaning of American history, not just to memorize facts. Both students and instructors have repeatedly told us how much they appreciate and enjoy our approach to the past.

As has been true since the first edition, each chapter opens with a dramatic vignette focusing on an individual or a group of people. These vignettes introduce key themes, which then frame the chapters in succinct introductions and summaries. Numerous maps, tables, graphs, and charts provide readers with the necessary geographical and statistical context for observations in the text. Carefully selected illustrations—many of them unique to this book—offer readers visual insight into the topics under discussion, especially because the authors have written the captions. In this edition, as in all previous ones, we have sought to incorporate up-to-date scholarship, readability, a clear structure, critical thinking, and instructive illustrative material on every page.

## Themes in This Book

Several themes and questions stand out in our continuing effort to integrate political, social, and cultural history. We study the many ways that Americans have defined themselves—gender, race, class, region, ethnicity, religion, sexual orientation—and the many subjects that have reflected their multidimensional experiences. We highlight the remarkably diverse everyday lives of the American people—in cities and on farms and ranches, in factories and in corporate headquarters, in neighborhoods and in legislatures, in love relationships and in hate groups, in recreation and in work, in the classroom and in military uniform, in secret national security conferences and in public foreign relations debates, in church and in voluntary associations, in polluted environments and in conservation areas. We pay particular attention to lifestyles, diet and dress, family life and structure, labor conditions, gender roles, migration and mobility, childbearing, and child rearing. We explore how Americans have entertained and informed themselves by discussing their music, sports, theater, print media, film, radio, television, graphic arts, and literature, in both "high" culture and popular culture. We study how technology has influenced Americans' lives, such as through the internal combustion engine and the computer.

Americans' personal lives have always interacted with the public realm of politics and government. To understand how Americans have sought to protect their different ways of life and to work out solutions to thorny problems, we emphasize their expectations of governments at the local, state, and federal levels; governments' role in providing answers; the lobbying of interest groups; the campaigns and outcomes of elections; and the hierarchy of power in any period. Because the United States has long been a major participant in world affairs, we explore America's participation in wars, interventions in other nations, empire-building, immigration patterns, images of foreign peoples, cross-national cultural ties, and international economic trends.

## What's New in This Edition

Planning for the eighth edition began at a two-day authors' meeting at the Houghton Mifflin headquarters in Boston. There we discussed the most recent scholarship in the field, the reviews of the seventh edition solicited from instructors, and the findings of our own continuing research. For this edition, we added a new colleague, Carol Sheriff, who experienced the intellectual exhilaration and rigor of such an authors' meeting for the first time. Sheriff, a member of the History Department at the College of William and Mary, has written extensively on antebellum America, especially in the North, and she has taken on the responsibility for those chapters in the eighth edition.

This edition builds on its immediate predecessor in continuing to enhance the global perspective on American history that has characterized the book since its first edition. From the "Atlantic world" context of European colonies in North and South America to the discussion of international terrorism, the authors have incorporated the most recent globally oriented scholarship throughout the volume. Significantly, the eighth edition includes an entirely new chapter on the American West in the years before the Civil War and the discussion of the West has been expanded throughout. The treatment of the history of children and childhood has been increased, as has the discussion of environmental history, including the devastating impact of hurricanes in North America and in the Caribbean from the earliest days of European settlement. As in the seventh edition, we have worked to strengthen our treatment of the diversity of America's people by examining differences within the broad ethnic categories commonly employed and by paying greater attention to immigration, cultural and intellectual infusions from around the world, and America's growing religious diversity. We have also stressed the incorporation of different peoples into the United States through territorial acquisition as well as through immigration. At the same time, we have integrated the discussion of such diversity into our narrative so as not to artificially isolate any group

from the mainstream. We have added three probing questions at the end of each chapter's introduction to guide students' reading of the pages that follow.

As always, the authors reexamined every sentence, interpretation, map, chart, illustration, and caption, refining the narrative, presenting new examples, and bringing to the text the latest findings of scholars in many areas of history, anthropology, sociology, and political science. More than one-third of the chapter-opening vignettes are new to this edition.

## "Legacies" and "Links to the World"

Each chapter contains two brief feature essays: "Legacies for a People and a Nation" (introduced in the sixth edition) and "Links to the World" (introduced in the seventh edition). Legacies appear toward the end of each chapter and offer compelling and timely answers to students who question the relevance of historical study by exploring the historical roots of contemporary topics. New subjects of Legacies are: Kennewick Man/Ancient One, Blue Laws, women's political activism, the township and range system, descendants of early Latino settlers, "Big Government," the Lost Cause, the Cowboy myth, recorded music, Guantánamo Bay, nuclear proliferation, and the all-volunteer force. Numerous other Legacies have been updated.

"Links to the World" examine both inward and outward ties between America (and Americans) and the rest of the world. The Links appear at appropriate places in each chapter to explore specific topics at considerable length. Tightly constructed essays detail the often little-known connections between developments here and abroad. The topics range broadly over economic, political, social, technological, medical, and cultural history, vividly demonstrating that the geographical region that is now the United States has never lived in isolation from other peoples and countries. New to this edition are Links on smallpox inoculations, the Amistad case, Russian Populism, European influence on American workers' compensation, and *National Geographic*. Each Link highlights global interconnections with unusual and lively examples that will both intrigue and inform students.

## Section-by-Section Changes in This Edition

**Mary Beth Norton,** who had primary responsibility for Chapters 1 through 8 and served as coordinating author, augmented her discussion of the age of European expansion with new information on Muslim power and the allure of exotic spices; she also expanded the treatment of Spanish colonization and settlements in the Caribbean. She incorporated extensive new scholarship on early Virginia into Chapter 2. In addition to reorganizing part of Chapter 3 to bring more coherence to the discussion of the origins of slavery in North America, she added demographic information about enslaved peoples (both Indians and Africans) and those who enslaved and transported them, stressing in particular the importance of African women in South Carolina rice cultivation. She added material on transported English convicts, Huguenot immigrants, Acadian exiles, iron-making, land riots, the Stono Rebellion, the Seven Years' War in western Pennsylvania, the experiences of common soldiers in the Revolution, Shays's Rebellion, and the Jay Treaty debates. In Chapter 8 she created new sections on Indians in the new nation and on revolutions at the end of the century, including among them the election of Thomas Jefferson.

**Carol Sheriff** completely reorganized the contents of Chapters 9, 11, and 12, clarifying chronological developments and including much new material. Chapter 9 now covers politics through 1823 in order to emphasize the impact of the War of 1812 in accelerating regional divisions. It has expanded coverage of popular political practice (including among non-voters), the separation of church and state, the Marshall Court, the First and Second Barbary Wars, and the incorporation of the Louisiana Territory and its residents into the United States. Chapter 11, retitled "The Modernizing North," consolidates information previously divided between two chapters and augments it with new discussions of daily life before commercial and industrial expansion, rural-urban contrasts, children and youth culture, male and female common laborers, and the origins of free-labor ideology. Chapter 12 focuses on reform and politics in the age of Jackson, with expanded attention to communitarian experiments, abolitionism (including African Americans in the movement), women's rights, and religion (including revivalism in general and the Second Great Awakening in particular). The entirely new Chapter 13, "The Contested West," combines material that was previously scattered in different locations with a great deal of recent scholarship on such topics as the disjunction between the ideal and reality of the West, exploration and migration, cultural diversity in the West, cooperation and conflict among the West's peoples, and the role of the federal government in regional development. In all of her reorganized chapters she relied on a base created by David M. Katzman, an original member of the author team who had responsibility for this section in the seven earlier editions.

**David W. Blight,** who had primary responsibility for Chapter 10 and Chapters 14 through 16, extensively reorganized Chapter 10 (previously Chapter 13), on the South, in part to reflect its new chronological placement in the book. The chapter now covers material beginning in 1815 rather than in 1830 and contains a section on Southern expansion and Indian removal. In his chapters he has added material on the Taos revolt, enslaved children, "Bleeding Kansas," Harriet Scott, Louisa May Alcott, union sentiment in the South, the conduct of the war, and economic and social conditions in the postwar North and South. He has revised Chapter 16 to emphasize economic as well as political change in the era of Reconstruction.

**Howard P. Chudacoff,** responsible for Chapters 17 through 21 and Chapter 24, has increased the coverage of Indians, Exodusters, and Hispanics in the West, and of western Progressivism. His treatment of popular culture now stresses its lower-class, bottom-to-top origins. He has added information on the history of childhood, vaudeville, and the movies; and he revised discussions of monetary policy, Progressivism, Populism, and urban and agrarian protests. He also has included more coverage of racism and those who combated it, such as Ida B. Wells, and of women and the Ku Klux Klan. Business operation and regulation receive new attention in his chapters, as do Calvin Coolidge, consumerism, and baseball.

**Fredrik Logevall,** with primary responsibility for Chapters 22, 23, 26, and 28, has continued to work to establish the wider international context for U.S. foreign affairs throughout his chapters. He has added considerable new material on the Middle East (especially in Chapter 28) and has incorporated recent scholarship on the Vietnam War. He also has updated the treatment of the Spanish-American War with new information on the sinking of the *Maine* and on the Philippine insurrection. His discussion of World War I now includes consideration of the antagonistic relationship of Woodrow Wilson and V. I. Lenin; and he has given more attention to American economic and cultural expansion in the 1920s and 1930s. Furthermore, he has expanded his treatment of American reactions to the Spanish Civil War.

**Beth Bailey,** primarily responsible for Chapters 25, 27, and 29, has added information on women, the left, and popular culture (especially film and the production code) during the 1930s. She has expanded coverage of the European front in World War II and of divisions within the United States during the war. In Chapter 29, she has thoroughly reorganized the section on civil rights to clarify the chronology and key points of development, and she also has included new information on emerging countercultures and the beats, union activities, and the Eisenhower administration.

Bailey and Logevall shared responsibility for Chapters 30 through 33. In Chapter 30 Freedom Summer is given enhanced attention and the section on civil rights has been reorganized to emphasize a clear chronology. These chapters contain new material on the women's movement and the barriers women faced before 1970s reforms, recent immigration, neoconservatism, anti-Vietnam War protests, Nixon's presidency, the Supreme Court, the 1982 Israeli invasion of Lebanon, and the 1991 Iraq War. Chapter 33, in particular, has been thoroughly revised to include the latest demographic data on Americans and their families, along with discussions of the struggles over science and religion, Hurricane Katrina, the Bush administration's domestic policies, and especially the Iraq War.

## Teaching and Learning Aids

The supplements listed here accompany the eighth edition of *A People and a Nation*. They have been created with the diverse needs of today's students and instructors in mind.

### For the Teacher

- Houghton Mifflin's **HistoryFinder** is a new online tool developed to help instructors create rich and exciting presentations for the U.S. history survey class. History-Finder offers thousands of online resources, including art, photographs, maps, primary sources, multimedia content, Associated Press interactive modules, and ready-made PowerPoint slides. HistoryFinder's assets can be searched easily by keyword topic, media type, or by textbook chapter. It is then possible to browse, preview, and download resources straight from the website into the instructor's own PowerPoint collection.

- **The Instructor Website** at HM HistorySPACE™, which is accessible by visiting college.hmco.com/pic/norton8e, includes a variety of resources that will help instructors engage their students in class and assess their understanding inside and outside the classroom. The Instructor Website includes the **Instructor's Resource Manual,** written by George C. Warren of Central Piedmont Community College. For each chapter there is a brief list of learning objectives, a comprehensive chapter outline, ideas for classroom activities, discussion questions, several suggested paper topics, and a lecture supplement. Also available on the Instructor Website is a complete set of PowerPoint slides created by Barney Rickman of Valdosta State University to assist in instruction and discussion of key topics and materials for each chapter.

- The **HM Testing™ CD-ROM** provides flexible test-editing capabilities for the test items written by George Warren of Central Piedmont Community College. Included in the Test Bank are multiple-choice, identification, geography, and essay questions.

- Houghton Mifflin's **Eduspace Course** for *A People and a Nation* offers a customizable course management system powered by Blackboard along with homework assignments that engage students and encourage in-class discussion. Assignments include gradable homework exercises, writing assignments, primary sources with questions, and Associated Press Interactives. Eduspace also provides a gradebook and communication capabilities, such as live chats, threaded discussion boards, and announcement postings. The Eduspace course also includes an interactive version of *A People and a Nation* with direct links to relevant primary sources, quizzes, and more.

### For the Student

- The **Student Website** at HM HistorySPACE™, also accessible by visiting college.hmco.com/pic/norton8e, contains a variety of review and self-assessment resources to help students succeed in the U.S. history survey course. ACE quizzes with feedback, interactive maps, primary sources, chronology exercises, flashcards, and other activities are available for each chapter. Audio files provide chapter summaries in MP3 format for downloading and listening to at any time.

- **Study Guides** (Volumes I and II), written by George Warren, provide learning objectives, vocabulary exercises, identification suggestions, skill-building activities, multiple-choice questions, essay questions, and map exercises in two volumes.

- A **Document-Based Question Workbook** accompanies the new edition providing extra practice for students ith writing essays that answer the DBQ question on the AP* US History Examination.

Please contact your local Houghton Mifflin sales representative for more information about these learning and teaching tools in addition to the **Rand McNally Atlas of American History,** WebCT and Blackboard cartridges, and transparencies for United States history. Your sales representative can also provide more information about **BiblioBase for U.S. History,** a database of hundreds of primary sources from which you can create a customized course pack.

||||||||||||||||||||||||||||||||||||||

## Acknowledgments

The authors would like to thank the following persons for their assistance with the preparation of this edition: Shawn Alexander, Marsha Andrews, Edward Balleisen, Philip Daileader, Katherine Flynn, John B. Heiser, Danyel Logevall, Daniel Mandell, Clark F. Norton, Mary E. Norton, Anna Daileader Sheriff, Benjamin Daileader Sheriff, Selene Sheriff, and Seymour Sheriff.

At each stage of this revision, a sizable panel of historian reviewers read drafts of our chapters. Their suggestions, corrections, and pleas helped guide us through this momentous revision. We could not include all of their recommendations, but the book is better for our having heeded most of their advice. We heartily thank:

**Marynita Anderson,** *Nassau Community College/SUNY*

**Stephen Aron,** *UCLA and Autry National Center*

**Gordon Morris Bakken,** *California State University, Fullerton*

**Todd Forsyth Carney,** *Southern Oregon University*

**Kathleen S. Carter,** *High Point University*

**Robert C. Cottrell,** *California State University, Chico*

**Lawrence Culver,** *Utah State University*

**Lawrence J. DeVaro,** *Rowan University*

**Lisa Lindquist Dorr,** *University of Alabama*

**Michelle Kuhl,** *University of Wisconsin, Oshkosh*

**Martin Halpern,** *Henderson State University*

**John S. Leiby,** *Paradise Valley Community College*

**Edwin Martini,** *Western Michigan University*

**Elsa A. Nystrom,** *Kennesaw State University*

**Chester Pach,** *Ohio University*

**Stephen Rockenbach,** *Northern Kentucky University*

**Joseph Owen Weixelman,** *University of New Mexico*

The authors once again thank the extraordinary Houghton Mifflin people who designed, edited, produced, and nourished this book. Their high standards and acute attention to both general structure and fine detail are cherished in the publishing industry. Many thanks, then, to Patricia Coryell, vice president and publisher, history and social science; Suzanne Jeans, publisher, history and political science; Sally Constable and Ann West, senior sponsoring editors; Ann Hofstra Grogg, freelance development editor; Jeff Greene, senior development editor; Jane Lee, senior project editor; Katherine Bates, senior marketing manager; Pembroke Herbert, photo researcher; Jill Haber, art and design manager; Charlotte Miller, art editor; and Evangeline Bermas, editorial assistant.

M. B. N.
C. S.
D. B.
H. C.
F. L.
B. B.

## Mary Beth Norton

Born in Ann Arbor, Michigan, Mary Beth Norton received her B.A. from the University of Michigan (1964) and her Ph.D. from Harvard University (1969). She is the Mary Donlon Alger Professor of American History at Cornell University. Her dissertation won the Allan Nevins Prize. She has written *The British-Americans* (1972), *Liberty's Daughters* (1980, 1996), *Founding Mothers & Fathers* (1996), which was one of three finalists for the 1997 Pulitzer Prize in History, and *In the Devil's Snare* (2002), which was one of five finalists for the 2003 *LA Times* Book Prize in History and which won the English-Speaking Union's Ambassador Book Award in American Studies for 2003. She has coedited *Women of America* (with Carol Berkin, 1979), *To Toil the Livelong Day* (with Carol Groneman, 1987), and *Major Problems in American Women's History* (with Ruth Alexander, 2007). She was general editor of the *American Historical Association's Guide to Historical Literature* (1995). Her articles have appeared in such journals as the *American Historical Review, William and Mary Quarterly,* and *Journal of Women's History*. Mary Beth has served as president of the Berkshire Conference of Women Historians, as vice president for research of the American Historical Association, and as a presidential appointee to the National Council on the Humanities. She has received four honorary degrees and in 1999 was elected a fellow of the American Academy of Arts and Sciences. She has held fellowships from the National Endowment for the Humanities, the Guggenheim, Rockefeller, and Starr Foundations, and the Henry E. Huntington Library. In 2005–2006, she was the Pitt Professor of American History and Institutions at the University of Cambridge and Newnham College.

## Carol Sheriff

Born in Washington, DC, and raised in Bethesda, Maryland, Carol Sheriff received her B.A. from Wesleyan University (1985) and her Ph.D. from Yale University (1993). Since 1993, she has taught history at the College of William and Mary, where she has won the Thomas Jefferson Teaching Award, the Alumni Teaching Fellowship Award, and the University Professorship for Teaching Excellence. Her publications include *The Artificial River: The Erie Canal and the Paradox of Progress* (1996), which won the Dixon Ryan Fox Award from the New York State Historical Association and the Award for Excellence in Research from the New York State Archives, and *A People at War: Civilians and Soldiers in America's Civil War, 1854–1877* (with Scott Reynolds Nelson, 2007). Carol has written sections of a teaching manual for the New York State history curriculum, given presentations to a Teaching American History grant project, consulted on an exhibit for the Rochester Museum and Science Center, appeared in the History Channel's Modern Marvels show on the Erie Canal, and is serving as a consultant for "The Inland Voyage," a forthcoming television documentary on the Erie Canal. At William and Mary, she teaches the U.S. history survey as well as upper-level classes on the Early Republic, the Civil War Era, and the American West.

## David W. Blight

Born in Flint, Michigan, David W. Blight received his B.A. from Michigan State University (1971) and his Ph.D. from the University of Wisconsin (1985). He is now professor of history and director of the Gilder Lehrman Center for the Study of Slavery, Resistance, and Abolition at Yale University. For the first seven years of his career, David was a public high school teacher in Flint. He has written *Frederick Douglass's Civil War* (1989) and *Race and Reunion: The Civil War in American Memory, 1863–1915* (2000). His most recent book is *A Slave No More: the Emancipation of John Washington and Wallace Turnage* (2007). His edited works include *When This Cruel War Is Over: The Civil War Letters of Charles Harvey Brewster* (1992), *Narrative of the Life of Frederick Douglass* (1993), W. E. B. Du Bois, *The Souls of Black Folk* (with Robert Gooding Williams, 1997), *Union and Emancipation* (with Brooks Simpson, 1997), and *Caleb Bingham, The Columbian Orator* (1997). David's essays have appeared in the *Journal of American History, Civil War History,* and Gabor Boritt, ed., *Why the Civil War Came* (1996), among others. In 1992–1993 he was senior Fulbright Professor in American Studies at the University of Munich, Germany. A consultant to several documentary films, David appeared in the 1998 PBS series, *Africans in America*. In 1999 he was elected to the Council of the American Historical Association. David also teaches summer seminars for secondary school teachers, as well as for park rangers and historians of the National Park Service. His book, *Race and Reunion: The Civil War in American Memory* (2000), received many honors in 2002, including The Bancroft Prize, Abraham Lincoln Prize, and the Frederick Douglass Prize. From the Organization of American Historians, he has received the Merle Curti Prize in Social History, the Merle Curti Prize in Intellectual History, the Ellis Hawley Prize in Political History, and the James Rawley Prize in Race Relations.

**Howard P. Chudacoff**

Howard P. Chudacoff, the George L. Littlefield Professor of American History and Professor of Urban Studies at Brown University, was born in Omaha, Nebraska. He earned his A.B. (1965) and Ph.D. (1969) from the University of Chicago. He has written *Mobile Americans* (1972), *How Old Are You?* (1989), *The Age of the Bachelor* (1999), *The Evolution of American Urban Society* (with Judith Smith, 2004), and *Children at Play: An American History* (2007). He has also co-edited with Peter Baldwin *Major Problems in American Urban History* (2004). His articles have appeared in such journals as the *Journal of Family History, Reviews in American History,* and *Journal of American History.* At Brown University, Howard has co-chaired the American Civilization Program, chaired the Department of History, and serves as Brown's faculty representative to the NCAA. He has also served on the board of directors of the Urban History Association. The National Endowment for the Humanities, Ford Foundation, and Rockefeller Foundation have given him awards to advance his scholarship.

**Fredrik Logevall**

A native of Stockholm, Sweden, Fredrik Logevall received his B.A. from Simon Fraser University (1986) and his Ph.D. from Yale University (1993). He is professor of history at Cornell University. He is the author of *Choosing War: The Lost Chance for Peace and the Escalation of War in Vietnam* (1999), which won three prizes, including the Warren F. Kuehl Book Prize from the Society for Historians of American Foreign Relations (SHAFR). His other publications include *The Origins of the Vietnam War* (2001), *Terrorism and 9/11: A Reader* (2002), as coeditor, the *Encyclopedia of American Foreign Policy* (2002), and, as co-editor, *The First Vietnam War: Colonial Conflict and Cold War Crisis* (2007). Fred is a past recipient of the Stuart L. Bernath article, book, and lecture prizes from SHAFR and is a member of the SHAFR Council, the Cornell University Press faculty board, and the editorial advisory board of the Presidential Recordings Project at the Miller Center of Public Affairs at the University of Virginia. In 2006–2007 he was Leverhulme Visiting Professor at the University of Nottingham and Mellon Senior Fellow at the University of Cambridge.

**Beth Bailey**

Born in Atlanta, Georgia, Beth Bailey received her B.A. from Northwestern University (1979) and her Ph.D. from the University of Chicago (1986). She is now a professor of history at Temple University. Her research and teaching fields include American cultural history (nineteenth and twentieth centuries), popular culture, and gender and sexuality. She is the author of *From Front Porch to Back Seat: Courtship in 20th Century America* (1988), a historical analysis of conventions governing the courtship of heterosexual youth; *The First Strange Place: The Alchemy of Race and Sex in WWII Hawaii* (with David Farber, 1992), which analyzes cultural contact among Americans in wartime Hawai'i; *Sex in the Heartland* (1999), a social and cultural history of the post-WWII "sexual revolution"; *The Columbia Companion to America in the 1960s* (with David Farber, 2001); and is co-editor of *A History of Our Time* (with William Chafe and Harvard Sitkoff, 6th ed., 2002). Beth has served as a consultant and/or on-screen expert for numerous television documentaries developed for PBS and the History Channel. She has received grants from the ACLS and NEH, was the Ann Whitney Olin scholar at Barnard College, Columbia University, from 1991 through 1994, where she was the director of the American Studies Program, and held a senior Fulbright lectureship in Indonesia in 1996. She teaches courses on sexuality and gender, war and American culture, research methods, and popular culture.

# A PEOPLE & A NATION

# Three Old Worlds Create a New

## 1492-1600

Lino Sanchez y Tapia

*Carancahueses*

ive years later, Alvar Nuñez Cabeza de Vaca still recalled the amazement he had encountered. "I reached four Christians on horseback who registered great surprise at seeing me so strangely dressed and in the company of Indians. They remained looking at me for a long time, so astonished that they neither spoke to me nor dared to ask anything."

The man whom the "four Christians" encountered in northern Mexico in mid-February 1536 was indeed astonishing. Cabeza de Vaca and three other men, one an enslaved North African named Estevan, had just walked across North America. They, along with about six hundred others, had left Spain in June 1527 on an ill-fated expedition under the command of Pánfilo de Narváez, newly named governor of Spanish territory bordering the Gulf of Mexico. After exploring territory near Tampa Bay, eighty of the men, including Cabeza de Vaca, were shipwrecked in late 1528 on the coast of modern Texas (probably near Galveston), at a place they named Isla de Malhado, or Island of Misfortune. Most of the survivors—alternately abused, aided, and enslaved by local Indians—died one by one. Cabeza de Vaca got to the mainland, where he survived as a traveling trader, exchanging seashells for hides and flint.

In January 1533 he stumbled on the other three. The Spaniards and Estevan—the slave of one of them—plotted to escape but could not do so until September 1534. They began by walking south; next they turned inland and headed north, exploring the upper reaches of the Rio Grande; then they walked west almost as far as the Pacific before turning south once more, all the while being guided by Indians who passed them from village to village. They convinced the people they encountered that they could heal the sick, earning food in exchange for their ministrations. Vaca described

◄ Cabeza de Vaca and his walk across North America in the 1530–1540s. Cabeza de Vaca lived with the Karankawas of the Texas Gulf coast for several years after the shipwreck of 1528. This is the only known depiction by an artist who actually saw them, the Spaniard Lino Sanchez y Tapia. *(Carancahusese-Gilcrease Museum, Tulsa, Oklahoma)*

## CHRONOLOGY

**12,000–10,000 B.C.E.** ■ Paleo-Indians migrate from Asia to North America across the Beringia land bridge

**7000 B.C.E.** ■ Cultivation of food crops begins in America

**C. 2000 B.C.E.** ■ Olmec civilization appears

**C. 300–600 C.E.** ■ Height of influence of Teotihuacán

**C. 600–900 C.E.** ■ Classic Mayan civilization

**1000 C.E.** ■ Ancient Pueblos build settlements in modern states of Arizona and New Mexico

**1001** ■ Norse establish settlement in "Vinland"

**1050–1250** ■ Height of influence of Cahokia
■ Prevalence of Mississippian culture in modern midwestern and southeastern United States

**14th century** ■ Aztec rise to power

**1450s–80s** ■ Portuguese explore and colonize islands in the Mediterranean Atlantic

**1477** ■ Marco Polo's *Travels* describe China

**1492** ■ Columbus reaches Bahamas

**1494** ■ Treaty of Tordesillas divides land claims between Spain and Portugal in Africa, India, and South America

**1496** ■ Last Canary Island falls to Spain

**1497** ■ Cabot reaches North America

**1513** ■ Ponce de León explores Florida

**1518–30** ■ Smallpox epidemic devastates Indian population of West Indies and Central and South America

**1519** ■ Cortés invades Mexico

**1521** ■ Aztec Empire falls to Spaniards

**1524** ■ Verrazzano sails along Atlantic coast of United States

**1534–35** ■ Cartier explores St. Lawrence River

**1534–36** ■ Vaca, Estevan, and two companions walk across North America

**1539–42** ■ Soto explores southeastern United States

**1540–42** ■ Coronado explores southwestern United States

**1587–90** ■ Raleigh's Roanoke colony vanishes

**1588** ■ Harriot publishes *A Briefe and True Report of the New Found Land of Virginia*

the diets, living arrangements, and customs of many of the villages they saw, thus providing modern historians and anthropologists with an invaluable record of native cultures as they first met Europeans. Little is known about Estevan's role en route, but that Vaca's account largely ignored him suggests that the Spaniards viewed him as a subordinate.

When the four travelers finally arrived in Mexico City in July 1536, their extraordinary feat won them unanimous praise. The other two Spaniards settled permanently in Mexico. Estevan was killed while accompanying an expedition northward into the modern United States. And Cabeza de Vaca himself was appointed governor of Paraguay, his fame forever established by the 1555 publication of his account of the remarkable journey.

For thousands of years before 1492, human societies in the Americas had developed in isolation from the rest of the world. The era that began in the Christian fifteenth century brought that long-standing isolation to an end. As Europeans sought treasure and trade, peoples from different cultures came into regular contact for the first time. All were profoundly changed. Their interactions involved cruelty and kindness, greed and deception, trade and theft, surprise and sickness, captivity and enslavement. By the time the three Spaniards and the African crossed North America, the age of European expansion and colonization was already well under way. Over the next 350 years, Europeans would spread their influence across the globe. The history of the tiny colonies that would become the United States must be seen in this broad context of European exploration and exploitation.

The continents that European sailors reached in the late fifteenth century had their own histories, which the intruders largely ignored. The residents of the Americas were the world's most skillful plant breeders; they developed vegetable crops more nutritious and productive than those grown in Europe, Asia, or Africa. They had invented systems of writing and mathematics, and created more accurate calendars than those used on the other side of the Atlantic. In the Americas, as in Europe, societies rose and fell as leaders succeeded or failed in expanding their political and economic power. But the arrival of Europeans immeasurably altered the Americans' struggles with one another.

After 1400 European nations not only warred on their own continent but also tried to acquire valuable colonies and trading posts elsewhere in the world. Initially interested primarily in Asia and Africa, Europeans eventually focused mostly on the Americas. Their contests for trade and conquest changed the course of history on four continents. Even as Europeans slowly achieved dominance, their fates were shaped by the strategies of Americans and Africans. In the Americas of the fifteenth and sixteenth centuries, three old worlds came together to produce a new.

- What were the key characteristics of the three worlds that met in the Americas?
- What impact did their encounter have on each of them?
- What were the crucial initial developments in that encounter?

## AMERICAN SOCIETIES

Human beings originated on the continent of Africa, where humanlike remains about 3 million years old have been found in what is now Ethiopia. Over many millennia, the growing population slowly dispersed to the other continents. Because the climate was then far colder than it is now, much of the earth's water was concentrated in huge rivers of ice called glaciers. Sea levels were accordingly lower, and land masses covered a larger proportion of the earth's surface than they do today. Scholars long believed that the earliest inhabitants of the Americas crossed a land bridge known as Beringia (at the site of the Bering Strait) approximately 12,000 to 14,000 years ago. Yet striking new archaeological discoveries in both North and South America suggest that parts of the Americas may have been settled much earlier, perhaps by seafarers. Some geneticists now theorize that three successive waves of migrants began at least 30,000 years ago. When, about 12,500 years ago, the climate warmed and sea levels rose, Americans were separated from the peoples living on the connected continents of Asia, Africa, and Europe.

The first Americans are called Paleo-Indians. Nomadic hunters of game and gatherers of wild plants, they spread throughout North and South America, probably moving as bands composed of extended families. By about 11,500 years ago the Paleo-Indians were making fine stone projectile points, which they attached to wooden spears and used to kill and butcher bison (buffalo), woolly mammoths, and other large mammals then living in the Americas. But as the Ice Age ended

**Ancient America**

and the human population increased, all the large American mammals except the bison disappeared. Scholars disagree about whether overhunting or the change in climate caused their demise. In either case, deprived of their primary source of meat, Paleo-Indians found new ways to survive.

By approximately 9,000 years ago, the residents of what is now central Mexico began to cultivate food crops, especially maize (corn), squash, beans, avocados, and peppers. In the Andes Mountains of South America, people started to grow potatoes. As knowledge of agricultural techniques improved and spread through the Americas, vegetables and maize proved a more reliable source of food than hunting and gathering. Except for those living in the harshest climates, most Americans started to adopt a more sedentary style of life so that they could tend fields regularly. Some established permanent settlements; others moved several times a year among fixed sites. They cleared forests through the use of controlled burning. The fires not only created cultivable lands by killing trees and fertilizing the soil with ashes but also opened meadows that attracted deer and other wildlife. All the American cultures emphasized producing sufficient food. Although they traded such items as shells, flint, salt, and copper, no society ever became dependent on another group for items vital to its survival.

Wherever agriculture dominated the economy, complex civilizations flourished. Such societies, assured of steady supplies of grains and vegetables, no longer had to devote all their energies to subsistence. Instead, they were able to accumulate wealth, produce ornamental objects, trade with other groups, and create elaborate rituals and ceremonies. In North America, the successful cultivation of nutritious crops, such as maize, beans, and squash, seems to have led to the growth and development of all the major civilizations: first the large city-states of Mesoamerica (modern Mexico and Guatemala) and then the urban clusters known collectively as the Mississippian culture and located in the present-day United States. Each of these societies, many historians and archaeologists now believe, reached its height of population and influence only after achieving success in agriculture. Each later declined and collapsed after reaching the limits of its food supply, with dire political and military consequences.

Archaeologists and historians still know little about the first major Mesoamerican civilization, the Olmecs, who about 4,000 years ago lived near the Gulf of Mexico in cities dominated by temple pyramids. The Mayas and Teotihuacán, which developed approximately 2,000 years later, are better recorded. Teotihuacán, founded in the Valley of Mexico about 300 B.C.E. (Before the Common

**Mesoamerican Civilizations**

Era), eventually became one of the largest urban areas in the world, housing perhaps 100,000 people in the fifth century C.E. (Common Era). Teotihuacán's commercial network extended hundreds of miles in all directions; many peoples prized its obsidian (a green glass), used to make fine knives and mirrors. Pilgrims traveled long distances to visit Teotihuacán's impressive pyramids and the great temple of Quetzalcoatl—the feathered serpent, primary god of central Mexico.

On the Yucatán Peninsula, in today's eastern Mexico, the Mayas built urban centers containing tall pyramids and temples. They studied astronomy and created an elaborate writing system. Their city-states, though, engaged in near-constant warfare with one another. Warfare and an inadequate food supply caused the collapse of the most powerful cities by 900 C.E., thus ending the classic era of Mayan civilization. By the time Spaniards arrived 600 years later, only a few remnants of the once-mighty society remained.

Ancient native societies in what is now the United States learned to grow maize, squash, and beans from Mesoamericans, but the exact nature of the relationship of the various cultures is unknown. (No Mesoamerican artifacts have been found north of the Rio Grande, but some items resembling Mississippian objects have been excavated in northern Mexico.) The Hohokam, Mogollon, and ancient Pueblo peoples of the modern states of Arizona and New Mexico subsisted by combining hunting and gathering with agriculture in an arid region of unpredictable rainfall. Hohokam villagers constructed extensive irrigation systems, but even so, they occasionally had to relocate their settlements when water supplies failed. Between 900 and 1150 C.E. in Chaco Canyon,

## Pueblos and Mississippians

the Pueblos built fourteen "Great Houses," multistory stone structures averaging two hundred rooms. The canyon, at the juncture of perhaps 400 miles of roads, served as a major regional trading and processing center for turquoise, used then as now to create beautiful ornamental objects. Yet the aridity eventually caused the Chacoans to migrate to other sites.

At almost the same time, the unrelated Mississippian culture flourished in what is now the midwestern and southeastern United States. Relying largely on maize, squash, nuts, pumpkins, and venison for food, the Mississippians lived in substantial settlements organized hierarchically. The largest of their urban centers was the City of the Sun (now called Cahokia), near modern St. Louis. Located on rich farmland close to the confluence of the Illinois, Missouri, and Mississippi Rivers, Cahokia, like Teotihuacán and Chaco Canyon, served as a focal point for both religion and trade. At its peak (in the eleventh and twelfth centuries C.E.), the City of the Sun covered more than 5 square miles and had a population of about twenty thousand—small by Mesoamerican standards but larger than any other northern community, and larger than London in the same era.

Although the Cahokians never invented a writing system, these sun-worshippers developed an accurate calendar, evidenced by their creation of a woodhenge—a large circle of tall timber posts aligned with the solstices and the equinox. The city's main pyramid (one of 120 of varying sizes), today called Monks Mound, was at the time of its

Pueblo Bonito in Chaco Canyon, ▶ in what is now the state of New Mexico. More than six hundred buildings were present on the well-defended site. The circular structures were kivas, used for food storage and religious rituals.

*(© Dewitt Jones/CORBIS)*

construction the third largest structure of any description in the Western Hemisphere; it remains the largest earthwork ever built anywhere in the Americas. It sat at the northern end of the Grand Plaza, surrounded by seventeen other mounds, some used for burials. Yet following 1250 C.E. the city was abandoned, several decades after a disastrous earthquake. Archaeologists believe that climate change and the degradation of the environment, caused by overpopulation and the destruction of nearby forests, contributed to the city's collapse.

The Aztecs' histories tell of the long migration of their people (who called themselves Mexica) into the Valley of Mexico during the twelfth cen-

||||||||||||||||||||||||||||||||||

**Aztecs**

tury. The uninhabited ruins of Teotihuacán, which by then had been deserted for at least two hundred years, awed and mystified the migrants. Their chronicles record that their primary deity, Huitzilopochtli—a war god represented by an eagle—directed them to establish their capital on an island where they saw an eagle eating a serpent, the symbol of Quetzalcoatl. That island city became Tenochtitlán, the center of a rigidly stratified society composed of hereditary classes of warriors, merchants, priests, common folk, and slaves.

The Aztecs conquered their neighbors, forcing them to pay tribute in textiles, gold, foodstuffs, and human beings who could be sacrificed to Huitzilopochtli. They also engaged in ritual combat, known as flowery wars, to obtain further sacrificial victims. The war god's taste for blood was not easily quenched. In the Aztec year Ten Rabbit (1502), at the coronation of Motecuhzoma II (the Spaniards could not pronounce his name correctly, so they called him Montezuma), thousands of people were sacrificed by having their still-beating hearts torn from their bodies.

The Aztecs believed that they lived in the age of the Fifth Sun. Four times previously, they wrote, the earth and all the people who lived on it had been destroyed. They predicted that their own world would end in earthquakes and hunger. In the Aztec year Thirteen Flint, volcanoes erupted, sickness and hunger spread, wild beasts attacked children, and an eclipse of the sun darkened the sky. Did some priest wonder whether the Fifth Sun was approaching its end? In time, the Aztecs learned that Thirteen Flint was called, by Europeans, 1492.

## NORTH AMERICA IN 1492

Over the centuries, the Americans who lived north of Mexico adapted their once-similar ways of life to very different climates and terrains, thus creating the diverse culture areas (ways of subsistence) that the Europeans encountered when they arrived (see Map 1.1). Scholars often refer to such culture areas by language group (such as Algonquian or Iroquoian) because neighboring Indian nations commonly spoke related languages. Bands that lived in environments not well suited to agriculture—because of inadequate rainfall or poor soil, for example—followed a nomadic lifestyle similar to that of the Paleo-Indians. Within the area of the present-day United States, these groups included the Paiutes and Shoshones, who inhabited the Great Basin (now Nevada and Utah). Because of the difficulty of finding sufficient food for more than a few people, such hunter-gatherer bands were small, usually composed of one or more related families. The men hunted small animals, and women gathered seeds and berries. Where large game was more plentiful and food supplies therefore more certain, as in present-day central and western Canada and the Great Plains, bands of hunters were somewhat larger.

In more favorable environments, larger groups combined agriculture with gathering, hunting, and fishing. Those who lived near the seacoasts, like the Chinooks of present-day Washington and Oregon, consumed fish and shellfish in addition to growing crops and gathering seeds and berries. Residents of the interior (for example, the Arikaras of the Missouri River valley) hunted large animals while also cultivating maize, squash, and beans. The peoples of what is now eastern Canada and the northeastern United States also combined hunting, fishing, and agriculture. They regularly used controlled fires both to open land for cultivation and to assist in hunting.

Societies that relied primarily on hunting large animals, such as deer and buffalo, assigned that task to

||||||||||||||||||||||||||||||||||

**Gendered Division of Labor**

men, allotting food preparation and clothing production to women. Before such nomadic bands acquired horses from the Spaniards, women—occasionally assisted by dogs—also carried the family's belongings whenever the band relocated. Such a sexual division of labor was universal among hunting peoples, regardless of their location. So, too, among seacoast peoples women gathered shellfish along the shore while men fished from boats. Yet agricultural societies assigned work in divergent ways. The Pueblo peoples, who lived in sixty or seventy autonomous villages and spoke five different languages, defined agricultural labor as men's work. In the east, large clusters of peoples speaking Algonquian, Iroquoian, and Muskogean languages by contrast allocated most agricultural chores to women, although men cleared the land. In all the farming societies, women gathered wild foods and

**Map 1.1  Native Cultures of North America**

The natives of the North American continent effectively used the resources of the regions in which they lived. As this map shows, coastal groups relied on fishing, residents of fertile areas engaged in agriculture, and other peoples employed hunting (often combined with gathering) as a primary mode of subsistence.

▲ Jacques Le Moyne, an artist accompanying the French settlement in Florida in the 1560s (see page 35), produced some of the first European images of North American peoples. His depiction of native agricultural practices shows the gendered division of labor: men breaking up the ground with fishbone hoes before women drop seeds into the holes. But Le Moyne's version of the scene cannot be accepted uncritically: unable to abandon a European view of proper farming methods, he erroneously drew plowed furrows in the soil.    *(Collection of Mary Beth Norton)*

prepared food for consumption or storage, whereas men were responsible for hunting.

Everywhere in North America, women cared for young children, while older youths learned adult skills from their same-sex parent. Children generally had a great deal of freedom. Young people commonly chose their own marital partners, and in most societies couples could easily divorce if they no longer wished to live together. In contrast to the earlier Mississippian cultures, populations in these societies remained at a level sustainable by existing food supplies, largely because of low birth rates. Infants and toddlers were nursed until the age of two or even longer, and taboos prevented couples from having sexual intercourse during that period.

The southwestern and eastern agricultural peoples had similar social organizations. They lived in villages,

||||||||||||||||||||||||||||||||||||||||

## Social Organization

sometimes with a thousand or more inhabitants. The Pueblos resided in multistory buildings constructed on terraces along the sides of cliffs or other easily defended sites. Northern Iroquois villages (in modern New York State) were composed of large, rectangular, bark-covered structures, or long houses; the name Haudenosaunee, which the Iroquois called themselves, means "People of the Long House." In the present-day southeastern United States, Muskogeans and southern Algonquians lived in large houses made of thatch. Most of the eastern villages were surrounded by wooden palisades and ditches to aid in fending off attackers.

In all the agricultural societies, each dwelling housed an extended family defined matrilineally (through a female line of descent). Mothers, their married daughters, and their daughters' husbands and children all lived together. Matrilineal descent did not imply matriarchy, or the wielding of power by women, but rather served as a means of reckoning kinship. Matrilineal ties also linked extended families into clans. The nomadic bands of the Prairies and Great Plains, by contrast, were most often related patrilineally (through the male line). They lacked settled villages and defended themselves from attack primarily through their ability to move to safer locations when necessary.

The defensive design of native villages discloses the significance of warfare in pre-Columbian America. Long

||||||||||||||||||||||||||||||||||

### War and Politics

before Europeans arrived, residents of the continent fought one another for control of the best hunting and fishing territories, the most fertile agricultural lands, or the sources of essential items, such as salt (for preserving meat) and flint (for making knives and arrowheads). Bands of Americans protected by wooden armor battled while standing in ranks facing each other, the better to employ their clubs and throwing spears, which were effective only at close quarters. They began to shoot arrows from behind trees only when they confronted European guns, which rendered their armor useless. People captured by the enemy in such wars were sometimes enslaved and dishonored by losing their previous names and identities, but slavery was never an important source of labor in pre-Columbian America.

American political structures varied considerably. Among Pueblos, the village council, composed of ten to thirty men, was the highest political authority; no government structure connected the villages. Nomadic hunters also lacked formal links among separate bands. The Iroquois, by contrast, had an elaborate political hierarchy incorporating villages into nations and nations into a confederation. A council comprising representatives from each nation made crucial decisions of war and peace for the entire confederacy. In all the North American cultures, civil and war leaders divided political power and wielded authority only so long as they retained the confidence of the people. Autocratic rule of the sort common in Europe was found only in southeastern chiefdoms descended from the Mississippians. Women more often assumed leadership roles among agricultural peoples, especially those in which females were the primary cultivators, than among nomadic hunters. Female sachems (rulers) led Algonquian villages in what is now Massachusetts, but women never became heads of hunting bands. Iroquois women did not become chiefs, yet clan matrons exercised political power. The older women of each village chose its chief and could both start wars (by calling for the capture of prisoners to

replace dead relatives) and stop them (by refusing to supply warriors with necessary foodstuffs).

All the American peoples were polytheistic, worshiping a multitude of gods. Each group's most important

||||||||||||||||||||||||||||||||||

### Religion

beliefs and rituals were closely tied to its means of subsistence. The major deities of agricultural peoples like the Pueblos and Muskogeans were associated with cultivation, and their chief festivals centered on planting and harvest. The most important gods of hunters like those living on the Great Plains and Prairies were associated with animals, and their major festivals were related to hunting. A band's economy and women's role in it helped to determine women's potential as religious leaders. Women held the most prominent positions in those agricultural societies in which they were also the chief food producers, whereas in hunting societies men took the lead in religious as well as political affairs.

A wide variety of cultures, comprising more than 10 million people, thus inhabited America north of Mexico when Europeans arrived. The hierarchical kingdoms of Mesoamerica bore little resemblance to the nomadic hunting societies of the Great Plains or to the agriculturalists of the Northeast or Southwest. The diverse inhabitants of North America spoke well over one thousand different languages. For obvious reasons, they did not consider themselves one people, nor did they—for the most part—think of uniting to repel the European invaders.

## AFRICAN SOCIETIES

Fifteenth-century Africa, like fifteenth-century America, housed a variety of cultures adapted to different terrains and climates (see Map 1.2). Many of these cultures were of great antiquity. In the north, along the Mediterranean Sea, lived the Berbers, who were Muslims, or followers of the Islamic religion founded by the prophet Mohammed in the seventh century C.E. On the east coast of Africa, Muslim city-states engaged in extensive trade with India, the Moluccas (part of modern Indonesia), and China. In these ports, sustained contact and intermarriage among Arabs and Africans created the Swahili language and culture. Through the East African city-states passed waterborne commerce between the eastern Mediterranean and East Asia; the rest followed the long land route across Central Asia known as the Silk Road.

South of the Mediterranean coast in the African interior lie the great Saharan and Libyan Deserts, vast expanses of nearly waterless terrain crisscrossed by trade routes passing through oases. The introduction of the camel in the fifth century C.E. made long-distance travel possible, and as Islam expanded after the ninth century,

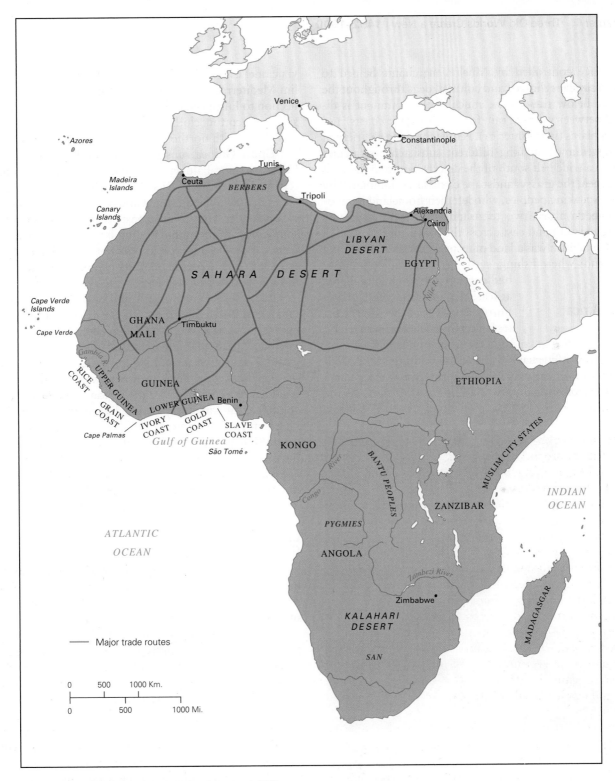

Map labels (within image):

Azores

Venice

Constantinople

Madeira
Islands

Tunis
Ceuta
BERBERS
Tripoli

Canary
Islands

Alexandria
Cairo

LIBYAN
DESERT

EGYPT

Red Sea

SAHARA DESERT

Cape Verde
Islands

Cape Verde

GHANA
MALI
Timbuktu

Gambia R.

Nile R.

ETHIOPIA

RICE COAST
UPPER GUINEA
GUINEA
GRAIN COAST
IVORY COAST
LOWER GUINEA
GOLD COAST
Benin
SLAVE COAST
Cape Palmas
Gulf of Guinea
São Tomé

KONGO

Congo River

BANTU PEOPLES

ZANZIBAR

MUSLIM CITY STATES

INDIAN
OCEAN

ATLANTIC

OCEAN

PYGMIES

ANGOLA

Zambezi River

Zimbabwe

MADAGASCAR

KALAHARI
DESERT

SAN

—— Major trade routes

0   500   1000 Km.

0   500   1000 Mi.

## Map 1.2   Africa and Its Peoples, c. 1400

On the African continent resided many different peoples in a variety of ecological settings and
political units. Even before Europeans began to explore Africa's coastlines, its northern regions were
linked to the Mediterranean (and thus to Europe) by a network of trade routes.

commerce controlled by Muslim merchants helped to spread similar religious and cultural ideas throughout the region. Below the deserts, much of the continent is divided between tropical rain forests (along the coasts) and grassy plains (in the interior). People speaking a variety of languages and pursuing different subsistence strategies lived in a wide belt south of the deserts. South of the Gulf of Guinea, the grassy landscape came to be dominated by Bantu-speaking peoples, who left their homeland in modern Nigeria about two thousand years ago and slowly migrated south and east across the continent.

West Africa was a land of tropical forests and savanna grasslands where fishing, cattle herding, and agriculture

|||||||||||||||||||||||||||||||||||

**West Africa (Guinea)**

had supported the inhabitants for at least ten thousand years before Europeans set foot there in the fifteenth century. The northern region of West Africa, or Upper Guinea, was heavily influenced by the Islamic culture of the Mediterranean. As early as the eleventh century C.E., many of the region's inhabitants had become Muslims. Trade via camel caravans between Upper Guinea and the Muslim Mediterranean was sub-Saharan Africa's major connection to Europe and West Asia. In return for salt, dates, silk, and cotton cloth Africans exchanged ivory, gold, and slaves with northern merchants.

Upper Guinea runs northeast-southwest from Cape Verde to Cape Palmas. The people of its northernmost region, the so-called Rice Coast (present-day Gambia, Senegal, and Guinea), fished and cultivated rice in coastal swamplands. The Grain Coast, the next region to the south, was thinly populated and not readily accessible from the sea because it had only one good harbor (modern Freetown, Sierra Leone). Its people concentrated on farming and raising livestock.

In Lower Guinea, south and east of Cape Palmas, most Africans were farmers who practiced traditional religions, not the precepts of Islam. Believing that spirits inhabited particular places, they invested those places with special significance. Like the agricultural peoples of the Americas, they developed rituals intended to ensure good harvests. Throughout the region, individual villages composed of kin groups were linked into hierarchical kingdoms. At the time of initial European contact, decentralized political and social authority characterized the region's polities.

The societies of West Africa, like those of the Americas, assigned different tasks to men and women. In general,

|||||||||||||||||||||||||||||||||||

**Complementary Gender Roles**

the sexes shared agricultural duties. Men also hunted, managed livestock, and did most of the fishing. Women were responsible for childcare, food preparation, manufacture, and trade. They managed the extensive local and regional networks through which families, villages, and small kingdoms exchanged goods.

Despite their different economies and the rivalries among states, the peoples of Lower Guinea had similar social systems organized on the basis of what anthropologists have called the dual-sex principle. In Lower Guinea, each sex handled its own affairs: just as male political and religious leaders governed men, so females ruled women. In the Dahomean kingdom, for example, every male official had his female counterpart; in the thirty little Akan states on the Gold Coast, chiefs inherited their status through the female line, and each male chief had a female assistant who supervised other women. Many West African societies practiced polygyny (one man's having several wives, each of whom lived separately with her children). Thus few adults lived permanently in marital households, but the dual-sex system ensured that their actions were subject to scrutiny by members of their own sex.

▲ This decorative brass weight, created by the Asante peoples of Lower Guinea, was used for measuring gold dust. It depicts a family pounding fu-fu, a food made by mashing together plantains (a kind of banana), yams, and cassava. The paste was then shaped into balls to be eaten with soup. This weight, probably used in trading with Europeans, shows a scene combining foods of African origin (plantains and yams) with an import from the Americas (cassava), thus bringing the three continents together in ways both symbolic and real. *(Trustees of the British Museum. Photo by Michael Holford)*

Throughout Guinea, religious beliefs stressed complementary male and female roles. Both women and men served as heads of the cults and secret societies that directed the spiritual life of the villages. Young women were initiated into the Sandé cult, young men into Poro. Neither cult was allowed to reveal its secrets to the opposite sex. Although West African women (unlike some of their Native American contemporaries) rarely held formal power over men, female religious leaders did govern other members of their sex within the Sandé cult, enforcing conformity to accepted norms of behavior and overseeing their spiritual well-being.

West African law recognized both individual and communal land ownership, but men seeking to accumulate wealth needed access to labor—wives, children, or slaves—who could work the land. West Africans enslaved for life therefore composed essential elements of the economy. Africans could be enslaved as punishment for crimes, but more often such slaves were enemy captives or people who voluntarily enslaved themselves or their children in payment for debts. An African who possessed bondspeople had a right to the products of their labor, although the degree to which slaves were exploited varied greatly, and slave status did not always descend to the next generation. Some slaves were held as chattel; others could engage in trade, retaining a portion of their profits; and still others achieved prominent political or military positions. All, however, found it difficult to overcome the social stigma of enslavement, and they could be traded or sold at the will of their owners.

**Slavery in Guinea**

West Africans, then, were agricultural peoples, skilled at tending livestock, hunting, fishing, and manufacturing cloth from plant fibers and animal skins. Both men and women worked communally, in family groups or alongside others of their own sex. They were accustomed to a relatively egalitarian relationship between the sexes, especially within the context of religion. Carried as captives to the Americas, they became essential to transplanted European societies that used their labor but had little respect for their cultural traditions.

## EUROPEAN SOCIETIES

In the fifteenth century, Europeans, too, were agricultural peoples. The daily lives of Europe's rural people had changed little for several hundred years. Split into numerous small, warring countries, Europe was divided linguistically, politically, and economically, yet in social terms Europeans' lives exhibited many similarities. In the hierarchical European societies, a few families wielded autocratic power over the majority of the people. English society in particular was organized as a series of interlocking hierarchies; that is, each person (except those at the very top or bottom) was superior to some, inferior to others. At the base of such hierarchies were people held in various forms of bondage. Although Europeans were not subjected to perpetual slavery, Christian doctrine permitted the enslavement of "heathens" (non-Christians), and some Europeans' freedom was restricted by such conditions as serfdom, which tied them to the land if not to specific owners. In short, Europe's kingdoms resembled those of Africa or Mesoamerica but differed greatly from the more egalitarian societies found in America north of Mexico (see Map 1.3).

Most Europeans, like most Africans and Americans, lived in small villages. Only a few cities dotted the landscape, most of them seaports or political capitals. European farmers, called peasants, owned or leased separate landholdings, but they worked the fields communally. Because fields had to lie fallow (unplanted) every second or third year to regain fertility, a family could not ensure itself a regular food supply unless all villagers shared annually the work and the crops. Men did most of the fieldwork; women helped out chiefly at planting and harvest. In some regions men concentrated on herding livestock. Women's duties consisted primarily of childcare and household tasks, including preserving food, milking cows, and caring for poultry. If a woman's husband was a city artisan or storekeeper, she might assist him in business. Because Europeans kept domesticated animals (pigs, goats, sheep, and cattle) for meat, hunting had little economic importance in their cultures. Instead, hunting was primarily a sport for male aristocrats.

**Work, Politics, and Religion**

Unlike in Africa or America, where women often played prominent roles in politics and religion, men dominated all areas of life in Europe. A few women—notably Queen Elizabeth I of England—achieved status or power by right of birth, but the vast majority were excluded from positions of political authority. European women also generally held inferior social, religious, and economic positions, yet they wielded power in their own households over children and servants. In contrast to the freedom children enjoyed in American families, European children were tightly controlled and subjected to harsh discipline.

Christianity was the dominant European religion. In the West, authority rested in the Catholic Church, based in Rome and led by the pope, who directed a wholly male clergy. Although Europeans were nominally Catholic, many adhered to local belief systems that the church

**Map 1.3    Europe in 1453**

The Europeans who ventured out into the Atlantic came from countries on the northwestern edge of the continent, which was divided into numerous competing nations.

deemed heretical and proved unable to extinguish. Kings would ally themselves with the church when it suited their needs but often acted independently. Yet even so, the Christian nations of Europe from the twelfth century on publicly united in a goal of driving nonbelievers (especially Muslims) not only from their own domains but also from the holy city of Jerusalem, which caused the series of wars known as the Crusades. Nevertheless, in the fifteenth century Muslims dominated the commerce and geography of the Mediterranean world, especially after they conquered Constantinople (capital of the Christian Byzantine empire) in 1453. Few would have predicted that Christian Europeans would ever be able to challenge that dominance.

When the fifteenth century began, European nations were slowly recovering from the devastating epidemic of plague known as the Black Death, which first struck them in 1346. The Black Death seems to have arrived in Europe from China, traveling with long-distance traders along the Silk Road to the eastern Mediterranean. The disease then recurred with particular severity in the 1360s and 1370s. Although no precise figures are available and the impact of the Black Death varied from region to region, the best estimate is that fully one-third of Europe's people died during those terrible years. A precipitous economic decline followed—in some regions more than half of the

**Effects of Plague and Warfare**

▲ Daily life in early sixteenth-century Portugal, as illustrated in a manuscript prayer book. At top a prosperous family shares a meal being served by an African slave. Other scenes show male laborers clearing land and hunting birds (left) and chopping wood (right), while at bottom a woman plants seeds in a prepared bed and in the top background female servants work in the kitchen.

*(Museu Nacional de Arte Antiga, Lisbon, Portugal)*

workers had died—as did severe social, political, and religious disruption because of the deaths of clergymen and other leading figures.

As plague ravaged the population, England and France waged the Hundred Years' War (1337–1453), initiated because English monarchs had claimed the French throne. The war interrupted overland trade routes connecting England and Antwerp (in modern Belgium) to Venice, a Christian trading center, and thence to India and China. England, on the periphery of the Mediterranean commercial core, exported wool and cloth to Antwerp in exchange for spices and silks from the East. Needing a new way to reach their northern trading partners, eastern Mediterranean merchants forged a maritime route to Antwerp. Using a triangular, or lateen, sail (rather than the then-standard square rigging) improved the maneuvera-

bility of ships, enabling vessels to sail out of the Mediterranean and north around the European coast. Also of key importance was the perfection of navigational instruments like the astrolabe and the quadrant, which allowed oceangoing sailors to estimate their position (latitude) by measuring the relationship of the sun, moon, or certain stars to the horizon.

After the Hundred Years' War, European monarchs forcefully consolidated their previously diffuse political

### Political and Technological Change

power and raised new revenues through increased taxation of an already hard-pressed peasantry. The long military struggle led to new pride in national identity, which eclipsed the prevailing regional and dynastic loyalties. In England, Henry VII in 1485 founded the Tudor dynasty and began uniting a previously divided land. In France, the successors of Charles VII unified the kingdom and levied new taxes. Most successful of all were Ferdinand of Aragón and Isabella of Castile, who married in 1469, founding a strongly Catholic Spain. In 1492 they defeated the Muslims, who had lived in Spain and Portugal for centuries, thereafter expelling all Jews and Muslims from their domain.

The fifteenth century also brought technological change to Europe. Movable type and the printing press, invented in Germany in the 1450s, made information more accessible than ever before. Printing stimulated the Europeans' curiosity about fabled lands across the seas, lands they could now read about in books. The most important such work was Marco Polo's *Travels*, first published in 1477, which recounted a Venetian merchant's adventures in thirteenth-century China and, most intriguing, described that nation as bordered on the east by an ocean. Polo's account circulated widely among Europe's educated elites, first in manuscript and later in print. The book led many Europeans to believe that they could trade directly with China in oceangoing vessels instead of relying on the Silk Road or the route through East Africa. A transoceanic route, if it existed, would allow northern Europeans to circumvent the Muslim and Venetian merchants who hitherto had controlled their access to Asian goods.

Technological advances and the growing strength of newly powerful national rulers made possible the Euro-

### Motives for Exploration

pean explorations of the fifteenth and sixteenth centuries. Each country craved easy access to African and Asian goods—silk, dyes, perfumes, jewels, sugar, gold, and especially spices, such as pepper, cloves, cinnamon, and nutmeg. Spices were desirable not only for seasoning food but also because they were believed to have medicinal and magical properties. Their allure stemmed largely from their rarity, their extraordinary cost, and their mysterious origins. They passed through so many hands en route to London or Seville that no European knew exactly where they came from. (Nutmeg, for example, grew only on nine tiny islands in the Moluccas, in what is now eastern Indonesia.) Avoiding intermediaries in Venice and Constantinople, and acquiring such valuable products directly, would improve a nation's income and its standing relative to other countries, in addition to supplying its wealthy leaders with coveted luxury items.

A concern for spreading Christianity around the world supplemented the economic motive. The linking of materialistic and spiritual goals perhaps seems contradictory today, but fifteenth-century Europeans saw no necessary conflict between the two. Explorers and colonizers—especially Roman Catholics—honestly sought to convert "heathen" peoples to Christianity. At the same time they hoped to increase their nation's wealth by establishing direct trade with Africa, China, India, and the Moluccas.

## EARLY EUROPEAN EXPLORATIONS

To establish that trade, European mariners first had to explore the oceans. To reach Asia, seafarers needed not just the maneuverable vessels and navigational aids increasingly used in the fourteenth century but also knowledge of the sea, its currents, and especially its winds. Wind would power their ships. But how did the winds run? Where would Atlantic breezes carry their square-rigged ships, which, even with the addition of a triangular sail, needed to run before the wind (that is, to have the wind directly behind the vessel)?

Europeans learned the answers to these questions in the region that has been called the Mediterranean Atlantic, the expanse of the Atlantic Ocean that is south and west of Spain and is bounded by the island groups of the Azores (on the west) and the Canaries (on the south), with the Madeiras in their midst (see Map 1.4). Europeans reached all three sets of islands during the fourteenth century—first the Canaries in the 1330s, then the Madeiras and the Azores. The Canaries proved a popular destination for mariners from Iberia, the peninsula that includes Spain and Portugal. Sailing to the Canaries from Europe was easy because strong winds known as the Northeast Trades blow southward along the Iberian and African coastlines. The voyage took

**Sailing the Mediterranean Atlantic**

about a week, and the volcanic peaks on the islands made them difficult to miss even with navigational instruments that were less than precise.

The problem was getting back. The Iberian sailor attempting to return home faced a major obstacle: the very winds that had brought him so quickly to the Canaries now blew directly at him. Rowing and tacking back and forth against the wind were similarly tedious and ineffectual. Confronted by contrary winds, mariners had usually waited for the wind to change, but the Northeast Trades blew steadily. So they developed a new technique: sailing "around the wind." That meant sailing as directly against the wind as was possible without being forced to tack. In the Mediterranean Atlantic, a mariner would head northwest into the open ocean, until—weeks later—he reached the winds that would carry him home, the so-called Westerlies. Those winds blow (we now know, although the seafarers at first did not) northward along the coast of North America before heading east toward Europe.

This solution must at first have seemed to defy common sense, but it became the key to successful exploration of both the Atlantic and the Pacific Oceans. Once a sailor understood the winds and their allied currents, he no longer feared leaving Europe without being able to return. Faced with a contrary wind, all he had to do was sail around it until he found a wind to carry him in the proper direction.

During the fifteenth century, armed with knowledge of the winds and currents of the Mediterranean Atlantic, Iberian seamen regularly visited the three island groups, all of which they could reach in two weeks or less. The uninhabited Azores were soon settled by Portuguese migrants who raised wheat for sale in Europe and sold livestock to passing sailors. The Madeiras also had no native peoples, and by the 1450s Portuguese colonists were employing slaves (probably Jews and Muslims brought from Iberia) to grow large quantities of sugar for export to the mainland. By the 1470s Madeira had developed into a colonial plantation economy. For the first time in world history, a region had been settled explicitly to cultivate a valuable crop—sugar—to be sold elsewhere. Moreover, because the work involved in large-scale plantation agriculture was so backbreaking, only a supply of enslaved laborers (who could not opt to quit) could ensure the system's continued success.

The Canaries did have indigenous residents—the Guanche people, who began trading animal skins and dyes with their European visitors. After 1402 the French,

**Islands of the Mediterranean Atlantic**

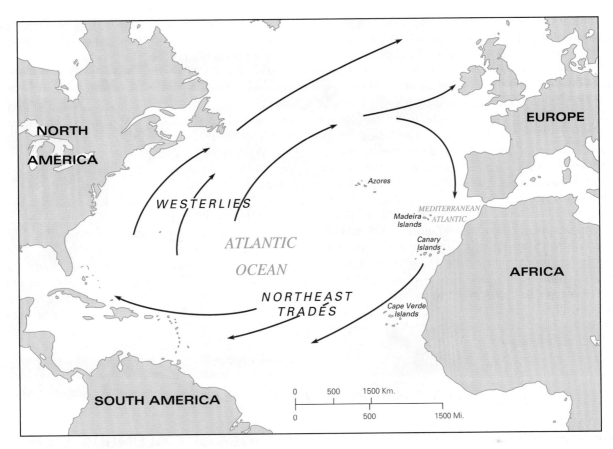

**Map 1.4    Atlantic Winds and Islands**
European mariners had to explore the oceans before they could find new lands. The first realm they discovered was that of Atlantic winds and islands.

Portuguese, and Spanish began sporadically attacking the islands. The Guanches resisted vigorously, even though they were weakened by their susceptibility to alien European diseases. One by one the seven islands fell to Europeans, who then carried off Guanches as slaves to the Madeiras or the Iberian Peninsula. Spain conquered the last island in 1496 and subsequently devoted the land to sugar plantations. Collectively, the Canaries and Madeira became known as the Wine Islands because much of their sugar production was directed to making sweet wines.

While some Europeans concentrated on exploiting the islands of the Mediterranean Atlantic, others used them as steppingstones to Africa.

**Portuguese Trading Posts in Africa**

In 1415 Portugal seized control of Ceuta, a Muslim city in North Africa (see Map 1.2). Prince Henry the Navigator, son of King John I of Portugal, knew that vast wealth awaited the first European nation to tap the riches of Africa and Asia directly. Repeatedly he dispatched ships southward along the African coast, attempting to discover an oceanic route to Asia. But not until after Prince Henry's death did Bartholomew Dias round the southern tip of Africa (1488) and Vasco da Gama finally reach India (1498), where at Malabar he located the richest source of peppercorns in the world.

Long before that, Portugal reaped the benefits of its seafarers' voyages. Although West African states successfully resisted European penetration of the interior, they allowed the Portuguese to establish trading posts along their coasts. Charging the traders rent and levying duties on goods they imported, the African kingdoms benefited considerably from their new, easier access to European manufactures. The Portuguese gained, too, for they no longer had to rely on trans-Saharan camel caravans. Their vessels earned immense profits by swiftly transporting African gold, ivory, and slaves to Europe. By bargaining with African masters to purchase their slaves and then

A relief carving of a square-rigged vessel, with a lateen sail at the rear for maneuverability. Fittingly, it is found on Vasco da Gama's tomb in the Jéronimos monastery in Belém, Portugal, which is located on the very spot whence he set sail in just such a ship on his voyage to India.

*(Collection of Mary Beth Norton)*

carrying those bondspeople to Iberia, the Portuguese introduced black slavery into Europe.

An island off the African coast, previously uninhabited, proved critical to Portuguese success. In the 1480s

### Lessons of Early Colonization

they colonized São Tomé, located in the Gulf of Guinea (see Map 1.2). By that time Madeira had already reached the limit of its capacity to produce sugar. The soil of São Tomé proved ideal for raising that valuable crop, and plantation agriculture there expanded rapidly. Planters imported large numbers of slaves from the mainland to work in the cane fields, thus creating the first economy based primarily on the bondage of black Africans.

By the 1490s, even before Christopher Columbus set sail to the west, Europeans had learned three key lessons of colonization in the Mediterranean Atlantic. First, they had learned how to transplant their crops and livestock successfully to exotic locations. Second, they had discovered that the native peoples of those lands could be either conquered (like the Guanches) or exploited (like the Africans). Third, they had developed a viable model of plantation slavery and a system for supplying nearly unlimited quantities of such workers. The stage was set for a pivotal moment in world history.

## VOYAGES OF COLUMBUS, CABOT, AND THEIR SUCCESSORS

Christopher Columbus was well schooled in the lessons of the Mediterranean Atlantic. Born in 1451 in the Italian city-state of Genoa, this largely self-educated son of a wool merchant was by the 1490s an experienced sailor and mapmaker. Like many mariners of the day, he was drawn to Portugal and its islands, especially Madeira, where he commanded a merchant vessel. At least once he voyaged to the Portuguese outpost on the Gold Coast. There he became obsessed with gold, and there he came to understand the economic potential of the slave trade.

Like all accomplished seafarers, Columbus knew the world was round. (So, indeed, did most educated people: the idea that his contemporaries believed the world to be flat is a myth.) But he differed from other cartographers in his estimate of the earth's size: he thought that China lay only 3,000 miles from the southern European coast. Thus, he argued, it would be easier to reach Asia by sailing west than by making the difficult voyage around the southern tip of Africa. Experts scoffed at this crackpot notion, accurately predicting that the two continents lay 12,000 miles apart. When Columbus in 1484 asked the

Portuguese rulers to back his plan to sail west to Asia, they rejected what appeared to be a crazy scheme.

Ferdinand and Isabella of Spain, jealous of Portugal's successes in Africa, were more receptive to Columbus's ideas. Urged on by some Spanish noblemen and a group of Italian merchants residing in Castile, the monarchs agreed to finance the risky voyage, in part because they hoped the profits would pay for a new expedition to conquer Muslim-held Jerusalem. And so, on August 3, 1492, in command of three ships—the *Pinta*, the *Niña*, and the *Santa Maria*—Columbus set sail from the Spanish port of Palos.

## Columbus's Voyage

The first part of the journey was familiar, for the ships steered down the Northeast Trades to the Canary Islands. There Columbus refitted his square-rigged ships, adding triangular sails to make them more maneuverable. On September 6, the ships weighed anchor and headed out into the unknown ocean.

Just over a month later, pushed by favorable trade winds, the vessels found land approximately where Colum-bus had predicted (see Map 1.5). On October 12, he and his men landed on an island in the Bahamas, which its inhabitants called Guanahaní but which he renamed San Salvador. (Because Columbus's description of his landfall can be variously interpreted, three different places—Samana, Plana, and Mayaguana—are today proposed as the most likely locations for his landing site.) Later he went on to explore the islands now known as Cuba and Hispaniola, which their residents, the Taíno people, called Colba and Bohío. Because he thought he had reached the East Indies, Columbus referred to the inhabitants of the region as "Indians."

Three themes predominate in Columbus's log, the major source of information on this first encounter. First,

## Columbus's Observations

he insistently asked the Taínos where he could find gold, pearls, and spices. Each time, his informants replied (via signs) that such products could be obtained on other islands, on the mainland, or in cities in the interior. Eventually he came to mistrust such answers, noting,

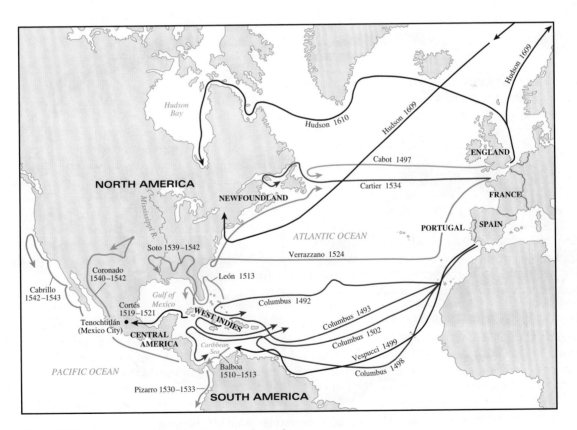

**Map 1.5    European Explorations in America**

In the century following Columbus's voyages, European adventurers explored the coasts and parts of the interior of North and South America.

"I am beginning to believe . . . they will tell me anything I want to hear."

Second, Columbus wrote repeatedly of the strange and beautiful plants and animals. "Here the fishes are so unlike ours that it is amazing. . . . The colors are so bright that anyone would marvel," he noted, and again, "The song of the little birds might make a man wish never to leave here. I never tire from looking at such luxurious vegetation." Yet Columbus's interest was not only aesthetic. "I believe that there are many plants and trees here that could be worth a lot in Spain for use as dyes, spices, and medicines," he observed, adding that he was carrying home to Europe "a sample of everything I can," so that experts could examine them.

Third, Columbus also described the islands' human residents, and he seized some to take back to Spain. The Taínos were, he said, very handsome, gentle, and friendly, though they told him of fierce people who lived on other nearby islands and raided their villages. The Caniba (today called Caribs), from whose name the word *cannibal*

is derived, were reported to eat their captives, but today scholars disagree about whether the tales were true. Columbus believed the Taínos to be likely converts to Catholicism, remarking that "if devout religious persons knew the Indian language well, all these people would soon become Christians." But he had more in mind than conversion. The islanders "ought to make good and skilled servants," Columbus declared. It would be easy to "subject everyone and make them do what you wished."

Thus the records of the first encounter between Europeans and America and its residents revealed themes that would be of enormous significance for centuries to come. Europeans wanted to extract profits from North and South America by exploiting their natural resources, including plants, animals, and peoples alike. Columbus made three more voyages to the west, exploring most of the major Caribbean islands and sailing along the coasts of Central and South America. Until the day he died in 1506 at the age of fifty-five, he believed he had reached Asia. Even before his death, others knew better. Because

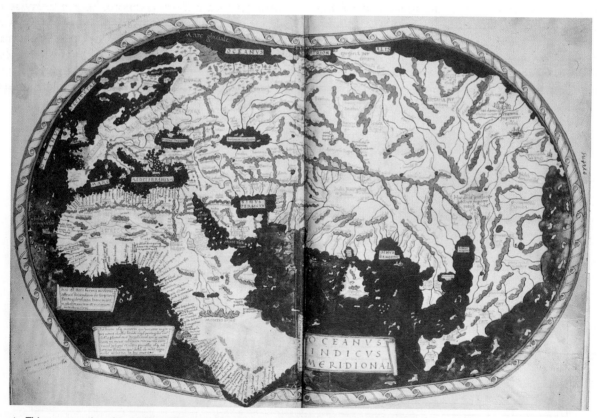

▲ This map, produced in 1489 by Henricus Marcellus, represents the world as Christopher Columbus knew it, for it incorporates information obtained after Bartholomew Dias, a Portuguese sailor, rounded the Cape of Good Hope at the southern tip of Africa in 1488. Marcellus did not try to estimate the extent of the ocean separating the west coast of Europe from the east coast of Asia. *(Trustees of the British Library)*

the Florentine Amerigo Vespucci, who explored the South American coast in 1499, was the first to publish the idea that a new continent had been discovered, Martin Waldseemüller in 1507 labeled the land "America," as is evident in his map (reproduced below). By then, Spain, Portugal, and Pope Alexander VI had signed the Treaty of Tordesillas (1494), confirming Portugal's dominance in Africa—and later Brazil—in exchange for Spanish preeminence in the rest of the Americas.

Five hundred years before Columbus, about the year 1001, the Norseman Leif Ericsson and other Norse people

### Norse and Other Northern Voyagers

had sailed to North America across the Davis Strait, which separated their villages in Greenland from Baffin Island (located northeast of Hudson Bay; see Map 1.1) by just 200 nautical miles, settling at a site they named "Vinland." Attacks by local residents forced them to depart hurriedly from Vinland after just a few years. In the 1960s, archaeologists determined that the Norse had established an outpost at what is now L'Anse aux Meadows, Newfoundland, but Vinland itself was probably located farther south.

Later Europeans did not know of the Norse explorers, but some historians argue that in the 1480s sailors probably located the rich fishing grounds off the coast of Newfoundland but kept the information secret. Whether or not fishermen crossed the entire width of the Atlantic, they thoroughly explored its northern reaches. Like the Portuguese in the Mediterranean Atlantic, fifteenth-century seafarers voyaged between the European continent, England, Ireland, and Iceland. The mariners who explored the region of North America that was to become the United States and Canada built on their knowledge.

The winds that the northern sailors confronted posed problems on their outbound rather than on their homeward journeys. The same Westerlies that carried Columbus and other southern voyagers back to Europe blew in the faces of northerners looking west. But mariners soon learned that the strongest winds shifted southward during the winter and that, by departing from northern ports in the spring, they could make adequate headway if they steered northward to catch sporadic easterly breezes. Thus, whereas the first landfall of most sailors to the south was somewhere in the Caribbean, those taking the northern route usually reached America along the coast of what is now Maine or the Canadian Maritime Provinces.

The European generally credited with "discovering" North America is Zuan Cabboto, known today as John

### John Cabot's Explorations

Cabot. More precisely, Cabot brought to Europe the first formal knowledge of the northern continental coastline and claimed the land for England. Like Columbus,

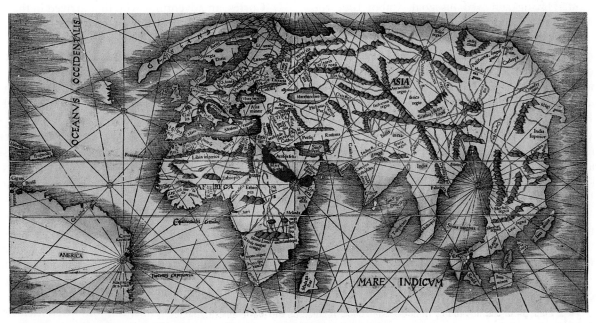

▲ In 1507 Martin Waldseemüller, a German mapmaker, was the first person to designate the newly discovered southern continent as "America." He named the continent after Amerigo Vespucci, the Italian explorer who realized that he had reached a "new world" rather than islands off the coast of Asia. *(John Carter Brown Library at Brown University)*

▲ Artifacts from L'Anse aux Meadows, Newfoundland, a site the Norse called Straumond. These inconspicuous items reveal a great deal to archaeologists investigating the Norse settlements in North America. The small circular object, a spindle whorl for use in spinning yarn, discloses women's presence at Straumond; the nut comes from a tree that grows only south of the St. Lawrence River, thus indicating the extent of Norse travel along the coast. *(L'Anse aux Meadows, Canada)*

Cabot was a master mariner from the Italian city-state of Genoa. Calculating that England—which traded with Asia only through a long series of intermediaries stretching from Antwerp to Venice to the Muslim world—would be eager to sponsor exploratory voyages, he gained financial backing from King Henry VII. He set sail from Bristol in late May 1497 in the *Mathew*, reaching his destination about a month later. Scholars disagree about the location of Cabot's landfall, but all recognize the importance of his month-long exploration of the coast of modern Newfoundland. Having achieved his goal, Cabot rode the Westerlies back to England, arriving just fifteen days after he left North America.

The voyages of Columbus, Cabot, and their successors finally brought the Eastern and Western Hemispheres together. The Portuguese explorer Pedro Álvares Cabral reached Brazil in 1500; John Cabot's son Sebastian followed his father to North America in 1507; France financed Giovanni da Verrazzano in 1524 and Jacques Cartier in 1534; and in 1609 and 1610 Henry Hudson explored the North American coast for the Dutch West India Company (see Map 1.5). All of these men were searching primarily for the legendary, nonexistent "Northwest Passage" through the Americas, hoping to find an easy route to the riches of Asia. Although they did not attempt to plant colonies in the Western Hemisphere, their discoveries interested European nations in exploring North and South America.

## SPANISH EXPLORATION AND CONQUEST

Only in the areas that Spain explored and claimed did colonization begin immediately. On his second voyage in 1493, Columbus brought to Hispaniola seventeen ships loaded with twelve hundred men, seeds, plants, livestock, chickens, and dogs—along with microbes, rats, and weeds. The settlement named Isabela (in the modern Dominican Republic) and its successors became the staging area for the Spanish invasion of America. On the islands of Cuba and Hispaniola the Europeans learned to adapt to the new environment, as did the horses, cattle, and hogs they imported. When the Spaniards moved on to explore the mainland, they rode island-bred horses and ate island-bred cattle and hogs.

At first, Spanish explorers fanned out around the Caribbean basin. In 1513 Juan Ponce de León reached Florida, and Vasco Núñez de Balboa crossed the Isthmus of Panama to the Pacific Ocean, followed by Pánfilo de Narváez and others who traced the coast of the Gulf of Mexico. In the 1530s and 1540s, conquistadors traveled farther, exploring many regions claimed by the Spanish monarchs: Francisco Vásquez de Coronado journeyed through the southwestern portion of what is now the United States at approximately the same time Hernán de Soto explored the Southeast. Juan Rodríguez Cabrillo sailed along the California coast; and Francisco Pizarro, who ventured into western South America, acquired the richest silver mines in the world by conquering the Incas. But the most important conquistador was Hernán Cortés, who in 1521 seized control of the Aztec Empire.

**Cortés and Other Explorers**

Cortés, an adventurer who first arrived in the Caribbean in 1506, landed a force on the Mexican mainland in 1519 to search for rumored wealthy cities. Near the coast, local Mayas presented him with a group of young enslaved women. One of them, Malinche (whom the Spaniards baptized as a Christian and renamed Doña Marina), had been sold into slavery by the Aztecs and raised by the Mayas. Because she became Cortés's translator, some modern Mexicans regard her as a traitor, but others suggest that she owed no loyalty to people who had enslaved her. In her own day, both Europeans and Aztecs accorded her great respect. Malinche bore Cortés a son, Martín— one of the first *mestizos,* or mixed-blood children—and eventually married one of his officers.

As he traveled toward the Aztec capital, Cortés, with Malinche's help, cleverly recruited peoples whom the Aztecs had long subjugated. The Spaniards' strange beasts (horses, livestock) and noisy weapons (guns, cannon) awed their new allies. Yet the Spaniards, too, were awed. Years later, Bernal Díaz del Castillo recalled his first sight of Tenochtitlán, situated in the midst of Lake Texcoco: "We were amazed and said that it was like the

**Capture of Tenochtitlán**

◀ An early illustration of a Carib lean-to shelter, with baskets, a pot, a loom (hanging at left), and a hammock—a novel place to sleep that fascinated European observers. The man at center has coated his skin with annatto, a plant extract that served as both insect repellent and sunscreen. *(1996 MAPes MONDe Ltd.)*

enchantments . . . on account of the great towers and cues [temples] and buildings rising from the water, and all built of masonry." Some soldiers asked, he remembered, "whether the things that we saw were not a dream."

The Spaniards came to Tenochtitlán not only with horses and steel weapons but also with smallpox, bringing an epidemic that had begun on Hispaniola. The disease peaked in 1520, fatally weakening Tenochtitlán's defenders. "It spread over the people as great destruction," as elderly Aztec later remembered. "Some it quite covered [with pustules] on all parts—their faces, their heads, their breasts. . . . There was great havoc. Very many died of it." Largely as a consequence, Tenochtitlán surrendered in 1521, and the Spaniards built Mexico City on its site. Cortés and his men seized a fabulous treasure of gold and silver. Thus, not long after Columbus's first voyage, the Spanish monarchs—who treated the American territories as their personal possessions—controlled the richest, most extensive empire Europe had known since ancient Rome.

Spain established the model of colonization that other countries later attempted to imitate, a model with three major elements. First, the Crown tried to maintain tight control over the colonies, imposing a hierarchical government that allowed little autonomy to American jurisdictions. That control included, for example, carefully vetting prospective emigrants and limiting their number, and insisting that the colonies import all their manufactured

### Spanish Colonization

goods from Spain. In order to encourage social stability, those settlers were then required to live in towns under the authorities' watchful eyes. Roman Catholic priests attempted to ensure the colonists' conformity with orthodox religious views.

Second, men constituted most of the first colonists. Although some Spanish women later immigrated to America, the men took primarily Indian—and, later, African—women as their wives or concubines, a development more often than not encouraged by colonial administrators. They thereby began creating the racially mixed population that characterizes much of Latin America to the present day.

Third, the colonies' wealth was based on the exploitation of both the native population and slaves imported from Africa. The Mesoamerican peoples were accustomed to autocratic rule. Spaniards simply took over the role once assumed by native leaders, who had exacted labor and tribute from their subjects. Cortés established the *encomienda system,* which granted Indian villages to individual conquistadors as a reward for their services, thus legalizing slavery in all but name.

In 1542, after an outcry from sympathetic Spaniards, a new code of laws reformed the system, forbidding the conquerors from enslaving Indians while still allowing them to collect money and goods from tributary villages. In response to the restrictions and to the declining Indian population, the *encomenderos,* familiar with slavery in Spain, began to import Africans in order to increase the labor force under their direct control. They employed Indians and Africans primarily in gold and silver mines, on sugar plantations, and on huge horse, cattle, and sheep ranches. African slavery was far more common in the Greater Antilles (the major Caribbean islands) than on the mainland.

Many demoralized residents of Mesoamerica accepted the Christian religion brought to New Spain by friars of the Franciscan and Dominican orders. The friars devoted their energies to persuading Mesoamerican people to move into towns and to build Roman Catholic churches. Spaniards leveled existing cities, constructing cathedrals and monasteries on sites once occupied by Aztec, Incan, and Mayan temples. In such towns, Indians were exposed to European customs and religious rituals designed to assimilate Catholic and pagan beliefs. Friars deliberately juxtaposed the cult of the Virgin Mary with that of the corn goddess, and the Indians adeptly melded aspects of their traditional world-view with Christianity, in a process called syncretism. Thousands of Indians residing in Spanish territory embraced Catholicism, at least partly because it was the religion of their new rulers and they were accustomed to obedience.

The New World's gold and silver, initially a boon, ultimately brought about the decline of Spain as a major

### Gold, Silver, and Spain's Decline

power. China, a huge country with silver coinage, insatiably demanded Spanish silver, gobbling up an estimated half of the total output of New World mines while paying twice the price current in Europe. Especially after the Spanish began in the 1570s to dispatch silver-laden galleons annually from Acapulco (on Mexico's west coast) to trade at their new settlement at Manila, in the Philippines, Spaniards acquired easy access to luxury Chinese goods, such as silk and Asian spices.

The influx of unprecedented wealth led to rapid inflation, which (among other adverse effects) caused Spanish products to be overpriced in international markets and imported goods to become cheaper in Spain. The once-profitable Spanish textile-manufacturing industry collapsed, as did scores of other businesses. The seemingly endless income from American colonies emboldened successive Spanish monarchs to spend lavishly on wars against the Dutch and the English. Several times in the late sixteenth and early seventeenth centuries the monarchs repudiated the state debt, wreaking havoc on the nation's finances. When the South American gold and silver mines started to give out in the mid-seventeenth century, Spain's economy crumbled and the nation lost its international importance.

## THE COLUMBIAN EXCHANGE

A broad mutual transfer of diseases, plants, and animals (called the Columbian Exchange by historian Alfred Crosby; see Figure 1.1) resulted directly from the European voyages of the fifteenth and sixteenth centuries and from Spanish colonization. The Eastern and Western Hemispheres had evolved separately for thousands of years, developing widely different forms of life. Many large mammals, such as cattle and horses, were native to the connected continents of Europe, Asia, and Africa, but the Americas contained no domesticated beasts larger than dogs and llamas. The vegetable crops of the Americas—particularly maize, beans, squash, cassava, and potatoes—were more nutritious and produced higher yields than those of Europe and Africa, such as wheat, millet, and rye. In time, native peoples learned to raise and consume European livestock, and Europeans and Africans became accustomed to planting and eating American crops. The diets of all three peoples were consequently vastly enriched. Partly as a result, the world's population doubled over the next three hundred years. About three-fifths of all crops cultivated in the world today were first grown in the Americas.

Diseases carried from Europe and Africa, though, had a devastating impact on the Americas. Indians fell

### Smallpox and Other Diseases

victim to microbes that had long infested the other continents and had repeatedly killed hundreds of thousands but had also often left survivors with some measure of immunity. The statistics are staggering. When Columbus landed on Hispaniola in 1492, approximately half a million people resided there. Fifty years later, that island had fewer than two thousand native inhabitants. Within thirty years of the first landfall at Guanahaní, not one Taíno survived in the Bahamas.

Although measles, typhus, influenza, malaria, and other illnesses severely afflicted the native peoples, as at Tenochtitlán the greatest killer was smallpox, spread primarily by direct human contact. Overall, historians estimate that the long-term effects of the alien microorganisms could have reduced the precontact American population by as much as 90 percent. The epidemics recurred at twenty- to thirty-year intervals, frequently appearing either in tandem or in quick succession, so that weakened survivors of one would be felled by a second or third. Large numbers of deaths also disrupted societies already undergoing severe strains caused by colonization, thus rendering native peoples more vulnerable to droughts, crop failures, or other challenging circumstances.

Even far to the north, where smaller American populations encountered only a few Europeans, disease also ravaged the countryside. A great epidemic, probably viral hepatitis, swept through the villages along the coast north of Cape Cod from 1616 to 1618. Again the mortality rate may have been as high as 90 percent. An English traveler several years later commented that the people had "died on heaps, as they lay in their houses," and that bones and skulls covered the ruins of villages. Because of

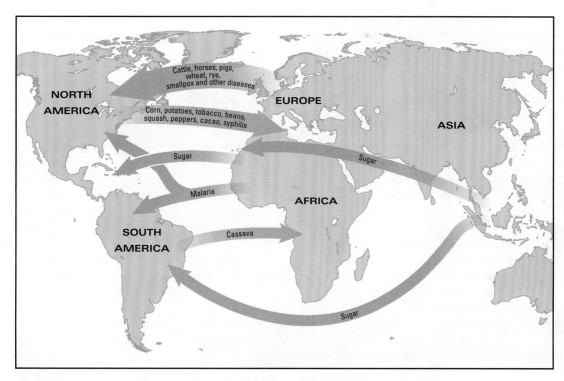

**Figure 1.1    Major Items in the Columbian Exchange**
As European adventurers traversed the world in the fifteenth and sixteenth centuries, they initiated the "Columbian Exchange" of plants, animals, and diseases. These events changed the lives of the peoples of the world forever, bringing new foods and new pestilence to both sides of the Atlantic.

▲ A male effigy dating from 200–800 C.E., found in a burial site in Nayarit, Mexico. The lesions covering the figurine suggest that the person it represents is suffering from syphilis, which, untreated, produces these characteristic markings on the body in its later stages. Such evidence as this pre-Columbian effigy has now convinced most scholars that syphilis originated in the Americas—a hypothesis in dispute for many years.    *(Typ 565.42.409F [B] p.825, Department of Printing and Graphic Arts, Houghton Library, Harvard College Library)*

this dramatic depopulation of the area, just a few years later English colonists were able to establish settlements virtually unopposed.

The Americans, though, seem to have taken a revenge of sorts. They probably gave the Europeans syphilis, a virulent venereal disease. The first recorded European case of the new ailment occurred in Barcelona, Spain, in 1493, shortly after Columbus's return from the Caribbean. Although less likely than smallpox to cause immediate death, syphilis was dangerous and debilitating. Carried by soldiers, sailors, and prostitutes, it spread quickly through Europe and Asia, reaching as far as China by 1505.

The exchange of three commodities had significant impacts on Europe and the Americas. Sugar, which was first domesticated in the East Indies, was being grown on the islands of the Mediterranean Atlantic by 1450. The ravenous European demand for sugar—which, after initially being regarded as a medicine, became a desirable luxury foodstuff—led Columbus to take Canary Island

## Sugar, Horses, and Tobacco

▲ A Spanish map from 1519 showing the coast of Hispaniola, focusing on what is now the modern nation of Haiti. The decorative figures, shown with tools for hunting and cultivation, appear to be African slaves imported as laborers to replace the Indian population, already being rapidly depleted by disease and mistreatment. *(Bibliothèque Nationale)*

sugar canes to Hispaniola on his 1493 voyage. By the 1520s, plantations in the Greater Antilles worked by African slaves regularly shipped cargoes of sugar to Spain. Half a century later, the Portuguese colony in Brazil (founded 1532) was producing sugar for the European market on an even larger scale, and after 1640 (see pages 40–41), sugar cultivation became the crucial component of English and French colonization in the Caribbean.

Horses—which, like sugar, were brought to America by Columbus in 1493—fell into the hands of North American Indians during the seventeenth century. Through trade and theft, horses spread among the peoples of the Great Plains, reaching most areas by 1750. Lakotas, Comanches, and Crows, among others, came to use horses for transportation and hunting, calculated their wealth

in number of horses owned, and waged war primarily on horseback. Women no longer had to carry the band's belongings on their backs. Some groups that previously had cultivated crops abandoned agriculture. Because of the acquisition of horses, a mode of subsistence that had been based on hunting several different animals, in combination with gathering and agriculture, became one focused almost wholly on hunting buffalo.

In America, Europeans encountered tobacco, which at first they believed to have beneficial medicinal effects. Smoking and chewing the "Indian weed" became a fad in Europe after it was planted in Turkey in the sixteenth century. Despite the efforts of such skeptics as King James I of England, who in 1604 pronounced smoking "loathsome to the eye, hatefull to the Nose, harmfull to the brain, [and]

# Maize

aize, to Mesoamericans, was a gift from Quetzalcoatl, the plumed serpent god. Cherokees told of an old woman whose blood produced the prized stalks after her grandson buried her body in a cleared, sunny field. For the Abenakis, the crop began when a beautiful maiden ordered a youth to drag her by the hair through a burned-over field. The long hair of the Cherokee grandmother and the Abenaki maiden turned into silk, the flower on the stalks that Europeans called Indian corn. Both tales' symbolic association of corn and women intriguingly supports archaeologists' recent suggestion that—in eastern North America at least—female plant breeders were responsible for substantial improvements in the productivity of maize.

Sacred to all the Indian peoples who grew it, maize was a cereal crop, a main part of their diet. They dried the kernels; ground into meal, maize was cooked as a mush or shaped into baked flat cakes, the forerunners of modern tortillas. Indians also heated the dried kernels until they popped open, just as is done today. Although the European invaders of North and South America initially disdained maize, they soon learned that it could be cultivated in a wide variety of conditions—from sea level to twelve thousand feet, from regions with abundant rainfall to dry lands with as little as twelve inches of rain a year. Corn was also highly productive, yielding almost twice as many calories per acre as wheat. So Europeans, too, came to rely on corn, growing it not only in their American settlements but also in their homelands.

Maize cultivation spread to Asia and Africa. Today China is second only to the United States in total corn production, and corn is more widely grown in Africa than any other crop. Still, the United States produces 45 percent of the world's corn—almost half of it in the three states of Illinois, Iowa, and Nebraska—and corn is the nation's single largest crop. More than half of American corn is consumed by livestock. Much of the rest is processed into syrup, which sweetens carbonated beverages and candies, or into ethanol, a gasoline additive that reduces both pollution and dependence on fossil fuels. Corn is an ingredient in light beer and toothpaste. It is used in the manufacture of tires, wallpaper, cat litter, and aspirin. Remarkably, of the ten thousand products in a modern American grocery store, about one-fourth rely to some extent on corn.

Today this crop bequeathed to the world by ancient American plant breeders provides one-fifth of all the calories consumed by the earth's peoples. The gift of Quetzalcoatl has linked the globe.

▲ **The earliest known European drawing of maize, the American plant that was to have such an extraordinary impact on the entire world.** *(Typ 565.42.409F [B] Department of Printing and Graphic Arts, Houghton Library, Harvard College Library)*

dangerous to the Lungs," tobacco's popularity climbed. Its addictive nicotine and its connection to lung cancer were discovered only in the twentieth century.

The European and African invasion of the Americas therefore had a significant biological component, for the invaders carried plants and animals with them. Some creatures, such as livestock, they brought deliberately. Others, including rats (which infested their ships), weeds, and diseases, arrived unexpectedly. And the same process occurred in reverse. When the Europeans returned home, they deliberately took back such crops as maize, potatoes, and tobacco, along with that unanticipated stowaway, syphilis.

## EUROPEANS IN NORTH AMERICA

Europeans were initially more interested in exploiting North America's natural resources than in the difficult task of establishing colonies there. John Cabot had reported that fish were extraordinarily plentiful near Newfoundland, so Europeans rushed to take advantage of abundant codfish, which were in great demand in their homelands as an inexpensive source of protein. The French, Spanish, and Portuguese dispatched vessels regularly to Newfoundland's waters throughout the sixteenth century. In the early 1570s, after Spain opened its markets to English shipping, the English (who previously had fished near Iceland for home consumption only) eagerly joined the Newfoundland fishery, thereafter selling salt cod to the Spanish in exchange for valuable Asian goods. The English soon became dominant in the region, which by the end of the century was the focal point of a European commerce more valuable than that with the Gulf of Mexico.

Fishermen quickly realized that they could increase their profits by exchanging cloth and metal goods, such as pots and knives, for native trappers' beaver pelts, used to make fashionable hats in Europe. Initially, Europeans traded from ships sailing along the coast, but later they set up outposts on the mainland to centralize and control the traffic in furs. Such outposts were inhabited chiefly by male adventurers, whose major aim was to send as many pelts as possible home to Europe.

**Trade Among Indians and Europeans**

The Europeans' demand for furs, especially beaver, was matched by the Indians' desire for European goods that could make their lives easier and establish their superiority over their neighbors. Some bands began to concentrate so completely on trapping for the European market that they abandoned their traditional economies. The Abenakis of Maine, for example, became partially dependent on food supplied by their neighbors to the south, the Massachusett tribe, because they devoted most of their energies to catching beaver to sell to French traders. The Massachusetts, in turn, intensified their production of foodstuffs, which they traded to the Abenakis in exchange for the European metal tools that they preferred to their own handmade stone implements. The intensive trade in pelts also had serious ecological consequences. In some regions beavers were wiped out. The disappearance of their dams led to soil erosion, which increased when European settlers cleared forests for farmland in later decades.

English merchants and political leaders watched enviously as Spain was enriched by its valuable American possessions. In the mid-sixteenth century, English "sea dogs" like John Hawkins and Sir Francis Drake began to raid Spanish treasure fleets sailing home from the Caribbean. Their actions caused friction between the two countries and helped foment a war that in 1588 culminated in the defeat of a huge invasion force—the Spanish Armada—off the English coast. As part of the contest with Spain, English leaders started to think about planting colonies in the Western Hemisphere, thereby gaining better access to valuable trade goods while simultaneously preventing their enemy from dominating the Americas.

**Contest Between Spain and England**

The first English colonial planners saw Spain's possessions as a model and a challenge. They hoped to reproduce Spanish successes by dispatching to America men who would exploit the native peoples for their own and their nation's benefit. In the mid-1570s, a group that included Sir Walter Raleigh began to promote a scheme to establish outposts that could trade with the Indians and provide bases for attacks on New Spain. Approving the idea, Queen Elizabeth I authorized Raleigh to colonize North America.

After two preliminary expeditions, in 1587 Sir Walter Raleigh sent 117 colonists to the territory he named Virginia, after Elizabeth, the "Virgin Queen." They established a settlement on Roanoke Island, in what is now North Carolina, but in 1590 a resupply ship—delayed in leaving England because of the Spanish Armada—could not find them. The colonists had vanished, leaving only the word *Croatoan* (the name of a nearby island) carved on a tree. Recent tree-ring studies have shown that the North Carolina coast experienced a severe drought between 1587 and 1589, which would have created a subsistence crisis for the settlers and could well have led them to abandon the Roanoke site.

**Roanoke**

▲ A watercolor by John White, an artist with Raleigh's second preliminary expedition (and who later was governor of the ill-fated 1587 colony). He identified his subjects as the wife and daughter of the chief of Pomeioc, a village near Roanoke. Note the woman's elaborate tattoos and the fact that the daughter carries an Elizabethan doll, obviously given to her by one of the Englishmen. *(©Trustees of the British Museum)*

Thus England's first attempt to plant a permanent settlement on the North American coast failed, as had similar efforts by Portugal on Cape Breton Island (early 1520s) and France in northern Florida (mid-1560s). All three enterprises collapsed because of the hostility of neighboring peoples and colonists' inability to be self-sustaining in foodstuffs. Spanish soldiers wiped out the French colony in 1565 (see page 35), and neither the Portuguese nor the English were able to maintain friendly relations with local Indians.

The explanation for such failings becomes clear in Thomas Harriot's *A Briefe and True Report of the New Found Land of Virginia,* published in 1588 to publicize Raleigh's colony. Harriot, a noted scientist who sailed with the second of the preliminary voyages to Roanoke, described the animals, plants, and people of the region for an English readership. His account revealed that, although the explorers depended on nearby villagers for most of their food, they needlessly antagonized their neighbors by killing some of them for what Harriot himself admitted were unjustifiable reasons.

## Harriot's *Briefe and True Report*

The scientist advised later colonizers to deal with the native peoples of America more humanely than his comrades had. But the content of his book suggested why that advice would rarely be followed. *A Briefe and True Report* examined the possibilities for economic development in America. Harriot stressed three points: the availability of commodities familiar to Europeans, such as grapes, iron, copper, and fur-bearing animals; the potential profitability of exotic American products, such as maize, cassava, and tobacco; and the relative ease of manipulating the native population to the Europeans' advantage. Should the Americans attempt to resist the English by force, Harriot asserted, the latter's advantages of disciplined soldiers and superior weaponry would quickly deliver victory.

Harriot's *Briefe and True Report* depicted for his English readers a bountiful land full of opportunities for quick profit. The people residing there would, he thought, "in a short time be brought to civilitie" through conversion to Christianity, admiration for European superiority, or conquest—if they did not die from disease, the ravages of which he witnessed. Thomas Harriot understood the key elements of the story, but his prediction was far off the mark. European dominance of North America would be difficult to achieve. Indeed, it never was fully achieved, in the sense Harriot and his compatriots intended.

## *Legacy* FOR A PEOPLE AND A NATION

### Kennewick Man/Ancient One

On July 28, 1996, Will Thomas, a college student wading in the Columbia River near Kennewick, Washington, felt something round underfoot. Shocked when he realized it was a skull, Thomas initially believed he had found a recent murder victim. Yet soon the antiquity of Thomas's find had been determined: it was about 9,200 years old. During the next decade, the skeleton dubbed "Kennewick Man" (by the press) or "Ancient One" (by local Indian tribes) was featured on CBS television's *60 Minutes* (October 1998), in *National Geographic* (December 2000), in a *Time* cover story (March 2006), and in several documentary films. The oldest nearly complete skeleton found in the United States, the remains became the subject of a major federal court case and numerous books and articles.

At issue in the lawsuit was the interpretation of the Native American Graves Protection and Repatriation Act (NAGPRA), adopted by Congress in 1990 to prevent the desecration of Indian gravesites and to provide for the return of bones and sacred objects to native peoples. It defined the term *Native American* as "of, or relating to, a tribe, people, or culture that is indigenous to the United States." Tribes in the area, led by the Umatillas, prepared to reclaim and rebury the remains with appropriate rituals. But then eight anthropologists filed suit in federal court, contending that bones of such antiquity were unlikely to be linked to modern tribes and requesting access to them for scientific study.

Although the U.S. government supported the tribes' claims, in late August 2002 a federal judge ruled in favor of the anthropologists, in a decision upheld on appeal two years later. He declared that the Interior Department had erred in concluding that all pre-1492 remains found in the United States should automatically be considered Native American under the NAGPRA definition. The Umatillas protested his decision, contending that it clearly contradicted Congress's intent in enacting NAGPRA and that "this treatment of Native American remains as scientific specimens deprives native people of the basic right to properly bury or care for these ancestors." In June 2006 Umatilla leaders visited the bones at a Seattle museum, where they were under study, to honor and pray for them.

The debate over the skeleton known alternately as Kennewick Man and Ancient One reveals one facet of the continuing legacy to the nation of the often-contentious relationship between its indigenous inhabitants and later immigrants.

## SUMMARY

The process of initial contact among Europeans, Africans, and Americans that ended with Thomas Harriot near the close of the sixteenth century began approximately 250 years earlier when Portuguese sailors first set out to explore the Mediterranean Atlantic and the West African coast. Those seamen established commercial ties that brought African slaves first to Iberia and then to the islands the Europeans conquered and settled. The Mediterranean Atlantic and its island sugar plantations nurtured the mariners who, like Christopher Columbus, ventured into previously unknown waters—those who sailed to India and Brazil as well as to the Caribbean and the North American coast. When Columbus first reached the Americas, he thought he had found Asia, his intended destination. Later explorers knew better but, except for the Spanish, regarded the Americas primarily as a barrier that prevented them from reaching their long-sought goal of an oceanic route to the riches of China and the Moluccas. Ordinary European fishermen were the first to realize that the northern coasts had valuable products to offer: fish and furs, both much in demand in their homelands.

The Aztecs had predicted that their Fifth Sun would end in earthquakes and hunger. Hunger they surely experienced after Cortés's invasion, and even if there were no earthquakes, their great temples tumbled to the ground nevertheless, as the Spaniards used their stones (and Indian laborers) to construct cathedrals honoring their God and his Son, Jesus, rather than Huitzilopochtli. The conquerors employed, first, American and, later, enslaved African workers to till the fields, mine the precious metals, and herd the livestock that earned immense profits for themselves and their mother country.

The initial impact of Europeans on the Americas proved devastating. Flourishing civilizations were markedly altered in just a few short decades. Europeans' diseases killed millions of the Western Hemisphere's inhabitants; and their livestock, along with a wide range of other imported animals and plants, irrevocably modified the American environment. Europe, too, was changed: American foodstuffs like corn and potatoes improved nutrition throughout the continent, and American gold and silver first enriched, then ruined, the Spanish economy.

By the end of the sixteenth century, fewer people resided in North America than had lived there before Columbus's arrival, even taking into account the arrival of many Europeans and Africans. And the people who did live there—Indian, African, and European—resided in a world that was indeed new—a world engaged in the unprecedented process of combining foods, religions, economies, ways of life, and political systems that had developed separately for millennia. Understandably, conflict and dissension permeated that process.

## SUGGESTIONS FOR FURTHER READING

Alfred W. Crosby, *The Columbian Exchange: Biological and Cultural Consequences of 1492* (1972)

John H. Elliott, *Empires of the Atlantic World: Britain and Spain in America, 1492–1830* (2006)

Alvin Josephy, Jr., ed., *America in 1492* (1992)

Charles C. Mann, *1491: New Revelations of the Americas Before Columbus* (2005)

D. W. Meinig, *Atlantic America, 1492–1800* (1986)

Samuel Eliot Morison, *The European Discovery of America: The Southern Voyages, A.D. 1492–1616* (1974); *The Northern Voyages, A.D. 1500–1600* (1971)

John Thornton, *Africa and Africans in the Making of the Atlantic World, 1400–1680* (1992)

*For a more extensive list for further reading, go to* college.hmco.com/pic/norton8e.

*C*aptain William Rudyerd seemed like the sort of man any Puritan colony in the Americas would prize, so when his older brother urged the planners of the new settlement to appoint him muster master general, they readily agreed. Rudyerd, a veteran of wars on the European continent, followed the new dissenting English faith, as did the planners and many of the settlers. In the first years of the colony, Rudyerd proved to be a vigorous soldier who worked hard to train the settlers to defend themselves from attack. But he also proved to be a vigorous defender of his own status, and his actions wreaked havoc in the fragile community. The captain beat to death a servant suffering from scurvy (Rudyerd thought the servant was merely lazy) and quarreled continually with other settlers, whom he believed failed to show the proper respect to a gentleman of noble birth.

One of Rudyerd's antagonists was the Reverend Lewis Morgan, with whom the captain argued about religious books and the conduct of church services. Rudyerd, traditional minded despite his Puritan beliefs, found Morgan's encouragement of congregational psalm singing scandalously radical. Their disagreements quickly escalated into exchanges of insults. "Your foul mouthed answer deserves rather sharp retribution than any equal respect from A gentleman," the captain once haughtily told the clergyman; "I have given you too Much respect; which has begot so much incivility."

Similar conflicts occurred in all the Anglo-American settlements, as gentlemen accustomed to unquestioning deference learned to their dismay that in a colonial setting their inherited social standing could be challenged by various upstarts. But in Rudyerd and Morgan's colony the disputes were especially dangerous, because the two lived on Providence Island, an isolated Puritan outpost off the coast of modern Nicaragua.

◀ This early eighteenth-century British map of the Caribbean and Central America vividly illustrates the precarious position of the seventeenth-century Providence Island settlers, on their tiny island surrounded by Spanish territory on the mainland to the east, south, and west, and the Spanish-dominated Greater Antilles to the north. *(Colonial Williamsburg Foundation)*

# CHRONOLOGY

1533 ■ Henry VIII divorces Catherine of Aragón
     ■ English Reformation begins

1558 ■ Elizabeth I becomes queen

1565 ■ Founding of St. Augustine (Florida), oldest permanent European settlement in present-day United States

1598 ■ Oñate conquers Pueblos in New Mexico for Spain

1603 ■ James I becomes king

1607 ■ Jamestown founded, first permanent English settlement in North America

1608 ■ Quebec founded by the French

1610 ■ Founding of Santa Fe, New Mexico

1611 ■ First Virginia tobacco crop

1614 ■ Fort Orange (Albany) founded by the Dutch

1619 ■ Virginia House of Burgesses established, first representative assembly in the English colonies

1620 ■ Plymouth colony founded, first permanent English settlement in New England

1622 ■ Powhatan Confederacy attacks Virginia

1624 ■ Dutch settle on Manhattan Island (New Amsterdam)
     ■ English colonize St. Kitts, first island in Lesser Antilles to be settled by Europeans
     ■ James I revokes Virginia Company's charter

1625 ■ Charles I becomes king

1630 ■ Massachusetts Bay colony founded

1634 ■ Maryland founded

1636 ■ Williams expelled from Massachusetts Bay, founds Providence, Rhode Island
     ■ Connecticut founded

1637 ■ Pequot War in New England

1638 ■ Hutchinson expelled from Massachusetts Bay, goes to Rhode Island

c. 1640 ■ Sugar cultivation begins on Barbados

1642 ■ Montreal founded by the French

1646 ■ Treaty ends hostilities between Virginia and Powhatan Confederacy

Providence Island, founded by a company of Puritan adventurers in 1630—the same year as the Massachusetts Bay colony—sought to establish an English beachhead in the fertile tropics, which could lead to successful colonization of the Central American mainland. Yet the outpost's perilous location amid Spanish settlements, its failure to establish a viable local economy, and, ultimately, its desperate attempts to stay afloat financially by serving as a base for English privateers caused its downfall. That decision led the Spaniards to conclude that the Puritans *had* to be removed. Twice, in 1635 and 1640, Providence Island fended off Spanish attacks. But in May 1641 a large Spanish fleet of seven ships carrying two thousand soldiers and sailors captured the island, and the survivors scattered to other Caribbean settlements, to English colonies on the mainland, or back to England.

By this time, though, Spain no longer predominated in the Americas. France, the Netherlands, and England all had permanent colonies in North America by the 1640s. The French and Dutch colonies, like the Spanish outposts, were settled largely by European men who interacted regularly with indigenous peoples, using their labor or seeking to convert them to Christianity. Like the conquistadors, French and Dutch merchants (on the mainland) and planters (in the Caribbean) hoped to make a quick profit and then perhaps return to their homelands. The English, as Thomas Harriot had made clear in the 1580s, were just as interested in profiting from North America. But they pursued those profits in a different way.

In contrast to other Europeans, most of the English settlers—including those of the failed Providence Island colony—came to America intending to stay. Along the northeast Atlantic coast of the continent, in the area that came to be known as New England, they arrived in family groups, sometimes accompanied by friends and relatives from neighboring villages back home. They re-created the European agricultural economy and family life to an extent impossible in the other colonies, where single men predominated. English colonies in the Chesapeake region and on the Caribbean islands, though, came to be based on large-scale agricultural production for the international market by a labor force composed of bonded servants and slaves.

Wherever they settled, the English, like other Europeans, prospered only after they learned to adapt to the alien environment, something the Providence Islanders never achieved. The first permanent English colonies survived because of contacts with nearby Indians. The settlers had to learn to grow such unfamiliar American crops as maize and squash. They also had to develop extensive trading relationships with native peoples and with colonies established by other European countries. Needing laborers for their fields, they first used English indentured servants, then later began to import African slaves, copying the example of the Spanish in the Atlantic and Caribbean islands, and the Portuguese in São Tomé and Brazil. Thus the early history of the region that became the United States and the English Caribbean is best understood not as an isolated story of English colonization but rather as a series of complex interactions among a variety of European, African, and American peoples and environments.

- Why did different groups of Europeans choose to migrate to the Americas?
- How did different native peoples react to their presence?
- In what ways did the English colonies in the Chesapeake and New England differ, and in what ways were they alike?

## SPANISH, FRENCH, AND DUTCH NORTH AMERICA

Spaniards established the first permanent European settlement within the boundaries of the modern United States, but others had initially attempted that feat. Twice in the 1560s Huguenots (French Protestants), who were seeking to escape persecution, planted colonies on the south Atlantic coast. A passing ship rescued the starving survivors of the first, located in present-day South Carolina. The second, near modern Jacksonville, Florida, was destroyed in 1565 by a Spanish expedition under the command of Pedro Menéndez de Avilés. To ensure Spanish domination of the strategically important region (located near sea-lanes used by Spanish treasure ships bound for Europe), Menéndez set up a small fortified outpost, which he named St. Augustine—now the oldest continuously inhabited European settlement in the United States.

The local Guale and Timucua nations initially allied themselves with the powerful newcomers and welcomed Franciscan friars into their villages. The relationship did not remain peaceful for long, though, for the natives resisted the imposition of Spanish authority. Still, the Franciscans offered the Indians spiritual solace for the diseases and troubles besetting them after the Europeans' invasion, and eventually they gained numerous converts at missions that stretched westward across Florida and northward into the islands along the Atlantic coast.

More than thirty years passed after the founding of St. Augustine before conquistadors ventured anew into the present-day United States. In 1598, drawn northward by rumors of rich cities, Juan de Oñate, a Mexican-born adventurer, led a group of about five hundred soldiers and settlers to New Mexico. At first, the Pueblo peoples greeted the newcomers cordially. But when the Spaniards began to use torture, murder, and rape to extort food and clothing from the villagers, the residents of Acoma killed several soldiers, among them Oñate's nephew, Juan de Zaldívar. The invaders responded ferociously, killing more than eight hundred people and

### New Mexico

▲ The women of Acoma pueblo have long been accomplished potters. Before the arrival of Europeans with iron utensils, residents of the pueblo stored food and water in pots like this. The unusual shape derived from its function: the low center of gravity allowed a woman to balance the pot easily on her head as she carried water from a cistern to the top of the mesa. *(The Field Museum, #A109998c)*

capturing the remainder. All the captives above the age of twelve were ordered enslaved for twenty years, and men older than twenty-five had one foot amputated. Not surprisingly, the other Pueblo villages surrendered.

Yet Oñate's bloody victory proved illusory, for New Mexico held little wealth. It also was too far from the Pacific coast to assist in protecting Spanish sea-lanes, which had been one of Oñate's aims (he, like others, initially believed the continent to be much narrower than it actually is). Many of the Spaniards returned to Mexico, but horses remained, transforming the lives of the indigenous inhabitants. Officials considered abandoning the isolated colony, which lay 800 miles north of the nearest Spanish settlement. Still, for defensive purposes the authorities decided to maintain a small military outpost and a few Christian missions in the area, with the capital at Santa Fe (founded in 1610) (see Map 3.3). As in regions to the south, Spanish leaders were granted *encomiendas* guaranteeing them control over the labor of Pueblo villagers. But in the absence of mines or fertile agricultural lands, such grants yielded small profit.

On the Atlantic coast, the French turned their attention northward, to the area that Jacques Cartier had explored in the 1530s. Several times they tried to establish permanent bases along the Canadian coast but failed until 1605, when they founded Port Royal. Then in 1608 Samuel de Champlain set up a trading post at an interior site that the local Iroquois had called Stadacona when Cartier spent the winter there seventy-five years earlier. Champlain renamed it Quebec. He had chosen well: Quebec was the most defensible spot in the entire St. Lawrence River valley, a stronghold that controlled access to the heartland of the continent. In 1642 the French established a second post, Montreal, at the falls of the St. Lawrence (and thus at the end of navigation by oceangoing vessels), a place the Indians called Hochelaga.

**Quebec and Montreal**

Before the founding of these settlements, fishermen served as the major transporters of North American beaver pelts to France, but the new posts quickly took over control of the lucrative trade in furs (see Table 2.1). Only a few Europeans resided in New France; most were men, some of whom married Indian women. The colony's leaders gave land grants along the river to wealthy seigneurs (nobles), who then imported tenants to work their farms. A small number of Frenchmen brought their wives and took up agriculture; even so, more than twenty-five years after Quebec's founding, it had just sixty-four resident families, along with traders and soldiers. With respect to territory occupied and farmed, northern New France never grew much beyond the confines of the river valley between Quebec and Montreal (see Map 2.1). Thus it differed significantly from New Spain, characterized by scattered cities and direct supervision of Indian laborers.

**Jesuit Missions in New France**

Missionaries of the Society of Jesus (Jesuits), a Roman Catholic order dedicated to converting nonbelievers to Christianity, also came to New France. First arriving in Quebec in 1625, the Jesuits, whom the Indians called Black Robes, tried to persuade indigenous peoples to live near French settlements and to adopt European agricultural methods. When that effort failed, the Jesuits concluded

| TABLE 2.1 | The Founding of Permanent European Colonies in North America, 1565–1640 | | |
|---|---|---|---|
| **Colony** | **Founder(s)** | **Date** | **Basis of Economy** |
| Florida | Pedro Menéndez de Avilés | 1565 | Farming |
| New Mexico | Juan de Oñate | 1598 | Livestock |
| Virginia | Virginia Co. | 1607 | Tobacco |
| New France | France | 1608 | Fur trading |
| New Netherland | Dutch West India Co. | 1614 | Fur trading |
| Plymouth | Separatists | 1620 | Farming, fishing |
| Maine | Sir Ferdinando Gorges | 1622 | Fishing |
| St. Kitts, Barbados, et al. | European immigrants | 1624 | Sugar |
| Massachusetts Bay | Massachusetts Bay Company | 1630 | Farming, fishing, fur trading |
| Maryland | Cecilius Calvert | 1634 | Tobacco |
| Rhode Island | Roger Williams | 1636 | Farming |
| Connecticut | Thomas Hooker | 1636 | Farming, fur trading |
| New Haven | Massachusetts migrants | 1638 | Farming |
| New Hampshire | Massachusetts migrants | 1638 | Farming, fishing |

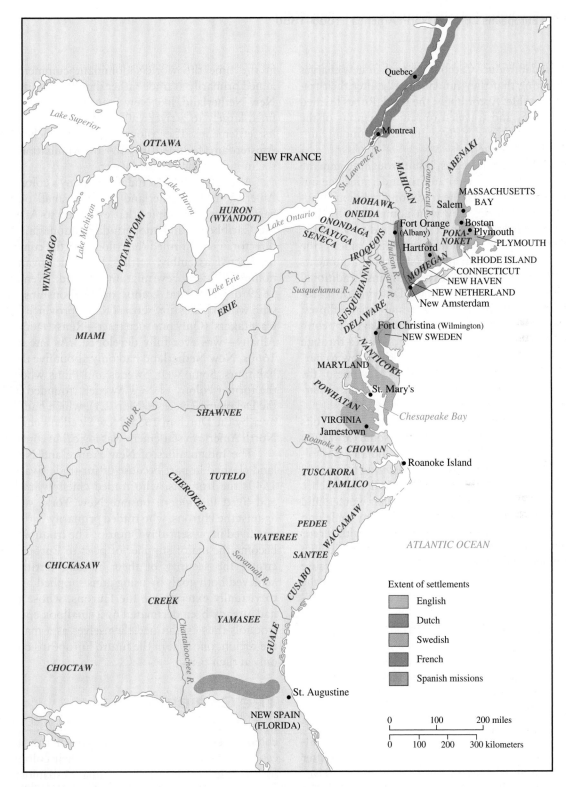

**Map 2.1    European Settlements and Indian Tribes in Eastern North America, 1650**

The few European settlements established in the East before 1650 were widely scattered, hugging the shores of the Atlantic Ocean and the banks of its major rivers. By contrast, America's native inhabitants controlled the vast interior expanse of the continent, and Spaniards had begun to move into the West.

that they could introduce Catholicism to their new charges without insisting that they fundamentally alter their traditional ways of life. Accordingly, the Black Robes learned Indian languages and traveled to remote regions of the interior, where they lived in twos and threes among hundreds of potential converts.

Using a variety of strategies, Jesuits sought to gain the confidence of influential men and to undermine the authority of village shamans, the traditional religious leaders. Trained in rhetoric, they won admirers with their eloquence. Immune to smallpox (for all had survived the disease already), they explained epidemics among the Indians as God's punishment for sin, their arguments aided by the ineffectiveness of the shamans' traditional remedies against the new pestilence. Drawing on European science, Jesuits predicted solar and lunar eclipses. Perhaps most important, they amazed the villagers by communicating with each other over long distances through marks on paper. The Indians' desire to learn how to harness the extraordinary power of literacy was one of the critical factors making them receptive to the missionaries' spiritual message.

Although the process took many years, the Jesuits slowly gained thousands of converts, some of whom moved to reserves set aside for Christian Indians. Catholicism offered women in particular the inspiring role model of the Virgin Mary, personified in Montreal and Quebec by communities of nuns who taught Indian women and children, and ministered to their needs. Many male and female converts followed Catholic teachings with fervor and piety, altering traditional native customs of allowing premarital sexual relationships and easy divorce, because Catholic doctrine prohibited both. Yet they resisted the Jesuits' attempts to have them adopt strict European child-rearing methods, instead retaining their more relaxed practices. Jesuits, unlike Franciscans in New Mexico, recognized that such aspects of native culture could be compatible with Christian beliefs. Their efforts to attract converts were further aided by their lack of interest in labor tribute or land acquisition.

Jesuit missionaries faced little competition from other Europeans for native peoples' souls, but French fur traders had to confront a direct challenge. In 1614, only five years after Henry Hudson explored the river that now bears his name, his sponsor, the Dutch West India Company, established an outpost (Fort Orange) on that river at the site of present-day Albany, New York. Like the French, the Dutch sought beaver pelts, and their presence so close to Quebec threatened French domination of the region. The Netherlands,

**New Netherland**

at the time the world's dominant commercial power, aimed primarily at trade rather than at colonization. Thus New Netherland, like New France, remained small, confined largely to a river valley that offered easy access to its settlements. The colony's southern anchor was New Amsterdam, founded in 1624 on Manhattan Island, at the mouth of the Hudson River.

As the Dutch West India Company's colony in North America, New Netherland was the small outpost of a vast commercial empire that extended to Africa, Brazil, the Caribbean, and modern-day Indonesia. Autocratic directors-general ruled the colony for the company; with no elected assembly, settlers felt little loyalty to their nominal leaders. Few migrants arrived. Even an offer in 1629 of large land grants, or patroonships, to people who would bring fifty settlers to the province failed to attract takers. (Only one such tract—Rensselaerswyck, near Albany—was ever fully developed.) As late as the mid-1660s, New Netherland had only about five thousand inhabitants. Some were Swedes and Finns who resided in the former colony of New Sweden (founded in 1638 on the Delaware River; see Map 2.1), which had been taken over by the Dutch in 1655. New Sweden's chief legacy to North American settlement was log cabin construction.

The Indian allies of New France and New Netherland clashed in part because of fur-trade rivalries. In the 1640s the Iroquois, who traded chiefly with the Dutch and lived in modern upstate New York, went to war against the Hurons, who traded primarily with the French and lived in present-day Ontario. The Iroquois wanted to become the major supplier of pelts to Europeans and to ensure the security of their hunting territories. They achieved both goals by using guns supplied by the Dutch to virtually exterminate the Hurons, whose population had already been decimated by a smallpox epidemic. The Iroquois thus established themselves as a major force in the region, one that in the future Europeans could ignore only at their peril.

## THE CARIBBEAN

In the Caribbean, France, the Netherlands, and England collided repeatedly in the first half of the seventeenth century. The Spanish concentrated their colonization efforts on the Greater Antilles—Cuba, Hispaniola, Jamaica, and Puerto Rico. They ignored many smaller islands, partly because of resistance by their Carib inhabitants, partly because the mainland offered greater wealth for less effort. But the tiny islands attracted other European powers: they could provide bases from which to attack Spanish vessels loaded with American gold and silver, and

## Wampum

When Europeans first came to North America, they quickly learned that native peoples highly valued small cylindrical beads made from whelk and quahog shells, known collectively as wampum. The white and purple beads had been strung on fibers for centuries to make necklaces and ornamental belts, but with the Europeans' arrival, wampum changed its character, becoming a currency widely employed by both groups.

The transformation of wampum occurred not only because the Indians prized it and would trade deerskins and beaver pelts to acquire the beads, but also because Dutch and English settlers lacked an equally handy medium of exchange. These settlers had limited access to currency from their homelands, yet they needed to do business with each other and with their native neighbors. Wampum filled a key need, especially in the first decades of settlement.

Whelk (white) and quahog (purple) shells were found primarily along the shores of Long Island Sound. Narragansetts, Montauks, Niantics, and other local peoples had long gathered the shells during the summers; women then fashioned the beads during the long northeastern winters. The shells were hard and brittle, so shaping them into hollow beads was a time-consuming task involving considerable skill. But Europeans' metal tools, including fine drills, allowed a rapid increase in the quantity and quality of wampum. Some villages gave up their hunter-gatherer modes of subsistence and settled permanently in shell-rich areas where they focused almost exclusively on the manufacture of wampum. What had been a seasonal task for women became their year-round work.

Wampum played a key role in the early economy of both New Netherland and New England. Dutch settlers in Manhattan traded such manufactured goods as guns and kettles, axes, or knives with the wampum makers, then transported wampum up the Hudson River to Fort Orange, where they used it to purchase furs and skins from the Iroquois. In 1627 Isaac de Rasière, a Dutch trader, introduced wampum to the English colonists at Plymouth when he offered it in exchange for corn. Ten years later, the Massachusetts Bay colony made wampum legal tender for the payment of debts under 12 pennies, at a rate of six white beads or three purple beads (which were rarer) to 1 penny. Wampum beads could be traded in loose handfuls but more often were strung on thin cords in set amounts worth English equivalents ranging from 1 penny to 5 shillings (60 pennies) in white beads, or 2 pennies to 10 shillings (120 pennies) in purple beads. People trading larger sums measured in wampum always feared being shortchanged. In 1660 one resident of New Netherland agreed to accept payment of a substantial debt in wampum only if his wife *personally* counted all the beads.

Wampum—originally with purely ornamental significance for its Indian makers—became an initial, indispensable link in the commerce between Europe and North America.

Before Europeans arrived in North America, wampum—requiring great skill to make—served primarily ceremonial purposes for native peoples, as in the "Four Huron Nations" wampum belt presented to Samuel de Champlain in 1611 to signify the alliance of France and the Hurons. But several decades later, after Dutch and English colonists came to rely on it as a medium of exchange and European tools made it easier to manufacture, wampum became far more utilitarian in design and appearance.

*(Below: American Museum of Natural History, photographed by Craig Chesek; Right: Musée de L'Homme)*

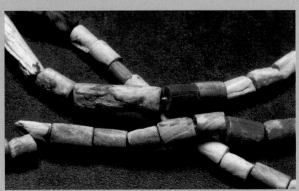

they could serve as sources of valuable tropical products such as dyes and fruits.

England was the first northern European nation to establish a permanent foothold in the smaller Caribbean islands (the Lesser Antilles), settling on St. Christopher (St. Kitts) in 1624, then later on other islands, such as Barbados (1627) and Providence (1630). France was able to colonize Guadeloupe and Martinique only by defeating the Caribs, whereas the Dutch more easily gained control of tiny St. Eustatius (strategically located near St. Kitts). In addition to indigenous inhabitants, Europeans had to worry about conflicts with Spaniards and with one another. Like Providence Island, many colonies changed hands during the seventeenth century. For example, the English drove the Spanish out of Jamaica in 1655, and the French soon thereafter took over half of Hispaniola, creating the colony of St. Domingue (modern Haiti).

## Warfare and Hurricanes

Another danger, too, confronted the new settlers: the great windstorms called by the Taíno people *hurakán*, or, in English, hurricanes. Just nine months after the establishment of the first English outpost on St Christopher, wrote one colonist, "came a Hericano and blew it away." Two years later, a second storm again devastated the infant colony, leaving the settlers "very miserable," without housing or adequate provisions. Almost every year in the late summer months one or two islands suffered significant damage from hurricanes. Survivors expressed awe at the destructive force of the storms, which repeatedly forced them to rebuild and replant. To withstand the winds, they designed one- or two-story brick and stone houses with low roofs and heavy wooden shutters over the windows.

Why did Europeans try to gain and retain control of such imperiled volcanic islands? The primary answer is sugar. Europeans loved sugar, which provided a sweet taste and a quick energy boost, and greatly

## Sugar Cultivation

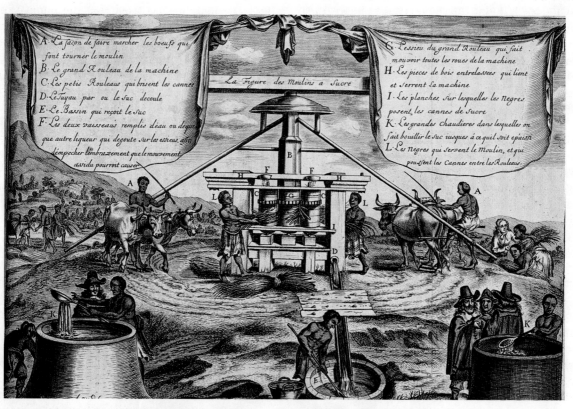

▲ In the 1660s, a French book illustrated the various phases of sugar processing for curious European readers. Teams of oxen (A) turned the mill, the rollers of which crushed the canes (C), producing the sap (D), which was collected in a vat (E), then boiled down into molasses (K). African slaves, with minimal supervision by a few Europeans (foreground), managed all phases of the process. *(Library Company of Philadelphia)*

enriched those who grew and processed it for international markets. Entering Europe in substantial quantities at approximately the same time as coffee and tea—the stimulating, addictive, and bitter Asian drinks improved by sweetening—sugar quickly became a crucial element of the European diet.

English residents of Barbados, after first experimenting with tobacco, cotton, and indigo, discovered in the early 1640s that the island's soil and climate were ideal for cultivating sugar cane. At the time, the world's supply of sugar came primarily from the Madeiras, the Canaries, São Tomé, and especially Brazil, where numerous farmers, each with a few servants or slaves, grew much of the crop. Sugar cane needed to be processed within two days of being harvested, or the juice would dry, so Brazilian producers quickly took their cane to central mills, where it was crushed, boiled down, and finally refined into brown and white sugars.

Barbadians, several of whom visited northeastern Brazil while it was briefly ruled by the Dutch in the 1630s and 1640s, initially copied both the Brazilians' machinery and their small-scale methods of production, which used an existing work force of servants and slaves. But—funded by wealthy English merchants and their own profits from raising tobacco and cotton—the more substantial planters expanded their enterprises dramatically by the mid-1650s. They increased the size of their landholdings, built their own sugar mills, and purchased growing numbers of laborers.

As other Caribbean planters embraced sugar-cane cultivation, Barbadians' profit margins were reduced. Even so, sugar remained the most valuable American commodity for more than one hundred years. In the eighteenth century, sugar grown by large gangs of slaves in British Jamaica and French St. Domingue dominated the world market. Yet, in the long run, the future economic importance of the Europeans' American colonies lay on the mainland rather than in the Caribbean.

# English Interest in Colonization

The failure of Raleigh's Roanoke colony ended English efforts to settle in North America for nearly two decades. When the English decided in 1606 to try once more, they again planned colonies that imitated the Spanish model. Yet, greater success came when they abandoned that model and founded settlements very different from those of other European powers. Unlike Spain, France, or the Netherlands, England eventually sent large numbers of men and women to set up agriculturally based colonies on the mainland. Two major developments prompted approximately 200,000 ordinary English men and women to move to North America in the seventeenth century and led their government to encourage their emigration.

The first was the onset of dramatic social and economic change. In the 150-year period after 1530, largely

**Social and Economic Change**

as a result of the introduction of nutritious American crops, England's population doubled. All those additional people needed food, clothing, and other goods. The competition for goods led to inflation, coupled with a fall in real wages as the number of workers increased. In these new economic and demographic circumstances, some English people—especially those with sizable landholdings that could produce food and clothing fibers for the growing population—substantially improved their lot. Others, particularly landless laborers and those with small amounts of land, fell into unremitting poverty. When landowners raised rents, took control of lands that peasants had long been allowed to use in common (enclosure), or decided to combine small holdings into large units, they forced tenants off the land. Consequently, geographical as well as social mobility increased, and the population of the cities swelled. London, for example, more than tripled in size by 1650, when 375,000 residents lived in its crowded buildings.

Wealthy English people reacted with alarm to what they saw as the disappearance of traditional ways of life. Steady streams of the landless and homeless filled the streets and highways. Obsessed with the problem of maintaining order, officials came to believe that England was overcrowded. They concluded that colonies established in North America could siphon off England's "surplus population," thus easing social strains at home. For similar reasons, many English people decided that they could improve their circumstances by migrating from a small, land-scarce, apparently overpopulated island to a large, land-rich, apparently empty continent and its nearby islands. Among those attracted by prospects for emigration were such younger sons of gentlemen as William Rudyerd, who were excluded from inheriting land by wealthy families' practice of primogeniture, which reserved all real estate for the eldest son. Such economic considerations were rendered even more significant in light of the second development: a major change in English religious practice.

The sixteenth century witnessed a religious transformation that eventually led large numbers of English dissenters to leave their homeland. In

**English Reformation**

1533 Henry VIII, wanting a male heir and infatuated with Anne Boleyn, sought to annul his marriage to his Spanish-born queen,

Catherine of Aragón, despite nearly twenty years of marriage and the birth of a daughter. When the pope refused to approve the annulment, Henry left the Roman Catholic Church. He founded the Church of England and—with Parliament's concurrence—proclaimed himself its head. In general, English people welcomed the schism, for many had little respect for the English Catholic Church. At first the reformed Church of England differed little from Catholicism in its practices, but under Henry's daughter Elizabeth I (child of his later marriage to Anne Boleyn), new currents of religious belief, which had originated on the European continent early in the sixteenth century, dramatically affected the English church.

These currents were the Protestant Reformation, led by Martin Luther, a German monk, and John Calvin, a French cleric and lawyer. Challenging the Catholic doctrine that priests were intermediaries between laypeople and God, Luther and Calvin insisted that people could interpret the Bible for themselves. That notion stimulated the spread of literacy: to understand and interpret the Bible, people had to learn how to read. Both Luther and Calvin rejected Catholic rituals, denying the need for an elaborate church hierarchy. They also asserted that the key to salvation was faith in God, rather than—as Catholic teaching had it—a combination of faith and good works. Calvin went further than Luther, stressing God's omnipotence and emphasizing the need for people to submit totally to God's will.

Elizabeth I tolerated diverse forms of Christianity as long as her subjects acknowledged her authority as head of the Church of England. During her long reign (1558–1603), Calvin's ideas gained influence within the English church, and some Catholics continued to practice their faith in private. By the late sixteenth century, many English Calvinists—those who came to be called Puritans, because they wanted to purify the church, or Separatists,

### Puritans and Separatists

because they wanted to leave it entirely—believed that the English Reformation had not gone far enough. Henry had simplified the church hierarchy; they wanted to abolish it altogether. Henry had subordinated the church to the interests of the state; they wanted a church free from political interference. And the Church of England, like the Catholic Church, continued to include all English people in its membership. Puritans and Separatists preferred a more restricted definition; they wanted to confine church membership to persons they believed to be "saved"—those God had selected for salvation before birth.

Paradoxically, though, a key article of their faith insisted that people could not know for certain if they were "saved" because mere mortals could not comprehend or affect their predestination to heaven or hell. Thus pious Puritans and Separatists daily confronted serious dilemmas: If the saved (or "elect") could not be identified with certainty, how could proper churches be constituted? If one was predestined and could not alter one's fate, why should one attend church or do good works? Puritans and Separatists dealt with the first dilemma by admitting that their judgments as to eligibility for church membership only approximated God's unknowable decisions. And they resolved the second by reasoning that God gave the elect the ability to accept salvation and to lead a good life. Therefore, even though one could not earn a place in heaven by piety and good works, such practices could indicate one's place in the ranks of the saved.

Elizabeth I's Stuart successors, her cousin James I (1603–1625) and his son Charles I (1625–1649), exhibited less tolerance for Puritans and Separatists. As Scots, they also had little respect for the traditions of representative government that had developed in England under the Tudors and their predecessors (see Table 2.2). The wealthy landowners who sat in Parliament had grown accustomed to having considerable influence on government policies, especially taxation. But James I, taking a position later endorsed by his son, publicly declared his belief in the divine right of kings. The Stuarts insisted that a monarch's power came directly from God and that his subjects had a duty to obey him. They likened the king's absolute authority to a father's authority over his children.

### Stuart Monarchs

Both James I and Charles I believed that their authority included the power to enforce religious conformity. Because Puritans and Separatists—and the remaining English Catholics—challenged many of the most important precepts of the English church, the Stuart monarchs authorized the removal of dissenting clergymen from their pulpits. In the 1620s and 1630s, some English Puritans,

| TABLE **2.2** | Tudor and Stuart Monarchs of England, 1509–1649 | | |
| --- | --- | --- | --- |
| Monarch | Reign | Relation to Predecessor | |
| Henry VIII | 1509–1547 | Son | |
| Edward VI | 1547–1553 | Son | |
| Mary I | 1553–1558 | Half-sister | |
| Elizabeth I | 1558–1603 | Half-sister | |
| James I | 1603–1625 | Cousin | |
| Charles I | 1625–1649 | Son | |

Separatists, and Catholics decided to move to America, where they hoped to put their religious beliefs into practice unhindered by the Stuarts or the church hierarchy. Some fled hurriedly to avoid arrest and imprisonment.

## THE FOUNDING OF VIRGINIA

The initial impulse that led to England's first permanent colony in the Western Hemisphere was, however, economic. A group of merchants and wealthy gentry in 1606 obtained a royal charter for the Virginia Company, organized as a joint-stock company, a forerunner of the modern corporation. Such enterprises, created for trading voyages, pooled the resources of many small investors through stock sales and spread out the risks. Investors usually received quick returns, but colonies required significant capital and commonly suffered from a chronic shortfall in financing. The lack of immediate returns made matters worse, generating tension between stockholders and colonists. Although at the outset investors in the Virginia Company anticipated great profits, the joint-stock company, then as later, proved to be a poor vehicle for establishing colonies, and neither settlement established by the Virginia Company—one in Maine that collapsed within a year and Jamestown—ever earned much.

In 1607 the company dispatched 104 men and boys to a region near Chesapeake Bay called Tsenacomoco by its

**Jamestown and Tsenacomoco**

native inhabitants. There in May they established the palisaded settlement called Jamestown on a swampy peninsula in a river they also named for their monarch. They quickly constructed small houses and a Church of England chapel. Ill equipped for survival in the unfamiliar environment, the colonists fell victim to dissension and disease as they attempted to maintain traditional English social and political hierarchies. Familiar with Spanish experience, the gentlemen and soldiers at Jamestown expected to rely on local Indians for food and tribute, yet the residents of Tsenacomoco refused to cooperate. Moreover, through sheer bad luck the settlers arrived in the midst of a severe drought (now known to be the worst in the region for 1,700 years), which persisted until 1612. The lack of rainfall not only made it difficult to cultivate crops but also polluted their drinking water.

The weroance (chief) of Tsenacomoco, Powhatan, had inherited rule over six Algonquian villages and later gained control of some twenty-five others (see Map 2.1). In late 1607 negotiations with Captain John Smith, one of the colony's leaders, the weroance tentatively agreed to an alliance with the Englishmen. In exchange for foodstuffs, Powhatan hoped to acquire guns, hatchets, and swords, which would give him a technological advantage over the enemies of his people. Each side in the alliance wanted to subordinate the other, but neither succeeded.

The fragile relationship soon foundered on mutual mistrust. The wereoance relocated his primary village in early 1609 to a place the newcomers could not access easily. Without Powhatan's assistance, the settlement experienced a "starving time" (winter 1609–1610), when many died and at least one colonist resorted to cannibalism. In spring 1610 the survivors packed up to leave on a newly arrived ship but en route out of the James River encountered a new governor, more settlers, and added supplies, so they returned to Jamestown. Sporadic skirmishes ensued as the standoff with the Powhatans continued. To gain the upper hand, the settlers in 1613 kidnapped Powhatan's daughter, Pocahontas, and held

▲ During her visit to London the Powhatan princess called "Pocahontas" in her childhood but Matoaka or Rebecca as an adult sat for her portrait by Simon Van de Passe, a young Dutch-German engraver. Her upright stance suggests her pride in her background. He depicted her wearing pearl earrings and an elaborate outfit topped by a gorgeous lace ruff. The ostrich fan she holds symbolizes royalty, but her hat is one worn more commonly by a Puritan man. Her features are clearly those of an indigenous Indian woman; Van de Passe did not "Europeanize" her looks. The portrait was originally reproduced in John Smith's *General Historie of Virginia* (1624).

*(National Portrait Gallery, Smithsonian Institution/Art Resource, NY)*

her hostage. In captivity, she agreed to convert to Christianity and to marry a colonist, John Rolfe. He had fallen in love with her, but she probably married him for diplomatic reasons; their union initiated a period of peace between the English and her people. Funded by the Virginia Company, she and Rolfe sailed to England to promote interest in the colony. She died at Gravesend in 1616, probably of dysentery, leaving an infant son who returned to Virginia as a young adult.

Although their royal charter nominally laid claim to a much wider territory, the Jamestown settlers saw their "Virginia" as essentially corresponding to Tsenacomoco. Powhatan's dominion was bounded on the north by the Potomac, on the south by the Great Dismal Swamp, and on the west by the fall line—the beginning of the upland Piedmont. Beyond those boundaries lay the Powhatans' enemies and (especially in the west) lands the Powhatans feared to enter. English people relied on the Powhatans as guides and interpreters, traveling along rivers and precontact paths in order to trade with the Powhatans' partners. For more than half a century, settlement in "Virginia" was confined to Tsenacomoco.

In Tsenacomoco and elsewhere on the North American coast, English settlers and local Algonquians focused on their cultural differences, not their similarities, although both groups held deep religious beliefs, subsisted primarily through agriculture, accepted social and political hierarchy, and observed well-defined gender roles. From the outset English men regarded Indian men as lazy because they did not cultivate crops and spent much of their time hunting (a sport, not work, in English eyes). Indian men thought English men effeminate because they did the "woman's work" of cultivation. In the same vein, the English believed that Algonquian women were oppressed because they did heavy field labor.

### Algonquian and English Cultural Differences

The nature of Algonquian and English hierarchies differed. Among Algonquians like the Powhatans, political power and social status did not necessarily pass directly through the male line, instead commonly flowing through sisters' sons. By contrast, English gentlemen inherited their position from their father. English political and military leaders tended to rule autocratically, whereas Algonquian leaders (even Powhatan) had limited authority over their people. Accustomed to the European concept of powerful kings, the English overestimated the ability of chiefs to make treaties that would bind their people.

Furthermore, Algonquians and English had different notions of property ownership. Most Algonquian villages held their land communally. It could not be bought or sold absolutely, although certain rights to use the land (for example, for hunting or fishing) could be transferred. Once, most English villagers, too, had used land in common, but because of enclosures in the previous century they had become accustomed to individual farms and to buying and selling land. The English also refused to accept the validity of Indians' claims to traditional hunting territories, insisting that only land intensively cultivated could be regarded as owned or occupied. As one colonist put it, "salvage peoples" who "rambled" over a region without farming it could claim no "title or propertye" in the land. Ownership of such "unclaimed" property, the English believed, lay with the English monarchy, in whose name John Cabot had laid claim to North America in 1497.

Above all, the English settlers believed unwaveringly in the superiority of their civilization. Although in the early years of colonization they often anticipated living peacefully alongside indigenous peoples, they always assumed that they would dictate the terms of such coexistence. Like Thomas Harriot at Roanoke, they expected native peoples to adopt English customs and to convert to Christianity. They showed little respect for the Indians when they believed English interests were at stake, as was demonstrated by developments in Virginia once the settlers had finally found the salable commodity they sought.

That commodity was tobacco, the American crop previously introduced to Europe by the Spanish and subsequently cultivated in Turkey. In 1611 John Rolfe planted seeds of a variety from the Spanish Caribbean, which was superior to the strain grown by Virginia Indians. Nine years later, Virginians exported 40,000 pounds of cured leaves, and by the late 1620s shipments had jumped dramatically to 1.5 million pounds. The great tobacco boom had begun, fueled by high prices and substantial profits for planters as they responded to escalating demand from Europe and Africa. The price later fell almost as sharply as it had risen, fluctuating wildly from year to year in response to increasing supply and international competition. Nevertheless, tobacco made Virginia prosper.

### Tobacco Cultivation

The spread of tobacco cultivation immeasurably altered life for everyone. Successful tobacco cultivation required abundant land, because the crop quickly drained soil of nutrients. Farmers soon learned that a field could produce only about three satisfactory crops before it had to lie fallow for several years to regain its fertility. Thus the once-small English settlements began to expand rapidly: eager applicants asked the Virginia Company for large land

▲ A comparison of the portrait of Sir Walter Raleigh and his son (left), with that of an Algonquian Indian drawn by John White, from Raleigh's Roanoke expedition (right), shows a dramatic difference in standard dress styles that, for many, must have symbolized the apparent cultural gap between Europeans and Americans. Yet the fact that both men (and the young boy) were portrayed in similar stances, with "arms akimbo," demonstrated that all were high-status individuals. In Europe, only aristocrats were represented in such a domineering pose.

*(Left: National Portrait Gallery, London; Right: Trustees of the British Museum)*

grants on both sides of the James River and its tributary streams. Lulled into a false sense of security by years of peace, Virginians established farms at some distance from one another along the riverbanks—a settlement pattern convenient for tobacco cultivation but dangerous for defense.

Opechancanough, Powhatan's brother and successor, watched the English colonists' expansion and witnessed their attempts to convert natives to Christianity. Recognizing the danger, the war leader launched coordinated attacks all along the James River on March 22, 1622. By the end of the day,

### Indian Assaults

347 colonists (about one-quarter of the total) lay dead, and only a timely warning from two Christian converts saved Jamestown itself from destruction.

Virginia reeled from the blow but did not collapse. Reinforced by new shipments of men and arms from England, the settlers repeatedly attacked Opechancanough's villages. A peace treaty was signed in 1632, but in April 1644 the elderly Opechancanough assaulted the invaders one last time, though he must have known he could not prevail. In 1646 survivors of the Powhatan Confederacy formally subordinated themselves to England. Although they continued to live in the region, their efforts to resist the spread of European settlement ended.

The 1622 assault that failed to destroy the colony did succeed in killing its parent. The Virginia Company never made any profits from the enterprise, for internal corruption and the heavy cost of supporting the settlers offset all its earnings. But before its demise the company developed two policies that set key precedents. First, to attract settlers, the company in 1617 established the "headright" system. Every new arrival paying his or her own way was promised a land grant of 50 acres; those who financed the passage of others received similar headrights for each person. To ordinary English farmers, many of whom owned little or no land, the headright system offered a powerful incentive to move to Virginia. To wealthy gentry, it promised even more: the possibility of establishing vast agricultural enterprises worked by large numbers of laborers. Two years later, the company introduced a second reform, authorizing the landowning men of the major Virginia settlements to elect representatives to an assembly called the House of Burgesses. English landholders had long been accustomed to electing members of Parliament and controlling their own local governments; therefore, they expected the same privilege in the nation's colonies.

**End of Virginia Company**

When James I revoked the charter in 1624, transforming Virginia into a royal colony, he continued the company's headright policy. Because he distrusted legislative bodies, though, James abolished the assembly. But Virginians protested so vigorously that by 1629 the House of Burgesses was functioning once again. Only two decades after the first permanent English settlement was planted in North America, the colonists successfully insisted on governing themselves at the local level. Thus the political structure of England's American possessions came to differ from those of the Spanish, Dutch, and French colonies, all of which were ruled autocratically.

## LIFE IN THE CHESAPEAKE

By the 1630s tobacco was firmly established as the staple crop and chief source of revenue in Virginia. It quickly became just as important in the second English colony planted on Chesapeake Bay: Maryland, given by Charles I to George Calvert, first Lord Baltimore, as a personal possession (proprietorship), which was settled in 1634. (Because Virginia and Maryland both border Chesapeake Bay—see Map 2.1—they are often referred to collectively as "the Chesapeake.") Members of the Calvert family intended the colony to serve as a haven for their persecuted fellow Catholics. Cecilius Calvert, second Lord Baltimore,

became the first colonizer to offer freedom of religion to all Christian settlers; he understood that protecting the Protestant majority could also ensure Catholics' rights. Maryland's Act of Religious Toleration codified his policy in 1649.

In everything but religion the two Chesapeake colonies resembled each other. In Maryland as in Virginia, tobacco planters spread out along the riverbanks, establishing isolated farms instead of towns. The region's deep, wide rivers offered dependable water transportation in an age of few and inadequate roads. Each farm or group of farms had its own wharf, where oceangoing vessels could take on or discharge cargo. Consequently, Virginia and Maryland had few towns, for their residents did not need commercial centers in order to buy and sell goods.

The planting, cultivation, harvesting, and curing of tobacco were repetitious, time-consuming, and labor-intensive tasks. Clearing land for new fields, necessary every few years, also demanded heavy labor. Above all else, then, successful Chesapeake farms required workers. But where and how could they be obtained? Nearby Indians, their numbers reduced by war and disease, could not supply such needs. Nor were enslaved Africans available: traders could more easily and profitably sell slaves to Caribbean sugar planters. Only a few people of African descent, some of them free, initially trickled into the Chesapeake. By 1650 about three hundred blacks lived in Virginia—a tiny fraction of the population.

**Demand for Laborers**

Chesapeake tobacco farmers thus looked primarily to England to supply their labor needs. Because of the headright system (which Maryland also adopted in 1640), a tobacco farmer anywhere in the Chesapeake could simultaneously obtain both land and labor by importing workers from England. Good management would make the process self-perpetuating: a farmer could use his profits to pay for the passage of more workers and thereby gain title to more land. Success could even bring movement into the ranks of the planter gentry that began to develop in the region.

Because men did the agricultural work in European societies, colonists assumed that field laborers should be men. Such male laborers, along with a few women, immigrated to America as indentured servants—that is, in return for their passage they contracted to work for periods ranging from four to seven years. Indentured servants accounted for 75 to 85 percent of the approximately 130,000 English immigrants to Virginia and Maryland during the seventeenth century. The rest tended to be young couples with one or two children.

Males between the ages of fifteen and twenty-four composed roughly three-quarters of the servants; only one immigrant in five or six was female. Most of these young men came from farming or laboring families, and many originated in regions of England experiencing severe social disruption. Some had already moved several times within England before relocating to America. Often they came from the middling ranks of society—what their contemporaries called the "common sort." Their youth indicated that most probably had not yet established themselves in their homeland.

For such people the Chesapeake appeared to offer good prospects. Servants who fulfilled the terms of their indenture earned "freedom dues"

### Conditions of Servitude

consisting of clothes, tools, livestock, casks of corn and tobacco, and sometimes even land. From a distance at least, America seemed to offer chances for advancement unavailable in England. Yet immigrants' lives were difficult. Servants typically worked six days a week, ten to fourteen hours a day, in a climate much warmer than England's. Their masters could discipline or sell them, and they faced severe penalties for running away. Even so, the laws did give them some protection. For example, their masters were supposed to supply them with sufficient food, clothing, and shelter, and they were not to be beaten excessively. Cruelly treated servants could turn to the courts for assistance, sometimes winning verdicts directing that they be transferred to more humane masters or released from their indenture.

Servants and their owners alike contended with epidemic disease. Immigrants first had to survive the process the colonists called "seasoning," a bout with disease (probably malaria) that usually occurred during their first Chesapeake summer. They then often endured recurrences of malaria, along with dysentery, typhoid fever, and other illnesses. Consequently, about 40 percent of male servants did not survive long enough to become freedmen. Even young men of twenty-two who successfully weathered their seasoning could expect to live only another twenty years.

For those who survived, though, the opportunities for advancement were real. Until the last decades of the seventeenth century, former servants often became independent farmers ("freeholders"), thereafter living a modest but comfortable existence. Some even assumed positions of political prominence, such as justice of the peace or militia officer. But in the 1670s tobacco prices entered a fifty-year period of stagnation and decline. Simultaneously, good land grew increasingly scarce and expensive. In 1681 Maryland dropped its legal requirement that servants receive land as part of their freedom dues, forcing large numbers of freed servants to live for years as wage laborers or tenant farmers. By 1700 the Chesapeake was no longer the land of opportunity it once had been.

Life in the early Chesapeake was hard for everyone, regardless of sex or status. Farmers (and sometimes their wives) toiled in the fields along-

### Standard of Living

side servants, laboriously clearing land, then planting and harvesting tobacco and corn. Because hogs could forage for themselves in the forests and needed little tending, Chesapeake households subsisted mainly on pork and corn, a filling diet but not sufficiently nutritious. Families supplemented this monotonous fare by eating fish, shellfish, and wildfowl, in addition to vegetables such as lettuce and peas, which they grew in small gardens. The near impossibility of preserving food for safe winter consumption magnified the health problems caused by epidemic disease. Salting, drying, and smoking, the only methods the colonists knew, did not always prevent spoilage.

Few households had many material possessions other than farm implements, bedding, and basic cooking and eating utensils. Chairs, tables, candles, and knives and forks were luxury items. Most people rose and went to bed with the sun, sat on crude benches or storage chests, and held plates or bowls in their hands while eating meat and vegetable stews with spoons. The ramshackle houses commonly had just one or two rooms. Colonists devoted their income to improving their farms, buying livestock, and purchasing more laborers instead of improving their standard of living. Rather than making such items as clothing and tools, tobacco-growing families imported necessary manufactured goods from England.

The predominance of males (see Figure 2.1), the incidence of servitude, and the high mortality rates combined to produce unusual patterns of fam-

### Chesapeake Families

ily life. Female servants normally could not marry during their term of indenture because masters did not want pregnancies to deprive them of workers. Many male ex-servants could not marry at all because of the scarcity of women; such men lived alone, in pairs, or as the third member of a household containing a married couple. In contrast, nearly every adult free woman in the Chesapeake married, and widows usually remarried within a few months of a husband's death. Yet because of high infant mortality and because almost all marriages were delayed by servitude or broken by death, Chesapeake women commonly reared only one to three healthy children, in contrast to English women, who normally had at least five.

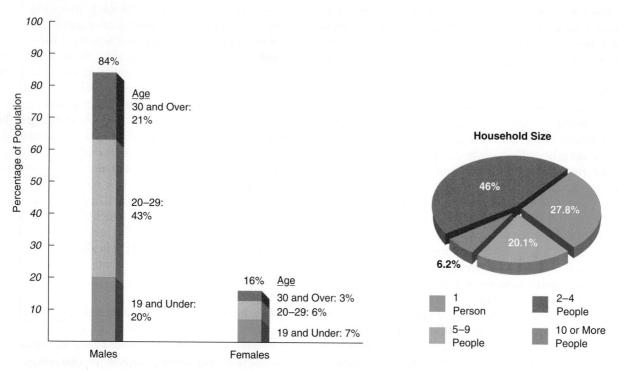

**Figure 2.1   Population of Virginia, 1625**

The only detailed census taken in the English mainland North American colonies during the seventeenth century was prepared in Virginia in 1625. It listed a total of 1,218 people, constituting 309 "households" and living in 278 dwellings—so some houses contained more than one family. The chart shows, on the left, the proportionate age and gender distribution of the 765 individuals for whom full information was recorded, and, on the right, the percentage variation in the sizes of the 309 households. The approximately 42 percent of the residents of the colony who were servants were concentrated in 30 percent of the households. Nearly 70 percent of the households had no servants at all.

*(Source of data: Robert V. Wells, The Population of the British Colonies in America Before 1776: A Survey of Census Data [Princeton: Princeton University Press, 1975], tables V-5 and V-6 and pp. 165–166.)*

Thus Chesapeake families were few, small, and short-lived. Youthful immigrants came to America as individuals free of familial control; they commonly died while their children were still young. In one Virginia county, for example, more than three-quarters of the children had lost at least one parent by the time they either married or reached age twenty-one. Those children were put to work as soon as possible on the farms of parents, stepparents, or guardians. Their schooling, if any, was haphazard; whether Chesapeake-born children learned to read or write depended largely on whether their parents were literate and took the time to teach them.

Throughout the seventeenth century, immigrants composed a majority of the Chesapeake population, with im-

## Chesapeake Politics

portant implications for regional political patterns. Most of the members of Virginia's House of Burgesses and Maryland's House of Delegates (established in 1635) were immigrants; they also dominated the governor's council, which simultaneously served as each colony's highest court, part of the legislature, and executive adviser to the governor. A cohesive, native-born ruling elite emerged only in the early eighteenth century.

Representative institutions based on the consent of the governed usually function as a major source of political stability. In the seventeenth-century Chesapeake, most property-owning white males could vote, and such freeholders chose as their legislators (burgesses) the local elites who seemed to be the natural leaders of their respective areas. But because most such men were immigrants lacking strong ties to one another or to the colonies, the assemblies' existence did not create political stability. Unusual demographic patterns thus contributed to the region's contentious politics.

## THE FOUNDING OF NEW ENGLAND

The economic motives that prompted English people to move to the Chesapeake and the Caribbean colonies also drew men and women to New England, the region known as North Virginia before Captain John Smith renamed it in 1616 after exploring its coast (see Map 2.2). But because Puritans organized the New England colonies and also because of environmental factors, the northern settlements turned out very differently from their counterparts to the south. The differences became apparent even as the would-be colonists left England.

Hoping to exert control over a migration that appeared disorderly (and which included dissenters seeking to flee the authority of the Church of England), royal bureaucrats in late 1634 ordered port officials in London to collect information on all travelers departing for the colonies. The resulting records for the year 1635 are a treasure trove for historians. They document the departure of 53 vessels in that year alone—20 to Virginia, 17 to New England, 8 to Barbados, 5 to St. Kitts, 2 to Bermuda, and 1 to Providence Island. On those ships sailed almost five thousand people, with two thousand departing for Virginia, about twelve hundred for New England, and the rest for island destinations. Nearly three-fifths of all the passengers were between fifteen and twenty-four years old, reflecting the predominance of young male servants among migrants to America.

**Contrasting Regional Demographic Patterns**

But among those bound for New England, such youths constituted less than one-third of the total; nearly 40 percent were older, and another third were younger. Whereas women made up just 14 percent of those going to Virginia, they composed almost 40 percent of the passengers to New England. Such composite figures show that New England migrants often traveled in family groups. They also brought more goods and livestock with them and tended to travel with other people from the same region. For example, aboard one vessel, more than half came from York; on another, nearly half came from Buckinghamshire. In short, people migrated to New England together with their close associates. Their lives in North America

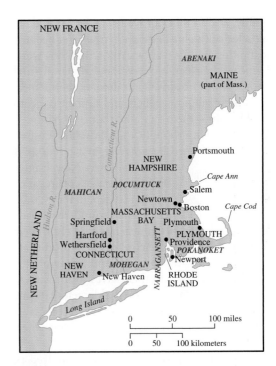

**Map 2.2   New England Colonies, 1650**
The most densely settled region of the mainland was New England, where English settlements and Indian villages existed side by side.

must have been more comfortable and less lonely than those of their southern counterparts.

Many of the people who colonized New England were inspired to migrate by religion, which elsewhere motivated chiefly the Catholics who moved to Maryland. Puritan congregations quickly became key institutions in colonial New England, whereas neither the Church of England nor Catholicism had much impact on the settlers or the early development of the Chesapeake colonies. Catholic and Anglican bishops in England paid little attention to their coreligionists in America, and Chesapeake congregations languished in the absence of sufficient numbers of properly ordained clergymen. (For example, in 1665 an observer noted that only ten of the fifty Virginia parishes had resident clerics.) Not until the 1690s did the Church of England begin to take firmer root in Virginia; by then it had also replaced Catholicism as the established church in Maryland.

**Contrasting Regional Religious Patterns**

By contrast, religion constantly affected the lives of pious Puritans, who regularly reassessed the state of their souls. Many devoted themselves to self-examination and

Bible study, and families prayed together each day under the guidance of the husband and father. Yet because even the most pious could never be certain that they were numbered among the elect, anxiety about their spiritual state troubled devout Puritans. That anxiety lent a special intensity to their religious beliefs and to their concern with proper behavior—their own and that of others.

Separatists who thought the Church of England too corrupt to be salvaged became the first religious dissen-

**Separatists**

ters to move to New England. In 1609 a Separatist congregation relocated to Leiden, in the Netherlands, where they found the freedom of worship denied them in Stuart England. But eventually the Netherlands worried them, for the nation that tolerated them also tolerated religions and behaviors they abhorred. Hoping to isolate themselves and their children from the corrupting influence of worldly temptations, these people, who came to be known as Pilgrims, received permission from the Virginia Company to colonize the northern part of its territory.

In September 1620 more than one hundred people, only thirty of them Separatists, set sail from England on the old and crowded *Mayflower*. Like a few English families that had settled permanently along the coast of Newfoundland during the previous decade, the Pilgrims expected to support their colony through profits from codfishery. In December they landed in America, but farther north than they had intended. Still, given the lateness of the season, they decided to stay where they were. They moved into the empty dwellings of an Indian village whose inhabitants had died in the epidemic of 1616–1618, at a fine harbor, named Plymouth by John Smith in 1616.

Even before they landed, the Pilgrims had to surmount their first challenge—from the "strangers," or non-Separatists, who sailed with them

**Pilgrims and Pokanokets**

to America. Because they landed outside the jurisdiction of the Virginia Company, some of the strangers questioned the authority of the colony's leaders. In response, the Mayflower Compact, signed in November 1620 on shipboard, established a "Civil Body Politic" as a temporary substitute for a charter. The male settlers elected a governor and initially made all decisions for the colony at town meetings. Later, after more towns had been founded and the population increased, Plymouth, like Virginia and Maryland, created an assembly to which the landowning male settlers elected representatives.

Like the Jamestown settlers before them, the residents of Plymouth were poorly prepared to subsist in the new environment. Only half of the *Mayflower*'s passengers lived to see the spring. That the others survived owed much to the Pokanokets (a branch of the Wampanoags), who controlled the area in which they had settled. Pokanoket villages had suffered terrible losses in the recent epidemic, so to protect themselves from the powerful Narragansetts of the southern New England coast (who had been spared the ravages of the disease), the Pokanokets allied themselves with the newcomers. In the spring of 1621, their leader, Massasoit, agreed to a treaty, and during the colony's first difficult years the Pokanokets supplied the settlers with essential foodstuffs. The colonists also relied on Squanto, an Indian who, like Malinche, served as a conduit between native peoples and Europeans. Captured by fishermen in the early 1610s and taken to Europe, Squanto had learned to speak English. Upon returning to North America, he discovered that his village had been wiped out by the epidemic. Squanto became the settlers' interpreter and a major source of information about the environment.

Before the 1620s ended, another group of Puritans (Congregationalists, who hoped to reform the Church of England from within) launched

**Massachusetts Bay Company**

the colonial enterprise that would come to dominate New England and would absorb Plymouth in 1691. Charles I, who became king in 1625, was more hostile to Puritans than his father had been. Under his leadership, the Church of England attempted to suppress Puritan practices, driving clergymen from their pulpits and forcing congregations to worship secretly. Some Congregationalist merchants, concerned about their long-term prospects in England, sent out a body of colonists to Cape Ann (north of Cape Cod) in 1628. The following year the merchants obtained a royal charter, constituting themselves as the Massachusetts Bay Company.

The new joint-stock company quickly attracted the attention of Puritans of the "middling sort" who were becoming increasingly convinced that they no longer would be able to practice their religion freely in their homeland. They remained committed to the goal of reforming the Church of England but concluded that they should pursue that aim in America. In a dramatic move, the Congregationalist merchants decided to transfer the Massachusetts Bay Company's headquarters to New England. The settlers would then be answerable to no one in the mother country and would be able to handle their affairs, secular and religious, as they pleased. Like the Plymouth settlers, they expected to profit from the codfishery; they also planned to export timber products.

▲ Some scholars now believe that this 1638 painting by the Dutch artist Adam Willaerts depicts the Plymouth colony about fifteen years after its founding. The shape of the harbor, the wooden gate, and the houses straggling up the hill all coincide with contemporary accounts of the settlement. No one believes that Willaerts himself visited Plymouth, but people returning from the colony to the Netherlands, where the Pilgrims had lived for years before emigrating, could well have described Plymouth to him. *(© J. D. Bangs, Courtesy of Leiden American Pilgrim Museum, The Netherlands)*

The most important recruit to the new venture was John Winthrop, a member of the lesser English gentry. In October 1629, the Massachusetts Bay Company elected Winthrop as its governor. (Until his death twenty years later, he served the colony continuously in one leadership post or another.) Winthrop organized the initial segment of the great Puritan migration to America. In 1630 over one thousand English men and women moved to Massachusetts—most of them to Boston. By 1643 nearly twenty thousand more had followed.

**Governor John Winthrop**

On board the *Arbella,* en route to New England in 1630, John Winthrop preached a sermon, "A Model of Christian Charity," laying out his expectations for the new colony. Above all, he stressed the communal nature of the endeavor on which he and his fellow settlers had embarked. God, he explained, "hath so disposed of the condition of mankind as in all times some must be rich, some poor, some high and eminent in power and dignity, others mean and in subjection." But differences in status did not imply differences in worth. On the contrary, God had planned the world so that "every man might have need of other, and from hence they might be all knit more nearly together in the bond of brotherly affection." In America, Winthrop asserted, "we shall be as a city upon a hill, the eyes of all people are upon us." If the Puritans failed to carry out their "special commission" from God, "the Lord will surely break out in wrath against us."

Winthrop's was a transcendent vision. He foresaw in Puritan America a true commonwealth, a community in which each person put the good of the whole ahead of his or her private concerns. Although, as in seventeenth-century England, that society would be characterized by social inequality and clear hierarchies of status and power, Winthrop hoped that its members would live according to the precepts of Christian love. Of course, such an ideal was beyond human reach. Early New England and its Caribbean counterpart, Providence Island, had their share of bitter quarrels and unchristian behavior. Remarkably, though, in New England the ideal persisted well into the third and fourth generations of the immigrants' descendants.

The Puritans expressed their communal ideal chiefly in the doctrine of the covenant. They believed God had

### Covenant Ideal

made a covenant—that is, an agreement or contract—with them when they were chosen for the special mission to America. In turn they covenanted with one another, promising to work together toward their goals. The founders of churches, towns, and even colonies in Anglo-America often drafted formal documents setting forth the principles on which their institutions would be based. The Pilgrims' Mayflower Compact was a covenant; so, too, was the Fundamental Orders of Connecticut (1639), which laid down the basic law for the settlements established along the Connecticut River valley in 1636 and thereafter.

The leaders of Massachusetts Bay likewise transformed their original joint-stock company charter into the basis for a covenanted community based on mutual consent. Under pressure from landowning male settlers, they gradually changed the General Court—officially the company's small governing body—into a colonial legislature. They also granted the status of freeman, or voting member of the company, to all property-owning adult male church members. Like the Virginians who won the reestablishment of the House of Burgesses after the king had abolished it, the male residents of Massachusetts insisted that their reluctant leaders allow them a greater voice in their government. Less than two decades after the first large group of Puritans arrived in Massachusetts Bay, the colony had a functioning system of self-government composed of a governor and a two-house legislature. The General Court also established a judicial system modeled on England's, although the laws they adopted differed from those of their homeland.

### New England Towns

The colony's method of distributing land helped to further the communal ideal. Unlike Virginia and Maryland, where individual applicants acquired headrights and sited their farms separately, in Massachusetts groups of men—often from the same English village—applied together to the General Court for grants of land on which to establish towns (novel governance units that did not exist in England). The men receiving such a grant determined how the land would be distributed. Understandably, the grantees copied the villages whence they had come. First they laid out lots for houses and a church. Then they gave each family parcels of land scattered around the town center: a pasture here, a woodlot there, an arable field elsewhere. They reserved the best and largest plots for the most distinguished among them, including the minister. People who had low status in England received smaller and less desirable allotments. Still, every man and

even a few single women obtained land, thus sharply differentiating these villages from their English counterparts. When migrants began to move beyond the territorial limits of the Massachusetts Bay colony into Connecticut (1636), New Haven (1638), and New Hampshire (1638), the same pattern of land grants and town formation persisted. (Only Maine, with coastal regions thinly populated by fishermen and their families, deviated from the standard practice.)

Town centers developed quickly, evolving in three distinctly different ways. Some, chiefly isolated agricultural settlements in the interior, tried to sustain Winthrop's vision of harmonious community life based on diversified family farms. A second group, the coastal towns like Boston and Salem, became bustling seaports, serving as focal points for trade and places of entry for thousands of new immigrants. The third category, commercialized agricultural towns, grew up in the Connecticut River valley, where easy water transportation made it possible for farmers to sell surplus goods readily. In Springfield, Massachusetts, for example, the merchant-entrepreneur William Pynchon and his son John began as fur traders and ended as large landowners with thousands of acres. Even in New England, then, the entrepreneurial spirit characteristic of the Chesapeake found expression. Yet the plans to profit from timber and fish exports did not materialize quickly or easily; the new settlements lacked the infrastructure necessary to support such enterprises.

Migration into the Connecticut valley ended the Puritans' relative freedom from clashes with nearby Indians.

### Pequot War and Its Aftermath

The first English people in the valley moved there from Massachusetts Bay under the direction of their minister, Thomas Hooker. Although their new settlements were remote from other English towns, the wide river promised ready access to the ocean. The site had just one problem: it fell within the territory controlled by the powerful Pequots.

The Pequots' dominance stemmed from their role as primary intermediaries in the trade between New England Algonquians and the Dutch in New Netherland. The arrival of English settlers signaled the end of the Pequots' power over such regional trading networks, for previously subordinate bands could now trade directly with Europeans. Clashes between Pequots and English colonists began even before the establishment of settlements in the Connecticut valley, but their founding tipped the balance toward war. The Pequots tried unsuccessfully to enlist other Indians in resisting English expansion. After two English traders were killed (not by Pequots), the English raided a Pequot village. In return, the Pequots attacked

▲ The Fairbanks house, in Dedham, Massachusetts, is one of the oldest surviving homes in New England. But only the central core (with the large chimney) was constructed in 1636; the other wings were added later. Early Massachusetts towns were filled with similar dwellings.

*(Photograph by Jeffrey Howe)*

the new town of Wethersfield in April 1637, killing nine and capturing two. To retaliate, a Massachusetts Bay expedition the following month attacked and burned the main Pequot town on the Mystic River. The Englishmen and their Narragansett allies slaughtered at least four hundred Pequots, mostly women and children, capturing and enslaving most of the survivors.

For the next four decades, New England Indians accommodated themselves to the European invasion. They traded with the newcomers and sometimes worked for them, but for the most part they resisted acculturation or incorporation into English society. Native Americans persisted in using traditional farming methods, which did not employ plows or fences, and women rather than men continued to be the chief cultivators. When Indian men learned "European" trades in order to survive, they chose those—like broom making, basket weaving, and shingle splitting—that most nearly accorded with their customary occupations and ensured both independence and income. The one European practice they adopted was

keeping livestock, for domesticated animals provided excellent sources of meat once earlier hunting territories had been turned into English farms and wild game had consequently disappeared.

Although the official seal of the Massachusetts Bay colony showed an Indian crying, "Come over and help us," most colonists showed little interest in converting the Algonquians to Christianity. Only a few Massachusetts clerics, most notably John Eliot and Thomas Mayhew, seriously undertook missionary work. Eliot insisted that converts reside in towns, farm the land in English fashion, assume English names, wear European-style clothing and shoes, cut their hair, and stop observing a wide range of their own customs. Because Eliot demanded a cultural transformation from his adherents—on the theory that Indians could not be properly Christianized unless they were also "civilized"—he understandably met with little success. At the peak of Eliot's efforts, only eleven hundred

**Missionary Activities**

▲ Among John Eliot's principal converts to Christianity was a young Native American named Daniel Takawampbartis. Ordained as a minister, he served at the head of the Indian congregation at Natick, Massachusetts, a "Praying Town," until his death in 1716. Members of his congregation made this desk for him in about 1677, incorporating elements of English design (brass pulls), Native American motifs (incised lines), and uniquely American hooved feet. The top, a hinged box, is intended to hold a Bible.

*(The Morse Institute, Natick, Massachusetts. Photo by Mark Sexton of the Peabody Essex Museum, Salem)*

▲ In 1664 an eight-year-old girl, Elizabeth Eggington, became the subject of the earliest known dated New England painting. Her mother died shortly after her birth, perhaps because of childbirth complications; the girl's rich clothing, elaborate jewelry, and feather fan not only reveal her family's wealth but also suggest that she was much loved by her father, a merchant and ship captain. Unfortunately, Elizabeth died about the time this portrait was painted; perhaps it—like some other colonial portraits of young children—was actually painted after her death to memorialize her.

*(Wadsworth Atheneum Museum of Art, Hartford, CT. Gift of Mrs. Walter H. Clark. Endowed by her daughter, Mrs. Thomas L. Archibald)*

Indians (out of many thousands) lived in the fourteen "Praying Towns" he established, and just 10 percent of those town residents had been formally baptized.

Eliot's failure to win many converts contrasted sharply with the successful missions in New France. Puritan services lacked Catholicism's beautiful ceremonies and special appeal for women, and the Calvinist Puritans could not offer pious believers assurances of a heavenly afterlife. Yet, on the island of Martha's Vineyard, Thomas Mayhew showed that it was possible to convert substantial numbers of Indians to Calvinist Christianity. He allowed Wampanoag Christians there to lead traditional lives, and he trained men of their own community to minister to them.

What attracted Indians to such religious ideas? Conversion often alienated new Christians (both Catholic and Puritan) from their relatives and traditions—a likely outcome that must have caused many potential converts to hesitate. But surely many hoped to use the Europeans' religion as a means of coping with the dramatic changes the intruders had wrought. The combination of disease, alcohol, new trading patterns, and loss of territory disrupted customary ways of life to an unprecedented extent. Shamans had little success in restoring traditional ways. Many Indians must have concluded that the Europeans' own ideas could provide the key to survival in the new circumstances.

John Winthrop's description of a great smallpox epidemic that swept through southern New England in the early 1630s reveals the relationship among smallpox, conversion to Christianity, and English land claims. "A great mortality among the Indians," he noted in his diary in 1633. "Divers of them, in their sickness, confessed that the Englishmen's God was a good God; and that if they recovered, they would serve him." But most did not recover: in January 1634 an English scout reported that smallpox had spread "as far as any Indian plantation was known to the west." By July, Winthrop observed that most of the Indians within a 300-mile radius of Boston had died of the disease. Therefore, he declared with satisfaction, "the Lord hath cleared our title to what we possess."

## LIFE IN NEW ENGLAND

New England's colonizers adopted modes of life that differed from those of both their Algonquian neighbors and their Chesapeake counterparts. Algonquian bands usually moved four or five times each year to take full advantage of their environment. In spring, women planted the fields, but once crops were established, the crops did not need regular attention for several months. Villages then divided into small groups, women gathering wild foods and men hunting and fishing. The villagers returned to their fields for harvest, then separated again for fall hunting. Finally, the people wintered together in a sheltered spot before returning to the fields to start the cycle anew the following spring. Women probably determined the timing of these moves, because their activities (gathering wild foods, including shellfish along the shore, and cultivating plants) used the nearby environment more intensively than did men's.

Unlike the mobile Algonquians, English people lived year-round in the same location. And, unlike residents of the Chesapeake, New Englanders constructed sturdy dwellings intended to last. (Some survive to this day.) Household furnishings resembled those of Chesapeake residents, but New Englanders' diets were somewhat more varied. They replowed the same fields, believing it was less arduous to employ manure as fertilizer than to clear new fields every few years. Furthermore, they fenced their croplands to prevent them from being overrun by the cattle, sheep, and hogs that were their chief sources of meat. Animal crowding more than human crowding caused New Englanders to spread out across the countryside; all their livestock constantly needed more pasturage.

Because Puritans commonly moved to America in family groups, the age range in early New England was wide; and because many more women migrated to New England than to the tobacco colonies, the population could immediately begin to reproduce itself. Lacking such tropical diseases as malaria, New England was also healthier than the Chesapeake and even the mother

**New England Families**

country, once settlements had survived the difficult first few years. Adult male migrants to the Chesapeake lost about a decade from their English life expectancy of fifty to fifty-five years; their Massachusetts counterparts gained five or more years.

Consequently, whereas Chesapeake population patterns gave rise to families that were few in number, small in size, and transitory, the demographic characteristics of New England made families there numerous, large, and long-lived. In New England most men married; immigrant women married young (at age twenty, on the average); and marriages lasted longer and produced more children, who were more likely to live to maturity. If seventeenth-century Chesapeake women could expect to rear one to three healthy children, New England women could anticipate raising five to seven.

The nature of the population had other major implications for family life. The presence of many children combined with Puritans' stress on the importance of reading the Bible led to widespread concern for the education of youth. That people lived in towns meant that small schools could be established; girls and boys were taught basic reading by their parents or a school "dame," and boys could then proceed to learn writing and eventually arithmetic and Latin. Further, New England in effect created grandparents, because in England people rarely lived long enough to know their children's children. And whereas early Chesapeake parents commonly died before their children married, New England parents exercised a good deal of control over their adult offspring. Young men could not marry without acreage to cultivate, and because of the communal land-grant system, they had to depend on their fathers for that land. Daughters, too, needed a dowry of household goods supplied by their parents. Parents relied on their children's labor and often seemed reluctant to see them marry and start their own households. These needs sometimes led to conflict between the generations. On the whole, though, children seem to have obeyed their parents' wishes, for they had few alternatives.

Puritans controlled the governments of Massachusetts Bay, Plymouth, Connecticut, and the other early northern colonies. Congregationalism was the only officially recognized religion; except in Rhode Island, founded by dissenters from Massachusetts, members of other sects had no freedom of worship. Some non-Puritans voted in town meetings, but in Massachusetts Bay and New Haven, church membership was a prerequisite for voting in colony elections. All the early colonies taxed residents

**Impact of Religion**

to build meetinghouses and pay ministers' salaries, but only in New England were provisions of criminal codes based on the Old Testament. Massachusetts's first bodies of law (1641 and 1648) incorporated regulations drawn from scriptures; New Haven, Plymouth, New Hampshire, and Connecticut later copied those codes. All colonists were required to attend religious services, whether or not they were church members, and people who expressed contempt for ministers or their preaching could be punished with fines or whippings.

The Puritan colonies attempted to enforce strict codes of moral conduct. Colonists there could be tried for drunkenness, card playing, dancing, or even idleness—although the frequent prosecutions for such offenses suggest that New Englanders often disobeyed the laws and thoroughly enjoyed such activities. Couples who had sex during their engagement (as revealed by the birth of a baby less than nine months after their wedding) were fined and publicly humiliated. Men, and a handful of women, who engaged in behaviors that today would be called homosexual were seen as especially sinful and reprehensible, and some were executed.

In New England, church and state were thus intertwined to a greater extent than in the Chesapeake, where few such prosecutions occurred. Puritans objected to secular interference in religious affairs but at the same time expected the church to influence the conduct of politics and the affairs of society. They also believed that the state was obliged to support and protect the one true church—theirs. As a result, although they came to America seeking freedom to worship as they pleased, they saw no contradiction in refusing to grant that freedom to others.

Roger Williams, a Separatist who migrated to Massachusetts Bay in 1631, quickly ran afoul of that Puritan orthodoxy. He told his fellow settlers that the king of England had no right to grant them land already occupied by Indians, that church and state should be kept entirely separate, and that Puritans should not impose their religious beliefs on others. Because Puritan leaders placed a heavy emphasis on achieving consensus in both religion and politics, they could not long tolerate significant dissent. In October 1635, the Massachusetts General Court tried Williams for challenging the validity of the colony's charter and for maintaining that New England Congregationalists had not separated themselves, their churches, or their polity sufficiently from England's corrupt institutions and practices.

**Roger Williams**

Convicted and banished, Williams journeyed in early 1636 to the head of Narragansett Bay, where he founded the town of Providence on land he obtained from the Narragansetts and Wampanoags. Because Williams believed that government should not interfere with religion in any way, Providence and other towns in what became Rhode Island adopted a policy of tolerating all religions, including Judaism. Along with Maryland, the tiny colony founded by Williams thus presaged the religious freedom that eventually became one of the hallmarks of the United States.

A dissenter who presented a more sustained challenge to Massachusetts' leaders was Mistress Anne Hutchinson. (The title *Mistress* revealed her high status.) A skilled medical practitioner popular with the women of Boston, she greatly admired John Cotton, a minister who stressed the covenant of grace, or God's free gift of salvation to unworthy human beings. By contrast, most Massachusetts clerics emphasized the need for Puritans to engage in good works, study, and reflection in preparation for receiving God's grace. (In its most extreme form, such a doctrine could verge on the covenant of works, or the idea that people could earn their salvation.) After spreading her ideas for months in the context of gatherings at childbirths—when no men were present—Mistress Hutchinson began holding women's meetings in her home to discuss Cotton's sermons. She emphasized the covenant of grace more than did Cotton himself, and she even asserted that the elect could be assured of salvation and communicate directly with God. Such ideas had an immense appeal for Puritans. Anne Hutchinson offered them certainty of salvation instead of a state of constant anxiety. Her approach also lessened the importance of the institutional church and its ministers.

**Anne Hutchinson**

Thus Hutchinson's ideas posed a dangerous threat to Puritan orthodoxy. So in November 1637, officials charged her with having maligned the colony's ministers by accusing them of preaching the covenant of works. For two days she defended herself cleverly, matching scriptural references and wits with John Winthrop himself. But then Anne Hutchinson triumphantly and boldly declared that God had spoken to her directly, explaining that he would curse the Puritans' descendants for generations if they harmed her. That assertion assured her banishment, for what member of the court could acknowledge the legitimacy of such a revelation? After she had also been excommunicated from the church, she and her family, along with some faithful followers, were exiled to Rhode Island in 1638. Several years later, after she moved to New Netherland, she and most of her children were killed by Indians.

The authorities in Massachusetts perceived Anne Hutchinson as doubly dangerous to the existing order:

she threatened not only religious orthodoxy but also traditional gender roles. Puritans believed in the equality before God of all souls, including those of women, but they considered actual women (as distinct from their spiritual selves) inferior to men. Christians had long followed Saint Paul's dictum that women should keep silent in church and submit to their husbands. Mistress Hutchinson did neither. The magistrates' comments during her trial reveal that they were almost as outraged by her "masculine" behavior as by her religious beliefs. Winthrop charged her with having set wife against husband, because so many of her followers were women. A minister at her church trial told her bluntly, "You have stepped out of your place, you have rather been a Husband than a Wife and a preacher than a Hearer; and a Magistrate than a Subject."

The New England authorities' reaction to Anne Hutchinson reveals the depth of their adherence to European gender-role concepts. To them, an orderly society required the submission of wives to husbands as well as the obedience of subjects to rulers and ordinary folk to gentry. English people intended to change many aspects of their lives by colonizing North America, but not the gendered division of labor, the assumption of male superiority, or the maintenance of social hierarchies.

## *Legacy* FOR A PEOPLE AND A NATION

### Blue Laws

The seventeenth-century New England colonies enacted statutes, now generally referred to as *blue laws,* preventing their residents from working or engaging in recreation on Sundays, when they were supposed to attend church. Although the laws were inconsistently enforced, over the years various colonists found themselves fined for such forbidden Sabbath activities as plowing their fields, pursuing wandering livestock, drinking in taverns, or playing such games as shuffleboard. More harshly treated were those thieves who took advantage of others' attendance at church services to break into their houses to steal food, clothing, and other items.

The term appears to have been coined by the Reverend Samuel Peters, a loyalist, in his *General History of Connecticut,* published in London in 1781. Peters—hardly an unbiased observer of the state that had forced him into exile—used *blue laws* to refer to Connecticut's early legal code in general, defining it as "bloody Laws; for they were all sanctified with whippings, cutting off the ears, burning the tongue, and death." Eventually, though, *blue laws* acquired its current primary meaning; that is, legislation regulating behavior on Sundays. States continued to enact such statutes after independence, especially in the nineteenth century, but just as in the colonial period, many of the laws were rarely enforced.

Still, they remained on the books, and some were rigorously applied. A 1961 Supreme Court decision, *McGowan v. Maryland,* upheld that state's law restricting what could be sold on Sundays because of its secular purpose—promoting the "health, safety, recreation, and general well-being" of the populace. Whereas colonial legislators were attempting to prevent Sunday work, modern Americans (like the Maryland legislature) seem more concerned about halting Sunday shopping. Not until 1991 did the last state (North Dakota) repeal a law requiring all stores to be closed on Sundays, and only in May 2003 did New York State remove its ban on Sunday liquor sales. Bergen County, New Jersey, still forbids the many shopping malls within its borders from opening on Sundays. Advocates of the ban cite the benefits of traffic reduction on that one day a week.

Today a web site, www.BlueLaws.net, urges readers to join its "Keep Sunday Special Campaign," arguing that Sunday closing laws are "pro-family, pro-environment and pro-labor"—and more necessary than ever. Its plea to "restore the observance of the Lord's Day in our nation" shows the continuing legacy of the seventeenth century for the American people.

## SUMMARY

By the middle of the seventeenth century, Europeans had come to North America and the Caribbean to stay, a fact that signaled major changes for the peoples of both hemispheres. These newcomers had indelibly altered not only their own lives but also those of native peoples. Europeans killed Indians with their weapons and diseases, and had varying success in converting them to Christianity. Contacts with indigenous peoples taught Europeans to eat new foods, speak new languages, and recognize—however reluctantly—the persistence of other cultural patterns. The prosperity and even survival of many of the European colonies depended heavily on the cultivation of American crops (maize and tobacco) and an Asian crop (sugar), thus attesting to the importance of post-Columbian ecological exchange.

Political rivalries once confined to Europe spread around the globe, as England, Spain, Portugal, France, and the Netherlands vied for control of the peoples and resources of Asia, Africa, and the Americas. In America, Spaniards reaped the benefits of their gold and silver mines, while French people earned their primary profits from the fur trade (in Canada) and cultivating sugar (in the Caribbean). Sugar also enriched the Portuguese. The Dutch concentrated on commerce—trading in furs and sugar as well as carrying human cargoes of enslaved Africans to South America and the Caribbean.

Although the English colonies, too, at first sought to rely on trade, they quickly took another form altogether when so many English people of the "middling sort" decided to migrate to North America. To a greater extent than their European counterparts, the English transferred the society and politics of their homeland to a new environment. Their sheer numbers, coupled with their need for vast quantities of land on which to grow their crops and raise their livestock, inevitably brought them into conflict with their Indian neighbors. New England and the Chesapeake differed in the sex ratio and age range of their immigrant populations, the nature of their developing economies, their settlement patterns, and the impact of religious beliefs. Yet they resembled each other in the internal and external conflicts their expansion engendered. In years to come, both regions would become embroiled in increasingly fierce rivalries besetting the European powers. Those rivalries would continue to affect Americans of all races until after the mid-eighteenth century, when France and England fought the greatest war yet known, and the Anglo-American colonies won their independence.

## SUGGESTIONS FOR FURTHER READING

Virginia DeJohn Anderson, *Creatures of Empire: How Domestic Animals Transformed Early America* (2004)

Richard S. Dunn, *Sugar and Slaves: The Rise of the Planter Class in the English West Indies, 1624–1713* (1972)

Alison Games, *Migration and the Origins of the English Atlantic World* (1999)

David D. Hall, *Worlds of Wonder, Days of Judgment: Popular Religious Belief in Early New England* (1989)

Karen O. Kupperman, *Indians & English: Facing off in Early America* (2000)

Mary Beth Norton, *Founding Mothers & Fathers: Gendered Power and the Forming of American Society* (1996)

Helen C. Rountree, *Pocahontas, Powhatan, Opechancanough: Three Indian Lives Changed by Jamestown* (2005)

David J. Weber, *The Spanish Frontier in North America* (1992)

Keith Wrightson, *English Society, 1580–1680* (1982)

*For a more extensive list for further reading, go to* college.hmco.com/pic/norton8e.

# North America in the Atlantic World *1650-1720*

NARRATIVE

OF THE

CAPTIVITY, SUFFERINGS AND REMOVES

OF

Mrs. *Mary Rowlandson,*

𝒮he was starving. Offered a piece of boiled horse's foot by a compassionate neighbor, the slave gulped it down. Desperate, she seized another piece from a small child, who "could not bite it . . . but lay sucking, gnawing, chewing and slobbering of it in the mouth and hand." Later, she recalled that "savoury it was to my taste. . . . Thus the Lord made that pleasant refreshing, which another time would have been an abomination." But Mary Rowlandson recorded that her mistress then threatened to kill her, telling her that she had "disgraced" the household by begging for food. The captive retorted, "they had as good knock me in the head as starve me to death."

What had brought the wife of the Reverend Joseph Rowlandson of Lancaster, Massachusetts, to such distress? On February 10, 1676, a force of Wampanoags, Narragansetts, and Nipmucks had killed fourteen townspeople (including her daughter) and captured twenty-three others, in the midst of the conflict that New Englanders called King Philip's War. Carried away by the attackers to be held for ransom, she endured their hardships as they fled through the wintry countryside of western Massachusetts and southern New Hampshire. She became the slave of Quinnapin, a Narragansett sachem, and his three wives, one of whom, Weetamoo, herself a Wampanoag sachem, was her mistress. Both were eventually killed by the colonists after the death of their leader, the Wampanoag known as King Philip, in August 1676. But months before that, in May, Mary Rowlandson had been ransomed from her captors for £20—roughly equivalent to $500 today. Her experience, the Puritan woman later wrote, had taught her an important religious lesson: "to look beyond present and smaller troubles, and to be quieted under them."

◀ Mary White Rowlandson's account of her experiences during King Philip's War, first published 1682, became the colonial equivalent of a best seller. Republished many times, it established a entire genre of popular literature: the captivity narrative. Generations of colonial readers were enthralled by tales of English settlers who spent months or years living with their native captors. *(Courtesy, American Antiquarian Society)*

## CHRONOLOGY

**1642–46** ■ English Civil War

**1649** ■ Charles I executed

**1651** ■ First Navigation Act passed to regulate colonial trade

**1660** ■ Stuarts (Charles II) restored to throne

**1663** ■ Carolina chartered

**1664** ■ English conquer New Netherland
■ New York founded
■ New Jersey established

**1670s** ■ Marquette, Jolliet, and La Salle explore the Great Lakes and Mississippi valley for France

**1675–76** ■ Bacon's Rebellion disrupts Virginia government; Jamestown destroyed

**1675–78** ■ King Philip's War devastates New England

**1680–1700** ■ Pueblo revolt temporarily drives Spaniards from New Mexico

**1681** ■ Pennsylvania chartered

**1685** ■ James II becomes king

**1686–88** ■ Dominion of New England established, superseding all charters of colonies from Maine to New Jersey

**1688–89** ■ James II deposed in Glorious Revolution
■ William and Mary ascend throne

**1689** ■ Glorious Revolution in America; Massachusetts, New York, and Maryland overthrow colonial governors

**1688–99** ■ King William's War fought on northern New England frontier

**1691** ■ New Massachusetts charter issued

**1692** ■ Witchcraft crisis in Salem; nineteen people hanged

**1696** ■ Board of Trade and Plantations established to coordinate English colonial administration
■ Vice-admiralty courts established in America

**1701** ■ Iroquois adopt neutrality policy toward France and England

**1702–13** ■ Queen Anne's War fought by French and English

**1711–13** ■ Tuscarora War (North Carolina) leads to capture or migration of most Tuscaroras

**1715** ■ Yamasee War nearly destroys South Carolina

**1718** ■ New Orleans founded in French Louisiana

Mary Rowlandson's famous narrative, *The Sovereignty and Goodness of God,* published in 1682, exposes more than the sufferings she shared with her captors; it also reveals that she had little understanding of, or sympathy for, their circumstances. When Weetamoo's baby died, she remarked coldly that "there was one benefit in it, that there was more room" in the wigwam. Even though Christian Indians served as go-betweens when her ransom was arranged, she distrusted them. Her narrative illustrates not only her own experiences as a captive but also the contentious relationships of Anglo New Englanders and their native neighbors. Much had changed since King Philip's father, Massasoit, had allied himself with the first settlers of Plymouth.

Many of those changes were directly related to the mainland colonies' involvement in a growing international network. Few developments demonstrated that fact more clearly than the postwar fate of many of King Philip's captured followers: they were sold into slavery in the Caribbean and elsewhere, some transported as far away as Tangier, in modern Morocco. North America, like England itself, was becoming embedded in a worldwide matrix of trade and warfare. The web woven by oceangoing vessels—once composed of only a few strands spun by Columbus and his successors—now crisscrossed the globe, carrying European goods to America and Africa, Caribbean sugar to New England and Europe, Africans to the Americas, and New England fish and wood products—and occasionally Indian slaves—to the Caribbean. Formerly tiny outposts, the North American colonies expanded their territorial claims and diversified their economies after the mid-seventeenth century.

Three developments shaped life in the mainland English colonies between 1640 and 1720: escalating conflicts with Indians and other European colonies in North America; the expansion of slavery, especially in the southern coastal regions; and changes in the colonies' political and economic relationships with England.

The explosive growth of the slave trade significantly altered the Anglo-American economy. Carrying human cargoes paid off handsomely, as many mariners and ship owners learned. Planters who could afford to buy slaves also reaped huge profits. At first involving primarily Indians and already enslaved Africans from the Caribbean, the trade soon came to focus on cargoes brought to the Americas directly from Africa. The arrival of large numbers of West African peoples thus pressed into labor expanded agricultural productivity, fueled the international trading system, and dramatically reshaped colonial society.

The burgeoning North American economy attracted new attention from colonial administrators. Especially after the Stuarts had been restored to the throne in 1660 (having lost it for a time because of the English Civil War), London bureaucrats attempted to supervise the American settlements more effectively and to ensure that the mother country benefited from their economic growth. By the early eighteenth century, following three decades of upheaval, a new stability characterized colonial political institutions.

Neither English colonists nor London administrators could ignore other peoples living on the North American continent. As English settlements expanded, they came into violent conflict not only with powerful Indian nations but also with the Dutch, the Spanish, and especially the French. Moreover, all the European colonies confronted significant crises during the decade of the 1670s. By 1720, war—between Europeans and Indians, among Europeans, and among Indians allied with different colonial powers—had become an all-too-familiar feature of American life. No longer isolated from one another or from Europe, the people and products of the North American colonies had become integral to the world trading system and inextricably enmeshed in its conflicts.

- What were the consequences of the transatlantic slave trade in North America and Africa?
- How did English policy toward the colonies change from 1650 to 1720?
- What were the causes and results of new friction between Europeans and native peoples?

## THE GROWTH OF ANGLO-AMERICAN SETTLEMENTS

Between 1642 and 1646 civil war between supporters of King Charles I and the Puritan-dominated Parliament engulfed the colonists' English homeland. Parliament triumphed, leading to the execution of the king in 1649 and interim rule by the parliamentary army's leader, Oliver Cromwell, during the so-called Commonwealth period.

| TABLE 3.1 | Restored Stuart Monarchs of England, 1660–1714 | |
| --- | --- | --- |
| **Monarch** | **Reign** | **Relation to Predecessor** |
| Charles II | 1660–1685 | Son |
| James II | 1685–1688 | Brother |
| Mary | 1688–1694 | Daughter |
| William | 1688–1702 | Son-in-law |
| Anne | 1702–1714 | Sister, Sister-in-law |

But after Cromwell's death, Parliament decided to restore the monarchy if Charles I's son and heir agreed to restrictions on his authority. Charles II did so, and the Stuarts were returned to the throne in 1660 (see Table 3.1). The new king subsequently rewarded nobles and others who had supported him during the Civil War with huge tracts of land on the North American mainland. The colonies thereby established made up six of the thirteen polities that eventually would form the American nation: New York, New Jersey, Pennsylvania (including Delaware), and North and South Carolina (see Map 3.1). Collectively, these became known as the Restoration colonies because they were created by the restored Stuart monarchy. All were proprietorships; in each of them one man or several men held title to the soil and controlled the government.

Charles's younger brother James, the duke of York, benefited quickly. In 1664 Charles II gave James the region between the Connecticut and Delaware Rivers, including the Hudson valley and Long Island. That the Dutch had settled there mattered little; the English and the Dutch were at the time engaged in sporadic warfare, and the English were also attacking other Dutch colonies. In August James's warships anchored off Manhattan Island, demanding New Netherland's surrender. The colony complied without resistance. Although in 1672 the Netherlands briefly retook the colony, the Dutch permanently ceded it in 1674.

**New York**

Thus James acquired a heterogeneous possession, which he renamed New York (see Table 3.2). In 1664 a significant minority of English people (mostly Puritan New Englanders on Long Island) already lived there, along with the Dutch and sizable numbers of Indians, Africans, Germans, Scandinavians, and a smattering of other European peoples. The Dutch West India Company had imported slaves into the colony, intending some for resale in the Chesapeake. Many, though, remained in New Netherland as laborers; at the time of the English conquest, almost one-fifth of Manhattan's approximately fifteen hundred free and enslaved inhabitants were of African

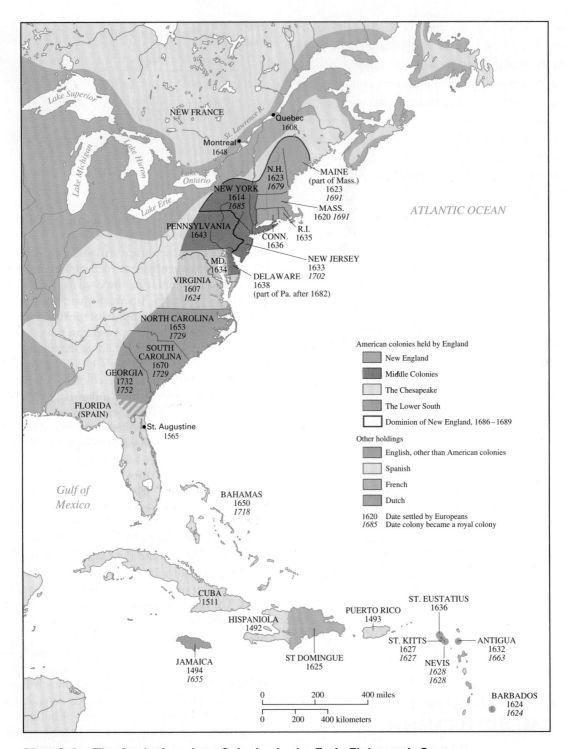

**Map 3.1** **The Anglo-American Colonies in the Early Eighteenth Century**

By the early eighteenth century, the English colonies nominally dominated the Atlantic coastline of North America. But the colonies' formal boundary lines are deceiving because the western reaches of each colony were still largely unfamiliar to Europeans and because much of the land was still inhabited by Native Americans.

| TABLE 3.2 | The Founding of English Colonies in North America, 1664–1681 | | |
|---|---|---|---|
| **Colony** | **Founder(s)** | **Date** | **Basis of Economy** |
| New York (formerly New Netherland) | James, duke of York | 1664 | Farming, fur trading |
| New Jersey | Sir George Carteret, John Lord Berkeley | 1664 | Farming |
| North Carolina | Carolina proprietors | 1665 | Tobacco, forest products |
| South Carolina | Carolina proprietors | 1670 | Rice, indigo |
| Pennsylvania (incl. Delaware) | William Penn | 1681 | Farming |

descent. Slaves then made up a higher proportion of New York's urban population than of the Chesapeake's rural people.

Recognizing the population's diversity, James's representatives moved cautiously in their efforts to establish English authority. The Duke's Laws, a legal code proclaimed in 1665, applied solely to the English settlements on Long Island, only later being extended to the rest of the colony. James's policies initially maintained Dutch forms of local government, confirmed Dutch land titles, and allowed Dutch residents to maintain customary legal practices. Each town was permitted to decide which church (Dutch Reformed, Congregational, or Church of England) to support with its tax revenues. Much to the dismay of English residents, the Duke's Laws made no provision for a representative assembly. Like other Stuarts, James distrusted legislative bodies, and not until 1683 did he agree to the colonists' requests for an elected legislature. Before then, an autocratic governor ruled New York.

The English takeover thus had little immediate effect on the colony. Its population grew slowly, barely reaching eighteen thousand by the time of the first English census in 1698. Until the second decade of the eighteenth century, New York City remained a commercial backwater within the orbit of Boston.

The English conquest brought so little change to New York primarily because the duke of York in 1664

### New Jersey

regranted the land between the Hudson and Delaware Rivers—East and West Jersey—to his friends Sir George Carteret and John Lord Berkeley. That grant left the duke's own colony hemmed in between Connecticut to the east and the Jerseys to the west and south, depriving it of much fertile land and hindering its economic growth. He also failed to promote migration. Meanwhile, the Jersey proprietors acted rapidly to attract settlers, promising generous land grants, limited freedom of religion, and—without authorization from the Crown—a representative assembly. In response, large numbers of Puritan New Englanders migrated southward to the Jerseys, along with some Barbadians and Dutch New Yorkers. New Jersey grew quickly; in 1726, at the time of its first census as a united colony, it had 32,500 inhabitants, only 8,000 fewer than New York.

Within twenty years, Berkeley and Carteret sold their interests in the Jerseys to separate groups of investors.

▲ About 1650 a Dutch artist produced this copper engraving of New Amsterdam. Dominated by a prominent windmill, tall government buildings, and European-style row houses, the small community closely resembled towns in the Netherlands. Note the many contrasts to the view of Plymouth on page 51. *(Museum of the City of New York. Gift of Dr. N. Sulzberber)*

The purchasers of all of Carteret's share (West Jersey) and portions of Berkeley's (East Jersey) were members of the Society of Friends, also called Quakers. That new, small sect rejected earthly and religious hierarchies. Quakers believed that anyone could be saved by directly receiving God's "inner light" and that all people were equal in God's sight. With no formally trained clergy, Quakers allowed anyone, male or female, to speak in meetings or become a "public Friend" and travel to spread God's word. Quakers proselytized throughout the Atlantic world in the 1650s, recruiting followers in all of England's colonies from a base in Barbados. Yet the authorities did not welcome the message of radical egalitarianism, and Quakers encountered persecution everywhere. Mary Dyer—who had followed Anne Hutchinson into exile—became a Quaker, returned to Boston as a missionary, and was hanged in 1660 (along with several men) for preaching Quaker doctrines.

The Quakers obtained their own colony in 1681, when Charles II granted the region between Maryland and New York to his close friend William Penn, a prominent member of the sect. Penn was then thirty-seven years old; he held the colony

## Pennsylvania

as a personal proprietorship, one that earned profits for his descendants until the American Revolution. Even so, Penn, like the Roman Catholic Calverts of Maryland before him, saw his province not merely as a source of revenue but also as a haven for persecuted coreligionists. Penn offered land to all comers on liberal terms, promised toleration of all religions (although only Christians were given the vote), guaranteed English liberties, such as the right to bail and trial by jury, and pledged to establish a representative assembly. He also publicized the ready availability of land in Pennsylvania through widely distributed promotional tracts printed in German, French, and Dutch.

Penn's activities and the Quakers' attraction to his lands gave rise to a migration whose magnitude equaled the Puritan exodus to New England in the 1630s. By mid-1683, more than three thousand people—among them Welsh, Irish, Dutch, and Germans—had already moved to Pennsylvania, and within five years the population reached twelve thousand. (By contrast, it had taken Virginia more than thirty years to achieve a comparable population.) Philadelphia, carefully sited on the easily navigable Delaware River and planned to be the major city in the province, drew merchants and artisans from

▲ William Penn, later the proprietor of Pennsylvania, as he looked during his youth in Ireland. In such pamphlets as the one shown here, Penn spread the word about his new colony to thousands of readers in England and its other colonial possessions.

*(Historical Society of Pennsylvania)*

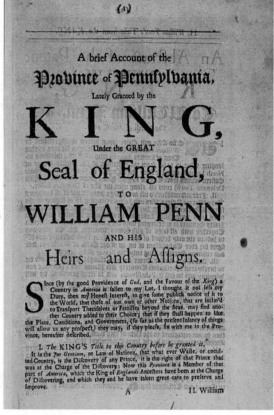

throughout the English-speaking world. From mainland and Caribbean colonies alike came Quakers seeking religious freedom; they brought with them years of experience on American soil and well-established trading connections. Pennsylvania's plentiful and fertile lands soon enabled its residents to begin exporting surplus flour and other foodstuffs to the West Indies. Practically overnight Philadelphia acquired more than two thousand citizens and started to challenge Boston's commercial dominance.

A pacifist with egalitarian principles, Penn attempted to treat native peoples fairly. He learned to speak the language of the Delawares (or Lenapes), from whom he purchased tracts of land to sell to European settlers. Penn also established strict regulations for trade and forbade the sale of alcohol to Indians. His policies attracted native peoples who moved to Pennsylvania near the end of the seventeenth century to escape repeated clashes with English colonists in Maryland, Virginia, and North Carolina. Most important were the Tuscaroras, whose experiences are described later in this chapter. Likewise, Shawnees and Miamis chose to move eastward from the Ohio valley. By a supreme irony, however, the same toleration that attracted Native Americans also brought non-Quaker Europeans who showed little respect for Indian claims to the soil. In effect, Penn's policy was so successful that it caused its own downfall. The Scots-Irish, Germans, and Swiss who settled in Pennsylvania in the first half of the eighteenth century clashed repeatedly over land with Indians who had also recently migrated to the colony.

The southernmost proprietary colony, granted by Charles II in 1663, encompassed a huge tract stretching

||||||||||||||||||||||||||||||||

### Carolina

from the southern boundary of Virginia to Spanish Florida. The area had great strategic importance: a successful English settlement there would prevent Spaniards from pushing farther north. The fertile, semitropical land also held forth the promise of producing such exotic and valuable commodities as figs, olives, wines, and silk. The proprietors named their new province Carolina in honor of Charles, whose Latin name was Carolus. The "Fundamental Constitutions of Carolina," which they asked the political philosopher John Locke to draft for them, set forth an elaborate plan for a colony governed by a hierarchy of landholding aristocrats and characterized by a carefully structured distribution of political and economic power.

But Carolina failed to follow the course the proprietors had laid out. Instead, it quickly developed two distinct population centers, which in 1729 split into separate colonies under direct royal rule. Virginia planters settled the Albemarle region that became North Carolina. They established a society much like their own, with an economy based on cultivating tobacco and exporting such forest products as pitch, tar, and timber. Because North Carolina lacked a satisfactory harbor, its planters relied on Virginia's ports and merchants to conduct their trade. The other population center, which eventually formed the core of South Carolina, developed at Charles Town, founded in 1670 near the juncture of the Ashley and Cooper Rivers. Many of its early residents migrated from overcrowded Barbados. These sugar planters expected to reestablish plantation agriculture and hoped to escape hurricanes. They were disappointed in both respects: they soon learned that sugar would not grow successfully in Carolina, and they experienced a "wonderfully horrid and destructive" hurricane in 1686.

The settlers began to raise corn and herds of cattle, which they sold to Caribbean planters hungry for foodstuffs. Like other colonists before them, they also depended on trade with nearby Indians to supply commodities they could sell elsewhere. In Carolina, those items were deerskins (almost as valuable as beaver pelts in Europe) and Indian slaves, which were shipped to the Caribbean and the northern colonies. Nearby Indian nations hunted deer with increasing intensity and readily sold captured enemies to the English settlers. During the first decade of the eighteenth century, South Carolina exported an average of 54,000 skins annually, and overseas shipments later peaked at 160,000 a year. Before 1715, Carolinians additionally exported an estimated 30,000 to 50,000 Indian slaves.

The English Civil War retarded the development of the earlier English settlements. In the Chesapeake, struggles

||||||||||||||||||||||||||||||||

### Chesapeake

between supporters of the king and Parliament caused military clashes in Maryland and political upheavals in Virginia. But once the war ended and immigration resumed, the colonies expanded once again. Some settlers, especially those on Virginia's eastern shore and along that colony's southern border, raised grain, livestock, and flax, which they sold to English and Dutch merchants. Tobacco growers began importing increasing numbers of English indentured servants to work on their farms, which had by then begun to develop into plantations. Freed from concerns about Indian attack by the final defeat of the Powhatan Confederacy in 1646, they—especially recent immigrants—eagerly sought to enlarge their landholdings.

Although they still depended primarily on English laborers, Chesapeake tobacco planters also started to acquire small numbers of slaves. Almost all came from a population that historian Ira Berlin has termed "Atlantic

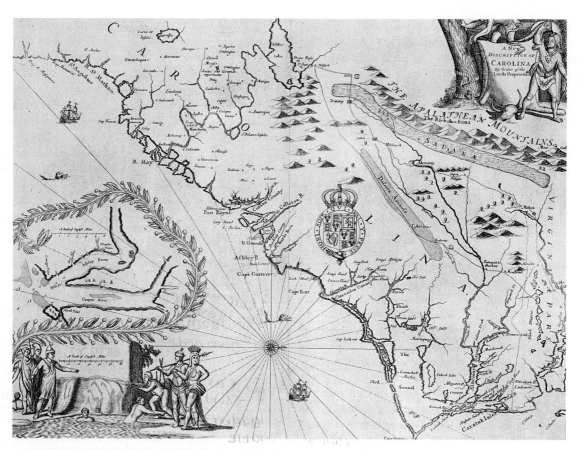

▲ Map from *A New Description of Carolina,* by John Ogilby, 1671 (with south at the top). Ogilby's tract, illustrated by a map drawn from information supplied by John Lederer, a German Indian trader, was intended to attract settlers to the new Carolina colony. He filled his text with information supplied by the Lords Proprietors, stressing the colony's pleasant climate, abundant resources, and friendly Native peoples, a message underscored by the peaceful scenes in the corner cartouches.

*(Colonial Williamsburg Foundation)*

creoles"—that is, people (perhaps of mixed race) who came from other European settlements in the Atlantic world, primarily from Iberian outposts. Not all the Atlantic creoles who came to the Chesapeake were bondspeople; some were free or indentured. With their arrival, the Chesapeake became what Berlin calls a "society with slaves," or one in which slavery does not dominate the economy but is one of a number of coexisting labor systems.

In New England, migration essentially ceased after the Civil War began in 1642. While Puritans were first challenging the king and then governing England as a commonwealth, they had little incentive to leave their homeland, and few migrated after the Restoration. Yet the Puritan colonies' population continued to grow dramatically because of natural increase. By the 1670s, New England's population had

## New England

more than tripled to reach approximately seventy thousand. Such a rapid expansion placed great pressure on available land. Colonial settlement spread far into the interior of Massachusetts and Connecticut, and many members of the third and fourth generations migrated— north to New Hampshire or Maine, south to New York or New Jersey, west beyond the Connecticut River—to find sufficient farmland for themselves and their children. Others abandoned agriculture and learned such skills as blacksmithing or carpentry to support themselves in the growing towns.

The people who remained behind in the small, yet densely populated older New England communities experienced a new phenomenon after approximately 1650: witchcraft accusations and trials. Other regions largely escaped such incidents, even though most seventeenth-century people believed that witches existed. These allies of the Devil were thought to harness invisible spirits for good or evil purposes. For example, a witch might engage in fortunetelling, prepare healing potions or charms, or harm others by causing the death of a child or valuable animals. Yet only New England witnessed many trials of accused witches (about one hundred in all before 1690). Most, though not all, of the accused were middle-aged women who had angered their neighbors. Historians have accordingly concluded that the dynamics of daily interactions in the close-knit communities, where the same families lived nearby for decades, fostered longstanding quarrels that led some colonists to believe that others had diabolically caused certain misfortunes. Even so, only a few of the accused were convicted, and fewer still were executed, because judges and juries remained skeptical of such charges.

That New England courts halted questionable prosecutions suggests the maturity of colonial institutions. By the last quarter of the

### Colonial Political Structures

seventeenth century, almost all the Anglo-American colonies had well-established political and judicial structures. In New England, property-holding men or the legislature elected the governors; in other regions, the king or the proprietor appointed such leaders. A council, either elected or appointed, advised the governor on matters of policy and served as the upper house of the legislature. Each colony had a judiciary with local justices of the peace, county courts, and, usually, an appeals court composed of the councilors.

Local political institutions also developed. In New England, elected selectmen initially governed the towns, but by the end of the seventeenth century, town meetings—held at least annually and attended by most free adult male residents—handled matters of local concern. In the Chesapeake colonies and both of the Carolinas, appointed magistrates ran local governments. At first the same was true in Pennsylvania, but by the early eighteenth century, elected county officials began to take over some government functions. And in New York, local elections were the rule even before the establishment of the colonial assembly in 1683.

## A DECADE OF IMPERIAL CRISES: THE 1670S

As the Restoration colonies were extending the range of English settlement, the first English colonies and French and Spanish settlements in North America faced crises caused primarily by their changing relationships with America's indigenous peoples. Between 1670 and 1680,

New France, New Mexico, New England, and Virginia experienced bitter conflicts as their interests collided with those of America's original inhabitants. All the early colonies changed irrevocably as a result.

In the mid-1670s Louis de Buade de Frontenac, the governor-general of Canada, decided to expand New

### New France and the Iroquois

France's reach into the south and west, hoping to establish a trade route to Mexico and to gain direct control of the valuable fur trade on which the prosperity of the colony rested. Accordingly, he encouraged the explorations of Father Jacques Marquette, Louis Jolliet, and René-Robert Cavelier de La Salle in the Great Lakes and

▲ Contemporary engraving of John Verelst's 1710 portrait of the Mohawk chief known as Hendrick to Europeans (his Indian name was rendered as "Dyionoagon" or "Tee Yee Neen Ho Ga Row"). Hendrick and three other Iroquois leaders visited London in 1710, symbolically cementing the Covenant Chain negotiated in 1677. His primarily European dress and the wampum belt in his hand accentuate his identity as a cross-cultural diplomatic emissary. *(John Carter Brown Library at Brown University)*

Mississippi valley regions. His goal, however, brought him into conflict with the powerful Iroquois Confederacy, composed of five Indian nations—the Mohawks, Oneidas, Onondagas, Cayugas, and Senecas. (In 1722 the Tuscaroras became the sixth.)

Under the terms of a unique defensive alliance forged early in the sixteenth century, a representative council made decisions of war and peace for the entire Iroquois Confederacy, although each nation still retained some autonomy and could not be forced to comply with a council directive against its will. Before the arrival of Europeans, the Iroquois waged wars primarily to acquire captives to replenish their population. Contact with foreign traders brought ravaging disease as early as 1633, intensifying the need for captives. Simultaneously, the Europeans' presence created an economic motive for warfare: the desire to dominate the fur trade and to gain unimpeded access to European goods. The war with the Hurons in the 1640s initiated a series of conflicts with other Indians known as the Beaver Wars, in which the Iroquois fought to achieve control of the lucrative peltry trade. Iroquois warriors did not themselves trap beaver; instead, they raided other villages in search of caches of pelts or attacked Indians from the interior as they carried furs to European outposts. Then the Iroquois traded that booty for European-made blankets, knives, guns, alcohol, and other desirable items.

In the mid-1670s, as Iroquois dominance grew, the French intervened, for an Iroquois triumph would have destroyed France's plans to trade directly with western Indians. Over the next twenty years the French launched repeated attacks on Iroquois villages. The English offered little assistance other than weapons to their trading partners, even though in 1677 New Yorkers and the Iroquois established a formal alliance known as the Covenant Chain. Its people and resources depleted by constant warfare, the confederacy in 1701 finally negotiated a neutrality treaty with France and other Indians. For the next half-century the Iroquois nations maintained their power through trade and skillful diplomacy rather than warfare, forming or abandoning alliances with Indian or European nations to best achieve their goals.

The wars against the Iroquois initiated in the 1670s were crucial components of French Canada's plan to penetrate the heartland of North America. Unlike Spaniards, French adventurers did not attempt to subjugate the Indians they encountered. Nor, at first, did they even formally claim large territories for France. Still, when France decided to strengthen its presence near the Gulf of Mexico by founding New Orleans in 1718—to counter both westward thrusts of the English colonies and eastward moves of the Spanish—the Mississippi posts became the glue of empire. *Coureurs de bois* (literally, "forest runners") used the rivers and lakes of the American interior to travel regularly between Quebec and Louisiana, carrying French goods to outposts such as Michilimackinac (at the junction of Lakes Michigan and Huron), Kaskaskia (in present-day Illinois), and Fort Rosalie (Natchez), on the lower Mississippi River (see Map 3.2).

### French Expansion

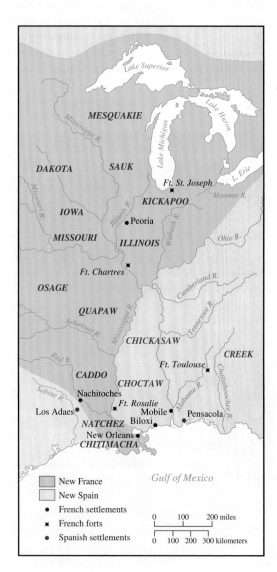

**Map 3.2   Louisiana, c. 1720**
By 1720 French forts and settlements dotted the Mississippi River and its tributaries in the interior of North America. Two isolated Spanish outposts were situated near the Gulf of Mexico.

*(Source: Adapted from* France in America, *by William J. Eccles. Copyright © 1972 by William J. Eccles. Reprinted by permission of HarperCollins Publishers, Inc. The New American Nation Series.)*

At such sites lived a small military garrison and a priest, surrounded by powerful nations such as the Choctaws, Chickasaws, and Osages. Indians gained easy access to valuable trade goods by tolerating the minimal European presence, and France's primarily political and economic aims did not include systematic missionary work. The largest French settlements in the region, known collectively as *le pays de Illinois* ("the Illinois country"), never totaled much above three thousand in population. Located along the Mississippi south of modern St. Louis and north of Fort Chartres, the settlements produced wheat for export to New Orleans. In all the French outposts, the shortage of European women led to interracial unions between French men and Indian women, and to the creation of mixed-race people known as *metís*.

In New Mexico, too, events of the 1670s led to a crisis with long-term consequences. Over the years un-

## Pueblo Peoples and Spaniards

der Spanish domination, the Pueblo peoples had added Christianity to their religious beliefs while still retaining traditional rituals, engaging in syncretic practices as had Mesoamericans. But as decades passed, Franciscans adopted increasingly brutal and violent tactics in order to erase all traces of the native religion. Priests and secular colonists who held *encomiendas* also placed heavy labor demands on the population. In 1680 the Pueblos revolted under the leadership of Popé, a respected shaman, successfully driving the Spaniards out of New Mexico (see Map 3.3). Even though Spain managed to restore its authority by 1700, imperial officials had learned their lesson. Afterward, Spanish governors stressed cooperation with native peoples, no longer attempting to violate their cultural integrity or to enslave them, though still relying on their labor. The

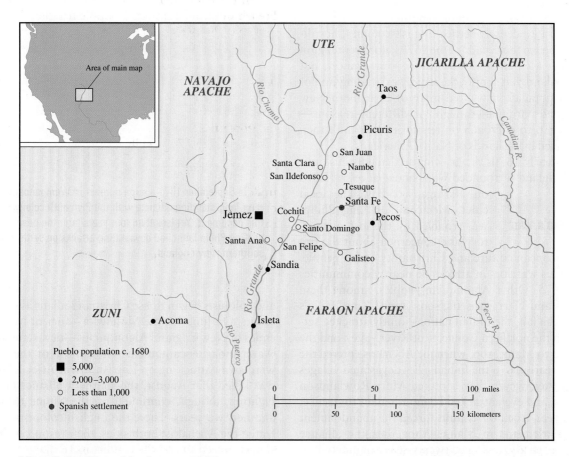

**Map 3.3   New Mexico, c. 1680**

In 1680, the lone Spanish settlement at Santa Fe was surrounded and vastly outnumbered by the many Pueblo villages nearby.

*(Source: Adapted from* Apache, Navaho, and Spaniard, *by Jack D. Forbes. Copyright © 1960 by the University of Oklahoma Press. Reprinted by permission of the University of Oklahoma Press.)*

Pueblo revolt constituted the most successful and longest-sustained Indian resistance movement in colonial North America.

When Spaniards expanded their territorial claims to the east and north, they followed the same strategy they had adopted in New Mexico, establishing their presence through military outposts (presidios) and Franciscan missions. The army maintained order among the subject Indians—to protect them from attack and ensure the availability of their labor—and guarded the boundaries of New Spain from possible incursions, especially by the French. The friars concentrated on conversions and allowed religious syncretism. By the late eighteenth century, Spain claimed a vast territory that stretched from California (first colonized in 1769 to prevent Russian sea-otter trappers from taking over the region) through Texas (settled after 1700) to the Gulf Coast. Throughout that region, the Spanish presence consisted of a mixture of missions and presidios dotting the countryside, sometimes at considerable distances from one another.

In the more densely settled English colonies, hostilities developed in the decade of the 1670s, not over religion (as in New Mexico) or trade (as in New France), but rather over land. Put simply, the rapidly expanding Anglo-American population wanted more of it. In both New England and Virginia—though for different reasons—settlers began to encroach on territories that until then had remained in the hands of Native Americans.

By the early 1670s the growing settlements in southern New England surrounded Wampanoag ancestral lands on Narragansett Bay. The local chief, Metacom, or King Philip, was troubled by the loss of territory and concerned about the impact of European culture and Christianity on his people. Philip led his warriors in attacks on nearby communities in June 1675. Other Algonquian peoples, among them Nipmucks and Narragansetts, soon joined King Philip's forces. In the fall, the Indian nations jointly attacked settlements in the northern Connecticut River valley, and the war spread to Maine, too, when the Abenakis entered the conflict. In early 1676 the Indian allies devastated villages like Lancaster, where they captured Mary Rowlandson and others, and even attacked Plymouth and Providence; later that year, Abenaki assaults forced the abandonment of most settlements in Maine. Altogether, the alliance wholly or partially destroyed twenty-seven of ninety-two towns and attacked forty others, pushing the line of English settlement back toward the east and south.

The tide turned in the south in the summer of 1676. The Indian coalition ran short of food and ammunition,

### King Philip's War

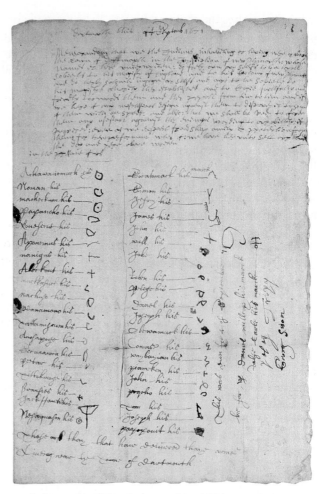

▲ In September 1671 a large number of Wampanoags renewed their long-standing alliance with the Plymouth colony by signing this document. Yet less than four years later the peace collapsed as King Philip launched devastating attacks on settlements in southern New England. *(Boston Athenaeum)*

and colonists began to use Christian Indians as guides and scouts. On June 12, the Mohawks—ancient Iroquois enemies of New England Algonquians—devastated a major Wampanoag encampment while most of the warriors were away attacking an English town. After King Philip was killed that August, the southern alliance crumbled. Fighting, though, continued on the Maine frontier for another two years. There the English colonists never defeated the Abenakis; both sides, their resources depleted, simply agreed to end the conflict in 1678.

In addition to the Wampanoags, Nipmucks, Narragansetts, and Abenakis who were captured and sold into slavery, still more died of starvation and disease. New Englanders had broken the power of the southern coastal tribes. Thereafter the southern Indians lived in small clusters, subordinated to the colonists and often working as servants or sailors. Only on the island of Martha's Vineyard did Christian Wampanoags preserve their cultural identity intact.

But the settlers paid a terrible price for their victory in King Philip's War: an estimated one-tenth of the able-bodied adult male population was killed or wounded. Proportional to population, it was the most costly conflict in American history. New Englanders did not fully rebuild abandoned interior towns for another three decades, and not until the American Revolution did the region's per capita income again reach pre-1675 levels.

Not coincidentally, conflict simultaneously wracked Virginia. In the early 1670s, ex-servants unable to acquire land avidly eyed the territory reserved by treaty for Virginia's Indians. Governor William Berkeley, the leader of an entrenched coterie of large landowners, resisted starting a war to further the aims of settlers who were challenging his authority. Dissatisfied colonists then rallied behind the leadership of a recent immigrant, the gentleman Nathaniel Bacon, who like other new arrivals had found that all the desirable land in settled areas had already been claimed. Using as a pretext the July 1675 killing of an indentured servant by some Doeg Indians, settlers attacked not only the Doegs but also the Susquehannocks, a more powerful nation. In retaliation, Susquehannock bands raided outlying farms early in 1676.

**Bacon's Rebellion**

Berkeley and Bacon soon clashed. The governor outlawed Bacon and his men; the rebels held Berkeley hostage until they won authorization to attack the Indians. As the chaotic summer of 1676 wore on, Bacon alternately pursued Indians and battled the governor. In September Bacon's forces attacked Jamestown itself, burning the capital to the ground. But when Bacon died of dysentery the following month, the rebellion began to collapse. Even so, the rebels had made their point, and a new treaty signed in 1677 opened much of the disputed territory to settlement. The end of Bacon's Rebellion thus pushed most of Virginia's Indians farther west, beyond the Appalachians.

# THE ATLANTIC TRADING SYSTEM

In the 1670s and 1680s, the prosperity of the Chesapeake rested on tobacco, and successful tobacco cultivation depended, as it always had, on an ample labor supply. But fewer and fewer English men and women proved willing to indenture themselves for long terms of service in Maryland and Virginia. Population pressures had eased in England, and the founding of the Restoration colonies meant that migrants could choose other American destinations. Furthermore, fluctuating tobacco prices in Europe and the growing scarcity of land made the Chesapeake less appealing to potential settlers. That posed a problem for wealthy Chesapeake tobacco growers. Where could they obtain the workers they needed? They found the answer in the Caribbean sugar islands, where Dutch, French, English, and Spanish planters were accustomed to purchasing African slaves.

**Why African Slavery?**

Slavery had been practiced in Europe and Islamic lands for centuries. European Christians—both Catholics and Protestants—believed that enslaving heathen peoples, especially those of exotic origin, was justifiable in religious terms. Muslims, too, thought that infidels could be enslaved, and they imported tens of thousands of black African bondspeople into North Africa and the Middle East. Some Christians argued, piously, that holding heathens in bondage would lead to their conversion. Others believed that any heathen taken prisoner in wartime could be enslaved. Consequently, when Portuguese mariners reached the sub-Saharan coast and encountered African societies holding slaves, they purchased bondspeople along with gold and other items. Starting in the 1440s, Portugal imported large numbers of slaves into the Iberian Peninsula; by 1500, enslaved Africans composed about one-tenth of the population of Lisbon and Seville, the chief cities of Portugal and Spain. In 1555 a few of them were taken to England, where—when others followed—residents of London and Bristol in particular became accustomed to seeing black slaves on the streets.

Iberians exported African slavery to their American possessions, New Spain and Brazil. Because the Catholic Church prevented the formal enslavement of Indians in those domains and free laborers saw no reason to work voluntarily in mines or on sugar plantations when they could earn better wages under easier conditions elsewhere, African bondspeople (who had no choice) became mainstays of the Caribbean and Brazilian economies. European planters on all the sugar islands began purchasing slaves—often from the Iberians—soon after they settled in the Caribbean. Accordingly, the first African slaves in the Americas were imported from Angola, Portugal's major early trading partner, and the Portuguese word *Negro* came into use as a common descriptor.

English people had few moral qualms about enslaving other humans. Slavery, after all, was sanctioned in the Bible, and it was widely practiced by their contemporaries.

▲ Nicholas Pocock made this engraving of the *Southwell* frigate, a former privateer from Bristol, England, turned into a slave-trading vessel, about 1760. The images at the bottom show the ship's company trading for slaves on the coast of West Africa. *(© Bristol City Museum and Art Gallery, UK/The Bridgeman Art Library Nationality/copyright status: English/out of copyright)*

Few at the time questioned the decision to hold Africans and their descendants—or captive Indians from New England or Carolina—in perpetual bondage. Yet their convoluted early attempts to define slave status nevertheless indicate that seventeenth-century English colonists initially lacked clear conceptual categories defining both "race" and "slave." For example, the 1670 Virginia law that first tried to define which people were enslaveable notably failed to employ the racial terminology that would later become commonplace. Instead, awkwardly seeking to single out imported Africans, it declared that "all servants not being christians imported into this colony by shipping shalbe slaves for their lives." Such nonracial phrasing reveals that Anglo-American settlers had not yet fully developed the meaning of *race* and *slave*, and that they did so in tandem over time, through their experience with the institution of slavery itself.

The planters of the North American mainland could not have obtained the enslaved workers they wanted had it not been for the rapid development of an Atlantic trading system, the linchpin of which was the traffic in enslaved human beings. Although this elaborate Atlantic economic system has been called the triangular trade, people and products did not move across the ocean in easily diagrammed patterns. Instead, their movements created a complicated web of exchange that inextricably tied the peoples of the Atlantic world together (see Map 3.4).

The oceanic slave trade was entirely new, though enslavement was not. The expanding network of commerce between Europe and its colonies was fueled by the sale and transport of slaves, the exchange of commodities produced by slave labor, and the need to feed and clothe so

## Atlantic Slave Trade

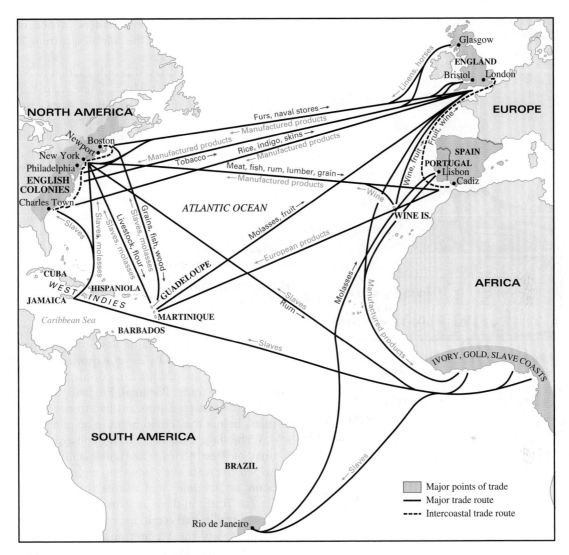

**Map 3.4   Atlantic Trade Routes**

By the late seventeenth century, an elaborate trade network linked the countries and colonies bordering the Atlantic Ocean. The most valuable commodities exchanged were enslaved people and the products of slave labor.

many bound laborers. The European economy, previously oriented toward the Mediterranean and Asia, shifted its emphasis to the Atlantic. By the late seventeenth century, commerce in slaves and the products of slave labor constituted the basis of the European economic system. The irony of Columbus's discoveries thus became complete: seeking the wealth of Asia, Columbus instead found the lands that—along with Africa—ultimately replaced Asia as the source of European prosperity.

The various elements of the trade had different relationships to one another and to the wider web of ex-

change. Chesapeake tobacco and Caribbean and Brazilian sugar were in great demand in Europe, so planters shipped their products directly to their home countries. The profits paid for both the African laborers who grew their crops and European manufactured goods. The African coastal rulers who ran the entrepôts where European slavers acquired their human cargoes received their payment in European manufactures and East Indian textiles; they had little need for most American products. Europeans purchased slaves from Africa for resale in their colonies and acquired sugar and tobacco from

▲ By the middle of the eighteenth century, American tobacco had become closely associated with African slavery. An English woodcut advertising tobacco from the York River in Virginia accordingly depicted not a Chesapeake planter but rather an African, shown with a hoe in one hand and a pipe in the other. Usually, of course, slaves would not have smoked the high-quality tobacco produced for export, although they were allowed to cultivate small crops for their own use.

*(Colonial Williamsburg Foundation)*

America, in exchange dispatching their manufactures everywhere.

European nations fought bitterly to control the lucrative trade. The Portuguese, who at first dominated the trade, were supplanted by the Dutch in the 1630s. In the Anglo-Dutch wars, the Dutch lost out to the English, who controlled the trade through the Royal African Company, a joint-stock company chartered by Charles II in 1672. Holding a monopoly on all English trade with sub-Saharan Africa, the company built and maintained seventeen forts and trading posts, dispatched to West Africa hundreds of ships carrying English manufactured goods, and transported about 100,000 slaves to England's Caribbean colonies. It paid regular dividends averaging 10 percent yearly, and some of its agents made fortunes. Yet even before the company's monopoly expired in 1712, many individual English and North American traders had illegally entered the market for slaves. By the early eighteenth century, such independent traders carried most of the Africans imported into the colonies, earning huge profits from successful voyages.

Most of the enslaved people carried to North America originated in West Africa. Some came from the Rice and Grain Coasts, especially the former, but even more had resided in the Gold and Slave Coasts and the Bight of Biafra (modern Nigeria) and Angola (see Map 1.2). Certain coastal rulers—for instance, the Adja kings of the Slave Coast—served as intermediaries, allowing the establishment of permanent slave-trading posts in their territories and supplying resident Europeans with slaves to fill ships that stopped regularly at coastal forts. Such rulers controlled Europeans' access to slaves and simultaneously controlled inland peoples' access to desirable trade goods, such as textiles, iron bars, alcohol, tobacco, guns, and cowry shells from the Maldive Islands (in the Indian Ocean), which were widely used as currency. Through Ouidah, Dahomey's major slave-trading port, passed at least 10 percent of all slaves exported to the Americas, and Ouidah's merchants earned substantial annual profits from the trade. Portugal, England, and France established forts there; Europeans had to pay fees to Ouidah's rulers before they could begin to acquire cargoes.

## West Africa and the Slave Trade

The slave trade had varying consequences for the nations of West Africa. The trade's centralizing tendencies helped to create such powerful eighteenth-century kingdoms as Dahomey and Asante (formed from the Akan States). Traffic in slaves destroyed smaller polities and disrupted traditional economic patterns, as goods once sent north toward the Mediterranean were redirected to the Atlantic and as local manufactures declined in the face of European competition. Agricultural production intensified, especially in rice-growing areas, because of the need to supply hundreds of slave ships with foodstuffs for transatlantic voyages. Because prisoners of war constituted the bulk of the exported slaves, the most active traders were also the most successful in battle. Some nations even initiated conflicts specifically to acquire valuable captives. For example, the state of Benin sold captive enemies to the Portuguese in the late fifteenth century; did not do so at the height of its power in the sixteenth and seventeenth centuries; and renewed the sale of prisoners in the eighteenth century when its waning power led to conflicts with neighboring states.

The trade therefore affected African regions unevenly. Rulers in parts of Upper Guinea, especially modern Gambia and Senegal, largely resisted involvement with the trade; the few slave vessels that departed from that area

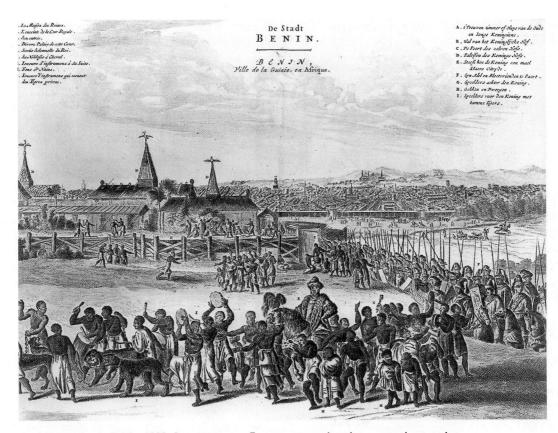

▲ A Procession in Benin, 1668. A contemporary European engraving shows a royal procession leaving the city of Benin, capital of the prosperous West African kingdom. During the seventeenth century, the power of Benin's rulers scared off would-be challengers, and so the kingdom did not engage in frequent warfare. In the fifteenth and eighteenth centuries, by contrast, when the kingdom was weaker, it did capture and sell its enemies. *(Library of Congress)*

were much more likely than others to experience onboard rebellions. Despite planters' preference for male slaves, women predominated in cargoes originating in the Bight of Biafra. In such regions as the Gold Coast, the trade had a significant impact on the sex ratio of the remaining population. There a relative shortage of men increased work demands on women, encouraged polygyny, and opened new opportunities to women and their children.

New England had the most complex relationship to the trading system. The region produced only one item England wanted: tall trees to serve as masts for sailing vessels. To buy English manufactures, New Englanders therefore needed profits earned elsewhere, especially in the Caribbean. Those islands lacked precisely the items that New England could produce in abundance: cheap food (primarily corn and salt fish) to feed the burgeoning slave population and wood for barrels to hold sugar and mo-

### New England and the Caribbean

lasses. By the late 1640s, decades before the Chesapeake economy became dependent on *production* by slaves, New England's already rested on *consumption* by slaves and their owners. The sale of foodstuffs and wood products to Caribbean sugar planters provided New England farmers and merchants with a major source of income. After the founding of Pennsylvania, New York, and New Jersey, those colonies, too, participated in the lucrative West Indian trade.

Shopkeepers in the interior of New England and the middle colonies bartered with local farmers for grains, livestock, and barrel staves, then traded those items to merchants located in port towns. Such merchants dispatched ships to the Caribbean, where they sailed from island to island, exchanging their cargoes for molasses, sugar, fruit, dyestuffs, and slaves. The system's sole constant was uncertainty, due to the weather, rapid shifts in supply and demand in the small island markets, and the delicate system of credit on which the entire structure depended. Once they had a full load, the ships returned to Boston, Newport, New York, or Philadelphia to dispose of their cargoes (often including a few slaves). Americans began to distill molasses into rum, a crucial aspect of the only part of the trade that could accurately be termed triangular. Rhode Islanders took rum to Africa and traded it for slaves, whom they carried to Caribbean islands to exchange for more molasses to produce still more rum.

Tying the system together was the voyage (commonly called the middle passage) that brought Africans

||||||||||||||||||||||||||||||||
### Slaving Voyages

to the Americas, where they cultivated the profitable crops and—in the Caribbean—consumed foods produced in North America. That voyage, always traumatic, could be fatal for the people who composed a ship's cargo. An average of 10 to 20 percent of the newly enslaved died en route; on long or disease-ridden voyages, mortality rates could be much

higher. In addition, another 20 percent or so of slaves died either before the ships left Africa or shortly after their arrival in the Americas. Europeans involved in the trade also died at high rates, chiefly through exposure to such diseases as yellow fever and malaria, which were endemic to Africa. To try to minimize such deaths, slaving vessels preferred to arrive on the African coast during the dry season, between November and May. But even so, one in every four or five European slave-ship sailors died on voyages, and just 10 percent of the men sent to run the Royal African Company's forts in Lower Guinea lived to return home to England.

Sailors signed on to slaving voyages reluctantly; indeed, many had to be coerced or tricked, because conditions on shipboard were difficult for the crew as well as the human cargo. Slave merchants were notoriously greedy and captains notoriously brutal—to sailors as well as to the slaves in the hold. Some crew members were them-

▲ The harbor of Christiansted, St. Croix, in the Danish West Indies. Although this view was painted over one hundred years after the events discussed in this chapter, the town had not changed much in the interim. Scenes like this would have been very familiar to seventeenth- and eighteenth-century colonial mariners, for such ports existed all over the Caribbean. Anchored merchant vessels await the hogsheads of molasses being prepared for shipment at the wharf. *(1996 MAPes MONDe Ltd.)*

selves slaves or freedmen. Unfortunately, the sailors, often the subject of abuse, in turn frequently abused the bondspeople in their charge. Yet at the same time, through intimate contact with the enslaved, they learned the value of freedom, and sailors became well known throughout the Atlantic world for their fierce attachment to personal independence.

## SLAVERY IN NORTH AMERICA AND THE CARIBBEAN

Barbados, America's first "slave society" (an economy wholly dependent on enslavement, as opposed to a "society with slaves"), spawned many others. As the island's population expanded and large planters consolidated their landholdings, about 40 percent of the early English residents dispersed to other colonies. The migrants carried their laws, commercial contacts, and slaveholding practices with them; the Barbados slave code of 1661, for example, served as the model for later codes in Jamaica, Antigua, Virginia, and South Carolina. Moreover, a large proportion of the first Africans imported into North America came via Barbados. In addition to the many Barbadians who settled in Carolina, others moved to the southern regions of Virginia (where they specialized in selling foodstuffs and livestock to their former island home), New Jersey, and New England, where they already had slave-trading partners.

Newly arrived Africans in the Chesapeake tended to be assigned to outlying parts of plantations (called quarters), at least until they learned some English and the routines of

||||||||||||||||||||||||||||||||

**African Enslavement in the Chesapeake**

American tobacco cultivation. By then, the crop that originated in the Americas was being grown in various locations in West Africa, so Chesapeake planters, who in the late seventeenth century were still experimenting with curing and processing techniques, could well have drawn on their slaves' expertise. Such Africans—the vast majority of them men—lived in quarters composed of ten to fifteen workers housed together in one or two buildings and supervised by an Anglo-American overseer. Each man was expected to cultivate about two acres of tobacco a year. Their lives must have been filled with toil and loneliness, for few spoke the same language, and all were expected to work for their owners six days a week. On Sundays, planters allowed them a day off. Many used that time to cultivate their own gardens or to hunt or fish to supplement their meager diet. Only rarely could they form families, because of the scarcity of women among newly imported Africans.

Slaves usually cost about two and a half times as much as indentured servants, but they repaid the greater investment with a lifetime of service, assuming they survived—which large numbers, weakened by the voyage and sickened by exposure to new diseases, did not. Many planters could not afford to purchase such expensive workers. Those with enough money could acquire slaves, accumulate greater wealth, and establish large plantations worked by tens, if not hundreds, of bondspeople, whereas the less affluent could not even buy indentured servants, whose price rose because of scarcity. As time passed, Anglo-American society in the Chesapeake thus became increasingly more stratified—that is, the gap between rich and poor planters steadily widened. The introduction of large numbers of Africans into the Chesapeake accordingly had a significant impact on the shape of Anglo-American society, in addition to reshaping the population as a whole.

So many Africans were imported into Virginia and Maryland so rapidly that, as early as 1690, those colonies contained more slaves than English indentured servants. By 1710 people of African descent composed one-fifth of the region's population. Even so, and despite sizable continuing imports, a decade later American-born slaves already outnumbered their African-born counterparts in the Chesapeake, and the native-born proportion of the slave population continued to increase thereafter.

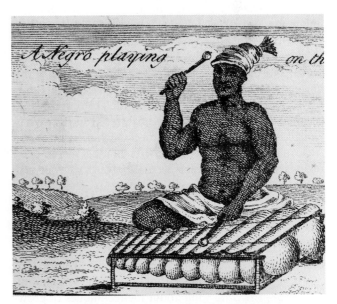

▲ In 1726, William Smith, an employee of the Royal African Company, sketched this musician playing a traditional marimba-like instrument called a *balafo*. Later in the eighteenth century Virginians described slaves playing the same instrument, thus showing that African music came to North America with the enslaved multitudes.

*(Joseph Regenstein Library)*

Africans who had lived in the Caribbean came with their masters to South Carolina from Barbados in 1670, composing one-quarter to one-third of the early population. The Barbadian slaveowners quickly discovered that African-born slaves had a variety of skills well suited to the semitropical environment of South Carolina. African-style dugout canoes became the chief means of transportation in the colony, which was crossed by rivers and included large islands just offshore. Fishing nets copied from African models proved more efficient than those of English origin. Baskets that enslaved laborers wove and gourds that they hollowed out came into general use as containers for food and drink. Africans' skill at killing crocodiles equipped them to handle alligators. And, finally, Africans adapted their traditional techniques of cattle herding for use in America. Because meat and hides numbered among the colony's chief exports in its earliest years, Africans contributed significantly to South Carolina's prosperity.

## African Enslavement in South Carolina

Not until after 1700 did South Carolinians begin to import slaves directly from Africa. Nevertheless, by 1710 African-born slaves already outnumbered those born in the Americas, and they constituted a majority of the enslaved population in South Carolina until about midcentury. By then, too, bondspeople composed a majority of the colony's residents. The similarity of the South Carolinian and West African environments, coupled with the substantial African-born population, ensured the survival of more aspects of West African culture than elsewhere on the North American mainland. Only in South Carolina did enslaved parents continue to give their children African names; only there did a dialect develop that combined English words with African terms. (Known as Gullah, it has survived to the present day in isolated areas.) African skills remained useful, so techniques lost in other regions when the migrant generation died were instead passed down to the migrants' children. And in South Carolina African women became the primary petty traders, dominating the markets of Charles Town as they did those of Guinea.

The importation of large numbers of Africans coincided with the successful introduction of rice in South Carolina. English people knew nothing about the techniques of growing and processing rice, but people from Africa's Rice Coast had spent their lives working with the crop. Although the evidence is circumstantial, the Africans' expertise almost certainly assisted their English masters in cultivating rice prof-

## Rice and Indigo

▲ Although this rice basket dates from nineteenth-century South Carolina, it is woven in traditional West African style. Enslaved women winnowed rice in such baskets, tossing the grains into the air after they had been pounded, so that the lighter pieces of hull would be blown away by the wind.

*(Rice Museum, Georgetown, South Carolina. Photograph by Craig Moran.)*

itably. Productive rice-growing techniques known in West Africa, especially cultivation in inland swamps and tidal rivers, both of which involved substantial water-control projects, were widely adopted. South Carolinians preferred to purchase slaves from the Rice Coast, and, unlike Chesapeake and Caribbean planters, they preferred women as well. Those preferences are most likely explained by women's crucial role in cultivating and processing rice in West Africa, where they were responsible for sowing and weeding the crop, as well as for pounding harvested rice with a mortar and pestle to remove the hulls and bran, then winnowing to separate the grains from the chaff. Because English grindstones damaged rice kernels (not until the late eighteenth century were new processes developed), South Carolinians continued to utilize the West African system of pounding rice by hand; planters assigned men as well as women to that task.

Every field worker on rice plantations, which were far larger than Chesapeake tobacco quarters, was expected to cultivate three to four acres of rice a year. Most of those field workers were female, because many enslaved men were assigned to jobs like blacksmithing or carpentry, which were not given to women. To cut expenses, planters also expected slaves to grow part of their own food. A universally adopted "task" system of predefined work assignments provided that, after bondspeople had finished their set tasks for the day, they could then rest or work in their own garden plots or on other projects. Experienced slaves could often complete their tasks by early afternoon; after that, as on Sundays, their masters had no legitimate claim on their time. One scholar has suggested that the unique task system, which gave bondspeople more freedom than gang labor, and which was in place in South Carolina by the early eighteenth century, resulted from negotiations between slaves familiar with rice cultivation and masters who desperately needed their expertise.

Developers of South Carolina's second cash crop also used the task system and drew on slaves' specialized skills. Indigo, the only source of blue dye for the growing English textile industry, was much prized. Eliza Lucas, a young woman managing her father's plantations, began to experiment with indigo cultivation during the early 1740s. Drawing on the knowledge of slaves and overseers from the Caribbean, she developed the planting and processing techniques later adopted throughout the colony. Indigo grew on high ground, and rice was planted in low-lying regions; rice and indigo also had different growing seasons. Thus the two crops complemented each other. South Carolina indigo never matched the quality of that from the Caribbean, but indigo plantations flourished because the crop was so valuable that Parliament offered Carolinians a bounty on every pound exported to Great Britain.

Among the people held in slavery in both Carolinas were Indian captives who had been retained rather than exported. In 1708 enslaved Indians composed as much as 14 percent of the South Carolina population. The

### Indian Enslavement in North and South Carolina

widespread and lucrative traffic in Indian slaves significantly affected South Carolina's relationship with its indigenous neighbors. Native Americans knew they could always find a ready market for captive enemies in Charles Town, so they took that means of ridding themselves of real or potential rivals. Yet native groups soon learned that Carolinians could not be trusted. As settlers and traders shifted their priorities, first one set of former allies, then another, found themselves enslaved rather than the enslavers.

The trade in Indian slaves began when the Westos (originally known as the Eries), migrated south from the Great Lakes region in the mid-1650s, fleeing their Iroquois enemies after the Beaver Wars. Expert in the use of European firearms, the Westos began raiding Spain's lightly defended Florida missions and selling the resulting Indian captives to Virginians. With the establishment of Carolina, the proprietors took for themselves a monopoly of trade with the Westos, which infuriated local settlers shut out of the profitable commerce in slaves and deerskins. The planters secretly financed attacks on the Westos, essentially wiping them out by 1682. Southeastern Indians reacted to such slave raids—continued by other native peoples after the defeat of the Westos—by trying to protect themselves either through subordination to the English or Spanish, or by coalescing into new, larger political units, such as those known later as Creeks, Chickasaws, or Cherokees.

At first the Carolinians themselves did not engage directly in conflicts with neighboring Indians. But in 1711 the Tuscaroras, an Iroquoian people, attacked a Swiss-German settlement at New Bern, North Carolina, which had expropriated their lands. South Carolinians and their Indian allies then combined to defeat the Tuscaroras in a bloody war. Afterward, more than a thousand Tuscaroras were enslaved, and the remainder drifted northward, where they joined the Iroquois Confederacy but were not allotted a seat on the council, instead being represented by the Oneidas.

Four years later, the Yamasees, who had helped to overcome the Tuscaroras, turned on their onetime English allies. In what seems to have been long-planned retaliation for multiple abuses by traders as well as threats to their own lands, the Yamasees enlisted the Creeks and other Muskogean peoples in coordinated attacks on outlying English settlements. In the spring and summer of 1715, English and African refugees by the hundreds streamed into Charles Town. The Yamasee-Creek offensive was eventually thwarted when reinforcements arrived from the north, colonists hastily armed their African slaves, and Cherokees joined the fight against the Creeks. After the war, Carolinian involvement in the Indian slave trade ceased, because all their native neighbors moved away for self-protection: Creeks migrated west, Yamasees went south, and other groups moved north. The abuses of the Carolina slave trade thus in effect caused its own destruction. And in the war's aftermath the native peoples of the Carolinas were able to regroup and rebuild their strength, for they were no longer subjected to slavers' raids.

Few Indians or Africans were enslaved in any of Spain's North American territories, which had no plantations or cash crops. In 1693, as slavery took deeper root in South Carolina, Florida officials offered freedom to fugitives who would convert to Catholicism. Hundreds of South Carolina runaways took

### Slaves in Spanish and French North America

advantage of the offer, although not all won their liberty. Many settled in a town founded for them near St. Augustine, Gracia Real de Santa Teresa de Mose, headed by a former slave, Francisco Menéndez.

In early Louisiana, too, slaves—some Indians, some Atlantic creoles—at first composed only a tiny proportion of the residents. But a growing European population demanded that the French government supply them with slaves, and in 1719 officials finally acquiesced, dispatching more than six thousand Africans, mostly from Senegal, over the next decade. The residents failed to develop a successful plantation economy, although they experimented with both tobacco and indigo. They did succeed in angering the Natchez Indians, whose lands they had usurped. In 1729 the Natchez, assisted by newly arrived slaves, attacked northern reaches of the colony, killing more than 10 percent of its European people. The French struck back, slaughtering the Natchez and their enslaved allies, but throughout much of the century Louisiana remained a society with slaves rather than a slave society.

Atlantic creoles from the Caribbean and native peoples from the Carolinas and Florida, along with local Indians

### Enslavement in the North

sentenced to slavery for crime or debt, constituted the bondspeople in the northern mainland colonies. The intricate involvement of northerners in the web of commerce surrounding the slave trade ensured that many people of African descent lived in America north of Virginia, and that "Spanish Indians" became an identifiable component of the New England population. Some bondspeople resided in urban areas, especially New York, which in 1700 had a larger black population than any other mainland city. Women tended to work as domestic servants, men as unskilled laborers on the docks. At the end of the seventeenth century, three-quarters of wealthy Philadelphia households included one or two slaves.

Yet even in the North most bondspeople worked in the countryside, the majority at agricultural tasks. Dutch farmers in the Hudson Valley and northern New Jersey were especially likely to rely on enslaved Africans, as were the owners of large landholdings in the Narragansett region of Rhode Island. Some bondsmen toiled in new rural enterprises, such as ironworks, working alongside hired laborers and indentured servants at forges and foundries. Although relatively few northern colonists owned slaves, those who did relied extensively on their labor. Therefore, even though slavery overall did not make a substantial contribution to the northern economy, certain individual

slaveholders benefited greatly from the institution and had good reason to want to preserve it.

As slavery became an integral part of the North American and Caribbean landscapes, so too did slaves'

### Slave Resistance

resistance to their masters. Most commonly that resistance took the form of malingering or running away, but occasionally bondspeople planned rebellions. Seven times before 1713 the English Caribbean experienced major revolts involving at least fifty slaves and causing the deaths of both whites and blacks. Twice, in 1675 and 1692, Barbados authorities thwarted plots shortly before they were to be implemented, afterward executing more than sixty convicted conspirators.

The first slave revolt in the mainland colonies took place in New York in 1712, at a time when enslaved people constituted about 15 percent of the population. The rebels, primarily recent arrivals from the Akan States of the Gold Coast, set a fire and then ambushed those who tried to put it out, killing eight and wounding another twelve. Some rebels committed suicide to avoid capture; of those caught and tried, eighteen were executed. Their decapitated bodies were left to rot outdoors as a warning to others.

## IMPERIAL REORGANIZATION AND THE WITCHCRAFT CRISIS

English officials seeking new sources of revenue decided to tap into the profits of the expanding Atlantic trading system in slaves and the products of slave labor. Chesapeake tobacco and Caribbean sugar had obvious value, but other colonial products also had considerable potential. Parliament and the Stuart monarchs accordingly drafted laws designed to harness the proceeds of the trade for the primary benefit of the mother country.

Like other European nations, England based its commercial policy on a series of assumptions about the

### Mercantilism and Navigation Acts

operations of the world's economic system, collectively called mercantilism. The theory viewed the economic world as a collection of national states, whose governments competed for shares of a finite amount of wealth. What one nation gained, another nation lost. Each nation sought to become as economically self-sufficient as possible while maintaining a favorable balance of trade with other countries by exporting more than it imported. Colonies played an important role, supplying the mother country

## Exotic Beverages

The seventeenth-century colonists developed a taste not only for tea (from China) but also for coffee (from Arabia), chocolate (from Mesoamerica), and rum (distilled from sugar, which also sweetened the bitter taste of the other three). The American and European demand for these once-exotic beverages helped reshape the world economy after the mid-seventeenth century. Indeed, one historian has estimated that approximately two-thirds of the people who migrated across the Atlantic before 1776 were involved in one way or another, primarily as slaves, in the production of tobacco, calico, and these four drinks for the world market. The exotic beverages had a profound impact, too, on custom and culture, as they moved swiftly from luxury to necessity.

Each beverage had its own pattern of consumption. Chocolate, brought to Spain from Mexico and enjoyed there for a century before spreading more widely throughout Europe, became the preferred drink of aristocrats, consumed hot at intimate gatherings in palaces and mansions. Coffee, by contrast, became the preeminent morning beverage of English and colonial businessmen, who praised its caffeine for keeping drinkers sober and focused. Coffee was served in new public coffeehouses, patronized only by men, where politics and business were the topics of conversation. The first coffeehouse opened in London in the late 1660s; Boston had several by the 1690s. By the mid-eighteenth century, though, tea had supplanted coffee as the preferred hot, caffeinated beverage in England and America. It was consumed in the afternoon in private homes at tea tables presided over by women. Tea embodied genteel status and polite conversation. In contrast, rum was the drink of the masses. This inexpensive, potent distilled spirit, made possible by new technology and the increasing production of sugar, was enthusiastically imbibed by free working people everywhere in the Atlantic world.

The American colonies played a vital role in the production, distribution, and consumption of each of these beverages. Chocolate, most obviously, originated in America, and cacao plantations in the South American tropics multiplied in size and number to meet the rising demand. Coffee and tea (particularly the latter) were as avidly consumed in the colonies as in England. And rum involved Americans in every phase of its production and consumption. The sugar grown on French and English Caribbean plantations was transported to the mainland in barrels and ships made from North American wood. There the syrup was turned into rum at 140 distilleries. The Americans themselves drank a substantial share of the distilleries' output—an estimated four gallons per person annually—but exported much of it to Africa. There the rum purchased more slaves to produce more sugar to make still more rum, and the cycle began again.

Thus new tastes and customs connected to four different beverages linked the colonies to the rest of the world and altered their economic and social development.

▲ The frontispiece of Peter Muguet, *Tractatus De Poto Caphe, Chinesium The et de Chocolata,* 1685. Muguet's treatise visually linked the three hot, exotic beverages recently introduced to Europeans. The drinks are being consumed by representatives of the cultures in which they originated: a turbaned Turk (with coffeepot in the foreground), a Chinese man (with teapot on the table), and an Indian drinking from a hollowed, handled gourd (with a chocolate pot and ladle on the floor in front of him). *(Library of Congress)*

with valuable raw materials to be consumed at home or sent abroad and serving as a market for the mother country's manufactured goods.

Parliament's Navigation Acts—passed between 1651 and 1673—established three main principles that accorded with mercantilist theory. First, only English or colonial merchants and ships could legally trade in the colonies. Second, certain valuable American products could be sold only in the mother country or in other English colonies. At first, these "enumerated" goods included wool, sugar, tobacco, indigo, ginger, and dyes; later acts added rice, naval stores (masts, spars, pitch, tar, and turpentine), copper, and furs to the list. Third, all foreign goods destined for sale in the colonies had to be shipped through England, paying English import duties. Some years later, new laws established a fourth principle: the colonies could not export items (such as wool clothing, hats, or iron) that competed with English products.

These laws adversely affected some colonies, like those in the Chesapeake, because planters there could not seek foreign markets for their staple crops. The statutes initially helped the sugar producers of the English Caribbean by driving Brazilian sugar out of the home market, but later prevented those English planters from selling their sugar elsewhere. In some places, the impact was minimal or even positive. Builders and owners of ships benefited from the monopoly on American trade given to English and colonial merchants; the laws stimulated the creation of a lucrative colonial shipbuilding industry, especially in New England. And the northern and middle colonies produced many unenumerated goods—for example, fish, flour, meat and livestock, and barrel staves. Such products could be traded directly to the French, Spanish, or Dutch Caribbean islands as long as they were carried in English or American ships.

The English authorities soon learned, though, that writing mercantilist legislation was far easier than enforcing it. The many harbors of the American coast provided ready havens for smugglers, and colonial officials often looked the other way when illegally imported goods were offered for sale. In ports like St. Eustatius in the Dutch West Indies, American merchants could easily dispose of enumerated goods and purchase foreign items on which duty had not been paid. Because American juries had already demonstrated a tendency to favor local smugglers over customs officers (a colonial customs service was instituted in 1671), Parliament in 1696 established several American vice-admiralty courts, which operated without juries and adjudicated violations of the Navigation Acts.

The Navigation Acts imposed regulations on Americans' international trade, but by the early 1680s mainland governments and their residents had become accustomed to a considerable degree of local governmental autonomy. The tradition of local rule was especially firmly established in New England, where Massachusetts, Plymouth, Connecticut, and Rhode Island operated essentially as independent entities, subject neither to the direct authority of the king nor to a proprietor. Whereas Virginia was a royal colony and New Hampshire (1679) and New York (1685) gained that status, all other mainland settlements were proprietorships, over which the nation exercised little control. Everywhere in the English colonies, free adult men who owned more than a minimum amount of property expected to have an influential voice in their governments, especially in decisions concerning taxation.

## Colonial Autonomy Challenged

After James II became king in 1685, such expectations clashed with those of the monarch. The new king and his successors sought to bring order to the apparently chaotic state of colonial administration by tightening the reins of government and by reducing the colonies' political autonomy. Most significantly, colonial administrators targeted Puritan New England. Reports from America convinced English officials that New England was a hotbed of smuggling. Moreover, Puritans refused to allow freedom of religion to non-Congregationalists and insisted on maintaining laws incompatible with English practice. New England thus seemed an appropriate place to exert English authority with greater vigor. The charters of all the colonies from New Jersey to Maine were revoked, and a Dominion of New England was established in 1686. (For the boundaries of the Dominion, see Map 3.1.) Sir Edmund Andros, the governor, had immense power: Parliament dissolved all the assemblies, and Andros needed only the consent of an appointed council to make laws and levy taxes.

## Glorious Revolution in America

New Englanders endured Andros's autocratic rule for more than two years. Then they learned that James II's hold on power was crumbling. James had angered his subjects by levying taxes without parliamentary approval and by announcing his conversion to Catholicism. In April 1689, Boston's leaders jailed Andros and his associates. The following month they received definite news of the bloodless coup known as the Glorious Revolution, in which James was replaced on

▲ Sir Edmund Andros (1637–1714), the much-detested autocratic governor of the Dominion of New England. In April 1689 he was overthrown by a coalition including some of the foremost leaders of the Bay Colony. He was imprisoned and eventually shipped back to England.

*(Massachusetts State Archives)*

the throne in late 1688 by his daughter Mary and her husband, the Dutch prince William of Orange. When Parliament offered the throne to the Protestants William and Mary, the Glorious Revolution affirmed the supremacy of both Parliament and Protestantism.

In other colonies, too, the Glorious Revolution emboldened people for revolt. In Maryland the Protestant Association overturned the government of the Catholic proprietor, and in New York a militia officer of German origin, Jacob Leisler, assumed control of the government. Bostonians, Marylanders, and New Yorkers alike allied themselves with the supporters of William and Mary. They saw themselves as carrying out the colonial phase of the English revolt against Stuart absolutism.

But, like James II, William and Mary believed that England should exercise tighter control over its unruly American possessions. Consequently, only the Maryland rebellion received royal sanction, primarily because of its anti-Catholic thrust. In New York, Leisler was hanged for treason, and Massachusetts (incorporating the formerly independent jurisdiction of Plymouth) became a royal colony with an appointed governor. The province retained its town meeting system of local government and continued to elect its council, but the new 1691 charter eliminated the traditional religious test for voting and office holding. A parish of the Church of England appeared in the heart of Boston. The "city upon a hill," as John Winthrop had envisioned it, had ended.

A war with the French and their Algonquian allies compounded New England's difficulties. King Louis XIV of France allied himself with the deposed James II, and England declared war on France in 1689. (In Europe, this conflict was known as the War of the League of Augsburg, but the colonists called it King William's War.) Even before war broke out in Europe, Anglo-Americans and Abenakis clashed over the English settlements in Maine that had been reoccupied after the 1678 truce and were once again expanding. Attacks wholly or partially destroyed a number of towns, including Schenectady, New York, and such Maine communities as Falmouth (now Portland), Salmon Falls (now Berwick), and York. Expeditions organized by the colonies against Montreal and Quebec in 1690 failed miserably, and throughout the rest of the conflict New England found itself on the defensive. Even the Peace of Ryswick (1697), which formally ended the war in Europe, failed to bring much respite from warfare to the northern frontiers. Maine could not be resettled for several decades because of the continuing conflict.

**King William's War**

During the hostilities, New Englanders understandably feared a repetition of the devastation of King Philip's War. For eight months in 1692, witchcraft accusations spread like wildfire through the rural communities of Essex County, Massachusetts— precisely the area most threatened by the Indian attacks in southern Maine and New Hampshire. Earlier incidents in which personal disputes occasionally led to isolated witchcraft charges bore little relationship to the witch fears that convulsed the region in 1692 while the war raged just to the north. Before the crisis ended, 14 women and 5 men were hanged, 1 man was pressed to death with heavy stones, 54 people confessed to being witches, and more than 140 people were jailed, some for many months.

**The 1692 Witchcraft Crisis**

The crisis began in late February when several children and young women in Salem Village (an outlying precinct of the bustling port of Salem) formally charged some older female neighbors with having tortured them in spectral form. Soon other accusers and confessors chimed in, some of them female domestic servants who had been orphaned in the Maine war. One had lost her grandparents in King Philip's War and other relatives in King

▲ The Reverend Cotton Mather of Boston, twenty-nine years old in 1692 at the time of the Salem witchcraft crisis, rushed this book—*The Wonders of the Invisible World*—into print shortly after the trials ended. He tried to explain to his fellow New Englanders the "Grievous Molestations by Daemons and Witchcrafts which have lately annoy'd the Countrey" by providing both brief trial narratives and examples of similar recent occurrences elsewhere, most notably in Mohra, Sweden.

*(Massachusetts Historical Society)*

William's War. These young women, perhaps the most powerless people in a region apparently powerless to affect its fate, offered their fellow New Englanders a compelling explanation for the seemingly endless chain of troubles afflicting them: their province was under direct assault not only by the Indians and their French allies but also by the Devil and his allied witches.

The so-called afflicted girls accused not just the older women commonly suspected of such offenses but also prominent men from the Maine frontier who had traded with or failed to defeat the Indians. The leader of the witch conspiracy, accusers and confessors alike declared, was the Reverend George Burroughs, a Harvard graduate who had ministered in both Maine and Salem Village and was suspected of bewitching the soldiers sent to combat the Abenakis. The colony's magistrates, who were also its political and military leaders, were all too willing to believe such accusations, because, if the Devil had caused New England's current troubles, they personally bore no responsibility for the terrible losses on the frontier.

In October, the worst phase of the crisis ended when the governor dissolved the special court established to try the suspects. He and several prominent clergymen began to regard the descriptions of spectral torturers as "the Devil's testimony"—and everyone knew the Devil could not be trusted. Most critics of the trials did not think the afflicted were faking, nor did they conclude that witches did not exist or that confessions were false. Rather, they questioned whether the guilt of the accused could be legally established by the evidence presented in court. Accordingly, during the final trials (ending in May 1693) in regular courts, almost all the defendants were acquitted, and the governor quickly reprieved the few found guilty.

In 1696 England took a major step in colonial administration by creating the fifteen-member Board of Trade and Plantations, which thereafter served as the chief organ of government concerned with the American colonies. The board gathered information, reviewed Crown appointments in America, scrutinized legislation passed by colonial assemblies, supervised trade policies, and advised successive ministries on colonial issues. Still, the Board of Trade did not have any direct powers of enforcement. It also shared jurisdiction over American affairs not only with the customs service and the navy but also with a member of the ministry. Although this reform improved the quality of colonial administration, supervision of the American provinces remained decentralized and haphazard.

## New Imperial Measures

That surely made it easier for Massachusetts and the rest of the English colonies in America to accommodate themselves to the new imperial order. Most colonists resented alien officials who arrived in America determined to implement the policies of king and Parliament, but they adjusted to their demands and to the trade restrictions imposed by the Navigation Acts. They fought another of Europe's wars—the War of the Spanish Succession, called Queen Anne's War in the colonies—from 1702 to 1713, without enduring the stresses of the first, despite the heavy economic burdens the conflict imposed. Colonists who allied themselves with the royal government received patronage in the form of offices and land grants, and composed "court parties" that supported English officials. Others, who were either less fortunate in their friends or more principled in defense of colonial autonomy, made up the opposition, or "country" interest. By the end of the first quarter of the eighteenth century, most men in both groups had been born in America. They were members of elite families whose wealth derived in the South from staple-crop production and in the North from commerce.

## *Legacy* FOR A PEOPLE AND A NATION

### Americans of African Descent

Before 1650, people of African descent composed only a tiny proportion of the population of the mainland North American colonies. After the 1670s, the rise of southern economies based largely on the enslavement of Africans, coupled with the widespread employment of enslaved Africans in northern colonies, dramatically altered the composition of the American population. By 1775, more than a quarter-million Africans had been imported into the territory that later became the United States, constituting about 20 percent of the population at the time of the Revolution.

According to the 2000 census, 12.5 percent of the American people now claim descent from African ancestors. Because the legal importation of African slaves ended in 1808 and because the United States attracted relatively few voluntary migrants of African descent until late in the twentieth century, most of today's African Americans have colonial ancestors—a claim few Americans of European descent can make. Most European Americans are descended at least in part from the massive European migrations of the nineteenth and early twentieth centuries.

The modern African American population includes people with many different skin colors, reflecting the large number of interracial sexual relationships (both coerced and voluntary) that have developed during the long African residence in mainland North America. African Americans, both free and enslaved, have had children with both Europeans and Indians since the colonial period; more recently, they have intermarried with Asian immigrants. In large part the mingling of different peoples of color resulted from state miscegenation laws, which from the early years of the American republic until 1967—when they were struck down by the Supreme Court—forbade legal marriages between people of European descent and those of other races. That forced the non-European groups to seek partners only among themselves.

Recently, increasing numbers of interracial unions have produced multiracial children. The 2000 census for the first time allowed Americans to define themselves simultaneously as members of more than one race. Opposition to this change came largely from leaders of the African American community, who feared a diminution of political clout. For years, state and federal laws defined people with any appreciable African ancestry as "black"; on census forms people of African descent have now proved less willing to define themselves as multiracial than do others. The racial self-definition of this large component of the American people thus continues to be influenced by a legacy of discrimination.

## SUMMARY

The seventy years from 1650 to 1720 established the basic economic and political patterns that were to structure subsequent changes in mainland colonial society. In 1650 just two isolated centers of English population, New England and the Chesapeake, existed along the seaboard, along with the tiny Dutch colony of New Netherland. In 1720 nearly the entire East Coast of North America was in English hands, and Indian control east of the Appalachian Mountains had largely been broken by the outcomes of King Philip's War, Bacon's Rebellion, the Yamasee and Tuscarora wars, and Queen Anne's War. To the west of the mountains, though, Iroquois power reigned supreme. What had been an immigrant population was now mostly American-born, except for the many African-born people in South Carolina and the Chesapeake; economies originally based on trade in fur and skins had become far more complex and more closely linked with the mother country; and a wide variety of political structures had been reshaped into a more uniform pattern. Yet at the same time the adoption of large-scale slavery in the Chesapeake and the Carolinas differentiated their societies from those of the colonies to the north. The production of tobacco, rice, and indigo for international markets distinguished the southern regional economies. They had become true slave societies, heavily reliant on a system of perpetual servitude, not societies with slaves, in which a few bondspeople mingled with indentured servants and free wage laborers.

Even the economies of the northern colonies, though, rested on profits derived from the Atlantic trading system, the key element of which was traffic in enslaved humans, primarily Africans but also including Indians. New England sold corn, salt fish, and wood products to the West Indies, where slaves consumed the foodstuffs and whence planters shipped sugar and molasses in barrels made from staves crafted by northern farmers. Pennsylvania and New York, too, found in the Caribbean islands a ready market for their livestock, grains, and wheat flour. The rapid growth of enslavement drove all the English colonial economies in these years.

Meanwhile, from a small outpost in Santa Fe, New Mexico, and missions in Florida, the Spanish had expanded their influence throughout the Gulf Coast region and, by just after midcentury, as far north as California.

The French had moved from a few settlements along the St. Lawrence to dominate the length of the Mississippi River and the entire Great Lakes region. Both groups of colonists lived near Indian nations and depended on the indigenous people's labor and goodwill. The Spanish could not fully control their Indian allies, and the French did not even try. The extensive Spanish and French presence to the south and west of the English settlements meant that future conflicts among the European powers in North America were nearly inevitable.

By 1720, the essential elements of the imperial administrative structure that would govern the English colonies until 1775 had been put firmly in place. The regional economic systems originating in the late seventeenth and early eighteenth centuries also continued to dominate North American life for another century—until after independence had been won. And Anglo-Americans had developed the commitment to autonomous local government that later would lead them into conflict with Parliament and the king.

## SUGGESTIONS FOR FURTHER READING

Wesley Frank Craven, *The Colonies in Transition, 1660–1713* (1968)

David Eltis, *The Rise of African Slavery in the Americas* (1998)

Alan Gallay, *The Indian Slave Trade: The Rise of the English Empire in the American South, 1670–1717* (2002)

Andrew Knaut, *The Pueblo Revolt of 1680* (1995)

Jill Lepore, *The Name of War: King Philip's War and the Origins of American Identity* (1998)

David S. Lovejoy, *The Glorious Revolution in America* (1972)

Edmund S. Morgan, *American Slavery, American Freedom: The Ordeal of Colonial Virginia* (1975)

Jennifer L. Morgan, *Laboring Women: Reproduction and Gender in New World Slavery* (2004)

Mary Beth Norton, *In the Devil's Snare: The Salem Witchcraft Crisis of 1692* (2002)

Betty Wood, *The Origins of American Slavery* (1997)

*For a more extensive list for further reading, go to* college.hmco.com/pic/norton8e.

# CHAPTER
# 4

# American Society
# Transformed
## *1720-1770*

as I in that Country I would not Stay one day longer in it," Alexander McAllister told his cousin in late 1770. "If god Spers [spares] you in this Cuntrie but a few years you will blis the day you left." McAllister, who as a youth had moved to North Carolina with his parents, clearly did bless the day he had left the Scottish Highlands. In many letters to friends and family back in Argyleshire, McAllister elaborated on the attractions of his adopted home at Cross Creek (near modern Fayetteville, North Carolina). Anyone could easily grow corn, wheat, barley, rye, oats, potatoes, and tobacco; "in truth it is the Best poor mans Cuntry I Ever heard of and I have had the opertunity of hearing from South & north." Lest his Scots correspondents think he exaggerated, McAllister assured them that other immigrants, too, were doing well. They had harvested "plenty of Corn for them Selves and famile and seemes to be very well Satisfied." Underscoring his point, he insisted that "ther is non but what is in a good way."

One historian has estimated that Alexander McAllister's letters were central to a network of correspondents that brought about five thousand of his fellow countrymen to North America in the two decades after the mid-1750s. His connections in the Highlands recognized that he was a ready source of advice, encouragement, and accurate information for potential emigrants. When Scots arrived in North Carolina with letters of introduction from people McAllister knew, he helped them find land and supplies. Although he understood that, as he told one correspondent, "the best [land] is taken up many years ago," and that newcomers' first two or three years would be hard, he never altered his recommendations. People should "take currage" and move to North America, McAllister asserted; "it will be of Benefitt to ther riseing generation." Certainly

◀ A farmer, probably an immigrant like Alexander McAllister, plows his field outside the town of Salem, North Carolina, in this 1787 painting by Ludwig G. von Redeken.

*(Collection of the Wachovia Historical Society)*

## CHRONOLOGY

**1690** ■ Locke's *Essay Concerning Human Understanding* published, a key example of Enlightenment thought

**1721–22** ■ Smallpox epidemic in Boston leads to first widespread adoption of inoculation in America

**1732** ■ Founding of Georgia

**1733** ■ John Peter Zenger is tried for and acquitted of "seditious libel" in New York

**1739** ■ Stono Rebellion (South Carolina) leads to increased white fears of slave revolts
■ George Whitefield arrives in America; Great Awakening broadens

**1739–48** ■ King George's War disrupts American economy

**1740s** ■ Black population of the Chesapeake begins to grow by natural increase, contributing to rise of large plantations

**1741** ■ New York City "conspiracy" reflects whites' continuing fears of slave revolts

**1747** ■ Princeton University founded, joining Harvard, Yale, and other earlier institutions of higher learning

**1751** ■ Franklin's *Experiments and Observations on Electricity* published, important American contribution to the Enlightenment science

**1760s** ■ Baptist congregations take root in Virginia

**1760–75** ■ Peak of eighteenth-century European and African migration to English colonies

**1765–66** ■ Hudson River land riots pit tenants and squatters against large landlords

**1767–69** ■ Regulator movement (South Carolina) tries to establish order in backcountry

**1771** ■ North Carolina Regulators defeated by eastern militia at Battle of Alamance

McAllister himself thrived in his new homeland; by the late 1780s, having fathered numerous children by two wives, he owned forty slaves and more than 2,500 acres of land. He served as an elder of the Presbyterian church, as a member of the colonial assembly, and as a state senator after independence was won. Although he was more successful than most migrants, his prosperity showed what some could achieve.

Alexander McAllister and other Highland Scots took part in a massive eighteenth-century migration of European and African peoples that by 1770 had changed the nature of the American population and the look of the American landscape. Ethnic diversity was especially pronounced in the small colonial cities, but the countryside, too, attracted settlers from many nations. Near McAllister's Cross Creek, for example, also resided large numbers of people from England, Germany, France, Wales, and the Scottish Lowlands. The British colonies south of New England drew by far the largest number of newcomers. Their arrival not only swelled the population but also altered political balances and affected the religious climate by introducing new sects. Unwilling immigrants (slaves and transported convicts), too, clustered primarily in the middle and southern colonies.

Several key themes marked colonial development in the mid-eighteenth century: not only population growth (through natural increase as well as immigration) and the new ethnic diversity, but also the increasing importance of colonial urban centers, the creation of a prosperous urban elite, rising levels of consumption for all social ranks, and the new significance of internal markets. In the French and British mainland colonies, exports continued to dominate the economy. Settlers along the Atlantic and Gulf coasts were tied to an international commercial system that fluctuated wildly for reasons having little to do with the colonies but inescapable in their effects. Yet expanding local populations demanded greater quantities and types of goods, and Europe could not supply all those needs. Therefore, in English and French America, as well as in the northern portions of New Spain known as the Borderlands (where exports were never an important element of the economy), colonists came increasingly to depend on exploiting and consuming their own resources (see Map 5.2).

Intermarried networks of wealthy families developed in each of Europe's American possessions by the 1760s. These well-off, educated colonists participated in transatlantic intellectual life, such as the movement known as the Enlightenment, whereas some colonists of the "lesser sort" could neither read nor write. The elites lived in comfortable houses and enjoyed leisure-time activities. Most colonists, whether free or enslaved, worked with their hands daily from dawn to dark. Such divisions were most pronounced in British America, the largest and most prosperous settlements on the continent. By the last half of the century, the social and economic distance among different ranks of Anglo-Americans had widened noticeably. As such stratification increased, so did conflicts—political, economic, and even religious—among people of diverse origins and social ranks.

In 1720 much of North America was still under Indian control. By 1770, in sharp contrast, settlements of Europeans and Africans ruled by Great Britain filled almost all of the region between the Appalachian Mountains and the Atlantic Ocean; and the British, following their victory over France in the Seven Years War (see pages 124–127), dominated the extensive system of rivers and lakes running through the heart of the continent. Spanish missions extended in a great arc from present-day northern California to the Gulf Coast. Such changes transformed the character of Europe's North American possessions.

- What were the effects of demographic and economic changes in the mainland colonies?
- What were the key elements of eighteenth-century colonial culture?
- What developments at midcentury began the process of political and religious change?

## POPULATION GROWTH AND ETHNIC DIVERSITY

Dramatic population growth characterized the British mainland colonies in the eighteenth century. Only about 250,000 European-Americans and African Americans resided in the colonies in 1700. Thirty years later, that number had more than doubled, and by 1775 it had become 2.5 million. Such rapid expansion appears even more remarkable when it is compared with the modest changes that occurred in French and Spanish North America. At the end of the eighteenth century, Texas had only about 2,500 Spanish residents and California even fewer; the largest Spanish colony, New Mexico, included just 20,000 or so. The total European population of the mainland French colonies expanded from approximately 15,000 in 1700 to about 70,000 in the 1760s, but only along the St. Lawrence River between Quebec and Montreal and in New Orleans were there significant concentrations of French settlers.

Although migration accounted for a considerable share of the growth in Anglo America, most of the gain resulted from natural increase. Once the difficult early decades of settlement had passed and the sex ratio evened out in the South (after 1700), the American population doubled approximately every twenty-five years. Such a rate of growth, unparalleled in human history until very recent times, had a variety of causes, chief among them women's youthful age at the onset of childbearing (early twenties for European-Americans, late teens for African Americans). Because married women became pregnant every two or three years, women normally bore five to ten children. Because the colonies, especially those north of Virginia, were relatively healthful places to live, a large proportion of children who survived infancy reached maturity and began families of their own. Consequently, about half of the American population was under sixteen years old in 1775. (By contrast, only about one-quarter of the American population was under sixteen in 2005.)

More Africans than Europeans came to the Americas, the overwhelming majority of them as slaves. Most

### Involuntary Migrants from Africa

went to Brazil or the Caribbean: of at least 11 million enslaved people brought to the Americas during the existence of slavery, only about 260,000 were imported by 1775 into the region that became the United States. The height of the trade occurred in the eighteenth century, when about half of all slaves were carried across the Atlantic, primarily in British or Portuguese vessels. Rice, indigo, tobacco, and sugar plantations expanded rapidly, thus steadily increasing the demand for bondspeople. Furthermore, in the slaveholding societies of South America and the Caribbean, a surplus of males over females and appallingly high mortality rates meant that only a large, continuing influx of slaves could maintain the work force at constant levels. On the mainland, only South Carolina, where rice cultivation was difficult and unhealthful (chiefly because malaria-carrying mosquitoes bred in the rice swamps), similarly required an inflow of Africans to sustain as well as expand its labor force.

The involuntary migrants came from many different ethnic groups and regions of Africa (see Map 4.1). More than 40 percent embarked from West Central Africa (modern Congo and Angola), nearly 20 percent from the Bight of Benin (modern Togo, Benin, and southwestern Nigeria), about 13 percent from the Bight of Biafra (today's Cameroon, Gabon, and southeastern Nigeria), and

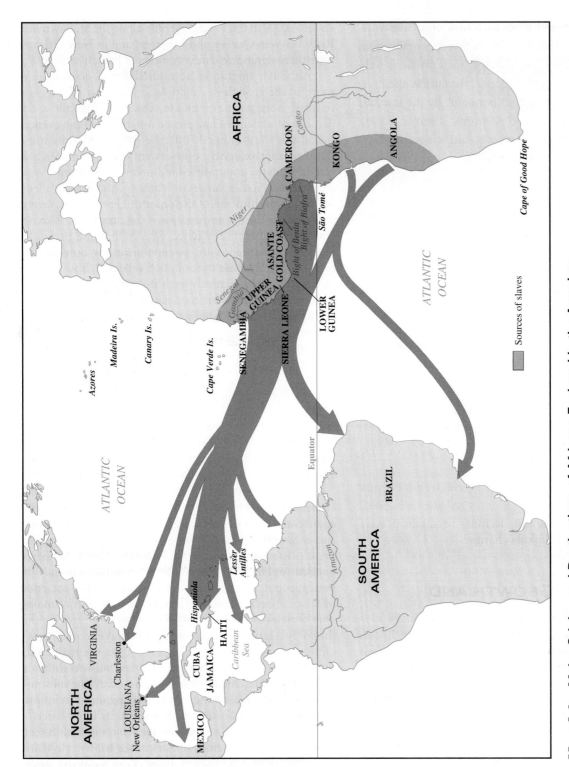

**Map 4.1    Major Origins and Destinations of Africans Enslaved in the Americas**
As this schematic map shows, enslaved Africans were drawn from many regions of western Africa (with some coming from the interior of the continent) and were shipped to areas throughout the Americas. (*Source: Joe W. Trotter, African-American Experience, 1st ed. Used by permission of Houghton Mifflin Company.*)

approximately 9 percent from the Gold Coast (modern Ghana and neighboring countries). Smaller proportions came from East Africa and the Windward and Rice Coasts (modern Senegal, Gambia, and Sierra Leone).

Standard slave-trading practice, in which a vessel loaded an entire cargo at one port and likewise sold them in one place, meant that people from the same area (enemies as well as allies) tended to be taken to the Americas together. That tendency was heightened by planter partiality for slaves of particular ethnic groups. Virginians, for example, purchased primarily Igbos from the Bight of Biafra, whereas South Carolinians and Georgians selected Senegambians and people from West Central Africa. Louisiana planters first chose slaves from the Bight of Benin but later bought many from West Central Africa. Rice planters' desire to purchase Senegambians, who had cultivated rice in their homeland, is easily explained, but historians disagree about the reasons for the other preferences.

*[handwritten annotation: chose Africans based on previous culture & skills]*

Thousands, possibly tens of thousands, of these enslaved Africans were Muslims. Some were literate in Arabic, and several came from aristocratic families. The discovery of noble birth could lead to slaves' being freed to return home. Job Ben Solomon, for example, arrived in Maryland in 1732. Himself a slave trader from Senegal, he had been captured by raiders while selling bondspeople in Gambia. A letter he wrote in Arabic so impressed his owners that he was liberated the next year. Abd al-Rahman, brought to Louisiana in 1788, was less fortunate. Known to his master as "Prince" because of his aristocratic origins, he was not freed until 1829, through the assistance of a European he had befriended in West Africa.

Despite the approximately 260,000 slaves brought to the mainland, American-born people of African descent came to dominate the enslaved population numerically because of high levels of natural increase, especially after 1740. Although about 40 percent of the Africans were male, women and children together composed a majority of slave imports; the girls and women were valued for their reproductive as well as productive capacities. A planter who owned adult female slaves could watch the size of his labor force expand steadily—through the births of their children, designated as slaves in all the colonies—without making additional major purchases of workers. The slaveholder Thomas Jefferson later pointed up the connections when he observed, "I consider a woman who brings a child every two years more profitable than the best man of the farm. What she produces is an addition to the capital, while his labors disappear in mere consumption."

In the Chesapeake, the number of bondspeople grew rapidly because the imports were added to an enslaved pop-

▲ In August 1753, the slave-trading firm of Austin & Laurens advertised the upcoming sale of slaves from the desirable locales of Angola and Gambia in Charleston's *South Carolina Gazette. (Library of Congress)*

*[handwritten annotation: more imports + natural increase = rapid growth]*

ulation that had begun to sustain itself through natural increase. The work routines involved in cultivating tobacco, coupled with a roughly equal sex ratio, reduced slave mortality and increased fertility. Even in unhealthful South Carolina, where substantial imports continued, American-born slaves outnumbered the African-born as early as 1750.

In addition to the new Africans, about 500,000 Europeans moved to British North America during the eighteenth century, most of them after 1730. Late in the seventeenth century, English officials decided to recruit German and French Protestants to prevent further large-scale emigration from England itself. Influenced by mercantilist thought, they had come to regard a large, industrious population at home as an asset rather than a liability. Thus they ordered the deportation to the colonies of such "undesirables" as vagabonds and Jacobite rebels (supporters of the deposed Stuart monarchs) but otherwise discouraged emigration. They offered foreign Protestants free lands and religious toleration, even financing the passage of some groups (for example, Germans sent to New York in the 1710s). After 1740 they relaxed citizenship (naturalization) requirements, insisting on only the payment of a small fee,

### Newcomers from Europe

seven years' residence, evidence of adherence to Protestant beliefs, and an oath of allegiance to the king. Such policies created an ethnic diversity in North America found only in Britain's possessions.

The patterns evident in Alexander McAllister's experience applied to better-off European migrants. Early arrivals wrote home, urging others to come; those contacts created chains of migration from particular regions. The most successful migrants came well prepared, having learned from their American correspondents that land and resources were abundant, especially in the inland areas known as the backcountry, but that they would need capital to take full advantage of the new opportunities. People who arrived penniless did less well;

approximately 40 percent of the newcomers fell into that category, for they immigrated as bound laborers of some sort.

Worst off of all were the 50,000 or so migrants who came as criminals convicted of such offenses as theft and murder, and sentenced to transportation for two to fourteen years instead of execution. Many unskilled and perhaps one-third female, they were dispatched most often to Maryland, where they were employed in the tobacco fields, or as ironworkers or household servants. Little is known about the ultimate fate of most, but some who committed further crimes in the colonies became notorious on both sides of the Atlantic, thanks to newspaper accounts of their exploits.

| TABLE 4.1 | Who Moved to America from England and Scotland in the Early 1770s, and Why? | | |
|---|---|---|---|
| | **English Emigrants** | **Scottish Emigrants** | **Free American Population** |
| **Destination** | | | |
| 13 British colonies | 81.1% | 92.7% | — |
| Canada | 12.1 | 4.2 | — |
| West Indies | 6.8 | 3.1 | — |
| **Age Distribution** | | | |
| Under 21 | 26.8 | 45.3 | 56.8% |
| 21–25 | 37.1 | 19.9 | 9.7 |
| 26–44 | 33.3 | 29.5 | 20.4 |
| 45 and over | 2.7 | 5.3 | 13.1 |
| **Sex Distribution** | | | |
| Male | 83.8 | 59.9 | — |
| Female | 16.2 | 40.1 | — |
| Unknown | 4.2 | 13.5 | — |
| **Traveling Alone or with Families** | | | |
| In families | 20.0 | 48.0 | — |
| Alone | 80.0 | 52.0 | — |
| **Known Occupation or Status** | | | |
| Gentry | 2.5 | 1.2 | — |
| Merchandising | 5.2 | 5.2 | — |
| Agriculture | 17.8 | 24.0 | — |
| Artisanry | 54.2 | 37.7 | — |
| Laborer | 20.3 | 31.9 | — |
| **Why They Left** | | | |
| Positive reasons (e.g., desire to better one's position) | 90.0 | 36.0 | — |
| Negative reasons (e.g., poverty, unemployment) | 10.0 | 64.0 | — |

*Note:* Between December 1773 and March 1776, the British government questioned individuals and families leaving ports in Scotland and England for the American colonies to learn who they were, where they were going, and why they were leaving. This table summarizes just a few of the findings of the official inquiries, which revealed a number of significant differences between the Scottish and English emigrants.

*Source of data* Bernard Bailyn, *Voyagers to the West* (New York: Knopf, 1986), Tables 4.1, 5.2, 5.4, 5.7, 5.23, and 6.1.

One of the largest groups of immigrants—over 150,000—came from Ireland or Scotland, largely in family units. About 70,000 Scots-Irish descendants of Presbyterian Scots who had settled in the north of Ireland during the seventeenth century joined some 35,000 people who, like Alexander McAllister, came directly to America from Scotland (see Table 4.1). Another 45,000, both Protestants and Catholics, migrated from southern Ireland (often as individuals). High rents, poor harvests, and religious discrimination (in Ireland) combined to push people from lands their families had long occupied. Many of the Irish migrants had supported themselves in Ireland by weaving linen cloth, but linen prices declined significantly in the late 1710s. Because the flax used for weaving was imported from Pennsylvania and flaxseed was exported to the same place, vessels with plenty of room for passengers regularly sailed from Ireland to Pennsylvania. By the 1720s, the migration route was well established, fueled by positive reports of prospects for advancement in North America.

**Scots-Irish, Scots, and Germans**

Such immigrants usually landed in Philadelphia or New Castle, Delaware. They moved into the backcountry of western Pennsylvania along the Susquehanna River, where the colonial government created a county named Donegal for them. Later migrants moved farther west and south, to the backcountry of Maryland, Virginia, and the Carolinas. Frequently unable to afford any acreage, they lived illegally on land belonging to Indians, land speculators, or colonial governments. In the frontier setting, they gained a reputation for lawlessness, hard drinking, and ferocious fighting, both among themselves and with neighboring Indians.

Migrants from Germany and German-speaking areas of Switzerland numbered about 85,000, most of them emigrating from the Rhineland between 1730 and 1755. They, too, usually came in family groups and landed in Philadelphia. Because about half of the migrants were youths when they arrived, late in the century they and their descendants accounted for one-third of Pennsylvania's residents. More important, they—like other ethnic groups—tended to settle together, so they composed up to half of the population of some counties. Many Germans moved west and then south into the backcountry of Maryland and Virginia. Others landed in Charles Town and settled in the southern interior. The Germans belonged to a wide variety of Protestant sects—primarily Lutheran, German Reformed, and Moravian—and therefore added to the already substantial religious diversity of Pennsylvania. So many Germans had arrived by 1751 that Benjamin

▲ In December 1729, probably in New York's Hudson Valley, an unknown artist portrayed J. M. Stolle, son of a Palatine immigrant who came to North America from Germany in 1709. The young man's fancy clothing and the column and balustrade in the background suggest that the artist wanted to convey an image of the family's economic success, though whether that image was accurate is unknown.

*(National Gallery of Art, Washington, D.C. Gift of Edgar William and Bernice Chrysler Garbisch)*

Franklin, for one, feared they would "Germanize" Pennsylvania. They "will never adopt our Language or Customs," he predicted inaccurately.

The most concentrated period of immigration to the colonies fell between 1760 and 1775. Tough economic times in Germany and the British Isles led many to decide to seek a better life in America; simultaneously, the slave trade burgeoned. In those fifteen years alone, more than 220,000 free and enslaved people arrived—nearly 10 percent of the entire population of British North America in 1775. Late-arriving free immigrants had little choice but to remain in the cities or move to the edges of settlement; land elsewhere was fully occupied (see Map 4.2). In the peripheries they became the tenants of, or bought property from, land speculators who had purchased giant tracts in the (usually vain) hope of making a fortune.

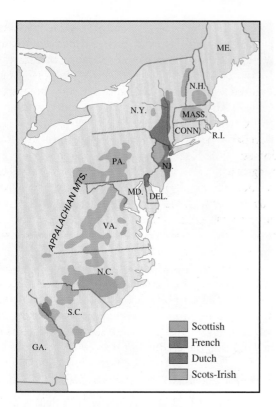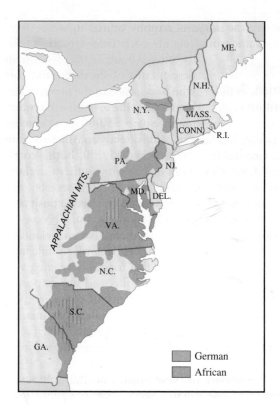

**Map 4.2    Non-English Ethnic Groups in the British Colonies, c. 1775**
Non-African immigrants arriving in the years after 1720 were pushed to the peripheries of settlement, as is shown by these maps. Scottish, Scots-Irish, French, and German newcomers had to move to the frontiers. The Dutch remained where they had originally settled in the seventeenth century. Africans were concentrated in coastal plantation regions.

Because of these migration patterns and the concentration of slaveholding in the South, half of the colonial population south of New England had non-English origins by 1775. Whether the migrants assimilated readily into Anglo-American culture depended on patterns of settlement, the size of the group, and the strength of the migrants' ties to their common culture. For example, in the late seventeenth century, the French Protestants (Huguenots) who migrated to Charles Town or New York City were unable to sustain either their language or their religious practices for more than two generations. Yet the Huguenots who created the rural communities of New Paltz and New Rochelle in the Hudson Valley remained recognizably French and Calvinist for a century. By contrast, the equally small group of colonial Jews maintained a distinct identity regardless of where they settled. Most were

## Maintaining Ethnic and Religious Identities

Sephardic, descended from persecuted Spanish and Portuguese Jews who had first fled to the Netherlands or its American colonies, then later migrated into English territory. In places like New York and Newport, Rhode Island, they established synagogues and worked actively to preserve their religion (for instance, by observing dietary laws and by trying to prevent their children from marrying Christians).

Members of the larger groups of migrants (Germans, Irish, and Scots) found it easier to sustain European ways. Some ethnic groups dominated certain localities. Near Frederick, Maryland, a visitor would have heard more German than English; in Anson and Cumberland Counties, North Carolina, the same visitor might have thought she was in Scotland. Where migrants from different countries settled in the same region, ethnic antagonisms often surfaced. One German clergyman in Pennsylvania, for example, claimed that Scots-Irish migrants were "lazy, dissipated and poor" and that "it is very seldom that German and English blood is happily united in wedlock." Anglo-American elites fostered such antagonisms in order to fracture opposition and maintain their political and economic power, and they frequently subverted the colonies' generous naturalization laws, thus depriving even long-resident immigrants of a voice in government.

The elites probably would have preferred to ignore the English colonies' growing racial and ethnic diversity, but ultimately they could not do so. When they moved toward revolution in the 1770s, they recognized that they needed the support of non-English Americans. Quite deliberately, they began to speak of "the rights of man," rather than "English liberties," when they sought recruits for their cause.

## ECONOMIC GROWTH AND DEVELOPMENT

The dramatic increase in the population of Anglo America caused colonial economies to grow, despite the vagaries of international markets. A comparison with French and Spanish America reveals significant differences. The population and economy of New Spain's northern Borderlands stagnated. The isolated settlements produced few items for export (notably, hides obtained from nearby Indians); residents more often exchanged goods illegally with French and English colonies than with Spanish Mexico or the Caribbean. French Canada exported large quantities of furs and fish, but the government's monopoly of trade ensured that most of the profits ended up in the home country instead of the colony. The Louisiana colony required substantial government subsidies to survive, despite its active internal trade and some agricultural exports. Of France's American possessions, only the Caribbean islands flourished economically.

In British North America, by contrast, each year the rising population generated ever-greater demands for

**Population and Economic Growth**

goods and services, leading to the development of small-scale colonial manufacturing and a complex network of internal trade. Roads, bridges, mills, and stores were built to serve the many new settlements. A lively coastal trade developed; by the late 1760s, more than half of the vessels leaving Boston harbor sailed to other mainland colonies. Such ships not only collected goods for export and distributed imports but also sold items made in America. The colonies thus began to move away from their earlier pattern of dependence on European manufactured goods. For the first time, the American population generated sufficient demand to encourage manufacturing enterprises.

Iron making became the largest indigenous industry. Located primarily in New Jersey, Pennsylvania, and the Chesapeake, ironworks required large investments and the coordination of substantial workforces—usually indentured servants, convicts, and slaves—who dug the ore; chopped and hauled trees, then fired them under controlled conditions to make charcoal; and finally used that charcoal to smelt and refine the ore into iron bars for domestic and foreign consumption. The work was dirty, dangerous, and difficult; convicts and servants often tried to run away, but it offered enslaved men new avenues to learn valuable skills and accumulate property, because supervisors compensated them for "overwork" (doing more than their assigned tasks). By 1775 Anglo America's iron production surpassed England's.

Foreign trade nevertheless constituted the major energizing, yet destabilizing, influence on the colonial economy. Colonial prosperity still depended heavily on overseas demand for American products like tobacco, rice, indigo, fish, and timber products. The sale of such items earned the colonists the credit they needed to purchase English and European imports. If demand for American exports slowed, the colonists' income dropped, as did their ability to buy imported goods. Merchants were particularly vulnerable to economic downswings, and bankruptcies were common.

Despite fluctuations, the American economy slowly grew during the eighteenth century. That growth, which

**Wealth and Poverty**

resulted partly from higher earnings from exports, in turn produced better standards of living for all property-owning Americans. Early in the century, as the price of British manufactures fell in relation to Americans' incomes, households began to acquire amenities such as chairs and earthenware dishes. Diet also improved as trading networks brought access to more varied foodstuffs. After 1750, luxury items like silver plate could be found in the homes of the wealthy, and the "middling sort" started to purchase imported English ceramics and teapots. Even the poorest property owners had more and better household goods. The differences lay not so much in *what* items people owned, but rather in the quality and quantity of those possessions.

Yet the benefits of economic growth were unevenly distributed: wealthy Americans improved their position relative to other colonists. The native-born elite families who dominated American political, economic, and social life by 1750 had begun the century with sufficient capital to take advantage of the changes caused by population growth. They were the urban merchants who exported raw materials and imported luxury goods, the large land-owners who rented small farms to immigrant tenants, the slave traders who supplied wealthy planters with their bondspeople, and the owners of rum distilleries. The rise of this group of moneyed families helped to make the social and economic structure of mid-eighteenth-century America more stratified than before.

New arrivals did not have the opportunities for advancement that had greeted their predecessors. Even so, few free settlers in rural areas (where about 95 percent of the colonists lived) appear to have been truly poor; at least two-thirds of rural householders owned their own land by 1750. But in the cities, families of urban laborers lived on the edge of destitution, and everywhere landless workers were available for hire. By the 1760s, applicants for assistance overwhelmed public urban poor-relief systems, and some cities began to build workhouses or alms-houses to shelter the growing number of poor people. Among them were recent immigrants, the elderly and infirm, and widows, especially those with small children.

Within this overall picture, different regional patterns can be identified. New England; the middle colonies (Pennsylvania, New York, and New Jersey); the Chesapeake (including North Carolina); and the Lower South (South Carolina and Georgia) each had its own economic rhythm derived from the nature of its export trade.

In New England, three elements combined to influence economic development: the nature of the landscape,

## New England and King George's War

New England's leadership in shipping, and the impact of imperial wars. New England's farms produced little to sell elsewhere, other than livestock and timber; the region also had the lowest average wealth per freeholder in the colonies. But New England had many wealthy merchants who earned substantial sums from trade with the Caribbean in items such as salt fish and molasses (see Figure 4.1).

Boston, by the 1730s a major shipbuilding center, soon felt the impact when warfare between European powers

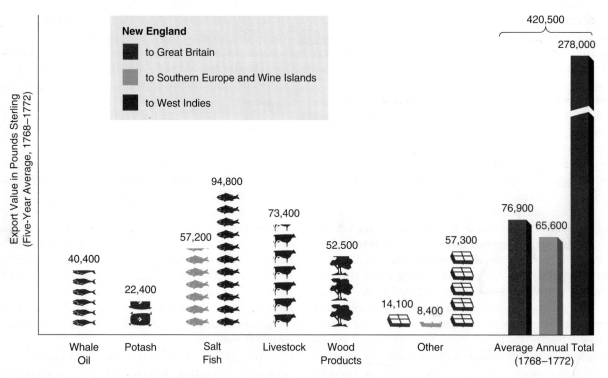

**Figure 4.1    Regional Trading Patterns: New England**
New England's major exports—salt fish, livestock, and wood products—were sold primarily in the West Indies.

*(Source: James F. Shepherd and Gary M. Walton,* Shipping, Maritime Trade, and the Economic Development of Colonial North America *[Cambridge: University Press, 1972]. Used by permission of Cambridge University Press.)*

resumed in 1739. British vessels clashed with Spanish ships in the Caribbean, sparking a conflict that became known in America as King George's War (Europeans called it the War of the Austrian Succession). The war initially energized Boston's economy, for ships—and sailors—were in great demand to serve as privateers. Merchants profited from contracts to supply military expeditions. But then New Englanders suffered major losses in Caribbean battles and forays against Canada. In 1745 a New England expedition captured the French fortress of Louisbourg (in modern Nova Scotia), which guarded the sea-lanes leading to New France. The expensive victory, though, led to heavy taxation of Massachusetts residents, and after the war unprecedented numbers of widows and children crowded Boston's relief rolls. The shipbuilding boom ended when the war did, the economy stagnated, and taxes remained high. Britain even returned Louisbourg to France in the Treaty of Aix-la-Chapelle (1748).

King George's War and its aftermath affected the middle colonies and the Chesapeake more positively because

|||||||||||||||||||||||||||||||||||||||
## Middle Colonies and Chesapeake

prosperous landlords and farmers could readily profit from the wartime demand for grain and flour, especially from the Caribbean (see Figure 4.2). In these colonies the soil was more fertile and growing seasons longer. An average Pennsylvania farm family consumed only 40 percent of what it produced, selling the rest. New York and New Jersey both had many tenant farmers who leased acreage, often paying their rent by sharing crops with their landlords. After the war, when a series of poor harvests in Europe caused flour prices to rise rapidly, Philadelphia and New York, which could draw on extensive grain- and livestock-producing areas, took the lead in the foodstuffs trade.

Increased European demand for grain had a significant impact on the Chesapeake as well. After 1745, when the price of grain began rising faster than that of tobacco, some planters began to convert tobacco fields to wheat and corn. By such diversification, they could avoid dependence on one product for their income (see Figure 4.3).

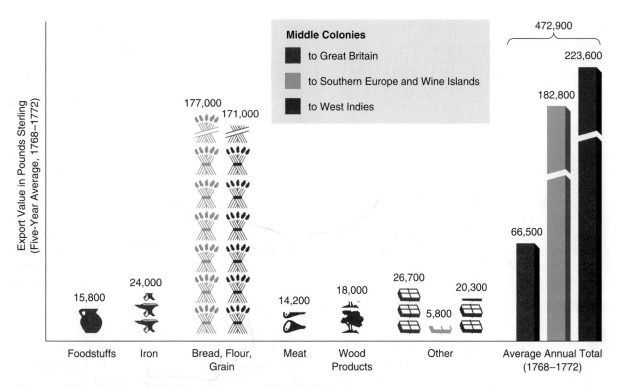

## Figure 4.2   Regional Trading Patterns: Middle Colonies
The middle colonies' major trading partners were the West Indies, the Wine Islands, and southern Europe. Bread, flour, and grains were the region's most valuable exports.

*(Source: James F. Shepherd and Gary M. Walton, Shipping, Maritime Trade, and the Economic Development of Colonial North America [Cambridge: University Press, 1972]. Used by permission of Cambridge University Press.)*

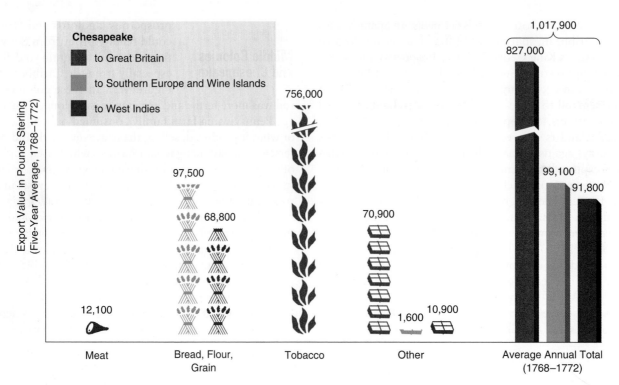

**Figure 4.3   Regional Trading Patterns: The Chesapeake**

Tobacco — legally exported only to Great Britain under the terms of the Navigation Acts — was the Chesapeake's dominant product. Grain made up an increasing proportion of the crops this region sold to other destinations.

*(Source: James F. Shepherd and Gary M. Walton,* Shipping, Maritime Trade, and the Economic Development of Colonial North America *[Cambridge: University Press, 1972]. Used by permission of Cambridge University Press.)*

Tobacco remained the largest single export from the mainland colonies, yet the beginnings of conversion to grain cultivation caused a significant change in Chesapeake settlement patterns by encouraging the development of port towns (like Baltimore), where merchants and shipbuilders established businesses to handle the new trade.

The Lower South, too, depended on staple crops and an enslaved labor force but had a distinctive pattern of economic growth. After Parliament in 1730 removed rice from the list of enumerated products, South Carolinians began to trade directly with continental Europe, especially the German states. Rice prices climbed steeply, doubling by the late 1730s (see Figure 4.4). But dependence on European sales had drawbacks, as planters discovered when the outbreak of King George's War disrupted trade with the continent. Rice prices plummeted, and South Car-

## Carolina and Georgia

olina entered a decade-long depression. Prosperity returned by the 1760s because of rapidly rising European demand for South Carolina's exports. But throughout the century the colony's rice and indigo crops — and sugar cane in the Caribbean islands — were periodically devastated by hurricanes. After such disasters, some overextended planters went bankrupt. Even so, the Lower South experienced more rapid economic growth than did the other colonial regions. Partly as a result, it had the highest average wealth per freeholder in mainland Anglo America by the time of the American Revolution.

Closely linked to South Carolina geographically, demographically, and economically was the newest settlement on the mainland: Georgia, chartered in 1732 as a haven for English debtors who were released from prison to relocate to the colony. Its founder, James Oglethorpe, envisioned Georgia as a garrison province peopled by sturdy farmers who would defend the southern flank of English

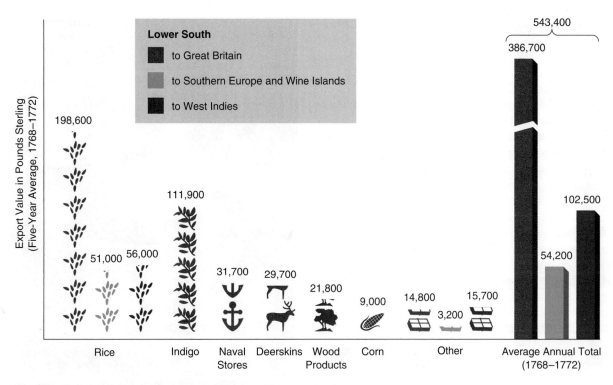

**Figure 4.4  Regional Trading Patterns: The Lower South**
Rice and indigo, sold primarily in the mother country, dominated the exports of the Lower South.

*(Source: James F. Shepherd and Gary M. Walton,* Shipping, Maritime Trade, and the Economic Development of Colonial North America *[Cambridge: University Press, 1972]. Used by permission of Cambridge University Press.)*

settlement against Spanish Florida. Accordingly, its charter prohibited slavery to ensure that all adult men in the colony could be its protectors. But Carolina rice planters won the removal of the restriction in 1751. Thereafter, they essentially invaded Georgia, which—despite remaining politically independent and becoming a royal colony in 1752—developed into a rice-planting slave society resembling South Carolina.

King George's War initially helped New England and hurt the Lower South, but in the long run those effects were reversed. In the Chesapeake and the middle colonies, the war ushered in a long period of prosperity. Such variations highlight the British mainland colonies' disparate experiences within the empire. Despite increasing coastal trade, the colonies' economic fortunes depended not on their neighbors in North America but rather on the shifting markets of Europe and the Caribbean. Had it not been for an unprecedented crisis in the British imperial system (discussed in Chapter 5), it is hard to see how they could have been persuaded to join in a common endeavor. Even with that impetus, they found unity difficult to maintain.

## COLONIAL CULTURES

By 1750, the population of Britain's American possessions was not only denser and more diverse than it had been a half-century earlier but also marked by new extremes of wealth and poverty, especially visible in the growing cities. Native-born colonial elites sought to distinguish themselves from ordinary folk in a variety of ways as they consolidated their hold on the local economy and political power.

One historian has termed these processes "the refinement of America." Colonists who acquired wealth through trade, agriculture, or manufacturing spent their money ostentatiously, dressing fashionably, traveling in horse-drawn carriages driven by uniformed servants, and entertaining one another at lavish parties. Most notably, they built large

**Genteel Culture**

houses containing rooms designed for such forms of socializing as dancing, cardplaying, or drinking tea. Sufficiently well-off to enjoy "leisure" time (a first for North America), they attended concerts and the theater, gambled at horse races, and played billiards and other games. They also cultivated polite manners, adopting stylized forms of address and paying attention to "proper" ways of behaving. Although the effects of accumulated wealth were most pronounced in Anglo America, elite families in New Mexico, Louisiana, and Quebec as well set themselves off from the "lesser sort." Together these wealthy families deliberately constructed a genteel culture quite different from that of ordinary colonists.

Men from such families prided themselves not only on their possessions and on their positions in the colonial political, social, and economic hierarchy, but also on their level of education and their intellectual connections to Europe. Many had been tutored by private teachers hired by their families; some even attended college in Europe or America. (Harvard, the first colonial college, founded in 1636, was joined by William and Mary in 1693, Yale in 1701, and later by several others—including Princeton in 1747.) In the seventeenth century, only aspiring clergymen attended college, studying a curriculum based on ancient languages and theology. But by the mid-eighteenth century, colleges broadened their curricula to include mathematics, the natural sciences, law, and medicine. Accordingly, a minuscule number of young men from elite or upwardly mobile families enrolled in college to study for careers other than the ministry. American women were mostly excluded from advanced education, with the exception of some who joined nunneries in Canada or Louisiana and could engage in sustained study within convent walls.

The intellectual current known as the Enlightenment deeply affected the learned clergymen who headed colonial colleges and their students. Around 1650, some European thinkers began to analyze nature in order to determine the laws governing the universe. They employed experimentation and abstract reasoning to discover general principles behind phenomena like the motions of planets and stars, the behavior of falling objects, and the characteristics of light and sound. Above all, Enlightenment philosophers emphasized acquiring knowledge through reason, taking particular delight in challenging previously unquestioned assumptions. John Locke's *Essay Concerning Human Understanding* (1690), for example, disputed the notion that human beings are born already imprinted with innate ideas. All knowledge, Locke asserted, derives from one's observations of the

## The Enlightenment

▲ Elizabeth Murray, the subject of this 1769 painting by John Singleton Copley, was the wife of James Smith, a wealthy rum distiller. Her fashionable dress and pose would seem to mark her as a lady of leisure, yet both before and during her marriage this Scottish immigrant ran a successful dry goods shop in Boston. She thus simultaneously catered to and participated in the new culture of consumption.

*(Gift of Joseph W. R. Rogers and Mary C. Rogers. Museum of Fine Arts, Boston. Reproduced with permission. © Museum of Fine Arts, Boston)*

external world. Belief in witchcraft and astrology, among other similar phenomena, thus came under attack.

The Enlightenment had an enormous impact on educated, well-to-do people in Europe and America. It supplied them with a common vocabulary and a unified view of the world, one that insisted that the enlightened eighteenth century was better, and wiser, than all previous ages. It joined them in a common endeavor, the effort to make sense of God's orderly creation. Thus American naturalists like John and William Bartram supplied European scientists with information about New World plants and animals for newly formulated universal classification systems. So, too, Americans interested in astronomy took part in an international effort to learn about the solar system by studying a rare occurrence, the transit of Venus

## Smallpox Inoculation

Smallpox, the world's greatest killer of human beings, repeatedly ravaged the population of North America, colonists and Indians alike. Thus, when the vessel *Seahorse* arrived in Boston from the Caribbean in April 1721 with smallpox-infected people on board, New Englanders feared the worst. The authorities ordered the ship and its passengers quarantined, but it was too late: smallpox escaped into the city, and by June several dozen people had caught the dread disease.

Yet there was perhaps some hope. The Reverend Cotton Mather, a member of London's Royal Society (an organization promoting Enlightenment approaches to science), had read in its journal several years earlier two accounts by physicians—one in Constantinople and one in Smyrna—of a medical technique previously unknown to Europeans but widely employed in North Africa and the Middle East. Called inoculation, it involved taking pus from the pustules (or poxes) of an infected person and inserting it into a small cut on the arm of a healthy individual. With luck, that person would experience a mild case of smallpox, thereafter gaining lifetime immunity from the disease. Mather's interest in inoculation was further piqued by his slave Onesimus, a North African who had been inoculated as a youth and who described the procedure in detail to his master.

With the disease coursing through the city, Mather circulated a manuscript among the local medical community, promoting inoculation as a solution to the current epidemic. But nearly all the city's doctors ridiculed his ideas, challenging his sources—and especially denigrating his reliance on information from Onesimus. Mather won only one major convert, Zabdiel Boylston, a physician and apothecary. The two men inoculated their own children and about two hundred others, despite bitter opposition, which included an attempt to bomb Mather's house. Yet after the epidemic ended, Bostonians could clearly see the results: of those inoculated, just 3 percent had died; among the thousands who took the disease "in the natural way," mortality was 15 percent. Even Mather's most vocal opponents were convinced, thereafter supporting inoculation as a remedy for the disease. Mather wrote reports for the Royal Society, and

following their publication even Britain's royal family was inoculated.

Thus, through transatlantic links forged by the Enlightenment and enslavement, American colonists learned how to combat the deadliest disease of all. Today, thanks to a successful campaign by the World Health Organization, smallpox has been wholly eradicated.

An Historical

# ACCOUNT

OF THE

# SMALL-POX

## INOCULATED

IN

## NEW ENGLAND,

Upon all Sorts of Persons, *Whites*, *Blacks*, and of all Ages and Constitutions.

With some Account of the Nature of the Infection in the NATURAL and INOCULATED Way, and their different Effects on HUMAN BODIES.

With some short DIRECTIONS to the UNEXPERIENCED in this Method of Practice.

Humbly dedicated to her Royal Highness the Princess of WALES, by *Zabdiel Boylston*, Physician.

LONDON:

*Printed for* S. CHANDLER, *at the* Cross-Keys *in the* Poultry. M.DCC.XXVI.

▲ Several years after he and Cotton Mather combated a Boston smallpox epidemic by employing inoculation, Zabdiel Boylston published this pamphlet in London to spread the news of their success. The dedication to the Princess of Wales was designed to indicate the royal family's support of the procedure. *(Private Collection)*.

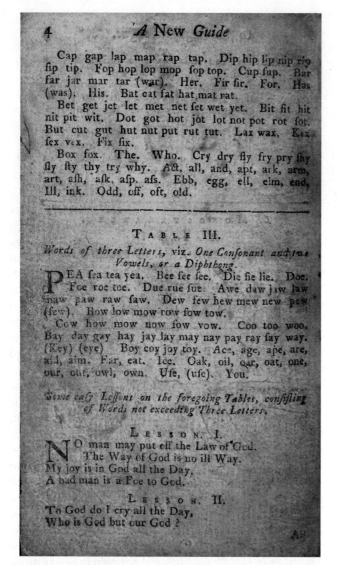

**▲** Thomas Dilworth's *A New Guide to the English Tongue,* first published in London in 1740 and reprinted by Benjamin Franklin in Philadelphia seven years later, was one of the most popular texts used to instruct colonial children in reading and spelling. It used what its author called a "step by step" approach, introducing words of two, then three, then four and more letters, taking care to exclude any words that might "excite loose and disorderly Thoughts."

*(Courtesy, American Antiquarian Society)*

across the face of the sun in 1769. A prime example of America's participation in the Enlightenment was Benjamin Franklin, who retired from a successful printing business in 1748 when he was just forty-two, thereafter devoting himself to scientific experimentation and public service. His *Experiments and Observations on Electricity* (1751) established the terminology and basic theory of electricity still used today.

Enlightenment rationalism affected politics as well as science. Locke's *Two Treatises of Government* (1691) and other works by French and Scottish philosophers challenged previous concepts of a divinely sanctioned, hierarchical political order originating in the power of fathers over families. Men created governments and so could alter them, Locke declared. A ruler who broke the social contract and failed to protect people's rights could legitimately be ousted from power by peaceful—or even violent—means. Government should aim at the good of the people, Enlightenment theorists proclaimed. A proper political order could prevent the rise of tyrants; God's natural laws governed even the power of monarchs.

The world in which such ideas were discussed was that of the few, not the many. Most residents of North America were illiterate. Even those who could read—a small proportion in French or Spanish America, about two-thirds of Anglo-Americans—often could not write. Books were scarce until the 1750s, and colonial newspapers did not begin publication until the 1720s or become commonly available for another three decades. Parents, older siblings, or local widows who needed extra income usually taught youngsters to read; several years later, the more fortunate boys (and genteel girls after the 1750s) might learn to write in private schools. Few Americans other than some Church of England missionaries in the South tried to instruct enslaved children. And only the most zealous Indian converts learned Europeans' literacy skills.

Thus the cultures of colonial North America were primarily oral, communal, and—at least through the first half of the eighteenth century—intensely local. Face-to-face conversation served as the major means of communication. Information tended to travel slowly and within relatively confined regions. Different locales developed divergent cultural traditions, and racial and ethnic variations heightened those differences. Public rituals served as the chief means through which the colonists forged their cultural identities.

Attendance at church was perhaps the most important such ritual. In Congregational (Puritan) churches, church leaders assigned seating to reflect standing in the community. In early New England, men and women sat on opposite sides of a central aisle, arranged in ranks according to age, wealth, and whether or not they had formally become church members. By the mid-eighteenth century, wealthy

## Oral Cultures

## Religious and Civic Rituals

Convicted criminals were publicly punished and shamed in front of their friends, relatives, and neighbors. A man might be put in the stocks for offenses such as contempt of authority, drunken and disorderly conduct, or theft. The intent was not simply to deter him from future misbehavior but to let his fate serve as a warning to all who saw his humiliating posture. *(Library of Congress)*

men and their wives sat in privately owned pews; their children, servants, slaves, and the less fortunate still sat in sex-segregated fashion at the rear, sides, or balcony of the church. In eighteenth-century Virginia, seating in Church of England parishes also conformed to the local status hierarchy. Planter families purchased their own pews, and in some parishes landed gentlemen customarily strode into church as a group just before the service, deliberately drawing attention to their exalted position. In Quebec City, formal processions of men into the parish church celebrated Catholic feast days; each participant's rank determined his place in the procession. By contrast, Quaker meetinghouses in Pennsylvania and elsewhere used an egalitarian but sex-segregated seating system. The varying rituals surrounding people's entrance into and seating in colonial churches thus symbolized their place in society and the values of the local community.

Communal culture also centered on the civic sphere. In New England, governments proclaimed official days of thanksgiving (for good harvests, military victories, and so forth) and days of fasting and prayer (when the colony was experiencing such difficulties as droughts or epidemics). Everyone was expected to participate in the public rituals held in churches on such occasions. Because all able-bodied men between the ages of sixteen and sixty were required to serve in local militias—the only military forces in the colonies—monthly musters also brought the community together.

In the Chesapeake, important rituals occurred on court and election days. When the county court met, men came to file lawsuits, appear as witnesses, or serve as jurors. Attendance at court functioned as a method of civic education; from watching the proceedings men learned what behavior their neighbors expected of them. Elections served the same purpose, for property-holding men voted in public. An election official, often flanked by the candidates for office, would call each man forward to declare his preference. The voter would then be thanked politely by the gentleman for whom he had cast his oral ballot. Traditionally, the candidates afterward treated their supporters to rum at nearby taverns.

Everywhere in colonial North America, the public punishment of criminals served not just to humiliate the offender but also to remind the community of proper behavioral standards. Public hangings and whippings, along with orders to sit in the stocks, expressed the community's outrage about crimes and restored harmony to its ranks. Judges often assigned penalties that shamed miscreants in especially appropriate ways. In San Antonio, Texas, for example, one cattle thief was sentenced to be led through the town's streets "with the entrails hanging from his neck"; and when a New Mexico man assaulted his father-in-law, he was directed not merely to pay medical expenses but also to kneel before him and beg his forgiveness publicly. New Englanders reprieved after being convicted of capital offenses did not thereby escape public humiliation: frequently they were ordered to wear a noose around their neck for years, as a constant reminder to themselves, their families, and their neighbors of their heinous violation of community norms.

## Rituals of Consumption

By 1770 Anglo-American households on average allocated one-quarter of their spending to purchasing consumer goods, which fostered new rituals centered on consumption. Such purchases established novel links among the various residents of North America, creating what historians have termed "an empire of goods." First came the acquisition of desirable items. In the seventeenth century, settlers acquired necessities by bartering with neighbors or ordering products from a home-country merchant. By the middle of the eighteenth century, specialized shops selling nonessentials had proliferated in cities like Philadelphia and New Orleans. In 1770 Boston alone had more than five hundred stores, which offered consumers a vast selection of millinery, sewing supplies, tobacco, gloves, tableware, and the like. Even small towns had one or two retail establishments. Colonists would set aside time to "go shopping," a novel and pleasurable leisure activity. The purchase of an object—for example, a ceramic bowl, a mirror, or a length of beautiful fabric— initiated the consumption rituals.

Consumers would deploy their purchases in an appropriate manner: hanging the mirror prominently on a wall, displaying the bowl on a table or sideboard, turning the fabric into a special piece of clothing. Colonists took pleasure in owning lovely objects, but they also proudly displayed their acquisitions (and thus their wealth and good taste) publicly to kin and neighbors. A rich man might even hire a artist to paint his family using the objects and wearing the clothing, thereby creating a pictorial record that also would be displayed for admiration.

Tea drinking, a consumption ritual dominated and controlled by women, played an especially important

## Tea and Madeira

role in Anglo America. Households with aspirations to genteel status sought to acquire the items necessary for the proper consumption of tea: not just pots and cups but also strainers, sugar tongs, bowls, and even special tables. Tea provided a focal point for socializing and, because of its cost, served as a crucial marker of status. Wealthy women regularly entertained their male and female friends at afternoon tea parties. A hot and mildly stimulating drink, tea also appeared healthful. Thus even poor households consumed tea, although they could not afford the fancy equipment used by their better-off neighbors. Some Mohawk Indians adopted the custom, much to the surprise of a traveler from Sweden, who observed them drinking tea in the late 1740s.

Another drink with connotations of gentility was Madeira wine, imported from the Portuguese islands by merchants with extensive transatlantic familial connections. By 1770 Madeira had become the favored drink of the elite, expensive to purchase and consume properly. Opening the bottle, letting it breathe, decanting and serving it with appropriate glassware were all accomplished with elaborate ceremony. Colonial consumers in different regions had varying tastes, to which producers and merchants responded; mainlanders tended to like their Madeira liberally

▲ This trade card (advertisement) issued by a Philadelphia tobacco dealer in 1770 shows a convivial group of wealthy men at a tavern. Both the leisurely activity depicted here and the advertisement itself were signs of the new rituals of consumption. Merchants began to advertise only when their customers could choose among different ways of spending money. *(Library Company of Philadelphia)*

laced with brandy, whereas residents of the Caribbean preferred sweeter and darker wines without added spirits. From the 1750s on, urban dwellers could buy such wines at specialized stores. And much of what they drank must have been smuggled, because more wines were advertised for sale than were recorded in customs records.

Other sorts of rituals allowed the disparate cultures of colonial North America to interact with one another.

||||||||||||||||||||||||||||||||

**Rituals on the "Middle Ground"**

Particularly important rituals developed on what the historian Richard White has termed the "middle ground"—that is, the psychological and geographical space in which Indians and Europeans encountered each other. Most of those cultural encounters occurred in the context of trade or warfare.

When Europeans sought to trade with Indians, they encountered an indigenous system of exchange that stressed gift giving rather than formalized buying and selling. Successful bargaining required French and English traders to present Indians with gifts (cloth, rum, gunpowder, and other items) before negotiating with them for pelts and skins. Eventually, those gifts would be reciprocated, and formal trading could then take place. To the detriment of Indian societies, rum became a crucial component of these intercultural trading rituals. Traders concluded that drunken Indians would sell their furs more cheaply, and some Indians refused to hunt or trade unless they first received rum. Alcohol abuse hastened the deterioration of villages already devastated by disease and dislocation.

Intercultural rituals also developed to deal with murders. Indians and Europeans both believed that murders required a compensatory act but differed over what that act should be. Europeans sought primarily to identify and punish the murderer. To Indians, such "eye for an eye" revenge was just one of many possible responses to murder. Compensation could also be accomplished by capturing another Indian or a colonist who could take the dead person's place, or by "covering the dead"—that is, by providing the family of the deceased with compensatory goods, a crucial strategy for maintaining peace on the frontiers. Eventually, the French and the Algonquians evolved an elaborate ritual for handling frontier murders which encompassed elements of both societies' traditions: murders were investigated and murderers identified, but by mutual agreement deaths were usually "covered" by trade goods rather than by blood revenge.

## COLONIAL FAMILIES

Families (rather than individuals) constituted the basic units of colonial society; never-married adults were extremely rare. People living together as families, commonly under the direction of a marital pair, everywhere constituted the chief mechanisms for both production and consumption. Yet family forms and structures varied widely in the mainland colonies, and not all were headed by couples.

As Europeans consolidated their hold on North America, Indians had to adapt to novel circumstances. Bands

||||||||||||||||||||||||||||||||

**Indian and Mixed-Race Families**

reduced in numbers by disease and warfare recombined into new units; for example, the Catawbas emerged in the 1730s in the western Carolinas from the coalescence of several earlier peoples, including Yamasees and Guales. Likewise, European secular and religious authorities reshaped Indian family forms. Whereas many Indian societies had permitted easy divorce, European missionaries frowned on such practices; and societies that had allowed polygynous marriages (including New England Algonquians) redefined such relationships, designating one wife as "legitimate" and others as "concubines."

Continued high mortality rates created Indian societies in which extended kin took on new importance, for when parents died, other relatives—even occasionally nonkin—assumed child-rearing responsibilities. Furthermore, once Europeans established dominance in any region, Indians there could no longer pursue traditional modes of subsistence. That led to unusual family structures as well as to a variety of economic strategies. In New England, for instance, Algonquian husbands and wives often could not live together, for adults supported themselves by working separately (perhaps wives as domestic servants, husbands as sailors). Some native women married African American men, unions encouraged by sexual imbalances in both populations. And in New Mexico, detribalized Navajos, Pueblos, and Apaches employed as servants by Spanish settlers clustered in the small towns of the Borderlands. Known collectively as *genizaros*, they lost contact with Indian cultures, instead living on the fringes of Latino society.

Wherever the population contained relatively few European women, sexual liaisons (both inside and outside marriage) occurred between European men and Indian women. The resulting mixed-race population of *mestizos* and *métis* worked as a familial "middle ground" to ease other cultural interactions. In New France and the Anglo-American backcountry, such families frequently resided in Indian villages and were enmeshed in trading networks. Often, children of these unions became prominent leaders of Native American societies. For example, Peter Chartier, son of a Shawnee mother and a French father, led a pro-French Shawnee band in western Pennsylvania in the 1740s. By contrast, in the Spanish Borderlands the offspring of

▲ In eighteenth-century Spain, the existence of mixed-race North American families aroused great curiosity, creating a market for so-called *casta* paintings, which illustrated different sorts of multiracial households. In 1763 the Mexican artist Miguel Cabrera depicted a Spanish father and an Indian mother, who have produced a *mestiza* daughter. Real families resembling this idealized picture would have been seen in New Mexico. *(Private Collection)*

Europeans and *genizaros* were treated as degraded individuals. Largely denied the privilege of legal marriage, they bore generations of "illegitimate" children of various racial mixtures, giving rise in Latino society to a wide range of labels describing degrees of skin color with a precision unknown in English or French America.

Eighteenth-century Anglo-Americans used the word *family* to mean all the people who occupied one household

## European American Families

(including any resident servants or slaves). The many European migrants to North America had more stable family lives than did Indian and *mestizo* peoples. European men or their widows headed households considerably larger than American families today. In 1790 the average home in the United States contained

5.7 free people; few such households included extended kin, such as grandparents. Family members—bound by ties of blood or servitude—worked together to produce goods for consumption or sale. The head of the household represented it to the outside world, voting in elections, managing the finances, and holding legal authority over the rest of the family—his wife, his children, and his servants or slaves.

In English, French, and Spanish America alike, the vast majority of European families supported themselves through agriculture, by cultivating crops and raising livestock. The scale and nature of the work varied: the production of indigo in Louisiana or tobacco in the Chesapeake required different sorts of labor from subsistence farming in New England or cattle ranching in New Mexico and Texas. Still, just as in the European, African, and Indian societies discussed in Chapter 1, household tasks were allocated by sex. The master, his sons, and his male servants or slaves performed one set of chores; the mistress, her daughters, and her female servants or slaves, a different set.

The mistress took responsibility for what Anglo-Americans called "indoor affairs." She and her female helpers prepared food, cleaned the house, did laundry, and often made clothing. Preparing food involved planting and cultivating a garden, harvesting and preserving vegetables, salting and smoking meat, drying apples and pressing cider, milking cows and making butter and cheese, not to mention cooking and baking. The head of the household and his male helpers, responsible for "outdoor affairs," also had heavy workloads. They planted and cultivated the fields, built fences, chopped wood for the fireplace, harvested and marketed crops, cared for livestock, and butchered cattle and hogs to provide the household with meat. So extensive was the work involved in maintaining a farm household that a married couple could not do it alone. If they had no children to help them, they turned to servants or slaves.

Most African American families lived as components of European American households—sometimes on plantations that masters perceived as one large family. More than 95 percent of colonial African Americans were held in perpetual bondage. Although many lived on farms with only one or two other slaves, others had the experience of living and working in a largely black setting. In South Carolina, a majority of the population was of African origin; in Georgia, about half; and in the Chesapeake, 40 percent. Portions of the Carolina low country were nearly 90 percent African American by 1790.

## African American Families

▲ William L. Breton's watercolor of "The Old London Coffee House" in eighteenth-century Philadelphia shows a slave auction taking place on its porch. That such a scene could have occurred in front of such a prominent and popular meeting place serves as a reminder of the ubiquity of slavery in the colonies, north as well as south. *(Historical Society of Pennsylvania)*

The setting in which African Americans lived determined the shape of their families, yet wherever possible slaves established strong family structures in which youngsters carried relatives' names or—in South Carolina—followed African naming patterns. In the North, the scarcity of other blacks often made it difficult for bondspeople to form stable households. In the Chesapeake, men and women who regarded themselves as married (slaves could not legally wed) frequently lived on different quarters or even on different plantations. Children generally resided with their mother, seeing their father only on Sundays. Simultaneously, the natural increase of the population created wide American-born kinship networks among Chesapeake slaves. On large Carolina and Georgia rice plantations, enslaved couples not only usually lived together with their children but also accumulated property through working for themselves after they had completed their daily "tasks." Some Georgia slaves sold their surplus produce at the market in Savannah, thereby earning money to buy nice clothing or such luxuries as tobacco or jewelry, but rarely enough to purchase their freedom.

Because all the British colonies legally permitted slavery, bondspeople had few options for escaping servi-

## Forms of Resistance

tude other than fleeing to Florida, where the Spanish offered protection. Some recently arrived Africans stole boats to try to return home or ran off in groups to frontier regions, to join the Indians or establish independent communities. Among American-born slaves, family ties strongly affected such decisions. South Carolina planters soon learned, as one wrote, that slaves "love their families dearly and none runs away from the other," so many owners sought to keep families together for practical reasons. In the Chesapeake, where family members often lived separately, affectionate ties could cause slaves to run away, especially if a family member had been sold or moved to a distant quarter.

Although colonial slaves rarely rebelled collectively, they often resisted enslavement in other ways. Bondspeople uniformly rejected attempts by their owners to commandeer their labor on Sundays without compensation. Extended-kin groups protested excessive punishment of relatives and sought to live near one another. The links that developed among African American families who had lived on the same plantation for several generations served as insurance against the uncertainties of existence under slavery. If parents and children were separated by sale, other relatives could help with child rearing. Among African Americans, just as among Indians, the extended family thus served a more important function than it did among European-Americans.

Most slave families managed to carve out a small measure of autonomy, especially in their working and spiritual lives, and particularly in the Lower South. Enslaved Muslims often clung to their Islamic faith, a pattern especially evident in Louisiana and Georgia. Some African Americans preserved traditional beliefs, and others converted to Christianity (often retaining some African elements), finding comfort in the assurances of their new religion that all people would be free and equal in heaven. Slaves in South Carolina and Georgia jealously guarded their customary ability to control their own time after completing their "tasks." Even on Chesapeake tobacco plantations, slaves planted their own gardens, trapped, or fished to supplement the minimal diet their masters supplied. Late in the century, some Chesapeake planters with a surplus of laborers began to hire slaves out to others, often allowing the workers to keep a small part of their earnings. Such accumulated property could buy desired goods or serve as a legacy for children.

Just as African-Americans and European-Americans resided together on plantations, so too they lived side by side in urban neighborhoods. (In 1760s Philadelphia, one-fifth of the work force was enslaved, and by 1775 blacks composed nearly 15 percent of the population of New York City.) Such cities were nothing but medium-sized towns by today's standards. In 1750 the largest, Boston and Philadelphia, had just seventeen thousand and thirteen thousand inhabitants, respectively. Life in the cities nonetheless differed considerably from that on northern farms, southern plantations, or southwestern ranches. City dwellers everywhere purchased food and wood in the markets. Urban residents lived by the clock rather than the sun, and men's jobs frequently took them away from their household. City people also had much more contact with the world beyond their own homes than did their rural counterparts.

By the 1750s, most major cities had at least one weekly newspaper, and some had two or three. Anglo-American newspapers printed the latest "advices from London" (usually two to three months old) and news from other colonies, as well as local reports. Newspapers were available (and often read aloud) at taverns and coffeehouses, so people who could not afford them, even illiterates, could learn the news. Contact with the outside world, however, had its drawbacks. Sailors sometimes brought deadly diseases into port. Boston, New York, Philadelphia,

**City Life**

and New Orleans endured terrible epidemics of smallpox and yellow fever, which Europeans and Africans in the countryside largely escaped.

## POLITICS: STABILITY AND CRISIS IN BRITISH AMERICA

Early in the eighteenth century, Anglo-American political life exhibited a new stability. Despite substantial migration from overseas, most residents of the mainland had been born in America. Men from genteel families dominated the political structures in each province, for voters (free male property holders) tended to defer to their well-educated "betters" on election days.

Throughout the Anglo-American colonies, political leaders sought to increase the powers of elected assemblies relative to the powers of the governors and other appointed officials. Assemblies began to claim privileges associated with the British House of Commons, such as the rights to initiate all tax legislation and to control the militia. The assemblies also developed effective ways of influencing British appointees, especially by threatening to withhold their salaries. In some colonies (Virginia and South Carolina, for example), elite members of the assemblies usually presented a united front to royal officials, but in others (such as New York), they fought among themselves long and bitterly. To win hotly contested elections, New York's genteel leaders began to appeal to "the people," competing openly for votes. Yet in 1733 the New York government imprisoned a newspaper editor, John Peter Zenger, who had too vigorously criticized its actions. Defending Zenger against the charge of "seditious libel," his lawyer argued that the truth could not be defamatory, thus helping to establish a free-press principle now found in American law.

**Colonial Assemblies**

Much of the business of colonial assemblies would today be termed administrative; only on rare occasions did they formulate new policies or pass significant laws. Assemblymen saw themselves as acting defensively to prevent encroachments on the colonists' liberties—for example, by preventing governors from imposing oppressive taxes. By midcentury, they were comparing the structure of their governments to Britain's balanced polity, reputedly a combination of monarchy, aristocracy, and democracy of the sort admired since the days of ancient Greece and Rome. Drawing rough analogies, political leaders equated their governors with the monarch, their councils with the aristocracy, and their assemblies with the House of Commons. All three were believed essential to good government, but Anglo-Americans did not regard

*not news = news*

them with the same degree of approval. They viewed governors and appointed councils as representatives of Britain who posed potential threats to customary colonial ways of life. Many colonists saw the assemblies, however, as the people's protectors. And in turn the assemblies regarded themselves as representatives of the people.

Yet such beliefs should not be equated with modern practice. The assemblies, many controlled by dominant families whose members were reelected year after year, rarely responded to the concerns of their poorer constituents. Although settlements continually expanded, assemblies failed to reapportion themselves, which led to serious grievances among backcountry dwellers, especially those from non-English ethnic groups. The colonial ideal of the assembly as the representative defender of liberty must therefore be distinguished from the colonial reality: the most dearly defended and ably represented were wealthy male colonists, particularly the assembly members themselves.

At midcentury, the political structures that had stabilized in a period of relative calm confronted a series of crises. None affected all the mainland colonies, but no colony escaped wholly untouched. The crises of various descriptions—ethnic, racial, economic, regional—exposed internal tensions building in the pluralistic American society, foreshadowing the greater disorder of the revolutionary era. Most important, they demonstrated that the political accommodations arrived at in the aftermath of the Glorious Revolution were no longer adequate to govern Britain's American empire. Once again, changes appeared necessary, and imminent.

One of the first crises occurred in South Carolina. Early on Sunday, September 9, 1739, about twenty enslaved men, most likely Catholics from Kongo, gathered near the Stono River south of Charles Town. September fell in the midst of the rice harvest (and thus at a time of great pressure for male Africans, less accustomed than women to rice cultivation), and September 8 was, to Catholics, the birthday of the Virgin Mary, venerated in Kongo with special fervor. Seizing guns and ammunition, the slaves killed storekeepers and nearby planter families. Then, joined by other local bondsmen, they headed toward Florida in hopes of finding refuge there. By midday, however, the alarm had been

### Slave Rebellions in South Carolina and New York

▲ In 1713 the colony of Massachusetts constructed its impressive State House in Boston. Here met the assembly and the council. The solidity and imposing nature of the building must have symbolized for its users the increasing consolidation of power in the hands of the Massachusetts legislature.

*(The Bostonian Society)*

sounded among slaveowners in the district. That afternoon a troop of militia attacked the fugitives, who then numbered about a hundred, killing some and dispersing the rest. More than a week later, most of the remaining conspirators were captured. The colony quickly executed the survivors, but for over two years rumors about escaped renegades haunted the colony.

The Stono Rebellion shocked slaveholding Carolinians as well as residents of other colonies. Throughout British America, laws governing the behavior of African Americans were stiffened. The most striking response came in New York City, the site of the first mainland slave revolt in 1712. There the news from the South, coupled with fears of Spain generated by the outbreak of King George's War, set off a reign of terror in the summer of 1741. Colonial authorities suspected a biracial gang of thieves and arsonists of conspiring to foment a slave uprising under the guidance of a white schoolteacher thought to be a priest in the pay of Spain. By summer's end, thirty-one blacks and four whites had been executed for participating in the alleged plot. The Stono Rebellion and the New York "conspiracy" not only exposed and confirmed Anglo-Americans' deepest fears about the dangers of slaveholding but also revealed the assemblies' inability to prevent serious internal disorder. Events of the next two decades confirmed that pattern.

By midcentury most of the fertile land east of the Appalachians had been purchased or occupied. Consequently, conflicts over land titles and conditions of landholding grew in number and frequency. In 1746, for example, some New Jersey farmers clashed violently with agents of the East Jersey proprietors. The proprietors claimed the farmers' land as theirs and demanded annual payments, called quit-rents, for the use of the property. Similar violence occurred in the 1760s in the region that later became Vermont. There, farmers holding land grants issued by New Hampshire battled with speculators claiming title to the area through grants from New York authorities.

**Rioters and Regulators**

The most serious land riots took place along the Hudson River in 1765–1766. Late in the seventeenth century, the governor of New York had granted huge tracts in the lower Hudson Valley to prominent families. The proprietors in turn divided these estates into small farms, which they rented chiefly to poor Dutch and German migrants who regarded tenancy as a step on the road to independent freeholder status. By the 1750s some proprietors had earned large sums annually from quit-rents and other fees.

After 1740, though, increasing migration from New England and Europe brought conflict to the great New York estates. Newcomers resisted the tenancy system. Many squatted on vacant portions of the manors, rejecting all attempts at eviction. In the mid-1760s the Philipse family sued farmers who had lived on Philipse land for two decades. New York courts upheld the Philipse claim, ordering squatters to make way for tenants with valid leases. Instead of complying, a diverse group of farmers rebelled, terrorizing proprietors and loyal tenants, freeing their friends from jail, and on one occasion battling a county sheriff and his posse. The rebellion lasted nearly a year, ending only when British troops finally captured its leaders.

Violent conflicts of a different sort soon erupted in the Carolinas as well. The Regulator movements of the late 1760s (South Carolina) and early 1770s (North Carolina) pitted backcountry farmers against wealthy eastern planters who controlled the colonial governments. In South Carolina, Scots-Irish settlers protested their lack of an adequate voice in colonial political affairs. For months they policed the countryside in vigilante bands known as Regulators, complaining of lax and biased law enforcement. North Carolina Regulators, who objected primarily to heavy taxation, fought and lost a battle with eastern militiamen at Alamance in 1771. Regional, ethnic, and economic tensions thus combined to create these disturbances, which ultimately arose from frontier people's dissatisfaction with the Carolina governments.

## A CRISIS IN RELIGION

The most widespread crisis, though, was religious. From the mid-1730s through the 1760s, waves of religious revivalism—today known collectively as the First Great Awakening—swept over various colonies, primarily New England (1735–1745) and Virginia (1750s–1760s). Orthodox Calvinists sought to combat Enlightenment rationalism, which denied innate human depravity. Simultaneously, the economic and political uncertainty accompanying King George's War made colonists receptive to evangelists' spiritual messages. Moreover, many recent immigrants and residents of the backcountry had no prior religious affiliation, thus presenting evangelists with many potential converts.

The Great Awakening began in New England, where descendants of the Puritan founding generation still composed the membership of Congregational churches. Whether in full or "halfway" communion—the latter, a category established in 1662 to ensure that people who had not experienced saving faith would still be subject to church discipline—such members were predominantly female. From the beginnings of the Awakening, though, men and women responded with equal fervor. In the mid-1730s, the Reverend Jonathan Edwards, a noted preacher and theologian, noticed a remarkable reaction among the youthful members of his church in Northampton, Massachusetts, to a message based squarely on Calvinist principles. Individuals could attain salvation, Edwards contended, only through recognition of their own depraved nature and the need to surrender completely to God's will. Such surrender brought to Congregationalists of both sexes an intensely emotional release from sin, coming to be seen as a single identifiable moment of conversion.

The effects of such conversions remained isolated until 1739, when George Whitefield, a Church of England clergyman already celebrated for leading revivals in England, arrived in America. For fifteen months he toured the British colonies, preaching to large audiences from Georgia to New England and concentrating his efforts in the major cities: Boston, New York, Philadelphia, Charles Town, and Savannah. A gripping orator, Whitefield in effect generated the Great Awakening. The historian Harry Stout has termed him "the first modern celebrity" because of his skillful self-promotion and clever manipulation of both his listeners and the newspapers. Everywhere he traveled, his fame preceded him. Readers snapped up books by and about him, the first colonial bestsellers. Thousands of free and enslaved folk turned out to listen—and to experience conversion. Whitefield's journey, the first such ever undertaken, created new interconnections among the previously distinct colonies.

**George Whitefield**

Regular clerics initially welcomed Whitefield and the American-born itinerant evangelist preachers who quickly imitated him. Soon, however, many clergymen began to realize that, although "revived" religion filled their churches, it ran counter to their own approach to doctrine and matters of faith. They disliked the emotional style of the revivalists, whose itinerancy also disrupted normal patterns of church attendance because it took churchgoers away from the services they usually attended. Particularly troublesome to the orthodox were the dozens of female exhorters who took to streets and pulpits, proclaiming their right (even duty) to expound God's word.

Opposition to the Awakening heightened rapidly, causing congregations to splinter. "Old Lights"—traditional clerics and their followers—engaged in bitter disputes with the "New Light" evangelicals. Already characterized by numerous sects, American Protestantism fragmented even further as the major denominations split into Old Light and New Light factions and as new evangelical sects—Methodists and Baptists—gained adherents. After 1771 Methodists sent "circuit riders" (preachers on horseback) to the far reaches of settlement, where they achieved wide-

**Impact of the Awakening**

▲ Reverend George Whitefield, the charismatic evangelist who sparked the First Great Awakening in the mainland British colonies, attracted harsh critics as well as avid admirers. Here an English cartoonist satirizes him as a money-grubbing charlatan who hoodwinks his gullible followers into believing that he is a "Pious Churchman" motivated by "Holy Zeal." Whitefield's crossed eyes, obvious in this image as in others, played a prominent role in contemporary depictions of him.

spread success in converting frontier dwellers. Paradoxically, the angry fights and the rapid rise in the number of distinct denominations eventually led to an American willingness to tolerate religious diversity. No single sect could make an unequivocal claim to orthodoxy, so they had to coexist if they were to exist at all.

Most significantly, the Awakening challenged traditional modes of thought, for the revivalists' message directly contested the colonial tradition of deference. Itinerant preachers, only a few of whom were ordained clergymen, claimed they understood the will of God better than did elite college-educated clerics. Moreover, they and their followers divided the world into two groups—

the saved and the damned—without respect to gender, age, or status, the previously dominant social categories. The revivalists' emphasis on emotion rather than learning undermined the validity of received wisdom, and New Lights questioned not only religious but also social and political orthodoxy. For example, New Lights began to defend the rights of groups and individuals to dissent from a community consensus, thereby challenging one of the fundamental tenets of colonial political life. The egalitarian themes of the Awakening simultaneously attracted ordinary folk and repelled the elite.

Nowhere was this trend more evident than in Virginia, where tax money supported the established Church of England, and the plantation gentry and their ostentatious lifestyle dominated society. By the 1760s Baptists had gained a secure foot-

**Virginia Baptists**

hold in Virginia; inevitably, their beliefs and behavior clashed with the way most genteel families lived. They rejected as sinful the horseracing, gambling, and dancing that occupied much of the gentry's leisure time. They dressed plainly, in contrast to the gentry's fashionable opulence. They addressed one another as "Brother" and "Sister" regardless of social status, and they elected the leaders of their congregations—more than ninety of them by 1776. Their monthly "great meetings," which attracted hundreds of people, introduced new public rituals that rivaled the weekly Anglican services.

Strikingly, almost all the Virginia Baptist congregations included both free and enslaved members. At the founding of the Dan River Baptist Church in 1760, for example, eleven of seventy-four members were African Americans, and some congregations had African American majorities. Church rules applied equally to all members;

# *Legacy* FOR A PEOPLE AND A NATION

## "Self-Made Men"

One of the most common American themes celebrates the "self-made man" (always someone explicitly *male*) of humble origins who gains wealth or prominence through extraordinary effort and talent. Those most commonly cited are such successful nineteenth-century businessmen as Andrew Carnegie (once a poor immigrant from Scotland) and John D. Rockefeller (born on a hardscrabble farm in upstate New York).

The initial exemplars of this tradition, though, lived in the eighteenth century. Benjamin Franklin's *Autobiography* chronicled his method for achieving success after beginning life as the seventeenth child of a Boston candle maker. From such humble origins Franklin became a wealthy, influential man active in science, politics, education, and diplomacy. Yet Franklin's tale is rivaled by that of a man apparently born a slave in South Carolina who subsequently worked as a sailor. He acquired literacy, purchased his freedom, became an influential abolitionist, married a wealthy Englishwoman, and published a popular autobiography that predated Franklin's in print. His first master called him Gustavus Vassa, the name he primarily used. But when publishing his *Interesting Narrative* in 1789, he called himself Olaudah Equiano.

In that *Narrative,* Equiano said he was born in Africa in 1745, kidnapped at the age of eleven, and transported to Barbados and then to Virginia, where a British naval officer purchased him. For years, scholars and students have relied on that account for its insights into the experience of the middle passage. But evidence recently uncovered by Vincent Carretta, although confirming the accuracy of much of Equiano's autobiography, shows that Equiano twice identified his birthplace as Carolina and was three to five years younger than he claimed. Why would Equiano conceal his origins and alter his age? Carretta speculates that the *Narrative* gained part of its credibility from Equiano's African birth and that admitting his real age would have raised questions about the account of his early life by revealing his youth at the time of the reputed kidnapping.

Equiano, or Vassa, thus truly "made himself," just as Benjamin Franklin and many others have done. (Franklin tended to omit, rather than alter, inconvenient parts of his personal history—for example, his having fathered an illegitimate son.) Equiano used information undoubtedly gleaned from acquaintances who *had* experienced the middle passage to craft an accurate depiction of the horrors of the slave trade. In the process he became one of the first Americans to explicitly reinvent himself.

interracial sexual relationships, divorce, and adultery were forbidden to all. In addition, congregations forbade masters' breaking up slave couples through sale. Biracial committees investigated complaints about church members' misbehavior. Churches excommunicated slaves for stealing from their masters, but they also excommunicated masters for physically abusing their slaves. One such slaveowner so dismissed in 1772 experienced a true conversion. Penalized for "burning" one of his slaves, Charles Cook apologized to the congregation and became a preacher in a largely African American church.

By injecting an egalitarian strain into Anglo-American life at midcentury, the Great Awakening had important social and political consequences, calling into question habitual modes of behavior in the secular as well as the religious realm.

## SUMMARY

Over the half-century before 1770, British North America was transformed. In part, that change occurred because of the many newcomers from Germany, Scotland, Ireland, and Africa, who brought their languages, customs, and religions with them. The European immigrants settled throughout the English colonies but were concentrated in the growing cities and in the backcountry. By contrast, enslaved migrants from Africa lived and worked primarily within 100 miles of the Atlantic coast. In many areas of the colonial South, 50 to 90 percent of the population was of African origin.

The economic life of Europe's North American colonies proceeded simultaneously on two levels. On the farms, plantations, and ranches on which most colonists resided, the daily, weekly, monthly, and yearly rounds of chores for men, women, and children alike dominated people's lives while providing the goods consumed by households and sold in markets. Simultaneously, an intricate international trade network affected the economies of the British, French, and Spanish colonies. The bitter wars fought by European nations during the eighteenth century inevitably involved the colonists by creating new opportunities for overseas sales or by disrupting their traditional markets. The volatile colonial economy fluctuated for reasons beyond Americans' control. Those fortunate few who—through skill, control of essential resources, or luck—reaped the profits of international commerce made up the wealthy class of merchants and landowners who dominated colonial political, intellectual, and social life. At the other end of the economic scale, poor colonists, especially city dwellers, struggled to make ends meet.

A century and a half after European peoples first settled in North America, the colonies mixed diverse European, American, and African traditions into a novel cultural blend that owed much to Europe but just as much, if not more, to North America itself. Europeans who interacted regularly with peoples of African and American origin—and with Europeans who came from nations other than their own—had to develop new methods of accommodating intercultural differences in addition to creating ties within their own potentially fragmenting communities. Yet at the same time the dominant colonists continued to identify themselves as French, Spanish, or British rather than as Americans. That did not change in Canada, Louisiana, or the Spanish Borderlands, but in the 1760s some Anglo-Americans began to realize that their interests did not necessarily coincide with those of Great Britain or its monarch. For the first time, they offered a direct challenge to British authority.

## SUGGESTIONS FOR FURTHER READING

Marilyn Baseler, "Asylum for Mankind": America 1607–1800 (1998)

Richard R. Beeman, The Varieties of Political Experience in Eighteenth-Century America (2004)

James F. Brooks, Captives and Cousins: Slavery, Kinship, and Community in the Southwest Borderlands (2002)

William E. Burns, Science and Technology in Colonial America (2005)

Richard Bushman, The Refinement of America: Persons, Houses, Cities (1992)

Rhys Isaac, The Transformation of Virginia, 1740–1790 (1982)

Jill Lepore, New York Burning: Liberty, Slavery, and Conspiracy in Eighteenth-Century Manhattan (2005)

John J. McCusker and Russell R. Menard, The Economy of British America, 1607–1789 (1985)

Harry S. Stout, The Divine Dramatist: George Whitefield and the Rise of Modern Evangelicalism (1991)

Stephanie G. Wolf, As Various as Their Land: The Everyday Lives of 18th Century Americans (1992)

*For a more extensive list for further reading, go to* college.hmco.com/pic/norton8e.

# Severing the Bonds of Empire

## 1754-1774

We the Ladys
of Edenton do
hereby Solemnly
Engage not to Conform
to that Pernicious Custom
of Drinking Tea, or that we the
aforesaid Ladys will not promote y wear
of any Manufacture from England
until such time that all Acts
which tend to Enslave this our
Native Country shall be Repealed

The well-born Scotswoman Janet Schaw chose an inopportune time to visit her older brother, who had moved to North America many years earlier. She and her companions set sail from Edinburgh in October 1774, arriving in the West Indies in January 1775 after a voyage plagued by storms. She enjoyed pleasant visits with the planter families of Antigua and St. Kitts, a number of whom were Scots like herself, and she did some shopping at the international free port of St. Eustatius, purchasing "excellent French gloves" and some "English thread-stockings" cheaper than at home. Then she sailed on to meet her brother in North Carolina. There she encountered indolent and unhealthy looking "rusticks" who had, in her opinion, a "rooted hatred" for the mother country and who were forming "schemes" detrimental to both Britain and America.

Janet Schaw soon learned that an American congress had forbidden "every kind of diversion, even card-playing." When Wilmington residents held a final ball before the ban went into effect, she found the event "laughable," comparing it to seventeenth-century Dutch paintings of comic, carousing peasants. She also reported that "the Ladies have burnt their tea in a solemn procession," but, she sniffed, "they had delayed however till the sacrifice was not very considerable, as I do not think any one offered above a quarter of a pound." All the "genteel" merchants, she observed, "disapprove of the present proceedings," and they were planning to leave as soon as they could. She pronounced the people "infatuated." Although insisting that "I am no politician," she concluded that the trouble in the colonies had been caused by "mistaken notions of moderation" in parliamentary policy. Janet herself returned to

◄ In 1775 an English cartoonist satirized American women's involvement in the resistance movement by depicting the women of Edenton, North Carolina, as grotesque, flirtatious figures. In his view, they neglected their responsibilities as mothers when they dared to enter the political arena by signing a statement in October 1774 pledging to do "every thing as far as lies in our power" to support the "publick good." In the background, he showed them discarding their tea, an action similar to that Janet Schaw described in the nearby town of Wilmington. *(Library of Congress)*

Scotland within the year; her brother's property was later confiscated by the state because he refused to take an oath of allegiance, but he remained in his new homeland until his death.

In retrospect, John Adams identified the period between 1760 and 1775 as the era of the true American Revolution. The Revolution, Adams declared, ended before the fighting started, for it was "in the Minds of the people," involving not the actual winning of independence but a fundamental shift of allegiance from Britain to America. Today, not all historians would concur with Adams that the shift he identified, and which Janet Schaw witnessed, constituted the Revolution. But none would deny the importance of the events of those crucial years, which divided the American population along political lines and set the colonies on the road to independence.

The story of the 1760s and early 1770s describes an ever-widening split between Great Britain and Anglo America, and among their respective supporters in the colonies. In the long history of British settlement in the Western Hemisphere, considerable tension had occasionally marred the relationship between individual provinces and the mother country. Still, that tension had rarely persisted for long, nor had it been widespread, except during the crisis following the Glorious Revolution in 1689. The primary divisions affecting the colonies had been internal rather than external. In the 1750s, however, a series of events began to draw the colonists' attention from domestic matters to their relations with Great Britain. It started with the Seven Years War.

Britain's overwhelming victory in that war, confirmed by treaty in 1763, forever altered the balance of power in North America. France was ousted from the continent and Spain from Florida, events with major consequences for both the indigenous peoples of the interior and the residents of the British colonies. Indians, who had become expert at playing European powers off against one another, lost one of their major diplomatic tools. Anglo-Americans no longer had to fear the French threat on their northern and western borders or the Spanish in the Southeast. The British colonies along the coast would never have dared to break with their mother country, some historians contend, had France still controlled the Mississippi River and the Great Lakes.

The British victory in 1763, then, dramatically affected all the residents of North America. That victory also had a significant impact on Great Britain, one that soon involved the colonies. Britain's massive war-related debt needed to be paid, so Parliament for the first time imposed revenue-raising taxes on the colonies in addition to the customs duties that had long regulated trade. That decision exposed differences in the political thinking of Americans and Britons—differences that until then had been obscured by a shared political vocabulary.

During the 1760s and early 1770s, a broad coalition of the residents of Anglo America, men and women alike, resisted new tax levies and attempts by British officials to tighten controls over provincial governments. The colonies' elected leaders became ever more suspicious of Britain's motives as the years passed. They laid aside old antagonisms to coordinate their responses to the new measures, and they slowly began to reorient their political thinking. As late as the summer of 1774, though, most were still seeking a solution within the framework of the empire; few harbored thoughts of independence.

- What were the causes and consequences of the Seven Years War?
- What British policies did Americans protest, and what theories and strategies did they develop to support those protests?
- Was a war for independence inevitable by the end of 1773? Why or why not?

## RENEWED WARFARE AMONG EUROPEANS AND INDIANS

In the mid-eighteenth century, the British colonies along the Atlantic seaboard were surrounded by hostile, or potentially hostile, neighbors: Indians everywhere, the Spanish in Florida and along the coast of the Gulf of Mexico, the French along the great inland system of rivers and lakes that stretched from the St. Lawrence to the Mississippi. The Spanish outposts posed little direct threat, for Spain's days as a major power had passed. The French were another matter. Their long chain of forts and settlements dominated the North American interior, facilitating trading partnerships and alliances with the Indians. In none of the three Anglo-French wars fought between 1689 and 1748 was Britain able to shake France's hold on the American frontier. Under the Peace of Utrecht, which ended Queen Anne's War in 1713, the English won control of such peripheral northern areas as Newfoundland, Hudson's Bay, and Acadia (Nova Scotia). But Britain made no territorial gains in King George's War (see Table 5.1 and Map 5.2).

During both Queen Anne's War and King George's War, the Iroquois Confederacy maintained the policy of

**Iroquois Neutrality**

neutrality that it first developed in 1701. While British and French forces vied for nominal control of the North American continent, the confederacy skillfully manipulated the Europeans, refusing to commit warriors fully to either side despite being showered with gifts by both. The Iroquois continued a long-standing conflict with Cherokees and Catawbas in the South, thus giving their young warriors combat experience and allowing the replacement of population losses

| TABLE 5.1 | The Colonial Wars, 1689–1763 | | | | |
|---|---|---|---|---|---|
| American Name | European Name | Dates | Participants | American Sites | Dispute |
| King William's War | War of the League of Augsburg | 1689–97 | England, Holland versus France, Spain | New England, New York, Canada | French power |
| Queen Anne's War | War of Spanish Succession | 1702–13 | England, Holland, Austria versus France, Spain | Florida, New England | Throne of Spain |
| King George's War | War of Austrian Succession | 1739–48 | England, Holland, Austria versus France, Spain, Prussia | West Indies, New England, Canada | Throne of Austria |
| French and Indian War | Seven Years War | 1756–63 | England versus France, Spain | Ohio country, Canada | Possession of Ohio country |

▲ An eighteenth-century Iroquois warrior as depicted by a European artist. Such men of the Six Nations confederacy dominated the North American interior before the Seven Years War. Lines drawn on maps by colonizing powers and the incursions of traders made little impact on their power.

*(Library of Congress, Rare Book and Special Collections Division)*

by acquiring new captives. They also cultivated peaceful relationships with Pennsylvania and Virginia, in part to obtain the colonists' imprimatur for their domination of the Shawnees and Delawares. And they forged friendly ties with Algonquians of the Great Lakes region, thereby thwarting potential assaults from those allies of the French and simultaneously making themselves indispensable go-betweens for commerce and communication between the Atlantic coast and the West. Thus the Iroquois consolidated their control over the entire American interior north of Virginia and south of the Great Lakes.

But even the Iroquois could not prevent the region inhabited by the Shawnees and Delawares (now western Pennsylvania and Virginia, and eastern Ohio) from providing the spark that set off a major war. In a significant reversal of previous patterns, that conflict spread from America to Europe, decisively resolving the contest for North America.

Trouble began in the 1740s, when at two treaty conferences Iroquois negotiators, claiming to speak for the Delawares and Shawnees, ceded large tracts of land to Pennsylvania officials. Squatters (mainly Scots-Irish and Germans, but also some Anglo-Americans) had already moved into parts of the region and had negotiated individual agreements with the Delawares for rights to settle there; some even paid rent to native "landlords." All resided on isolated farms in Delaware territory and coexisted peacefully with their native neighbors. But the agreements reached by agents of the Penn family and the Iroquois ignored both the local Indians and the squatters, all of whom were told to move. Disgruntled Delawares and Shawnees migrated west, where they joined other displaced eastern Indians and nursed their grievances.

The region to which they moved, claimed by both Virginia and Pennsylvania, was coveted by wealthy Virginians, who, organized as the Ohio Company, received a huge land grant in 1749. As a first step, the company's agents established trading posts in the west, with the goal of controlling the crucial area where the Allegheny and Monongahela Rivers join to form the Ohio (see Map 5.1). But that "Ohio country" was also vital to the French. Because the Ohio River offered direct access by water to French posts on the Mississippi, a permanent British presence in the Ohio country would challenge France's prominence along the western rivers. Thus, in the early 1750s, Pennsylvania fur traders, Ohio Company representatives, the French military, squatters, Iroquois, Delawares, and Shawnees all jostled for position in the region. A 1752 raid by the French and their native allies on a trading outpost sited at modern Cleveland rid the region of Pennsylvanians, but the Virginians posed a more serious challenge. Accordingly, in 1753 the French pushed southward from Lake Erie, building fortified outposts at strategic points.

In response to the French threat, delegates from seven northern and middle colonies gathered in Albany, New York, in June 1754. With the backing of London officials, they sought

**Albany Congress**

two goals: to persuade the Iroquois to abandon their traditional neutrality and to coordinate the defenses of the colonies. They succeeded in neither. The Iroquois listened politely to the colonists' arguments but saw no reason to change a policy that had served them well for half a century. And although the Albany Congress delegates adopted a Plan of Union (which would have established an elected intercolonial legislature with the power to tax), their provincial governments uniformly rejected the plan—primarily because those governments feared a loss of autonomy.

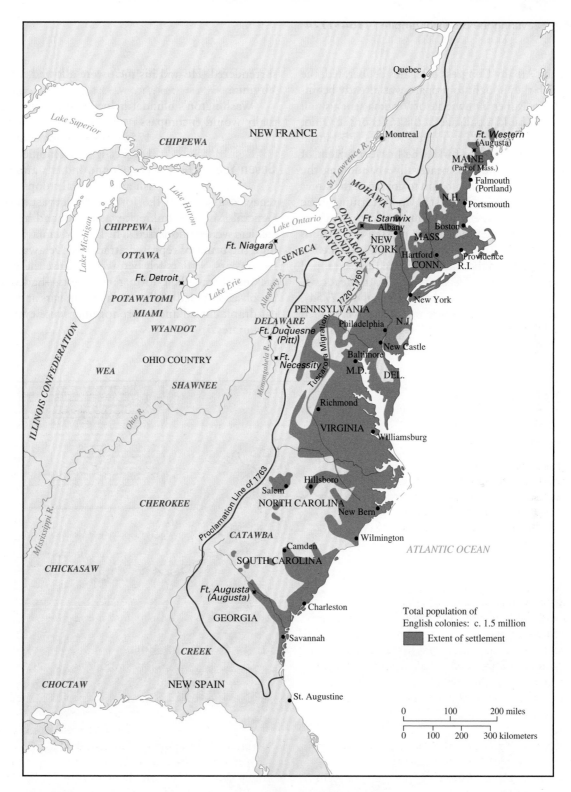

## Map 5.1 European Settlements and Indians, 1754

By 1754 Europeans had expanded the limits of the English colonies to the eastern slopes of the Appalachian Mountains. Few independent Indian nations still existed in the East, but beyond the mountains they controlled the countryside. Only a few widely scattered English and French forts maintained the Europeans' presence there.

While the Albany Congress delegates deliberated, the war for which they sought to prepare was already beginning. Governor Robert Dinwiddie of Virginia sent a small militia troop to build a palisade at the forks of the Ohio, then later dispatched reinforcements. When a substantial French force arrived at the forks, the first contingent of Virginia militia surrendered, peacefully abandoning the strategic site. The French then began to construct the larger and more elaborate Fort Duquesne. Upon learning of the confrontation, the inexperienced young officer who commanded the Virginia reinforcements pressed onward instead of awaiting further instructions. He attacked a French detachment and then allowed himself to be trapped in his crudely built Fort Necessity at Great Meadows, Pennsylvania. After a day-long battle (on July 3, 1754), during which more than one-third of his men were killed or wounded, twenty-two-year-old George Washington surrendered. He and his men were allowed to return to Virginia.

Washington's blunder helped ignite a war that eventually would encompass nearly the entire world. In July

|||||||||||||||||||||||||||||||||

**Seven Years War**

1755, a few miles south of Fort Duquesne, a combined force of French and Indians attacked British and colonial troops readying a renewed assault on the fort. In the devastating defeat, General Edward Braddock was killed, and his surviving soldiers were demoralized. The Pennsylvania frontier then bore the brunt of repeated attacks by Delawares for two more years. Settlers felt betrayed because the Indians attacking them—their former neighbors—had once been (an observer noted) "allmost dayly familiars at their houses eat drank cursed and swore together were even intimate play mates."

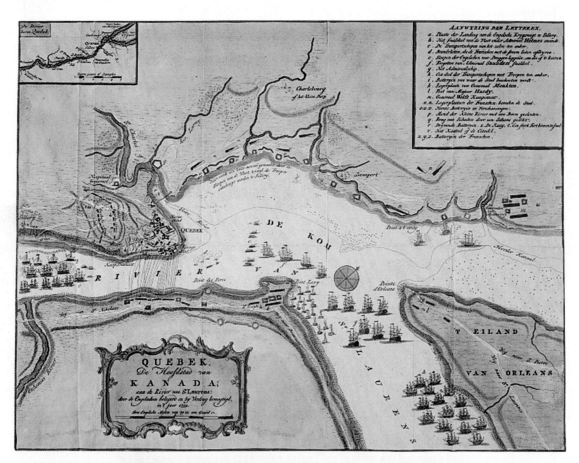

▲ A 1769 Dutch atlas charted the successful British attack on Quebec ten years earlier. Ships of the British fleet fill the St. Lawrence River. Cannon on the southern shore bombard the fortified town (indicated by the lines across the river). And to the left of the city, on the Plains of Abraham, the string of small red blocks represents the British troops who had stealthily climbed the heights at night to confront Quebec's French defenders (the blue blocks). *(Collection of Mary Beth Norton)*

## The First Worldwide War

Today we call two twentieth-century conflicts world wars, but the first worldwide war predated them by more than a century. The contest that historians term the "Great War for the Empire" began in spring 1754 in southwestern Pennsylvania, over a seemingly local quarrel—whether Britain or France would build a fort at the forks of the Ohio. That it eventually involved combatants around the world attests not only to the growing importance of European nations' overseas empires but also to the increasing centrality of North America to their struggles for dominance.

Previous wars among Europeans had taken place mostly in Europe, though overseas colonies occasionally got involved. But the contest at the forks of the Ohio helped to reinvigorate a conflict between Austria and Prussia that sent European nations scrambling for allies. Eventually England, Hanover, and Prussia lined up against France, Austria, and Russia, joined by Sweden, Saxony, and, later, Spain. The war in Europe would last seven years. In 1763 these nations signed a peace treaty that returned the continent to the prewar status quo, but elsewhere, in the rest of the world, Britain had decisively vanquished both France and Spain.

"Elsewhere" included a mind-boggling list of battles. In the Caribbean, Britain seized the French islands of Guadeloupe and Martinique, and took Havana from Spain. In North America, the British recaptured the French fortress of Louisbourg and at last conquered Quebec. In Africa, Britain overwhelmed France's slave-trading posts in Senegambia. In India, British forces won control of Bengal by defeating both a local ruler and French soldiers stationed there. Three years later, the British beat a French army at Pondicherry; four months after France lost Canada, its influence in India was also extinguished. At the very end of the war, a British expedition took Manila in the Philippines from Spain. The commander did not know that his nation had declared war on Britain, so the assault caught him unawares.

Thus the war that started in the American backcountry revealed the steadily growing links between North America and the rest of the world. And the aftermath exposed an unexpected additional link. Both winners and losers had to pay for this first worldwide war. Financial struggles in Britain and France, though separate, ultimately produced similar outcomes: revolutions abroad (for Britain, in America) and at home (for France).

◀ In 1771 the artist Dominic Serres, the Elder, depicted British naval vessels attacking the French fortress at Chandernagore in India in 1757 (at left in background). Cannon fire from the warships was critical to the British victory, one of the keys to the conquest of India during the Seven Years War.

*(National Maritime Museum, London)*

After news of the debacle reached London, Britain declared war on France in 1756, thus formally beginning the Seven Years War. Even before then, Britain, poised for renewed conflict with old enemies, took a fateful step. Britons and New Englanders feared that France would try to retake Nova Scotia, where most of the population was descended from seventeenth-century French settlers who had intermarried with local Mikmaqs. Afraid that in the event of an attack the approximately twelve thousand French Nova Scotians would abandon the policy of neutrality they had followed since the early years of the century, British commanders in 1755 forced about seven thousand of them from their homeland—the first large-scale modern deportation, now called ethnic cleansing. Ships crammed with Acadians sailed to each of the mainland colonies, where the exiles encountered hostility and discrimination as they were dispersed into widely scattered communities. Many families were separated, some forever. After 1763 the survivors relocated: some returned to Canada, others traveled to France or its Caribbean is-

lands, and many eventually settled in Louisiana, where they became known as Cajuns (derived from *Acadian*).

For three years, one disaster followed another. British officers tried without much success to coerce the colonies into supplying men and materiel to the army. Then, led by William Pitt, the civilian official placed in charge of the war effort in 1757, Britain finally pursued a successful military strategy. Pitt agreed to reimburse the colonies for their wartime expenditures and placed recruitment in local hands, thereby gaining greater American support for the war. Large numbers of colonial militiamen served alongside equally large numbers of red-coated regulars sent to North America from Britain; the two groups nevertheless had an antagonistic relationship, lacking mutual respect.

In July 1758, British forces recaptured the fortress at Louisbourg, winning control of the entrance to the St. Lawrence River and cutting the major French supply route. In the fall, the Delawares and Shawnees accepted British peace overtures, and the French abandoned Fort Du-

**Map 5.2    European Claims in North America**

The dramatic results of the British victory in the Seven Years (French and Indian) War are vividly demonstrated in these maps, which depict the abandonment of French claims to the mainland after the Treaty of Paris in 1763.

quesne. Then, in a stunning attack in September 1759, General James Wolfe's regulars defeated the French on the Plains of Abraham and took Quebec. Sensing a British victory, the Iroquois abandoned their traditional neutrality, hoping to gain a postwar advantage by allying themselves with Britain. A year later, the British captured Montreal, the last French stronghold on the continent, and the American phase of the war ended.

In the Treaty of Paris (1763), France ceded its major North American holdings to Britain. Spain, an ally of France toward the end of the war, gave Florida to the victors. France, meanwhile, ceded Louisiana west of the Mississippi to Spain, in partial compensation for its ally's losses elsewhere. The British thus gained control of the continent's fur trade. No longer would the English seacoast colonies have to worry about the threat to their existence posed by France's extensive North American territories (see Map 5.2).

The overwhelming British triumph stimulated some Americans to think expansively. Men like Benjamin Franklin, who had long touted the colonies' wealth and potential, predicted a glorious new future for British North America—a future that included not just geographical expansion but also economic development and population growth. Such men were to lead the resistance to British measures in the years after 1763. They uniformly opposed any laws that would retard America's growth and persistently supported steps to increase Americans' control over their own destiny. Many of them also speculated in western lands.

# 1763: A TURNING POINT

The great victory over France had an irreversible impact on North America, felt first by the indigenous peoples of the interior. With France excluded from the continent altogether and Spanish territory now confined to west of the Mississippi, the diplomatic strategy of playing Europeans off against one another, which the Indians had long adopted, became obsolete. The consequences were immediate and devastating.

Even before the Treaty of Paris, southern Indians had to adjust to new circumstances. After Britain gained the upper hand in the American war in 1758, Creeks and Cherokees lost their ability to force concessions by threatening to turn instead to France or Spain. In desperation, and in retaliation for British atrocities, Cherokees attacked the Carolina and Virginia frontiers in 1760. Though initially victorious, the Indians were defeated the following year by a force of British regulars and colonial militia. Late in 1761 the two sides concluded a treaty under which the Cherokees allowed the construction of British forts in their territories and opened a large tract to European settlement.

The fate of the Cherokees in the South portended events in the Ohio country. There, the Ottawas, Chippewas, and Potawatomis reacted angrily when Great Britain, no longer facing French competition, raised the price of trade goods and ended traditional gift-giving practices. Settlers rapidly moved into the Monongahela and Susquehanna valleys. A shaman named Neolin (also known as the Delaware Prophet) urged Indians to oppose the incursion on their lands and European influence on their culture. For the first time since King Philip in 1675, an influential native leader called for the unity of all tribes in the face of an Anglo-American threat. Contending that Indian peoples were destroying themselves by dependence on European goods (especially alcohol), Neolin advocated resistance, both peaceful and armed. If all Indians west of the mountains united to reject the invaders, Neolin declared, the Master of Life would replenish the depleted deer herds and once again look kindly upon his people. Yet, ironically, Neolin's call for a return to native traditions itself revealed European origins; his reference to a single Master of Life showed the influence on his thinking of a syncretic Christianity.

**Neolin and Pontiac**

Pontiac, war chief of an Ottawa village near Detroit, became the leader of a movement based on Neolin's precepts. In spring 1763, Pontiac forged an unprecedented alliance among Hurons, Chippewas, Potawatomis, Delawares, Shawnees, and Mingoes (Pennsylvania Iroquois). Pontiac then besieged Fort Detroit while war parties attacked other British outposts in the Great Lakes. Detroit withstood the siege, but by late June all the other forts west of Niagara and north of Fort Pitt (formerly Fort Duquesne) had fallen to the alliance. Indians then raided the Virginia and Pennsylvania frontiers throughout the summer, slaying at least two thousand settlers. Still, they could not take Niagara, Fort Pitt, or Detroit. In early August, colonial militiamen soundly defeated a combined Indian force at Bushy Run, Pennsylvania. Conflict ceased when Pontiac broke off the siege of Detroit in late October. A treaty ending the war was finally negotiated three years later.

The warfare on the Pennsylvania frontier in 1755–1757 and 1763 ended what had once been a uniquely peaceful relationship between European settlers and Indians in that province. For nearly eighty years the residents of "Penn's Woods" had avoided major conflicts with each other. But first the Indian attacks and then the settlers'

▲ Benjamin West, the first well-known American artist, engraved this picture of a prisoner exchange at the end of Pontiac's Uprising, with Colonel Henry Bouquet supervising the return of settlers abducted during the war. In the foreground, a child resists leaving the Indian parents he had grown to love. Many colonists were fascinated by the phenomenon West depicted—the reluctance of captives to abandon their adoptive Indian families.

*(Ohio Historical Society)*

response—especially the massacre of several families of defenseless Conestoga Indians in December 1763 by fifty Scots-Irish men known as the Paxton Boys—revealed that violence in the region would subsequently become endemic.

Pontiac's war demonstrated that the huge territory Britain had acquired from France would be difficult to gov-

**Proclamation of 1763**

ern. London officials had no experience managing such a vast area, particularly one inhabited by restive peoples: the remaining French settlers along the St. Lawrence and the many Indian communities. In October the ministry issued the Proclamation of 1763, which designated the headwaters of rivers flowing into the Atlantic from the Appalachians as the temporary western boundary for colonial settlement (see Map 5.1). Its promulgators expected the proclamation to prevent clashes by forbidding colonists to move onto Indian lands until land cessions had been negotiated. But it infuriated two distinct groups of colonists: those who had already squatted west of the line (among them many Scots-Irish immigrants) and land speculation companies from Pennsylvania and Virginia.

In the years after 1763, the latter groups (which included such men as George Washington, Thomas Jefferson, Patrick Henry, and Benjamin Franklin) lobbied vigorously to have their claims validated by colonial governments and London administrators. At a treaty conference at Fort Stanwix, New York, in 1768, they negotiated with Iroquois representatives to push the boundary line farther west and south, opening Kentucky to their speculations. The Iroquois, still claiming to speak for the Delawares and the Shawnees—who used Kentucky as their hunting grounds—agreed to the deal, which brought them valuable trade goods and did not affect their own territories. Yet even though the Virginia land companies eventually gained the support of the House of Burgesses for their claims, they never made any headway where it really mattered—in London—because administrators there realized that significant western expansion would require the expenditure of funds they did not have.

The hard-won victory in the Seven Years War had cost Britain millions of pounds and created an immense

**George III**

war debt. The problem of paying it, and of finding the money to defend the newly acquired territories, bedeviled King George III, who in 1760 succeeded his grandfather, George II. The twenty-two-year-old monarch, an intelligent, passionate man with a mediocre education, was unfortunately an erratic judge of character. During the crucial years between 1763 and 1770, when the rift with the colonies grew ever wider and a series of political crises beset England, the king replaced ministries with bewildering rapidity. Although determined to assert the power of the monarchy, George III was immature and unsure of himself. He stubbornly regarded adherence to the status quo as the hallmark of patriotism.

The man he selected as prime minister in 1763, George Grenville, believed that the American colonies could be more tightly administered. Grenville confronted a financial crisis: England's burden of indebtedness had nearly doubled since 1754, from £73 million to £137 million. Annual expenditures before the war had amounted to no more than £8 million; now the yearly interest on the debt alone came to £5 million. Grenville's ministry had to find new sources of funds, and the British people themselves were already heavily taxed. Because the colonists had benefited greatly from wartime expenditures, Grenville concluded that Anglo-Americans should be asked to pay a larger share of the cost of running the empire.

Grenville did not question Great Britain's right to levy taxes on the colonies. Like all his countrymen, he

## Theories of Representation

believed that government's legitimacy derived ultimately from the consent of the people, but he defined consent differently than the colonists. Americans had come to

believe that they could be represented only by men who lived nearby and for whom they or their property-holding neighbors actually voted; otherwise, they could not count on legislators to represent their interests properly. Grenville and his English contemporaries, however, believed that Parliament—king, lords, and commons acting together—by definition represented all British subjects, wherever they resided (even overseas) and whether or not they could vote.

Parliament saw itself as collectively representing the entire nation; the particular constituency that chose a member of the House of Commons had no special claim on that member's vote, nor did the member have to live near his constituents. According to this theory, called virtual representation, all Britons—including colonists—were represented in Parliament. Thus their consent to acts of Parliament could be presumed. In the colonies, by contrast, members of the lower houses of the assemblies were viewed as specifically representing the regions that had elected them. Before Grenville proposed to tax the colonists, the two notions coexisted because no conflict exposed the central contradiction. But events of the 1760s revealed the incompatibility of the two definitions of representation.

The same events threw into sharp relief Americans' attitudes toward political power. The colonists had be-

## Real Whigs

come accustomed to a central government that wielded limited authority over them, affecting their daily lives very little. Consequently,

they believed that a good government was one that largely left them alone, a view in keeping with the theories of a group of British writers known as the Real Whigs. Drawing on a tradition of dissenting thought that reached back to John Locke and even to the English Civil War, the Real Whigs stressed the dangers inherent in a powerful government, particularly one headed by a monarch. Some of them even favored republicanism, which proposed to eliminate monarchs altogether and rest political power more directly on the people. Real Whigs

warned the people to guard constantly against government's attempts to encroach on their liberty and seize their property. Political power was always to be feared, wrote John Trenchard and Thomas Gordon in their essay series *Cato's Letters* (originally published in London in 1720–1723 and reprinted many times thereafter in the colonies). The people had to exercise perpetual vigilance to prevent rulers' attempts to corrupt and oppress them.

Britain's efforts to tighten the reins of government and to raise revenues from the colonies in the 1760s and early 1770s convinced many Americans that the Real Whigs' reasoning applied to their circumstances, especially because of the link between liberty and property rights. Excessive and unjust taxation, they believed, could destroy their freedoms. They eventually interpreted British measures in light of the Real Whigs' warnings and saw oppressive designs behind the actions of Grenville and his successors. Historians disagree over the extent to which those perceptions were correct, but by 1775 a large number of colonists believed they were. In the mid-1760s, however, colonial leaders did not immediately accuse Grenville of conspiring to oppress them. Rather, they questioned the wisdom of the laws he proposed.

Parliament passed the first such measures, the Sugar and Currency Acts, in 1764. The Sugar Act (also known

## Sugar and Currency Acts

as the Revenue Act) revised existing customs regulations and laid new duties on some foreign imports into the colonies. Its key provisions,

strongly advocated in London by influential Caribbean planters, aimed at discouraging American rum distillers from smuggling French West Indian molasses, thereby improving the market for British sugar. It also established a vice-admiralty court at Halifax, Nova Scotia, to adjudicate violations of the law, along with other maritime offenses. Although the Sugar Act appeared to resemble the Navigation Acts, which the colonies had long accepted as legitimate, it broke with tradition in being explicitly designed to raise revenue, not to channel American trade through Britain. The Currency Act effectively outlawed most colonial issues of paper money, because British merchants had long complained that Americans were paying their debts in inflated local currencies. Americans could accumulate little sterling because they imported more than they exported; colonists complained that the act deprived them of a useful medium of exchange.

The Sugar and Currency Acts were imposed on an economy already in the midst of depression. A business boom accompanied the Seven Years War, but the brief spell of prosperity ended abruptly in 1760 when the war shifted overseas. Atlantic trade routes were disrupted; urban merchants found few buyers for imported goods; and the loss of the military's demand for foodstuffs hurt American farmers. The bottom dropped out of the European tobacco market, threatening the livelihood of Chesapeake planters. Sailors were thrown out of work, and artisans had few customers. In such circumstances, the prospect of increased import duties and inadequate supplies of currency aroused merchants' hostility.

Individual American essayists and incensed colonial governments protested the new policies. But, lacking any precedent for a united campaign against acts of Parliament, Americans in 1764 took only hesitant and uncoordinated steps. Eight colonial legislatures sent separate petitions to Parliament requesting the Sugar Act's repeal. They argued that its commercial restrictions would hurt Britain as well as the colonies and that they had not consented to its passage. The protests had no effect. The law remained in force, and Grenville proceeded with another revenue plan.

## THE STAMP ACT CRISIS

The Stamp Act (1765), Grenville's most important proposal, was modeled on a law that had been in effect in Britain for almost a century. It touched nearly every colonist by requiring tax stamps on most printed materials, but it placed the heaviest burden on merchants and other members of the colonial elite, who used printed matter more frequently than did ordinary folk. Anyone who purchased a newspaper or pamphlet, made a will, transferred land, bought dice or playing cards, applied for a liquor license, accepted a government appointment, or borrowed money would have to pay the tax, which was doubled for foreign-language newspapers. Never before had a revenue measure of such scope been proposed for the colonies. The act also required that tax stamps be purchased with scarce sterling coin. Violators would be tried by vice-admiralty courts, in which judges alone rendered decisions, leading Americans to fear the loss of their right to trial by a jury of their peers. Finally, such a law would break decisively with the colonial tradition of self-imposed taxation.

The most important colonial pamphlet protesting the Sugar Act and the proposed Stamp Act was *The*

**James Otis's**
***Rights of the***
***British Colonies***

*Rights of the British Colonies Asserted and Proved,* by James Otis Jr., a brilliant young Massachusetts attorney. Otis starkly exposed the dilemma that confounded the colonists for the next decade. How

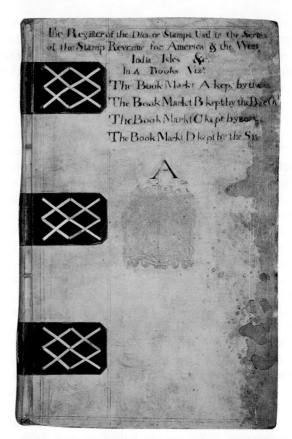

▲ In 1765 a clerk in the offices of British tax officials prepared this register to contain examples of the tax stamps intended for use in the American colonies. But because the law was never enforced and soon repealed, the register is largely empty, and the other volumes the clerk anticipated were never readied at all. *(The British Library Philatelic Section, Inland Revenue Archives)*

could they justify their opposition to certain acts of Parliament without questioning Parliament's authority over them? On the one hand, Otis asserted, Americans were "entitled to all the natural, essential, inherent, and inseparable rights" of Britons, including the right not to be taxed without their consent. "No man or body of men, not excepting the parliament . . . can take [those rights] away," he declared. On the other hand, Otis admitted that, under the British system established after the Glorious Revolution, "the power of parliament is uncontrollable but by themselves, and we must obey. . . . Let the parliament lay what burthens they please on us, we must, it is our duty to submit and patiently bear them, till they will be pleased to relieve us."

Otis's first contention, drawing on colonial notions of representation, implied that Parliament could not constitutionally tax the colonies, because Americans were not represented in its ranks. Yet his second point both acknowledged political reality and accepted the prevailing theory of British government: that Parliament was the sole, supreme authority in the empire. Even unconstitutional laws enacted by Parliament had to be obeyed until Parliament decided to repeal them.

According to orthodox British political theory, there could be no middle ground between absolute submission to Parliament and a frontal challenge to its authority. Otis tried to find such a middle ground by proposing colonial representation in Parliament, but his idea was never taken seriously on either side of the Atlantic. The British believed that colonists were already virtually represented in Parliament, and Anglo-Americans quickly realized that a handful of colonial delegates to London would be outvoted. Otis published his pamphlet before the Stamp Act was passed. When Americans first learned of the act's adoption in the spring of 1765, they reacted indecisively. Few colonists—even appointed government officials—publicly favored the law. But colonial petitions had already failed to prevent its adoption, and further lobbying appeared futile. Perhaps Otis was correct: the only course open to Americans was to pay the stamp tax, reluctantly but loyally. Acting on that assumption, colonial agents in London sought the appointment of their American friends as stamp distributors so that the law would at least be enforced equitably.

Not all the colonists resigned themselves to paying the new tax. A twenty-nine-year-old lawyer serving his first term in the Virginia House of Burgesses was appalled by his fellow legislators' unwillingness to oppose the Stamp Act. Patrick Henry later recalled that he was "young, inexperienced, unacquainted with the forms of the house and the members that composed it"—but he decided to act. "Alone, unadvised, and unassisted, on a blank leaf of an old law book," he wrote the Virginia Stamp Act Resolves.

### Patrick Henry and the Virginia Stamp Act Resolves

Little in Henry's earlier life foreshadowed his success in the political arena that he entered so dramatically. The son of a prosperous Scots immigrant to western Virginia, Henry had little formal education. After marrying at eighteen, he failed at both farming and storekeeping before turning to the law as a means of supporting his wife and their six children. Henry lacked legal training, but his oratorical skills made him an effective advocate, first for his clients and later for his political beliefs. A prominent Virginia lawyer observed, "He is by far the most powerful speaker I ever heard. Every word he says not only engages, but commands the attention."

▲ In 1795 the artist Lawrence Sully painted the only known life portrait of Patrick Henry. The old man's fierce gaze reflects the same intensity that marked his actions thirty years earlier, when he introduced the Virginia Stamp Act Resolves in the House of Burgesses.

*(Mead Art Museum, Amherst College. Bequest of Herbert L. Pratt, Class of 1985)*

Patrick Henry introduced his seven proposals near the end of the legislative session, when many burgesses had already departed for home. Henry's fiery speech led the Speaker of the House to accuse him of treason. (Henry denied the charge, contrary to the nineteenth-century myth that he exclaimed, "If this be treason, make the most of it!") The few burgesses remaining in Williamsburg adopted five of Henry's resolutions by a bare majority. Although they repealed the most radical of the five the next day, their action had far-reaching effects. Some colonial newspapers printed Henry's seven original resolutions as if they had been uniformly passed by the House, even though one was rescinded and two others were never debated or voted on at all.

The four propositions adopted by the burgesses repeated Otis's arguments, asserting that colonists had never forfeited the rights of British subjects, among which was consent to taxation. The other three resolutions went much further. The repealed resolution claimed for the burgesses "the only exclusive right" to tax Virginians, and the final two (those never considered) asserted that Virginians need not obey tax laws passed by other legislative bodies (namely, Parliament), terming any opponent of that opinion "an Enemy to this his Majesty's Colony."

The burgesses' decision to accept only the first four of Henry's resolutions anticipated the position most Americans would adopt throughout the following decade. Though willing to contend for their rights, the colonists did not seek independence. The Maryland lawyer Daniel Dulany, whose *Considerations on the Propriety of Imposing Taxes on the British Colonies* was the most widely read pamphlet of 1765, expressed the consensus: "The colonies are dependent upon Great Britain, and the supreme authority vested in the king, lords, and commons, may justly be exercised to secure, or preserve their dependence." But, warned Dulany, a superior did not have the right "to seize the property of his inferior when he pleases"; there was a crucial distinction between a condition of "dependence and inferiority" and one of "absolute vassalage and slavery."

### Continuing Loyalty to Britain

Over the next ten years, America's political leaders searched for a formula that would enable them to control their internal affairs, especially taxation, but remain under British rule. The chief difficulty lay in British officials' inability to compromise on the issue of parliamentary power. The notion that Parliament could exercise absolute authority over all colonial possessions inhered in the British theory of government. Even the harshest British critics of the ministries of the 1760s and 1770s questioned only the wisdom of specific policies, not the principles on which they rested. In effect, the Americans wanted British leaders to revise their fundamental understanding of the workings of their government. That was simply too much to expect.

The ultimate effectiveness of Americans' opposition to the Stamp Act rested on more than ideological arguments over parliamentary power. The decisive and inventive actions of some colonists during the late summer and fall of 1765 gave the resistance its primary force.

In August, the Loyal Nine, a Boston social club of printers, distillers, and other artisans, organized a demonstration against the Stamp Act. Hoping to show that people of all ranks opposed the act, they approached the leaders of the city's rival laborers' associations, based in Boston's North End and South End neighborhoods. The two gangs, composed of unskilled workers and poor

### Anti–Stamp Act Demonstrations

tradesmen, often battled each other, but the Loyal Nine convinced them to lay aside their differences to participate in the demonstration. All colonists, not just affluent ones, would have to pay the stamp taxes.

Early on August 14, the demonstrators hung an effigy of Andrew Oliver, the province's stamp distributor, from a tree on Boston Common. That night a large crowd led by a group of about fifty well-dressed tradesmen paraded the effigy around the city. The crowd tore down a small building they thought was intended as the stamp office, making a bonfire near Oliver's house with wood from the structure. Beheading the effigy, they added it to the flames. Demonstrators broke most of Oliver's windows and threw stones at officials who tried to disperse them. In the midst of the melee, the North End and South End leaders drank a toast to their successful union. The Loyal Nine achieved success when Oliver publicly promised not to fulfill the duties of his office. One Bostonian jubilantly wrote to a relative, "I believe people never was more Universally pleased not so much one could I hear say he was sorry, but a smile sat on almost every ones countinance."

But another crowd action twelve days later, aimed this time at Oliver's brother-in-law, Lieutenant Governor Thomas Hutchinson, drew no praise from Boston's respectable citizens. On the night of August 26, a mob reportedly led by the South End leader Ebenezer MacIntosh attacked the homes of several customs officers. The crowd then completely destroyed Hutchinson's elaborately furnished townhouse in one of Boston's most fashionable districts. The lieutenant governor reported that by the next morning "one of the best finished houses in the Province had nothing remaining but the bare walls and floors." His trees and garden were ruined, his valuable library was lost, and the mob "emptied the house of every thing whatsoever except a part of the kitchen furniture." But Hutchinson took some comfort in the fact that "the encouragers of the first mob never intended matters should go this length and the people in general express the utmost detestation of this unparalleled outrage."

The differences between the two Boston mobs of August 1765 exposed divisions that would continue to characterize subsequent colonial protests. Few colonists sided with Britain during the 1760s, but various colonial groups had divergent goals. The skilled craftsmen who composed the Loyal Nine and merchants, lawyers, and other members of the educated elite preferred orderly demonstrations confined to political is-

### Americans' Divergent Interests

## Map 5.3    Sites of Major Demonstrations Against the Stamp Act

Every place named on these maps was the site of a demonstration against the Stamp Act of 1765; British colonies outside the eventual United States joined in the nearly universal opposition to the hated measure.

*(Source: From Lester J. Cappon et al., eds., Atlas of Early American History: The Revolutionary Era, 1760–1790. Copyright © 1976 by Princeton University Press, 2004 renewed Princeton University Press. Reprinted by permission of Princeton University Press.)*

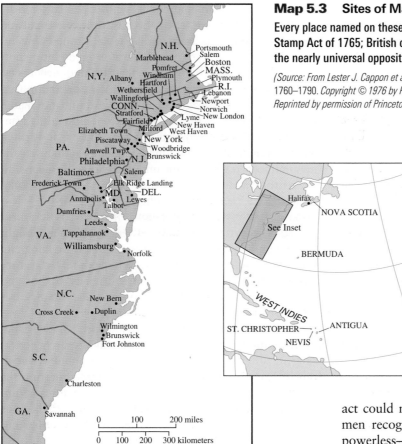

The entry of unskilled workers, slaves, and women into the realm of imperial politics both threatened and aided the elite men who wanted to mount effective opposition to British measures. On the one hand, crowd action could have a stunning impact. Anti-Stamp Act demonstrations occurred in cities and towns stretching from Halifax in the north to the Caribbean island of Antigua in the south (see Map 5.3). They were so successful that, by November 1, when the law was scheduled to take effect, not one stamp distributor was willing to carry out his duties. Thus the act could not be enforced. On the other hand, wealthy men recognized that mobs composed of the formerly powerless—whose goals were not always identical to theirs (as the Boston experience showed)—could endanger their own dominance of the society. What would happen, they wondered, if the "hellish Fury" of the crowd turned against them?

They therefore attempted to channel resistance into acceptable forms by creating an intercolonial association, the Sons of Liberty. New Yorkers organized the first such group in early November, and branches spread rapidly through the coastal cities. Composed of merchants, lawyers, and prosperous tradesmen, the Sons of Liberty by early 1766 linked protest leaders from Charleston, South Carolina, to Portsmouth, New Hampshire. Not surprisingly, in light of the central role of taverns as settings for the exchange of news and opinions, a considerable number of members were tavern owners.

**Sons of Liberty**

The Sons of Liberty could influence events but not control them. In Charleston (formerly Charles Town) in October 1765, an informally organized crowd shouting, "Liberty Liberty and stamp'd paper" forced the resignation of the South Carolina stamp distributor. The victory celebration a few days later—the largest demonstration

sues. For the city's laborers, by contrast, economic grievances may have been paramount. Certainly, their "hellish Fury" as they wrecked Hutchinson's house suggests resentment against his ostentatious display of wealth.

Colonists, like Britons, had a long tradition of crowd action in which disfranchised people took to the streets to redress deeply felt local grievances. But the Stamp Act controversy for the first time drew ordinary urban folk into transatlantic politics, including recent non-English-speaking immigrants targeted by the double taxation of foreign-language newspapers. Matters that previously had been of concern only to the gentry or to members of colonial legislatures were now discussed on every street corner and in every tavern. Benjamin Franklin's daughter observed as much when she informed her father, then serving as a colonial agent in London, that "nothing else is talked of, the Dutch [Germans] talk of the stompt act the Negroes of the tamp, in short every body has something to say."

the city had ever known—featured a British flag with the word "Liberty" emblazoned on it. But the new Charleston chapter of the Sons of Liberty was horrified when in January 1766 local slaves paraded through the streets similarly crying, "Liberty!" Freedom from slavery was not the sort of liberty elite slaveowners had in mind.

In Philadelphia, too, resistance leaders were dismayed when an angry mob threatened to attack Benjamin Franklin's house. The city's laborers believed Franklin to be partly responsible for the Stamp Act because he had obtained the post of stamp distributor for a close friend. But Philadelphia's artisans—the backbone of the opposition movement there and elsewhere—were fiercely loyal to Franklin, one of their own who had made good. They gathered to protect his home and family from the crowd. The house was saved, but the resulting split between Philadelphia's better-off tradesmen and common laborers prevented the establishment of an alliance as successful as Boston's.

During the fall and winter of 1765–1766, opponents of the Stamp Act pursued several different strategies. Co-

### Opposition and Repeal

lonial legislatures petitioned Parliament to repeal the hated law, and courts closed because they could not obtain the stamps now required for all legal documents. In October, nine colonies sent delegates to a general congress, the first since the 1754 Albany Congress. The Stamp Act Congress met in New York to draft a statement of protest that stressed the law's adverse economic effects rather than its perceived violations of Americans' rights. At the same time, the Sons of Liberty held mass meetings, attempting to rally public support for the resistance movement. Finally, American merchants organized nonimportation associations to pressure British exporters. By the 1760s, one-quarter of all British exports went to the colonies, and American merchants

reasoned that London merchants whose sales suffered severely would lobby for repeal. Because times were bad and American merchants were finding few customers for imported goods anyway, a general moratorium on future purchases would also help to reduce their bloated inventories.

In March 1766, Parliament repealed the Stamp Act. The nonimportation agreements had had the anticipated effect, creating allies for the colonies among wealthy London merchants. But boycotts, formal protests, and crowd actions were less important in winning repeal than was the appointment of a new prime minister, chosen by George III for reasons unrelated to colonial politics. Lord Rockingham, who replaced Grenville in the summer of 1765, had opposed the Stamp Act, not because he believed Parliament lacked power to tax the colonies, but because he thought the law unwise and divisive. Thus, although Rockingham proposed repeal, he linked it to passage of a Declaratory Act, which asserted Parliament's authority to tax and legislate for Britain's American possessions "in all cases whatsoever."

News of the repeal arrived in Newport, Rhode Island, in May, and the Sons of Liberty quickly dispatched messengers to carry the welcome tidings throughout the colonies. They organized celebrations commemorating the glorious event, all of which stressed the Americans' unwavering loyalty to Britain. Their goal achieved, the Sons of Liberty dissolved. Few colonists saw the ominous implications of the Declaratory Act.

In August 1766, after William Pitt ▶ became prime minister, a British artist depicted "The Triumph of America" as an impending disaster. America (an Indian) rides in a carriage driven by Pitt, heading directly for a chasm into which Britannia has already fallen. The six horses represent the members of Pitt's new ministry.

*(Library of Congress)*

# RESISTANCE TO THE TOWNSHEND ACTS

The colonists had accomplished their immediate aim, but the long-term prospects were unclear. In the summer of 1766, another change in the ministry in London revealed how fragile their victory had been. The new prime minister, William Pitt, had fostered cooperation between the colonies and Britain during the Seven Years War. But Pitt fell ill, and another man, Charles Townshend, became the dominant force in the ministry. An ally of Grenville and a supporter of colonial taxation, Townshend decided to renew the attempt to obtain additional funds from Britain's American possessions (see Table 5.2).

The duties Townshend proposed in 1767 were to be levied on trade goods like paper, glass, and tea; thus they seemed to extend the existing Navigation Acts. But the Townshend duties differed from previous customs levies in two ways. First, they applied to items imported into the colonies from Britain, not to those from foreign countries. Accordingly, they violated mercantilist theory. Second, the revenues would be used to pay some royal officials in the colonies. Assemblies, in short, would no longer be able to threaten to withhold salaries in order to win those officials' cooperation. Additionally, Townshend's scheme established an American Board of Customs Commissioners and vice-admiralty courts at Boston, Philadelphia, and Charleston. Both moves angered merchants, whose profits would be threatened by more vigorous enforcement of the Navigation Acts.

In 1765, months passed before the colonists protested the Stamp Act. The passage of the Townshend Acts, however, drew a quick response. One series of essays in particular,

**John Dickinson's Farmer's Letters**

*Letters from a Farmer in Pennsylvania*, by the prominent lawyer John Dickinson, expressed a broad consensus. Eventually all but four colonial newspapers printed Dickinson's essays; in pamphlet form they went through seven American editions. Dickinson contended that Parliament could regulate colonial trade but could not exercise that power to raise revenue. By distinguishing between trade regulation and unacceptable commercial taxation, Dickinson avoided the sticky issue of consent and how it affected colonial subordination to Parliament. But his argument created a different, and equally knotty, problem. In effect it obligated the colonies to assess Parliament's motives in passing any law pertaining to trade before deciding whether to obey it. That was unworkable in the long run.

The Massachusetts assembly responded to the Townshend Acts by drafting a letter to circulate among the other colonial legislatures, calling for unity and suggesting a joint petition of protest. Not the letter itself but the ministry's reaction to it united the colonies. When Lord Hillsborough, recently named to the new post of secretary of state for America, learned of the circular letter, he ordered Governor Francis Bernard of Massachusetts to insist that the assembly recall it. He also directed other governors to prevent their assemblies from discussing the letter. Hillsborough's order gave colonial assemblies an incentive to join forces to oppose this new threat to their prerogatives. In late 1768, the Massachusetts legislature met, debated, and resoundingly rejected recall by a vote of 92 to 17. Bernard immediately dissolved the assembly, and other governors followed suit when their legislatures debated the circular letter.

The number of votes cast against recalling the circular letter—92—assumed ritual significance for the supporters of resistance. The number 45 already had symbolic meaning because John Wilkes, a radical Londoner sympathetic to the American cause, had been jailed for libel for publishing an essay entitled *The North Briton*, No. 45. In Boston, the silversmith Paul Revere made a punchbowl weighing 45 ounces that held 45 gills (half-cups) and was engraved with the names of opposition legislators; James Otis, John Adams, and others publicly drank 45 toasts from it. In Charleston the city's tradesmen decorated a tree with 45 lights and set off 45 rockets. Carrying 45 candles, they adjourned to a tavern where 45 tables were set with 45 bowls of wine, 45 bowls of punch, and 92 glasses.

**Rituals of Resistance**

Such public rituals served important unifying and educational functions. Just as the pamphlets by Otis, Dulany, Dickinson, and others acquainted literate colonists with the issues raised by British actions, so public rituals taught illiterate Americans about the reasons for resistance and familiarized them with the terms of the argument. When

| TABLE 5.2 | British Ministries and Their American Policies |
|---|---|
| **Head of Ministry** | **Major Acts** |
| George Grenville | Sugar Act (1764) |
|  | Currency Act (1764) |
|  | Stamp Act (1765) |
| Lord Rockingham | Stamp Act repealed (1766) |
|  | Declaratory Act (1766) |
| William Pitt/ Charles Townshend | Townshend Acts (1767) |
| Lord North | Townshend duties (except for the tea tax) repealed (1770) |
|  | Tea Act (1773) |
|  | Coercive Acts (1774) |
|  | Quebec Act (1774) |

Boston's revived Sons of Liberty invited hundreds of city residents to dine with them each August 14 to commemorate the first Stamp Act demonstration, and the Charleston Sons of Liberty held their meetings in public, crowds gathered to watch and listen. Likewise, the public singing of songs supporting the American cause helped to spread the word. The participants in such events openly expressed their commitment to the cause of resistance and encouraged others to join them.

The Sons of Liberty and other American leaders made a deliberate effort to involve ordinary folk in the campaign against the Townshend duties. Most important, they urged colonists of all ranks and both sexes to sign agreements not to purchase or consume British products. The new consumerism that previously had linked colonists economically now linked them politically as well, supplying them with a ready method of displaying their allegiance. As "A Tradesman" wrote in a Philadelphia paper in 1770, it was essential "for the Good of the Whole, to strengthen the Hands of the Patriotic Majority, by agreeing not to purchase British Goods."

**Daughters of Liberty**

As the primary purchasers of textiles and household goods, women played a central role in the nonconsumption movement. More than three hundred Boston matrons publicly promised not to buy or drink tea, "Sickness excepted." As Janet Schaw later noted, the women of Wilmington, North Carolina, burned their tea after walking through town in a solemn procession. Women throughout the colonies exchanged recipes for tea substitutes or drank coffee instead. The best known of the protests, the so-called Edenton Ladies Tea Party, actually had little to do with tea. It was a meeting of prominent North Carolina women who pledged formally to work for the public good

and to support resistance to British measures. (See the satirical cartoon on page 118.)

Women also encouraged home manufacturing. In many towns, young women calling themselves Daughters of Liberty met to spin in public squares to try to persuade other women to make homespun and to encourage colonists to wear homespun clothing, thereby ending the colonies' dependence on British cloth. These symbolic displays of patriotism—publicized by newspapers and broadsides—served the same purpose as the male rituals involving the numbers 45 and 92. When young ladies from well-to-do families sat outdoors at spinning wheels all day, eating only American food, drinking local herbal tea, and listening to patriotic sermons, they served as political instructors. Many women took great satisfaction in their newfound role. When a satirist hinted that women discussed only "such triffling subjects as Dress, Scandal and Detraction" during their spinning bees, three Boston women replied angrily, "Inferior in abusive sarcasm, in personal invective, in low wit, we glory to be, but inferior in veracity, sincerity, love of virtue, of liberty and of our country, we would not willingly be to any."

But the colonists were by no means united in support of nonimportation and nonconsumption. If the Stamp

**Divided Opinion over Boycotts**

Act protests had occasionally (as in Boston and Philadelphia) revealed a division between artisans and merchants on the one side and common laborers on the other, resistance to the Townshend Acts exposed new splits in American ranks. The most significant—which arose from

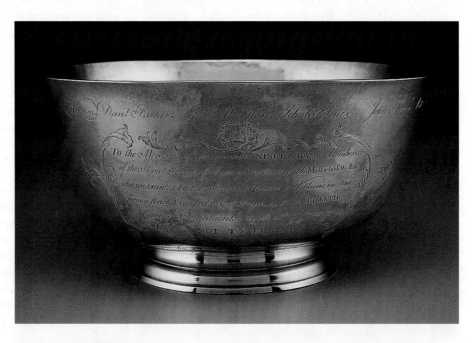

Paul Revere crafted a punchbowl ▶ to commemorate the 92 members of the Massachusetts Assembly who in 1768 voted against rescinding the circular letter. The bowl was also linked symbolically to John Wilkes by its size and weight, and through its use in rituals incorporating the number 45.

*(Courtesy, Museum of Fine Arts, Boston. Gift by Subscription and Francis Bartlett Fund. Reproduced with permission. © 1999 Museum of Fine Arts, Boston. All rights reserved.)*

a change in economic circumstances—divided urban artisans and merchants, allies in 1765.

The Stamp Act boycotts had helped to revive a depressed economy by creating a demand for local products and reducing merchants' inventories. But in 1768 and 1769, merchants were enjoying boom times and had no financial incentive to support a boycott. Consequently, merchants signed the agreements reluctantly and sometimes secretly violated them. In contrast, artisans supported nonimportation enthusiastically, recognizing that the absence of British goods would create a ready market for their own manufactures. Thus tradesmen formed the core of the crowds that coerced both importers and their customers by picketing stores, publicizing offenders' names, and sometimes destroying property.

Such tactics were effective: colonial imports from England dropped dramatically in 1769, especially in New York, New England, and Pennsylvania. But the tactics also aroused heated opposition, dividing opinion in another way. Some Americans who supported resistance to British measures began to question the use of violence to force others to join the boycott. In addition, the threat to private property inherent in the campaign frightened wealthier and more conservative men and women. Political activism by ordinary colonists challenged the ruling elite's domination, just as its members had feared in 1765.

Disclosures that leading merchants had violated the nonimportation agreement caused dissension in the ranks of the boycotters, so Americans were relieved when news arrived in April 1770 that the Townshend duties had been repealed, with the exception of the tea tax. A new prime minister, Lord North, persuaded Parliament that duties on trade within the empire were ill-advised. Although some colonial leaders argued that nonimportation should continue until the tea tax was repealed, merchants quickly resumed importing. The other Townshend Acts remained in force, but repealing the duties made the provisions for paying officials' salaries and tightening customs enforcement appear less objectionable.

▲ A 1769 Boston broadside commended the spinners, "Rich and Poor," who had "Compassion for their Country" and promoted "Frugality" during the Townshend Act crisis. The poet put into verse precisely the message the spinners intended to convey. *(Massachusetts Historical Society)*

## CONFRONTATIONS IN BOSTON

Initially the new ministry did nothing to antagonize the colonists. Yet on the very day Lord North proposed repeal of the Townshend duties, a confrontation between civilians and soldiers in Boston led to five Americans' deaths. The origins of the event that patriots called the Boston Massacre lay in repeated clashes between customs officers and the people of Massachusetts. The decision to base the American Board of Customs Commissioners in Boston ultimately caused the confrontation.

Mobs targeted the customs commissioners from the day they arrived in November 1767. In June 1768 their seizure of the patriot leader John Hancock's sloop *Liberty* on suspicion of smuggling caused a riot in which prominent customs officers' property was destroyed. The riot in turn helped to convince the ministry that troops were needed to maintain order in the unruly port. The assignment of two regiments of regulars to their city confirmed Bostonians' worst fears; the redcoats constantly reminded city dwellers of the oppressive potential of British power. Guards on Boston Neck, the entrance to the city, checked all travelers and their goods. Redcoat patrols roamed the city day and night, questioning and sometimes harassing passersby. Military parades on Boston

Common were accompanied by martial music and often the public whipping of deserters and other violators of army rules. Parents began to fear for the safety of their daughters, who were subjected to soldiers' coarse sexual insults. But the greatest potential for violence lay in the uneasy relationship between the soldiers and Boston laborers. Many redcoats sought employment in their off-duty hours, competing for unskilled jobs with the city's workingmen. Members of the two groups brawled repeatedly in taverns and on the streets.

Early on the evening of March 5, 1770, a crowd of laborers began throwing hard-packed snowballs at soldiers guarding the Customs House.

**Boston Massacre**

Goaded beyond endurance, the sentries acted against express orders and fired on the crowd, killing four and wounding eight, one of whom died a few days later. Reportedly the first to die was Crispus Attucks, a sailor of mixed Nipmuck and African origins. Resistance leaders idealized Attucks and the other dead rioters as martyrs for the cause of liberty, holding a solemn funeral and later commemorating March 5 annually with patriotic orations. Paul Revere's engraving of the massacre was part of the propaganda campaign.

Leading patriots wanted to ensure that the soldiers did not become martyrs as well. Despite the political benefits the patriots derived from the massacre, they probably did not approve the crowd action that provoked it. Ever since the destruction of Hutchinson's house in August 1765, men allied with the Sons of Liberty had supported orderly demonstrations and expressed distaste at such uncontrolled riots as the one that provoked the Boston Massacre. Thus, when the soldiers were tried for the killings in November, John Adams and Josiah Quincy Jr., both unwavering patriots, acted as their defense attorneys. Almost all the accused were acquitted, and the two men convicted were released after being branded on the thumb. Undoubtedly the favorable outcome of the trials persuaded London officials not to retaliate against the city.

For more than two years after the Boston Massacre and the repeal of the Townshend duties, a superficial calm descended on the colonies. In June 1772, Rhode Islanders angry

**A British Plot?**

with overzealous customs enforcement by the British naval schooner *Gaspée* attacked and burned it as it lay aground at low tide in Narragansett Bay near Providence, but because a subsequent investigation failed to identify the perpetrators, no adverse consequences followed for the colonists. The most outspoken newspapers, such as the *Boston Gazette*, the *Pennsylvania Journal*, and the *South Carolina Gazette*,

published essays drawing on Real Whig ideology and accusing Great Britain of deliberately scheming to oppress the colonies. After the Stamp Act's repeal, the protest leaders had praised Parliament; following repeal of the Townshend duties, they warned of impending tyranny. What had seemed to be an isolated mistake, a single ill-chosen stamp tax, now appeared to be part of a plot against American liberties. Essayists pointed to Parliament's persecution of the British radical John Wilkes, the stationing of troops in Boston, and the growing number of vice-admiralty courts as evidence of plans to enslave the colonists. Indeed, patriot writers played repeatedly on the word *enslavement*. Most free colonists had direct knowledge of slavery (either as slaveholders themselves or as neighbors of slaveowners), and the threat of enslavement by Britain must have hit them with peculiar force.

Still, no one yet advocated independence from the mother country. Although some colonists were becoming increasingly convinced that they should seek freedom from parliamentary authority, they continued to acknowledge their British identity and allegiance to George III. They began, therefore, to envision a system that would enable them to be ruled by their own elected legislatures while remaining subordinate to the king. But any such scheme violated Britons' conception of the nature of their government, which posited that Parliament wielded sole, undivided sovereignty over the empire. Furthermore, in the British mind, Parliament encompassed the king as well as lords and commons, so separating the monarch from the legislature was impossible.

Then, in the fall of 1772, the North ministry began to implement the Townshend Act that provided for governors and judges to be paid from customs revenues. In early November, voters at a Boston town meeting established a Committee of Correspondence to publicize the decision by exchanging letters with other Massachusetts towns. Heading the committee was Samuel Adams, who had proposed its formation.

Fifty-one in 1772, Samuel Adams was about a decade older than the other leaders of American resistance, including his distant cousin John.

**Samuel Adams and Committees of Correspondence**

He had been a Boston tax collector, a member and clerk of the Massachusetts assembly, an ally of the Loyal Nine, and one of the Sons of Liberty. Unswerving in his devotion to the American cause, Adams drew a sharp contrast between a corrupt, vice-ridden Britain and the colonies, peopled by simple, liberty-loving folk. An experienced political organizer, Adams continually stressed the necessity of prudent collective action in speeches in

▲ Shortly after the Boston Massacre, Paul Revere printed this illustration of the confrontation near the customs house on March 5, 1770. Offering visual support for the patriots' version of events, it showed the British soldiers firing on an unresisting crowd (instead of the aggressive mob described at the soldiers' trial) and—even worse—a gun firing from the building itself, which has been labeled "Butchers Hall." *(Courtesy of the John Carter Brown Library at Brown University)*

the Boston town meeting. His Committee of Correspondence thus undertook the task of creating an informed consensus among the residents of Massachusetts.

Such committees, which were eventually established throughout the colonies, represented the next logical step in the organization of American resistance. Until 1772, the protest movement was confined largely to the seacoast and primarily to major cities and towns (see Map 5.3). Adams realized that the time had come to widen the movement's geographic scope, to attempt to involve more colonists in the struggle. Accordingly, the Boston town meeting directed the Committee of Correspondence "to state the Rights of the Colonists and of this Province in particular"; to list "the Infringements and Violations thereof

that have been, or from time to time may be made"; and to send copies to the other towns in the province. In return, Boston requested "a free communication of their Sentiments on this Subject."

The statement of colonial rights prepared by the Bostonians declared that Americans had absolute rights to life, liberty, and property. The idea that "a British house of commons, should have a right, at pleasure, to give and grant the property of the colonists" was "irreconcileable" with "the first principles of natural law and Justice . . . and of the British Constitution in particular." The list of grievances complained of taxation without representation, the presence of unnecessary troops and customs officers on American soil, the use of imperial revenues to pay colonial officials, the expanded jurisdiction of vice-admiralty courts, and even the nature of the instructions given to American governors by their superiors in London.

The entire document, which was printed as a pamphlet for distribution to the towns, exhibited none of the hesitation that had characterized colonial claims against Parliament in the 1760s. No longer were resistance leaders—at least in Boston—preoccupied with defining the precise limits of parliamentary authority. No longer did they mention the necessity of obedience to Parliament. They were committed to a course that placed American rights first, loyalty to Great Britain a distant second.

The response of the Massachusetts towns to the committee's pamphlet must have caused Samuel Adams to rejoice. Some towns disagreed with Boston's assessment of the state of affairs, but most aligned themselves with the city. From Braintree came the assertion that "all civil officers are or ought to be Servants to the people and dependent upon them for their official Support, and every instance to the Contrary from the Governor downwards tends to crush and destroy civil liberty." The town of Holden declared that "the People of New England have never given the People of Britain any Right of Jurisdiction over us." The citizens of Petersham commented that resistance to tyranny was "the first and highest social Duty of this people." And Pownallborough warned, "Allegiance is a relative Term and like Kingdoms and commonwealths is local and has its bounds." Beliefs like these made the next crisis in Anglo-American affairs the last.

## TEA AND TURMOIL

The tea tax was the only Townshend duty still in effect by 1773. In the years after 1770, some Americans continued to boycott English tea, while others resumed drinking it either openly or in secret. As was explained in Chapter 4, tea figured prominently in both the colonists' diet and their social lives, so observing the boycott required them not only to forgo a favorite beverage but also to alter habitual forms of socializing. Tea thus retained an explosively symbolic character even though the boycott began to disintegrate after 1770.

In May 1773, Parliament passed an act designed to save the East India Company from bankruptcy. The company, which held a monopoly on British trade with the East Indies, was critically important to the British economy and to the financial well-being of many prominent Brit-

|||||||||||||||||||||||||||||||

**Reactions to the Tea Act**

ish politicians who had invested in its stock. According to the Tea Act, legal tea would henceforth be sold in America only by the East India Company's designated agents, which would enable the company to avoid intermediaries in both Britain and the colonies, and to price its tea competitively with that offered by smugglers. The net result would be cheaper tea for American consumers. Resistance leaders, however, interpreted the new measure as a pernicious device to make them admit Parliament's right to tax them, for the less expensive tea would still be taxed under the Townshend law. Others saw the Tea Act as the first step in the establishment of an East India Company monopoly on all colonial trade. Residents of the four cities designated to receive the first shipments of tea accordingly prepared to respond to what they perceived as a new threat to their freedom.

In New York City, tea ships never arrived. In Philadelphia, Pennsylvania's governor persuaded the captain to sail back to Britain. In Charleston, the tea was unloaded and stored; some was destroyed, the rest sold in 1776 by the new state government. The only confrontation occurred in Boston, where both sides—the town meeting, including participants from nearby towns, and Governor Thomas Hutchinson, two of whose sons were tea agents—rejected compromise.

The first of three tea ships, the *Dartmouth,* entered Boston harbor on November 28. The customs laws required cargo to be landed and the appropriate duty paid by its owners within twenty days of a ship's arrival; otherwise, the cargo had to be seized by customs officers and sold at auction. After a series of mass meetings, Bostonians voted to post guards on the wharf to prevent the tea from being unloaded. Hutchinson refused to permit the vessels to leave the harbor.

On December 16, one day before the cargo would have been confiscated, more than five thousand people (nearly a third of the city's population) crowded into Old South Church. The meeting, chaired by Samuel Adams, made a final attempt to convince Hutchinson to send the tea back to England. But the governor remained adamant. In the early evening Adams reportedly announced "that he could think of nothing further to be done—that they had now done all they could for the Salvation of their Country." Cries then rang out from the back of the crowd: "Boston harbor a tea-pot tonight! The Mohawks are come!" Small groups pushed their way out of the meeting. Within a few minutes, about sixty men crudely disguised as Indians assembled at the wharf, boarded the three ships, and dumped the cargo into the harbor. By 9 P.M. their work was done: 342 chests of tea worth approximately £10,000 floated in splinters on the water.

GREEN DRAGON TAVERN

Where we met to Plan the Consignment of few Shiploads of Tea. Dec 16 1773

John Johnson Water Street Boston Mass. 1773

◀ The planners of the Boston Tea Party met here, at the Green Dragon Tavern, sketched later by one of their number, the portrait painter John Johnson.

*(Courtesy, American Antiquarian Society)*

Among the "Indians" were many representatives of Boston's artisans, including the silversmith Paul Revere. Five masons, eleven carpenters and builders, three leatherworkers, a blacksmith, two barbers, a coachmaker, a shoemaker, and twelve apprentices have been identified as participants. That their ranks also included four farmers from outside Boston, ten merchants, two doctors, a teacher, and a bookseller illustrated the widespread support for the resistance movement. The next day John Adams exulted in his diary that the Tea Party was "so bold, so daring, so firm, intrepid and inflexible" that "I cant but consider it as an Epocha in history."

The North administration reacted with considerably less enthusiasm when it learned of the Tea Party. In March 1774, Parliament adopted the first of four laws that became known as the Coercive, or Intolerable, Acts.* It ordered the port of Boston closed until the tea was paid for, prohibiting all but coastal trade in food and firewood. Later in the spring, Parliament passed three other punitive measures. The Massachusetts Government Act altered the province's charter, substituting an appointed council for the elected one, increasing the governor's powers, and forbidding most town meetings. The Justice Act provided that a person accused of committing murder in the course of suppressing a riot or enforcing the laws could be tried

**Coercive and Quebec Acts**

* in response to Tea Party

outside the colony where the incident had occurred. Finally, the Quartering Act allowed military officers to commandeer privately owned buildings to house their troops. Thus the Coercive Acts punished not only Boston but also Massachusetts as a whole, alerting other colonies to the possibility that their residents, too, could be subject to retaliation if they opposed British authority.

After passing the last of the Coercive Acts, Parliament turned its attention to much-needed reforms in the government of Quebec. The Quebec Act thereby became linked with the Coercive Acts in the minds of the patriots. Intended to ease strains that had arisen since the British conquest of the formerly French colony, the Quebec Act granted greater religious freedom to Catholics—alarming Protestant colonists, who equated Roman Catholicism with religious and political despotism. It also reinstated French civil law, which had been replaced by British procedures in 1763, and it established an appointed council (rather than an elected legislature) as the governing body of the colony. Finally, in an attempt to provide northern Indians with some protection against Anglo-American settlement, the act annexed to Quebec the area west of the Appalachians, east of the Mississippi River, and north of the Ohio River. That region, still with few European inhabitants, was thus removed from the jurisdiction of the seacoast colonies. The wealthy colonists who hoped to develop the Ohio country to attract additional settlers now faced the prospect of dealing with officials in Quebec.

Members of Parliament who voted for the punitive legislation believed that at long last they had solved the problem posed by the troublesome Americans. But resistance leaders showed little inclination to bow to Parliament's authority. In their eyes, the Coercive Acts and the Quebec Act proved what they had feared since 1768: that Britain had embarked on a deliberate plan to oppress them. If the port of Boston could be closed, why not the ports of Philadelphia or New York? If the royal charter of Massachusetts could be changed, why not the charter of South Carolina? If certain people could be transferred to distant colonies for trial, why not any violator of any law? If troops could be forcibly quartered in private houses, did that not portend the occupation of all America? If the Catholic Church could receive favored status in Quebec, why not everywhere? It seemed as though the full dimensions of the plot against American rights and liberties had at last been revealed.

The Boston Committee of Correspondence urged all colonies to join an immediate boycott of British goods.

But other provinces hesitated to take such a drastic step. Rhode Island, Virginia, and Pennsylvania each suggested that another intercolonial congress be convened to consider an appropriate response, and in mid-June 1774 Massachusetts acquiesced. Few people wanted to take hasty action; even the most ardent patriots remained loyal Britons and hoped for reconciliation. Despite their objections to British policy, they continued to see themselves as part of the empire. Americans were approaching the brink of confrontation, but they had not committed themselves to an irrevocable break. So the colonies agreed to send delegates to Philadelphia in September to attend a Continental Congress.

## *Legacy* FOR A PEOPLE AND A NATION

### Women's Political Activism

In the twenty-first century, female citizens of the United States participate at every level of American politics. In 1984 Geraldine Ferraro was nominated for vice president by the Democratic Party; Nancy Pelosi was elected Speaker of the House, third in line for the presidency, in January 2007; and shortly thereafter Hillary Rodham Clinton announced her candidacy in the presidential election of 2008. Eighty-seven women sit in the House and Senate; many serve as governors and in other state offices. But before the 1760s, American women as a group were seen as having no political role—to the extent that they often felt it necessary to apologize for even talking about political issues with their friends. A male essayist expressed the consensus in the mid-1730s: "Poli[ti]cks is what does not become them; the Governing Kingdoms and Ruling Provinces are Things too difficult and knotty for the fair Sex, it will render them grave and serious, and take off those agreeable Smiles that should always accompany them."

But that changed when colonists began to resist the imposition of new British taxes and laws in the mid- to late 1760s. Supporters of American resistance, men and women alike, realized that traditional forms of protest (for example, assemblies' petitions to Parliament) were too limited. Because women made purchasing decisions for American households, and because in the case of spinning and cloth manufacture their labor could replace imported clothing, it was vital for them to participate in the cause. For the first time in American history, women began to take formal political stands. Women of all ranks had to decide whether they would join or oppose the movement to boycott British goods. The groups they established to promote home manufactures—dubbed "Daughters of Liberty"—constituted the first American women's political organizations, tentative and informal though they were.

Since then, American women have taken part in many political movements, among them antislavery societies, pro- and anti-woman suffrage organizations, the Women's Christian Temperance Union, and the civil rights movement. The legacy of revolutionary-era women for the nation continues today in such groups as the National Women's Political Caucus and Concerned Women for America. Indeed, contemporary Americans would undoubtedly find it impossible to imagine their country without female activists of all political and partisan affiliations.

## SUMMARY

Just twenty years earlier, at the outbreak of the Seven Years War in the wilderness of western Pennsylvania, no one could have predicted that the future would bring such swift and dramatic change to Britain's mainland colonies. Yet that conflict simultaneously removed France from North America and created a huge debt that Britain had to find means to pay, developments with major implications for the imperial relationship.

In the years after the war ended in 1763, momentous changes occurred in the ways colonists thought about themselves and their allegiances. The number of colonists who defined themselves as political actors increased substantially. Once linked unquestioningly to Great Britain, they began to develop a sense of their own identity as Americans, including a recognition of the cultural and social gulf that separated them from Britons. They started to realize that their concept of the political process differed from that held by people in the mother country. Most important, they held a different definition of what constituted representation and appropriate consent to government actions. They also came to understand that their economic interests did not necessarily coincide with those of Great Britain. Colonial political leaders reached such conclusions only after a long train of events, some of them violent, had altered their understanding of their relationship with the mother country. Parliamentary acts such as the Stamp Act and the Townshend Acts elicited colonial responses—both ideological and practical—that produced further responses from Britain. Tensions escalated until they climaxed when Bostonians destroyed the East India Company's tea. From that point on, there would be no turning back.

In the late summer of 1774, Americans were committed to resistance but not to independence. Even so, they had started to sever the bonds of empire. During the next decade, they would forge the bonds of a new American nationality to replace those rejected Anglo-American ties.

## SUGGESTIONS FOR FURTHER READING

Fred Anderson, *The War That Made America: A Short History of the French and Indian War* (2005)

Bernard Bailyn, *The Ideological Origins of the American Revolution* (1967)

T. H. Breen, *The Marketplace of Revolution: How Consumer Politics Shaped American Independence* (2004)

Gregory Dowd, *War Under Heaven: Pontiac, the Indian Nations, and the British Empire* (2002)

Marc Egnal, *A Mighty Empire: The Origins of the American Revolution* (1988)

Merrill Jensen, *The Founding of a Nation: A History of the American Revolution, 1763–1776* (1968)

Pauline R. Maier, *From Resistance to Revolution: Colonial Radicals and the Development of American Opposition to Britain, 1765–1776* (1972)

Gary B. Nash, *The Unknown American Revolution: The Unruly Birth of Democracy and the Struggle to Create America* (2005)

William A. Pencak and Daniel K. Richter, eds., *Friends & Enemies in Penn's Woods: Indians, Colonists, and the Racial Construction of Pennsylvania* (2004)

Timothy Shannon, *Indians and Colonists at the Crossroads of Empire: The Albany Congress of 1754* (1999)

*For a more extensive list for further reading, go to* college.hmco.com/pic/norton8e.

# A Revolution, Indeed *1774-1783*

𝒯he Shawnee chief Blackfish named his new captive Sheltowee, or Big Turtle, and adopted him as his son. Blackfish's warriors had easily caught the lone hunter, who was returning with a slaughtered buffalo to an encampment of men making salt at the briny spring known as Blue Licks. The captive then persuaded his fellow frontiersmen to surrender to the Shawnees (allies of the British) without a fight. It was February 1778. The hunter, Daniel Boone, had moved his family from North Carolina to Kentucky about three years before, just as the Revolutionary War began. Both his contemporaries and some historians have wondered about Boone's allegiances during the American Revolution. His encounter with the Shawnees in 1778, which can be interpreted in several ways, highlights many ambiguities of revolutionary-era loyalties.

The Shawnees were seeking captives to cover the death of their chief, Cornstalk, who had been killed several months earlier while a prisoner of American militiamen in the Ohio country. Of the twenty-six men taken at the spring, about half were adopted into Shawnee families; the others— less willing to conform to Indian ways—were dispatched as prisoners to the British fort at Detroit. Boone, who assured Blackfish that in the spring he would negotiate the surrender of the women and children remaining at his home settlement of Boonesborough, watched and waited, outwardly content with his new life. In June 1778 he escaped, hurrying home to warn the Kentuckians of an impending attack.

When Blackfish's Shawnees and their British allies appeared outside the Boonesborough stockade in mid-September, Boone proved amenable to negotiations. Although the settlers adamantly refused to move back across the mountains, fragmentary evidence

◀ A statue of George III standing in the Bowling Green in New York City was one of the first casualties of the American Revolution, as colonists marked the adoption of the Declaration of Independence by pulling it down. Much of the metal was melted to make bullets, but in the twentieth century the head—largely intact—was unearthed in Connecticut.

*(Lafayette College Art Collection, Easton, Pennsylvania)*

## CHRONOLOGY

**1774** ■ First Continental Congress meets in Philadelphia, adopts Declaration of Rights and Grievances
■ Continental Association implements economic boycott of Britain; committees of observation established to oversee boycott

**1774–75** ■ Provincial conventions replace collapsing colonial governments

**1775** ■ Battles of Lexington and Concord; first shots of war fired
■ Second Continental Congress begins
■ Washington named commander-in-chief
■ Dunmore's proclamation offers freedom to patriots' slaves who join British forces

**1776** ■ Paine publishes *Common Sense,* advocating independence
■ British evacuate Boston
■ Declaration of Independence adopted
■ New York City falls to British

**1777** ■ British take Philadelphia
■ Burgoyne surrenders at Saratoga

**1778** ■ French alliance brings vital assistance to America
■ British evacuate Philadelphia

**1779** ■ Sullivan expedition destroys Iroquois villages

**1780** ■ British take Charleston

**1781** ■ Cornwallis surrenders at Yorktown

**1782** ■ Peace negotiations begin

**1783** ■ Treaty of Paris signed, granting independence to the United States

suggests that they agreed to swear allegiance to the British in order to avert a bloody battle. But the discussions dissolved into a melee, with the Indians futilely besieging the fort for a week before withdrawing. With the threat gone, Boone was charged with treason and court-martialed by the Kentucky militia. Although he was cleared, questions about the incident at Blue Licks and its aftermath haunted him for the rest of his life.

Where did Daniel Boone's loyalties lie? To the British? to the Americans? to other Kentuckians? His actions could be viewed in all three lights. Had he betrayed the settlers to Shawnees and sought to establish British authority in Kentucky? Had he—as he later claimed—twice deceived the Shawnees? Or had he rather made the survival of the fragile settlements his highest priority? Kentucky was a borderland—a region where British, Indians, and various groups of American settlers all vied for control. Boone and other residents of the Appalachian backcountry did not always face clear-cut choices as they struggled to establish themselves securely under such precarious circumstances.

Daniel Boone was not the only American of uncertain or shifting allegiances in the 1770s. As a civil war that affected much of North America east of the Mississippi River, the American Revolution uprooted thousands of families, disrupted the economy, reshaped society by forcing many colonists into permanent exile, led Americans to develop new conceptions of politics, and created a nation from thirteen separate colonies. Much more than a series of clashes between the British and patriot armies, it marked a significant turning point in Americans' collective history.

The struggle for independence required revolutionary leaders to accomplish three separate but closely related tasks. The first was political and ideological: transforming a consensus favoring loyal resistance into a coalition supporting independence. Pursuing a variety of measures (ranging from persuasion to coercion) to enlist all European-Americans in the patriot cause, the colonies' elected leaders also tried to ensure the neutrality of Indians and slaves in the impending conflict.

The second task involved foreign relations. To win independence, patriot leaders knew they needed international recognition and aid, particularly from France. Thus they dispatched to Paris the most experienced American diplomat, Benjamin Franklin, who had served for years as a colonial agent in London. Franklin skillfully negotiated the Franco-American alliance of 1778, which was to prove crucial to winning independence.

Only the third task directly involved the British. George Washington, commander-in-chief of the American army, soon recognized that his primary goal should be, not to win battles, but to avoid losing them decisively. The outcome of any one battle was less important than ensuring that his army survived to fight another day.

Consequently, the story of the Revolutionary War reveals British action and American reaction, British attacks and American defenses and withdrawals. The American war effort was aided by British military planners' failure to analyze the problem confronting them accurately. Until it was too late, they treated the war against the colonists as they treated wars against other Europeans: they concentrated on winning battles and did not consider the difficulties of achieving their main goal, retaining the colonies' allegiance. In the end, the Americans' triumph owed more to their own endurance and to Britain's mistakes than to their military prowess.

- What choices of allegiance confronted residents of North America after 1774? Why did people of various descriptions make the choices they did?
- What military strategies did the British and American forces adopt?
- Why did the Americans win the war?

## GOVERNMENT BY CONGRESS AND COMMITTEE

When the fifty-five delegates to the First Continental Congress convened in Philadelphia in September 1774, they knew that any measures they adopted were likely to enjoy widespread support. That summer, well-publicized open meetings held throughout the colonies had endorsed the idea of another nonimportation pact. Participants in such meetings promised (in the words of the freeholders of Johnston County, North Carolina) to "strictly adhere to, and abide by, such Regulations and Restrictions as the Members of the said General Congress shall agree to." Most of the congressional delegates were selected by extralegal provincial conventions whose members were chosen at local gatherings, because governors had forbidden regular assemblies to conduct formal elections. Thus the very act of designating delegates to attend the Congress involved Americans in open defiance of British authority.

The colonies' leading political figures—most of them lawyers, merchants, and planters representing every colony but Georgia—attended the Philadelphia Congress. The Massachusetts delegation included both Samuel Adams, the experienced organizer of Boston resistance, and his younger cousin John, an ambitious lawyer. Among others, New York sent John Jay, a talented young attorney.

**First Continental Congress**

From Pennsylvania came the conservative Joseph Galloway and his long-time rival, John Dickinson. Virginia elected Richard Henry Lee and Patrick Henry, both noted for their patriotic zeal, as well as George Washington. Most of these men had never met, but in the weeks, months, and years that followed they became the chief architects of the new nation.

The congressmen faced three tasks when they convened at Carpenters' Hall on September 5. The first two were explicit: defining American grievances and developing a plan for resistance. The third—articulating their constitutional relationship with Great Britain—was less clear-cut and proved troublesome. The most radical congressmen, like Lee of Virginia, argued that colonists owed allegiance only to George III and that Parliament had no legitimate authority over the colonies. The conservatives—Joseph Galloway and his allies—proposed a formal plan *wanted in between plan.* of union that would have required Parliament and a new American legislature to consent jointly to all laws pertaining to the colonies. After heated debate, delegates narrowly rejected Galloway's proposal, but they were not prepared to embrace the radicals' position either.

Finally, they accepted wording proposed by John Adams. The crucial clauses in the Congress's Declaration of Rights and Grievances declared that Americans would obey Parliament, but only voluntarily, and that they would resist all taxes in disguise, like the Townshend duties. Remarkably, such a position—which only a few years before would have been regarded as radical—represented a compromise in the fall of 1774. The Americans had come a long way since their first hesitant protests against the Sugar Act ten years earlier.

With the constitutional issue resolved, the delegates readily agreed on the laws they wanted repealed (notably the Coercive Acts) and decided to implement an economic boycott while petitioning the king for relief. They adopted the Continental Association, which called for nonimportation of British goods (effective December 1, 1774), nonconsumption of British products (effective March 1, 1775), and nonexportation of American goods to Britain and the British West Indies (effective September 10, 1775).

**Continental Association**

The provisions of the Association—far more comprehensive than any previous economic measure adopted by the colonies—were carefully designed to appeal to different groups and regions. For example, the inclusive language of the nonimportation agreement banned commerce in slaves as well as manufactures, which accorded with a long-standing desire of the Virginia gentry to halt, or at least to slow, the arrival of enslaved Africans on their shores. (Leading Virginians believed that continuing slave importations had discouraged the immigration to their colony of free Europeans with useful skills.) Delaying nonconsumption until three months after implementing nonimportation allowed northern urban merchants time to sell items they had acquired legally before December 1. And both the novel tactic of nonexportation and its postponement for nearly a year served other interests. In 1773 small farmers in Virginia had already vowed to stop exporting tobacco, to raise prices in a then-glutted market. The next year, they enthusiastically welcomed an Association that accomplished the same end while permitting them to profit from higher prices for their 1774 crop, which needed to be dried and cured before shipment. Postponing the nonexportation agreement also benefited the northern exporters of wood products and foodstuffs to the Caribbean, giving them a final season of sales before the embargo began.

To enforce the Continental Association, Congress recommended the election of committees of observation and inspection in every American locality. By specifying that committee members be chosen by all men qualified to vote for members of the lower houses of assembly, Congress guaranteed the committees a broad popular base. The seven to eight thousand committeemen—some experienced officeholders, some new to politics—became the local leaders of American resistance.

### Committees of Observation

Such committees were officially charged only with overseeing implementation of the boycott, but in the course of the next six months they became de facto governments. They examined merchants' records, publishing the names of those who continued to import British goods. They promoted home manufactures, encouraging Americans to adopt simple modes of dress and behavior to symbolize their commitment to liberty and virtuous conduct. Because expensive leisure-time activities were believed to reflect vice and corruption, Congress (as Janet Schaw learned) urged Americans to forgo dancing, gambling, horseracing, cardplaying, cockfighting, and other forms of "extravagance and dissipation." Some committees extracted apologies from people caught gambling, drinking to excess, or racing. Thus private activities acquired public significance.

The committees gradually extended their authority over many aspects of American life. They attempted to identify opponents of American resistance, developing elaborate spy networks, circulating copies of the Continental Association for signatures, and investigating reports of questionable remarks and activities. Suspected dissent-

ers were urged to support the colonial cause publicly; if they refused, the committees had them watched, restricted their movements, or tried to force them to leave the area. People engaging in casual political exchanges with friends one day could find themselves charged with "treasonable conversation" the next. One Massachusetts man, for example, was called before his local committee for maligning the Congress as "a Pack or Parcell of Fools" that was "as tyrannical as Lord North and ought to be opposed & resisted." When he refused to recant, the committee put him under surveillance.

While the committees of observation were expanding their power during the winter and early spring of 1775, the regular colonial governments were collapsing. Only a few legislatures continued to meet without encountering challenges to their authority. In most colonies, popularly elected provincial conventions took over the task of running the government, sometimes entirely replacing the legislatures and at other times holding concurrent sessions. In late 1774 and early 1775, these conventions approved the Continental Association, elected delegates to the Sec-

### Provincial Conventions

▲ In 1775 a British cartoonist demonstrated his contempt for the pronouncements of the Continental Congress by setting his satire in a privy, or "necessary house," and showing a politician who has used a torn congressional resolution as toilet paper. The person at right is poring over a political pamphlet while portraits of John Wilkes and a man who has been tarred and feathered decorate the walls.

*(Library of Congress)*

ond Continental Congress (scheduled for May), organized militia units, and gathered arms and ammunition. Unable to stem the tide of resistance, the British-appointed governors and councils watched helplessly as their authority crumbled.

Royal officials suffered humiliation after humiliation. Courts were prevented from meeting; taxes were paid to the conventions' agents rather than to provincial tax collectors; sheriffs' powers were challenged; and militiamen would muster only when committees ordered. In short, during the six months preceding the battles at Lexington and Concord, independence was being won at the local level, but without formal acknowledgment and for the most part without bloodshed. Not many Americans fully realized what was happening. The vast majority still proclaimed their loyalty to Great Britain, denying that they sought to leave the empire.

## CONTEST IN THE BACKCOUNTRY

While the committees of observation were consolidating their authority in the East, some colonists were heading west. Ignoring the Proclamation of 1763, pronouncements by colonial governors, and the threat of Indian attacks alike, land-hungry folk—many of them recent immigrants from Ireland and soldiers who demobilized in North America after the Seven Years War—swarmed onto lands along the Ohio River and its tributaries after the mid-1760s. Sometimes they purchased property from opportunists with grants of dubious origin; often, they simply surveyed and claimed land, squatting on it in hopes that their titles would eventually be honored. Britain's 1771 decision to abandon (and raze) Fort Pitt removed the final restraints on settlement in the region, for the withdrawal rendered the Proclamation of 1763 unenforceable. By late 1775, thousands of new homesteads dotted the landscape of the backcountry from western Pennsylvania south through Virginia and eastern Kentucky into western North Carolina.

Few of the backcountry folk viewed the region's native peoples positively. (Rare exceptions were the Moravian missionaries who settled with their Indian converts in three small frontier communities in the upper Ohio valley.) The frontier dwellers had little interest in the small-scale trade that had once helped to sustain an uneasy peace in the region; they wanted only land on which to grow crops and pasture their livestock.

In 1774 Virginia, headed by a new governor, Lord Dunmore, moved vigorously to assert its title to the rapidly developing backcountry. During the spring and early summer, tensions mounted as Virginians surveyed land in Kentucky on the south side of the Ohio River—territory claimed by the Shawnees, who rejected the Fort Stanwix treaty of 1768. "Lord Dunmore's war" consisted of one large-scale confrontation between Virginia militia and some Shawnee warriors. Neither side won a clear-cut victory, but in the immediate aftermath thousands of settlers—including Daniel Boone and his associates—flooded across the mountains.

When the Revolutionary War began just as large numbers of people were migrating into Kentucky, the loyalties of Indians and settlers in the backcountry remained, like Boone's, fluid and uncertain. They were hostile to each other, but which side should either take in the imperial struggle? The answer might well depend on which could better serve their interests. Understanding that, the Continental Congress moved to reoccupy the site of Fort Pitt and to establish other garrisons in the Ohio country. Relying on such protection, as many as twenty thousand settlers poured into Kentucky and western Pennsylvania by 1780. Yet frontier affiliations were not clear: the growing town of Pittsburgh, for example, harbored many active loyalists.

The native peoples' grievances against the European American newcomers predisposed many toward an alliance with Great Britain. Yet some chiefs urged caution: after all, the British abandonment of Fort Pitt (and them) suggested that Britain lacked the will and ability to protect them in the future. Furthermore, Britain hesitated to make full, immediate use of its potential native allies. Officials on the scene understood that neither the Indians' style of fighting nor their war aims necessarily coincided with British goals and methods. Accordingly, they at first sought from Indians only a promise of neutrality.

Recognizing their poor standing with native peoples, patriots also sought Indians' neutrality. In 1775 the Second Continental Congress sent a general message to Indian communities, describing the war as "a family quarrel between us and Old England" and requesting that they "not join on either side" because "you Indians are not concerned in it." The Iroquois responded with a pledge of neutrality. But a group of Cherokees led by Chief Dragging Canoe decided to take advantage of the "family quarrel" to regain some land. In summer 1776, they attacked settlements in western Virginia and the Carolinas. After a militia campaign destroyed many Cherokee towns, along with crops and supplies, Dragging Canoe and his die-hard followers fled to the West, establishing new villages. Other Cherokees agreed to a treaty that ceded still more of their land.

||||||||||||||||||||||||||||||||

**Distrust and Warfare**

▲ An eighteenth-century watercolor, by an unknown artist, showing the village and fort at Detroit. Once a French stronghold, it had been taken over by the British after the Seven Years War. American forces tried but failed to capture the fort during the Revolutionary War. *(William L. Clements Library)*

*natives & colonists still fought even after war over.*

Bands of Shawnees and Cherokees continued to attack settlements in the backcountry throughout the war, but dissent in their own ranks crippled their efforts. The British victory over France in 1763 had destroyed the Indian nations' most effective means of maintaining their independence: playing European powers off against one another. Successful strategies were difficult to envision under these new circumstances, and Indian leaders no longer concurred on a unified course of action. Communities split asunder as older and younger men, or civil and war leaders, disagreed vehemently over what policy to adopt. Only a few communities (among them the Stockbridge Indians of New England and the Oneidas in New York) unwaveringly supported the American revolt; most other native villages either tried to remain neutral or sporadically aligned themselves with the British. And the settlers fought back: in 1778 and early 1779 a frontier militia force under George Rogers Clark captured British posts in modern Illinois (Kaskaskia) and Indiana (Vincennes). Still, the revolutionaries could never mount an effective attack against the redcoats' major stronghold at Detroit.

Warfare between settlers and Indians persisted in the backcountry long after fighting between patriot and red-

**Frontier Hostilities**

coat armies had ceased. Indeed, the Revolutionary War itself constituted a brief chapter in the ongoing struggle for control of the region west of the Appalachians, which began in 1763 and continued into the next century.

## CHOOSING SIDES

In 1765 protests against the Stamp Act had won the support of most colonists in the Caribbean and Nova Scotia as well as in the future United States. Demonstrations occurred in Halifax (the major Nova Scotian port, founded 1748) as well as in Boston, New York, and Charleston. Although provisions of the 1764 Sugar Act benefited Britain's Caribbean possessions, the Stamp Act levied higher duties on them than on the mainland colonies; the residents of St. Christopher and Nevis in particular joined mainlanders in demonstrating against the law (see Map 5.3). When the act went into effect, though, islanders loyally paid the stamp duties until repeal. And eventually a significant number of colonists in North America and the West Indies began to question both the aims and the tactics of the resistance movement. Doubts arose with particular urgency in Nova Scotia and the Caribbean.

Both the northern mainland and the southern island colonies depended heavily on Great Britain militarily and

## Nova Scotia and The Caribbean

*[margin note: support the mother country]*

economically. Despite the over-whelming British victory in the Seven Years War, they believed themselves vulnerable to French counterattack and eagerly sought regular troops and naval vessels stationed within their borders. Additionally, sugar planters—on some islands outnumbered by their bondspeople twenty-five to one—feared the potential for slave revolts in the absence of British troops. Neither region had a large population of European descent, nor were local political structures very strong. Fewer people lived in Halifax in 1775 than in the late 1750s, and the sugar islands had only a few resident planters to provide leadership, because successful men headed to England to buy great manors, leaving supervision of their property to hired managers.

Both Nova Scotians and West Indians had major economic reasons for ultimately choosing to support the mother country. In the mid-1770s the northerners finally broke into the Caribbean market with their cargoes of dried and salted fish. They also began to reduce New England's domination of the northern coastal trade, and once the shooting started they benefited greatly from Britain's retaliatory measures against the rebels' commerce. British sugar producers relied for their profits primarily on their monopoly of trade within the empire, for more efficient French planters were able to sell their sugar for one-third less. Further, the West Indian planters' effective lobbyists in London won the islands' exclusion from some provisions of the Townshend Acts. Accordingly, they could well have concluded that their interests could be adequately protected within the empire. Neither islanders nor Nova Scotians had reason to believe that they would be better off independent.

## Patriots

*[margin note: support Revolution]*

*[margin note: 2/5]*

Many residents of the thirteen colonies—especially members of the groups that dominated colonial society numerically or politically—reached different conclusions, choosing to support resistance, then independence. Active revolutionaries accounted for about two-fifths of the European American population. Among them were small and middling farmers, members of dominant Protestant sects (both Old and New Lights), Chesapeake gentry, merchants dealing mainly in American commodities, city artisans, elected office-holders, and people of English descent. Wives usually adopted their husbands' political beliefs, but not always. Although all these patriots supported the Revolution, they pursued divergent goals within the broader coalition, as they had in the 1760s. Some sought limited political reform; others, extensive political change; and still others,

social and economic reforms. (The ways their concerns interacted are discussed in Chapter 7.)

Some colonists, though, found that they could not in good conscience endorse independence. Like their more radical counterparts, most objected to parliamentary policies, but they preferred the remedy of imperial constitutional reform. The events of the crucial year between the passage of the Coercive Acts and the outbreak of fighting in Massachusetts crystallized their thinking. Their objections to violent protest, their desire to uphold legally constituted government, and their fears of anarchy combined to make them sensitive to the dangers of resistance.

*[margin note: no violence]*

*[margin note: 1/5]*

## Loyalists

About one-fifth of the European American population remained loyal to Great Britain, firmly rejecting independence. Most loyalists had long opposed the men who became patriot leaders, though for varying reasons. British-appointed government officials; Anglican clergy everywhere and lay Anglicans in the North, where their denomination was in the minority; tenant farmers, particularly those whose landlords sided with the patriots; members of persecuted religious sects; many of the backcountry southerners who had rebelled against eastern rule in the late 1760s and early 1770s; and non-English ethnic minorities, especially Scots—all these groups feared the power wielded by those who controlled the colonial assemblies and who had shown little concern for their welfare in the past. Joined by merchants whose trade depended on imperial connections and by former officers and enlisted men from the British army who had settled in America after 1763, they formed a loyalist core that remained true to a self-conception that revolutionaries proved willing to abandon.

During the war, loyalists congregated in cities held by the British army. When those posts were evacuated at war's end, loyalists scattered to different parts of the British Empire—Britain, the Bahamas, and especially Canada. In the provinces of Nova Scotia, New Brunswick, and Ontario they re-created their lives as colonists, laying the foundations of British Canada. All told, perhaps as many as seventy thousand Americans preferred exile to life in a nation independent of British rule.

*[margin note: wouldn't give up Br. rule]*

Between the patriots and the loyalists, there remained in the middle perhaps two-fifths of the European American population. Some who tried to avoid taking sides were sincere pacifists, such as Quakers. Others opportunistically shifted their allegiance to whatever side currently happened to be winning. Still others simply wanted to be left alone; they cared little about politics and usually obeyed whoever

*[margin note: 2/5]*

## Neutrals

▲ Governor John Wentworth of New Hampshire, as painted by John Singleton Copley in 1769. Wentworth, a New Hampshire native, sympathized with early colonial protests against British policies, but ultimately remained loyal to the crown. He was one of the leaders of the loyalist exiles who gathered in London during the war, and in 1792 was named governor of Nova Scotia, serving until 1808.

*(Hood Museum of Art, Dartmouth College, Hanover, New Hampshire; gift of Mrs. Esther Lowell Abbott in memory of her husband, Gordon Abbott)*

was in power. Such colonists also resisted British and Americans alike when the demands on them seemed too heavy—when taxes became too high or when calls for militia service came too often. Their attitude might best be summed up as "a plague on both your houses." Such people made up an especially large proportion of the population in the backcountry (including Boone's Kentucky), where Scots-Irish settlers had little love for either the patriot gentry or the English authorities.

To patriots, apathy or neutrality was as heinous as loyalism: those who were not for them were surely against them. By the winter of 1775–1776, the Second Continental Congress was recommending that all "disaffected" persons be disarmed and arrested. State legislatures passed laws prescribing severe penalties for suspected loyalists or neutrals. Many began to require all voters (or, in some cases, all free adult men) to take oaths of allegiance; the penalty for refusal was usually banishment to England or extra taxes. After 1777 many states confiscated the property of banished persons, using the proceeds for the war effort.

The patriots' policies helped to ensure that their scattered and persecuted opponents could not band together to threaten the revolutionary cause. But loyalists and neutrals were not the patriots' only worry, for revolutionaries could not assume that their slaves would support them.

In New England, with few resident bondspeople, revolutionary fervor was widespread, and free African Americans enlisted in local patriot militias. The middle colonies, where slaves constituted a small but substantial proportion of the population, were more divided but still largely revolutionary. In Virginia and Maryland, where free people constituted a slender majority, the potential for slave revolts raised occasional but not disabling fears. By contrast, South Carolina and Georgia, where slaves composed more than half of the population, were noticeably less enthusiastic about resistance to Britain. Georgia sent no delegates to the First Continental Congress and reminded its representatives at the second one to consider its circumstances, "with our blacks and tories [loyalists] within us," when voting on the question of independence. On the mainland as well as in the Caribbean islands, therefore, colonists feared the potential enemy in their midst.

## Slaves

Bondspeople themselves faced a dilemma during the Revolution. Above all, their goal was *personal* independence. But how best could they escape from slavery? Should they fight with or against their masters? African Americans made different decisions, but to most slaves, supporting the British appeared more promising. In late 1774 and early 1775, groups of slaves began to offer to assist the British army in return for freedom. The most serious incident occurred in 1775 in Charleston, where Thomas Jeremiah, a free black harbor pilot, was brutally executed after being convicted of attempting to foment a slave revolt.

The slaveowners' worst fears were realized in November 1775, when Virginia's royal governor, Lord Dunmore, offered to free any slaves and indentured servants who would leave their patriot masters to join the British forces. Dunmore hoped to use African Americans in his fight against the revolutionaries and to disrupt the economy by depriving planters of their labor force. About one thousand African Americans initially rallied to the British standard; although many of them perished in a smallpox epidemic, three hundred survived to reach occupied

## New Nations

The American Revolution not only created the United States but led directly to the formation of three other nations: English-dominated Canada, Sierra Leone, and Australia.

In northern North America before the Revolution, only Nova Scotia had a sizable number of English-speaking settlers. Those people, largely New Englanders, had been recruited after 1758 to repopulate the region forcibly taken from the exiled Acadians. During and after the Revolution, however, many loyalist families, especially those from the northern and middle colonies, moved to the region that is now Canada, which remained under British rule. The provinces of New Brunswick and Upper Canada (later Ontario) were established to accommodate them, and some exiles settled in Quebec as well. In just a few years, the loyalist refugees transformed the sparsely populated former French colony, laying the foundation of the modern bilingual (but majority English-speaking) Canadian nation.

Sierra Leone, too, was founded by colonial exiles—African Americans who had fled to the British army during the war, many of whom ended up in London. Seeing the refugees' poverty, a group of charitable merchants—calling themselves the Committee for Relief of the Black Poor—developed a plan to resettle the African Americans elsewhere. After the refugees refused to be sent to the Bahamas, fearing that in the Caribbean they would be reenslaved, they concurred in a scheme to return them to the land of their ancestors. In early 1787, vessels carrying about four hundred settlers reached Sierra Leone in West Africa, where representatives of the Black Poor Committee acquired land from local rulers. The first years of the new colony were difficult, and many of the newcomers died of disease and deprivation. But in 1792 they were joined by several thousand other loyalist African Americans who had originally moved to Nova Scotia. The influx ensured the colony's survival; it remained a part of the British Empire until achieving its independence in 1961.

While the Sierra Leone migrants were preparing to sail from London in late 1786, the first prison ships were simultaneously being readied for Australia. At the Paris peace negotiations in 1782, American diplomats adamantly rejected British suggestions that the United States continue to serve as a dumping ground for convicts, as had been true throughout the eighteenth century. Britain thus needed another destination for the convicts sentenced in its courts to transportation for crimes such as theft, assault, and manslaughter. It decided to send them halfway round the world, to the continent Captain James Cook had explored and claimed in 1770. Britain continued to dispatch convicts to some parts of Australia until 1868, but long before then voluntary migrants had also begun to arrive. The modern nation was created from a federation of separate colonial governments on January 1, 1901.

Thus the founding event in the history of the United States links the nation to the formation of its northern neighbor and to new nations in West Africa and the Asian Pacific.

▲ An early view of the settlement of black loyalists in West Africa, the foundation of the modern nation of Sierra Leone.

*(Miriam and Ira D. Wallach Division of Art, Prints and Photographs, The New York Public Library. Astor, Lenox, and Tilden)*

◀ Thomas Rowlandson, an English artist, sketched the boatloads of male and female convicts as they were being ferried to the ships that would take them to their new lives in the prison colony of Australia. Note the gibbet on the shore with two hanging bodies—symbolizing the fate these people were escaping.

*(National Library of Australia)*

New York City under British protection. Because other commanders later renewed Dunmore's proclamation, tens of thousands of runaway slaves eventually joined the British, and at the end of the war at least nine thousand left with the redcoats.

Although slaves did not pose a serious threat to the revolutionary cause in its early years, the patriots turned rumors of slave uprisings to their own advantage. In South Carolina, resistance leaders argued that unity under the Continental Association would protect masters from their slaves at a time when royal government was unable to muster adequate defense forces. Undoubtedly many wavering Carolinians were drawn into the revolutionary camp by fear that an overt division among the colony's free people would encourage rebellion by the bondspeople.

Patriots could never completely ignore the threats posed by loyalists, neutrals, slaves, and Indians as well, but only rarely did fear of these groups seriously hamper the revolutionary movement. Occasionally backcountry militiamen refused to turn out for duty on the seacoast because they feared Indians would attack at home in their absence. Sometimes southern troops refused to serve in the North because they (and their political leaders) were unwilling to leave their regions unprotected against a slave insurrection. But the practical impossibility of a large-scale slave revolt, coupled with dissension in Indian communities and the patriots' successful campaign to disarm and neutralize loyalists, ensured that the revolutionaries would by and large remain firmly in control of the countryside as they fought for independence.

## WAR AND INDEPENDENCE

On January 27, 1775, Lord Dartmouth, secretary of state for America, addressed a fateful letter to General Thomas Gage in Boston, urging him to take a decisive step. Opposition could not be "very formidable," Dartmouth wrote, and even if it were, "it will surely be better that the Con-

▲ In 1775 an unknown artist painted the redcoats entering Concord. The fighting at North Bridge, which occurred just a few hours after this triumphal entry, signaled the start of open warfare between Britain and the colonies.   *(Photography Courtesy of Concord Museum, Concord, Mass.)*

flict should be brought on, upon such ground, than in a riper state of Rebellion."

After Gage received Dartmouth's letter on April 14, he sent an expedition to confiscate colonial military supplies stockpiled at Concord. Bostonians dispatched two messengers, William Dawes and Paul Revere (later joined by Dr. Samuel Prescott), to rouse the countryside. So, when the British vanguard of several hundred men approached Lexington at dawn on April 19, they found a ragtag group of seventy militiamen—about half of the adult male population of the town—mustered on the common. Realizing they could not halt the redcoats' advance, the Americans' commander ordered his men to withdraw. But as they began to disperse, a shot rang out; the British soldiers then fired several volleys. When they stopped, eight Americans lay dead, and another ten had been wounded. The British moved on to Concord, 5 miles away.

## Battles of Lexington and Concord

There the contingents of militia were larger, Concord residents having been joined by groups of men from nearby towns. An exchange of gunfire at the North Bridge spilled the first British blood of the Revolution: three men were killed and nine wounded. Thousands of militiamen then fired from houses and from behind trees and bushes at the British forces as they retreated to Boston. By the end of the day, the redcoats had suffered 272 casualties, including 70 deaths. Only the arrival of reinforcements and the American militia's lack of coordination prevented much heavier British losses. The patriots suffered just 93 casualties.

By the evening of April 20, thousands of American militiamen had gathered around Boston, summoned by local committees that spread the alarm across the countryside. Many did not stay long (they went home for spring planting), but those who remained, along with newer recruits, were organized into formal units. Officers under the command of General Artemas Ward of the Massachusetts militia ordered that latrines be dug, the water supply protected, supplies purchased, military discipline enforced, regular drills held, and defensive fortifications constructed.

## First Year of War

*need to prepare for war*

▲ The plight of the redcoat soldiers besieged in Boston during the fall and winter of 1775–1776 attracted the sympathies of a British cartoonist. For "Six-Pence a Day," he noted, soldiers were exposed to "Yankees, Fire and Water, Sword and Famine," while their wives and children begged for assistance at home. The artist hoped to persuade men not to enlist in the British army.

*(Courtesy of the British Museum, Department of Prints and Drawings, Satires)*

For nearly a year the two armies sat and stared at each other across those siege lines. The redcoats attacked their besiegers only once, on June 17, when they drove the Americans from trenches atop Breed's Hill in Charlestown. In that misnamed Battle of Bunker Hill, the British incurred their greatest losses of the entire war: over 800 wounded and 228 killed. The Americans, though forced to abandon their position, lost less than half that number.

During the same eleven-month period, patriots captured Fort Ticonderoga, a British fort on Lake Champlain, acquiring much-needed cannon. Trying to bring Canada into the war on the American side, they also mounted a northern campaign that ended in disaster at Quebec in early 1776 after their troops were ravaged by smallpox. But the chief significance of the war's first year lay in the long lull in fighting between the main armies at Boston. The delay gave both sides a chance to regroup, organize, and plan their strategies.

Lord North and his new American secretary, Lord George Germain, made three central assumptions about the war they faced. First, they con-

### British Strategy

cluded that patriot forces could not withstand the assaults of trained British regulars. They and their generals were convinced that the 1776 campaign would be the first and last of the war. Accordingly, they dispatched to America the largest force Great Britain had ever assembled anywhere: 370 transport ships carrying 32,000 troops and tons of supplies, accompanied by 73 naval vessels and 13,000 sailors. Such an extraordinary effort, they thought, would ensure a quick victory. Among the troops were thousands of German mercenaries (many from the state of Hesse); eighteenth-century armies were often composed of such professional soldiers who hired out to the highest bidder.

Second, British officials and army officers treated this war as comparable to conflicts in Europe. They adopted a conventional strategy of capturing major American cities and defeating the rebel army decisively without suffering serious casualties themselves. Third, they assumed that a clear-cut military victory would achieve their goal of retaining the colonies' allegiance.

All three assumptions proved false. North and Germain vastly underestimated Americans' commitment to armed resistance. Battlefield defeats did not lead patriots to abandon their political aims and sue for peace. London officials also failed to recognize the significance of the American population's dispersal over an area 1,500 miles long and more than 100 miles wide. Although Britain would control each of the largest American ports at some time during the war, less than 5 percent of the population lived in those cities. Furthermore, the coast offered so many excellent harbors that essential commerce was easily rerouted. In other words, the loss of cities did little to damage the American cause, while British generals repeatedly squandered their resources to capture such ports.

Most of all, London officials did not initially understand that military triumph would not necessarily lead to political victory. Securing the colonies permanently would require hundreds of thousands of Americans to return to their original allegiance. After 1778 the ministry adopted a strategy designed to achieve that goal through the expanded use of loyalist forces and the restoration of civilian authority in occupied areas. But the new policy came too late. Britain's leaders never fully realized that they were fighting, not a conventional European war, but rather an entirely new kind of conflict: the first modern war of national liberation.

At least Great Britain had a bureaucracy ready to supervise the war effort. The Americans had only the

### Second Continental Congress

Second Continental Congress, originally intended simply to consider the ministry's response to the Continental Association. Instead, the delegates who convened in Philadelphia on May 10, 1775, had to assume the mantle of intercolonial government. "Such a vast Multitude of objects, civil, political, commercial and military, press and crowd upon us so fast, that we know not what to do first," John Adams wrote a close friend early in the session. Yet as the summer passed, Congress slowly organized the colonies for war. It authorized the printing of money with which to purchase necessary goods, established a committee to supervise relations with foreign countries, and took steps to strengthen the militia. Most important, it created the Continental Army and appointed its generals.

Until Congress met, the Massachusetts provincial congress had supervised Ward and the militiamen encamped at Boston. But that army, composed of men from all over New England, constituted a heavy drain on limited local resources. Consequently, Massachusetts asked the Continental Congress to assume the task of directing the army. As a first step, Congress had to choose a commander-in-chief, and many delegates recognized the importance of naming someone who was not a New Englander. John Adams later recalled that in mid-June he proposed the appointment of a Virginian "whose Skill and Experience as an Officer, whose independent fortune, great Talents and excellent universal Character, would command the Approbation of all America": George Washington. The Congress unanimously concurred.

Neither fiery radical nor reflective political thinker, Washington had not participated prominently in the

### George Washington

pre-revolutionary agitation. Devoted to the American cause, he was dignified, conservative, and respectable—a man of unimpeachable integrity. The younger son of a Virginia planter, Washington did not expect to inherit substantial property and planned to work as a surveyor. But the early death of his older brother and his marriage to the wealthy widow Martha Custis made George Washington one of the largest slaveholders in Virginia. Though an aristocrat, he was unswervingly committed to representative government. After his mistakes at the beginning of the Seven Years War, he had repaired his reputation by rallying the troops and maintaining a calm demeanor under fire during Braddock's defeat in 1755.

Washington also had remarkable stamina. In over eight years of war, he never had a serious illness and took only one brief leave of absence. Moreover, he both looked and acted like a leader. More than six feet tall in an era when most men were five inches shorter, he displayed a stately and commanding presence. Other patriots praised his judgment, steadiness, and discretion, and even a loyalist admitted that Washington could "atone for many demerits by the extraordinary coolness and caution which distinguish his character."

### British Evacuate Boston

Washington needed all the coolness and caution he could muster when he took command of the army outside Boston in July 1775. The new general continued Ward's efforts to organize and sustain those troops. By March 1776, when the arrival of cannon from Ticonderoga finally enabled him to put direct pressure on the redcoats in the city, the army was prepared to act. Yet an assault on Boston proved unnecessary. Sir William Howe, the new commander, had been considering an evacuation; he wanted to transfer his men to New York City. The patriots' cannon decided the matter. On March 17, the British and more than a thousand of their loyalist allies abandoned Boston forever.

That spring of 1776, as the British fleet left Boston for the temporary haven of Halifax, the colonies were moving inexorably toward independence. Although they had been at war for months, American leaders denied seeking a break with Great Britain until a pamphlet published in January 1776 advocated such a step.

### Common Sense

Thomas Paine's *Common Sense* exploded on the American scene, quickly selling tens of thousands of copies. The author, a radical English printer who had lived in America only since 1774, called stridently for independence. Paine also challenged many common American assumptions about government and the colonies' relationship to Britain. Rejecting the notion that only a balance of monarchy, aristocracy, and democracy could preserve freedom, he advocated the establishment of a republic, a government by the people with no king or nobility. Instead of acknowledging the benefits of links to the mother country, Paine insisted that Britain had exploited the colonies unmercifully. And for the frequently heard assertion that an independent America would be weak and divided he substituted an unlimited confidence in America's strength once freed from European control.

He expressed these striking sentiments in equally striking prose. Scorning the rational style of most other pamphleteers, Paine adopted an enraged tone, describing the king as a "royal brute," a "wretch" unconcerned for the

*risky but effective*

▲ That America's patriot leaders read Thomas Paine's inflammatory *Common Sense* soon after it was published in early 1776 is indicated by this first edition, owned by George Washington himself. *(Boston Athenaeum)*

colonists' welfare. His pamphlet reflected the oral culture of ordinary folk. Couched in everyday language, its primary source of authority was the Bible, the only book familiar to most Americans. No wonder the pamphlet had a wider distribution than any other political publication of its day.

It is unclear how many people were converted to the cause of independence by reading *Common Sense*. But by late spring, independence had become inevitable. On May 10, the Second Continental Congress formally recommended that individual colonies form new governments, replacing their colonial charters with state constitutions. Perceiving the trend, the few loyalists still connected with Congress severed their ties to that body.

Then on June 7 came confirmation of the movement toward independence. Richard Henry Lee of Virginia, seconded by John Adams of Massachusetts, introduced the crucial resolution: "that these United Colonies are, and of right ought to be, free and independent States, that they are absolved of all allegiance to the British Crown, and that all political connection between them and the State of Great Britain is, and ought to be, totally dissolved." Congress debated but did not immediately adopt Lee's resolution. Instead, it postponed a vote until early July, to allow time for consultation and public reaction. In the meantime, a five-man committee—including Thomas Jefferson, John Adams, and Benjamin Franklin—was directed to draft a declaration of independence.

The committee assigned primary responsibility for writing the declaration to Jefferson, who was well known for his eloquent style. Years later John Adams recalled that Jefferson had modestly protested his selection, suggesting that Adams prepare the initial draft. The Massachusetts revolutionary recorded his frank response: "You can write ten times better than I can."

Thirty-four-year-old Thomas Jefferson, a Virginia lawyer, had been educated at the College of William and Mary

**Jefferson and the Declaration of Independence**

and in the law offices of a prominent attorney. A member of the House of Burgesses, he had read widely in history and political theory. That broad knowledge was evident not only in the declaration but also in his draft of the Virginia state constitution, completed just a few days before his appointment to the committee. Jefferson, an intensely private man, loved his home and family deeply. This early stage of his political career was marked by his beloved wife Martha's repeated difficulties in childbearing. While he wrote and debated in Philadelphia, she suffered a miscarriage at their home, Monticello. Not until after her death in 1782, from complications following the birth of their sixth (but only third

surviving) child in ten years of marriage, did Jefferson fully commit himself to public service.

The draft of the declaration was laid before Congress on June 28, 1776. The delegates officially voted for independence four days later, then debated the wording of the declaration for two more days, adopting it with some changes on July 4. Since Americans had long ago ceased to see themselves as legitimate subjects of Parliament, the Declaration of Independence concentrated on George III (see the appendix), who provided an identifiable villain. The document accused the king of attempting to destroy representative government in the colonies and of oppressing Americans through the unjustified use of excessive force.

The declaration's chief long-term importance, however, did not lie in its lengthy catalogue of grievances against George III (including, in a section deleted by Congress, Jefferson's charge that the British monarchy had forced slavery on America). It lay instead in the ringing statements of principle that have served ever since as the ideal to which Americans aspire: "We hold these truths to be self-evident: That all men are created equal; that they are endowed by their Creator with certain unalienable rights; that among these are life, liberty and the pursuit of happiness; that, to secure these rights, governments are instituted among men, deriving their just powers from the consent of the governed; that whenever any form of government becomes destructive of these ends, it is the right of the people to alter or to abolish it, and to institute new government." These phrases have echoed down through American history like no others.

The delegates in Philadelphia who voted to accept the Declaration of Independence could not predict the consequences of their audacious act. When they adopted the declaration, they were committing treason. Therefore, when they concluded with the assertion that they "mutually pledge[d] to each other our lives, our fortunes, and our sacred honor," they spoke no less than the truth. The real struggle still lay before them, and few had Thomas Paine's boundless confidence in success.

## THE STRUGGLE IN THE NORTH

In late June 1776, the first ships carrying Sir William Howe's troops from Halifax appeared off the coast of New York (see Map 6.1). On July 2, the day Congress voted for independence, redcoats landed on Staten Island. Washington marched his army of seventeen thousand south from Boston to defend Manhattan. Because Howe waited until more troops arrived from England before attacking, Americans could prepare to defend the city.

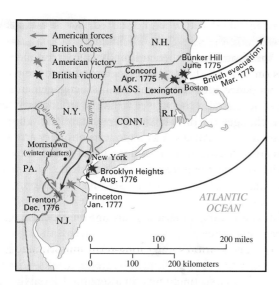

**Map 6.1    The War in the North, 1775–1777**

The early phase of the Revolutionary War was dominated by British troop movements in the Boston area, the redcoats' evacuation to Nova Scotia in the spring of 1776, and the subsequent British invasion of New York and New Jersey.

▲ George Washington at the Battle of Princeton, 1779, by Charles Willson Peale. Two years after the battle, Peale created this heroic image of the Continental Army's commander, intended (as were all his portraits of revolutionary leaders) to instill patriotic sentiments and pride in its viewers.

*(Courtesy of the Pennsylvania Academy of Fine Arts, Philadelphia. Gift of Maria McKean Allen and Phoebe Warren)*

But Washington and his men, still inexperienced in fighting and maneuvering, made major mistakes, losing battles at Brooklyn Heights and on Manhattan Island. The city fell to the British, who captured nearly three thousand American soldiers. (Those men spent most of the rest of the war on British prison ships anchored in New York harbor, where many died of smallpox and other diseases.) Washington slowly retreated across New Jersey into Pennsylvania, and British forces took control of most of New Jersey. Occupying troops met little opposition; the revolutionary cause appeared to be in disarray. "These are the times that try men's souls," wrote Thomas Paine in his pamphlet *The Crisis*. "The summer soldier and the sunshine patriot will, in this crisis, shrink from the service of his country; . . . yet we have this consolation with us, that the harder the conflict, the more glorious the triumph."

## New York and New Jersey

The British then forfeited their advantage as redcoats stationed in New Jersey went on a rampage of rape and plunder. Washington determined to strike back. Moving quickly, he crossed the Delaware River at night to attack a Hessian encampment at Trenton early on the morning of December 26, while the Germans were still recuperating from celebrating Christmas. The patriots captured more than nine hundred Hessians and killed another thirty; only three Americans were wounded. A few days later, Washington attacked again at Princeton. Having gained command of the field and buoyed American spirits with the two swift victories, Washington set up winter quarters at Morristown, New Jersey.

British strategy for 1777, sketched in London over the winter, aimed to cut New England off from the other colonies. General John Burgoyne, a subordinate of Howe and one of the planners, would lead an invading force of redcoats and Indians

## Campaign of 1777

down the Hudson River from Canada to rendezvous near Albany with a similar force that would move east along the Mohawk River valley. The combined forces would then presumably link up with Howe's troops in New York City. But in New York Howe simultaneously prepared his own plan to capture Philadelphia. Consequently, in 1777 the British armies in America would operate independently; the result would be disaster (see Map 6.2).

Howe took Philadelphia, but he did so in inexplicable fashion, delaying for months before beginning the campaign, then taking six weeks to transport his troops by sea instead of marching them overland. Incredibly, at the end of the lengthy voyage, he ended up only 40 miles closer to Philadelphia than when he started. By the time Howe advanced on Philadelphia, Washington had had time to prepare its defenses. Twice, at Brandywine Creek and again at Germantown, the two armies clashed near the patriot capital. Although the British won both engagements, the Americans handled themselves well. The redcoats captured Philadelphia in late September, but to little effect. The campaign season was nearly over; the revolutionary army had gained confidence in itself and its leaders; and, far to the north, Burgoyne was going down to defeat.

Burgoyne and his men had set out from Montreal in mid-June, traveling first by boat on Lake Champlain, then later marching slowly overland toward the Hudson, forced as they went to clear giant trees felled across their path by patriot militiamen. An easy triumph at Fort Ticonderoga in July was followed in August by two setbacks—the redcoats and Indians marching east along the Mohawk River turned back after a battle at Oriskany, New York; and in a clash near Bennington, Vermont, American militiamen nearly wiped out eight hundred of Burgoyne's German mercenaries. The general's dawdling had given American troops time to prepare for his arrival. After several skirmishes with an American army commanded by General

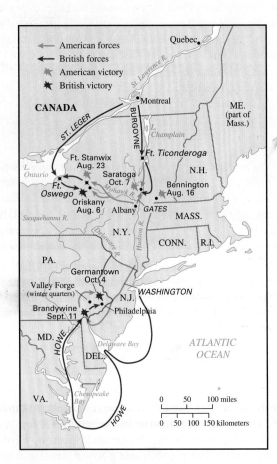

**Map 6.2   Campaign of 1777**

The crucial campaign of 1777 was fought on two fronts: along the upper Hudson and Mohawk River valleys, and in the vicinity of Philadelphia. The rebels won in the north; the British triumphed—at least nominally—in the south. The capture of Philadelphia, however, did the redcoats little good, and they abandoned the city the following year.

▲ Joseph Brant, the Iroquois leader who helped to persuade the Mohawks, Senecas, and Cayugas to support the British in the latter stages of the Revolution, as painted by Charles Willson Peale in 1797. *(Independence National Historic Park Collection)*

Horatio Gates, Burgoyne was surrounded near Saratoga, New York. On October 17, 1777, he surrendered his entire force of more than six thousand men.

The August 1777 battle at Oriskany divided the Iroquois Confederacy. Although the Six Nations had formally

||||||||||||||||||||||||||||||||||

**Iroquois
Confederacy
Splinters**

pledged to remain neutral in the war, two influential Mohawk leaders, the siblings Mary and Joseph Brant, believed that the Iroquois should ally themselves with the British to protect their territory from land-hungry colonists. The Brants won over the Senecas, Cayugas, and Mohawks, all of whom contributed warriors to the 1777 expedition. But the Oneidas—who had been converted to Christianity by Protestant missionaries—preferred the American side and brought the Tuscaroras with them. The Onondagas split into three factions, one on each side and one supporting neutrality. At Oriskany, some Oneidas and Tuscaroras joined patriot militiamen in fighting their Iroquois brethren, shattering a three-hundred-year-old league of friendship.

The collapse of Iroquois unity and the confederacy's abandonment of neutrality had significant consequences. In 1778 Iroquois warriors allied with the British raided frontier villages in Pennsylvania and New York. To retaliate, the Americans the following summer dispatched an expedition under General John Sullivan to burn Iroquois crops, orchards, and settlements. The resulting devastation led many bands to seek food and shelter north of the Great Lakes during the winter of 1779–1780. A large number of Iroquois people never returned to New York but settled permanently in Canada.

Burgoyne's surrender at Saratoga brought joy to patriots, discouragement to loyalists and Britons. In exile in London, Thomas Hutchinson wrote of "universal dejection" among loyalists there. "Everybody in a gloom," he commented, "most of us expect to lay our bones here." The disaster prompted Lord North to authorize a peace commission to offer the Americans what they had requested in 1774—in effect, a return to the imperial system of 1763. That proposal came far too late: the patriots rejected the overture, and the peace commission sailed back to England empty-handed in mid-1778.

Most important, the American victory at Saratoga drew France formally into the conflict. Ever since 1763, the French had sought to avenge their defeat in the Seven Years War, and the American Revolution gave them that opportunity. Even before Benjamin Franklin arrived in Paris in late 1776, France covertly supplied the revolutionaries with military necessities. Indeed, 90 percent of the gunpowder used by the Americans during the war's first

two years came from France, transported via the French Caribbean island of Martinique.

Benjamin Franklin worked tirelessly to strengthen ties between the two nations. He adopted a plain style of

||||||||||||||||||||||||||||||||||

**Franco-American
Alliance of 1778**

dress that made him conspicuous amid the luxury of the court of King Louis XVI. Presenting himself as a representative of American simplicity, Franklin played on the French image of Americans as virtuous farmers. His efforts culminated in 1778 when the countries signed two treaties. In the Treaty of Amity and Commerce, France recognized American independence, establishing trade ties with the new nation. In the Treaty of Alliance, France and the United States promised—assuming that France would declare war on Britain, which it soon did—that neither would negotiate peace with the enemy without consulting the other. France also formally abandoned any claim to Canada and to North American territory east of the Mississippi River. In the years that followed, the most visible symbol of Franco-American cooperation was the Marquis de Lafayette, a young nobleman who volunteered for service with George Washington in 1777 and fought with American forces until the conflict ended.

The French alliance had two major benefits for the patriot cause. First, France began to aid the Americans openly, sending troops and naval vessels in addition to arms, ammunition, clothing, and blankets. Second, Britain could no longer focus solely on the American mainland, for it had to fight France in the Caribbean and elsewhere. Spain's entry into the war in 1779 as an ally of France (but not of the United States) magnified Britain's problems, for the Revolution then became a global war. The French aided the Americans throughout the conflict, but in its last years that assistance proved vital.

## LIFE IN THE ARMY AND ON THE HOME FRONT

Only in the first months of the war was the revolutionaries' army manned primarily by the semi-mythical "citizen-soldier," the militiaman who exchanged his plow for a gun to defend his homeland. After a few months or at most a year, the early arrivals went home. They reenlisted only briefly and only if the contending armies neared their farms and towns. In such militia units, elected officers and the soldiers who chose them reflected existing social hierarchies in their regions of origin, yet also retained a freedom and flexibility absent from the Continental Army, composed of men in formally organized statewide units led by appointed officers.

*French on Americans's side*

Continental soldiers, unlike militiamen, were primarily young, single, or propertyless men who enlisted for

||||||||||||||||||||||||||||||

**Continental Army**

long periods or for the war's duration, in part to earn monetary bonuses or allotments of land after the war. They responded to calls for "manly resistance" to Britain, seeing in military service an opportunity to protect homes and families, assert their masculine identity, and claim postwar citizenship and property-owning rights. As the fighting dragged on, the bonuses grew larger and more enticing. To meet their quotas, towns and states eagerly recruited everyone they could. Regiments from the middle states contained an especially large proportion of recent immigrants; about 45 percent of Pennsylvania soldiers were of Irish origin, and about 13 percent were German, some serving in German-speaking regiments.

Dunmore's proclamation led Congress in January 1776 to modify an earlier policy that had prohibited the enlistment of African Americans in the regular American army, and recruiters in northern states turned increasingly to slaves, who were often promised freedom after the war. Enslaved substitutes for their masters constituted about 10 percent of eastern Connecticut enlistees, for example, along with another 5 percent identified as free blacks, who earned enlistment bounties. Southern states initially resisted the trend, but later all except Georgia and South Carolina also enlisted black soldiers. Approximately five thousand African Americans eventually served in the Continental Army. They commonly served in racially integrated units but were assigned tasks that others shunned, such as burying the dead, foraging for food, and driving wagons. Overall, at any given time they composed about 10 percent of the regular army, although they seldom served in militia units.

Also attached to the American forces were a number of women, the wives and widows of poor soldiers, who came to the army with their menfolk because they were too impoverished to survive alone. Such camp followers—estimated to be about 3 percent of the total number of troops—worked as cooks, nurses, and launderers in return for rations and low wages. The women, along with civilian commissaries and militiamen who floated in and out of camp at irregular intervals, made up an unwieldy assemblage that officers found difficult to manage, especially because none of them could be subjected to the same military discipline as regular soldiers. Yet the army's shapelessness also reflected its greatest strength: an almost unlimited reservoir of manpower and womanpower.

The officers of the Continental Army developed an intense sense of pride and commitment to the revolution-

▲ Barzillai Lew, a free African American born in Groton, Massachusetts, in 1743, served in the Seven Years War before enlisting with patriot troops in the American Revolution. An accomplished fifer, Lew fought at the Battle of Bunker Hill. Like other freemen in the north, he cast his lot with the revolutionaries, in contrast to southern bondspeople, who tended to favor the British.

*(Courtesy of Mae Theresa Bonitto)*

||||||||||||||||||||||||||||||

**Officer Corps**

ary cause. The hardships they endured, the battles they fought, the difficulties they overcame all helped to forge an esprit de corps that outlasted the war. The realities of warfare were often dirty, messy, and corrupt, but the officers drew strength from a developing image of themselves as professionals who sacrificed personal gain for the good of the entire nation. When Benedict Arnold, an officer who fought heroically for the patriot cause early in the war, defected to the British, they made his name a metaphor for villainy. "How black, how despised, loved by none, and hated by all," wrote one officer.

The officers' wives, too, prided themselves on their and their husbands' service to the nation. Unlike poor

*[handwritten: wives made things more comfortable]*

women, they did not travel with the army but instead came for extended visits while the troops were in camp (usually during the winters). Martha Washington and other officers' wives, for example, lived at Valley Forge in the winter of 1777–1778. They brought with them food, clothing, and household furnishings to make their stay more comfortable, and they entertained each other and their menfolk at teas, dinners, and dances. Socializing and discussing current events created friendships later renewed in civilian life when some of their husbands became the new nation's leaders.

Life in the American army was difficult for everyone, although ordinary soldiers endured more hardships than their officers. Wages were small, and often the army could not meet the payroll. Rations (a daily standard allotment of bread, meat, vegetables, milk, and beer) did not always appear, and men had to forage for their own food. Clothing and shoes the army supplied were often of poor quality; soldiers had to make do or find their own. While in camp, soldiers occasionally hired themselves out as laborers to nearby farmers to augment their meager rations or earnings. When conditions deteriorated, troops threatened mutiny (though only a few carried out that threat) or, more often, simply deserted. Punishments for desertion or other offenses such as theft and assault were harsh; convicted soldiers were sentenced to hundreds of lashes, whereas officers were publicly humiliated, deprived of their commission, and discharged in disgrace.

### Hardship and Disease

*[handwritten margin: disease]*

Endemic disease in the camps—especially dysentery, various fevers, and, early in the war, smallpox—made matters worse, sometimes discouraging recruiting. Most native-born colonists had neither been exposed to smallpox nor inoculated against the disease, so soldiers and civilians were vulnerable when smallpox spread through the northern countryside after the early months of 1774. The disease ravaged residents of Boston during the British occupation, the troops attacking Quebec in 1775–1776, and the African Americans who fled to join Lord Dunmore (1775) or Lord Cornwallis (1781). Because most British soldiers had already survived smallpox (which was endemic in Europe), it did not pose a significant threat to redcoat troops.

Washington recognized that smallpox could potentially decimate the revolutionaries' ranks, especially after it helped cause the failure of the 1775 Quebec expedition. Thus, in Morristown in early 1777, he ordered that entire regular army and all new recruits be inoculated, although some would die from the risky procedure and survivors would be incapacitated for weeks. Those dramatic meas-

*[handwritten bottom: Washington took charge b/c didn't want his troops dying off.]*

*[handwritten top: foreign born men helped soldiers b/c they were immune]*

ures, coupled with the increasing numbers of foreign-born (and mostly immune) men who enlisted, helped to protect Continental soldiers later in the war, contributing significantly to the eventual American victory.

Men who enlisted in the army or served in Congress were away from home for long periods of time. In their absence their womenfolk, who previously had handled only the "indoor affairs" of the household, shouldered the responsibility for "outdoor affairs" as well. As the wife of a Connecticut soldier later recalled, her husband "was out more or less during the remainder of the war [after 1777], so much so as to be unable to do anything on our farm. What was done, was done by myself." Similarly, John and Abigail Adams took great pride in Abigail's developing skills as a "farmeress." Like other female contemporaries, Abigail Adams stopped calling the farm "yours" in letters to her husband and began referring to it as "ours"—a revealing change of pronoun. Most women did not work in the fields themselves, but they supervised field workers and managed their families' resources.

### Home Front

*[handwritten margin: Women step up and keep things running smoothly crucial!]*

*[handwritten margin: "yours" ↓ "ours"]*

Wartime disruptions affected the lives of all Americans. Even far from the battlefields, people suffered from shortages of necessities like salt, soap, and flour. Small luxuries like new clothing or even ribbons or gloves were essentially unavailable. Severe inflation added to the country's woes, eroding the value of any income. For those who lived near the armies' camps or lines of march, difficulties were compounded. Soldiers of both sides plundered farms and houses, looking for food or salable items; they burned fence rails in their fires and took horses and oxen to transport their wagons. Moreover, they carried smallpox and other diseases with them wherever they went. In such circumstances and in the absence of their husbands, women had to make the momentous decision whether to deliberately risk their children's lives by inoculating them with smallpox or to take the chance of the youngsters' contracting the disease "in the natural way," with its even greater risk of death. Many, including Abigail Adams, chose the former course of action and were relieved when their children survived.

## VICTORY IN THE SOUTH

In early 1778, in the wake of the Saratoga disaster, Lord George Germain and British military leaders reassessed their strategy. The loyalist exiles in London persuaded them to shift the field of battle southward, contending that loyal southerners would welcome the redcoat army as liberators. Once the South had been pacified and returned

*[handwritten margin: Amer. secretary of state]*

to friendly civilian control, it could then serve as a base for once again attacking the middle and northern states.

Sir Henry Clinton, who replaced Sir William Howe, oversaw the regrouping of British forces in America. He ordered the evacuation of Philadelphia in June 1778 and sent a convoy that successfully captured the French Caribbean island of St. Lucia, which thereafter served as a key base for Britain. He also dispatched a small expedition to Georgia at the end of the year. When Savannah and then Augusta fell easily into British hands, Clinton became convinced that a southern strategy would succeed. In late 1779 he sailed down the coast from New York to besiege Charleston, the most important city in the South (see Map 6.3). Although afflicted by smallpox, the Americans trapped in the city held out for months. Still, on May 12, 1780, General Benjamin Lincoln was forced to surrender the entire southern army—5,500 men—to the invaders. In the following weeks, the redcoats spread through South Carolina, establishing garrisons at key points in the interior. Hundreds of South Carolinians renounced allegiance to the United States, proclaiming their renewed loyalty to the Crown. Clinton organized loyalist regiments, and the process of pacification began.

Yet the triumph was less complete than it appeared. The success of the southern campaign depended on control of the seas, for the British armies were so widely dispersed and travel by land was so difficult that only through British naval vessels could the armies coordinate their efforts. For the moment, the Royal Navy safely dominated the American coastline, but French naval power posed a threat to the entire southern enterprise. American privateers infested Caribbean waters, seizing valuable cargoes bound to and from the British islands. Furthermore, after late 1778 France picked off those islands one by one, including Grenada—second only to Jamaica in sugar production—and, in 1781, St. Christopher as well. Even though in early 1781 the British captured and plundered St. Eustatius (the Dutch island that after French entry into the war served as the main conduit for the movement of military supplies from Europe to America), the victory did them little good. Indeed, it might well have cost them the war, for Admiral Sir George Rodney, occupied with securing the victory (and his personal profits from the plunder), failed to pursue the French fleet under Admiral François de Grasse when it subsequently sailed from the Caribbean to Virginia, where it played a major role in the battle at Yorktown.

Then, too, the redcoats never managed to establish full control of the areas they seized in South Carolina or Georgia. Patriot bands operated freely, and loyalists could

||||||||||||||||||||||||||||||

## South Carolina and the Caribbean

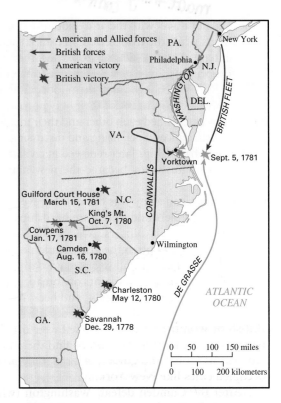

**Map 6.3   The War in the South**

The southern war—after the British invasion of Georgia in late 1778—was characterized by a series of British thrusts into the interior, leading to battles with American defenders in both North and South Carolina. Finally, after promising beginnings, Cornwallis's foray into Virginia ended with disaster at Yorktown in October 1781.

not be adequately protected. The fall of Charleston failed to dishearten the patriots; instead, it spurred them to greater exertions. As one Marylander declared confidently, "The Fate of America is not to be decided by the Loss of a Town or Two." Patriot women in four states formed the Ladies Association, which collected money to purchase shirts for needy soldiers. Recruiting efforts were stepped up.

Nevertheless, the war in South Carolina went badly for the patriots throughout most of 1780. At Camden in August, forces under Lord Cornwallis, the new British commander in the South, crushingly defeated a reorganized southern army led by Horatio Gates. Thousands of enslaved African Americans joined the redcoats, seeking the freedom promised by Lord Dunmore and later by Sir Henry Clinton. Running away from their patriot masters individually and as families, they seriously disrupted planting and harvesting in the Carolinas and Georgia in 1780 and 1781. Tens of thousands of slaves were lost to their owners as a result of the war. Not all of them joined the

▲ "A View from the Two-Gun Battery," St. Lucia, 1780, by Charles Forrest. Forrest, a British officer stationed in the West Indies during the Revolution, sketched this scene showing some of the island's defenses against a possible attack by the American or French Navy. *(William L. Clements Library)*

British or won their freedom if they did, but their flight had exactly the effect the British sought. Many served the redcoats as scouts and guides, or as laborers in camps or occupied cities like New York.

After the Camden defeat, Washington (who had to remain in the North to contain the British army occupying New York) appointed General Nathanael Greene to command the southern campaign. Appalled by conditions in South Carolina, Greene told a friend that "the word difficulty when applied to the state of things here . . . is almost without meaning, it falls so far short" of reality. His troops needed clothing, blankets, and food, but "a great part of this country is already laid waste and in the utmost danger of becoming a desert." Incessant guerrilla warfare had, he commented, "so corrupted the principles of the people that they think of nothing but plundering one another."

In such dire circumstances, Greene had to move cautiously. He adopted a conciliatory policy toward the many Americans who had switched sides, an advantageous move in a region in which people could well have altered their allegiance up to seven times in less than two years. He also ordered his troops to treat captives fairly and not to loot loyalist property. Recognizing that the patriots needed to convince a war-weary populace that they could bring stability to the region, he helped the shattered provincial congresses of Georgia and South Carolina to reestablish civilian authority in the interior—a goal the British were never able to accomplish. Because he had so few regulars (only sixteen hundred when he took command), Greene had to rely on western volunteers and could not afford to

### Greene and the Southern Campaign

have frontier militia companies occupied in defending their homes from Indian attack. He accordingly pursued diplomacy aimed at keeping the Indians out of the war. Although royal officials cooperating with the redcoat invaders initially won some Indian allies, Greene's careful maneuvers eventually proved successful. By war's end, only the Creeks remained allied with Great Britain.

Even before Greene took command of the southern army in December 1780, the tide had begun to turn. In October, at King's Mountain, a force from the backcountry defeated a large party of redcoats and loyalists. Then in January 1781 Greene's trusted aide Daniel Morgan brilliantly routed the British regiment Tarleton's Legion at Cowpens. Greene himself confronted the main body of British troops under Lord Cornwallis at Guilford Court House, North Carolina, in March. Although Cornwallis controlled the field at the end of the day, most of his army had been destroyed. He had to retreat to Wilmington, on the coast, to receive supplies and fresh troops from New York by sea. Meanwhile, Greene returned to South Carolina, where, in a series of swift strikes, he forced the redcoats to abandon their interior posts and retire to Charleston.

Cornwallis headed north into Virginia, where he joined forces with a detachment of redcoats commanded by the American traitor Benedict Arnold. Instead of acting decisively with his new army of 7,200 men, Cornwallis withdrew to the peninsula between the York and James Rivers, where he fortified Yorktown and awaited supplies and reinforcements. Seizing the opportunity, Washington quickly moved more than 7,000 French and American troops south from New York City. When De Grasse's fleet

### Surrender at Yorktown

*officers unappreciative*

arrived from the Caribbean just in time to defeat the Royal Navy vessels sent to relieve Cornwallis, the British general was trapped (see Map 6.3). On October 19, 1781, Cornwallis surrendered.

When news of the defeat reached London, Lord North's ministry fell. Parliament voted to cease offensive operations in America, authorizing peace negotiations. Washington returned with the main army to the environs of New York, where his underpaid—and, they thought, underappreciated—officers grew restive. In March 1783 they threatened to mutiny unless Congress guaranteed them adequate compensation for their services. Washington, warned in advance of the so-called Newburgh Conspiracy, met the challenge brilliantly. Summoning his officers, he defused the crisis with a well-reasoned but emotional speech drawing on their patriotism. How could they, he asked, "open the flood Gates of Civil discord, and deluge our rising Empire in Blood"? When at one point he fumbled for glasses, remarking in passing that "I have grown gray in your service and now find myself growing blind," eye-

witnesses reported that many of the rebellious officers began to cry. At the end of the year, he stood before Congress and formally resigned his commission as commander-in-chief. Through such actions at the end of the conflict, Washington established an enduring precedent: civilian control of the American military.

The war had been won, but at terrible cost. More than 25,000 American men died in the war, only about one-quarter of them from wounds suffered in battle. The rest were declared missing in action or died of disease or as prisoners of war. In the South, years of guerrilla warfare and the loss of thousands of runaway slaves shattered the economy. Indebtedness soared, and local governments were crippled for lack of funds, as few people could afford to pay their taxes. In the 1780s in Charles County, Maryland, for example, men commonly refused to serve in elective or appointive office because their personal estates would become liable for any taxes or fines they were unable to collect. Many of the county's formerly wealthy planters descended into insolvency, and in the 1790s a traveler

# *Legacy* FOR A PEOPLE AND A NATION

## Revolutionary Origins

The United States was created in an event universally termed the American Revolution. Yet many historians today would contend that it was not truly "revolutionary," if *revolution* means overturning an earlier power structure. The nation won its independence and established a republic, both radical events in the context of the eighteenth century, but essentially the same men who had led the colonies also led the new country (with the exception of British officials and appointees). In sharp contrast, the nearly contemporary French Revolution witnessed the execution of the monarch and many aristocrats, and consequently a significant redistribution of authority. So the legacy of the American Revolution appears ambiguous, at once radical and conservative.

Throughout the more than two hundred years since the "Revolution," groups of widely varying political views have claimed to represent its true meaning. From far left to far right, Americans frequently declare that they are acting in the spirit of the Revolution. People protesting discriminatory policies against women and minorities (usually "liberals") invoke the "created equal" language of the Declaration of Independence. Left-wing organizations rail

against concentrations of wealth and power in the hands of a few, again citing the Revolution's egalitarian thrust. Those protesting higher taxes (usually "conservatives" wanting a reduced role for government) often adopt the symbolism of the Boston Tea Party. Right-wing militias arm themselves, preparing to defend their homes and families against a malevolent government, just as they believe the minutemen did in 1775. Indeed, in 2006 so-called minutemen formed vigilante groups to guard the United States–Mexico border against illegal aliens. The message of the Revolution can be invoked to support extralegal demonstrations of any description, from invasions of military bases by antiwar protesters to demonstrations outside abortion clinics, all of which may be analogized to the demonstrations against British policies in the 1760s. But the Revolution can also be invoked to oppose such street protests, because—some would argue—in a republic, change should come peacefully, via the ballot box and not in the streets.

Just as Americans in the eighteenth century disagreed over the meaning of their struggle against the mother country, so the legacy of revolution remains contested early in the twenty-first century, both for the nation thus created and for today's American people.

observed that the countryside "wears a most dreary aspect," remarking on the "old dilapidated mansions" that had once housed well-to-do slaveowners.

Yet Charles County residents and Americans in general "all rejoiced" when they learned of the signing of the preliminary peace treaty at Paris in November 1782. The American

||||||||||||||||||||||||||||||||

**Treaty of Paris**          diplomats—Benjamin Franklin, John Jay, and John Adams—ignored their instructions from Congress to be guided by France and instead negotiated directly with Great Britain. Their instincts were sound: the French government was more an enemy to Britain than a friend to the United States. In fact, French ministers worked secretly behind the scenes to try to prevent the establishment of a strong, unified government in America. Spain's desire to lay claim to the region between the Appalachian Mountains and the Mississippi River further complicated the negotiations. But the American delegates proved adept at power politics, achieving their main goal: independence as a united nation. Weary of war, the new British ministry, headed by Lord Shelburne (formerly an outspoken critic of Lord North's American policies), made numerous concessions—so many, in fact, that Parliament ousted the ministry shortly after peace terms were approved.

The treaty, signed formally on September 3, 1783, granted unconditional independence to a nation named "the United States of America." Generous boundaries delineated that new nation: to the north, approximately the present-day boundary with Canada; to the south, the 31st parallel (about the modern northern border of Florida); to the west, the Mississippi River. Florida, which Britain had acquired in 1763, reverted to Spain (see Map 7.2). The Americans also gained unlimited fishing rights off Newfoundland. In ceding so much land to the United States, Great Britain ignored the territorial rights of its Indian allies, sacrificing their interests to the demands of European politics. British diplomats also poorly served loyalists and British merchants. The treaty's ambiguously worded clauses pertaining to the payment of prewar debts and the postwar treatment of loyalists caused trouble for years to come, proving impossible to enforce.

*should have been patriots!*

## SUMMARY

The long war finally over, the victorious Americans could look back on their achievement with satisfaction and awe. Having unified the disparate mainland colonies, they had claimed their place in the family of nations and forged a successful alliance with France. With an inexperienced army composed of militia and regulars, they had defeated the professional soldiers of the greatest military power in the world. They accomplished their goal more through persistence and commitment than through brilliance on the battlefield, a persistence that involved wives and families on the home front as well as soldiers. They had won only a few actual victories—most notably, at Trenton, Saratoga, and Yorktown—but their army always survived defeats to fight again, even after the devastating losses at Manhattan and Charleston. Ultimately, the Americans simply wore their enemy down.

In winning the war, the Americans reshaped the physical and mental landscapes in which they lived. They abandoned the British identity once so important to them, excluding from their new nation their loyalist neighbors who were unwilling to make a break with the mother country. They established republican governments at state and national levels. In the families of Continental Army soldiers in particular they began the process of creating new national loyalties. They also laid claim to most of the territory east of the Mississippi River and south of the Great Lakes, thereby greatly expanding the land potentially open to their settlements and threatening the traditional Indian dominance of the continent's interior.

In achieving independence, Americans surmounted formidable challenges. But in the future they faced perhaps an even greater one: ensuring the survival of their republican polity in a world dominated by the bitter rivalries among Britain, France, and Spain.

## SUGGESTIONS FOR FURTHER READING

Robert McCluer Calhoon, *The Loyalists in Revolutionary America, 1760–1781* (1973)

Colin Calloway, *The American Revolution in Indian Country* (1995)

Stephen Conway, *The War of American Independence, 1775–1783* (1995)

Sylvia Frey, *Water from the Rock: Black Resistance in a Revolutionary Age* (1991)

Pauline Maier, *American Scripture: Making the Declaration of Independence* (1997)

Charles Niemeyer, *America Goes to War: A Social History of the Continental Army* (1997)

Mary Beth Norton, *Liberty's Daughters: The Revolutionary Experience of American Women, 1750–1800* (2d ed., 1996)

Cassandra Pybus, *Epic Journeys of Freedom: Runaway Slaves of the American Revolution and their Global Quest for Liberty* (2006)

Charles Royster, *A Revolutionary People at War: The Continental Army and American Character, 1775–1783* (1980)

Richard W. Van Alstyne, *Empire and Independence: The International History of the American Revolution* (1965)

# Forging a National Republic *1776-1789*

*O*n December 26, 1787, a group of Federalists—supporters of the proposed Constitution—gathered in Carlisle, a Pennsylvania frontier town. The men planned to fire a cannon to celebrate their state convention's ratification vote two weeks earlier, but a large crowd of Antifederalists prevented them from doing so. First the Antis stood in front of the cannon, refusing to budge. Then, moving from passive to active resistance, they attacked the Federalists, who fled the scene as the angry Antis publicly burned a copy of the Constitution.

The next day, the Federalists returned to fire their cannon and to read the convention's ratification proclamation. Choosing to avoid another violent confrontation, Antifederalists instead paraded and then burned effigies of two Federalists. When Federalist officials later arrested several demonstrators on riot charges, the Antifederalist-dominated militia broke the men out of jail. Only a flaw in the warrant—which freed the arrestees legally—prevented another bloody brawl.

For several weeks thereafter, participants in these events argued in the Carlisle newspaper about the meaning of the demonstrations. Federalist authors proclaimed that the respectable initial celebrants acted with "good order and coolness," in contrast to their Antifederalist opponents, who were "obscure" men, "a few worthless ragamuffins." Replying, "one of the People" pronounced the Federalists "an unhallowed riotous mob." Although the Constitution's supporters had declared themselves to be "friends of government," they were not: through their advocacy of government that aimed to suppress the people's liberties, they had revealed their true identity as secret aristocrats.

◄ Detail of *The Ramsay-Polk Family at Carpenter's Point, Cecil County, Maryland,* painted by James Peale about 1793. The sumptuous dresses and elaborate hats and hairdos mark these republican women as ladies of leisure. On the river wharf in the background, ready for shipping, are the hogsheads of tobacco (produced by slave labor) that made their leisure possible. *(Courtesy, Hirschl & Adler Galleries, New York)*

## CHRONOLOGY

**1776** ■ Second Continental Congress directs states to draft constitutions
   ■ Abigail Adams advises her husband to "Remember the Ladies"

**1777** ■ Articles of Confederation sent to states for ratification
   ■ Vermont becomes first jurisdiction to abolish slavery

**1781** ■ Articles of Confederation ratified

**1783** ■ Treaty of Paris signed, formalizing American independence

**1784** ■ Diplomats sign treaty with Iroquois at Fort Stanwix, but Iroquois repudiate it two years later

**1785** ■ Land Ordinance of 1785 provides for surveying and sale of national lands in Northwest Territory

**1785–86** ■ United States negotiates treaties at Hopewell, South Carolina, with Choctaws, Chickasaws, and Cherokees

**1786** ■ Annapolis Convention meets, discusses reforming government

**1786–87** ■ Shays's Rebellion in western Massachusetts raises questions about future of the republic

**1787** ■ Royall Tyler's *The Contrast,* first successful American play, performed
   ■ Northwest Ordinance organizes territory north of Ohio River and east of Mississippi River
   ■ Constitutional Convention drafts new form of government

**1788** ■ Hamilton, Jay, and Madison write *The Federalist* to urge ratification of the Constitution by New York
   ■ Constitution ratified

**1789** ■ William Hill Brown publishes *The Power of Sympathy,* first American novel
   ■ Massachusetts orders towns to support public schools

**1800** ■ Weems publishes his *Life of Washington*

The Carlisle riots presaged violent disputes over the new Constitution in Albany (New York), Providence (Rhode Island), and other cities. In an ongoing struggle that began in 1775 and persisted until the end of the century, Americans argued continually—in print and in person—over how to implement republican principles and over who best represented the people. Easterners debated with westerners; in both regions, elites contended with ordinary folk. Public celebrations like those in the small Pennsylvania town played an important part in the struggle. After all, in a world in which only relatively few property-holding men had the right to vote, other people (even voters themselves) expressed their political opinions in the streets.

Republicanism—the idea that governments should be based wholly on the consent of the people—originated with political theorists in ancient Greece and Rome. Republics, theorists declared, were desirable yet fragile forms of government. Unless their citizens were especially virtuous—that is, sober, moral, and industrious—and largely in agreement on key issues, republics were doomed to failure. When Americans left the British Empire, they abandoned the idea that the best system of government balanced monarchy, aristocracy, and democracy—or, to put it another way, that a stable polity required participation by a king, the nobility, and the people. They substituted a belief in the superiority of republicanism, in which the people, not Parliament, were sovereign. During and after the war, Americans had to deal with the potentially unwelcome consequences of that decision, such as those evident in the Carlisle demonstrations. How could they ensure political stability? How could they foster consensus among the populace? How could they create and sustain a virtuous republic?

America's political and intellectual leaders attempted to inculcate virtue in their fellow countrymen and countrywomen. After 1776, American literature, theater, art, architecture, and education all pursued explicitly moral goals. Women's education was considered particularly important, for the mothers of the republic's children were primarily responsible for ensuring the nation's future. On such matters Americans could agree, but they disagreed on many other critical issues. Almost all white men assumed that women, African Americans, and Indians should have no formal role in politics; men saw the first two groups as household dependents, the last as outside the polity. Still, they found it difficult to reach a consensus on how many of their own number should be included in the political process, how often elections should be held, or how their new governments should be structured.

Republican citizens had to make many other decisions as well. Should a republic's diplomacy differ from that of other nations? (For example, should the United States work to advance the cause of republicanism elsewhere?) And then there were Thomas Jefferson's words in the Declaration of Independence: "all men are created equal." Given that bold statement of principle, how could white republicans justify holding African Americans in perpetual bondage? Some answered that question by freeing their slaves or by voting for state laws that abolished slavery. Others responded by denying that blacks were "men" in the same sense as whites.

The most important task facing Americans in these years was constructing a unified national government. Before 1765 the British mainland colonies had rarely cooperated on common endeavors. Many circumstances separated them: diverse economies, varying religious traditions and ethnic compositions, competing western land claims, and different polities. But fighting the Revolutionary War brought them together, creating a new nationalistic spirit, especially among those who served in the Continental Army or the diplomatic corps. Wartime experiences dissolved at least some of the boundaries that previously had divided Americans, replacing loyalties to state and region with loyalties to the nation.

Still, forging a national republic (as opposed to a set of loosely connected states) was neither easy nor simple. America's first such government, under the Articles of Confederation, proved too weak and decentralized. But political leaders tried another approach when they drafted the Constitution in 1787. Some historians have argued that the Articles of Confederation and the Constitution reflect opposing political philosophies, the Constitution representing an "aristocratic" counterrevolution against the "democratic" Articles. The two documents are more accurately viewed as successive attempts to solve the same problems—for instance, the relationship of states and nation, and the extent to which authority should be centralized. Both applied theories of republicanism to practical problems of governance; neither was entirely successful in resolving those difficulties.

- What were the elements of the new national identity? How did women, Indians, and African Americans fit into that identity?
- What problems confronted the new nation's leaders as they attempted to establish the first modern republic?
- How and why were those problems resolved differently at different times?

## CREATING A VIRTUOUS REPUBLIC

When the colonies declared independence, John Dickinson recalled many years later, "there was no question concerning forms of Government, no enquiry whether a Republic or a limited Monarchy was best. . . . We knew that the people of this country must unite themselves under some form of Government and that this could be no other than the republican form"—in short, self-government by the people. But how should that goal be implemented?

Three different definitions of republicanism emerged in the new United States. Ancient history and political theory informed the first, held chiefly by members of the educated elite (such as the Adamses of Massachusetts). The histories of popular governments in Greece and Rome suggested that republics could succeed only if they were small in size and homogeneous in population. Unless a republic's citizens were willing to sacrifice their own private interests for the good of the whole, the government would collapse. A truly virtuous man, classical republican theory insisted, had to forgo personal profit and work solely for the best interests of the nation. In return for sacrifices, though, a republic offered its citizens equality of opportunity. Under such a government, rank would be based on merit rather than on inherited wealth and status. Society would be governed by members of a "natural aristocracy," men whose talent had elevated them from what might have been humble beginnings to positions of power and privilege. Rank would not be abolished but instead would be founded on merit.

**Varieties of Republicanism**

A second definition, advanced by other members of the elite but also by some skilled craftsmen, drew more on economic theory than on political thought. Instead of perceiving the nation as an organic whole composed of people nobly sacrificing for the common good, this version of

▲ When the great French sculptor Jean-Antoine Houdon prepared this bust of George Washington in 1785, he chose to show the revolutionary leader in classical garb rather than in contemporary clothing. Such images linked the aspirations of the new nation to the ancient republics American thinkers revered.

*(Collection of Dr. Gary Milan)*

republicanism followed the Scottish theorist Adam Smith in emphasizing individuals' pursuit of rational self-interest. The huge profits some men reaped from patriotism by selling supplies to the army underscored such an approach. The nation could only benefit from aggressive economic expansion, argued men such as Alexander Hamilton. When republican men sought to improve their own economic and social circumstances, the entire nation would benefit. Republican virtue would be achieved through the pursuit of private interests, rather than through subordination to communal ideals. Such thinking decisively abandoned the old notion of the Puritan covenant, which the first definition perpetuated in its emphasis on consensus, though not in its stress on an aristocracy of talent rather than birth.

The third notion of republicanism was less influential but more egalitarian than the other two, both of which contained considerable potential for inequality. Many of its illiterate or barely literate proponents could write little to promote their beliefs. Men who advanced the third

version of republicanism, the most prominent of whom was Thomas Paine, called for widening men's participation in the political process. They also wanted government to respond directly to the needs of ordinary folk, rejecting any notion that the "lesser sort" should automatically defer to their "betters." They were, indeed, democrats in more or less the modern sense. For them, the untutored wisdom of the people embodied republican virtue.

Despite the differences, the three strands of republicanism shared many of the same assumptions. All three contrasted the industrious virtue of America with the corruption of Britain and Europe. In the first version, that virtue manifested itself in frugality and self-sacrifice; in the second, it would prevent self-interest from becoming vice; in the third, it was the justification for including propertyless free men in the ranks of voters. "Virtue, Virtue alone . . . is the basis of a republic," asserted Dr. Benjamin Rush of Philadelphia, an ardent patriot, in 1778. His fellow Americans concurred, even if they defined virtue differently. Most agreed that a virtuous country would be composed of hard-working citizens who would dress simply and live plainly, elect wise leaders to public office, and forgo the conspicuous consumption of luxury goods.

As citizens of the United States set out to construct their republic, they believed they were embarking on an unprecedented enterprise. With great pride in their new nation, they expected to replace the vices of monarchical Europe—immorality, selfishness, and lack of public spirit—with the sober virtues of republican America. They sought to embody republican principles not only in their governments but also in their society and culture, expecting painting, literature, drama, and architecture to convey messages of nationalism and virtue to the public.

### Virtue and the Arts

Americans faced a crucial contradiction at the outset of their efforts. To some republicans, fine arts were manifestations of vice. Their presence in a virtuous society, many contended, signaled the existence of luxury and corruption. Why did a frugal farmer need a painting or a novel? Why should anyone spend hard-earned wages to see a play in a lavishly decorated theater? The first American artists, playwrights, and authors confronted an impossible dilemma. They wanted to produce works embodying virtue, but many viewed those very works as corrupting, regardless of their content.

Still, authors and artists tried. William Hill Brown's *The Power of Sympathy* (1789), the first novel written in the United States, related a lurid tale of seduction as a warning to young women. In Royall Tyler's *The Contrast* (1787), the first successful American play, the virtuous

## Novels

He citizens of the United States, fiercely patriotic and proud of achieving political independence from Great Britain, also sought intellectual and cultural independence. In novels, poems, paintings, plays, and histories they explored aspects of their new national identity. Ironically, though, the standards against which they measured themselves and the models they followed were European, primarily British.

That was especially true of the most widely read form of literature in the new United States: the novel. Susanna Haswell Rowson's *Charlotte: A Tale of Truth,* the most popular early "American" novel, was actually composed in England, where the novel originated as a literary form. In the mid-eighteenth century, Samuel Richardson had composed the first works of fiction that today are called novels, the very name revealing their "newness," or novelty. Written in epistolary style (that is, through letters drafted by the various characters) Richardson's novels—*Pamela* (1740), *Clarissa* (1748), and *Sir Charles Grandison* (1753)—all revolved around the courtship and sexual relationships of young adults. The same themes permeated *Charlotte* and Richardson's other American imitators, and for good reason. Changing social mores in the late eighteenth century largely freed English and American young people from parental supervision of their marital decisions. While giving them greater individual choice, that freedom also rendered girls particularly vulnerable to new dangers of deception and seduction by unscrupulous suitors. And these same young women, as a group, were the most avid readers of novels, especially as expanded women's education increased female literacy rates.

William Hill Brown's *Power of Sympathy* (1789) and Hannah Foster's *Coquette* (1797), fictional versions of true "seduction and abandonment" tales, had avid readerships, but neither matched the sales of *Charlotte,* which despite its subtitle, *A Tale of Truth,* had no known factual basis. Rowson, born in England but raised in Massachusetts as the daughter of a customs officer in the British service, lived with her family in England during the Revolution but permanently returned to the United States in 1793. Her popular novel, first published in London in 1791, was reprinted in Philadelphia three years later and eventually went through more than 160 editions. *Charlotte* (later titled *Charlotte Temple*) narrates the story of a naive young woman who elopes, pregnant and unmarried, with her seducer, only to be deserted when a beautiful, rich, and virtuous rival appears on the scene. After giving birth to her baby, Charlotte dies in her father's arms, with her last breath directing him to care for the child. "Oh my dear girls," Rowson cautions her readers, "pray for fortitude to resist the impulses of inclination, when it runs counter to the precepts of religion and virtue."

Generations of young American women sobbed over Charlotte's fate, visiting Trinity churchyard in lower Manhattan, where a real-life counterpart of the fictional heroine was reputed to be buried. Their tears and women's preference on both sides of the Atlantic for such sentimental novels linked the young readers and their nation to the former mother country from which they were nominally so eager to separate.

This "Eighth American Edition" (such statements on the title pages of early novels can rarely be trusted because some printings were pirated) of Susanna Rowson's *Charlotte Temple* included a "portrait" of its entirely fictional heroine. That engraving thus reinforced the subtitle, *A Tale of Truth.*

*(AC7.R7997.79lc 1809 Houghton Library, Harvard University)*

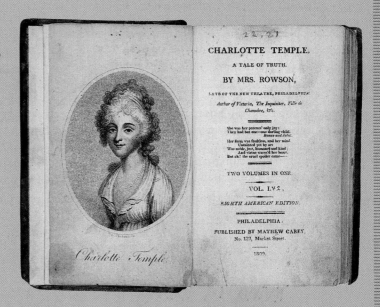

conduct of Colonel Manly was contrasted (hence the title) with the reprehensible behavior of the fop Billy Dimple. The most popular book of the era, Mason Locke Weems's *Life of Washington,* published in 1800 shortly after George Washington's death, was intended by its author to "hold up his great Virtues . . . to the imitation of Our Youth." Weems could hardly be accused of subtlety. The famous tale he invented—six-year-old George bravely admitting cutting down his father's favorite cherry tree—ended with George's father exclaiming, "Run to my arms, you dearest boy. . . . Such an act of heroism in my son, is worth more than a thousand trees, though blossomed with silver, and their fruit of purest gold."

Painting and architecture, too, were expected to exemplify high moral standards. Two of the most prominent artists of the period, Gilbert Stuart and Charles Willson Peale, painted innumerable portraits of upstanding republican citizens. John Trumbull's vast canvases depicted such milestones of American history as the Battle of Bunker Hill and Cornwallis's surrender at Yorktown. Such portraits and historical scenes were intended to instill patriotic sentiments in their viewers. Architects likewise hoped to convey in their buildings a sense of the young republic's ideals. When the Virginia government asked Thomas Jefferson, then minister to France, for advice on the design of the state capitol in Richmond, Jefferson unhesitatingly recommended copying a Roman building, the Maison Carrée at Nîmes. "It is very simple," he explained, "but it is noble beyond expression." Jefferson set forth ideals that would guide American architecture for a generation to come: simplicity of line, harmonious proportions, a feeling of grandeur.

Despite the artists' efforts (or, some would have said, because of them), some Americans began to detect signs of luxury and corruption by the mid-1780s. The resumption of European trade after the war brought a return to up-to-date imported fashions for both men and women. Elite families again attended balls and concerts. Parties no longer seemed complete without gambling and cardplaying. Social clubs for young people multiplied; Samuel Adams worried in print about the opportunities for corruption lurking behind plans for tea drinking and genteel conversation among Boston youths. Especially alarming to fervent republicans was the establishment in 1783 of the Society of the Cincinnati, a hereditary association for Revolutionary War officers and their firstborn male descendants. Although the organizers hoped to advance the notion of the citizen-soldier, opponents feared that the group would become the nucleus of a native-born aristocracy. All these developments directly challenged the United States' self-image as a virtuous republic.

Americans' deep-seated concern for the future of the infant republic focused their attention on children, the "rising generation." Education had previously been seen as a private means to personal advancement, the concern of individual families. Now schooling would serve a public purpose. If young people were to resist the temptations of vice and become useful citizens prepared for self-government, they would need a good education. In fact, the very survival of the nation depended on it. The 1780s and 1790s thus witnessed two major changes in educational practice.

### Educational Reform

First, some northern states began to use tax money to support public elementary schools. In 1789 Massachusetts became one of the first states to require towns to offer their citizens free public elementary education. Second, schooling for girls was improved. Recognizing the importance of the rising generation led Americans to conclude that mothers would have to be properly educated if they were to instruct their children adequately. Therefore, Massachusetts insisted that town elementary schools teach girls as well as boys. Throughout the United States, private academies were founded to give teenage girls from well-to-do families an opportunity for advanced schooling. No one yet proposed opening colleges to women, but a few fortunate girls could study history, geography, rhetoric, and mathematics. The academies also trained female students in fancy needlework—the only artistic endeavor considered appropriate for genteel women.

### Judith Sargent Murray

Judith Sargent Murray of Gloucester, Massachusetts, became the chief theorist of early women's education in the early republic. Murray argued in several essays that women and men had equal intellectual capacities, although women's inadequate education might make them seem less intelligent. "We can only reason from what we know," she declared, "and if an opportunity of acquiring knowledge hath been denied us, the inferiority of our sex cannot fairly be deduced from thence." Therefore, concluded Murray, boys and girls should be offered equivalent schooling. She further contended that girls should be taught to support themselves by their own efforts: "Independence should be placed within their grasp."

Murray's direct challenge to the traditional colonial belief that, as one man put it, girls "knew quite enough if they could make a shirt and a pudding" was part of a general rethinking of women's position that occurred as a result of the Revolution. Both men and women realized that

▲ Judith Sargent Stevens (later Murray), by John Singleton Copley, c. 1770–1772. The eventual author of tracts advocating improvements in women's education sat for this portrait two decades earlier, during her first marriage. Her clear-eyed gaze suggests both her intelligence and her seriousness of purpose.

*(Terra Museum of American Art, Chicago, Illinois. Daniel J. Terra Collection)*

female patriots had made vitally important contributions to the American independence movement. Consequently, Americans began to develop new ideas about the roles women should play in a republican society.

The best-known expression of those new ideas appeared in a letter Abigail Adams addressed to her husband in March 1776. "In the new Code of Laws which I suppose it will be necessary for you to make I desire you would Remember the Ladies," she wrote. "Remember all Men would be tyrants if they could. . . . If perticuliar care and attention is not paid to the Laidies [sic] we are determined to foment a Rebelion, and will not hold ourselves bound by any Laws in which we have no voice, or Representa-

### Women and the Republic

tion." With these words, Abigail Adams took a step that would be duplicated by other disfranchised Americans. She deliberately applied the ideology developed to combat parliamentary supremacy to purposes revolutionary leaders had never intended. They assumed that wives had no interests different from those of their husbands. Yet Abigail Adams argued that, because men were "Naturally Tyrannical," the United States should reform colonial marriage laws, which subordinated wives to their husbands, giving men control of family property and denying wives the right to independent legal action.

Abigail Adams did not ask for woman suffrage, but others claimed that right. The drafters of the New Jersey state constitution in 1776 defined voters carelessly as "all free inhabitants" who met certain property qualifications. They thereby unintentionally gave the vote to property-holding white spinsters and widows, as well as to free black landowners. Qualified women and African Americans regularly voted in New Jersey's local and congressional elections until 1807, when they were disfranchised by the state legislature, which falsely charged them with widespread vote fraud. Yet the fact that women voted at all was evidence of their altered perception of their place in the political life of the country.

Such dramatic episodes were unusual. After the war, European-Americans still viewed women in traditional terms, affirming that women's primary function was to be good wives, mothers, and mistresses of households. They perceived significant differences between male and female character, which eventually enabled a resolution of the conflict between the two most influential strands of republican thought and led to new roles for some women. Because wives could not own property or participate directly in economic life, women came to be seen as the embodiment of self-sacrificing, disinterested republicanism. Through new female-run charitable associations founded after the war, better-off women assumed public responsibilities, in particular through caring for poor widows and orphaned children. Thus men were freed from the naggings of conscience as they pursued their economic self-interest (that other republican virtue), secure in the knowledge that their wives and daughters were fulfilling the family's obligation to the common good. The ideal republican man, therefore, was an individualist, seeking advancement for himself and his family. The ideal republican woman, by contrast, always put the well-being of others ahead of her own.

Together, European American men and women established the context for the creation of a virtuous republic. But nearly 20 percent of the American population was of

African descent. How did approximately 700,000 African Americans fit into the developing national plan?

## THE FIRST EMANCIPATION AND THE GROWTH OF RACISM

Revolutionary ideology exposed one of the primary contradictions in American society. Both European-Americans and African Americans saw the irony in slaveholders' claims that they sought to prevent Britain from "enslaving" them. Many revolutionary leaders voiced the theme. In 1773 Dr. Benjamin Rush called slavery "a vice which degrades human nature," warning ominously that "the plant of liberty is of so tender a nature that it cannot thrive long in the neighborhood of slavery." Common folk also pointed out the contradiction. When Josiah Atkins, a Connecticut soldier, saw Washington's plantation, he observed in his journal: "Alas! That persons who pretend to stand for the rights of mankind for the liberties of society, can delight in oppression, & that even of the worst kind!"

African Americans did not need revolutionary ideology to tell them that slavery was wrong, but they quickly took advantage of that ideology. In 1779 a group of slaves from Portsmouth, New Hampshire, asked the state legislature "from what authority [our masters] assume to dispose of our lives, freedom and property," pleading "that the name of slave may not more be heard in a land gloriously contending for the sweets of freedom." The same year, several bondsmen in Fairfield, Connecticut, petitioned the legislature for their freedom, characterizing slavery as a "dreadful Evil" and "flagrant Injustice." How could men who were "nobly contending in the Cause of Liberty," they asked, continue "this detestable Practice"?

Both legislatures responded negatively, but the postwar years witnessed the gradual abolition of slavery in the North, a process that has become known as "the first emancipation."

**Emancipation and Manumission**

Vermont, still an independent jurisdiction, banned slavery in its 1777 constitution. Responding to lawsuits filed by enslaved men and women, Massachusetts courts decided in 1783 that the state constitution prohibited slavery. Other states north of Maryland adopted gradual emancipation laws between 1780 (Pennsylvania) and 1804 (New Jersey). New Hampshire did not formally abolish slavery, but only eight slaves were reported on the 1800 census and none in 1810. Although no southern state adopted general emancipation laws, the legislatures of Virginia (1782), Delaware (1787), and Maryland (1790 and 1796) altered laws that earlier had restricted slaveowners' ability to free their bondspeople. Yet South Caro-

▲ A sailor of African descent posed proudly for this portrait around 1790. Unfortunately, neither the name of the sailor nor the name of the artist is known today.

*(Private collection, photograph courtesy of Hirschl & Adler Galleries, New York)*

lina and Georgia never considered adopting such acts, and North Carolina insisted that all manumissions (emancipations of individual slaves) be approved by county courts.

Revolutionary ideology thus had limited impact on the well-entrenched economic interests of large slaveholders. Only in the northern states—societies with slaves, not slave societies—could state legislatures vote to abolish slavery. Even there, legislators' concern for the property rights of owners of human chattel—the Revolution, after all, was fought for *property* as well as for life and liberty—led them to favor gradual emancipation over immediate abolition. For example, New York's law freed children born into slavery after July 4, 1799, but only after they had reached their mid-twenties (by then having through their labor more than paid back the cost of their upbringing). The laws failed to emancipate the existing slave population, thereby leaving the owners' current human property largely intact. For decades, then, African Americans in the North lived in an intermediate stage between slavery and freedom. Although the emancipation laws forbade the sale of slaves to jurisdictions in which the institution remained legal, slaveowners regularly circumvented such provisions. The 1840 census recorded the presence of slaves in several northern states; not until later that decade did Rhode Island and Connecticut, for instance, abolish all vestiges of slavery.

Despite the slow progress of abolition, the number of free people of African descent in the United States grew dramatically in the first years after the Revolution. Before the war they had been few in number; in 1755, for example, only 4 percent of African Americans in Maryland were free. Most slaves emancipated before the war were mulattos, born of unions between bondswomen and their masters, who then manumitted the children. But wartime disruptions radically augmented the freed population. Wartime escapees from plantations, slaves who had served in the American army, and still others who had been emancipated by their owners or by state laws were now free. By 1790 nearly 60,000 free people of color lived in the United States; ten years later they numbered more than 108,000, nearly 11 percent of the total African American population.

### Growth of Free Black Population

In the Chesapeake, manumissions were speeded by economic changes, such as declining soil fertility and the shift from tobacco to grain production, as well as by the rising influence of antislavery Baptists and Methodists. One prominent Baptist convert, the immensely wealthy planter Robert Carter, manumitted all of his bondspeople after he became convinced that slaveowning was sinful. Because grain cultivation was less labor-intensive than tobacco growing, planters began to complain about "excess" slaves. They occasionally solved that problem by freeing some of their less productive or more favored bondspeople. The enslaved also seized the opportunity to negotiate agreements with their owners allowing them to live and work independently until they could purchase themselves with their accumulated earnings. The free black population of Virginia more than doubled between 1790 and 1810, and by the latter year nearly one-quarter of Maryland's African American population was no longer in legal bondage.

In the 1780s and thereafter, freedpeople from rural areas often made their way to northern port cities, such as Boston and Philadelphia. Women outnumbered men among the migrants by a margin of three to two, for they had better employment opportunities in the cities, especially

### Freedpeople's Lives

in domestic service. Some freedmen also worked in domestic service, but larger numbers were employed as unskilled laborers and sailors. A few of the women and a sizable proportion of men (nearly one-third of those in Philadelphia in 1795) were skilled workers or retailers. These people chose new names for themselves, exchanging the surnames of former masters for names like Newman or Brown, and as soon as possible they established independent two-parent families instead of continuing to live in their employers' households. They also began to occupy distinct neighborhoods, probably as a result of discrimination.

Emancipation did not bring equality. Even whites who recognized African Americans' right to freedom were unwilling to accept them as equals. Laws discriminated against freedpeople as they had against slaves. Several states—among them Delaware, Maryland, and South Carolina—quickly adopted laws denying property-owning black men the vote. South Carolina forbade free blacks from testifying against whites in court. New Englanders used indenture contracts to control freed youths, who were also often denied education in public schools. Freedmen found it difficult to purchase property and find good jobs. And though in many areas African Americans were accepted as members—even ministers—of evangelical churches, they were rarely allowed an equal voice in church affairs.

Gradually, freedpeople developed their own institutions, often based in their own neighborhoods. In Charleston, mulattos formed the Brown Fellowship Society, which provided insurance coverage for its members, financed a school, and helped to support orphans. In 1794 former slaves in Philadelphia and Baltimore, led by the Reverend Richard Allen, founded societies that eventually formed the African Methodist Episcopal (AME) denomination. AME churches later sponsored schools and, along with African Baptist, African Episcopal, and African Presbyterian churches, became cultural centers of the free black community. Freedpeople quickly learned that, to survive and prosper, they had to rely on collective effort rather than on the goodwill of their white compatriots.

Their endeavors were all the more important because the postrevolutionary years witnessed the development of formal racist theory in the United States. European-Americans had long regarded their slaves as inferior, but the most influential writers attributed that inferiority to environmental factors. They argued that African slaves' seemingly debased character derived from their enslavement, rather than enslavement's being the consequence of inherited inferiority. In the Revolution's aftermath, though,

### Development of Racist Theory

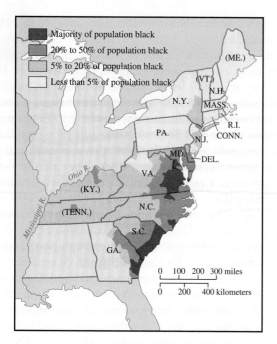

Map 7.1   **African American Population, 1790: Proportion of Total Population**

The first census clearly indicated that the African American population was heavily concentrated in just a few areas of the United States, most notably in coastal regions of South Carolina, Georgia, and Virginia. Although there were growing numbers of blacks in the backcountry—presumably taken there by migrating slaveowners—most parts of the North and East, with the exception of the immediate vicinity of New York City, had few African American residents.

*(**Source**: From Lester J. Cappon et al., eds.,* Atlas of Early American History: The Revolutionary Era, 1760–1790. *Copyright © 1976 by Princeton University Press. Reprinted by permission of Princeton University Press.)*

slaveowners needed to defend holding other human beings in bondage against the proposition that "all men are created equal." Consequently, they began to argue that people of African descent were less than fully human and that the principles of republican equality applied only to European-Americans. In other words, to avoid having to confront the contradiction between their practice and the egalitarian implications of revolutionary theory, they redefined the theory so that it would not apply to African Americans.

Simultaneously, the very notion of "race" appeared in coherent form applied to groups defined by skin color as "whites," "reds," and "blacks." The rise of egalitarian thinking among European-Americans both downplayed status distinctions within their own group and differentiated all "whites" from people of color—Indians and African Americans. (That differentiation soon manifested itself in new miscegenation laws adopted in both northern and southern states to forbid intermarriage between whites and blacks or Indians.) Indians from disparate nations, especially in the southeastern United States, had decades earlier begun to refer to themselves as "red." Meanwhile, experience as slaves on American soil forged the identity "African" or "black" from the various ethnic and national affiliations of people who had survived the transatlantic crossing. Strikingly, among the first to term themselves "Africans" were oceanic sailors—men whose wide-ranging contacts with Europeans caused them to construct a unified (and separate) identity for themselves. Thus in the revolutionary era "whiteness," "redness," and "blackness"—along with the superiority of the first, the inferiority of the latter two—developed in tandem as contrasting terms.

Such racism had several intertwined elements. First came the assertion that, as Thomas Jefferson insisted in 1781, blacks were "inferior to the whites in the endowments both of body and mind." (He was less certain about the inferiority of Indians.) There followed the belief that blacks were congenitally lazy and disorderly. Even though owners had often argued, conversely, that slaves were "natural" workers, no one seemed to notice the inherent contradiction. Third was the notion that all blacks were sexually promiscuous and that African American men lusted after European American women. The specter of interracial sexual intercourse involving black men and white women haunted early American racist thought. Significantly, the more common reverse circumstance—the sexual exploitation of enslaved women by their masters—aroused little comment or concern.

African Americans did not allow these developing racist notions to go unchallenged. Benjamin Banneker, a free black mathematical genius, directly disputed Thomas Jefferson's belief in Africans' intellectual inferiority. In 1791 Banneker sent Jefferson a copy of his latest almanac (which included his astronomical calculations) as an example of blacks' mental powers. Jefferson's response admitted Banneker's intelligence but indicated that he regarded Banneker as exceptional; Jefferson insisted that he needed more evidence before he would change his mind about people of African descent generally.

At its birth, then, its leaders defined the republic as a white male enterprise. Even though men of African descent served with honor in the Continental Army, laws from the 1770s on linked "whiteness" and male citizenship rights. Indeed,

## A White Men's Republic

some historians have argued that the subjugation of blacks, Indians, and women was a necessary precondition for theoretical equality among white men. They have pointed out that identifying common racial antagonists helped to create white solidarity and to lessen the threat to gentry power posed by the enfranchisement of poorer men. Moreover, excluding women from the political realm reserved all power for men, specifically those of the "better sort." That was perhaps one reason why after the Revolution the division of American society between slave and free was transformed into a division between blacks—some of whom were free—and whites. The white male wielders of power ensured their continued dominance in part by substituting race for enslavement as the primary determinant of African Americans' status.

# DESIGNING REPUBLICAN GOVERNMENTS

In May 1776, even before adoption of the Declaration of Independence, the Second Continental Congress directed states to devise new republican governments to replace the popularly elected provincial conventions and committees that had met since colonial governments collapsed in 1774 and 1775. Thus American men initially concentrated on drafting state constitutions and devoted little attention to their national government—an oversight they later had to remedy.

At the state level, political leaders immediately faced the problem of defining a "constitution." Americans

### State Constitutions

wanted to create tangible documents specifying the fundamental structures of government, but at first legislators could not decide how to accomplish that goal. States eventually concluded that regular legislative bodies should not draft their constitutions. Following the lead established by Vermont in 1777 and Massachusetts in 1780, they began to elect conventions for the sole purpose of drafting constitutions. Thus states sought direct authorization from the people—the theoretical sovereigns in a republic—before establishing new governments. After preparing new constitutions, delegates submitted them to voters for ratification.

The framers of state constitutions concerned themselves primarily with outlining the distribution of and limitations on government power—both crucial to the survival of republics. If authority was not confined within reasonable limits, the states might become tyrannical, as Britain had. Americans' experience with British rule permeated every provision of their new constitutions. States experimented with different solutions to the problems the framers perceived, and the early constitutions varied considerably in specifics while remaining broadly comparable in outline.

Under their colonial charters, Americans had learned to fear the power of the governor—usually the appointed agent of the king or proprietor—and to see the legislature as their defender. Accordingly, the first state constitutions typically provided for the governor to be elected annually (commonly by the legislature), limited the number of terms he could serve, and gave him little independent authority. Simultaneously, the constitutions expanded the legislature's powers. Every state except Pennsylvania and Vermont retained a two-house structure, with members of the upper house having longer terms and required to meet higher property-holding standards than members of the lower house. But they also redrew electoral districts to more accurately reflect population patterns, and they increased the number of members in both houses. Finally, most states lowered property qualifications for voting. As a result, the legislatures came to include some members who before the war would not have been eligible to vote. Thus the revolutionary era witnessed the first deliberate attempt to broaden the base of American government, a process that has continued to the present day.

But the state constitutions' authors knew that governments designed to be responsive to the people would

### Limiting State Governments

not necessarily provide sufficient protection if tyrants were elected to office. They consequently included explicit limitations on government authority in the documents they composed, attempting to protect what they regarded as the inalienable rights of individual citizens. Seven constitutions contained formal bills of rights, and others had similar clauses. Most guaranteed citizens freedom of the press, rights to fair trials and to consent to taxation, and protection against general search warrants. An independent judiciary was charged with upholding such rights. Most states also guaranteed freedom of religion, but with restrictions. For example, seven states required that all officeholders be Christians, and some continued to support churches with tax money. (Not until 1833 did Massachusetts become the last state to remove all vestiges of a religious establishment.)

In general, the constitution makers put greater emphasis on preventing state governments from becoming tyrannical than on making them effective wielders of political authority. Their approach to shaping governments was understandable, given the American experience with Great Britain. But establishing such weak political units, especially in wartime, practically ensured that the constitutions would need revision. Soon some states began to rewrite constitutions they had drafted in 1776 and 1777.

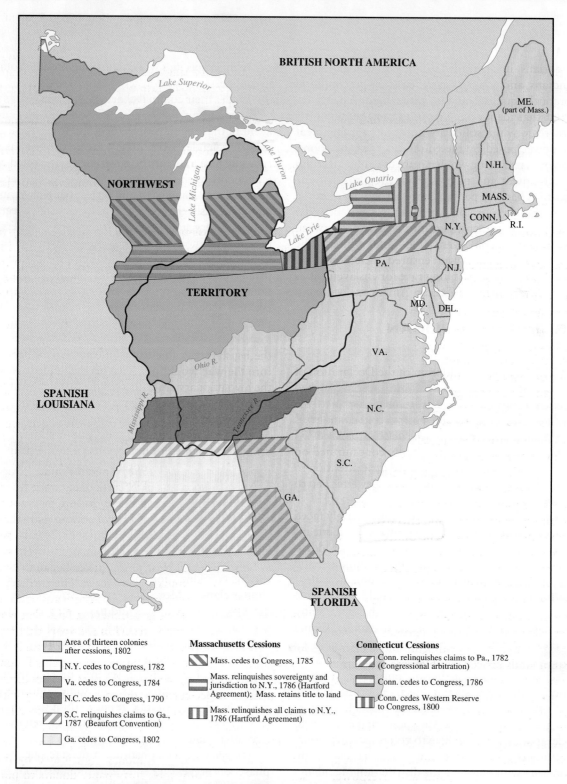

**BRITISH NORTH AMERICA**

Lake Superior

Lake Michigan

Lake Huron

Lake Ontario

Lake Erie

**NORTHWEST**

**TERRITORY**

ME.
(part of Mass.)

N.H.

MASS.

CONN.

R.I.

N.Y.

PA.

N.J.

MD.

DEL.

VA.

Ohio R.

**SPANISH
LOUISIANA**

Mississippi R.

Tennessee R.

N.C.

S.C.

GA.

**SPANISH
FLORIDA**

| | |
|---|---|
| Area of thirteen colonies after cessions, 1802 | |
| N.Y. cedes to Congress, 1782 | |
| Va. cedes to Congress, 1784 | |
| N.C. cedes to Congress, 1790 | |
| S.C. relinquishes claims to Ga., 1787 (Beaufort Convention) | |
| Ga. cedes to Congress, 1802 | |

**Massachusetts Cessions**

Mass. cedes to Congress, 1785

Mass. relinquishes sovereignty and jurisdiction to N.Y., 1786 (Hartford Agreement); Mass. retains title to land

Mass. relinquishes all claims to N.Y., 1786 (Hartford Agreement)

**Connecticut Cessions**

Conn. relinquishes claims to Pa., 1782 (Congressional arbitration)

Conn. cedes to Congress, 1786

Conn. cedes Western Reserve to Congress, 1800

## Map 7.2   Western Land Claims and Cessions, 1782–1802

After the United States achieved independence, states competed with one another for control of valuable lands to which they had possible claims under their original charters. That competition led to a series of compromises among the states or between individual states and the new nation, indicated on this map.

Invariably, the revised versions increased the powers of the governor and reduced the scope of the legislature's authority. By the mid-1780s, some American political leaders had concluded that the best way to limit government power was to balance legislative, executive, and judicial powers, a design called checks and balances. The national Constitution that they drafted in 1787 also embodied that principle.

**Revising State Constitutions**

Yet the constitutional theories that Americans applied at the state level did not immediately influence their conception of national government. Because American officials initially focused on organizing the military struggle against Britain, the powers and structure of the Continental Congress evolved by default. Not until late 1777 did Congress send the Articles of Confederation—the document outlining a national government—to the states for ratification, and those Articles simply wrote into law the unplanned arrangements of the Continental Congress.

The chief organ of national government was a unicameral (one-house) legislature in which each state had one vote. Its powers included conducting foreign relations, mediating interstate disputes, controlling maritime affairs, regulating Indian trade, and valuing state and national coinage. The Articles did not give the national government the ability to raise revenue effectively or to enforce a uniform commercial policy. The United States of America was described as "a firm league of friendship" in which each state "retains its sovereignty, freedom and independence, and every Power, Jurisdiction and right, which is not by this confederation expressly delegated to the United States, in Congress assembled."

**Articles of Confederation**

The Articles required unanimous consent of state legislatures for ratification or amendment, and a clause concerning western lands proved troublesome. The draft accepted by Congress allowed states to retain all land claims derived from their original charters. But states with definite western boundaries in their charters (such as Maryland and New Jersey) wanted other states to cede to the national government their landholdings west of the Appalachian Mountains. Otherwise, they feared, states with large claims could expand and overpower their smaller neighbors. Maryland refused to accept the Articles until 1781, when Virginia finally promised to surrender its western holdings to national jurisdiction (see Map 7.2). Other states followed suit, establishing the principle that unorganized lands would be held by the nation as a whole.

The capacity of a single state to delay ratification for three years portended the fate of American government under the Articles of Confederation. The unicameral legislature, whether it was called the Second Continental Congress (until 1781) or the Confederation Congress (thereafter), was too inefficient and unwieldy to govern effectively. The Articles' authors had not given adequate thought to the distribution of power within the national government or to the relationship between the Confederation and the states. The Congress they created was simultaneously a legislative body and a collective executive (there was no judiciary), but it had no independent income and no authority to compel the states to accept its rulings. Under the Articles, national government lurched from crisis to crisis. (See the appendix for the text of the Articles of Confederation.)

## TRIALS OF THE CONFEDERATION

Finance posed the most persistent problem faced by both state and national governments. Because legislators at all levels levied taxes only reluctantly, both Congress and the states at first tried to finance the war simply by printing currency. Even though the money was backed only by good faith, it circulated freely and without excessive depreciation during 1775 and most of 1776. Demand for military supplies and civilian goods was high, stimulating trade (especially with France) and local production. Indeed, the amount of money issued in those years was probably no more than what a healthy economy required as a medium of exchange.

But in late 1776, as the American army suffered reverses in New York and New Jersey, prices began to rise, and inflation set in. The currency's value rested on Americans' faith in their government, a faith that was sorely tested in the years that followed, especially during the dark days of British triumphs in the South (1779 and 1780). State governments fought inflation by controlling wages and prices and requiring acceptance of paper currency on an equal footing with specie (coins). States also borrowed funds, established lotteries, and levied taxes. Their efforts were futile. So, too, was Congress's attempt to stop printing currency altogether and to rely solely on money contributed by the states. By early 1780 it took forty paper dollars to purchase one silver dollar. Soon Continental currency was worthless (see Figure 7.1).

**Financial Affairs**

In 1781, faced with total collapse of the monetary system, Congress undertook ambitious reforms. After establishing a department of finance under the wealthy Philadelphia merchant Robert Morris, it asked the states

*buying not selling*

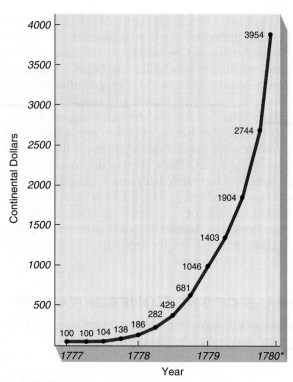

Year

* Currency abandoned in April 1780

**Figure 7.1    Depreciation of Continental Currency, 1777–1780**

The depreciation of Continental currency accelerated in 1778, as is shown in this graph measuring its value against one hundred silver dollars. Thereafter, its value dropped almost daily.

*( Source: Data from John J. McCusker, "How Much Is That in Real Money? A Historical Price Index for Use as a Deflator of Money Values in the Economy of the United States,"* Proceedings of the American Antiquarian Society, *Vol. 101, Pt. 2 [1991], Table C-1.)*

*refusing taxes*

to amend the Articles of Confederation to allow a national duty of 5 percent on imported goods. Morris put national finances on a solid footing, but the customs duty was never adopted. First Rhode Island and then New York refused to agree to the tax. The states' resistance reflected fear of a too-powerful central government. As one worried citizen wrote in 1783, "If permanent Funds are given to Congress, the aristocratical Influence, which predominates in more than a major part of the United States, will fully establish an arbitrary Government."

Because the Articles denied Congress the power to establish a national commercial policy, the realm of for-

**Foreign Affairs**

eign trade also exposed the new government's weaknesses. Immediately after the war, Britain, France,

and Spain restricted American trade with their colonies. Americans, who had hoped independence would bring about trade with all nations, were outraged but could do little to change matters. Members of Congress watched helplessly as British manufactured goods flooded the United States while American produce could no longer be sold in the British West Indies, once its prime market. Although Americans reopened commerce with other European countries and started a profitable trade with China in 1784, neither substituted for access to closer and larger markets.

Congress furthermore had difficulty dealing with the Spanish presence on the nation's southern and western borders. Determined to prevent the republic's expansion, Spain in 1784 closed the Mississippi River to American navigation, thereby depriving the growing settlements west of the Appalachians of access to the Gulf of Mexico. Congress, through its Department of Foreign Affairs, opened negotiations with Spain in 1785, but even John Jay, one of the nation's most experienced diplomats, could not win the necessary concessions. The talks collapsed the following year after Congress divided sharply: southerners and westerners insisted on navigation rights on the Mississippi, whereas northerners were willing to abandon that claim in order to win commercial concessions in the West Indies. The impasse made some congressmen question the possibility of a national consensus on foreign affairs.

Provisions of the 1783 Treaty of Paris, too, caused serious problems. Article Four, which promised payment

**Peace Treaty Provisions**

of prewar debts (most of them owed by Americans to British merchants), and Article Five, which recommended that states allow loyalists to recover their confiscated property, aroused considerable opposition. States passed laws denying British subjects the right to sue for recovery of debts or property in American courts, and town meetings decried the loyalists' return. As residents of Norwalk, Connecticut, put it, few Americans wanted to permit the "Tory Villains" to return "while filial Tears are fresh upon our Cheeks and our Murdered Brethren scarcely cold in their Graves." State governments also had reason to oppose enforcement of the treaty. Sales of loyalists' land, houses, and other possessions had helped finance the war. Because many purchasers were prominent patriots, states hesitated to raise questions about the legitimacy of their property titles.

The refusal of state and local governments to comply with Articles Four and Five gave Britain an excuse to maintain military posts on the Great Lakes long after its troops were supposed to have withdrawn. Furthermore,

THE COMMISSIONERS

▲ A British cartoon ironically reflected Americans' hopes for post-war trade, hopes that were dashed after 1783. The Indian woman symbolizing America sits on a pile of tobacco bales, with rice and indigo casks bound for Europe nearby. The artist was satirizing the failed 1778 British peace commission and Britons' willingness to make concessions to the rebellious colonies, but his image captured Americans' belief in the importance of their produce.

*(Chicago Historical Society)*

Congress's inability to convince states to implement the treaty disclosed its lack of power, even in an area—foreign affairs—in which it had authority under the Articles. Concerned nationalists argued publicly that failure to enforce the treaty, however unpopular, challenged the republic's credibility. "Will foreign nations be willing to undertake anything with us or for us," asked Alexander Hamilton, "when they find that the nature of our governments will allow no dependence to be placed on our engagements?"

## ORDER AND DISORDER IN THE WEST

Congressmen also confronted knotty problems when they considered the status of land beyond the Appalachians. Although British and American diplomats did not discuss tribal claims, the United States assumed that the Treaty of Paris cleared its title to all land east of the Mississippi except the area still held by Spain. Still, recognizing that land cessions should be obtained from the most powerful tribes, Congress initiated negotiations with both northern and southern Indians (see Map 7.3).

At Fort Stanwix, New York, in 1784, American diplomats negotiated a treaty with chiefs who claimed to represent the Iroquois; and at Hopewell, South Carolina, in late 1785 and early 1786, they did the same with emissaries from the Choctaw, Chickasaw, and Cherokee nations. In 1786 the Iroquois formally repudiated the Fort Stanwix treaty, denying that the men who attended the negotiations had been authorized to speak for the Six Nations. The confederacy threatened new attacks on frontier settlements, but everyone knew the threat was empty; the flawed treaty stood by default. At intervals until the end of the

**Indian Relations**

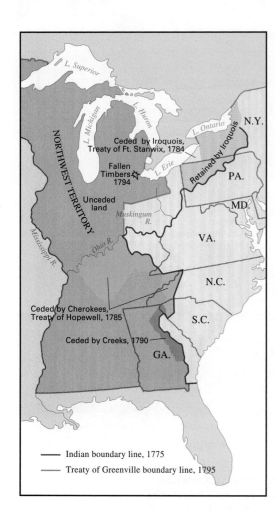

**Map 7.3   Cession of Tribal Lands to the United States, 1775–1790**

The land claims of the United States meant little as long as Indian nations still controlled vast territories within the new country's formal boundaries. A series of treaties in the 1780s and 1790s opened some lands to white settlement.

(Source: From Lester J. Cappon et al., eds., Atlas of Early American History: The Revolutionary Era, 1760–1790. Copyright © 1976 by Princeton University Press. Reprinted by permission of Princeton University Press.)

Creeks—who had not agreed to the Hopewell treaties—to defend their territory by declaring war. Only in 1790 did they come to terms with the United States.

Western nations, such as the Shawnees, Chippewas, Ottawas, and Potawatomis, had already started to reject Iroquois hegemony as early as the 1750s. After the collapse of Iroquois power, they formed their own confederacy and demanded direct negotiations with the United States. They intended to present a united front so as to avoid the piecemeal surrender of land by individual bands and villages. But they faced a difficult task. In the postwar world, Indian nations could no longer pursue the diplomatic strategy that had worked so well for so long: playing off European and American powers against one another. France was gone; Spanish territory lay far to the west and south; and British power was confined to Canada, north of the Great Lakes. Only the United States remained.

At first the national government ignored the western confederacy. Shortly after state land cessions were completed, Congress began to organize the Northwest Territory, bounded by the Mississippi River, the Great Lakes, and the Ohio River (see Map 7.2). Ordinances passed in 1784, 1785, and 1787 outlined the process through which the land could be sold to settlers and formal governments organized.

**Ordinance of 1785**

To ensure orderly development, Congress in 1785 directed that the land be surveyed into townships 6 miles square, each divided into thirty-six sections of 640 acres (1 square mile). Revenue from the sale of the sixteenth section of each township was to be reserved for the support of public schools—the first instance of federal aid to education in American history. One dollar was the minimum price per acre; the minimum sale was one section. Thus Congress showed little concern for the small farmer: the resulting minimum outlay, $640, lay beyond the reach of ordinary Americans, except those veterans who received part of their army pay in land warrants. Proceeds from western land sales constituted the first independent revenues available to the national government.

The most important of the three land policies—the Northwest Ordinance of 1787—contained a bill of rights guaranteeing settlers freedom of religion and the right to a jury trial, forbidding cruel and unusual punishments, and nominally prohibiting slavery. Eventually, that prohibition became an important symbol for antislavery northerners, but at the time it had little effect. Some residents of the territory already held slaves, and Congress did not intend to deprive them of their property. More-

**Northwest Ordinance**

decade, New York purchased large tracts of land from individual Iroquois nations. By 1790 the once-dominant confederacy was confined to a few scattered reservations. In the South, too, the United States took the treaties as confirmation of its sovereignty, authorizing settlers to move onto the territories in question. European-Americans poured over the southern Appalachians, provoking the

▲ In 1784 Thomas Jefferson proposed a scheme for organizing the new nation's western lands. His plan would have divided the region on a grid pattern, yielding fourteen new states (with names such as "Metropotamia" and "Pelisipia") composed of 10-mile-square "hundreds." After a year of debate, Jefferson's plan was replaced by the one adopted in the Land Ordinance of 1785, which is described in the text. *(Clements Library, University of Michigan)*

over, the ordinance also contained a provision allowing slaveowners to "lawfully reclaim" runaway bondspeople who took refuge in the territory—the first national fugitive slave law. The ordinance prevented slavery from taking deep root by discouraging slaveholders from moving into the territory with their human chattel, but not until 1848 was enslavement abolished throughout the region, known as the Old Northwest. And by omission Congress implied that slavery was legal in the territories south of the Ohio River.

The ordinance of 1787 also specified the process by which territorial residents could organize state governments and seek admission to the Union "on an equal footing with the original States." Early in the nation's history, therefore, Congress laid down a policy of admitting new states on the same basis as the old and assuring residents of the territories the same rights held by citizens of the original states. Having suffered under the rule of a colonial power, congressmen understood the importance of preparing the new nation's first "colony" for eventual self-government. Nineteenth- and twentieth-century Americans were to be less generous in their attitudes toward residents of later territories, many of whom were non-European or non-Protestant. But the nation never fully lost sight of the egalitarian principles of the Northwest Ordinance.

In a sense, though, in 1787 the ordinance was purely theoretical. Miamis, Shawnees, and Delawares in the region refused to acknowledge American sovereignty. They opposed settlement violently, attacking unwary pioneers who ventured too far north of the Ohio River. In 1788 the Ohio Company, to which Congress had sold a large tract of land at reduced rates, established the town of Marietta at the juncture of the Ohio and Muskingum Rivers. But Indians prevented the company from extending settlement very far into the interior.

The problems the United States encountered in ensuring safe settlement of the Northwest Territory revealed the basic weakness of the Confederation government. Not until after the Articles of Confederation were replaced with a new constitution could the United States muster sufficient force to implement the Northwest Ordinance. Thus, although the ordinance is often viewed as one of the few lasting accomplishments of the Confederation Congress, it must be seen within a context of political impotence.

## FROM CRISIS TO THE CONSTITUTION

Americans involved in finance, overseas trade, and foreign affairs became acutely aware of the inadequacies of the Articles of Confederation. Congress could not levy taxes, nor could it impose its will on the states to establish a uniform commercial policy or ensure the enforcement of treaties. Partly as a result, the American economy slid into a depression less than a year after war's end. Exporters of staple crops (especially tobacco and rice) and importers of manufactured goods suffered from the postwar restrictions that European powers imposed on American commerce. Although recovery began by 1786, the war's effects proved impossible to erase, particularly in the Lower South. Some estimates suggest that between 1775 and 1790 America's per capita gross national product declined by nearly 50 percent.

The war wrought permanent change in the American economy. The near-total cessation of foreign commerce in nonmilitary items during the war stimulated domestic manufacturing. Consequently, despite the influx of European goods after 1783, the postwar period witnessed the stirrings of American industrial development. For example, the first American textile mill began production in Pawtucket, Rhode Island, in 1793. Because of continuing population growth, the domestic market assumed greater relative importance in the overall economy. Moreover, foreign trade patterns shifted from Europe and toward the West Indies, continuing a trend that had begun before the war. Foodstuffs shipped to the French and Dutch Caribbean islands became America's largest single export, replacing tobacco (and thus accelerating the Chesapeake's conversion from tobacco to grain production). South Carolina resumed importing slaves on a large scale, as planters sought to replace workers lost to wartime disruptions. Yet without British subsidies American indigo could not compete with that produced in the

**Economic Change and Commercial Reform**

Caribbean, and even rice planters struggled to find new markets.

Recognizing the Confederation Congress's inability to deal with commercial matters, representatives of Virginia and Maryland met at Mt. Vernon (George Washington's plantation) in March 1785 to negotiate an agreement about trade on the Potomac River, which divided the two states for much of its length. The successful meeting led to an invitation to other states to discuss trade policy generally at a convention in Annapolis, Maryland. Although nine states named representatives to the meeting in September 1786, only five delegations attended. Those present realized that so few people could not have any significant impact on the political system. They issued a call for another convention, to be held in Philadelphia nine months later, "to devise such further provisions as shall . . . appear necessary to render the constitution of the federal government adequate to the exigencies of the Union."

The other states did not respond immediately. But then an armed rebellion in Massachusetts did what a polite invitation could not: convince doubters that reform was needed. Men from several western counties, many of them veterans from leading families, violently opposed high taxes levied by the eastern-dominated legislature to pay off war debts. Such obligations consisted largely of securities issued during the war to soldiers in lieu of pay and to others in return for supplies and loans. But during the hard times immediately following the war, many veterans and creditors were forced to sell the securities at heavy discounts to a relative handful of speculators. The state legislature nevertheless levied taxes to pay off the securities (plus interest) at full price in specie before the end of the decade. Men with little prospect of obtaining specie without selling their land responded furiously when the state moved to collect the new taxes.

**Shays's Rebellion**

Daniel Shays, a former officer in the Continental Army, assumed nominal leadership of the disgruntled westerners. On January 25, 1787, he led about fifteen hundred troops in an assault on the federal armory at Springfield, attempting to capture the military stores housed there. The militiamen mustered to defend the armory fired on their former comrades-in-arms, who withdrew after suffering twenty-four casualties. Some (including Shays) fled the state, never to return; two were hanged; and most escaped punishment by paying small fines and taking oaths of allegiance to Massachusetts. The state legislature, for its part, soon dramatically reduced the burden on landowners by enacting new import duties and by easing tax collections.

Even so, the words of the Shaysites reverberated around the new nation. Terming Massachusetts "tyrannical" and styling themselves "Regulators" (like backcountry Carolinians in the 1760s), they had insisted that "whenever any encroachments are made either upon the liberties or properties of the people, if redress cannot be had without, it is virtue in them to disturb government." Thus they linked their rebellion to the earlier independence struggle.

Such explosive assertions convinced many political leaders that the nation's problems extended far beyond trade policy. To some, the rebellion confirmed the need for a much stronger federal government. After most of the states had already appointed delegates, the Confederation Congress belatedly endorsed the proposed convention, "for the sole and express purpose of revising the Articles of Confederation." In mid-May 1787, fifty-five men, representing all the states but Rhode Island, assembled in Philadelphia to begin deliberations. *ALL THERE!*

## Constitutional Convention

The vast majority of delegates to the Constitutional Convention were substantial men of property. They all favored reform; otherwise, they would not have come to Philadelphia. Most wanted to give the national government new authority over taxation and foreign commerce. Yet simultaneously they sought to advance their states' interests. Many had been state legislators, and some had helped to draft state constitutions. Their understanding of the success or failure of those constitutions influenced their Philadelphia deliberations. Their ranks included merchants, planters, physicians, generals, governors, and especially lawyers—twenty-three had studied the law. Most had been born in America; many came from families that had arrived a century earlier. Most were Congregationalists, Presbyterians, or Anglicans. In an era when only a tiny handful of men had advanced education, more than half had attended college. A few had been educated in Britain, but most had graduated from American institutions: Princeton, with ten, counted the most alumni participants. The youngest delegate was twenty-six, the oldest—Benjamin Franklin—eighty-one. Like George Washington, whom they elected their presiding officer, most were in their vigorous middle years. A dozen men did the bulk of the convention's work. Of those, James Madison of Virginia most fully deserves the title "Father of the Constitution."

The frail, shy James Madison was thirty-six years old in 1787. A Princeton graduate raised in western Virginia, he served on the local Committee of Safety and was elected successively to the provincial convention, the state's lower and upper houses, and the Continental Congress (1780–1783). Although Madison returned to Virginia to serve in the state legislature in 1784, he remained

## Madison and the Constitution

▲ **James Madison (1751–1836),** the youthful scholar and skilled politician who earned the title "Father of the Constitution."

*(Library of Congress)*

← *pretty diverse group*

in touch with national politics, partly through continuing correspondence with his close friend Thomas Jefferson. A promoter of the Annapolis Convention, he strongly supported its call for further reform.

Madison stood out among the delegates for his systematic preparation for the Philadelphia meeting. Through Jefferson in Paris he bought more than two hundred books on history and government, carefully analyzing their accounts of past confederacies and republics. A month before the Constitutional Convention began, he summed up the results of his research in a lengthy paper entitled "Vices of the Political System of the United States." After listing the flaws he perceived in the current structure of the government (among them "encroachments by the states on the federal authority" and lack of unity "in matters where common interest requires it"), Madison revealed the conclusion that would guide his actions over the next few months. What the government most needed, he declared, was "such a modification of the sovereignty as will render it sufficiently neutral between the different interests and factions, to controul one part of the society from invading

*prepared & well-educated*

the rights of another, and at the same time sufficiently controuled itself, from setting up an interest adverse to that of the whole Society."

Madison thus believed that government had to be constructed in such a way that it could not become tyrannical or fall wholly under the influence of a particular faction. He regarded the large size of a potential national republic as an advantage in that respect. Rejecting the common assertion that republics had to be small to survive, Madison asserted that a large, diverse republic should be preferred. Because the nation would include many different factions, no one of them would be able to control the government. Political stability would result from compromises among the contending parties.

The so-called Virginia Plan, introduced on May 29 by Edmund Randolph, embodied Madison's conception of national government. The plan

### Virginia and New Jersey Plans

provided for a two-house legislature, the lower house elected directly by the people and the upper house selected by the lower; representation in both houses proportional to property or population; an executive elected by Congress; a national judiciary; and congressional veto over state laws. The Virginia Plan gave Congress the broad power to legislate "in all cases to which the separate states are incompetent." Had it been adopted intact, it would have created a government in which national authority reigned unchallenged and state power was greatly diminished. Proportional representation in both houses (however reckoned) would also have given large states a dominant voice in the national government.

The convention included many delegates who recognized the need for change but believed the Virginia Plan went too far in the direction of national consolidation. After two weeks of debate on Randolph's proposal, disaffected delegates—particularly those from small states—united under the leadership of William Paterson of New Jersey. On June 15 Paterson presented an alternative scheme, the New Jersey Plan, calling for strengthening the Articles rather than completely overhauling the government. Paterson proposed retaining a unicameral Congress in which each state had an equal vote, but giving Congress new powers of taxation and trade regulation. Earlier Paterson had made his position clear in debate. Asserting that the Articles were "the proper basis of all the proceedings of the convention," he contended that the delegates' proper task was "to mark the orbits of the states with due precision and provide for the use of coercion" by the national government. Although the convention initially rejected Paterson's position, he and

his allies won a number of victories in the months that followed.

The delegates began their work by discussing the structure and functions of Congress. They readily agreed that

### Debates over Congress

the new national government should have a two-house (bicameral) legislature. Further, in accordance with Americans' long-standing opposition to virtual representation, they concurred that "the people" (however that term was defined) should be directly represented in at least one house of Congress. But they discovered that they differed widely in their answers to three key questions: Should representation in both houses of Congress be proportional to population? How was representation in either or both houses to be apportioned among the states? And, finally, how were the members of the two houses to be elected?

The last issue proved the easiest to resolve. To quote John Dickinson, the delegates thought it "essential" that members of the lower branch of Congress be elected directly by the people and "expedient" that members of the upper house be chosen by state legislatures. Because legislatures had selected delegates to the Confederation Congress, they would expect a similar privilege in the new government. If the convention had not agreed to allow state legislatures to elect senators, the Constitution would have run into significant opposition among state political leaders. The plan also had the virtue of placing the election of one house of Congress one step removed from the "lesser sort," whose judgment the wealthy convention delegates did not wholly trust.

The possibility of representation proportional to population in the Senate caused considerably greater disagreement. The delegates accepted without much debate the principle of proportional representation in the House of Representatives. But small states, through their spokesman Luther Martin of Maryland, argued for equal representation in the Senate. Such a scheme, they rightly supposed, would give them relatively more power at the national level. Large states, on the other hand, supported a proportional plan, for they would then be allotted more votes in the upper house. For weeks the convention deadlocked, neither side able to obtain a majority. A committee appointed to work out a compromise recommended equal representation in the Senate, coupled with a proviso that all appropriation bills originate in the lower house. But not until the convention accepted a suggestion that a state's two senators vote as individuals rather than as a unit was a breakdown averted.

The remaining critical question divided the nation along sectional lines rather than by size of state: how was

## Slavery and the Constitution

representation in the lower house to be apportioned among states? Delegates concurred that a census should be conducted every ten years to determine the nation's actual population, and they agreed that Indians who paid no taxes should be excluded for purposes of representation. Delegates from states with large numbers of slaves wanted African and European inhabitants to be counted equally; delegates from states with few slaves wanted only free people counted. Slavery thus became inextricably linked to the foundation of the new government. Delegates resolved the dispute by using a formula developed by the Confederation Congress in 1783 to allocate financial assessments among states: three-fifths of slaves would be included in population totals. (The formula reflected delegates' judgment that slaves were less efficient producers of wealth than free people, not that they were 60 percent human and 40 percent property.) The three-fifths compromise on representation won unanimous approval. Only two delegates, Gouverneur Morris of New York and George Mason of Virginia, later spoke out against the institution of slavery.

Although the words *slave* and *slavery* do not appear in the Constitution (the framers used such euphemisms as "other persons"), the document contained both direct and indirect protections for slavery. The three-fifths clause, for example, assured white southern male voters not only congressional representation out of proportion to their numbers but also a disproportionate influence on the selection of the president, because the number of each state's votes in the electoral college (see below) was determined by the size of its congressional delegation. In return for southerners' agreement that commercial regulations could be adopted by a simple majority vote in Congress (rather than two-thirds), New Englanders agreed that Congress could not end the importation of slaves for at least twenty years. Further, the fugitive slave clause required all states to return runaways to their masters. By guaranteeing that the national government would aid any states threatened with "domestic violence," the Constitution promised aid in putting down future slave revolts, as well as incidents like Shays's Rebellion.

Once delegates agreed on the knotty, conjoined problems of slavery and representation, they readily achieved consensus on the other issues confronting them. All concurred that the national government needed the authority to tax and to regulate foreign and interstate commerce. But instead of giving Congress the

## Congressional and Presidential Powers

nearly unlimited scope proposed in the Virginia Plan, delegates enumerated congressional powers and then provided for flexibility by granting it all authority "necessary and proper" to carry out those powers. Discarding the congressional veto contained in the Virginia Plan, the convention implied but did not explicitly authorize a national judicial veto of state laws. The Constitution plus national laws and treaties would constitute "the supreme law of the land; and the judges in every state shall be bound thereby," Article VI declared ambiguously. As another means of circumscribing state powers, delegates drafted a long list of actions forbidden to states. And—contrary to many state constitutions—they provided that religious tests could never be required of U.S. officeholders.

The convention placed primary responsibility for conducting foreign affairs in the hands of a new official, the president, who was also designated commander-in-chief of the armed forces. That decision raised the question, left unspecified in the Constitution's text, of whether the president (or Congress, for that matter) acquired special powers in times of war. With the consent of the Senate, the president could appoint judges and other federal officers. To select the president, delegates established an elaborate mechanism, the electoral college, whose members would be chosen in each state by legislatures or qualified voters. If a majority of electors failed to unite behind one candidate, the House of Representatives (voting as states, not as individuals) would choose the president. Delegates also agreed that the chief executive would serve for four years but be eligible for reelection, rejecting proposals that he serve one longer term.

The final document still showed signs of its origins in the Virginia Plan, but compromises created a system of government less powerful at the national level than Madison and Randolph had envisioned. The key to the Constitution was the distribution of political authority—that is, separation of powers among executive, legislative, and judicial branches of the national government, and division of powers between states and nation (called *federalism*). Two-thirds of Congress and three-fourths of the states, for example, had to concur on amendments. The branches balanced one another, their powers deliberately entwined to prevent each from acting independently. The president could veto congressional legislation, but that veto could be overridden by two-thirds majorities in both houses, and his treaties and major appointments required the Senate's consent. Congress could impeach the president and federal judges, but courts appeared to have the final say on interpreting the Constitution. These checks and balances would make it difficult for the government to become tyrannical. At the same time, though, the elaborate system would sometimes prevent the government from acting quickly and decisively. Furthermore, the Constitution drew such a vague line between state and national powers that the United States fought a civil war in the next century over that very issue.

The convention held its last session on September 17, 1787. Of the forty-two delegates present (others had returned home weeks earlier), only three refused to sign the Constitution, two of them in part because of the lack of a bill of rights. Benjamin Franklin had written a speech calling for unity; because his weak voice could not be heard, another delegate read it for him. "I confess that there are several parts of this constitution which I do not at present approve," Franklin admitted. Yet he urged its acceptance "because I expect no better, and because I am not sure, that it is not the best." Only then was the Constitution made public. The convention's proceedings had been entirely secret—and remained so until the delegates' private notes were published in the nineteenth century. (See the appendix for the full text of the Constitution.)

## OPPOSITION AND RATIFICATION

Later the same month, the Confederation Congress submitted the Constitution to the states. The ratification clause provided for the new system to take effect once it was approved by special conventions in at least nine states, with delegates being elected by qualified voters. Thus the national Constitution, unlike the Articles of Confederation, would rest directly on popular authority (and the presumably hostile state legislatures would be circumvented).

As states began to elect delegates to the special conventions, discussion of the proposed government grew more heated. Newspaper essays and pamphlets vigorously defended or attacked the Philadelphia convention's decisions. The extent of the debate was unprecedented. Every newspaper in the country printed the full text of the Constitution, and most supported its adoption. It quickly became apparent, though, that disputes within the Constitutional Convention had been mild compared to divisions of opinion within the populace as a whole. Although most citizens concurred that the national government should have more power over taxation and foreign and interstate commerce, some believed that the proposed

In August 1787 a first draft of the Constitution was secretly printed in Philadelphia for the use of convention members. Wide margins left room for additions and amendments, such as those made on this copy by the South Carolina delegate Pierce Butler. Note that in this early version the preamble does not yet read "We the people of the United States," but instead begins by listing the individual states.

*(The Gilder Lehrman Collection, © Collection of the New York Historical Society, courtesy of the Gilder Lehrman Institute of American History at the New York Historical Society.)*

*opposite*

government held the potential for tyranny. As happened in Carlisle, Pennsylvania, the vigorous debate between the two sides frequently spilled out into the streets.

Those supporting the proposed Constitution called themselves Federalists. They built on the notions of clas-

## Federalists and Antifederalists

sical republicanism, holding forth a vision of a virtuous, collectivist, self-sacrificing republic vigorously led by a manly aristocracy of talent.
Claiming that the nation did not need to fear centralized authority when good men drawn from the elite were in charge, they argued that the carefully structured government would preclude the possibility of tyranny. A republic could be large, they declared, if the government's design prevented any one group from controlling it. The separation of powers among legislative, executive, and judicial branches, and the division of powers between states and nation, would accomplish that goal. Thus people did not need to be protected in a formal way from the powers of the new government. Instead, their liberties would be guarded by "distinguished worthies"—men of the "better sort" whose only goal (said George Washington) was "to merit the approbation of good and virtuous men."

The Federalists termed those who opposed the Constitution Antifederalists, thus casting them in a negative light. Antifederalists, while recognizing the need for a national source of revenue, feared a too-powerful central government. They saw the states as the chief protectors of individual rights; consequently, weakening the states could bring the onset of arbitrary power. Antifederalist arguments against the Constitution often consisted of lists of potential abuses of government authority.

Heirs of the Real Whig ideology of the late 1760s and early 1770s, Antifederalists stressed the need for constant popular vigilance to avert oppression. Indeed, some of the Antifederalists had originally promulgated those ideas—Samuel Adams, Patrick Henry, and Richard Henry Lee led the opposition to the Constitution. Such older Americans, whose political opinions had been shaped prior to the centralizing, nationalistic Revolution, peopled the Antifederalist ranks. Joining them were small farmers preoccupied with guarding their property against excessive taxation, backcountry Baptists and Presbyterians, and ambitious, upwardly mobile men who would benefit from an economic and political system less tightly controlled than that the Constitution envisioned. Federalists denigrated such men as disorderly, licentious, and even "unmanly" and "boyish" because they would not follow the elites' lead in supporting the Constitution.

As public debate continued, Antifederalists focused on the Constitution's lack of a bill of rights. Even if the

## Bill of Rights

new system weakened the states, critics believed, people could still be protected from tyranny by specific guarantees of rights. The Constitution did contain some prohibitions on congressional power. For example, the writ of habeas corpus, which prevented arbitrary imprisonment, could not be suspended except in "cases of rebellion or invasion." But Antifederalists found such constitutional provisions to be few and inadequate. Nor were they reassured by Federalist assertions that the new government could not violate people's rights because

*YES*

FEDERAL HALL·

LET Trumpets found, and fwift wing'd Fame,
Thefe glorious tidings far proclaim ;
On Virtue's bafe, by Wifdom plann'd ;
And rear'd by Union's facred hand ;
The FEDERAL DOME, is rais'd fublime :
Its PILLARS folid, ftrong as time ;
Rife ! Commerce ! rife ! unfurl the fail,
Rich Golden harvefts blefs the vale :
Arts ! Science ! Genius ! fpring to light ;
And Freedom burft on realms of Night

▲ *The Federal Almanack* for 1789 trumpeted the virtues of the new Constitution. Not all Americans were so certain that the national government, here symbolized as an edifice supported by thirteen pillars, was as "solid, strong as time" as the printer proclaimed. *(American Antiquarian Society)*

it had only limited powers. Opponents wanted the national governing document to incorporate a bill of rights, as had most state constitutions.

*Letters of a Federal Farmer,* perhaps the most widely read Antifederalist pamphlet, listed the rights that should be protected: freedom of the press and religion, trial by jury, and guarantees against unreasonable searches. From Paris, Thomas Jefferson added his voice to the chorus. Replying to Madison's letter conveying a copy of the Constitution, Jefferson declared, "I like much the general idea" but not "the omission of a bill of rights. . . . A bill of rights is what the people are entitled to against every government on earth, general or particular, and what no just government should refuse, or rest on inference."

As state conventions considered ratification, delegates tended to put state and local interests first. Thus many were persuaded when Federalists argued that the establishment of a national government with the power to tax foreign commerce

### Ratification

would lessen the financial burdens that had prompted Shays's Rebellion and localized protests in other states. Yet the lack of a bill of rights loomed ever larger as a flaw in the proposed government. Four of the first five states to ratify did so unanimously, but serious disagreements then surfaced. Massachusetts, in which Antifederalist forces had been bolstered by a backlash against the state government's heavy-handed treatment of the Shays rebels, ratified by a majority of only 19 votes out of 355 cast and recommended amendments identifying rights. In June 1788, when New Hampshire ratified, the requirement of nine states was satisfied. But New York and Virginia had not yet voted, and everyone realized the new Constitution could not succeed unless those key states accepted it.

Despite a valiant effort by the Antifederalist Patrick Henry, pro-Constitution forces won by 10 votes in the Virginia convention, which likewise recommended the addition of specifications of rights. In New York, James Madison, John Jay, and Alexander Hamilton, writing collectively as "Publius," published *The Federalist,* a series of

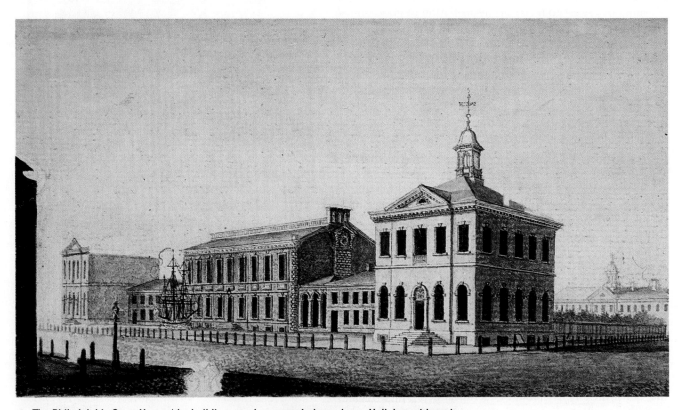

▲ The Philadelphia State House (the building now known as Independence Hall, but without its familiar tower), on the left; and, to its right, Congress Hall, where Congress met when Philadelphia served as the U.S. capital. Portrayed in front of the state house in this 1792 watercolor is the 33-foot-long vessel *Union,* an elaborately constructed ship carried through the city streets in the grand ratification parade of July 4, 1788. *(Philadelphia Museum of Art, Lent by the Dietrich American Foundation)*

eighty-five political essays explaining the theory behind the Constitution and masterfully answering its critics. Their reasoned arguments, coupled with Federalists' promise to add a bill of rights to the Constitution, helped win the battle. On July 26, 1788, New York ratified the Constitution by the slim margin of 3 votes. Although the last states—North Carolina and Rhode Island—did not join the Union until November 1789 and May 1790, respectively, the new government was a reality.

Americans in many cities celebrated ratification (somewhat prematurely) with a series of parades on July 4, 1788, ritualistically linking the acceptance of the Constitution to the formal adoption of the Declaration of Independence. The carefully planned processions dramatized the history and symbolized the unity of the new nation, seeking to counteract memories of the dissent that had so recently engulfed such towns as Carlisle, Pennsylvania. Like pre-Revolution protest meetings, the parades served as polit-

**Celebrating Ratification**

ical lessons for literate and illiterate Americans alike. The processions aimed to educate men and women about the significance of the new Constitution and to instruct them about political leaders' hopes for industry and frugality on the part of a virtuous American public.

Symbols expressing those goals filled the Philadelphia parade, planned by the artist Charles Willson Peale. About five thousand people participated in the procession, which featured floats portraying such themes as "The Grand Federal Edifice" and stretched for a mile and a half. Marchers representing the first pioneers and Revolutionary War troops paraded with groups of farmers and artisans dramatizing their work. More than forty groups of tradesmen, including barbers, hatters, printers, cloth manufacturers, and clockmakers, sponsored floats. Lawyers, doctors, clergymen of all denominations, and congressmen followed the artisans. A final group of marchers symbolized the nation's future: students from the University of Pennsylvania and other city schools bore a flag labeled "The Rising Generation."

## *Legacy* FOR A PEOPLE AND A NATION

### The Township and Range System

Anyone flying over the American countryside west of the Appalachians today can see the impact of the township and range system inscribed on the landscape. Roads cross the land in straight lines, meeting at 90-degree angles, carving the terrain into a checkerboard pattern. That system of land surveys originated in the Land Ordinance of 1785, developed to organize land sales in the Northwest Territory.

Both English and native peoples traditionally bounded their lands by using such natural landmarks as hills, streams, large trees, and prominent rock outcroppings. That system, known as *metes and bounds,* produced such property descriptions as this one from 1667 in Maine: a "certen Parcell of upland . . . lying on the South West side of the . . . island, next [to] the Mussell Ridge & soe to the Sea Wall, & soe Joyneing to the Marsh." Even in the colonies' earliest days, though, some settlers employed surveyors, who created lots of varying sizes divided by lines laid out abstractly on the soil. Sometimes those lines related to natural features, such as the long, narrow lots in French Canada that fronted on the St. Lawrence River; other times they bore little relationship to

the land. But because North America was settled in piecemeal fashion at various times and using different methods of land distribution, no one system dominated—not, at least, until the Land Ordinance of 1785. From then on, the system the ordinance described became the template for all land distributions by the U.S. government.

After a surveyor established an east-west baseline and a north-south meridian on a particular tract, he laid out rectangular townships composed of thirty-six numbered square-mile sections. He paid no attention to natural features; potential buyers were supposed to learn for themselves which sections had rivers, hills, or desirable assets like salt licks. The initial policy of selling sections as units, all priced the same, gave way by 1832 to a system in which individuals could purchase as few as 40 acres and, after 1854, to price variations. As the United States expanded its reach westward across the continent, the township and range system followed, democratizing access to land and methodically opening land for settlement.

The legacy of the Land Ordinance of 1785 for the American people and nation still marks the landscape everywhere west of the Ohio River.

## SUMMARY

During the 1770s and 1780s the nation took shape as a political union. It began to develop an economy independent of the British Empire and attempted to chart its own course in the world in order to protect the national interest, defend the country's borders, and promote beneficial trade. Some Americans prescribed guidelines for the cultural and intellectual life they thought appropriate for a republic, outlining artistic and educational goals for a properly virtuous people. An integral part of the formation of the Union was the systematic formulation of American racist thought. Emphasizing race (rather than status as slave or free) as a determinant of African Americans' standing in the nation allowed men who now termed themselves "white" to define republicanism to exclude most men but themselves and to ensure that they would dominate the country for the foreseeable future. White women, viewed primarily as household dependents, had a limited role to play in the republic, as mothers of the next generation and as selfless contributors to the nation's welfare.

The experience of fighting a war and struggling for survival as an independent nation altered the political context of American life in the 1780s. In 1775 most Americans believed that "that government which governs best governs least," but by the late 1780s many had changed their minds. They were the drafters and supporters of the Constitution, who concluded from the republic's vicissitudes under the Articles of Confederation that a more powerful central government was needed. During ratification debates they contended that their proposals were just as "republican" in conception as (if not more so than) the Articles.

Both sides concurred in a general adherence to republican principles, but they emphasized different views of republicanism. Federalists advanced a position based on the principles of classical republicanism, stressing the community over the individual. Antifederalists, fearing that elected leaders would not subordinate personal gain to the good of the whole, wanted a weak central government, formal protection of individual rights, and a loosely regulated economy. The Federalists won their point when the Constitution was adopted, however narrowly. The process of consolidating the states into a national whole was thereby formalized. The 1790s, the first decade of government under the Constitution, would witness hesitant steps toward the creation of a true nation, the United States of America.

## SUGGESTIONS FOR FURTHER READING

Richard Beeman et al., eds., *Beyond Confederation: Origins of the Constitution and American National Identity* (1987)

Carol Berkin, *A Brilliant Solution: Inventing the American Constitution* (2002)

Ira Berlin and Ronald Hoffman, eds., *Slavery and Freedom in the Age of the American Revolution* (1983)

Cathy N. Davidson, *Revolution and the Word: The Rise of the Novel in America* (1987)

Edith Gelles, *Portia: The World of Abigail Adams* (1992)

Peter S. Onuf, *Statehood and Union: A History of the Northwest Ordinance* (1987)

Jack N. Rakove, *Original Meanings: Politics and Ideas in the Making of the Constitution* (1996)

Leonard L. Richards, *Shays's Rebellion: The American Revolution's Final Battle* (2002)

David Waldstreicher, *In the Midst of Perpetual Fetes: The Making of American Nationalism, 1776–1820* (1997)

Gordon S. Wood, *The Creation of the American Republic, 1776–1787* (1969)

*For a more extensive list for further reading, go to* college.hmco.com/pic/norton8e.

# The Early Republic: Conflicts at Home and Abroad *1789-1800*

𝓘n the last months of 1798, wealthy Philadelphia matron Deborah Norris Logan became the target of widespread public criticism. Her husband, Jefferson supporter Dr. George Logan, had undertaken a personal peace mission to France, fearing the looming prospect of war between the United States and its former ally. In her husband's absence, Logan's wife loyally defended his actions, and she in turn had to endure a campaign unlike any an American woman had previously experienced. That such an episode could occur at all suggests simultaneously the political symbolism now embodied by women, the growing division between the factions known as Federalists and Republicans, and the significance of foreign affairs in the early republic.

First to attack was "Peter Porcupine," the Federalist newspaper editor William Cobbett, who observed with sly sexual innuendo in his *Porcupine's Gazette* in July that "it is said that JEFFERSON went to his friend Doctor Logan's farm and spent three days there, soon after the Doctor's departure for France. *Query:* What did he do there? Was it to arrange the Doctor's *valuable manuscripts?*" Later Cobbett suggested that both George and Deborah Logan should be placed in a pillory and publicly shamed for their actions—him, presumably, for treason (for that was the crime of which Federalists accused him) and her, Cobbett implied, for adultery. Understanding the symbolic significance of women's virtuous conduct in the fragile young republic, Republican newspapers leaped to Deborah's defense. They attacked the vulgarity of the suggestions about her and Vice President Jefferson, and insisted that not even a corrupt Londoner could have written "a greater libel upon public virtue or national morals."

◀ George and Deborah Logan, whose activities caused so much political controversy in 1798. Their elegant house, Stenton, where Jefferson visited her in her husband's absence, is still preserved as a historic site.

*(Left: Historical Society of Pennsylvania. Collection Atwater Kent Museum of Philadelphia. Right: Courtesy of the National Society of Colonial Dames of America in the Commonwealth of Pennsylvania at Stenton, Philadelphia)*

## CHRONOLOGY

1789 ■ Washington inaugurated as first president
 ■ Judiciary Act of 1789 organizes federal court system
 ■ French Revolution begins

1790 ■ Hamilton's *Report on Public Credit* proposes assumption of state debts

1791 ■ First ten amendments (Bill of Rights) ratified
 ■ First national bank chartered

1793 ■ France declares war on Britain, Spain, and the Netherlands
 ■ Washington's neutrality proclamation keeps the United States out of war
 ■ Democratic-Republican societies founded, the first grassroots political organizations

1794 ■ Wayne defeats Miami Confederacy at Fallen Timbers
 ■ Whiskey Rebellion in western Pennsylvania protests taxation

1795 ■ Jay Treaty with England resolves issues remaining from the Revolution
 ■ Pinckney's Treaty with Spain establishes southern boundary of the United States
 ■ Treaty of Greenville with Miami Confederacy opens Ohio to settlement

1796 ■ First contested presidential election: Adams elected president, Jefferson vice president

1798 ■ XYZ affair arouses American opinion against France
 ■ Sedition Act penalizes dissent
 ■ Virginia and Kentucky Resolutions protest suppression of dissent

1798–99 ■ Quasi-War with France
 ■ Fries's Rebellion in Pennsylvania protests taxation

1800 ■ Franco-American Convention ends Quasi-War
 ■ Gabriel's Rebellion threatens Virginia slave-owners

1801 ■ Thomas Jefferson elected president by the House of Representatives after stalemate in electoral college

Deborah Logan remained resolute in the face of such publicity. Although at first she secluded herself at her country estate, on Jefferson's advice she returned to Philadelphia to prove to the world George's "innocence and honor" and to show that she was "not afraid nor ashamed to meet the public eye." As reports emerged that her husband had been cordially received by French leaders and that he had had some success in quelling hostilities, she reveled in the praise subsequently showered on him, later recalling that "almost every day, wishes for his safety and speedy return greeted my ears." George Logan was indeed enthusiastically welcomed home, at least by Jeffersonian partisans. Congress, controlled by Federalists, was less impressed. In January 1799 it adopted the so-called Logan Act, still in effect, which forbids private citizens from undertaking diplomatic missions.

The controversy caused by the Logans' actions was but one of many such battles in the 1790s. The fight over ratifying the Constitution turned out to presage an even wider division over the major political, economic, and diplomatic questions confronting the young republic: the extent to which authority (especially fiscal authority and taxation) should be centralized in the national government; the relationship between national power and states' rights; the formulation of foreign policy in an era of continual warfare in Europe; and the limits of dissent. Americans had not anticipated the acrimonious disagreements that rocked the 1790s. Believing that the Constitution would resolve the problems that had arisen under the Confederation, they mistakenly expected the new government to rule largely by consensus. And no one predicted the difficulties that would develop as the United States attempted to deal with Indian nations now wholly encompassed within its borders.

Most important, perhaps, Americans could not understand or fully accept the division of the nation's citizens into two competing factions. In republics, they believed, the rise of such factions signified decay and corruption. Yet on numerous occasions, as happened with Deborah and George Logan, Federalist and Republican leaders sought to mobilize their respective supporters through publications and public gatherings, thereby reworking the nation's political practice if not its theory. As the decade closed, Americans still had not come to terms with the implications of partisan politics, as was vividly illustrated by the fierce debates accompanying the election of 1800.

- What major challenges confronted the new republic?
- What issues caused disputes among the nation's citizens?
- How did Americans react to those disputes?

## BUILDING A WORKABLE GOVERNMENT

At first, consensus appeared possible, as the nationalistic spirit expressed in the processions celebrating ratification of the Constitution carried over to the first session of Congress. Only a few Antifederalists ran for office in the congressional elections held late in 1788, and even fewer were elected. Thus the First Congress consisted chiefly of men who supported a strong national government. The drafters of the Constitution had deliberately left many key issues undecided, so the nationalists' domination of Congress meant that their views on those points quickly prevailed.

Congress faced four immediate tasks when it convened in April 1789: raising revenue to support the new

**First Congress**

government, responding to states' calls for a bill of rights, setting up executive departments, and organizing the federal judiciary. The last task was especially important. The Constitution established a Supreme Court but left it to Congress to decide whether to have other federal courts.

James Madison, representing Virginia in the House of Representatives, soon became as influential in Congress as he had been at the Constitutional Convention. A few months into the first session, he persuaded Congress to adopt the Revenue Act of 1789, imposing a 5 percent tariff on certain imports. Thus the First Congress quickly achieved what the Confederation Congress never had: an effective national tax law. The new government would have problems in its first years, but lack of revenue would not be one of them.

Madison also took the lead with respect to constitutional amendments. During and after the convention, he

**Bill of Rights**

had opposed additional limitations on the national government. He believed it unnecessary to guarantee people's rights explicitly when the government had limited powers. But Madison recognized that Congress should respond to amendments proposed in state ratifying conventions. Accordingly, he introduced

nineteen amendments, based on those presented in the states. The states formally ratified ten, which officially became part of the Constitution on December 15, 1791 (see the appendix for the Constitution and all amendments, including the Twenty-seventh, which was one of Madison's nineteen). Their adoption defused Antifederalist opposition and rallied support for the new government.

The First Amendment prohibited Congress from passing any law restricting the right to freedom of religion, speech, press, peaceable assembly, or petition. The next two amendments arose directly from the former colonists' fear of standing armies. The Second Amendment guaranteed the right "to keep and bear arms," because of the need for a "well-regulated Militia." Thus the constitutional right to bear arms was based on the expectation that most able-bodied men would serve the nation as citizen-soldiers, and there would be little need for a permanent army. The Third Amendment limited the conditions under which troops could be quartered in private homes. The next five pertained to judicial procedures. The Fourth Amendment prohibited "unreasonable searches and seizures"; the Fifth and Sixth established the rights of accused persons; the Seventh specified the conditions for jury trials in civil (as opposed to criminal) cases; and the Eighth forbade "cruel and unusual punishments." The Ninth and Tenth Amendments reserved to the people and the states other unspecified rights and powers. In short, the amendments' authors insisted that, in listing some rights, they did not mean to preclude the exercise of others.

While debating proposed amendments, Congress also considered the organization of the executive branch.

**Executive and Judiciary**

It readily agreed to continue the three administrative departments established under the Articles of Confederation: War, Foreign Affairs (renamed State), and Treasury. Congress instituted two lesser posts: the attorney general—the nation's official lawyer—and the postmaster general. Controversy arose over whether the president alone could dismiss officials whom he had originally appointed with the Senate's consent. After some debate, the House and Senate agreed that he had such authority. That established the important principle that the heads of executive departments are accountable solely to the president.

The most far-reaching law that the First Congress adopted, the Judiciary Act of 1789, defined the jurisdiction of the federal judiciary and established a six-member Supreme Court, thirteen district courts, and three circuit courts of appeal. Its most important provision, Section 25, allowed appeals from state to federal courts when cases raised certain types of constitutional questions.

The act presumed that Article VI of the Constitution, which stated that federal statutes and treaties were to be considered "the supreme Law of the Land," implied the right of appeal from state to federal courts, yet the Constitution did not explicitly permit such actions. In the nineteenth century, judges and legislators committed to states' rights would challenge the constitutionality of Section 25.

During its first decade, the Supreme Court handled few cases of any importance, and several members resigned. (John Jay, the first chief justice, served only six years.) But in a significant 1796 decision, *Ware v. Hylton,* the Court for the first time declared a state law unconstitutional. That same year it also reviewed the constitutionality of an act of Congress, upholding its validity in the case of *Hylton v. U.S.* The most important case of the decade, *Chisholm v. Georgia* (1793), established that states could be sued in federal courts by citizens of other states. Five years later, the Eleventh Amendment to the Constitution overturned that decision, which was unpopular with state governments.

Despite the constitutional provisions forbidding Congress from prohibiting the importation of slaves for twenty years, in early 1790 three groups of Quakers submitted petitions to Congress favoring abolition and calling for an end to slave importations. In the ensuing debates, the nation's first political leaders directly addressed the questions they had suppressed in euphemisms in the Constitution. Southerners vigorously asserted that Congress should not only reject the petitions, but also not even discuss them. Had southern states thought that the federal government would consider interfering with the institution of slavery, such congressmen argued, they would never have ratified the Constitution. The legislators developed a positive defense of slavery that forecast most of the arguments offered on the subject during the next seven decades. They insisted that slavery was integral to the Union and that abolition would cause more problems than it solved, primarily by confronting the nation with the question of how to deal with a sizable population of freed people.

**Debate over Slavery**

Some northern congressmen—and, in his last published essay, Benjamin Franklin—contested the southerners' position, but a consensus soon emerged to quash such discussions in the future. Congress accepted a committee report denying it the power either to halt slave importations before 1808 or to emancipate slaves at any time, that authority "remaining with the several States alone." The precedent that Congress could not abolish slavery held until the Civil War.

## DOMESTIC POLICY UNDER WASHINGTON AND HAMILTON

George Washington did not seek the presidency. In 1783 he returned to Mount Vernon eager for the peaceful life of a Virginia planter. But his fellow countrymen never regarded Washington as just another private citizen. Unanimously elected to preside at the Constitutional Convention, he did not participate in debates but consistently voted for a strong national government. After the adoption of the new governmental structure, Americans concurred that only George Washington had sufficient stature to serve as the republic's first president, an office designed largely with him in mind. The unanimous vote of the electoral college merely formalized that consensus.

Reluctant to return to public life, George Washington nevertheless knew he could not ignore his country's call. Awaiting the summons to New York City, the nation's capital, he wrote to an old friend, "My movements to the chair of Government will be accompanied by feelings not unlike those of a culprit who is going to the place of his execution. . . . I am sensible, that I am embarking the voice of my Countrymen and a good name of my own, on this voyage, but what returns will be made for them, Heaven alone can foretell." Symbolically he donned a suit of homespun for the inaugural ceremony.

Washington acted cautiously during his first months in office in 1789, knowing that whatever he did would set precedents for the future. When the title by which he should be addressed aroused controversy (Vice President John Adams favored "His Highness, the President of the United States of America, and Protector of their Liberties"), Washington said nothing. The accepted title soon became a plain "Mr. President." By using the heads of the executive departments collectively as his chief advisers, he created the cabinet. As the Constitution required, he sent Congress an annual State of the Union message. Washington also concluded that he should exercise his veto power over congressional legislation sparingly—only, indeed, if he became convinced a bill was unconstitutional.

**Washington's First Steps**

Early in his term, Washington undertook elaborately organized journeys to all the states. At each stop, he was ritually welcomed by uniformed militia units, young women strewing flowers in his path, local leaders, groups of Revolutionary War veterans, and respectable citizens who presented him with formal addresses reaffirming their loyalty to the United States. The president thus personally came to embody national unity, simultaneously drawing ordinary folk into the sphere of national politics.

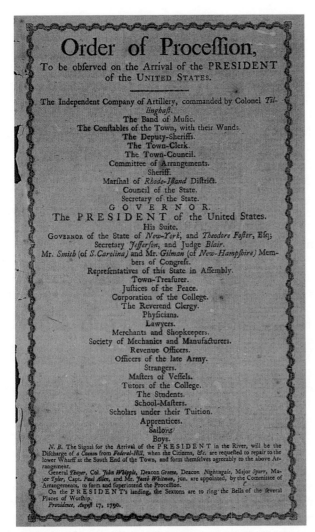

## Order of Procession,

To be observed on the Arrival of the PRESIDENT of the UNITED STATES.

The Independent Company of Artillery, commanded by Colonel *Tillinghaft*.
The Band of Mufic.
The Conftables of the Town, with their Wands.
The Deputy-Sheriffs.
The Town-Clerk.
The Town-Council.
Committee of Arrangements.
Sheriff.
Marfhal of *Rhode-Ifland* Diftrict.
Council of the State.
Secretary of the State.
G O V E R N O R.
The P R E S I D E N T of the United States.
His Suite.
GOVERNOR of the State of *New-York*, and *Theodore Fofter*, Efq;
Secretary *Jefferfon*, and Judge *Blair*.
Mr. *Smith* (of *S. Carolina*) and Mr. *Gilman* (of *New-Hampfhire*) Members of Congrefs.
Reprefentatives of this State in Affembly.
Town-Treafurer.
Juftices of the Peace.
Corporation of the College.
The Reverend Clergy.
Phyficians.
Lawyers.
Merchants and Shopkeepers.
Society of Mechanics and Manufacturers.
Revenue Officers.
Officers of the late Army.
Strangers.
Mafters of Veffels.
Tutors of the College.
The Students.
School-Mafters.
Scholars under their Tuition.
Apprentices.
Sailors.
Boys.
*N. B.* The Signal for the Arrival of the P R E S I D E N T in the River, will be the Difcharge of *a Cannon* from *Federal-Hill*, when the Citizens, &c. are requefted to repair to the lower Wharf at the South End of the Town, and form themfelves agreeably to the above Arrangement.
General *Thayer*, Col. *John Whipple*, Deacon *Greene*, Deacon *Nightingale*, Major *Spurr*, Major *Tyler*, Capt. *Paul Allen*, and Mr. *Jacob Whitman*, jun. are appointed, by the Committee of Arrangements, to form and fuperintend the Procession.
On the P R E S I D E N T's landing, the Sextons are to ring the Bells of the feveral Places of Worfhip.
*Providence, Auguft* 17, 1790.

▲ When George Washington toured the nation during his first term in office, he was greeted by local leaders in elaborately orchestrated rituals. The organizers of the ceremony at Providence, Rhode Island, on August 17, 1790, issued this broadside to inform participants of their plans for a formal procession. While some Americans gloried in such displays of pomp, others feared they presaged the return of monarchy.

*(The Huntington Library & Art Collections, San Marino, California)*

Washington's first major task as president was to choose the heads of the executive departments. For the War Department he selected an old comrade-in-arms, Henry Knox of Massachusetts, who had been his reliable general of artillery during much of the Revolution. His choice for the State Department was his fellow Virginian Thomas Jefferson, who had just returned to the United States from his post as minister to France. And for the crucial position of secretary of the treasury, the president chose the brilliant, intensely ambitious Alexander Hamilton.

The illegitimate son of a Scottish aristocrat and a woman whose husband had divorced her for adultery and desertion, Hamilton was born in the British West Indies in 1757. His early years were spent in poverty; after his mother's death when he was eleven, he worked as a clerk for a mercantile firm. In 1773 Hamilton enrolled at King's College (later Columbia University) in New York City. Only eighteen months later, in late 1774, the precocious seventeen-year-old contributed a pamphlet to the prerevolutionary publication wars. Devoted to the patriot cause, Hamilton volunteered for service in the American army, where he came to Washington's attention. In 1777 Washington appointed the young man as one of his aides, and the two developed great mutual affection.

### Alexander Hamilton

The general's patronage helped the poor youth of dubious background to marry well. At twenty-three he wed Elizabeth Schuyler, daughter of a wealthy New York family. After the war, Hamilton practiced law in New York City and served as a delegate to the Annapolis Convention and later the Constitutional Convention. Although he exerted little influence at either gathering, his contributions to *The Federalist* in 1788 revealed him as one of the chief political thinkers in the republic.

In his dual role as treasury secretary and presidential adviser, Hamilton exhibited two traits distinguishing him from most of his contemporaries. First, his primary loyalty lay with the nation. Caribbean-born, Hamilton had no natal ties to any state; he neither sympathized with nor fully understood demands for local autonomy. His fiscal policies always aimed at consolidating national power. Hamilton never feared the exercise of centralized executive authority, as did older compatriots who had clashed repeatedly with colonial governors, and he openly favored maintaining close political and economic ties with Britain.

Second, Hamilton regarded his fellow humans with unvarnished cynicism. Perhaps because of his difficult early life and his own overriding ambition, Hamilton believed people to be motivated primarily by self-interest—particularly economic self-interest. He placed no reliance on people's capacity for virtuous, self-sacrificing behavior. This outlook set him apart from those Americans who foresaw a rosy future in which public-spirited citizens would pursue the common good rather than their own private advantage. Although other Americans (for instance, James Madison) also stressed the role of private interests in a republic, Hamilton went further in his emphasis on self-interest as the major motivator of human

▲ John Trumbull, known primarily for his larger-than-life portraits of patriot leaders, painted this miniature (c. 1792–1794) of George Washington, who posed for it during his presidency.

*(Division of Political History, Smithsonian Institution, Washington, D.C.)*

▲ Alexander Hamilton, by James Sharpless, about 1796. This profile of Hamilton, painted near the end of Washington's presidency, shows the secretary of the treasury as he looked during the years of his first heated partisan battles with Thomas Jefferson and James Madison.

*(National Portrait Gallery, Smithsonian Institution/Art Resource, NY)*

behavior. Those beliefs significantly influenced the way he tackled the monumental task before him: straightening out the new nation's tangled finances.

Congress ordered the new secretary of the treasury to assess the public debt and to submit recommendations for supporting the government's credit. Hamilton found that the country's remaining war debts fell into three categories: those owed by the nation to foreign governments and investors, mostly to France (about $11 million); those owed by the national government to merchants, former soldiers, holders of revolutionary bonds, and the like (about $27 million); and, finally, similar debts owed by state governments (roughly $25 million). With respect to the national debt, few disagreed: Americans recognized that, if their new government was to succeed, it would have to repay at full face value those financial obligations the nation had incurred while winning independence.

The state debts were another matter. Some states—notably, Virginia, Maryland, North Carolina, and Georgia—had already paid off most of their war debts

**National and State Debts**

by levying taxes and handing out land grants in lieu of monetary payments. They would oppose the national government's assumption of responsibility for other states' debts because their citizens would be taxed to pay such obligations. Massachusetts, Connecticut, and South Carolina, by contrast, still had sizable unpaid debts and would welcome a system of national assumption. The possible assumption of state debts also had political implications. Consolidating the debt in the hands of the national government would help to concentrate economic and political power at the national level. A contrary policy would reserve greater independence of action for the states.

Hamilton's first *Report on Public Credit,* sent to Congress in January 1790, stimulated lively debate. The treasury secretary proposed that Congress assume outstanding state debts, combine them with national obligations, and issue new securities covering both principal and accumulated unpaid interest. Hamilton thereby hoped to ensure that holders of the public debt—many of them wealthy merchants and speculators—had a significant fi-

**Hamilton's Financial Plan**

nancial stake in the new government's survival. The opposition coalesced around James Madison, who opposed the assumption of state debts for two reasons. First, his state of Virginia had already paid off most of its obligations, and second, he wanted to avoid rewarding wealthy speculators who had purchased state and national debt certificates at a small fraction of their face value from needy veterans and farmers.

Prompted in part by Madison, the House initially rejected the assumption of state debts. The Senate, however, adopted Hamilton's plan largely intact. A series of compromises followed, in which the assumption bill became linked to the other major controversial issue of that congressional session: the location of the permanent national capital. Several related political deals were struck. A southern site on the Potomac River (favored by Washington and close to Mount Vernon) was selected for the capital, and the first part of Hamilton's financial program became law in August 1790.

Four months later, Hamilton submitted to Congress a second report on public credit, recommending the chartering of a national bank modeled on the Bank of England. This proposal, too, aroused much opposition, primarily after Congress had already voted to establish the bank.

**First Bank of the United States**

The Bank of the United States, to be chartered for twenty years, was to be capitalized at $10 million. Just $2 million would come from public funds, while private investors supplied the rest. The bank would act as collecting and disbursing agent for the Treasury, and its notes would circulate as the nation's currency. Most political leaders recognized that such an institution would be beneficial, especially because it would solve the problem of America's perpetual shortage of an acceptable medium of exchange. But another issue loomed large: did the Constitution give Congress the power to establish such a bank?

James Madison answered that question with a resounding no. He pointed out that Constitutional Convention delegates had specifically rejected a clause authorizing Congress to issue corporate charters. Consequently, he argued, that power could not be inferred from other parts of the Constitution. Madison's contention disturbed President Washington, who decided to request other opinions before signing the bill into law. Edmund Randolph, the attorney general, and Thomas Jefferson, the secretary of state, agreed with Madison that the bank was unconstitutional. Jefferson referred to Article I, Section 8, of the Constitution, which gave Congress the power

**Interpreting the Constitution**

"to make all Laws which shall be necessary and proper for carrying into Execution the foregoing Powers." The key word, Jefferson argued, was *necessary*: Congress could do what was needed, but without specific constitutional authorization could not do what was merely desirable. Thus Jefferson formulated the strict-constructionist interpretation of the Constitution.

Washington asked Hamilton to reply to the negative assessments of his proposal. Hamilton's *Defense of the Constitutionality of the Bank*, presented to the president in February 1791, brilliantly expounded a broad-constructionist view of the Constitution. Hamilton argued forcefully that Congress could choose any means not specifically prohibited by the Constitution to achieve a constitutional end. He reasoned thus: if the end was constitutional and the means was not *un*constitutional, then the means was constitutional.

Washington concurred, and the bill became law. The bank proved successful, as did the scheme for funding the national debt and assuming the states' debts. The new nation's securities became desirable investments for its own citizens and for wealthy foreigners, especially those in the Netherlands, who rushed to purchase American debt certificates. The influx of new capital, coupled with the high prices that American grain now commanded in European markets, eased farmers' debt burdens and contributed to a new prosperity. But two other aspects of Alexander Hamilton's wide-ranging financial scheme did not fare so well.

In December 1791, Hamilton presented to Congress his *Report on Manufactures*, the third and last of his prescriptions for the American economy. It outlined an ambitious plan for encouraging and protecting the United States' infant industries, such as shoemaking and textile manufacturing. Hamilton argued that the nation could never be truly independent as long as it relied heavily on Europe for manufactured goods. He urged Congress to promote the immigration of technicians and laborers, and to support industrial development through a limited use of protective tariffs. Many of Hamilton's ideas were implemented in later decades, but few congressmen in 1791 could see much merit in his proposals. They firmly believed that America's future lay in agriculture and the carrying trade, and that the mainstay of the republic was the yeoman farmer. Congress therefore rejected the report.

**Report on Manufactures**

That same year Congress accepted another feature of Hamilton's financial program, levying an excise tax on whiskey distilled within the United States. Although proceeds from the Revenue Act of 1789 covered the interest on

PAPER STAINING MANUFACTORY

BOSTON   1800.

Eben. Clough
Paper Stainer
near
Charles Riv. Bridge
– BOSTON. –
Manufactures &
keeps constantly
for sale a
great variety of
Paper Hangings

Americans, Encourage the Manufactories of your Country, if you wish for its prosperity.

▲ Although Congress did not react positively to the arguments in Hamilton's *Report on Manufactures*, the owners of America's burgeoning industries recognized the importance of the policy Hamilton advocated. Ebenezer Clough, a Boston maker of wallpaper, incorporated into his letterhead the exhortation "Americans, Encourage the Manufactories of your Country, if you wish for its prosperity." *(American Antiquarian Society)*

the national debt, the decision to fund state debts meant that the national government required additional income. A tax on whiskey affected relatively few westerners—the farmers who grew corn and the small and large distillers who turned that corn into whiskey—and might also reduce the consumption of whiskey. (Eighteenth-century Americans, notorious for their heavy drinking, consumed about twice as much alcohol per capita as today's rate.) Moreover, Hamilton knew that those western farmers and distillers were Jefferson's supporters, and he saw the benefits of taxing them rather than the merchants who favored his own policies.

News of the tax set off protests in frontier areas of Pennsylvania, where residents were dissatisfied with the army's defense of their region from threats of Indian attack. To their minds, the same government that protected them inadequately was now proposing to tax them disproportionately. Unrest continued for two years on the frontiers of Pennsylvania, Maryland, and Virginia. Large groups of men drafted petitions

**Whiskey Rebellion**

protesting the tax, deliberately imitated crowd actions of the 1760s, and occasionally harassed tax collectors.

President Washington responded with restraint until violence erupted in July 1794, when western Pennsylvania farmers resisted two excisemen trying to collect the tax. About seven thousand rebels convened on August 1 to plot the destruction of Pittsburgh but decided not to face the heavy guns of the fort guarding the town. Washington then took decisive action to prevent a crisis reminiscent of Shays's Rebellion. On August 7, he called on the insurgents to disperse and summoned nearly thirteen thousand militia from Pennsylvania and neighboring states. By the time federal forces marched westward in October and November (led at times by Washington himself), the disturbances had ceased. The troops met no resistance and arrested only twenty suspects. Two, neither of them prominent leaders of the rioters, were convicted of treason, but—continuing his policy of restraint—Washington pardoned both. The leaderless and unorganized rebellion ended with little bloodshed.

The importance of the Whiskey Rebellion lay not in military victory over the rebels—for there was none—but in the forceful message it conveyed to the American people. The national government, Washington had demonstrated, would not allow violent resistance to its laws. In the republic, change would be effected peacefully, by legal means. People dissatisfied with the law should try to amend or repeal it, not take extralegal action as they had during the colonial era.

## THE FRENCH REVOLUTION AND THE DEVELOPMENT OF PARTISAN POLITICS

By 1794 some Americans were already beginning to seek change systematically through electoral politics, even though traditional political theory regarded organized opposition—especially in a republic—as illegitimate. In a monarchy, formal opposition groups, commonly called factions, were to be expected. In a government of the people, by contrast, sustained factional disagreement was taken as a sign of corruption and subversion. Such negative judgments, though widely held, still did not halt the growth of partisan sentiment.

Jefferson and Madison became convinced as early as 1792 that Hamilton's policies of favoring wealthy commercial interests at the expense of agriculture aimed at imposing a corrupt, aristocratic government on the United States. Characterizing themselves as the true heirs of the Revolution, they charged that Hamilton was plotting to subvert republican principles. To dramatize their point, Jefferson, Madison, and their followers in Congress began calling themselves Republicans. Hamilton in turn accused Jefferson and Madison of the same crime: attempting to destroy the republic. Hamilton and his supporters began calling themselves Federalists, to legitimize their claims and link themselves with the Constitution. Each group accused the other of being an illicit faction working to sabotage the republican principles of the Revolution. Newspapers aligned with the two sides fanned the flames of partisanship, publishing virulent attacks on their political opponents.

**Republicans and Federalists**

At first, President Washington tried to remain aloof from the political dispute that divided Hamilton and Jefferson, his chief advisers. The growing controversy did help persuade him to promote political unity by seeking office again in 1792. But in 1793 and thereafter, developments in foreign affairs magnified the disagreements, for France (America's wartime ally) and Great Britain (America's most important trading partner) re-

▲ A Federalist political cartoon from the 1790s shows "Mad Tom" Paine "in a rage," trying to destroy the federal government as carefully constructed (in classical style) by President Washington and Vice President Adams. That Paine is being aided by the Devil underscores the hostility to partisanship common in the era.

*(The Huntington Library & Art Collections, San Marino, California)*

sumed the periodic hostilities that had originated a century earlier.

In 1789 Americans had welcomed the news of the French Revolution. The French people's success in limiting, and then overthrowing, an oppressive monarchy seemed to vindicate the United States' own revolution. Americans saw themselves as the vanguard of an inevitable historical trend that would reshape the world in a republican mold. But by the early 1790s the reports from France were disquieting. Outbreaks of violence continued, and political leaders succeeded each other with bewildering rapidity. Executions mounted; the king himself was beheaded in early 1793. Although many Americans, including Jefferson and Madison, retained sympathy for the revolution, others—among

**French Revolution**

▲ The violence of the French Revolution, especially the guillotining of King Louis XVI, shocked Americans, causing many to question whether the United States should remain that nation's ally.

*(Erich Lessing/Art Resource, NY)*

them Alexander Hamilton—began to cite France as a prime example of the perversion of republicanism.

Debates within the United States intensified when the newly republican France became enmeshed in conflict with other European nations. Both because French leaders feared that neighboring monarchies would intervene to crush the revolution and because they sought to spread the republican gospel throughout the continent, they declared war first on Austria and then, in 1793, on Britain, Spain, and Holland. That confronted the Americans with a dilemma. The 1778 Treaty of Alliance with France bound them to that nation "forever," and a mutual commitment to republicanism created ideological bonds. Yet the United States was connected to Great Britain as well. In addition to their shared history and language, America and Britain had again become important economic partners. Americans still purchased most of their manufactured goods from Great Britain. Indeed, because the revenues of the United States depended heavily on import tariffs, the na-

tion's economic health in effect required uninterrupted trade with the former mother country.

The political and diplomatic climate grew even more complicated in April 1793, when Edmond Genêt, a representative of the French government, arrived in Charleston, South Carolina. As Genêt made his way north to New York City, he recruited Americans for expeditions against British and Spanish colonies in the Western Hemisphere, freely distributing privateering commissions. Genêt's arrival raised troubling questions for President Washington. Should he receive Genêt, thus officially recognizing the French revolutionary government? Should he acknowledge an obligation to aid France under the terms of the 1778 Treaty of Alliance? Or should he proclaim American neutrality?

**Edmond Genêt**

Washington resolved his dilemma by receiving Genêt but also issuing a proclamation informing the world that the United States would adopt "a conduct friendly and impartial toward the belligerent powers." Federalist newspapers vociferously defended the proclamation, and partisan leaders organized rallies to praise the president's action. Republicans who favored assisting France reluctantly accepted the neutrality policy, which had overwhelming popular support.

Genêt's faction fell from power in Paris, and he subsequently sought political asylum in the United States. But his disappearance from the diplomatic scene did not diminish the impact of the French Revolution in America. The domestic divisions Genêt helped to widen were perpetuated by clubs called Democratic societies, formed by Americans sympathetic to the French Revolution and worried about the policies of the Washington administration. Such societies reflected a growing grassroots concern about the same developments that troubled Jefferson and Madison.

More than forty Democratic societies organized between 1793 and 1800. Their members saw themselves

**Democratic Societies**

as heirs of the Sons of Liberty, seeking the same goal as their predecessors: protection of people's liberties against encroachments by corrupt and self-serving rulers. To that end, they publicly protested government fiscal and foreign policy, and repeatedly proclaimed their belief in "the equal rights of man," particularly the rights to free speech, free press, and assembly. Like the Sons of Liberty, the Democratic societies comprised chiefly artisans and craftsmen, although professionals, farmers, and merchants also joined. Although locally based, they communicated effectively through a network of newspapers and allied themselves nationally with congressional Republicans.

The rapid spread of such citizens' groups, outspokenly critical of the administration, disturbed Hamilton and Washington. Federalist writers charged that the organizations were dangerously subversive, because elected officials, not "self-created societies," should formulate public policy. The groups' "real design," a newspaper asserted, was "to involve the country in war, to assume the reins of government and tyrannize over the people." The counterattack climaxed in the fall of 1794, when Washington accused the societies of fomenting the Whiskey Rebellion. Republican leaders and newspaper editors responded by defending the societies but condemning the insurgents.

In retrospect, Washington and Hamilton's reaction to the Democratic societies seems disproportionately hostile. But factional disputes were believed to endanger the survival of republics. As the first organized political dissenters in the United States, the Democratic societies alarmed administration officials, who had not yet accepted the idea that one component of a free government was an organized loyal opposition.

## PARTISAN POLITICS AND RELATIONS WITH GREAT BRITAIN

In 1794 George Washington dispatched Chief Justice John Jay to London to negotiate several unresolved questions in Anglo-American relations. The British had recently seized some American merchant ships trading in the French West Indies. The United States wanted to establish the countervailing principle of freedom of the seas and to assert its right, as a neutral nation, to trade freely with both combatants. Further, Great Britain still held posts in the American Northwest, thus violating the 1783 peace treaty. Settlers there believed that the British were responsible for renewed warfare with neighboring Indians, and they wanted that threat removed. The Americans also hoped for a commercial treaty and sought compensation for the slaves who left with the British army at the end of the war.

The negotiations in London proved difficult, because Jay had little to offer in exchange for the concessions he

**Jay Treaty Debate**

sought. Britain did agree to evacuate the western forts and ease restrictions on American trade to England and the West Indies. (Some limitations were retained, however, violating the Americans' desire for open commerce.) The treaty established two arbitration commissions—one to deal with prewar debts Americans owed to British creditors and the other to hear claims for captured American merchant ships—but Britain adamantly refused slaveowners compensation for their lost bondspeople. Under the circumstances, Jay had probably done the best he could. Nevertheless, most Americans, including the president, at first expressed dissatisfaction with at least some clauses of the treaty.

The Senate debated the Jay Treaty in secret. Not until after ratification in late June 1795 (by 20 to 10, the exact two-thirds the Constitution required) did members of the public learn its provisions. Immediate protests followed, in the form of both newspaper essays and popular gatherings that adopted resolutions asking Washington to reject the treaty. Especially vehement opposition arose in the South, as planters criticized the lack of compensation for runaway slaves and objected to the commission on prewar debts, which might make them pay off obligations to British merchants dating back to the 1760s. But Federalists countered with meetings and publications of their own, contending that, upon careful examination, the

Jay Treaty would prove preferable to the alternative—no treaty at all. The president, displeased by the Republicans' organized vocal opposition and convinced by pro-treaty arguments, signed the pact in mid-August. Just one opportunity remained to prevent it from going into effect: Congress had to appropriate funds to carry out the treaty, and, according to the Constitution, appropriation bills had to originate in the House of Representatives.

Washington delayed submitting the treaty to the House until March 1796, futilely hoping that by then the opposition would have dissipated. During the debate, Republicans argued loudly against approving the appropriations, and they won a vote asking Washington to submit to the House all documents pertinent to the negotiations. In successfully resisting the request, Washington established a power still used today—executive privilege, in which the president may withhold information from Congress if he deems it necessary.

The treaty's opponents initially commanded a congressional majority, but pressure for appropriating the necessary funds built as time passed, fostered by an especially vigorous Federalist campaign of publications and petitions targeting middle-state congressmen whose districts would benefit from approval. Constituent petitions contended that failure to fund the treaty would lead to war with Britain, thus endangering Pennsylvania frontier settlements and New York and New Jersey commercial interests alike. Further, Federalists successfully linked the Jay Treaty with another, more popular pact. In 1795 Thomas Pinckney of South Carolina had negotiated a treaty with Spain giving the United States navigation privileges on the Mississippi River and the right to land and store goods at New Orleans tax free, thus boosting the nation's economy. The overwhelming support for Pinckney's Treaty (the Senate ratified it unanimously) helped to overcome opposition to the Jay Treaty. In late April, the House appropriated the money by the narrow margin of 51 to 48. The vote divided along partisan and regional lines: all but 2 southerners opposed the treaty; all but 3 congressional Federalists supported it; and a majority of middle-state representatives also voted yes.

Despite the Federalists' success in the treaty dispute, their campaign to sway public opinion had ironically violated their fundamental philosophy of government. They believed that ordinary people should defer to the judgment of elected leaders, yet in this instance, in order to persuade the House to follow the president's lead, they had actively engaged in grassroots politicking. The Federalists had won the battle, but in the long run they lost the war, for Republicans ultimately proved far more effective in appealing to the citizenry at large.

To describe the growing partisanship in Congress and the nation is easier than to explain such divisions in the electorate. The terms used by Jefferson and Madison (the people versus aristocrats) or by Hamilton and Washington (true patriots versus subversive rabble) do not adequately explain the growing divisions. Simple economic differences between agrarian and commercial interests do not provide the answer either, as more than 90 percent of Americans still lived in rural areas. Moreover, Jefferson's vision of a prosperous agrarian America rested on commercial farming, not rural self-sufficiency. Nor did the divisions in the 1790s simply repeat the Federalist-Antifederalist debate of 1787–1788. Even though most Antifederalists became Republicans, the party's leaders, Madison and Jefferson, had supported the Constitution.

## Bases of Partisanship

Yet certain distinctions can be made. Republicans, especially prominent in the southern and middle states, tended to be self-assured, confident, and optimistic about both politics and the economy. Southern planters, in control of their region and dominating a class of enslaved laborers, foresaw a prosperous future based partly on continued westward expansion, a movement they expected to dominate. Republicans employed democratic rhetoric to win the allegiance of small farmers south of New England. Members of non-English ethnic groups—especially Irish, Scots, and Germans—found Republicans' words attractive. Artisans also joined the coalition; they saw themselves as the urban equivalent of small farmers, cherishing their independence from domineering bosses. Republicans of all descriptions emphasized developing America's own resources, worrying less than Federalists did about the nation's place in the world. Republicans also remained sympathetic to France in international affairs.

By contrast, Federalists, concentrated among the commercial interests of New England, came mostly from English stock. Insecure, they stressed the need for order, hierarchy, and obedience to political authority. Wealthy New England merchants aligned themselves with the Federalists, but so, too, did the region's farmers who, prevented from expanding agricultural production because of New England's poor soil, gravitated toward the more conservative party. Federalists, like Republicans, assumed that southern and middle-state interests would dominate western lands, so they had little incentive to work actively to develop that potentially rich territory. In Federalist eyes, potential enemies—both internal and external—perpetually threatened the nation, which required a continuing alliance with Great Britain for its own protection. Given the dangers posed to the nation by European warfare, Federalists' vision of international affairs may have been accurate, but it was also unappealing. Because the Federalist view held out little hope of a better future to the voters of any region, it is not surprising that the Republicans prevailed in the end.

After the treaty debate, wearied by the criticism to which he had been subjected, George Washington decided

**Washington's Farewell Address**

to retire. (Presidents had not yet been limited to two terms, as they have been since the adoption of the Twenty-second Amendment in 1951.) In September Washington published his Farewell Address, most of which had been written by Hamilton. In it Washington outlined two principles that guided American foreign policy at least until the late 1940s: to maintain commercial but not political ties to other nations and to enter no permanent alliances. He also drew sharp distinctions between the United States and Europe, stressing America's uniqueness—its exceptionalism—and the need for independent action in foreign affairs, today called unilateralism.

Washington lamented the existence of factional divisions among his countrymen. Some historians have interpreted his call for an end to partisan strife as the statement of a man who could see beyond political affiliations to the good of the whole. But in the context of the impending presidential election, the Farewell Address appears rather as an attack on the legitimacy of the Republican opposition. Washington advocated unity behind the Federalist banner, which he viewed as the only proper political stance. The Federalists (like the Republicans) continued to see themselves as the sole guardians of the truth and the only true heirs of the Revolution. Both sides perceived their opponents as misguided, unpatriotic troublemakers who sought to undermine revolutionary ideals.

The two organized groups actively contending for office made the presidential election of 1796 the first serious

**Election of 1796**

contest for the position. To succeed Washington, the Federalists in Congress put forward Vice President John Adams, with the diplomat Thomas Pinckney as his running mate. Congressional Republicans chose Thomas Jefferson as their presidential candidate; the lawyer, Revolutionary War veteran, and active Republican politician Aaron Burr of New York agreed to run for vice president.

That the election was contested does not mean that the people decided its outcome. In most states, legislatures appointed electors, some even before Federalists and Republicans designated their nominees. Moreover, the method of voting in the electoral college did not take into account the possibility of party slates. The Constitution's drafters had not foreseen the development of competing national political organizations, so the Constitution provided no way to express support for one person for president and another for vice president. The electors simply voted for two people. The man with the highest total became president; the second highest, vice president.

This procedure proved to be the Federalists' undoing. Adams won the presidency with 71 votes, but a number of Federalist electors (especially those from New England) failed to cast ballots for Pinckney. Thomas Jefferson won 68 votes, 9 more than Pinckney, to become vice president. The incoming administration was thus politically divided. During the next four years the new president and vice president, once allies and close friends, became bitter enemies.

## JOHN ADAMS AND POLITICAL DISSENT

John Adams took over the presidency peculiarly blind to the partisan developments of the previous four years. As president he never abandoned an outdated notion discarded by George Washington as early as 1794: that the president should be above politics, an independent and dignified figure who did not seek petty factional advantage. Thus Adams kept Washington's cabinet intact, despite its key members' allegiance to his chief Federalist rival, Alexander Hamilton. Adams often adopted a passive posture, letting others (usually Hamilton) take the lead when the president should have acted decisively. As a result, his administration gained a reputation for inconsistency. But Adams's detachment from Hamilton's maneuverings did enable him to weather the greatest international crisis the republic had yet faced: the Quasi-War with France.

The Jay Treaty improved America's relationship with Great Britain, but it provoked the French government

**XYZ Affair**

to retaliate by ordering its ships to seize American vessels carrying British goods. In response, Congress increased military spending, authorizing the building of ships and the stockpiling of weapons and ammunition. President Adams also sent three commissioners to Paris to negotiate a settlement. For months, the American commissioners sought talks with Talleyrand, the French foreign minister, but Talleyrand's agents demanded a bribe of $250,000 before negotiations could begin. The Americans retorted, "No, no; not a sixpence" and reported the incident in dispatches that the president received in early March 1798. Adams informed Congress of the impasse and recommended further increases in defense appropriations.

Convinced that Adams had deliberately sabotaged the negotiations, congressional Republicans insisted that the dispatches be turned over to Congress. Adams complied, aware that releasing the reports would work to his advantage. He withheld only the names of the French agents, referring to them as X, Y, and Z. The revelation that the Americans had been treated with contempt stimulated a wave of anti-French sentiment in the United States. A journalist's version of the commissioners' reply, "Millions for defense, but not a cent for tribute," became the national slogan. Cries for war filled the air. Congress formally abrogated the Treaty of Alliance and authorized American ships to seize French vessels.

Thus began an undeclared war with France fought in Caribbean waters between warships of the U.S. Navy and French privateers. Although Americans initially suffered heavy losses of merchant shipping, by early 1799 the U.S. Navy had established its superiority in the West Indies. Its ships captured eight French privateers and

**Quasi-War with France**

naval vessels, easing the threat to America's vital Caribbean trade.

The Republicans, who opposed war and continued to sympathize with France, could do little to stem the tide of anti-French feelings. Because Agent Y had boasted of the existence of a "French party in America," Federalists flatly accused Republicans (including the eccentric envoy George Logan) of traitorous designs. A New York newspaper declared that anyone who remained "lukewarm" after reading the XYZ dispatches was a "criminal—and the man who does not warmly reprobate the conduct of the French must have a soul black enough to be fit for treason Strategems and spoils." John Adams wavered between calling the Republicans traitors and acknowledging their right to oppose administration measures. His wife was less tolerant. "Those whom the French boast of as their Partizans," Abigail Adams declared, should be "adjudged traitors to their country." If Jefferson had been president, she added, "we should all have been sold to the French."

Federalists saw this climate of opinion as an opportunity to deal a death blow to their Republican opponents.

▲ This cartoon drawn during the XYZ affair depicts the United States as a maiden being victimized by the five leaders of the French government's directorate. In the background, John Bull (England) watches from on high, while other European nations discuss the situation.

*(The Lilly Library, Indiana University, Bloomington, Indiana)*

## Alien and Sedition Acts

Now that the country seemed to see the truth of what they had been saying ever since the Whiskey Rebellion in 1794—that Republicans were subversive foreign agents—Federalists sought to codify that belief into law. In 1798 the Federalist-controlled Congress adopted a set of four laws known as the Alien and Sedition Acts, intended to suppress dissent and to prevent further growth of the Republican faction.

Three of the acts targeted recently arrived immigrants, whom Federalists accurately suspected of being Republican in their sympathies. The Naturalization Act lengthened the residency period required for citizenship and ordered all resident aliens to register with the federal government. The two Alien Acts, though not immediately implemented, provided for the detention of enemy aliens in time of war and gave the president authority to deport any alien he deemed dangerous to the nation's security.

The fourth statute, the Sedition Act, sought to control both citizens and aliens. It outlawed conspiracies to prevent the enforcement of federal laws, setting the maximum punishment for such offenses at five years in prison and a $5,000 fine. The act also tried to control speech. Writing, printing, or uttering "false, scandalous and malicious" statements against the government or the president "with intent to defame . . . or to bring them or either of them, into contempt or disrepute" became a crime punishable by as much as two years' imprisonment and a fine of $2,000. Today, any such law punishing speech alone would be unconstitutional. But in the eighteenth century, when organized political opposition was by definition

▲ In 1798, in hopes of appealing to the American market, a potter in Liverpool, England, created this pitcher with President John Adams's portrait on one side and an eagle on the other, surrounded by 16 rings representing the states.

*(Left and Right: National Museum of American History, Smithsonian Institution, Washington, D.C.)*

suspect, many Americans supported the Sedition Act's restrictions on free speech.

The Sedition Act led to fifteen indictments and ten convictions, including one congressman, Matthew Lyons of Vermont, and several outspoken Republican newspaper editors who failed to mute their criticism of the administration. One was James Callender, a Scots immigrant and scandalmonger, who relentlessly attacked Federalists while being subsidized by Thomas Jefferson. Callender's exposé forced Alexander Hamilton to admit to an extramarital affair. After turning his attention to President Adams, Callender was convicted, fined, and jailed for nine months, but he continued to produce pro-Jeffersonian writings from the Richmond prison.

Faced with prosecutions of their political allies, Jefferson and Madison sought an effective means of combating the acts. Petitioning the Federalist-controlled Congress to repeal the laws would clearly fail. Furthermore, Federalist judges refused to allow accused individuals to question the Sedition Act's constitutionality. Accordingly, the Republican leaders turned to the only other forum available for protest: state legislatures. Carefully concealing their own role—the vice president and congressman wanted to avoid being indicted for sedition—Jefferson and Madison drafted different sets of resolutions that were introduced into the Kentucky and Virginia legislatures, respectively, in the fall of 1798. Because a compact among the states had created the Constitution, the resolutions contended, people speaking through their states had a legitimate right to judge the constitutionality of actions taken by the federal government. Both pronounced the Alien and Sedition Acts unconstitutional, and thus (declared Kentucky) "void and of no force," advancing the doctrine later known as nullification.

**Virginia and Kentucky Resolutions**

Although no other state endorsed them, the Virginia and Kentucky Resolutions nevertheless had considerable influence. First, they constituted superb political propaganda, rallying Republican opinion throughout the country. They placed the opposition party squarely in the revolutionary tradition of resistance to tyrannical authority. Second, the theory of union that they proposed inspired the Hartford Convention of 1814 and southern states' rights advocates in the 1830s and thereafter. Jefferson and Madison had identified a key constitutional issue: How far could states go in opposing the national government? How could a conflict between the two be resolved? These questions would not be definitively answered until the Civil War.

Just as the Sedition Act was being implemented and northern state legislatures were rejecting the Virginia and Kentucky Resolutions, Federalists split over the course of action the United States should take toward France. Hamilton and his supporters called for a declaration legitimizing the undeclared naval war. Adams, though, received a number of private signals—among them George Logan's report—that the French government regretted its treatment of the American commissioners.

**Convention of 1800**

Acting on such assurances, Adams dispatched the envoy William Vans Murray to Paris to negotiate with Napoleon Bonaparte, France's new leader, who was consolidating his hold on the country and eager to end messy foreign conflicts. The United States sought two goals: compensation for ships the French had seized since 1793 and abrogation of the treaty of 1778. The Convention of 1800, which ended the Quasi-War, provided for the latter but not the former. Still, it freed the United States from its only permanent alliance, thus allowing it to follow the independent diplomatic course George Washington had urged in his Farewell Address.

## THE WEST IN THE NEW NATION

By the end of the eighteenth century, the nation had added three states (Vermont, Kentucky, and Tennessee) to the original thirteen and more than 1 million people to the nearly 4 million counted by the 1790 census. It also nominally controlled all the land east of the Mississippi River and north of Spanish Florida, divided by the Ohio River. Control of the land north of the Ohio was achieved only after considerable bloodshed, for initially the land was dominated by a powerful western confederacy of eight Indian nations led by the Miamis.

General Arthur St. Clair, first governor of the Northwest Territory, futilely tried to open more land to settlement through failed treaty negotiations with the western confederacy in early 1789. Subsequently, Little Turtle, the confederacy's able war chief, defeated forces led by General Josiah Harmar (1790) and by St. Clair himself (1791) in major battles near the present border between Indiana and Ohio. More than six hundred of St. Clair's men died, and scores more were wounded, in the United States' worst defeat in the entire history of the American frontier.

**War in the Northwest Territory**

In 1793 the Miami Confederacy declared that peace could be achieved only if the United States recognized the Ohio River as its northwestern boundary. But the national government refused to relinquish its claims in the region. A reorganized and newly invigorated army under the com-

▲ The two chief antagonists at the Battle of Fallen Timbers and negotiators of the Treaty of Greenville (1795). On the left, Little Turtle, the leader of the Miami Confederacy; on the right, General Anthony Wayne. Little Turtle, in a copy of a portrait painted two years later, appears to be wearing a miniature of Wayne on a bear-claw necklace.

*(Left: Courtesy, Chicago Historical Society. Right: Independence National Historic Park)*

mand of General Anthony Wayne, a Revolutionary War hero, attacked and defeated the confederacy in August 1794 at the Battle of Fallen Timbers (near present-day Toledo, Ohio; see Map 7.3). Peace negotiations then began.

In August 1795, Wayne reached agreement with the Miami Confederacy. The Treaty of Greenville gave each side a portion of what it wanted. The United States gained the right to settle much of what was to become Ohio, the indigenous peoples retaining only the northwest corner of the region. Indians, though, received the acknowledgment they had long sought: American recognition of their rights to the soil. At Greenville, the United States formally accepted the principle of Indian sovereignty, by virtue of residence, over all lands the native peoples had not ceded. Never again would the U.S. government claim that it had acquired Indian territory solely through negotiation with a European or North American country.

South of the Ohio, Pinckney's Treaty with Spain that same year established the 31st parallel as the boundary be-tween the United States and Florida. Nevertheless, Spanish influence in the Old Southwest continued to raise questions about the loyalty of American settlers in the region, much of it still unceded and occupied by Creeks, Cherokees, and other Indian nations. A Southwest Ordinance (1790) attempted to organize the territory; by permitting slavery, it made the region attractive to slaveholders.

Increasingly, even Indian peoples who lived independent of federal authority came within the orbit of U.S. influence. The nation's stated goal was to "civilize" them. "Instead of exterminating a part of the human race," Henry Knox, Washington's secretary of war, contended in 1789, the government should "impart our knowledge of cultivation and the arts to the aboriginals of the country." The first step in such a project, Knox suggested, should be to introduce to Indian peoples "a love for exclusive property"; to that end, he proposed that the government give

### "Civilizing" the Indians

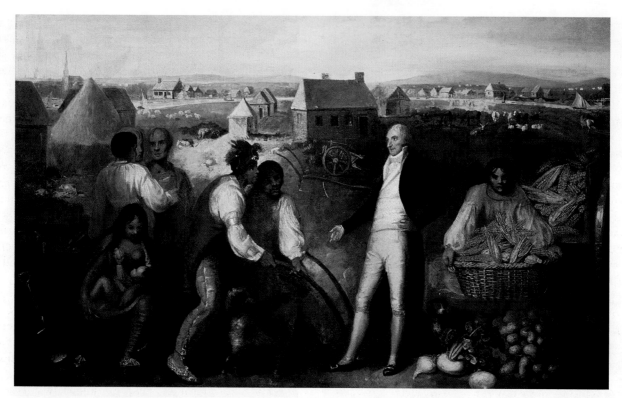

▲ In 1805, an unidentified artist painted Benjamin Hawkins, a trader and U.S. agent to the Indians of the Southeast, at the Creek agency near Macon, Georgia. Hawkins introduced European-style agriculture to the Creeks, who are shown here with vegetables from their fields. Throughout the eastern United States, Indian nations had to make similar adaptations of their traditional lifestyles in order to maintain their group identity.   *(Collection of the Greenville County Art Museum, South Carolina)*

livestock to individual Indians. Four years later, the Indian Trade and Intercourse Act of 1793 codified Knox's plan, promising that the federal government would supply Indians with animals and agricultural implements, and also provide appropriate instructors.

The well-intentioned plan reflected federal officials' blindness to the realities of native peoples' lives. Not only did it incorrectly posit that the Indians' traditional commitment to communal notions of landowning could easily be overcome, it also ignored the centuries-long agricultural experience of eastern Indian peoples. The policymakers focused only on Indian men: because they hunted, male Indians were "savages" who had to be "civilized" by being taught to farm. That in these societies women traditionally did the farming was irrelevant because, in the eyes of the officials, Indian women—like those of European descent—should properly confine themselves to child rearing, household chores, and home manufacturing.

Indian nations at first responded cautiously to the "civilizing" plan. The Iroquois Confederacy had been devastated by the war; its people in the 1790s lived in what one historian has called "slums in the wilderness." Restricted to small reservations increasingly surrounded by Anglo-American farmlands, men could no longer hunt and often spent their days in idle carousing. Quaker missionaries started a demonstration farm among the Senecas, intending to teach men to plow, but they quickly learned that women showed greater interest in their message. The same was true among the Cherokees of Georgia, where Indian agents found that women eagerly sought to learn both new farming methods and textile-manufacturing skills. As their southern hunting territories were reduced, Cherokee men did begin to raise cattle and hogs, but they startled the reformers by treating livestock like wild game, allowing the

### Iroquois and Cherokees

Revolutions" at the End of the Century

animals to run free in the woods and simply shooting them when needed, in the same way they had once killed deer. Men also started to plow the fields, although Cherokee women continued to bear primary responsibility for cultivation and harvest.

Iroquois men became more receptive to the Quakers' lessons after the spring of 1799, when a Seneca named Handsome Lake experienced a remarkable series of visions. Like other prophets stretching back to Neolin in the 1760s, Handsome Lake preached that Indian peoples should renounce alcohol, gambling, and other destructive European customs. Even though he directed his followers to reorient men's and women's work assignments as the Quakers advocated, Handsome Lake aimed above all to preserve Iroquois culture by doing so. He recognized that, because men could no longer obtain meat through hunting, only by adopting a sexual division of labor that had originated in Europe could the Iroquois retain an autonomous existence.

## "REVOLUTIONS" AT THE END OF THE CENTURY

Three events in the last two years of the eighteenth century can be deemed real or potential revolutions: Fries's Rebellion, Gabriel's Rebellion, and the election of Thomas Jefferson. Although they differed significantly, all these events mirrored the tensions and uncertainties of the young republic. The Fries rebels resisted national authority to tax. Gabriel and his followers directly challenged the slave system that was crucial to the Chesapeake economy. And the venomous, hard-fought presidential election of 1800 exposed a structural flaw in the Constitution that would have to be corrected by amendment.

The tax resistance movement known by the name of one of its prominent leaders, the militia captain and Revolutionary War veteran John Fries,

**Fries's Rebellion**

arose in Pennsylvania's Lehigh Valley in 1798–1799, among German American farmers. To finance the Quasi-War, Congress had enacted taxes on land, houses, and legal documents. German Americans, imbued with revolutionary ideals (at least two-fifths of them were veterans, like Fries), saw in the taxes a threat to their liberties and livelihoods, as well as an echo of the hated Stamp Act of 1765. Asserting a right of resistance to unconstitutional laws, they raised liberty poles, signed petitions to Congress, and nonviolently prevented assessors from evaluating their homes. They voiced repeated threats but harmed no one.

Even so, a federal judge in Philadelphia ordered the arrest of 20 resisters. In response, in March 1799 Fries led a troop of 120 militiamen to Bethlehem, where they surrounded the tavern that temporarily housed the prisoners. Lengthy negotiations failed to win their release, but eventually, fearing a violent confrontation, a federal marshal let the men go. President Adams described the militiamen's actions as "treason, being overt acts of levying war against the United States." Fries and many of his neighbors were arrested and tried; he and 2 others were convicted of treason; 32 more, of violating the Sedition Act. Although Fries and the other "traitors" were sentenced to hang, Adams pardoned them (and all the others) just two days before their scheduled execution, having concluded that they were rioters rather than traitors. Despite clemency from a Federalist president, the region's residents became, and remained, Republican partisans.

Like their white compatriots in the Lehigh Valley and elsewhere, African Americans both slave and free became

**Gabriel's Rebellion**

familiar with concepts of liberty and equality during the Revolution. They, too, witnessed the benefits of fighting collectively for freedom, rather than resisting individually or running away—a message reinforced by the dramatic news of the successful slave revolt in St. Domingue in 1793. Gabriel, an enslaved Virginia blacksmith who planned the second end-of-the-century revolution, drew on both Haitian and American experiences as well as his religious beliefs.

For months, often accompanied by his preacher brother, Martin, Gabriel visited Sunday services at black Baptist and Methodist congregations, where bondspeople gathered free of the watchful eyes of their owners. Gabriel first recruited to his cause other skilled African Americans who like himself lived in semi-freedom under minimal supervision. Next he enlisted rural slaves. The rebels planned to attack Richmond on the night of August 30, 1800; set fire to the city; seize the state capitol; and capture the governor, James Monroe. At that point, Gabriel believed, other slaves and perhaps poor whites would join in.

The plan showed considerable political sophistication, but heavy rain forced a postponement. Several planters then learned of the plot from informers and spread the alarm. Gabriel avoided arrest for weeks, but militia troops quickly apprehended and interrogated most of the other leaders of the rebellion. Twenty-six rebels, including Gabriel himself, were hanged. Ironically, only those slaves who betrayed their fellows won freedom as a result of the rebellion.

▲ Richmond, Virginia, at the time of Gabriel's Rebellion. This was the city as Gabriel knew it. The state capitol, the rebels' intended target, dominates the city's skyline as it dominated Gabriel's thinking. *(Maryland Historical Society)*

At his trial, one of Gabriel's followers made explicit the links that so frightened Chesapeake slaveholders. He told his judges that, like George Washington, "I have adventured my life in endeavouring to obtain the liberty of my countrymen, and am a willing sacrifice in their cause." Southern state legislatures responded to such claims by increasing the severity of the laws regulating slavery. Before long, all talk of emancipation ceased in the South, and slavery became even more firmly entrenched as an economic institution and way of life.

The third end-of-the-century revolution was a Republican "takeover"—the election of Thomas Jefferson as president and a Congress dominated by Republicans—and the culmination of a decade of increasing partisanship. Prior to November 1800, Federalists and Republicans not only campaigned for congressional seats but also maneuvered furiously to control the outcome in the electoral college. Each side feared victory by the other, and both wanted to avoid reproducing the divided results of 1796. Republicans again nominated Thomas Jefferson and Aaron Burr; Federal-

**Election of 1800**

ists named John Adams, with Charles Cotesworth Pinckney of South Carolina as vice president. When the votes were counted, Jefferson and Burr had tied with 73 (no Republican elector wanted to chance omitting Burr's name from his ballot), while Adams had 64 and Pinckney 63. Under Article II, Section 1, of the Constitution, the election had to be decided in the existing House of Representatives; the newly elected Jeffersonians would not take office until the president did.

Balloting continued for six days and thirty-five ballots, with Federalists uniformly supporting Burr, whereas Republicans held firm for Jefferson. Finally, James Bayard, a Federalist and the sole congressman from Delaware, concluded (perhaps correctly) that "we must risk the Constitution and a civil war or take Mr. Jefferson." He brokered a deal that gave the Virginian the presidency on the thirty-sixth ballot. A crucial consequence of the election was the adoption of the Twelfth Amendment, which provided that electors would henceforth cast separate ballots for president and vice president.

The defeated Federalists turned to strengthening their hold on the judiciary while they could. President Adams

## Haitian Refugees

Although many European-Americans initially welcomed the news of the French Revolution in 1789, few expressed similar sentiments about the slave rebellion that broke out soon thereafter in the French colony of St. Domingue (later Haiti), which shared the island of Hispaniola with Spanish Santo Domingo. The large number of refugees who soon flowed into the new United States from that nearby revolt brought with them consequences deemed undesirable by most political leaders. Less than a decade after winning independence, the new nation confronted its first immigration crisis.

Among the approximately 600,000 residents of St. Domingue in the early 1790s were about 100,000 free people, almost all of them slaveowners; half were whites, the rest mulattos. When in the wake of the French Revolution those free mulattos split the slaveholding population by seeking greater social and political equality, the slaves seized the opportunity to revolt. By 1793 they had triumphed under the leadership of a former slave, Toussaint L'Ouverture, and in 1804 they finally ousted the French, thereafter establishing the republic of Haiti. Thousands of whites and mulattos, accompanied by as many slaves as they could readily transport, sought asylum in the United States during those turbulent years.

Although willing to offer shelter to refugees from the violence, American political leaders nonetheless feared the consequences of their arrival. Southern plantation owners shuddered at the thought that slaves so familiar with ideas of freedom and equality would mingle with their own bondspeople. Many were uncomfortable with the immigration of numerous free people of color, even though the immigrants were part of the slaveholding class. Most of the southern states adopted laws forbidding the entry of Haitian slaves and free mulattos, but the laws were difficult if not impossible to enforce, as was a later congressional act to the same effect. So, more than 15,000 refugees—white, black, and of mixed-race origins—flooded into the United States and Spanish Louisiana. Many ended up in Virginia (which did not pass an exclusion law) or the cities of Charleston, Savannah, and New Orleans.

There they had a considerable impact on the existing population. In both New Orleans and Charleston, the influx of mulattos gave rise to a heightened color consciousness that placed light-skinned people at the top of a hierarchy of people of color. Not coincidentally, the Charleston Brown Fellowship Society, composed exclusively of free mulattos, was founded in 1793. After the United States purchased Louisiana in 1803, the number of free people of color in the territory almost doubled in three years, largely because of a final surge of immigration from the new Haitian republic. And in Virginia, stories of the successful revolt helped to inspire local slaves in 1800 when they planned the action that has become known as Gabriel's Rebellion.

The Haitian refugees thus linked both European-Americans and African Americans to current events in the West Indies, indelibly affecting both groups of people.

▲ A free woman of color in Louisiana early in the nineteenth century, possibly one of the refugees from Haiti. Esteban Rodriguez Miró, named governor of Spanish Louisiana in 1782, ordered all slave and free black women to wear head wraps rather than hats—which were reserved for whites—but this woman and many others subverted his order by nominally complying, but nevertheless creating elaborate headdresses. *(Louisiana State Museum)*

## SUMMARY

As the nineteenth century began, inhabitants of the United States faced changed lives in the new republic. Indian peoples east of the Mississippi River found that they had to surrender some aspects of their traditional culture to preserve others. Some African Americans struggled unsuccessfully to free themselves from the inhuman bonds of slavery, then subsequently confronted more constraints than ever because of increasingly restrictive laws.

European-Americans, too, adjusted to changed circumstances. The first eleven years of government under the Constitution established many enduring precedents for congressional, presidential, and judicial action—among them establishment of the cabinet, interpretations of key clauses of the Constitution, and stirrings of judicial review of state and federal legislation. Building on successful negotiations with Spain (Pinckney's Treaty), Britain (the Jay Treaty), and France (the Convention of 1800), the United States developed its diplomatic independence, striving to avoid entanglement with European countries and their continental wars.

Yet especially after 1793 internal political consensus proved elusive. The 1790s spawned vigorous debates over foreign and domestic policy, and saw the beginnings of a system of organized factionalism and grassroots politicking, if not yet formal parties. The Whiskey and Fries Rebellions showed that regional conflicts persisted even under the new government. The waging of an undeclared war against France proved extremely contentious, splitting one faction and energizing another. In 1801, after more than a decade of struggle, the Jeffersonian view of the future of agrarian, decentralized republicanism prevailed over Alexander Hamilton's vision of a powerful centralized economy and a strong national government.

## SUGGESTIONS FOR FURTHER READING

Joyce Appleby, *Capitalism and a New Social Order: The Republican Vision of the 1790s* (1984)

Douglas Egerton, *Gabriel's Rebellion: The Virginia Slave Conspiracies of 1800 and 1802* (1993)

Stanley Elkins and Eric McKitrick, *The Age of Federalism, 1788–1800* (1993)

Joseph J. Ellis, *Founding Brothers: The Revolutionary Generation* (2000)

Ronald Hoffman and Peter J. Albert, eds., *Launching the "Extended Republic": The Federalist Era* (1998)

James Horn, Jan Ellen Lewis, and Peter S. Onuf, eds., *The Revolution of 1800: Democracy, Race, and the New Republic* (2002)

Thomas P. Slaughter, *The Whiskey Rebellion* (1986)

*For a more extensive list for further reading, go to* college.hmco.com/pic/norton8e.

# Defining the Nation *1801-1823*

$\mathcal{E}$ager to set himself apart from the allegedly aristocratic ways of his Federalist predecessors, President Thomas Jefferson displayed impatience, even disdain, for ceremony. But on his first New Year's Day in office, the third president eagerly awaited the ceremonial presentation of a much-heralded tribute to his commitment, in the words of one of the gift's bearers, to "defend Republicanism and baffle all the arts of Aristocracy." Crafted in Massachusetts, the belated inaugural gift had been nearly a month en route, traveling amid much fanfare for more than 400 miles by sleigh, boat, and wagon. Weighing more than twelve hundred pounds and measuring four feet in diameter, it bore the inscription "THE GREATEST CHEESE IN AMERICA—FOR THE GREATEST MAN IN AMERICA."

The idea for the "mammoth cheese," as it became known, had been born the previous July in a small farming community in western Massachusetts. The "Ladies" of Cheshire—a town as resolutely Jeffersonian-Republican as it was Baptist—had made the cheese from the milk of nine hundred cows as "a mark of the exalted esteem" in which the town's residents held the Republican president. As members of a religious minority in New England, where Congregationalists still dominated the pulpits and statehouses, the Cheshire Baptists had much to celebrate in the election of a president whose vision for the nation's future featured not just agrarianism but also separation of church and state. Their fiery pastor, John Leland, presented the cheese to the president and, two days later, preached the Sunday sermon in the House of Representatives, where at least one genteel listener dismissed his brand of evangelicalism as "horrid."

◀ Federalists derided the Cheshire cheese as the "mammoth" cheese, after the mastodon (similar to the "woolly mammoth") unearthed by naturalist Charles Willson Peale in 1801. Partially funded by the Jefferson administration, Peale's expedition was considered a boondoggle by Federalists.

*(Courtesy of the Maryland Historical Society)*

Americans and their African American slaves; and helped spur revolutions in transportation and industry.

Although contemporary observers noted that the postwar nationalism heralded an "Era of Good Feelings," it would soon become apparent that those good feelings had their limits. When economic boom turned to bust, the postwar bubble of nationalistic optimism and ostensible unity may not have popped, but it would never again prove quite so buoyant. No issue proved more divisive than the future of slavery in the West, as Missouri's petition to be admitted to the Union revealed.

- What characterized the two main competing visions for national development?
- How did America's relationship with Europe influence political and economic developments?
- In what ways did nonvoting Americans—most blacks, women, and Native Americans—take part in defining the new nation?

## POLITICAL VISIONS

In his inaugural address, Jefferson reached out to his opponents. Standing in the Senate chamber, the only completed part of the Capitol, he appealed to the electorate not as party members but as citizens with common beliefs: "We are all republicans, we are all federalists." Nearly a thousand people strained to hear his vision of a restored republicanism. "A wise and frugal government, which shall restrain men from injuring one another, which shall leave them free to regulate their pursuits of industry and improvement, and shall not take from the mouth of labor the bread it had earned. This is the sum of good government," he concluded.

But outgoing president John Adams was not there to hear Jefferson's call for unity. He had left Washington before dawn to avoid the Republican takeover. He and Jefferson had once been close friends but had grown to dislike each other intensely. Despite the spirit of Jefferson's inaugural address, the Democratic-Republicans—as the Republicans of the 1790s now called themselves, after the Democratic societies of the 1790s—and the Federalists remained bitter opponents. These parties held different visions of how society and government should be organized. The Federalists advocated a strong national government with centralized authority to promote economic development. The Democratic-Republicans, by contrast, sought to restrain the national government, believing that limited government would foster Republican virtue. The Jeffersonians believed that virtue derived from agricultural endeavors. Nearly two decades later, Jefferson would refer to his election as "the revolution of 1800," which was "as real a revolution in the principles of our government as that of 1776 was in its form."

When the Cheshire farmers sent Jefferson a mammoth cheese, they did so in large part to express gratitude for his commitment to the separation of church and state. On the very day he received the overripe cheese, Jefferson reciprocated by penning a letter to the Baptist association in Danbury, Connecticut, proclaiming that the Constitution's First Amendment supported a "wall of separation between church and state." Jefferson's letter articulated a core component of his vision of limited government. The president declared that "religion is a matter which lies solely between Man & his God." It lay beyond the purview of the government. New England Baptists

### Separation of Church and State

▲ This portrait of President Thomas Jefferson was painted by Rembrandt Peale in 1805. Charles Willson Peale (Rembrandt's father) and his five sons helped establish the reputation of American art in the new nation. Rembrandt Peale achieved fame for his presidential portraits; here he has captured Jefferson in a noble pose without the usual symbols of office or power, befitting the Republican age.

*(© Collection of the New-York Historical Society)*

hailed Jefferson as a hero, but New England Federalists felt their worst fears had been confirmed. During the election of 1800, Federalists had waged a venomous campaign against Jefferson, incorrectly labeling him an atheist. Their rhetoric proved so effective that, after Jefferson's election, some New England women hid their Bibles in their gardens and wells to foil Democratic-Republicans allegedly bent on confiscating them. Jefferson's letter to the Danbury Baptists seemingly vindicated such hysteria.

Jefferson came to office during a period of religious revivalism, particularly among Methodists and Baptists, whose democratic preaching—all humans, they said, were equal in God's eyes—fed into a growing democratic political culture. Emboldened by a combination of secular and religious ideologies about human equality, society's non-elites articulated their own political visions in the early republic. They did not simply take stands in debates defined by their social and political betters. They worked, too, to reshape the debates. When the Cheshire Baptists sent their cheese to President Jefferson, for example, they pointedly informed the Virginia planter that it had been made "without a single slave to assist."

### Political Mobilization

The revolution of 1800, which gave the Democratic-Republicans majorities in both houses of Congress in addition to the presidency, resulted from an electorate that was limited largely, but not exclusively, to property-holding men. The Constitution left the regulation of voting to the individual states. In no state but New Jersey could women vote even if they met property qualifications, and in New Jersey that right was granted inadvertently and later revoked in 1807. In 1800 free black men who met property qualifications had the right to vote in all states but Delaware, Georgia, South Carolina, and Virginia, but local custom often kept them from exercising that right. Yet partisan politics nonetheless captured nearly all Americans' imaginations, and politicians actively courted nonvoters as well as voters. Most political mobilization took place locally, where partisans rallied popular support for candidates and their ideologies on militia training grounds, in taverns and churches, at court gatherings, and during holiday celebrations. Voters and nonvoters alike expressed their views by marching in parades, signing petitions, singing songs, and debating politically charged sermons. Perhaps most important, they devoured a growing print culture that included pamphlets, broadsides (posters), almanacs, and—especially—newspapers.

Newspapers provided a forum for a sustained political conversation. Read aloud in taverns, artisans' work-

### The Partisan Press

shops, and homes, newspapers helped give national importance to local events. Without newspaper publicity, Cheshire's mammoth cheese would have been little more than a massive hunk of curdled milk. With it, a cheese became worthy of presidential response. In 1800 the nation had 260 newspapers; by 1810 it had 396, virtually all of which were unabashedly partisan.

The parties adopted official organs. Shortly after his election, Jefferson persuaded the *National Intelligencer* to move from Philadelphia to the new capital of Washington, where it became the voice of the Democratic-Republicans. In 1801 Alexander Hamilton launched the *New York Evening Post* as the Federalist vehicle. It boosted Federalists while frequently calling Jefferson a liar and depicting him as the head of a slave harem. The party organs—published six or seven times a week, year in and year out—helped ensure that the growing American obsession with partisan politics was not limited to electoral campaigns.

Jefferson needed public servants as well as supporters. To bring into his administration men who shared his vision of individual liberty, an agrarian republic, and limited government, Jefferson refused to recognize appointments that Adams had made in the last days of his presidency and dismissed Federalist customs collectors from ports. He awarded vacant treasury and judicial offices to Republicans. Federalists accused Jefferson of "hunting the Federalists like wild beasts" and abandoning the peaceful overtures of his inaugural address.

### Limited Government

Even a government filled with Democratic-Republicans should be limited, Jeffersonians believed, so the president, his cabinet, and Congress worked to make the government leaner. If Alexander Hamilton had viewed the national debt as the engine of economic growth, Jefferson saw it as the source of government corruption. Secretary of the Treasury Albert Gallatin cut the army budget in half and reduced the 1802 navy budget by two-thirds. He then moved to reduce the national debt from $83 million to $57 million, as part of a plan to retire it altogether by 1817. Jefferson's austerity led him to close two of the nation's five diplomatic missions abroad, at The Hague and in Berlin. Jeffersonians attacked taxes as well as spending: the Democratic-Republican–controlled Congress oversaw the repeal of all internal taxes, including the despised whiskey tax of 1791.

In addition to frugality, ideas of liberty distinguished Democratic-Republicans from Federalists. The Alien and

Sedition Acts of 1798 had helped unite the Republicans in opposition. Jefferson now declined to use the acts against his opponents and pardoned those who had been convicted under the provisions. Congress let the Sedition Act expire in 1801 and the Alien Act in 1802. Congress also repealed the Naturalization Act of 1798, which had required fourteen years of residency for citizenship. The 1802 act that replaced it, while stipulating the registration of aliens, required of would-be citizens only five years of residency, loyalty to the Constitution, and the forsaking of foreign allegiances and titles. The new act would remain the basis of naturalized American citizenship into the twentieth century.

To many Democratic-Republicans, the judiciary represented a centralizing and undemocratic force, especially

### Judicial Politics

as judges were appointed rather than elected and served for life. Partisan Democratic-Republicans thus targeted opposition judges. At Jefferson's prompting, the House impeached (indicted) and the Senate convicted Federal District Judge John Pickering of New Hampshire. Allegedly deranged and alcoholic, Pickering made an easy mark. On the same day in 1803 that Pickering was ousted from office, the House impeached Supreme Court Justice Samuel Chase for judicial misconduct. A staunch Federalist, Chase had pushed for prosecutions under the Sedition Act, had actively campaigned for Adams in 1800, and had repeatedly denounced Jefferson's administration from the bench. But in the Senate the Democratic-Republicans failed to muster the two-thirds majority necessary for conviction. The failure to remove Chase preserved the Court's independence and established the precedent that criminal actions, not political disagreements, justified impeachment.

Although Jefferson appointed three new Supreme Court justices during his two administrations, the Court

### The Marshall Court

nonetheless remained a Federalist stronghold under the leadership of his distant cousin John Marshall. Marshall adopted some outward trappings of Republicanism—opting for a plain black gown over the more colorful academic robes of his fellow justices—but he adhered steadfastly to Federalist ideology. Even after the Democratic-Republicans achieved a majority of Court seats in 1811, Marshall remained extremely influential during his tenure as chief justice (1801–1835). Under the Marshall Court, the Supreme Court consistently upheld federal supremacy over the states while protecting the interests of commerce and capital.

Marshall made the Court an equal branch of the government in practice as well as theory. Previously re-

garded lightly, judicial service became a coveted honor for ambitious and talented men. Marshall, moreover, strengthened the Court by having it speak with a more unified voice; rather than issuing a host of individual concurring judgments, the justices now issued joint majority opinions. Marshall himself became the voice of the majority: from 1801 through 1805 he wrote twenty-four of the Court's twenty-six decisions; through 1810 he wrote 85 percent of the opinions, including every important one.

One of the most important involved Adams's midnight appointments. In his last hours in office, Adams

### Judicial Review

had named Federalist William Marbury a justice of the peace in the District of Columbia. But Jefferson's secretary of state, James Madison, declined to certify the appointment, so that the new president could appoint a Democratic-Republican instead. Marbury sued, requesting a writ of mandamus (a court order forcing the president to appoint him). *Marbury v. Madison* presented a political dilemma. If the Supreme Court ruled in Marbury's favor, the president probably would not comply with the writ, and the Court had no way to force him to do so. Yet, if the Federalist-dominated bench refused to issue the writ, it would hand the Democratic-Republicans a victory.

Marshall brilliantly recast the issue to avoid both pitfalls. Writing for the Court, he ruled that Marbury had a right to his appointment but that the Supreme Court could not compel Madison to honor the appointment because the Constitution did not grant the Court power to issue a writ of mandamus. In the absence of any specific mention in the Constitution, Marshall ruled, the section of the Judiciary Act of 1789 that authorized the Court to issue writs was unconstitutional. Thus the Supreme Court denied itself the power to issue writs of mandamus but established its far greater power to judge the constitutionality of laws passed by Congress. In doing so, Marshall fashioned the theory of judicial review. Because the Constitution was "the supreme law of the land," Marshall wrote, any federal or state act contrary to the Constitution must be null and void. The Supreme Court, whose duty it was to uphold the law, would decide whether a legislative act contradicted the Constitution. "It is emphatically the province and duty of the judicial department," Marshall ruled, "to say what the law is." This power of the Supreme Court to determine the constitutionality of legislation and presidential acts permanently enhanced the independence of the judiciary and breathed life into the Constitution. "Marshall found the Constitution paper and made it power," President James A. Garfield later observed.

In the first election after the Twelfth Amendment's ratification, Jefferson took no chances: he dropped Burr as his running mate and, in keeping with the already established convention of having a North-South balance on the ticket, chose George Clinton of New York. Their ticket swamped their opponents—South Carolinian Charles Cotesworth Pinckney and New Yorker Rufus King—in the electoral college by 162 votes to 14, carrying fifteen of the seventeen states.

**Election of 1804**

That 1804 election escalated the long-standing animosity between Burr and Hamilton, who supported Burr's rival in the New York gubernatorial election. When Hamilton called Burr a liar, Burr challenged Hamilton to a duel. Believing his honor was at stake, Hamilton accepted the challenge even though his son Philip had died in 1801 from dueling wounds. Because New York had outlawed dueling, the encounter took place across the Hudson River in New Jersey. Hamilton decided not to fire and paid for the decision with his life. In New York and New Jersey, prosecutors indicted Burr for murder.

Facing arrest if he returned to either state and with his political career in ruins, Burr fled to the West, where he and Brigadier General James Wilkinson schemed to create a new empire by using military force to acquire what is now Texas and by persuading already existing western territories to leave the United States and join the new empire. The plan fizzled when Wilkinson, fearful of the negative repercussions for himself, revealed the plot to Jefferson. The president personally assisted the prosecution in Burr's 1807 trial for treason, which was overseen by Jefferson's political rival Chief Justice Marshall. (At the time, Supreme Court justices presided over circuit courts.) Prompted by Marshall to interpret treason in a very narrow sense, the jury acquitted Burr, who fled to Europe.

## NATIONAL EXPANSION WESTWARD

Little excited the popular imagination more than the West and its seeming abundance of unoccupied land. By 1800 hundreds of thousands of white Americans had settled in the rich Ohio River and Mississippi River valleys, intruding on Indian lands. In the Northwest they raised foodstuffs, primarily wheat, and in the Southwest they cultivated cotton. At the time of the American Revolution, cotton production was profitable only for the Sea Island planters in South Carolina and Georgia, who grew the long-staple variety. Short-staple cotton, which grew readily in the interior and in all kinds of soil, was unmarketable because its sticky seeds could be removed only by hand. After a young New England inventor named Eli

Whitney designed a cotton gin (short for "engine") in 1793, allowing one person to remove the same number of seeds that previously required fifty people working by hand, the cultivation of short-staple cotton spread rapidly westward into the fertile lands of Louisiana, Mississippi, Alabama, Arkansas, and Tennessee. By exponentially increasing the efficiency with which cotton fiber could be extracted from raw cotton, the cotton gin greatly increased the demand for slaves, who seeded, tended, and harvested cotton fields.

Whatever crops they marketed, American settlers depended on free access to the Mississippi River and its Gulf port, New Orleans. "The Mississippi," wrote Secretary of State James Madison, "is to them [western settlers] everything. It is the Hudson, the Delaware, the Potomac and all navigable rivers of the Atlantic States formed into one stream." Whoever controlled the port of New Orleans had a hand on the throat of the American economy.

Spain, which had acquired France's territory west of the Mississippi in the settlement of the Seven Years War (1763), secretly transferred it back to France in 1800 and 1801. American officials learned of the transfer only in 1802, when Napoleon seemed poised to rebuild a French empire in the New World. "Every eye in the United States is now focused on the affairs of Louisiana," Jefferson wrote to Robert R. Livingston, the American minister in Paris. American concerns intensified when Spanish officials, on the eve of ceding control to the French, violated Pinckney's treaty by denying Americans the privilege of storing their products (or exercising their "right of deposit") at New Orleans prior to transshipment to foreign markets. Western farmers and eastern merchants, who traded through New Orleans, thought a devious Napoleon had closed the port; they talked war.

**New Orleans**

To relieve the pressure for war and win western farmers' support, Jefferson urged Congress to authorize the call-up of eighty thousand militiamen but at the same time sent Virginia Governor James Monroe to join Robert Livingston in France with instructions to buy the port of New Orleans and as much of the Mississippi valley as possible. Arriving in Paris in April 1803, Monroe learned with astonishment that France had already offered to sell all 827,000 square miles of Louisiana to the United States for a mere $15 million. With St. Domingue torn from French control by revolution and slave revolt, Napoleon gave up dreams of a New World empire and no longer needed Louisiana as its breadbasket. His more urgent need was for money to wage war against Britain. On April 30, Monroe and Livingston signed a treaty buying the vast terri-

UNDER MY WINGS EVERY THING PROSPERS

▲ At the time of the Louisiana Purchase in 1803, New Orleans was already a bustling port, though boosters predicted an even brighter future under American "wings."

*(Historic New Orleans Collection)*

tory whose exact borders and land remained uncharted (see Map 9.1).

## Louisiana Purchase

The Louisiana Purchase appealed to Americans with divergent ideas about how best to achieve national greatness and personal prosperity. The purchase ensured that the United States would control the Mississippi's mouth, giving peace of mind to western settlers who relied on the river to market their goods. It also inspired the commercial visions of those who imagined the United States as the nexus of international trade networks reaching between Europe and Asia. Louisiana promised to fulfill the dreams of easterners seeking cheap, fertile lands. Its vast expanse meant, too, that land could be set aside for Indians displaced by the incursion of white settlers and their black slaves, soothing the consciences of those white Americans who preferred to "civilize" rather than to exterminate the continent's first settlers. The purchase had its critics, though: some doubted its constitutionality (even Jefferson agonized over it); others worried that it belied the Democratic-Republicans' commitment to debt reduction; and some New England Federalists complained that it under-

mined their commercial interests and threatened the sustainability of the republic itself by spreading the population beyond the bounds of where it could be properly controlled. Overall, though, the Louisiana Purchase was the most popular achievement of Jefferson's presidency.

Louisiana was not, however, the "vast wilderness" that some Federalists lamented and most Republicans coveted. When the United States acquired the territory, hundreds of thousands of people who had not been party to the agreement became American subjects. These included Native Americans from scores of nations who made their homes within the enormous territory, as well as people of European and African descent—or, often, a mixture of the two—who congregated primarily along the Gulf Coast. Around New Orleans, Louisiana's colonial heritage was reflected in its people: creoles of French and Spanish descent, slaves of African descent, free people of color, and Acadians, or Cajuns (descendants of French settlers in eastern Canada), as well as some Germans and English. The 1810 census, the first taken after the purchase, reported that 97,000 non-Indians lived in the Louisiana Purchase area, of whom the great majority (77,000) lived in what is now the state of Louisiana. Not all these new Americans

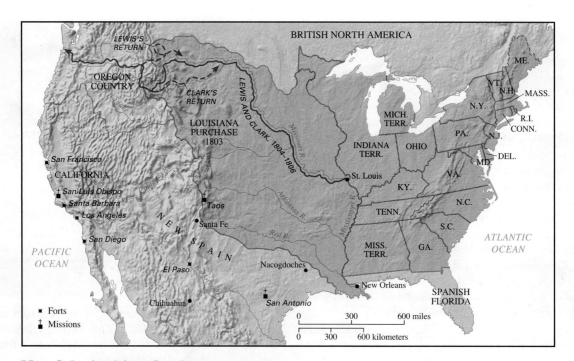

**Map 9.1    Louisiana Purchase**

The Louisiana Purchase (1803) doubled the area of the United States and opened the trans-Mississippi West for American settlement.

welcomed their new national identity. Although Jefferson imagined the West as an "empire of liberty," free blacks and slaves soon discovered that they lost some rights accorded them under French and Spanish law.

Jefferson had a long-standing interest in the trans-Mississippi West, envisioning it as punctuated with volcanoes and mountains of pure salt, where llamas and mammoths roamed and Welshmen settled. He felt an urgent need to explore it, fearing that, if Americans did not claim it as their own, the British, who still controlled the northern reaches of the continent (in present-day Canada) and parts of the Pacific Northwest, surely would. He lost no time in launching a military-style mission that would chart the region's commercial possibilities—its water passages to the Pacific as well as its trading opportunities with Indians—while cataloguing its geography, flora, and fauna.

## Lewis and Clark Expedition

The expedition, headed by Meriwether Lewis and William Clark, began in May 1804 and lasted for more than two years; it traveled up the Missouri River, across the Rockies, and then down the Columbia to the Pacific Ocean—and back. Along the way, the expedition's members "discovered" (as they saw it) dozens of previously unknown Indian tribes, many of whom had long before discovered Europeans. Lewis and Clark found the Mandans and Hidatsas already well supplied with European trade goods, such as knives, corduroy trousers, and rings. Although the Corps of Discovery, as the expedition came to be called, expected to find Indians and prepared for possible conflict, its goal was peaceable: to foster trade relations, win political allies, and take advantage of Indians' knowledge of the landscape. Accordingly, Lewis and Clark brought with them twenty-one bags of gifts for Native American leaders, both to establish goodwill and to stimulate interest in trading for American manufactured goods. Most of the corps' interactions with native peoples were cordial, but when Indians failed to be impressed by Lewis and Clark's gifts, tensions arose. After an encounter with the Lakota (or Sioux), Lewis denounced them as "the vilest miscreants of the savage race."

Although military in style, the Corps of Discovery proved unusually democratic in seating enlisted men on courts-martial and allowing Clark's black slave York as well as the expedition's female guide and translator Sacagawea to vote on where to locate winter quarters in 1805. But, unlike the expedition's other members, neither York nor Sacagawea drew wages, and when York later demanded his freedom for his services, Clark repaid him with—in Clark's own words—"a severe trouncing."

Lewis and Clark failed to discover a Northwest Passage to the Pacific, and the route they mapped across the Rockies proved more perilous than practical. But their federally sponsored expedition helped set the stage for additional government-sponsored exploration, capturing the imagination of white Americans seeking land for farming and profit.

In seeking land, white Americans mostly ignored the presence of Native Americans. Although Jefferson had more sympathy for Indians than did many of his contemporaries—he took interest in their cultures and believed Indians to be intellectually equal to whites—he nonetheless lobbied, unsuccessfully, for a constitutional amendment that would transport them west of the Mississippi into the newly acquired Louisiana Territory. He became personally involved in efforts to pressure the Chickasaws to sell their land, and in the event that legal methods for removing Indians should fail, he advocated trickery. Traders, he suggested, might run the "good and influential individuals" into debt, which they would have to repay "by a cessation of lands."

Some Indian nations decided to deal with white intruders by adopting white customs as a means of survival

▲ This Charles M. Russell painting of the Lewis and Clark expedition depicts Sacagawea talking with Chinook Indians. A Shoshone, Sacagawea knew the land and the languages of the mountain Indians, and helped guide the Corps of Discovery.

*(Courtesy, Montana Historical Society, Gift of the artist)*

### Divisions Among Indian Peoples

and often agreeing to sell their lands and move west. These "accommodationists" (or "progressives") were opposed by "traditionalists," who urged adherence to native ways and refused to relinquish their lands. Distinctions between accommodationists and traditionalists were not always so clear-cut, however, as the Seneca Handsome Lake had demonstrated just a few years before.

In the early 1800s, two Shawnee brothers, Tenskwatawa (1775–1837) and Tecumseh (1768–1813), led a traditionalist revolt against American encroachment by fostering a pan-Indian federation that centered in the Old Northwest and reached into parts of the South. During the two brothers' own lifetimes, the Shawnees had lost most of their Ohio land; by the 1800s they occupied only scattered sites in Ohio and in the Michigan and Louisiana territories. Despondent, Lalawethika—as Tenskwatawa had been called as a youth—had turned to a combination of European remedies (particularly whiskey) and Native American ones, becoming a shaman in 1804. But when European diseases ravaged his village, he despaired.

Lalawethika emerged from his own battle with illness in 1805 as a new man, renamed Tenskwatawa ("the Open Door") or—by whites— "the Prophet." Claiming to have died and been resurrected, he traveled widely in the Ohio River valley as a religious leader, attacking the decline of moral values among Native Americans, warning against whiskey, condemning intertribal battles, and stressing harmony and respect for elders. He urged Indians to return to the old ways and to abandon white ways: to hunt with bows and arrows, not guns; to stop wearing hats; and to give up bread for corn and beans. Tenskwatawa was building a religious movement that offered hope to the Shawnees, Potawatomis, and other displaced western Indians.

### Tenskwatawa and Tecumseh

By 1808 Tenskwatawa and his older brother Tecumseh talked less about spiritual renewal and more about resisting American aggression. They invited Indians from all nations to settle in pan-Indian towns in Indiana, first at Greenville (1806–1808) and then at Prophetstown (1808–1812), near modern-day Lafayette. The new towns challenged the treaty-making process by denying the claims of Indians who had been guaranteed the same land as part of the Treaty of Greenville of 1795 in exchange for enormous

▲ During the War of 1812, British forces and their Indian allies seized Fort Shelby in Wisconsin, renaming it Fort McKay. After the Treaty of Ghent (1814) restored the installation to American hands, British Captain W. Andrew Bulger bid farewell to his Indian allies before withdrawing and burning the fort. (*Captain W. Andrew Bulger Saying Farewell at Fort McKay, Prairie du Chien, Wisconsin, 1815* by Peter Rindis-bacher; 1815 watercolor and ink wash on paper, no. 1968.262. Amon Carter Museum, Fort Worth, Texas.)

cessions. Younger Indians, in particular, flocked to Tecumseh, the more politically oriented of the two brothers.

Convinced that only an Indian federation could stop the advance of white settlement, Tecumseh sought to unify northern and southern Indians by preaching Indian resistance across a wide swath of territory, ranging from Canada to Georgia. Among southern Indians, only one faction of the Creek nation welcomed him, but his efforts to spread his message southward nonetheless alarmed white settlers and government officials. In November 1811, while Tecumseh was in the South, Indiana governor William Henry Harrison moved against Tenskwatawa and his followers. During the battle of Tippecanoe, the army burned their town; as they fled, the Indians exacted revenge on white settlers. "What other course is left for us to pursue," asked Harrison, "but to make a war of extirpation upon them." With the stakes raised, Tecumseh entered a formal alliance with the British, who maintained forts in southern Ontario. This alliance, along with issues over American neutral rights on the high seas, were already propelling the United States toward war with Britain.

## THE NATION IN THE ORBIT OF EUROPE

A decade earlier, in 1801, when Jefferson had sought to set a new course for the nation, he tried to put tensions with France to rest. "Peace, commerce, and honest friendship with all nations, entangling alliances with none," he had proclaimed in his first inaugural address. Yet the economy of the early republic relied heavily on both fishing and the carrying trade, in which the American merchant marine transported commodities between nations. Merchants in Boston, Salem, and Philadelphia traded with China, sending cloth and metal to swap for furs with Chinook Indians on the Oregon coast, and then sailing to China to trade for porcelain, tea, and silk. The slave trade lured American ships to Africa. America's commercial interests were clearly focused on the seas, and not long after Jefferson's first inaugural address, the United States was at war with Tripoli—a state along the Barbary Coast of North Africa—over a principle that would long be a cornerstone of American foreign policy: freedom of the seas. In other words, outside of national territorial waters, the high seas should be open for free transit of all vessels.

In 1801 the bashaw (pasha) of Tripoli declared war on the United States for its refusal to pay tribute for safe

### First Barbary War

passage of its ships, sailors, and passengers through the Mediterranean. Jefferson deployed a naval squadron to protect American ships. After two years of stalemate, Jefferson declared a blockade of Tripoli, but when the American frigate *Philadelphia* ran aground in the harbor, its three hundred officers and sailors were imprisoned. Jefferson refused to ransom them, and a small American force accompanied by Arab, Greek, and African mercenaries marched from Egypt to the "shores of Tripoli" (memorialized to this day in the Marine Corps anthem) to seize the port of Derne. A treaty ended the war in 1805, but the United States continued to pay tribute to the three other Barbary states—Algiers, Morocco, and Tunis—until 1815. In the intervening years, the United States became embroiled in European conflicts.

At first Jefferson managed to distance the nation from the turmoil in Europe in the wake of the French Revolution. After the Senate ratified the Jay Treaty in 1795, the United States and Great Britain appeared to reconcile their differences. Britain withdrew from its western forts on American soil (while still retaining those in Canada and the Pacific Northwest) and interfered less in American trade with France. Then, in May 1803, two weeks after Napoleon sold Louisiana to the United States, France was at war against Britain and, later, Britain's continental allies, Prussia, Austria, and Russia. The Napoleonic wars again trapped the United States between belligerents on the high seas. But at first the United States—as the world's largest neutral shipping carrier—actually benefited from the conflict, and American merchants gained control of most of the West Indian trade. After 1805, however, when Britain defeated the French and Spanish fleets at Trafalgar, Britain's Royal Navy tightened its control of the oceans. Two months later, Napoleon crushed the Russian and Austrian armies at Austerlitz. Stalemated, France and Britain launched a commercial war, blockading each other's trade. As a trading partner of both countries, the United States paid a high price.

One British tactic in particular threatened American sovereignty. To replenish their supply of sailors, British

### Threats to American Sovereignty

vessels stopped American ships and impressed (forcibly recruited) British deserters, British-born naturalized American seamen, and other sailors suspected of being British. Perhaps six to eight thousand Amer-

icans were seized in this way between 1803 and 1812. Moreover, alleged deserters—many of them American citizens—faced British courts-martial. Americans saw impressment as a direct assault on their nation's independence. The principle of "once a British subject, always a British subject" mocked U.S. citizenship and sovereignty. Americans also resented the British interfering with their West Indian trade as well as their searching and seizing American vessels within U.S. territorial waters.

In April 1806 Congress responded with the Non-Importation Act, barring British manufactured goods from entering American ports. Because the act exempted most cloth and metal articles, it had little impact on British trade; instead, it warned the British what to expect if they continued to violate American neutral rights. In November Jefferson suspended the act temporarily while William Pinkney, a Baltimore lawyer, joined James Monroe in London to negotiate a settlement. But the treaty they carried home violated Jefferson's instructions—it did not so much as mention impressment—and the president never submitted it to the Senate for ratification.

Anglo-American relations steadily deteriorated, coming to a head in June 1807 when the USS *Chesapeake*, sailing out of Norfolk for the Mediterranean, was stopped by the British frigate *Leopard*, whose officers demanded to search the ship for British deserters. Refused, the *Leopard* opened fire, killing three Americans and wounding eighteen others, including the captain. The British then seized four deserters, three of whom held American citizenship; one of them was hanged. The *Chesapeake* affair outraged Americans while also exposing American military weakness.

Had the United States been better prepared militarily, public indignation over the incident might have resulted

### The Embargo of 1807

in a declaration of war. Instead, Jefferson opted for what he called "peaceable coercion." In July, the president closed American waters to British warships and soon thereafter increased military and naval expenditures. In December 1807, Jefferson again put economic pressure on Great Britain by invoking the Non-Importation Act, followed eight days later by a new restriction, the Embargo Act. Jefferson and his congressional supporters saw the embargo, which forbade all exports from the United States to any country, as a short-term measure to avoid war by pressuring Britain and France to respect American rights and by preventing confrontation between American merchant vessels and European warships.

The embargo's biggest economic impact, however, fell on the United States. Exports declined by 80 percent in 1808, squeezing New England shippers and their workers

▲ *Boarding and Taking of the American Ship* Chesapeake (1816) portrays crew from the British frigate *Leopard* fighting to search the USS *Chesapeake* for British navy deserters. The sailors of the *Chesapeake* resisted, but the British overpowered them and seized four deserters, three of them American citizens. Americans were humiliated and angered by the British violation of American rights. *(William L. Clements Library)*

as economic depression set in. Manufacturers, by contrast, received a boost, as the domestic market became theirs exclusively, and merchants began to shift their capital from shipping to manufacturing. In 1807 there were twenty cotton and woolen mills in New England; by 1813 there were more than two hundred. Meanwhile, merchants who were willing to engage in smuggling profited enormously.

They had only to look at the vibrant slave trade to see how scarcity bred demand. With Jefferson's encouragement, Congress had voted in 1807 to abolish the international slave trade as of January 1, 1808—the earliest date permissible under the Constitution. South Carolina alone still allowed the legal importation of slaves, but most of the state's influential planters favored a ban on the trade, nervous (having seen what happened in St. Domingue) about adding to the black population of a state in which whites were already outnumbered. Congressional debate focused not on whether it was a good idea to abolish the trade but on what should become of any Africans imported illegally after the ban took effect. The final bill provided

### International Slave Trade

that smuggled slaves would be sold in accordance with the laws of the state or territory in which they arrived. It underscored, in other words, that slaves (even illegal ones) were property. Had the bill not done so, threatened one Georgia congressman, the result might have been "resistance to the authority of the Government," even civil war. Although the debate over the slave trade did not fall along strictly sectional (or regional) lines, sectional tensions never lay far beneath the surface in this era of heated partisan conflict.

In anticipation of the higher prices that their human property would fetch once the law took effect, traders temporarily withheld their slaves from the market in the months after the law's passage. During the last four months of 1807 alone, sixteen thousand African slaves arrived at Gadsden Wharf in Charleston, where they were detained by merchants eager to wait out the January 1 deadline. Although many of these slaves—hundreds, if not thousands—died in the cramped, disease-ridden holding pens before they could be sold, merchants calculated that the increased value of those who survived until the ban took effect would outweigh the losses. Not that January 1, 1808, brought an end to the international slave trade; a brisk—and profitable—illegal trade took over. As Justice Joseph Story noted in 1819, the slave trade "is still carried on with all the implacable ferocity and insatiable rapacity of former times. Avarice has grown more subtle in its evasions; and watches and seizes its prey with an appetite quickened rather than suppressed by its guilty vigils." In 1819 Congress passed a law authorizing the president to use force to intercept slave ships along the African coast, but the small American navy could not halt the illicit trade in human beings.

As discussion of the international slave trade subsided, debate over the embargo heated up, especially with the approach of the 1808 presidential election. Democratic-Republicans suffered from factional dissent and dissatisfaction in seaboard states hobbled by the trade restrictions. Although nine state legislatures passed resolutions urging Jefferson to run again, the president followed George Washington's lead in declining a third term. He supported James Madison, his secretary of state, as the Democratic-Republican standard-bearer. For the first time, however, the Democratic-Republican nomination was contested. Madison won the endorsement of the party's congressional caucus, but Virginia Democratic-Republicans put forth James Monroe, who later withdrew, and some easterners supported Vice President George Clinton. Madison and Clinton headed the ticket. Charles Cotesworth Pinckney and Rufus King again ran on the Federalist ticket, but with new vigor.

### Election of 1808

The younger Federalists, led by Harrison Gray Otis and other Bostonians, made the most of the widespread disaffection with Democratic-Republican policy, especially the embargo. Pinckney received only 47 electoral votes to Madison's 122, but he carried all of New England except Vermont, won Delaware, and carried some electoral votes in two other states. Federalists also gained seats in Congress and captured the New York State legislature. Although the Federalist future looked promising, the transition from one Democratic-Republican administration to the next went smoothly.

This transition was eased, in part, by the wives of elected and appointed officials in the new capital, who encouraged political and diplomatic negotiation. Such negotiations often took place in social settings, even private homes, where people with divergent interests could bridge their ideological divides through personal relationships. Women played crucial roles, fostering conversation, providing an ear or a voice for unofficial messages, and—in

### Women and Politics

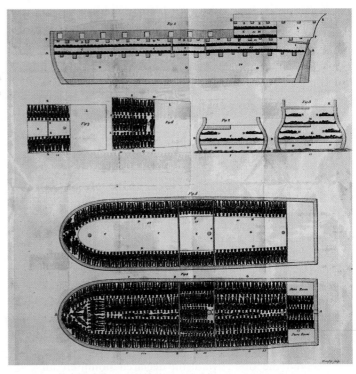

▲ In an effort to win support for measures to end the international slave trade and slavery itself, abolitionists published drawings of the inhumanely cramped slave ships, where each person was allotted a space roughly the size of a coffin. Disease spread rapidly under such conditions, causing many slaves to die before reaching American shores. *(The Huntington Library & Art Collections, San Marino, California)*

the case of international affairs—standing as surrogates for their nation. Elite women hosted events that muted domestic partisan rivalries, events at which Federalists and Democratic-Republicans could find common ground in civility, if not always politics. Political wives' interactions among themselves served political purposes, too: when First Lady Dolley Madison visited congressmen's wives, she cultivated goodwill for her husband while collecting recipes that allowed her to serve regionally diverse cuisine at White House functions. Mrs. Madison hoped her menus would help keep simmering sectional tensions from reaching a boiling point.

But it was women's buying power that may have proved most influential in the era of the embargo. Recalling women's support of revolutionary-era boycotts, Jeffersonians appealed directly for women's support of their embargo. Sympathetic women responded by spurning imported fabric and making (or directing their slaves to make) homespun clothing for themselves and their families. Federalists, however, encouraged women to "keep commerce alive," and sympathetic women bought smuggled goods.

Under the pressure of domestic opposition, the embargo eventually collapsed. In its place, the Non-Intercourse Act of 1809 reopened trade with all nations except Britain and France, and authorized the president to resume trade with those two nations once they respected American neutral rights. The new act solved only the problems created by the embargo; it did not prevent further British and French interference with American commerce. For one brief moment it appeared to work. In June 1809, President Madison reopened trade with Britain after its minister to the United States offered assurances that Britain would repeal restrictions on American trade. His Majesty's government in London, though, repudiated the minister's assurances, and Madison reverted to nonintercourse.

When the Non-Intercourse Act expired in 1810, Congress substituted a variant, Macon's Bill Number 2, which reopened trade with both Great Britain and France but provided that, when either nation stopped violating American commercial rights, the president would suspend American commerce with the other. When Napoleon accepted the offer, Madison declared nonintercourse on Great Britain in 1811. Although the French continued to seize American ships, Britain became the main focus of American hostility because its Royal Navy dominated the seas.

In spring 1812, the British admiralty ordered its ships not to stop, search, or seize American warships, and in June Britain reopened the seas to American shipping. But Britain's response came too late. Before word of the change in British policy reached American shores, Congress declared war.

The vote was sharply divided. The House voted 79 to 49 for war; the Senate, 19 to 13. Democratic-Republicans favored war by a vote of 98 to 23; Federalists opposed it 39 to 0.

**Mr. Madison's War**

Those who favored war, including President Madison, pointed to impressment, violation of neutral trading rights, British alliances with western Indians, and affronts to American independence and honor. The British, in other words, had assaulted American sovereignty. Others saw in the war an opportunity to conquer and annex British Canada. Most militant were land-hungry southerners and westerners—the "War Hawks"—led by John C. Calhoun of South Carolina and first-term congressman and House Speaker Henry Clay of Kentucky. John Randolph of Virginia, an opponent of war, charged angrily, "Agrarian cupidity, not maritime rights, urges war!" He heard "but one word" in Congress: "Canada! Canada! Canada!" Most representatives from the coastal states, and especially from the Northeast, feared disruption to commerce and opposed what they called "Mr. Madison's War."

The War of 1812 did not begin badly for the Federalists, who benefited from antiwar sentiment. They joined renegade Democratic-Republicans in supporting New York City mayor DeWitt Clinton for president in the election of 1812. Clinton lost to President Madison by 128 to 89 electoral votes—a respectable showing against a wartime president—and the Federalists gained some congressional seats and carried many local elections. But the South and the West—areas that favored the war—remained solidly Democratic-Republican.

## THE WAR OF 1812

For lack of a better term, the war has come down to us as the War of 1812. It lasted until 1815, unfolding in a series of scuffles and skirmishes (see Map 9.2), for which the U.S. armed forces, kept lean by Jeffersonian fiscal policies, were ill prepared. Officers executed campaigns poorly, and full-scale battles were rare. Although the U.S. Navy had a corps of experienced officers, it was no match for the Royal Navy. The U.S. Army had neither an able staff nor an adequate force of enlisted men. By 1812 the U.S. Military Academy at West Point, founded in 1802, had produced only eighty-nine regular officers. Senior army officers were aged Revolutionary War veterans or political appointees.

Nor did the United States succeed at mustering sufficient forces. The government's efforts to lure recruits—with sign-up bonuses and promises of three months' pay and rights to purchase 160 acres of western land upon discharge—met with mixed success. At first, recruitment went well among westerners, who were motivated by civic spirit, desire for land, strong anti-Indian sentiment, and fears of Tecumseh's pan-Indian organization. But after word spread of delays in pay, as well as inadequate supplies and rations, recruitment dwindled. In New England, raising an army was even more difficult. Federalists discouraged enlistments, and even some New England Democratic-Republicans declined to raise volunteer companies. Others promised their men that they would serve only in defensive roles, as in Maine, where they would guard the coastline. Militias in New England and New York often refused to fight outside their own states. Desperate for soldiers, New York offered freedom to slaves who enlisted, and compensation to their owners, and the U.S. Army made the same offer to slaves in the Old

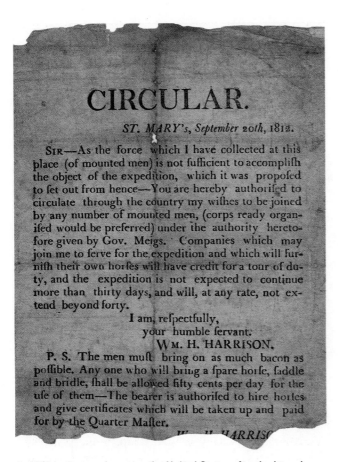

## CIRCULAR.

**ST. MARY's, September 20th, 1812.**

SIR—As the force which I have collected at this place (of mounted men) is not sufficient to accomplish the object of the expedition, which it was proposed to set out from hence—You are hereby authorized to circulate through the country my wishes to be joined by any number of mounted men, (corps ready organized would be preferred) under the authority heretofore given by Gov. Meigs. Companies which may join me to serve for the expedition and which will furnish their own horses will have credit for a tour of duty, and the expedition is not expected to continue more than thirty days, and will, at any rate, not extend beyond forty.

I am, respectfully,
your humble servant,
WM. H. HARRISON,

P. S. The men must bring on as much bacon as possible. Any one who will bring a spare horse, saddle and bridle, shall be allowed fifty cents per day for the use of them—The bearer is authorized to hire horses and give certificates which will be taken up and paid for by the Quarter Master.

W. H. HARRISO

▲ With a tiny regular army, the United States often had to rely upon short-term recruits to wage war on the British. Because inadequate transportation made it difficult to supply soldiers with necessities, this poster calls upon recruits to bring as much bacon with them as possible and offers a bounty if they bring their own equipped horses.

*(Chicago Historical Society)*

Northwest and in Canada. In Philadelphia, black leaders formed a "Black Brigade" to defend the city. But in the Deep South, fear of arming slaves kept them out of the military except in New Orleans, where a free black militia dated back to Spanish control of Louisiana. The British, on the other hand, recruited slaves by promising freedom in exchange for service. In the end, British forces—made up of British regulars, their Indian allies, fugitive slaves, and Canadians, many of whom were loyalists who had fled to Canada during the American Revolution—outnumbered the Americans overall.

Despite their recruitment problems, Americans had expected to take Canada easily. Canada's population was sparse, its army small, and the Great Lakes inaccessible

### Invasion of Canada

to the Royal Navy in the Atlantic. Americans hoped, too, that the French in Canada might welcome U.S. forces.

American strategy aimed to split Canadian forces and isolate pro-British Indians, especially Tecumseh, whom the British had promised an Indian nation in the Great Lakes region. In July 1812, U.S. general William Hull, territorial governor of Michigan, marched his troops into Upper Canada (modern Ontario), hoping to conquer Montreal. Although his forces outnumbered those of the British and their allies, Hull waged a timid campaign, retreating more than he attacked. His abandonment of Mackinac Island and Fort Dearborn and his surrender of Fort Detroit left the entire Midwest exposed to the enemy. The only bright spot was the September 1812 defense of Fort Harrison in Indiana Territory by Captain Zachary Taylor, who provided the Americans with their first land victory. By the winter of 1812–1813, the British controlled about half of the Old Northwest. The United States had no greater success on the Niagara Front, where New York borders Canada, in large part because New York militiamen refused to leave their state to join the invasion of Canada.

### Naval Battles

Despite victories on the Atlantic by the USS *Constitution* (nicknamed "Old Ironsides" after its rout of the HMS *Guerrière*), the USS *Wasp*, and the USS *United States,* the American navy—which began the war with just seventeen ships—could not match the powerful Royal Navy. The Royal Navy blockaded the Chesapeake and Delaware Bays in December 1812, and by 1814 the blockade covered nearly all American ports along the Atlantic and Gulf coasts. After 1811, American trade overseas declined by nearly 90 percent, and the decline in revenue from customs duties threatened to bankrupt the federal government and prostrate New England.

The contest for control of the Great Lakes, the key to the war in the Northwest, evolved as a shipbuilding race. Under Master Commandant Oliver Hazard Perry and shipbuilder Noah Brown, the United States outbuilt the British on Lake Erie and defeated them at the bloody Battle of Put-in-Bay on September 10, 1813, gaining control of Lake Erie.

### Burning Capitals

General William Henry Harrison then began what would be among the United States' most successful land campaigns. A ragged group of Kentucky militia volunteers, armed only with swords and knives, marched

**Map 9.2    Major Campaigns of the War of 1812**
The land war centered on the U.S.-Canadian border, the Chesapeake Bay, and the Louisiana and Mississippi Territories.

20 to 30 miles a day to join Harrison's forces in Ohio. Now 4,500 strong, Harrison's forces attacked and took Detroit before crossing into Canada, where at the Battle of the Thames they defeated British, Shawnee, and Chippewa forces in October 1813. Among the fallen was Tecumseh. The Americans went on to raze the Canadian capital of York (now Toronto), looting and burning the Parliament building before withdrawing.

After defeating Napoleon in Europe in April 1814, the British launched a land counteroffensive against the United States, concentrating on the Chesapeake Bay region. In retaliation for the burning of York—and to divert American troops from Lake Champlain, where the British planned a new offensive—royal troops occupied Washington, D.C., in August and set it ablaze, leaving the presidential mansion and parts of the city burning all night. Chaos ruled.

The president and cabinet fled. Dolley Madison stayed in town long enough to oversee the removal of cabinet documents and, famously, to save a Gilbert Stuart portrait of George Washington.

The British intended the attack on the capital only as a diversion. The major battle occurred in September 1814 at Baltimore, where the Americans held firm. Francis Scott Key, detained on a British ship, watched the bombardment of Fort McHenry from Baltimore harbor and the next morning wrote the verses of "The Star-Spangled Banner" (which became the national anthem in 1931). Although the British inflicted heavy damage, they achieved little militarily; their offensive on Lake Champlain proved equally unsuccessful when American ships turned back a British flotilla at Plattsburgh. The British halted their offensive; the war had reached a stalemate.

To the south, the war's final campaign began with an American attack on the Red Stick Creeks along the Gulf of Mexico and the British around New Orleans. The Red Sticks had responded to Tecumseh's call (his mother was a Creek) to resist U.S. expansion. Some had died in Indiana Territory, when General Harrison's troops routed Shawnee forces at Tippecanoe in 1811. In 1813 the Red Sticks attacked Fort Mims, about 40 miles from Mobile, killing hundreds of white men, women, and children who had sought protection there. Seeking revenge, General Andrew Jackson of Tennessee rallied his militiamen as well as Indian opponents of the Red Sticks (including other Creeks who favored accommodation with whites) and crushed the Red Sticks at Horseshoe Bend (in present-day Alabama) in March 1814. The victory helped clear additional land for white American settlement. In the 1814 Treaty of Fort Jackson, the Creeks ceded 23 million acres of their land, or about half of their holdings, and withdrew to the southern and western part of Mississippi Territory.

### War in the Old Southwest

Jackson became a major general in the regular army and continued south toward the Gulf of Mexico, with his eye on New Orleans. After seizing Pensacola (in Spanish Florida) and then securing Mobile, Jackson's forces continued on to New Orleans, where for three weeks they played a game of cat-and-mouse with the British soldiers. Finally, on January 8, 1815, the two forces met head-on. In fortified positions, Jackson's poorly trained army held its ground against two British frontal assaults. At day's end, more than two thousand British soldiers lay dead or wounded (a casualty rate of nearly one-third), while the Americans suffered only twenty-one casualties.

The Battle of New Orleans took place two weeks after the war's official conclusion: word had not yet reached

▲ Americans rejoiced that the War of 1812 had reaffirmed their independence from the British monarchy. The sailor's foot here steps upon the crown while broken chains of bondage lie nearby.

*(Picture Research Consultants & Archives)*

the United States that British and American diplomats had signed the Treaty of Ghent on December 24, 1814. Although militarily unnecessary, the Battle of New Orleans helped catapult General Andrew Jackson to national political prominence, and a soon legendary victory over a formidable foe inspired a sense of national pride.

The Treaty of Ghent essentially restored the prewar status quo. It provided for an end to hostilities with the British and with Native Americans, release of prisoners, restoration of conquered territory, and arbitration of boundary disputes. But the United States received no satisfaction on impressment, blockades, or other maritime rights for neutrals, and the British demands for territorial cessions from Maine to Minnesota went unmet. The British dropped their promise to Tecumseh of an independent Indian nation.

### Treaty of Ghent

Why did the negotiators settle for so little? Napoleon's defeat allowed the United States to discard its prewar demands, because peace in Europe made impressment and interference with American commerce moot issues. Similarly, war-weary Britain—its treasury nearly depleted—stopped pressing for military victory.

Yet the War of 1812 had significant consequences for America's status in the world. It affirmed the indepen-

American
Sovereignty
Reasserted

dence of the American republic and ensured Canada's independence from the United States. Although conflict with Great Britain over trade and territory continued, it never again led to war. The experience strengthened America's resolve to steer clear of European politics.

The return of peace with Europe also allowed the United States to again turn its attention to the Barbary Coast, where the dey (governor) of Algiers had taken advantage of the American preoccupation with British forces to declare his own war on the United States. In the Second Barbary War, U.S. forces seized prisoners, as the bashaw of Tripoli had done in 1801, holding hundreds of Algerians captive while negotiating a treaty in the summer of 1815 that forever freed the United States from having to pay tributes for passage in the Mediterranean. The Second Barbary War helped reaffirm American sovereignty, as well as its commitment to the principle of freedom of the seas.

The War of 1812 had profound domestic consequences, too. The Federalists' hopes of once again be-

Domestic
Consequences

coming a national party all but evaporated with the Hartford Convention. With the war stalemated and the New England economy shattered by embargo and war, delegates from New England met in Hartford, Connecticut, for three weeks in the winter of 1814–1815 to dis-
cuss revising the national compact or pulling out of the republic. Moderates prevented a resolution of secession—a resolution to withdraw from the Union—but the twenty-six convention delegates condemned the war and the embargo while endorsing changes in the Constitution that would weaken the South's power vis-à-vis the North and make it harder to declare war. When news arrived in upcoming weeks of, first, Jackson's victory in New Orleans and, then, the Treaty of Ghent, the Hartford Con-
vention made the Federalists look wrong-headed, if not treasonous. Although the Federalists survived in a handful of states until the 1820s, the party faded from the na-
tional scene.

With the death of Tecumseh, midwestern Indians lost their most powerful political and military leader; with the withdrawal of the British, they lost their strongest ally. In the South, the Red Sticks had ceded vast tracts of fertile land. The war did not bring disaster to all Indians—some accommodationists, such as the Cherokees, tempo-

rarily flourished in its aftermath—but it effectively disarmed traditionalists bent on resisting American expansion. Although the Treaty of Ghent pledged the United States to end hostilities with Indians and to restore their prewar "possessions, rights, and privileges," Indians did not have the power to make the United States live up to the terms of the agreement.

For American farmers, the war opened vast tracts of formerly Indian land for the cultivation of cotton in the Old Southwest and wheat in the Old Northwest. For young industries, the war also, in the end, proved a stim-
ulant, as Americans could no longer rely on overseas im-
ports to fill their demands for manufactured goods, particularly textiles. The War of 1812 thus fueled the de-
mand for raw cotton, and the newly acquired lands in the Southwest beckoned southerners who migrated there either with their slaves or with expectations of someday owning slaves.

The conclusion of the war accelerated three trends that would dominate U.S. history for upcoming decades: west-
ward expansion, industrial takeoff, and the entrenchment of slavery. Increasingly, political elites, including Democratic-Republicans, came to believe that the federal government ought to give direction to the American economy.

## THE NATIONALIST PROGRAM

In his last year as president, James Madison and the Democratic-Republicans embraced a nationalist agenda, absorbing the Federalist idea that the federal government should encourage economic growth. In his December 1815 message to Congress, Madison recommended economic development and military expansion. His agenda, which Henry Clay later called the American System, included a national bank, improved transportation, and a protective tariff—a tax on imported goods that was designed to protect American manufacturers from foreign competition. Yet Madison did not stray entirely from his Jeffersonian roots; only a constitutional amendment, he argued, could authorize the federal government to build local roads and canals.

Clay and other leaders in Congress, such as Calhoun of South Carolina, thought that the American System

American System

would unify the nation as it ex-
panded, bridging sectional divides. The tariff would stimulate New England industry. Goods produced in New England would find markets in the South and West. At the same time, the agricultural products of the South and West—cotton and foodstuffs—would feed New England mills and their workers. Manufactured goods

and agricultural products would move in all directions along roads and canals—what contemporaries called internal improvements—which tariff revenues would fund. A national bank would handle the transactions.

In the last year of Madison's administration, the Democratic-Republican Congress enacted much of the nationalist program. In 1816 it chartered the Second Bank of the United States (the charter on the first bank had expired in 1811) to serve as a depository for federal funds and to issue currency, collect taxes, and pay the government's debts. The Second Bank of the United States was responsible, too, for overseeing state and local banks, making certain that their paper money had backing in specie (precious metals). Like its predecessor, the bank mixed public and private ownership; the government provided one-fifth of the bank's capital and appointed one-fifth of its directors.

Congress also passed a protective tariff to aid industries that had flourished during the War of 1812 but were now threatened by the resumption of overseas trade. The Tariff of 1816 levied taxes on imported woolens and cottons, as well as on iron, leather, hats, paper, and sugar. Foreshadowing a growing trend, though, the tariff served more to divide than to unify the nation. New England as well as the western and Middle Atlantic states stood to benefit from it and thus applauded it, whereas many in the South opposed it because it raised the price on goods they purchased while also raising the possibility that Britain would retaliate with a tariff on cotton.

Some southerners did press for internal improvements. Calhoun vocally promoted roads and canals to "bind the republic together." However, on March 3, 1817, the day before he left office, President Madison, citing constitutional scruples, stunned Congress by vetoing Calhoun's "Bonus Bill," which would have authorized federal funding for such public works.

Constitutional scruples aside, Federalists and Democratic-Republicans agreed on the need for internal improvements. Improved transportation was necessary for both parties' vision of the nation's route to prosperity. Federalists saw roads and canals as a way to spur the nation's commercial development; Jeffersonians, as the route to the nation's western expansion and agrarian growth. In 1806 Congress had passed (and Jefferson had signed into law) a bill authorizing federal funding for the Cumberland Road (later, the National Road) running between Cumberland, Maryland, and Wheeling, Virginia (now West Virginia). Construction on the road began in 1811, stretching the 130 miles to Wheeling in 1818. In

## Early Internal Improvements

1820 Congress authorized a survey of the National Road to Columbus, Ohio, a project that was funded in 1825 and completed in 1833; the road would ultimately extend into Indiana.

After President Madison's veto of the Bonus Bill, though, most transportation initiatives received funding from states, private investors, or a combination of the two. In 1817 the State of New York began construction on the Erie Canal, linking the Great Lakes to the Atlantic seaboard; the project would be completed in 1825. Although modest canals were built in southern states, the South relied mostly on rivergoing steamboats that quickly dominated river trade following Robert Fulton's successful trial of a steam-powered vessel in 1807. In 1815 a steamboat made the first upriver voyage on the Mississippi; by 1817, steamboats began making the trip regularly. Canals and steamboats greatly reduced the time and costs involved in transporting western agricultural products to market, and fueled the nation's westward expansion. Unlike steamboats, though, canals expanded commercial networks into regions that did not have natural waterways. Although the Mississippi provided the great commercial highway of the Early Republic, canals would begin to reorient midwestern commerce through the North.

James Monroe, Madison's successor, continued Madison's domestic program, supporting tariffs and vetoing the Cumberland Road Bill (for repairs) in 1822. Monroe was the last president to have attended the Constitutional Convention and the third Virginian elected president since 1801. A former senator and twice governor of Virginia, he had served under Madison as secretary of state and of war, and had used his close association with Jefferson and Madison to attain the presidency. In 1816 he and his running mate, Daniel Tompkins, trounced the last Federalist presidential nominee, Rufus King, garnering all the electoral votes except those of the Federalist strongholds of Massachusetts, Connecticut, and Delaware. A Boston newspaper dubbed this one-party period the "Era of Good Feelings."

## The Era of Good Feelings

Led by Federalist chief justice John Marshall, the Supreme Court became the bulwark of the nationalist point of view. In *McCulloch v. Maryland* (1819), the Court struck down a Maryland law taxing banks within the state that were not chartered by the Maryland legislature—a law aimed at hindering the Baltimore branch of the federally chartered Second Bank of the United States. The bank had refused to pay the tax and sued. At issue was state versus federal jurisdiction. Writing for a unanimous Court, Marshall asserted the supremacy of the federal government over the states. "The Constitution and the laws thereof are supreme," he declared. "They control the constitution and laws of the respective states and cannot be controlled by them." The Court also unanimously ruled that Congress had the power to charter banks under the Constitution's clause that endowed it with the authority to pass "all laws which shall be necessary and proper for carrying into execution" the enumerated powers of government. The Marshall Court thus provided a bulwark for the Federalist view that the federal government could promote interstate commerce.

### Government Promotion of Market Expansion

Later Supreme Court cases validated government promotion of economic development and encouraged business enterprise and risk taking. In *Gibbons v. Ogden* (1824), the Supreme Court overturned the New York law that had given Robert Fulton and Robert Livingston (and their successor, Aaron Ogden) a monopoly on the New York–New Jersey steamboat trade. Chief Justice John Marshall ruled that the federal power to license new enterprises took precedence over New York's grant of monopoly rights and declared that Congress's power under the commerce clause of the Constitution extended to "every species of commercial intercourse," including transportation. The *Gibbons v. Ogden* ruling built on earlier Marshall Court decisions, such as those in *Dartmouth College v. Woodward* (1819), which protected the sanctity of contracts against state interference, and *Fletcher v. Peck* (1810), which voided a Georgia law that violated individuals' rights to make contracts. Within two years of *Gibbons v. Ogden*, the number of steamboats operating in New York increased from six to forty-three. A later ruling under Chief Justice Roger Taney, *Charles River Bridge v. Warren Bridge* (1837), encouraged new enterprises and technologies by favoring competition over monopoly and the public interest over implied privileges in old contracts.

Federal and state courts, in conjunction with state legislatures, also encouraged the proliferation of corporations—organizations entitled to hold property and transact business as if they were individuals. Corporation owners, called shareholders, were granted limited liability, or freedom from personal responsibility for the company's debts beyond their original investment. Limited liability encouraged investors to back new business ventures.

The federal government assisted the development of a commercial economy in other ways. The U.S. Post Office fostered the circulation of information, a critical element of the market economy. The number of post offices grew from three thousand in 1815 to fourteen thousand in 1845. To create an atmosphere conducive to economic growth and individual creativity, the government protected inventions and domestic industries. Patent laws gave inventors a seventeen-year monopoly on their inventions, and tariffs protected American industry from foreign competition.

### Boundary Settlements

Monroe's secretary of state, John Quincy Adams, matched the self-confident Marshall Court in assertiveness and nationalism. Adams, the son of John and Abigail Adams, managed the nation's foreign policy from 1817 to 1825, stubbornly pushing for expansion, fishing rights for Americans in Atlantic waters, political distance from Europe, and peace. An ardent expansionist, he nonetheless believed that expansion must come through negotiations, not war, and that newly acquired territories must bar slavery.

Under Adams's leadership, the United States settled outstanding points of conflict with both Britain and Spain. In 1817 the United States and Great Britain agreed in the Rush-Bagot Treaty to limit their naval forces to one ship each on Lake Champlain and Lake Ontario, and to two ships each on the four other Great Lakes. This first disarmament treaty of modern times led to the demilitarization of the border between the United States and Canada. Adams then pushed for the Convention of 1818, which fixed the U.S.-Canadian border from Lake of the Woods in Minnesota westward to the Rockies along the 49th parallel. When they could not agree on the boundary west of the Rockies, Britain and the United States settled on joint occupation of Oregon for ten years (renewed indefinitely in 1827).

Adams's negotiations resulted in the Adams-Onís Treaty, in which the United States gained Florida, already occupied by General Andrew Jackson under pretext of suppressing Seminole raids against American settlements across the border during the First Seminole War of 1817–1818. Although the Louisiana Purchase had omitted reference to Spanish-ruled West Florida, the United States claimed the territory as far east as the Perdido River (the present-day Florida-Alabama border). During the War of 1812, the United States had seized Mobile and the remainder of West Florida, and after the war—with Spain preoccupied with its own domestic and colonial troubles—Adams had laid claim to East Florida. In 1819 Don Luís de Onís, the Spanish minister to the United States, agreed to cede Florida to the United States without payment if the United States renounced its dubious claims to northern Mexico (Texas) and assumed $5 million of claims by

American citizens against Spain. The Adams-Onís (or Transcontinental) Treaty also defined the southwestern boundary of the Louisiana Purchase and set the line between Spanish Mexico and Oregon Country at the 42nd parallel.

John Quincy Adams's desire to insulate the United States and the Western Hemisphere from European conflict brought about his greatest achievement: the Monroe Doctrine. The immediate issue was the recognition of the new governments in Latin America. Between 1808 and 1822, the United Provinces of Río de la Plata (present-day northern Argentina, Paraguay, and Uruguay), Chile, Peru, Colombia, and Mexico all broke free from Spain. In 1822, shortly after the ratification of the Adams-Onís Treaty, the United States became the first nation outside Latin America to recognize the new states, including Mexico. But in Europe, reactionary regimes were in the ascendancy, and with France now occupying Spain to suppress a liberal rebellion, the United States feared that continental powers would attempt to return the new Latin American states to colonial rule. Having withdrawn from an alliance with continental nations, Britain proposed a joint declaration with the United States against European intervention in the Western Hemisphere. But Adams rejected Britain's offer as just the kind of entanglement he sought to avoid, despite clear advantages to allying with the British and their powerful navy.

Monroe presented to Congress in December 1823 what became known as the Monroe Doctrine. His message announced that the American continents "are henceforth not to be considered subjects for future colonization by any European power." This principle addressed American anxiety not only about Latin America but also about Russian expansion beyond Alaska and its settlements in California. Monroe demanded nonintervention by Europe in the affairs of independent New World nations, and he pledged noninterference by the United States in European affairs, including those of Europe's existing New World colonies. Although Monroe's words carried no force—European nations stayed out of New World affairs because they feared the Royal Navy, not the United States' proclamations—they proved popular at home, tapping American nationalism as well as anti-British and anti-European feelings.

**Monroe Doctrine**

## SECTIONALISM EXPOSED

The embargo, the War of 1812, and the postwar spurt of internal improvements encouraged the southern and northern economies to develop in different but interre-lated ways. While the South would become ever more dependent on cotton, the North saw an acceleration of industrial development, whose groundwork had been laid two decades earlier. Although Jeffersonians, committed to frugal government and an agrarian nation, did not promote industry, a small number of entrepreneurs did.

For all of their efforts to define themselves as a separate nation, Americans relied on British technology to bring together the many steps of textile manufacturing—carding (or disentangling) fibers, spinning yarn, and weaving cloth—under one factory roof. The first American water-powered spinning mill was established in 1790 by Samuel Slater, a British immigrant who reconstructed from memory the complex machines he had used as an apprentice and then as a supervisor in a British cotton-spinning factory. But Slater's mill only carded and spun yarn; that yarn still needed to be hand-woven into cloth, work that was often done by farm women seeking to earn extra cash. In 1810 Bostonian Francis Cabot Lowell, determined to introduce water-powered mechanical weaving in the United States, visited the British textile center of Manchester, where he toured factories during the day and at night sketched from memory what he had seen. In 1813 he and his business associates, calling themselves the Boston Manufacturing Company, brought together all phases of textile manufacturing under one roof in Waltham, Massachusetts. A decade later, the Boston Manufacturing Company established what it saw as a model industrial village—named for its now-deceased founder—along the banks of the Merrimack River. At Lowell, Massachusetts, there would be boarding houses for workers, a healthy alternative to the tenements and slums of Manchester. American industrialists envisioned that America would industrialize without the poverty and degradation associated with European industrialization.

**Early Industrial Development**

The American textile factory had been born in the midst of the War of 1812. When the British began flooding the American market with cheap textiles after the Treaty of Ghent, Lowell realized the market now needed to be protected. He lobbied hard for the inclusion of cotton textiles in the Tariff of 1816, playing a crucial role in persuading reluctant South Carolinians to support the provision.

The growth of early industry, primarily in the northern states, was inextricably linked to slavery. Much of the capital behind early industrialization came from merchants who had made their fortunes at least in part through the trade in African slaves, and two of the most

## Industrial Piracy

Although Americans pride themselves on inventiveness and hard work, their start in industrial development depended on importing technology, sometimes by stealth. Great Britain, which in the late eighteenth century had pioneered the invention of mechanical weaving and power looms, knew the value of its head start in the industrial revolution and prohibited the export of textile technology. But the British-born brothers Samuel and John Slater, their Scottish-born power-loom-builder William Gilmore, and Bostonians Francis Cabot Lowell and Nathan Appleton evaded British restrictions and patents to establish America's first textile factories.

As an apprentice and then a supervisor in a British cotton-spinning factory, Samuel Slater had mastered the machinery and the process. Britain forbade the export of textile technology, so Slater emigrated to the United States disguised as a farmer. In 1790 in Pawtucket, Rhode Island, he opened the first water-powered spinning mill in America on the Blackstone River, rebuilding the complex machines from memory. With his brother John and their Rhode Island partners—Moses and Obadiah Brown and William Almy—Slater later built and oversaw mills in Rhode Island and Massachusetts. In 1815 he hired a recent immigrant, William Gilmore, to build a water-powered loom like those used in Britain. Later in the 1820s, the Slaters introduced British steam-powered looms. Spinning and weaving would now be done in New England factories organized along British models.

In 1810 Francis Cabot Lowell had the same idea as the Slaters: to build modern mills with mechanical, water-powered looms. Lowell took a family vacation to Britain, and in Edinburgh, Scotland, he met fellow Bostonian Nathan Appleton. Impressed by the textile mills they had seen in Britain, they laid plans to introduce water-powered mechanical weaving into the United States. They knew they had to acquire the "improved manufactures" from Britain that had made Manchester famous as a textile center. Lowell went to Manchester, during the day visiting and observing the factories, and meeting the factory managers. At night he returned to his hotel to sketch from memory the power looms and processes that he had seen. Back in the United States, he and others formed the Boston Associates, which created the Waltham-Lowell Mills based on Lowell's industrial piracy. Within a few years, textiles would be a major American industry, and the Boston Associates would dominate it.

Thus the modern American industrial revolution began with international links, not homegrown American inventions. Ingenuity and industrial piracy put the United States on the road to industrial advancement.

This contemporary painting shows the Boston Manufacturing Company's 1814 textile factory at Waltham, Massachusetts. All manufacturing processes were brought together under one roof, and the company built its first factories in rural New England to tap roaring rivers as a power source.

*(Courtesy of Gore Place Society, Waltham, Massachusetts)*

prominent industries—textiles and shoes—expanded in tandem with a growing southern cotton economy. Southern cotton fed northern textile mills, and northern shoe factories sold their "Negro brogans" (work shoes) to southern planters. Even in an older form of northern industrial labor which took place in private homes—outwork—the connections to the slave South were strong: New England farm girls wove palm-leaf hats for merchants who sold them to southern planters for their slaves.

Immediately after the war, the American economy boomed. The demand for (and price of) American commodities on the international market reached new heights. Poor weather in Europe led to crop failures and thus to an increased demand for northern agricultural exports, and European textile manufacturers clamored for the South's raw cotton. The demand for American wheat and cotton touched off western land speculation. Speculators raced to buy large tracts of land at modest, government-established prices and then to resell it at a hefty profit to would-be settlers. This American expansion was built on easy credit. With easily obtained loans and paper money, farmers and speculators bought land, while manufacturers established new enterprises or enlarged existing ones.

**Panic of 1819**

Prosperity proved short-lived. Now recovered from war as well as weather, by the late 1810s Europeans could grow their own food, and Britain's new Corn Laws established a high tariff on imported foodstuffs—further lessening demand for American agricultural exports. Cotton prices fell in England. Wars in Latin America interfered with mining and reduced the supply of precious metals, leading European nations to hoard specie; in response, American banks furiously printed paper money and expanded credit even further. Fearful of inflation, the Second Bank of the United States, which had itself issued more loans than it could back in hard currency, demanded in 1819 that state banks repay loans in specie. State banks in turn called in the loans and mortgages they had made to individuals and companies. The falling prices of commodities meant that farmers could not pay their mortgages, and the decline of land values—from 50 to 75 percent in portions of the West—meant they could not meet their debts even by selling their farms. The nation's banking system collapsed. The 1819 financial panic reminded Americans all too starkly that they still lived within the economic orbit of Europe.

Hard times came to countryside and city alike. Foreclosures soared. Unemployment skyrocketed, even in older manufacturing areas that had focused on industries like iron making and tobacco processing. In Philadelphia it reached 75 percent. The contraction devastated workers and their families. As a Baltimore physician noted in 1819, working people felt hard times "a thousand fold more than the merchants." They could not build up savings during boom times to get them through the hard times; often they could not make it through the winter without drawing on charity for food, clothing, and firewood.

The depression sent tremors throughout American society. Americans from all regions contemplated the virtues and hazards of rapid market expansion, disagreeing most intensely on where to place the blame for its shortcomings. Westerners blamed easterners; farmers and workers blamed bankers. Even as the nation's economy began to rebound in the early 1820s, amid a flurry of internal improvement projects, no one could predict with confidence where—in what region, in what sector—the nation's economic and political fortunes would lie.

Just as financial panic struck the nation in 1819, so, too, did political crisis. The issue was slavery's westward expansion. Although economic connections abounded between North and South, slavery had long been politically explosive. Since the drafting of the Constitution, Congress had tried to avoid the issue; the one exception had been debates over the international slave trade. In 1819, however, slavery once again burst onto the national political agenda when residents of the Missouri Territory—carved out of the Louisiana Territory—petitioned Congress for admission to the Union with a constitution permitting slavery. At stake was more than the future of slavery in an individual state. Missouri's admission to the Union would give the slaveholding states a two-vote majority in the Senate, and what happened in Missouri would surely set a precedent for all the new western states created from the vast Louisiana Purchase. "This momentous question," wrote former President Jefferson, fearful for the life of the Union, "like a fire bell in the night, awakened and filled me with terror."

**Missouri Compromise**

Following the Louisiana Purchase and especially after the end of the War of 1812, the American population had surged westward, leading five new states to join the Union: Louisiana (1812), Indiana (1816), Mississippi (1817), Illinois (1818), and Alabama (1819). Of these, Louisiana, Mississippi, and Alabama permitted slavery. Because Missouri was on the same latitude as free Illinois, Indiana, and Ohio (a state since 1803), its admission as a

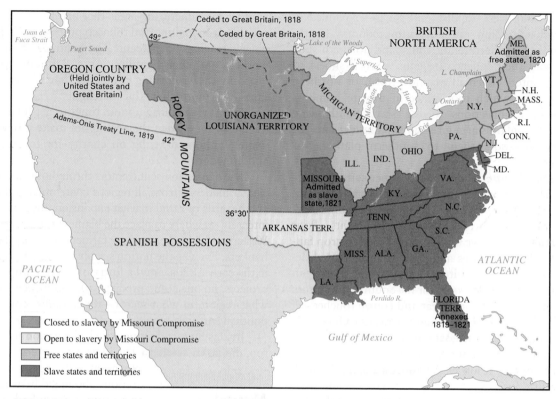

**Map 9.3   Missouri Compromise and the State of the Union, 1820**
The compromise worked out by House Speaker Henry Clay established a formula that avoided debate over whether new states would allow or prohibit slavery. In the process, it divided the United States into northern and southern regions.

slave state would thrust slavery not just westward but also farther northward, as well as tilt the uneasy balance in the Senate.

For two and a half years the issue dominated Congress, with the fiery debate transcending the immediate issue of slavery in Missouri. When Representative James Tallmadge Jr. of New York proposed gradual emancipation in Missouri, some southerners accused the North of threatening to destroy the Union. "If you persist, the Union will be dissolved," Thomas W. Cobb of Georgia shouted at Tallmadge. Only "seas of blood" could extinguish the fire Tallmadge had ignited, warned Cobb. "Let it come," retorted Tallmadge. The House, which had a northern majority, passed the Tallmadge Amendment, but the Senate rejected it.

House Speaker Henry Clay—himself a western slaveholder—put forward a compromise in 1820. Maine, carved out of Massachusetts, would enter as a free state, followed by Missouri as a slave state, maintaining the balance between slave and free states—at twelve to twelve. In the rest

of the Louisiana Territory north of Missouri's southern border of 36°30′, slavery would be prohibited forever (see Map 9.3).

The compromise carried but almost unraveled when Missouri submitted a constitution barring free blacks from entering the state, a provision that opponents contended would violate the federal constitutional provision that citizens of each state were "entitled to all privileges and immunities of citizens in the several States." Proponents countered that many states, North and South, already barred free blacks from entering. In 1821 Clay proposed a second compromise: Missouri would guarantee that none of its laws would discriminate against citizens of other states. (The compromise carried, but once admitted to the Union, Missouri twice adopted laws barring free blacks.) For more than three decades, the Missouri Compromise would govern congressional policy toward admitting new slave states. But the compromise masked rather than suppressed the simmering political conflict over slavery's westward expansion.

*Legacy* FOR A PEOPLE AND A NATION

## States' Rights and Nullification

When the Constitution replaced the Articles of Confederation, the United States had a much stronger central government, but the exact nature of the relationship between the states and the federal government was ambiguous, because Constitutional Convention delegates could not agree on whether states or nation should prevail in the event of irreconcilable conflict. The Tenth Amendment to the Constitution offered only a slight clarification: powers not delegated to the central government, it said, were reserved to the states or to the people. The exact nature of the federal system's shared power, as well as who would determine which powers had been delegated to which authority, remained to be defined.

When New England Federalists met in Hartford at the end of 1814 to prepare a list of grievances against "Mr. Madison's War," they drew on the doctrine of nullification, first announced sixteen years earlier in the Kentucky and Virginia Resolutions, written by Thomas Jefferson and James Madison, respectively. Opposing the Alien and Sedition Acts, these founding fathers had asserted that, if the national government assumed powers not delegated to it by the Constitution, states could nullify federal actions—that is, declare them inoperative within state borders. At Hartford, Federalist representatives of New England states discussed taking nullification a step further by seceding. They backed away from this extreme step, but their formulation of states' rights to evaluate and nullify federal authority left a legacy for dissent that would be played out in crises up to the present day.

In the following decade, South Carolina nullified federal tariffs that it opposed, and in 1861 southern states threatened by Abraham Lincoln's election to the presidency claimed the right of secession. Although the Civil War supposedly settled the issue—states could neither nullify federal law nor secede—southern states opposing the Supreme Court's 1954 ruling in favor of school integration again claimed the right to nullify "unauthorized" federal policy within their borders. In the 1990s, some western states sought to nullify federal environmental laws. In the early twenty-first century, the issue of gay marriage once again exposed discord between the federal and state governments, though this time the states turned to neither secession nor nullification. Instead, as the U.S. Congress failed to muster a two-thirds majority to propose a constitutional amendment banning gay marriage, dozens of states asserted their rights by ratifying their own constitutional amendments banning gay marriage. The Hartford Convention's legacy for a people and a nation provides Americans who dissent from national policy with a model for using state governments as vehicles for their protests.

## SUMMARY

The partisanship of the 1790s, though alarming to the nation's political leaders, captured Americans' imaginations, making the early republic a period of pervasive and vigorous political engagement. Troubled by vicious partisanship, President Jefferson sought both to unify the nation and to solidify Democratic-Republican control of the government. With a vision of an agrarian nation that protected individual liberty, Jeffersonians promoted a limited national government—one that stayed out of religious affairs and spent little on military forces, diplomatic missions, and economic initiatives. The rival Federalists, who exerted most of their influence through the judiciary, declared federal supremacy over the states even as the judiciary affirmed its own supremacy over other branches of the government.

Federalists hoped a strengthened federal government would help promote commerce and industry.

Despite his belief in limited government, Jefferson considered the acquisition of the Louisiana Territory and the commissioning of the Corps of Discovery among his most significant presidential accomplishments. The enormous expanse of fertile lands fueled the Jeffersonian dream of an agrarian republic: Americans soon streamed into the Louisiana Territory. Even more would have done so, had it not been for the Indians (and their British allies) who stood in their way and for poorly developed transportation routes.

Jefferson's vision rested, too, on American disentanglement from foreign affairs. But with its economy so focused on international shipping, the United States soon found that its greatest threats came from abroad, not from partisan or sectional divisions. In its wars with the Barbary states, the United States sought to guard its commerce and ships on the high seas. The second war with Britain—the War of 1812—was fought for similar reasons but against a much more formidable power. Although a military stalemate, the war helped to inspire a new sense of nationalism and to launch a new era of American development.

The Treaty of Ghent reaffirmed American independence; thereafter the nation was able to settle disputes with Great Britain at the bargaining table. The war also dealt a serious blow to Indian resistance in the Midwest and Southwest. At the same time, embargoes and war accelerated the pace of American industrial growth. Because the Federalists' opposition to the war undermined their political credibility, their party all but disappeared from the national political scene by 1820. The absence of well-organized partisan conflict created what contemporaries called an Era of Good Feelings.

Although overt tension was muted in the heady postwar years, competing visions of America's route to prosperity and greatness endured. Under Chief Justice John Marshall, the Supreme Court supported the Federalist agenda, issuing rulings that stimulated commerce and industry through economic nationalism. The Democratic-Republicans looked, instead, toward the South and West, the vast and fertile Louisiana Territory. Whether they supported agrarian or industrial development, almost all Americans could agree on the need for improved transportation, though most internal improvements took place in the North.

During the first quarter of the nineteenth century, the United States vastly expanded its territorial reach, not just through the Louisiana Purchase but also with the acquisition of Florida. Fearful of European intentions to reassert their influence in the Americas and emboldened by the nation's expanding boundaries, President Monroe proclaimed that the United States would not tolerate European intervention in American affairs. But even as its expanding boundaries strengthened the United States' international presence, that same territorial expansion would threaten the nation's newfound political unity at home.

That threat became most apparent in 1819, when the postwar economic boom came to a grinding halt and when congressmen predicted dire consequences if they could not settle the dispute over whether to admit Missouri as a slave state. The compromise brokered by Henry Clay removed the issue of slavery's expansion from political center stage, but—by addressing only those territories already owned by the United States—it did not permanently settle the issue.

## SUGGESTIONS FOR FURTHER READING

Catherine Allgor, *A Perfect Union: Dolley Madison and the Creation of the American Nation* (2006)

Stephen Aron, *American Confluence: The Missouri Frontier from Borderland to Border State* (2006)

David Edmunds, *Tecumseh and the Quest for Indian Leadership* (2006)

Morton J. Horowitz, *The Transformation of American Law, 1780–1860* (1977)

Reginald Horsman, *The Diplomacy of the Early Republic* (1985)

John Lauritz Larson, *Internal Improvement: National Public Works and the Promise of Popular Government in the United States* (2001)

Peter Onuf and Leonard J. Sadosky, *Jeffersonian America* (2002)

Jeffrey Ostler, *The Plains Sioux and U.S. Colonialism from Lewis and Clark to Wounded Knee* (2004)

Jeffrey Pasley, Andrew Robertson, and David Waldstreicher, eds., *Beyond the Founders: New Approaches to the Political History of the Early American Republic* (2004)

*For a more extensive list for further reading, go to* college.hmco.com/pic/norton8e.

# The Rise of
# the South *1815-1860*

𝛼 slaveholder in debt was a dangerous man, and Pierce Butler was broke. It was late winter 1859, fear of disunion dominated national life, and Butler's slave auction had all of coastal Georgia and South Carolina talking. Butler was the grandson of Major Pierce Butler, a framer of the Constitution, a South Carolina senator, and a wealthy planter. Butler the younger divided his time between the family's ostentatious home in Philadelphia and fifteen hundred acres of cotton plantations, worked by eight hundred slaves, on Butler Island and St. Simons Island in Georgia. His marriage to the famous British actress Fanny Kemble had ended in divorce; she could not bear the realities of slavery on her husband's cotton plantations, and he could not bear her protests. By 1859 Butler had squandered a fortune of $700,000 through speculation and gambling. Allegedly, he squandered $25,000 on one hand of cards.

Most of Butler's properties and possessions in Philadelphia were sold to satisfy his creditors. Then came the largest slave auction in American history. In the last week of February, 436 Butler slaves were taken to Savannah by railroad and steamboat. They were housed for several days in horse-and-carriage sheds at the Ten Broeck racetrack. People of all ages—infants, husbands, wives, children, grandparents—huddled in fearful expectation. Joseph Bryan, a slave broker and auctioneer, managed the sale. Among the planters and speculators who were there to buy was an undercover *New York Tribune* reporter who left a detailed account of the event. The auction, held in the racecourse's grandstand, lasted an agonizing two days in a driving rainstorm.

If possible, families were sold intact for group prices; thus the old and infirm could still be liquidated, while the closest kin stayed together. A seventeen-year-old "Prime

◀ *Slave Market,* painting by unknown American artist, ca. 1850–1860. The scene condemns the cruelty and brutality of traders and planters at a slave auction, which was one of the most widely depicted images of slavery in antislavery culture. A young woman is separated from her lover and a child from the mother. *(Carnegie Museum of Art, Pittsburgh. Gift of Mrs. W. Fitch Ingersoll [detail])*

249

## CHRONOLOGY

**1810–20** ■ 137,000 slaves are forced to move from the Upper South to Alabama, Mississippi, and other western regions

**1822** ■ Vesey's insurrection plot is discovered in South Carolina

**1830s** ■ Vast majority of African American slaves are native-born in America

**1830s–40s** ■ Cotton trade grows into largest source of commercial wealth and America's leading export

**1831** ■ Turner leads a violent slave rebellion in Virginia

**1832** ■ Virginia holds the last debate in the South about the future of slavery; gradual abolition is voted down
■ Publication of Dew's proslavery tract *Abolition of Negro Slavery*

**1836** ■ Arkansas gains admission to the Union as a slave state

**1839** ■ Mississippi's Married Women's Property Act gives married women some property rights

**1845** ■ Florida and Texas gain admission to the Union as slave states
■ Publication of Douglass's *Narrative of the Life of Frederick Douglass, an American Slave, Written by Himself*

**1850** ■ Planters' share of agricultural wealth in the South is 90 to 95 percent

**1850–60** ■ Of some 300,000 slaves who migrate from the Upper to the Lower South, 60 to 70 percent go by outright sale

**1857** ■ Publication of Hinton R. Helper's *The Impending Crisis,* denouncing the slave system
■ Publication of George Fitzhugh's *Southern Thought,* an aggressive defense of slavery

**1860** ■ 405,751 mulattos in the United States, 12.5 percent of the African American population
■ Three-quarters of all southern white families own no slaves
■ South produces largest cotton crop ever

woman" named Dorcas and her three-month-old son, Joe, went for $2,200. A nineteen-year-old "prime young man," Abel, netted $1,295. Some families of four, such as Goin, Cassander, and their two daughters, Emiline and Judy, brought only $1,600 together. At the end of the second day of what blacks in the region called the "weeping time," Butler had amassed $303,850 by selling 436 human beings. It would have been impossible to convince the numbed and despairing African Americans who traveled away from Savannah in wagons or railcars that their enslavement was not at the heart of the crisis dividing the nation.

But in 1815 a quest for national unity dominated sectional division, and the southern tier of states and territories, with fertile soil and a growing labor force of enslaved people to cultivate it, was poised for growth, prosperity, and power. New lands were settled, new states were peopled, and steadily the South emerged as the world's most extensive and vigorous commercial agricultural economy, linked to an international cotton trade and textile industry. It was also an economy rooted in a system of slavery with far-reaching influence on all of southern society. The Old South's wealth came from export crops, land, and slaves, and its population was almost wholly rural. In the land where cotton became king, racial slavery affected not only economics but also values, customs, laws, class structure, and the region's relationship to the nation and the world. On the ground in the South, as slaves' bodies, labor, and lives came to be defined more and more as chattel, they struggled increasingly not only to survive but also to resist, sometimes overtly, but more often in daily life and cultural expression. By 1860 white Southerners not only asserted the moral and economic benefits of slavery with a vigorous defense of the system, but also sought to sustain and advance their political power over the national government.

- How and why was the Old South a "slave society," with slavery permeating every class and group within it, free or unfree?

- How and why did white southerners come to see cotton as "king" of a global economy, and how did the cotton trade's international reach shape southern society from 1815 to 1860?

- How did African American slaves build and sustain a meaningful life and a sense of community amid the potential chaos and destruction of their circumstances?

- How would you weigh the comparative significance of the following central themes in the history of the Old South: class, race, migration, power, liberty, wealth?

## THE "DISTINCTIVE" SOUTH

Not until the first half of the 1800s did the region of slaveholding states from the Chesapeake and Virginia to Missouri, and from Florida across to Texas, come to be designated as the South. Today many still consider it America's most distinctive region. Historians have long examined how the Old South was like and unlike the rest of the nation. Because of its unique history, has the South, in the words of poet Allen Tate, always been "Uncle Sam's other province"? Or, as southern writer W. J. Cash said in 1940, is the South "a tree with many age rings, with its limbs and trunk bent and twisted by all the winds of the years, but with its tap root in the Old South?" Analyzing just why the South seems more religious, more conservative, or more tragic than other regions of America has been an enduring practice in American culture and politics.

Certain American values, such as materialism, individualism, and faith in progress, have been associated with the North and values such as tradition, honor, and family loyalty, with the South. The South, so the stereotype has it, was static, even "backward," and the North was dynamic in the decades leading up to the Civil War. There are many measures of just how different South was from North in the antebellum era. At the same time, there were many Souths: low-country rice and cotton regions with dense slave populations; mountainous regions of small farmers and subsistence agriculture; semitropical wetlands in the Southeast; plantation culture in the Cotton Belt and especially the Mississippi valley; Texas grasslands; tobacco- and wheat-growing regions in Virginia and North Carolina; cities with bustling ports; wilderness areas with only the rare homestead of hillfolk.

The South was distinctive because of its commitment to slavery, but it also shared much in common with the rest of the nation. The geographic sizes of the South and the North were roughly the same. In 1815 white southerners shared with their fellow free citizens in the North a heritage of heroes and ideology from the era of the American Revolution and the War of 1812. With varying accents, southerners spoke the same language and worshiped the same Protestant God as northerners. Southerners lived under the same Constitution as northerners, and they shared a common mixture of nationalism and localism in their attitudes toward government. Down to the 1840s, northerners and southerners invoked with nearly equal frequency the doctrine of states' rights against federal authority. A sense of American mission and dreams inspired by the westward movement were as much a part of southern as of northern experience.

Indeed, some of the most eloquent visions of America as a land of yeomen—independent, self-sufficient farmers—expanding westward had come from a southerner, Thomas Jefferson. Jefferson believed that "virtue" rested in those who tilled the soil, that farmers made the best citizens. In 1804 Jefferson declared his "moral and physical preference of the agricultural over the manufacturing man." But as slavery and the plantation economy expanded (see Map 10.1), the South did not become a land of individual opportunity in the same manner as the North.

During the forty-five years before the Civil War, the South shared in the nation's economic booms and busts. Research has shown that, despite its enormous cruelties, slavery was a profitable labor system for planters. Southerners and northerners shared an expanding capitalist economy. As it grew, the slave-based economy of money-crop agriculture reflected the rational choices of planters. More land and more slaves generally converted into more wealth.

By the eve of the Civil War in 1860, the distribution of wealth and property in the two sections was almost identical: 50 percent of free adult males owned only 1 percent of real and personal property, and the richest 1 percent owned 27 percent of the wealth. One study comparing Texas and Wisconsin in 1850 shows that the richest 2 percent of families in each state owned 31 to 32 percent of the wealth. So, both North and South had ruling classes, even if their wealth was invested in different kinds of property. Entrepreneurs in both sections whether forging plantations out of Mississippi Delta land or shoe factories and textile mills in New England river towns, sought their fortunes in an expanding market economy. The southern "master class" was, in fact, more likely than propertied northerners to move west to make a profit.

There were important differences between the North and the South. The South's climate and longer growing

**South-North Similarity**

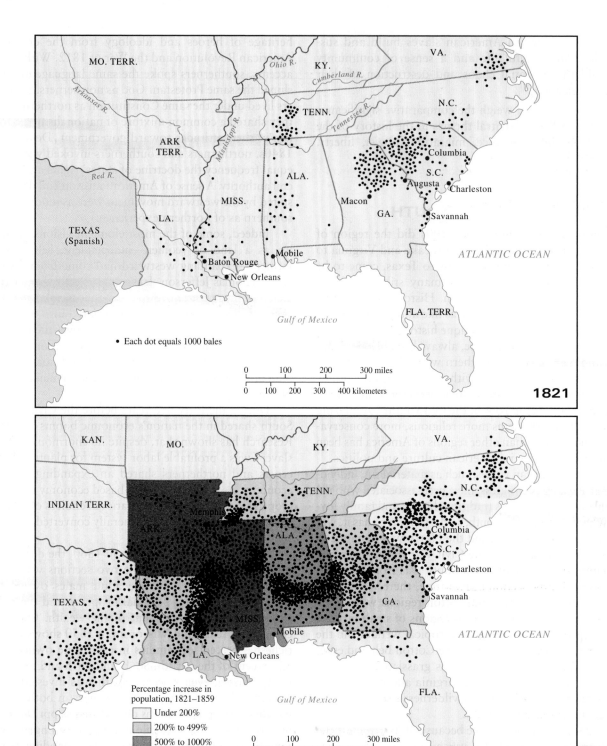

**Map 10.1    Cotton Production in the South**

These two maps reveal the rapid westward expansion of cotton production and its importance
to the antebellum South.

## South-North Dissimilarity

season gave it an unmistakably rural and agricultural destiny. Many great rivers provided rich soil and transportation routes to market. The South's people, white and black, developed an intense attachment to place, to the ways people were related to the land and to one another. The South developed as a biracial society of brutal inequality, where the liberty of one race depended directly on the enslavement of another. White wealth was built on highly valued black labor.

Cotton growers spread out over as large an area as possible to maximize production and income. As a result, population density in the South was low; by 1860 there were only 2.3 people per square mile in vast and largely unsettled Texas, 15.6 in Louisiana, and 18.0 in Georgia. By contrast, population density in the nonslaveholding states east of the Mississippi River was almost three times higher. The Northeast had an average of 65.4 people per square mile. Massachusetts had 153.1 people per square mile, and New York City compressed 86,400 people into each square mile. When, in the 1850s, young Frederick Law Olmsted of Connecticut, later renowned as a landscape architect, toured the South as a journalist, he traveled mostly on horseback along primitive trails. Between Columbus, Georgia, and Montgomery, Alabama, Olmsted found "a hilly wilderness, with a few dreary villages, and many isolated cotton farms." For one who would design Central Park in New York City, this was just too much ruralness.

Where people were scarce, it was difficult to finance and operate schools, churches, libraries, and even inns and restaurants. Similarly, the rural character of the South and the significance of the plantation as a self-sufficient social unit meant that the section put few resources into improving disease control and public health. Southerners were strongly committed to their churches, and some believed in the importance of universities, but all such institutions were far less developed than those in the North. Factories were rare, because planters invested most of their capital in slaves. A few southerners did invest in iron or textiles on a small scale. But the largest southern "industry" was lumbering, and the largest factories used slave labor to make cigars. More decisively, the South was slower than the North to develop a unified market economy and a regional transportation network. Despite concerted efforts, the South had only 35 percent of the nation's railroad mileage in 1860.

The Old South never developed its own banking and shipping capacity to any degree. If it had, its effort to be an international cartel might have succeeded longer. Most

▲ *America, 1841,* lithograph and watercolor by Edward Williams Clay. An idealized portrayal of loyal and contented slaves, likely distributed by northern apologists for slavery. All is well on the plantation as well-dressed slaves dance and express their gratitude to their master and his perfect family. The text includes the old slave saying: "God bless you master! You feed and clothe us. When we are sick you nurse us, and when too old to work, you provide for us!" The master replies piously: "These poor creatures are a sacred legacy from my ancestors and while a dollar is left me, nothing shall be spared to increase their comfort and happiness."

*(Library of Congress)*

southern bank deposits, like those of Pierce Butler, were in the North, and southern cotton planters became ever more dependent on New York for shipping. As early as 1822, one-sixth of all southern cotton cleared for Liverpool or Le Havre from the port of New York and constituted two-fifths of all that city's exports. Many New York merchants and bankers developed deep interests in the fate of slavery and cotton prices. In a series of economic conventions held from 1837 to 1839, southern delegates debated the nature of foreign trade, dependence on northern importers and financiers, and other alleged threats to their commercial independence and security. But nothing, save rhetoric, came of these conventions; it was the last time southern planters would organize to break from their Yankee middlemen and shippers.

The South lagged far behind the North in nearly any measure of industrial growth. Its urban centers were mostly ports like New Orleans and Charleston, which became crossroads of commerce and small-scale manufacturing. In the interior were small market towns dependent on agricultural trade—"urbanization without cities," as one historian has said. Slavery slowed urban growth. As a system of racial control, slavery did not work well in cities. Likewise, because of a lack of manufacturing jobs, the South did not attract immigrants as readily as did the North. By 1860 only 13 percent of the nation's foreign-born population lived in the slave states.

Like most northerners, antebellum southerners were adherents to evangelical Christianity. Americans from all regions held in common a faith in a personal God and in conversion and piety as the means to salvation. But southern evangelicalism was distinct from its northern practice. In the South, Baptists and Methodists concentrated on personal rather than social improvement. By the 1830s in the North, evangelicalism was a major wellspring of reform movements (see Chapter 9); but in states where blacks were so numerous and unfree, and where the very social structure received increasingly aggressive attacks from abolitionists, religion, as one scholar has written, preached "a hands-off policy concerning slavery." Although slaves began to convert to Christianity in the early-nineteenth-century South, many southern whites feared a reform impulse that would foster what one historian has called an "interracial communion" in their churches. Moreover, those women who may have been reform minded were prevented from developing frequent associations with other reformers because of distance and sparse population. The only reform movements that did take hold in the emerging Bible Belt of the South, such as that for temperance, focused on personal behavior, not social reform.

The slave system made it inevitable that the interests and social structures of the North and the South would diverge after 1815. Because of its inherently conservative social structure, antebellum southern law restricted the authority of the courts, reinforcing a tradition of planter control. Penitentiaries tended to house only whites, as most blacks were under the authority of personal masters. Law-breaking in the South tended to involve crimes of violence rather than crimes against property.

Perhaps in no way was the South more distinctive than in its embrace of a particular world-view, a system of thought and meaning held especially by the planter class, but also influencing the entire society. Like those of all people, southerners' justifications for slavery were not so different from those of any other civilization trying to defend the institutions it inherits. But at the heart of the proslavery argument was a deep and abiding racism. The persistence of modern racism in all sections of the United States is all the more reason to comprehend antebellum southerners' rationalizations for human slavery.

## A Southern World-View and the Proslavery Argument

In the wake of the American Revolution, the Enlightenment ideas of natural rights and equality did stimulate antislavery sentiment in the Upper South, produced a brief flurry of manumissions, and led to considerable hope for gradual emancipation. In 1796 Virginian St. George Tucker argued that "slavery not only violates the laws of nature and of civil society, it also wounds the best forms of government." But confidence that the exercise of reason among gentlemen might end such a profitable system as slavery waned in the new nation. As slavery spread, southerners soon vigorously defended it. In 1816 George Bourne, a Presbyterian minister exiled from Virginia for his anti-slavery sermons and for expulsion of slaveholders from his church, charged that, whenever southerners were challenged on slavery, "they were fast choked, for they had a Negro stuck fast in their throats." After walking home with South Carolina statesman and proslavery advocate John C. Calhoun from an 1820 cabinet meeting, John Quincy Adams confided to his diary that too many southerners "writhe in agonies of fear at the very mention of human rights as applicable to men of color."

By the 1820s white southerners went on the offensive, actively justifying slavery as a "positive good" and not merely a "necessary evil." They used the antiquity of slavery, as well as the Bible's many references to slaveholding, to foster a historical argument for bondage. Slavery, they deemed, was the natural status of blacks. Whites were the more intellectual race, and blacks the race more inherently physical and therefore destined for labor. Whites were the creators of civilizations, blacks the appointed hewers of wood and drawers of water. Proslavery writers did not mince words. In a proslavery tract written in 1851, John Campbell confidently declared that "there is as much difference between the lowest tribe of negroes and the white Frenchman, Englishman, or American, as there is between the monkey and the negro."

Some southerners defended slavery in practical terms; they simply saw their bondsmen as economic necessities and symbols of their quest for prosperity. In 1845 James Henry Hammond of South Carolina argued that slave-holding was essentially a matter of property rights. Unwilling to "deal in abstractions" about the "right and wrong" of slavery, Hammond considered property sacred and protected by the Constitution, because slaves were legal property—end of argument. The deepest root of the pro-slavery argument was a hierarchical view of the social order as slavery's defenders believed God or nature had prescribed it. Southerners cherished tradition, duty, and honor, believing social change should come only in slow increments, if at all. As the Virginia legislature debated the gradual abolition of slavery in 1831–1832, in the wake of Nat Turner's rebellion, Thomas R. Dew, a slaveholder and professor of law and history at the College of William and Mary, contended that "that which is the growth of *ages* may require ages to remove." Dew's widely read work *Abolition of Negro Slavery* (1832) ushered in an outpouring of proslavery writing that would intensify over the next thirty years. Until Turner's bloody rebellion, Dew admitted, emancipation in the South had "never been seriously discussed." But as slavery expanded westward and fueled national prosperity, Dew cautioned southerners that any degree of gradual abolition threatened the whole region's "irremediable ruin." Dew declared black slavery part of the "order of nature," an indispensable part of the "deep and solid foundations of society" and the basis of the "well-ordered, well-established liberty" of white Americans. Dew's well-ordered society also included his conception of the proper division of men and women into separate spheres and functions.

Proslavery advocates held views very different from those of northern reformers on the concepts of freedom, progress, and equality. They turned natural-law doctrine to their favor, arguing that the natural state of humankind was inequality of ability and condition, not equality. A former U.S. senator in South Carolina, William Harper, charged in 1837 that Jefferson's famous dictum about equality in the Declaration of Independence was no more than a "sentimental phrase." "Is it not palpably nearer the truth to say that no man was ever born free," Harper argued, "and that no two men were ever born equal?" Proslavery writers believed that people were born to certain stations in life; they stressed dependence over autonomy and duty over rights as the human condition. As Virginia writer George Fitzhugh put it in 1854, "Men are not born entitled to equal rights. It would be far nearer the truth to say, that some were born with saddles on their backs, and others booted and spurred to ride them."

Many slaveholders believed that their ownership of people bound them to a set of paternal obligations as guardians of a familial relationship between masters and slaves. Although contradicted by countless examples of slave resistance and escape, as well as by slave sales, planters needed to believe in and exerted great energy in constructing the idea of the contented slave. The slaveholders who promoted their own freedom and pursued personal profits through the bondage of blacks had to justify themselves endlessly.

Slavery and race affected everything in the Old South.

▲ A slave woman with an inventory number; unidentified photographer, c. 1860. This woman's humanity seems to survive in her expression, despite the dehumanization represented by her worn clothing and her number. *(The Burns Archive)*

## A Slave Society

Whites and blacks alike grew up, were socialized, married, reared children, worked, conceived of property, and honed their most basic habits of behavior under the influence of slavery. This was true of slaveholding and nonslaveholding whites, as well as of blacks who were slave and free. Slavery shaped the social structure of the South, fueled almost anything meaningful in its economy, and came to dominate its politics. Rudolphe Lucien Desdunes, a Louisiana sugar planter, remembered growing up in a society where "slavery was the pivot around which everything revolved."

The South was interdependent with the North, the West, and even with Europe in a growing capitalist market system. To keep the cotton trade flowing, southerners relied on northern banks, on northern steamship companies working the great western rivers, and on northern merchants. But there were elements of that system that southerners increasingly rejected during the antebellum era, especially urbanism, the wage labor system, a broadening right to vote, and any threat to their racial and class order.

In the antebellum era, as later, there were many Souths, but Americans have always been determined to define what one historian called the "Dixie difference." "The South is both American and something different," writes another historian, "at times a mirror or magnifier of national traits and at other times a counterculture." This was most acutely true in the decades before the Civil War.

Culturally, the South developed a proclivity to tell its own story. Its ruralness and its sense of tradition may have given southerners a special habit of telling tales. "Southerners . . . love a good tale," said Mississippi writer Eudora Welty. "They are born reciters, great memory retainers, diary keepers, letter exchangers, and letter savers, history tracers, and debaters, and—outstaying all the rest—great talkers." The South's story is both distinctive and national, and it begins in what we have come to call the Old South, a term only conceivable after the eviction of native peoples from the region.

## SOUTHERN EXPANSION, INDIAN RESISTANCE AND REMOVAL

Americans were a restless, moving people when the trans-Appalachian frontier opened in the wake of the War of 1812. Some 5 to 10 percent of the booming population moved each year, usually westward. In the first two decades of the century, they poured into the Ohio valley; by the 1820s, after the death of the Shawnee chief Tecumseh and the collapse of the pan-Indian federation, they were migrating into the Mississippi River valley and beyond. By 1850 two-thirds of Americans lived west of the Appalachians.

As much as in any other region, this surging westward movement was a southern phenomenon. After 1820

**A Southern Westward Movement**

the heart of cotton cultivation and the slave-based plantation system shifted from the coastal states to Alabama and the newly settled Mississippi valley—Tennessee, Louisiana, Arkansas, and Mississippi. Southern slaveholders forced slaves to move with them to the newer areas of the South, and yeoman farmers followed, also hoping for new wealth through cheap land and the ownership of other people.

A wave of migration was evident everywhere in the Southeast. As early as 1817, Georgian Samuel McDonald observed a "disease prevalent" in his region. "The patient," he said, first exhibited a "great love" of talking about "the new country" to the west. Then he tried to "make sale of his stock" and "lastly . . . to sell his plantation." Once attacked by this "Alabama fever," most never recovered

and were carried "off to the westward." That same year, a Charleston, South Carolina, newspaper reported with alarm that migration out of that state had already reached "unprecedented proportions." Indeed, almost half of the white people born in South Carolina after 1800 left the state, most for the Southwest. And by 1833, Tyrone Power, an Irish actor riding a stagecoach from Georgia into Alabama, encountered many "camps of immigrants" and found the roads "covered" by such pilgrims.

The way to wealth for seaboard planters in the South was to go west to grow cotton for the booming world markets, by purchasing ever more land and slaves. The population of Mississippi soared from 73,000 in 1820 to 607,000 in 1850, with African American slaves in the majority. Across the Mississippi River, the population of Arkansas went from 14,000 in 1820 to 210,000 in 1850. By 1835 the American immigrant population in Texas reached 35,000, including 3,000 slaves, and outnumbering Mexicans two to one. Aggressive American settlers declared Texas's independence from Mexico in 1836, spurring further American immigration into the region. By 1845 "Texas fever" had boosted the Anglo population to 125,000. Statehood that year opened the floodgates to more immigrants from the east and to a confrontation with Mexico that would lead to war.

As the cotton kingdom grew to what southern political leaders dreamed would be national and world dominion, this westward migration, fueled at first by an optimistic nationalism, ultimately made migrant planters more sectional and more southern. In 1817 Congressman John C. Calhoun embraced national expansion as the means to "bind the Republic together," as he provided the process its unquestioned assumption: "Let us conquer space." In time, political dominance in the South migrated westward into the Cotton Belt as well. By the 1840s and 1850s, these energetic capitalist planters, ever mindful of world markets and fearful that their slave-based economy was under attack, sought to protect and expand their system. Increasingly, they saw themselves, as one historian has written, less as "landowners who happened to own slaves" than as "slaveholders who happened to own land."

Before all this expansion could take place, other, older groups of Americans already occupied much of this land. Before 1830 large swaths of upper Georgia belonged to the Cherokees, and huge regions of Alabama and Mississippi were either Creek, Choctaw, or Chickasaw land. Indians were also on the move, but in forced migrations. The indigenous cultures of the eastern and southern woodlands had to be uprooted to make way for white expansion. For the vast majority of white Americans, the Indians were in the way of their growing empire. Taking Indian land, so the reasoning went, merely reflected the

# The Amistad Case

In April 1839 a Spanish slave ship, *Tecora,* sailed from Lomboko, the region of West Africa that became Sierre Leone. On board were Mende people, captured and sold by their African enemies. In June they arrived in Havana, Cuba, a Spanish colony. Two Spaniards purchased 53 of the Mende and set sail aboard *La Amistad* for their plantations elsewhere in Cuba. After three days at sea, the Africans revolted. Led by a man the Spaniards called Joseph Cinque, they killed the captain and seized control of the vessel. They ordered the two Spaniard owners to take them back to Africa, but the slaveholders sailed east by day and north by night, trying to reach the shores of the American South. Far off course, the *Amistad* was seized by the USS *Washington* in Long Island Sound and brought ashore in Connecticut.

The "Amistad Africans" were soon a celebrated moral and legal cause for abolitionists and slaveholders, as well as in U.S.-Spanish relations. The Africans were imprisoned in New Haven, and a prolonged dispute ensued around many questions: Were they slaves and murderers, and the property of their Cuban owners, or were they free people exercising their natural rights? Were they Spanish property, seized on the high seas in violation of a 1795 treaty? If a northern state could "free" captive Africans, what did it mean for enslaved African Americans in the South? Connecticut abolitionists immediately went to court, where a U.S. Circuit Court judge dismissed the charges of mutiny and murder but refused to release the Africans because their Spanish owners claimed them as property.

Meanwhile, the Mende were desperate to tell their own story. A Yale professor of ancient languages, Josiah Gibbs, visited the captives and learned their words for numbers. In New York he walked up and down the docks repeating the Mende words until an African seaman, James Covey, responded. Covey journeyed to New Haven, conversed with the jubilant Africans, and soon their harrowing tale garnered sympathy all over Yankee New England.

In a new trial, the judge ruled that the Africans were illegally enslaved and ordered them returned to their homeland. Although slavery might be legal in Cuba, the slave trade between Africa and the Americas had been outlawed in a treaty between Spain and Great Britain. Spain's lawyers demanded the return of their "merchandise." In need of southern votes to win reelection, President Martin Van Buren supported the Spanish claims and advocated the Africans' return to a likely death in Cuba.

The administration appealed the case to the Supreme Court in February 1841. Arguing the abolitionists' case, former president John Quincy Adams famously pointed to a copy of the Declaration of Independence on the wall of the court chambers, invoked the natural rights to life and liberty, and chastised the Van Buren administration for its "immense array of power . . . on the side of injustice." In a 7-to-1 decision, the Court ruled that the Africans were "freeborn" with the right of self-defense, while remaining silent on slavery's legality in the United States.

Fund-raising and speaking tours featuring Cinque made the return voyage possible. On November 27, 1841, thirty-five survivors and five American missionaries disembarked for Africa. They arrived in Sierre Leone on January 15, 1842, whereupon Cinque wrote a letter to the Amistad Committee. "I thank all 'merican people," he said, "I shall never forget 'merican people." But the international meanings of the Amistad case would endure. Sarah Magru, one of the child captives on the *Amistad,* stayed in America to attend Oberlin College and later returned to work at the Mende mission in Sierre Leone.

The Amistad case showed how intertwined slavery was with freedom, and the United States with the world. It poisoned diplomatic relations between America and Spain for a generation, and stimulated Christian mission work in Africa.

◀ *Return to Africa of the Amistad Captives,* by Hale Woodruff, depicting the repatriated Amistad Africans back on the shores of their native continent. The figures are Cinque, the missionaries, and the young black woman, Marsgue, who in later years had a son who returned to graduate from Yale University with a Ph.D.

*(Slavery Library Archives, Talladega College, Gift of George W. Crawford, 1973 NHCH© 1973.20c)*

natural course of history: the "civilizers" had to displace the "children of the forest" in the name of progress. National leaders provided all the rhetoric and justification needed. "Nothing," said General Andrew Jackson as early as 1816, "can promote the welfare of the United States, and particularly the southwestern frontier so much as bringing into market . . . the whole of this fertile country." As president in 1830, Jackson spoke with certainty about why the Indians must go. "What good man would prefer a country," he asked, "covered with forests and ranged by a few thousand savages to our extensive Republic, studded with cities, towns, and prosperous farms?"

### Indian Treaty Making

In theory, under the U.S. Constitution, the federal government recognized Indian sovereignty and treated Indian peoples as foreign nations. Indeed, the United States received Indian delegations with pomp and ceremony, exchanging gifts as tokens of friendship. Agreements between Indian nations and the United States were signed, sealed, and ratified like other international treaties. In practice, however, swindle and fraud dominated the government's approach to treaty making and Indian sovereignty. The United States imposed conditions on Indian representatives, and as the country expanded, new treaties replaced old ones, shrinking Indian land holdings.

Indians could delay but rarely thwart removal. Although Indian resistance persisted against such pressure after the War of 1812, it only slowed the process. In the 1820s, native peoples in the middle West, Ohio valley, Mississippi valley, and other parts of the cotton South ceded lands totaling 200 million acres for a pittance.

Increasingly, Indian nations east of the Mississippi sought to survive through accommodation. In the first three decades of the century, the Choctaw, Creek, and Chickasaw peoples in the lower Mississippi became suppliers and traders in the nation's expanding market economy.

### Indian Accommodation

Under treaty provisions, Indian commerce took place through trading posts and stores that provided Indians with supplies, and purchased or bartered Indian-produced goods. The trading posts extended credit to chiefs, who increasingly fell into debt that they could pay off to the federal government only by selling their land.

By 1822 the Choctaw nation had sold 13 million acres but still carried a debt of $13,000. The Indians struggled to adjust, increasing agricultural production and hunting, working as farmhands and craftsmen, and selling produce at market stalls in Natchez and New Orleans. As the United States expanded westward, white Americans promoted their assimilation, through education and conversion to Christianity, with renewed urgency. "Put into the hand of [Indian] children the primer and the hoe," the House Committee on Indian Affairs recommended in 1818, "and they will naturally, in time, take hold of the plough; and, as their minds become enlightened and expand, the Bible will be their book, and they will grow up in habits of morality and industry." In 1819, in response to missionary lobbying, Congress appropriated $10,000 annually for "civilization of the tribes adjoining the frontier settlements." Protestant missionaries administered the "civilizing fund" and established mission schools.

Within five years, thirty-two boarding schools enrolled Indian students. They substituted English for American Indian languages and taught agriculture alongside the Christian gospel. But this emphasis on agriculture and the value of private property did not deter settlers eyeing Indian land; assimilation through education seemed too slow a process. Wherever native peoples lived, illegal settlers disrupted their lives. The federal government only halfheartedly enforced the integrity of treaties, as legitimate Indian land rights gave way to the advance of white civilization.

Over time, however, the Indians could not prevent the spread of the cotton economy that arose all around them, and they could not cede enough acreage to satisfy land-hungry whites. With loss of land came dependency. The Choctaws came to rely on white Americans not only for manufactured goods but even for food. Dependency, coupled with disease, facilitated removal of American Indian peoples to western lands. While the population of other groups increased rapidly, the Indian population fell, some nations declining by 50 percent in only three decades. The French traveler and author Alexis de Tocqueville noticed the contrast. "Not only have these wild tribes receded, but they are destroyed," Tocqueville concluded, after personally observing the tragedy of forced removal in 1831, "and as they give way or perish, an immense and increasing people fill their place. There is no instance upon record of so prodigious a growth or so rapid a destruction." As many as 100,000 eastern and southern Indian peoples were removed between 1820 and 1850; about 30,000 died in the process.

The wanderings of the Shawnees, the people of the Prophet and Tecumseh (see pages 229–230), illustrate the uprooting of Indian peoples. After giving up 17 million acres in Ohio in a 1795 treaty, the Shawnees scattered to Indiana and eastern Missouri. After the War of 1812, some Shawnees sought protection from either the British in Canada or from Mexico. Yet another group moved to the Kansas territory in 1825. By 1854 Kansas was open to white settlement, and the Shawnees had to cede seven-eighths of their land, or 1.4 million acres.

Removal had a profound impact on all Shawnees. The men lost their traditional role as providers; their methods of hunting and their knowledge of woodland animals were useless on the prairies of Kansas. As grain became the tribe's dietary staple, Shawnee women played a greater role as providers, supplemented by government aid under treaty provisions. Remarkably, the Shawnees preserved their language and culture in the face of these devastating dislocations.

Attention focused on southeastern tribes—Cherokees, Creeks, Choctaws, Chickasaws, and Seminoles—because

## Indian Removal as Federal Policy

much of their land had remained intact after the War of 1812, and they had aggressively resisted white encroachment. In his last annual message to Congress in late 1824, President James Monroe proposed that all Indians be moved beyond the Mississippi River. Monroe described his proposal as an "honorable" one that would protect Indians from invasion and provide them with independence for "improvement and civilization." Force would be unnecessary, he believed; Indians would willingly accept western land free from white encroachment.

Monroe's proposition targeted the Cherokees, Creeks, Choctaws, and Chickasaws, and they unanimously rejected it. Between 1789 and 1825 the four nations had negotiated thirty treaties with the United States, and they had reached their limit. Most wished to remain on what little was left of their ancestral land.

Pressure from Georgia had prompted Monroe's policy. In the 1820s, the state had accused the federal government of not fulfilling its 1802 promise to remove the Cherokees and Creeks from northwestern Georgia in return for the state's renunciation of its claim to western lands. Georgia remained unsatisfied by Monroe's removal messages and by the Creeks' recalcitrance. In 1826, under federal pressure, the Creek nation ceded all but a small strip of its Georgia acreage, but Georgians remained unmoved. Only the complete removal of the Georgia Creeks to the West could resolve the conflict between the state and the federal government.

For the Creeks the outcome was devastating. In an ultimately unsuccessful attempt to hold fast to the remainder of their traditional lands, which were in Alabama, they radically altered their political structure. In 1829, at the expense of traditional village autonomy, they centralized tribal authority and forbade any chief from ceding land. In the end, they lost not only their land but also their traditional forms of social and political organization.

In 1830, after extensive debate and a narrow vote in both houses, Congress passed the Indian Removal Act, authorizing the president to negotiate treaties of removal with all tribes living east of the Mississippi. The bill, which provided federal funds for such relocations, would likely not have passed the House without the additional representation afforded slave states due to the three-fifths clause in the Constitution.

Adapting to American ways seemed no more successful than resistance in forestalling removal. No people

## Cherokees

met the challenge of assimilating to American standards more thoroughly than the Cherokees, whose traditional home centered on eastern Tennessee and northern Alabama and Georgia. Between 1819 and 1829 the tribe became economically self-sufficient and politically self-governing; during this Cherokee renaissance the nearly fifteen thousand adult Cherokees came to think of themselves as a

◀ Southern Indians attempted to remain in their ancestral lands in the South. Karl Bodmer's watercolor portrayed a Choctaw camp on the Mississippi River near Natchez, before the Indians were forced out of Mississippi and Alabama in 1830.

*(Joslyn Art Museum, Omaha, Nebraska. Gift of the Enron Art Foundation)*

nation, not a collection of villages. In 1821 and 1822, Sequoyah, a self-educated Cherokee, devised an eighty-six-character phonetic alphabet that made possible a Cherokee-language Bible and a bilingual tribal newspaper, *Cherokee Phoenix* (1828). Between 1820 and 1823, the Cherokees created a formal government with a bicameral legislature, a court system, and a salaried bureaucracy. In 1827 they adopted a written constitution modeled after that of the United States.

Cherokee land laws, however, differed from U.S. law. The nation collectively owned all Cherokee land and forbade land sales to outsiders. Nonetheless, economic change paralleled political adaptation. Many became individual farmers and slaveholders; by 1833 they held fifteen hundred black slaves. They transformed their economy from hunting, gathering, and subsistence agriculture to commodity trade based on barter, cash, and credit.

But Cherokees' political and economic changes failed to win respect or acceptance from white southerners. In the 1820s, Georgia pressed them to sell the 7,200 square miles of land they held in the state. Congress appropriated $30,000 in 1822 to buy the Cherokee land in Georgia, but the Cherokees resisted. Impatient with their refusals to negotiate cession, Georgia annulled the Cherokees' constitution, extended the state's sovereignty over them, prohibited the Cherokee National Council from meeting except to cede land, and ordered their lands seized. Then, the discovery of gold on Cherokee land in 1829 further whetted Georgia's appetite for Cherokee territory.

Backed by sympathetic whites but not by President Andrew Jackson, the Cherokees under Chief John Ross turned to the federal courts to defend their treaty with the United States. Their legal strategy reflected their growing political sophistication. In *Cherokee Nation v. Georgia* (1831), Chief Justice John Marshall ruled that under the federal Constitution an Indian tribe was neither a foreign nation nor a state and therefore had no standing in federal courts. Indians' relationship with the United States was "marked," said Marshall, "by cardinal and peculiar distinctions which exist nowhere else." They were deemed "domestic, dependent nations." Legally, they were in but not of the United States. Nonetheless, said Marshall, the Indians had an unquestionable right to their lands; they could lose title only by voluntarily giving it up.

A year later, in *Worcester v. Georgia,* Marshall defined the Cherokee position more clearly. The Indian nation was, he declared, a distinct political community in which "the laws of Georgia can have no force" and into which Georgians could not enter without permission or

**Cherokee Nation v. Georgia**

treaty privilege. The Cherokees cheered. *Phoenix* editor Elias Boudinot called the decision "glorious news." Jackson, however, whose reputation had been built as an Indian fighter, did his best to usurp the court's action. Newspapers widely reported that Jackson had said, "John Marshall has made his decision: now let him enforce it." Keen to open up new lands for settlement, Jackson favored expelling the Cherokees.

Georgians, too, refused to comply; they would not tolerate a sovereign Cherokee nation within their borders, and they refused to hear the pleas of Indian people to share their American dream. A Cherokee census indicated that they owned 33 grist mills, 13 sawmills, 1 powder mill, 69 blacksmith shops, 2 tanneries, 762 looms, 2,486 spinning wheels, 172 wagons, 2,923 plows, 7,683 horses, 22,531 cattle, 46,732 pigs, and 2,566 sheep. "You asked us to throw off the hunter and warrior state," declared the Cherokee leader, John Ridge, in 1832. "We did so— you asked us to form a republican government: We did so—adopting your own as a model. You asked us to cultivate the earth, and learn the mechanic arts: We did so. You asked us to learn to read: We did so. You asked us to cast away our idols, and worship your God: We did so." But neither the plow nor the Bible earned the Cherokees respect in the face of the economic, imperial, and racial quests of their fellow southerners (see Map 10.2).

The Choctaws went first; they made the forced journey from Mississippi and Alabama to the West in the winter of 1831 and 1832. Alexis de Tocqueville was visiting Memphis when they passed through: "The wounded, the sick, newborn babies, and the old men on the point of death. . . . I saw them embark to cross the great river," he wrote, "and the sight will never fade from my memory. Neither sob nor complaint rose from that silent assembly. Their afflictions were of long standing, and they felt them to be irremediable." Other tribes soon joined the forced march. The Creeks in Alabama resisted removal until 1836, when the army pushed them westward. A year later the Chickasaws followed.

**Trail of Tears**

Having fought removal in the courts, the Cherokees were divided. Some believed that further resistance was hopeless and accepted removal as the only chance to preserve their civilization. The leaders of this minority agreed in 1835 to exchange their southern home for western land, in the Treaty of New Echota. Most, though, wanted to stand firm. John Ross, with petitions signed by fifteen thousand Cherokees, lobbied the Senate against ratification of the treaty. He lost. But when the time for evacuation came in 1838, most Cherokees refused to move. President

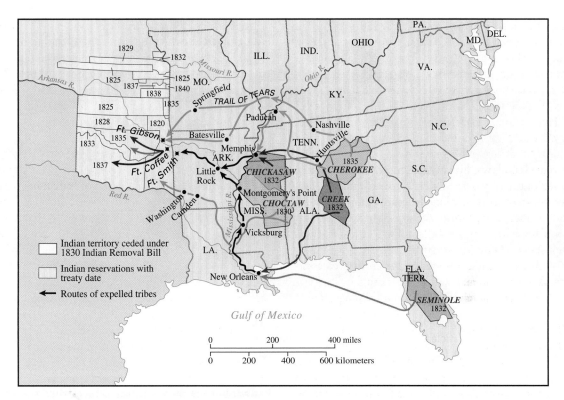

**Map 10.2    Removal of Native Americans from the South, 1820–1840**

Over a twenty-year period, the federal government and southern states forced Native Americans to exchange their traditional homes for western land. Some tribal groups remained in the South, but most settled in the alien western environment.

*(© Martin Gilbert, 2002,* Routledge Atlas of American History, *4th edition. Published by Routledge 2002. Reproduced by permission of Taylor & Francis Books UK)*

Martin Van Buren sent federal troops to round them up. About twenty thousand Cherokees were evicted, held in detention camps, and marched under military escort to Indian Territory in present-day Oklahoma. Nearly one-quarter of them died of disease and exhaustion on what came to be known as the Trail of Tears.

When the forced march to the West ended, the Indians had traded about 100 million acres east of the Mississippi for 32 million acres west of the river plus $68 million. Only a few scattered remnants, among them the Seminoles in Florida and the Cherokees in the southern Appalachian Mountains, remained east of the Mississippi River.

Forced removal had a disastrous impact on the Cherokees and other displaced Indian nations. In the West they encountered an alien environment; lacking traditional ties, few felt at peace with the land. Unable to live off the land, many became dependent on government payments for survival. Removal also brought new internal conflicts. The Cherokees in particular struggled over their tribal gov-ernment. In 1839 followers of John Ross assassinated the leaders of the protreaty faction. Violence continued sporadically until a new treaty in 1846 imposed a temporary truce. In time the Cherokees managed to reestablish their political institutions and a governing body in Tahlequah, in northeastern Oklahoma.

In Florida a small band of Seminoles continued to resist. Some Seminole leaders agreed in the 1832 Treaty of Payne's Landing to relocate to the West within three years, but others opposed the treaty, and some probably did not know it existed.

### Seminole Wars

A minority under Osceola, a charismatic leader, refused to vacate their homes and fought the protreaty group. When federal troops were sent to impose removal in 1835, Osceola waged a fierce guerrilla war against them.

The Florida Indians were a varied group that included many Creeks and mixed Indian–African Americans (ex-slaves or descendants of runaway slaves). The U.S. Army,

▲ *The Trail of Tears,* by twentieth-century Pawnee artist Brummet Echohawk. About twenty thousand Cherokees were evicted in 1838–1839, and about one-quarter of them died on the forced march to present-day Oklahoma. *(Thomas Gilcrease Institute of American History and Art)*

however, considered them all Seminoles, subject to removal. General Thomas Jesup believed that the runaway slave population was the key to the war. "This, you may be assured, is a Negro, not an Indian war," he wrote a friend in 1836, "and if it be not speedily put down, the South will feel the effects of it on their slave population before the end of the next season."

Osceola was captured under a white flag of truce and died in an army prison in 1838, but the Seminoles fought on under Chief Coacoochee (Wild Cat) and other leaders. In 1842 the United States abandoned the removal effort. Most of Osceola's followers agreed to move west to Indian Territory after another war in 1858, but some Seminoles remained in the Florida Everglades, proud of having resisted conquest.

## LIMITS OF MOBILITY IN A HIERARCHICAL SOCIETY

As Indians increasingly were forced westward, their lands were now open to restless and mobile white settlers. A large majority of white southern families (three-quarters in 1860) owned no slaves. Some lived in towns and ran stores or businesses, but most were yeoman farmers who owned their own land and grew their own food. The social distance between poorer whites and the planter class could be great, although the line between slaveholder and non-slaveholder was fluid. Still greater was the distance between

whites and blacks with free status. White yeomen, landless whites, and free blacks occupied the broad base of the social pyramid in the Old South.

Many of the white farmers who pioneered the southern wilderness, moving into undeveloped regions or Indian land after removal, owned no slaves. After the War of 1812 they moved in successive waves down the southern Appalachians into the Gulf lands or through the Cumberland Gap into Kentucky and Tennessee. In large sections of the South, especially inland from the coast and away from large rivers, small, self-sufficient farms were the norm. Lured by stories of good land, many men repeatedly uprooted their wives and children. So many shared the excitement over new lands that one North Carolinian wrote in alarm, "The Alabama Fever rages here with great violence. . . . I am apprehensive if it continues to spread as it has done, it will almost depopulate the country."

### Yeoman Farmers

These farmers were individualistic and hard working. Unlike their northern counterparts, their lives were not transformed by improvements in transportation. They could be independent thinkers as well, but their status as a numerical majority did not mean that they set the political or economic direction of the slave society. Self-reliant and often isolated, absorbed in the work of their farms, they operated both apart from and within the slave-based staple-crop economy.

▲ Eastman Johnson's *Fiddling His Way* (1866) depicts rural life by representing the visit of an itinerant black musician to a farm family. Expressions and gestures suggest a social mixing between the races at the yeoman level of southern society.

*(The Chrysler Museum of Art, Norfolk, Virginia. Bequest of Walter P. Chrysler, Jr.)*

On the southern frontier, men cleared fields, built log cabins, and established farms, while their wives labored in the household economy and patiently re-created the social ties—to relatives, neighbors, fellow churchgoers—that enriched everyone's experience. Women seldom shared the men's excitement about moving. They dreaded the isolation and loneliness of the frontier. "We have been [moving] all our lives," lamented one woman. "As soon as ever we git comfortably settled, it is time to be off to something new."

Some yeomen acquired large tracts of level land, purchased slaves, and became planters. They forged part of the new wealth of the cotton boom states of Mississippi and Louisiana, where mobility into the slaveowning class was possible. Others clung to familiar mountainous areas or sought self-sufficiency as farmers because, as one frontiersman put it, they disliked "seeing the nose of my neighbor sticking out between the trees." As one historian has written, though they owned no slaves, yeomen were jealous of their independence, and "the household grounded their own claims to masterhood." Whatever the size of their property, they wanted control over their economic and domestic lives.

The yeomen enjoyed a folk culture based on family, church, and local region. Their speech patterns and inflections recalled their Scots-Irish and Irish backgrounds. They flocked to religious revivals called camp meetings, and in between they got together for house-raisings, logrollings, quilting bees, corn-shuckings, and hunting for both food and sport. Such occasions combined work with fun and fellowship, offering food and liquor in abundance.

### Yeoman Folk Culture

A demanding round of work and family responsibilities shaped women's lives in the home. They worked in the fields to an extent that astonished travelers like Frederick Law Olmsted and British writer Frances Trollope, who believed yeomen had rendered their wives "slaves of the soil." Throughout the year, the care and preparation of food consumed much of women's time. Household tasks continued during frequent pregnancies and childcare. Primary nursing and medical care also fell to mothers, who often relied on folk wisdom. Women, too, wanted to be masters of their household, the only space and power over which they could claim domain, although it came at the price of their health.

Among the men, many aspired to wealth, eager to join the scramble for slaves and cotton profits. North Carolinian John F. Flintoff kept a diary of his struggle for success. At age eighteen in 1841, Flintoff went to Mississippi to seek his fortune. Like other aspiring yeomen, he worked as an overseer of slaves but often found it impossible to please his employers. At one point he gave up and returned to North Carolina, where he married and lived for a while in his parents' house. But Flintoff was "impatient to get along in the world," so he tried Louisiana next and then Mississippi again.

### Yeomen's Livelihoods

Flintoff's health suffered in the Gulf region and, routinely, "first rate employment" alternated with "very low wages." Moreover, as a young man working on isolated plantations, Flintoff often felt lonely. Even a revival meeting in 1844 proved "an extremely cold time" with "little warm feeling." His uncle and other employers found fault with his work, and in 1846 Flintoff concluded in despair that "managing negroes and large farms is soul destroying."

But a desire to succeed kept him going. At twenty-six, even before he owned any land, Flintoff bought his first slave, "a negro boy 7 years old." Soon he had purchased two more children, the cheapest slaves available. Conscious of his status as a slaveowner, Flintoff resented the low wages he was paid. In 1853, with nine young slaves and a growing family, Flintoff faced "the most unhappy time of my life." Fired by his uncle, he returned to North Carolina, sold some of his slaves, and purchased 124 acres with help from his in-laws. By 1860 he owned animal stock and several slaves and was paying off his debts. As the Civil War approached, he looked forward to freeing his wife from labor and possibly sending his sons to college. Although Flintoff demonstrated that a farmer could move in and out of the slaveholding class, he never achieved the cotton planter status (owning roughly twenty or more slaves) that he desired.

Probably more typical of the southern yeoman was Ferdinand L. Steel, who as a young man moved from North Carolina to Tennessee to work as a river boatman but eventually took up farming in Mississippi. Steel rose every day at 5 a.m. and worked until sundown. He and his family raised corn and wheat, though cotton was his cash product: he sold five or six bales (about two thousand pounds) a year to obtain money for sugar, coffee, salt, calico, gunpowder, and a few other store-bought goods.

Thus Steel entered the market economy—the broader commercial exchange of goods—as a small farmer, but with mixed results. He picked his own cotton and complained that it was brutal work and not profitable. He felt like a serf in cotton's kingdom. When cotton prices fell, a small grower like Steel could be driven into debt and lose his farm.

Steel's life in Mississippi in the 1840s retained much of the flavor of the frontier and survived on a household economy. He made all the family's shoes; his wife and sister sewed dresses, shirts, and "pantaloons." The Steel women also rendered their own soap and spun and wove cotton into cloth; the men hunted game. Steel doctored his illnesses with boneset tea and other herbs. As the nation fell deeper into crisis over the future of free or slave labor, this independent southern farmer never came close to owning a slave.

The focus of Steel's life was family and religion. Family members prayed together daily, and he studied Scripture for an hour after lunch. "My Faith increases, & I enjoy much of that peace which the world cannot give," he wrote in 1841. Seeking to prepare himself for Judgment Day, Steel

▲ **This formal photograph, c. 1855, of a black woman attending to two mulatto children, indicates how common mixed-race children were in domestic relations in the Old South.** *(Photograph by James P. Bau; collection of Matthew Isenburg)*

borrowed histories, Latin and Greek grammars, and religious books from his church. Eventually he became a traveling Methodist minister. "My life is one of toil," he reflected, "but blessed be God that it is as well with me as it is."

Toil with even less security was the lot of two other groups of free southerners: landless whites and free blacks.

## Landless Whites

A sizable minority of white southern workers—from 25 to 40 percent, depending on the state—were hired hands who owned no land and worked for others in the countryside and towns. Their property consisted of a few household items and some animals—usually pigs—that could feed themselves on the open range. The landless included some immigrants, especially Irish, who did heavy and dangerous work, such as building railroads and digging ditches.

In the countryside, white farm laborers struggled to purchase land in the face of low wages or, if they rented, unpredictable market prices for their crops. By scrimping, saving, and finding odd jobs, some managed to climb into the ranks of yeomen. When James and Nancy Bennitt of North Carolina succeeded in their ten-year struggle to buy land, they decided to avoid the unstable market in cotton; thereafter they raised extra corn and wheat as sources of cash. People like the Bennitts were both participants in and victims of an economy dominated by cotton producers who relied on slave labor.

Herdsmen with pigs and other livestock had a desperate struggle to succeed. By 1860, as the South anticipated war to preserve its society, between 300,000 and 400,000 white people in the four states of Virginia, North and South Carolina, and Georgia—approximately one-fifth of the total white population—lived in genuine poverty. Their lives were harsh. An early antebellum traveler in central South Carolina described the white folk he encountered in the countryside: they "looked yellow, poor, and sickly. Some of them lived the most miserably I ever saw any poor people live." Land and slaves determined wealth in the Old South, and many whites possessed neither.

Class tensions emerged in the western, nonslaveholding parts of the seaboard states by the 1830s. There,

## Yeomen's Demands and White Class Relations

yeoman farmers resented their underrepresentation in state legislatures and the corruption in local government. After vigorous debate, the reformers won many battles. Voters in the more recently settled states of the Old Southwest adopted white manhood suffrage and other electoral reforms, including popular election of governors, legislative apportionment based on white population only, and locally chosen county government. Slaveowners with new wealth, however, knew that a more open government structure could permit troubling class conflicts and were determined to hold the ultimate reins of power.

Given such tensions, it was perhaps remarkable that slaveholders and nonslaveholders did not experience more overt conflict. Historians have offered several explanations. One of the most important factors was race. The South's racial ideology stressed the superiority of all whites to blacks. Thus slavery became the basis of equality among whites, and white privilege inflated the status of poor whites and gave them a common interest with the rich. At the same time, the dream of upward mobility blunted some class conflict. The Old South was to some extent a fluid society in which some people rose in status by acquiring land or slaves and those who did not wished that they could.

Most important, before the Civil War most yeomen were able to pursue their independent lifestyle largely unhindered by slaveholding planters. They worked their farms, avoided debt, and marked progress for their families in rural habitats of their own making. Likewise, slaveholders pursued their goals quite independently of yeomen. Planters farmed for the market but also for themselves. Suppression of dissent also played an increasing role. After 1830 white southerners who criticized the slave system out of moral conviction or class resentment were intimidated, attacked, legally prosecuted, or rendered politically powerless in a society held together in part by white racial solidarity.

Still, there were signs that the relative lack of conflict between slaveholders and nonslaveholders was coming to an end in the late antebellum period. As cotton lands filled up, nonslaveholders faced narrower economic prospects; meanwhile, wealthy planters enjoyed expanding profits. The risks of entering cotton production were becoming too great and the cost of slaves too high for many yeomen to rise in society. From 1830 to 1860 the percentage of white southern families holding slaves declined steadily from 36 to 25 percent. Although slaveowners were a distinct minority in the white population, planters' share of the South's agricultural wealth remained at between 90 and 95 percent.

Anticipating possible secession and the prospect of a war to defend slavery, slaveowners expressed growing fear about the loyalty of nonslaveholders during the late antebellum years. But for the moment slaveowners stood secure. In the 1850s they occupied from 50 to 85 percent of the seats in state legislatures and a similarly high percentage of the South's congressional seats. And planters' interests controlled all the other major social institutions, such as churches and colleges.

The nearly quarter-million free blacks in the South in 1860 also yearned for mobility. But their condition was

### Free Blacks

generally worse than the yeoman's and often little better than the slave's. The free blacks of the Upper South were usually descendants of men and women manumitted by their owners in the 1780s and 1790s. A remarkable number of slaveholders in Virginia and the Chesapeake region had freed their slaves because of religious principles and revolutionary ideals in the wake of American independence (see Chapter 7). Many free blacks also became free as runaways, especially by the 1830s, disappearing into the southern population; a few made their way northward.

White southerners were increasingly desperate to restrict this growing free black presence in their midst. "It seems the number of free Negroes," complained a Virginia slaveholder, "always exceeds the number of Negroes freed." Some free blacks worked in towns or cities, but most lived in rural areas and struggled to survive. They usually did not own land and had to labor in someone else's fields, often beside slaves. By law, free blacks could not own a gun, buy liquor, violate curfew, assemble except in church, testify in court, or (throughout the South after 1835) vote. Despite these obstacles, a minority bought land, and others found jobs as skilled craftsmen, especially in cities.

A few free blacks prospered and bought slaves. In 1830 there were 3,775 free black slaveholders in the South; 80 percent lived in the four states of Louisiana, South Carolina, Virginia, and Maryland, and approximately half of the total lived in the two cities of New Orleans and Charleston. Most of them purchased their own wives and children, whom they nevertheless could not free, because laws required newly emancipated blacks to leave their state. In order to free family members whom they had purchased, hundreds of black slaveholders petitioned for exemption from the antimanumission laws passed in most southern states. At the same time, a few mulattos in New Orleans were active slave traders in its booming market. The complex world of southern free blacks received new attention through Edward P. Jones's *The Known World*, a hugely successful novel published in 2003 about a Virginia family that rises from slavery to slaveownership. Although rare in the United States, the greed and the tragic quest for power that lay at the root of slavery could cross any racial or ethnic barrier.

In the Cotton Belt and Gulf regions, a large proportion of free blacks were mulattos, the privileged offspring of wealthy white planters. Not all planters freed their mixed-race off-

### Free Black Communities

spring, but those who did often recognized the moral obligation of giving their children a good education and financial backing. In a few cities like New Orleans, Charleston, and Mobile, extensive interracial sex, as well as migrations from the Caribbean, had produced a mulatto population that was recognized as a distinct class.

In many southern cities by the 1840s, free black communities formed, especially around an expanding number of churches. By the late 1850s, Baltimore had fifteen churches, Louisville nine, and Nashville and St. Louis four each—most of them African Methodist Episcopal. Class and race distinctions were important to southern free blacks, but outside a few cities, which developed fraternal orders of skilled craftsmen and fellowships of light-skinned people, most mulattos experienced hardship. In the United States, "one drop" of black "blood" (any observable racial mixture to white people's eyes) made them black, and potentially enslaveable.

## THE PLANTERS' WORLD

At the top of the southern social pyramid were slaveholding planters. As a group they lived well, but most lived in comfortable farmhouses, not on the opulent scale that legend suggests. The grand plantation mansions, with fabulous gardens and long rows of outlying slave quarters, are an enduring symbol of the Old South. But a few statistics tell the fuller story: in 1850, 50 percent of southern slaveholders had fewer than five slaves; 72 percent had fewer than ten; 88 percent had fewer than twenty. Thus the average slaveholder was not a wealthy aristocrat but an aspiring farmer.

Louisiana cotton planter Bennet Barrow, a newly rich planter of the 1840s, was preoccupied with moneymaking.

### The Newly Rich

He worried constantly over his cotton crop, filling his diary with weather reports and gloomy predictions of his yields. Yet Barrow also strove to appear above such worries. He hunted frequently and had a passion for racing horses and raising hounds. He could report the loss of a slave without feeling, but emotion broke through his laconic manner when illness afflicted his sporting animals. "Never was a person more unlucky than I am," he mourned. "My favorite pup never lives." His strongest feelings surfaced when his horse Jos Bell—equal to "the best Horse in the South"—"broke down running a mile . . . ruined for Ever." The same day, the distraught Barrow gave his human property a "general Whipping." In 1841 diary entries he worried about a rumored slave insurrection. He gave a "severe whipping" to several of his slaves when they disobediently killed a hog. And when a slave named Ginney Jerry "sherked" his cotton-picking duties and was rumored "about to run off," Barrow whipped him one day and the next, recorded matter-of-factly: "took my gun found him in the Bayou behind the Quarter, shot him in his thigh—etc. raining all around."

The richest planters used their wealth to model genteel sophistication. Extended visits, parties, and balls to which women wore the latest fashions provided opportunities for friendship, courtship, and display. Such parties were held during the Christmas holidays, but also on such occasions as molasses stewing, a bachelors' ball, a horserace, or the crowning of the May queen. These entertainments were especially important as diversions for plantation women, and at the same time they sustained a rigidly gendered society. Young women relished social events to break the monotony of their domestic lives. In 1826 a Virginia girl was ecstatic about the "week . . . I was in Town. . . . There were five beaux and as many belles in the house constantly," she declared, and all she and her companions did was "eat, visit, romp, and sleep."

Most of the planters in the cotton-boom states of Alabama and Mississippi were newly rich by the 1840s. As one historian put it, "a number of men mounted from log cabin to plantation mansion on a stairway of cotton bales, accumulating slaves as they climbed." And many did not live like rich men. They put their new wealth into cotton acreage and slaves even as they sought refinement and high social status.

William Faulkner immortalized the new wealthy planter in a fictional character, Thomas Sutpen, in his novel *Absalom, Absalom!* (1936). After a huge win at riverboat gambling, Sutpen arrives in a Mississippi county in the 1830s, buys a huge plantation which he calls Sutpen's Hundred, and with his troop of slaves converts it into a wealthy enterprise. Sutpen marries a local woman, and although he is always viewed as a mysterious outsider by earlier residents of the county, he becomes a pillar of the slaveholding class, eventually an officer in the Confederate Army. But Sutpen is a self-made man of indomitable will and slave-based wealth. Although his ambition is ultimately his undoing, one of the earliest lessons he learns about success in the South is that "you got to have land and niggers and a fine house."

The cotton boom in the Mississippi valley created one-generation aristocrats. A nonfictional case in point is Greenwood Leflore, a Chocktaw chieftain who owned a plantation in Mississippi with four hundred slaves. After selling his cotton on the world market, he spent $10,000 in France to furnish a single room of his mansion with handwoven carpets, furniture upholstered with gold leaf,

tables and cabinets ornamented with tortoise-shell inlay, a variety of mirrors and paintings, and a clock and candelabra of brass and ebony.

Slave ownership was the main determinant of wealth in the South, and slave labor was the primary means of cultivating cotton and other cash crops on a large scale. Slaves were a commodity and an investment, much like gold; people bought them on speculation, hoping for a steady rise in their market value. Across the South, variations in wealth from county to county corresponded very closely to variations in slaveholding. Wealth in slaves also translated into political power: a solid majority of political officeholders were slaveholders, and the most powerful were usually large-scale planters.

## Social Status and Planters' Values

Slavery's influence spread throughout the social system, until even the values and mores of nonslaveholders bore its imprint. The availability of slave labor tended to devalue free labor: where strenuous work under supervision was reserved for an enslaved race, few free people relished it. When Alexis de Tocqueville crossed from Ohio into Kentucky in his travels of 1831, he observed "the effect that slavery produces on society. On the right bank of the Ohio [River] everything is activity, industry; labor is honoured; there are no slaves. Pass to the left bank and the scene changes so suddenly that you think yourself on the other side of the world; the enterprising spirit is gone. There, work is not only painful; it is shameful." Tocqueville's own class impulses found a home in the South, however. There he found a "veritable aristocracy which . . . combines many prejudices with high sentiments and instincts."

The values of the aristocrat—lineage, privilege, pride, honor, and refinement of person and manner—commanded respect throughout the South. Many of those qualities were in short supply, however, in the recently settled portions of the cotton kingdom, where frontier values of courage and self-reliance ruled during the 1820s and 1830s. By the 1850s, a settled aristocratic group of planters did rule, however, in much of the Mississippi valley. In this geographically mobile society, independence and codes of honor motivated both planter and frontier farmer alike.

Instead of gradually disappearing, as it did in the North, the Code Duello, which required men to defend their honor through violence, lasted much longer in the South. In North Carolina in 1851, wealthy planter Samuel Fleming sought to settle disputes with lawyer William Waightstill Avery by "cowhiding" him on a public street. According to the code, Avery had two choices: to redeem his honor violently or to brand himself a coward through inaction. Three weeks later, he shot Fleming dead at point-blank range during a session of the Burke County Superior

Court. A jury took only ten minutes to find Avery not guilty, and the spectators gave him a standing ovation.

In their pride, aristocratic planters expected not only to wield power but also to receive deference from poorer whites. But the sternly independent yeoman class resented infringements of their rights, and many belonged to evangelical faiths that exalted values of simplicity and condemned the planters' love of wealth. Yeomen sometimes challenged the political pretensions of planters. Much of the planters' power and their claims to leadership, after all, were built on their assumption of a monopoly on world cotton and on a foundation of black slave labor.

Planters always had their eyes on the international growth of the cotton markets. Cash crops such as cotton

### King Cotton in a Global Economy

were for export; the planters' fate depended on world trade, especially with Europe. The American South so dominated the world's supply of cotton that southern planters gained enormous confidence that the cotton boom was permanent and that the industrializing nations of England and France in particular would always bow to King Cotton.

American cotton production doubled in yield each decade after 1800 and provided three-fourths of the world's supply by the 1840s. Southern staple crops were fully three-fifths of all American exports by 1850, and one of every seven workers in England depended on American cotton for his job. Indeed, cotton production made slaves the single most valuable financial asset in the United States—greater in dollar value than all of America's banks, railroads, and manufacturing combined. In 1860 dollars, the slaves' total value as property came to an estimated $3.5 billion. In early-twenty-first-century dollars, that would be approximately $70 billion.

"Cotton is King," the *Southern Cultivator* declared in 1859, "and wields an astonishing influence over the world's commerce." Until 1840 the cotton trade furnished much of the export capital to finance northern economic growth. After that date, however, the northern economy expanded without dependence on cotton profits. Nevertheless, southern planters and politicians continued to boast of King Cotton's supremacy. "Our cotton is the most wonderful talisman in the world," announced a planter in 1853. "By its power we are transmuting whatever we choose into whatever we want." "No power on earth dares . . . to make war on cotton," James Hammond lectured the U.S. Senate in 1858; "Cotton is king." Although the South produced 4.5 million bales in 1861, its greatest cotton crop ever, such world dominance was about to collapse. Thereafter, cotton was more a shackle to the South than a king.

Slaveholding men often embraced a paternalistic ideology that justified their dominance over both black slaves and white women. Instead

### Paternalism

of stressing the profitable aspects of commercial agriculture, they stressed their obligations, viewing themselves as custodians of the welfare of society in general, and of the black families they owned in particular. The paternalistic planter saw himself not as an oppressor but as the benevolent guardian of an inferior race.

Paul Carrington Cameron, who was North Carolina's largest slaveholder, exemplifies this mentality. After a period of sickness among his one thousand North Carolina slaves (he had hundreds more in Alabama and Mississippi), Cameron wrote, "I fear the Negroes have suffered much from the want of proper attention and kindness under this late distemper no love of lucre shall ever induce me to be cruel." On another occasion he described to his sister the sense of responsibility he felt: "Do you remember a cold & frosty morning, during [our mother's] illness, when she said to me 'Paul my son the people ought to be shod' this is ever in my ears, whenever I see any ones shoes in bad order; and in my ears it will be, so long as I am master."

It was comforting to rich planters to see themselves in this way, and slaves—accommodating to the realities of power—encouraged their masters to think that their benevolence was appreciated. Paternalism also served as a defense against abolitionist criticism. Still, paternalism was often a matter of self-delusion, a means of avoiding some harsh dimensions of slave treatment. In reality, paternalism grew as a give-and-take relationship between masters and slaves, each extracting from the other what they desired—owners took labor from the bondsmen, while slaves obligated masters to provide them a measure of autonomy and living space. As one historian has argued, paternalism "grew out of the necessity to discipline and morally justify a system of exploitation, . . . a fragile bridge across the intolerable contradictions inherent" in a slave society dependent on "the willing reproduction and productivity of its victims."

Even Paul Cameron's benevolence vanished with changed circumstances. After the Civil War, he bristled at African Americans' efforts to be free and made sweeping economic decisions without regard for their welfare. Writing on Christmas Day 1865, Cameron showed little Christian charity (but a healthy profit motive) when he declared, "I am convinced that the people who gets rid of the free negro first will be the first to advance in improved agriculture. Have made no effort to retain any of mine." With that he turned off his land nearly a thousand black people, rented his fields to several white farmers, and invested in industry.

Relations between men and women in the planter class were similarly defined by paternalism. The upper-class southern woman was raised and educated to be a wife, mother, and subordinate companion to men. South Carolina's Mary Boykin Chesnut wrote of her husband, "He is master of the house. To hear is to obey.... All the comfort of my life depends upon his being in a good humor." In a social system based on the coercion of an entire race, women found it very difficult to challenge society's rules on sexual or racial relations.

Planters' daughters usually attended one of the South's rapidly multiplying boarding schools. There they formed friendships with other girls and received an education. Typically, the young woman could entertain suitors whom her parents approved. But very soon she had to choose a husband and commit herself for life to a man whom she generally had known for only a brief time. Young women were often alienated and emotionally unfulfilled. They had to follow the wishes of their family, especially their father. "It was for me best that I yielded to the wishes of papa," wrote a young North Carolinian in 1823. "I wonder when my best will cease to be painful and when I shall begin to enjoy life instead of enduring it."

Upon marriage, a planter-class woman ceded to her husband most of her legal rights, becoming part of his family. Most of the year she was isolated on a large plantation, where she had to oversee the cooking and preserving of food, manage the house, supervise care of the children, and attend sick slaves. All these realities were more rigid and confining on the frontier, where isolation was even greater. Women sought refuge in their extended family and associations with other women. In 1821 a Georgia woman wrote to her brother of the distress of a cousin's wife: "They are living . . . in the frontiers of the state and [a] perfectly uncivilized place. Cousin W. gets a good practice [the husband] but she is almost crazy to get to Alabama where one of her sisters is living." Men on plantations could occasionally escape into the public realm—to town, business, or politics. Women could retreat from rural plantation culture only into kinship.

It is not surprising that a perceptive young white woman sometimes approached marriage with anxiety. Women could hardly help viewing their wedding day, as one put it in 1832, as "the day to fix my fate." Lucy Breckinridge, a wealthy Virginia girl of twenty, lamented the autonomy she surrendered at the altar. In her diary she recorded this unvarnished observation on marriage: "If [husbands] care for their wives at all it is only as a sort of servant, a being made to attend to their comforts and to keep the children out of the way. A woman's life after she is married, unless there is an immense amount of love, is nothing but suffering and hard work."

## Marriage and Family Among Planters

Lucy loved young children but knew that childbearing often involved grief, poor health, and death. In 1840 the birth rate for white southern women in their childbearing years was almost 30 percent higher than the national average. The average southern white woman could expect to bear eight children in 1800; by 1860 the figure had decreased to only six, with one or more miscarriages likely. Complications of childbirth were a major cause of death, occurring twice as often in the hot, humid South as in the Northeast.

Sexual relations between planters and slaves were another source of problems that white women had to endure

◀ Portrait of a planter's family and slave, New Market, Virginia; photographer unidentified, c. 1859–1864. The structure of life on a small plantation is vividly indicated here: the young black woman holding the baby, the white mistress with shawl and fan, and the planter as patriarch. *(Collection of William A. Turner)*

but were not supposed to notice. "Violations of the moral law . . . made mulattos as common as blackberries," protested a woman in Georgia, but wives had to play "the ostrich game." "A magnate who runs a hideous black harem," wrote Mrs. Chesnut, ". . . poses as the model of all human virtues to these poor women whom God and the laws have given him."

Southern men tolerated little discussion by women of the slavery issue. In the 1840s and 1850s, as abolitionist attacks on slavery increased, southern men published a barrage of articles stressing that women should restrict their concerns to the home. The *Southern Quarterly Review* declared, "The proper place for a woman is at home. One of her highest privileges, to be politically merged in the existence of her husband."

But some southern women were beginning to seek a larger role. A study of women in Petersburg, Virginia, a large tobacco-manufacturing town, revealed behavior that valued financial autonomy. Over several decades before 1860, the proportion of women who never married, or did not remarry after the death of a spouse, grew to exceed 33 percent. Likewise, the number of women who worked for wages, controlled their own property, and ran dressmaking businesses increased. In managing property, these and other women benefited from legal changes enacted to protect families from the husband's indebtedness during business panics and recessions. These reforms gave married women some property rights.

Planters forged a society around their domestic lives and local mores. But they did so through the energies and lives of generations of enslaved African Americans who helped them extract great wealth from southern soil.

## SLAVE LIFE AND LABOR

For African Americans, slavery was a burden that destroyed some people and forced others to develop modes of survival. Slaves knew a life of poverty, coercion, toil, and resentment. They provided the physical strength, and much of the know-how, to build an agricultural empire. But their daily lives embodied the nation's most basic contradiction: in the world's model republic, they were on the wrong side of a brutally unequal power relationship.

Southern slaves enjoyed few material comforts beyond the bare necessities. Although they generally had enough

||||||||||||||||||||||||||||||||

**Slaves' Everyday Conditions**

to eat, their diet was monotonous and nonnutritious. Clothing, too, was plain, coarse, and inexpensive. Few slaves received more than one or two changes of clothing for hot

and cold seasons, and one blanket each winter. Children of both sexes ran naked in hot weather and wore long cotton shirts in winter. Many slaves had to go without shoes until December, even as far north as Virginia. The bare feet of slaves were often symbolic of their status and one reason why, after freedom, many black parents were so concerned with providing their children with shoes. These conditions were generally better in cities, where slaves frequently lived in the same dwelling as their owners and were hired out to employers on a regular basis, enabling them to accumulate their own money.

Some of the richer plantations provided substantial houses, but the average slave lived in a crude, one-room cabin. The gravest drawback of slave cabins was not lack of comfort but unhealthfulness. Each dwelling housed one or two entire families. Crowding and lack of sanitation fostered the spread of infection and such contagious diseases as typhoid fever, malaria, and dysentery. White plantation doctors were hired to care for sick slaves on a regular basis, but some "slave doctors" attained a degree of power in the quarters and with masters by practicing health care and healing through herbalism and spiritualism.

Hard work was the central fact of slaves' existence. The long hours and large work gangs that characterized

||||||||||||||||||||||||||||||||

**Slave Work Routines**

Gulf Coast cotton districts operated almost like factories in the field. Overseers rang the morning bell before dawn, and black people of varying ages, tools in hand, walked toward the fields. Slaves who cultivated tobacco in the Upper South worked long hours picking the sticky, sometimes noxious, leaves under harsh discipline. And, as one woman recalled when interviewed in the 1930s, "it was way after sundown fore they could stop that field work. Then they had to hustle to finish their night work [such as watering livestock or cleaning cotton] in time for supper, or go to bed without it."

Working "from sun to sun" became a norm in much of the South. As one planter put it, slaves were the best labor because "you could command them and make them do what was right." Profit took precedence over paternalism. Slave women did heavy fieldwork, often as much as the men and even during pregnancy. Old people were kept busy caring for young children, doing light chores, or carding, ginning, and spinning cotton. The black abolitionist orator Frances Ellen Watkins captured the grinding economic reality of slavery in an 1857 speech, charging that slaveholders had "found out a fearful alchemy by which . . . blood can be transformed into gold. Instead of listening to the cry of agony, they listen to the ring of dollars and stoop down to pick up the coin."

By the 1830s slaveowners found that labor could be similarly motivated by the clock. Incentives had to be part of the labor regime and the master-slave relationship as well. Planters in the South Carolina and Georgia low country used a task system whereby slaves were assigned measured amounts of work to be performed in a given amount of time. So much cotton on a daily basis was to be picked from a designated field, so many rows hoed or plowed in a particular slave's specified section. When their tasks were finished, slaves' time was their own for working garden plots, tending hogs, even hiring out their own extra labor. From this experience and personal space, many slaves developed their own sense of property ownership. When the task system worked best, slaves and masters alike embraced it, fostering a degree of reciprocal trust.

Slave children were the future of the system and widely valued as potential labor. Of the 1860 population of 4 million slaves, fully half were under the age of sixteen. "A child raised every two years," wrote Thomas Jefferson, "is of more profit than the crop of the best laboring man." And in 1858 a slaveowner writing in an agricultural mag-

azine calculated that a slave girl he purchased in 1827 for $400 had borne three sons now worth $3,000 as his working field hands. Slave children gathered kindling, carried water to the fields, swept the yard, lifted cut sugar-cane stalks into carts, stacked wheat, chased birds away from sprouting rice plants, and labored at many levels of cotton and tobacco production. "Work," wrote one historian, "can be rightly called the thief who stole the childhood of youthful bond servants."

As slave children matured, they faced many psychological traumas. They faced a feeling of powerlessness as they became aware that their parents ultimately could not protect them. They had to muster strategies to fight internalizing what whites assumed was their inferiority. Thomas Jones, who grew up in North Carolina, remembered that his greatest struggle with the sense of "suffering and shame" as he "was made to feel . . . degraded." Many former slaves resented foremost their denial of education. "There is one sin that slavery committed against me which I will never forgive," recollected the minister James Pennington. "It robbed me of my education." And for girls reaching maturity, the potential trauma of sexual abuse loomed over their lives.

▲ George Fuller, an itinerant painter from Massachusetts, worked from 1856 to 1858 in Alabama, where he made this sketch in ink and pencil of a mistress joining her slave at work on washday.

*(Pocumtuck Valley Memorial Association)*

Slaves could not demand much autonomy, of course, because the owner enjoyed a monopoly on force and violence. Whites throughout the South believed that slaves "can't be governed except with the whip." One South Carolinian frankly explained to a northern journalist that he whipped his slaves regularly, "say once a fortnight; . . . the fear of the lash kept them in good order." Evidence suggests that whippings were less frequent on small farms than on large plantations. But beatings symbolized authority to the master and tyranny to the slaves, who made them a benchmark for evaluating a master. In the words of former slaves, a good owner was one who did not "whip too much," whereas a bad owner "whipped till he's bloodied you and blistered you."

### Violence and Intimidation Against Slaves

As these reports suggest, terrible abuses could and did occur. The master wielded virtually absolute authority on his plantation, and courts did not recognize the word of chattel. Slaveholders rarely had to answer to the law or to the state. Pregnant women were whipped, and there were burnings, mutilation, torture, and murder. Yet physical cruelty may have been less prevalent in the United States than in other slaveholding parts of the New World. Especially in some of the sugar islands of the Caribbean, treatment was so poor and death rates so high that the heavily male slave population shrank in size. In the United States, by contrast, the slave population experienced a steady natural increase, as births exceeded deaths and each generation grew larger.

The worst evil of American slavery was not its physical cruelty but the nature of slavery itself: coercion, belonging to another person, virtually no hope for mobility or change. Recalling their time in bondage, some former slaves emphasized the physical abuse, or the "bullwhip days," as one woman described her past. But memories of physical punishment focused on the tyranny of whipping as much as the pain. Delia Garlic made the essential point: "It's bad to belong to folks that own you soul an' body. I could tell you 'bout it all day, but even then you couldn't guess the awfulness of it." Thomas Lewis put it this way: "There was no such thing as being good to slaves. Many people were better than others, but a slave belonged to his master and there was no way to get out of it." To be a slave was to be the object of another person's will and material gain, to be owned, as the saying went, "from the cradle to the grave."

Most American slaves retained their mental independence and self-respect despite their bondage. Contrary to popular belief at the time, they were not loyal partners in their own oppression. They had to be subservient and speak honeyed words to their masters, but they talked and behaved quite differently among themselves. In *Narrative of the Life of Frederick Douglass, an American Slave, Written by Himself* (1845), Douglass wrote that most slaves, when asked about "their condition and the character of their masters, almost universally say they are contented, and that their masters are kind." Slaves did this, said Douglass, because they were governed by the maxim that "a still tongue makes a wise head," especially in the presence of unfamiliar people. Because they were "part of the human family," slaves often quarreled over who had the best master. But at the end of the day, Douglass remarked, when one had a bad master, he sought a better master; and when he had a better one, he wanted to "be his own master."

Some former slaves remembered warm feelings between masters and slaves, but the prevailing attitudes were distrust and antagonism. Slaves saw through acts of kindness. One woman said her mistress was "a mighty good somebody to belong to" but only "'cause she was raisin' us to work for her." A man recalled that his owners took good care of their slaves, "and Grandma Maria say, 'Why shouldn't they—it was their money.'" Slaves also resented being used as beasts of burden. One man observed that his master "fed us reg'lar on good, 'stantial food, just like you'd tend to your horse, if you had a real good one."

### Slave-Master Relationships

Slaves were alert to the thousand daily signs of their degraded status. One man recalled the general rule that slaves ate cornbread and owners ate biscuits. If blacks did get biscuits, "the flour that we made the biscuits out of was the third-grade sorts." A former slave recalled, "Us catch lots of 'possums," but "the white folks at [ate] 'em." If the owner took his slaves' garden produce to town and sold it for them, the slaves often suspected him of pocketing part of the profits.

Suspicion often grew into hatred. When a yellow fever epidemic struck in 1852, many slaves saw it as God's retribution. An elderly ex-slave named Minnie Fulkes cherished the conviction that God was going to punish white people for their cruelty to blacks. She described the whippings that her mother had to endure, and then she exclaimed, "Lord, Lord, I hate white people and the flood waters goin' to drown some more." On the plantation, of course, slaves had to keep such thoughts to themselves. Often they expressed one feeling to whites, another within their own household. In their daily lives slaves created many ways to survive and to sustain their humanity in this world of repression.

## SLAVE CULTURE AND RESISTANCE

A people is always "more than the sum of its brutalization," wrote African American novelist Ralph Ellison in 1967. What people create in the face of hard luck and oppression is what provides hope. The resource that enabled slaves to maintain such defiance was their culture: a body of beliefs, values, and practices born of their past and maintained in the present. As best they could, they built a community knitted together by stories, music, a religious world-view, leadership, the smells of their cooking, the sounds of their own voices, and the tapping of their feet. "The values expressed in folklore," wrote African American poet Sterling Brown, provided a "wellspring to which slaves . . . could return in times of doubt to be refreshed." That they endured and found loyalty and strength among themselves is a tribute to their courage and to the triumph of the human spirit.

Slave culture changed significantly after 1808, when Congress banned further importation of slaves and the

**African Cultural Survival**

generations born in Africa died out. For a few years South Carolina reopened the international slave trade, but by the 1830s, the vast majority of slaves in the South were native-born Americans. Many blacks, in fact, can trace their American ancestry back further than most white Americans.

Yet African influences remained strong, despite lack of firsthand memory, especially in appearance and forms of expression. Some slave men plaited their hair into rows and fancy designs; slave women often wore their hair "in string"—tied in small bunches secured by a string or piece of cloth. A few men and many women wrapped their heads in kerchiefs of the styles and colors of West Africa. Some could remember the names of African ancestors passed on to them by family lore. In burial practices, slaves used jars and other glass objects to decorate graves, following similar African traditions.

Music, religion, and folktales were parts of daily life for most slaves. Borrowing partly from their African background, as well as forging new American folkways, they developed what scholars have called a sacred world-view, which affected all aspects of work, leisure, and self-understanding. Slaves made musical instruments with carved motifs that resembled African stringed instruments. Their drumming and dancing followed African patterns that made whites marvel. One visitor to Georgia in the 1860s described a ritual dance of African origin: "A ring of singers is formed. . . . They then utter a kind of melodious chant, which gradually increases in strength, and in noise, until it fairly shakes the house, and it can be heard for a long distance." This observer of the "ring shout" also noted the agility of the dancers and the African call-and-response pattern in their chanting.

Many slaves continued to believe in spirit possession. Whites, too, believed in ghosts and charms, but the slaves' belief resembled the African concept of the living dead—the idea that deceased relatives visit the earth for many years until the process of dying is complete. Slaves also practiced conjuration and quasi-magical root medicine. By the 1850s the most notable conjurers and root doctors were reputed to live in South Carolina, Georgia, Louisiana, and other isolated coastal areas with high slave populations.

These cultural survivals provided slaves with a sense of their separate past. Such practices and beliefs were not static "Africanisms" or mere "retentions." They were cultural adaptations, living traditions re-formed in the Americas in response to new experience. African American slaves in the Old South were a people forged by two centuries of cultural mixture in the Atlantic world, and the South itself was a melding of many African and European cultural forces.

As they became African Americans, slaves also developed a sense of racial identity. In the colonial period, Africans had arrived in America from many different states and kingdoms, represented in distinctive languages, body markings, and traditions. Planters had used ethnic differences to create occupational hierarchies. By the early antebellum period, however, old ethnic identities gave way as American slaves increasingly saw themselves as a single group unified by race. Africans had arrived in the New World with virtually no concept of "race"; by the antebellum era, their descendants had learned through bitter experience that race was now the defining feature of their lives. They were a transplanted and transformed people.

As African culture gave way to a maturing African American culture, more and more slaves adopted Christi-

**Slaves' Religion and Music**

anity. But they fashioned Christianity into an instrument of support and resistance. Theirs was a religion of justice and deliverance, quite unlike their masters' religious propaganda directed at them as a means of control. "You ought to have heard that preachin'," said one man. "'Obey your master and mistress, don't steal chickens

Drawing by Lewis Miller of a "Lynchburg Negro Dance," Lynchburg, Virginia, August 18, 1853. This work of art shows the slaves' use of elaborate costumes, string instruments, and "the bones"—folk percussion instruments of African origin, held between the fingers and used as clappers.

*(Abby Aldrich Rockefeller Folk Art Collection, Colonial Williamsburg Foundation)*

and eggs and meat,' but nary a word about havin' a soul to save." Slaves believed that Jesus cared about their souls and their plight. In their interpretations of biblical stories, as one historian has said, they were "literally willing themselves reborn."

For slaves, Christianity was a religion of personal and group salvation. Devout men and women worshiped every day, "in the field or by the side of the road" or in special "prayer grounds" that afforded privacy. Some slaves held fervent secret prayer meetings that lasted far into the night. Many slaves nurtured an unshakable belief that God would enter history and end their bondage. This faith—and the joy and emotional release that accompanied worship—sustained them.

Slaves also adapted Christianity to African practices. In West African belief, devotees are possessed by a god so thoroughly that the god's own personality replaces the human personality. In the late antebellum era, Christian slaves experienced possession by the Protestant "Holy Spirit." The combination of shouting, singing, and dancing that seemed to overtake black worshipers formed the heart of their religious faith. "The old meeting house caught fire," recalled an ex-slave preacher. "The spirit was there. . . . God saw our need and came to us. I used to wonder what made people shout but now I don't. There is a joy on the inside and it wells up so strong that we can't keep still. It is fire in the bones. Any time that fire touches a man, he will jump." Out in brush arbors or in meetinghouses, slaves took in the presence of God, thrust their arms to heaven, made music with their feet, and sang away their woes. Some travelers observed "bands" of "Fist and Heel Worshippers." Many postslavery black choirs could not perform properly without a good wooden floor to use as their "drum."

Rhythm and physical movement were crucial to slaves' religious experience. In black preachers' chanted sermons, which reached out to gather the sinner into a narrative of meanings and cadences along the way to conversion, an American tradition was born. The chanted sermon was both a message from Scripture and a patterned form that required audience response punctuated by "yes sirs!" and "amens!" But it was in song that the slaves left their most sublime gift to American culture.

Through the spirituals, slaves tried to impose order on the chaos of their lives. Many themes run through the lyrics of slave songs. Often referred to later as the "sorrow songs," they also anticipate imminent rebirth. Sadness could immediately give way to joy: "Did you ever stan' on a mountain, wash yo hands in a cloud?" Rebirth was at the heart as well of the famous hymn "Oh, Freedom": "Oh, Oh, Freedom / Oh, Oh, Freedom over me— / But before I'll be a slave, / I'll be buried in my grave, / And go home to my Lord, / And Be Free!"

This tension and sudden change between sorrow and joy animates many songs: "Sometimes I feel like a motherless chile . . . / Sometimes I feel like an eagle in the air, / . . . Spread my wings and fly, fly, fly!" Many songs also express a sense of intimacy and closeness with God. Some songs display an unmistakable rebelliousness, such as the enduring "He said, and if I had my way / If I had my way, if I had my way, / I'd tear this building down!" And some spirituals reached for a collective sense of hope in the black community as a whole.

▲ This photograph of five generations of a slave family, taken in Beaufort, South Carolina, in 1862, is silent but powerful testimony to the importance that enslaved African Americans placed on their ever-threatened family ties. *(Library of Congress)*

O, gracious Lord! When shall it be,
That we poor souls shall all be free;
Lord, break them slavery powers—
Will you go along with me?
Lord break them slavery powers,
Go sound the jubilee!

In many ways, American slaves converted the Christian God to themselves. They sought an alternative world to live in—a home other than the one fate had given them on earth. In a thousand variations on the Br'er Rabbit folktales—in which the weak survive by wit and power is reversed—and in the countless refrains of their songs, they fashioned survival and resistance out of their own cultural imagination.

American slaves clung tenaciously to the personal relationships that gave meaning to life. Although American

## The Black Family in Slavery

law did not recognize slave families, masters permitted them; in fact, slaveowners *expected* slaves to form families and have children. As a result, even along the rapidly expanding edge of the cotton kingdom, there was a normal ratio of men to women, young to old. Studies have shown that, on some of the largest cotton plantations of South Carolina, when masters allowed their slaves increased autonomy through work on the task system, the property accumulation in livestock, tools, and garden produce thus fostered led to more stable and healthier families.

Following African kinship traditions, African Americans avoided marriage between cousins (commonplace among aristocratic slaveowners). By naming their children after relatives of past generations, African Americans emphasized their family histories. Kinship networks and broadly extended families are what held life together in many slave communities.

For slave women, sexual abuse and rape by white masters were ever-present threats to themselves and their family life. By 1860 there were 405,751 mulattos in the United States, comprising 12.5 percent of the African American population. White planters were sometimes open with their behavior toward slave women, but not in the way they talked about it. As Mary Chesnut remarked, sex between slaveholding men and their slave women was "the thing we can't name." Buying slaves for sex was all too common at the New Orleans slave market. In what was called the "fancy trade" (a "fancy" was a young, attractive slave girl or woman), females were often sold for prices as much as 300 percent higher than the average. At such auctions for young women, slaveholders exhibited some of the ugliest values at the heart of the slave system—patriarchal dominance demonstrated by paying $3,000 to $5,000 for female "companions."

Slave women had to negotiate this confused world of desire, threat, and shame. Harriet Jacobs, who spent much of her youth and early adult years dodging her owner's relentless sexual pursuit, described this circumstance as "the war of my life." In recollecting her desperate effort to protect her children and help them find a way north to freedom, Jacobs asked a haunting question that many slave women carried with them to their graves: "Why does the slave ever love? Why allow the tendrils of the heart to twine around objects which may at any moment be wrenched away by the hand of violence?"

Separation by violence from those they loved, sexual appropriation, and sale were what slave families most feared and hated. Many struggled for years to keep their children together and, after emancipation, to reestablish contact with loved ones lost by forced migration and sale. Between 1820 and 1860, an estimated 2 million slaves were moved into the region extending from western Georgia to eastern Texas. When the Union Army registered thousands of black marriages in Mississippi and Louisiana in 1864 and 1865, fully 25 percent of the men over forty reported that they had been forcibly separated from a previous wife. Thousands of black families were disrupted every year to serve the needs of the expanding cotton economy. The Butler auction of 1859, described in the chapter-opening vignette, was only one in a gruesome series.

Many antebellum white southerners made their living from the slave trade. In South Carolina alone by the 1850s, there were over one hundred slave-trading firms

## The Domestic Slave Trade

selling an annual average of approximately 6,500 slaves to southwestern states. Although southerners often denied it, vast numbers of slaves moved west by outright sale and not by migrating with their owners. A typical trader's advertisement read, "NEGROES WANTED. I am paying the highest cash prices for young and likely NEGROES, those having good front teeth and being otherwise sound." One estimate from 1858 indicated that slave sales in Richmond, Virginia, netted $4 million that year alone. A market guide to slave sales that same year in Richmond listed average prices for "likely ploughboys," ages twelve to fourteen, at $850 to $1,050; "extra number 1 fieldgirls" at $1,300 to $1,350; and "extra number 1 men" at $1,500.

Slave traders were practical, roving businessmen. They were sometimes considered degraded by white planters, but many slaveowners did business with them. Market forces, as the Butler auction indicates, drove this commerce in humanity. At slave "pens" in cities like New Orleans, traders promoted "a large and commodious showroom . . . prepared to accommodate over 200 Negroes for sale." Traders did their utmost to make their slaves appear young, healthy, and happy, cutting gray whiskers off men, using paddles as discipline so as not to scar their merchandise, and forcing people to dance and sing as buyers arrived for an auction. When transported to the southwestern markets, slaves were often chained together in "coffles," which made journeys of 500 miles or more on foot.

The complacent mixture of racism and business among traders is evident in their own language. "I refused a girl 20 year[s] old at 700 yesterday," one trader wrote to another in 1853. "If you think best to take her at 700 I can still get her. She is very badly whipped but good teeth." Some sales were transacted at owners' requests, often for tragically inhumane reasons. "Bought a cook yesterday that was to go out of state," wrote a trader; "she just made the people mad that was all." Some traders demonstrated how deeply slavery and racism were intertwined. "I have bought the boy Isaac for 1100," wrote a trader in 1854 to his partner. "I think him very prime. . . . He is a . . . house servant . . . first rate cook . . . and splendid carriage driver. He is also a fine painter and varnisher and . . . says he can make a fine panel door. . . . Also he performs well on the violin. . . . He is a genius and its strange to say I think he is smarter than I am."

Slaves brought to their efforts at resistance the same common sense and determination that characterized their struggle to secure their family lives.

## Strategies of Resistance

The scales weighed heavily against overt revolution, and they knew it. But they seized opportunities to alter their work conditions. They

◀ A slave coffle on the march toward newly settled states of the Southwest.

*(Collection of William Loren Katz)*

accounts of these resistant slaves who gave the lie to the image of the docile bondsman. The price they paid was high. Such lonely rebels were customarily secured and flogged, sold away, or hanged.

Many individual slaves attempted to run away to the North, and some received assistance from the loose network known as the Underground Railroad (see page 378). But it was more common for slaves to run off temporarily to hide in the woods. Approximately 80 percent of runaways were male; women simply could not flee as readily because of their responsibility for children. Fear, disgruntlement over treatment, or family separation might motivate slaves to risk all in flight. Only a minority of those who tried such escapes ever made it to freedom in the North or Canada, but these fugitives made slavery a very insecure institution by the 1850s.

But American slavery also produced some fearless revolutionaries. Gabriel's Rebellion involved as many as a thousand slaves when it was discovered in 1800, just before it would have exploded in Richmond, Virginia (see pages 215–216). According to controversial court testimony, a similar conspiracy existed in Charleston in 1822, led by a free black named Denmark Vesey. Born a slave in the Caribbean, Vesey won a lottery of $1,500 in 1799, bought his own freedom, and became a religious leader in the black community. According to one long-argued interpretation, Vesey was a heroic revolutionary determined to free his people or die trying. But, in a recent challenge, historian Michael Johnson points out that the court testimony is the only reliable source on the alleged insurrection. Might the testimony reveal less of reality than of white South Carolina's fears of slave rebellion? The court, says Johnson, built its case on rumors and intimidated witnesses, and "conjured into being" an insurrection that was not about to occur in reality. Whatever the facts, when the arrests and trials were over, thirty-seven "conspirators" were executed, and more than three dozen others were banished from the state.

The most famous rebel of all, Nat Turner, struck for freedom in Southampton County, Virginia, in 1831. The

sometimes slacked off when they were not being watched. Thus owners complained that slaves "never would lay out their strength freely."

Daily discontent and desperation were also manifest in sabotage of equipment; in wanton carelessness about work; in theft of food, livestock, or crops; or in getting drunk on stolen liquor. Some slaves who were hired out might show their anger by hoarding their earnings. Or they might just fall into recalcitrance. "I have a boy in my employ called Jim Archer," complained a Vicksburg, Mississippi, slaveholder in 1843. "Jim does not want to be under anyones control and says . . . he wants to go home this summer." A woman named Ellen, hired as a cook in Tennessee in 1856, quietly put mercury poison into a roasted apple for her unsuspecting mistress. And some slave women resisted as best they could by trying to control their own pregnancy, either by avoiding it or by seeking it as a way to improve their physical conditions.

Many male, and some female, slaves acted out their defiance by violently attacking overseers or even their owners. Southern court records and newspapers contain

▲ A bill of sale documents that this slave woman, Louisa, was owned by the young child whom she holds on her lap. In the future, Louisa's life would be subject to the child's wishes and decisions.

*(Missouri Historical Society, St. Louis)*

## Nat Turner's Insurrection

son of an African woman who passionately hated her enslavement, Nat Turner was a precocious child who learned to read when he was very young. Encouraged by his first owner to study the Bible, he enjoyed certain privileges but also endured hard work and changes of masters. His father successfully escaped to freedom.

Young Nat eventually became a preacher with a reputation for eloquence and mysticism. After nurturing his plan for several years, Turner led a band of rebels from farm to farm in the predawn darkness of August 22, 1831. The group severed limbs and crushed skulls with axes or killed their victims with guns. Before alarmed planters stopped them, Nat Turner and his followers had in forty-eight hours slaughtered sixty whites of both sexes and all ages. The rebellion was soon put down, and in retaliation whites killed slaves at random all over the region, including in adjoining states. Turner was eventually caught and then hanged. As many as two hundred African Americans, including innocent victims of marauding whites, lost their lives as a result of the rebellion.

Nat Turner remains one of the most haunting symbols in America's unresolved history with racial slavery and discrimination. While in jail awaiting execution, Turner was interviewed by a Virginia lawyer and slaveholder, Thomas R. Gray. Their intriguing creation, *The Confessions of Nat Turner,* became a bestseller within a month of Turner's hanging. Turner told of his early childhood, his religious visions, his zeal to be free; Gray called the rebel a "gloomy fanatic," but in a manner that made him fascinating and produced one of the most remarkable documents in the annals of American slavery. In the wake of Turner's insurrection, many states passed stiffened legal codes against black education and religious practice.

Most importantly, in 1832 the state of Virginia, shocked to its core, held a full-scale legislative and public debate over gradual emancipation as a means of ridding itself of slavery and of blacks. The plan debated would not have freed any slaves until 1858, and it provided that eventually all blacks would be colonized outside Virginia. But when the House of Delegates voted, gradual abolition lost, 73 to 58. In the end, Virginia opted to do nothing except reinforce its own moral and economic defenses of slavery. It was the last time white southerners would debate any kind of emancipation until war forced their hand.

## SUMMARY

During the four decades before the Civil War, the South grew in land, wealth, and power along with the rest of the country. Although the southern states were deeply enmeshed in the nation's heritage and political economy, they also developed as a distinctive region, ideologically and economically, because of slavery. Far more than the North, the antebellum South was a biracial society; whites grew up directly influenced by black folkways and culture; and blacks, the vast majority of whom were slaves, became predominantly native-born Americans and the cobuilders with whites of a rural, agricultural society. From the Old South until modern times, white and black southerners have always shared a tragic mutual history.

With the sustained cotton boom, as well as state and federal policies of Indian Removal, the South grew into a huge slave society. The coercive influence of slavery af-

# *Legacy* FOR A PEOPLE AND A NATION

## Reparations for Slavery

How should the United States come to terms with 250 years of racial slavery? Is this period best forgotten as a terrible passage that African Americans as well as the country transcended over time? Or does the nation owe a long-overdue debt to black people for their oppression? In the wake of emancipation in 1865, and rooted in vague federal promises, many former slaves believed they were entitled to "forty acres and a mule," but these never materialized.

In 1897 Callie House, a poor mother of four who had been born in 1865 in a contraband camp for ex-slaves, organized the National Ex-Slave Pension and Bounty Association, modeled after the pension system established for soldiers. House traveled all over the South, recruiting 250,000 members at 10-cent dues. Her lobbying of the federal government for slave pensions failed; she was accused of mail fraud and imprisoned for one year in 1916.

More recently, a widespread debate over "reparations" for slavery has emerged. In the rewriting of slavery's history since the 1960s, Americans have learned a great deal about how slave labor created American wealth: how insurance companies insured slaves, how complicit the U.S. government was in slavery's defense and expansion, and how slaves built the U.S. Capitol while their owners received $5 a month for their labor.

The debate is fueled by a wealth of analogies: the reparations paid to Japanese Americans interned during World War II; the reparations paid to several Native American tribes for their stolen land; the reparations paid to thousands of Holocaust survivors and victims of forced labor; and a suit settled in 1999 that will pay an estimated $2 billion to some twenty thousand black farmers for discrimination practiced by the Agriculture Department in the early twentieth century.

On the other side, some argue that, because there are no living former slaves or slaveholders, reparations for slavery can never take the form of money. But in 2002 a lawsuit was filed against three major corporations who allegedly profited from slavery, and the National Reparations Coordinating Committee promises a suit against the U.S. government itself. Indeed, some city councils have passed resolutions forcing companies that do business in their jurisdictions to investigate their possible past complicity with slave trading or ownership, which has prompted some banks and other firms to establish scholarship programs for African Americans.

Critics argue that resources would be better spent "making sure black kids have a credible education" and rebuilding inner cities. Advocates contend that, when "government participates in a crime against humanity," it is "obliged to make the victims whole." The movement for reparations has strong support in grassroots black communities, and the issue has become the subject of broad public debate. The legacy of slavery for a people and a nation promises to become America's most traumatic test of how to reconcile its history with justice.

---

fected virtually every element of southern life and politics, and increasingly produced a leadership determined to preserve a conservative, hierarchical social and racial order. Despite the white supremacy that united them, the democratic values of yeomen often clashed with the profit motives of aristocratic planters. The benevolent self-image and paternalistic ideology of slaveholders ultimately had to stand the test of the slaves' own judgments. African American slaves responded by fashioning over time a rich, expressive folk culture and a religion of personal and group deliverance. Their experiences could be profoundly different from one region and kind of labor to another. Some blacks were crushed by bondage; many others transcended it in an epic of survival and resistance.

By 1850, through their own wits and on the backs of African labor, white southerners had aggressively built one of the last profitable, expanding slave societies on earth. North of them and deeply intertwined with them in the same nation, economy, constitutional system, and history, a different kind of society had grown even faster—driven by industrialism and free labor. The clash of these two deeply connected, yet mutually fearful and divided societies would soon explode in political storms over the nation's future.

## SUGGESTIONS FOR FURTHER READING

Ira Berlin, *Generations of Captivity: A History of African American Slaves* (2003)

David Brion Davis, *Inhuman Bondage: The Rise and Fall of Slavery in the New World* (2006)

Steven Deyle, *Carry Me Back: The Domestic Slave Trade in American Life* (2005)

Drew G. Faust, ed., *The Ideology of Slavery: Proslavery Thought in the Antebellum South, 1830–1860* (1981)

Walter Johnson, *Soul by Soul: Life Inside the Antebellum Slave Market* (1999)

Charles Joyner, *Down by the Riverside: A South Carolina Slave Community* (1984)

James D. Miller, *South by Southwest: Planter Emigration and Identity in the Slave South* (2002)

James Oakes, *Slavery and Freedom: An Interpretation of the Old South* (1991)

Michael O'Brien, *Conjectures of Order: Intellectual Life and the American South, 1810–1860* (2004)

Daniel H. Usner Jr., *American Indians in the Lower Mississippi Valley* (1998)

Jean Fagan Yellin, *Harriet Jacobs: A Life* (2004).

*For a more extensive list for further reading, go to* college.hmco.com/pic/norton8e.

𝒯he four children, all under the age of ten, struggled to find their land legs. It was April 17, 1807, and they had spent the last twenty-five days on a stormy voyage from Scotland to New York. Their parents, Mary Ann and James Archbald, had left their ancestral homeland reluctantly, but envisioning a future in which their children would be beholden to no one—neither landlord nor employer. They had set sail in search of the Jeffersonian dream of republican independence.

The Archbalds bought a farm in central New York, along a tributary of the Hudson River, where they raised a large flock of sheep, grew hay and vegetables, skinned rabbits for their meat and fur—and then sold whatever food or fur the family did not need to feed or clothe itself. From the wool shorn by her husband and sons, Mary Ann and her daughters spun thread and wove cloth for their own use and for sale. They used the cash to pay their mortgage. Twenty-one years after leaving Scotland, Mary Ann Archbald, in anticipation of making their last payment, declared herself wealthy: "being out of debt is, in my estimation, being rich." By then, though, her sons were young adults and had their own visions of wealth. Theirs centered on water, not land.

Eleven years earlier, on April 17, 1817—a decade to the day after the Archbalds had stepped onto American shores—the New York State legislature authorized construction of a canal that would connect Lake Erie to the Hudson River, and surveyors mapped a route that ran through the Archbalds' farm. The sons (one in his early twenties, the other a teenager) helped dig the canal, while Mary Ann and her daughters cooked and cleaned for the twenty Irish laborers whom the sons hired. Bitten by canal fever, the Archbald sons soon tried their hands at commercial speculation, borrowing money to buy wheat

◀ Farm families transported their surplus produce and handicrafts to local marketplaces, where merchants purchased them for resale.

*(Nathaniel Currier,* Preparing for Market, *1856, hand-colored lithograph. Gift of Lenore B. and Sidney A. Alpert, supplemented with Museum of Fine Arts Collections Funds, Springfield Museums Association. Detail used with permission.)*

## CHRONOLOGY

1825 ■ Erie Canal completed

1830 ■ Railroad era begins

1830s–50s ■ Urban riots commonplace

1834 ■ Women workers strike at Lowell textile mills

1835 ■ Arkansas passes first women's property law

1836 ■ Second Bank of the United States closes

1837 ■ Panic of 1837 begins economic downturn

1839–43 ■ Economic depression

1842 ■ *Commonwealth v. Hunt* declares strikes lawful

1844 ■ Federal government grant sponsors first telegraph line
　　 ■ Lowell Female Reform Association formed

and lumber in western New York with the idea of reselling it at substantial profits to merchants in Albany and New York City. This was not the future Mary Ann had envisioned for her sons, and their ventures distressed, but did not surprise, her. As early as 1808 she had reached an unpleasant conclusion about her new home: "We are a nation of traders in spite of all Mr. Jefferson can say or do."

The United States may have already been a "nation of traders" as early as 1808, but in the years after the War of 1812, the market economy took off in ways few could have anticipated when the Archbald family decided to seek its independence in America. In the North, steamboats, canals, and then railroads remapped the young republic's geography and economy, setting off booms in westward migration, industry, commerce, and urban growth which fueled optimism among commercially minded Americans.

Although the transportation revolution would foster commercial exchange, technology alone could not make it happen. Even after the War of 1812, the United States'

financial connections to Europe, particularly Britain, remained profound. When Europeans suffered hard times, so, too, did American merchants, manufacturers, farmers, workers—and their families. Particularly for those Americans who relied on wages for their livelihood, economic downturns often meant unemployment and destitution.

Economic downswings could shake even the most commercially minded northerners, as could other consequences of the economy's rapid expansion in the years after the War of 1812. Market expansion, some worried, threatened the nation's very moral fiber if not properly controlled. It upset traditional patterns of family organization, and it relied heavily on the labor of unskilled workers—many of whom were immigrants and free African Americans—who at best seemed unfit for republican citizenship and at worst seemed threatening. The burgeoning cities spawned by market expansion seemed to bear out Thomas Jefferson's opinion that they were "pestilential to the morals, the health and the liberties of man." Like Jefferson, who also acknowledged that cities nourished the arts, commercially minded Americans could see cities as both exemplars of civilization and breeding grounds of depravity and conflict. Only by maintaining a strong faith in improvement, progress, and upward mobility could these Americans remain hopeful that the nation's greatness lay down the path of commercial expansion. They did so in part by articulating a free-labor ideology that at once rationalized the negative aspects of market expansion while promoting the northern labor system as superior to the South's.

- What factors contributed to the commercialization of northern society, and why did they have less of an influence on the South?

- How did the daily lives—work, family, leisure—of northerners change between 1815 and 1860?

- What factors contributed to rapid urbanization, and how did urban and rural life in the North compare with that in the South?

# OR IS IT THE NORTH THAT WAS DISTINCTIVE?

Historian James McPherson has proposed a new twist to the old question of southern distinctiveness: perhaps it was the *North*—New England, the Middle Atlantic, and the Old Northwest—that diverged from the norm. At the republic's birth, the two regions had much in common, with some similarities persisting for decades: slavery, ethnic homogeneity, an overwhelming proportion of the population engaged in agricultural pursuits, a small urban population. As late as the War of 1812, the regions were more similar than dissimilar. But all that started to change with postwar economic development. Although often couched in nationalist terms, such development was undertaken mostly by state and local governments as well as private entrepreneurs, and it took place much more extensively and rapidly in the North. As the North embraced economic progress, it—rather than the South—diverged from the international norm. The North, writes McPherson, "hurtled forward toward a future that many Southerners found distasteful if not frightening."

While the South expanded as a slave society, the North changed rapidly and profoundly. It transformed, as one historian has put it, from a society with markets to a market society. In the colonial era, settlers lived in a society with markets, one in which they engaged in long-distance trade—selling their surpluses to merchants, who in turn sent raw materials to Europe, using the proceeds to purchase finished goods for resale—but in which most settlers remained self-sufficient. During and after the War of 1812, the North became more solidly a market society, one in which participation in long-distance commerce fundamentally altered people's aspirations and activities. With trade with Europe largely cut off during the war, entrepreneurs invested in domestic factories, setting off a series of changes in the organization of daily life. More men, women, and children began working for others in exchange for wages—rather than for themselves on a family farm—making the domestic demand for foodstuffs soar. The result was a transformation of agriculture itself. Farming became commercialized, with individual farmers abandoning self-sufficiency and specializing instead in crops that would yield cash on the market. With the cash that farmers earned when things went well, they now bought goods that they had once made for themselves, such as cloth, candles, and soap, as well as some luxuries. Unlike the typical southern yeoman, they were not self-reliant, and isolation was rare. In the North, market expansion altered, sometimes dramatically, virtually every aspect of life. Some historians see these rapid and pervasive changes as a market revolution.

At the beginning of the nineteenth century, few yeoman farmers, North or South, were entirely independent. Most practiced what is called mixed agriculture: they raised a variety of crops and livestock. Their goal was to procure what they called a "competence": everyday comforts and economic opportunities for their children. When they produced more than they needed, they traded the surplus with neighbors or sold it to local storekeepers. Such transactions often took place without money; farmers might trade eggs for shoes, or they might labor in their neighbor's fields in exchange for bales of hay. Even farmers like James and Mary Ann Archbald, whose main goals were to secure their own independence and seek opportunities for their children, engaged in long-distance market exchange. They did not simply trade their farm goods with neighbors but rather sold them for cash to merchants, who then sent the goods on their way to people whom the Archbalds would never meet, living perhaps hundreds of miles away. The Archbalds practiced mixed agriculture—they grew rye, corn, barley, peas, oats, and potatoes in addition to raising livestock—while also producing cloth to sell. But for Mary Ann Archbald, the main reason to earn cash was not to accumulate wealth but to pay off the family's land debt. Families like the Archbalds indulged in the occasional luxury—for Mary Ann Archbald, that meant buying books—but security mattered more than profit.

## Preindustrial Farms

The main source of farm labor was family members, though some yeoman farmers, North and South, also relied on slaves or indentured servants. Work generally divided along gender lines. Men and boys worked in the fields, herded livestock, chopped firewood, fished, and hunted. Women and girls tended gardens, milked cows, spun and wove, processed and preserved food, prepared meals, washed clothes, and looked after infants and toddlers.

In their quest for independence, farmers cooperated with one another. They lent each other farm tools, harvested each other's fields, bartered goods, and raised their neighbors' barns and husked their corn. Little cash exchanged hands, in large part because money was in short supply. Still, New England farmers often kept elaborate account books in which they recorded what they owed and were owed (without assigning monetary value), whereas most farmers in the South rejected such formalities and simply made mental notes of debts. In both regions, years might pass without debts being repaid, and when they were, they were not always repaid directly. A farmer who owed a neighbor two days' labor might bring the local storekeeper his eggs, to be credited to the neighbor's account.

Many farmers engaged simultaneously in this local economy and in long-distance trade. In the local economy—where they exchanged goods with people whom they knew—a system of "just price" prevailed, in which neighbors calculated value in terms of how much labor was involved in producing a good or providing a service. When the same farmers engaged in long-distance trade—when they sold their goods to merchants who resold it to other merchants before the goods eventually traveled as far away as coastal cities or even Europe—they set prices based on what the market would bear. In the long-distance market, credit and debt were reckoned in monetary value.

Farmers who lived near towns or villages often purchased crafted goods from local cobblers, saddlers, black-

## Preindustrial Artisans

smiths, gunsmiths, silversmiths, and tailors. Most artisans, though, lived in the nation's seaports, where master craftsmen (independent businessmen who owned their own shops and tools) oversaw workshops that employed apprentices and journeymen. Although the vast majority of craftsmen, North and South, were white, free blacks were well represented in some cities' urban trades, such as tailoring and carpentry in Charleston, South Carolina. Teenage apprentices lived with their masters, who taught them a craft, lodged and fed them, and offered parental oversight in exchange for labor. The master's wife, assisted by her daughters, cooked, cleaned, and sewed for her husband's workers. The relationship between a master craftsmen and his workers was often familial in nature, if not always harmonious. When the term of their apprenticeship expired, apprentices became journeymen who

▲ Although separating flax fibers from their woody base could be arduous work, flax-scutching bees—much like corn-husking bees—brought together neighbors for frivolity as well as work.

*(National Gallery of Art, Washington, D.C. Gift of Edgar William and Bernice Chrysler Garbisch)*

earned wages, usually with an eye toward saving money to open their own shops. The workplace had little division of labor or specialization. A tailor measured, designed, and sewed an entire suit; a cobbler did the same with shoes.

Men, women, and children worked long days on farms and in workshops, but the pace of work was generally uneven and unregimented. During busy periods, they worked dawn to dusk; the pace of work slowed after the harvest or after a large order had been completed. Market and court days were as much about exchanging gossip and offering toasts as exchanging goods and watching justice unfold. Husking bees and barn raisings brought people together to shuck corn and raise buildings, but also to eat, drink, dance, and flirt. Busy periods did not stop artisans from punctuating the day with grog breaks or from taking turns reading the newspaper aloud; they might even close their shops entirely to attend a political meeting. Nor did each workday adhere to a rigid schedule; journeymen craftsmen often staggered in late on Monday mornings, if they showed up at all, after a long night of carousing on their day off. Although the master craftsman remained the boss, his workers exerted a good deal of influence over the workplace.

By the War of 1812, these preindustrial habits had already changed, more noticeably in some places than in others. Early industry in the United States reorganized daily work routines and market relationships. Women and children had long made the clothing, hats, soap, candles, and other goods on which their families relied for their daily existence. In the late eighteenth and early nineteenth centuries, a "putting-out" system—similar to one that existed in parts of western Europe—began to develop in the Northeast, particularly in Massachusetts, New Jersey, and Pennsylvania. Women and children continued to produce goods as they always had but now did so in much greater quantities and for the consumption of people beyond their own families and communities. A merchant supplied them with raw materials, paid them a wage (usually a price for each piece they produced), and sold their wares in distant markets, pocketing the profit for himself. "Outwork," as it is sometimes called, appealed to women eager to earn cash, whether to secure some economic independence or to save money for additional land on which their children could set up their own farms. Particularly in New England—where population density, small farms, and tired soil conspired to constrict farming opportunities and thus to create a surplus labor pool—the putting-out system provided opportunities to earn money

### Early Industrialization

with which to buy cheaper, more fertile western lands without requiring that family members seek employment away from home.

The earliest factories grew up in tandem with the putting-out system. When Samuel Slater helped set up the first American water-powered spinning mill in Rhode Island in 1790—using children to card and spin raw cotton into thread—he sent the spun thread to nearby farm families who wove it into cloth before sending it back to Slater, from whom they received a wage. Early shoe factories relied on a similar system: factory workers cut cowhide into uppers and bottoms that were sent to rural homes. There, women sewed the uppers while men lasted (or shaped) and pegged the bottoms, a process that also sometimes took place in small workshops. The change was subtle but significant: although the work remained familiar, women now operated their looms for wages and produced cloth for the market, not primarily for their families, while male cobblers made shoes for feet that would never walk into their shops or homes.

## THE TRANSPORTATION REVOLUTION

In order to market goods at substantial distances from where they were produced, internal improvements were needed. Before the War of 1812, natural waterways provided the most readily available and cheapest transportation routes for people and goods, but their limitations were readily apparent. Boatmen poled bateaux (cargo boats) down shallow rivers or floated flatboats down deep ones. Cargo generally moved in one direction only—downstream—and most boats were broken up for lumber once they reached their destination. On portions of a few rivers, including the Mississippi and the Hudson, sailing ships could tack their way upstream under the right wind conditions, but upstream commerce was very limited.

Overland transport was limited, too. Although some roads had been built during the colonial and revolutionary eras, they often became obstructed by fallen trees, soaked by mud, or clouded in dust. To reduce mud and dust, some turnpike companies built "corduroy" roads, whose tightly lined-up logs resembled the ribbed cotton fabric. But passengers complained of nausea from being continually jolted, and merchants remained wary of transporting fragile wares by wagon. Land transportation was slow and expensive, demanding a good deal of human and animal power. In 1800, according to a report commissioned by the federal

### Roads

government, it cost as much to ship a ton of goods 30 miles into the country's interior as to ship the same goods from New York to England. The lack of cheap, quick transportation impeded the westward expansion of the population as well as industrial growth. Fed up with the frigid winters in upstate New York, the Archbald family considered moving to Ohio in 1810 but decided against it because, as Mary Ann Archbald explained, "it is at a great distance from markets."

After the American Revolution, some northern states chartered private stock companies to build turnpikes (toll roads). These roads expanded commercial possibilities in southern New England and the Middle Atlantic, but during the War of 1812 the nation's lack of a road system in its more northerly and southerly reaches impeded the movement of troops and supplies, prompting renewed interest—in the name of defense—in building roads. Aside from the National Road, the financing fell on the states and private investors, and generally the enthusiasm for building turnpikes greatly outpaced the money and manpower expended. The new turnpike companies that emerged did sometimes adopt improvements, such as laying hard surfaces made of crushed stone and gravel, but many of the newly built roads suffered from the old problems. With natural water routes unpredictable and roads predictably bad, an urgent need arose not just for more, but also for better transportation.

The first major innovation was the steamboat. In 1807 Robert Fulton's *Clermont* traveled between New York and Albany on the Hudson River in thirty-two hours, demonstrating the feasibility of using steam engines to power boats. After the Supreme Court's 1814 ruling against steamboat monopolies in *Gibbons v. Ogden* (1824), steamboat companies flourished on eastern rivers and, to a lesser extent, on the Great Lakes. These boats carried more passengers than freight, transporting settlers to the Midwest, where they would grow grain and raise pigs that fed northeastern factory workers. Along western rivers like the Mississippi and the Ohio, steamboats played a more direct commercial role, carrying midwestern timber and grain, and southern cotton, to New Orleans, where they were transferred to oceangoing vessels destined for northern and international ports. In the 1850s, steamboats began plying rivers as far west as California and Washington Territory. Steamboats were privately owned and operated but became subject to federal regulations after frequent and deadly accidents in which boilers exploded, fires ignited, and boats collided.

**Steamboats**

To travel between Ohio and New Orleans by flatboat in 1815 took several months; in 1840 the same trip by steamboat took just ten days. But the steamboat did not supplant the flatboat. Rather, the number of flatboats traveling downstream to New Orleans more than doubled between 1816 and 1846. Now that flatboat crews could return upstream by steamboat rather than by foot, the greatest investment in flatboat travel—time—had been greatly reduced.

In the late eighteenth and early nineteenth centuries, private companies (sometimes with state subsidies) built small canals to transport goods and produce to and from interior locations previously accessible only by difficult-to-navigate rivers or by poorly maintained roads. These projects rarely reaped the substantial profits for which investors hoped, making it difficult to court investors for other projects. In 1815 only three canals in the United States measured more than 2 miles long; the longest was 27 miles. After Madison's veto of the Bonus Bill dashed commercially minded New Yorkers' hopes for a canal connecting Lake Erie to the port of New York, Governor DeWitt Clinton pushed hard and successfully for a state-sponsored initiative. What later became known as the Erie Canal was to run 363 miles between Buffalo and Albany, and was to be 4 feet deep. Skeptics derided it as "Clinton's Big Ditch."

**Canals**

But the optimists prevailed. Construction began—amid much symbolism and fanfare—on July 4, 1817. The canal, its promoters emphasized, would help the nation fulfill its revolutionary promises. It would demonstrate how American ingenuity and hard work could overcome any obstacle, including imposing natural ones, such as the combined ascent and descent of 680 feet between Buffalo and Albany. By so doing, it would help unify the nation and secure its commercial independence from Europe.

Over the next eight years, nearly nine thousand laborers felled forests, shoveled and piled dirt, picked at tree roots, blasted rock, heaved and hauled boulders, rechanneled streams, and molded the canal bed. Stonemasons and carpenters built aqueducts and locks. The work was dangerous. Much of it took place in malaria- and rattlesnake-infested swamps. Where the landscape was rock-solid, gunpowder explosions blew up some workers along with the rock. Collapsing canal beds smothered yet others, while some fell to their death from aqueducts and locks.

The canal's promoters celebrated the waterway as the work of "republican free men," a tribute to the nation's republican heritage. But few of those involved in the canal's construction would have perceived their work as fulfilling Jefferson's notion of republican freedom. Although farmers and artisans provided important labor, unskilled laborers—including many immigrants and some convicts—outnumbered them. Once completed, the Erie Canal relied heavily on the labor of children. Boys led the horses who pulled the canal boats between the canal's eighty-three locks, while girls cooked and cleaned on the boats. When the canal froze shut during winter, many canal workers found themselves with neither employment nor shelter. Some tried, successfully, to get themselves imprisoned as vagrants; many of the rest experienced destitution.

After its completion in November 1825, the Erie Canal became an immediate commercial success. Horse-drawn boats, stacked high with bushels of wheat, barrels of oats, and piles of logs, streamed steadily eastward from western New York and Buffalo, where shipments from ports all around Lake Erie were transferred to canal boat. Tens of thousands of passengers—forty thousand in 1825 alone—traveled on the new waterway each year. The canal shortened the journey between Buffalo and New York City from twenty to six days and reduced freight charges by nearly 95 percent—thus securing New York City's position as the nation's preeminent port. Goods that previously had not been readily available in the nation's interior now could be had easily and cheaply. Home production of cloth, for example, fell sharply after canal boats began carrying factory-made fabric from the eastern seaboard to central New York.

Other states rushed to construct their own canals. By 1840 canals crisscrossed the Northeast and Midwest, and total canal mileage reached 3,300. Many fewer canals were dug in the South, where the region's easily navigable rivers made them less necessary. None of the new canals, North or South, enjoyed the Erie's financial success. As the high cost of construction combined with an economic contraction, investment in canals slumped in the 1830s. Several midwestern states could not repay their canal loans, leading them to bankruptcy or near-bankruptcy. By midcentury more miles were abandoned than built. The canal era had ended, though the Erie Canal (by then twice enlarged and rerouted) continued to prosper and remained in commercial operation until the late twentieth century.

The future belonged to railroads. Trains moved faster than canal boats and could operate year-round. Unlike canals, railroads did not need to be built near natural sources of water and could therefore connect even the most remote locations to

## Railroads

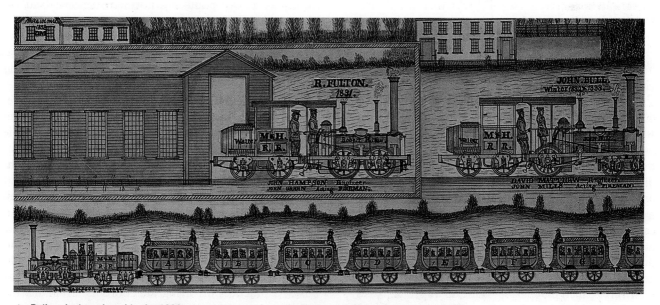

▲ Railroads, introduced in the 1830s, soon surpassed canals. Easier, quicker, and cheaper to build than canals, they moved goods and people faster. David Matthews, the engineer of the Mohawk & Hudson's John Bull, drew this picture of his early locomotive. The Mohawk & Hudson offered competition to the slower Erie Canal boats. *(© Collection of the New York Historical Society)*

national and international markets. The "improvement" in travel and shipping made possible by the expansion of railroads, noted the editor of the *American Farmer* in 1839, is "truly astonishing." By 1860 the United States had 60,000 miles of track, most of it in the North, and railroads had dramatically reduced the cost and the time involved in shipping goods by land—and they had excited the popular imagination in the process.

The railroad era in the United States began in 1830 when Peter Cooper's locomotive, Tom Thumb, first steamed along 13 miles of Baltimore & Ohio Railroad track. In 1833 the nation's second railroad ran 136 miles from Charleston to Hamburg in South Carolina. Not until the 1850s, though, did railroads offer long-distance service at reasonable rates. Even then, the lack of a common standard for the width of track thwarted development of a national system. Pennsylvania and Ohio railroads, for example, had no fewer than seven different track widths. A journey from Philadelphia to Charleston involved eight different gauges, which meant that passengers and freight had to change trains seven times. Only at Bowling Green, Kentucky, did northern and southern railroads connect to one another. Although northerners and southerners alike raced to construct internal improvements, the nation's canals and railroads did little to unite the regions and promote nationalism, as the earliest proponents of government-sponsored internal improvements had hoped.

Northern state and local governments and private investors spent substantially more on internal improvements

### Government Promotion of Internal Improvements

than did southerners. Pennsylvania and New York together accounted for half of all state monies invested. Southern states did invest in railroads, but—with smaller free populations—they collected fewer taxes, leaving them with less to spend.

For capitalists seeking dividends, southern railroads often seemed a poor bet. To be both profitable for investors and affordable for shippers, trains could not ship only one way; if they took agricultural products to market, their cars had to be filled with manufactured or finished goods for the return trip. But slaves and cash-strapped farmers did not provide much of a consumer base. Although planters did buy northern ready-made clothes and shoes for their slaves, such purchases—made on an annual basis—did not constitute a regular source of incoming freight. Because the wealthiest men lived along rivers and could send their cotton to market on steamboats, they sometimes saw little need for railroads. Many continued to reinvest in land

and slaves, believing them a surer bet than risky railroad ventures.

The North and South laid roughly the same amount of railroad track per person before the Civil War, but when measured in terms of overall mileage, the more populous North had a web of tracks that stretched considerably farther, forming an integrated system of local lines branching off major trunk lines. In the South, though, railroads remained local in nature. Southern travelers had to patch together trips that involved railroads, stagecoaches, and boats. Neither people nor goods moved easily across the South, unless they traveled via steamboat or flatboat along the Mississippi River system—and even then, flooded banks disrupted passage for weeks at a time.

Unlike southern investments in river improvements and steamboats, which disproportionately benefited the

### Regional Connections

planters whose lands bordered the region's riverbanks, the North's frenzy of canal and railroad building expanded transportation networks far into the hinterlands, proving not only more democratic but also more unifying. In 1815 nearly all the produce from the Old Northwest floated down the Mississippi to New Orleans, tying that region's fortunes to the South. By the 1850s, though, canals and railroads had strengthened the economic, cultural, and political links between the Old Northwest—particularly the more densely populated northern regions—and the Northeast.

Internal improvements hastened the population's westward migration. They eased the journey itself while also making western settlement more appealing by providing easy access to eastern markets and the comforts of home. News, visitors, and luxuries now traveled regularly to previously remote areas of the Northeast and Midwest. Delighted that the Erie Canal made fresh seafood available in central New York, hundreds of miles from the sea, Mary Archbald explained that "distance . . . is reduced to nothing here."

With Samuel F. B. Morse's invention of the telegraph in 1844, the compression of distance and time became even starker. News traveled almost instantaneously along telegraph wires. By 1852 more than 23,000 miles of lines had been strung across the nation. With time reduced to "nothing," the telegraph made possible the birth of modern business practices involving the coordination of market conditions, production, and supply across great distances. Together, internal improvements and the telegraph allowed people in previously isolated areas to proclaim themselves—as did one western New Yorker—a "citizen of the world."

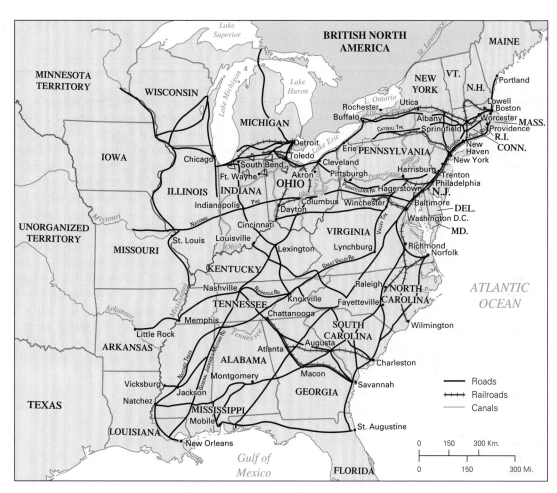

**Map 11.1    Major Roads, Canals, and Railroads, 1850**
A transportation network linked the seaboard to the interior. Settlers followed those routes westward, and they sent back grain, grain products, and cotton to the port cities.

Many northerners hailed internal improvements as symbols of progress. One New York farmer likened the construction of the Erie Canal to "building castles in the air." Northerners proclaimed that, by building canals and railroads, they had completed God's design for the North American continent. On a more practical level, canals and railroads would allow them to seek better opportunities for themselves and their children in the West.

But people who welcomed such opportunities could find much to lament. Mary Ann Archbald savored her fresh seafood dinners but regretted that her sons turned to speculation. Others decried the presence of enormous numbers of Irish canal diggers and railroad track layers,

## Ambivalence Toward Progress

whom they deemed depraved and racially inferior. Still others worried that, by promoting urban growth, transportation innovations fostered social ills.

The degradation of the natural world proved worrisome, too. When streams were rerouted, swamps drained, and forests felled, natural habitats were disturbed, even destroyed. Humans soon felt the consequences. Deprived of water power, mills no longer ran. Without forests to sustain them, wild animals—on which many rural people (Native American and European American) had relied for protein—sought homes elsewhere. Fishermen, too, found their sources of protein (and cash) dried up when natural waterways were dammed or rerouted to feed canals. If many northerners embraced progress, they also regretted its costs.

## The United States as a Developing Nation

In the early nineteenth century, the United States was a "developing nation," as its economy slowly shifted from dependence on agriculture and raw materials to producing manufactured goods. In order to develop, the United States imported capital to finance international trade, internal improvements, and early factories.

American political and economic leaders in the early nineteenth century talked as if they were masters of their own fate. In many ways, however, the United States remained economically dependent on Great Britain. The political independence that the United States won in the Revolutionary War and affirmed in the War of 1812 was not matched in the economic sphere.

Following the War of 1812, Americans depended on Britain for capital investment: 90 percent of all U.S. foreign capital came from Britain, and around 60 percent of all British capital exports flowed to the United States. Americans used British capital to develop, first, the canals, then the railroads that facilitated American industrial development. For instance, from 1817 to 1825 the British invested $7 million in New York State bonds to finance the Erie Canal.

Altogether, European investors provided 80 percent of the money to build the Erie.

The United States imported more goods than it exported. In other words, Americans consumed more than they produced. Imported capital balanced the trade deficit. As in most developing countries, exports were concentrated in agricultural commodities; 50 percent of the value of all exports was in cotton. And British credit financed cotton sales.

U.S. dependency on international capital was highlighted when imported capital was interrupted, as in the Panics of 1819 and 1837. Although these financial crises began in the United States, the hard times were exacerbated in both cases when British investors and creditors squeezed Americans. Economic crises in England led investors to pull out capital from the United States while merchants demanded that Americans pay what they owed to British creditors. Money became tight, and the economy declined.

Thus both economic development and hard times revealed the significance of international capital links to the United States, a developing nation.

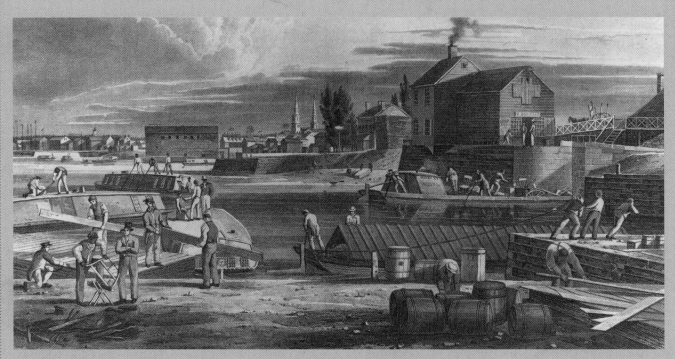

▲ Workers near the entrance of the Erie Canal into the Hudson River prepare to ship agricultural products from western New York and the Midwest to the international port of New York.

*(© Collection of the New York Historical Society)*

# FACTORIES AND INDUSTRIALIZATION

By dramatically lowering transportation costs, internal improvements made possible the Northeast's rapid manufacturing and commercial expansion. After canals and railroads opened up the trans-Appalachian West for wide-scale settlement, western farmers supplied raw materials and foodstuffs for northeastern factories and their workers. They also created a larger domestic market for goods manufactured in the Northeast. With most of their time devoted to cultivating their lands, western settlers preferred to buy rather than make cloth, shoes, and other goods. They needed northeastern iron, too—for farm implements (plows, pitchforks, scythes), for nails (to build houses and other buildings, particularly in the Midwest's rapidly burgeoning cities), and for railroad tracks.

One of the oldest industries in North America, iron production was centered in the Middle Atlantic states, especially Pennsylvania, but stretched as far south as Richmond and as far north as Albany. Iron forges, which tended to be small enterprises, flourished wherever ore deposits lay and sources of fuel abounded. During the 1840s, ironworks, which previously heated their furnaces with charcoal, turned increasingly to coal and then steam. But production methods in iron making changed little, with smaller firms remaining more efficient than larger ones. Although the industry expanded, daily work stayed largely the same.

But in many other industries, daily life changed dramatically. Much early industrialization involved processing raw materials—milling flour, turning hogs into packaged meat, sawing lumber—and the pork-packing industry illustrates strikingly how specialization turned skilled craftsmen into laborers. Traditionally, each butcher cut up an entire pig. Under the new industrial organization, each worker was assigned a particular task—such as cutting off the right front leg or scooping out the entrails—as the pig made it way down a "disassembly line."

## Factory Work

The impersonal nature and formal rules of factory work contrasted sharply with the informal atmosphere of artisan shops and farm households. The bell, the steam whistle, or the clock governed the flow of work. In large factories, laborers never saw owners, working instead under paid supervisors, nor did they see the final product of their labor. Factory workers lost their sense of autonomy as impersonal market forces seemed to dominate their lives. Their jobs were insecure, as competition—particularly from European immigrants, who arrived in enormous numbers starting in the 1840s—frequently led to layoffs and replacement by cheaper, less-skilled workers or children. Perhaps most demoralizing, opportunities for advancement in the new system were virtually nil.

Machinery made mass production possible in some industries. Although at first Americans imported machines or copied British designs, they soon built their own. The American System of manufacturing, as the British called it, used precision machinery to produce interchangeable parts that did not require individual adjustment to fit. Eli Whitney, the cotton gin's inventor, promoted the idea of interchangeable parts in 1798, when he contracted with the federal government to make ten thousand rifles in twenty-eight months. In the 1820s the United States Ordnance Department contracted with private firms to introduce machine-made interchangeable parts for firearms. The American System quickly spread beyond the arsenals, producing the machine-tool industry—the manufacture of machines for the purpose of mass production. With the time and skill involved in manufacturing greatly reduced, the new system permitted mass production at low costs: Waltham watches, Yale locks, and other goods became inexpensive but high-quality household items.

In no industry was mechanization more dramatic than in textiles, whose production was centered in New England, near sources of water to power the spinning machines and looms.

## Textile Mills

After 1815 the rudimentary cotton mills of New England developed into modern factories in which machines mass-produced goods. Cotton cloth production rose from 4 million yards in 1817 to 323 million in 1840. Mechanization did not make workers obsolete; rather, more workers were needed to monitor the machines. In the mid-1840s, the cotton mills employed approximately eighty thousand "operatives," more than half of them women. Mill owners employed a resident manager to run the mills, thus separating ownership from management. Workers received wages, and the cloth they produced was sold throughout the United States.

Unable to find enough laborers in the vicinity of their mills, managers recruited New England farm daughters, whom they paid wages and housed in dormitories and boarding houses in what became known as the Waltham or Lowell plan of industrialization. People who made their living off the land often harbored suspicions of those who did not—particularly in the young United States, where an agrarian lifestyle was often associated with virtue itself—so some rural parents hesitated to send their daughters to textile mills. To ease such concerns, mill owners offered paternalistic oversight to the mill girls; they enforced curfews, prohibited alcohol, and required church attendance.

▲ This young mill girl at Waltham or Lowell, probably in the late 1840s, posed for an early daguerreotype. Her swollen and rough hands contrast with her youth, neat dress, and carefully tied, beribboned hair. Her hands suggest that she worked, as did most twelve- and thirteen-year-olds, as a warper, straightening the strands of cotton or wool as they entered the looms. *(Courtesy of Jack Naylor)*

Despite its restrictions, the system in Waltham offered farm girls opportunities to socialize with women of the same age and to gain a sense of independence that came from living away from home and earning wages. Workers wrote literary pieces for the owner-subsidized *Lowell Offering* and attended educational lectures in the evenings.

Most women imagined their factory stints as temporary, and the conditions of the work itself—the deafening roar of the power looms, the long hours, the regimentation—made few change their minds. They nonetheless welcomed the social and cultural opportunities as well as the wages, which they used to help their families buy land or send a brother to college, to save for their own dowries or education, or to spend on personal items, such as fashionable clothing. The average girl arrived at sixteen and stayed only five years, usually leaving to get married— often to men they met in town rather than to farm boys

at home. When they left the mills, other younger women took their places.

Although the Waltham plan drew international attention for its novelty, more common was the Rhode Island (or Fall River) plan employed by Samuel Slater, among others. Mills hired entire families, whom they lodged in company boarding houses. Men often worked farm plots around the factories while their wives and children worked in the mills, though as the system developed, men were more likely to work in the factories full-time, directly supervising the labor of their wives and children in small, family-based work units.

Life in the textile mills got harder over time, especially during the depression of 1837 to 1843, when demand for cloth declined and most mills ran only part-time. To increase productivity, managers sped up the machines and required each worker to operate more machines. Between 1836 and 1850 the number of spindles and looms in Lowell increased 150 and 140 percent, respectively, whereas the number of workers increased by only 50 percent. In the race for profits, owners lengthened hours, cut wages, tightened discipline, and packed the boarding houses.

### Labor Protests

Workers organized, accusing their bosses of treating them like wage slaves. In 1834, in reaction to a 25 percent wage cut, they unsuccessfully "turned out" (struck) against the Lowell mills. Two years later, when boarding house fees increased, they turned out again. As conditions continued to worsen and as strikes continued to fail, workers resisted in new ways. In 1844 Massachusetts mill women formed the Lowell Female Reform Association and joined forces with other workers to press, without success, for state legislation mandating a ten-hour day—as opposed to the fourteen-hour days that some workers endured.

Women aired their complaints in worker-run newspapers: in 1842, the *Factory Girl* appeared in New Hampshire, the *Wampanoag and Operatives' Journal* in Massachusetts. Two years later, mill workers founded the *Factory Girl's Garland* and the *Voice of Industry*, nicknamed "the factory girl's voice." Even the *Lowell Offering*, the owner-sponsored paper that was the pride of mill workers and managers alike, became embroiled in controversy when workers charged that its editors had suppressed articles criticizing working conditions.

The women's organizational efforts were weakened by worker turnover. Few militant native-born mill workers stayed on to fight the managers and owners, and gradually, fewer New England daughters entered the mills. In the 1850s, Irish immigrant women replaced them. Technological improvements in the looms and other machinery had made the work less skilled and more routine. The mills could thus pay lower wages and draw from a reservoir of unskilled labor.

Male workers, too, protested the changes wrought by the market economy and factories. But, unlike women, they could vote. Labor political parties first formed in Pennsylvania, New York, and Massachusetts in the 1820s, and then spread elsewhere; they advocated free public education and an end to imprisonment for debt, and opposed banks and monopolies. Some advocated for free homesteads, a reminder that most early industrial workers still aspired to land ownership.

Organized labor's greatest achievement came through the courts, with protection from conspiracy laws. When

### Labor Unions

journeyman shoemakers organized during the first decade of the century, their employers accused them of criminal conspiracy. The cordwainers' (shoemakers') cases between 1806 and 1815 left labor organizations in an uncertain position. Although the courts acknowledged the journeymen's right to organize, judges viewed strikes as illegal until a Massachusetts case, *Commonwealth v. Hunt* (1842), ruled that Boston journeyman bootmakers could strike "in such manner as best to subserve their own interests."

The first unions arose among urban journeymen in printing, woodworking, shoemaking, and tailoring. They tended to be local; the strongest resembled medieval guilds, in that members sought protection against competition from inferior workmen by regulating apprenticeships and establishing minimum wages. Umbrella organizations composed of individual craft unions, like the National Trade Union (1834), arose in several cities in the 1820s and 1830s. But the movement fell apart amid wage reductions and unemployment in the hard times of 1839–1843.

Workers found permanent labor organizations difficult to sustain. Skilled craftsmen looked down on unskilled and semiskilled workers. Moreover, workers divided along ethnic, religious, racial, and gender lines.

## CONSUMPTION AND COMMERCIALIZATION

By producing inexpensive cloth, the New England mills spawned the ready-made clothing industry. Before the 1820s, women sewed most clothing at home, and some people purchased used clothing. Tailors and seamstresses made wealthy men's and women's clothing to order. By the 1820s and 1830s, much clothing was mass-produced for sale in retail clothing stores. The process often involved little more than the reorganization of work; instead of a

tailor's performing every task in the process of making an article of clothing—from measuring to finishing work—the process was now divided. Measuring was replaced by standard sizes, and efficiency was created by a division of labor. One worker cut patterns all day, another sewed hems, another affixed buttons, still another attached collars. The invention of the sewing machine in 1846 sped the process along, especially after it became widely available in the 1850s. Many farm families continued to make their own clothing, but when they could afford to do so, they often bought their clothes, creating more time for raising both crops and children.

Market expansion created a demand for mass-produced clothing. Rural girls who left farms for factories

### The Garment Industry

no longer had time to sew clothes. Young immigrant men—often separated by thousands of miles from mothers and sisters—had to buy the crudely made, loose-fitting clothing. But the biggest market for ready-made clothes, at least initially, was in the cotton South. With the success of the textile industry driving up the demand and price for raw cotton, planters in the cotton kingdom bought ready-made shoes and clothes for slaves, in whose hands they would rather place a hoe than a needle and thread. Doing so made good economic sense.

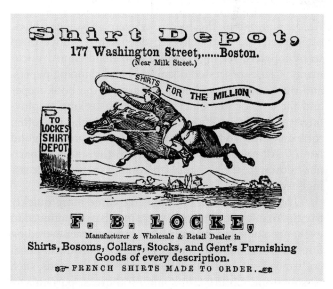

▲ F. B. Locke adapted to the new market for ready-made clothing by becoming a manufacturer, wholesaler, and retailer of men's shirts. Although he continued to make shirts to order, the staple of his Shirt Depot was mass-produced shirts, as this advertisement from the *Boston Directory* for 1848–1849 indicates.

*(Warshaw Collection of Business Americana, Smithsonian Institution, Washington, D.C.)*

Retailers often bought goods wholesale, though many manufactured shirts and trousers in their own factories. Lewis and Hanford of New York City boasted of cutting more than 100,000 garments in the winter of 1848–1849. The New York firm did business mostly in the South and owned its own retail outlet in New Orleans. Paul Tulane, a New Orleans competitor, owned a New York factory that made goods for his Louisiana store. In the Midwest, Cincinnati became the center of the new men's clothing industry. But although southerners and westerners became involved in the clothing trade, its center remained in New York.

Commerce expanded with manufacturing. Commercial specialization transformed some traders in big cities, especially New York, into virtual merchant princes. After the Erie Canal opened, New York City became a stop on every major trade route from Europe, southern ports, and the West. New York traders were the intermediaries for southern cotton and western grain. Merchants in other cities played a similar role. Traders in turn sometimes invested their profits in factories, further stimulating urban manufacturing. Some cities specialized: Rochester became a milling center ("The Flour City"), and Cincinnati ("Porkopolis") became the first meatpacking center.

### Specialization of Commerce

Merchants who engaged in complex commercial transactions required large office staffs, mostly all male. At the bottom of the hierarchy were messenger boys, often preteens, who delivered documents. Above them were copyists, on high stools, who hand-copied documents. Clerks processed documents and shipping papers, and did translations. Above them were the bookkeeper and the confidential chief clerk. Those seeking employment in such an office, called a countinghouse, often took a course from a writing master to acquire a "good hand." All hoped to rise someday to the status of partner, although their chances of doing so grew increasingly slim.

The specialization of commerce came more quickly to cities than to small towns, where merchants continued to exchange some goods with local farm women—trading flour or pots and pans for eggs and other produce. Local craftsmen continued to sell their own finished goods, such as shoes and clothing. In some rural areas, particularly newly settled ones, peddlers acted as general merchants. But as transportation improved and towns grew, small-town merchants also began to specialize.

Even amid the boom in manufacturing and commerce, agriculture remained the backbone of the nation's economy, North and South. But the expansion of southern cotton production in the Southwest did little to bring about economic change in other parts of the South; instead, profitable farmers reinvested their capital in the slave economy, and poorer farmers continued to farm much as they had before. In the North, by contrast, the transportation revolution and market expansion transformed formerly semisubsistence farms into commercial enterprises. Many families stopped practicing mixed agriculture and began to specialize in cash crops. Although most northerners continued to farm on the eve of the Civil War, their daily lives and relationships often looked very different from those of their parents and grandparents.

### Commercial Farming

By the 1820s, eastern farmers had cultivated nearly all the land available to them, and small farms and their uneven terrains did not lend themselves to the new labor-saving farm implements introduced in the 1830s, such as mechanical sowers, reapers, and threshers. As a result, many northern farmers either moved west or gave up farming for jobs in merchants' houses and factories. Those farmers who remained, however, proved as adaptable on the farm as were their children working at water-powered looms or in countinghouses, their efforts encouraged by state governments that energetically promoted agricultural innovation. Massachusetts in 1817 and New York in 1819 began to subsidize agricultural prizes and county fairs. To spread innovation, New York published the winners' essays about how they grew their prize crops.

In 1820 about one-third of all northern produce was intended for the market, but by 1850 the amount surpassed 50 percent. As farmers shifted toward specialization and market-oriented production, they often invested in additional land (buying the farms of neighbors who moved west), new farming equipment (such as improved iron and steel plows), and new sources of labor (hired hands). Many New England and Middle Atlantic farm families faced steep competition from midwestern farmers after the opening of the Erie Canal and began abandoning the production of wheat and corn. Instead, they raised livestock, especially cattle, and specialized in vegetable and fruit production. Much of what they produced ended up in the stomachs of the North's rapidly growing urban and manufacturing populations.

Farmers financed innovations through land sales and debts. Indeed, increasing land values, not the sale of agricultural products, promised the greatest profit. Farm families who owned their own land flourished, but it became harder to take up farming in the first place. By the 1840s it took more than ten years for a rural laborer in the Northeast to save enough money to buy a farm. The number of tenant farmers and hired hands increased, and provided labor to drive commercial expansion. Farmers who had previously relied mostly on the labor of unpaid family members and enslaved workers now leased portions of their farms or hired waged labor to help raise their livestock and crops.

As the commercial economy expanded, rural women took on additional responsibilities that added to their already substantial farm and domestic chores. Some took in outwork.

### Farm Women's Changing Labor

Many increased their production of eggs, dairy products, and garden produce for sale; others raised bees or silkworms.

With the New England textile mills producing more and more finished cloth, farm women and children often abandoned time-consuming spinning and weaving, bought factory-produced cloth, and dedicated the saved time to producing additional products, such as butter and cheese, for the market. Women had always made butter and cheese; now they produced it in large quantities with intentions of profiting from its sale. Some mixed-agriculture farms converted entirely to dairy production, with men taking over formerly female tasks. Canals and railroads carried cheese to eastern ports, where wholesalers sold it around the world, shipping it to California, England, and China. In 1844 Britain imported more than 5 million pounds of cheese from the United States.

Although agricultural journals and societies exhorted farmers to manage their farms like time-efficient businesses, not all farmers abandoned the old practices of gathering at market, general stores, taverns, and church. They did not forgo barn raisings and husking bees, but by the 1830s there were fewer young people at such events to dance and flirt. Many young women had gone to work in textile mills, and young men often worked as clerks or factory hands. Those who stayed behind were more likely to come dressed in store-bought clothing and to consume pies made with store-bought flour.

### Rural Communities

Even as they continued to swap labor and socialize with neighbors, farmers became more likely to reckon debts in dollars. They kept tighter accounts and watched national and international markets more closely. When financial panics hit, shortages of cash almost halted business activity, casting many farmers further into debt, not infrequently to the point of bankruptcy. Faced with the possibility of losing their land, farmers did what many would have considered unthinkable before: they called in debts with their neighbors, sometimes causing fissures in long-established relationships.

The expansion of the market economy led to a cycle of booms and busts. Prosperity stimulated demand for finished goods, such as clothing and furniture. Increased demand in turn led not only to higher prices and still higher production, but also, because of business optimism and expectation of higher prices, to speculation in land.

### Cycles of Boom and Bust

Investment money was plentiful as Americans saved and foreign, mostly British, investors bought U.S. bonds and securities. Then production surpassed demand, causing prices and wages to fall; in response, land and stock values collapsed, and investment money flowed out of the United States. This boom-and-bust cycle influenced every corner of the country, but particularly the Northeast, where even the smallest localities became enmeshed in regional and national markets.

Although the 1820s and 1830s were boom times, financial panic triggered a bust cycle in 1837, the year after the Second Bank of the United States closed. Economic contraction remained severe through 1843. Internal savings and foreign investments declined sharply. Many banks could not repay their depositors, and states, facing deficits because of the decline in the economy, defaulted on their bonds. European, especially British, investors became suspicious of all U.S. loans and withdrew money from the United States.

Hard times had come. Philadelphia took on an eerie aura. "The streets seemed deserted," Sidney George Fisher observed in 1842. "The largest [merchant] houses are shut up and to rent, there is no business . . . no money, no confidence." New York countinghouses closed their doors. Former New York mayor Philip Hone later observed, "a deadly calm pervades this lately flourishing city. No goods are selling, no businesses stirring." The hungry formed bread lines in front of soup societies, and beggars crowded the sidewalks. Some workers looted. Crowds of laborers demanding their deposits gathered at closed banks. Sheriffs sold seized property at one-quarter of pre-hard-time prices. In smaller cities like Lynn, Massachusetts, shoemakers weathered the hard times by fishing and tending gardens, while laborers became scavengers, digging for clams and harvesting dandelions. Once-prosperous businessmen—some victims of the market, others of their own reckless-ness—lost nearly everything, prompting Congress to pass the Federal Bankruptcy Law of 1841; by the t the law was repealed two years later, 41,000 bankrupts had sought protection under its provisions.

## FAMILIES IN FLUX

Anxieties about economic fluctuations reverberated beyond factories and countinghouses into northern homes. Sweeping changes in the household economy, rural as well as urban, led to new ideals of the family. In the preindustrial era, families had been primarily economic units; now they became a moral and cultural institution, though in reality few families could live up to the new ideal.

In the North, the market economy increasingly separated the home from the workplace, leading to a new

As they strove to live according to new domestic ideals, middle-ss families often relied on African American or immigrant servants, sacrificed time with their own children in order to care for their oyers' children.

*Louis Art Museum, Bequest of Edgar William and Bernice Chrysler Garbisch)*

### The "Ideal" Family

middle-class ideal in which men functioned in the public sphere, while women oversaw the private or domestic sphere. The home became, in theory, an emotional retreat from the competitive, selfish world of business, where men increasingly focused on their work, equally eager to prosper and fearful of failure in the unpredictable market economy. At the home's center was a couple that married for love rather than for economic convenience or advantage. Men provided and protected, while women nurtured and guarded the family's morality, making sure that the excesses of the capitalist world did not invade the private sphere. Childhood became focused more on education than on work, and the definition of childhood itself expanded: children were to remain at home until their late teens or early twenties. This ideal came to be known as separate-sphere ideology, or sometimes the cult of domesticity or the cult of true womanhood. Although it rigidly separated the male and female spheres, this ideology gave new standing to domestic responsibilities. In her widely read *Treatise on Domestic Economy* (1841), Catharine Beecher approached housekeeping as a science even as she trumpeted mothers' role as their family's moral guardian. Although Beecher advocated the employment of young, single women as teachers, she believed that, once married, women belonged in the home. She maintained that women's natural superiority as moral, nurturing caregivers made them especially suited for teaching (when single) and parenting (once married). Although Beecher saw the public sphere as a male domain, she insisted that the private sphere be elevated to the same status as the public.

These new domestic ideals depended on smaller families in which parents, particularly mothers, could give children more attention, better education, and more financial help.

### Shrinking Families

With the market economy, parents could afford to have fewer children because children no longer played a vital economic role. Urban families produced fewer household goods, and commercial farmers, unlike self-sufficient ones, did not need large numbers of workers year-round, turning instead to hired laborers during peak work periods. Although smaller families resulted in part from first marriages' taking place at a later age—shortening the period of potential childbearing—they also resulted from planning, made easier when cheap rubber condoms became available in the 1850s. Some women chose, too, to end accidental pregnancies with abortion.

In 1800 American women bore seven or eight children; by 1860 the figure had dropped to five or six. This decline occurred even though many immigrants with large-family traditions were settling in the United States; thus the birth rate among native-born women declined even more sharply. Although rural families remained larger than urban ones, birth rates among both groups declined comparably.

Yet, even as birth rates fell, few northern women could fulfill the middle-class ideal of separate spheres. Most wage-earning women provided essential income for their families and could not stay home. They often saw domestic ideals as oppressive, as middle-class reformers mistook poverty for immorality, condemning working mothers for letting their children work or scavenge rather than attend school. Although most middle-class women could stay home, new standards of cleanliness and comfort weighed heavily on their time. These women's contributions to their families were generally assessed in moral terms, even though their economic contributions were significant. When they worked inside their homes, they provided, without remuneration, the labor for which wealthier women paid when they hired domestic servants to perform daily chores. Without servants, moreover, women could not devote themselves primarily to their children's upbringing, placing the ideals of the cult of domesticity beyond the reach of even many middle-class families.

In working-class families, women left their parental home as early as age twelve, earning wages most of their life, with only short respites for bearing and rearing children. Un-

**Women's Paid Labor**

married girls and women worked primarily as domestic servants or in factories; married and widowed women worked as laundresses, seamstresses, and cooks. Some hawked food and wares on city streets; other did piecework at home, earning wages in the putting-out system; and some became prostitutes. Few of these occupations enabled women to support themselves or a family at a comfortable level.

Middle-class Americans sought to keep women closer to home. If young girls left the home to work—in New England's textile mills, in new urban stores as clerks—it was only for a brief interval before marriage. Otherwise, teaching was the only occupation consistent with genteel notions of femininity. In 1823 the Beecher sisters, Catharine and Mary, established the Hartford Female Seminary and offered history and science in addition to the traditional women's curriculum of domestic arts and religion. A decade later, Catharine Beecher successfully campaigned for teacher-training schools for women. She argued in part for women's moral superiority and in part for their economic value; because these women would be single, she

contended, they did not need to earn as much as their male counterparts, whom she presumed to be married, though not all were. Unmarried women earned about half the salary of male teachers. By 1850 schoolteaching had become a woman's profession. Many women worked for a time as teachers, usually for two to five years.

The proportion of single women in the population increased significantly in the nineteenth century. In the East, some single women would have preferred to marry but found market and geographic expansion working against them: more and more young men headed west in search of opportunity, leaving some eastern communities with a disproportionate number of young women. But other women chose to remain independent, hoping to take advantage of opportunities opened by the market economy and urban expansion. Because women's work was generally poorly paid, those who forswore marriage and a family faced serious challenges, and many single women found it difficult to support themselves without charitable or family assistance.

## THE GROWTH OF CITIES

To many contemporary observers, cities came to symbolize what market expansion had wrought—for better or for worse—on northern society. No period in American history saw more rapid urbanization than the years between 1820 and 1860. The percentage of people living in urban areas (defined as a place with a population of 2,500 or more) grew from just over 7 percent in 1820 to nearly 20 percent in 1860. Most of this growth took place in the Northeast and the Midwest. Although most northerners continued to live on farms or in small villages, the population of individual cities boomed. Many of those residents were temporary—soon moving on to another city or the countryside—and many came from foreign shores.

Even as new cities sprang up, existing cities saw a tremendous growth in their population (see Map 11.2). In 1820 the United States had 13 places with a population of 10,000 or more; in 1860 it had 93. New York City, already the nation's largest city in 1820, saw its population grow from 123,709 people in that year to 813,669 in 1860—a growth factor of six and a half times. Philadelphia, the nation's second-largest city in both 1820 and 1860, saw the size of its population multiply ninefold during that same forty-year period. In 1815 Rochester, New York, had a population of just 300 persons. By 1830, the Erie Canal had turned the sleepy agricultural town into a bustling manufacturing center; it was now the nation's twenty-fifth-largest city,

**Urban Boom**

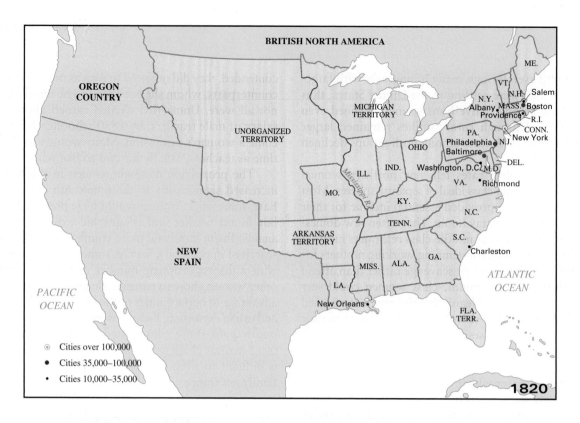

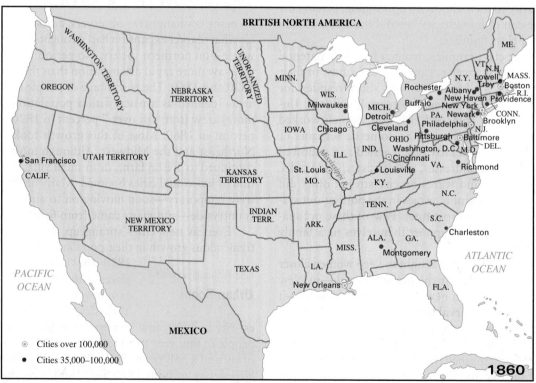

**Map 11.2** **Major American Cities in 1820 and 1860**

The number of Americans who lived in cities increased rapidly between 1820 and 1860, and the number of large cities grew as well. In 1820 only New York City had a population exceeding 100,000; forty years later, eight more cities had surpassed that level.

with a population of just over 9,000. Its population continued to multiply at fantastic rates, even doubling in a single decade. By 1860 it had more than 50,000 residents.

Cities experienced geographic expansion as well as population growth. New York City, for example, had burst its boundaries by around 1830. Until then, New Yorkers could walk from one end of the city to the other in an hour. In 1825 Fourteenth Street was the city's northern boundary. By 1860, 400,000 people lived above that divide, and Forty-second Street was the city's northern limit. Gone were the cow pastures, kitchen gardens, and orchards. Public transit made city expansion possible. Horse-drawn omnibuses appeared in New York in 1827, and the Harlem Railroad, completed in 1832, ran the length of Manhattan. By the 1850s, all big cities had horse-drawn streetcars, allowing wealthier residents who could afford the fare to settle on larger plots of land on the cities' outskirts.

Cities helped sustain the North's market revolution by serving as transportation hubs, commercial centers, and—in some cases—manufacturing sites.

## Market-Related Development

Some cities grew up with manufacturing. The Boston Manufacturing Company selected the site for Lowell, Massachusetts, because of its proximity to the Merrimack River, whose rapidly flowing waters could power their textile mill. Incorporated in 1826, by the 1850s it was the second-largest city in New England. Although most early manufacturing took place in rural areas, some commercial cities, such as New York, experienced what historians sometimes call metropolitan industrialization, a form that relied not on mechanization but on a reorganization of labor, similar to the earlier putting-out system. Much of the early production of ready-made clothing, for example, took place not in factories but in tenements throughout New York City, where women performed an urban form of outwork, spending hour after hour sewing on buttons for a piece of ready-made clothing, while others sewed hem after hem. In 1860, 25,000 women worked in manufacturing jobs in New York City, where they constituted a quarter of the waged labor force. Two-thirds of them worked in the garment industry.

The North urbanized more quickly than the South, but what was most striking about northern urbanization was where it took place. With only a few exceptions, southern cities were seaports, whereas the period between 1820 and 1860 saw the creation of many inland cities in the North—usually places that sprang to life with the creation of transportation lines or manufacturing establishments.

Northern cities developed elaborate systems of municipal services but lacked adequate taxing power to provide services for all. At best, they could tax property adjoining new sewers, paved streets, and water mains. New services and basic sanitation depended on residents' ability to pay. Another solution was to charter private companies to sell basic services, such as providing gas for lights. Baltimore first chartered a private gas company in 1816. By mid-century every major city was lit by a private gas supplier. Private firms lacked the capital to build adequate water systems, though, and they laid pipe only in commercial and well-to-do residential areas, bypassing the poor. The task of supplying water ultimately fell on city governments.

Throughout the United States, wealth was becoming concentrated in the hands of a relatively small number of

## Extremes of Wealth

people. By 1860 the top 5 percent of American families owned more than half of the nation's wealth, and the top 10 percent owned nearly three-quarters. In the South, the extremes of wealth were most apparent on rural plantations, but in the North, cities provided the starkest evidence of economic inequities.

Despite the optimistic forecasts of early textile manufacturers that American industrialization need not engender the poverty and degradation associated with European industrialization, America's industrial cities soon resembled European ones. A number of factors contributed to widespread poverty: poor wages, the inability of many workers to secure full-time employment, and the increasingly widespread employment of women and children, which further drove down wage rates for everyone. Women and children, employers rationalized, did not need a living wage because they were—in the employers' way of thinking—dependent by nature, meaning that they could rely on men to support them and did not need to earn a wage that allowed self-sufficiency. In reality, though, not all women or children had men to support them, nor did men's wages always prove adequate to support a family comfortably.

New York provides a striking example of the extremes of wealth accompanying industrialization. Where workers lived, conditions were crowded, unhealthy, and dangerous. Houses built for two families often held four; tenements built for six families held twelve. Some of those families took in lodgers to pay the rent, adding to the unbearably crowded conditions that encouraged poorer New Yorkers to spend as much time as possible outdoors. But streets in poor neighborhoods were filthy. Excess sewage from outhouses drained into ditches that carried urine and

This gouache, attributed to Nicholino Calyo, depicts the Haight family in their drawing room in 1848. Richard K. Haight was a wealthy New York City merchant, trading internationally, as the globe in the foreground suggests. Sarah Rogers Haight was a famous beauty and socialite, and the family's clothing, art, library, and furniture all stand in sharp contrast to the poverty, homelessness, and orphans found on the city's streets.

*(Museum of the City of New York. Bequest of Elizabeth Cushing Iselin)*

fecal matter into the streets. People piled garbage into gutters or left it to accumulate in backyards or alleys. Pigs, geese, dogs, and vultures scavenged the streets, while enormous rats roamed under cities' wooden sidewalks and through large buildings. Disease thrived. Typhoid, dysentery, malaria, and tuberculosis regularly visited the poorer sections of cities. Epidemics of cholera struck in 1831, 1849, and again in 1866, claiming thousands of victims.

But within walking distance of poverty-stricken neighborhoods grew up neighborhoods that boasted lavish mansions, whose residents could escape to their country estates during the summer's brutal heat or during epidemics. Much of this wealth was inherited. For every John Jacob Astor, who became a millionaire in the western fur trade after beginning life in humble circumstances, ten others had inherited or married money. These rich New Yorkers were not idle, though; they worked at increasing their fortunes and power by investing in commerce and manufacturing.

Between the two extremes of wealth sat a distinct middle class, larger than the wealthy elite but substantially smaller than the working classes. They were businessmen, traders, and professionals, and the rapid turn toward industrialization and commercial specialization made them a much larger presence in northern cities than in southern ones. Middle-class families enjoyed new consumer items: wool carpeting, fine wallpaper, and rooms full of furniture replaced the bare floors, whitewashed walls, and relative sparseness of eighteenth-century homes. Houses were large, often having from four to six rooms. Middle-class children slept one to a bed, and by the 1840s and 1850s, middle-class families used indoor toilets that were mechanical, though not yet flushing. Middle-class families formed the backbone of urban clubs and societies, filled the family pews in church, and sent their sons to college. They were as distinct from the world of John Jacob Astor as they were from the milieu of the working class and the poor.

Many of the urban poor were immigrants. The 5 million immigrants who came to the United States between 1830 and 1860 outnumbered the country's entire population in 1790.

## Immigration

The vast majority were Europeans, primarily from Ireland and the German states (see Figure 11.1). During the peak period of pre–Civil War immigration (1847–1857), 3.3 million immigrants entered the United States, including 1.3 million Irish and 1.1 million Germans. By 1860, 15 percent of the white population was foreign-born, with 90 percent of immigrants living in northern states. Not all planned to stay permanently, and many, like the Irish, saw themselves as exiles from their homeland.

A combination of factors "pushed" Europeans from their homes and "pulled" them to the northern United States. In Ireland, the potato famine (1845–1850)—a period of widespread starvation caused by a diseased potato crop—drove millions from their homeland. Although economic conditions pushed most Germans as well, some were political refugees—liberals, freethinkers, Socialists, communists, and anarchists—who fled after the abortive revolu-

▲ Visible signs of urban poverty in the 1850s were the homeless and orphaned children, most of them immigrants, who wandered the streets of New York City. The Home for the Friendless Orphanage, at Twenty-ninth Street and Madison Avenue, provided shelter for some of the orphan girls. *(© Collection of the New York Historical Society)*

tions of 1848. Europeans' awareness of the United States grew as employers, states, and shipping companies promoted opportunities across the Atlantic. Often the message was stark: work and prosper in America, where everyone could aspire to be an independent farmer, or starve in Europe. Although boosters promised immigrants a land of milk and honey, many soon became disillusioned, and hundreds of thousands returned home.

Many early immigrants lived or worked in rural areas. Like the Archbalds, a few settled immediately on farms and eventually bought land. Others, unable to afford even a modest down payment on a farm, worked as hired farm hands, canal diggers, or railroad track layers—often with the hope of buying land later. Pádraig Cúndún was among the lucky. The Irishman used his earnings as a canal laborer to buy land in western New York, proclaiming proudly in 1834 that "I have a fine farm of land now, which I own outright. No one can demand rent from me. My family and I can eat our fill of bread and meat, butter and milk any

day we like throughout the year, so I think being here is better than staying in Ireland, landless and powerless, without food or clothing." By the 1840s and 1850s—when the steady stream of immigration turned into a flood—the prospects of buying land became more remote.

By 1860 most immigrants settled in cities, often the port at which they arrived. The most destitute among them could not afford the canal or railroad fare to places farther inland. Others arrived with resources but fell victim to the swindlers who preyed on newly arrived immigrants. The ethnic flair of urban life induced still others to stay put. In 1855, 52 percent of New York's 623,000 inhabitants were immigrants, 28 percent from Ireland and 16 percent from the German states. Boston, another major entry port for the Irish, took on a European tone; throughout the 1850s the city was about 35 percent foreign-born, of whom more than two-thirds were Irish.

Most of the new immigrants from Ireland were young, poor, from rural districts, and Roman Catholic.

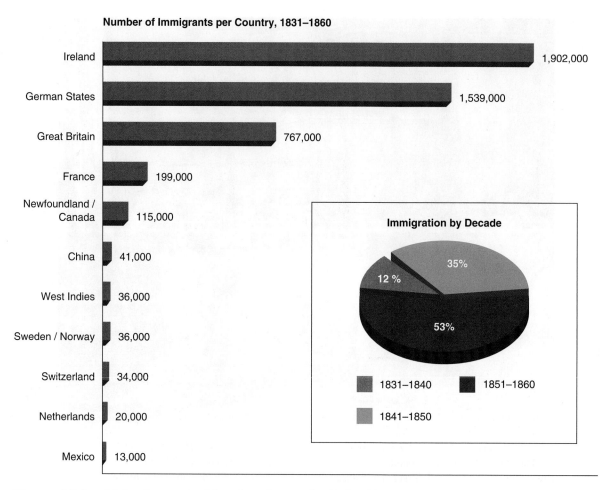

**Figure 11.1   Major Sources of Immigration to the United States, 1831–1860**

Most immigrants came from two areas: Great Britain, of which Ireland was a part, and the German states. These two areas sent more immigrants between 1830 and 1860 than the inhabitants of the United States enumerated at the first census in 1790. By 1860, 15 percent of the white population was of foreign birth.

*(Source: Data from Stephan Thernstrom, ed.,* Harvard Encyclopedia of American Ethnic Groups *[Cambridge, Mass., and London: Harvard University Press, 1980], 1047.)*

Women found work as domestic servants or mill hands, while men worked in construction or transportation. Very few Germans settled in New England; most of them came with enough resources to head to the upper Mississippi and Ohio valleys, to states such as Ohio, Illinois, Wisconsin, and Missouri. Although some southern cities like Charleston and Savannah had significant numbers of Irish immigrants, the vast majority of European immigrants, many of whom arrived with aversions to slavery and to semitropical heat, settled in the Northeast or Midwest.

Tension—often resulting from anxieties over the era's economic changes—characterized the relationship between native-born Americans and immigrants, particularly Irish Catholics. Native-born workers blamed immigrants for scarce job opportunities and low wages. Middle-class whites blamed them for poverty and crime. As they saw it, immigrants' moral depravity—not poor wages—led to poverty.

Native-born Americans often associated the Irish with another group whom they deemed morally inferior: African Americans. White northerners often portrayed Irish immigrants as nonwhite, as African in appearance. But Irish and African Americans did not develop a sense of solidarity. Instead, some of the era's most virulent

## Ethnic Tensions

▲ Poverty usually "pushed" immigrants from Ireland while the promise of economic and political opportunity lured them to America. Although ethnic prejudice often stifled their prospects in the United States, many Irish immigrants hoped for better futures for their children.

*(Left: Museum of the City of New York; Right: © Collection of the New York Historical Society)*

riots erupted between Irish immigrants and African Americans.

Closely related to racial stereotyping was anti-Catholicism, which became strident in the 1830s. In Boston anti-Catholic riots occurred frequently. Nearby Charlestown, Massachusetts, saw a mob burn a convent in 1834. In Philadelphia a crowd attacked priests and nuns, and vandalized churches in 1844, and in Lawrence, Massachusetts, a mob leveled the Irish neighborhood in 1854. Anti-Catholic violence was not limited to urban areas—riots between native-born and Irish workers erupted along the nation's canals and railroads—but urban riots usually attracted more newspaper attention, fueling fears that cities were violent, depraved places.

German immigrants, at least the majority who were Protestants, mostly fared better than the Irish. In part because Germans generally arrived with some resources and skills, Americans stereotyped them as hard working, self-reliant, and intelligent. But non-Protestant Germans—Catholics and Jews (whom white Americans considered a separate race) frequently encountered hostility fed by racial and religious prejudice.

Immigrants often lived in ethnic enclaves. Intolerance between Protestants and Catholics ran both ways, and Irish Catholics tended to live in their own neighborhoods, where they set up Catholic churches and schools. In larger cities, immigrants from the same German states clustered together. Immigrants set up social clubs and mutual-aid societies, such as the Hibernian Society and Sons of Erin (Irish), and B'nai B'rith (Jewish).

African Americans also forged their own communities and culture. As late as the 1830s, significant numbers

### People of Color

of them remained enslaved in New York and New Jersey, but the numbers of free African Americans grew steadily, and by 1860 nearly 250,000 (many of them refugees from southern slavery) lived in the urban North. Despite differences in status, occupation, wealth, education, and religion, African Americans often felt a sense of racial solidarity. African Methodist Episcopal churches and preachers helped forge communities. Chapels and social halls functioned as town halls and school buildings. Ministers were political leaders, and their halls housed political forums, conventions, and protest meetings.

But white racism impinged on every aspect of northern African Americans' lives. Streetcars, hotels, restaurants, and theaters could turn away African Americans with no legal penalty. City laws barred African Americans from entering public buildings. Even where laws were more liberal, popular attitudes among whites constrained African Americans' opportunities. In Massachusetts, for example, African Americans enjoyed more legal rights than anywhere else in the country. Yet laws protecting civil and political rights could not make whites shop at black businesses. "Colored men in business in Massachusetts receive more respect, and less patronage than in any place I know of," proclaimed a prominent African American lawyer.

African Americans were excluded from factory and clerical jobs. Women worked as house servants, cooks, washerwomen, and child nurses. Most African American men worked as construction workers, porters, longshoremen, or day laborers—all jobs subject to frequent periods of unemployment. Others found employment in the lower-paying but more stable service industry, working as servants, waiters, cooks, barbers, and janitors. Many African American men hired on as sailors and merchant seamen, as commercial sailing offered regular employment and opportunities for advancement, though not protection from racial taunts.

In the growing cities, African Americans turned service occupations into businesses, opening their own restaurants, taverns, hotels, barber shops, and employment agencies for domestic servants. Some became caterers. Others sold used clothing or were junk dealers or small-job contractors. A few became wealthy, invested in real estate, and loaned money. With professionals—ministers, teachers, physicians, dentists, lawyers, and newspaper editors—they formed a small but growing African American middle class.

In cities large and small, African Americans became targets of urban violence. Philadelphia experienced the most violence, with five major riots in the 1830s and 1840s, and major riots occurred in Providence and New York as well. White rioters clubbed and stoned African Americans,

▲ Although African Americans could not make much money as news vendors, the job provided more stability and independence than many of the other jobs for which European-Americans were willing to hire them.

*(The Fine Arts Museums of San Francisco, Mildred Anna Williams Collection)*

and destroyed their houses, churches, and businesses—in some cases, sending African Americans fleeing for their lives. By 1860 many hundreds had died in urban riots.

Living in cramped, squalid conditions, working-class families—white and black, immigrant and native-born—spent little time indoors. In the 1840s, a working-class youth culture developed on the Bowery, one of New York's entertainment strips. The lamp-lit promenade, lined with theaters, dance halls, and cafés, became an urban midway. Older and more elite New Yorkers often feared the "Bowery boys and gals."

### Urban Culture

The Bowery boys' greased hair, distinctive clothing, and swaggering gait frightened many middle-class New Yorkers, as did the Bowery girls' colorful costumes and ornate hats, which contrasted with genteel ladies' own modest veils and bonnets. Equally scandalous to an older generation were the middle-class clerks who succumbed to the city's temptations, most notably prostitution.

Gangs of garishly dressed young men and women—flaunting their sexuality, using foul language, sometimes speaking in foreign tongues, and drinking to excess—drove self-styled respectable citizenry to establish private clubs and associations. Some joined the Masonic order, which offered everything the bustling, chaotic city did not: an elaborate hierarchy, an older code of deference between ranks, harmony, and shared values. Although the Masons admitted men only, women organized their own associations, including literary clubs and benevolent societies.

Increasingly, urban recreation and sports became formal commodities to be purchased. One had to buy a ticket to go to the theater, the circus, P. T. Barnum's American Museum in New York City, the racetrack, or the ballpark. Horseracing, walking races, and, in the 1850s, baseball began to attract large urban male crowds. Starting in 1831, enthusiasts could read the all-sports newspaper, *Spirit of the Times*. A group of Wall Street office workers formed the Knickerbocker Club in 1842 and in 1845 drew up rules for the game of baseball. By 1849 news of boxing was so much in demand that a round-by-round account of a Maryland boxing match was telegraphed throughout the East.

A theater was often the second public building constructed in a town, after a church. Large cities boasted two or more theaters catering to different classes, though some plays cut across class lines; Shakespeare was performed so often and appreciated so widely that even illiterate theatergoers knew his plays well. In the 1840s, singing groups, theater troupes, and circuses traveled from city to city. Particularly popular were minstrel shows, in which white men (often Irish) in burnt-cork makeup imitated African Americans in song, dance, and patter. In the early 1830s, Thomas D. Rice of New York became famous for his role as Jim Crow, an old southern slave. In ill-fitting patched clothing and torn shoes, the blackface Rice shuffled, danced, and sang. Minstrel performers told jokes mocking economic and political elites, and evoked nostalgia for preindustrial work habits and morality, as supposedly embodied by carefree black men. At the same time, though, the antics of blackface actors encouraged a racist stereotyping of African Americans as sensual and lazy.

Many northerners saw cities—with their mixtures of people, rapid growth, municipal improvements, and violence—as symbolizing at once progress and decay. On the one hand, cities represented economic advancement; new ones grew at the crossroads of transportation and commerce. Cities nurtured churches, schools, civil governments, and museums—all signs of civilization and culture. As canals and railroads opened the West for mass settlement, many white northerners applauded the appearance of what they called "civilization"—church steeples, public buildings—in areas that had recently been what they called "savage wilderness"; that is, territory controlled by Native Americans. One Methodist newspaper remarked in 1846 that the nation's rapid expansion westward would

### Cities as Symbols of Progress

◀ Thomas D. Rice playing "Jim Crow" in blackface at the Bowery Theater in New York City, 1833. The rowdy audience climbed onto the stage, leaving Rice little room to perform. In representing African Americans on stage, Rice and other minstrels contributed to establishing both black and white as racial categories.

*(© Collection of the New York Historical Society)*

outpace "our means of moral and intellectual improvement." But the remedies, the editor noted, were evident: bring churches, schools, and moral reform societies to the West. "Cities, civilization, religion, mark our progress," he declared. To many nineteenth-century white Americans, cities represented the moral triumph of civilization over savagery and heathenism.

Yet some of the same Americans deplored the everyday character of the nation's largest cities, which they saw as havens of disease, poverty, crime, and vice. To many middle-class observers, disease combined with crime to represent moral decline. They considered epidemics to be divine scourges, which struck primarily those who were filthy, intemperate, and immoral. Many middle-class and wealthy people believed that epidemics resulted from the moral degradation of the urban poor. Theft and prostitution provided evidence of moral vice, and wealthy observers perceived these crimes not as by-products of poverty but

as signs of individual failing. They responded by pressing for laws against vagrancy and disturbing the peace, and by pushing city officials to establish the nation's first police forces. Boston hired uniformed policemen in 1837 to supplement its part-time watchmen and constables, and New York hired its own police force in 1845.

How did northerners reconcile the vices and depravity of the city with their view of cities as symbols of progress? Middle-class reformers focused on purifying cities of their disease and vice. If disease was a divine punishment—rather than an offshoot of cramped conditions engendered by economic change—then it was within Americans' power to fix things. Middle-class reformers took to the streets and back alleys, trying to convince the urban working classes that life would improve if they gave up alcohol, worked even harder, and prayed frequently. They talked about how the northern working poor—unlike southern slaves—could improve their condition through hard work and virtuous

## *Legacy* FOR A PEOPLE AND A NATION

### A Mixed Economy

How active should the U.S. government be? Should it run, regulate, or leave to the market system healthcare, Social Security and private pensions, corporate concentration, and stock trading and investments? To what degree should the government be responsible for the well-being of the economy and individuals?

The Articles of Confederation limited government, the Constitution empowered it, and the Bill of Rights restricted it in specific areas. Although Americans have continuously debated the appropriate role of government, the United States has generally occupied a middle ground: a mixed economy.

In the early nineteenth century, government played an active role in economic expansion. Federal and state governments built roads and canals, developed harbors, and operated post offices and the early telegraph. More commonly the government intervened to stimulate and regulate the private sector. In chartering corporations and banks and in land sales and grants, the United States created an infrastructure that laid the way for the market economy and industrialization.

In the late nineteenth century, advocates of laissez-faire or hands-off government challenged the pre-Civil War traditions of an active government. Laissez faire dom-

inated briefly until the 1880s and 1890s, when large corporations and trusts accumulated so much power that governments stepped in to regulate railroads and business concentration. After the turn of the century, the federal government extended regulation to food, drugs, the environment, working conditions, and fair business practices. Probably the most innovative example of a combination of federal regulation and private initiative was the creation in 1913 of the Federal Reserve System—a public system for overseeing currency and banking which left control in private hands. After a revival of laissez faire in the 1920s, the crisis of the Great Depression of the 1930s and World War II would lead the federal government to establish the modern welfare state, which operates through a mixed public/private structure.

Americans today still debate the appropriate role of government. Conservatives view government as the problem rather than the solution, arguing that government regulation hampers individual freedom and distorts the law of supply and demand. Advocates of an activist government argue that only government has the power and resources to check economic concentration and to protect health, safety, and the environment. The framework of this debate is a legacy from before the Civil War.

habits. This belief in upward mobility became central to many northerners' ideas about progress.

Belief in upward mobility related to the idea of free labor, the concept that, in a competitive marketplace, those who worked hard and lived virtuous lives could improve their status. Free-labor ideology appealed especially to manufacturers and merchants eager to believe that their own success emerged from hard work and moral virtue—and eager as well to encourage their factory hands and clerks to work hard and live virtuously, to remain optimistic despite current hardships. Many laborers initially rejected free-labor ideology, seeing it as little more than a veiled attempt to tout industrial work habits, to rationalize poor wages, and to quell worker protest. But by the 1850s, when the question of slavery's westward expansion returned to the political foreground, more and more northerners would embrace free-labor ideology and come to see slavery as antithetical to the modernizing, free-labor ideology of the North. It was this way of thinking, perhaps more than anything else, that made the North distinctive.

## SUMMARY

During the first half of the nineteenth century, the North became rapidly enmeshed in a commercial culture. Northern states and capitalists invested heavily in internal improvements, helping to propel the North down a new development track. Most northerners now turned either toward commercial farming or, in smaller numbers, toward industrial wage labor. Farmers gave up mixed agriculture and specialized in cash crops, while their children often went to work in factories or countinghouses.

To many northerners, the market economy symbolized progress, in which they found much to celebrate: easier access to cheap western lands, employment for surplus farm laborers, and the ready commercial availability of goods that had once been time-consuming to produce. At the same time, though, the market economy led to increased specialization, a less personal workplace, complex market relationships, more regimentation, a sharper divide between work and leisure, and a degradation of natural resources. Northerners' involvement in the market economy also tied them more directly to fluctuating national and international markets, and during economic downturns, many northern families experienced destitution.

With parents relying less directly on children's labor, northerners began producing smaller families. Even as working-class children continued to work as canal drivers and factory hands (or to scavenge urban streets), middle-class families began to create a sheltered model of childhood in which they tried to shield children from the perceived dangers of the world outside the family. Their mothers, in theory, became moral guardians of the household, keeping the home safe from the encroachment of the new economy's competitiveness and selfishness. Few women, though, had the luxury to devote themselves entirely to nurturing their children and husbands.

Immigrants and free African Americans performed much of the lowest-paying work in the expanding economy, and many native-born whites blamed them for the problems that accompanied the era's rapid economic changes. Anti-immigrant (especially anti-Catholic) and anti-black riots became commonplace. At the same time, immigrants and African Americans worked to form their own communities.

Cities came to symbolize for many Americans both the possibilities and the limits of market expansion. Urban areas were marked by extremes of wealth, and they fostered vibrant working-class cultures even as they encouraged poverty and crime. To reconcile the seeming contradictions of progress—the coexistence, for example, of abundance and destitution—middle-class northerners articulated an ideology of free labor, touting the possibility for upward mobility in a competitive marketplace. This ideology would become increasingly central to northern regional identity.

## SUGGESTIONS FOR FURTHER READING

Hal Barron, *Those Who Stayed Behind: Rural Society in Nineteenth-Century New England* (1984)

Jeanne Boydston, *Home and Work: Housework, Wages, and the Ideology of Labor in the Early Republic* (1990)

Christopher Clark, *The Roots of Rural Capitalism: Western Massachusetts, 1780–1860* (1990)

Nancy Cott, *The Bonds of Womanhood: "Women's Sphere" in New England, 1780–1835* (1977)

Bruce Laurie, *Artisans into Workers: Labor in Nineteenth-Century America* (1989)

Winifred Barr Rothenberg, *From Market-Places to Market Economy: The Transformation of Rural Massachusetts, 1750–1850* (1994)

Mary Ryan, *Cradle of the Middle Class: The Family in Oneida County, New York, 1790–1865* (1981)

Carol Sheriff, *The Artificial River: The Erie Canal and the Paradox of Progress, 1817–1862* (1996)

Christine Stansell, *City of Women: Sex and Class in New York, 1789–1860* (1986)

George Rogers Taylor, *The Transportation Revolution, 1815–1860* (1951)

*For a more extensive list for further reading, go to* college.hmco.com/pic/norton8e.

# Reform and Politics in the Age of Jackson *1824-1845*

THE WONDERFUL LEAPS OF SAM PATCH

The twenty-eight-year-old mill hand steadied himself atop a cliff in Paterson, New Jersey; peered down the seventy-foot precipice to the river below; and then leapt feet first, bending his knees to his chest before entering the water straight as an arrow, with legs extended and arms clasped to his sides. He resurfaced to cheers for his death-defying stunt—and what it symbolized. It was September 1827, and Sam Patch—a textile spinner who had worked in mills since he was seven or eight years old—wanted to make a point.

Jumping from waterfalls had long been a pastime among boys who labored in the nation's earliest textile mills; Sam Patch had made his own first leaps as a youth in Pawtucket, Rhode Island. But to Patch jumping was more than a pastime: he considered it an "art" imbued with political meaning. He timed his Paterson leap to steal the show from Timothy B. Crane, an entrepreneur who had dreamed up Forest Garden, a pleasure park designed to provide "respectable" ladies and gentlemen a respite from the mill town. To get to the park, which had formerly been open to everyone, they would need to cross a toll bridge. The toll would raise revenue to sustain the park, but, more important, it would keep out those Paterson residents who could not afford it. To Crane that meant keeping out the riffraff.

Patch and the mill hands understood that the riffraff meant *them,* and they saw in Forest Garden all that was wrong with the modernizing North. Forest Garden symbolized a world in which manual labor was devalued, in which artisans were turning into workers, in which industrialists and entrepreneurs increasingly held themselves to be morally superior to those who drew wages. In previous months, town residents had attacked (physically and verbally) the park, its workers, its buildings, and Timothy Crane himself. Then, when Crane planned elaborate celebrations to mark the completion of his

◀ **Sam Patch and his daring exploits captured Americans' imaginations into the late nineteenth century.** *(University of Delaware Library, Newark, Delaware)*

## CHRONOLOGY

**1790s–1840s** ■ Second Great Awakening spreads religious fervor

**1820s** ■ Reformers in New York and Pennsylvania establish model penitentiaries

**1824** ■ No presidential candidate wins a majority in electoral college

**1825** ■ House of Representatives elects Adams president

**1826** ■ American Society for the Promotion of Temperance founded

**1828** ■ Tariff of Abominations passed
■ Jackson elected president

**1830s–40s** ■ Democratic-Whig competition gels in second party system

**1831** ■ Garrison begins abolitionist newspaper *The Liberator*
■ Antimasons are first political party to hold national convention

**1832** ■ Jackson vetoes rechartering Second Bank of the United States
■ Jackson reelected president

**1832–33** ■ South Carolina nullifies Tariffs of 1828 and 1832, prompting nullification crisis

**1836** ■ Specie Circular ends credit purchase of public lands
■ Van Buren elected president

**1837** ■ *Caroline* affair sparks tension with Britain
■ Financial panic ends boom of the 1830s

**1838–39** ■ United States and Canada mobilize militias over Maine–New Brunswick border dispute

**1839–43** ■ Hard times spread unemployment and deflation

**1840** ■ Whigs win presidency under Harrison

**1841** ■ Tyler assumes presidency after Harrison's death

**1848** ■ Woman's Rights Convention at Seneca Falls, New York, calls for female suffrage.

toll bridge, Sam Patch determined that he would use the occasion to assert the pride of those workers who made the industrial revolution possible in the first place.

In the two years following his Paterson leap—before making his last, and fatal, jump at the 125-foot Genesee Falls in Rochester, New York—Sam Patch would become a professional waterfall jumper, taking on falls in some of the North's most rapidly industrializing areas. Even as some observers dismissed his leaps as mere drunken stunts, he costumed himself in the symbolic clothing of the textile spinner and associated socially and politically with a raucous crowd of skilled operatives. (As a boss spinner, Patch's job was highly skilled.) His flaunting of respectable, middle-class values, along with his leaps themselves, caught the attention of the political press. Members of the era's two main political parties—the Whigs and the Jacksonian Democrats—saw Patch through very different lenses. To Whigs, Patch exemplified what was, in one editor's words, "wrong with democracy," whereas Jacksonians hailed Patch as a heroic artisan. Patch captured the fancy of none other than President Andrew Jackson himself. When in 1833 the city of Philadelphia presented Jackson with a horse, the president named him Sam Patch. The horse became the president's favorite and would ultimately be buried with full military honors.

Many Americans joined Sam Patch in trying to reaffirm control over their lives in an era of rapid economic and social changes. The market economy, growing wealth and inequality, immigration, the westward thrust of settlement and slavery, and territorial expansion all contributed simultaneously to Americans' hopes and fears. Many Americans embraced progress even as they hoped to limit what they saw as its unpleasant side effects. These same Americans, though, often divided sharply among themselves over what defined progress, what constituted a social ill, and how those ills should be remedied.

Anxious about their personal status in a rapidly changing world, many Americans turned to evangelical religion, which in turn launched many of the era's myriad reform movements, most of them centered in the North. Believing in the notion of human perfectibility, reformers worked to free individuals and society from sin. In the Northeast and Midwest in particular, women and men organized to end the abuses of prostitution and alcohol, to improve conditions in prisons and asylums, and to establish public schools. Some reformers, instead of trying to fix society, established separate experimental communities that might model a new form of social relations. Opponents of slavery and proponents of women's rights, meanwhile, worked within the existing system but sought to radically alter Americans' premises about the practical implications of the revolutionary declaration that "all men are created equal."

Evangelical reformers generally aligned themselves with the Whig Party, but the Jacksonian Democrats, too, were concerned with what they saw as social problems, mostly class inequities. They grew suspicious of middle-class reformers who told working-class men and women how to live their lives, and they opposed special privileges bestowed by government policies and institutions, such as the Second Bank of the United States. Yet when it came to the era's most pressing issue—slavery—the national parties often remained silent, hoping to keep sectional conflict submerged.

The new system of political rivalry that emerged between the Democrats and Whigs did lay out distinct positions, however, on most other salient issues. Democrats emphasized that the best government is that which governs least, whereas the Whigs championed a strong federal government to promote economic development and maintain social order. Democrats saw the nation's agricultural expansion to the west as an urgent need, whereas Whigs actively promoted the nation's industrial and commercial growth in the East. They hoped to bring about that growth through their American System of high protective tariffs, centralized banking, and federal funding for internal improvements. Together, Democrats and Whigs constituted what is often called the second party system, characterized by strong organizations, intense loyalty, and religious and ethnic voting patterns.

- What were the "evils" in society that reformers hoped to eliminate, and what motivated them to do so?
- What was the relationship between reform and politics?
- What were the main issues dividing Democrats and Whigs?

## FROM REVIVAL TO REFORM

A series of religious revivals in the late eighteenth and early nineteenth centuries—sometimes called the Second Great Awakening for their resemblance to revivals of the Great Awakening of the eighteenth century—raised people's hopes for the Second Coming of the Christian messiah and the establishment of the Kingdom of God on earth. Revivalists resolved to speed the millennium, or the thousand years of peace on earth that would accompany Christ's Second Coming, by combating sin. Some believed that the United States had a special mission in God's design and a special role in eliminating evil. If sin and evil could be eliminated, individuals and society could be perfected. Revivalists called on individuals to renounce personal sins, such as drinking, swearing, and licentiousness. They also called on individuals to combat social evils, including—most prominently—slavery, but also dueling and desecration of the Sabbath. Not until all Americans had been converted, and all social evils suppressed, would Christ make his Second Coming.

Because it was not enough for an individual to embrace God and godliness, revivalists strove for large-scale conversions. Rural women, men, and children traveled long distances to camp meetings, where they listened to fiery sermons preached day and night from hastily constructed platforms and tents in forests or open fields. In cities, women in particular attended daily church services and prayer meetings, sometimes for months on end. Converts renounced personal sin, vowed to live sanctified lives, and committed themselves to helping others see the light.

The most famous revival was at Cane Ridge, Kentucky, in August 1801. One report estimated that 25,000 people attended, including men and women, free and enslaved, at a time when Kentucky's largest city, Lexington, had fewer than 2,000 inhabitants. The call to personal repentance and conversion invigorated Protestantism throughout the South, giving churches an evangelical base. Although laws often restricted or outlawed black churches and preachers, particularly after Nat Turner's bloody revolt in 1831, in practice black and mixed churches often flourished on the local level, with black and white evangelicals forging a united front against their profane neighbors. During the 1840s and 1850s, though, as the slavery issue increasingly worked itself into public debate, southern Presbyterian, Baptist, and Methodist churches seceded from their denominations' national conferences. For the white leaders of these secessionist churches, slavery did not impede human perfectibility but rather ensured it; the paternal guidance of

**Revivals**

benevolent masters, they reasoned, would bring Africans to Christ.

All revivalists shared a belief in individual self-improvement, but northern revivalists also emphasized communal improvement, making them missionaries for both individual salvation and social reform. Wherever they preached, northern evangelists generated new religious groups and voluntary reform societies. Preachers like Lyman Beecher, who made his base in New England before moving to Cincinnati, and Charles Finney, who traveled the canals and roads that linked the Northeast to the Midwest, argued that evil was avoidable, that Christians were not doomed by original sin, and that anyone could achieve salvation. In everyday language, Finney—a former lawyer—preached that "God has made man a moral free agent." Finney's brand of revivalism transcended sects, class, and race. At first a Presbyterian, he eventually found his home in Methodism. Revivalism had a particularly strong base among Methodists and Baptists, whose denominational structures maximized democratic participation and drew their ministers from ordinary folk.

Finney experienced his greatest successes in the area of western New York that had experienced rapid changes in transportation and industrialization—in what he called the "Burned-Over District" because of the intensity of the region's evangelical fires. Rapid change raised fears of the social evils that might accompany economic progress—the dissolution of the family, drinking, swearing, and prostitution. Many individuals worried, too, whether their status would improve or decline in an economy that cycled through booms and busts.

When northern revivalist preachers emphasized the importance of good works—that is, good deeds and piety—they helped ignite many of the era's social reform movements, which began in the Burned-Over District and spread eastward to New England and the Middle Atlantic, and westward to the upper Midwest. Evangelically inspired reform associations together constituted what historians call the "benevolent empire." Even as they advocated for distinct causes, these associations shared an overall commitment to human perfectibility, and they often turned to the same wealthy men for financial resources and advice.

Those resources allowed them to make good use of the era's new technologies—steam presses and railroads—to spread the evangelical word.

## Moral Reform

By mass-producing pamphlets and newspapers for distribution far into the interior of the country, reformers spread their message throughout the Northeast and Midwest, strengthening the cultural connections between regions increasingly tied together economically. With ca-

▲ Samuel Waldo and William Jewett's oil portrait of Charles Finney around 1834 captures Finney at his peak. The charismatic Finney mesmerized his audiences, and contemporaries credited him with converting 500,000 people. *(Oberlin College Archives, Oberlin, OH)*

nals and railroads making travel easier, reformers could attend annual conventions and contact like-minded people personally, and local reform societies could host speakers from distant places. Most reform organizations, like political parties, sponsored weekly newspapers, creating a virtual community of reformers.

While the new wealth of industrialists and merchants provided financial resources for evangelical reform, their wives and daughters did the everyday work of soliciting new members and circulating petitions. Women more than men tended to feel personally responsible for counteracting the social evils of the expanding market economy. The cult of domesticity, which arose in tandem with industrialization and the revivals, assigned women the role of moral guardianship of their families; evangelical reformers expanded that role beyond the domestic sphere into the public realm. Women undertook to do more than provide moral guidance to their own children; they would help run reformatories for wayward youth or establish asylums for orphans. Participation in reform movements thus allowed some women to exercise their moral authority outside the household, giving them a new sense of purpose. Their influence might both improve people's lives and hasten the millennium. Women also enjoyed the friendships with other women that came from participation in benevolent societies. Although some elite women in Upper South cities also formed and joined reform societies, moral reform was primarily a northeastern and midwestern phenomenon.

For women and some men, reform represented their primary form of political involvement at a time when the vote was restricted to property-owning men. The aftermath of an 1830 exposé of prostitution in New York City illustrates how reform led to political action. Even as female reformers organized a shelter for the city's prostitutes and tried to secure respectable employment for them, they publicized the names of brothel clients in an effort to shame the men who contributed to the women's waywardness. The New York women organized themselves into the Female Moral Reform Society and soon expanded their geographic scope and activities. By 1840 the society had 555 affiliated chapters across the nation. In the next few years, it entered the political sphere by lobbying successfully for criminal sanctions in New York State against men who seduced women into prostitution. If only prostitutes could be freed from the corrupting reach of the men who preyed on them, reformers believed, so-called fallen women might be morally uplifted.

A similar belief in perfectibility led reformers to establish institutions to impose discipline on criminals and delinquents. Rather than simply punishing criminals, reformers tried to transform them into productive members of society. Their model penitentiaries aimed to rehabilitate criminals through disciplined regimens.

### Penitentiaries and Asylums

Other reformers sought to reform treatment of the mentally ill, who were frequently imprisoned, often alongside criminals, and put in cages or dark dungeons, chained to walls, brutalized, or held in solitary confinement. Dorothea Dix, the leader of this crusade, exemplifies the early-nineteenth-century reformer who started with a religious belief in individual self-improvement and human perfectibility, and moved into social action by advocating collective responsibility. Investigating asylums, petitioning the Massachusetts legislature, and lobbying other states and Congress, Dix moved from reform to politics and helped create a new public role for women. In response to Dix's efforts, twenty-eight of thirty-three states had built public institutions for the mentally ill by 1860.

Advocates of temperance, who pushed for either partial or full abstinence from alcoholic beverages, likewise crossed from the personal into the political sphere. Drinking was widespread in the early nineteenth century, when men like Sam Patch frequently gathered in public houses and rural inns to drink whiskey, rum, and hard cider while they gossiped, talked politics, and played cards. Contracts were sealed, celebrations commemorated, and harvests toasted with liquor. "Respectable" women did not drink in public, but many regularly tippled alcohol-based patent medicines promoted as cure-alls.

### Temperance

Evangelicals considered drinking sinful, and in many denominations, forsaking alcohol was part of conversion.

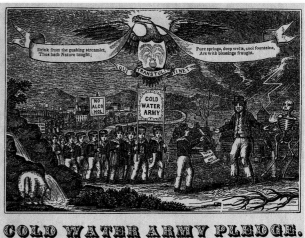

▲ Children became active in the "Cold Water Army," or temperance societies, and advocated complete abstinence from alcoholic beverages. On holidays such as George Washington's birthday and the Fourth of July, they marched at public gatherings, carrying banners and singing temperance songs.

(© Collection of the New York Historical Society)

Preachers condemned alcohol for violating the Sabbath—the only day workers had off, which some spent at the public house. Factory owners condemned alcohol for making their workers unreliable. Civic leaders connected alcohol with crime. Middle-class reformers, often women, condemned it for squandering wages, diverting men from their family responsibilities, and making them more likely to be abusive when they came home from the tavern. In the early 1840s, thousands of ordinary women formed Martha Washington societies to protect families by reforming alcoholics, raising children as teetotalers, and spreading the temperance message. Abstinence from alcohol, reformers believed, would help achieve both religious perfectibility and secular progress. They hoped to stamp out the raucous drinking culture of the likes of Sam Patch.

As the temperance movement gained momentum, its goal shifted from moderation to voluntary abstinence and finally to prohibition. By the mid-1830s, five thousand state and local temperance societies touted teetotalism, and more than a million people had taken the pledge of abstinence, including several hundred thousand children who enlisted in the Cold Water Army. Per capita consumption of alcohol fell from five gallons per year in 1800 to below two gallons in the 1840s. The American Society for the Promotion of Temperance, organized in 1826 to promote pledges of abstinence, became a pressure group for legislation that would end alcohol manufacture and sale. In 1851 Maine became the first state to ban alcohol except for medicinal purposes, and by 1855 similar laws had been enacted throughout New England and in New York, Pennsylvania, and the Midwest.

The temperance campaign had a nativist—or anti-immigrant and anti-Catholic—strain to it. The Irish and Germans, complained the *American Protestant Magazine* in 1849, "bring the grog shops like the frogs of Egypt upon us." Along the nation's canals, reformers lamented the hundreds of taverns that catered to the largely Irish work force, and in the cities, they expressed outrage at the Sunday tradition of urban German families' gathering at beer gardens to eat and drink, to dance and sing, and sometimes to play cards. Their efforts had some success, as Catholics took the pledge of abstinence and formed their own organizations, such as the St. Mary's Mutual Benevolence Total Abstinence Society in Boston.

But temperance spawned strong opposition, too. Many workers—Protestants as well as Catholics—rejected what they saw as middle-class efforts to impose middle-class values on people whose lives they did not understand, and they steadfastly defended their right to drink whatever they pleased. Workers agreed that poverty and crime were indeed problems but that poor wages, not drinking habits, were to blame. Even some who abstained from alcohol opposed prohibition, believing that drinking should be a matter of self-control, not state coercion.

Protestants and Catholics often came into conflict over education as well. Public education almost always included religious education, but when teachers taught Protestant beliefs and used the King James version of the Bible, Catholics established their own schools, which taught Catholic doctrines. This move led some Protestants to fear that Catholics would never be assimilated into American culture, and some charged Catholics with being exclusionists, plotting to undermine the republic and impose papal control. Yet, even as these conflicts brewed, public education touched the lives of more Americans than did any other reform movement.

## Public Schools

The leader of this movement was Horace Mann, a Massachusetts lawyer and reformer who came from humble beginnings. He advocated free, tax-supported education to replace church schools and the private schools set up by untrained, itinerant young men. Universal education, Mann proposed, would end misery and crime, and would help Americanize immigrants. "If we do not prepare children to become good citizens," he argued, "if we do not develop their capacities, imbue their hearts with the love of truth and duty, and a reverence for all things sacred and holy, then our republic must go down to destruction."

During Mann's tenure as secretary of the Massachusetts Board of Education from 1837 to 1848, Massachusetts led the "common school" movement which established training for teachers, lengthened the school year, and raised teachers' salaries to make the profession more attractive. In keeping with the era's notions that women had special claims to morality and with the practical advantage that they could be paid less, Mann envisioned a system in which women would prepare future clerks, farmers, and workers with a practical curriculum that deemphasized classics in favor of geography, arithmetic, and science. Like so many other reform movements, educational reform rested on the notions of progress and perfectibility; given the proper guidance, individuals could educate themselves out of their circumstances, material and moral alike.

Thanks to the expansion of public education, by 1850 every state offered some publication of its own, and the vast majority of native-born white Americans were literate. Newspapers and magazines proliferated, and bookstores spread. Power printing presses and better transportation made possible wide distribution of books and periodicals. The religious press—of both traditional sects and revivalists—produced pamphlets, hymnals, Bibles, and religious newspapers. Americans also read secular publications. Newspapers and magazines—political organs, literary journals, and the voices of working groups like the mill girls at Lowell—abounded in the 1830s and after.

## COMMUNITARIAN EXPERIMENTS

While moral reformers tried to perfect American society, some idealists dreamed of an entirely new social order. They established dozens of utopian communities—ideal communities that could then serve as models for broader society—based on either religious principles, a desire to resist what they saw as the excessive individualism of the market economy, or a combination of the two. Some groups, like the Shakers, had originated in eighteenth-century Europe, while others, like the Mormons, arose in the wake of the religious ferment of the Second Great Awakening. Utopian communities attempted to recapture what they perceived as the more communal nature of the past, even as they offered sometimes-radical departures from established practices of marriage and child rearing.

The Shakers, the largest of the communal utopian experiments, reached their peak between 1820 and 1860, when six thousand members lived in twenty settlements in eight states. Shaker communities emphasized agriculture and handcrafts, selling their produce and manufactured goods beyond the bounds of their own community; most managed to become self-sufficient and profitable enterprises. The community's craft tradition contrasted with the new factory regime. But the Shakers were essentially a spiritual community. Founded in England in 1772 by Mother Ann Lee, they got their name from their worship service, which included shaking their entire bodies as well as singing, dancing, and shouting. Ann Lee's children had died in infancy, and she believed that their deaths were retribution for her sin of intercourse; thus she advocated celibacy. After imprisonment in England in 1773–1774, she fulfilled a vision by settling in America.

**Utopian Communities**

In religious practice and social relations, Shakers offered an alternative to the era's rapid changes in urban and rural life. Shakers lived communally, with men and women

▲ This bucolic image of New Harmony, painted several years after the experiment's collapse, belies the rancorous history of the short-lived community, which attracted many settlers who proved unwilling or unable to commit themselves fully to communitarian life. Pictured here on the far left is the "Hive," which housed the kitchen, office, and meeting rooms; along the hilltop are buildings that housed residents, a laundry, and printing presses.

*(Joslyn Art Museum, Omaha, Nebraska, Gift of Enron Art Foundation)*

in separate quarters; individual families were abolished. Leadership was shared equally between men and women. Many Shaker settlements became temporary refuges for orphans, widows, runaways, abused wives, and unemployed workers during hard times. Their settlements depended on constant enlistment of new recruits, not only because the practice of celibacy meant that they could not reproduce themselves, but also because some members soon left, unsuited to either communal living or the Shakers' spiritual message.

Other influential utopian communities also sought to resist the social changes brought about by industrialism. John Humphrey Noyes, a lawyer who had been converted by Finney's revivals, established two perfectionist communities: first in Putney, Vermont, in 1835, and then—after being indicted for adultery—in Oneida, New York, in 1848. Noyes decried individualism and instead advocated communal ownership of property, communal child rearing, and "complex marriage," in which all men in the community were married to all women, but in which a woman was free to accept or reject a sexual proposition. In the Oneida Colony, exclusive sexual relationships were forbidden, and men were to practice "male continence," or intercourse without ejaculation, in order to promote relationships built on more than sexual fulfillment. All pregnancies were to be planned; couples would apply to Noyes for permission to have a child, or Noyes would assign two people to reproduce with each other. Robert Dale Owen's community in New Harmony, Indiana (1825–1828), also abolished private property and advocated communal child rearing. The Fourierists, named after French philosopher Charles Fourier, established more than two dozen communities in the Northeast and Midwest; these communities, too, resisted the individualism of market society and promoted equality between the sexes.

The most famous Fourier community was Brook Farm, in West Roxbury, Massachusetts, near Boston. Inspired by transcendentalism—the belief that the physical world is secondary to the spiritual realm, which human beings can reach not by custom and experience but only by intuition—Brook Farm's members rejected materialism. Their rural communalism combined spirituality, manual labor, intellectual life, and play. Originally founded in 1841 by the Unitarian minister George Ripley, a literary critic and friend of transcendentalist lecturer and essayist Ralph Waldo Emerson, Brook Farm attracted farmers, craftsmen, and writers, among them the novelist Nathaniel Hawthorne. Although the Unitarians were not evangelicals, their largely middle- and upper-class followers had a long-standing "devotion to progress," as one of their most influential ministers put it. The Brook Farm school drew students from outside the community, and Brook Farm residents contributed regularly to the *Dial*, the leading transcendentalist journal. In 1845 Brook Farm's hundred members organized themselves into model phalanxes (working-living units) along the model suggested by Fourier. As rigid regimentation replaced individualism, membership dropped. A year after a disastrous fire in 1846, the experiment collapsed.

Though short-lived, Brook Farm played a significant role in the flowering of a national literature. During these

### American Renaissance

years, Hawthorne, Emerson, and *Dial* editor Margaret Fuller joined Henry David Thoreau, Herman Melville, and others in a literary outpouring known today as the American Renaissance. In philosophical intensity and moral idealism, their work was both distinctively American and an outgrowth of the European romantic movement. Their themes were universal, their settings and characters American. Hawthorne, for instance, used Puritan New England as a backdrop, and Melville wrote of great spiritual quests as seafaring adventures.

Essayist Ralph Waldo Emerson was the prime mover of the American Renaissance and a pillar of the transcendental movement. Emerson had followed his father and grandfather into the ministry but quit his Boston Unitarian pulpit in 1831. After a two-year sojourn in Europe, he returned to lecture and write, preaching individualism and self-reliance. "We live in succession, in division, in parts, in particles," Emerson wrote. "We see the world piece by piece, as the sun, the moon, the animal, the tree; but the whole, of which these are the shining parts, is the soul." Intuitive experience of God is attainable, insisted Emerson, because "the Highest dwells" within every individual in the form of the "Over-soul." What gave Emerson's writings force was, for his times, a simple, direct prose. In his first book, *Nature* (1836), and in "The American Scholar" (1837), a Phi Beta Kappa address at Harvard, Emerson explored human nature and American culture. Widely admired, he influenced Thoreau, Fuller, Hawthorne, and other members of Brook Farm.

No communitarian experiment had a more lasting influence than the Church of Jesus Christ of Latter-day Saints,

### Mormons

whose members were known as the Mormons. During the religious ferment of the 1820s in western New York, Joseph Smith, a young farmer, reported that an angel called Moroni had given him divinely engraved gold plates. Smith published his revelations as the *Book of Mormon* and organized a church in 1830. The next year, the community moved west to Ohio to build a "New Jerusalem" and await the Second Coming of Jesus.

▲ Violence stalked the Mormons until they found safety in the Great Salt Lake valley. Here a Mormon family—a father, three wives, and five children—poses for a photographer in Salt Lake City in the 1850s.

*(Church of Jesus Christ of Latter-day Saints)*

But angry mobs drove the Mormons from Ohio, and they settled in Missouri. Anti-Mormons charged that Mormonism was fraudulent, a scam by Joseph Smith. Opponents feared Mormon economic and political power. In 1838 the governor of Missouri charged Smith with fomenting insurrection and gathered evidence to indict him and other leaders for treason.

Smith and his followers resettled in Nauvoo, Illinois. The state legislature gave them a city charter that made them self-governing and authorized a local militia. But again the community met antagonism, especially after Smith introduced the practice of polygamy in 1841, allowing men to have several wives at once. The next year Smith became mayor, and this consolidation of religious and political power, as well as Nauvoo's petition to the federal government to be a self-governing territory, further antagonized opponents, who now included some former Mormons. In 1844, after Smith and his brother were charged with treason and jailed, and then murdered, the Mormons left Illinois to seek security in the western wilderness. Under the leadership of Brigham Young, they set up a cooperative community in the Great Salt Lake valley.

There, the Mormons distributed agricultural land according to family size. An extensive irrigation system, constructed by men who contributed their labor in proportion to the quantity of land they received and the amount of water they expected to use, transformed the arid valley into a rich oasis. As the colony developed, the church el-

ders gained control of water, trade, industry, and eventually the territorial government of Utah.

## ABOLITIONISM

While moral reformers tried to eliminate individual sin and utopians established model communities apart from mainstream society, evangelical abolitionists tried to eradicate what they saw as a communal sin suffusing American society: slavery. Inspired by the Second Great Awakening, their efforts built on those of an earlier generation of antislavery activists.

From the nation's earliest days—in places like Philadelphia, New York, Albany, Boston, and Nantucket—free blacks formed societies to petition legislatures, seek judicial redress, stage public marches, and, especially, publish tracts that chronicled the horrors of life in bondage. African American abolitionists wrote about slavery's devastating impact on both black and white families, advocated an immediate end to slavery, offered assistance to fugitive slaves, and promoted legal equality for free blacks. By 1830 there were fifty African American abolitionist societies in the United States. But it was the writings of one man, David Walker, that captured white Americans' attention like none other. In his *Appeal ... to the Colored Citizens* (1829), Walker—a southern-born free African American—advocated the violent overthrow of slavery, sending shock waves of fear throughout the white South and much of the North as well.

**Early Abolitionism and Colonization**

Violent overthrow could not have been further from the goals of the white abolitionists who, in the years after the American Revolution, had come together in places like Boston and, especially, Philadelphia, with its large population of Quakers, whose religious beliefs emphasized human equality. These early antislavery advocates pressed for slavery's gradual abolition and an end to the international slave trade. Although they aided African Americans who sought freedom through judicial decisions, their assumptions about blacks' racial inferiority made them stop short of advocating for equal rights. These early white abolitionists tended to be wealthy, socially prominent men who excluded women, African Americans, and less elite men from their societies.

Elites were more likely to support the colonization movement, which crystallized in 1816 with the organization of the American Colonization Society. Its members planned to purchase and then relocate American slaves, as well as free blacks, to Africa or the Caribbean. Among its supporters were Thomas Jefferson, James Madison, James

▲ After purchasing his own freedom in 1829, Gilbert Hunt left Virginia for Liberia under the auspices of the American Colonization Society. Although Hunt admired much he saw in Africa, he quickly became disillusioned with colonization and returned to Richmond, where he worked as a blacksmith and became a deacon in the First African Baptist Church. *(Virginia Historical Society)*

Monroe, and Henry Clay, as well as many lesser-known men and women who came from the North and, especially, the Upper South. In 1824 the society founded Liberia, on the west coast of Africa, and began to establish a settlement for African Americans who were willing to go. The society had resettled nearly twelve thousand people in Liberia by 1860. Some colonizationists aimed to strengthen slavery by ridding the South of troublesome slaves or to purge the North of African Americans altogether. Others hoped colonization would improve African Americans' conditions. Although some African Americans supported the movement, black abolitionists generally denounced it.

In the early 1830s, a new group of more radical white abolitionists—most prominently, William Lloyd Garrison—rejected both the violent overthrow advocated by David Walker and the gradual approaches of white legal reformers and colonizationists. Instead, they demanded immediate, complete, and uncompensated emancipation. In the first issue of *The Liberator*, which he began publishing in 1831, Garrison declared, "I am in earnest—I will not equivocate—I will not excuse—I will not retreat a single inch—and *I will be heard.*" Two years later, he founded the American Antislavery Society, which became the era's largest abolitionist organization.

Immediatists, as they came to be called, believed that slavery was an absolute sin needing urgent eradication.

### Immediatism

They were influenced by African American abolitionist societies and by evangelicals' notion that humans, not God, determined their own spiritual fate by deciding whether to choose good or evil. In that sense, all were equal before God's eyes. When all humans had chosen good over evil, the millennium would come. Slavery, however, denied enslaved men and women the ability to make such choices, the ability to act as what Finney called "moral free agents." For every day that slavery continued, then, the millennium was also delayed.

Because the millennium depended on *all* hearts having been won over to Christ, because it depended on the perfectibility of all human beings, including slaveowners, Garrison's brand of abolitionism focused on "moral suasion." He and his followers hoped to bring about emancipation, not through coercion, but rather by winning over the hearts of slaveowners as well as other white Americans who supported or tolerated slavery. Evangelical abolitionism depended, then, on large numbers of ministers and laypeople spreading the evangelical message to all corners of the nation.

In 1829 Congregationalists and Presbyterians founded the Lane Seminary in Cincinnati to train ministers who

### The Lane Debates

would carry the evangelical message into the West. With Lyman Beecher as president, it drew students from North and South, and encouraged "people of color" to apply. Not long after Theodore Weld, one of Charles Finney's most faithful converts, arrived at the Lane Seminary in 1833, he organized what became known as the Lane Debates, eighteen days of discussion among the school's students and faculty about the relative merits of colonization and immediatism. Immediatism won.

Led by Weld, the Lane students and faculty next founded an antislavery society, and began reaching out more fully to the growing African American population

# The International Antislavery Movement

he heart of the international antislavery movement had been in Great Britain, but in the 1830s many of Britain's local antislavery societies thought that they had accomplished their mission and disbanded. Over the previous three decades, the international slave trade had greatly diminished, and in 1833 Parliament ended slavery in the British Empire. At the same time, however, abolitionism in the United States was on the rise, and now American abolitionists extended their work across the Atlantic. They revived the international movement to end slavery where it still existed—in Spanish possessions like Cuba, in independent and colonial South America, in Africa and Asia, and in the United States.

American abolitionism in the 1830s was invigorated by the militancy of black abolitionists and by the conversion of William Lloyd Garrison to immediatism. Seeking to raise money and to put international pressure on the United States to abolish slavery, African American abolitionists in the 1840s toured Britain regularly. On the lecture circuit and in published narratives, they appealed for support. Especially effective were ex-slaves, who recounted their firsthand experiences of slavery and bared their scarred bodies.

Black abolitionists spoke in small towns and villages, and in Britain's industrial centers. After fugitive slave Moses Gandy toured England, he published his autobiography, the first of dozens of slave narratives published in London. The next year, 1845, Frederick Douglass began a nineteen-month tour, giving three hundred lectures in Britain.

In 1849 black abolitionists William Wells Brown, Alexander Crummell, and J. W. C. Pennington were among the twenty American delegates at the international Paris Peace Conference. There, Brown likened war to slavery, telling the eight hundred delegates from western Europe and the United States that "it is impossible to maintain slavery without maintaining war." His scheduled brief lecture tour in Britain turned into a five-year exile because, after passage of the 1850 Fugitive Slave Law, he feared being seized and sent back to slavery if he returned to the United States. In 1854 he became free when British abolitionists purchased his freedom from his former master.

Gandy, Douglass, Brown, and dozens of other former slaves helped revive abolitionism as an international issue.

They energized the British and Foreign Anti-Slavery Society, founded in 1839, and hundreds of more militant local societies. By the early 1850s, national abolitionist movements succeeded in abolishing slavery in Colombia, Argentina, Venezuela, and Peru. Although the United States continued to resist internal and international pressure, its black abolitionists were instrumental not only in reviving the worldwide antislavery movement, but also, as advocates of women's rights, international peace, temperance, and other reforms, in linking Americans to reform movements around the world.

▲ William Wells Brown's autobiography stirred abolitionists in the United States and England. In 1849 Brown was among the American delegates to the Paris Peace Conference, then spent the next five years as an exile in Britain, fearing being sent back to slavery under the 1850 Fugitive Slave Act. He returned to the United States only after British abolitionists purchased his freedom from his former master. *(Southern Historical Collection, the Library of the University of North Carolina, Chapel Hill)*

of Cincinnati, who in 1829 had been the target of a brutal attack by white people. Fearful that Weld and his students would provoke renewed disorder, white business leaders protested the creation of the antislavery society. Lane's trustees responded by banning antislavery organizations on campus and barring further debate on the topic of slavery. Beecher supported the trustees. Weld and the other "Lane Rebels" publicly broke from the seminary and the following year enrolled in a new seminary at Oberlin, a town in northern Ohio founded as a Christian perfectionist settlement. The new seminary, which was dedicated to immediatism, would become the first college to admit women and one of the first to admit African Americans. Weld turned down a faculty post at Oberlin, preferring instead to carry the abolitionist message directly into the western countryside as an agent for the American Antislavery Society.

By 1838, at its peak, the society had 2,000 local affiliates and a membership of over 300,000. In stark contrast to an earlier generation of white abolitionists, the immediatists welcomed men and women of all racial and class backgrounds into their organizations. Lydia Maria Child, Maria Chapman, and Lucretia Mott served on its executive committee; Child edited its official paper, the *National Anti-Slavery Standard,* from 1841 to 1843, and Chapman coedited it from 1844 until 1848. The society sponsored black and female speakers, and women undertook most of the day-to-day conversion efforts.

### The American Antislavery Society

In rural and small-town northern and midwestern communities, women addressed mail, collected signatures, raised money, organized boycotts of textiles made from slave-grown cotton, and increased awareness of their cause. With the "great postal campaign," launched in 1835, the society's membership flooded the mails with antislavery tracts. Women went door to door collecting signatures on antislavery petitions; by 1838 more than 400,000 petitions, each with numerous signatures, had been sent to Congress. Abolitionist-minded women met in "sewing circles," where they made clothes for fugitive slaves while organizing future activities, such as antislavery fairs at which they sold goods—often items they had made themselves—and later donated the proceeds to antislavery causes, such as abolitionist publications. These fairs also increased the visibility of abolitionism itself and drew more Americans into direct contact with abolitionists and their ideas.

Even as white abolitionist societies opened membership to African Americans and sponsored speaking tours

### African American Abolitionists

by former slaves, African Americans continued into the 1840s and 1850s their independent efforts to end slavery and to improve the status of free African Americans. Former slaves—most famously, Frederick Douglass, Henry Bibb, Harriet Tubman, and Sojourner Truth—dedicated their lives to ending slavery through their speeches, publications, and participation in a secret network known as the Underground Railroad, which spirited enslaved men, women, and children to freedom. By the thousands, less famous African Americans continued the work of the postrevolutionary generation and established their own churches, founded their own moral reform societies, published their own newspapers, created schools and orphanages for African American children, and held conventions to consider tactics for improving African Americans' status within the free states.

Although genuine friendships emerged among white and black abolitionists, many white abolitionists treated blacks as inferiors, driving some African Americans to reject white antislavery organizations and to strike out on their own. Others lacked the patience for the supposed immediatism of William Lloyd Garrison; they did not ob-

▲ Women played an activist role in reform, especially in abolitionism. A rare daguerreotype from August 1850 shows women and men, including Frederick Douglass, on the podium at an abolitionist rally in Cazenovia, New York.

*(Collection of J. Paul Getty Museum, Los Angeles, California)*

ject to moral suasion, but they thought there were even more immediate solutions, such as legislation, to the problems African Americans faced in both the South and the North.

African American abolitionists nonetheless took heart in the immediatists' success at winning converts. But that very success also gave rise to a virulent, even violent, opposition. In the South, mobs blocked the distribution of antislavery tracts. The state of South Carolina intercepted and burned abolitionist literature, and in 1835 proslavery assailants killed four abolitionists in South Carolina and Louisiana, as well as forty people allegedly plotting a slave rebellion in Mississippi and Louisiana that summer.

## Opposition to Abolitionism

White northerners had their own reasons for opposing abolition: they recognized cotton's vital role in the nation's economy, and they feared that emancipation would prompt an enormous influx of freed slaves into their own region. Like many southerners, they questioned the institution's morality but not its practicality: They believed blacks to be inherently inferior and incapable of acquiring the attributes—virtue and diligence—required of freedom and citizenship. Some northerners, too, objected to white women's involvement in abolitionism, believing that women's proper role lay within the home.

The North saw its share of anti-abolitionist violence. In Boston, David Walker died under mysterious circumstances in 1830, after a bounty had apparently been put on his head. Among those northerners who despised abolitionists most were "gentlemen of property and standing"— a nineteenth-century term for commercial and political elites—who often had strong economic connections to the southern cotton economy and who maintained political connections to leading southerners. Northern gentlemen incited anti-abolitionist riots. In Utica, New York, in 1835 merchants and professionals broke up the state Anti-Slavery Convention, which had welcomed blacks and women. Mob violence peaked that year, with more than fifty riots aimed at abolitionists or African Americans. In 1837 in Alton, Illinois, a mob murdered abolitionist editor Elijah P. Lovejoy, and rioters sacked his printing office. The following year, rioters in Philadelphia hurled stones and insults at three thousand black and white women attending the Anti-Slavery Convention of American Women held in the brand-new Pennsylvania Hall, a building constructed to house abolitionist meetings and an abolitionist bookstore. The following day, a mob burned the building to the ground, just three days after its dedication.

The violent reaction to abolitionism made some immediatists question whether moral suasion was a realistic tactic. Among them was James G. Birney, the son of a Kentucky slaveowner, who embraced immediatism but sought to end slavery by electing abolitionists who would push for a legislative end to slavery. Those who favored a more practical, political solution saw little room for women within the abolitionist movement. The end of slavery, they believed, could be brought about only in the male sphere of politics. To involve women violated the natural order of things while detracting from the ultimate goal: freedom for slaves.

## Moral Suasion Versus Political Action

Thus, when William Lloyd Garrison, an ardent supporter of women's rights, endorsed the appointment of Abby Kelly to the business committee of the American Anti-Slavery Society in 1840, he provoked an irreparable split in the abolitionist movement. Arthur Tappan and Theodore Weld led a dissident group that formed the new American and Foreign Anti-Slavery Society. That society in turn established a new political party: the Liberty Party, which nominated Birney for president in 1840 and 1844.

Although committed to immediate abolitionism, members of the Liberty Party doubted the federal government had the authority to abolish slavery where it already existed. It was up to the states, not the federal government, to determine the legality of slavery within their bounds. Where the government could act, they felt, was in the western territories, and they demanded that all new territories prohibit slavery. Some prominent black abolitionists, including Frederick Douglass, endorsed the party, whose leaders emphasized the need to combat not just southern slavery but also northern prejudice.

# WOMEN'S RIGHTS

Frustrated by their treatment within the abolitionist movement, some female abolitionists took the lead in advocating women's rights. At the first World Anti-Slavery Convention in London in 1840, abolitionists Lucretia Mott and Elizabeth Cady Stanton first met, united in their dismay that female abolitionists were denied seats in the convention's main hall; eight years later, the two would help organize the first American women's rights convention. Angelina and Sarah Grimké had been born to a slaveholding family in South Carolina but later moved north and became active in the abolitionist movement. After critics attacked them for speaking to audiences that included men, they rejected claims that women should obey, not

▲ Elizabeth Cady Stanton posed in 1848 with two of her sons, Henry Jr., left, and Neil. Stanton, one of the organizers of the Seneca Falls Woman's Rights Convention, traveled widely and agitated for women's equality while raising five children.

*(Collection of Rhoda Jenkins)*

lecture, men, and the sisters took the lead in advocating for women's legal and social equality.

Religious revivalism and moral reform led other women to reexamine their positions in society. Revivals helped women to see themselves as inherently equal to men, and reform movements brought middle-class women outside the home and into the public sphere. Female reformers' lobbying had helped to effect legal change, and some women believed the next step was obvious: women should be granted full citizenship rights.

There were a great many legal obstacles to overcome. After independence, American states carried over traditional English marriage law, which gave husbands absolute control over the family. Men owned their wives' personal property, were legal guardians of their children, and owned whatever family members produced or earned. A father had the legal authority to oppose his daughter's choice of husband, though by 1800 most American women chose their own marriage partner.

### Legal Rights

Married women made modest gains in property and spousal rights from the 1830s on. Arkansas in 1835 passed the first married women's property law, and by 1860 sixteen more states had followed. In those states, women—singled, married, or divorced—could own and convey property. When a wife inherited property, it was hers, not her husband's, though money that she earned or acquired in some other way continued to belong to her husband. Women could also write wills. Such laws were particularly popular among wealthy Americans, South and North, who hoped to protect their family fortunes during periods of economic boom and bust; property in a woman's name was safe from her husband's creditors. In the 1830s, states also liberalized divorce laws, adding cruelty and desertion as grounds for divorce, but divorce remained rare.

Despite these changes, a few radical reformers argued that marriage constituted a form of bondage. Among the most outspoken critics of marriage was Lucy Stone, who finally consented to marry fellow abolitionist Henry Blackwell, but only under the condition that she not take a vow of obedience and that she keep her own name. The term "Lucy Stoner" entered common parlance as a reference to married women who did not adopt their husband's name.

By the time Lucy Stone and Harry Blackwell married in 1855, both had become active in the organized movement to secure women's political rights. That movement had been launched in July 1848, when Elizabeth Cady Stanton, Lucretia Mott, Mary Ann McClintock, Martha Wright, and Jane Hunt—all abolitionists and, except Stanton, Quakers—organized the first Woman's Rights Convention at Seneca Falls, New York. Three hundred women and men gathered to demand social and economic equality for women, and some added political equality to the list of demands. They protested women's legal disabilities as well as their social restrictions, such as exclusion from advanced schooling and many occupations. Their Declaration of Sentiments, modeled on the Declaration of Independence, broadcast the injustices suffered by women and launched the women's rights movement. "All men and women are created equal," the declaration proclaimed. The similar premises of abolitionism and women's rights led many reformers, including former slaves like Sojourner Truth, to work simultaneously for both movements in the 1850s. Even among those who supported the movement's general aims, the question of female suffrage became divisive. Some men were supporters, notably William Lloyd Garrison and Frederick Douglass, but most men actively opposed women's right to vote. At Seneca Falls, the resolution on woman suffrage passed only after Frederick Douglass spoke passionately for it, but

### Political Rights

even then some participants refused to sign. In 1851 Elizabeth Cady Stanton joined forces with Susan B. Anthony, a temperance advocate, to become the most vocal and persistent activists for women's voting rights. Despite their best efforts, Stanton and Anthony won relatively few converts and many critics.

## JACKSONIANISM AND PARTY POLITICS

No less than reformers, politicians sought to control the direction of change in the expanding nation. With changes to suffrage laws, they reframed their political visions to appeal to an increasingly broad-based electorate. Hotly contested elections helped make politics the great nineteenth-century American pastime, drawing the interest and participation of voters and nonvoters alike.

Property restrictions for voters, which states began abandoning during the 1810s, remained in only seven of twenty-six states by 1840. Some states even allowed foreign nationals who had officially declared their intention of becoming American citizens to vote. The net effect was a sharply higher number of votes cast in presidential elections. Between 1824 and 1828 that number increased threefold, from 360,000 to over 1.1 million. In 1840, 2.4 million men cast votes. The proportion of eligible voters who cast ballots also grew, from about 27 percent in 1824 to more than 80 percent in 1840.

**Expanding Political Participation**

At the same time, the method of choosing presidential electors became more democratic. Previously, a caucus of party leaders had done so in most states, but by 1824 eighteen out of twenty-four states chose electors by popular vote, compared to just five of sixteen in 1800. As a result, politicians augmented their direct appeals to voters, and the election of 1824 saw the end of the congressional caucus, when House and Senate members of the same political party came together to select their candidate.

As a result, five candidates, all of whom identified as Democratic-Republicans, came forward to run for president in 1824. The poorly attended Republican caucus chose William H. Crawford of Georgia, secretary of the treasury, as its presidential candidate. But other Democratic-Republicans boycotted the caucus as undemocratic, ending Congress's role in nominating presidential candidates. Instead, state legislatures nominated candidates, offering the expanded electorate a slate of sectional candidates. John Quincy Adams drew support from New England, while westerners backed

**Election of 1824**

House Speaker Henry Clay of Kentucky. Some southerners at first supported Secretary of War John C. Calhoun, who later dropped his bid for the presidency and ran for the vice presidency instead. The Tennessee legislature nominated Andrew Jackson, a military hero whose political views were unknown.

Among the four candidates who remained in the presidential race until the election, Jackson led in both electoral and popular votes, but no candidate received a majority in the electoral college. Adams finished second, and Crawford and Clay trailed far behind. Under the Constitution, the House of Representatives, voting by state delegation, one vote to a state, would select the next president from among the three leaders in electoral votes. Clay, who had the fewest votes, was dropped, but the three others courted his support, hoping he would influence his electors to vote for them. Crawford, disabled from a stroke that he suffered before the election, never received serious consideration. Clay backed Adams, who won with thirteen of the twenty-four state delegations and thus became president (Map 12.1). Adams named Clay to the cabinet position of secretary of state, the traditional steppingstone to the presidency.

Angry Jacksonians denounced the election's outcome as a "corrupt bargain," claiming that Adams had stolen the election from their candidate by offering Clay a cabinet

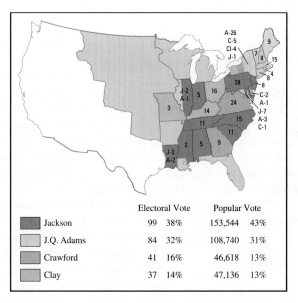

| | | Electoral Vote | | Popular Vote | |
|---|---|---|---|---|---|
| | Jackson | 99 | 38% | 153,544 | 43% |
| | J.Q. Adams | 84 | 32% | 108,740 | 31% |
| | Crawford | 41 | 16% | 46,618 | 13% |
| | Clay | 37 | 14% | 47,136 | 13% |

**Map 12.1   Presidential Election, 1824**

Andrew Jackson led in both electoral and popular votes but failed to win a majority of electoral college votes. The House elected John Quincy Adams president.

position in exchange for his votes. Jackson's bitterness fueled his later emphasis on the people's will. The Republican Party split. The Adams wing emerged as the National Republicans, and the Jacksonians became the Democrats; they immediately began planning for 1828.

After taking the oath of office, Adams proposed a strong nationalist policy incorporating Henry Clay's American System, a program of protective tariffs, a national bank, and internal improvements. Adams believed the federal government's active role should extend to education, science, and the arts. He proposed a national university in Washington, D.C. Brilliant as a diplomat and secretary of state, Adams fared less well as chief executive. He underestimated the lingering effects of the Panic of 1819 and the resulting staunch opposition to a national bank and a protective tariff.

The 1828 election pitted Adams against Jackson in a rowdy campaign. Nicknamed "Old Hickory" after the toughest of American hardwood, Andrew Jackson was a rough-and-tumble, ambitious man. Born in South Carolina in 1767, he rose from humble beginnings to become a wealthy Tennessee planter and slaveholder. Jackson was the first American president from the West and the first born in a log cabin; he was at ease among both frontiersmen and planters. Having served in the Revolution as a boy, Jackson claimed a

### Election of 1828

connection to the founding generation. In the Tennessee militia, General Jackson led the campaign to remove Creeks from the Alabama and Georgia frontier. He burst onto the national scene in 1815 as the hero of the Battle of New Orleans and in 1818 enhanced his glory in an expedition against Seminoles in Spanish Florida. Jackson also served as a congressman and senator from Tennessee, and as the first territorial governor of Florida (1821), before running for president in 1824.

Voters and nonvoters, too, displayed their enthusiasm for Jackson with badges, medals, and other campaign paraphernalia, which were mass-produced for the first time. The contest was also intensely personal. Jackson's supporters accused Adams of stealing the 1824 election and, when he was envoy to Russia, of having secured prostitutes for the czar. Anti-Jacksonians published reports that Jackson's wife, Rachel, had married Jackson before her divorce from her first husband was final; she was, they sneered, an adulterer and a bigamist. In 1806 Jackson, in an attempt defend Rachel's integrity, had killed a man during a duel, and the cry of "murderer!" was revived in the election.

Although Adams kept the states he had won in 1824, his opposition was now unified behind a single candidate, and Jackson swamped him, polling 56 percent of the popular vote and winning in the electoral college by 178 to 83 votes (Map 12.2). Jacksonians believed that the will of

▲ Presidential candidate Andrew Jackson is portrayed on a trinket or sewing box in 1824. This is an example both of how campaigns entered popular culture and of the active role of women, excluded from voting, in politics. *(Collection of David J. and Janice L. Frent)*

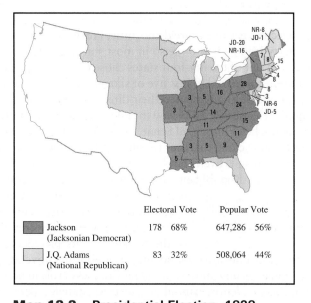

| | | Electoral Vote | | Popular Vote | |
|---|---|---|---|---|---|
| ■ | Jackson (Jacksonian Democrat) | 178 | 68% | 647,286 | 56% |
| ▢ | J.Q. Adams (National Republican) | 83 | 32% | 508,064 | 44% |

**Map 12.2   Presidential Election, 1828**
Andrew Jackson avenged his 1824 loss of the presidency, sweeping the election in 1828.

the people had finally been served. Through a lavishly financed coalition of state parties, political leaders, and newspaper editors, a popular movement had elected the president. The Democratic Party became the first well-organized national political party in the United States, and tight party organization became the hallmark of nineteenth-century American politics.

The Democrats represented a wide range of views but shared a fundamental commitment to the Jeffersonian

#### Democrats

concept of an agrarian society. They viewed a strong central government as the enemy of individual liberty, and they believed that government intervention in the economy benefited special-interest groups and created corporate monopolies that favored the rich. They sought to restore the independence of the individual—the artisan and the ordinary farmer—by ending federal support of banks and corporations, and by restricting the use of paper currency. Jackson and his supporters also opposed reform movements. They believed, for instance, that public schools restricted individual liberty by interfering with parental responsibility and undermined freedom of religion by replacing church schools. When it came to westward expansion, though, Jackson and his followers called for federal intervention. It was Jackson who initiated Indian removal despite the protests of northeastern reformers.

By restraining government and emphasizing individualism, Jacksonians sought to restore traditional republican virtues, such as self-discipline and self-reliance, traits supposedly undermined by economic and social change. Jackson looked to Jefferson and the founding generation as models of traditional values. "My political creed," Jackson wrote to Tennessee congressman James K. Polk in 1826, "was formed in the old republican school." Jackson rejected elitism and advocated for popular government. Time and again he declared that sovereignty resided with the people, not with the states or the courts. In this respect Jackson himself was a reformer; he sought government by majority, not elite, rule.

Like Jefferson, Jackson strengthened the executive branch of government even as he advocated limited government. In combining the roles of party leader and chief of state, he centralized power in the White House. He relied on political friends, his "Kitchen Cabinet," for advice, only rarely consulting his official cabinet. Jackson commanded enormous loyalty and rewarded his followers handsomely. Rotating officeholders, Jackson claimed, made government more responsive to the public will and allowed him to appoint loyal Democrats to office, a practice that his critics called the spoils system, in which the victor gives the spoils of victory to his supporters. Although Jackson was not the first president to do so—Jefferson had replaced many of Adams's appointees—his own outcry against corrupt bargains made him an easy target for inflammatory rhetoric. The spoils system, opponents charged, corrupted the government itself because appointments were based on loyalty, not competency.

Opponents mocked Jackson as "King Andrew I," charging him with abuse of power by ignoring the Supreme

#### King Andrew

Court's ruling on Cherokee rights, by sidestepping his cabinet, and by removing experienced officeholders in favor of his own political cronies. They rejected his claim of restoring republican virtue and accused him of recklessly destroying the economy.

▲ Whigs, who named themselves after the loyal opposition in Britain, delighted in portraying Andrew Jackson as a power-hungry leader eager to turn a republic into a monarchy.

*(© Collection of the New York Historical Society)*

▲ Even as his critics portrayed him as monarchical, Jackson presented himself as the president of the common man. Here he sits atop his prized horse, Sam Patch, named after the disgruntled factory worker and daring waterfall jumper.

*(The Hermitage: Home of President Andrew Jackson, Nashville, TN)*

Perhaps nothing rankled Jackson's critics more than his frequent use of the veto, which he used to promote his vision of a limited government. In 1830 he vetoed the Maysville Road bill, which would have funded construction of a 60-mile turnpike from Maysville to Lexington, Kentucky. A federally subsidized internal improvement confined to one state was unconstitutional, he insisted; states bore responsibility for such projects. The veto undermined Henry Clay's American System and personally embarrassed Clay because the project was in his home district.

From George Washington to John Quincy Adams, the first six presidents had vetoed nine bills; Jackson alone vetoed twelve. Previous presidents believed that vetoes were justified only on constitutional grounds, but Jackson considered policy disagreements legitimate grounds as well. He made the veto an effective weapon for controlling Congress, because representatives and senators had to weigh the possibility of a presidential veto as they deliberated.

## FEDERALISM AT ISSUE: THE NULLIFICATION AND BANK CONTROVERSIES

Soon after the Maysville Road veto, Jackson directly faced the question of state versus federal power. The slave South feared federal power and no state more so than South Carolina, where the planter class was the strongest and slavery the most concentrated. Southerners also resented protectionist tariffs, one of the foundations of Clay's American System, which in 1824 and 1828 protected manufactures by imposing import duties on manufactured cloth and iron. But in protecting northern factories, the tariff raised the costs of manufactured goods to southerners, who quickly labeled the high tariff of 1828 the Tariff of Abominations.

South Carolina's political leaders rejected the 1828 tariff, invoking the doctrine of nullification, according to which a state had the right to overrule, or nullify, federal legislation.

**Nullification**

Nullification was based on the idea expressed in the Virginia and Kentucky Resolutions of 1798—that the states, representing the people, have a right to judge the constitutionality of federal actions. Jackson's vice president, John C. Calhoun of South Carolina, argued in his unsigned *Exposition and Protest* that, in any disagreement between the federal government and a state, a special state convention—like the conventions called to ratify the Constitution—should decide the conflict by either nullifying or affirming the federal law. Only the power of nullification, Calhoun asserted, could protect the minority against the tyranny of the majority.

As Jackson's running mate in 1828, Calhoun had avoided endorsing nullification and thus embarrassing the Democratic ticket; he also hoped to win Jackson's support as the Democratic presidential heir apparent. Thus, in early 1830, Calhoun presided silently over the Senate and its packed galleries when Senator Daniel Webster of Massachusetts and Senator Robert Y. Hayne of South Carolina debated states' rights. The debate started over a resolution to restrict western land sales but soon touched on the tariff. From there, it focused on the nature of the Union, with nullification a subtext. Hayne charged that the North was threatening to bring disunity. For two days Webster eloquently defended New England and the republic, as he kept supporters of nullification on the defensive. Although debating Hayne, he aimed his remarks at Calhoun. At the climax of the debate, Webster invoked two powerful images. One was the outcome of nullification: "states dissevered, discordant, belligerent; on a land rent with civil feuds, or drenched . . . in fraternal blood!" The other was a patriotic vision of a great nation flourishing under the motto "Liberty and Union, now and forever, one and inseparable."

Though sympathetic to states' rights and distrustful of the federal government, Jackson rejected the idea of state sovereignty. He strongly believed that sovereignty rested with the people. Believing deeply in the Union, he shared Webster's dread of nullification. Soon after the Webster-Hayne debate, the president made his position clear at a Jefferson Day dinner with the toast "Our Federal Union, it must and shall be preserved." Vice President Calhoun, when his turn came, toasted "The Federal Union—next to our liberty the most dear," revealing his adherence to states' rights. Calhoun and Jackson grew apart, and Jackson looked to Secretary of State Martin Van Buren, not Calhoun, as his successor.

Tension resumed when Congress passed a new tariff in 1832, reducing some duties but retaining high taxes on imported iron, cottons, and woolens. Although a majority of southern representatives supported the new tariff, South Carolinians refused to go along. In their eyes, the constitutional right to control their own destiny had been sacrificed to the demands of northern industrialists. They feared the act could set a precedent for congressional legislation on slavery. In November 1832 a South Carolina state convention nullified both the 1828 and the 1832 tariffs, declaring it unlawful for federal officials to collect duties in the state.

Privately, Jackson threatened to invade South Carolina and hang Vice President Calhoun; publicly, he took measured steps. In December Jackson issued a proclamation opposing nullification. He moved troops to federal forts in South Carolina and prepared U.S. marshals to collect the required duties. At Jackson's request, Congress passed the Force Act, authorizing the president to call up troops but also offering a way to avoid force by collecting duties before foreign ships reached Charleston's harbor. At the same time, Jackson extended an olive branch by recommending tariff reductions.

**The Force Act**

Calhoun, disturbed by South Carolina's drift toward separatism, resigned as vice president and soon won election to represent South Carolina in the U.S. Senate. There he worked with Henry Clay to draw up the compromise Tariff of 1833. Quickly passed by Congress and signed by the president, the new tariff lengthened the list of duty-free items and reduced duties over nine years. Satisfied, South Carolina's convention repealed its nullification law. In a final salvo, it also nullified Jackson's Force Act. Jackson ignored the gesture.

Nullification offered a genuine debate on the nature and principles of the republic. Each side believed it was upholding the Constitution and opposing special privilege and subversion of republican values. South Carolina's leaders opposed the tyranny of the federal government and manufacturing interests. Jackson fought the tyranny of South Carolina, whose refusal to bow to federal authority threatened to split the republic. Neither side won a clear victory, though both claimed to have done so. It took another crisis, over a central bank, to define the powers of the federal government more clearly.

At stake was survival of the Second Bank of the United States, whose twenty-year charter was scheduled to expire in 1836. The bank served as a depository for federal funds and provided credit for businesses. Its bank notes circulated as currency throughout the country; they could be readily exchanged for gold, and the federal government accepted them as payment in all transactions. Through its twenty-five branch offices, the Second Bank acted as a clearing-house for state banks, refusing to accept bank notes of any state bank lacking sufficient gold in reserve. Most state banks resented the central bank's police role: by presenting a state bank's notes for redemption all at once, the Second Bank could easily ruin a state bank. Moreover, with less money in reserve, state banks found themselves unable to compete on an equal footing with the Second Bank.

**Second Bank of the United States**

Many state governments also regarded the national bank as unresponsive to local needs. Westerners and urban workers remembered with bitterness the bank's conservative credit policies during the Panic of 1819. As a private, profit-making institution, its policies reflected the interest of its owners, especially its president, Nicholas Biddle, who controlled the bank completely. An eastern patrician, Biddle symbolized all that westerners found wrong with the bank. The bank became the prime issue in the presidential campaign of 1832, the first in which political parties held conventions.

The national political convention was the innovation of the Antimason Party, which had started in upstate New York in the mid-1820s as a grass-roots movement against Freemasonry, a secret male fraternity that attracted middle- and upper-class men prominent in commerce and civic affairs. Opponents of Masonry claimed the fraternity to be unrepublican; Masons colluded to bestow business and political favors on each other, and—in the incident that sparked the organized Antimasonry movement—Masons had obstructed justice in the investigation of the 1826 disappearance of a disgruntled former member who had written an exposé of the society. Evangelicals considered Masons sacrilegious, claiming that they talked of being Christians but behaved in unchristian ways. Masonry, they said, encouraged men to neglect their families for alcohol and ribald entertainment at Masonic lodges. Antimasonry soon developed into a vibrant political movement in the Northeast and parts of the Midwest. In the 1828 presidential election, the Antimasons had opposed Jackson, himself a Mason. With their confidence bolstered by strong showings in gubernatorial elections in 1830, the Antimasons held the first national political convention in Baltimore in 1831, nominating William Wirt of Maryland for president and Amos Ellmaker of Pennsylvania for vice president.

**Anti-Masonry**

Following the Antimasons' lead, the Democrats and National Republicans held their own conventions. The Democrats reaffirmed the choice of Jackson, who had already been nominated by state legislatures, for president and nominated Martin Van Buren of New York for vice president. The National Republican convention selected Clay and John Sergeant of Pennsylvania. The Independent Democrats ran John Floyd and Henry Lee of Virginia; as governor of Virginia, Floyd had supported nullification, winning him the hearts of many South Carolinians.

**Election of 1832**

Jacksonians denounced the bank as a vehicle for special privilege and economic power, while the Republicans supported it as a pillar of their plan for economic nationalism. The bank's charter was valid until 1836, but as part of his campaign strategy, Clay persuaded Biddle to ask Congress to approve an early rechartering. If Jackson signed the rechartering bill, then Clay could attack the president's inconsistency on the issue. If he vetoed it, then—Clay reasoned—the voters would give the nod to Clay. The plan backfired. The president vetoed the bill and issued a pointed veto message appealing to those voters who feared that the era's rapid economic development spread its ad-

vantages undemocratically. Jackson acknowledged that prosperity could never be evenly dispersed, but he took a strong stand against special interests that tried to use the government to their own unfair advantage. "It is to be regretted," he wrote, "that the rich and powerful too often bend the acts of government to their selfish purposes." The message was powerful and successful. Jackson won 54 percent of the popular vote to Clay's 37 percent; he fared even better in the electoral college, where he captured 76 percent of electors. Although the Antimasons won just one state, Vermont, they nonetheless helped galvanize the anti-Jackson opposition.

After his sweeping victory and second inauguration, Jackson moved in 1833 to dismantle the Second Bank. He deposited federal funds in state-chartered banks (critics called them his "pet banks"). Without federal money, the Second Bank shriveled. When its federal charter expired in 1836, it became just another Pennsylvania-chartered private bank. Five years later it closed its doors.

**Jackson's Second Term**

As Congress allowed the Bank of the United States to die, it passed the Deposit Act of 1836 with Jackson's support. The act authorized the secretary of the treasury to designate one bank in each state and territory to provide services formerly performed by the Bank of the United States. The act provided that the federal surplus in excess of $5 million be distributed to the states as interest-free loans beginning in 1837. These loans were never repaid—a fitting Jacksonian restraint on the federal purse.

The surplus had derived from wholesale speculation in public lands: speculators borrowed money to purchase public land, used the land as collateral for credit to buy additional acreage, and repeated the cycle. Between 1834 and 1836, federal receipts from land sales rose from $5 million to $25 million. The state banks providing the loans issued bank notes. Jackson, an opponent of paper money, feared that the speculative craze threatened the stability of state banks and undermined the interests of settlers, who could not compete with speculators in bidding for the best land.

In keeping with his opposition to paper currency, the president ordered Treasury Secretary Levi Woodbury to issue the Specie Circular. It provided that after August 1836 only specie—gold or silver—or Virginia scrip (paper money) would be accepted as payment for land. By ending credit sales, it significantly reduced purchases of public land and the federal budget surplus. As a result, the government suspended payments to the states.

**Specie Circular**

The policy was a disaster. Although federal land sales fell sharply, speculation continued as land available for sale became scarce. The increased demand for specie squeezed banks, and many suspended the redemption of bank notes for specie. Credit contracted further as banks issued fewer notes and made fewer loans. Jackson aggravated the situation by pursuing a tight money policy. More important, the Specie Circular was similar to a bill defeated in the Senate just three months earlier, so Jackson used presidential powers to override the legislative will. Jackson's opponents thus saw King Andrew at work. In the waning days of Jackson's administration, Congress voted to repeal the circular, but the president pocket-vetoed the bill by holding it unsigned until Congress adjourned. Finally, in May 1838, a joint resolution of Congress overturned the circular. Sales of land resumed, and the speculative fervor ended.

## THE WHIG CHALLENGE AND THE SECOND PARTY SYSTEM

In the 1830s, opponents of the Democrats, including remnants of the National Republican and Antimason Parties, joined together to become the Whig Party. Resentful of Jackson's domination of Congress, the Whigs borrowed the name of the eighteenth-century British party that opposed the tyranny of Hanoverian monarchs. They, too, were the loyal opposition. From 1834 through the 1840s, the Whigs and the Democrats competed on nearly equal footing, and each drew supporters from all regions. The era's political competition—the second party system—was more intense and better organized than what scholars have labeled as the first party system of Democratic-Republicans versus Federalists.

Whigs favored economic expansion through an activist government. They supported corporate charters, a

**Whigs and Reformers**

national bank, and paper currency; Democrats opposed all three. Whigs generally professed a strong belief in progress and perfectibility, and they favored social reforms, including public schools, prison and asylum reform, and temperance. Whigs did not object to helping special interests if doing so promoted the general welfare. The chartering of corporations, they argued, expanded economic opportunity for everyone, laborers and farmers alike. Democrats, distrustful of concentrated economic power and of moral and economic coercion, held fast to the Jeffersonian principle of limited government.

Whigs stressed a "harmony of interests" among all classes and interests. Their philosophy was one of equal opportunity. Democrats tended to see society as divided

into the "haves" and the "have nots," and they embraced a motto of "equal rights." They championed "heroic artisans" like Sam Patch, whereas Whigs remained wary of the "excesses of democracy" and preferred to see society ruled from the top down. Whigs believed in free-labor ideology and thought that society's wealthy and powerful had risen by their own merits. Democrats alleged that, instead, their political opponents had benefited from special favors.

But religion and ethnicity, as much as class, influenced party affiliation. The Whigs' support for energetic government and moral reform won the favor of evangelical Protestants. Methodists and Baptists were overwhelmingly Whigs, as were the small number of free black voters. In many locales the membership rolls of reform societies overlapped those of the party. Indeed, Whigs practiced a kind of political revivalism. Their rallies resembled camp meetings; their speeches employed pulpit rhetoric; their programs embodied reformers' perfectionist beliefs.

In their appeal to evangelicals, Whigs alienated members of other faiths. The evangelicals' ideal Christian state had no room for nonevangelical Protestants, Catholics, Mormons, or religious freethinkers. Those groups opposed Sabbath laws and temperance legislation in particular, and state interference in moral and religious questions in general. In fact, they preferred to keep religion and politics separate. As a result, more than 95 percent of Irish Catholics, 90 percent of Reformed Dutch, and 80 percent of German Catholics voted Democratic.

The parties' platforms thus attracted what might seem to be an odd coalition of voters. Whigs appealed more to those who benefited from the era's rapid economic changes, whereas Democrats often remained wary of those changes and committed to agrarian expansion. The Whigs drew antislavery supporters as well as northern businessmen and workers pledged to maintaining good relations with the South. Well-settled slave owners, especially in the Upper South, often voted Whig, as did black New Englanders. Both groups favored halting slavery's westward expansion—the former, to protect their own investments from cheap western competition and the latter, to undercut slavery itself. Democrats' promises to open additional lands for settlement attracted yeoman farmers, wage earners, frontier slaveowners, and immigrants. With such broad coalitions of voters, there was room within each party for a broad spectrum of beliefs, particularly when it came to slavery.

Politicians recognized, however, the potentially divisive nature of slavery, and some went to extremes to keep it out of the national political debate. In response to the American Anti-Slavery Society's petitioning campaign, the House of Representatives in 1836 adopted what abolitionists labeled the "gag rule," which automatically tabled abolitionist petitions, effectively preventing debate on them. In a dramatic defense of the right of petition, former president John Quincy Adams, now a representative from Massachusetts, took to the floor again and again to speak against the gag rule, which was ultimately repealed in 1844.

Vice President Martin Van Buren, handpicked by Jackson, headed the Democratic ticket in the 1836 presidential election. Van Buren was a career politician who had built a political machine—the Albany Regency—in New York and then left to join Jackson's cabinet in 1829, first as secretary of state and then as American minister to Great Britain.

### Election of 1836

Because the Whigs in 1836 had not yet coalesced into a national party, they entered three sectional candidates: Daniel Webster (New England), Hugh White (the South), and William Henry Harrison (the West). By splintering the vote, they hoped to throw the election into the House of Representatives. Van Buren, however, comfortably captured the electoral college even though he had only a 25,000-vote edge out of a total of 1.5 million votes cast. No vice-presidential candidate received a majority of electoral votes, and for the only time in American history, the Senate decided a vice-presidential race, selecting Democratic candidate Richard M. Johnson of Kentucky.

Van Buren took office just weeks before the American credit system collapsed. In response to the Specie Circular, New York banks stopped redeeming paper currency with gold in mid-1837. Soon all banks suspended payments in hard coin. A downward economic spiral began, curtailing bank loans and strangling business confidence. Credit contraction made things worse. After a brief recovery, hard times persisted from 1839 until 1843.

### Van Buren and Hard Times

Van Buren followed Jackson's hard-money policies. He cut federal spending, causing prices to drop further, and he opposed a national bank, which would have expanded credit. The president proposed, too, a new regional treasury system for government deposits. The proposed treasury branches would accept and disperse only gold and silver coin; they would not accept paper currency or checks drawn on state banks. Van Buren's independent treasury bill became law in 1840. By increasing the demand for hard coin, it deprived banks of gold and accelerated price deflation. Whigs and Democrats faced off at the state level over these issues. Whigs favored new banks, more paper currency, and readily available corporate and bank charters. As the party of hard money, Democrats favored eliminating

paper currency altogether. Increasingly the Democrats became distrustful even of state banks, and by the mid-1840s a majority favored eliminating all bank corporations.

Amid hard times came a renewal of Anglo-American tensions. One of the most troublesome disputes arose from the *Caroline* affair. After the privately owned steamer *Caroline* carried supplies to aid an unsuccessful Canadian uprising against Great Britain, a group of British loyalists burned the ship, killing an American citizen in the process. Britain refused to apologize, and American newspapers called for revenge. Fearing that popular support for the Canadian rebels would ignite war, President Van Buren posted troops under General Winfield Scott at the border to discourage Americans from seeking vigilante retaliation. Tensions subsided in late 1840 when New York arrested a Canadian deemed responsible for the American's death aboard the *Caroline*. The alleged murderer was acquitted. Had the verdict gone otherwise, Lord Palmerston, the British foreign minister, might have sought war.

### Anglo-American Tensions

At almost the same time, an old border dispute between Maine and New Brunswick disrupted Anglo-American relations. Great Britain had accepted an 1831 arbitration decision fixing a new boundary, but the U.S. Senate rejected it. Thus, when Canadian lumbermen cut trees in the disputed region in the winter of 1838–1839, a posse of Maine citizens assembled to expel them. The lumbermen captured the posse, both sides mobilized their militias, and Congress authorized a call-up of fifty thousand men. General Scott was now dispatched to Aroostook, Maine, where he arranged a truce. The Webster-Ashburton Treaty (1842) settled the boundaries between Maine and New Brunswick, and along the Great Lakes, but it left unresolved the still-disputed northern boundary of Oregon, joint occupancy of which had been renewed in 1827.

With the nation in the grip of hard times, the Whigs faced the election of 1840 with confidence. Their strategy was simple: maintain loyal supporters and win over independents by blaming hard times on the Democrats. The Whigs rallied behind a military hero, General William Henry Harrison, conqueror of the Shawnees at Tippecanoe Creek in 1811. The Democrats renominated President Van Buren, and the newly formed Liberty Party ran James Birney.

### William Henry Harrison and the Election of 1840

Harrison, or "Old Tippecanoe," and his running mate, John Tyler of Virginia, ran a "log cabin and hard cider" campaign—a people's crusade—against the aristocratic president in "the Palace." Although descended from a

▲ Even as the Whigs opposed the Democrats, they adopted many of the Democrats' campaign techniques, appealing to the common man with their "log cabin and cider" campaign of 1840. The band in this street scene is riding a wagon decorated with a log-cabin painting. The campaign's excitement appealed to nonvoters as well as voters, and eighty percent of eligible voters cast ballots. *(F. D. R. Library)*

Virginia plantation family, Harrison presented himself as an ordinary farmer. Party hacks bluntly blamed hard times on the Democrats, but Harrison himself remained silent, earning himself the nickname "General Mum." The Whigs wooed voters with huge rallies, parades, songs, posters, campaign mementos, and a party newspaper, *The Log Cabin.* They reached out to voters as well as non-voters, including women, who attended their rallies and speeches. One Virginia woman's support for the Whigs led her to publish two pamphlets backing Harrison's candidacy. In a huge turnout, 80 percent of eligible voters cast ballots. Harrison won the popular vote by a narrow margin but swept the electoral college by 234 to 60.

Immediately after taking office in 1841, President Harrison convened a special session of Congress to pass the Whig program: repeal of the independent treasury system, a new national bank, and a higher protective tariff.

But the sixty-eight-year-old Harrison caught pneumonia and died within a month of his inauguration. His vice president, John Tyler, who had left the Democratic Party to protest Jackson's nullification proclamation, now found himself the first vice president whose president had died in office. The Constitution did not stipulate what should happen in such circumstances, but Tyler quickly took full possession of executive powers and set a crucial precedent that would not be codified in the Constitution until the latter part of the twentieth century with the Twenty-fifth Amendment.

In office, Tyler became more a Democrat than a Whig. He repeatedly vetoed Clay's protective tariffs, internal improvements, and bills aimed at reviving the Bank of the United States. Two days after Tyler's second veto of a bank bill, the entire cabinet except Secretary of State Daniel Webster resigned; Webster, once done negotiating the Webster-Ashburton treaty, followed. Tyler became a president without a party, and the Whigs lost the presidency without losing an election. Disgusted Whigs referred to Tyler as "His Accidency."

**President Tyler**

Like Jackson, Tyler expanded presidential powers and emphasized westward expansion. His expansionist vision contained Whig elements, though: he had his eye on commercial markets in Hawaii and China. During his presidency, the United States negotiated its first treaties with China, and Tyler expanded the Monroe Doctrine to include Hawaii (or the Sandwich Islands). But, more than anything else, Tyler's vision for the nation's path to greatness fixed on Texas and the westward expansion of slavery.

## SUMMARY

Religion and reform shaped politics from 1824 through the 1840s. Driven by a belief in human perfectibility, many evangelicals, especially women, worked tirelessly to right the wrongs of American society. By doing so, they hoped to trigger the millennium, the thousand years of peace on earth that would accompany Christ's Second Coming. Reformers battled the evils of prostitution and alcohol, and sought to reform criminals and delinquents, improve insane asylums, and establish public schools. Some rejected the possibility of reforming American society from within and instead joined experimental communities that modeled radical alternatives to the social and economic order. Abolitionists combined the reformers' and utopians' approaches; they worked to perfect American society from within but through radical means—the eradication of slavery. As women entered the public sphere as advocates of reform and, especially, abolitionism, some of them

# *Legacy* FOR A PEOPLE AND A NATION

## The Bible Belt

Had an eighteenth-century visitor to North America asked for the Bible belt, she would have been directed to New England, all of whose colonies were founded for religious purposes. Early southerners tended to be more secular than religious. By the 1830s, even as revivalist preachers lit evangelical fires in the Northeast and Midwest, the South was the most churched region, and southerners were the most devout. The Second Great Awakening, beginning with the Cane Ridge revival in 1801, spread quickly through the South. By the 1830s, more than half of white and one-quarter of black southerners had undergone a conversion experience, and religion and the South formed a common identity. Embracing the Bible as the revealed word of God, the South became known as the Bible belt.

Religion helped define southern distinctiveness. Southern Protestant liturgy and cadences were as much African as European; thus southern and northern denominations grew apart. They formally separated in the 1840s, when Southern Baptists and Methodists withdrew from the national organizations that had barred slaveowners from church offices. Presbyterians withdrew later. After the Civil War, evangelical denominations remained divided in northern and southern organizations.

Southern religion maintained tradition and resisted modern ways. Protestantism dominated, making the South more religiously homogeneous than other regions. Mostly evangelical, southern religion emphasized conversion and a personal battle against sin. By the twentieth century, fundamentalism, which stressed a literal reading of the Bible, reinforced resistance to modernism. Yet southern Protestantism lost ground as a political force in opposing evolution and in alliances with nativist, anti-immigrant groups.

But evangelicalism rose again in the 1960s, especially after a Catholic—John F. Kennedy—won the Democratic nomination for president. Many evangelicals began to vote their religion, moving to the Republican Party, and in 1964 Republican Barry Goldwater won the Bible belt states, breaking up the solid Democratic block. His conservative rhetoric resonated with southerners concerned about desegregation and erosion of religious values. *Time* called 1976 the "Year of the Evangelical" when born-again Southern Baptist Jimmy Carter was elected president.

In the 1980s and 1990s, the Bible belt became the base of mobilized evangelical political action led by the Moral Majority. Religious and cultural issues rallied southern evangelicals defending the traditional family, advocating prayer in schools, and opposing abortion, the Equal Rights Amendment, and gay rights legislation. In the midterm elections of 2006, even as dissatisfaction with the Iraq war cost the Republicans control of both houses of Congress, most Bible belt states still stuck tenaciously to the party most associated with conservative, Christian values. Thus the revivals that began in Kentucky in 1801 have rippled in ever wider circles across the South for two centuries, shaping the distinctive southern blend of culture and politics.

turned toward the equally radical proposition of full legal and political rights for women.

Reform remade politics, and politicians reshaped public discourse to appeal to the broadening electorate. As did reformers, President John Quincy Adams raised expectations about an expanded governmental role. The struggles between the National Republicans and the Democrats, then between the Democrats and the Whigs, stimulated even greater interest in campaigns and political issues. The Democrats, who rallied around Andrew Jackson, and Jackson's opponents, who found shelter under the Whig tent, competed almost equally for the loyalty of voters. Both parties built strong organizations that faced off in national and local elections. And both parties favored economic expansion but by different means: The Whigs advocated centralized government initiative to spur commercial growth, whereas Democrats advocated limited government and sought agricultural expansion. Jackson did not hesitate, however, to use presidential authority, and his opponents called him King Andrew. The controversies over the Second Bank of the United States and nullification exposed different interpretations of the nation's founding principles.

The late 1830s and early 1840s would be a period of uncertainty: the economy once again cycled through a period of bust; tensions with the British resurfaced; and—for the first time—a president died in office. As John Tyler, derided by his critics as "His Accidency," took office, he tenaciously articulated a vision of American greatness that depended on its westward expansion.

## SUGGESTIONS FOR FURTHER READING

Michael F. Holt, *The Rise and Fall of the American Whig Party: Jacksonian Politics and the Onset of the Civil War* (1999)

Julie Roy Jeffrey, *The Great Silent Army of Abolitionism: Ordinary Women in the Antislavery Movement* (1998)

Curtis D. Johnson, *Redeeming America: Evangelicals and the Road to Civil War* (1993)

Paul E. Johnson, *Sam Patch, the Famous Jumper* (2003)

Steven Mintz, *Moralists and Modernizers: America's Pre-Civil War Reformers* (1995)

Richard S. Newman, *The Transformation of American Abolitionism: Fighting Slavery in the Early Republic* (2002)

Harry L. Watson, *Liberty and Power: The Politics of Jacksonian America* (2006)

Sean Wilentz, *The Rise and Fall of American Democracy: Jefferson to Lincoln* (2005)

*For a more extensive list for further reading, go to* college.hmco.com/pic/norton8e.

# The Contested West *1815-1860*

*T*o eight-year-old Henry Clay Bruce, moving west was an adventure. In April 1844, the Virginia boy set out on a 1,500-mile, two-month trip to his new home in Missouri. Henry marveled at the newness of it all—beautiful natural terrain, impressive towns, different styles of dress. Nothing fascinated him more, though, than the steamboat ride from Louisville to St. Louis; it was like being on "a house floating on the water." As soon as he landed in Missouri, Henry was struck by just how much the West differed from the East. The farms lay at much greater distances from one another, and the countryside abounded with berries, wild fruits, game, and fish. But it was not all paradise. Rattlesnakes, wolves, and vicious hogs roamed the countryside, keeping Henry and his playmates from straying too far from home.

Only one thing matched the ferocity of the wildlife: Jack Perkinson, the man who owned the plantation on which Henry now lived. For Henry was a slave boy and had been moved there, along with his mother and siblings, because his master had decided to seek a new beginning in the West. Pettis Perkinson (Jack's brother and Henry's owner) and three other white Virginians had crammed their families, their slaves, and whatever belongings they could fit into three wagons—two for the slaves, one for the whites. Upon their arrival in Missouri, Pettis took up residence with Jack Perkinson, who—according to Henry—showed no compunction about yelling at and whipping his own slaves.

Henry's first year in Missouri was as carefree as a slave child's life could be. The boy fished, hunted (with dogs, not guns), and gathered the eggs of prairie chickens. But as he approached his ninth birthday, Henry was hired out, first to a brickmaker, then to the owner of a tobacco factory. He worked sunup to sundown, and when he failed to live up to his bosses' expectations, he was whipped.

◀ **Like Henry Clay Bruce, many emigrants in the 1840s traveled west by steamboat for part of their journey, making the rest of the trip on foot, horseback, wagon, canal boat, or—often—by some combination of means.** *(The Steamboat Napoleon, 1833 by Karl Bodmer [detail]; Joslyn Art Museum, Omaha, Nebraska)*

## CHRONOLOGY

1812 ■ Congress establishes General Land Office

1820 ■ Congress lowers price of public lands

1821 ■ William Becknell charts Santa Fe Trail
  ■ Mexico becomes independent nation

1823 ■ Mexico allows Stephen Austin to settle U.S. citizens in Mexico

1824 ■ Congressional General Survey Act empowers military to chart transportation routes
  ■ Jedediah Smith publicizes the South Pass to the Far West
  ■ Indian Office (later Bureau of Indian Affairs) established

1825–1832 ■ *Empresario* contracts signed for American settlement of Texas

1826 ■ Failed Fredonia rebellion in Texas

1830 ■ Indian Removal Act (see Chapter 10)

1832 ■ Black Hawk War

1834 ■ Cyrus McCormick patents mechanical reaper

1836 ■ Lone Star Republic founded
  ■ U.S. Army Corps of Topographical Engineers established

1840–1860 ■ 250,000 to 500,000 migrants travel overland to the Far West

1841 ■ Log Cabin Bill allows settlers to claim 160 acres of public land on credit

1844 ■ Presidential campaign features annexation of Texas

1845 ■ Democratic editor coins "manifest destiny"
  ■ Texas annexed by joint resolution of Congress (March 1) and becomes twenty-eighth state (December 29)

1846–1848 ■ War with Mexico (see Chapter 14)

1847 ■ Mormons settle in Great Salt Lake valley

1848 ■ Gold discovered in California

1849–50s ■ Farmers and prospectors stream into the Great Plains and Far West

1855 ■ Massacre of Indians at Ash Hollow triggers warfare between the Lakota and the United States

1857–1858 ■ Mormons and U.S. Army engage in armed conflict

1862 ■ Homestead Act allots 160 acres of free land to those who improve it

Meanwhile, Pettis Perkinson decided that he preferred life in Virginia and went home, only later sending for some of his slaves, including Henry, who returned "contrary to our will." A less rigorous work routine awaited the Perkinson slaves in Virginia, but that was small compensation for having to leave behind loved ones who stayed in Missouri.

Once again Pettis Perkinson soon grew weary of the tired, rocky soil in his part of Virginia, and he renewed his determination to seek opportunity in the West, this time in Mississippi, where he had a sister. But life on a cotton plantation suited neither Henry nor his master, who now decided—much to his slaves' joy—to give Missouri a second chance.

Henry's master remained restless and two years later set his eyes farther west, on Texas. Henry, now in his late teens, and his brothers announced that they would not go. Although livid, Pettis Perkinson apparently did not wish to contend with recalcitrant slaves and so abandoned his plans. After being hired out several more times, Henry became the foreman on Perkinson's Missouri farm, where he remained until escaping amid the turmoil of civil war to the free state of Kansas in 1864. More than twenty years after first leaving Virginia, Henry Clay Bruce found the opportunity and freedom that so many had sought when they first set out for the West.

In 1820 about 20 percent of the nation's population lived west of the Appalachian Mountains. By 1860 nearly 50 percent did. Most white people and free blacks moved west because they—or their heads of household—thought that better opportunities awaited them there. When easterners thought about the West, they generally envisioned enormous tracts of fertile and uncultivated land. Or, beginning in the late 1840s, they imagined the West as a place whose gold or silver mines would allow them to get rich quick. Some saw opportunities for lumbering or ranching, or for selling goods or services to farmers, miners, lumbermen, and cattlemen.

Many of those who headed west had no say in the matter. Men often made the decision without consulting their wives and children, and their slaves' wishes received even less consideration. Nor did western settlers give much, if any, thought to how their migration would affect the lives of the Indian peoples who already lived in the West—on lands they had occupied in some cases for generations and, in other cases, since being relocated there by the U.S. government.

The federal government's involvement in westward expansion extended far beyond removing Indians from lands coveted by white settlers. The government sponsored exploration, made laws regulating settlement and the establishment of territorial governments, surveyed and fixed prices on public lands, sold those lands, invested in transportation routes, and established a military presence to assist white settlers.

The Mexican government, too, played a role in Anglo-American settlement in the West—one it would later regret—when it encouraged immigration to its northern borderlands in the 1820s. From the United States came settlers who vied with the region's other inhabitants—Indians, Hispanics, and people of mixed heritage—for land and other natural resources. A decade later, Texas, one of Mexico's northern provinces, declared its independence and sought annexation by the United States. Thus began an era of heightened tensions—not only between the United States and Mexico, but also within the United States, as Texas's future became entangled with the thorny issue of slavery.

For some white Americans, mostly from the South, the ability to own slaves in the West signaled the epitome of their own freedom. For others, from both the North and the South, slavery's westward expansion frustrated dreams for a new beginning in a region free from what they saw as slavery's degrading influence on white labor. Northerners, in particular, often set their sights on the Oregon Territory, which they reached only after an arduous transcontinental journey. They believed the sacrifices would be outweighed by the rewards: agricultural prosperity in a land free from blacks, whether enslaved or free.

Even as the nation's main political parties tried to avoid the slavery issue, they took distinct stands on the role of westward expansion in the nation's economic development. Once the national spotlight trained on Texas, the nation's political leaders would find it increasingly difficult to disentangle the issues of westward expansion and slavery.

Human interactions in the West were characterized by both cooperation and conflict, but with each passing decade conflict—between expectations and reality, between people with different aspirations and world-views—increasingly defined daily life. By the mid-1840s, events in the West would, in turn, aggravate long-simmering discord between southern and northern interests in the national political realm.

- How did tensions in the modernizing North and the slave South influence western migration and settlement?
- How did public, private, and individual initiatives work together to shape the West's development?
- What motivated cooperation in the West, and what spurred conflict?

# THE WEST IN THE AMERICAN IMAGINATION

For historian Frederick Jackson Turner, writing in the late nineteenth century, it was the West, not the South or the North, that was distinctive. With its abundance of free land, the western frontier—what he saw as the "meeting point between savagery and civilization"—bred American democracy, shaped the American character, and made the United States exceptional among nations. Modern historians generally eschew the notion of American exceptionalism, stressing instead the deep and complex connections between the United States and the rest of the world. But although today's scholars also reject the racialist assumptions of Turner's definition of *frontier*, some do see continued value in the term when it is understood as a meeting place of different cultures. Others see the West as fundamentally a place, not a process, though they offer conflicting definitions of what delineates it.

For early-nineteenth-century Americans of European descent, the West would have included anything west of the Appalachian Mountains. But it was, first and foremost, a place that **Defining the West** represented the future—a place where they might seek economic and social betterment for themselves and their children. For many, that betterment would come through land ownership; the West seemed to have such an abundance of land that even the poor could hope to own a farm and achieve economic and political independence. Men who already owned land, like Pettis Perkinson, looked westward for cheaper, bigger, and more fertile landholdings. With the discovery of gold in California in 1848, the West became a place to strike it rich and then return home, where one might live in increased comfort or even opulence.

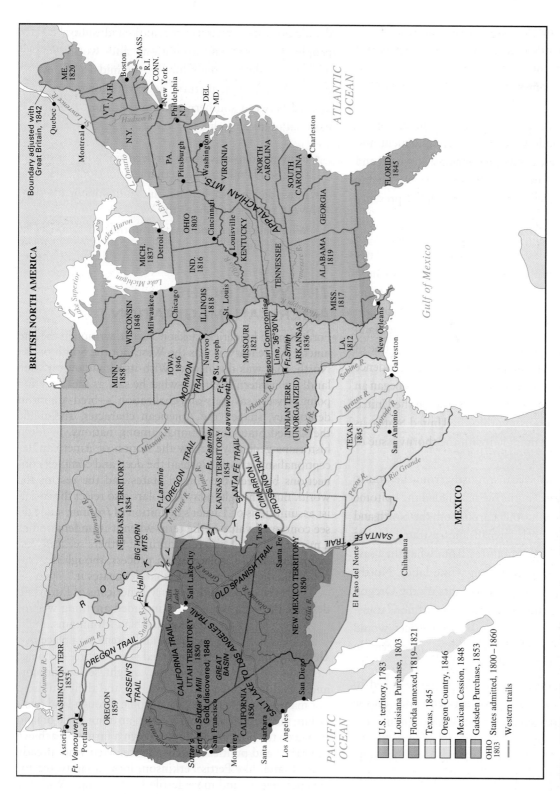

**Map 13.1 Westward Expansion, 1800–1860**

Through exploration, purchase, war, and treaty, the United States became a continental nation, stretching from the Atlantic to the Pacific.

Many people arrived in the West only under the threat of force. These included enslaved men, women, and children whose owners moved them, often against their will, as well as Indians removed from their eastern homelands by the U.S. military under the provisions of the Indian Removal Act of 1830.

To others, the very notion of the West would have been baffling. Emigrants from Mexico and Central or South America traveled north to get to what European-Americans called the West. The 25,000 or so Chinese who went to California during the 1850s traveled from the East. Many Indians simply considered it home. Other Indians and French Canadians journeyed southward to the West. All these people, much like European-Americans, arrived in the western portion of the North American continent because of a combination of factors that pushed and pulled them.

For European-Americans, Daniel Boone became the archetypal frontiersman, a man whose daring individualism opened the Eden-like West for virtuous and hard-working freedom lovers from the East and Europe.

### Frontier Literature

Through biographies published by John Filson during Boone's lifetime and by Timothy Flint after Boone's death, Boone became a familiar figure in American and European households. The mythical Boone lived in the wilderness, became "natural" himself, and shrank from society, feeling the need to move on as soon as he saw smoke billowing from a neighboring cabin. He single-handedly overpowered bears and Indians. Even as he took on the ways of the wilderness, according to legend, Boone became the pathfinder for civilization. As a friend wrote shortly after Boone's death, he "has been the instrument of opening the road to millions of the human family from the pressure of sterility and want, to a Land flowing with milk and honey." By borrowing the language of the Bible—the land of milk and honey referred to the Promised Land, the idyllic place that God promised to the beleaguered Israelites—Boone's friend suggested that Boone was a sort of Moses leading his people to a land of abundance.

Stories about Boone mythologized the West as much as they did the man. The Indian-fighting Boone, according to Flint's bestselling biography, had wrested for civilized society "the great west—the garden of the earth." Little matter that the real Boone regretted having killed any Indians and had often struggled to support his own family. When Boone became the heroic model for James Fenimore Cooper's *Leatherstocking Tales*—set on the frontier of western New York—he came to symbolize not only American adventure but also individualism and freedom.

With the invention of the steam press in the early 1830s, western adventure stories were cheap and widely read. Davy Crockett, another real-life figure turned into mythical hero, was featured in many of them. In real life, Crockett had first fought the Creeks under Andrew Jackson but later came to champion Indian rights, rebuking the Indian removal bill. After he lost his life defending the Alamo mission during Texas's fight for independence (1836), though, Crockett often appeared in stories that portrayed the West as violent, a place where one escaped from civilized society and instead fought Indians and Mexicans. But even in this version of the western myth, the American West symbolized what white Americans saw as their nation's core value: freedom.

Inspired in part by such literature, many easterners yearned to see the West and its native peoples, and artists hastened to accommodate them. Yet the images they produced often revealed more about white Americans' ideals than about the West itself. In these portrayals, the West was sometimes an untamed wilderness inhabited by savages (noble or otherwise), and sometimes a cultivated garden, a land of milk and honey where the Jeffersonian agrarian dream was realized.

### Western Art

The first Anglo-American artists to travel west were Samuel Seymour and Titian Ramsay Peale, whom the federal government hired to accompany explorer Stephen H. Long on his expedition to the Rocky Mountains in 1820. They pioneered an influential genre of art: facsimiles in government reports. Between 1840 and 1860, Congress published nearly sixty works on western exploration, featuring hundreds of lithographs and engravings of the region's plants, animals, and people. Some of these reports became bestsellers. The most popular was the twelve-volume Pacific Railway Survey (1855–1860), chronicling expeditions to explore four competing routes for a western railroad. The government distributed more than 53,000 copies of that single volume, helping easterners to visualize for themselves the continent's western reaches.

Although government reports often faithfully reproduced original paintings, they sometimes made telling alterations. When Richard Kern accompanied explorer James H. Simpson in 1849 to the Southwest, for example, he painted a Navajo man in a submissive pose. The reproduction of his painting for general distribution transformed the man's pose into a rebellious one. In other cases, the government reports transformed artists' depictions of Indian-occupied landscapes into empty terrain seemingly free for the taking.

Yet the original paintings and sketches did not necessarily offer an accurate view of the West either. Artists pictured their subjects through the lens of their own cultural

▲ In one of his most famous portraits, George Catlin painted Wi-Jun-Jon, an Assiniboine Indian, both before and after he had mingled with white men. In the "before" stance, the Indian is a dignified, peace-pipe-bearing warrior; in the "after" portrait, the "corrupted" Indian has abandoned dignity for vanity and his peace pipe for a cigar.

*(Smithsonian American Art Museum, Washington, DC /Art Resource, NY)*

assumptions, and commercial artists produced what they thought the public craved. When George Catlin traveled west in the early 1830s, he may have genuinely hoped to paint what he saw as the Indians' vanishing way of life. But he also aimed to attract a paying public of easterners to his exhibitions. Traveling and painting in the immediate aftermath of the Indian Removal Act of 1830, Catlin painted the West with a moral in mind. Indians came in two varieties—those who had preserved their original, almost noble qualities, characterized by freedom and moderation, and those who, after coming in contact with whites, had become "dissolute." Indians, he implied, would benefit from removal from the corrupting influence of white Americans.

Western artwork became familiar to Americans as facsimiles appeared in magazines and books, and even on banknotes. Such images nurtured easterners' curiosities and fantasies—and sometimes their itch to move westward.

But the western reality often clashed with promoters' promises, and disappointed settlers sometimes tried to clarify matters for future migrants. From Philadelphia in the 1850s came a song parodying the familiar call of "to the West":

### Countering the Myths

> At the west they told me there was wealth to be won,
> The forest to clear, was the work to be done;
> I tried it—couldn't do it—gave it up in despair,
> And just see if you'll ever again catch me there.
> The little snug farm I expected to buy,
> I quickly discovered was just all in my eye,
> I came back like a streak—you may go—but I'm bless'd
> If you'll ever again, sirs, catch me at the west.

Rebecca Burlend, an English immigrant who settled in Illinois, encountered hardships aplenty—intemperate weather, difficult working conditions, swindlers—and with her son wrote an autobiographical account, *A True Picture of Emigration* (1831), which alerted her countrymen to what awaited them in the American West. The Burlends had themselves been lured to Illinois by an Englishman's letters extolling "a land flowing with milk and honey." Burlend reckoned that he must have "gathered his honey rather from thorns than flowers." Her account did not seek to discourage emigration, but to substitute a realistic for a rosy description.

## EXPANSION AND RESISTANCE IN THE OLD NORTHWEST

Americans had always been highly mobile, but never as much as they became after the War of 1812 weakened Indian resistance and set off a flurry of transportation projects. In the 1820s and 1830s, settlers streamed into the Old Northwest and the Old Southwest. They traveled by foot, horseback, wagon, canal boat, steamboat, or—often—by some combination of means. Many people, like Pettis Perkinson and his slaves, moved several times, pulling up their stakes in search of better opportunities, and when opportunities failed to materialize, some returned home.

The Northwest Territory grew at phenomenal rates in the early nineteenth century. In the first federal census of 1790, the region had a white population that numbered just a few hundred people. By 1860 nearly 7 million people

**Map 13.2    Settlement in the Old Southwest and Old Northwest, 1820 and 1840**

Removal of Indians and a growing transportation network opened up land to white and black settlers in the regions known as the Old Southwest and the Old Northwest, as the U.S. population grew from 9.6 million in 1820 to 17.1 million in 1840.

called the region home. Between 1810 and 1830, the population of Ohio more than quadrupled, while Indiana and Illinois grew fourteenfold and thirteenfold, respectively. Michigan's population multiplied by fifty times in the thirty years between 1820 and 1850. Migration rather than birth rates accounted for most of this growth, and once in the Old Northwest, people did not stay put. By the 1840s, more people left Ohio than moved into it. Geographic mobility,

the search for more and better opportunities, and connections to the market economy came to define the region that became known as the Midwest following the acquisition of U.S. territory farther to the west. This region came to symbolize, for many northerners, the heart of American values: freedom and upward mobility, both of which could be achieved (for European immigrants and white Americans) through hard work and virtuous behavior.

The decision to move west—and then to move on again—was often difficult to make. Moving west meant leaving behind worn-out soil and

||||||||||||||||||||||||||||||||

**Deciding Where to Move**

settled areas where little land was available for purchase, but it also meant leaving behind family, friends, and communities. The trip itself promised to be arduous and expensive, as did the backbreaking labor of clearing new lands for cultivation. The West was a land of opportunity but also of uncertainty. What if the soil proved less fertile than anticipated? What if neighbors—white as well as Indian—proved unfriendly, or even worse? What if homesickness became simply unbearable?

Given all that settlers risked when moving west, they understandably tried to control as many variables as possible. Like Pettis Perkinson, people often relocated to communities where they had relatives or friends, and they often made the journey with people they knew from home. They sought out areas with climates similar to those they left behind. Massachusetts farmers headed to western New York or Ohio, Virginians and North Carolinians went to

Missouri, Georgians populated Mississippi and Texas, and Europeans—mostly Germans and Irish—headed to the Old Northwest in much larger numbers than to the Old Southwest. Migrants settled in ethnic communities or sought out people of similar religious values and affiliations. As a result, the Midwest was—in the words of two of its historians—"more like an ethnic and cultural checkerboard than the proverbial melting pot."

When westward-bound Americans fixed on particular destinations, their decisions rested in no small part on the status of slavery in those places. Some white southerners, tired of the undue social and political power wielded by the planter elite, sought homes in areas free from slavery—or at least where plantations did not dominate the landscape. Many others, though, went west to increase their chances of owning slaves, or of owning more slaves. White northerners mostly hoped to distance themselves from slavery, but rarely out of sympathy for slaves themselves. Rather, they, too, had grown to detest the economic and political power exerted by elite slaveowners. The thought of planters appropriating more lands farther west concerned them, as did the thought of black laborers'

▲ In 1834 Karl Bodmer painted a farm on the Illinois Prairie, depicting the more permanent, if still modest, structures that farmers built after the initial urgency to clear fields for cultivation had subsided. *(Joslyn Art Museum, Omaha, Nebraska, Gift of Enron Art Foundation)*

working those lands. Many northerners hoped to settle in areas free from slavery—and, better yet, free from *any* black people. In the 1850s, many midwestern states passed "black laws" prohibiting African Americans, free as well as enslaved, from living within their boundaries. (In the Far West, Oregon would do the same.) Ironically, many free blacks had themselves migrated west believing that the region would be freer from prejudice than the East.

Between 1815 and 1860, few western migrants settled on the Great Plains, a region reserved for Indians and closed to white settlement until the 1850s, and relatively few easterners risked the overland journey to California and Oregon before the completion of the transcontinental railroad in 1869. Although at first the Southwest seemed to hold the edge in attracting new settlers, the Midwest—with its better-developed transportation routes, its more democratic access to economic markets, its smaller African American population, its smaller and cheaper average landholding, and its climatic similarity to New England and northern Europe—proved considerably more attractive in the decades after 1820. The Midwest's thriving transportation hubs also made good first stops for western migrants, American and foreign-born, lacking cash to purchase land. They found work unloading canal boats, planting and harvesting wheat on nearby farms, grinding wheat into flour, or sawing trees into lumber—or, more often, they cobbled together a combination of these seasonal jobs. The South offered fewer such opportunities. With the Old Northwest's population growing at a much faster rate, white southerners became increasingly worried about congressional representation and laws regarding slavery.

In both the Midwest and the Southwest, the expansion of white settlement depended on the removal of the region's Indians. Even as the U.S.

### Indian Removal and Resistance

Army escorted Indians out of the Old Southwest, the federal government also arranged treaties in which northeastern Indian nations relinquished their land titles in exchange for lands west of the Mississippi River. Between 1829 and 1851, eighty-six treaties were signed between the U.S. government and northern Indian tribes.

Some northern Indians managed to evade removal, including the Miamis in Indiana, the Ottawas and Chippewas in the upper Midwest, and the Winnebagos in southern Wisconsin. In 1840, for example, chiefs of the Miamis had acceded to pressure to exchange 500,000 acres of land in Indiana for an equivalent number of acres in Indian Country. Under the terms of the treaty, their people had five years to move. When they failed to do so, federal

troops arrived to escort them west. But about half of the Miami nation managed to dodge the soldiers—and many of those who did make the trek to Indian Country later returned unauthorized. In Wisconsin, some Winnebagos similarly eluded removal or returned to Wisconsin after being escorted by soldiers to points west of the Mississippi.

The Sauks (or "Sacs") and Fox fared much less well. In a series of treaties between 1804 and 1830, their leaders exchanged their tribes' lands in

### Black Hawk War

northwestern Illinois and southwestern Wisconsin for lands across the Mississippi River in Iowa Territory. Black Hawk, a Sauk warrior who had sided with the British during the War of 1812, disputed the validity of the treaties and vowed his people would return to their ancestral lands. In 1832 he led a group of Sauk and Fox families to Illinois, causing panic among white settlers. The state's governor called up the militia, who were later joined in their pursuit of Black Hawk by militia units from surrounding states and territories, as well as by U.S. Army regular soldiers. Over the next several months, hundreds of Indians and dozens of whites died under often-gruesome circumstances in what is known as the Black Hawk War. As the Sauks and Fox tried to flee across the Mississippi River, they were fired on indiscriminately by American soldiers on steamboats and on land. Those men, women, and children who managed to survive the river crossing were met with gunfire on the western shore by Lakota (Sioux), their longtime enemies now allied with the Americans.

Black Hawk survived to surrender, and U.S. officials undertook to impress on him and the uprising's other leaders the futility of resistance. After being imprisoned, then sent to Washington, D.C., along a route meant to underscore the immense size and population of the United States, and then imprisoned again, the Indians were returned to their homes. The Black Hawk War marked the end of militant Indian uprisings in the Old Northwest, adding to the region's appeal to white settlers.

Land speculators, developers of "paper towns" (which existed on paper only), steamboat companies, and manufacturers of farming implements

### Selling the West

did their best to promote the Midwest as tranquil place of unbounded opportunity. Land proprietors emphasized the region's connections to eastern ways of life and markets. They knew that, when families uprooted themselves to relocate in the West, they did not—the mythical Daniel Boone and Davy Crockett aside—seek to escape civilization. When Michael D. Row, the proprietor of Rowsburg in northern Ohio, sought to sell town lots in 1835, he emphasized that Rowsburg was in

In his advertisements, Cyrus McCormick portrayed his reapers as making the West into a place of prosperity and leisure.

*(Wisconsin Historical Society)*

a "thickly settled" area, stood at the crossroads of public transportation leading in every direction, and had established mills and tanning yards.

Settlement in the West generally followed rather than preceded connections to national and international markets. Eastern farmers, seeking to escape tired soil or tenancy, sought fertile lands on which to grow commercial crops. Labor-saving devices, such as Cyrus McCormick's reaper (1834) and John Deere's steel plow (1837), made the West more alluring. McCormick, a Virginia inventor, patented a horse-drawn reaper that allowed two men to harvest the same number of acres of wheat that would previously have required between four and sixteen men, depending on the type of hand-held tool they wielded. Because the reaper's efficiency achieved its greatest payoffs on the prairies, where tracts of land were larger and flatter than in the Shenandoah valley, McCormick relocated his factory to Chicago in 1847 and began a dogged campaign to sell his reaper—which at $100 was an expensive investment for the average farmer—and, along with it, the West itself. Without John Deere's steel plow, which unlike wooden and iron plows could break through tough grass and roots, and did not require constant cleaning, "breaking the plains" might not have been possible at all.

Most white Americans who went west intended to farm. After locating a suitable land claim, they immediately

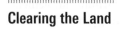

### Clearing the Land

constructed a rudimentary cabin if one did not already exist. Time did not permit more elaborate structures, for—contrary to McCormick reaper ads—few western settlers found plowed fields awaiting them. First they had to clear the land.

For those who settled in wooded areas, the quickest and easiest way to get crops in the ground was to girdle, or to cut deep notches with an ax around a tree's base, cutting off the flow of sap. A few weeks later, the trees would lose their leaves, which farmers burned for fertilizer. As soon as enough light came through, settlers would plant corn—a durable and nutritious crop. Eventually the dead trees would fall and could be chopped for firewood and fences, leaving stumps whose removal was a backbreaking task in itself. At the rate of five to ten acres a year, depending on a family's size, the average family needed ten years to fully clear a farm, assuming they did not move on earlier. Prairie land took less time. Throughout the 1850s, though, many farmers dismissed lands free of timber as the equivalent of deserts, unfit for cultivation.

Whereas farming attracted families, lumbering and mining appealed mostly to single young men. By the 1840s, the nation's timber industry was centered around the Great Lakes. As forests became depleted in the eastern United States and Canada, northeastern lumber companies and their laborers migrated to Wisconsin, Michigan, and Minnesota. Recently arrived Scandinavians and French Canadians also worked in the booming lumber industry, which provided construction materials for growing cities and wooden ties for expanding railroads. As the Great Lakes forests thinned, lumbermen moved on once again—some to the Gulf States' pine forests, some to Canada, and some to the Far West, where Mexicans in California and British in Canada had already established flourishing lumber industries. With the rapid growth of California's cities following the Gold Rush of 1849, the demand for timber soared, drawing midwestern lumbermen farther west.

The Midwest's own cities nurtured the settlement of the surrounding countryside. Steamboats turned river settlements like Louisville and Cincinnati into rapidly growing commercial centers, while Chicago, Detroit, and

Cleveland grew up on the banks of the Great Lakes. By the mid-nineteenth century, Chicago, with its railroads, stockyards, and grain elevators, was positioned to dominate the region's economy; western farmers transported their livestock and grain by rail to that city, where pigs became packed meat and grain became flour before being shipped farther east. The promise of future flour and future pigs gave rise to commodities markets. Some of the most sophisticated and speculative economic practices in the world took place in Chicago.

## THE FEDERAL GOVERNMENT AND WESTWARD EXPANSION

Few white Americans considered settling in the West before the region had been explored, surveyed, secured, and "civilized," by which they meant not only the removal of native populations but also the establishment of churches, businesses, and American legal structures. Although some individuals did head west in advance of European civilization, wide-scale settlement became possible only with the sponsorship of the federal government.

No figure better represents the mythical westerner than the mountain man: the loner who wandered the mountains, trapping beaver, living off the land, casting off all semblance of civilization, and daring to go where no white person had ever trod. Fur trappers were, in fact, among the first white Americans in the trans-Appalachian West, but in reality, their lives bore only faint resemblance to the myth. Although many had little contact with American society, they interacted regularly with the West's native peoples. Fur trappers lived among Indians, became multilingual, and often married Indian women, who also became their business partners. Indian women did the arduous work of transforming an animal carcass into a finished pelt, and they also helped smooth trade relations between their husbands and their own native communities. The children of such marriages—métis or mestizos (people of mixed Indian and European heritage)—often became involved in the fur trade themselves and added to the cultural complexity of the West.

The fur trade was an international business, with many pelts from deep in the American interior finding their way to Europe and to Asia. Until the 1820s, it was dominated by British companies, but American ventures prospered in the 1820s and 1830s. The American Fur Company made John Jacob Astor the wealthiest man in the United States. While Astor lived lavishly in his mansion in New York City, his business employed hundreds

### The Fur Trade

▲ Artist Alfred Jacob Miller portrayed a marriage *à la façon du pays* (in the custom of the country) in which an Indian woman is given in marriage by her father to a *métis* man at a Rocky Mountain *rendezvous* in 1837.

*(Courtesy of the Eiteljorg Museum of American Indians and Western Art, Indianapolis)*

of trappers and traders who lived and worked among native peoples in the Great Lakes and Pacific Northwest regions. From its base in Astoria on the Columbia River, just a few miles from the Pacific Ocean in present-day Oregon, the American Fur Company made millions by sending furs to China.

Even for the great majority of trappers who never made it to Astoria, the fur trade had an international dimension. Beginning in the 1820s, they came together annually for a "rendezvous"—a multiday gathering at which they traded fur for guns, tobacco, and beads that they could later exchange with Indians while also sharing stories and alcohol, and gambling. Modeled on similar Indian gatherings that had occurred for generations, the rendezvous brought together Americans, Indians, Mexicans, and people of mixed heritage from all over the West—from

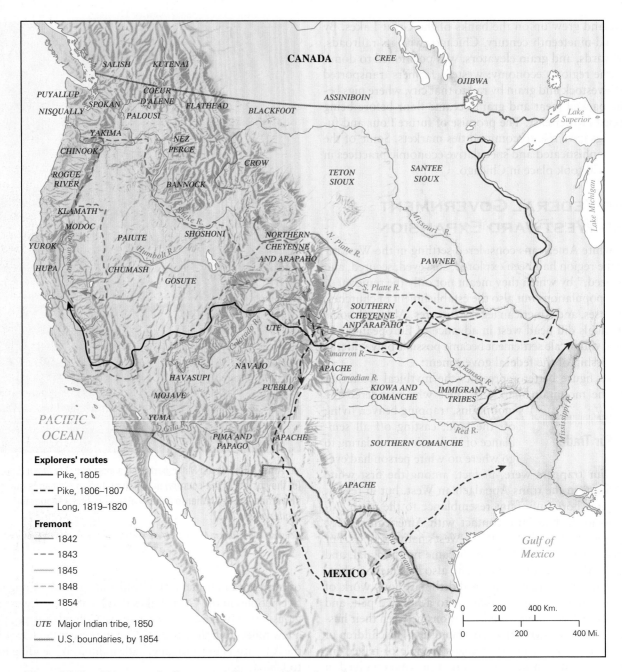

**Map 13.3   Western Indians and Routes of Exploration**

Although western explorers believed they were discovering new routes and places, Indians had long lived in most of the areas through which explorers traveled.   *(Robert Utley,* The Indian Frontier of the American West, 1846–1890, *University of New Mexico Press, 1984. p. 5. Reprinted by permission of the University of New Mexico Press.)*

as far north as Canada and as far south as Mexico. Rendezvous took place in remote mountain locations, but they were cosmopolitan affairs.

By the 1840s, the American fur trade was in decline. Beavers had been overhunted, and fashions had shifted, with silk supplanting beaver fur as the preferred material

for hats. The traders' legacy includes setting a pattern of resource extraction and depletion (and boom and bust); introducing native peoples to devastating diseases; and developing trails across the trans-Mississippi West.

A desire for quicker and safer routes for transporting furs and other goods to trading posts drove much early

## Gold in California

hen James Marshall discovered gold in Sutter's Mill, California, in January 1848, word spread quickly—and quite literally around the world. Within a year, tens of thousands of adventurers from other countries rushed to California, making it the most cosmopolitan place in North America, and perhaps the entire world.

In an era before the telegraph crossed the oceans, it is surprising how fast the news traveled. Mexicans heard of the gold strike first. Next, word spread to Chile, Peru, and throughout South America; then across the Pacific to Hawai'i, China, and Australia; and then to Europe—Ireland, France, and the German states. How did the news travel? Overland travelers brought the news south to Baja California and Sonora in Mexico. By spring 1849 some six thousand Mexicans were panning for gold around the newly established town of Sonora, California. Many of the Mexicans came north seasonally to seek gold, spreading news of California on every trip home.

Sailing ships brought news of California gold to Hawai'i. The newspaper *Honolulu Polynesian* announced it in the kingdom on June 24, 1848. "Honolulu has never before witnessed such an excitement as the gold fever has created," the *Polynesian* reported later that summer. Gold seekers and merchants sailed from Hawai'i to California, and their letters home recruited others to come. The constant traffic led to regular steamship service between Hawai'i and California as early as 1853.

A ship brought news of California gold discoveries to Valparaiso, Chile, in August 1848. More dramatically, a few weeks later, another sailing vessel landed with $2,500 in gold dust aboard. Although Chilean newspapers initially ignored the discovery, people in Chile's cities talked feverishly about gold. By November, newspapers were reporting rumors of overnight riches in California. Before year's end, two thousand Chileans had left for California, and many Chilean merchants opened branch stores in San Francisco.

Word of gold and California reached Australia in December 1848. Gold seekers quickly made travel arrangements, and by 1850 every ship in Sydney Harbour was destined for California. News had already reached China in mid-1848. A San Francisco merchant headed for the gold fields, Chum Ming, had written a cousin about his hopes for wealth. Four months later, the cousin arrived in San Francisco, with fellow villagers whom he had recruited. Widespread poverty and the allure of gold prompted many other Chinese to follow. By the mid-1850s, one in five gold miners was Chinese.

Californians, new and old, foreign and native-born, expressed amazement at the ethnic variety. One described it as "the most curious Babel of a place imaginable." In 1850 the new state of California had nearly 40 percent foreign-born inhabitants, the majority non-European. Through word of mouth, rumor, letters home, and newspaper reports, the discovery of gold in 1848 linked California to millions of ordinary people around the globe.

◀ This 1855 Frank Marryat drawing of a San Francisco saloon dramatizes the international nature of the California gold rush. Like theater performers, the patrons of the saloon dress their parts as Yankees, Mexicans, Asians, and South Americans.

*(© Collection of the New York Historical Society)*

## Transcontinental Exploration

exploration. William Becknell, an enterprising merchant, helped in 1821 to chart the Santa Fe Trail running between Missouri and Santa Fe, New Mexico, where it connected to the Chihuahua Trail running southward into Mexico, allowing American and Mexican merchants to develop a vibrant exchange of American manufactured goods for furs and other items. Fur trader Jedediah Smith rediscovered in 1824 the South Pass; this 20-mile break in the Rocky Mountains in present-day Wyoming had previously been known only to Native Americans and a handful of fur trappers from the Pacific Fur Company who had passed through in 1812. The South Pass became the route followed by most people headed overland to California and Oregon. Less well-known traders, trappers, missionaries, and gold seekers, often assisted by Native American guides, also discovered traveling routes throughout the West, and some—most famously, mountain man Kit Carson—aided government expeditions.

Lewis and Clark's Corps of Discovery was only the first of many federally sponsored expeditions to chart the trans-Mississippi West. These expeditions often had diplomatic goals, aiming to establish cordial relations with Indian groups with whom Americans might trade or enter military alliances. Some had scientific missions, charged with recording information about the region's native inhabitants, flora, and fauna. But they were always also commercial in purpose. Just as Lewis and Clark had hoped to find what proved to be an elusive Northwest Passage to the Pacific, so, too, did later explorers hope to locate land, water, and rail routes that would allow American businessmen and farmers to engage in national and international trade.

In 1805 the U.S. Army dispatched Zebulon Pike to find the source of the Mississippi and a navigable route west. Along the way, he was to collect information on natural resources and native peoples, and foster diplomatic relationships with Indian leaders whom he encountered. He was also to purchase land from Indians; before the Supreme Court ruled in *Johnson v. M'Intosh* (1823) that Indians did not own land but rather had only a "right of occupancy," government officials instructed Pike and other explorers to identify and purchase lands suitable for military garrisons.

Although Pike failed to identify the source of the Mississippi and had only limited success in cultivating relationships and purchasing land, he nonetheless gathered important information about the terrain he covered. Shortly after returning from present-day Minnesota, he set out for what are now Missouri, Nebraska, Kansas, and Colorado. After Pike and his men wandered into

Spanish territory to the south, military officials held Pike captive for several months in Mexico, inadvertently giving him a tour of areas that he might not have explored on his own. After his release, Pike wrote an account of his experiences that described a potential market in southwestern cities, as well as bountiful furs and precious metals. The province of Tejas (Texas), with its fertile soil and rich grasslands, enchanted him. At the same time, Pike dismissed the other northern provinces of Mexico, whose boundaries stretched to the northern borders of present-day Nevada and Utah, as unsuitable for human habitation. Although nomadic Indians might sustain themselves there, he explained, the region was unfit for cultivation by civilized people.

Stephen Long, another army explorer, similarly declared in 1820 that the region comprising modern-day Oklahoma, Kansas, and Nebraska was "the Great American Desert," incapable of cultivation. Until the 1850s, when a transcontinental railroad was planned, this "desert" was reserved for Indian settlement, and most army-sponsored exploration focused on other parts of the West.

In 1838 Congress established the U.S. Army Corps of Topographical Engineers to systematically explore the West in advance of widespread settlement. As a second lieutenant in that corps, John C. Frémont undertook three expeditions to the region between the upper Mississippi and Missouri rivers, the Rockies, the Great Basin, Oregon, and California. He helped survey the Oregon Trail. With the assistance of his wife, Jessie Benton Frémont, Frémont published bestselling accounts of his explorations, earning him the nickname "The Pathfinder" and paving the way for a political career. The Corps of Topographical Engineers' most significant contributions came in the 1850s with its surveying of possible routes for a transcontinental railroad.

The federal government spent millions publicizing the results of its explorations, much more than it allotted for exploration itself. Westward migrants often carried two books with them: the Bible and Frémont's account of his army explorations.

The army did more than explore the West. It also helped ready it for settlement. With the General Survey

## A Military Presence

Act of 1824, Congress empowered the military to chart transportation improvements deemed vital to the nation's military protection or commercial growth. In addition to working on federally funded projects, army engineers helped design state- and privately-sponsored roads, canals, and railroads, and its soldiers did the laborious work of clearing forests and laying roadbeds. A related bill, also

▲ Charles Koppel portrayed the Colorado Desert and Signal Mountain for the *Pacific Railway Reports* (1853). The desert appears vast and unlimited, and those who travel through it seem to be advancing into the unknown.

*(The Center for American History, The University of Texas at Austin)*

in 1824, authorized the army to help improve the Ohio and Mississippi rivers, and a later amendment did the same for the Missouri.

By the 1850s, 90 percent of the U.S. military was stationed west of the Mississippi River. When Indians refused to relinquish their lands, the army escorted them westward; when they inflicted harm on whites or their property, the army waged war. The army sometimes destroyed the crops and buildings of white squatters who refused to vacate lands they had settled without legal title. But, primarily, the army presence assisted overland migration. Army forts on the periphery of Indian Country intimidated Indians, defended settlers and migrants from Indian attacks, and supplied them with information and provisions. In theory, the army was also supposed to protect Indians by driving settlers off Indian lands and enforcing laws prohibiting the sale of alcohol to Indians. Yet the army's small size compared to the territory it regulated

made it virtually impossible to enforce such policies even when officers were disposed to do so.

The Office of Indian Affairs handled the government's other interactions with Indians, including the negotiation of treaties, the management of schools, and the oversight of trade. Created in 1824 as part of the War Department, the Indian Office cooperated with the military in removing Indians from lands that stood in the way of American expansion and in protecting those citizens who staked their future in the West. In 1849 the Indian Office became part of the newly established Department of the Interior, and it soon shifted its focus from removal to civilization, through a reservation system. Whereas some Indians accepted reservations as the best protection from white incursion, others rejected them, sometimes setting off deadly intratribal disagreements.

The federal government controlled vast tracts of land, procured either from the states' cessions of their western

### Public Lands

claims after the Revolution or through treaties with foreign powers, including Indian nations. The General Land Office, established in 1812 as part of the Treasury Department, handled the distribution of those lands. Its earliest policies, crafted with an eye toward raising revenue, divided western lands into 640-acre tracts to be sold at public auction at a minimum price of $2 an acre. These policies favored speculators over individual, cash-poor farmers. Speculators bought up millions of acres of land. Unable to afford federal lands, many settlers became squatters, prompting Congress in 1820 to lower the price of land to $1.25 per acre and to make available tracts as small as 80 acres. Twelve years later, it began selling 40 acre tracts. Yet it also demanded that the land be bought outright, and in a cash-poor society (particularly in the aftermath of the Panic of 1819), few would-be western settlers had enough cash to purchase a farm from the government. Because speculators sold land on credit, many small-time farmers bought from them instead, but at inflated prices.

Farmers pressed for a federal policy of preemption—that is, the right to settle on land without obtaining title, to improve it, and to buy it later at the minimum price ($1.25 an acre) established by law. Although some states offered their lands through preemption, and although Congress authorized preemption of federal lands in particular instances in the 1820s and 1830s, a more general preemption law did not come until 1841 with the so-called Log Cabin Bill, and even then, it applied to surveyed land only. The right of preemption extended to unsurveyed lands with the Homestead Act of 1862, which provided that land would be provided free to any U.S. citizen (or foreigner who had declared his or her intention of becoming a citizen), provided he or she resided on it for five years and improved it. Alternatively, settlers could buy the land outright at $1.25 an acre after six months of living on it, an arrangement that allowed them to use the land as collateral for loans with which to purchase additional land, farming supplies, or machinery. By the time of the Homestead Act, though, much of the land left in the federal domain was arid, and 160 acres was not always enough for an independent farm.

## THE SOUTHWESTERN BORDERLANDS

Along the southwestern border of the Louisiana Territory were vast provinces that fell under the domain not of the United States but of different national governments, first Spain and then—after 1821—the newly independent nation of Mexico. New Mexico, with its bustling commercial centers of Albuquerque and Santa Fe, remained under Mexican federal control until the United States conquered the territory during its War with Mexico. Texas, by contrast, had a much more attenuated relationship with the Mexican government; in 1824 it became an autonomous state, giving it substantially more political independence from federal authorities in Mexico City than New Mexico enjoyed. This situation would help foster Texas's struggle for national independence and then annexation to the United States, which in turn would return the divisive issue of slavery to the center of the American political agenda.

By the time Anglo-Americans became interested in the northern reaches of Mexico, slavery had existed in the Southwest for centuries. Yet

### Southwestern Slavery

slavery as practiced there by indigenous peoples—the Apaches, Comanches, Kiowas, Navajos, Utes, and Pueblos—and Spaniards differed from the chattel slavery of Africans and African Americans in the American South. Southwestern slavery was no less violent, but it centered on capturing women and children, who were then assimilated into their captors' communities, where they provided labor but also status. Captives also fostered economic and diplomatic exchanges with the communities from which they had been captured.

This system of "captives and cousins," as one scholar has put it, was built on racial mixing—a practice that was anathema to most white Americans. As white slaveholders from the Southeast pushed their way into Mexican territory during the 1820s and 1830s, they often justified their conquest in racial terms. Even the region's Hispanic settlers, they reasoned, had been rendered lazy and barbarous by racial intermixing and were thus destined to be supplanted, whether peaceably or otherwise.

When Mexico gained independence from Spain in 1821, the population of the province of New Mexico was

### The New Mexican Frontier

dominated by Hispanic peoples, who outnumbered the indigenous Pueblo peoples by three to one. There were 28,000 Hispanics, including people born in Spain and, especially, criollos, people born in New Spain to parents of Spanish descent. Whether Spanish, Indian, criollo, or mestizo, most New Mexicans engaged in irrigated agriculture. To the north of Santa Fe, they worked small plots of land, but to that settlement's south, larger farms and ranches predominated. Rancheros' wealth came from selling their wool and corn in distant markets, and from relying on laborers whom they did not need to pay: farm hands,

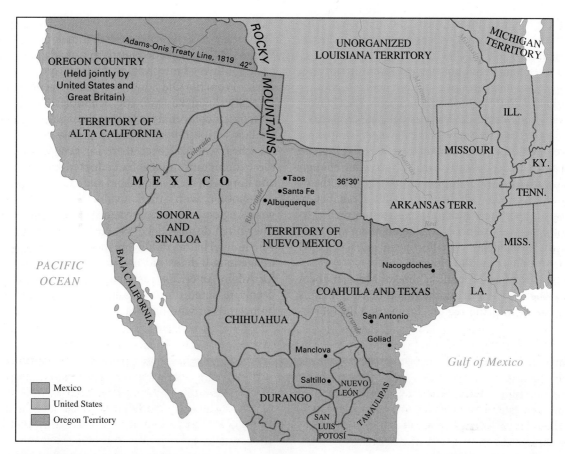

**Map 13.4    Mexico's Far North**
What is now considered the American Southwest was made up of the northern provinces of Mexico until the United States conquered the territory during the Mexican War (1846–1848). *(From Andres Resendez,* Changing National Identities and the Frontier: Texas and New Mexico, 1800–1850, *p. 19. Copyright © 2005 Cambridge University Press. Reprinted with the permission of Cambridge University Press.)*

often their own relatives, bound to the rancheros by debt. United by a threat from the province's raiding Indian tribes—the Apaches, Utes, Navajos, and sometimes the Comanches—Hispanics, Pueblos, and mestizos sometimes came together in common defense. But relations among Hispanics and the sedentary Pueblos were not always peaceful. Their numerical superiority allowed Hispanics to take over many of the Pueblos' villages and lands in the rich northern river valleys of an otherwise arid region.

The Santa Fe Trail caused a commercial explosion in New Mexico, doubling the value of imports in just two years. Whereas the Spanish had tried to keep foreigners out, the Mexican government offered enormous land grants to Anglo-American and French entrepreneurs, sometimes in partnership with the region's Hispanic residents, in the hope that they would develop the region's industry and agriculture, and strengthen commercial ties with the United States.

Although commercial ties did in fact strengthen, very few Americans settled permanently in New Mexico during the 1820s and 1830s. Most of the best lands had already been taken by Indians and Hispanics. And Americans in search of cheap, fertile land did not need to travel that far west; they could find what they were looking for in Texas.

That they would do so, however, was not evident at the time of Mexican independence. Unlike those in New Mexico, indigenous Indians remained the dominant group in

## The Texas Frontier

Texas in 1821, although the population also included immigrant Indians, Hispanics, Anglos, and mestizos. Of the thirty thousand indigenous people, most were Comanches, but there were also Jumanos, Coahuiltecans, Tonkawas, Karankawas, Apaches, Caddos, and Wichitas. To identify distinctive Indian groups, though, belies the intermarriage and cultural exchange among them. Indians married Indians from other nations, as well as Europeans and African Americans.

Cultural exchange did not prevent intermittent warfare, however, as Indian groups competed with one another for the region's resources. Mounted on horses, the Comanches hunted bison or stole horses, livestock, and crops from their enemies, among whom were the Pawnees, Arapahos, and Cheyennes. Other, smaller Indian groups, such as the Wichitas and Caddos, mostly farmed, growing enough corn, beans, squash, and pumpkin not only to feed themselves but also to trade with the more mobile Comanches. When crops failed, these Indian farmers often turned to bison hunting as well, sometimes bringing them into conflict with the Comanches. But European diseases killed many more Indians than did violence.

Tensions increased around the time of Mexican independence, when the first of another ten thousand Indians began migrating into the region. From the Old Northwest came Shawnees and Kickapoos—former members of Tecumseh's confederacy—who after their defeat during the War of 1812 had headed north to Canada before heading back southward into Kansas, Indian Territory, and then Texas. From the Old Southwest came Cherokees, Creeks, Choctaws, Chickasaws, and Seminoles. As these Indian newcomers competed for land and animals, they came into conflict with established Indian groups, such as the Comanches, who had been there for generations. Many of these immigrant Indians had adopted European clothing and European ideas about land and race. They saw land as a commodity with a market value. Some had intermarried with Anglos, and some owned African American slaves. They often dismissed as "savage" the indigenous Indians who hunted buffalo and wore their skins. But contempt for indigenous Indians did not necessarily mean an affinity for Anglo-Americans, as many of the immigrant Indians deeply resented those who had evicted them from their homelands or who had waged war on them.

▲ This depiction of San Antonio residents going to a ball, circa 1848, represents the lively cultural life in early Texas society. *(Daughters of the Republic of Texas Library)*

Hispanic peoples had been in Texas since the 1500s, establishing missions and presidios, but by 1820 they numbered only five thousand. Most

**Tejanos**

raised livestock on ranches, while others made their living from trading with Indians. Because they were so distant from the Spanish colonial capital in Mexico City, they formed a distinctive identity, seeing themselves as Tejanos (or Texans) rather than as Spaniards. Many intermarried with Indians.

In the years after the War of 1812, Anglo-Americans began entering Texas, where they sought furs, silver, or adventure. They traded manufactured goods—such as guns, ammunition, and kettles—for animal hides, horses, and mules. Although some Anglos settled in Texas, often among Indians, many more Anglos simply traveled along the Santa Fe and Chihuahua trails without settling. These Anglo newcomers largely supplanted the Tejanos as the Indians' trading partners, and the economic fortunes of the region's indigenous and immigrant tribes became increasingly oriented toward the United States and, in particular, the New Orleans market.

In the 1820s, Americans began settling in Texas under an *empresario* system. The first arrangement was made

**American Empresarios**

by Moses Austin, a miner and trader from Missouri, who approached Spanish authorities in Mexico City in January 1821 with a plan to settle the area. The Spanish were interested because they thought of Texas as a buffer between hostile Indians and the United States, and they wanted to see it populated. But they also wanted the newcomers to be assimilated, so they gave Austin an enormous land grant of approximately 200,000 acres along the Brazos River in exchange for his promise to bring three hundred Catholic families—and no slaves—with him. Before Austin could act, though, he died, and Mexico won its independence from Spain in September 1821.

Austin's son, Stephen, took up his father's scheme and pressed the new Mexican government to honor the grant, which it did in 1823, provided that the younger Austin give up his American citizenship and become a Mexican national. By 1825 Stephen Austin had brought in three hundred families (two thousand white people) and, despite the promise of no slaves, four hundred "contract laborers" of African descent. With contracts that ran for ninety-nine years, these African Americans were slaves by another name. Still, Austin's success at luring settlers to Texas encouraged the Mexican government to sign three more contracts granting Austin land in exchange for his bringing nine hundred additional families.

Generally satisfied with the Austin experiment, in 1824 Mexico passed a Colonization Law providing land and tax incentives to future foreign settlers and leaving the details of colonization up to the individual Mexican states. Coahuila y Texas specified that the head of a family could obtain as much as 4,428 acres of grazing land or 177 acres of farming land. The land was cheap, and—unlike land in the United States—could be paid for in installments over six years, with no money due until the fourth year. To be eligible, foreigners had to be upstanding Christians with "good habits," and they had to establish permanent residency. Eager for these new settlers to assimilate into Mexican society, the Coahuila y Texas government provided additional land incentives to those settlers who married Mexican women.

Most U.S. citizens who settled in Mexico did so under the auspices of an *empresario*, or immigration agent, who took responsibility for selecting "moral" colonists, distributing lands, and enforcing regulations. In exchange, he received nearly 25,000 acres of grazing land and 1,000 acres of farming land for every hundred families that he settled. Between 1825 and 1832, approximately twenty-four *empresario* contracts (seventeen of which went to Anglo-Americans) had been signed, with the *empresarios* agreeing to bring eight thousand families total. The land grants were so vast that together they covered almost all of present-day Texas.

During the 1820s, Anglo-Americans emigrated, with their slaves, to Texas, motivated by a combination of push and pull factors. Some were pushed from the United States in large part by the hard times following the Panic of 1819; at the same time, they were drawn by cheap land and, especially, generous terms of credit. Despite Mexican efforts to encourage assimilation with Mexicans of Spanish origin living in Texas, these Americans tended to settle in separate communities and to interact little with the Tejanos. Even more troubling to the Mexican government, the Anglo-Americans outnumbered the Tejanos two to one. Authorities worried that the transplanted Americans would try to make Texas part of the United States.

In 1826 their fears seemed to materialize when an *empresario* named Haden Edwards called for an independent Texas, which he called the

**Texas Politics**

"Fredonia Republic." Other *empresarios*, reasoning that they had more to gain than to lose from peaceful relations with the Mexican government, resisted Edwards's secessionist movement. Austin even sent militia to help put down the rebellion. Although the Fredonia revolt failed, Mexican authorities dreaded what it might foreshadow.

The answer to the secessionist threat, Mexican authorities thought, was to weaken the American presence in Texas. In 1830 they terminated legal immigration from the United States while simultaneously encouraging immigration from Europe and other parts of Mexico as a way of diluting the American influence. They also prohibited American slaves from entering Texas, a provision that brought Texas in line with the rest of Mexico—where slavery had been outlawed the previous year—and that was also meant to repel American slaveholders. Yet these laws did little to discourage Americans and their slaves from coming; soon they controlled most of the Texas coastline and its border with the United States. Mexican authorities repealed the anti-immigration law in 1833, reasoning that it discouraged upstanding settlers but did nothing to stem the influx of those whom they considered undesirable. By 1835 the population of Texas was nearly thirty thousand, with Americans outnumbering Tejanos seven to one.

White Texans divided into two main factions. There were those, like Stephen Austin, who favored staying in Mexico but demanding more autonomy, the legalization of slavery, and free trade with the United States. Others pushed for Texas to secede from Mexico and asked to be annexed to the United States. In 1835 the secessionists overtook a Mexican military installation charged with collecting taxes at Galveston Bay. Austin advocated a peaceful resolution to the crisis, but Mexican authorities nonetheless considered him suspicious and jailed him for eighteen months, an act that helped convert him to the cause of independence. But it would be Sam Houston and Davy Crockett—newly arrived Americans—who would lead the movement.

With discontent over Texas increasing throughout Mexico, Mexican president General Santa Anna declared himself dictator and marched his army toward Texas. Fearing that Santa Anna would free their slaves, and citing similarities between their own cause and that of the American colonies in the 1770s, Texans staged an armed rebellion. After initial defeats at the Alamo mission in San Antonio and at Goliad in March 1836, the Texans easily won the conflict by the end of the year. They declared themselves the Lone Star Republic and elected Sam Houston as president. The Texas constitution legalized slavery and banned free blacks from living within Texas.

### The Lone Star Republic

Texas then faced the challenge of nation building, which to its leaders involved Indian removal. When the Indians refused to leave, Mirabeau Lamar, the nation's second president, mobilized the Texas Rangers—mounted

▲ Like George Allen, many Texas settlers relied on slave labor to work their fields and maintain their households. *(The Center for American History, The University of Texas at Austin)*

non-uniformed militia—to drive them out through terror. Sanctioned by the Texas government, but sometimes acting on their own, the Rangers raided Indian villages, where they robbed, raped, and murdered. Although some Texas officials tried to negotiate with the Indians and Tejanos, it was what one historian has called "ethnic cleansing" that cleared the land of its native settlers to make room for white Americans and their African American slaves.

## MIGRATION TO THE FAR WEST

In the following decade, as Texas's future remained uncertain, more and more Americans took the gamble of a lifetime and moved to the Far West, even though California and Utah were part of Mexico. Although some sought religious freedom or to convert others to Christianity, most were looking for fertile farmland.

Catholic missionaries—Americans, Europeans, and converted Indians—maintained a strong presence in the Far West even after a Mexican law secularized the California missions in 1833, removing them from ecclesiastical control and using them primarily to organize Indian labor. The missionaries ministered to Catholic immigrants, worked—with some success—to convert Indians, and encouraged specifically Roman Catholic colonies. Missionaries founded schools and colleges, introduced medical services, and even aided in railroad explorations.

**Western Missionaries**

In the Pacific Northwest, Catholics vied directly with Protestant missionaries for Indian souls. Although evangelicals focused on the Midwest, a few sought to bring Christianity to the Indians of the Far West. Under the auspices of the American Board of Commissioners for Foreign Missions, two missionary couples—generally credited as being the first white migrants along the Oregon Trail—traveled to the Pacific Northwest in 1836. Narcissa and Marcus Whitman built a meetinghouse for Cayuse Indians in Waiilatpu, near present-day Walla Walla, Washington, while Eliza and Henry Spalding worked to convert the Nez Percé at Lapwai, in what is now Idaho. With their air of cultural superiority, the Whitmans did little to endear themselves to the Cayuses, none of whom converted to Christianity. The Whitmans turned their efforts instead toward the ever-increasing stream of white migrants flowing into Oregon beginning in the 1840s.

The arrival of these migrants escalated tensions with the Cayuses, and when a devastating measles epidemic struck in 1847, the Cayuses saw it as a calculated assault on their people. They retaliated by murdering the Whitmans and twelve other missionaries. After the Whitmans'

violent deaths, the Spaldings abandoned their own, more successful mission; blamed Catholics for inciting the massacre; and became farmers in Oregon, not returning to Lapwai for another fifteen years.

The Mormons, who had been persecuted in Missouri and Illinois, went west to seek a religious sanctuary. In 1847 Brigham Young led them to their "Promised Land" in the Great Salt Lake valley, still under Mexican control but soon to become part of the unorganized U.S. territory of Utah. As non-Mormons began to settle in Utah, Brigham Young worked to dilute their influence by attracting new Mormon settlers to what he called the state of Deseret. In 1849 Young and his associates set up the Perpetual Emigration Fund, which sponsored "handcart companies" of poor migrants, particularly from Europe, who put all their belongings in small handcarts that they pushed to Utah.

**Mormons**

Although Mormons prospered from providing services, such as ferries, and supplies to tens of thousands of California-bound settlers and miners who passed by their settlements, Young discouraged "gentiles" (his term for non-Mormons) from settling in Deseret and advocated boycotts of gentile businesses. When in 1852 the Mormons openly sanctioned polygamy, which some of its followers had practiced for more than a decade, animosity toward them increased throughout the nation. After some young Mormons vandalized federal offices in Utah, President James Buchanan—hoping to divert Americans' attention from the increasingly divisive issue of slavery—dispatched 2,500 federal troops in June 1857 to suppress an alleged Mormon rebellion.

Anxious over their own safety and eager to maintain peaceful relations with neighboring Indians, a group of Mormons joined some Paiutes in attacking a passing wagon train of non-Mormon migrants from Arkansas and Missouri. Approximately 120 men, women, and children died in the so-called Mountain Meadows Massacre in August 1857. In the next two years, the U.S. Army and the Mormons engaged in armed conflict, resulting in much property destruction but no fatalities. As these events indicate, western violence often emerged from complex interactions and alliances which cannot be understood as simply pitting natives against newcomers.

Not all encounters between natives and newcomers were violent. In the twenty years after 1840, between 250,000 and 500,000 people, many of them children, walked across much of the continent on foot, a trek that took seven months on average. Although they traveled armed

**Oregon and California Trails**

for conflict, most of their encounters with Indians were peaceful, if tense.

Overlanders began their journeys at one of the so-called jumping-off points—towns such as Independence, St. Joseph, and Westport Landing—along the Missouri River, where they bought supplies for the 2,000-mile trip still ahead of them. After cramming supplies into wagons already overflowing with household possessions, they set out either in organized wagon trains or on their own. While miners frequently traveled alone or in groups of fortune-seeking young men, farmers—including many women migrating only at their husbands' insistence—often traveled with their relatives, neighbors, church members, and other acquaintances.

They timed their departures to be late enough that they could find forage grass for their oxen and livestock, but not so late that they would encounter the treacherous snows that came early to the Rockies and the Sierra Nevada. Not all were successful. In 1846–1847 the Donner Party took a wrong turn, got caught in a blizzard, and resorted to cannibalism. More fortunate overland migrants trudged alongside their wagons, beginning their days well before dawn, pausing only for a short midday break, and walking until late afternoon. They covered on average 15 miles a day, in weather ranging from freezing cold to blistering heat. In wagon trains composed of families, men generally tended livestock during the day, while women—after an energy-draining day on the trail—set up camp, prepared meals, and tended small children. Trail life was exhausting, both physically and emotionally. Overlanders worried about Indian attack, getting lost, running out of provisions or water, and losing loved ones, who would have to be buried along the trail, in graves never again to be visited. But for most adults, trail life did not prove particularly dangerous, with Indian attacks rare and death rates approximating those of society at large. Children, though, had a greater risk than adults of being crushed by wagon wheels or drowning during river crossings.

Indians were usually peaceful, if cautious. Particularly during the trails' early days, Indians provided migrants with food and information, or they ferried them across rivers; in exchange, migrants offered wool blankets, knives, metal pots, tobacco, ornamental beads, and other items in short supply in Indian societies. When exchanges went bad—when one of the parties misunderstood the other's cultural practices or tried to swindle the other—relationships grew tense, not just between the particular persons involved, but between Indians and migrants more generally. Indians grew suspicious of all white people, just as migrants failed to distinguish different native bands or tribes.

A persistent aggravation among migrants was the theft of their livestock, which they tended to blame on Indians even though white thieves stole livestock, too. Indians who took livestock often did so when whites failed to offer gifts in exchange for grazing rights. One such incident that resulted in human bloodshed, the so-called Mormon Cow Incident (or the Grattan Massacre), forever altered relationships along the Oregon Trail.

In August 1854, a Lakota in present-day Wyoming slaughtered a cow that had strayed from a nearby Mor-

This rare stereocard shows an ▶ emigrant train, including two women and possibly a child, dwarfed by the natural landscape in Strawberry Valley, Califonia, in the 1860s.

*(Library of Congress)*

mon camp. When Lakota leaders offered compensation for the cow, U.S. Army Lieutenant John Grattan, intent on making an example of the incident, refused the offer. Tempers flared, Grattan ordered his men to shoot, and after a Lakota chief fell dead, the Indians returned the fire, killing Grattan and all twenty-nine of his men. In retaliation, the following year General William Harney led six hundred soldiers to a village near Ash Hollow, where migrants and Indians had traded peaceably for many years. When Indian leaders refused to surrender any of their people to Harney, the general ordered his men to fire. Thirty minutes later, eighty-seven Indians lay dead, and seventy women and children had been taken prisoner. The event disrupted peaceful exchange along the trail and laid the groundwork for nearly two decades of warfare between the Lakotas and the U.S. Army.

Even as the U.S. Army became embroiled in armed conflict with the Lakotas, the Indian Office worked to negotiate treaties aimed to keep Indians—and their intertribal conflicts—from interfering with western migration and commerce. The Fort Laramie Treaty of 1851 (or the Horse Creek Council Treaty) was signed by the United States and eight northern

## Indian Treaties

Plains tribes—the Lakotas, Cheyennes, Arapahos, Crows, Assiniboines, Gros-Ventres, Mandans, and Arrickaras—who occupied the Platte River valley through which the three great overland routes westward—the Oregon, California, and Mormon Trails—all passed. Two years later, in 1853, the United States signed a treaty with three southwestern nations, the Comanches, Kiowas, and Apaches, who lived in the vicinity of the Sante Fe Trail. Under the terms of both treaties, the Indians agreed to maintain peace among themselves, to recognize government-delineated tribal boundaries, to allow the United States to construct roads and forts within those boundaries, to refrain from depredations against western migrants, and to issue restitution for any depredations nonetheless committed. In return, they would receive annual allotments from the U.S. government for ten years, to be paid with provisions, domestic animals, and agricultural implements. These allotments could be renewed for another five years at the discretion of the president of the United States.

But these treaties often meant different things to their Indian signatories than to the U.S. officials who brokered them. Contrary to U.S. expectations, Indian chiefs did not believe such treaties to be perpetually binding. Government officials, meanwhile, promised allotments but did little to ensure their timely arrival, often leaving Indians starving and freezing as they waited. The treaties did not mark the end of intratribal warfare, nor did they fully secure the safety of overlanders. But they did represent the U.S. government's continued

◀ Established in 1834, Fort Laramie—pictured here three years later by Alfred Jacob Miller—served as a fur-trading site, where Indians and trappers of European or mixed heritage came together not only to exchange goods but also to socialize. In 1849, as interactions between Indians and overland migrants to Oregon grew increasingly tense, the U.S. Army took over the fort, now designed to protect overland emigrants. Located in eastern Wyoming, the fort stood at the beginning of the Oregon Trail.

*(The Walters Art Museum, Baltimore)*

effort to promote expansion and to protect those citizens who caught the western fever.

Armed conflict along the trails took relatively few lives compared to cholera, smallpox, and other maladies. The trails' jumping-off points, where migrants camped in close quarters while preparing for their journeys, bred disease, which migrants carried with them, inadvertently infecting Indians with whom they traded. Fearful of infection, Indians and migrants increasingly shied away from trading relationships.

### Ecological Consequences of Cultural Contact

The disappearance of the buffalo (American bison) from the trails' environs further inflamed tensions. The buffalo not only provided protein to Plains Indians; they also held great spiritual significance. Many Native Americans blamed the migrants for the buffalo's disappearance, even though most overlanders never laid eyes on a buffalo. By the time the overland migration reached its peak in the late 1840s and 1850s, the herds had already been overhunted, in part by Native Americans eager to trade their hides. As traffic picked up on the trail, the surviving buffalo scattered to areas where the grass was safe from the voracious appetites, and trampling feet, of the overlanders' livestock. But on those rare occasions when wagon trains did stumble upon bison herds, men rushed to live out their frontier fantasies—nurtured by the literature they had read—and shot the animals; buffalo chases also provided diversions from the drudgery and anxiety of the trail. Overlanders hunted other animals for sport, too, leaving behind rotting carcasses of antelopes, wolves, bears, and birds—animals that held spiritual significance for many Native Americans.

Overland migrants also caused prairie fires. Indians had long used fire to clear farm land,

to stimulate the growth of grasslands, and to create barren zones that would discourage bison from roaming into a rival nation's territory. But now emigrants—more accustomed to cooking over stoves than over open fires—often started fires that got out of control and swept across the prairies, killing animals and the vegetation on which they survived. On rarer occasions, Indians started fires in the hope of capturing the migrants' fleeing livestock. Stories about intentionally lit fires were more prevalent than the events themselves, but they, too, contributed to increasing hostility among Indians and overlanders.

Nowhere did migrants intrude on Indian life more deeply than near the gold strikes in California. In January 1848, John Wilson Marshall discovered gold in a shallow tributary to the American River near present-day Sacramento, California. During the next year, tens of thousands of "forty-niners" rushed to California, where they practiced what is called placer mining, panning and dredging for gold in the hope of instant riches.

### Gold Rush

And some did indeed make fortunes. Peter Brown, a black man from Ste. Genevieve, Missouri, wrote his wife in 1851 that "California is the best country in the world to make money. It is also the best place for black folks on

The vibrant trade in buffalo hides ▶ prompted both Indians and whites to over hunt the American bison, leading to near extinction for the animal by the latter part of the nineteenth century. *(Library of Congress)*

the globe." He had earned $300 in two months. Most forty-niners, however, never found enough gold to pay their expenses. "The stories you hear frequently in the States," one gold seeker wrote home, "are the most extravagant lies imaginable—the mines are a humbug." With their dreams dashed—and too poor or embarrassed to return home—many forty-niners took wage-paying jobs with large mining companies that used dangerous machinery to cut deep into the earth's surface to reach mineral veins.

The discovery of gold forever changed the face of California. As a remote Mexican province, California had a chain of small settlements surrounded by military forts (presidios) and missions, and it was inhabited mostly by Indians, along with a small number of Mexican rancheros, who raised cattle and sheep on enormous landholdings worked by coerced Indian laborers. With the arrival of forty-niners, who did not have time to grow their own food, came the great California agricultural boom. Wheat became the preferred crop; it required minimal investment, was easily planted, and offered a quick return at the end of a relatively short growing season. In contrast to the Midwest and Oregon, where family farms were the basic unit of production, in California large-scale wheat farming relied largely on bonded Indian laborers. Even as California agriculture thrived overall, the immediate vicinity of mines became barren, when hydraulic mining washed away the surface soil to expose buried lodes.

Mining areas experienced a commercial and industrial boom, as enterprising merchants rushed to supply, feed, and clothe the new settlers.

### Mining Settlements

Among them was Levi Strauss, a German Jewish immigrant, whose tough mining pants found a ready market among the prospectors. Because men greatly outnumbered women, women's skills (and company) were in great demand. Even as men set up all-male households and performed tasks that bent prevailing notions of gender propriety, women received high fees for cooking, laundering, and sewing. Women also ran boarding houses, hotels, and brothels.

Cities sprang up. In 1848 San Francisco had been a small mission settlement of about 1,000 Mexicans, Anglos, soldiers, friars, and Indians. With the gold rush, it became an instant city, ballooning to 35,000 people in 1850. It was the West Coast gateway to the interior, and ships bringing people and supplies continuously jammed the harbor. A French visitor in that year wrote, "At San Francisco, where fifteen months ago one found only a half-dozen large cabins, one finds today a stock exchange, a theater, churches of all Christian cults, and a large number of quite beautiful homes."

Yet as the Anglo-American, European, Hispanic, Asian, and African American populations swelled, the Indian population experienced devastation. Although California was admitted into the Union as a free state in 1850, its legislature soon passed "An Act for the Government and Protection of Indians" that essentially legalized the enslavement of Indians. The practice of using enslaved Indians in the California mines between 1849 and 1851 ended only when newly arrived miners brutally attacked the Indian workers, believing they degraded white labor and gave an unfair advantage to established miners. Those slaves who survived the violence were sent to work instead as field workers and house servants. Between 1821 and 1860, the Indian population of California fell from 200,000 to 30,000, as Indians died from disease, starvation, and violence. Because masters separated male and female workers, even Indians who survived failed to reproduce in large numbers.

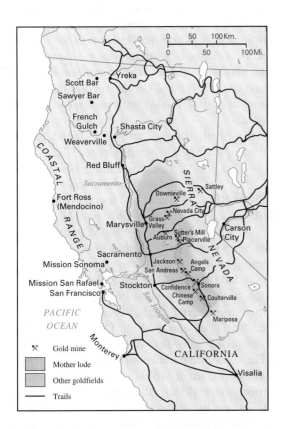

### Map 13.5   The California Gold Rush

Gold was discovered at Sutter's Mill in 1848, sparking the California gold rush that took place mostly along the western foothills of the Sierra Nevada mountains. *(Warren A. Beck and Ynez D. Haase,* Historical Atlas of California, *University of Oklahoma Press, 1974, map 50, p. 407. Copyright © 1974 by the University of Oklahoma Press. Reprinted by permission of the University of Oklahoma Press.)*

# THE POLITICS OF TERRITORIAL EXPANSION

With Americans moving west in numbers that would shift the locus of political power, Democratic and Whig politicians did their best to keep the slavery issue out of the politics of territorial expansion. But they could not. Westward expansion was central to Democratic ideology, which saw the West's fertile and abundant lands as essential for creating a society in which white men could establish independent livelihoods and receive equal rights, freed from the undue influence of established slaveholders or urban elites. Whigs were more suspicious of rapid westward expansion, though they welcomed the commercial opportunities it might bring. Instead, they pushed harder for industrial and commercial development within the nation's current boundaries.

The Texas issue, however, made it impossible for politicians to disentangle westward expansion and slavery. Soon after establishing the Lone Star Republic, Sam Houston approached American authorities to propose annexation as a state. But a new slave state would upset the balance of slave and free states in the Senate which had been maintained since before the time of the Missouri Compromise. Neither the Whigs nor the Democrats, wary of causing sectional divisions within their ranks, were inclined to confront the issue. In the 1830s, Democratic presidents Andrew Jackson and Martin Van Buren—one a strong proponent of slavery, the other a mild opponent—sidestepped the issue. But by the mid-1840s—with cotton cultivation expanding rapidly—some Democratic politicians began to equate the annexation of Texas with the nation's manifest destiny.

The belief that American expansion westward and southward was inevitable, just, and divinely ordained

**Manifest Destiny** dated to the nation's founding but was first labeled "manifest destiny" in 1845, by John L. O'Sullivan, editor of the *United States Magazine and Democratic Review*. O'Sullivan claimed that Texas annexation would be "the fulfillment of our manifest destiny to overspread the continent allotted by Providence for the free development of our yearly multiplying millions." The nation's destiny, he and others believed, was to encompass the continent. Manifest destiny implied that Americans had a God-given right, perhaps even an obligation, to expand their republican and Christian institutions to less fortunate and less civilized peoples. Manifest destiny motivated few Americans to pack their wagons and head westward. It did, however, provide a political rationale for territorial expansion.

Implicit in the idea of manifest destiny was the belief that American Indians and Hispanics, much like people of African descent, were inferior peoples best controlled or conquered. White racial theorists believed that, unlike white people, pure-blooded Indians and blacks were not capable of self-improvement. Nor, according to these racial theorists, were Hispanics, because intermarriage with Indians had left them incapable of improvement. Lansford Hastings, an Ohio native who ventured west and authored *The Emigrants' Guide to Oregon and California* (1845) noted that a *Californio* (a Mexican living in California) was "scarcely a visible grade, in the scale of intelligence, above the barbarous tribes by whom he is surrounded." Hastings hoped that, if enough Anglo-Saxons migrated to California, they could conquer the Mexicans with sheer numbers. And if they did so, they could congratulate themselves for carrying out God's will.

In June 1846, less patient expansionists, including John C. Frémont, staged an armed rebellion against Mexican authorities and declared California an independent republic. Because the U.S. military soon conquered California in its War with Mexico, the "Bear Flag Rebellion"—so named for the symbol on the revolutionaries' flag—was short-lived but further inflamed racial tensions in California.

To the north, Britain and the United States had jointly occupied the disputed Oregon Territory since 1818. Beginning with John Quincy Adams's administration, the United

**Fifty-Four Forty or Fight** States had tried to fix the boundary at the 49th parallel, but Britain was determined to maintain access to Puget Sound and the Columbia River. As migrants began streaming into Oregon in the early 1840s, expansionists demanded the entire Oregon Country for the United States, up to its northernmost border at latitude 54°40'. Soon "fifty-four forty or fight" became their rallying cry.

President Tyler wanted both Oregon and Texas, but he was obsessed with Texas and pursued the issue tirelessly. He argued that there was little to fear from slavery's expansion, for it would spread the nation's black population more thinly, allowing for the institution's gradual demise. But when word leaked out that Secretary of State John Calhoun had written to the British minister in Washington to justify Texas annexation as a way of protecting slavery—"a political institution essential to the peace, safety, and prosperity of those States in which it exists"—the Senate rejected annexation in 1844 by a vote of 35 to 16.

Worried southern Democrats persuaded their party's 1844 convention to adopt a rule requiring that the pres-

▲ This 1845 portrayal of Oregon City, the western terminus of the Oregon Trail, was provided by a British army officer sent to investigate the influence of large-scale American immigration into a territory jointly occupied by Great Britain and the United States. After the Oregon Treaty (1846) drew the boundary between British and American territory at the forty-ninth parallel, Oregon City became the capital of the Oregon Territory from 1848 to 1851.

*(Library of Congress)*

## Polk and the Election of 1844

idential nominee receive two-thirds of the convention votes, effectively giving the southern states a veto and allowing them to block the nomination of Martin Van Buren, an opponent of annexation. Instead, the party ran "Young Hickory," House Speaker James K. Polk, an avid expansionist and slaveholding cotton planter from Tennessee. The Democratic platform, designed to appeal to voters across regional lines, called for occupation of the entire Oregon Territory and annexation of Texas. The Whigs, who ran Henry Clay as their nominee, argued that the Democrats' belligerent nationalism would lead the nation into war with Great Britain or Mexico or both. Clay favored expansion through negotiation, whereas many northern Whigs opposed annexation altogether, fearful that it would lead to additional slave states as well as strained relations with vital trading partners.

Polk and the Democrats won the election by 170 electoral votes to 105, though with a margin of just 38,000 out of 2.7 million votes cast. Polk won New York's 36 electoral votes by just 6,000 popular votes. Abolitionist James G. Birney, the Liberty Party candidate, had drawn almost 16,000 votes away from Clay by running on a Free-Soil platform. Without Birney, Clay might have won New York, giving him an edge of 141 to 134 in the electoral college. Abolitionist forces thus unwittingly helped elect a slaveholder as president.

Interpreting Polk's victory as a mandate for annexation, President Tyler proposed that Texas be admitted by joint resolution of Congress. The usual method of annexation, by treaty negotiation, required a two-thirds vote in the Senate—which expansionists clearly did not have, because there were sufficient opponents to slavery who would vote against annexation. Joint resolution required only a simple majority in each house. On March 1, 1845, the resolution passed the House by 120 to 98 and the Senate by 27 to 25. Three days before leaving office, Tyler signed the measure. Mexico, which had never recognized Texas independence, immediately broke relations with the United States. In October the citizens of Texas ratified annexation, and Texas joined the Union, with a constitution permitting slavery, in December 1845. The nation was on the brink of war with Mexico. That conflict—like none other before it—would lay bare the inextricable relationships among westward expansion, slavery, and sectional discord.

## Annexation of Texas

## *Legacy* FOR A PEOPLE AND A NATION

### Descendants of Early Latino Settlers

Today, the American news media are filled with stories about Latinos in the United States, for current census figures identify them as the largest racial or ethnic minority in the country. Newspapers, magazines, television, and radio focus on such topics as the growing number of documented and undocumented Latino immigrants, the increasing impact of Latinos in the communities where they live and work, and the occasionally difficult relationships of such immigrants and African Americans. Yet all the attention devoted to recent arrivals overlooks a considerable proportion of the Latino population: those who are descended not from immigrants but from people whose residency in North America predated the existence of the United States.

When the region stretching from eastern Texas to California was acquired by the United States in the 1840s, its population included not only the members of indigenous Indian nations, but also scattered settlements composed of thousands of people with at least partial European ancestry, primarily Spanish or Portuguese. Their descendants have included such U.S. senators as Dennis Chávez (who served from 1936 to 1962) and such congressmen as Manuel Luján (1969–1988). Today, when asked about their immigrant ancestors, they commonly reply that the country came to them rather than the reverse. Their families have resided in what is now U.S. territory for as long as twelve or fourteen generations.

Intriguingly, persuasive evidence suggests that many of the early Iberian settlers in New Mexico were *conversos,* or of New Christian descent—that is, people whose Jewish ancestors formally converted to Catholicism in the fifteenth century in order to avoid religious persecution. After Jews were expelled from Spain and Portugal in 1492, many fled to the far corners of the Spanish empire. Some participated in Juan de Oñate's 1598 expedition to New Mexico, and others subsequently moved to the remote settlement. There, some secretly continued to follow such Jewish customs as Sabbath observances and food restrictions (not eating pork, for example). When the Inquisition took note of these practices in the 1660s, among those charged with such offenses were a former governor of the colony and his wife. Today, some Latino residents of New Mexico have acknowledged their *converso* roots and reclaimed a Jewish identity.

All the long-standing Latino citizens of the United States, not just those of *converso* descent, have given the nation and its people an important multicultural legacy.

## SUMMARY

Encouraged by literary and artistic images of the frontier, easterners often viewed the West as a place of natural abundance, where hard-working individuals could seek security, freedom, and perhaps even fortune. By the millions they poured into the Old Southwest and Old Northwest in the early decades of the nineteenth century. Although the federal government promoted westward expansion—in the form of support for transportation improvements, surveying, cheap land, and protection from Indians—western migrants did not make the decision to head west lightly. Nor did they always find what they were looking for. Some returned home, some moved to new locations, and some—too poor or too embarrassed—stayed in the West, where they reluctantly abandoned their dreams of economic independence. Others found what they were looking for in the West, though often the road to success proved much slower and more circuitous than they had anticipated.

Not everyone who went west did so voluntarily, nor did everyone in the West think of it as an expanding region. African American slaves were moved westward by their owners in enormous numbers in the years between 1820 and 1860. Native Americans saw their lands and their livelihoods constrict, and their environments so altered that their economic and spiritual lives were threatened. Some Indians responded to the white incursion through accommodation and peaceful overtures; others resisted, sometimes forcefully. If their first strategy failed, then they tried another. But the sheer force of numbers favored whites. For Indians in Texas and California, white incursions brought devastation.

Although their belief in Native Americans' inferiority allowed many white Americans to rationalize the Indians' fate, it was white attitudes toward black people and slavery that drove their decisions about where to locate in the West. Those who believed that slavery degraded white labor headed along a northern trajectory, whereas those who dreamed of slave ownership headed southward, where they clashed with yet another group of people whom they deemed racially inferior: Mexicans. When American settlers in Texas achieved their independence from Mexico, legalized slavery, and applied for annexation by the United States, they brought the divisive issue of slavery's westward expansion to the surface of American politics. Although Democratic politicians at first tried to maintain a geographic equilibrium by proposing an ambitious territorial agenda in Oregon as well, it would be Texas annexation that set the stage for military conflict, the addition of vast territories in the Southwest, and reinvigorated sectional conflict.

## SUGGESTIONS FOR FURTHER READING

Gary Clayton Anderson, *The Conquest of Texas: Ethnic Cleansing in the Promised Land, 1820–1875* (2005)

Stuart Banner, *How the Indians Lost Their Land: Law and Power on the Frontier* (2005)

James F. Brooks, *Captives and Cousins: Slavery, Kinship, and Community in the Southwest Borderlands* (2002)

Andrew R. L. Cayton and Peter S. Onuf, *The Midwest and the Nation: Rethinking the History of an American Region* (1990)

Robert V. Hine and John Mack Faragher, *The American West: A New Interpretive History* (2000)

Albert L. Hurtado, *Indian Survival on the California Frontier* (1998)

Susan L. Johnson, *Roaring Camp: The Social World of the California Gold Rush* (2000)

Andrés Reséndez, *Changing National Identities at the Frontier: Texas and New Mexico, 1800–1850* (2005)

Michael L. Tate, *Indians and Emigrants: Encounters on the Overland Trails* (2006)

Richard White, *"It's Your Misfortune and None of My Own": A New History of the American West* (1991)

*For a more extensive list for further reading, go to* college.hmco.com/pic/norton8e.

# Slavery and America's Future: The Road to War *1845-1861*

*O*n a stiflingly hot evening, June 16, 1858, former one-term congressman Abraham Lincoln stepped onto the raised platform of the legislative chamber in the state house at Springfield, Illinois, to accept the Republican Party's nomination to run for the U.S. Senate against the most famous Democrat in America—the incumbent, Stephen A. Douglas. At six feet, four inches, Lincoln towered over the packed hall, his head nearly level with the edge of the balcony. The nation was at a historic crossroads, and he had worked on this speech for weeks. He loved to recite poetry and delivered his poetic prose with unmatched intellectual power. His body angular, his hands large and awkward, his voice strong but high-pitched, Lincoln quickly gained his audience's attention. "Slavery agitation" had convulsed American politics and exploded in guerrilla war in Kansas. "In my opinion," ventured Lincoln, "it will not cease, until a crisis shall have been reached, and passed." Then, in imagery familiar to his Bible-reading listeners, he gave the crisis its unforgettable metaphor.

"A house divided against itself cannot stand." I believe this government cannot endure permanently half slave and half free. I do not expect the Union to be dissolved—I do not expect the house to *fall*—but I *do* expect it will cease to be divided. It will become *all* one thing, or *all* the other. Either the *opponents* of slavery will arrest the further spread of it, and place it where the public mind shall rest in the belief that it is in the course of ultimate extinction; or its *advocates* will push it forward, till it shall become alike lawful in *all* the States, *old* as well as *new*—North as well as South.

In much of the remainder of the thirty-minute speech, Lincoln contended that a conspiracy—a "design" led by the Democratic Party's "chief bosses"—sought to make slavery a *national* institution. With partisan fervor, he charged Douglas with not caring

◄ **Abraham Lincoln at the Lincoln-Douglas debates, undated image. Stephen Douglas stands immediatley behind Lincoln, and the picture depicts the crowds, brass bands, and political banners that were part of each debate.** *(© Bettmann/Corbis)*

## CHRONOLOGY

**1846** ■ War with Mexico begins
- Oregon Treaty negotiated
- Wilmot Proviso inflames sectional divisions

**1847** ■ Cass proposes idea of popular sovereignty

**1848** ■ Treaty of Guadalupe Hidalgo gives United States new territory in the Southwest
- Free-Soil Party formed
- Taylor elected president
- Gold discovered in California, which later applies for admission to Union as free state

**1850** ■ Compromise of 1850 passes, containing controversial Fugitive Slave Act

**1852** ■ Stowe publishes *Uncle Tom's Cabin*
- Pierce elected president

**1854** ■ Publication of "Appeal of the Independent Democrats"
- Kansas-Nebraska Act wins approval and ignites controversy
- Republican Party formed
- Return of fugitive Burns to slavery in Virginia

**1856** ■ Bleeding Kansas troubles nation
- Brooks attacks Sumner in Senate chamber
- Buchanan elected president, but Republican Frémont wins most northern states

**1857** ■ *Dred Scott v. Sanford* endorses southern views on black citizenship and slavery in territories
- Economic panic and widespread unemployment begin

**1858** ■ Kansas voters reject Lecompton Constitution
- Lincoln-Douglas debates attract attention
- Douglas contends popular sovereignty prevails over *Dred Scott* decision in territories

**1859** ■ Brown raids Harpers Ferry

**1860** ■ Democratic Party splits in two; southern Democrats demand constitutional guarantee for the territories
- Lincoln elected president in divided, sectional election
- Crittenden Compromise fails
- South Carolina secedes from Union

**1861** ■ Six more Deep South states secede
- Confederacy established at Montgomery, Alabama
- Attack on Fort Sumter begins Civil War
- Four states in the Upper South join the Confederacy

"whether slavery be voted down or voted up." For Lincoln this was a choice history would no longer allow Americans to avoid.

In the ensuing campaign, Lincoln and Douglas squared off over the great issues dividing the country: the westward expansion of slavery, the meaning of abolitionism, the character of federal authority over property in slaves, whether the Declaration of Independence had signaled some form of racial equality, and ultimately the moral integrity and future existence of the American republic. Both candidates crisscrossed Illinois, with Lincoln traveling 4,350 miles and delivering some 63 major speeches, and Douglas logging over 5,000 miles and speaking 130 times. Reluctantly, Douglas agreed to seven debates, one in each congressional district of Illinois, with the exception of Chicago and Springfield, where the candidates had already appeared.

The format for the Lincoln-Douglas debates inspires envy in twenty-first-century Americans: they were three-hour marathons of direct confrontation, political analysis, and theater, with the candidates alternately speaking in long addresses and rebuttals. Tens of thousands of people attended these outdoor events, arriving by foot, by wagon, on trains, and accompanied by brass bands. Perhaps never before or since have Americans demonstrated such an appetite for democratic engagement. "The prairies are on fire," wrote an eastern journalist. "It is astonishing how deep an interest in politics this people takes."

Over and over, Douglas accused his opponent and all Republicans of radicalism, of being "abolitionists" and favoring racial equality. Lincoln was forced to admit that he opposed social equality between whites and blacks, but he embraced the natural-rights doctrine of the Declaration of Independence and morally condemned slavery as an "evil" that must be constrained. Lincoln insisted on stopping slavery's expansion, while maintaining that the federal government could not legally end it in the South. He accused Douglas of a dangerous neutrality, even indifference, about slavery's future.

A foot shorter than Lincoln, better dressed, and resplendent in oratorical manner, Douglas appealed to racial prejudice and to a vague, if eloquent, unionism. Lincoln cast the election as a moral choice between free-labor–Free-Soil doctrine and a republic ultimately dominated by an oligarchy of slaveholders and their abettors, determined to snuff out the liberties of ordinary citizens. In 1858 Lincoln and Douglas debated the nature of American democracy. Both appealed to fear and to hope; the citizens of Illinois listened, learned, and voted for different futures.

Of the quarter-million votes cast, Lincoln received four thousand more than Douglas. But senators were elected by state legislatures in the nineteenth century; due to an outdated apportionment, Democrats maintained a 54-to-46 margin and returned Douglas to the U.S. Senate. Lincoln would be heard from again, however. "I am glad I made the late race," he said. "It gave me a hearing on the great and durable question of the age."

Well before 1858, a larger drama of conflict and violence had begun to envelop the nation. In Kansas Territory, open warfare had exploded between proslavery and antislavery settlers. On the floor of the U.S. Senate, a southern representative had beaten a northern senator senseless. A new fugitive slave law had sent thousands of free and fugitive blacks fleeing into Canada in fear for their liberty and their lives. The tradition of compromise on political problems related to slavery teetered on the brink of collapse. The Supreme Court had just issued a dramatic decision about slavery's constitutionality in westward expansion, as well as the status of African American citizenship—to the delight of most southerners and the dread of many northerners. And abolitionist John Brown was planning a raid into Virginia to start a slave rebellion.

The political culture of the American republic was disintegrating. As the 1850s advanced, slavery pulled Americans, North and South, into a maelstrom of dispute that its best statesmen ultimately could not subdue. Divergent economic and political aims, which had long been held in check, now flew apart over the issue of slavery. The old nationwide political parties fractured, and a realignment that reinforced sectional interests took their place. What began as a dark cloud over the western territories became a storm engulfing the nation. Each time the nation expanded, it confronted a thorny issue: should new territories and states be slave or free?

A feeling grew in both North and South that America's future was at stake—the character of its economy, its labor system, its definition of constitutional liberty, and its racial self-definition. For blacks, the growing dispute brought both hope and despair. They could take heart that political strife over slavery might somehow lead to their liberation. But in a nation now trying to define its future, blacks had to wonder whether they had a future at all in America. In 1855 Frederick Douglass spoke for the enslaved when he wrote that "the thought of only being a creature of the present and the past, troubled me, and I longed to have a future—a future with hope in it." In those words Douglass spoke as well to the nation's central dilemma.

- After 1845, how and why did westward expansion become so intertwined with the future of slavery and freedom?
- During the 1850s, why did Americans (white males, virtually all of whom could vote, and blacks, few of whom had the franchise) seem to care so deeply about electoral politics?
- What were the long-term and immediate causes of the Civil War?

## THE WAR WITH MEXICO AND ITS CONSEQUENCES

In the 1840s, territorial expansion surged forward under the leadership of President James K. Polk of North Carolina. The annexation of Texas just before his inauguration did not necessarily make war with Mexico inevitable, but through a series of calculated decisions, Polk brought the conflict on. Mexico broke off relations with the United States, and during the annexation process, Polk urged Texans to seize all land to the Rio Grande and claim the river as their southern and western border. Mexico held that the Nueces River was the border; hence, the stage was set for conflict. Nothing could weaken Polk's determination to fulfill the nation's manifest destiny to rule the continent. He wanted Mexico's territory all the way to the Pacific, and all of Oregon Country as well. He and his expansionist cabinet achieved their goals but were largely unaware of the price in domestic harmony that expansion would exact.

During the 1844 campaign, Polk's supporters had threatened war with Great Britain to gain all of Oregon.

**Oregon**

As president, however, Polk turned first to diplomacy. Not wanting to fight Mexico and Great Britain at the same time, he tried to avoid bloodshed in the Northwest, where America and Britain had since 1819 jointly occupied disputed territory. Dropping the demand for a boundary at latitude 54°40', he pressured the British to accept the 49th parallel. In 1846 Great Britain agreed. The Oregon Treaty gave the United States all of present-day Oregon, Washington, and Idaho, and parts of Wyoming and Montana (see Map 14.1). Thus a new era of land acquisition and conquest had begun under the eleventh president of the United States, the sixth to be a slaveholder and one who, through an agent, secretly bought and sold slaves from the White House.

### "Mr. Polk's War"

Toward Mexico Polk was more aggressive. In early 1846 he ordered American troops under "Old Rough and Ready," General Zachary Taylor, to march south and defend the contested border of the Rio Grande across from the town of Matamoros, Mexico (see Map 14.2). Polk especially desired California as the prize in his expansionist strategy, and he attempted to buy from Mexico a huge tract of land extending to the Pacific. When that effort failed, Polk waited for war. Negotiations between troops on the Rio Grande were awkwardly conducted in French because no American officer spoke Spanish and no Mexican spoke English. After a three-week standoff, the tense situation came to a head. On April 24, 1846, Mexican cavalry ambushed a U.S. cavalry unit on the north side of the river; eleven Americans were killed, and sixty-three were taken captive. On April 26, Taylor sent a dispatch overland to Washington, D.C., which took two weeks to arrive, announcing, "Hostilities may now be considered as commenced."

Polk now drafted a message to Congress: Mexico had "passed the boundary of the United States, had invaded our territory and shed American blood on American soil." In the bill accompanying the war message, Polk deceptively declared that "war exists by the act of Mexico itself" and summoned the nation to arms. Two days later, on May 13, the House recognized a state of war with Mexico by a vote of 174 to 14, and the Senate, by 40 to 2, with numerous abstentions. Some antislavery Whigs had tried to oppose the war in Congress but were barely allowed to speak. Because Polk withheld key facts, the full reality of what had happened on the distant Rio Grande was not known. But the theory and practice of manifest destiny had launched the United States into its first major war on foreign territory.

### Foreign War and the Popular Imagination

The idea of war unleashed great public celebrations. Huge crowds gathered in southern cities, such as Richmond and Louisville, to voice support for the war effort. Twenty thousand Philadelphians and even more New Yorkers rallied in the same spirit. After news came of General Taylor's first two battlefield victories at Palo Alto and Resaca de la Palma, volunteers swarmed recruiting stations. From his home in Lansingburgh, New York, writer Herman Melville remarked that "the people here are all in a state of delirium. . . . A military ardor pervades all ranks. . . . Nothing is talked of but the 'Halls of the Montezumas.'" Publishers rushed books about Mexican geography into print; "Palo Alto" hats and root beer went on sale. And new daily newspapers, now printed on rotary presses, boosted their sales by giving the war a romantic appeal.

Here was an adventurous war of conquest in a far-off, exotic land. Here was the fulfillment of an Anglo-Saxon–Christian destiny to expand and possess the North American continent, and to take civilization to the "semi-Indian" Mexicans. For many, racism fueled the expansionist spirit. In 1846 an Illinois newspaper justified the war on the basis that Mexicans were "reptiles in the path of progressive democracy." For those who read newspapers, the War with Mexico became the first national event experienced with immediacy. The battles south of

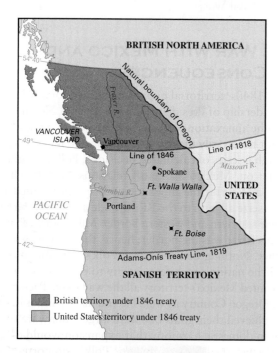

**Map 14.1   American Expansion in Oregon**

The slogan of Polk's supporters had been "fifty-four forty or fight," but negotiation of a boundary at the 49th parallel avoided the danger of war with Great Britain.

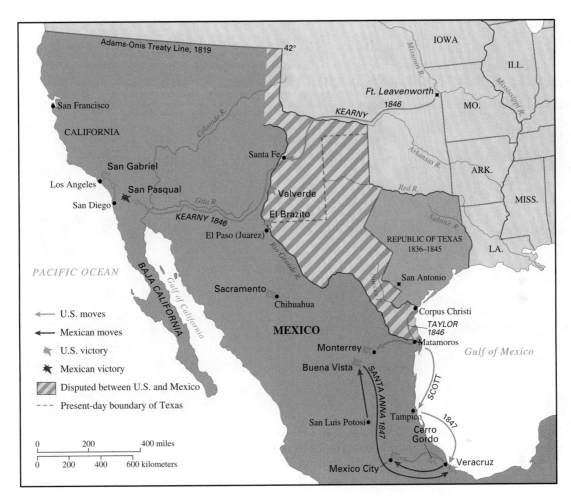

**Map 14.2    The War with Mexico**

This map shows the territory disputed between the United States and Mexico. After U.S. gains in northeastern Mexico, in New Mexico, and in California, General Winfield Scott captured Mexico City in the decisive campaign of the war.

the border were reported by war correspondents. From Vera Cruz on the Gulf Coast of Mexico, ships carried news dispatches to New Orleans, whose nine daily newspapers ran a faster steamer out to meet them. With stories set in type before they even reached shore, riders carried the news to the North. Near the end of the war, news traveled by telegraph in only three days from New Orleans to Washington, D.C.

The war spawned an outpouring of poetry, song, drama, travel literature, and lithographs that captured the popular imagination and glorified the conflict. New lyrics to the tune of "Yankee Doodle" proclaimed: "They attacked our men upon our land / and crossed our river too sir / now show them all with sword in hand / what yankee

boys can do sir." Most of the war-inspired flowering of the popular arts was patriotic. But not everyone cheered. Abolitionist James Russell Lowell considered the war a "national crime committed in behoof of slavery, our common sin." Ralph Waldo Emerson confided to his journals in 1847, "The United States will conquer Mexico, but it will be as the man swallows arsenic, which brings him down in turn. Mexico will poison us." Even proslavery spokesman John C. Calhoun saw the perils of expansionism. Mexico, he said, was "the forbidden fruit; the penalty of eating it would be to subject our institutions to political death."

The troops proved unruly and undisciplined, and their politically ambitious commanders often quarreled among

▲ Enthusiastic publishers vied to furnish the American public with up-to-date news of the War with Mexico. This is one of three lithographs issued by Currier and Ives in 1846 to celebrate U.S. forces' capture of Mexico's General La Vega during the Battle of Resaca de la Palma, fought near the border of Texas and Mexico. *(Amon Carter Museum, Fort Worth, Texas)*

## Conquest

themselves. Nevertheless, early in the war, U.S. forces made significant gains. In May 1846 Polk ordered Colonel Stephen Kearny and a small detachment to invade the remote and thinly populated provinces of New Mexico and California. Taking Santa Fe largely without opposition, Kearny pushed into California, where he joined forces with two U.S. naval units and rebellious American settlers led by Captain John C. Frémont. General Zachary Taylor's forces attacked and occupied Monterrey, which surrendered in September, securing northeastern Mexico (see Map 14.2).

New Mexico did not prove easy for U.S. forces to subdue, however. In January 1847, in Taos, northwest of Santa Fe, Hispanics and Indians led by Pablo Montoya and Tomas Romero rebelled against the Americans and killed numerous government officials. In what came to be known as the Taos Revolt, some 500 Mexican and Indian insurgents laid siege to a mill in Arroyo Hondo, outside Taos. The U.S. command acted swiftly to suppress the revolt with 300 heavily armed troops. The growing band of insurgents eventually retreated to Taos Pueblo and held out in a thick-walled church. With cannon, the U.S. Army succeeded in killing some 150 and capturing 400 of the rebels. After many arrests, approximately 28 insurgent leaders were hanged in the Taos plaza, ending the bloody resistance to U.S. occupation of lands still claimed by Mexican and Indian peoples.

Before the end of 1846, American forces had also established dominion over California. Because losses on the periphery of their large country had not broken Mexican resistance, General Winfield Scott carried the war to the enemy's heartland. Landing at Veracruz, he led 14,000 men toward Mexico City. This daring invasion proved the decisive campaign of the war. Scott's men, outnumbered and threatened by yellow fever, encountered a series of formidable Mexican defenses, but engineers repeatedly discovered flanking routes around their foes. After a series of hard-fought battles, U.S. troops captured the Mexican capital.

Representatives of both countries signed the Treaty of Guadalupe Hidalgo in February 1848. The United States

**Treaty of Guadalupe Hidalgo**

gained California and New Mexico (including present-day Nevada, Utah, and Arizona, and parts of Colorado and Wyoming), and recognition of the Rio Grande as the southern boundary of Texas. In return, the American government agreed to settle the claims of its citizens (mostly Texans) against Mexico ($3.2 million) and to pay Mexico a mere $15 million. On the day Polk received the treaty from the Senate, a mob in Paris forced Louis Philippe to abdicate the throne of France, and a German writer, Karl Marx, published a pamphlet, *The Communist Manifesto,* in London. The enormous influence of Marx's work would be many years away, but as the 1848 nationalistic revolutions against monarchy spread to Italy, Austria, Hungary, and Germany, republican America seized a western empire.

The costs of the war included the deaths of thirteen thousand Americans (mostly from disease) and fifty thousand Mexicans. Moreover, enmity between Mexico and the United States endured into the twentieth century. The domestic cost to the United States was even higher. Public opinion was sharply divided. Southwesterners were enthusiastic about the war, as were most southern planters; New Englanders strenuously opposed it. Whigs in Congress charged that Polk, a Democrat, had "provoked" an unnecessary war and "usurped the power of Congress." The aged John Quincy Adams denounced the war, and an Illinois Whig named Abraham Lincoln called Polk's justifications the "half insane mumbling of a fever-dream." Abolitionists and a small minority of antislavery Whigs charged that the war was a plot to extend slavery. Congressman Joshua Giddings of Ohio charged that Polk's purpose was "to render slavery secure in Texas" and to extend slavery's dominion over the West.

These charges fed northern fear of the "Slave Power." Abolitionists had long warned of a slaveholding oligarchy that intended to dominate the

**"Slave Power Conspiracy"**

nation through its hold on federal power. Slaveholders had gained control of the South by suppressing dissent. They had forced the gag rule on Congress in 1836 and threatened northern liberties. To many white northerners, even those who saw nothing wrong with slavery, it was the battle over free speech that first made the idea of a Slave Power credible. The War with Mexico deepened such fears. Had this questionable war, asked antislavery northerners, not been launched for vast, new slave territory?

Northern opinion on slavery's expansion began to shift, but the impact of the war on southern opinion was even more dramatic. At first, some southern Whigs attacked the Democratic president for causing the war, and few southern congressmen saw slavery as the paramount issue. Many whites in both North and South feared that large land seizures would bring thousands of nonwhite Mexicans into the United States and upset the racial order. An Indiana politician did not want "any mixed races in our Union, nor men of any color except white, unless they be slaves." And the *Charleston* (South Carolina) *Mercury* asked if the nation expected "to melt into our population eight millions of men, at war with us by race, by language, by religion, manners and laws." Yet, despite their racism and such numerical exaggerations, many statesmen soon saw other prospects in the outcomes of a war of conquest in the Southwest.

In August 1846, David Wilmot, a Pennsylvania Democrat, proposed an amendment, or proviso, to a military

**Wilmot Proviso**

tary appropriations bill: that "neither slavery nor involuntary servitude shall ever exist" in any territory gained from Mexico. Although the proviso never passed both houses of Congress, its repeated introduction by northerners transformed the debate over the expansion of slavery. Southerners suddenly circled their wagons to protect the future of a slave society. Alexander H. Stephens, only recently "no defender of slavery," now declared that slavery was based on the Bible and above moral criticism, and John C. Calhoun took an aggressive stand. The territories, Calhoun insisted, belonged to all the states, and the federal government could do nothing to limit the spread of slavery there. Southern slaveholders had a constitutional right rooted in the Fifth Amendment, Calhoun claimed, to take their slaves (as property) anywhere in the territories.

This position, often called "state sovereignty," which quickly became a test of orthodoxy among southern politicians, was a radical reversal of history. In 1787 the Confederation Congress had discouraged if not fully excluded slavery from the Northwest Territory; Article IV of the U.S. Constitution had authorized Congress to make "all needful rules and regulations" for the territories; and the Missouri Compromise had barred slavery from most of the Louisiana Purchase. Now, however, southern leaders demanded future guarantees for slavery.

In the North, the Wilmot Proviso became a rallying cry for abolitionists. Eventually the legislatures of fourteen northern states endorsed it—and not because all of its supporters were abolitionists. David Wilmot, significantly, was

| TABLE 14.1 | **New Political Parties** | | |
|---|---|---|---|
| **Party** | **Period of Influence** | **Area of Influence** | **Outcome** |
| Liberty Party | 1839–1848 | North | Merged with other antislavery groups to form Free-Soil Party |
| Free-Soil Party | 1848–1854 | North | Merged with Republican Party |
| Know-Nothings (American Party) | 1853–1856 | Nationwide | Disappeared, freeing most to join Republican Party |
| Republican Party | 1854–present | North (later nationwide) | Became rival of Democratic Party and won presidency in 1860 |

neither an abolitionist nor an antislavery Whig. He denied having any "squeamish sensitiveness upon the subject of slavery" or "morbid sympathy for the slave." Instead, his goal was to defend "the rights of white freemen" and to obtain California "for free white labor." Wilmot's involvement in antislavery controversy is a measure of the remarkable ability of the territorial issue to alarm northerners of many viewpoints.

As Wilmot demonstrated, it was possible, however, to be both a racist and an opponent of slavery. The vast majority of white northerners were not active abolitionists, and their desire to keep the West free from slavery was often matched by their desire to keep blacks from settling there. Fear of the Slave Power was thus building a potent antislavery movement that united abolitionists and antiblack voters. At stake was an abiding version of the American Dream: the free individual's access to social mobility through acquisition of land in the West. This sacred ideal of free labor, and its dread of concentrated power, fueled a new political persuasion in America. A man's ownership and sale of his own labor, wrote British economist Adam Smith, was "the most sacred and inviolable foundation of all property." Slave labor, thousands of northerners had come to believe, would degrade the honest toil of free men and render them unemployable. The West must therefore be kept free of slaves.

The divisive slavery question now infested national politics. After Polk renounced a second term as president, the Democrats nominated Senator Lewis Cass of Michigan for president and General William Butler of Kentucky for vice president. Cass, a party loyalist who had served in Jackson's cabinet, had devised in 1847 the idea of "popular sovereignty"— letting residents in the western territories decide the question of slavery for themselves. His party's platform declared that Congress lacked the power to interfere with

**The Election of 1848 and Popular Sovereignty**

slavery's expansion. The Whigs nominated General Zachary Taylor, a southern slaveholder and war hero; Congressman Millard Fillmore of New York was his running mate. The Whig convention similarly refused to assert that Congress had power over slavery in the territories.

But the issue could not be avoided. Many southern Democrats distrusted Cass and eventually voted for Taylor because he was a slaveholder. Among northerners, concern over slavery led to the formation of a new party. New York Democrats committed to the Wilmot Proviso rebelled against Cass and nominated former president Martin Van Buren. Antislavery Whigs and former supporters of the Liberty Party then joined them to organize the Free-Soil Party, with Van Buren as its candidate (see Table 14.1). This party, which sought to restrict slavery expansion to any western territories and whose slogan was "Free Soil, Free Speech, Free Labor, and Free Men," won almost 300,000 northern votes. For a new third party to win 10 percent of the national vote was unprecedented. Taylor polled 1.4 million votes to Cass's 1.2 million and won the White House, but the results were more ominous than decisive.

American politics had split along sectional lines as never before. Religious denominations, too, severed into northern and southern wings. Many Protestants, North and South, began to fear that God had an appointment with America, either to destroy the national sin of slavery or to help the South defend it as part of his divine order. As the 1850s dawned, the legacies of the War with Mexico and the conflicts of 1848 dominated national life and threatened the nature of the Union itself.

## 1850: COMPROMISE OR ARMISTICE?

The first sectional battle of the new decade involved California. More than eighty thousand Americans flooded into California during the gold rush of 1849. With Congress unable to agree on a formula to govern the territories, President Taylor urged these settlers to apply directly for admission to the Union. They promptly did so, proposing a state constitution that did not allow for slavery. Because California's admission as a free state would upset the sectional balance of power in the Senate (the ratio of slave to free states was fifteen to fifteen), southern politicians wanted to postpone admission and make California a slave territory, or at least extend the Missouri Compromise line west to the Pacific.

Henry Clay, the venerable Whig leader, sensed that the Union was in peril. Twice before—in 1820 and 1833—

## Debate over Slavery in the Territories

Clay, the "Great Pacificator," had taken the lead in shaping sectional compromise; now he struggled one last time to preserve the nation. To hushed Senate galleries Clay presented a series of compromise measures in the winter of 1850. At one point he held up what he claimed was a piece of George Washington's coffin as a means of inspiring unity. Over the weeks that followed, he and Senator Stephen A. Douglas of Illinois, the "Little Giant," steered their compromise package through debate and amendment.

The problems to be solved were numerous and difficult. Would California, or part of it, become a free state? How should the territory acquired from Mexico be organized? Texas, which allowed slavery, claimed large portions of the new land as far west as Santa Fe. Southerners complained that fugitive slaves were not being returned as the Constitution required, and northerners objected to the sale of human beings in the nation's capital. Eight years earlier, in *Prigg v. Pennsylvania* (1842), the Supreme Court had ruled that enforcement of the fugitive slave clause in the Constitution was a federal, not a state, obligation, buttressing long-standing southern desires to bring this issue to a head. The Court further ruled that states could not exact measures, often called "personal liberty laws," banning the seizure and removal of a fugitive. Most troublesome of all, however, was the status of slavery in the territories.

Clay and Douglas hoped to avoid a specific formula, and in Lewis Cass's idea of popular sovereignty they discovered what one historian called a "charm of ambiguity." Ultimately Congress would have to approve statehood for a territory, but "in the meantime," said Cass, it should allow the people living there "to regulate their own concerns in their own way."

Those simple words proved all but unenforceable. When could settlers prohibit slavery? To avoid dissension within their party, northern and southern Democrats explained Cass's statement to their constituents in two incompatible ways. Southerners claimed that neither Congress nor a territorial legislature could bar slavery. Only late in the territorial process, when settlers were ready to draft a state constitution, could they take that step, thus allowing time for slavery to take root. Northerners, however, insisted that Americans living in a territory were entitled to local self-government and thus could outlaw slavery at any time.

The cause of compromise gained a powerful supporter when Senator Daniel Webster committed his prestige and eloquence to Clay's bill. "I wish to speak today," Webster declaimed on March 7 in a scene of high drama, "not as a Massachusetts man, nor as a Northern man, but as an American. I speak today for the preservation of the Union." Abandoning his earlier support for the Wilmot Proviso, Webster urged northerners not to "taunt or reproach" the South with antislavery measures. To southern firebrands he issued a warning that disunion inevitably would cause violence and destruction. For his efforts at compromise, Webster was condemned by many former abolitionist friends in New England who accused him of going over to the "devil."

Only three days earlier, with equal drama, Calhoun had been carried from his sickbed to deliver a speech opposing the compromise. As Calhoun was unable to stand and speak, Senator James Mason of Virginia read his address for him. Grizzled and dying, the South's intellectual defender warned that the "cords which bind these states" were "already greatly weakened." Calhoun did not address the specific measures in the bill; he predicted disunion if southern demands were not met, thereby frightening some into support of compromise.

Yet rising fear and Webster's influence were not enough. After months of labor, Clay and Douglas finally brought their legislative package to a vote, and lost. With Clay sick and absent from Washington, Douglas reintroduced the compromise measures one at a time. Although there was no majority for compromise, Douglas shrewdly realized that different majorities might be created for the separate measures. Because southerners favored some bills and northerners the rest, the small majority for compromise could be achieved on each distinct issue. The strategy worked, and Douglas's resourcefulness alleviated the crisis as the Compromise of 1850 became law.

The compromise had five essential measures:

1. California became a free state.

## Compromise of 1850

2. The Texas boundary was set at its present limits (see Map 14.3), and the United States paid Texas $10 million in compensation for the loss of New Mexico Territory.

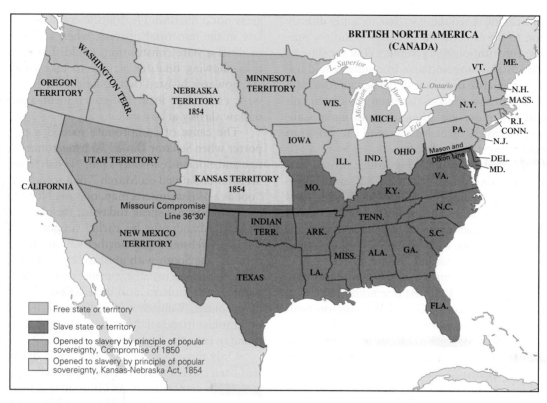

**Map 14.3 The Kansas-Nebraska Act and Slavery Expansion, 1854**
The vote on the Kansas-Nebraska Act in the House of Representatives (see also Table 14.2 on page 380) demonstrates the sectionalization of American politics due to the slavery question.

3. The territories of New Mexico and Utah were organized on a basis of popular sovereignty.

4. The fugitive slave law was strengthened.

5. The slave trade was abolished in the District of Columbia.

Jubilation greeted passage of the compromise; crowds in Washington and other cities celebrated the happy news. "On one glorious night," records a modern historian, "the word went abroad that it was the duty of every patriot to get drunk. Before the next morning many a citizen had proved his patriotism."

In reality, there was less cause for celebration than people hoped. At best, the Compromise of 1850 was an artful evasion. As one historian has argued, the legislation was more an "armistice," delaying greater conflict, than a compromise. Douglas had found a way to pass the five proposals without convincing northerners and southerners to agree on fundamentals. The compromise bought time for the nation, but it did not provide a real settlement of the territorial questions.

Furthermore, the compromise had two basic flaws. The first concerned the ambiguity of popular sovereignty. Southerners insisted there would be no prohibition of slavery during the territorial stage, and northerners declared that settlers could bar slavery whenever they wished. The compromise even allowed for the appeal of a territorial legislature's action to the Supreme Court. One witty politician remarked that the legislators had enacted a lawsuit instead of a law.

The second flaw lay in the Fugitive Slave Act, which gave new—and controversial—protection to slavery. The law empowered slaveowners to go into court in their own states to present evidence that a slave who owed them service had escaped. The resulting transcript and a description of the fugitive would then serve as legal proof of a person's slave status, even in free states and territories. Specially appointed court officials adjudicated the identity of the person described, not whether he or she was indeed a slave. Penalties made it a felony to harbor fugitives, and the law

**Fugitive Slave Act**

stated that northern citizens could be summoned to hunt fugitives. The fees paid to U.S. marshals favored slaveholders: $10 if the alleged fugitive was returned to the slaveowner, $5 if not returned.

Abolitionist newspapers quickly attacked the Fugitive Slave Act as a violation of fundamental American rights. Why were alleged fugitives denied a trial by jury? Why were they given no chance to present evidence or cross-examine witnesses? Why did the law give authorities a financial incentive to send suspected fugitives into bondage, and why would northerners now be arrested if they harbored runaways? These arguments convinced some northerners that all free blacks were vulnerable to kidnapping and enslavement. The "free" states were no longer a safe haven for black folk, whatever their origins; an estimated 20,000 fled to Canada in the wake of the Fugitive Slave Act.

Between 1850 and 1854, protests and violent resistance to slave catchers occurred in dozens of northern towns. Sometimes a captured fugitive was broken out of jail or from the clutches of slave agents by abolitionists, as in the 1851 Boston case of Shadrach Minkins, who was spirited by a series of wagons and trains across Massachusetts, up through Vermont, to Montreal, Canada. Also in 1851, a fugitive named Jerry McHenry was freed by an abolitionist mob in Syracuse, New York, and hurried to Canadian freedom. That same year as well, the small black community in Lancaster County, Pennsylvania, rose up in arms to defend four escaped slaves from a federal posse charged with reenslaving them. At this "Christiana riot," the fugitives shot and killed Edward Gorsuch, the Maryland slaveowner who sought the return of his "property." Amid increasing border warfare over fugitive slaves, a headline reporting the Christiana affair screamed, "Civil War, The First Blow Struck!"

Many abolitionists became convinced by their experience of resisting the Fugitive Slave Act that violence was a legitimate means of opposing slavery. In an 1854 column entitled "Is It Right and Wise to Kill a Kidnapper?" Frederick Douglass said that the only way to make the fugitive slave law "dead letter" was to make a "few dead slave catchers."

At this point, a novel portrayed the humanity and suffering of slaves in a way that touched millions of northerners. Harriet Beecher Stowe, whose New England family had

||||||||||||||||||||||||||||||||

**Uncle Tom's Cabin**

produced many prominent ministers, wrote *Uncle Tom's Cabin* out of deep moral conviction. Her story, serialized in 1851 and published as a book in 1852, conveyed the agonies faced by slave families and described a mother's dash to

▲ **The Webb Family toured the North, presenting dramatic readings of** *Uncle Tom's Cabin.* **Performances by the Webbs and others deepened the already powerful impact of Harriet Beecher Stowe's novel.** *(Harriet Beecher Stowe Center, Hartford, Connecticut)*

freedom with her child across the frozen Ohio River. Stowe also portrayed slavery's evil effects on slaveholders, indicting the institution itself more harshly than she indicted the southerners caught in its web. Moreover, Stowe exposed northern racism and complicity with slavery by making the worst slaveholder a man of New England birth and a visiting relative on a plantation a squeamish Vermont woman who could hardly cope with the near presence of blacks.

In nine months the book sold over 300,000 copies and by mid-1853 over 1 million. Countless people saw *Uncle Tom's Cabin* performed as a stage play, heard the story in dramatic readings, or read similar novels inspired by it. Stowe brought home the evil of slavery to many who had never given it much thought. Indeed, for generations, the characters in *Uncle Tom's Cabin*—Eliza, Little Eva, Simon Legree, and Uncle Tom himself—entered the American imagination as symbols of slavery and its demise.

The popularity of *Uncle Tom's Cabin* alarmed anxious southern whites. In politics and now in popular literature they saw threats to their way of life. Behind the South's aggressive claims about territorial rights lay the fear that, if nearby areas outlawed slavery, they would be used as bases from which to spread abolitionism into the slave states. To most white southerners, a moral condemnation of slaveholding anywhere meant the same thing everywhere.

To protect slavery in the arena of ideas, southerners needed to counter indictments of the institution as a moral wrong. Accordingly, some fifteen to twenty proslavery novels were published in the 1850s as responses to *Uncle Tom's Cabin.* Most of these paled in comparison to Mrs. Stowe's masterpiece, but southern writers continued to defend their system as more humane than wage labor, and they blamed the slave trade on the "outside interference" of Yankee speculators. In awkward stories, such as J. W. Page's *Uncle Robin in His Cabin and Tom Without One in Boston,* slaves were induced to run away by visiting abolitionists, and then all but starved in northern cities.

In reality, slaveholders were especially disturbed by the 1850s over what was widely called the Underground

### The Underground Railroad

Railroad. This loose, illegal network of civil disobedience, spiriting runaways to freedom, had never been very organized. Thousands of slaves did escape by these routes, but largely through their own wits and courage, and through the assistance of blacks in some northern cities. Lewis Hayden in Boston, David Ruggles in New York, William Still in Philadelphia, John Parker in Ripley, Ohio, and Jacob Gibbs in Washington, D.C., were only some of the many black abolitionists who managed fugitive slave escapes through their regions.

Moreover, Harriet Tubman, herself an escapee in 1848, returned to her native Maryland and to Virginia at least a dozen times, and through clandestine measures helped possibly as many as three hundred slaves, some of them her own family members, to freedom. Maryland planters were so outraged at her heroic success that they offered a $40,000 reward for her capture.

In Ohio, numerous white abolitionists, often Quakers, joined with blacks as agents of slave liberation at various points along the river border between slavery and freedom. The Underground Railroad also had numerous maritime routes, as coastal slaves escaped aboard ship out of Virginia or the Carolinas, or from New Orleans, and ended up in northern port cities, the Caribbean, or England. Many fugitive slaves from the Lower South and Texas escaped to Mexico, which had abolished slavery in 1829. Some slaves escaped by joining the Seminole communities in Florida, where they fought with them against the U.S. Army in the Seminole Wars of 1835–1842 and 1855–1858.

▲ In *Still Life of Harriet Tubman with Bible and Candle,* we see the youthful, calm, determined leader of the Underground Railroad. Appearing gentle, Tubman was in her own way a revolutionary who liberated nearly three hundred of her people.   *(© 2000 Louis Psihoyos/Matrix)*

This constant, dangerous flow of humanity was a testament to human courage and the will for freedom. It never reached the scale believed by some angry slaveholders or that of the countless safe houses and hideaways claimed by hundreds of northern towns and local historical societies today. But, in reality and in legend, the Underground Railroad applied pressure to the institution of slavery and provided slaves with a focus for hope.

The 1852 election gave southern leaders hope that slavery would be secure under the administration of a

### Election of 1852 and the Collapse of Compromise

new president. Franklin Pierce, a Democrat from New Hampshire, won an easy victory over the Whig presidential nominee, General Winfield Scott. Pierce defended each section's rights as essential to the nation's unity, and southerners hoped that his firm support for the Compromise of 1850 might end the season of crisis. Because Scott's views on the compromise had been unknown and the Free-Soil candidate, John P. Hale of New Hampshire, had openly rejected it, Pierce's victory suggested widespread support for the compromise.

Pierce's victory, however, derived less from his strengths than from the Whig Party's weakness. The Whigs had never achieved much success in presidential politics, and by 1852 sectional discord had rendered it all but dead. President Pierce's embrace of the compromise appalled many northerners. His vigorous enforcement of the Fugitive Slave Act provoked outrage and fear of the Slave Power, especially in the case of the fugitive slave Anthony Burns, who had fled Virginia by stowing away on a ship in 1852. In Boston, thinking he was safe in a city known for abolitionism, Burns began a new life. But in 1854 federal marshals found and placed him under guard in Boston's courthouse. An interracial crowd of abolitionists attacked the courthouse, killing a jailer in an unsuccessful attempt to free Burns, whose case attracted nationwide attention.

Pierce moved decisively to enforce the Fugitive Slave Act. He telegraphed local officials to "incur any expense to insure the execution of the law" and sent marines, cavalry, and artillery to Boston. U.S. troops marched Burns to Boston harbor through streets that his supporters had draped in black and hung with American flags at half-mast. At a cost of $100,000, a single black man was returned to slavery through the power of federal law.

The national will to sustain the future of slavery was now tested at every turn. This demonstration of federal support for slavery radicalized opinion, even among many conservatives. Textile manufacturer Amos A. Lawrence observed that "we went to bed one night old fashioned, conservative, Compromise Union Whigs & waked up stark mad Abolitionists." Juries refused to convict the abolitionists who had stormed the Boston courthouse, and New England states began to pass personal liberty laws designed to impede or block federal enforcement. In such laws, local judges were absolved from enforcing the Fugitive Slave Act, in effect nullifying federal authority. What northerners now saw as evidence of a dominating Slave Power, outraged slaveholders saw as the legal defense of their rights.

Pierce confronted sectional conflict at every turn. His proposal for a transcontinental railroad derailed when congressmen fought over its location, North or South. His attempts to acquire foreign territory stirred more trouble. An annexation treaty with Hawai'i failed because southern senators would not vote for another free state, and efforts to acquire slaveholding Cuba angered northerners. Events in the Pacific also caused division at home over just how far American expansion should extend. With two orchestrated landings in the Bay of Tokyo, in 1853 and 1854, Commodore Matthew Perry established U.S. intentions to trade with Japan, whether that country sought such contact or not. Offended and intrigued, the Japanese were impressed with Perry's steam-powered warships, the first such black smoke–belching, floating machines they had seen. Perry's Treaty of Kanagawa in March 1854 negotiated two ports as coaling stations for American ships. The much sought-after trading arrangements were slow in coming, although this did not stop merchants and bankers from lavishing on Perry a hero's honors when he returned to the United States. In his meetings with the Japanese, the pompous Perry had given his hosts, whom he considered an inferior people, a telegraph system, a quarter-scale railroad train, a bound history of the War with Mexico, and one hundred gallons of Kentucky whiskey.

Soon, back home, another territorial bill threw Congress and the nation into even greater turmoil, and the Compromise of 1850 fell into complete collapse.

## SLAVERY EXPANSION AND COLLAPSE OF THE PARTY SYSTEM

The new controversy began in a surprising way. Stephen A. Douglas, one of the architects of the Compromise of 1850, introduced a bill to establish the Kansas and Nebraska Territories. Talented and ambitious for the presidency, Douglas was known for compromise, not sectional quarreling. But he did not view slavery as a fundamental problem, and he was willing to risk some controversy to win economic benefits for Illinois, his home state. A transcontinental railroad would encourage settlement of the Great Plains and stimulate the economy of Illinois, but no company would build such a railroad before Congress organized the territories it would cross. Thus interest in promoting the construction of such a railroad drove Douglas to introduce a bill that inflamed sectional passions.

The Kansas-Nebraska Act exposed the conflicting interpretations of popular sovereignty. Douglas's bill left

**The Kansas-Nebraska Act**

"all questions pertaining to slavery in the Territories . . . to the people residing therein." Northerners and southerners, however, still disagreed violently over what territorial settlers could constitutionally do. Moreover, the Kansas and Nebraska Territories lay within the Louisiana Purchase, and the Missouri Compromise prohibited slavery in all that land from latitude 36°30' north to the Canadian border. If popular sovereignty were to mean anything in Kansas and Nebraska, it had to mean that the Missouri Compromise was no longer in effect and that settlers could establish slavery there.

Southern congressmen, anxious to establish slaveholders' right to take slaves into any territory, pressed Douglas to concede this point. They demanded an explicit repeal of the 36°30' limitation as the price of their support. During a carriage ride with Senator Archibald Dixon of Kentucky, Douglas debated the point at length. Finally he made an impulsive decision: "By God, Sir, you are right. I will incorporate it in my bill, though I know it will raise a hell of a storm."

Perhaps Douglas underestimated the storm because he believed that conditions of climate and soil would keep slavery out of Kansas and Nebraska. Nevertheless, his bill threw open to slavery land from which it had been prohibited for thirty-four years. Opposition from Free-Soilers and antislavery forces was immediate and enduring; many considered this turn of events a betrayal of a sacred trust. The titanic struggle in Congress lasted three and a half months. Douglas won the support of President Pierce and eventually prevailed: the bill became law in May 1854 by a vote that demonstrated the dangerous sectionalization of American politics (see Map 14.3 and Table 14.2).

But the storm was just beginning. Abolitionists charged sinister aggression by the Slave Power, and northern fears of slavery's influence deepened. Opposition to the Fugitive Slave Act grew dramatically; between 1855 and 1859, Connecticut, Rhode Island, Massachusetts, Michigan, Maine, Ohio, and Wisconsin passed personal-liberty laws. These laws enraged southern leaders by providing counsel for alleged fugitives and requiring trial by jury. More important was the devastating impact of the Kansas-Nebraska Act on political parties. The weakened Whig Party broke apart into northern and southern wings that could no longer cooperate nationally. The Democrats survived, but their support in the North fell drastically in the 1854 elections. Northern Democrats lost sixty-six of their ninety-one congressional seats and lost control of all but two free-state legislatures.

The beneficiary of northern voters' wrath was a new political party. During debate on the Kansas-Nebraska Act,

**Birth of the Republican Party**

six congressmen had published an "Appeal of the Independent Democrats." Joshua Giddings, Salmon Chase, and Charles Sumner—the principal authors of this protest— attacked Douglas's legislation as a "gross violation of a sacred pledge" (the Missouri Compromise) and a "criminal betrayal of precious rights" that would make free territory a "dreary region of despotism." Their appeal tapped a reservoir of deep concerns in the North, cogently expressed by Illinois's Abraham Lincoln.

Although Lincoln did not personally condemn southerners—"They are just what we would be in their situa-

| TABLE 14.2 | The Vote on the Kansas-Nebraska Act | |
|---|---|---|
| The vote was 113 to 100 in favor. | | |
| | **Aye** | **Nay** |
| Northern Democrats | 44 | 42 |
| Southern Democrats | 57 | 2 |
| Northern Whigs | 0 | 45 |
| Southern Whigs | 12 | 7 |
| Northern Free-Soilers | | 4 |

tion"—he exposed the meaning of the Kansas-Nebraska Act. Lincoln argued that the founders, from love of liberty, had banned slavery from the Northwest Territory, kept the word *slavery* out of the Constitution, and treated it overall as a "cancer" on the republic. Rather than encouraging liberty, the Kansas-Nebraska Act put slavery "on the high road to extension and perpetuity," and that constituted a "moral wrong and injustice." America's future, Lincoln warned, was being mortgaged to slavery and all its influences.

Thousands of ordinary white northerners agreed. During the summer and fall of 1854, antislavery Whigs and Democrats, Free-Soilers, and other reformers throughout the Old Northwest met to form the new Republican Party, dedicated to keeping slavery out of the territories. The influence of the Republicans rapidly spread to the East, and they won a stunning victory in the 1854 elections. In their first appearance on the ballot, Republicans captured a majority of northern House seats. Antislavery sentiment had created a new party and caused roughly a quarter of northern Democrats to desert their party.

For the first time, too, a sectional party had gained significant power in the political system. Now the Whigs were gone, and only the Democrats struggled to maintain national membership. The Republicans absorbed the Free-Soil Party and grew rapidly in the North. Indeed, the emergence of the Republican coalition of antislavery interests is the most rapid transformation in party allegiance and voter behavior in American history.

Republicans also drew into their coalition a fast-growing nativist movement that called itself the American

**Know-Nothings**

Party, or Know-Nothings (because its first members kept their purposes secret, answering, "I know nothing" to all questions). This group exploited fear of foreigners and Catholics. Between 1848 and 1860, nearly 3.5 million immigrants entered the United States—proportionally the heaviest inflow of foreigners ever in American history. Democrats courted the votes of these new citizens, but many native-born Anglo-Saxon Protestants believed that Irish and German Cath-

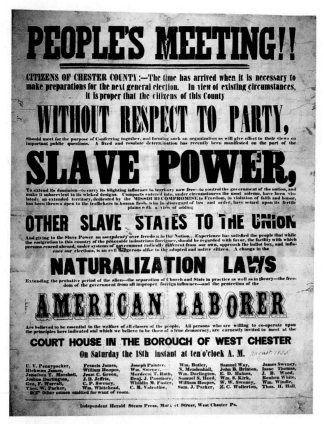

## PEOPLE'S MEETING!!

CITIZENS OF CHESTER COUNTY:—The time has arrived when it is necessary to make preparations for the next general election. In view of existing circumstances, it is proper that the citizens of this County

### WITHOUT RESPECT TO PARTY,

Should meet for the purpose of Conferring together, and forming such an organization as will give effect to their views on important public questions. A fixed and resolute determination has recently been manifested on the part of the

## SLAVE POWER,

To extend its dominion—to carry its blighting influence to territory now free—to control the government of the nation, and make it subservient to its wicked designs. Compacts entered into, under circumstances the most solemn, have been violated; an extended territory, dedicated by the MISSOURI COMPROMISE to Freedom, in violation of faith and honor, has been thrown open to the traffickers in human flesh, who in disregard of law and order, have seized upon its fertile plains with a view of adding

### OTHER SLAVE STATES TO THE UNION

And giving to the Slave Power an ascendency over freedom in the Nation. Experience has satisfied the people that while the principles of the peaceable industrious foreigner, should be regarded with favor, the facility with which persons reared abroad, under systems of government radically different from our own, approach the ballot box, and influence our elections, is an evil dangerous alike to the adopted and native citizens. A change in the

## NATURALIZATION LAWS

Extending the probative period of the alien—the separation of Church and State in practice as well as in theory—the freedom of the government from all improper foreign influence—and the protection of the

## AMERICAN LABORER

Are believed to be essential to the welfare of all classes of the people. All persons who are willing to co-operate upon the principles here indicated and which we believe to be those of a true democracy, are earnestly invited to meet at the

### COURT HOUSE IN THE BOROUGH OF WEST CHESTER

On Saturday the 18th instant at ten o'clock A. M.

| | | | | |
|---|---|---|---|---|
| U. V. Pennypacker, | Francis James, | Joseph Painter, | Wm. Butler, | Samuel Way, |
| Hickman James, | William Hoopes, | Wm. Sweney, | N. Mendenhall, | James Sweney, |
| Jonathan T. Marshall, | Jesse C. Green, | Mordecai T. Ruth, | Wm. Darlington, | Isaac Thomas, |
| Joshua Darlington, | J.B. Jeffris, | Benj. A. Passmore, | Samuel S. Heed, | J. B. Wood, |
| Geo. F. Worrall, | C.P. Sweney, | Whildin M. Foster, | William Hoopes, | Wm. B. Kirk, |
| Thos. W. Parker, | Wm. Whitehead, | C. M. Valentine, | Sam. J. Parker, | Reuben White, |
| | | | | W. W. Sweney, |

Other names omitted for want of room.

Independent Herald Steam Press, Market Street, West Chester Pa.

▲ Throughout the North, the Kansas-Nebraska Act kindled fires of alarm over the Slave Power's "determination to extend its dominion" and "control the government of the nation." Public meetings like the one announced here, held in West Chester, Pennsylvania, aided the new Republican Party.

*(American Antiquarian Society)*

olics would owe primary allegiance to the pope in Rome and not to the American nation.

In 1854 anti-immigrant fears gave the Know-Nothings spectacular success in some northern states. They triumphed especially in Massachusetts, electing 11 congressmen, a governor, all state officers, all state senators, and all but 2 of 378 state representatives. The temperance movement also gained new strength early in the 1850s with its promises to stamp out the evils associated with liquor and immigrants (a particularly anti-Irish campaign). In this context the Know-Nothings strove to reinforce Protestant morality and to restrict voting and office holding to the native-born. As the Whig Party faded from the scene, the Know-Nothings temporarily filled the void. But, like the Whigs, the Know-Nothings could not keep their northern and southern wings together in the face of the slavery expansion issue, and they dissolved after 1856. The growing Republican coalition wooed the nativists with

temperance ordinances and laws postponing suffrage for naturalized citizens (see Table 14.1).

With nearly half of the old electorate up for grabs, the demise of the Whig Party ensured a major realignment

### Party Realignment and the Republicans' Appeal

of the political system. The remaining parties made appeals to various segments of the electorate. Immigration, temperance, homestead bills, the tariff, internal improvements—all played important roles in attracting voters during the 1850s. The Republicans appealed strongly to those interested in the economic development of the West. Commercial agriculture was booming in the Ohio–Mississippi–Great Lakes area, but residents of that region desired more canals, roads, and river and harbor improvements. Because credit was scarce, a homestead program—the idea that western land should be free to individuals who would farm it and make a home on it—attracted many voters. The Republicans seized on these political desires, promising internal improvements and land grants, as well as backing higher tariffs to protect industry.

Partisan ideological appeals became the currency of the realigned political system. As Republicans preached, "Free Soil, Free Labor, Free Men," they captured a self-image of many northerners. These phrases resonated with traditional ideals of equality, liberty, and opportunity under self-government—the heritage of republicanism. Invoking that heritage also undercut charges that the Republican Party was radical and abolitionist.

The northern economy was booming, and thousands of migrants had moved west to establish productive farms and growing communities. Midwesterners multiplied their yields by using new machines, such as mechanical reapers. Railroads were carrying their crops to urban markets. And industry was beginning to perform wonders of production, making available goods that only recently had been beyond the reach of the average person. As northerners surveyed the general growth and prosperity, they thought they saw a reason for it.

The key to progress appeared, to many people, to be free labor—the dignity of work and the incentive

### Republican Ideology

of opportunity. Any hard-working and virtuous man, it was thought, could improve his condition and achieve economic independence by seizing the main chance. Republicans argued that the South, with little industry and slave labor, was backward by comparison. Their arguments captured the spirit of the age in the North.

Traditional republicanism hailed the virtuous common man as the backbone of the country. In Abraham

## Annexation of Cuba

One of the most contentious issues in antebellum American foreign relations was the annexation of Cuba. As a strategic bulwark against Britain and France in the Western Hemisphere, for its massive sugar wealth, and as a slave society that might reinforce the security of southern slavery, the Spanish-controlled island fired the imagination of manifest destiny. In the early republic, Presidents Thomas Jefferson and James Madison explored acquisition. "I have ever looked on Cuba as the most interesting addition which could . . . be made to our system of states," wrote Jefferson. John Quincy Adams, speaking as secretary of state in 1823, considered Cuba "indispensable to the continuance . . . of the Union."

Until the 1840s, the United States officially supported Spanish rule for stability and the preservation of slavery. Southerners feared a "second Haiti" if Cuba became independent through revolution. The prospect of slave insurrection and the spread of abolitionism throughout the upper Caribbean and the rim of the Deep South drove many southerners and three Democratic administrations to shift course and pursue acquisition of Cuba. Slaveholding politicians viewed Cuba as critical to expansion; human bondage, they believed, had to expand southward and westward, or it might die.

In 1848 President Polk authorized $100 million to purchase Cuba. The Spanish foreign minister, however, told Polk's emissary that his government would rather see Cuba "sunk in the ocean" than sell it to the United States. During the crisis over the Kansas-Nebraska Act in 1854, as President Pierce revived the annexation scheme, some southerners planned to seize Cuba by force. Although the expedition never embarked, its prospect outraged antislavery Republicans eager to halt slavery's expansion and protect their claims for free labor as the basis of America's future.

Yet another aggressive American design on Cuba emerged in the Ostend Manifesto in October 1854. Written after a meeting among the American foreign ministers to Britain, France, and Spain, the document advocated conquest of Cuba if it could not be purchased. The ministers predicted that Cuba "would be Africanized and become a second St. Domingo, with all its attendant horrors to the white race." But antislavery northerners saw schemes of the Slave Power, whose "will is the law of this administration." The Ostend controversy forced temporary abandonment of annexation efforts, but as the fires in Bleeding Kansas subsided in 1858, President Buchanan reignited Cuba fever. A fierce Senate debate over yet another purchase offer in early 1859 ended in bitter division over the extension of slavery's domain.

The failure of Cuban annexation was deeply intertwined with the meaning of the United States as a slaveholding republic. "I want Cuba, and I know that sooner or later we must have it . . . for the planting or spreading of slavery," said Mississippian Albert G. Brown in 1858. Too many northerners, however, understood Brown's intentions. In America's links to the world—in this case only 90 miles from the Florida coast—just as in domestic affairs, the expansion of slavery poisoned the body politic.

▲ Despite the failure of filibustering expeditions, the effort to annex Cuba continued throughout James Buchanan's presidential administration. This cartoon portrays Sam Houston, the famed Texan and proponent of American expansion, rowing the boat for a harpoonist in quest of the whale, Cuba. The dream of appropriating Cuba to the United States died very hard in the antebellum era. *Vanity Fair,* New York, June 1860. *(© Bettmann/Corbis)*

Lincoln, a man of humble origins who had become a successful lawyer and political leader, Republicans had a symbol of that tradition. They portrayed their party as the guardian of economic opportunity, giving individuals a chance to work, acquire land, and attain success. In the words of an Iowa Republican, the United States was thriving because its "door is thrown open to all, and even the poorest and humblest in the land, may, by industry and application, gain a position which will entitle him to the respect . . . of his fellow-men."

At stake in the crises of the 1850s were thus two competing definitions of "liberty": southern planters' claims to protection of their liberty in the possession and transport of their slaves anywhere in the land, and northern workers' and farmers' claims to protection of their liberty to seek a new start on free land, unimpeded by a system that defined labor as slave and black.

Opposition to the extension of slavery had brought the Republicans into being, but party members carefully broadened their appeal by adopting the causes of other groups. Their coalition ideology consisted of many elements: resentment of southern political power, devotion to unionism, antislavery based on free-labor arguments, moral revulsion to slavery, and racial prejudice. As *New York Tribune* editor Horace Greeley wrote in 1856, "It is beaten into my bones that the American people are not yet anti-slavery." Four years later, Greeley again observed that "an Anti-Slavery man per se cannot be elected." But, he added, "a Tariff, River-and-Harbor, Pacific Railroad, Free Homestead man, may succeed although he is Anti-Slavery." As these elements placed their hopes in the Republican Party, they also grew to fear slavery even more.

In the South, the disintegration of the Whig Party had left many southerners at loose ends politically; they in-

### Southern Democrats

cluded a good number of wealthy planters, smaller slaveholders, and urban businessmen. Some gravitated to the American Party, but not for long. In the increasingly tense atmosphere of sectional crisis, these people were highly susceptible to strong states' rights positions and the defense of slavery. The security of their own communities seemed at stake, and in the 1850s, most formerly Whig slaveholders converted to the Democratic Party.

Since Andrew Jackson's day, however, nonslaveholding yeomen had been the heart of the Democratic Party. Democratic politicians, though often slaveowners themselves, lauded the common man and argued that their policies advanced his interests. According to the southern version of republicanism, white citizens in a slave society enjoyed liberty and social equality because black people were enslaved. As Jefferson Davis put it in 1851, in other societies distinctions were drawn "by property, between the rich and the poor." But in the South, slavery elevated every white person's status and allowed the nonslaveholder to "stand upon the broad level of equality with the rich man." To retain the support of ordinary whites, southern Democrats appealed to racism, warning starkly of the main issue: "shall negroes govern white men, or white men govern negroes?"

Southern leaders also portrayed sectional controversies as matters of injustice and insult to the honor of the South. The rights of all southern whites were in jeopardy, they argued, because antislavery and Free-Soil forces threatened an institution protected in the Constitution. The stable, well-ordered South was the true defender of constitutional principles; the rapidly changing North, their destroyer.

Racial fears and traditional political loyalties helped keep the political alliance between yeoman farmers and planters largely intact through the 1850s. Across class lines, white southerners joined together in the interest of community security against what they perceived as the Republican Party's capacity to cause slave unrest in their midst. In the South, no viable party emerged to replace the Whigs, and as in the North, political realignment sharpened sectional identities.

Political leaders of both sections used race in their arguments about opportunity, but northerners and southerners saw different futures. The *Montgomery* (Alabama) *Mail* warned southern whites in 1860 that the Republicans intended "to free the negroes and force amalgamation between them and the children of the poor men of the South. The rich will be able to keep out of the way of the contamination." Republicans warned northern workers that, if slavery entered the territories, the great reservoir of opportunity for ordinary citizens would be poisoned.

The Kansas-Nebraska Act spawned hatred and violence as land-hungry partisans in the sectional struggle

### Bleeding Kansas

clashed repeatedly in Kansas Territory. Abolitionists and religious groups sent in armed Free-Soil settlers; southerners sent in their reinforcements to establish slavery and prevent "northern hordes" from stealing Kansas away. Conflicts led to vicious bloodshed, and soon the whole nation was talking about "Bleeding Kansas."

Politics in the territory resembled war more than democracy. During elections for a territorial legislature in 1855, thousands of proslavery Missourians—known as Border Ruffians—invaded the polls and ran up a large but fraudulent majority for proslavery candidates. They

▲ Proslavery advocates and Free-Soilers clashed in open battle in Kansas Territory on September 13, 1856, as captured in this sketch by eyewitness S. J. Reader. *(Kansas State Historical Society)*

murdered and intimidated free state settlers. At one rally of such ruffians with other southerners, flags flapped in the breeze with the mottoes "Southern Rights," "Supremacy of the White Race," and "Alabama for Kansas." The resulting legislature legalized slavery, and in response Free-Soilers held an unauthorized convention at which they created their own government and constitution. Kansas was a tinderbox. By the spring of 1856, newspapers screamed for violence. "In a fight, let our motto be 'War to the knife, and knife to the hilt," demanded the proslavery *Squatter Sovereign.* Slavery's advocates taunted their adversaries as cowards and likened "abolitionists" to "infidels" worthy only of "total extermination."

In May, a proslavery posse sent to arrest the Free-Soil leaders sacked the Kansas town of Lawrence, killing several people and destroying a hotel with cannon shot. In revenge, John Brown, a radical abolitionist with a band of followers, murdered five proslavery settlers living along Pottawatomie Creek. The victims were taken in the dark of night from the clutches of their families, their heads and limbs hacked to pieces by heavy broadswords, their bodies heaved into dead brush. Brown himself did not wield the swords, but he did fire a single shot into the head of one senseless foe to assure his death. Soon, armed bands of guerrillas roamed the territory, battling over land claims as well as slavery.

These passions brought violence to the U.S. Senate in May 1856, when Charles Sumner of Massachusetts de-nounced "the Crime against Kansas." Radical in his anti-slavery views, Sumner bitterly assailed the president, the South, and Senator Andrew P. Butler of South Carolina. Soon thereafter, Butler's cousin, Representative Preston Brooks, approached Sumner at the latter's Senate desk, raised his cane, announced the defense of his kin's honor, and mercilessly beat Sumner on the head. The senator collapsed, bleeding, on the floor while unsympathetic colleagues watched.

Shocked northerners recoiled from what they saw as another case of wanton southern violence and an assault on free speech. William Cullen Bryant, editor of the *New York Evening Post,* asked, "Has it come to this, that we must speak with bated breath in the presence of our southern masters?" As if in reply, the *Richmond Enquirer* de-nounced "vulgar Abolitionists in the Senate" who "have been suffered to run too long without collars. They must be lashed into submission." Popular opinion in Massachusetts strongly supported Sumner; South Carolina voters reelected Brooks and sent him dozens of commemorative canes.

The election of 1856 showed how extreme such polarization had become. For Republicans, "Bleeding Sumner" and "Bleeding Kansas" had become rallying cries. When Democrats met to select a nominee, they shied away from prominent leaders whose views on the territorial question would invite controversy. Instead, they chose James Buchanan of

**Election of 1856**

Pennsylvania, whose chief virtue was that for the past four years he had been ambassador to Britain, uninvolved in territorial controversies. Superior party organization helped Buchanan win 1.8 million votes and the election, but he owed his victory to southern support. Hence, he was tagged with the label "a northern man with southern principles."

Eleven of sixteen free states voted against Buchanan, and Democrats did not regain ascendancy in those states for decades. The Republican candidate, John C. Frémont, famous as a western explorer, won those eleven free states and 1.3 million votes; Republicans had become the dominant party in the North after only two years of existence. The Know-Nothing candidate, Millard Fillmore, won almost 1 million votes, but this election was that party's last hurrah. The coming battle would pit a sectional Republican Party against an increasingly divided Democratic Party. With huge voter turnouts, as high as 75 to 80 percent in many states, Americans were about to learn that elections really matter.

## SLAVERY AND THE NATION'S FUTURE

For years the issue of slavery in the territories had convulsed Congress, and Congress had tried to settle the issue with vague formulas. In 1857 the Supreme Court stepped into the fray, took up this emotionally charged subject, and attempted to silence controversy with a definitive verdict.

A Missouri slave named Dred Scott and his wife, Harriet Robinson Scott, had sued for their freedom. Scott

### Dred Scott Case

based his claim on the fact that his former owner, an army surgeon, had taken him for several years into Illinois, a free state, and to Fort Snelling in the Minnesota Territory, from which slavery had been barred by the Missouri Compromise. Scott first won and then lost his case as it moved on appeal through the state courts into the federal system and, finally, after eleven years, to the Supreme Court.

The impetus for the lawsuit likely came as much from Harriet as from Dred Scott. They were legally married at Fort Snelling (free territory) in 1836 when Dred was forty and Harriet seventeen. She had already lived as a slave on free soil for at least five years and had given birth to four children, also born on free soil: two sons who died in infancy and two daughters, Eliza and Lizzie, who lived. In all likelihood, the quest to achieve "freedom papers" through a lawsuit—begun in 1846 as two separate cases, one in his name and one in hers—came as much from Harriet's desire to sustain her family and pro-

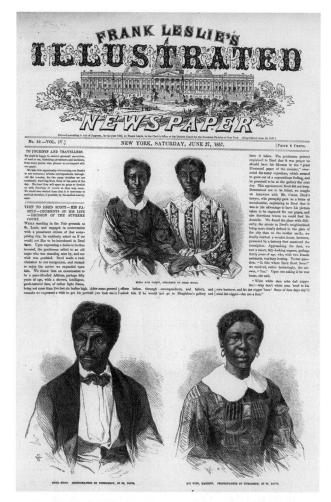

▲ Frank Leslie's *Illustrated Newspaper*, June 27, 1857. Dred Scott and his wife Harriet, below, and their two children, Eliza and Lizzie, above. Such dignified pictures and imformative articles provided Americans broadly with images of the otherwise mysterious Dred Scott and his family in the landmark Supreme Court case.

*(Library of Congress)*

tect her two teenage daughters from potential sale and sexual abuse as from the aging and sickly Dred. Indeed, her legal case for freedom may have been even stronger than Dred's, but their lawyers subsumed her case into his during the long appeal process.

Normally, Supreme Court justices were reluctant to inject themselves into major political issues. An 1851 decision had declared that state courts determined the status of blacks who lived within their jurisdictions. The Supreme Court had only to follow this precedent to avoid ruling on substantive, and very controversial, issues: Was a black person like Dred Scott a citizen of the United States and thus eligible to sue in federal court?

Had residence in a free state or territory made him free? Did Congress have the power to prohibit or promote slavery in a territory?

After hesitation, the Supreme Court agreed to hear *Dred Scott v. Sanford* and decided to rule on the Missouri Compromise after all. Two northern justices indicated that they would dissent from the assigned opinion and argue for Scott's freedom and the constitutionality of the Missouri Compromise. Their decision emboldened southerners on the Court, who were growing eager to declare the 1820 geographical restriction on slavery unconstitutional. Southern sympathizers in Washington were pressing for a proslavery verdict, and several justices felt they should simply try to resolve sectional strife once and for all.

In March 1857, Chief Justice Roger B. Taney of Maryland delivered the majority opinion of a divided Court (the vote was 7 to 2). Taney declared that Scott was not a citizen of either the United States or Missouri; that residence in free territory did not make Scott free; and that Congress had no power to bar slavery from any territory. The decision not only overturned a sectional compromise that had been honored for thirty-seven years, it also invalidated the basic ideas of the Wilmot Proviso and popular sovereignty.

The Slave Power seemed to have won a major constitutional victory. African Americans were especially dismayed, for Taney's decision asserted that the founders had never intended for black people to be citizens. At the nation's founding, the chief justice wrote, blacks had been regarded "as beings of an inferior order" with "no rights which the white man was bound to respect." Taney was mistaken, however. African Americans had been citizens in several of the original states and had in fact voted.

Nevertheless, the ruling seemed to shut the door permanently on black hopes for justice. After 1857, African Americans lived in the land of the *Dred Scott* decision. In northern black communities, rage and despair prevailed. Many who were still fugitive slaves sought refuge in Canada; others considered emigration to the Caribbean or even to Africa. Mary Ann Shadd Cary, who was free and the leader of an emigration movement to Canada, advised her fellow blacks, "Your national ship is rotten and sinking, why not leave it?" Another black abolitionist said that the *Dred Scott* decision had made slavery "the supreme law of the land and all descendants of the African race denationalized." In this state of social dislocation and fear, blacks contemplated whether they had any future in the United States.

Northern whites who rejected the decision's content were suspicious of the circumstances that had produced it. Five of the nine justices were southerners; three of the northern justices actively dissented or refused to concur in parts of the decision. The only northerner who supported Taney's opinion, Justice Robert Grier of Pennsylvania, was known to be close to President Buchanan. In fact, Buchanan had secretly brought to bear improper but effective influence.

A storm of angry reaction broke in the North. The decision seemed to confirm every charge against the aggressive Slave Power. "There is such a thing as the slave power," warned the *Cincinnati Daily Commercial*. "It has marched over and annihilated the boundaries of the states. We are now one great homogenous slaveholding community." The *Cincinnati Freeman* asked, "What security have the Germans and the Irish that their children will not, within a hundred years, be reduced to slavery in this land of their adoption?" Poet James Russell Lowell expressed the racial and economic anxieties of poor northern whites when he had his Yankee character Ezekiel Biglow say, in the language of the day,

> Wy, it's just ez clear ez figgers,
> Clear ez one an' one make two,
> Chaps thet make black slaves o' niggers,
> Want to make wite slaves o' you.

Republican politicians used these fears to strengthen their antislavery coalition. Abraham Lincoln stressed

### Abraham Lincoln and the Slave Power

that the territorial question affected every citizen. "The whole nation," he had declared as early as 1854, "is interested that the best use shall be made of these Territories. We want them for homes of free white people. This they cannot be, to any considerable extent, if slavery shall be planted within them." The territories must be reserved, he insisted, "as an outlet for free white people everywhere" so that immigrants could come to America and "find new homes and better their condition in life."

More important, Lincoln warned of slavery's increasing control over the nation. The founders had created a government dedicated to freedom, Lincoln insisted. Admittedly they had recognized slavery's existence, but the public mind, he argued in the "House Divided" speech of 1858, had always rested in the belief that slavery would die either naturally or by legislation. The next step in the unfolding Slave Power conspiracy, Lincoln alleged, would be a Supreme Court decision "declaring that the Constitution does not permit a State to exclude slavery from its limits. . . . We shall lie down pleasantly, dreaming that the people of Missouri are on the verge of making their State free; and we shall awake to the reality instead, that the Supreme Court has made Illinois a slave State." This charge was not hyperbole, for lawsuits soon challenged state laws that freed slaves brought within their borders. Countless northerners heeded Lincoln's warnings, as events convinced them that slaveholders were intent on making slavery a national institution. Southerners, fatefully, never forgot Lincoln's use of the direct words "ultimate extinction."

Politically, Republicans were now locked in conflict with the *Dred Scott* decision. By endorsing the South's doctrine of state sovereignty, the Court had in effect declared that the central position of the Republican Party—no extension of slavery—was unconstitutional. Republicans could only repudiate the decision, appealing to a "higher law," or hope to change the personnel of the Court. They did both and gained politically as fear of the Slave Power grew. But fear also deepened among free blacks. Frederick Douglass continued to try to fashion hope among his people but concluded a speech in the wake of the *Dred Scott* decision bleakly: "I walk by faith, not by sight."

For northern Democrats like Stephen Douglas, the Court's decision posed an awful dilemma. Northern voters were alarmed by the prospect that the territories would be opened to slavery. To retain their support, Douglas had to find some way to reassure these voters. Yet, given his presidential ambitions, Douglas could not afford to alienate southern Democrats.

### The Lecompton Constitution and Disharmony Among Democrats

Douglas chose to stand by his principle of popular sovereignty, even if the result angered southerners. In 1857 Kansans voted on a proslavery constitution that had been drafted at Lecompton. It was defeated by more than ten thousand votes in a referendum boycotted by most proslavery voters. The evidence was overwhelming that Kansans did not want slavery, yet President Buchanan tried to force the Lecompton Constitution through Congress in an effort to hastily organize the territory.

Never had the Slave Power's influence over the government seemed more blatant; the Buchanan administration and southerners demanded a proslavery outcome, contrary to the majority will in Kansas. Breaking with the administration, Douglas threw his weight against the Lecompton Constitution. But his action infuriated southern Democrats. After the *Dred Scott* decision, southerners like Senator Albert G. Brown of Mississippi believed that slavery was protected in the territories: "The Constitution as expounded by the Supreme Court awards it. We demand it; we mean to have it." Increasingly, though, many southerners believed that their sectional rights and slavery would be safe only in a separate nation. And north-

ern Democrats, led by Douglas, found it harder to support the territorial protection for slavery that southern Democrats insisted was theirs as a constitutional right. Thus in North and South the issue of slavery in the territories continued to destroy moderation and promote militancy.

## DISUNION

It is worth remembering that, in the late 1850s, most Americans were not always caught up daily in the slavery crisis. They were preoccupied with personal affairs, especially coping with the effects of the economic panic that had begun in the spring of 1857. They were worried about widespread unemployment, the plummeting price of wheat, the declining wages at a textile mill, or sons who needed land. In the Midwest, clerks, mechanics, domestics, railroad hands, and lumber camp workers lost jobs by the thousands. Bankers were at a loss for what to do about a weak credit system caused by frenzied western land speculation that began early in the decade. In parts of the South, such as Georgia, the panic intensified class divisions between upcountry yeomen and coastal slaveholding planters. Farmers blamed the tight money policies of Georgia's budding commercial banking system on wealthy planters who controlled the state's Democratic Party.

The panic had been caused by several shortcomings of the unregulated American banking system, by frenzies of speculation in western lands and railroads, and by a weak and overburdened credit system. By 1858 Philadelphia had 40,000 unemployed workers and New York City, nearly 100,000. Fear of bread riots and class warfare gripped many cities in the North. True to form, blame for such economic woe became sectionalized, as southerners saw their system justified by the temporary collapse of industrial prosperity and northerners feared even more the incursions of the Slave Power on an insecure future.

Soon, however, the entire nation's focus would be drawn to a new dimension of the slavery question—

### John Brown's Raid on Harpers Ferry

armed rebellion, led by the abolitionist who had killed proslavery settlers along Pottawatomie Creek in "Bleeding Kansas." Born in Connecticut in 1800, John Brown had been raised by staunchly religious antislavery parents. Between 1820 and 1855, he engaged in some twenty business ventures, including farming, nearly all of them failures. But Brown had a distinctive vision of abolitionism. He relied on an Old Testament conception of justice—"an eye for an eye"—and he had a puritanical obsession with the wickedness of others, especially southern slaveowners. Brown believed that slavery was an "unjustifiable" state of

▲ The earliest known photograph of John Brown, probably taken in 1846 in Massachusetts, shows him pledging his devotion to an unidentified flag, possibly an abolitionist banner. Already Brown was aiding runaway slaves and pondering ways to strike at slavery.

*(Ohio Historical Society)*

war conducted by one group of people against another. He also believed that violence in a righteous cause was a holy act, even a rite of purification for those who engaged in it. To Brown, the destruction of slavery in America required revolutionary ideology and revolutionary acts.

On October 16, 1859, Brown led a small band of eighteen whites and blacks in an attack on the federal arsenal at Harpers Ferry, Virginia. Hoping to trigger a slave rebellion, Brown failed miserably and was quickly captured. In a celebrated trial in November and a widely publicized execution in December, in Charles Town, Virginia, Brown became one of the most enduring martyrs, as well as villains, of American history. His attempted insurrection struck fear into the South.

Then it became known that Brown had received financial backing from several prominent abolitionists. When such northern intellectuals as Ralph Waldo Emerson and Henry David Thoreau praised Brown as a holy warrior who "would make the gallows as glorious as the cross," white southerners' outrage intensified. The South almost universally interpreted Brown's attack at Harpers Ferry

as an act of midnight terrorism, as the fulfillment of their long-stated dread of "abolition emissaries" who would infiltrate the region to incite slave rebellion.

Perhaps most telling of all was the fact that the pivotal election of 1860 was less than a year away when Brown went so eagerly to the gallows, handing a note to his jailer with the famous prediction "I John Brown am now quite certain that the crimes of this guilty land will never be purged away, but with blood." Most troubling to southerners, perhaps, was their awareness that, though Republican politicians condemned Brown's crimes, they did so in a way that deflected attention onto the still-greater crime of slavery.

Many Americans believed that the election of 1860 would decide the fate of the Union. The Democratic Party was the only party that was truly national in scope. "One after another," wrote a Mississippi editor, "the links which have bound the North and South together, have been severed . . . [but] the Democratic party looms gradually up . . . and waves the olive branch over the troubled waters of politics." But, fatefully, at its 1860 convention in Charleston, South Carolina, the Democratic Party split.

### Election of 1860

Stephen Douglas wanted his party's presidential nomination, but he could not afford to alienate northern voters by accepting the southern position on the territories. Southern Democrats, however, insisted on recognition of their rights—as the *Dred Scott* decision had defined them—and they moved to block Douglas's nomination. When Douglas obtained a majority for his version of the platform, delegates from the Deep South walked out of the convention. After efforts at compromise failed, the Democrats presented two nominees: Douglas for the northern wing, and Vice President John C. Breckinridge of Kentucky for the southern.

The Republicans nominated Abraham Lincoln at a rousing convention in Chicago. The choice of Lincoln reflected the growing power of the Midwest, and he was perceived as more moderate on slavery than the early front runner, Senator William H. Seward of New York. A Constitutional Union Party, formed to preserve the nation but strong only in the Upper South, nominated John Bell of Tennessee.

Bell's only issue in the ensuing campaign was the urgency of preserving the Union; Constitutional Unionists hoped to appeal to history, sentiment, and moderation to hold the country together. Douglas desperately sought to unite his northern and southern supporters, while Breckinridge quickly backed away from the appearance of extremism, and his supporters in several states stressed his

| TABLE 14.3 | Presidential Vote in 1860 (by State) |
|---|---|
| Lincoln (Republican)* | Carried all northern states and all electoral votes except 3 in New Jersey |
| Breckinridge (Southern Democrat) | Carried all slave states except Virginia, Kentucky, Tennessee, Missouri |
| Bell (Constitutional Union) | Carried Virginia, Kentucky, Tennessee |
| Douglas (Northern Democrat) | Carried only Missouri |

*Lincoln received only 26,000 votes in the entire South and was not even on the ballot in ten slave states. Breckinridge was not on the ballot in three northern states.

unionism. Although Lincoln and the Republicans denied any intent to interfere with slavery in the states where it existed, they stood firm against the extension of slavery into the territories.

The election of 1860 was sectional in character, and the only one in American history in which the losers refused to accept the result. Lincoln won, but Douglas, Breckinridge, and Bell together received a majority of the votes. Douglas had broad-based support but won few states. Breckinridge carried nine southern states, all in the Deep South. Bell won pluralities in Virginia, Kentucky, and Tennessee. Lincoln prevailed in the North, but in the four slave states that ultimately remained loyal to the Union (Missouri, Kentucky, Maryland, and Delaware—the border states) he gained only a plurality, not a majority (see Table 14.3). Lincoln's victory was won in the electoral college. He polled only 40 percent of the total vote and was not even on the ballot in ten slave states.

Opposition to slavery's extension was the core issue for Lincoln and the Republican Party. Moreover, abolitionists and Free-Soil supporters in the North worked to keep the Republicans from compromising on their territorial stand. Meanwhile, in the South, proslavery advocates and secessionists whipped up public opinion and demanded that state conventions assemble to consider secession.

Lincoln made the crucial decision not to soften his party's position on the territories. He wrote of the necessity of maintaining the bond of faith between voter and candidate, and of declining to set "the minority over the majority." Although many conservative Republicans—eastern businessmen and former Whigs who did not feel strongly about slavery—hoped for a compromise, the original and most committed Republicans—old Free-Soilers and antislavery Whigs—held the line on slavery expansion.

In the winter of 1860–1861, Senator John J. Crittenden of Kentucky tried to craft a late-hour compromise. Hoping to don the mantle of Henry Clay and avert dis-

union, Crittenden proposed that the two sections divide the territories between them at the Missouri Compromise line, 36°30'. But this well-worn and controversial idea did not work. When Lincoln ruled out concessions on the territorial issue, Crittenden's peacemaking effort, based on old and discredited measures, collapsed.

Meanwhile, the Union was being destroyed. On December 20, 1860, South Carolina passed an ordinance of secession amid jubilation and cheering. Secession strategists concentrated their efforts on the most extreme proslavery state, hoping that South Carolina's bold act would induce other states to follow, with each decision building momentum for disunion.

## Secession and the Confederate States of America

By reclaiming its independence, South Carolina raised the stakes in the sectional confrontation. No longer was secession an unthinkable step; the Union was broken. Secessionists now argued that other states should follow South Carolina and that those who favored compromise could make a better deal outside the Union than in it. Moderates found it difficult to dismiss such arguments, since most of them—even those who felt deep affection for the Union—were committed to defending southern rights and institutions.

Southern extremists soon got their way in the Deep South. Overwhelming their opposition, they called separate state conventions and passed secession ordinances in Mississippi, Florida, Alabama, Georgia, Louisiana, and Texas. By February 1861 these states had joined South Carolina to form a new government in Montgomery, Alabama: the Confederate States of America. The delegates at Montgomery chose Jefferson Davis of Mississippi as their president, and the Confederacy began to function independently of the United States.

This apparent unanimity of action was deceiving. Confused and dissatisfied with the alternatives, many

R. H. Howell, after Henry Cleenewerck, ▶
*The First Flag of Independence Raised in the South.* Lithograph, Savannah, Georgia, 1860. On the night of November 8, 1860, a huge crowd gathered in Johnson Square, Savannah, to protest Lincoln's election victory. The special banner on the obelisk reads "Our Motto Southern Rights, Equality of the States, Don't Tread on Me," drawing on traditions from the Revolutionary War.

*(Library of Congress)*

southerners who in 1860 had voted in the U.S. presidential election stayed home a few months later rather than vote for delegates who would decide on secession. Even so, in some state conventions the secession vote was close, and decided by overrepresentation of plantation districts. Four states in the Upper South—Virginia, North Carolina, Tennessee, and Arkansas—flatly rejected secession and did not join the Confederacy until after fighting had begun. In the border states, popular sentiment was deeply divided; minorities in Kentucky and Missouri tried to secede, but these slave states ultimately came under Union control, along with Maryland and Delaware (see Map 14.4).

Such misgivings were not surprising. Secession posed new and troubling issues for southerners, especially the possibility of war, where it would be fought, and who would die. Analysis of election returns from 1860 and 1861 indicates that slaveholders and nonslaveholders were beginning to part company politically. Heavily slaveholding counties strongly supported secession. But nonslaveholding areas that had favored Breckinridge in the presidential election proved far less willing to support secession: most counties with few slaves took an antisecession position or were staunchly Unionist (see Figure 14.1). With war on the horizon, yeomen were beginning to consider their class interests and to ask themselves how far they would go to support slavery and slaveowners.

As for why the Deep South bolted, we need look no further than the speeches and writings of the secession commissioners sent out by the seven seceded states to try to convince the other slave states to join them. Repeatedly they stressed independence as the only way to preserve white racial security and the slave system against the hostile Republicans. Upon "slavery," said the Alabama commissioner, Stephen Hale, to the Kentucky legislature, rested "not only the wealth and prosperity of the southern peo-

ple, but their very existence as a political community." Only secession, Hale contended, could sustain the "heaven-ordained superiority of the white over the black race."

The dilemma facing President Lincoln on inauguration day in March 1861 was how to maintain the authority of the federal government without provoking war. Proceeding cautiously, he sought only to hold onto forts in the states that had left the Union, reasoning that in this way he could assert federal sovereignty while waiting for a restoration. But Jefferson Davis, who could not claim to lead a sovereign nation if the Confederate ports were under foreign (that is, U.S.) control, was unwilling to be so patient. A collision soon came.

## Fort Sumter and Outbreak of War

It arrived in the early morning hours of April 12, 1861, at Fort Sumter in Charleston harbor. A federal garrison there ran low on food, and Lincoln notified the South Carolinians that he was sending a ship to resupply the fort. For the Montgomery government, the alternatives were to attack the fort or to acquiesce to Lincoln's authority. After the Confederate cabinet met, the secretary of war ordered local commanders to obtain a surrender or attack the fort. After two days of heavy bombardment, the federal garrison finally surrendered. No one died in battle, though an accident during post-battle ceremonies killed two Union soldiers. Confederates permitted the U.S. troops to sail away on unarmed vessels while Charlestonians celebrated wildly. The Civil War—the bloodiest war in America's history—had begun.

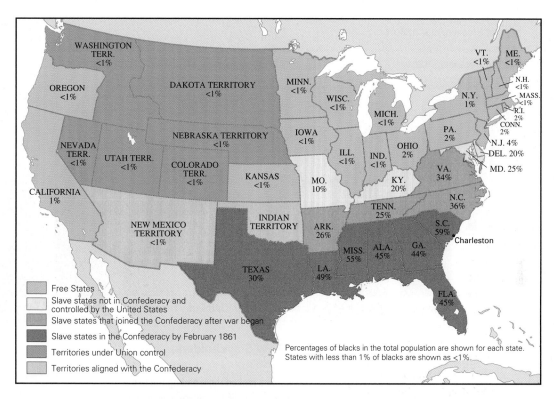

**Map 14.4    The Divided Nation—Slave and Free Areas, 1861**

After fighting began, the Upper South joined the Deep South in the Confederacy. How does the nation's pattern of division correspond to the distribution of slavery and the percentage of blacks in the population?

## Causation

Historians have long debated the immediate and long-term roots of the Civil War. Some have interpreted it as an "irrepressible conflict," the clash of two civilizations on divergent trajectories of history. Another group saw the war as "needless," the result of a "blundering generation" of irrational politicians and activists who trumped up an avoidable conflict. But the issues dividing Americans in 1861 were fundamental to the future of the republic. The logic of Republican ideology tended in the direction of abolishing slavery, even though Republicans denied any such intention. The logic of southern arguments led to establishing slavery everywhere, though southern leaders, too, denied such a motive.

These positions hardened in American political life during the decade and a half before secession. Lincoln put these facts succinctly. In a postelection letter to his old friend Alexander Stephens of Georgia, soon to be vice president of the Confederacy, Lincoln offered assurance that Republicans would not attack slavery in the states where it existed. But Lincoln continued, "You think slavery is right and ought to be expanded; while we think it is wrong and ought to be restricted. That I suppose is the rub." Frederick Douglass demonstrated that he understood this in a postwar speech in which he declared that the "fight" had not been between "rapacious birds and ferocious beasts, a mere display of brute courage . . . but it was a war between men of thought, as well as of action, and in dead earnest for something beyond the battlefield."

Directly or indirectly, Douglass's "something" had almost everything to do with slavery. Without slavery, there would have been no war. Many Americans still hold to a belief that the war was about states' rights, the theory and practice of the proper relationship of state to federal authority. But the significance of states' rights, then as now, is always in the cause in which it is employed. If secession was an exercise in states' rights—to what end? To borrow from Douglass, it is the meaning within the fight that we must understand.

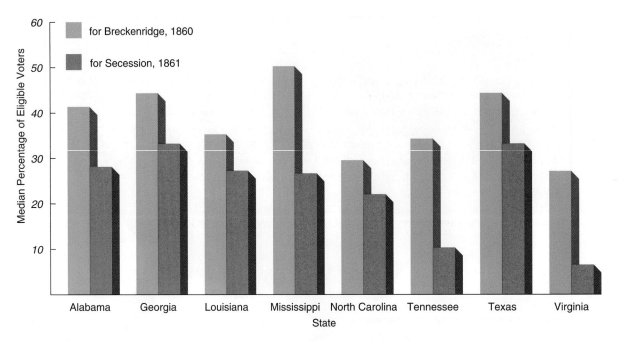

**Figure 14.1**   **Voting Returns of Counties with Few Slaveholders, Eight Southern States, 1860 and 1861**

This graph depicts voting in counties whose percentage of slaveholders ranked them among the lower half of the counties in their state. How does voters' support for secession in 1861 compare with support for John Breckinridge, the southern Democratic candidate in 1860? Why was their support for secession so weak? At this time counties with many slaveholders were giving increased support to secession.

## SUMMARY

Events often seem inevitable after they have occurred. We should never fall into the trap of seeing big events in history only through a lens of inevitability. The events and ideas that Americans clashed over were links in a chain leading to conflict; humans made choices all along the way and to go to war.

The War with Mexico fostered massive land acquisition, which in turn forced an open debate about slavery in the West. The Compromise of 1850 attempted to settle the dispute but only added fuel to the fires of sectional contention, leading to the fateful Kansas-Nebraska Act of 1854, which tore asunder the political party system and gave birth to a genuine antislavery coalition. With Bleeding Kansas and the *Dred Scott* decision by 1857, Americans North and South faced clear and dangerous choices about the future of labor and the meaning of liberty in an ambitious and expanding society. And finally, by 1859, when radical abolitionist John Brown attacked Harpers Ferry to foment a slave insurrection, southerners and northerners came to see each other in conspiratorial terms. Meanwhile, African Americans, slave and free, fled from slave catchers in unprecedented numbers and grew to ex-

pect violent if uncertain resolutions to their dreams of freedom in America. No one knew the future, but all knew that the issues and conflicts were real.

Throughout the 1840s and 1850s, many able leaders had worked to avert the outcome of disunion. As late as 1858, even Jefferson Davis had declared, "This great country will continue united," saying that "to the innermost fibers of my heart I love it all, and every part." Secession dismayed northern editors and voters, and it also plunged some planters into depression. Paul Cameron, the largest slaveowner in North Carolina, confessed that he was "very unhappy. I love the Union." Many blacks, however, shared Frederick Douglass's outlook. "The contest must now be decided," he wrote in March 1861, "and decided forever, which of the two, Freedom or Slavery, shall give law to this Republic. Let the conflict come."

Why had war broken out? Why had all efforts to prevent it failed? The emotions bound up in attacking and defending slavery's future were too powerful, and the interests it affected too vital for a final compromise. Advocates of compromise anticipated that the tradition of conciliation and sectional adjustment would yet again save the Union in 1860, but their hopes were dashed.

## Terrorist or Freedom Fighter?

The greatest significance of John Brown's raid on Harpers Ferry in 1859 rests in its long aftermath in American memory. "Men consented to his death," wrote Frederick Douglass of Brown, "and then went home and taught their children to honor his memory." Brown is as important as a symbol as he is for his deeds. He has been at once one of the most beloved and most loathed figures in American history. In the song that bears his name, "John Brown's Body," a popular marching tune during the Civil War, his "soul goes marching on." As poet Stephen Vincent Benét wrote: "You can weigh John Brown's body well enough, / But how and in what balance weigh John Brown?"

In the wake of his execution, in painting, song, and poetry people constructed a John Brown mythology. Was he a Christ-like figure who died for the nation's sins, who had to commit crimes in order to expose the nation's larger crime? Or was he a terrorist, who murdered in the name of his own vision of God's will? Brown can be inspiring and disturbing, majestic and foolish, a warrior saint and a monster. He represents the highest ideals and the most ruthless deeds. He killed for justice and was hanged as a traitor. Perhaps Brown was one of the avengers of history who does the work the rest of us will not, could not, or should not.

Over the years many organizations have adopted John Brown as their justifying symbol, from left-wing students opposing American foreign policy to current anti-abortion groups who target clinics and doctors. In today's world, terrorism and revolutionary violence are more often in the news. Suicide bombers attack buses and restaurants in Israel; a federal building explodes in Oklahoma City; Al Qaeda operatives blow up trains in Madrid; American embassies are attacked in Africa and Europe; on September 11, 2001, four hijacked passenger airplanes become weapons of death that bring terrorism to American soil as never before; and in Iraq a lethal insurgency resists the American occupation, as a country falls into sectarian civil war between Shi'ites and Sunnis. The story of John Brown's raid in 1859 continues to force us to ask when and how revolutionary violence—violence in the name of a political or spiritual end—is justified. That is his legacy for a people and a nation.

---

During the 1850s, every southern victory in territorial expansion increased fear of the Slave Power, and each new expression of Free-Soil sentiment prompted slaveholders to harden their demands. In the profoundest sense, slavery was the root of the war. But as the fighting began, the war's central issue was shrouded in confusion. How would the Civil War affect slavery, its place in the law, and African Americans' place in society? Would the institution survive a short war, but not a long war? As a people and a nation, Americans had reached the most fateful turning point in their history. Answers would now come from the battlefield and from the mobilization of two societies to wage war on a scale they had not imagined.

## SUGGESTIONS FOR FURTHER READING

Edward L. Ayers, *What Caused the Civil War: Reflections on the South and Southern History* (2005)

Richard J. Carwardine, *Lincoln* (2003)

Charles Dew, *Apostles of Disunion: Southern Secession Commissioners and the Causes of the Civil War* (2001)

Nicole Etcheson, *Bleeding Kansas: Contested Liberty in the Civil War Era* (2004)

Don E. Fehrenbacher, *The Slaveholding Republic: An Account of the United States Government's Relations to Slavery* (2001)

Eric Foner, *Free Soil, Free Labor, Free Men: The Ideology of the Republican Party* (1970)

Robert W. Johannsen, *To the Halls of the Montezumas: The Mexican War and the American Imagination* (1985)

Michael A. Morrison, *Slavery and the American West: The Eclipse of Manifest Destiny and the Coming of the Civil War* (1997)

David S. Reynolds, *John Brown, Abolitionist: The Man Who Killed Slavery, Sparked the Civil War, and Seeded Civil Rights* (2005)

Richard H. Sewell, *Ballots for Freedom: Antislavery Politics in the United States* (1976)

*For a more extensive list for further reading, go to* college.hmco.com/pic/norton8e.

# Transforming Fire: The Civil War *1861-1865*

*S*lave pens were the dark and ugly crossroads of American history. To see, hear, and smell one was to understand why the Civil War happened. Wallace Turnage, a seventeen-year-old slave from a cotton plantation in Pickens County, Alabama, entered wartime Mobile in December 1862 through the slave traders' yard; he would leave Mobile from that same yard a year and eight months later.

Turnage had been born on a remote tobacco farm near Snow Hill, North Carolina, in 1846. In mid-1860, as the nation teetered on the brink of disunion, he was sold to a Richmond, Virginia, slave trader named Hector Davis. Turnage worked in Davis's three-story slave jail, organizing daily auctions until he was himself sold for $1,000 in early 1861 to a cotton planter from Pickens County, Alabama. Frequently whipped and longing for escape, the desperate teenager tried four times over the next two years to run away to Mississippi, seeking the lines of the Union armies. Although he remained at large for months, he was captured each time and returned to his owner in southeastern Alabama.

In frustration, his owner took Turnage to the Mobile slave traders' yard, where the youth was sold for $2,000 to a wealthy merchant in the port city. During 1864, as Union Admiral David Farragut prepared his fleet for an assault on Mobile Bay and the city came under siege, its slaves were enlisted to build elaborate trenchworks. Meanwhile, Turnage labored at all manner of urban tasks for his new owner's family, including driving their carriage on errands.

One day in early August, Turnage crashed the old carriage on a Mobile street. In anger, his owner took him to the slave pen and hired the jailer to administer thirty lashes in the pen's special "whipping house." Stripped naked, his hands tied in ropes, Turnage was hoisted up on a hook on the wall. At the end of the gruesome ritual, his owner instructed

◀ Lithograph of a runaway slave, which was one of the most common depictions of slavery generally in northern popular culture. Part of Wallace Turnage's final excape occurred in a setting much like this image. *(Library of Congress)*

## CHRONOLOGY

1861 ■ Battle of Bull Run
    ■ McClellan organizes Union Army
    ■ Union blockade begins
    ■ U.S. Congress passes first confiscation act
    ■ *Trent* affair

1862 ■ Union captures Fort Henry and Fort Donelson
    ■ U.S. Navy captures New Orleans
    ■ Battle of Shiloh shows the war's destructiveness
    ■ Confederacy enacts conscription
    ■ McClellan's Peninsula Campaign fails to take Richmond
    ■ U.S. Congress passes second confiscation act, initiating emancipation
    ■ Confederacy mounts offensive in Maryland and Kentucky
    ■ Battle of Antietam ends Lee's drive into Maryland in September
    ■ British intervention in the war on Confederate side is averted

1863 ■ Emancipation Proclamation takes effect
    ■ U.S. Congress passes National Banking Act
    ■ Union enacts conscription
    ■ African American soldiers join Union Army
    ■ Food riots occur in southern cities
    ■ Battle of Chancellorsville ends in Confederate victory but Jackson's death
    ■ Union wins key victories at Vicksburg and Gettysburg
    ■ Draft riots take place in New York City

1864 ■ Battles of the Wilderness and Spotsylvania produce heavy casualties on both sides
    ■ Battle of Cold Harbor continues carnage in Virginia
    ■ Sherman captures Atlanta
    ■ Confederacy begins to collapse on home front
    ■ Lincoln wins reelection, eliminating any Confederate hopes for negotiated end to war
    ■ Jefferson Davis proposes arming slaves
    ■ Sherman marches through Georgia to the sea

1865 ■ Sherman marches through Carolinas
    ■ U.S. Congress approves Thirteenth Amendment
    ■ Lee abandons Richmond and Petersburg
    ■ Lee surrenders at Appomattox Court House
    ■ Lincoln assassinated
    ■ Death toll in war reaches 620,000

Wallace to walk home. Instead, Turnage "took courage," as he wrote in his postwar narrative, "prayed faithfully," and walked steadfastly southwest, right through the Confederate encampment and trenchworks. The soldiers took the bloodied and tattered black teenager for simply one among the hundreds of slaves who did camp labor.

For the next three weeks, Turnage crawled and waded for twenty-five miles through the snake-infested swamps of the Foul River estuary, down the west edge of Mobile Bay. Nearly starved and narrowly escaping Confederate patrols, Turnage made it all the way to Cedar Point, where he could look out at the forbidding mouth of Mobile Bay to Dauphin Island, now occupied by Union forces. Alligators swam in their wallows nearby, delta grass swayed waist-high in the hot breezes, and the laughing gulls squawked around him as Turnage hid from Confederate lookouts in a swampy den. He remembered his choices starkly: "It was death to go back and it was death to stay there and freedom was before me; it could only be death to go forward if I was caught and freedom if I escaped."

Turnage barely survived a desperate attempt to ride a log out into the ocean and narrowly made it back to shore. Then, one day at the water's edge, he noticed an old rowboat that had rolled in with the tide. The veteran runaway now took a "piece of board" and began to row out into the bay. As a squall with "water like a hill coming" at him nearly swamped him, he suddenly "heard the crash of oars and behold there was eight Yankees in a boat." Following the rhythm of the oars, Turnage jumped into the Union gunboat. For a stunning few moments, he remembered, the oarsmen in blue "were struck with silence" as they contemplated the frail young black man crouched in front of them. Turnage turned his head and looked back at Confederate soldiers on the shore and measured the distance of his bravery at sea. Then he took his first breaths of freedom.

The Civil War brought astonishing changes to individuals everywhere in North and South. It obliterated the normal patterns of life. Millions of men were swept away into training camps and regiments. Armies numbering in the hundreds of thousands marched over the South, devastating the countryside. Families struggled to survive without their men; businesses tried to cope with the loss of workers. Women in both North and South took on extra responsibilities in the home and moved into new jobs in the work force. Many women joined the ranks of nurses and hospital workers. No sphere of life went untouched.

But southern soldiers and their families also experienced what few other groups of Americans have—utter defeat. For most of them, wealth changed to poverty and hope to despair as countless southern farms were ruined. Late in the war, many southerners yearned only for an end to inflation, to shortages, to the escape of their slaves, and to the death that visited nearly every family. Even the South's slaves, who eventually placed great hope in the war, did not always encounter sympathetic liberators such as those who took Turnage from his drowning boat, fed and clothed him in a tent, and took him before a Union general, where the freedman was given two choices: join a black regiment or become a camp servant for a white officer. For the remainder of the war Turnage cooked for a Maryland captain.

In the North, farm boys and mechanics from all regions would be asked for heretofore unimagined sacrifices. Businessmen, however, found untold new profits in war. The conflict ensured vast government expenditures and lucrative federal contracts. *Harper's Monthly* reported that an eminent financier expected a long war, fostering huge purchases, active speculation, and rising prices. "The battle of Bull Run," predicted the financier, "makes the fortune of every man in Wall Street who is not a natural idiot."

Change was most drastic in the South, where secessionists had launched a conservative revolution for their section's national independence. Born of states' rights doctrine, the Confederacy now had to be transformed into a centralized nation to fight a vast war. Never were men more mistaken: their revolutionary means were fundamentally incompatible with their conservative purpose. Southern whites had feared that a peacetime government of Republicans would interfere with slavery and ruin plantation life. Instead, their own actions led to a war that turned southern society upside down and imperiled the very existence of slavery.

The war created social strains in both North and South. Northern workers lost ground to inflation, but the economy hummed. To the alarm of many, the powers of the federal government and of the president increased during the war.

Disaffection was strongest, though, in the Confederacy, where poverty and class resentment threatened the South from within as federal armies assailed it from without. In the North, dissent also flourished, and antiwar sentiment occasionally erupted into violence.

Ultimately, the Civil War forced on the nation a social and political revolution regarding race. Its greatest effect was to compel leaders and citizens to finally face the great question of slavery. And blacks themselves embraced what was for them the most fundamental turning point in their experience as Americans.

- How and why did the Civil War bring social transformations to both South and North?
- How did the war to preserve the Union or for southern independence become the war to free the slaves?
- By 1865, when Americans on all sides searched for the *meaning* of the war they had just fought, what might some of their answers have been?

## AMERICA GOES TO WAR, 1861–1862

Few Americans understood what they were getting into when the war began. The onset of hostilities sparked patriotic sentiments, optimistic speeches, and joyous ceremonies in both North and South. Northern communities raised companies of volunteers eager to save the Union and sent them off with fanfare. In the South, confident recruits boasted of whipping the Yankees and returning home before Christmas. Southern women sewed dashing uniforms for men who would soon be lucky to wear drab gray or butternut homespun. Americans went to war in 1861 with decidedly romantic notions of what they would experience.

Through the spring of 1861, both sides scrambled to organize and train their undisciplined armies. On July 21,

**First Battle of Bull Run**

1861, the first battle took place outside Manassas Junction, Virginia, near a stream called Bull Run. General Irvin McDowell and 30,000 Union troops attacked General P. G. T. Beauregard's 22,000 southerners (see Map 15.1). As raw recruits struggled amid the confusion of their first battle, federal forces began to gain ground. Then they ran

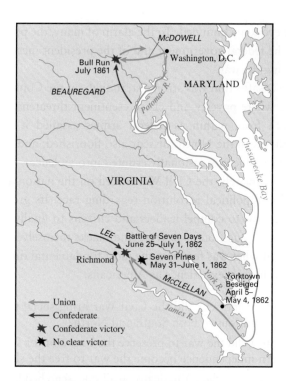

**Map 15.1    McClellan's Campaign**

The water route chosen by McClellan to threaten Richmond during the peninsular campaign.

into a line of Virginia troops under General Thomas Jackson. "There is Jackson standing like a stone wall," shouted one Confederate. "Stonewall" Jackson's line held, and the arrival of 9,000 Confederate reinforcements by train won the day for the South. Union troops fled back to Washington, observed by shocked northern congressmen and spectators who had watched the battle; a few sightseers were actually captured for their folly.

The unexpected rout at Bull Run gave northerners their first hint of the nature of the war to come. Although the United States enjoyed an enormous advantage in resources, victory would not be easy. Pro-Union feeling was growing in western Virginia, and loyalties were divided in the four border slave states—Missouri, Kentucky, Maryland, and Delaware. But the rest of the Upper South—the states of North Carolina, Virginia, Tennessee, and Arkansas—had joined the Confederacy in the wake of the attack on Fort Sumter. Moved by an outpouring of regional loyalty, half a million southerners volunteered to fight—so many that the Confederate government could hardly arm them all. The United States therefore undertook a massive mobilization of troops around Washington, D.C.

Lincoln gave command of the army to General George B. McClellan, an officer who proved to be better

at organization and training than at fighting. McClellan put his growing army into camp and devoted the fall and winter of 1861 to readying a formidable force of a quarter-million men whose mission would be to take Richmond, established as the Confederate capital by July 1861. "The vast preparation of the enemy," wrote one southern soldier, produced a "feeling of despondency" in the South for the first time. But southern morale remained high early in the war. Most Americans still possessed a rather romantic conception of the war looming on their horizon.

While McClellan prepared, the Union began to implement other parts of its overall strategy, which called for a blockade of southern ports and eventual capture of the Mississippi River. Like a constricting snake, this "Anaconda plan" would strangle the Confederacy (see Map 15.2). At first the Union Navy had too few ships to patrol 3,550 miles of coastline and block the Confederacy's avenues of supply. Gradually, however, the navy increased the blockade's effectiveness, though it never stopped southern commerce completely.

## Grand Strategy

The Confederate strategy was essentially defensive. A defensive posture was not only consistent with the South's claim of independence, but also reasonable in light of the North's advantage in resources (see Figure 15.1). But Jefferson Davis called the southern strategy an "offensive defensive," taking advantage of opportunities to attack and using its interior lines of transportation to concentrate troops at crucial points. In its war aims, the Confederacy did not need to conquer the North; the Union effort, however, as time would tell, required conquest of the South.

Strategic thinking on both sides slighted the importance of the West, that vast expanse of territory between Virginia and the Mississippi River and beyond. Guerrilla warfare broke out in 1861 in the politically divided state of Missouri, and key locations along the Mississippi and other major western rivers would prove to be crucial prizes in the North's eventual victory. Beyond the Mississippi River, the Confederacy hoped to gain an advantage by negotiating treaties with the Creeks, Choctaws, Chickasaws, Cherokees, Seminoles, and smaller groups of Plains Indians. Meanwhile, the Republican U.S. Congress carved the West into territories in anticipation of state making. For most Indians west of the Mississippi, what began during the Civil War was nearly three decades of offensive warfare against them, an enveloping strategy of conquest, relocation, and slaughter. They, with all Americans, soon knew they were in a war the scale of which few people had ever imagined.

The last half of 1861 brought no major land battles, but the North made gains by sea. Late in the summer,

▲ In *Departure of the Seventh Regiment* (1861), flags and the spectacle of thousands of young men from New York marching off to battle give a deceptively gay appearance to the beginning of the Civil War. *(Museum of Fine Arts, Boston; M. and M. Karolik Collection)*

## Union Naval Campaign

Union naval forces captured Cape Hatteras and then Hilton Head, one of the Sea Islands off Port Royal, South Carolina. A few months later, similar operations secured vital coastal points in North Carolina, as well as Fort Pulaski, which defended Savannah. Federal naval operations established significant beachheads along the Confederate coastline (see Map 15.2).

The coastal victories off South Carolina foreshadowed a revolution in slave society. At the federal gunboats' approach, planters abandoned their land and fled. For a while, Confederate cavalry tried to round up slaves and move them to the interior as well. But thousands of slaves greeted what they hoped to be freedom with rejoicing and broke the hated cotton gins. Some entered their masters' homes and took clothing and furniture, which they conspicuously displayed. A growing stream of runaways poured into Union lines. Unwilling at first to wage a war against slavery, the federal government did not acknowledge the slaves' freedom—though it began to use their labor in the Union cause. This swelling tide of emancipated slaves, defined by many Union officers as "contra-band" of war (confiscated enemy property), forced first a bitter and confused debate within the Union Army and government over how to treat the freedmen, and then a forthright attempt to harness their labor and military power.

The coastal incursions worried southerners, but the spring of 1862 brought even stronger evidence of the war's gravity. In March, two ironclad ships—the *Monitor* (a Union warship) and the *Merrimack* (a Union ship seized by the Confederacy)—fought each other for the first time off the coast of Virginia. Their battle, though indecisive, ushered in a new era in naval design. In April, Union ships commanded by Admiral David Farragut smashed through log booms blocking the Mississippi River and fought their way upstream to capture New Orleans. The city at the mouth of the Mississippi, the South's greatest seaport and slave-trading center, was now in federal hands.

Farther west, three full Confederate regiments were organized, mostly of Cherokees, from Indian Territory, but

## War in the Far West

a Union victory at Elkhorn Tavern, Arkansas, shattered southern control of the region. Thereafter, dissension within Native American groups and a Union victory the following

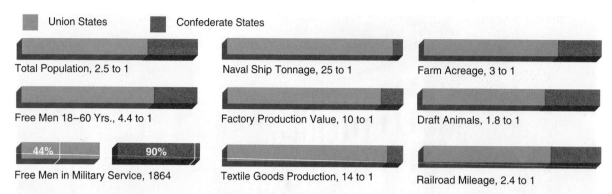

**Figure 15.1   Comparative Resources, Union and Confederate States, 1861**

The North had vastly superior resources. Although the North's advantages in manpower and industrial capacity proved very important, the South still had to be conquered, its society and its will crushed. *(Source:* The Times Atlas of World History. *Used with permission.)*

year at Honey Springs, Arkansas, reduced Confederate operations in Indian Territory to guerrilla raids.

In the westernmost campaign of the war, from February to May 1862, some three thousand Confederate and four thousand Union forces fought for control of New Mexico Territory. The military significance of the New Mexico campaign was limited, but the Confederate invasion had grander aims: access to the trade riches of the Santa Fe Trail and possession of gold mines in Colorado and California. If the campaign had endured long enough, the Confederacy would have been much stronger with a western empire. But Colorado and New Mexico Unionists fought for their region, and in a series of battles at Glorieta Pass, 20 miles east of Santa Fe, on March 26 through 28, they blocked the Confederate invasion. By May 1, Confederate forces straggled down the Rio Grande River back into Texas, ending their effort to take New Mexico.

Meanwhile, in February 1862, land and river forces in northern Tennessee won significant victories for the Union. A Union commander named Ulysses S. Grant saw the strategic importance of Fort Henry and Fort Donelson, the Confederate outposts guarding the Tennessee and Cumberland Rivers. If federal troops could capture these forts, Grant realized, they would open two prime routes into the heartland of the Confederacy. In just ten days he seized the forts, completely cutting off the Confederates and demanding "unconditional surrender" of Fort Donelson. A path into Tennessee, Alabama, and Mississippi now lay open before the Union

**Grant's Tennessee Campaign and the Battle of Shiloh**

Army. Grant's achievement of such a surrender from his former West Point roommate, Confederate commander Simon Bolivar Buckner, inspired northern public opinion.

Grant moved on into southern Tennessee and the first of the war's shockingly bloody encounters, the Battle of Shiloh (see Map 15.2). On April 6, Confederate general Albert Sidney Johnston caught federal troops with their backs to the water awaiting reinforcements along the Tennessee River. The Confederates attacked early in the morning and inflicted heavy damage all day. Close to victory, General Johnston was shot from his horse and killed. Southern forces almost achieved a breakthrough, but Union reinforcements arrived that night. The next day the tide of battle turned, and after ten hours of terrible combat, Grant's men forced the Confederates to withdraw.

Neither side won a decisive victory at Shiloh, yet the losses were staggering, and the Confederates were forced to retreat into northern Mississippi. Northern troops lost 13,000 men (killed, wounded, or captured) out of 63,000; southerners sacrificed 11,000 out of 40,000. Total casualties in this single battle exceeded those in all three of America's previous wars combined. Now both sides were beginning to sense the true nature of the war. "I saw an open field," Grant recalled, "over which Confederates had made repeated charges . . . so covered with dead that it would have been possible to walk across the clearing, in any direction, stepping on dead bodies, without a foot touching the ground." Shiloh utterly changed Grant's thinking about the war. He had hoped that southerners would soon be "heartily tired" of the conflict. After Shiloh, "I gave up all idea of saving the Union except by complete conquest." Memories of the Shiloh bat-

▲ Both armies experienced religious revivals during the war. This photograph shows members of a largely Irish regiment from New York celebrating Mass at the beginning of the war. Notice the presence of some female visitors in the left foreground. *(Library of Congress)*

tlefield, and many others to come, would haunt the soldiers who survived for the rest of their lives. Herman Melville's "Shiloh, A Requiem" captures the pathos of that spring day when armies learned the truth about war.

Skimming lightly, wheeling still,
The swallows fly low
Over the field in clouded days,
The forest-field of Shiloh—
Over the field where April rain
Solaced the parched ones stretched in pain
Through the pause of night
That followed the Sunday fight
Around the church of Shiloh—
The church so lone, the log-built one,
That echoed to many a parting groan
And natural prayer
Of dying foemen mingled there—
Foemen at morn, but friends at eve—
Fame or country least their care:

(What like a bullet can undeceive!)
But now they lie low,
While over them the swallows skim,
And all is hushed at Shiloh.

On the Virginia front, President Lincoln had a different problem. General McClellan was slow to move.

### McClellan and the Peninsula Campaign

Only thirty-six, McClellan had already achieved notable success as an army officer and railroad president. Habitually overestimating the size of enemy forces, he called repeatedly for reinforcements and ignored Lincoln's directions to advance. McClellan advocated war of limited aims that would lead to a quick reunion. He intended neither disruption of slavery nor war on noncombatants. McClellan's conservative vision of the war was practically outdated before he even moved his army into Virginia. Finally he chose to move by a water route, sailing his troops down the Chesapeake, landing them on the peninsula between the York and James Rivers, and advancing on Richmond from the east (see Map 15.1).

After a bloody but indecisive battle at Fair Oaks on May 31 through June 1, the federal armies moved to within 7 miles of the Confederate capital. They could see the spires on Richmond churches. The Confederate commanding general, Joseph E. Johnston, was badly wounded at Fair Oaks, and President Jefferson Davis placed his chief military adviser, Robert E. Lee, in command. The fifty-five-year-old Lee was an aristocratic Virginian, a life-long military officer, and a veteran of distinction from the War with Mexico. Although he initially opposed secession, Lee loyally gave his allegiance to his state and became a staunch Confederate nationalist. He soon foiled McClellan's legions.

First, Lee sent Stonewall Jackson's corps of 17,000 northwest into the Shenandoah valley behind Union forces, where they threatened Washington, D.C., and with rapid-strike mobility drew some federal troops away from Richmond to protect their own capital. Further, in mid-June, in an extraordinary four-day ride around the entire Union Army, Confederate cavalry under J. E. B. Stuart, a self-styled Virginia cavalier with red cape and plumed hat, confirmed the exposed position of a major portion of McClellan's army north of the rain-swollen Chickahominy River. Then, in a series of engagements known as the Seven Days Battles, from June 26 through July 1, Lee struck at McClellan's army. Lee never managed to close his pincers around the retreating Union forces, but the daring move of taking the majority of his army northeast and attacking the Union right flank, while leaving only a small force to defend Richmond, forced

McClellan (always believing he was outnumbered) to retreat toward the James River.

During the sustained fighting of the Seven Days, the Union forces suffered 20,614 casualties and the Confederates, 15,849. After repeated rebel assaults against entrenched positions on high ground at Malvern Hill, an officer concluded, "It was not war, it was murder." By August 3, McClellan withdrew his army back to the Potomac and the environs of Washington. Richmond remained safe for almost two more years.

Buoyed by these results, Jefferson Davis conceived an ambitious plan to turn the tide of the war and gain recognition of the Confederacy by European nations. He ordered a general offensive, sending Lee north into Maryland and Generals Kirby Smith and Braxton Bragg into Kentucky. Calling on residents of Maryland and Kentucky, still slave states, to make a separate peace with his government, Davis also invited northwestern states like Indiana, which sent much of their trade down the Mississippi to New Orleans, to leave the Union. This was a coordinated effort to take the war to the North and to try to force both a military and a political turning point.

The plan was promising, but in the end the offensive failed. Lee's forces achieved a striking success at the bat-

## Confederate Offensive in Maryland and Kentucky

In October 1862 in New York City, photographer Mathew Brady opened an exhibition of photographs from the Battle of Antietam. Although few knew it, Brady's vision was very poor, and this photograph of Confederate dead was actually made by his assistants, Alexander Gardner and James F. Gibson.

*(Library of Congress)*

tle of Second Bull Run, August 29 through 30, just southwest of Washington, D.C. On the same killing fields along Bull Run Creek where federal troops had been defeated the previous summer, an entire Union army was sent in retreat back into the federal capital. Thousands of wounded occupied schools and churches, and 2,000 suffered on cots in the rotunda of the U.S. Capitol.

But in the bloodiest day of the entire war, September 17, 1862, McClellan turned Lee back from Sharpsburg, Maryland. In this Battle of Antietam, 5,000 men died, and another 18,000 were wounded. Lee was lucky to escape destruction, for McClellan had intercepted a lost battle order, wrapped around cigars for each Confederate corps commander and inadvertently dropped by a courier. But McClellan moved slowly, failed to use his larger forces in simultaneous attacks, and allowed Lee's stricken army to retreat to safety across the Potomac. In the wake of Antietam, Lincoln removed McClellan from command.

In Kentucky, Generals Smith and Bragg secured Lexington and Frankfort, but their effort to force the Yankees back to the Ohio River was stopped at the Battle of Perryville on October 8. Bragg's army retreated back into Tennessee, where on December 31, 1862, to January 2, 1863, they fought an indecisive but much bloodier battle at Murfreesboro. Casualties exceeded even those of Shiloh, and many lives were sacrificed on a bitter winter landscape.

Confederate leaders had marshaled all their strength for a breakthrough but had failed. Outnumbered and disadvantaged in resources, the South could not continue the offensive. Profoundly disappointed, Davis admitted to a committee of Confederate representatives that southerners were entering "the darkest and most dangerous period we have yet had."

But 1862 also brought painful lessons to the North. Confederate general J. E. B. Stuart executed a daring cavalry raid into Pennsylvania in October. Then, on December 13, Union general Ambrose Burnside, now in command of the Army of the Potomac, unwisely ordered his soldiers to attack Lee's army, which held fortified positions on high ground at Fredericksburg, Virginia. Lee's men performed so efficiently in killing northerners that Lee was moved to say, "It is well that war is so terrible. We should grow too fond of it." Burnside's repeated assaults up Marye's Heights shocked even the opponents. "The Federals had fallen like the steady dripping of rain from the eaves of a house," remarked Confederate general James Longstreet. And a Union officer observed of the carnage of 1,300 dead and 9,600 wounded Union soldiers, "The whole plain was covered with men, prostrate and dropping. . . . I had never before seen fighting like

that . . . the next brigade coming up in succession would do its duty, and melt like snow coming down on warm ground." The scale of carnage now challenged people on both sides to search deeply for the meaning of such a war. The rebellion was far from being suppressed, and people on both home fronts now had to decide just what they would endure to win such an all-out civil war.

## WAR TRANSFORMS THE SOUTH

The war caused tremendous disruptions in civilian life and altered southern society beyond all expectations. One of the first traditions to fall was the southern preference for local and limited government. States' rights had been a formative ideology for the Confederacy, but state governments were weak operations. The average citizen, on whom the hand of government had rested lightly, probably knew county authorities best. To withstand the massive power of the North, however, the South needed to centralize; like the colonial revolutionaries, southerners faced a choice of joining together or dying separately. Jefferson Davis quickly saw the necessity of centralization and moved to thwart the separate aims of states.

Davis moved promptly to bring all arms, supplies, and troops under his control. But by early 1862 the scope and duration of the conflict required something more. Tens of thousands of Confederate soldiers had volunteered for just one year's service, planning to return home in the spring to plant their crops. More recruits were needed constantly to keep southern armies in the field. However, as one official admitted, "the spirit of volunteering had died out." Finally, faced with a critical shortage of troops, in April 1862 the Confederate government enacted the first national conscription (draft) law in American history. Thus the war forced unprecedented change on states that had seceded out of fear of change.

**The Confederacy and Centralization**

Davis adopted a firm leadership role toward the Confederate Congress, which raised taxes and later passed a tax-in-kind—paid in farm products. Nearly 4,500 agents dispersed to collect the tax. Where opposition arose, the government suspended the writ of habeas corpus (which prevented individuals from being held without trial) and imposed martial law. Despite Davis's unyielding stance, this tax system proved inadequate for the South's war effort.

To replace the food that men in uniform would have grown, Davis exhorted state governments to require farmers to switch from cash crops to food crops. But the army remained short of food and labor. The War Department resorted to impressing slaves to work on fortifications, and after 1861 the government relied heavily on confiscation of food to feed the troops. Officers swooped down on farms in the line of march and carted away grain, meat, wagons, and draft animals. Such raids caused increased hardship and resentment for women managing farms in the absence of husbands and sons.

Soon the Confederate administration in Richmond gained virtually complete control over the southern economy. The Confederate Congress also gave the central government almost complete control of the railroads. A large bureaucracy sprang up to administer these operations: over 70,000 civilians staffed the Confederate administration. By the war's end, the southern bureaucracy was larger in proportion to population than its northern counterpart.

Historians have long argued over whether the Confederacy itself was a "rebellion," a "revolution," or the creation of a genuine "nation."

## Confederate Nationalism

Whatever label we apply, Confederates created a culture and an ideology of nationalism. Southerners immediately tried to forge their own national symbols and identity. In flags, songs, language, seals, school readers, and other national characteristics, Confederates created their own story.

In its conservative crusade to preserve states' rights, the social order, and racial slavery, southerners believed that the Confederacy was the true legacy of the American Revolution—a bulwark against centralized power that was in keeping with the war for independence and a bulwark against centralized power. In this view, southern "liberty" was no less a holy cause than that of the patriots of 1776. To southerners, theirs was a continuing revolution against the excesses of Yankee democracy, and George Washington (a Virginian) on horseback formed the center of the official seal of the Confederacy.

Also central to Confederate nationalism was a refurbished defense of slavery as a benign, protective institution. In wartime schoolbooks, children were instructed in the divinely inspired, paternalistic character of slavery. And the idea of the "faithful slave" was key to southerners' nationalist cause. A poem popular among whites captured an old slave's rejection of the Emancipation Proclamation.

> Now, Massa, dis is berry fine, dese words
> You've spoke to me,
> No doubt you mean it kindly, but ole Dinah
> Won't be free . . .
> Ole Massa's berry good to me—and though I am
> His slave,
> He treats me like I'se kin to him—and I would
> Rather have
> A home in Massa's cabin, and eat his black
> Bread too,
> Dan leave ole Massa's children and go and
> Lib wid you.

In the face of defeat and devastation, this and other forms of Confederate nationalism collapsed in the final year of the war. But much of the spirit and substance of Confederate nationalism would revive in the postwar period in a new ideology of the Lost Cause.

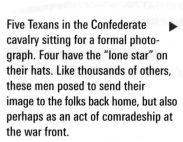

Five Texans in the Confederate cavalry sitting for a formal photograph. Four have the "lone star" on their hats. Like thousands of others, these men posed to send their image to the folks back home, but also perhaps as an act of comradeship at the war front.

*(The Panhandle-Plains Historical Society, Canyon, Texas)*

Clerks and subordinate officials crowded the towns and cities where Confederate departments set up their offices. Clerks had always been males, but now "government girls" staffed the Confederate bureaucracy. The sudden urban migration that resulted overwhelmed the housing supply and stimulated new construction. The pressure was especially great in Richmond, whose population increased 250 percent. Mobile's population jumped from 29,000 to 41,000; Atlanta, too, began to grow; and 10,000 people poured into war-related industries in little Selma, Alabama.

### Southern Cities and Industry

As the Union blockade disrupted imports of manufactured products, the traditionally agricultural South forged new industries. Many planters shared Davis's hope that industrialization would bring "deliverance, full and unrestricted, from all commercial dependence" on the North or the world. Indeed, beginning almost from scratch, the Confederacy achieved tremendous feats of industrial development. Chief of Ordnance Josiah Gorgas increased the capacity of Richmond's Tredegar Iron Works and other factories to the point that by 1865 his Ordnance Bureau was supplying all Confederate small arms and ammunition. Meanwhile, the government constructed new railroad lines and ironworks, much of the labor for which consisted of slaves relocated from farms and plantations.

### Changing Roles of Women

White women, restricted to narrow roles in antebellum society, gained substantial new responsibilities in wartime. The wives and mothers of soldiers now headed households and performed men's work, including raising crops and tending animals. Women in nonslaveowning families cultivated fields themselves, while wealthier women suddenly had to perform as overseers and manage field work. In the cities, white women—who had been largely excluded from the labor force—found a limited number of respectable paying jobs, often in the Confederate bureaucracy, where some found clerks' jobs as "government girls." And female schoolteachers appeared in the South for the first time.

Women experienced both confidence and agony from their new responsibilities. Among them was Janie Smith, a young North Carolinian. Raised in a rural area by prosperous parents, she now faced grim realities as the war reached her farm and troops turned her home into a hospital. "It makes me shudder when I think of the awful sights I witnessed that morning," she wrote to a friend. "Ambulance after ambulance drove up with our wounded. . . . Under every shed and tree, the tables were carried for amputating the limbs. . . . The blood lay in puddles in the grove; the groans of the dying . . . were horrible." But Janie Smith learned to cope with crisis. She ended her account with the proud words "I can dress amputated limbs now and do most anything in the way of nursing wounded soldiers."

Patriotic sacrifice appealed to some women, but others resented their new burdens. A Texas woman who had struggled to discipline slaves pronounced herself "sick of trying to do a man's business." Others grew angry over shortages and resented cooking and unfamiliar contact with lower-class women. Some women grew scornful of the war and demanded that their men return to help provide for their families.

### Human Suffering, Hoarding, and Inflation

For millions of ordinary southerners, the war brought privation and suffering. Mass poverty descended for the first time on a large minority of the white population. Many yeoman families had lost their breadwinners to the army. As a South Carolina newspaper put it, "The duties of war have called away from home the sole supports of many, many families. . . . Help must be given, or the poor will suffer." Women on their own sought help from relatives, neighbors, friends, anyone. Sometimes they pleaded their case to the Confederate government. "In the name of humanity," begged one woman, "discharge my husband he is not able to do your government much good and he might do his children some good . . . my poor children have no home nor no Father." To the extent that the South eventually lost the will to fight in the face of defeat, women played a role in demanding an end to the war.

The South was in many places so sparsely populated that the conscription of one skilled craftsman could wreak hardship on the people of an entire county. Often they begged in unison for the exemption or discharge of the local miller, or the neighborhood tanner or wheelwright. Physicians were also in short supply. Most serious, however, was the loss of a blacksmith. As a petition from Alabama explained, "Our Section of County [is] left entirely Destitute of any man that is able to keep in order any kind of Farming Tules."

The blockade of Confederate shipping created shortages of important supplies—salt, sugar, coffee, nails—and speculation and hoarding made the shortages worse. Greedy businessmen cornered the supply of some commodities; prosperous citizens stocked up on food. The *Richmond Enquirer* criticized a planter who purchased so many wagonloads of supplies that his "lawn and paths looked like a wharf covered with a ship's loads." North Carolina's Governor Zebulon Vance worried about "the cry of distress . . . from the poor wives and children of our soldiers. . . . What will become of them?"

Inflation raged out of control, fueled by the Confederate government's heavy borrowing and inadequate taxes, until prices had increased almost 7,000 percent. Inflation particularly imperiled urban dwellers without their own sources of food. As early as 1861 and 1862, newspapers reported that "want and starvation are staring thousands in the face," and troubled officials predicted that "women and children are bound to come to suffering if not starvation." Hoarding continued to cause local conflict, and a rudimentary relief program organized by the Confederacy failed to meet the need.

As their fortunes declined, people of once-modest means looked around and found abundant evidence that all classes were not sacrificing equally. The Confederate government enacted policies that decidedly favored the upper class. Until the last year of the war, for example, prosperous southerners could avoid military service by hiring substitutes. Prices for substitutes skyrocketed until it cost a man $5,000 or $6,000 to send someone to the front in his place. Well over fifty thousand upper-class southerners purchased such substitutes. Mary Boykin Chesnut knew of one young aristocrat who "spent a fortune in substitutes. . . . He is at the end of his row now, for all able-bodied men are ordered to the front. I hear he is going as some general's courier."

**Inequities of the Confederate Draft**

Anger at such discrimination exploded in October 1862, when the Confederate Congress exempted from military duty anyone who was supervising at least twenty slaves. "Never did a law meet with more universal odium," observed one representative. "Its influence upon the poor is most calamitous." Protests poured in from every corner of the Confederacy, and North Carolina's legislators formally condemned the law. Its defenders argued, however, that the exemption preserved order and aided food production, and the statute remained on the books.

This "twenty Negro" law is indicative of the racial fears many Confederates felt as the war threatened to overturn southern society. But it also fueled desertion and stimulated new levels of overt Unionism in nonslaveholding regions of the South. In Jones County, Mississippi, an area of piney woods and few slaves or plantations, Newt Knight, a Confederate soldier, led a band of renegades who took over the county, declared their allegiance to the Union, and called their district the "Free State of Jones."

They held out for the remainder of the war as an enclave of independent Union sympathizers.

The bitterness of letters to Confederate officials suggests the depth of the dissension and class anger. "If I and my little children suffer [and] die while there Father is in service," threatened one woman, "I invoke God Almighty that our blood rest upon the South." Another woman swore to the secretary of war that, unless help was provided to poverty-stricken wives and mothers, "an allwise god . . . will send down his fury . . . [on] those that are in power." War magnified existing social tensions in the Confederacy, and created a few new ones.

## WARTIME NORTHERN ECONOMY AND SOCIETY

With the onset of war, a tidal wave of change rolled over the North as well. Factories and citizens' associations geared up to support the war, and the federal government and its executive branch gained new powers. The energies of an industrializing society were harnessed to serve the cause of the Union. Idealism and greed flourished together, and the northern economy proved its awesome productivity. Unlike the experience in the South, northern farms and factories came through the war unharmed.

At first the war was a shock to business. Northern firms lost their southern markets, and many companies had to change their products and find new customers in order to remain open. Southern debts became uncollectible, jeopardizing not only northern merchants but also many western banks. In farming regions, families struggled with an aggravated shortage of labor caused by army enlistments. A few enterprises never pulled out of the tailspin caused by the war. Cotton mills lacked cotton; construction declined; shoe manufacturers sold few of the cheap shoes that planters had bought for their slaves.

**Northern Business, Industry, and Agriculture**

But certain entrepreneurs, such as wool producers, benefited from shortages of competing products, and soaring demand for war-related goods swept some businesses to new success. To feed the hungry war machine, the federal government pumped unprecedented sums into the economy. The Treasury issued $3.2 billion in bonds and paper money called "greenbacks," and the War Department spent over $360 million in revenues from new taxes, including the nation's first income tax. Government contracts soon totaled more than $1 billion.

Secretary of War Edwin M. Stanton's list of the supplies needed by the Ordnance Department indicates the

▲ Despite initial problems, the task of supplying a vast war machine kept the northern economy humming. This photograph shows businesses on the west side of Hudson Street in New York City in 1865. *(© Collection of The New York Historical Society)*

scope of government demand: "7,892 cannon, 11,787 artillery carriages, 4,022,130 small-arms, . . . 1,022,176,474 cartridges for small-arms, 1,220,555,435 percussion caps, . . . 26,440,054 pounds of gunpowder, . . . and 90,416,295 pounds of lead." Stanton's list covered only weapons; the government also purchased huge quantities of uniforms, boots, food, camp equipment, saddles, ships, and other necessities. War-related spending revived business in many northern states. In 1863 a merchants' magazine examined the effects of the war in Massachusetts: "Seldom, if ever, has the business of Massachusetts been more active or profitable than during the past year. . . . In every department of labor the government has been, directly or indirectly, the chief employer and paymaster." Government contracts saved Massachusetts shoe manufacturers from ruin.

Nothing illustrated the wartime partnership between business and government better than the work of Jay Cooke, a wealthy New York financier. Cooke threw himself into the marketing of government bonds to finance the war effort. With imagination and energy, he convinced both large investors and ordinary citizens to invest enormous sums, in the process earning hefty commissions for himself. But the financier's profit served the Union cause, as the interests of capitalism and government merged in American history's first era of "big government."

War aided some heavy industries in the North as well, especially iron and steel production. Although new railroad construction slowed, the manufacture of rails actually increased with demand for repairs. Of considerable significance for the future was the railroad industry's adoption of a standard gauge (width) for track, which eliminated the unloading and reloading of boxcars, and created a unified transportation system.

The northern economy also grew because of a complementary relationship between agriculture and industry. Mechanization of agriculture had begun before the war. Wartime recruitment and conscription, however, gave western farmers an added incentive to purchase labor-saving machinery. The shift from human labor to machines created new markets for industry and expanded the food supply for the urban industrial work force. The boom in the sale of agricultural tools was tremendous. Cyrus and William McCormick built an industrial empire in Chicago from the sale of their reapers. Between 1862 and 1864, the manufacture of mowers and reapers doubled to 70,000 yearly; by war's end, 375,000 reapers were in use, triple the number in 1861. Thus northern farm families whose breadwinners went to war did not suffer as much as did their counterparts in the South. "We have seen," one magazine observed, "a stout matron whose sons are in the army, cutting hay with her team . . . and she cut seven acres with ease in a day, riding leisurely upon her cutter."

Northern industrial and urban workers did not fare as well. After the initial slump, jobs became plentiful, but inflation ate up much of a worker's paycheck. The price of coffee had tripled; rice and sugar had doubled; and clothing, fuel, and rent had all climbed. Between 1860 and 1864, consumer prices rose at least 76 percent, while daily wages rose only 42 percent. Workers' families consequently suffered a substantial decline in their standard of living.

### Northern Workers' Militancy

As their real wages shrank, industrial workers lost job security. To increase production, some employers replaced workers with labor-saving machines. Other employers urged the government to promote immigration to secure cheap labor. Workers responded by forming unions and sometimes by striking. Skilled craftsmen organized to combat the loss of their jobs and status to machines; women and unskilled workers, who were excluded by the craftsmen, formed their own unions. Indeed, thirteen occupational groups—including tailors, coal miners, and railway engineers—formed national unions during the Civil War, and the number of strikes climbed steadily.

Employers reacted with hostility to this new labor independence. Manufacturers viewed labor activism as a threat to their freedom of action and accordingly formed statewide or craft-based associations to cooperate and pool information. These employers shared blacklists of union members and required new workers to sign "yellow dog" contracts (promises not to join a union). To put down strikes, they hired strikebreakers from among blacks, immigrants, and women, and sometimes used federal troops to break the unions' will.

Labor militancy, however, prevented employers neither from making profits nor from profiteering on government contracts. Unscrupulous businessmen took advantage of the suddenly immense demand for army supplies by selling clothing and blankets made of "shoddy"—wool fibers reclaimed from rags or worn cloth. Shoddy goods often came apart in the rain; most of the shoes purchased in the early months of the war were worthless. Contractors sold inferior guns for double the usual price and passed off tainted meat as good. Corruption was so widespread that it led to a year-long investigation by the House of Representatives. These realities of everyday economic life eroded what remained of any romance for war among most Americans.

Legitimate enterprises also made healthy profits. The output of woolen mills increased so dramatically that dividends in the industry nearly tripled. Some cotton mills made record profits on what they sold, even though they reduced their output. Brokerage houses worked until midnight and earned unheard-of commissions. Railroads carried immense quantities of freight and passengers, increasing their business to the point that railroad stocks skyrocketed in value.

### Economic Nationalism and Government-Business Partnership

Railroads were also a leading beneficiary of government largesse. With southern representatives absent from Congress, the northern route of the transcontinental railroad quickly prevailed. In 1862 and 1864, Congress chartered two corporations, the Union Pacific Railroad and the Central Pacific Railroad, and assisted them financially in connecting Omaha, Nebraska, with Sacramento, California. For each mile of track laid, the railroads received a loan of from $16,000 to $48,000 in government bonds plus 20 square miles of land along a free 400-foot-wide right of way. Overall, the two corporations gained approximately 20 million acres of land and nearly $60 million in loans.

Other businessmen benefited handsomely from the Morrill Land Grant Act (1862). To promote public education in agriculture, engineering, and military science, Congress granted each state 30,000 acres of federal land for each of its congressional districts. The states could sell the land as long as they used the income for the purposes Congress had intended. The law eventually fostered sixty-nine colleges and universities, but one of its immediate effects was to enrich a few prominent speculators. At the same time, the Homestead Act of 1862 offered cheap, and sometimes free, land to people who would settle the West and improve their property.

Before the war, there were no adequate national banking, taxation, or currency. Banks operating under state charters issued no fewer than seven thousand different kinds of notes, which were difficult to distinguish from forgeries. During the war, Congress and the Treasury Department established a national banking system empowered to issue national bank notes, and by 1865 most state banks were forced by a prohibitive tax to join the national system. This process created sounder currency, but also inflexibility in the money supply and an eastern-oriented financial structure that, later in the century, pushed farmers in need of credit and cash to revolt.

Republican economic policies expanded the scope of government and bonded people to the nation as never before. Experience with economic nationalism and the marked expansion of presidential power eventually helped buttress public opinion for the controversial cause of slave emancipation.

Yet ostentation coexisted with idealism. In the excitement of wartime moneymaking, an eagerness to display one's wealth flourished in the largest cities. *Harper's Monthly* reported that "the suddenly enriched contractors, speculators, and stock-jobbers . . . are spending money with a profusion never before witnessed in our country. . . . The men button their waistcoats with diamonds . . . and the women powder their hair with gold and silver dust." The *New York Herald* summarized that city's atmosphere: "This war has entirely changed the American character. . . . The individual who makes the most money—no matter how—and spends the most—no matter for what—is considered the greatest man."

In thousands of self-governing towns and communities, northern citizens felt a personal connection to representative government. Secession threatened to destroy their system, and northerners rallied to its defense. In the first two years of the war, northern morale remained remarkably high for a cause that today may seem abstract—the Union—but at the time meant the preservation of a social and political order that people cherished.

## The Union Cause

Secular and church leaders supported the cause, and even ministers who preferred to separate politics and pulpit denounced "the iniquity of causeless rebellion." Many churches endorsed the Union cause as God's cause. One Methodist newspaper described the war as a contest between "equalizing, humanizing Christianity" and "disunion, war, selfishness, [and] slavery." Abolitionists campaigned to turn the war into a crusade against slavery. Free black communities and churches both black and white responded to the needs of slaves who flocked to the Union lines, sending clothing, ministers, and teachers to aid the freedpeople. Indeed, northern blacks gave wholehearted

▲ Union women's volunteer defense unit, ca. 1864. The soldiers' cap and muskets make this a rare image of women's lives on the homefront during the Civil War. *(National Archives)*

support to the war, volunteering by the thousands at first and in spite of the initial rejection they received from the Lincoln administration.

Thus northern society embraced strangely contradictory tendencies. Materialism and greed flourished alongside idealism, religious conviction, and self-sacrifice. In decades to come, Americans would commemorate and build monuments to soldiers' sacrifice and idealism, not to opportunism and sometimes not even to the causes for which they fought, which was a way of forgetting the deeper nature of the conflict.

Northern women, like their southern counterparts, took on new roles. Those who stayed home organized

### Northern Women on Home Front and Battlefront

over ten thousand soldiers' aid societies, rolled bandages, and raised $3 million to aid injured troops. Women were instrumental in pressing for the first trained ambulance corps in the Union Army, and they formed the backbone of the U.S. Sanitary Commission, a civilian agency officially recognized by the War Department in 1861. The Sanitary Commission provided crucial nutritional and medical aid to soldiers. Although most of its officers were men, the bulk of the volunteers who ran its seven thousand auxiliaries were women. Women organized elaborate "Sanitary Fairs" all across the North to raise money and awareness for soldiers' health and hygiene.

Approximately 3,200 women also served as nurses in frontline hospitals, where they pressed for better care of the wounded. Yet women had to fight for a chance to serve at all; the professionalization of medicine since the Revolution had created a medical system dominated by men, and many male physicians did not want women's aid. Even Clara Barton, famous for her persistence in working in the worst

hospitals at the front, was ousted from her post in 1863. But along with Barton, women such as the stern Dorothea Dix, well known for her efforts to reform asylums for the insane, and an Illinois widow, Mary Ann Bickerdyke, who served tirelessly in Sherman's army in the West, established a heroic tradition for Civil War nurses. They also advanced the professionalization of nursing, as several schools of nursing were established in northern cities during or after the war.

Women also wrote popular fiction about the war. In sentimental war poetry, short stories, and novels, and in printed war songs that reached thousands of readers, women produced a commercial literature in illustrated weeklies, monthly periodicals, and special "story papers." In many stories, female characters seek recognition for their loyalty and service to the Union, while others probe the suffering and death of loved ones at the front. One woman writer was Louisa May Alcott, who arrived at her job as a nurse in Washington, D.C., just after the horrific Union defeat at Fredericksburg, in December 1862. From her six weeks' experience (she had to quit because of illness), she later wrote *Hospital Sketches* (1863), a widely selling book in which she described shattered men, "riddled with shot and shell," who had "borne suffering for which we have no name." Alcott provided northern readers a clear-eyed view of the hospitals in which so many of their loved ones agonized and perished.

At its heart, in what one historian has called a "feminized war literature," woman writers explored the re-

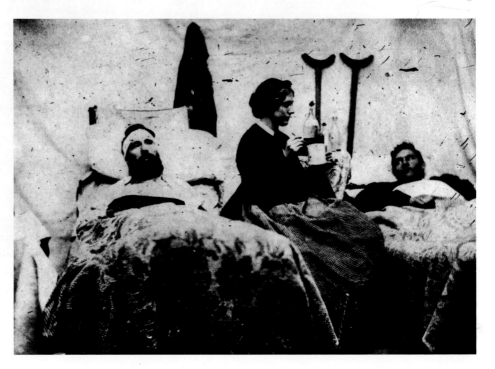

**Nurse Anne Bell tending to wounded soldiers in a federal hospital, Nashville, Tennessee, ca. 1863. The distant gaze of the man on the left and the grateful gaze of the one on the right realistically represent agonies of military hospitals.**

*( U.S. Army Center of Military History)*

lationship between individual and national needs, between home and "the cause." And by 1863 many women found the liberation of slaves an inspiring subject, as Julia Ward Howe did in her immortal "Battle Hymn of the Republic: "As He died to make men holy / Let us die to make men free."

The poet Walt Whitman also left a record of his experiences as a volunteer nurse in Washington, D.C. As

**Walt Whitman's War**

he dressed wounds and tried to comfort suffering and lonely men, Whitman found "the marrow of the tragedy concentrated in those Army Hospitals." But despite "indescribably horrid wounds," he also found inspiration in such suffering and a deepening faith in American democracy. Whitman celebrated the "incredible dauntlessness" and sacrifice of the common soldier who fought for the Union. As he had written in the preface to his great work *Leaves of Grass* (1855), "The genius of the United States is not best or most in its executives or legislatures, but always most in the common people." Whitman worked this idealization of the common man into his poetry, which also explored homoerotic themes and rejected the lofty meter and rhyme of European verse to strive for a "genuineness" that would appeal to the masses.

In "The Wound Dresser," Whitman meditated unforgettably on the deaths he had witnessed on both sides:

> On, on I go, (open doors of time! open hospital
>      doors!)
> The crush'd head I dress, (poor crazed hand
>      tear not
> the bandage away,)
> The neck of the cavalry-man with the bullet
>      through
> and through I examine,
> Hard the breathing rattles, quite glazed already
>      the eye,
> yet life struggles hard,
> (Come sweet death! be persuaded O beautiful
>      death!
> In mercy come quickly.)

Whitman mused for millions in the war who suffered the death of a husband, brother, father, or friend. Indeed, the scale of death in this war shocked many Americans into believing that the conflict had to be for purposes larger than themselves.

## THE ADVENT OF EMANCIPATION

Despite the sense of loyalty to cause that animated soldiers and civilians on both sides, the governments of the United States and the Confederacy lacked clarity about the purpose of the war. Throughout the first several months of the struggle, both Davis and Lincoln studiously avoided references to slavery. Davis realized that emphasis on the issue could increase class conflict in the South. To avoid identifying the Confederacy only with the interests of slaveholders, he articulated a broader, traditional ideology. Davis told southerners that they were fighting for constitutional liberty: northerners had betrayed the founders' legacy, and southerners had seceded to preserve it. As long as Lincoln also avoided making slavery an issue, Davis's strategy seemed to work.

Lincoln had his own reasons for avoiding slavery. It was crucial at first not to antagonize the Union's border slave states, whose loyalty was tenuous. Also, for many months Lincoln hoped that a pro-Union majority would assert itself in the South. It might be possible, he thought, to coax the South back into the Union and stop the fighting, short of what he later called "the result so fundamental and astounding"—emancipation. Raising the slavery issue would severely undermine both goals. Powerful political considerations also dictated Lincoln's reticence. The Republican Party was a young and unwieldy coalition. Some Republicans burned with moral outrage over slavery; others were frankly racist, dedicated to protecting free whites from the Slave Power and the competition of cheap slave labor. No Republican, or even northern, consensus on what to do about slavery existed early in the war.

The president's hesitancy ran counter to some of his personal feelings. Lincoln's compassion, humility, and

**Lincoln and Emancipation**

moral anguish during the war were evident in his speeches and writings. But as a politician, Lincoln distinguished between his own moral convictions and his official acts. His political positions were studied and complex, calculated for maximum advantage.

Many blacks attacked Lincoln furiously during the first year of the war for his refusal to convert the struggle into an "abolition war." When Lincoln countermanded General John C. Frémont's order of liberation for slaves owned by disloyal masters in Missouri in September 1861, the *Anglo-African* declared that the president, by his actions, "hurls back into the hell of slavery thousands . . . rightfully set free." As late as July 1862, Frederick Douglass condemned Lincoln as a "miserable tool of traitors and rebels," and characterized administration policy as reconstruction of "the old union on the old and corrupting basis of compromise, by which slavery shall retain all the power that it ever had." Douglass wanted the old Union destroyed and a new one created in the crucible of

▲ A group of "contrabands" (liberated slaves), photographed at Cumberland Landing, Virginia, May 14, 1862, at a sensitive point in the war when their legal status was still not fully determined. The faces and generations of the women, men, and children represent the human drama of emancipation. *(Library of Congress)*

a war that would destroy slavery and rewrite the Constitution in the name of human equality. To the black leader's own amazement, within a year, just such a profound result began to take place.

Lincoln first broached the subject of slavery in a substantive way in March 1862, when he proposed that the states consider emancipation on their own. He asked Congress to promise aid to any state that decided to emancipate, appealing especially to border state representatives. What Lincoln proposed was gradual emancipation, with compensation for slaveholders and colonization of the freed slaves outside the United States. To a delegation of free blacks in August 1862 he explained that "it is better for us both . . . to be separated."

Until well into 1864, Lincoln's administration promoted an impractical scheme to colonize blacks in Central America or the Caribbean. Lincoln saw colonization as one option among others in dealing with the impending freedom of America's 4.2 million slaves. He was as yet unconvinced that America had any prospect as a biracial society, and he desperately feared that white northerners might not support a war for black freedom. Led by Fred-

erick Douglass, black abolitionists vehemently opposed these machinations by the Lincoln administration.

Other politicians had much greater plans for a struggle against slavery. A group of Republicans in Congress, known as the Radicals and led by men such as George Julian, Charles Sumner, and Thaddeus Stevens, dedicated themselves to a war for emancipation. They were instrumental in creating a special House-Senate committee on the conduct of the war, which investigated Union reverses, sought to make the war effort more efficient, and prodded the president to take stronger measures against slavery.

In August 1861, at the Radicals' instigation, Congress passed its first confiscation act. Designed to punish

**Confiscation Acts**

the Confederates, the law confiscated all property used for "insurrectionary purposes." Thus, if the South used slaves in a hostile action, those slaves were seized and liberated as "contraband" of war. A second confiscation act (July 1862) went much further: it confiscated the property of anyone who supported the rebellion, even those who merely resided in the South and paid Confederate taxes. Their slaves were declared "forever free of their servitude." These acts stemmed from the logic that, in order to crush the southern rebellion, the government had to use extraordinary powers.

Lincoln refused to adopt that view in the summer of 1862. He stood by his proposal of voluntary gradual emancipation by the states and made no effort at first to enforce the second confiscation act. His stance provoked a public protest from Horace Greeley, editor of the powerful *New York Tribune*. In an open letter to the president entitled "The Prayer of Twenty Millions," Greeley pleaded with Lincoln to "execute the laws" and declared, "On the face of this wide earth, Mr. President, there is not one . . . intelligent champion of the Union cause who does not feel that all attempts to put down the Rebellion and at the same time uphold its inciting cause are preposterous and futile." Lincoln's reply was an explicit statement of his calculated approach to the question. He disagreed, he said, with all those who would make slavery the paramount issue of the war. "I would save the Union," announced Lincoln. "If I could save the Union without freeing any slave I would do it, and if I could save it by freeing all the slaves I would do it; and if I could save it by freeing some and leaving others alone I would also do that. What I do about slavery, and the colored race, I do because I believe it helps to save the Union." Lincoln closed with a personal disclaimer: "I have here stated my purpose according to my view of official duty; and I intend no modification of my oft-expressed personal wish that all men everywhere could be free."

When he wrote those words, Lincoln had already decided to boldly issue a presidential Emancipation Proclamation. He was waiting, however, for a Union victory so that it would not appear to be an act of desperation. Yet the letter to Greeley was not simply an effort to stall; it was an integral part of Lincoln's approach to the future of slavery, as the text of the Emancipation Proclamation would show. Lincoln was concerned with conditioning public opinion as best he could for the coming social revolution, and he needed to delicately consider international opinion as well.

On September 22, 1862, shortly after Union success at the Battle of Antietam, Lincoln issued the first part of his two-part proclamation. In-

**Emancipation Proclamations**

voking his powers as commander-in-chief of the armed forces, he announced that on January 1, 1863, he would emancipate the slaves in the states "in rebellion." Lincoln made plain that he would judge a state to be in rebellion in January if it lacked legitimate representatives in the U.S. Congress. Thus his September 1862 proclamation was less a declaration of the right of slaves to be free than a threat to southerners: unless they put down their arms and returned to Congress, they would lose their slaves. "Knowing the value that was set on the slaves by the rebels," said Garrison Frazier, a black Georgia minister, "the President thought that his proclamation would stimulate them to lay down their arms . . . and their not doing so has now made the freedom of the slaves a part of the war." Lincoln had little expectation that southerners would give up their effort, but he was careful to offer them the option and compel a reply.

In the fateful January 1, 1863, proclamation, Lincoln declared that "all persons held as slaves" in areas in rebellion "shall be then, thenceforward, and forever free." But he excepted (as areas in rebellion) every Confederate county or city that had fallen under Union control. Those areas, he declared, "are, for the present, left precisely as if this proclamation were not issued." Nor did Lincoln liberate slaves in the border slave states that remained in the Union. "The President has purposely made the proclamation inoperative in all places where . . . the slaves [are] accessible," charged the anti-administration *New York World*. "He has proclaimed emancipation only where he has notoriously no power to execute it." Partisanship aside, even Secretary of State Seward said sarcastically, "We show our sympathy with slavery by emancipating slaves where we cannot reach them and holding them in bondage where we can set them free."

But Lincoln was worried about the constitutionality of his acts, and he anticipated that after the war southerners might sue in court for restoration of their "property." Making the liberation of the slaves "a fit and necessary war measure" raised a variety of legal questions: How long did a war measure remain in force? Did it expire with the suppression of a rebellion? The proclamation did little to clarify the status or citizenship of the freed slaves, although it did open the possibility of military service for blacks. How, indeed, would this change the character and purpose of the war?

Thus the Emancipation Proclamation was an ambiguous document. But if as a legal document it was wanting, as a moral and political document it had great meaning. Because the proclamation defined the war as a war against slavery, Congressional Radicals could applaud it. Yet at the same time it protected Lincoln's position with conservatives, leaving him room to retreat if he chose and forcing no immediate changes on the border slave states. It was a delicate balancing act, but one from which there was no real turning back.

Most important, though, thousands of slaves had already reached Union lines in various sections of the South.

They had "voted with their feet" for emancipation, as many said, well before the proclamation. And now, every advance of federal forces into slave society was a liberating step. This Lincoln knew in taking his own initially tentative, and then forthright, steps toward emancipation.

Across the North and in Union-occupied sections of the South, blacks and their white allies celebrated the Emancipation Proclamation with unprecedented fervor. Full of praise songs, these celebrations demonstrated that, whatever the fine print of the proclamation, black folks knew that they had lived to see a new day. At a large "contraband camp" in Washington, D.C., some six hundred black men, women, and children gathered at the superintendent's headquarters on New Year's Eve and sang through the night. In chorus after chorus of "Go Down, Moses" they announced the magnitude of their painful but beautiful exodus. One newly supplied verse concluded with "Go down, Abraham, away down in Dixie's land, tell Jeff Davis to let my people go!"

The need for men soon convinced the administration to recruit northern and southern blacks for the Union Army. By the spring of 1863, Afri-

### African American Recruits

can American troops were answering the call of a dozen or more black recruiters barnstorming the cities and towns of the North. Lincoln came to see black soldiers as "the great available and yet unavailed of force for restoring the Union."

African American leaders hoped that military service would secure equal rights for their people. Once the black soldier had fought for the Union, wrote Frederick Douglass, "there is no power on earth which can deny that he has earned the right of citizenship in the United States." If black soldiers turned the tide, asked another man, "would the nation refuse us our rights?"

In June 1864, with thousands of black former slaves in blue uniforms, Lincoln gave his support to a constitutional ban on slavery. On the eve of the Republican national convention, Lincoln called on the party to "put into the platform as the keystone, the amendment of the Constitution abolishing and prohibiting slavery forever." The party promptly called for the Thirteenth Amendment. Republican delegates probably would have adopted such a plank without his urging, but Lincoln demonstrated his commitment by lobbying Congress for quick approval of the measure. The proposed amendment passed in early 1865 and was sent to the states for ratification. The war to save the Union had also become the war to free the slaves.

It has long been debated whether Abraham Lincoln deserved the label (one he never claimed for himself) of

### Who Freed the Slaves?

"Great Emancipator." Was Lincoln ultimately a reluctant emancipator, following rather than leading Congress and public opinion? Or did Lincoln give essential presidential leadership to the most transformative and sensitive aspect of the war by going slow on emancipation but, once moving, never backpedaling on black freedom? Once he had realized the total character of the war and decided to prosecute it to the unconditional surrender of the Confederates, Lincoln made the destruction of slavery central to the war's purpose.

Others have argued, however, that the slaves themselves are the central story in the achievement of their own freedom. When they were in proximity to the war zones or had opportunities as traveling laborers, slaves fled for their freedom by the thousands. Some worked as camp laborers for the Union armies, and eventually more than 180,000 black men served in the Union Army and Navy. Sometimes freedom came as a combination of confusion, fear, and joy in the rural hinterlands of the South. Some found freedom as individuals in 1861, and some not until 1865, as members of trains of refugees trekking great distances to reach contraband camps.

However freedom came to individuals, emancipation was a historical confluence of two essential forces: one, a policy directed by and dependent on the military authority of the president in his effort to win the war; and the other, the will and courage necessary for acts of self-emancipation. Wallace Turnage's escape in Mobile Bay in 1864 demonstrates that emancipation could result from both a slave's own extraordinary heroism and the liberating actions of the Union forces. Most blacks comprehended their freedom as both given and taken, but also as their human right. "I now dreaded the gun and handcuffs . . . no more," remembered Turnage of his liberation. "Nor the blowing of horns and running of hounds, nor the threats of death from rebels' authority." He was free in body and mind. "I could now speak my opinion" Turnage concluded, "to men of all grades and colors."

Before the war was over, the Confederacy, too, addressed the issue of emancipation. Jefferson Davis himself offered a proposal for black

### A Confederate Plan of Emancipation

freedom of a kind. Late in the war he was willing to sacrifice slavery to achieve independence. He proposed that the Confederate government purchase 40,000 slaves to work for the army as laborers, with a promise of freedom at the end of their service. Soon Davis upgraded the idea, calling for the recruitment and arming of slaves as soldiers, who likewise would gain their freedom at war's end. The wives and children of these soldiers, he made plain, must also receive freedom from the states. Davis and his advisers envisioned an "intermediate" status for ex-slaves of "serfage or peonage." Thus, at the bitter end, a few southerners were willing to sacrifice some of the racial, if not class, destiny for which they had launched their revolution.

Bitter debate over Davis's plan resounded through the Confederacy. When the Confederate Congress finally approved slave enlistments in March 1865, owners had to comply only on a "voluntary" basis. In sheer desperation for manpower, General Lee also supported the idea of slave soldiers. Against the reality all around them of slaves fleeing to Union lines, some southern leaders mistakenly hoped that they could still count on the "loyalty" of their bondsmen. Most Confederate slaveholders and editors vehemently opposed the enlistment plan; those who did support it acknowledged that the war had already freed some portion of the slave population. Their aim was to fight to a stalemate, achieve independence, and control the postwar racial order through their limited wartime emancipation schemes. It was too late. As a Mississippi planter wrote to his state's governor, the plan seemed "like a drowning man catching at straws."

By contrast, Lincoln's Emancipation Proclamation stimulated a vital infusion of forces into the Union armies. Before the war was over, 134,000 former slaves (and 52,000 free blacks) had fought for freedom and the Union. Their participation was pivotal in northern victory. As both policy and process, emancipation had profound practical and moral implications for the new nation to be born out of the war.

## THE SOLDIERS' WAR

The intricacies of policymaking and social revolutions were far from the minds of most ordinary soldiers. Military service completely altered their lives. Enlistment took young men from their homes and submerged them in large organizations whose military discipline ignored their individuality. Army life meant tedium, physical hardship, and separation from loved ones. Yet the military experience had powerful attractions as well. It molded men on both sides so thoroughly that they came to resemble one another far more than they resembled civilians back home. Many soldiers forged amid war a bond with their fellows and a connection to a noble purpose that they cherished for years afterward.

Union soldiers may have sensed most clearly the massive scale of modern war. Most were young; the average soldier was between eighteen and twenty-one. Many went straight from small towns and farms into large armies supplied by extensive bureaucracies. By late 1861 there were 640,000 volunteers in arms, a stupendous increase over the regular army of 20,000 men.

Soldiers benefited from certain new products, such as canned condensed milk, but blankets, clothing, and arms were often of poor quality. Hospitals were badly managed at first.

**Hospitals and Camp Life**

Rules of hygiene in large camps were scarcely enforced; latrines were poorly made or carelessly used. One investigation turned up "an area of over three acres, encircling the camp as a broad belt, on which is deposited an almost perfect layer of human excrement." Water supplies were unsafe and typhoid epidemics common. About 57,000 men died from dysentery and diarrhea; in fact, 224,000 Union troops died from disease or accidents, far more than the 110,100 who died as a result of battle. Confederate troops were less well supplied, especially in the latter part of the war, and they had no sanitary commission. Still, an extensive network of hospitals, aided by many white female volunteers and black woman slaves, sprang up to aid the sick and wounded.

On both sides, troops quickly learned that soldiering was far from glorious. "The dirt of a camp life knocks all its poetry into a cocked hat," wrote a North Carolina volunteer in 1862. One year later he marveled at his earlier innocence. Fighting had taught him "the realities of a soldier's life. We had no tents after the 6th of August, but slept on the ground, in the woods or open fields. . . . I learned to eat fat bacon raw, and to like it. . . . Without time to wash our clothes or our persons . . . the whole army became lousy more or less with body lice." Union troops "skirmished" against lice by boiling their clothes, but, reported one soldier, "I find some on me in spite of all I can do."

Few had seen violent death before, but war soon exposed them to the blasted bodies of their friends and comrades. "Any one who goes over a battlefield after a battle," wrote one Confederate, "never cares to go over another. . . . It is a sad sight to see the dead and if possible more sad to see the wounded—shot in every possible way you can imagine." Many men died gallantly; there were innumerable striking displays of courage. But often soldiers gave up their lives in mass sacrifice, in tactics that made little sense.

Still, Civil War soldiers developed deep commitments to each other and to their task. As campaigns dragged on, most soldiers who did not desert grew determined to see the struggle through. "We now, like true Soldiers go determined not to yield one inch," wrote a New York corporal. When at last the war was over, "it seemed like breaking up a family to separate," one man observed. Another admitted, "We shook hands all around, and laughed and seemed to make merry, while our hearts were heavy and our eyes ready to shed tears."

Advances in technology made the Civil War particularly deadly. By far the most important were the rifle and the "minie ball." Bullets fired from

### The Rifled Musket

a smoothbore musket tumbled and wobbled as they flew through the air, and thus were not accurate at distances over eighty yards. Cutting spiraled grooves inside the barrel gave the projectile a spin and much greater accuracy, but rifles remained difficult to load and use until the Frenchman Claude Minie and the American James Burton developed a new kind of bullet. Civil War bullets were lead slugs with a cavity at the bottom that expanded on firing so that the bullet "took" the rifling and flew accurately. With these bullets, rifles were deadly at four hundred yards and useful up to one thousand yards.

This meant, of course, that soldiers assaulting a position defended by riflemen were in greater peril than ever before; the defense thus gained a significant advantage. While artillery now fired from a safe distance, there was no substitute for the infantry assault or the popular turning movements aimed at an enemy's flank. Thus advancing soldiers had to expose themselves repeatedly to accurate rifle fire. Because medical knowledge was rudimentary, even minor wounds often led to amputation and death through infection. Never before in Europe or America had such massive forces pummeled each other with weapons of such destructive power. As losses mounted, many citizens wondered at what Union soldier (and future Supreme Court justice) Oliver Wendell Holmes Jr. called "the butcher's bill."

At the outset of the war, racism in the Union Army was strong. Most white soldiers wanted nothing to do with black people and regarded

### The Black Soldier's Fight for Manhood

them as inferior. "I never came out here for to free the black devils," wrote one soldier, and another objected to fighting beside African Americans, because "We are a too superior race for that." For many, acceptance of black troops grew only because they could do heavy labor and "stop Bullets as well as white people." A popular song celebrated "Sambo's Right to Be Kilt" as the only justification for black enlistments.

But among some, a change occurred. While recruiting black troops in Virginia in late 1864, Massachusetts soldier Charles Brewster sometimes denigrated the very

▲ Company E, Fourth U.S. Colored Infantry, photographed at Fort Lincoln, Virginia, in 1864. Nothing so symbolized the new manhood and citizenship among African Americans in the midst of the war as such young black men in blue. *(Chicago Historical Society)*

1863: The Tide of Battle Turns

men he sought to enlist. But he was delighted at the sight of a black cavalry unit because it made the local "secesh" furious, and he praised black soldiers who "fought nobly" and filled hospitals with "their wounded and mangled bodies." White officers who volunteered to lead segregated black units only to gain promotion found that experience altered their opinions. After just one month with black troops, a white captain informed his wife, "I have a more elevated opinion of their abilities than I ever had before. I know that many of them are vastly the superiors of those . . . who would condemn them all to a life of brutal degradation." One general reported that his "colored regiments" possessed "remarkable aptitude for military training," and another observer said, "They fight like fiends."

Black troops created this change through their own dedication. They had a mission to destroy slavery and demonstrate their equality. "When Rebellion is crushed," wrote a black volunteer from Connecticut, "who will be more proud than I to say, 'I was one of the first of the despised race to leave the free North with a rifle on my shoulder, and give the lie to the old story that the black man will not fight.'" Corporal James Henry Gooding of Massachusetts's black Fifty-fourth Regiment explained that his unit intended "to live down all prejudice against its color, by a determination to do well in any position it is put." After an engagement, he was proud that "a regiment of white men gave us three cheers as we were passing them," because "it shows that we did our duty as men should."

Through such experience under fire, the blacks and whites of the Fifty-fourth Massachusetts forged deep bonds. Just before the regiment launched its costly assault on Fort Wagner in Charleston harbor, in July 1863, a black soldier called out to abolitionist Colonel Robert Gould Shaw, who would perish that day, "Colonel, I will stay by you till I die." "And he kept his word," noted a survivor of the attack. "He has never been seen since." Indeed, the heroic assault on Fort Wagner was celebrated for demonstrating the valor of black men. This bloody chapter in the history of American racism proved many things, not least of which that black men had to die in battle to be acknowledged as men.

Such valor emerged despite persistent discrimination. Off-duty black soldiers were sometimes attacked by northern mobs; on duty, they did most of the heavy labor. The Union government, moreover, paid white privates $13 per month plus a clothing allowance of $3.50, whereas black privates earned only $10 per month less $3 for clothing. Outraged by this injustice, several regiments refused to accept any pay whatsoever, and Congress eventually remedied the inequity. In this instance at least, the majority of legislators agreed with a white private that black troops

had "proved their title to manhood on many a bloody field fighting freedom's battles."

## 1863: THE TIDE OF BATTLE TURNS

The fighting in the spring and summer of 1863 did not settle the war, but it began to suggest the outcome. The campaigns began in a deceptively positive way for Confederates, as Lee's army performed brilliantly in battles in central Virginia.

For once, a large Civil War army was not slow and cumbersome, but executed tactics with speed and precision.

**Battle of Chancellorsville**

On May 2 and 3, west of Fredericksburg, Virginia, some 130,000 members of the Union Army of the Potomac bore down on fewer than 60,000 Confederates. Boldly, Lee and Stonewall Jackson divided their forces, ordering 30,000 men under Jackson on a day-long march westward to prepare a flank attack.

This classic turning movement was carried out in the face of great numerical disadvantage. Arriving at their position late in the afternoon, Jackson's seasoned "foot cavalry" found unprepared Union troops laughing, smoking, and playing cards. The Union soldiers had no idea they were under attack until frightened deer and rabbits bounded out of the forest, followed by gray-clad troops. The Confederate attack drove the entire right side of the Union Army back in confusion. Eager to press his advantage, Jackson rode forward with a few officers to study the ground. As they returned at twilight, southern troops mistook them for federals and fired, fatally wounding their commander. The next day, Union forces left in defeat. Chancellorsville was a remarkable southern victory, but costly because of the loss of Stonewall Jackson, who would forever remain a legend in Confederate memory.

July brought crushing defeats for the Confederacy in two critical battles—Vicksburg and Gettysburg—that severely damaged Confederate hopes for independence. Vicksburg was a vital western citadel, the last major fortification on the Mississippi River in southern hands (see Map 15.2). After months of searching through swamps and bayous, General Ulysses S. Grant found an advantageous approach to the city. He laid siege to Vicksburg in May, bottling up the defending army of General John Pemberton. If Vicksburg fell, Union forces would control the river, cutting the Confederacy in two and gaining an open path into its interior. To stave off such a result, Jefferson Davis gave command of all other forces in the

**Siege of Vicksburg**

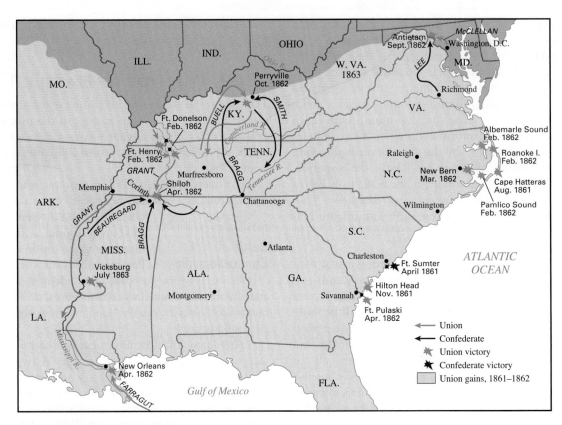

**Map 15.2    War in the West, 1861–1863**

Here is an overview of the Union's successful campaigns in the West and its seizure of key points on the Mississippi River, as well as along the Atlantic coast in 1862 and 1863. These actions were decisive in paving the way for ultimate northern victory.

area to General Joseph E. Johnston and beseeched him to go to Pemberton's aid. Meanwhile, at a council of war in Richmond, General Robert E. Lee proposed a Confederate invasion of the North. Although such an offensive would not relieve Vicksburg directly, it could stun and dismay the North and, if successful, possibly even lead to peace. By invading the North a second time, Lee hoped to take the war out of war-weary Virginia, garner civilian support in Maryland, win a major victory on northern soil, threaten major cities, and thereby force a Union capitulation on his terms.

As Lee's emboldened army advanced through western Maryland and into Pennsylvania, Confederate prospects to the south along the Mississippi darkened. Davis repeatedly wired General Johnston, urging him to concentrate his forces and attack Grant's army. Johnston, however, did little, telegraphing back, "I consider saving Vicksburg hopeless." Grant's men, meanwhile, were supplying themselves from the abundant crops of the Mississippi River valley and could continue their siege indefinitely.

Their rich meat-and-vegetable diet became so tiresome, in fact, that one day, as Grant rode by, a private looked up and muttered, "Hardtack," referring to the dry biscuits that were the usual staple of soldiers' diets. Soon a line of soldiers was shouting, "Hardtack! Hardtack!" demanding respite from turkey and sweet potatoes.

In such circumstances the fall of Vicksburg was inevitable, and on July 4, 1863, its commander surrendered. The same day, a battle that had been raging for three days concluded at Gettysburg, Pennsylvania (see Map 15.3). On July 1, Confederate forces hunting for a supply of shoes had collided with part of the Union Army. Heavy fighting on the second day over two steep hills left federal forces in possession of high ground along Cemetery Ridge, running more than a mile south of the town. There they enjoyed the protection of a stone wall and a clear view of their foe across almost a mile of open field.

**Battle of Gettysburg**

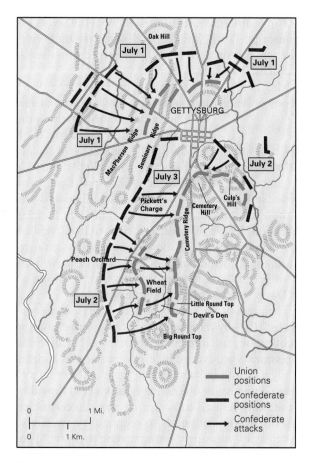

**Map 15.3    Battle of Gettysburg**
In the war's greatest battle, fought around a small market town in southern Pennsylvania, Lee's invasion of the North was repulsed. Union forces had the advantage of high ground, shorter lines, and superior numbers. The casualties for the two armies—dead, wounded, and missing—exceeded 50,000 men.

Undaunted, Lee believed that his reinforced troops could break the Union line, and on July 3 he ordered a direct assault. Full of foreboding, General James Longstreet warned Lee that "no 15,000 men ever arrayed for battle can take that position." But Lee stuck to his plan. Virginians under General George E. Pickett and North Carolinians under General James Pettigrew methodically marched up the slope in a doomed assault known as Pickett's Charge. For a moment, a few hundred Confederates breached the enemy's line, but most fell in heavy slaughter. On July 4 Lee had to withdraw, having suffered almost 4,000 dead and about 24,000 missing and wounded. The Confederate general reported to President Davis that "I am alone to blame" and offered to resign. Davis replied that to find a more capable commander was "an impossibility." The

Confederacy had reached what many consider its "high water mark" on that ridge at Gettysburg.

Southern troops displayed unforgettable courage and dedication at Gettysburg, and under General George G. Meade, the Union Army, which suffered 23,000 casualties (nearly one-quarter of the force), exhibited the same bravery in stopping the Confederate invasion. But the results there and at Vicksburg were disastrous for the South. The Confederacy was split in two; west of the Mississippi, General E. Kirby Smith had to operate on his own, virtually independent of Richmond. Moreover, the heartland of Louisiana, Tennessee, and Mississippi lay exposed to invasion. Far to the north, Lee's defeat spelled the end of major southern offensive actions. Too weak to prevail in attack, the Confederacy henceforth would have to conserve its limited resources and rely on a prolonged defense. By refusing to be beaten and by wearing down northern morale, the South might yet win, but its prospects were darker than before.

## DISUNITY: SOUTH, NORTH, AND WEST

Both northern and southern governments waged the final two years of the war in the face of increasing opposition at home. Dissatisfactions that had surfaced earlier grew more intense and sometimes violent. The gigantic costs of a civil war that neither side seemed able to win fed the unrest. But protest also arose from fundamental stresses in the social structures of North and South.

Wherever Union forces invaded they imposed a military occupation consisting roughly of three zones: garrisoned towns, with large numbers of troops in control of civilian and economic life; the Confederate frontier, areas still under southern control but also with some federal military penetration; and "no man's land," the land between the two armies, beyond Confederate authority and under frequent Union patrols.

**Union Occupation Zones**

As many as one hundred southern towns were garrisoned during the war, causing severe disruption to the social landscape. Large regions of Tennessee, Virginia, Louisiana, Mississippi, and Georgia fell under this pattern of occupation and suffered food shortages, crop and property destruction, disease, roadway banditry, guerrilla warfare, summary executions, and the random flow of escaped slaves. After two years of occupation, a southern white woman wrote to a kinsman about their native Clarksville, Tennessee. "You would scarcely know the place," she lamented, "it is nothing but a dirty hole filled . . . with niggers and Yankees."

Vastly disadvantaged in industrial capacity, natural resources, and labor, southerners felt the cost of the war more directly and more painfully than northerners. But even more fundamental were the Confederacy's internal problems; the southern class system threatened the Confederate cause.

### Disintegration of Confederate Unity

One ominous development was the planters' increasing opposition to their own government. Along with new taxation, Confederate military authorities also impressed slaves to build fortifications. And when Union forces advanced on plantation areas, Confederate commanders burned stores of cotton that lay in the enemy's path. Many planters bitterly complained about such interference with their agricultural production and financial interests.

Nor were the centralizing policies of the Davis administration popular. The increasing size and power of the Richmond government alarmed planters. In fact, the Confederate constitution had granted substantial powers to the central government, especially in time of war. But many planters took the position articulated by R. B. Rhett, editor of the *Charleston Mercury*, that the Confederate constitution "leaves the States untouched in their Sovereignty, and commits to the Confederate Government only a few simple objects, and a few simple powers to enforce them." Governor Joseph E. Brown of Georgia took a similar states' rights position, occasionally prohibiting supplies and that state's soldiers from leaving its borders.

Years of opposition to the federal government within the Union had frozen southerners in a defensive posture. Now they erected the barrier of states' rights as a defense against change, hiding behind it while their capacity for creative statesmanship atrophied. Planters sought, above all, a guarantee that their plantations and their lives would remain untouched. As secession revolutionized their world and hard war took so many lives, some could never fully commit to the cause.

Confused and embittered planters struck out at Jefferson Davis. Conscription, thundered Governor Brown, was "subversive of [Georgia's] sovereignty, and at war with all the principles for the support of which Georgia entered into this revolution." Searching for ways to frustrate the law, Brown ordered local enrollment officials not to cooperate with the Confederacy. The *Charleston Mercury* told readers that "conscription . . . is . . . the very embodiment of Lincolnism, which our gallant armies are today fighting." In a gesture of stubborn selfishness, Robert Toombs of Georgia, a former U.S. senator, refused to switch from cotton to food crops, defying the wishes of the government, the newspapers, and his neighbors' petitions.

The southern courts ultimately upheld Davis's power to conscript. Davis was deeply devoted to southern independence, but some of his actions earned him the hatred of influential and elite citizens.

Meanwhile, for ordinary southerners, the dire predictions of hunger and suffering were becoming a reality. Food riots occurred in the spring of 1863 in Atlanta, Macon, Columbus, and Augusta, Georgia, and in Salisbury and High Point, North Carolina. On April 2 a crowd assembled in Richmond to demand relief. A passerby, noticing the excitement, asked a young girl, "Is there some celebration?" "We celebrate our right to live," replied the girl. "We are starving. As soon as enough of us get together we are going to the bakeries and each of us will take a loaf of bread." Soon they did just that, sparking a riot that Davis ordered quelled at gunpoint.

### Food Riots in Southern Cities

Throughout the rural South, ordinary people resisted more quietly—by refusing to cooperate with conscription, tax collection, and impressments of food. "In all the States impressments are evaded by every means which ingenuity can suggest, and in some openly resisted," wrote a high-ranking commissary officer. Farmers who did provide food for the army refused to accept payment in certificates of credit or government bonds, as required by law. Conscription officers increasingly found no one to draft. "The disposition to avoid military service is general," observed one of Georgia's senators in 1864. In some areas, tax agents were killed in the line of duty.

Jefferson Davis was ill equipped to deal with such discontent. Austere and private by nature, he failed to communicate with the masses. Often he buried himself in military affairs or administrative details. His class perspective also distanced him from the sufferings of the common people. While his social circle in Richmond dined on duck and oysters, ordinary southerners recovered salt from the drippings on their smokehouse floors and went hungry. Davis failed to reach out to the plain folk and thus lost their support.

Such discontent was certain to affect the Confederate armies. "What man is there that would stay in the army and no that his family is sufring at home?" an angry citizen wrote anonymously to the secretary of war. Worried about their loved ones and resentful of what they saw as a rich man's war, large numbers of men did indeed leave the armies. Their friends and neighbors gave them support. Mary Chesnut observed a man being dragged back to the army as his wife looked on. "Desert agin, Jake!" she cried openly. "You desert

### Desertions from the Confederate Army

▲ Refugees driven from their homes in the South as armies, seen in the distant camp in the background, move through the countryside. Hundreds of thousands of southerners, white and black, were displaced people by 1864–1865. *(National Archives)*

agin, quick as you kin. Come back to your wife and children."

Desertion did not become a serious problem for the Confederacy until mid-1862, and stiffer policing solved the problem that year. But from 1863 on, the number of men on duty fell rapidly. By mid-1863, John A. Campbell, the South's assistant secretary of war, wondered whether "so general a habit" as desertion could be considered a crime. Campbell estimated that 40,000 to 50,000 troops were absent without leave and that 100,000 were evading duty in some way. Furloughs, amnesty proclamations, and appeals to return had little effect; by November 1863, Secretary of War James Seddon admitted that one-third of the army could not be accounted for.

The defeats at Gettysburg and Vicksburg dealt a heavy blow to Confederate morale. When the news reached Josiah Gorgas, the genius of Confederate ordnance operations, he confided to his diary, "Today absolute ruin seems our portion. The Confederacy totters to its destruction." In desperation President Davis and several state governors resorted to threats and racial scare tactics to drive southern whites to further sacrifice. Defeat, Davis warned, would mean "extermination of yourselves, your wives, and children." Governor Charles Clark of Mississippi predicted "elevation of the black race to a position of equality—aye, of superiority, that will make them your masters and rulers."

From this point on, the internal disintegration of the Confederacy quickened. A few newspapers began to call openly for peace. "We are for peace," admitted the *Raleigh* (North Carolina) *Daily Progress,* "because there has been enough of blood and carnage, enough of widows and orphans." Similar proposals were made in several state legislatures, though they were presented as plans for independence on honorable terms. Confederate leaders began to realize that they were losing the support of the common people. It is, indeed, remarkable how long and how effectively the Confederacy sustained a military effort in the face of such internal division.

In North Carolina, a peace movement grew under the leadership of William W. Holden, a popular Democratic politician and editor. Over one hundred public meetings in support of peace negotiations took place during the summer of 1863, and Holden may have had the majority of the people behind him. In Georgia early in 1864, Governor Brown and Alexander H. Stephens, vice president of the Confederacy, led a similar effort. Ultimately, however, these movements

**Antiwar Sentiment, South and North**

came to naught. The lack of a two-party system threw into question the legitimacy of any criticism of the government; even Holden and Brown could not entirely escape the taint of dishonor and disloyalty.

The results of the 1863 congressional elections strengthened dissent in the Confederacy. Everywhere secessionists and supporters of the administration lost seats to men not identified with the government. In the last years of the war, Davis's support in the Confederate Congress dwindled. Some newspaper editors and a core of courageous, determined soldiers, especially in Lee's Army of Northern Virginia, kept the Confederacy alive in spite of disintegrating popular support.

By 1864 much of the opposition to the war had moved entirely outside the political sphere. Southerners were simply giving up the struggle. Deserters dominated some whole towns and counties. Active dissent was particularly common in upland and mountain regions, where support for the Union had always been genuine. "The condition of things in the mountain districts of North Carolina, South Carolina, Georgia, and Alabama," admitted Assistant Secretary of War Campbell, "menaces the existence of the Confederacy as fatally as either of the armies of the United States." The government was losing the support of its citizens.

Opposition to the war, though less severe, existed in the North as well. Alarm intensified over the growing centralization of government, and by 1863 war-weariness was widespread. Resentment of the draft sparked protest, especially among poor citizens, and the Union Army, too, struggled with a troubling desertion rate. But the Union was so much richer than the South in human resources that none of these problems ever threatened the effectiveness of the government. Fresh recruits were always available, especially after black enlistments in 1863.

Moreover, Lincoln possessed a talent that Davis lacked: he knew how to stay in touch with the ordinary citizen. Through public letters to newspapers and private ones to soldiers' families he reached the common people. The daily carnage, the tortuous political problems, and the ceaseless criticism weighed heavily on him. But this president—a self-educated man of humble origins—was able to communicate his suffering. His moving words helped to contain northern discontent, though they could not remove it.

Much of the wartime protest in the North was political in origin. The Democratic Party fought to regain power by blaming Lincoln for the war's death toll, the expansion of federal powers, inflation and the high tariff, and the emancipation

## Peace Democrats

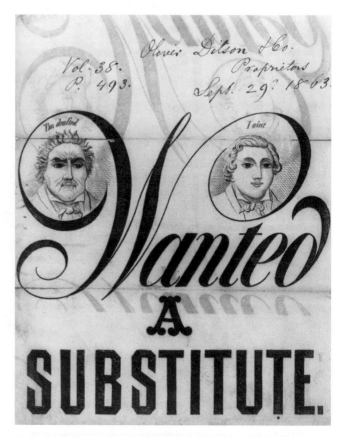

▲ In the Union government's conscription system, a draftee could hire a "substitute" to replace him in the army, lending credence to the claim by some that the conflict became a "rich man's war but a poor man's fight." Less than 7 percent of all Union soldiers were draftees, but this practice caused problems in northern morale. *(Library of Congress)*

of blacks. Appealing to tradition, its leaders called for an end to the war and reunion on the basis of "the Constitution as it is and the Union as it was." The Democrats denounced conscription and martial law, and defended states' rights. They charged repeatedly that Republican policies were designed to flood the North with blacks, depriving white males of their status, their jobs, and their women. In the 1862 congressional elections, the Democrats made a strong comeback, with peace Democrats wielding influence in New York State and majorities in the legislatures of Illinois and Indiana.

Led by outspoken men like Representative Clement L. Vallandigham of Ohio, the peace Democrats became highly visible. Vallandigham criticized Lincoln as a "dictator" who had suspended the writ of habeas corpus without congressional authority and arrested thousands of innocent citizens. He condemned both conscription and emancipation, and urged voters to use their power at the polls to depose "King Abraham." Vallandigham stayed carefully within legal bounds, but his attacks seemed so damaging to the war effort that military authorities arrested him for treason. Lincoln wisely decided against punishment—and martyr's status—for the Ohioan and exiled him to the Confederacy. (Eventually Vallandigham returned to the North through Canada.)

Lincoln believed that antiwar Democrats were linked to secret organizations that harbored traitorous ideas. These societies, he feared, encouraged draft resistance, discouraged enlistment, sabotaged communications, and plotted to aid the Confederacy. Likening such groups to a poisonous snake, Republicans sometimes branded them—and by extension the peace Democrats—as "Copperheads." Although some Confederate agents were active in the North and Canada, they never genuinely threatened the Union war effort.

More violent opposition to the government arose from ordinary citizens facing the draft, which became law in 1863. Although many soldiers risked their lives willingly out of a desire to preserve the Union or extend freedom, others openly sought to avoid service. Under the law, a draftee could stay at home by providing a substitute or paying a $300 commutation fee. Many wealthy men chose these options, and in response to popular demand, clubs, cities, and states provided the money for others to escape conscription. In all, 118,000 substitutes were provided and 87,000 commutations paid before Congress ended the commutation system in 1864.

### New York City Draft Riots

The urban poor and immigrants in strongly Democratic areas were especially hostile to conscription. Federal enrolling officers made up the lists of eligibles, a procedure open to personal favoritism and prejudice. The North's poor viewed the system as discriminatory, and many immigrants suspected (wrongly, on the whole) that they were called in disproportionate numbers. (Approximately 200,000 men born in Germany and 150,000 born in Ireland served in the Union Army.)

As a result, there were scores of disturbances. Enrolling officers received rough treatment in many parts of the North, and riots occurred in New Jersey, Ohio, Indiana, Pennsylvania, Illinois, and Wisconsin. By far the most serious outbreak of violence occurred in New York City in July 1863. The war was unpopular in that Democratic stronghold, and racial, ethnic, and class tensions ran high. Shippers had recently broken a longshoremen's strike by hiring black strikebreakers to work under police protection. Working-class New Yorkers feared an inflow of black labor from the South and regarded blacks as the cause of the war. Poor Irish workers resented being forced to serve in the place of others who could afford to avoid the draft.

Military police officers came under attack first, and then mobs crying, "Down with the rich" looted wealthy homes and stores. But blacks became the special target. The mob rampaged through African American neighborhoods, beating and murdering people in the streets, and burning an orphan asylum. At least seventy-four people died in the violence, which raged out of control for three days. Only the dispatch of army units directly from Gettysburg ended this tragic episode of racism and class resentment.

East and West, over race, land, and culture, America was a deeply divided country. A civil war of another kind raged on the Great Plains and in the Southwest. By 1864 U.S. troops under the command of Colonel John Chivington waged full-scale war against the Sioux, Arapahos, and Cheyennes in order to eradicate Indian title to all of eastern Colorado. Indian chiefs sought peace, but American commanders had orders to "burn villages and kill Cheyennes whenever and wherever found." A Cheyenne chief, Lean Bear, was shot from his horse as he rode toward U.S. troops, holding in his hand papers given him by President Lincoln during a visit to Washington, D.C. Another chief, Black Kettle, was told by the U.S. command that, by moving his people to Sand Creek, Colorado, they would find a safe haven. But on November 29, 1864, 700 cavalrymen, many drunk, attacked the Cheyenne village. With most of the men absent hunting, the slaughter included 105 Cheyenne women and children and 28 men. American soldiers scalped and mutilated their victims, carrying women's body parts on their saddles or hats back to Denver. The Sand Creek Massacre, and the retaliation against white ranches and stagecoaches by Indians in 1865, would live in western historical memory forever.

### War Against Indians in the Far West

In New Mexico and Arizona Territories, an authoritarian and brutal commander, General James Carleton, waged war on the Apaches and the Navajos. Both tribes had engaged for generations in raiding the Pueblo and Hispanic peoples of the region to maintain their security and economy. During the Civil War years, Anglo-American farms also became Indian targets. In 1863 the New Mexico Volunteers, commanded in the field by former mountain man Kit Carson, defeated the Mescalero Apaches and forced them onto a reservation at Bosque Redondo in the Pecos River valley.

But the Navajos, who lived in a vast region of canyons and high deserts, resisted. In a "scorched earth" campaign,

Carson destroyed the Navajos' livestock, orchards, and crops. On the run, starving and demoralized, the Navajos began to surrender for food in January 1864. Three-quarters of the 12,000 Navajos were rounded up and forced to march 400 miles (the "Long Walk") to the Bosque Redondo Reservation, suffering malnutrition and death along the way. When General William T. Sherman visited the reservation in 1868, he found the Navajos "sunk into a condition of absolute poverty and despair." Permitted to return to a fraction of their homelands later that year, the Navajos carried with them searing memories of the federal government's ruthless policies of both removal and eradication of Indian peoples.

Back east, war-weariness reached a peak in the summer of 1864, when the Democratic Party nominated the popular general George B. McClellan

**Election of 1864**

for president and inserted a peace plank into its platform. The plank, written by Vallandigham, called for an armistice and spoke vaguely about preserving the Union. The Democrats made racist appeals to white insecurity, calling Lincoln "Abe the nigger-lover" and "Abe the widow-maker." Lincoln concluded that it was "exceedingly probable that this Administration will not be reelected." No incumbent president had been reelected since 1832, and no nation had ever held a general election in the midst of all-out civil war. Some Republicans worked to dump Lincoln from their ticket in favor of either Salmon P. Chase or John C. Frémont, although little came of either effort. Even a relatively unified Republican Party, declaring itself for "unconditional surrender" of the Confederacy and a constitutional amendment abolishing slavery, had to contend with the horrible casualty lists and the battlefield stalemate of the summer of 1864.

The fortunes of war soon changed the electoral situation. With the fall of Atlanta and Union victories in the Shenandoah Valley by early September, Lincoln's prospects rose. Decisive in the election was that eighteen states allowed troops to vote at the front; Lincoln won an extraordinary 78 percent of the soldier vote. In taking 55 percent of the total popular vote, Lincoln's reelection—a referendum on the war and emancipation—had a devastating impact on southern morale. Without such a political outcome in 1864, a Union military victory and a redefined nation might never have been possible.

## 1864–1865: THE FINAL TEST OF WILLS

During the final year of the war, the Confederates could still have won their version of victory if military stalemate and northern antiwar sentiment had forced a negotiated settlement. But events and northern determination prevailed, as Americans endured the bloodiest nightmare in their history.

The North's long-term diplomatic strategy succeeded in 1864. From the outset, the North had pursued one

**Northern Diplomatic Strategy**

paramount goal: to prevent recognition of the Confederacy by European nations. Foreign recognition would belie Lincoln's claim that the United States was fighting an illegal rebellion and would open the way to the financial and military aid that could ensure Confederate independence. Both England and France stood to benefit from a divided and weakened America. Thus, to achieve their goal, Lincoln and Secretary of State Seward needed to avoid both serious military defeats and controversies with the European powers.

Aware that the textile industry employed one-fifth of the British population directly or indirectly, southerners banked on British recognition of the Confederacy. But at the beginning of the war, British mills had a 50 percent surplus of cotton on hand, and they later found new sources of supply in India, Egypt, and Brazil. And throughout the war, some southern cotton continued to reach Europe, despite the Confederacy's embargo on cotton production, an ill-fated policy aimed at securing British support. The British government flirted with recognition of the Confederacy but awaited battlefield demonstrations of southern success. France, though sympathetic to the South, was unwilling to act independently of Britain. Confederate agents managed to purchase valuable arms and supplies in Europe and obtained loans from European financiers, but they never achieved a diplomatic breakthrough.

More than once the Union strategy nearly broke down. An acute crisis occurred in 1861 when the overzealous commander of an American frigate stopped the British steamer *Trent* and removed two Confederate ambassadors, James Mason and John Slidell, sailing to Britain. When they were imprisoned in Boston, northerners cheered, but the British interpreted the capture as a violation of freedom of the seas and demanded the prisoners' release. Lincoln and Seward waited until northern public opinion cooled and then released the two southerners. The incident strained U.S.-British relations.

Then the sale to the Confederacy of warships constructed in England sparked vigorous protest from U.S. ambassador Charles Francis Adams. A few English-built ships, notably the *Alabama,* reached open water to serve the South. Over a period of twenty-two months, without entering a southern port (because of the Union blockade),

▲ Both General Grant *(left)* and General Lee *(right)* were West Point graduates and had served in the U.S. Army during the War with Mexico. Their bloody battles against each other in 1864 stirred northern revulsion to the war even as they brought its end in sight. *(National Archives)*

the *Alabama* destroyed or captured more than sixty U.S. ships, leaving a bitter legal legacy to be settled in the postwar period.

On the battlefield, northern victory was far from won in 1864. General Nathaniel Banks's Red River campaign, designed to capture more of Louisiana and Texas, fell apart, and the capture of Mobile Bay in August did not cause the fall of Mobile. Union general William Tecumseh Sherman commented that the North had to "keep the war South until they are not only ruined, exhausted, but humbled in pride and spirit." Sherman soon brought total war to the southern heartland. On the eastern front during the winter of 1863–1864, the two armies in Virginia settled into a stalemate awaiting yet another spring offensive by the North.

## Battlefield Stalemate and a Union Strategy for Victory

Military authorities throughout history have agreed that deep invasion is very risky: the farther an army penetrates enemy territory, the more vulnerable are its own communications and supply lines. Moreover, observed the Prussian expert Karl von Clausewitz, if the invader encounters a "truly national" resistance, his troops will be "everywhere exposed to attacks by an insurgent population." The South's vast size and a determined resistance could yet make a northern victory elusive.

General Grant, by now in command of all the federal armies, decided to test southern will with a strategic innovation of his own: raids on a massive scale. Less tied to tradition and textbook maneuver than most other Union commanders, Grant proposed to use armies to destroy Confederate railroads, thus ruining the enemy's transportation and economy. Abandoning their lines of support, Union troops would live off the land while laying waste all resources useful to the military and to the civilian population of the Confederacy. After General George H. Thomas's troops won the Battle of Chattanooga in November 1863, the heartland of Georgia lay open. Grant entrusted General Sherman with 100,000 men for an invasion deep into the South, toward the rail center of Atlanta.

Jefferson Davis countered by positioning the army of General Joseph E. Johnston in Sherman's path. Davis's

# The Civil War in Britain

So engaged was the British public with America's disunion and war that an unemployed weaver, John Ward, frequently trekked many miles from Britain's Low Moor to Clitheroe just to read newspaper accounts of the strife.

Because of the direct reliance of the British textile industry on southern cotton (cut off by the war), as well as the many ideological and familial ties between the two nations, the American war was significant in Britain's economy and domestic politics. The British aristocracy and most cotton mill owners were solidly pro-Confederate and proslavery, whereas a combination of clergymen, shopkeepers, artisans, and radical politicians worked for the causes of Union and emancipation. Most British workers saw their future at stake in a war for slave emancipation. "Freedom" to the huge British working class (who could not vote) meant basic political and civil rights, as well as the bread and butter of secure jobs in an industrializing economy, now damaged by a "cotton famine" that threw millhands out of work.

English aristocrats saw Americans as untutored, wayward cousins and took satisfaction in America's troubles. Conservatives believed in the superiority of the British system of government and looked askance at America's leveling tendencies. And some aristocratic British Liberals also saw Americans through their class bias and sympathized with the Confederacy's demand for "order" and independence. English racism also intensified in these years, exemplified by the popularity of minstrelsy and the employment of science in the service of racial theory.

The intensity of the British propaganda war over the American conflict is evident in the methods of their debate: public meetings organized by both sides were huge affairs, with cheering and jeering, competing banners, carts and floats, orators and resolutions. In a press war the British argued over when rebellion is justified, whether secession was right or legal, whether slavery was at the heart of the conflict, and especially over the democratic image of America itself. This bitter debate about America's trial became a test of reform in Britain: those eager for a broadened franchise and increased democracy were pro-Union, and those who preferred to preserve Britain's class-ridden political system favored the Confederacy.

The nature of the internal British debate was no better symbolized than by the dozens of African Americans who served as pro-Union agents in England. The most popular was William Andrew Jackson, Confederate president Jefferson Davis's former coachman, who had escaped from Richmond in September 1862. Jackson's articulate presence at British public meetings countered pro-Confederate arguments that the war was not about slavery.

In the end, the British government did not recognize the Confederacy, and by 1864 English cotton lords had found new sources of the crop in Egypt and India. But in this link between America and its English roots at its time of greatest travail, we can see that the Civil War was a transformation of international significance.

▲ Some southern leaders pronounced that cotton was king and would bring Britain to their cause. This British cartoon shows King Cotton brought down in chains by the American eagle, anticipating the cotton famine to follow and the intense debate in Great Britain over the nature and meaning of the American Civil War. *(Granger Collection)*

## Fall of Atlanta

entire political strategy for 1864 was based on demonstrating Confederate military strength and successfully defending Atlanta. Davis hoped that southern resolve would lead to the political defeat of Lincoln and the election of a president who would sue for peace. When General Johnston slowly but steadily fell back toward Atlanta, Davis grew anxious and sought assurances that Atlanta would be held. From a purely military point of view, Johnston maneuvered skillfully. But when Johnston fell silent and continued to retreat, Davis replaced him with the one-legged General John Hood, who knew his job was to fight. "Our all depends on that army at Atlanta," wrote Mary Chesnut. "If that fails us, the game is up."

For southern morale, the game *was* up. Hood attacked but was beaten, and Sherman's army occupied Atlanta on September 2, 1864. The victory buoyed northern spirits and ensured Lincoln's reelection. A government clerk in Richmond wrote, "Our fondly-cherished visions of peace have vanished like a mirage of the desert." Davis exhorted

southerners to fight on and win new victories before the federal elections, but he had to admit that "two-thirds of our men are absent...most of them absent without leave." In a desperate diversion, Hood's army marched north to cut Sherman's supply lines and force him to withdraw, but Sherman began to march sixty thousand of his men straight to the sea, planning to live off the land and destroying Confederate resources as he went (see Map 15.4).

Sherman's army was an unusually formidable force, composed almost entirely of battle-tested veterans and officers who had risen through the ranks from the midwestern states.

## Sherman's March to the Sea

Before the march began, army doctors weeded out any men who were weak or sick. Weathered, bearded, and tough, the remaining veterans were determined, as one put it, "to Conquer this Rebelien or Die." They believed "the South are to blame for this war" and were ready to make the South pay. Although many harbored racist attitudes, most had come to support emancipation because, as one said, "Slavery stands in the way of putting down

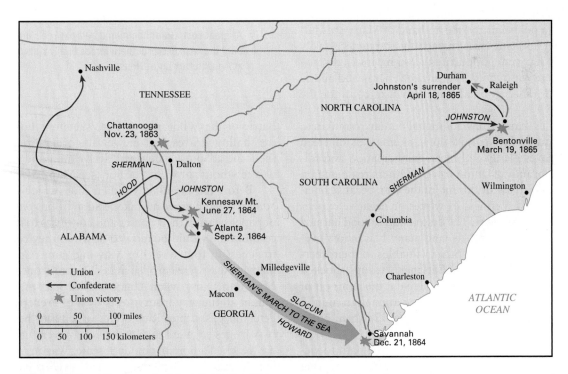

## Map 15.4   Sherman's March to the Sea

The Deep South proved a decisive theater at the end of the war. From Chattanooga, Union forces drove into Georgia, capturing Atlanta. Following the fall of Atlanta, General Sherman embarked on his march of destruction through Georgia to the coast and then northward through the Carolinas.

the rebellion." Confederate General Johnston later commented, "There has been no such army since the days of Julius Caesar."

As Sherman's men moved across Georgia, they cut a path 50 to 60 miles wide and more than 200 miles long. The totality of the destruction they caused was awesome; indeed, it was Sherman's campaign that later prompted many historians to deem this the first modern "total war." A Georgia woman described the "Burnt Country" this way: "The fields were trampled down and the road was lined with carcasses of horses, hogs, and cattle that the invaders, unable either to consume or to carry with them, had wantonly shot down to starve our people. . . . The stench in some places was unbearable." Such devastation diminished the South's material resources and sapped its will to resist.

After reaching Savannah in December, Sherman marched his armies north into the Carolinas. To his soldiers, South Carolina was "the root of secession." They burned and destroyed as they marched, encountering little resistance. The opposing army of General Johnston was small, but Sherman's men should have been prime targets for guerrilla raids and harassing attacks by local defense units. The absence of both led South Carolina's James Chesnut Jr. (a politician and the husband of Mary Chesnut) to write that his state "was shamefully and unnecessarily lost. . . . We had time, opportunity and means to destroy him. But there was wholly wanting the energy and ability required." Southerners had lost the will to continue the struggle.

Sherman's march drew additional human resources to the Union cause. In Georgia alone, as many as nineteen thousand slaves gladly embraced emancipation and followed the marauding Union troops. Others remained on the plantations to await the end of the war, because of either an ingrained wariness of whites or negative experiences with federal soldiers. The destruction of food harmed slaves as well as white rebels, and many blacks lost livestock, clothing, crops, and other valuables to their liberators. In fact, the brutality of Sherman's troops shocked some liberated slaves. "I've seen them cut the hams off of a live pig or ox and go off leavin' the animal groanin'," recalled one man. "The master had 'em kilt then, but it was awful."

It was awful, too, in Virginia, where the path to victory proved protracted and ghastly. Throughout the spring and summer of 1864, intent on capturing Richmond, Grant hurled his troops at Lee's army and suffered appalling losses: almost eighteen thousand casualties in the

||||||||||||||||||||||||||||||||||

## Virginia's Bloody Soil

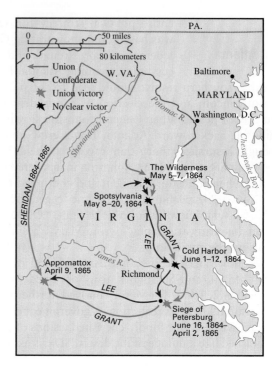

**Map 15.5   The War in Virginia, 1864–1865**

At great cost, Grant hammered away at Lee's army until the weakened southern forces finally surrendered at Appomattox Court House.

Battle of the Wilderness, where skeletons poked out of the shallow graves dug one year before; more than eight thousand at Spotsylvania; and twelve thousand in the space of a few hours at Cold Harbor (see Map 15.5).

Before the assault at Cold Harbor (which Grant later admitted was a grave mistake), Union troops pinned scraps of paper bearing their names and addresses to their backs, certain they would be mowed down as they rushed Lee's trenches. In four weeks in May and June, Grant lost as many men as were enrolled in Lee's entire army. From early May until July, when Union forces had marched and fought all the way from forests west of Fredericksburg to Petersburg, south of Richmond, which they besieged, the two armies engaged each other nearly every day. The war had reached a horribly modern scale. Wagon trains carrying thousands of Union wounded crawled back toward Washington. "It was as if war," wrote historian Bruce Catton, "the great clumsy machine for maiming people, had at last been perfected. Instead of turning out its grist spasmodically, with long waits between each delivery, it was at last able to produce every day, without any gaps at all."

▲ At the war's end, the U.S. flag flew over the state capitol in Richmond, Virginia, which bore many marks of destruction. *(National Archives)*

Undaunted, Grant kept up the pressure, saying, "I propose to fight it out along this line if it takes all summer." Although costly, and testing northern morale to its limits, these battles prepared the way for eventual victory: Lee's army shrank until offensive action was no longer possible, while Grant's army kept replenishing its forces with new recruits. The siege of Petersburg, with the armies facing each other in miles of trenches, lasted throughout the winter of 1864–1865.

The end finally came in the spring of 1865. Grant kept battering Lee, who tried but failed to break through the Union line. With the numerical superiority of Grant's army now greater than two to one, Confederate defeat was inevitable. On April 2, Lee abandoned Richmond and Petersburg. On April 9, hemmed in by Union troops, short of rations, and with fewer than thirty thousand men left, he surrendered at Appomattox Court House. Grant treated his rival with respect and paroled the defeated troops, allowing cavalrymen to keep their horses and take them home. The war was over at last. Within weeks, Confederate forces under Johnston surrendered to Sherman in North Carolina, and Davis, who had fled Richmond but wanted the war to continue, was captured in Georgia. The North rejoiced, and most southerners fell into despair, expecting waves of punishment.

### Surrender at Appomattox

In the profound relief and stillness of the surrender field at Appomattox, no one could know the harrowing tasks of healing and justice that lay ahead.

With Lee's surrender, Lincoln knew that the Union had been preserved, yet he lived to see but a few days of war's aftermath. On the evening of Good Friday, April 14, he accompanied his wife to Ford's Theatre in Washington to enjoy a popular comedy. There John Wilkes Booth, an embittered southern sympathizer, shot the president in the head at point-blank range. Lincoln died the next day. Twelve days later, troops tracked down and killed Booth. The Union had lost its wartime leader, and millions publicly mourned the martyred chief executive along the route of the funeral train that took his body home to Illinois. Relief at the war's end mingled hauntingly with a renewed sense of loss and anxiety about the future. Millions never forgot where they were and how they felt at the news of Lincoln's assassination.

Property damage and financial costs were enormous, though difficult to tally. U.S. loans and taxes during the conflict totaled almost $3 billion, and interest on the war debt was $2.8 billion. The Confederacy borrowed over $2 billion but lost far more in the destruction of homes, crops, livestock, and other property. In southern war zones the landscape was desolated. Over wide regions fences and crops were

### Financial Tally

The death of President Lincoln ▶ caused a vast outpouring of grief in the North. As this Currier & Ives print shows, his funeral train stopped at several cities on its way to Illinois, to allow local services to be held.

*(Anne S. K. Brown Military Collection, John Hay Library, Brown University)*

destroyed; houses, barns, and bridges burned; and fields abandoned and left to erode. Union troops had looted factories and put two-thirds of the South's railroad system out of service.

Estimates of the total cost of the war exceed $20 billion—five times the total expenditures of the federal government from its creation until 1861. By 1865 the federal government's spending had soared to twenty times the prewar level and accounted for over 26 percent of the gross national product. Many of these changes were more or less permanent, as wartime measures left the government more deeply involved in manufacturing, banking, and transportation. If southerners had hoped to remove government from the economy, the war had now irrevocably bound them together.

The human costs of the Civil War were especially staggering. The total number of military casualties on both sides exceeded 1 million—a frightful toll for a nation of 31 million people.

**Death Toll**

Approximately 360,000 Union soldiers died, 110,000 of them from wounds suffered in battle. Another 275,175 Union soldiers were wounded but survived. On the Confederate side, an estimated 260,000 lost their lives, and almost as many suffered wounds. More men died in the Civil War than in all other American wars combined until Vietnam. Of an estimated 194,743 northerners in southern prisons, 30,218 died; of 214,865 southerners in northern prisons, 25,976 died. The prison story from the war was one in which neither side could claim pride, and it caused embittered debate for decades over mutual accusations of willful starvation and brutal treatment.

These unprecedented losses (approximately 620,000 total dead) flowed from fundamental strife over the nature of the Union and the liberty of black people. Both sides saw vital interests in the struggle. As Julia Ward Howe wrote in her famous "Battle Hymn," they had heard "the trumpet that shall never call retreat." And so the war took its horrifying course.

## *Legacy* FOR A PEOPLE AND A NATION

### "Big Government"

n 1995 President Bill Clinton declared that "the era of big government is over." Before him, President Ronald Reagan had achieved considerable political success denouncing "big government" programs. Whether the federal government ought to be the agent of social change, citizen welfare, and legal protection has been one of the most polarizing questions in American political culture since at least the New Deal of the 1930s. But when did "big government" really begin?

One good answer is in the Lincoln administration and Republican policies during the Civil War. In response to the demands of war, the Republicans created an activist federal government, rooted in a theory they called the "harmony of interests" among capitalism, free labor, and government power. They converted the sale of war bonds into a crusade, believing that the country could absorb any level of debt or expense for the cause of Union. Indeed, with agricultural legislation, an income tax, land grant colleges, higher tariffs, the Homestead Act, and railroad subsidies, the federal government entered the nation's economy forever.

The powers of the federal government and the president grew steadily during the crisis. In one striking exercise of executive power, Lincoln suspended the writ of habeas corpus for everyone living between Washington, D.C., and Philadelphia. He had scant legal justification, but the president's motive was practical: to ensure the loyalty of Maryland, which surrounded the capital on three sides. Later in the war, with congressional approval, Lincoln repeatedly suspended habeas corpus and invoked martial law. Between fifteen and twenty thousand U.S. citizens were arrested on suspicion of disloyal acts and speech. Through such measures Lincoln expanded the powers of wartime presidents.

Above all, the Emancipation Proclamation and the Union military's prosecution of a war to destroy slavery was the most aggressive use of federal power yet. It caused the largest government confiscation of property in American history. The active way in which Lincoln and the Republicans pushed for the Thirteenth Amendment to abolish slavery also stood as stark evidence of the advance of federal over state authority.

Today, Lincoln's legacy is richly controversial because of his exercise of such power in the Civil War. His many admirers have long honored him for his vision in taking the nation to a "new birth" of freedom in the crucible of total war. But his critics have attacked him, some viciously, as the "great centralizer," the father of the leviathan, "big government." One modern Lincoln hater has accused the Civil War president of inventing the current "welfare-warfare state." And ironically, twenty-first-century conservative Republicans crave the mantle of "the party of Lincoln" while denouncing the idea of activist, regulatory government that Lincoln championed. As long as Americans debate the meaning of the size and function of their federal government, they are playing out a chief legacy of the Civil War.

## SUMMARY

The Civil War altered American society forever. The first great legacy of the war in the lives of its survivors was, therefore, death itself. Although precise figures on enlistments are unavailable, it appears that 700,000 to 800,000 men served in the Confederate armies. Far more, possibly 2.3 million, served in the Union armies. All of these men were taken from home, family, and personal goals; their lives, if they survived, were disrupted in ways that were never repaired. During the war, in both North and South, women, too, took on new roles as they struggled to manage the hardships of the home front, to grieve, and to support the war effort.

Industrialization and economic enterprises grew exponentially in tandem with the war. Ordinary citizens found that their futures were increasingly tied to huge organizations. The character and extent of government power, too, changed markedly. Under Republican leadership, the federal government expanded its power not only to preserve the Union but also to extend freedom. A social revolution and government authority emancipated the slaves, and Lincoln called for "a new birth of freedom" in

America. A republic desperately divided against itself had survived, but in new constitutional forms yet to take shape during Reconstruction.

It was unclear at the end of the war how or whether the nation would use its power to protect the rights of the former slaves. Secession was dead, but whether Americans would continue to embrace a centralized nationalism remained to be seen. The war ended decisively after tremendous sacrifice, but it left many unanswered questions: How would white southerners, embittered and impoverished, respond to efforts to reconstruct the nation? How would the country care for the maimed, the orphans, the farming women without men to work their land, and all the dead who had to be found and properly buried? What would be the place of black men and women in American life?

In the West, two civil wars had raged: one between Union and Confederate forces, and the other resulting in a conquest of southwestern Indians by U.S. troops and land-hungry settlers. On the diplomatic front, the Union government had delicately managed to keep Great Britain and other foreign powers out of the war. Dissent flourished in both North and South, playing a crucial role in the ultimate collapse of the Confederacy, and the Union cause was only marginally affected by sabotage and draft riots.

In the Civil War Americans had undergone an epic of destruction and survival—a transformation like nothing else in their history. White southerners had experienced defeat that few other Americans had ever faced. Blacks were moving proudly but anxiously from slavery to freedom. White northerners were, by and large, self-conscious victors in a massive war for the nation's existence and for new definitions of freedom. The war, with all of its drama, sacrifice, and social and political change, would leave a compelling memory in American hearts and minds for generations.

## SUGGESTIONS FOR FURTHER READING

Stephen V. Ash, *When the Yankees Came: Conflict and Chaos in the Occupied South* (1995)

Edward L. Ayers, *In the Presence of Mine Enemies: War in the Heart of America, 1859–1863* (2002)

Ira Berlin et al., eds., *Freedom: A Documentary History of Emancipation, 1861–1867*, 3 vols. (1979–1982)

David W. Blight, *Frederick Douglass' Civil War: Keeping Faith in Jubilee* (1989)

Alice Fahs, *The Imagined Civil War: Popular Literature of the North and South* (2001)

Drew G. Faust, *Mothers of Invention: Women of the Slave-holding South in the Civil War* (1996)

William W. Freehling, *The South vs. the South* (2001)

Gary W. Gallagher, *The Confederate War* (1997)

Bruce Levine, *Confederate Emancipation: Southern Plans to Free and Arm Slaves During the Civil War* (2006)

James M. McPherson, *Battle Cry of Freedom: The Civil War Era* (1987)

Philip S. Paludan, *"A People's Contest": The Union and the Civil War* (1989)

Heather Cox Richardson, *The Greatest Nation on Earth: Republican Economic Policies During the Civil War* (1997)

*For a more extensive list for further reading, go to* college.hmco.com/pic/norton8e.

# Reconstruction: An Unfinished Revolution
## *1865-1877*

The lower half of the city of Charleston, South Carolina, the seedbed of secession, lay in ruin when most of the white population evacuated on February 18, 1865. A prolonged bombardment by Union batteries and gunboats around Charleston harbor had already destroyed many of the lovely town homes of the low-country planters. Then, as the city was abandoned, fires broke out everywhere, ignited in bales of cotton left in huge stockpiles in public squares. To many observers the flames were the funeral pyres of a dying civilization.

Among the first Union troops to enter Charleston was the Twenty-first U.S. Colored Regiment, which received the surrender of the city from its mayor. For black Charlestonians, most of whom were former slaves, this was a time of celebration. In symbolic ceremonies they proclaimed their freedom and announced their rebirth. Whatever the postwar order would bring, the freedpeople of Charleston converted Confederate ruin into a vision of Reconstruction based on Union victory and black liberation.

Still, in Charleston as elsewhere, death demanded attention. During the final year of the war, the Confederates had converted the planters' Race Course, a horseracing track, and its famed Jockey Club, into a prison. Union soldiers were kept in terrible conditions in the interior of the track, without shelter. The 257 who died there of exposure and disease were buried in a mass grave behind the judges' stand. After the fall of the city, Charleston's blacks organized to create a proper burial ground for the Union dead. During April, more than twenty black workmen reinterred the dead in marked graves and built a high fence around the cemetery. On the archway over the cemetery's entrance they painted the inscription "Martyrs of the Race Course."

◀ "Entrance of the 55th Massachusetts (Colored) Regiment into Charleston, S. C., February 21, 1865." Thomas Nast, pencil, oil, and wash on board, 1865. Black troops celebrated as they marched into the Confederate stronghold, hoisting their caps on their bayonets, and singing "John Brown's Body" as they marched up Meeting Street, Charleston's main thoroughfare. *(Museum of Fine Arts, Boston)*

## CHRONOLOGY

**1865** ■ Johnson begins rapid and lenient Reconstruction
- ■ White southern governments pass restrictive black codes
- ■ Congress refuses to seat southern representatives
- ■ Thirteenth Amendment ratified, abolishing slavery

**1866** ■ Congress passes Civil Rights Act and renewal of Freedmen's Bureau over Johnson's veto
- ■ Congress approves Fourteenth Amendment
- ■ In *Ex parte Milligan* the Supreme Court reasserts its influence

**1867** ■ Congress passes First Reconstruction Act and Tenure of Office Act
- ■ Constitutional conventions called in southern states

**1868** ■ House impeaches and Senate acquits Johnson
- ■ Most southern states readmitted to Union under Radical plan
- ■ Fourteenth Amendment ratified
- ■ Grant elected president

**1869** ■ Congress approves Fifteenth Amendment (ratified in 1870)

**1871** ■ Congress passes second Enforcement Act and Ku Klux Klan Act
- ■ Treaty with England settles *Alabama* claims

**1872** ■ Amnesty Act frees almost all remaining Confederates from restrictions on holding office
- ■ Grant reelected

**1873** ■ *Slaughter-House* cases limit power of Fourteenth Amendment
- ■ Panic of 1873 leads to widespread unemployment and labor strife

**1874** ■ Democrats win majority in House of Representatives

**1875** ■ Several Grant appointees indicted for corruption
- ■ Congress passes weak Civil Rights Act
- ■ Democratic Party increases control of southern states with white supremacy campaigns

**1876** ■ *U.S. v. Cruikshank* further weakens Fourteenth Amendment
- ■ Presidential election disputed

**1877** ■ Congress elects Hayes president

And then they planned an extraordinary ceremony. On the morning of May 1, 1865, a procession of ten thousand people marched around the planters' Race Course, led by three thousand children carrying armloads of roses and singing "John Brown's Body." The children were followed by black women with baskets of flowers and wreaths, and then by black men. The parade concluded with members of black and white Union regiments, along with white missionaries and teachers led by James Redpath, the supervisor of freedmen's schools in the region. All who could fit assembled at the gravesite; five black ministers read from Scripture, and a black children's choir sang "America," "We'll Rally 'Round the Flag," "The Star-Spangled Banner," and Negro spirituals. When the ceremony ended, the huge crowd retired to the Race Course for speeches, picnics, and military festivities.

The war was over in Charleston, and "Decoration Day"—now Memorial Day, the day to remember the war dead and decorate their graves with flowers—had been founded by African Americans. Black people—by their labor, their words, their songs, and their marching feet on the old planters' Race Course—had created an American tradition. In their vision, they were creating the Independence Day of a Second American Revolution.

Reconstruction would bring revolutionary circumstances, but revolutions can also go backward. The Civil War and its aftermath wrought unprecedented changes in American society, law, and politics, but the underlying realities of economic power, racism, and judicial conservatism limited Reconstruction's revolutionary potential. As never before, the nation had to determine the nature of federal-state relations, whether confiscated land could be redistributed, and how to bring justice to both freedpeople and aggrieved white southerners whose property and lives had been devastated. Americans faced the harrowing challenge of psychological healing from a bloody and fratricidal war. How they would negotiate the tangled relationship between healing and justice would determine the extent of change during Reconstruction.

Nowhere was the turmoil of Reconstruction more evident than in national politics. Lincoln's successor, Andrew Johnson, fought bitterly with Congress over the shaping of Reconstruction policies. Although a southerner,

Johnson had always been a foe of the South's wealthy planters, and his first acts as president suggested that he would be tough on "traitors." Before the end of 1865, however, Johnson's policies changed direction, and he became the protector of southern interests. Jefferson Davis stayed in prison for two years, but Johnson quickly pardoned other rebel leaders and allowed them to occupy high offices. He also ordered the return of plantations to their original owners, including abandoned coastal lands of Georgia and South Carolina on which forty thousand freed men and women had settled early in 1865, by order of General William Tecumseh Sherman.

Johnson imagined a lenient and rapid "restoration" of the South to the Union rather than the fundamental "reconstruction" that Republican congressmen favored. Between 1866 and 1868, the president and the Republican leadership in Congress engaged in a bitter power struggle over how to put the United States back together again. Before the struggle ceased, Congress had impeached the president, enfranchised freedmen, and given them a role in reconstructing the South. The nation also adopted the Fourteenth and Fifteenth Amendments, ushering equal protection of the law, a definition of citizenship, and universal manhood suffrage into the Constitution. But little was done to open the doors of economic opportunity to black southerners, and the cause of equal rights for African Americans fell almost as fast as it had risen.

By 1869 the Ku Klux Klan employed extensive violence and terror to thwart Reconstruction and undermine black freedom. As white Democrats in the South took control of state governments, they encountered little opposition from the North. Moreover, the wartime industrial boom had created new opportunities and priorities. The West, with its seemingly limitless potential and its wars against Indians, drew American resources and consciousness like never before. Political corruption became a nationwide scandal, and bribery a way of doing business.

Thus Reconstruction became a revolution eclipsed. The white South's desire to reclaim control of its states and of race relations overwhelmed the national interest in stopping it. But Reconstruction left enduring legacies with which the nation has struggled ever since.

- Should the Reconstruction era be considered the Second American Revolution? By what criteria should we make such a judgment?

- What were the origins and meanings of the Fourteenth Amendment in the 1860s? What is its significance today?

- Reconstruction is judged to have "ended" in 1877. Over the course of the 1870s, what caused its end?

## WARTIME RECONSTRUCTION

Civil wars leave immense challenges of healing, justice, and physical rebuilding. Anticipating that process, reconstruction of the Union was an issue as early as 1863, well before the war ended. Many key questions loomed on the horizon when and if the North succeeded on the battlefield: How would the nation be restored? How would southern states and leaders be treated—as errant brothers or as traitors? What was the constitutional basis for readmission of states to the Union, and where, if anywhere, could American statesmen look for precedence or guidance? More specifically, four vexing problems compelled early thinking and would haunt the Reconstruction era throughout. One, who would rule in the South once it was defeated? Two, who would rule in the federal government—Congress or the president? Three, what were the dimensions of black freedom, and what rights under law would the freedmen enjoy? And four, would Reconstruction be a preservation of the old republic or a second Revolution, a reinvention of a new republic?

Abraham Lincoln had never been anti-southern, though he had become the leader of an antislavery war.

**Lincoln's 10 Percent Plan**

He lost three brothers-in-law, killed in the war on the Confederate side. His worst fear was that the war would collapse at the end into guerrilla warfare across the South, with surviving bands of Confederates carrying on resistance. Lincoln insisted that his generals give lenient terms to southern soldiers once they surrendered. In his Second Inaugural Address, delivered only a month before his assassination, Lincoln promised "malice toward none; with charity for all," as Americans strove to "bind up the nation's wounds."

Lincoln planned early for a swift and moderate Reconstruction process. In his "Proclamation of Amnesty and Reconstruction," issued in December 1863, he proposed to replace majority rule with "loyal rule" as a means of reconstructing southern state governments. He proposed pardons to all ex-Confederates except the highest-ranking military and civilian officers. Then, as soon as 10 percent of the voting population in the 1860 general election in a given state had taken an oath to the United States and established a government, the new state would be recognized. Lincoln did not consult Congress in these plans, and "loyal" assemblies (known as "Lincoln governments") were created in Louisiana, Tennessee, and Arkansas in 1864, states largely occupied by Union troops. These governments were weak and dependent on northern armies for survival.

Congress responded with great hostility to Lincoln's moves to readmit southern states in what seemed such a premature manner. Many Radical Republicans, strong proponents of emancipation and of aggressive prosecution of the war against the South, considered the 10 percent plan a "mere mockery" of democracy. Led by Thaddeus Stevens of Pennsylvania in the House and Charles Sumner of Massachusetts in the Senate, congressional Republicans locked horns with Lincoln and proposed a longer and harsher approach to Reconstruction. Stevens advocated a "conquered provinces" theory, arguing that southerners had organized as a foreign nation to make war on the United States and, by secession, had destroyed their status as states. They therefore must be treated as "conquered foreign lands" and returned to the status of "unorganized territories" before any process of readmission could be entertained by Congress.

**Congress and the Wade-Davis Bill**

In July 1864, the Wade-Davis bill, named for its sponsors, Senator Benjamin Wade of Ohio and Congressman Henry W. Davis of Maryland, emerged from Congress with three specific conditions for southern readmission.

1. It demanded a "majority" of white male citizens participating in the creation of a new government.

2. To vote or be a delegate to constitutional conventions, men had to take an "iron-clad" oath (declaring that they had never aided the Confederate war effort).

3. All officers above the rank of lieutenant, and all civil officials in the Confederacy, would be disfranchised and deemed "not a citizen of the United States."

The Confederate states were to be defined as "conquered enemies," said Davis, and the process of readmission was to be harsh and slow. Lincoln, ever the adroit politician, pocket-vetoed the bill and issued a conciliatory proclamation of his own, announcing that he would not be inflexibly committed to any "one plan" of Reconstruction.

This exchange came during Grant's bloody campaign against Lee in Virginia, when the outcome of the war and Lincoln's reelection were still in doubt. On August 5, Radical Republicans issued the "Wade-Davis Manifesto" to newspapers. An unprecedented attack on a sitting president by members of his own party, it accused Lincoln of usurpation of presidential powers and disgraceful leniency toward an eventually conquered South. What emerged in 1864–1865 was a clear debate and a potential constitutional crisis. Lincoln saw Reconstruction as a means of weakening the Confederacy and winning the war; the Radicals saw it as a longer-term transformation of the political and racial order of the country.

In early 1865, Congress and Lincoln joined in two important measures that recognized slavery's centrality to the war. On January 31, with strong administration backing, Congress passed the Thirteenth Amendment, which had two provisions: first, it abolished involuntary servitude everywhere in the United States; second, it declared that Congress shall have the power to enforce this outcome by "appropriate legislation." When the measure passed by 119 to 56, a mere 2 votes more than the necessary two-thirds, rejoicing broke out in Congress. A Republican recorded in his diary, "Members joined in the shouting and kept it up for some minutes. Some embraced one another, others wept like children. I have felt ever since the vote, as if I were in a new country."

**Thirteenth Amendment**

But the Thirteenth Amendment had emerged from a long congressional debate and considerable petitioning and public advocacy. One of the first and most remarkable petitions for a constitutional amendment abolishing slavery was submitted early in 1864 by Elizabeth Cady Stanton, Susan B. Anthony, and the Women's Loyal National League. Women throughout the Union accumulated thousands of signatures, even venturing into staunchly pro-Confederate regions of Kentucky and Missouri to secure supporters. It was a long road from the Emancipation Proclamation to the Thirteenth Amendment—through treacherous constitutional theory about individual "property rights," a bedrock of belief that the sacred document ought never to be altered, and partisan politics. But the logic of winning the war by crushing slavery, and of securing a new beginning under law for the nation that so many had died to save, won the day.

Potentially as significant, on March 3, 1865, Congress created the Bureau of Refugees, Freedmen, and Abandoned Lands—the Freedmen's Bureau, an unprecedented agency of social uplift necessitated by the ravages of the war. Americans had never engaged in federal aid to cit-

**Freedmen's Bureau**

izens on such a scale. With thousands of refugees, white and black, displaced in the South, the government continued what private freedmen's aid societies had started as early as 1862. In the mere four years of its existence, the Freedmen's Bureau supplied food and medical services, built several thousand schools and some colleges, negotiated several hundred thousand employment contracts between freedmen and their former masters, and tried to manage confiscated land.

The Bureau would be a controversial aspect of Reconstruction—within the South, where whites generally hated it, and within the federal government, where politicians divided over its constitutionality. Some Bureau agents were devoted to freedmen's rights, whereas others were opportunists who exploited the chaos of the postwar South. The war had forced into the open an eternal question of republics: what are the social welfare obligations of the state toward its people, and what do people owe their governments in return? Apart from their conquest and displacement of the eastern Indians, Americans were relatively inexperienced at the Freedmen's Bureau's task—social reform through military occupation.

In 1865, due to the devastation of the war, America was now a land with ruins. Like the countries of Europe,

**Ruins and Enmity**

it now seemed an older, more historic landscape. It had torn itself asunder—physically, politically, spiritually. Some of its cities lay in rubble, large stretches of the southern countryside were depopulated and defoliated, and thousands of people, white and black, were refugees. Some of this would in time seem romantic to northern travelers in the postwar South.

Thousands of yeoman farmer-soldiers, some paroled by surrenders and others who had abandoned Confederate ranks earlier, walked home too late in the season to plant a crop in a collapsed economy. Many white refugees faced genuine starvation. Of the approximately 18,300,000 rations distributed across the South in the first three years of the Freedmen's Bureau, 5,230,000 went to whites. In early 1866, in a proud agricultural society, the legislature of South Carolina issued $300,000 in state bonds to purchase corn for the destitute.

In October 1865, just after a five-month imprisonment in Boston, former Confederate Vice President Alexander H. Stephens rode a slow train southward. In Virginia he found "the desolation of the country . . . was horrible to behold." When Stephens reached northern Georgia, his native state, his shock ran over: "War has left a terrible impression. . . . Fences gone, fields all a-waste, houses burnt." A northern journalist visiting Richmond that same fall observed a city "mourning for her sins . . . in dust and ashes." The "burnt district" was a "bed of cinders . . . broken and blackened walls, impassable streets deluged with debris." Above all, every northern traveler encountered a wall of hatred among white southerners for their conquerors. An innkeeper in North Carolina told a journalist that Yankees had killed his sons in the war, burned his house, and stolen his slaves. "They left me one inestimable privilege," he said, "to hate 'em. I git up at half-past four in the morning, and sit up 'til twelve at night, to hate 'em."

## THE MEANINGS OF FREEDOM

Black southerners entered into life after slavery with hope and circumspection. A Texas man recalled his father's telling him, even before the war was over, "Our forever was going to be spent living among the Southerners, after they got licked." Freed men and women tried to gain as much as they could from their new circumstances. Often the changes they valued the most were personal—alterations in location, employer, or living arrangements.

For America's former slaves, Reconstruction had one paramount meaning: a chance to explore freedom. A

**The Feel of Freedom**

southern white woman admitted in her diary that the black people "showed a natural and exultant joy at being free." Former slaves remembered singing far into the night after federal troops, who confirmed rumors of their emancipation, reached their plantations. The slaves on a Texas plantation shouted for joy, their leader proclaiming, "We is free—no more whippings and beatings." A few people gave in to the natural desire to do what had been impossible before. One angry grandmother dropped her hoe and ran to confront her mistress. "I'm free!" she yelled. "Yes, I'm free! Ain't got to work for you no more! You can't put me in your pocket now!" Another man recalled that he and others "started on the move," either to search for family members or just to exercise the human right of mobility.

Many freed men and women reacted more cautiously and shrewdly, taking care to test the boundaries of their new condition. "After the war was over," explained one man, "we was afraid to move. Just like terrapins or turtles after emancipation. Just stick our heads out to see how the land lay." As slaves they had learned to expect hostility from white people, and they did not presume it would instantly disappear. Life in freedom might still be a matter of what was possible, not what was right. Many freedpeople evaluated potential employers with shrewd caution.

▲ *The Armed Slave,* William Sprang, oil on canvas, c. 1865. This remarkable painting depicts an African American veteran soldier, musket with fixed bayonet leaning against the wall, cigar in hand indicating a new life of safety and leisure, reading a book to demonstrate his embrace of education and freedom. The man's visage leaves the impression of satisfaction and dignity. *(The Civil War Library and Museum, Philadelphia)*

"Most all the Negroes that had good owners stayed with 'em, but the others left. Some of 'em come back and some didn't," explained one man. After considerable wandering in search of better circumstances, a majority of blacks eventually settled as agricultural workers back on their former farms or plantations. But they relocated their houses and did their utmost to control the conditions of their labor.

Throughout the South, former slaves devoted themselves to reuniting their families, separated during slavery by sale or hardship, and during the war by dislocation and the emancipation process. With only shreds of information to guide them, thousands of freedpeople embarked on odysseys in search of a husband, wife, child, or parent. By relying on the black community for help and information, and by placing ads

### Reunion of African American Families

that continued to appear in black newspapers well into the 1880s, some succeeded in their quest, while others searched in vain.

Husbands and wives who had belonged to different masters established homes together for the first time, and, as they had tried under slavery, parents asserted the right to raise their own children. A mother bristled when her old master claimed a right to whip her children. She informed him that "he warn't goin' to brush none of her chilluns no more." The freed men and women were too much at risk to act recklessly, but, as one man put it, they were tired of punishment and "sure didn't take no more foolishment off of white folks."

Many black people wanted to minimize contact with whites because, as Reverend Garrison Frazier told General Sherman in January 1865, "There is a prejudice against us . . . that will take years to get over." To avoid contact with overbearing whites who were used to supervising them, blacks abandoned the slave quarters and fanned out to distant corners of the land they worked. "After the war my stepfather come," recalled Annie Young, "and got my mother and we moved out in the piney woods." Others described moving "across the creek" or building a "saplin house . . . back in the woods." Some rural dwellers established small, all-black settlements that still exist along the back roads of the South.

### Blacks' Search for Independence

Even once-privileged slaves desired such independence and social separation. One man turned down his master's offer of the overseer's house and moved instead to a shack in "Freetown." He also declined to let the former owner grind his grain for free because it "make him feel like a free man to pay for things just like anyone else."

In addition to a fair employer, what freed men and women most wanted was the ownership of land. Land represented self-sufficiency and a chance to gain compensation for generations of bondage. General Sherman's special Field Order Number 15, issued in February 1865, set aside 400,000 acres of land in the Sea Islands region for the exclusive settlement of freedpeople. Hope swelled among ex-slaves as forty-acre plots, mules, and "possessary titles" were promised to them. But President Johnson ordered them removed in October and the land returned to its original owners under army enforcement. A northern observer noted that slaves freed in the Sea Islands of South Carolina and Georgia made "plain, straight-forward" inquiries as they settled on new land. They wanted to be

### Freedpeople's Desire for Land

sure the land "would be theirs after they had improved it." Everywhere, blacks young and old thirsted for homes of their own.

But most members of both political parties opposed genuine land redistribution to the freedmen. Even northern reformers who had administered the Sea Islands during the war showed little sympathy for black aspirations. The former Sea Island slaves wanted to establish small, self-sufficient farms. Northern soldiers, officials, and missionaries of both races brought education and aid to the freedmen but also insisted that they grow cotton. They emphasized profit, cash crops, and the values of competitive capitalism.

"The Yankees preach nothing but cotton, cotton!" complained one Sea Island black. "We wants land," wrote another, but tax officials "make the lots too big, and cut we out." Indeed, the U.S. government eventually sold thousands of acres in the Sea Islands, 90 percent of which went to wealthy investors from the North. At a protest against evictions from a contraband camp in Virginia in 1866, freedman Bayley Wyatt made black desires and claims clear: "We has a right to the land where we are located. For why? I tell you. Our wives, our children, our husbands, has been sold over and over again to purchase the lands we now locates upon; for that reason we have a divine right to the land."

Ex-slaves everywhere reached out for education. Blacks of all ages hungered for the knowledge in books

### Black Embrace of Education

that had been permitted only to whites. With freedom, they started schools and filled classrooms both day and night. On log seats and dirt floors, freed men and women studied their letters in old almanacs and in discarded dictionaries. Young children brought infants to school with them, and adults attended at night or after "the crops were laid by." Many a teacher had "to make herself heard over three other classes reciting in concert" in a small room. The desire to escape slavery's ignorance was so great that, despite their poverty, many blacks paid tuition, typically $1 or $1.50 a month. These small amounts constituted major portions of a person's agricultural wages and added up to more than $1 million by 1870.

The federal government and northern reformers of both races assisted this pursuit of education. In its brief life the Freedmen's Bureau founded over four thousand schools, and idealistic men and women from the North established others funded by private northern philanthropy. The Yankee schoolmarm—dedicated, selfless, and religious—became an agent of progress in many southern

▲ African Americans of all ages eagerly pursued the opportunity to gain an education in freedom. This young woman in Mt. Meigs, Alabama, is helping her mother learn to read.

*(Smithsonian Institution, photo by Rudolf Eickemeyer)*

communities. Thus did African Americans seek a break from their past through learning. More than 600,000 were enrolled in elementary school by 1877.

Blacks and their white allies also saw the need for colleges and universities to train teachers, ministers, and professionals for leadership. The American Missionary Association founded seven colleges, including Fisk and Atlanta Universities, between 1866 and 1869. The Freedmen's Bureau helped to establish Howard University in Washington, D.C., and northern religious groups, such as the Methodists, Baptists, and Congregationalists, supported dozens of seminaries and teachers' colleges.

During Reconstruction, African American leaders often were highly educated individuals; many were from the prewar elite of free people of color. Francis Cardozo, who held various offices in South Carolina, had attended universities in Scotland and England. P. B. S. Pinchback, who became lieutenant governor of Louisiana, was the son of a planter who had sent him to school in Cincinnati. Both of the two black senators from Mississippi, Blanche K. Bruce and Hiram Revels, possessed privileged educations. Bruce was the son of a planter who had provided tutoring at home; Revels was the son of free North Carolina blacks who had sent him to Knox College in Illinois. These men and many self-educated former slaves brought to political office not only fervor but education.

Freed from the restrictions and regulations of slavery, blacks could build their own institutions as they saw fit. The secret churches of slavery came into the open; in countless communities throughout the South, ex-slaves "started a brush arbor."

### Growth of Black Churches

A brush arbor was merely "a sort of . . . shelter with leaves for a roof," but the freed men and women worshiped in it enthusiastically. "Preachin' and shouting sometimes lasted all day," they recalled, for the opportunity to worship together freely meant "glorious times."

Within a few years, independent branches of the Methodist and Baptist denominations had attracted the great majority of black Christians in the South. By 1877 in South Carolina alone, the African Methodist Episcopal (A.M.E.) Church had 1,000 ministers, 44,000 members, and its own school of theology, while the A.M.E. Zion Church had 45,000 members. In the rapid growth of churches, some of which became the wealthiest and most autonomous institutions in black life, the freedpeople demonstrated their most secure claim on freedom and created enduring communities.

Churches became a center of African American life, both social and political, during and after Reconstruction. Churches large and small, like this one, Faith Memorial Church in Hagley Landing, South Carolina, became the first black-owned institutions for the postfreedom generation. ▶

*(Aunt Phebe, Uncle Tom and Others: Character Studies Among the Old Slaves of the South Fifty Years After by Essie Collins Matthews)*

The desire to gain as much independence as possible also shaped the former slaves' economic arrangements.

### Rise of the Sharecropping System

Since most of them lacked money to buy land, they preferred the next best thing: renting the land they worked. But the South had a cash-poor economy with few sources of credit, and few whites would consider renting land to blacks. Most blacks had no means to get cash before the harvest, so other alternatives had to be tried.

Black farmers and white landowners therefore turned to sharecropping, a system in which farmers kept part of their crop and gave the rest to the landowner while living on his property. The landlord or a merchant "furnished" food and supplies, such as draft animals and seed, needed before the harvest, and he received payment from the crop. Although landowners tried to set the laborers' share at a low level, black farmers had some bargaining power, at least at first. Sharecroppers would hold out, or move and

▲ Sharecropping became an oppressive system in the postwar South. At plantation stores like this one, photographed in Mississippi in 1868, merchants recorded in their ledger books debts that few sharecroppers were able to repay.

*(Amistad Center for Art & Culture, Hartford, Connecticut, Simpson Collection.)*

try to switch employers from one year to another. As the system matured during the 1870s and 1880s, most share-croppers worked "on halves"—half for the owner and half for themselves.

The sharecropping system, which materialized as early as 1868 in parts of the South, originated as a desirable compromise between former slaves and white landown-ers. It eased landowners' problems with cash and credit, and provided them a permanent, dependent labor force; blacks accepted it because it gave them freedom from daily supervision. Instead of working in the hated gangs under a white overseer, as in slavery, they farmed their own plots of land in family groups. But sharecropping later proved to be a disaster. Owners and merchants developed a monopoly of control over the agricultural economy, as sharecroppers found themselves riveted in ever-increasing debt (see page 576).

The fundamental problem, however, was that southern farmers as a whole still concentrated on cotton. In free-dom, black women often chose to stay away from the fields and cotton picking, to concentrate on domestic chores. Given the diminishing incentives of the system, they placed greater value on independent choices about gender roles and family organization than on reaching higher levels of production. By 1878 the South had recovered its prewar share of British cotton purchases. But even as southerners grew more cotton than ever, their reward diminished. Cot-ton prices began a long decline, as world demand fell off.

Thus southern agriculture slipped deeper and deeper into depression. Black sharecroppers struggled under a growing burden of debt which reduced their independence and bound them to landowners and to furnishing mer-chants almost as oppressively as slavery had bound them to their masters. Many white farmers became debtors, too; gradually lost their land; and joined the ranks of share-croppers. By the end of Reconstruction, over one-third of all southern farms were worked by sharecropping ten-ants, white and black. This economic transformation took place as the nation struggled to put its political house back in order.

## JOHNSON'S RECONSTRUCTION PLAN

When Reconstruction began under President Andrew Johnson, many expected his policies to be harsh. Throughout his career in Tennessee he had criticized the wealthy planters and championed the small farmers.

When an assassin's bullet thrust Johnson into the presidency, many former slaveowners shared the dismay of a North Carolina woman who wrote, "Think of Andy Johnson [as] the president! What will become of us—'the aristocrats of the South' as we are termed?" Northern Radicals also had reason to believe that Johnson would deal sternly with the South. When one of them suggested the exile or execution of ten or twelve leading rebels to set an example, Johnson replied, "How are you going to pick out so small a number? . . . Treason is a crime; and crime must be punished."

Like his martyred predecessor, Johnson followed a path in antebellum politics from obscurity to power. With

**Andrew Johnson of Tennessee**

no formal education, he became a tailor's apprentice. But from 1829, while in his early twenties, he held nearly every office in Tennessee politics: alderman, state representative, congressman, two terms as governor, and U.S. senator by 1857. Although elected as a southern Democrat, Johnson

▲ Combative and inflexible, President Andrew Johnson contributed greatly to the failure of his own Reconstruction program.

*(Library of Congress)*

was the only senator from a seceded state who refused to follow his state out of the Union. Lincoln appointed him war governor of Tennessee in 1862; hence his symbolic place on the ticket in the president's bid for reelection in 1864.

Although a Unionist, Johnson's political beliefs made him an old Jacksonian Democrat. And, as they said in the mountainous region of east Tennessee, where Johnson established a reputation as a stump speaker, "Old Andy never went back on his 'raisin'." Johnson was also an ardent states' rightist. Before the war, he had supported tax-funded public schools and homestead legislation, fashioning himself as a champion of the common man. Although he vehemently opposed secession, Johnson advocated limited government. He shared none of the Radicals' expansive conception of federal power. His philosophy toward Reconstruction may be summed up in the slogan he adopted: "The Constitution as it is, and the Union as it was."

Through 1865 Johnson alone controlled Reconstruction policy, for Congress recessed shortly before he became president and did not reconvene until December. In the following eight months, Johnson formed new state governments in the South by using his power to grant pardons. He advanced Lincoln's leniency by extending even easier terms to former Confederates.

Johnson had owned house slaves, although he had never been a planter. He accepted emancipation as a result

**Johnson's Racial Views**

of the war, but he did not favor black civil and political rights. Johnson believed that black suffrage could never be imposed on a southern state by the federal government, and that set him on a collision course with the Radicals. When it came to race, Johnson was a thoroughgoing white supremacist. He held what one politician called "unconquerable prejudices against the African race." In perhaps the most blatantly racist official statement ever delivered by an American president, Johnson declared in his annual message of 1867 that blacks possessed less "capacity for government than any other race of people. No independent government of any form has ever been successful in their hands; . . . wherever they have been left to their own devices they have shown a constant tendency to relapse into barbarism."

Such racial views had an enduring effect on Johnson's policies. Where whites were concerned, however, Johnson seemed to be pursuing changes in class relations. He proposed rules that would keep the wealthy planter class at least temporarily out of power.

White southerners were required to swear an oath of loyalty as a condition of gaining amnesty or pardon, but

**Johnson's
Pardon Policy**

Johnson barred several categories of people from taking the oath: former federal officials, high-ranking Confederate officers, and political leaders or graduates of West Point or Annapolis who joined the Confederacy. To this list Johnson added another important group: all ex-Confederates whose taxable property was worth more than $20,000. These individuals had to apply personally to the president for pardon and restoration of their political rights. The president, it seemed, meant to take revenge on the old planter elite and thereby promote a new leadership of deserving yeomen.

Johnson appointed provisional governors, who began the Reconstruction process by calling state constitutional conventions. The delegates chosen for these conventions had to draft new constitutions that eliminated slavery and invalidated secession. After ratification of these constitutions, new governments could be elected, and the states would be restored to the Union with full congressional representation. But only those southerners who had taken the oath of amnesty and had been eligible to vote on the day the state seceded could participate in this process. Thus unpardoned whites and former slaves were not eligible.

If Johnson intended to strip former aristocrats of their power, he did not hold to his plan. The old white leadership proved resilient and influential; prominent Confederates won elections and turned up in various appointive offices. Then Johnson started pardoning planters and leading rebels. He hired additional clerks to prepare the necessary documents and then began to issue pardons to large categories of people. By September 1865, hundreds were being issued in a single day. These pardons, plus the rapid return of planters' abandoned lands, restored the old elite to power and quickly gave Johnson an image as the South's champion.

**Presidential
Reconstruction**

Why did Johnson allow the planters to regain power? Personal vanity may have played a role, as he turned proud planters into pardon seekers. He was also determined to achieve a rapid Reconstruction in order to deny the Radicals any opportunity for the more thorough racial and political changes they desired in the South. And Johnson needed southern support in the 1866 elections; hence, he declared Reconstruction complete only eight months after Appomattox. Thus, in December 1865, many Confederate congressmen traveled to Washington to claim seats in the U.S. Congress. Even Alexander Stephens, vice president of the Confederacy, returned to Capitol Hill as a senator-elect from Georgia.

The election of such prominent rebels troubled many northerners. Some of the state conventions were slow to repudiate secession; others admitted only grudgingly that slavery was dead and wrote new laws to show it.

Furthermore, to define the status of freed men and women and control their labor, some legislatures merely revised large sections of the slave codes by substituting the word *freedmen* for *slaves*. The new black codes compelled former slaves to carry passes, observe a curfew, live in housing provided by a landowner, and give up hope of entering many desirable occupations. Stiff vagrancy laws and restrictive labor contracts bound freedpeople to plantations, and "anti-enticement" laws punished anyone who tried to lure these workers to other employment. State-supported schools and orphanages excluded blacks entirely.

**Black Codes**

It seemed to northerners that the South was intent on returning African Americans to servility and that Johnson's Reconstruction policy held no one responsible for the terrible war. But memories of the war—not yet even a year over—were still raw and would dominate political behavior for several elections to come. Thus the Republican majority in Congress decided to call a halt to the results of Johnson's plan. On reconvening, the House and Senate considered the credentials of the newly elected southern representatives and decided not to admit them. Instead, they bluntly challenged the president's authority and established a joint committee to study and investigate a new direction for Reconstruction.

## THE CONGRESSIONAL RECONSTRUCTION PLAN

Northern congressmen were hardly unified, but they did not doubt their right to shape Reconstruction policy. The Constitution mentioned neither secession nor reunion, but it gave Congress the primary role in the admission of states. Moreover, the Constitution declared that the United States shall guarantee to each state a "republican form of government." This provision, legislators believed, gave them the authority to devise policies for Reconstruction.

They soon found that other constitutional questions affected their policies. What, for example, had rebellion done to the relationship between southern states and the Union? Lincoln had always believed secession impossible—the Confederate states had engaged in an "insurrection" within the Union in his view. Congressmen who favored vigorous Reconstruction measures argued that the war had broken the Union and that the South was subject to the victor's will. Moderate congressmen held that the states had forfeited their rights through rebellion and thus had come under congressional supervision.

These theories mirrored the diversity of Congress itself. Northern Democrats, weakened by their opposition to the war in its final year, denounced any idea of racial equality and supported Johnson's policies.

### The Radicals

Conservative Republicans, despite their party loyalty, favored a limited federal role in Reconstruction. The Radical Republicans, led by Thaddeus Stevens, Charles Sumner, and George Julian, wanted to transform the South. Although a minority in their party, they had the advantage of clearly defined goals. They believed it was essential to democratize the South, establish public education, and ensure the rights of the freedpeople. They favored black suffrage, supported some land confiscation and redistribution, and were willing to exclude the South from the Union for several years if necessary to achieve their goals.

Born of the war and its outcome, the Radicals brought a new civic vision to American life; they wanted to create an activist federal government and the beginnings of racial equality. A large group of moderate Republicans, led by Lyman Trumbull, opposed Johnson's leniency but wanted to restrain the Radicals. Trumbull and the moderates were, however, committed to federalizing the enforcement of civil, if not political, rights for the freedmen.

One overwhelming political reality faced all four groups: the 1866 elections. Ironically, Johnson and the Democrats sabotaged the possibility of a conservative coalition. They refused to cooperate with conservative or moderate Republicans and insisted that Reconstruction was over, that the new state governments were legitimate, and that southern representatives should be admitted to Congress. Among the Republicans, the Radicals' influence grew in proportion to Johnson's intransigence and outright provocation.

Trying to work with Johnson, Republicans believed a compromise had been reached in the spring of 1866. Under its terms Johnson would agree to two modifications of his program: extension of the Freedmen's Bureau for another year and passage of a civil rights bill to counteract the black codes. This bill would force southern courts to practice equality under the ultimate scrutiny of the federal judiciary. Its provisions applied to public, not private, acts of discrimination. The Civil Rights Bill of 1866 was the first statutory definition of the rights of American citizens and is still on the books today.

### Congress Versus Johnson

Johnson destroyed the compromise, however, by vetoing both bills (they later became law when Congress overrode the president's veto). Denouncing any change in his program, the president condemned Congress's action and

▲ The Memphis race riots during Reconstruction. Unarmed blacks are gunned down by well-armed whites in this scene, reinforced by a Congressional investigation. *(Library of Congress)*

revealed his own racism. Because the civil rights bill defined U.S. citizens as native-born persons who were taxed, Johnson claimed that it discriminated against "large numbers of intelligent, worthy, and patriotic foreigners . . . in favor of the negro." The bill, he said, operated "in favor of the colored and against the white race."

All hope of presidential-congressional cooperation was now dead. In 1866 newspapers reported daily violations of blacks' rights in the South and carried alarming accounts of antiblack violence—notably in Memphis and New Orleans, where police aided brutal mobs in their attacks. In Memphis, forty blacks were killed and twelve schools burned by white mobs, and in New Orleans, the toll was thirty-four African Americans dead and two hundred wounded. Such violence convinced Republicans, and the northern public, that more needed to be done. A new Republican plan took the form of the Fourteenth Amendment to the Constitution.

Of the five sections of the Fourteenth Amendment, the first would have the greatest legal significance in later

||||||||||||||||||||||||||||||||||||

**Fourteenth Amendment**

years. It conferred citizenship on "all persons born or naturalized in the United States" and prohibited states from abridging their constitutional "privileges and immunities" (see the Appendix for the Constitution and all amendments). It also barred any state from taking a person's life, liberty, or property "without due process of law" and from denying "equal protection of the laws." These resounding phrases have become powerful guarantees of African Americans' civil rights—indeed, of the rights of all citizens, except for Indians, who were not granted citizenship rights until 1924.

Nearly universal agreement emerged among Republicans on the amendment's second and third sections. The fourth declared the Confederate debt null and void, and guaranteed the war debt of the United States. Northerners rejected the notion of paying taxes to reimburse those who had financed a rebellion, and business groups agreed on the necessity of upholding the credit of the U.S. government. The second and third sections barred Confederate leaders from holding state and federal office. Only Congress, by a two-thirds vote of each house, could remove the penalty. The amendment thus guaranteed a degree of punishment for the leaders of the Confederacy.

The second section of the amendment also dealt with representation and embodied the compromises that produced the document. Northerners disagreed about whether blacks should have the right to vote. As a citizen of Indiana wrote to a southern relative, "Although there is a great deal [of] profession among us for the relief of the darkey yet I think much of it is far from being sincere. I guess we

want to compel you to do right by them while we are not willing ourselves to do so." Those arched words are indicative not only of how revolutionary Reconstruction had become, but also of how far the public will, North and South, lagged behind the enactments that became new constitutional cornerstones. Many northern states still maintained black disfranchisement laws during Reconstruction.

Emancipation finally ended the three-fifths clause for the purpose of counting blacks, which would increase southern representation. Thus the postwar South stood to gain power in Congress, and if white southerners did not allow blacks to vote, former secessionists would derive the political benefit from emancipation. That was more irony than most northerners could bear. So Republicans determined that, if a southern state did not grant black men the vote, their representation would be reduced proportionally. If they did enfranchise black men, their representation would be increased proportionally. This compromise avoided a direct enactment of black suffrage but would deliver future black southern voters to the Republican Party.

The Fourteenth Amendment specified for the first time that voters were "male" and ignored female citizens, black and white. For this reason it provoked a strong reaction from the women's rights movement. Advocates of women's equality had worked with abolitionists for decades, often subordinating their cause to that of the slaves. During the drafting of the Fourteenth Amendment, however, female activists demanded to be heard. Prominent leaders, such as Elizabeth Cady Stanton and Susan B. Anthony, ended their alliance with abolitionists and fought for women, while others remained committed to the idea that it was "the Negro's hour." Thus the amendment infused new life into the women's rights movement and caused considerable strife among old allies. Many male former abolitionists, white and black, were willing to delay the day of woman suffrage in favor of securing freedmen the right to vote in the South.

In 1866, however, the major question in Reconstruction politics was how the public would respond to the

||||||||||||||||||||||||||||||||||||

**The South's and Johnson's Defiance**

congressional initiative. Johnson did his best to block the Fourteenth Amendment in both North and South. Condemning Congress for its refusal to seat southern representatives, the president urged state legislatures in the South to vote against ratification. Every southern legislature except Tennessee's rejected the amendment by a wide margin.

To present his case to northerners, Johnson organized a National Union Convention and took to the stump himself. In an age when active personal campaigning was rare for a president, Johnson boarded a special train for a "swing around the circle" that carried his message into the Northeast, the Midwest, and then back to Washington. In city after city, he criticized the Republicans in a ranting, undignified style. Increasingly, audiences rejected his views, hooting and jeering at him. In this whistle-stop tour, Johnson began to hand out American flags with thirty-six rather than twenty-five stars, declaring the Union already restored. At many towns he likened himself to a "persecuted" Jesus who might now be martyred "upon the cross" for his magnanimity toward the South. And, repeatedly, he labeled the Radicals "traitors" for their efforts to take over Reconstruction.

The elections of 1866 were a resounding victory for Republicans in Congress. Radicals and moderates whom Johnson had denounced won reelection by large margins, and the Republican majority grew to two-thirds of both houses of Congress. The North had spoken clearly: Johnson's official policies of states' rights and white supremacy were prematurely giving the advantage to rebels and traitors. Although the Radicals may have been out ahead

of public opinion, most northerners feared Johnson's approach more. Thus Republican congressional leaders won a mandate to pursue their Reconstruction plan.

But Johnson and southern intransigence had brought the plan to an impasse. Nothing could be accomplished as long as the "Johnson governments" existed and the southern electorate remained exclusively white. Republicans resolved to form new state governments in the South and enfranchise the freedmen.

After some embittered debate in which Republicans and the remaining Democrats in Congress argued over the meaning and memory of the Civil War itself, the First Reconstruction Act passed in March 1867. This plan, under which the southern states were actually readmitted to the Union, incorporated only a part of the Radical program. Union generals, commanding small garrisons of troops and charged with supervising elections, assumed control in five military districts in the

## Reconstruction Acts of 1867–1868

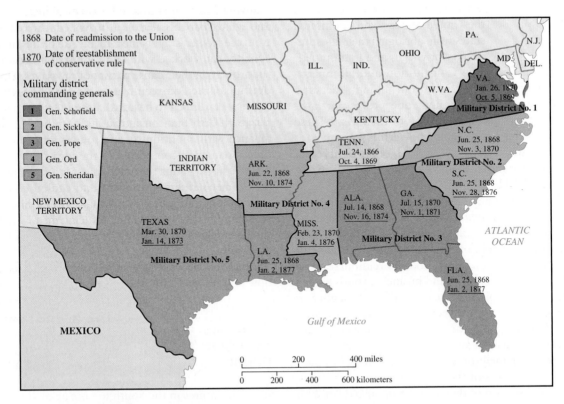

**Map 16.1    The Reconstruction**

This map shows the five military districts established when Congress passed the Reconstruction Act of 1867. As the dates within each state indicate, conservative Democratic forces quickly regained control of government in four southern states. So-called Radical Reconstruction was curtailed in most of the others, as factions within the weakened Republican Party began to cooperate with conservative Democrats.

South (see Map 16.1). Confederate leaders designated in the Fourteenth Amendment were barred from voting until new state constitutions were ratified. The act guaranteed freedmen the right to vote in elections for as well as serve in state constitutional conventions and in subsequent elections. In addition, each southern state was required to ratify the Fourteenth Amendment, to ratify its new constitution by majority vote, and to submit it to Congress for approval (see Table 16.1).

Thus African Americans gained an opportunity to fight for a better life through the political process, and ex-Confederates were given what they interpreted as a bitter pill to swallow in order to return to the Union. The Second, Third, and Fourth Reconstruction Acts, passed between March 1867 and March 1868, provided the details of operation for voter registration boards, the adoption of constitutions, and the administration of "good faith" oaths on the part of white southerners.

In the words of one historian, the Radicals succeeded in "clipping Johnson's wings." But they had hoped Congress could do much more. Thad-

### Failure of Land Redistribution

deus Stevens, for example, argued that economic opportunity was essential to the freedmen. "If we do not furnish them with homesteads from forfeited and rebel property," Stevens declared, "and hedge them around with protective laws . . . we had better left them in bondage." Stevens therefore drew up a plan for extensive confiscation and redistribution of land, but it was never realized.

Racial fears among whites and an American obsession with the sanctity of private property made land redistribution unpopular. Northerners were accustomed to a limited role for government, and the business community staunchly opposed any interference with private-property rights, even for former Confederates. Thus black farmers were forced to seek work in a hostile environment in which landowners opposed their acquisition of land.

Congress's quarrels with Andrew Johnson grew still worse. To restrict Johnson's influence and safeguard its

### Constitutional Crisis

plan, Congress passed a number of controversial laws. First, it limited Johnson's power over the army by requiring the president to issue military orders through the General of the Army, Ulysses S. Grant, who could not be dismissed without the Senate's consent. Then Congress passed the Tenure of Office Act, which gave the Senate power to approve changes in the president's cabinet. Designed to protect Secretary of War Stanton, who sympathized with the Radicals, this law violated the tradition that a president controlled appointments to his own cabinet.

All of these measures, as well as each of the Reconstruction Acts, were passed by a two-thirds override of presidential vetoes. The situation led some to believe that the federal government had reached a stage of "congressional tyranny" and others to conclude that Johnson had become an obstacle to the legitimate will of the people in reconstructing the nation on a just and permanent basis.

| TABLE 16.1 | Plans for Reconstruction Compared | | | |
|---|---|---|---|---|
| | **Johnson's Plan** | **Radicals' Plan** | **Fourteenth Amendment** | **Reconstruction Act of 1867** |
| **Voting** | Whites only; high-ranking Confederate leaders must seek pardons | Give vote to black males | Southern whites may decide but can lose representation if they deny black suffrage | Black men gain vote; whites barred from office by Fourteenth Amendment cannot vote while new state governments are being formed |
| **Officeholding** | Many prominent Confederates regain power | Only loyal white and black males eligible | Confederate leaders barred until Congress votes amnesty | Fourteenth Amendment in effect |
| **Time out of Union** | Brief | Several years; until South is thoroughly democratized | Brief | 3–5 years after war |
| **Other change in southern society** | Little; gain of power by yeomen not realized; emancipation grudgingly accepted, but no black civil or political rights | Expand public education; confiscate land and provide farms for freedmen; expansion of activist federal government | Probably slight, depending on enforcement | Considerable, depending on action of new state governments |

Johnson took several belligerent steps of his own. He issued orders to military commanders in the South, limiting their powers and increasing the powers of the civil governments he had created in 1865. Then he removed military officers who were conscientiously enforcing Congress's new law, preferring commanders who allowed disqualified Confederates to vote. Finally, he tried to remove Secretary of War Stanton. With that attempt the confrontation reached its climax.

Impeachment is a political procedure provided for in the Constitution as a remedy for crimes or serious abuses of power by presidents, federal judges, and other high government officials. Those who are impeached (judged or politically indicted) in the House are then tried in the Senate. Historically, this power has generally not been used as a means to investigate and judge the private lives of presidents, although in recent times it was used in this manner in the case of President Bill Clinton.

## Impeachment of President Johnson

Twice in 1867, the House Judiciary Committee had considered impeachment of Johnson, rejecting the idea once and then recommending it by only a 5-to-4 vote. That recommendation was decisively defeated by the House. After Johnson tried to remove Stanton, however, a third attempt to impeach the president carried easily in early 1868. The indictment concentrated on his violation of the Tenure of Office Act, though many modern scholars regard his efforts to obstruct enforcement of the Reconstruction Act of 1867 as a far more serious offense.

Johnson's trial in the Senate lasted more than three months. The prosecution, led by Radicals, attempted to prove that Johnson was guilty of "high crimes and misdemeanors." But they also argued that the trial was a means to judge Johnson's performance, not a judicial determination of guilt or innocence. The Senate ultimately rejected such reasoning, which could have made removal from office a political weapon against any chief executive who disagreed with Congress. Although a majority of senators voted to convict Johnson, the prosecution fell one vote short of the necessary two-thirds majority. Johnson remained in office, politically weakened and with less than a year left in his term. Some Republicans backed away from impeachment because they had their eyes on the 1868 election and did not want to hurt their prospects of regaining the White House.

In the 1868 presidential election, Ulysses S. Grant, running as a Republican, defeated Horatio Seymour, a New York Democrat. Grant was not a Radical, but his platform supported congressional Reconstruction and endorsed black suffrage in the South.

## Election of 1868

▲ Thomas Waterman Wood, who had painted portraits of society figures in Nashville before the war, sensed the importance of Congress's decision in 1867 to enfranchise the freedmen. This oil painting, one in a series on suffrage, emphasizes the significance of the ballot for the black voter. *(Cheekwood Museum of Art, Nashville, Tennessee)*

(Significantly, Republicans stopped short of endorsing black suffrage in the North.) The Democrats, meanwhile, vigorously denounced Reconstruction and preached white supremacy. Indeed, in the 1868 election, the Democrats conducted the most openly racist campaign to that point in American history. Both sides waved the "bloody shirt," accusing each other as the villains of the war's sacrifices. By associating themselves with rebellion and with Johnson's repudiated program, the Democrats went down to defeat in all but eight states, though the popular vote was fairly close. Participating in their first presidential election ever on a wide scale, blacks decisively voted en masse for General Grant.

In office Grant acted as an administrator of Reconstruction but not as its enthusiastic advocate. He vacillated

▲ A Republican Party brass band in action during the 1868 election campaign in Baton Rouge, Louisiana. The Union regimental colors and soldiers' caps demonstrate the strong federal presence in the South at this pivotal moment in radical Reconstruction.

*(Andrew D. Lytle Collection, Louisiana and Lower Mississippi Valley Collections, LSU Libraries, Louisiana State University, Baton Rouge, Louisiana.)*

in his dealings with the southern states, sometimes defending Republican regimes and sometimes currying favor with Democrats. On occasion Grant called out federal troops to stop violence or enforce acts of Congress. But he never imposed a true military occupation on the South. Rapid demobilization had reduced a federal army of more than 1 million to 57,000 within a year of the surrender at Appomattox. Thereafter, the number of troops in the South continued to fall, until in 1874 there were only 4,000 in the southern states outside Texas. The later legend of "military rule," so important to southern claims of victimization during Reconstruction, was steeped in myth.

In 1869 the Radicals pushed through the Fifteenth Amendment, the final major measure in the constitutional revolution of Reconstruction. This measure forbade states to deny the right to vote "on account of race, color, or previous condition of servitude." Such wording did not guarantee the right to vote. It deliberately left states free to restrict suffrage on other grounds so that northern states could continue to deny suffrage to women and certain groups of men—Chinese immigrants, illiterates, and those too poor to pay poll taxes.

**Fifteenth Amendment**

Although several states outside the South refused to ratify, three-fourths of the states approved the measure, and the Fifteenth Amendment became law in 1870. It, too, had been a political compromise, and though African Americans rejoiced all across the land at its enactment, it left open the possibility for states to create countless qualification tests to obstruct voting in the future.

With passage of the Fifteenth Amendment, many Americans, especially supportive northerners, considered Reconstruction essentially completed. "Let us have done with Reconstruction," pleaded the *New York Tribune* in April 1870. "The country is tired and sick of it. . . . Let us have Peace!" But some northerners, like abolitionist Wendell Phillips, worried. "Our day," he warned, "is fast slipping away. Once let public thought float off from the great issue of the war, and it will take . . . more than a generation to bring it back again."

## POLITICS AND RECONSTRUCTION IN THE SOUTH

From the start, Reconstruction encountered the resistance of white southerners. In the black codes and in private attitudes, many whites stubbornly opposed emancipation, and the former planter class proved especially unbending because of their tremendous financial loss in slaves. In 1866 a Georgia newspaper frankly observed that "most of the white citizens believe that the institution of slavery was right, and . . . they will believe that the condition, which comes nearest to slavery, that can now be established will be the best." And for many poor whites who had never owned slaves and yet had sacrificed enormously in the war, destitution, plummeting agricultural prices, disease, and the uncertainties of a growing urban industrialization, drove them off land, toward cities, and into hatred of the very idea of black equality.

Fearing loss of control over their slaves, some planters attempted to postpone freedom by denying or misrepresenting events. Former slaves reported that their owners "didn't tell them it was freedom" or "wouldn't let [them] go." Agents of the Freedmen's Bureau reported that "the old system of slavery [is] working with even more rigor than formerly at a few miles distant from any point where U.S. troops are stationed." To hold onto their workers, some landowners claimed control over black children and used guardianship and apprentice laws to bind black families to the plantation.

**White Resistance**

Whites also blocked blacks from acquiring land. A few planters divided up plots among their slaves, but most condemned the idea of making blacks landowners. A Georgia woman whose family was known for its support of religious education for slaves was outraged that two property owners planned to "rent their lands to the Negroes!" Such action was, she declared, "injurious to the best interest of the community."

Adamant resistance by whites soon manifested itself in other ways, including violence. In one North Carolina town, a local magistrate clubbed a black man on a public street, and in several states bands of "Regulators" terrorized blacks who displayed any independence. Amid their defeat, many planters believed, as a South Carolinian put it, that blacks "can't be governed except with the whip." And after President Johnson encouraged the South to resist congressional Reconstruction, many white conserva-

tives worked hard to capture the new state governments, while others boycotted the polls in an attempt to defeat Congress's plans.

Very few black men stayed away from the polls. Enthusiastically and hopefully, they voted Republican. Most agreed with one man who felt he should "stick to the end with the party that freed me." Illiteracy did not prohibit blacks (or uneducated whites) from making intelligent choices. Although Mississippi's William Henry could read only "a little," he testified that he and his friends had no difficulty selecting the Republican ballot. "We stood around and watched," he explained. "We saw D. Sledge vote; he owned half the county. We knowed he voted Democratic so we voted the other ticket so it would be Republican." Women, who could not vote, encouraged their husbands and sons, and preachers exhorted their congregations to use the franchise. Zeal for voting spread through entire black communities.

**Black Voters and the Southern Republican Party**

▲ Southern blacks attempting to vote are halted by White Leaguers in this engraving by J. H. Wares. The black man doffing his cap holds a "Republican ticket" but it will not get him to the ballot box, guarded by the election judge with a loaded pistol.

*(Granger Collection)*

Thanks to a large black turnout and the restrictions on prominent Confederates, a new southern Republican Party came to power in the constitutional conventions of 1868–1870. Republican delegates consisted of a sizable contingent of blacks (265 out of the total of just over 1,000 delegates throughout the South), some northerners who had moved to the South, and native southern whites who favored change. The new constitutions drafted by this Republican coalition were more democratic than anything previously adopted in the history of the South. They eliminated property qualifications for voting and holding office, and they turned many appointed offices into elective posts. They provided for public schools and institutions to care for the mentally ill, the blind, the deaf, the destitute, and the orphaned.

The conventions broadened women's rights in property holding and divorce. Usually the goal was not to make women equal with men but to provide relief to thousands of suffering debtors. In white families left poverty-stricken by the war and weighed down by debt, it was usually the husband who had contracted the debts. Thus giving women legal control over their own property provided some protection to their families.

Under these new constitutions the southern states elected Republican-controlled governments. For the first

**Triumph of Republican Governments**

time, the ranks of state legislators in 1868 included black southerners. It remained to be seen now how much social change these new governments would foster. Contrary to what white southerners would later claim, the Republican state governments did not disfranchise ex-Confederates as a group. James Lynch, a leading black politician from Mississippi, explained why African Americans shunned the "folly" of disfranchising whites. Unlike northerners who "can leave when it becomes too uncomfortable," landless former slaves "must be in friendly relations with the great body of the whites in the state. Otherwise . . . peace can be maintained only by a standing army." Despised and lacking material or social power, southern Republicans strove for acceptance, legitimacy, and safe ways to gain a foothold in a depressed economy.

Far from being vindictive toward the race that had enslaved them, most southern blacks treated leading rebels with generosity and appealed to white southerners to adopt a spirit of fairness. In this way the South's Republican Party condemned itself to defeat if white voters would not cooperate. Within a few years most of the fledgling Republican parties in the southern states would be struggling for survival against violent white hostility. But for a

time some propertied whites accepted congressional Reconstruction as a reality.

Reflecting northern ideals and southern necessity, the Reconstruction governments enthusiastically promoted

**Industrialization and Mill Towns**

industry. Accordingly, Reconstruction legislatures encouraged investment with loans, subsidies, and short-term exemptions from taxation. The southern railroad system was rebuilt and expanded, and coal and iron mining made possible Birmingham's steel plants. Between 1860 and 1880, the number of manufacturing establishments in the South nearly doubled.

This emphasis on big business, however, produced higher state debts and taxes, drew money away from schools and other programs, and multiplied possibilities for corruption in state legislatures. The alliance between business and government took firm hold, often at the expense of the needs of common farmers and laborers. It also locked Republicans into a conservative strategy and doomed them to failure in building support among poorer whites.

Poverty remained the lot of vast numbers of southern whites. On a daily basis during the Reconstruction years, they had to subordinate politics to the struggle for livelihood. The war had caused a massive one-time loss of income-producing wealth, such as livestock, and a steep decline in land values. From 1860 to 1880, the South's share of per capita income fell from nearly equal to only 51 percent of the national average. In many regions the old planter class still ruled the best land and access to credit or markets.

As many poor whites and blacks found farming less tenable, they moved to cities and new mill towns. Industrialization did not sweep the South as it did the North, but it certainly laid deep roots. Attracting textile mills to southern towns became a competitive crusade. "Next to God," shouted a North Carolina evangelist, "what this town needs is a cotton mill!" In 1860 the South counted some 10,000 mill workers; by 1880, the number grew to 16,741 and by the end of the century, to 97,559. In thousands of human dramas, poor southerners began the multigenerational journey from farmer to mill worker and other forms of low-income urban wage earner.

Policies appealing to African American voters never went beyond equality before the law. In fact, the whites who

**Republicans and Racial Equality**

controlled the southern Republican Party were reluctant to allow blacks a share of offices proportionate to their electoral strength. Aware of their weakness, black leaders

▲ One notable success in Reconstruction efforts to stimulate industry was Birmingham, Alabama.
Here workers cast molten iron into blocks called pigs. *(Birmingham Public Library)*

did not push very far for revolutionary economic or social change. In every southern state, they led efforts to establish public schools, although they did not press for integrated facilities. In 1870 South Carolina passed the first comprehensive school law in the South. By 1875, 50 percent of black school-age children in that state were enrolled in school, and approximately one-third of the three thousand teachers were black.

Some African American politicians did fight for civil rights and integration. Many were from cities such as New Orleans or Mobile, where large populations of light-skinned free blacks had existed before the war. Their experience in such communities had made them sensitive to issues of status, and they spoke out for open and equal public accommodations. Laws requiring equal accommodations won passage, but they often went unenforced.

The vexing questions of land reform and enforcement of racial equality, however, all but overwhelmed the Republican governments. Land reform largely failed because in most states whites were in the majority, and former slaveowners controlled the best land and other sources of economic power. Economic progress was uppermost in the minds of most freedpeople. Black southerners needed land,

and much land did fall into state hands for nonpayment of taxes. Such land was offered for sale in small lots. But most freedmen had too little cash to bid against investors or speculators. South Carolina established a land commission, but it could help only those with money to buy. Any widespread redistribution of land had to arise from Congress, which never supported such action.

Within a few years, as centrists in both parties met with failure, white hostility to congressional Reconstruction began to dominate. Some conservatives had always wanted to fight Reconstruction through pressure and racist propaganda. They put economic and social pressure on blacks: one black Republican reported that "my neighbors will not employ me, nor sell me a farthing's worth of anything." Charging that the South had been turned over to ignorant blacks, conservatives deplored "black domination," which became a rallying cry for a return to white supremacy.

## Myth of "Negro Rule"

Such attacks were inflammatory propaganda and part of the growing myth of "Negro rule," which would serve as a central theme in battles over the memory of Reconstruction. African Americans participated in politics but hardly dominated or controlled events. They were a majority in only two out of ten state constitutional writing conventions (transplanted northerners were a majority in one). In the state legislatures, only in the lower house in South Carolina did blacks ever constitute a majority. Sixteen blacks won seats in Congress before Reconstruction was over, but none was ever elected governor. Only eighteen served in a high state office, such as lieutenant governor, treasurer, superintendent of education, or secretary of state.

In all, some four hundred blacks served in political office during the Reconstruction era, a signal achievement by any standard. Although they never dominated the process, they established a rich tradition of government service and civic activism. Elected officials, such as Robert Smalls in South Carolina, labored tirelessly for cheaper land prices, better healthcare, access to schools, and the enforcement of civil rights for their people. For too long the black politicians of Reconstruction were the forgotten heroes of this seedtime of America's long civil rights movement.

Conservatives also assailed the allies of black Republicans. Their propaganda denounced whites from the

**Carpetbaggers and Scalawags**

North as "carpetbaggers," greedy crooks planning to pour stolen tax revenues into their sturdy luggage made of carpet material. Immigrants from the North, who held the largest share of Republican offices, were all tarred with this rhetorical brush.

In fact, most northerners who settled in the South had come seeking business opportunities, as schoolteachers, or to find a warmer climate; most never entered politics. Those who did enter politics generally wanted to democratize the South and to introduce northern ways, such as industry and public education. Carpetbaggers' ideals were tested by hard times and ostracism by white southerners.

In addition to tagging northern interlopers as carpetbaggers, conservatives invented the term *scalawag* to discredit any native white southerner who cooperated with the Republicans. A substantial number of southerners did so, including some wealthy and prominent men. Most scalawags, however, were yeoman farmers, men from mountain areas and nonslaveholding districts who had been Unionists under the Confederacy. They saw that they could benefit from the education and opportunities promoted by Republicans. Sometimes banding together with freedmen, they pursued common class interests and hoped to make headway against the power of long-dominant planters. Such cooperation led to genuine hopes for black-white

coalitions, but most of these efforts in the long run floundered in the quicksand of racism.

Taxation was a major problem for the Reconstruction governments. Republicans wanted to repair the war's

**Tax Policy and Corruption as Political Wedges**

destruction, stimulate industry, and support such new ventures as public schools. But the Civil War had destroyed much of the South's tax base. One category of valuable property—slaves—had disappeared entirely. And hundreds of thousands of citizens had lost much of the rest of their property—money, livestock, fences, and buildings—to the war. Thus an increase in taxes (sales, excise, and property) was necessary even to maintain traditional services. Inevitably, Republican tax policies aroused strong opposition, especially among the yeomen.

Corruption was another serious charge levied against the Republicans. Unfortunately, it was often true. Many carpetbaggers and black politicians engaged in fraudulent schemes, sold their votes, or padded expenses, taking part in what scholars recognize was a nationwide surge of corruption in an age ruled by "spoilsmen" (see pages 566–567). Corruption carried no party label, but the Democrats successfully pinned the blame on unqualified blacks and greedy carpetbaggers among southern Republicans.

All these problems hurt the Republicans, whose leaders also allowed factionalism along racial and class lines

**Ku Klux Klan**

to undermine party unity. But in many southern states the deathblow came through violence. The Ku Klux Klan (its members altered the Greek word for "circle," *kuklos*), a secret veterans' club that began in Tennessee in 1866, spread through the South and rapidly evolved into a terrorist organization. Violence against African Americans occurred from the first days of Reconstruction but became far more organized and purposeful after 1867. Klansmen sought to frustrate Reconstruction and keep the freedmen in subjection. Nighttime harassment, whippings, beatings, rapes, and murders became common, as terrorism dominated some counties and regions.

Although the Klan tormented blacks who stood up for their rights as laborers or individuals, its main purpose was political. Lawless nightriders made active Republicans the target of their attacks. Leading white and black Republicans were killed in several states. After freedmen who worked for a South Carolina scalawag started voting, terrorists visited the plantation and, in the words of one victim, "whipped every . . . [black] man they could lay their hands on." Klansmen also attacked Union League

IF HE IS A UNION MAN OR A FREEDMAN.

"VERDICT", HANG THE D— YANKEE AND NIGGER."

▲ During Reconstruction, especially the years 1868–1871, the Ku Klux Klan, and other groups like them, terrorized and murdered blacks as well as white unionists or Republicans. Their goals were to destroy black community development and Republican political power.   *(Harper's Weekly, March 23, 1867)*

▲ Albion Winegar Tourgée, a former Union soldier severely wounded at the Battle of Bull Run in 1861, became a carpetbagger and was elected a district judge in North Carolina during Reconstruction. In 1879 he published a bestselling novel, *A Fool's Errand,* which told his own story of travail as a Yankee immigrant in the South confronting the Ku Klux Klan and implementing freedmen's rights.

*(Chautauqua County Historical Society, Westfield, N.Y.)*

clubs—Republican organizations that mobilized the black vote—and schoolteachers who were aiding the freedmen.

Klan violence was not a spontaneous outburst of racism; very specific social forces shaped and directed it. In North Carolina, for example, Alamance and Caswell Counties were the sites of the worst Klan violence. Slim Republican majorities there rested on cooperation between black voters and white yeomen, particularly those whose Unionism or discontent with the Confederacy had turned them against local Democratic officials. Together, these black and white Republicans had ousted officials long entrenched in power. The wealthy and powerful men in Alamance and Caswell who had lost their accustomed political control

were the Klan's county officers and local chieftains. They organized a deliberate campaign of terror, recruiting members and planning atrocities. By intimidation and murder, the Klan weakened the Republican coalition and restored a Democratic majority.

Klan violence injured Republicans across the South. One of every ten black leaders who had been delegates to the 1867–1868 state constitutional conventions was attacked, seven fatally. In one judicial district of North Carolina, the Ku Klux Klan was responsible for twelve murders, over seven hundred beatings, and other acts of violence, including rape and arson. A single attack on Alabama Republicans in the town of Eutaw left four blacks dead and fifty-four wounded. In South Carolina, five hundred masked Klansmen lynched eight black prisoners at the Union County jail, and in nearby York County, the Klan committed at least eleven murders and hundreds of whippings. According to historian Eric Foner, the Klan "made it virtually impossible for Republicans to campaign or vote in large parts of Georgia."

Thus a combination of difficult fiscal problems, Republican mistakes, racial hostility, and terror brought down the Republican regimes. In most southern states, Radical Reconstruction lasted only a few years (see Map 16.1). The most enduring failure of Reconstruction, however, was not political; it was social and economic. Reconstruction failed to alter the South's social structure or its distribution of wealth and power.

# RETREAT FROM RECONSTRUCTION

During the 1870s, northerners increasingly lost the political will to sustain Reconstruction in the South, as a vast economic and social transformation occurred in their own region as well as in the West. Radical Republicans like Albion Tourgée, a former Union soldier who moved to North Carolina and was elected a judge, condemned Congress's timidity. Turning the freedman out on his own without protection, said Tourgée, constituted "cheap philanthropy." Indeed, many African Americans believed that, during Reconstruction, the North "threw all the Negroes on the world without any way of getting along." As the North underwent its own transformations and lost interest in the South's dilemmas, Reconstruction collapsed.

In one southern state after another, Democrats regained control, and they threatened to defeat Republicans in the North as well. Whites in the old Confederacy referred to this decline of Reconstruction as "southern redemption," and during the 1870s, "redeemer" Democrats claimed to be the saviors of the South from alleged "black domination" and "carpetbag rule." And for one of only a few times in American history, violence and terror emerged as a tactic in normal politics.

**Political Implications of Klan Terrorism**

In 1870 and 1871 the violent campaigns of the Ku Klux Klan forced Congress to pass two Enforcement Acts and an anti-Klan law. These laws made actions by individuals against the civil and political rights of others a federal criminal offense for the first time. They also provided for election supervisors and permitted martial law and suspension of the writ of habeas corpus to combat murders, beatings, and threats by the Klan. Federal prosecutors used the laws rather selectively. In 1872 and 1873, Mississippi and the Carolinas saw many prosecutions; but in other states where violence flourished, the laws were virtually ignored. Southern juries sometimes refused to convict Klansmen; out of a total of 3,310 cases, only 1,143 ended in convictions. Although many Klansmen (roughly 2,000 in South Carolina alone) fled their state to avoid prosecution, and the Klan officially disbanded, the threat of violence did not end. Paramilitary organizations known as Rifle Clubs and Red Shirts often took the Klan's place.

Klan terrorism openly defied Congress, yet even on this issue there were ominous signs that the North's commitment to racial justice was fading. Some conservative but influential Republicans opposed the anti-Klan laws. Rejecting other Republicans' arguments that the Thirteenth, Fourteenth, and Fifteenth Amendments had made the federal government the protector of the rights of citizens, these dissenters echoed an old Democratic charge that Congress was infringing on states' rights. Senator Lyman Trumbull of Illinois declared that the states remained "the depositories of the rights of the individual." If Congress could punish crimes like assault or murder, he asked, "what is the need of the State governments?" For years Democrats had complained of "centralization and consolidation"; now some Republicans seemed to agree with them. This opposition foreshadowed a more general revolt within Republican ranks in 1872.

Both immigration and industrialization surged in the North. Between 1865 and 1873, 3 million immigrants entered the country, most settling in the industrial cities of the North and West. Within only eight years, postwar industrial production increased by 75 percent. For the first time, nonagricultural workers outnumbered farmers, and wage earners outnumbered independent craftsmen. And by 1873 only Britain's industrial output was greater than that of the United States. Government financial policies did much to bring about this rapid growth. Low taxes on investment and high tariffs on manufactured goods aided the growth of a new class of powerful industrialists, especially railroad entrepreneurs.

**Industrial Expansion and Reconstruction in the North**

Railroads became the symbol of and the stimulus for the American age of capital. From 1865 to 1873, 35,000 miles of new track were laid, a total exceeding the entire national rail network of 1860. Railroad building fueled the banking industry and made Wall Street the center of American capitalism. Eastern railroad magnates, such as Thomas Scott of the Pennsylvania Railroad, the largest corporation of its time, created economic empires with the assistance of huge government subsidies of cash and land. Railroad corporations also bought up mining operations, granaries, and lumber companies. In Congress and in every state legislature, big business now employed lobbyists to curry favor with government. Corruption ran rampant, with some congressmen and legislators were paid annual retainers by major companies.

This soaring capitalist-political alliance led as well to an intensified struggle between labor and capital. As captains of industry amassed unprecedented fortunes in an age with no income tax, gross economic inequality polarized American society. The work force, worried a prominent Massachusetts business leader, was in a "transition state . . . living in boarding houses" and becoming a "permanent factory population." In Cincinnati, three large factories employed as many workers as the city's thousands of small shops. In New York or Philadelphia, workers increasingly lived in dark, unhealthy tenement housing. Thousands would list themselves on the census as "common laborer" or "general jobber." Many of the free labor maxims of the Republican Party were now under great duress. Did the individual work ethic guarantee social mobility in America or erode, under the pressure of profit making, into a world of unsafe factories, child labor, and declining wages? In 1868 the Republicans managed to pass an eight-hour workday bill in Congress that applied to federal workers. The "labor question" (see Chapter 18) now preoccupied northerners far more than the "southern" or the "freedmen" question.

Then the Panic of 1873 ushered in over five years of economic contraction. Three million people lost their jobs as class attitudes diverged, especially in large cities. Debtors and the unemployed sought easy-money policies to spur economic expansion (workers and farmers desperately needed cash). Businessmen, disturbed by the widespread strikes and industrial violence that accompanied the panic, fiercely defended property rights and demanded "sound money" policies. The chasm between farmers and workers on the one hand, and wealthy industrialists on the other, grew ever wider.

Disenchanted with Reconstruction, a largely northern group calling itself the Liberal Republicans bolted the party in 1872 and nominated Horace Greeley, the famous editor of the *New York Tribune,* for president. The Liberal Republicans were a varied group, including foes of corruption and advocates of a lower tariff. Normally such disparate elements would not cooperate with one another, but two popular and widespread attitudes united them: distaste for federal intervention in the South and an elitist desire to let market forces and the "best men" determine policy and events.

**Liberal Republican Revolt**

The Democrats also gave their nomination to Greeley in 1872. The combination was not enough to defeat Grant, who won reelection, but it reinforced Grant's desire to avoid confrontation with white southerners. Greeley's campaign for North-South reunion, for "clasping hands across the bloody chasm," was a bit premature to win at the polls but was a harbinger of the future in American politics. Organized Blue-Gray fraternalism (gatherings of Union and Confederate veterans) began as early as 1874. Grant continued to use military force sparingly and in 1875 refused a desperate request from the governor of Mississippi for troops to quell racial and political terrorism in that state.

Dissatisfaction with Grant's administration grew during his second term. Strong-willed but politically naive, Grant made a series of poor appointments. His secretary of war, his private secretary, and officials in the Treasury and Navy Departments were involved in bribery or tax-cheating scandals. Instead of exposing the corruption, Grant defended the culprits. In 1874, as Grant's popularity and his party's prestige declined, the Democrats recaptured the House of Representatives, signaling the end of the Radical Republican vision of Reconstruction.

The effect of Democratic gains in Congress was to weaken legislative resolve on southern issues. Congress had already lifted the political disabilities of the Fourteenth Amendment from many former Confederates. In 1872 it had adopted a sweeping Amnesty Act, which pardoned most of the remaining rebels and left only five hundred barred from political office holding. In 1875 Congress passed a Civil Rights Act, partly as a tribute to the recently deceased Charles Sumner, purporting to guarantee black people equal accommodations in public places, such as inns and theaters, but the bill was watered down and contained no effective provisions for enforcement. (The Supreme Court later struck down this law; see page 573.)

**General Amnesty**

Democrats regained control of four state governments before 1872 and a total of eight by the end of January 1876 (see Map 16.1). In the North, Democrats successfully stressed the failure and scandals of Reconstruction governments. As opinion shifted, many Republicans sensed that their constituents were tiring of southern issues and the legacies of the war. Sectional reconciliation now seemed crucial for commerce. The nation was expanding westward rapidly, and the South was a new frontier for investment.

Nowhere did the new complexity and violence of American race relations play out so vividly as in the West. As the Fourteenth Amendment and other enactments granted to blacks the beginnings of citizenship, other nonwhite peoples faced continued persecution. Across the West, the federal government pursued a policy of containment against Native Americans. In California, where white farmers and ranchers often forced Indians into captive labor, some civilians practiced a more violent form of "Indian hunting." By 1880,

**The West, Race, and Reconstruction**

## The Grants' Tour of the World

On May 17, 1877, two weeks after his presidency ended, Ulysses S. Grant and his wife Julia embarked from Philadelphia on a grand tour of the world that would last twenty-six months. Portrayed as a private vacation, the trip was a very public affair. The taint of corruption in Grant's second term could be dissipated only in the air of foreign lands reached by steamship. The small entourage included John Russell Young, a reporter for the *New York Herald* who recorded the journey in the two-volume, illustrated *Around the World with General Grant.* The Grants' expenses were paid by banker friends and by Grant's personal resources, accumulated in gifts.

The Grants spent many months in England attending a bewildering array of banquets, one with Queen Victoria. In Newcastle, thousands of workingmen conducted a massive parade in Grant's honor. He was received as the odd American cousin, simple and great, the conqueror and warrior statesman. In an age that worshiped great men, Grant was viewed as the savior of the American nation, the liberator of slaves, and a celebrity—a measure of the American presence on the world stage.

On the European continent the pattern continued, as every royal or republican head of state hosted the Grants. In Belgium, France, Switzerland, Italy, Russia, Poland, Austria, and Spain, the Grants reveled in princely attentions. In Berlin, Grant met Otto von Bismarck, the chancellor of Germany. The two got along well discussing war, world politics, and the abolition of slavery.

The Grants next went to Egypt, where they rode donkeys into remote villages along the Nile and then traveled by train to the Indian Ocean, where they embarked for India. They encountered British imperialism in full flower in Bombay, and that of the French in Saigon. Northward in Asia, the grand excursion went to China and Japan. In Canton, Grant passed before an assemblage of young men who, according to a reporter, "looked upon the barbarian with . . . contempt in their expression, very much as our young men in New York would regard Sitting Bull or Red Cloud." In Japan, the Grants had a rare audience with Emperor Mutsuhito in the imperial palace. Grant found Japan "beautiful beyond description," and the receptions there were the most formal of all.

"I am both homesick and dread going home," Grant wrote in April 1879. Sailing across the Pacific, the Grants landed in San Francisco in late June. Why had Grant taken such a prolonged trip? Travel itself had its own rewards, but the tour became an unusual political campaign. Grant sought publicity abroad to convince his countrymen back home that they should reelect him president in 1880. But the strategy failed; Grant had developed no compelling issue or reason why Americans should choose him again. He would spend his final years, however, a war hero and a national symbol. No American president would again establish such personal links to the world until Woodrow Wilson at the end of World War I.

▲ On their tour of the world, Ulysses and Julia Grant sat here with companions and guides in front of the Great Hypostyle Hall at the Temple of Amon-Ra in Karnak at Luxor, Egypt, 1878. The Grants' extraordinary tour included many such photo opportunities, often depicting the plebeian American president's presence in exotic places with unusual people. Whether he liked it or not, Grant was a world celebrity. *(Library of Congress)*

▲ Anti-Chinese cartoon, "Every Dog (No Distinction of Color) Has His Day." The imagery here links Native Americans, African Americans, and Chinese immigrants in the same racist and xenophobic fear. *(Granger Collection)*

thirty years of such violence left an estimated 4,500 California Indians dead at the hands of white settlers.

In Texas and the Southwest, the rhetoric of national expansion still deemed Mexicans and other mixed-race Hispanics to be debased, "lazy," and incapable of self-government. And in California and other states of the Far West, thousands of Chinese immigrants became the victims of brutal violence. Few whites had objected to the Chinese who did the dangerous work of building railroads through the Rocky Mountains. But when the Chinese began to compete for urban, industrial jobs, great conflict emerged. Anti-coolie clubs appeared in California in the 1870s, seeking laws against Chinese labor, fanning the flames of racism, and organizing vigilante attacks on Chinese workers and the factories that employed them. Western politicians sought white votes by pandering to prejudice, and in 1879 the new California constitution denied the vote to Chinese.

If we view America from coast to coast, and not merely on the North-South axis, the Civil War and Reconstruction years both dismantled racial slavery and

fostered a volatile new racial complexity, especially in the West. During the same age when early anthropologists employed elaborate theories of "scientific" racism to determine a hierarchy of racial types, the West was a vast region of racial mixing and conflict. Some African Americans, despite generations of mixture with Native Americans, asserted that they were more like whites than the nomadic, "uncivilized" Indians, while others, like the Creek freedmen of Indian Territory, sought an Indian identity. In Texas, whites, Indians, blacks, and Hispanics had mixed for decades, and by the 1870s forced reconsideration in law and custom of who was white and who was not.

During Reconstruction, America was undergoing what one historian has called a reconstruction of the very idea of race itself. As it did so, tumbling into some of the darkest years of American race relations, the turbulence of the expanding West reinforced the new nationalism and the reconciliation of North and South based on a resurgent white supremacy.

Following the Civil War, pressure for expansion reemerged (see Chapter 22), and in 1867 Secretary of State William H. Seward arranged a vast addition of territory to the national domain through the purchase of Alaska from Russia. Opponents ridiculed Seward's $7.2 million venture, calling Alaska "Frigidia," "the Polar Bear Garden," and "Walrussia." But Seward convinced important congressmen of Alaska's economic potential, and other lawmakers favored the dawning of friendship with Russia.

**Foreign Expansion**

Also in 1867 the United States took control of the Midway Islands, a thousand miles northwest of Hawai'i. And in 1870 President Grant tried unsuccessfully to annex the Dominican Republic. Seward and his successor, Hamilton Fish, also resolved troubling Civil War grievances against Great Britain. Through diplomacy they arranged a financial settlement of claims on Britain for damage done by the *Alabama* and other cruisers built in England and sold to the Confederacy. They recognized that sectional reconciliation in Reconstruction America would serve new ambitions for world commerce and expansion.

Meanwhile, the Supreme Court played its part in the northern retreat from Reconstruction. During the Civil War, the Court had been cautious and inactive. Reaction to the *Dred Scott* decision (1857) had been so vehement, and the Union's wartime emergency so great, that the Court had avoided interference with government actions. The justices breathed a collective sigh of relief, for example, when legal technicalities prevented them from reviewing the case of Clement Vallandigham,

**Judicial Retreat from Reconstruction**

a Democratic opponent of Lincoln's war effort who had been convicted by a military tribunal of aiding the enemy. But in 1866 a similar case, *Ex parte Milligan,* reached the Court.

Lambdin P. Milligan of Indiana had plotted to free Confederate prisoners of war and overthrow state governments. For these acts a military court sentenced Milligan, a civilian, to death. Milligan challenged the authority of the military tribunal, claiming that he had a right to a civil trial. The Supreme Court declared that military trials were illegal when civil courts were open and functioning, and its language indicated that the Court intended to reassert its authority.

In the 1870s the Court successfully renewed its challenge to Congress's actions when it narrowed the meaning and effectiveness of the Fourteenth Amendment. The *Slaughter-House* cases (1873) began in 1869, when the Louisiana legislature granted one company a monopoly on the slaughtering of livestock in New Orleans. Rival butchers in the city promptly sued. Their attorney, former Supreme Court justice John A. Campbell, argued that Louisiana had violated the rights of some of its citizens in favor of others. The Fourteenth Amendment, Campbell contended, had revolutionized the constitutional system by bringing individual rights under federal protection. Campbell thus articulated an original goal of the Republican Party: to nationalize civil rights and guard them from state interference.

But in the *Slaughter-House* decision, the Supreme Court dealt a stunning blow to the scope and vitality of the Fourteenth Amendment. Refusing to accept Campbell's argument, the Court declared state citizenship and national citizenship separate. National citizenship involved only matters such as the right to travel freely from state to state, and only such narrow rights, held the Court, were protected by the Fourteenth Amendment.

The Supreme Court also concluded that the butchers who sued had not been deprived of their rights or property in violation of the due-process clause of the amendment. Shrinking from a role as "perpetual censor upon all legislation of the States, on the civil rights of their own citizens," the Court's majority declared that the framers of the recent amendments had not intended to "destroy" the federal system, in which the states exercised "powers for domestic and local government, including the regulation of civil rights." Thus the justices severely limited the amendment's potential for securing and protecting the rights of black citizens—its original intent.

The next day the Court decided *Bradwell v. Illinois,* a case in which Myra Bradwell, a female attorney, had been denied the right to practice law in Illinois because she was a married woman, and hence not considered a free

agent. Pointing to the Fourteenth Amendment, Bradwell's attorneys contended that the state had unconstitutionally abridged her "privileges and immunities" as a citizen. The Supreme Court rejected her claim, declaring a woman's "paramount destiny . . . to fulfill the noble and benign offices of wife and mother."

In 1876 the Court weakened the Reconstruction era amendments even further by emasculating the enforcement clause of the Fourteenth Amendment and revealing deficiencies inherent in the Fifteenth Amendment. In *U.S. v. Cruikshank* the Court overruled the conviction under the 1870 Enforcement Act of Louisiana whites who had attacked a meeting of blacks and conspired to deprive them of their rights. The justices ruled that the Fourteenth Amendment did not give the federal government power to act against these whites. The duty of protecting citizens' equal rights, the Court said, "rests alone with the States." Such judicial conservatism had a profound impact down through the next century, blunting the revolutionary potential in the Civil War amendments.

As the 1876 elections approached, most political observers saw that the nation was increasingly focused on economic issues and that the North was no longer willing to pursue the goals of Reconstruction. The results of a disputed presidential election confirmed this fact. Samuel J. Tilden, the Democratic governor of New York, ran strongly in the South and needed only one more electoral vote to triumph over Rutherford B. Hayes, the Republican nominee. Nineteen electoral votes from Louisiana, South Carolina, and Florida (the only southern states not yet under Democratic rule) were disputed; both Democrats and Republicans claimed to have won in those states despite fraud committed by their opponents (see Map 16.2).

## Disputed Election of 1876 and Compromise of 1877

To resolve this unprecedented situation Congress established a fifteen-member electoral commission. Membership on the commission was to be balanced between Democrats and Republicans. Because the Republicans held the majority in Congress, they prevailed, 8 to 7, on every attempt to count the returns, with commission members voting along strict party lines. Hayes would become president if Congress accepted the commission's findings.

Congressional acceptance was not certain. Democrats controlled the House and could filibuster to block action on the vote. Many citizens worried that the nation would slip once again into civil war, as some southerners vowed, "Tilden or Fight!" The crisis was resolved when Democrats acquiesced in the election of Hayes based on a "deal" cut in a Washington hotel between Hayes's supporters and southerners who wanted federal aid to railroads,

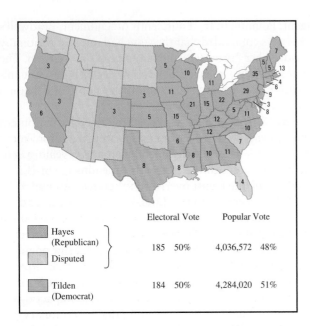

**Map 16.2    Presidential Election of 1876 and the Compromise of 1877**

In 1876 a combination of solid southern support and Democratic gains in the North gave Samuel Tilden the majority of popular votes, but Rutherford B. Hayes won the disputed election in the electoral college, after a deal satisfied Democratic wishes for an end to Reconstruction.

|  | Electoral Vote | | Popular Vote | |
|---|---|---|---|---|
| Hayes (Republican) | 185 | 50% | 4,036,572 | 48% |
| Disputed | | | | |
| Tilden (Democrat) | 184 | 50% | 4,284,020 | 51% |

internal improvements, federal patronage, and removal of troops from southern states. Northern and southern Democrats simply decided not to contest the election of a Republican who was not going to continue Reconstruction policies in the South. Thus Hayes became president, inaugurated privately inside the White House to avoid any threat of violence. Southerners relished their promises of economic aid, and Reconstruction was unmistakably over.

Southern Democrats rejoiced, but African Americans grieved over the betrayal of their hopes for equality. The Civil War had brought emancipation, and Reconstruction had guaranteed their rights under law. But events and attitudes in larger white America were foreboding. In a Fourth of July speech in Washington, D.C., in 1875, Frederick Douglass anticipated this predicament. He reflected anxiously on the American centennial to be celebrated the following year. The nation, Douglass feared, would "lift to the sky its million voices in one grand Centennial hosanna of peace and good will to all the white race . . . from gulf to lakes and from sea to sea." Douglass looked back on fifteen years of unparalleled change for his people and worried about the hold of white supremacy on America's historical memory: "If war among the whites brought peace and liberty to the blacks, what will peace among the whites bring?" Douglass's question would echo down through American political culture for decades.

## SUMMARY

Reconstruction left a contradictory record. It was an era of tragic aspirations and failures but also of unprecedented legal, political, and social change. The Union victory brought about an increase in federal power, stronger nationalism, sweeping federal intervention in the southern states, and landmark amendments to the Constitution. But northern commitment to make these changes endure had eroded, and the revolution remained unfinished. The mystic sense of promise for new lives and liberties among the freedpeople, demonstrated in that first Decoration Day in Charleston, had fallen into a new, if temporary, kind of ruin.

The North embraced emancipation, black suffrage, and constitutional alterations strengthening the central government. But it did so to defeat the rebellion and secure the peace. As the pressure of these crises declined, Americans, especially in the North, retreated from Reconstruction. The American people and the courts maintained a preference for state authority and a distrust of federal power. The ideology of free labor dictated that property should be respected and that individuals should be self-reliant. Racism endured and transformed into the even more virulent forms of Klan terror and theories of black degeneration. Concern for the human rights of African Americans was strongest when their plight

# *Legacy* FOR A PEOPLE AND A NATION

## The Lost Cause

All major wars and their aftermath compel a struggle over their memory. Sometimes losers prevail over winners in contests to shape historical memory. After the Civil War, white southerners and their northern allies constructed a "Lost Cause" tradition, a potent and racially exclusive version of the war and Reconstruction which persists in American culture today.

The Lost Cause emerged among ex-Confederates as a mourning ritual and a psychological response to the trauma of defeat. But with time it also took root in selective reinterpretations of the war's causes, in southern resistance to Reconstruction, in doctrines of white supremacy, and in a mythic, nostalgic popular culture enjoyed and promoted by northerners and southerners alike. Lost Cause advocates—from high-ranking officers to common soldiers writing reminiscences to women leading memorial associations—argued that the war had never been about slavery, that the Confederates had only lost to Yankee numbers and resources, and that the nation should reconcile by equally honoring both southern and northern sacrifice. In the industrial, urban, multi-ethnic America of the emerging twentieth century, an Old South of benevolent masters and faithful slaves, of Robert E. Lee portrayed as America's truest Christian soldier, provided a romantic, sentimentalized road to reunion. These images reverberated in the very heartbeat of Jim Crow America, and they endure in modern tastes for Civil War memorabilia, such as the epic *Gone with the Wind,* the 2003 film *Gods and Generals,* and uses of the Confederate flag to oppose civil rights and affirmative action.

From 1865 to the 1880s, this Confederate legend had been forged by wartime participants determined to vindicate the Confederacy. By the 1890s, however, Lost Cause culture emerged especially with the United Daughters of the Confederacy. Elite southern white women built monuments, lobbied congressmen, delivered lectures, ran essay contests for schoolchildren, and strove to control the content of history textbooks, all in the service of an exalted South. Above all, Lost Causers advocated a story not at all about loss, but about what one historian has called a "victory narrative." This new victory was the nation's triumph over the racial revolution and constitutional transformations of Reconstruction. In his 1881 memoir, Jefferson Davis argued that slavery "was in no wise the cause of the conflict" and that slaves had been "contented with their lot." He also declared the Lost Cause not lost: "Well may we rejoice in the regained possession of self-government. . . . This is the great victory . . . a total non-interference by the Federal government in the domestic affairs of the States."

threatened to undermine the interests of whites, and reform frequently had less appeal than moneymaking in an individualistic, industrializing society.

New challenges to American society and values began to overwhelm the aims of Reconstruction. How would the country develop its immense resources in an increasingly interconnected national economy? Could farmers, industrial workers, immigrants, and capitalists co-exist in harmony? Industrialization not only promised prosperity but also wrought increased exploitation of labor. Moreover, industry increased the nation's power and laid the foundation for an enlarged American role in international affairs. The American imagination again turned to the conquest of new frontiers.

In the wake of the Civil War, Americans faced two profound tasks—the achievement of healing and the dispensing of justice. Both had to occur, but they never developed in historical balance. Making sectional reunion compatible with black freedom and equality overwhelmed the imagination in American political culture, and the nation still faced much of this dilemma more than a century later.

## SUGGESTIONS FOR FURTHER READING

David W. Blight, *Race and Reunion: The Civil War in American Memory* (2001)

W. E. B. Du Bois, *Black Reconstruction in America* (1935)

Eric Foner, *Reconstruction: America's Unfinished Revolution, 1863–1877* (1988)

William Gillette, *Retreat from Reconstruction, 1869–1879* (1980)

Steven Hahn, *A Nation Under Our Feet: Black Political Struggles in the Rural South from Slavery to the Great Migration* (2003)

Gerald Jaynes, *Branches Without Roots: The Genesis of the Black Working Class in the American South, 1862–1882* (1986)

Michael Perman, *The Road to Redemption* (1984)

George Rable, *But There Was No Peace* (1984)

Heather Richardson, *The Death of Reconstruction* (2001)

Elliot West, "Reconstructing Race," *Western Historical Quarterly* (Spring 2003)

*For a more extensive list for further reading, go to* college.hmco.com/pic/norton8e.

# The Development of the West *1865-1900*

*I*n 1893 a young historian named Frederick Jackson Turner delivered a stunning lecture at the Columbian Exposition in Chicago. In it, Turner expounded a theory that would shape views of the American West for several generations. Titled "The Significance of the Frontier in American History," the paper argued that the existence of "free land, its continuous recession, and the advancement of American settlement westward" had created a distinctive spirit of democracy and egalitarianism. The settlement of a succession of frontier Wests from colonial times onward, in other words, explained American progress and character.

At a covered arena across the street from the Chicago world's fair, the folk character Buffalo Bill Cody staged two performances daily of an extravaganza called "The Wild West." Although Cody also dramatized the conquest of frontiers and the creation of an American identity, his perspective differed markedly from Turner's. Whereas Turner described a relatively peaceful settlement of largely empty western land, Cody portrayed violent conquest of territory occupied by savage Indians. Turner's heroes were persevering farmers who tamed the wilderness with axes and plows. Buffalo Bill's heroes were rugged scouts who braved danger and vanquished Indians with firepower and blood. Turner used images of log cabins, wagon trains, and wheat fields to argue that the frontier fashioned a new, progressive people. Cody, who employed a cast of actual Indians and soldiers (plus himself) to stage scenes of clashes between native warriors and white cavalry, depicted the West as a place of brutal aggression and heroic victory.

Turner's thesis and Cody's spectacle contained exaggerations and inaccuracies, yet both Turner and Cody were to some degree correct. The American West inspired material

◀ Thomas Moran (1837–1926) painted numerous scenes like this one of a lone Indian dwarfed by nature. Yet the West's raw bounty was luring countless white settlers even as Moran depicted the region's wilderness and immensity.

(Mist in Kanab Canyon, Utah, *Thomas Moran, 1892, oil, Smithsonian American Art Museum, Bequest of Mrs. Bessie B. Croffut*)

## CHRONOLOGY

1862 ■ Homestead Act grants free land to citizens who live on and improve the land
     ■ Morrill Land Grant Act gives states public land to sell in order to finance agricultural and industrial colleges

1864 ■ Chivington's militia massacres Black Kettle's Cheyennes at Sand Creek

1869 ■ First transcontinental railroad completed

1872 ■ Yellowstone becomes first national park

1876 ■ Lakotas and Cheyennes ambush Custer's federal troops at Little Big Horn, Montana

1877 ■ Nez Percé Indians under Young Joseph surrender to U.S. troops

1878 ■ Timber and Stone Act allows citizens to buy timberland cheaply but also enables large companies to acquire huge tracts of forest land

1879 ■ Carlisle School for Indians established in Pennsylvania

1880–81 ■ Manypenny's Our Indian Wards and Jackson's A Century of Dishonor influence public conscience about poor government treatment of Indians

1881–82 ■ Chinese Exclusion Acts prohibit Chinese immigration to the United States

1883 ■ National time zones established

1884 ■ U.S. Supreme Court first denies Indians as wards under government protection

1887 ■ Dawes Severalty Act ends communal ownership of Indian lands and grants land allotments to individual native families

1887–88 ■ Devastating winter on Plains destroys countless livestock and forces farmers into economic hardship

1890 ■ Final suppression of Plains Indians by U.S. Army at Wounded Knee
     ■ Census Bureau announces closing of the frontier
     ■ Yosemite National Park established

1892 ■ Muir helps found Sierra Club

1902 ■ Newlands Reclamation Act passed

progress, and it also witnessed the forceful domination of one group of humans over another and over the environment. Both Turner and Cody believed that by the 1890s the frontier era had come to an end. In fact, Turner's essay had been sparked by an announcement from the superintendent of the 1890 census that "at present the unsettled area [of the West] has been so broken into by isolated bodies of settlement that there can be hardly said to be a frontier line." Over time, Turner's theory was abandoned (even by Turner himself) as too simplistic, and Buffalo Bill was relegated to the gallery of rogues and showmen. Yet the depictions of both Wests persist in the romance of American history, even while they obscured the complex story of western development in the late nineteenth century.

One fact is certain. Much of the West was never empty, and its inhabitants built communities and utilized its resources in quite different ways. Indians had managed the environment and sustained their needs long before white settlers arrived on the scene. On the Plains, for example, the Pawnees planted crops in the spring, left their fields in summer to hunt buffalo, then returned for harvesting. They sometimes battled with Cheyennes and Arapahos, who wanted hunting grounds and crops for their own purposes. The technology of Plains Indians was simple. Although they sometimes splurged, feasting on buffalo, they survived by developing and using natural resources in limited ways. In what now is the American Southwest, including southern California, natives shared the land and sometimes integrated with Hispanic people, who were descendants of Spanish colonists. Most Hispanics farmed small plots or worked for large landowners who had only limited access to outside markets.

As white immigrants built new communities in the West in the late nineteenth century, however, they exploited the environment for profit far more extensively than did Indians. They excavated deep into the earth to remove minerals, felled forests for timber to construct homes, pierced the countryside with railroads to carry goods and link markets, and dammed rivers and plowed soil with machines to grow crops. Their goal was not mere survival; it included buying and selling in regional, national, and international markets. As they transformed the landscape, the triumph of their market economies transformed the nation.

The West, which by 1870 referred to the expanse between the Mississippi River and the Pacific Ocean, actually consisted of several regions and a variety of economic potential. Abundant rainfall along the northern Pacific coast fed huge forests. Farther south into California, woodlands and grasslands provided fertile valleys suitable for vegetable fields and orange groves. Eastward, from the Cascades and the Sierra Nevada to the Rocky Mountains, is a series of deserts and plateaus known as the Basin and Range province, where gold, silver, and other minerals lay buried. East of the Rockies, the Great Plains divided into a semiarid western side of few trees and tough buffalo grass and an eastern sector of ample rainfall and tall grasses which could support grain crops and livestock.

Much of the West had long been the scene of migrations. Before contact with whites, Indian peoples had moved around and through the region. As they searched for food and shelter, they warred, traded, and negotiated with one another. In parts of the Southwest, Hispanics had moved north and south between Mexican and American territory, and they built towns, farms, and ranches. After the Civil War, white Americans flooded into the West, overwhelming the native and Hispanic peoples. Between 1870 and 1890, the white population living in the region swelled from 7 million to nearly 17 million.

The West's abundance of exploitable land and raw materials filled white Americans with faith that anyone eager and persistent enough could succeed. But this confidence rested on a belief that white people were somehow superior, and individual advantage often asserted itself at the expense of people of color as well as the environment. Although eventually some people came to realize the benefits of protecting the environment, Americans rarely thought about conserving resources because there always seemed to be more territory to develop and bring into the market economy.

By 1890 communities of farms, ranches, mines, towns, and cities could be found in almost every corner of the present-day continental United States, but vast stretches of land remained unsettled. Although it may have been of symbolic importance to Frederick Jackson Turner, the fading of the frontier had little direct impact on people's behavior. Pioneers who failed in one locale rarely perished; they moved on and tried again elsewhere. Although life in the West could be challenging, a surplus of seemingly uninhabited land gave Americans a feeling that they would always have a second chance. It was this belief in an infinity of second chances, more than Turner's theory of frontier democracy or Cody's reenactments of heroic battles, that left a deep imprint on the American character.

- How did the interaction between people and the environment shape the physical landscape of the West and the lives of the region's inhabitants?
- How did the U.S. government's relations with Native Americans change over time throughout the late nineteenth century?
- Describe the societal and technological changes that revolutionized the lives of farmers and ranchers on the Great Plains.

## THE ECONOMIC ACTIVITIES OF NATIVE PEOPLES

Native Americans settled the West long before other Americans migrated there. Neither passive nor powerless in the face of nature, Indians had been shaping their environment—for better and for worse—for centuries. Nevertheless, almost all native economic systems weakened in the late nineteenth century. Several factors explain why and how these declines happened.

Western Indian communities varied. Some natives inhabited permanent settlements; others lived in a series of temporary camps. Seldom completely isolated, most Indians were

**Subsistence Cultures**

both participants and recipients in a large-scale flow of goods, culture, language, and disease carried by bands that migrated from one region to another. Regardless of their type of community, all Indians based their economy to differing degrees on four activities: crop growing; livestock raising; hunting, fishing, and gathering; and trading and raiding. Corn was the most common crop; sheep and horses, acquired from Spanish colonizers and from other Indians, were the livestock; and buffalo (American bison) were the primary prey of hunts. Indians raided one another for food, tools, hides, and horses, which in turn they used in trading with other Indians and with whites. They also attacked to avenge wrongs and to drive out competitors from hunting grounds. To achieve their

▲ Using buffalo hides to fashion garments, Indians often exhibited artistic skills in decorating their apparel. This Ute Indian hide dress shows symbolic as well as aesthetic representations.
*(Denver Art Museum)*

standards of living, Indians tried to balance their economic systems. When a buffalo hunt failed, they subsisted on crops. When crops failed, they could still hunt buffalo and steal food and horses in a raid or trade livestock and furs for necessities.

For Indians on the Great Plains, whether nomads, such as the Lakotas (or "Sioux"), or village dwellers, such as the Pawnees, everyday life focused on the buffalo. They cooked and preserved buffalo meat; fashioned hides into clothing, shoes, and blankets; used sinew for thread and bowstrings; and carved tools from bones and horns. Buffalo were so valuable that the Pawnees and Lakotas often fought over access to herds. Plains Indians also depended on horses, which they used for transportation and hunting, and as symbols of wealth. To provide food for their herds, Plains Indians altered the environment by periodi-

cally setting fire to tall-grass prairies. The fires burned away dead plants, facilitating the growth of new grass in the spring so that horses could feed all summer.

In the Southwest, Indians were herders and placed great value on sheep, goats, and horses. Old Man Hat, a Navajo, explained, "The herd is money. . . . You know that you have some good clothing; the sheep gave you that. And you've just eaten different kinds of food; the sheep gave that food to you. Everything comes from the sheep." He was not speaking of money in a business sense, though. To Navajos, the herds provided status and security. Like many Indians, the Navajos emphasized generosity and distrusted private property and wealth. Within the family, sharing was expected; outside the family, gifts and reciprocity governed personal relations. Southwestern Indians, too, altered the environment, building elaborate irrigation systems to maximize use of scarce water supplies.

What buffalo were to Plains Indians and sheep were to southwestern Indians, salmon were to Indians of the Northwest. Before the mid-nineteenth century, the Columbia River and its tributaries supported the densest population of native peoples in North America, all of whom fished the river for salmon in the summer and stored dried fish for the winter. To harvest fish, the Clatsops, Klamath, and S'Klallams developed technologies of stream diversion, platform construction over the water, and special baskets. Like natives of other regions, many of these Indians traded for horses, buffalo robes, beads, cloth, and knives.

On the Plains and in parts of the Southwest, this native world began to dissolve after 1850, when white migrants entered and competed with Indians for access to and control over natural resources. Perceiving buffalo and Indians as hindrances to their ambitions, whites endeavored to eliminate both. The U.S. Army refused to enforce treaties that reserved hunting grounds for exclusive Indian use, so railroads sponsored buffalo hunts in which eastern sportsmen shot at the bulky targets from slow-moving trains. Some hunters collected from $1 to $3 from tanneries for hides that were sent east for use mainly as belts to drive industrial machinery; others did not even stop to pick up their kill.

Unbeknownst to both Indians and whites, however, a complex combination of circumstances had already doomed the buffalo before the slaughter of the late 1800s. Natives themselves were contributing to the depletion of the herds by increasing their kills, especially to trade hides with whites and other Indians. Also, a period of generally dry years in the 1840s and 1850s had forced Indians to

**Slaughter of Buffalo**

◀ Horses, sometimes numbering more than one hundred, and women and children, usually twenty or thirty, were a liability as well as a help to a Plains Indian camp. The horses competed with buffalo for valuable pasturage, and the women and children made camps vulnerable when white soldiers attacked.

*(Denver Public Library, Western History Division)*

set up camps in river basins, where they competed with buffalo for space and water. As a result, the buffalo were pushed out of nourishing grazing territory and faced threats of starvation. When whites arrived on the Plains, they, too, sought to settle in the same river basin areas, thereby further forcing buffalo away from nutritious grasslands. At the same time, lethal animal diseases, such as anthrax and brucellosis, brought in by white-owned livestock, decimated buffalo already weakened by malnutrition and drought. Increased numbers of horses, oxen, and sheep, owned by white newcomers as well as by some Indians, also upset the buffalo's grazing patterns by devouring grasses that they depended on at certain times of the year. In sum, human and environmental shocks created vulnerability among the buffalo, to which mass killing only struck the final blow. By the 1880s only a few hundred of the 25 million buffalo estimated on the Plains in 1820 remained.

In the Northwest, the basic wild source of Indian food supply, salmon, suffered a fate similar to that of the buffalo, but for different reasons.

**Decline of Salmon**

White commercial fishermen and canneries moved into the Columbia and Willamette River valleys during the 1860s and 1870s, and they harvested increasing numbers of salmon running upriver to spawn before laying their eggs, so the fish supply was not being replenished. By the 1880s they had greatly diminished the salmon runs on the Columbia, and by the early 1900s, the construction of dams on the river and its tributaries further impeded the salmon's ability to reproduce. The U.S. government protected Indian fishing rights, but not the supply of fish on the river. Hatcheries helped restore some of this supply, but dams built to provide power, combined with overfishing and pollution, diminished salmon stocks.

## THE TRANSFORMATION OF NATIVE CULTURES

Buffalo slaughter and salmon reduction undermined Indian subsistence, but a unique mix of human demography contributed as well. For most of the nineteenth century, the white population that migrated into western lands inhabited by Indians was overwhelmingly young and male. In 1870 white men outnumbered white women by three to two in California, two to one in Colorado, and two to one in Dakota Territory. By 1900, preponderances of men remained throughout these places. Most of these males were unmarried and in their twenties and thirties, the stage of life when they were most prone to violent behavior. In other words, the whites with whom Indians were most likely to come into contact first were explorers, traders, trappers, soldiers, prospectors, and cowboys—almost all of whom possessed guns and had few qualms about using their weapons against animals and humans who got in their way.

Moreover, these men subscribed to prevailing attitudes that Indians were primitive, lazy, devious, and cruel.

**Western Men**

Such contempt made exploiting and killing natives all the easier, and whites often justified violence against Indians by claiming preemptive defense of threats to life and property. When Indians raided white settlements, they sometimes mutilated bodies, burned buildings, and kidnapped women, acts that were embellished in campfire stories, pamphlets, and popular fiction—all of which reinforced images of Indians as savages. Among the bachelor society of saloons and cabins, men boasted of their exploits in Indian fighting and showed off trophies of scalps and other body parts taken from victims.

Indian warriors, too, were young, armed, and prone to violence. Valuing bravery and vengeance, they boasted of fighting white interlopers. But Indian communities contrasted with those of whites in that they contained excesses of women and children, making native bands less mobile and therefore vulnerable to attack. They also were susceptible to the bad habits of bachelor white society. Indians copied white behavior of bingeing on cheap whiskey and indulging in prostitution. The syphilis and gonorrhea that Indian men contracted from Indian women infected by white men killed many and reduced natives' ability to reproduce, a consequence that their populations, already declining from smallpox and other diseases spread by whites, could not afford. Thus the age and gender structure of the white frontier population, combined with attitudes of racial contempt, created a further threat to Indian existence in the West.

Government policy reinforced efforts to remove Indians from the path of white ambitions. North American natives were organized not so much into tribes, as whites believed, as into hundreds of bands and confederacies in the Plains and into villages in the Southwest and Northwest. Some two hundred languages and dialects separated these groups, making it difficult for Indians to unite against white invaders. Although a language group could be defined as a tribe, separate bands and clans within each language group had their own leaders, and seldom did a tribal chief hold widespread power. Moreover, bands often spent more time quarreling among themselves than with white settlers.

**Lack of Native Unity**

Nevertheless, the U.S. government needed some way of categorizing Indians so as to fashion a policy toward them. It did so by imputing more meaning to tribal organization than was warranted. After the Treaty of Greenville in 1795, American officials considered Indian tribes to be separate nations with which they could make treaties that ensured peace and defined boundaries between Indian and white lands. But the government did not understand that a chief or chiefs

**Territorial Treaties**

who agreed to a treaty did not speak for all members of a band and that the group would not necessarily abide by an agreement. Moreover, white settlers seldom accepted treaties as guarantees of Indians' future land rights. In the Northwest, whites considered treaties protecting Indians' fishing rights on the Columbia River to be nuisances and ousted Indians from the best locations so that they could use mechanical devices that harvested thousands of fish a day. On the Plains, whites assumed that they could settle wherever they wished, and they rarely hesitated to commandeer choice farmland along river basins. As white migrants pressed into Indian territories, treaties made one week were violated the next.

Prior to the 1880s, the federal government tried to force western Indians onto reservations, where, it was thought, they could be "civilized." Reservations usually consisted of those areas of a group's previous territory that were least desirable to whites. When assigning Indians to such parcels, the government promised protection from white encroachment and agreed to provide food, clothing, and other necessities.

**Reservation Policy**

The reservation policy helped make way for the market economy. In the early years of contact in the West, trade had benefited both Indians and whites and had taken place on a nearly equal footing, much as it had between eastern Indians and whites in the years before the American Revolution. Indians acquired clothing, guns, and horses from whites in return for furs, jewelry, and, sometimes, military assistance against other Indians. In the West, however, whites' needs and economic power grew disproportionate to Indians' needs and power. Indians became more dependent, and whites increasingly dictated what was to be traded and on what terms. For example, white traders persuaded Navajo weavers in the Southwest to produce heavy rugs suitable for eastern customers and to adopt new designs and colors to boost sales. Meanwhile, Navajos raised fewer crops and were forced to buy food because the market economy undermined their subsistence agriculture. Soon they were selling land and labor to whites as well, and their dependency made it easier to force them onto reservations.

Reservation policy had degrading consequences. First, Indians had no say over their own affairs on reservations. Supreme Court decisions in 1884 and 1886 defined them as wards (falling, like helpless children, under government protection) and denied them the right to become U.S. citizens. Thus they were unprotected by the Fourteenth and Fifteenth Amendments, which had extended to African Americans the privileges and legal protections of citizenship. Second, pressure from white farmers, miners, and herders who continually sought Indian lands made it difficult for the government to preserve reservations intact. Third, the government ignored native history, even combining on the same reservation Indian bands that habitually had waged war against each other. Rather than serving as civilizing communities, reservations weakened every aspect of Indian life, except the resolve to survive.

Not all Indians succumbed to market forces and reservation restrictions. Apache tribes in the Southwest

### Native Resistance

long had raided settlers and migrants passing through their lands and continued to battle whites even after most of their people had been forced onto reservations. Their raiding ended only after the last of their leaders, the Chiricahua insurgent Geronimo, was captured in 1886. Pawnees in the Midwest resisted the disadvantageous deals that white traders tried to impose on them. In the Northwest, Nez Percé Indians tried to prevent being forced onto a reservation by fleeing to Canada in 1877. They successfully eluded U.S. troops and their Crow and Cheyenne scouts over 1,800 miles of rugged terrain, but when they reached Montana, their leader, Young Joseph, decided that they could not succeed, and he ended the flight. Sent to a reservation, Joseph repeatedly petitioned the government for a return of his ancestral lands, but his appeals went unheeded.

As they had done earlier in the East, whites responded to western Indian defiance with military aggression. In

### Indian Wars

1860, for example, Navajos, reacting to U.S. military pressure, carried out a destructive raid on Fort Defiance in Arizona Territory. In reprisal, the army eventually attacked and starved the Navajo into submission, destroying their fields, houses, and livestock, and in 1863–1864 forced them on a "Long Walk" from their homelands to a reservation at Bosque Redondo in New Mexico. Also in 1864, in order to eliminate Indians who blocked white ambitions in the Sand Creek region of Colorado, a militia led by Methodist minister John Chivington attacked a Cheyenne band under Black Kettle, killing almost every Indian. In 1879, 4,000 U.S. soldiers forced a surrender from Utes who already had given up most of their ancestral territory in western Colorado but were resisting further concessions.

▲ Plains Indians did not write books or letters as whites did, but they did tell stories and spread news through art. They painted scenes in notebooks and on hides, like this one which depicts the Indians' annihilation of General George A. Custer's soldiers at Little Big Horn in 1876.

*(Smithsonian Institution, Western History Division)*

The most publicized of Indian battles occurred in June 1876, when 2,500 Lakotas and Cheyennes led by Chiefs Rain-in-the-Face, Sitting Bull, and Crazy Horse surrounded and annihilated 256 government troops led by the rash Colonel George A. Custer near the Little Big Horn River in southern Montana. Although Indians consistently demonstrated military skill in such battles, shortages of supplies and relentless pursuit by U.S. soldiers, including all–African American units of Union Army veterans called Buffalo Soldiers (so named by the Cheyennes and Comanches they fought), eventually overwhelmed armed Indian resistance. Native Americans were not so much conquered in battle as they were harassed and starved into submission.

In the 1870s and 1880s, government officials and reformers sought more purposely than in the past to "civilize" and "uplift" natives through landholding and education. This meant changing their identities and outlawing customs deemed to be "savage and barbarous." In this regard, the United States copied imperialist policies of other nations, such as the French, who banned native religious ceremonies in their Pacific island colonies, and the British, who jailed African religious leaders. The American government determined to persuade Indians to abandon their traditional cultures and adopt American values of ambition, thrift, and materialism.

**Reform of Indian Policy**

At the same time, other groups argued for sympathetic—and sometimes patronizing—treatment. Reform treatises, such as George Manypenny's *Our Indian Wards* (1880) and Helen Hunt Jackson's *A Century of Dishonor* (1881), and unfavorable comparison with Canada's management of Indian affairs aroused the American conscience. Canada had granted native peoples the rights of British subjects and proceeded more slowly than the United States in efforts to acculturate Indians. A high rate of intermarriage between Indians and Canadian whites also promoted smoother relations.

In the United States, the two most active Indian reform organizations were the Women's National Indian Association (WNIA) and the Indian Rights Association (IRA). The WNIA, composed mainly of white women who sought to use domestic skills to help people in need, urged gradual assimilation of Indians. The IRA, which was more influential but numbered few Native Americans among its members, advocated citizenship and landholding by individual Indians. Most reformers believed Indians were culturally inferior to whites and assumed Indians could succeed economically only if they embraced middle-class values of diligence and education.

Reformers particularly deplored Indians' sexual division of labor. Women seemed to do all the work—tending crops, raising children, cooking, curing hides, making tools and clothes—while being servile to men, who hunted but were otherwise idle. Ignoring the fact that white men sometimes mistreated white women, groups such as the WNIA and IRA wanted Indian men to bear more responsibilities, to treat Indian women more respectfully, and to resemble male heads of white middle-class households. But when Indian men and women adopted the model of white society, in which women were supposed to be submissive and private, Indian women lost much of the economic independence and power over daily life that they once had.

**Zitkala-Sa**

Some exceptional Indians managed to use white-controlled education to their advantage. Zitkala-Sa (Red Bird) was a Yankton Sioux born on the Pine Ridge reservation in South Dakota in 1876. At age twelve, she was sent to a Quaker boarding school in Indiana and later attended Earlham College and the Boston Conservatory of Music. She became an accomplished orator and violinist, but her major contribution was her writing on behalf of her people's needs and the preservation of their cultures. In 1901 Zitkala-Sa published a work of fiction titled *Old Indian Legends,* in which she translated Sioux oral tradition into stories. She wrote other pieces for *Harper's* and *Atlantic Monthly,* and served in various capacities on the Standing Rock and Ute reservations. Zitkala-Sa married a Sioux who had taken the name Ray Bonnin and became known as Gertrude Bonnin. Subsequently, she was elected the first full-blooded Indian secretary of the Society of American Indians (see page 606) and served as editor of *American Indian Magazine,* all the while advocating for Indian rights and cultural respect.

**Dawes Severalty Act**

In 1887 Congress reversed its reservation policy and passed the Dawes Severalty Act. The act, supported by reformers, authorized dissolution of community-owned Indian property and granted land allotments to individual Indian families. The government held that land in trust for twenty-five years, so families could not sell their allotments. The law also awarded citizenship to all who accepted allotments (an act of Congress in 1906 delayed citizenship for those Indians who had not yet taken their allotment). It also entitled the government to sell unallocated land to whites.

Indian policy, as implemented by the Interior Department, now took on two main features, both of which aimed at assimilating Indians into white American culture.

▲ White reformers believed children at Indian boarding schools needed to adopt "civilized" dress as necessary to their education. Thus the eleven Chirachua Apache girls and boys who were wearing native dress when they reached the Carlisle (Pennsylvania) School in November 1883 (top) had their hair cut and wore uniforms and dresses for the (bottom) photograph taken after their supposed transformation four months later.

*(Both photos: Cumberland County Historical Society, Carlisle, PA)*

First and foremost, as required by the Dawes Act, the government distributed reservation land to individual families in the belief that the American institution of private property would create productive citizens and integrate Indians into the larger society. As one official stated, the goal was to "weaken and destroy [Indians'] tribal relations and individualize them by giving each a separate home and having them subsist by industry." Second, officials believed that Indians would abandon their "barbaric" habits more quickly if their children were educated in boarding schools away from the reservations.

The Dawes Act reflected a Euro-American and Christian world-view, an earnest but narrow belief that a society of families headed by men was the most desired model.

Government agents and reformers were joined by educators who viewed schools as tools to create a patriotic, industrious citizenry. Using the model of Hampton Institute, founded in Virginia in 1869 for the education of newly freed slaves, educators helped establish the Carlisle School in Pennsylvania in 1879, which served as the flagship of the government's Indian school system. In keeping with European American custom, the boarding schools imposed white-defined sex roles: boys were taught farming and carpentry, and girls learned sewing, cleaning, and cooking.

In 1890 the government made one last show of force. With active resistance having been suppressed, some Lakotas and other groups turned to the religion of the Ghost Dance as a spiritual means of preserving native culture. Inspired by a Paiute prophet named Wovoka, the Ghost Dance consisted of movement in a circle until the dancers reached a trancelike state and envisioned dead ancestors. Some dancers believed these ancestral visitors heralded a day when buffalo would return to the Plains and all elements of white civilization, including guns and whiskey, would be buried. The Ghost Dance expressed this messianic vision in a ritual involving several days of dancing and meditation.

**Ghost Dance**

Ghost Dancers forswore violence but appeared threatening when they donned sacred shirts that they believed would repel the white man's bullets. As the religion spread, government agents became alarmed about the possibility of renewed Indian uprisings. Charging that the cult was anti-Christian, they began arresting Ghost Dancers. Late in 1890, the government sent the Seventh Cavalry, Custer's old regiment, to detain Lakotas moving toward Pine Ridge, South Dakota. Although the Indians were starving and seeking shelter, the army assumed they were armed for revolt. Overtaking the band at a creek called Wounded Knee, the troops massacred an estimated three hundred men, women, and children in the snow.

The Indian wars and the Dawes Act effectively accomplished what whites wanted and Indians feared: it reduced native control over land. Eager speculators induced Indians to sell their newly acquired property, in spite of federal safeguards against such practices. Between 1887 and the 1930s, Indian landholdings dwindled from 138 million acres to 52 million. Land-grabbing whites were particularly cruel to the Ojibwas of the northern plains. In 1906 Senator Moses E. Clapp of Minnesota attached to an Indian appropriations bill a rider declaring that mixed-blood adults on the White Earth reservation were "competent" (meaning educated in white ways)

**The Losing of the West**

enough to sell their land without having to observe the twenty-five-year waiting period stipulated in the Dawes Act. When the bill became law, speculators duped many Ojibwas into signing away their land in return for counterfeit money and worthless merchandise. The Ojibwas lost more than half their original holdings, and economic ruin overtook them.

The government's policy had other injurious effects on Indians' ways of life. The boarding-school program enrolled thousands of children and tried to teach them that their inherited customs were inferior, but most returned to their families demoralized rather than ready to assimilate into white society. Polingaysi Qoyawayma, a Hopi woman forced to take the Christian name Elizabeth Q. White, recalled after four years spent at the Sherman Institute in Riverside, California, "As a Hopi, I was misunderstood by the white man; as a convert of the missionaries, I was looked upon with suspicion by the Hopi people."

Ultimately, political and ecological crises overwhelmed most western Indian groups. White violence and military superiority alone did not defeat them. Their economic systems had started to break down before the military campaigns occurred. Buffalo extinction, enemy raids, and disease, as well as force, combined to hobble subsistence culture to the point where Native Americans had no alternative but to yield their lands to market-oriented whites. Believing their culture to be superior, whites determined to transform Indians into successful farmers by teaching them the value of private property, educating them in American ideals, and eradicating their "backward" languages, lifestyles, and religions. Although Indians tried to retain their culture by both adapting to the various demands they faced, by the end of the century they had lost control of the land and were under increasing pressure to shed their group identity. The West was won at their expense, and to this day they remain casualties of an aggressive age.

## THE EXTRACTION OF NATURAL RESOURCES

In contrast to Indians, who used natural resources to meet subsistence needs and small-scale trading, most whites who migrated to the West and the Great Plains were driven by the desire for material success. To their eyes, the vast stretches of territory lay as untapped sources of wealth that could bring about a better life (see Map 17.1). Extraction of these resources advanced settlement and created new markets at home and abroad; it also fueled revolutions in transportation, agriculture, and industry that swept across the United States in the late nineteenth century.

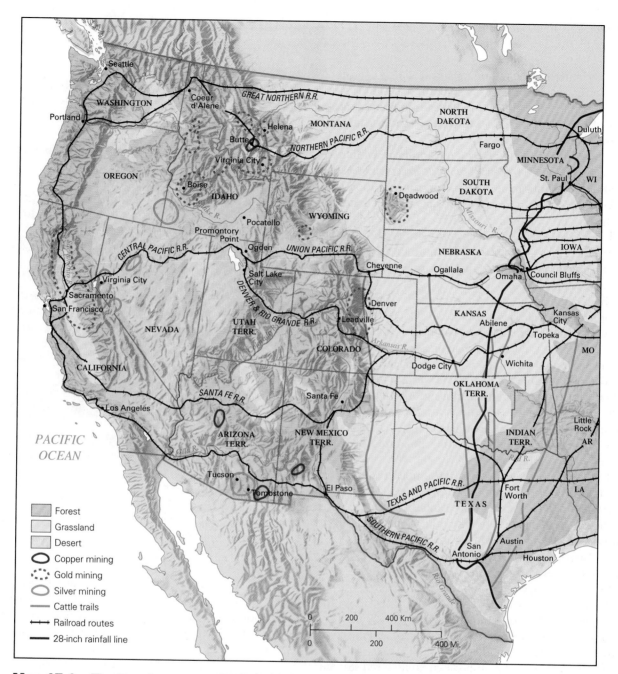

**Map 17.1** **The Development and Natural Resources of the West**

By 1890, mining, lumbering, and cattle ranching had penetrated many areas west of the Mississippi River, and railroad construction had linked together the western economy. These activities, along with the spread of mechanized agriculture, altered both the economy and the people who were involved in them.

This same extraction of nature's wealth also gave rise to wasteful interaction with the environment and fed habits of racial and sexual oppression.

In the mid-1800s, eager prospectors began to comb western forests and mountains for gold, silver, copper, and

## Mining and Lumbering

other minerals. The mining frontier advanced rapidly, drawing thousands of people to Nevada, Idaho, Montana, Utah, and Colorado. California, where a gold rush helped populate a thriving state by 1850, furnished many of the miners, who traveled to nearby states in search of riches. Others seeking mineral riches followed traditional routes, moving from the East and Midwest to western mining regions.

Prospectors tended to be restless optimists, willing to climb mountains and trek across deserts in search of a telltale glint of precious metal. They shot game for food and financed their explorations by convincing merchants to advance credit for equipment in return for a share of the as-yet-undiscovered lode. Unlucky prospectors whose credit ran out took jobs and saved up for another search.

Digging for and transporting minerals was extremely expensive, so prospectors who did discover veins of metal seldom mined them. Instead, they sold their claims to large mining syndicates, such as the Anaconda Copper Company. Financed by eastern capital, these companies brought in engineers, heavy machinery, railroad lines, and work crews, and helped boost populations in cities such as El Paso and Tucson. In doing so, they made western mining corporate just like eastern manufacturing. Although discoveries of gold and silver first drew attention to the West and its resources, mining companies usually exploited less romantic but equally lucrative bonanzas of lead, zinc, tin, quartz, and copper.

Unlike mining, cutting trees for lumber to satisfy the demand for construction and heating materials required vast tracts of forest land to be profitable. Because tree supplies in the upper Midwest and South had been depleted—aided by such inventions as bandsaws and feeding machines, which quickened the pace of timber cutting—lumber corporations moved into the forests of the Northwest. They often grabbed millions of acres under the Timber and Stone Act, passed by Congress in 1878 to stimulate settlement in California, Nevada, Oregon, and Washington. It allowed private citizens to buy, at a low price, 160-acre plots "unfit for cultivation" and "valuable chiefly for timber." Lumber companies hired seamen from waterfront boarding houses to register claims to timberland and then transfer those claims to the companies. By 1900 private citizens had bought over 3.5 million acres, but most of that land belonged to corporations.

While mining corporations were excavating western mineral deposits and lumber corporations were cutting down Northwest timberlands, oil companies were beginning to drill wells in the Southwest. In 1900 most of the nation's petroleum still came from the Appalachians and the Midwest, but rich oil reserves had been discovered in southern California and eastern Texas, creating not only new wealth but also boosting boom cities, such as Los

▲ By the 1880s, large-scale operations had replaced solitary prospectors in the extraction of minerals from western territories. Here, powerful sprays of water are being used to wash silver from a deposit in Alma, Colorado. *(Colorado Historical Society)*

Angeles and Houston. Although oil and kerosene were still used mostly for lubrication and lighting, oil discovered in the Southwest later became a vital new source of fuel.

As the West developed, it became a rich multiracial society, including not only Native Americans and native-born white migrants but also Mexicans, African Americans, and Asians, all involved in a process of community building. A crescent of territory, a borderland stretching from western Texas through New Mexico and Arizona to northern California, supported Mexicano ranchers and sheepherders, descendants of the Spanish who had originally claimed the land. In New Mexico, Spaniards mixed with Indians to form a mestizo population of small farmers and ranchers. All along the Southwest frontier, Mexican immigrants moved into American territory to find work. Some returned to Mexico seasonally; others stayed.

**Complex Communities**

Although the Treaty of Guadalupe Hidalgo (1848) had guaranteed property rights to Hispanics, "Anglo" (the Mexican name for a white American) miners, speculators, and railroads used fraud and other means to steal much of Hispanic landholdings. As a result, many Mexicanos moved to cities such as San Antonio and Tucson, and became wage laborers.

Before the Chinese Exclusion Act of 1882 prohibited the immigration of Chinese laborers, some 200,000 Chinese—mostly young, single males—came to the United States and built communities in California, Oregon, and Washington. Many came with five-year contracts to work on railroad construction, then return home, presumably with resources for a better life. They also worked in the fields. By the 1870s, Chinese composed half of California's agricultural work force. The state's farms and citrus groves demanded a huge migrant work force, and Chinese laborers moved from one ripening crop to another, working as pickers and packers. In cities such as San Francisco, they labored in textile and cigar factories, and lived in large boarding houses. Few married because Chinese women were scarce.

Like Chinese and Mexicans, Japanese and European immigrants moved from place to place as they worked in mining and agricultural communities. The region consequently developed its own migrant economy, with workers shifting communities within a large geographical area as they took short-term jobs in mining, farming, and railroad construction.

African Americans tended to be more settled, many of them "exodusters" who built all-black western towns. Nicodemus, Kansas, for example, was founded in 1877 by black migrants from Lexington, Kentucky, and grew to 600 residents within two years. Early experiences were challenging, but eventually the town developed newspapers, shops, churches, a hotel, and a bank. When attempts to obtain railroad connections failed, however, the town declined, as many of its businesses moved across the Solomon River to the town of Bogue, where a Union Pacific Railroad camp was located.

The major exodus occurred in 1879, when some 6,000 blacks, many of them former slaves, moved from the South to Kansas, aided by the Kansas Freedmen's Relief Association. Other migrants, encouraged by newspaper editors and land speculators, went to Oklahoma Territory. In the 1890s and early 1900s, African American settlers founded thirty-two all-black communities in Oklahoma, and the territory boasted several successful black farmers.

Although unmarried men numerically dominated the western natural-resource frontier, many communities

## Western Women

contained populations of white women who had come for the same reason as men: to make their fortune. But on the mining frontier as elsewhere, women's independence was limited; they usually accompanied a husband or father and seldom prospected themselves. Even so, many women used their labor as a resource and earned money by cooking and laundering, and in some cases providing sexual services for the miners in houses of prostitution. In the Northwest, they worked in canneries, cleaning and salting the fish that their husbands caught. Mexicano women took jobs in cities as laundresses and seamstresses.

A number of white women helped to bolster family and community life as members of the home mission movement. Protestant missions had long sponsored benevolent activities abroad, such as in China, and had aided the settlement of Oregon in the 1830s and 1840s. But in the mid-nineteenth century, a number of women broke away from male-dominated missionary organizations. Using the slogan "Woman's work for women," they sought to help women wherever polygamy and female infanticide existed. In the West, they exerted moral authority by establishing missionary societies and aiding women—unmarried mothers, Mormons, Indians, and Chinese—who they believed had fallen prey to men or who had not yet accepted the principles of Christian virtue.

To control labor and social relations within this complex population, white settlers made race an important distinguishing characteristic. They usually classified people into five races: Caucasians (themselves), Indians, Mexicans (both Mexican Americans, who had originally inhabited western lands, and Mexican immigrants), "Mongolians" (a term applied to Chinese), and "Negroes." In applying these categories, whites imposed racial distinctions on people who, with the possible exception of African Americans, had never before considered themselves to be a "race." Whites using these categories ascribed demeaning characteristics to all others, judging them to be permanently inferior. In 1878, for example, a federal judge in California ruled that Chinese could not become U.S. citizens because they were not "white persons."

Racial minorities in western communities occupied the bottom half of a two-tiered labor system. Whites dominated the top tier of managerial and skilled labor positions, while Irish, Chinese, Mexican, and African American laborers held unskilled positions. All non-Anglo groups, in addition to the Irish, encountered prejudice,

## Significance of Race

▲ Born in China, Polly Bemis, pictured here, came to America when her parents sold her as a slave. An Idaho saloonkeeper bought her, and she later married a man named Charlie Bemis, who won her in a card game. Her life story was common among the few Chinese women who immigrated to the United States in the 1860s and 1870s (most Chinese immigrants were men). Unlike many Chinese, however, she lived peacefully after her marriage until her death in 1933.

*(Idaho Historical Society Library and Archives)*

especially as dominant whites tried to reserve for themselves whatever riches the West might yield. Anti-Chinese violence erupted during hard times. When the Union Pacific Railroad tried to replace white workers with lower-waged Chinese in Rock Springs, Wyoming, in 1885, whites invaded and burned down the Chinese part of town, killing twenty-eight. Mexicans, many of whom had been the original owners of the land in California and elsewhere, saw their property claims ignored or stolen by white miners and farmers.

The multiracial quality of western communities, however, also included a cross-racial dimension. Because so many white male migrants were single, intermarriage with Mexican and Indian women was common. Such intermarriage was acceptable for white men, but not for white women, especially where Asian immigrants were involved. Most miscegenation laws passed by western legislatures were intended to prevent Chinese and Japanese men from marrying white women.

As whites were wresting control of the land from the Indian and Mexican inhabitants of the West, questions

## Conservation Movement

arose over control of the nation's animal, mineral, and timber resources. Much of the remaining undeveloped territory west of the Mississippi was in the public domain, and some people believed that the federal government, as its owner, should limit its exploitation. Others, however, believed that their own and the nation's prosperity depended on unlimited use of the land.

Questions about natural resources caught Americans between a desire for progress and a fear of spoiling nature. After the Civil War, people eager to protect the natural landscape began to organize a conservation movement. Sports hunters, concerned about loss of wildlife, opposed market hunting and lobbied state legislatures to pass hunting regulations. Artists and tourists in 1864 persuaded Congress to preserve the beautiful Yosemite Valley by granting it to the state of California, which reserved it for public use. Then, in 1872, Congress designated the Yellowstone River region in Wyoming as the first national park. And in 1891 conservationists, led by naturalist John Muir, pressured Congress to authorize President Benjamin Harrison to create forest reserves—public lands protected from private-interest cutting.

Such policies met with strong objections from lumber companies, lumber dealers, railroads, and householders accustomed to cutting timber freely for fuel and building material. Despite Muir's activism and efforts by the Sierra Club (which Muir helped found in 1892) and by such corporations as the Southern Pacific Railroad, which supported rational resource development, opposition was loudest in the West, where people remained eager to take advantage of nature's bounty. Ironically, however, by prohibiting trespass in areas such as Yosemite and Yellowstone, conservation policy deprived Indians and white settlers of the wildlife, water, and firewood that they had previously taken from federal lands.

## Admission of New States

Development of mining and forest regions, as well as of farms and cities, brought western territories to the economic and population threshold of statehood (see Map 17.2). In 1889 Republicans seeking to solidify control of Congress passed an omnibus bill granting statehood to North Dakota, South Dakota, Washington, and Montana. Wyoming and Idaho, both of which allowed women to vote, were admitted the following year. Congress denied statehood to Utah until 1896, wanting assurances from the Mormons, who constituted a majority of the territory's population and controlled its government, that they would give up polygamy.

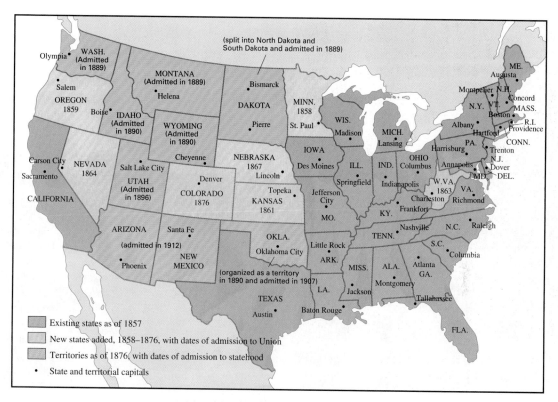

**Map 17.2    The United States, 1876–1912**

A wave of admissions between 1889 and 1912 brought remaining territories to statehood and marked the final creation of new states until Alaska and Hawai'i were admitted in the 1950s.

Western states' varied communities spiced American folk culture and fostered a "go-getter" optimism that distinguished the American spirit. The lawlessness and hedonism of places such as Deadwood, in Dakota Territory, and Tombstone, in Arizona Territory, gave their region notoriety and romance. Legends grew up almost immediately about characters whose lives both typified and magnified the western experience, and promoters such as Buffalo Bill enhanced the appeal of western folklore.

Arizona's mining towns, with their free-flowing cash and loose law enforcement, attracted gamblers, thieves, and opportunists whose names came to stand for the Wild West. Near Tombstone, the infamous Clanton family and their partner John Ringgold (known as Johnny Ringo) engaged in smuggling and cattle rustling. Inside the town, the Earp brothers—Wyatt, Jim, Morgan, Virgil, and Warren—and their friends William ("Bat") Masterson and John Henry ("Doc") Holliday operated on both sides of the law as gunmen, gamblers, and politicians. A feud between the Clantons and the Earps climaxed on October 26, 1881, in a shootout at the OK Corral, where three Clantons were killed and Holliday and Morgan Earp were wounded. These characters and their exploits provided material for countless future novels, movies, and television programs.

Writers Mark Twain, Bret Harte, and others captured the flavor of western life, and characters such as Buffalo Bill, Annie Oakley, Wild Bill Hickok, and Poker Alice became western folk heroes. But violence and eccentricity were far from common. Most miners and lumbermen worked long hours, often for corporations rather than as rugged individuals, and had little time, energy, or money for gambling, carousing, or gunfights. Women worked as long or longer as teachers, laundresses, storekeepers, and housewives. Only a few were sharpshooters or dance-hall queens. For most, western life was a matter of adapting and surviving.

## IRRIGATION AND TRANSPORTATION

Glittering gold, tall trees, and gushing oil shaped popular images of the West, but water gave it life. If western territories and states promised wealth from mining, cutting,

▲ Water, aided by human resolve, coaxed crops from the dry soil and helped make the West habitable for whites. On this Colorado farm, a windmill pumps water for irrigation.

*(Longmont Museum, Longmont, Colorado)*

and drilling, their agricultural potential promised more— but only if settlers could find a way to bring water to the arid land. Western economic development is the story of how public and private interests used technology and organization to develop the region's river basins and make the land agriculturally productive. Just as control of land was central to western development, so, too, was control of water.

For centuries, Indians irrigated southwestern lands to sustain their subsistence farming. When the Spanish arrived, they began tapping the Rio Grande River to irrigate farms in southwest Texas and New Mexico. Later they channeled water to the California mission communities of San Diego and Los Angeles. The first Americans of northern European ancestry to practice extensive irrigation were the Mormons. Arriving in Utah in 1847, they quickly diverted streams and rivers into networks of canals, whose water enabled them to farm the hard-baked soil. By 1890 Utah boasted over 263,000 irrigated acres supporting more than 200,000 people.

Efforts at land reclamation through irrigation in Colorado and California sparked conflict over rights to

## Rights to Water

the precious streams that flowed through the West. Americans had inherited the English common-law principle of riparian rights, which held that only those who owned land along a river's banks could appropriate from the water's flow. The stream itself, according to riparianism, belonged to God; those who lived near it could take water for normal needs but were not to diminish the river. This principle, intended to protect nature, discouraged economic development because it prohibited each property owner from damming or diverting water at the expense of others who lived downstream.

Americans who settled the West rejected riparianism in favor of the doctrine of prior appropriation, which awarded a river's water to the first person who claimed it. Westerners, taking cues in part from eastern Americans who had diverted waterways to power mills and factories, asserted that water, like timber, minerals, and other natural resources, existed to serve human needs and advance profits. They argued that anyone intending a "reasonable" or "beneficial" (economically productive) use of river water should have the right to appropriation, and the courts generally agreed.

Under appropriation, those who dammed and diverted water often reduced the flow of water downstream. People disadvantaged by such action could protect their interests either by suing those who deprived them of water or by establishing a public authority to regulate water usage. Thus in 1879 Colorado created several water divisions, each with a commissioner to determine and regulate water rights. In 1890 Wyoming enlarged the concept of control with a constitutional provision declaring that the state's rivers were public property subject to state supervision.

Destined to become the most productive agricultural state, California devised a dramatic response to the problem of water rights, sometimes called the California Solution. In the 1860s, a few individuals controlled huge tracts of land in the fertile Sacramento and San Joaquin River valleys, which they used for speculating in real estate, raising cattle, and growing wheat. But around the edges of the wheat fields lay unoccupied lands that could profitably support vegetable and fruit farming if irrigated properly.

Unlike western states that had favored appropriation rights over riparian rights, California maintained a mixed legal system that upheld riparianism while allowing for some appropriation. This system disadvantaged irrigators and prompted them to seek to change state law. In 1887 the legislature passed a bill permitting farmers to organize into districts that would construct and operate irrigation projects. An irrigation district could use its public authority to purchase water rights, seize private property to build irrigation canals, and finance projects through taxation or by issuing bonds. As a result of this legislation, California became the nation's leader in irrigated acreage, with more than 1 million irrigated acres by 1890, making the state's fruit and vegetable agriculture the most profitable in the country.

Although state irrigation provisions stimulated development, the federal government still owned most of

|||||||||||||||||||||||||||||||||||||

**Newlands Reclamation Act**

western lands in the 1890s, ranging from 64 percent of California to 96 percent of Nevada. Prodded by land-hungry developers, states wanted the federal government to transfer to them at least part of the public domain lands. States claimed that they could make these lands profitable through reclamation—providing them with irrigated water. Congress generally refused such assignments because of the controversies they raised. If one state sponsored irrigation to develop its own land, who would regulate waterways that flowed through more than one state? If, for example, California assumed control of the Truckee River, which flowed westward out of Lake Tahoe on the California-Nevada border, how would Nevadans be assured that California would give them sufficient water? Only the federal government, it seemed, had the power to regulate regional water development.

In 1902, after years of debates, Congress passed the Newlands Reclamation Act. Named for Nevada congressman Francis Newlands, the law allowed the federal government to sell western public lands to individuals in parcels not to exceed 160 acres and to use proceeds from such sales to finance irrigation projects. The Newlands Act provided for control but not conservation of water, because three-fourths of the water used in open-ditch irrigation, the most common form, was lost to evaporation. Thus the legislation fell squarely within the tradition of development of nature for human profit. Often identified as an example of sensitivity to natural-resource conservation, the Newlands Reclamation Act in fact represented a decision by the federal government to aid the agricultural and general economic development of the West, just as state and federal subsidies to railroads during the 1850s and 1860s aided western settlement.

Between 1865 and 1890, railroad expansion boomed, as total track in the United States grew from 35,000 to

|||||||||||||||||||||||||||||||||||||

**Railroad Construction**

200,000 miles, mostly from construction west of the Mississippi River (see Map 17.1). By 1900 the United States contained one-third of all railroad track in the world. A diverse mix of workers made up construction crews. The Central Pacific, built eastward from San Francisco, employed thousands of Chinese to build its tracks; the Union Pacific, extending westward from Omaha, Nebraska, used mainly Irish construction gangs. Workers lived in shacks and tents that were dismantled, loaded on flatcars, and relocated each day.

Railroad construction had powerful economic effects. After 1880, when steel rails began to replace iron rails, railroads helped to boost the nation's steel industry to international leadership. Railroad expansion also spawned related industries, including coal production, passenger- and freight-car manufacture, and depot construction. Influential and essential, railroads also gave important impetus to western urbanization. With their ability to transport large loads of people and freight, lines such as the Union Pacific and the Southern Pacific accelerated the growth of western hubs, such as Chicago, Omaha, Kansas City, Cheyenne, Los Angeles, Portland, and Seattle.

Railroads accomplished these feats with help from some of the largest government subsidies in American

# The Australian Frontier

America's frontier West was not unique. Australia, founded like the United States as a European colony, had a frontier society that resembled the American West in several ways, especially in its mining development, its folk society, and its treatment of indigenous people. Australia experienced a gold rush in 1851, just two years after the United States did, and large-scale mining companies quickly moved into its western regions to extract lucrative mineral deposits. In 1897 future U.S. president Herbert Hoover, who at that time was a twenty-two-year-old geology graduate, went to work in Australia and began his successful career as a mining engineer.

A promise of mineral wealth lured thousands of immigrants to Australia in the late nineteenth century. Many of the newcomers arrived from China, and, as in the United States, these immigrants, most of them men, encountered abusive treatment. Anti-Chinese riots erupted in debarkation ports in New South Wales in 1861 and 1873, and beginning in 1854, the Australian government passed several laws restricting Chinese immigration. When the country became an independent British federation in 1901, one of its first acts applied a strict literacy test that virtually terminated Chinese immigration for over fifty years.

As in the American West, the Australian frontier bred folk heroes who came to symbolize white masculinity. In a society where men vastly outnumbered women, Australians glorified the tough, aggressive individual who displayed self-reliance and quick judgment. As an ethos of freedom and opportunity intertwined with the idea of masculine ruggedness, the Australian backcountry man soon became as idealized as the American cowboy. Australian outlaws (called "bushrangers") such as Ned Kelly, an infamous bandit who was hanged in 1880, achieved the same notoriety as Americans Jesse James and Billy the Kid.

Although Australians lauded white men who brought a spirit of personal liberty and opportunism to a new country, they also considered indigenous peoples, whom they called "Aborigines" rather than Indians, as savages needing to be conquered and civilized. Christian missionaries viewed aborigines as lost in pagan darkness and tried to convert them. In 1869 the government of Victoria Province passed an Aborigine Protection Act that, like American policy toward Indians, encouraged removal of native children from their families so they could learn European customs in schools run by whites. Aborigines adapted in their own ways. They formed cricket teams, and those with light skin sometimes hid their identity by telling a census taker they were white. In the end, though, assimilation did not work, and Australians resorted to reservations as a means of "protecting" Aborigines, just as Americans isolated native peoples on reserved land. Like the Americans, white Australians could not find a place for indigenous people in a land of opportunity.

Much like the American counterpart, the Australian frontier was populated by natives before Anglo colonists arrived. The Aborigines, as the Australian natives were called, lived in villages and utilized their own culture to adapt to the environment. This photo shows a native camp in the Maloga Reserve.
*(National Library of Australia)*

▲ This ad from 1882 shows a steam engine of the Illinois Central Railroad pulling into a station and admired by all. The ad boasts of how the I.C.R.R. not only linked the growing city of Chicago with numerous places all the way south to New Orleans but also replaced old methods of transportation such as the stagecoach and barge pictured in the small insets on the right side of the illustration. *(Library of Congress)*

### Railroad Subsidies

history. Promoters argued that, because railroads were a public benefit, the government should aid them by giving them land from the public domain, which they could then sell to finance construction. During the Civil War, Congress, dominated by business-minded Republicans and in the absence of representatives from the seceded southern states, was sympathetic, as it had been when it aided steamboat companies earlier in the nineteenth century. As a result, the federal government granted railroad corporations over 180 million acres, mostly for interstate routes. These grants usually consisted of a right of way, plus alternate sections of land in a strip 20 to 80 miles wide along the right of way. Railroads funded construction by using the land as security for bonds or by selling it for cash. States and localities heaped on further subsidies. State legislators, many of whom had financial interests in a railroad's success, granted some 50 million acres. Cities and towns also assisted, usually by offering loans or by purchasing railroad bonds or stocks.

Government subsidies had mixed effects. Although capitalists often opposed government involvement in the economic affairs of private companies, privately owned railroads nevertheless accepted public aid and pressured governments into meeting their needs. The Southern Pacific, for example, threatened to bypass Los Angeles unless the city paid a bonus and built a depot. Localities that could not or would not pay suffered. Without public help, few railroads could have prospered sufficiently to attract private investment, yet such aid was not always salutary.

During the 1880s, the policy of generosity haunted communities whose zeal had prompted them to commit too much to railroads that were never built or that defaulted on loans. Some laborers and farmers fought subsidies, arguing that companies such as the Southern Pacific would become too powerful. Many communities boomed, however, because they had linked their fortunes to the iron horse. Moreover, railroads helped attract investment into the West and drew farmers into the market economy.

Railroad construction brought about important techological and organizational reforms. By the late, 1880s, almost all lines had adopted standard-gauge rails so that their

### Standard Gauge, Standard Time

tracks could connect with one another. Air brakes, automatic car couplers, standardized handholds on freight cars, and other devices made rail transportation safer and more efficient. The need for gradings, tunnels, and bridges spurred the growth of the American engineering profession. Organizational advances included systems for coordinating passenger and freight schedules, and the adoption of uniform freight-classification systems. Railroads also, however, helped reinforce racial segregation by separating black from white passengers on railroad cars and in stations.

Rail transportation altered conceptions of time and space. First, by surmounting physical barriers to travel, railroads transformed space into time. Instead of expressing the distance between places in miles, people began to refer to the amount of time it took to travel from one place to another. Second, railroad scheduling required nationwide standardization of time. Before railroads, local church bells and clocks struck noon when the sun was directly overhead, and people set clocks and watches accordingly. But because the sun was not overhead at exactly the same moment everywhere, time varied from place to place. Boston's clocks, for instance, differed from those in New York by almost twelve minutes. To impose regularity, railroads created their own time zones. In 1883, without authority from Congress, the nation's railroads agreed to establish four standard time zones for the country. Most communities adjusted their clocks accordingly, and railroad time became national time.

## FARMING THE PLAINS

While California emerged as the nation's highest-yielding agricultural state, extraordinary development occurred in the Great Plains. There, farming in the late nineteenth century exemplified two important achievements: the transformation of arid, windswept prairies into arable land that would yield crops to benefit humankind, and the transformation of agriculture into big business by means of mechanization, long-distance transportation, and scientific cultivation. These feats did not come easily. The climate and terrain of the Great Plains presented formidable challenges, and overcoming them did not guarantee success. Irrigation and the mechanization of agriculture enabled farmers to feed the nation's burgeoning population and turned the United States into the world's breadbasket, but the experience also scarred the lives of countless men and women who made that accomplishment possible.

During the decades of the 1870s and 1880s, more acres were put under cultivation in states such as Kansas, Nebraska, and Texas than in the

### Settlement of the Plains

entire country during the previous 250 years. The number of farms tripled from 2 million to over 6 million between 1860 and 1910, as hundreds of thousands of hopeful farmers streamed into the Plains region. The Homestead Act of 1862 and other measures to encourage western settlement offered cheap or free plots to people who would reside on and improve their property. Land-rich railroads were especially aggressive, advertising cheap land, arranging credit terms, offering reduced fares, and promising instant success. Railroad agents—often former immigrants—traveled to Denmark, Sweden, Germany, and other European nations to recruit settlers and greeted newcomers at eastern ports.

Most families who settled western farmlands migrated because opportunities in the West seemed to promise a second chance, a better existence than their previous one. Railroad expansion gave farmers in remote regions a way to ship produce to market, and the construction of grain elevators eased problems of storage. As a result of worldwide as well as national population growth, demand for farm products burgeoned, and the prospects for commercial agriculture—growing crops for profit and for shipment to distant, including international, markets—became more favorable than ever.

Life on the farm, however, was much harder than advertisements and railroad agents insinuated. Migrants often encountered scarcities of es-

### Hardship on the Plains

sentials that they had once taken for granted, and they had to adapt to the environment. The prairies contained insufficient lumber for housing and fuel, so pioneer families had to build houses of sod and burn buffalo dung for heat. Water for cooking and cleaning was sometimes scarce also. Machinery for drilling wells was expensive, as were windmills for drawing water to the surface.

**Map 17.3   Agricultural Regions of the United States, 1890**

In the Pacific Northwest and east of the twenty-eight-inch-rainfall line, farmers could grow a greater variety of crops. Territory west of the line was either too mountainous or too arid to support agriculture without irrigation. The grasslands that once fed buffalo herds could now feed beef cattle.

The weather was even more formidable than the terrain. The climate between the Missouri River and the Rocky Mountains divides along a line running from Minnesota southwest through Oklahoma, then south, bisecting Texas. West of this line, annual rainfall averages less than twenty-eight inches, not enough for most crops or trees (see Map 17.3), and even that scant life-giving rain was never certain. Heartened by adequate water one year, farmers gagged on dust and broke plows on hardened limestone soil the next.

Weather seldom followed predictable cycles. Weeks of torrid summer heat and parching winds suddenly gave way to violent storms that washed away crops and property. The wind of frigid winter blizzards piled up mountainous snowdrifts that halted outdoor movement. During the Great Blizzard that struck Nebraska, Wyoming, and the Dakota Territory in the winter of 1886–1887, the temperature plunged to 36 degrees below zero. In springtime, melting snow swelled streams, and floods threatened millions of acres. In fall, a week without rain turned dry grasslands into tinder, and the slightest spark could ignite a raging prairie fire. A severe drought in Texas between 1884 and 1886 drove many farmers off the land, and a more widespread drought in 1886 struck areas as diverse as Dakota, Wyoming, and California

Nature could be cruel even under good conditions. Weather that was favorable for crops was also good for breeding insects. Worms and flying pests ravaged fields. In the 1870s and 1880s, grasshopper swarms virtually ate up entire farms. Heralded only by the din of buzzing wings, a mile-long cloud of insects would smother the land and devour everything: plants, tree bark, and clothing. As one farmer lamented, the "hoppers left behind nothing but the mortgage."

Settlers also had to cope with social isolation. In New England and Europe, farmers lived in villages and traveled daily to nearby fields. This pattern of community building was rare in the vast expanses of the Plains—and in the Far West and

**Social Isolation**

Evelyn Cameron was a British-born ▶ Montana settler whose diaries and photographs portrayed the hardship and beauty of the frontier in the 1890s and early 1900s. Here she depicted two homesteaders and their simple dwelling with its dirt floor, wood stove, and boxes serving as furniture.
*(Montana Historical Society)*

South as well—where peculiarities of land division compelled rural dwellers to live apart from each other. Because most plots were rectangular—usually encompassing 160 acres—at most four families could live near one another, but only if they built homes around their shared four-corner intersection. In practice, farm families usually lived back from their boundary lines, and at least a half-mile separated farmhouses. Men might find escape by working in distant fields and taking occasional trips to sell crops or buy supplies. Women were more isolated, confined by domestic chores to the household. They visited and exchanged food and services with neighbor women when they could, but, as one writer observed, a farm woman's life was "a weary, monotonous round of cooking and washing and mending."

Letters that Ed Donnell, a young Nebraska homesteader, wrote to his family in Missouri reveal how time and circumstances could dull optimism. In the fall of 1885, Donnell rejoiced to his mother, "I like Nebr first rate. . . . I have saw a pretty tuff time a part of the time since I have been out here, but I started out to get a home and I was determined to win or die in the attempt. . . . Have got a good crop of corn, a floor in my house and got it ceiled overhead." Already, though, Donnell was lonely. He went on, "There is lots of other bachelors here but I am the only one I know who doesn't have kinfolks living handy. . . . You wanted to know when I was going to get married. Just as quick as I can get money ahead to get a cow."

A year and a half later, Donnell's dreams were dissolving and, still a bachelor, he was beginning to look for a second chance elsewhere. He wrote to his brother, "The rats eat my sod stable down. . . . I may sell out this summer, land is going up so fast. . . . If I sell I am going west and grow up with the country." By fall, conditions had worsened. Donnell lamented, "We have been having wet weather for 3 weeks. . . . My health has been so poor this summer and the wind and the sun hurts my head so. I think if I can sell I will . . . move to town for I can get $40 a month working in a grist mill and I would not be exposed to the weather." Donnell's doubts and hardships, shared by thousands of other people, fed the cityward migration of farm folk that fueled late-nineteenth-century urban growth (see Chapter 19).

Farm families survived by sheer resolve and by organizing churches and clubs where they could socialize a few times a month. By 1900 two developments had brought rural settlers who lived east of the rainfall line into closer contact with modern consumer society.

## Mail-Order Companies and Rural Free Delivery

First, mail-order companies, such as Montgomery Ward and Sears, Roebuck, made new products attainable by the 1870s and 1880s. Emphasizing personal attention to customers, Ward and Sears received letters that often reported family news and sought advice on needs from gifts to childcare. A Washington man

▲ By the late nineteenth century, the industrial revolution was having a significant impact on farming. This scene from a Colorado wheat farm shows a harvest aided by a steam tractor and a belt-driven thresher, equipment that made large-scale commercial crop production possible.

*(Colorado Historical Society)*

wrote to Mr. Ward, "As you advertise everything for sale that a person wants, I thought I would write you, as I am in need of a wife, and see what you could do for me." Another reported, "I suppose you wonder why we haven't ordered anything from you since the fall. The cow kicked my arm and broke it and besides my wife was sick, and there was the doctor bill. But now, thank God, that is paid, and we are all well again, and we have a fine new baby boy, and please send plush bonnet number 29d8077."

Second, after farmers petitioned Congress for extension of the postal service, in 1896 the government made Rural Free Delivery (RFD) widely available. Farmers previously had to go to town to pick up mail. Now they could receive letters, newspapers, and catalogues in a roadside mailbox nearly every day. In 1913 the postal service inaugurated parcel post, which enabled people to receive packages, such as orders from Ward and Sears, more cheaply.

As with industrial production (see Chapter 18), the late-nineteenth-century agricultural revolution was driven

## Mechanization of Agriculture

by the expanded use of machinery. When the Civil War drew men away from farms in the upper Mississippi River valley, women and older men who remained behind began using reapers and other mechanical implements to satisfy demand for food and take advantage of high grain prices. After the war, continued demand encouraged farmers to utilize machines, and inventors developed new implements to facilitate planting and harvesting. Seeders, combines, binders, mowers, and rotary plows, carried westward by railroads, improved grain growing on the Plains and in California. Technology also aided dairy and poultry farming. The centrifugal cream separator, patented in 1879, sped the process of skimming cream from milk, and a mechanized incubator, invented in 1885, made chicken raising more profitable.

For centuries, the acreage of grain a farmer planted was limited by the amount that could be harvested by hand. Machines—driven first by animals, then by steam—significantly increased productivity. Before mechanization, a farmer working alone could harvest about 7.5 acres of wheat. Using an automatic binder that cut and bundled the grain, the same farmer could harvest 135 acres. Machines dramatically reduced the time and cost of farming other crops as well.

Meanwhile, Congress and scientists worked to improve existing crops and develop new ones. The 1862

## Legislative and Scientific Aids

Morrill Land Grant Act gave each state federal lands to sell in order to finance agricultural research at educational institutions. The act prompted establishment of public universities in Wisconsin, Illinois, Minnesota, California, and other states. A second Morrill Act in 1890 aided more

| TABLE 17.1 | Summary: Government Land Policy |
| --- | --- |
| Railroad land grants (1850–1871) | Granted 181 million acres to railroads to encourage construction and development |
| Homestead Act (1862) | Gave 80 million acres to settlers to encourage settlement |
| Morrill Act (1862) | Granted 11 million acres to states to sell to fund public agricultural colleges |
| Other grants | Granted 129 million acres to states to sell for other educational and related purposes |
| Dawes Act (1887) | Allotted some reservation lands to individual Indians to promote private property and weaken tribal values among Indians and offered remaining reservation lands for sale to whites (by 1906, some 75 million acres had been acquired by whites) |
| Various laws | Permitted direct sales of 100 million acres by the Land Office |

*Source:* Goldfield, David; Abbott, Carl; Anderson, Virginia Dejohn; Argersinger, Jo Ann; Argersinger, Peter H.; Barney, William L.; and Weir, Robert M., *The American Journey, Volume II,* 3rd ed., © 2004. Reproduced by permission of Pearson Education, Inc., Upper Saddle River, New Jersey.

schools, including several all-black colleges. The Hatch Act of 1887 provided for agricultural experiment stations in every state, further encouraging the advancement of farming science and technology.

Science also enabled farmers to use the soil more efficiently. Researchers developed dry farming, a technique of plowing and harrowing that minimized evaporation of precious moisture. Botanists perfected varieties of "hard" wheat whose seeds could withstand northern winters, and millers invented a process for grinding the tougher wheat kernels into flour. Agriculturists also adapted new varieties of alfalfa from Mongolia, corn from North Africa, and rice from Asia. Horticulturist Luther Burbank developed hundreds of new food plants and flowers at a garden laboratory in Sebastopol, California. George Washington Carver, a son of slaves who became a chemist and taught at Alabama's Tuskegee Institute, created hundreds of new products from peanuts, soybeans, and sweet potatoes. Other scientists developed means of combating plant and animal diseases. Just as in mining and manufacturing, science and technology provided American farming with means for expanding productivity in the market economy.

## THE RANCHING FRONTIER

While commercial farming was overspreading the West, it ran headlong into one of the region's most romantic industries—ranching. Beginning in the sixteenth century, Spanish landholders had engaged in cattle raising in Mexico and what would become the American Southwest.

They employed Indian and Mexican cowboys, known as *vaqueros,* who tended the herds and rounded up cattle to be branded and slaughtered. Anglo ranchers moving into Texas and California in the early nineteenth century hired *vaqueros,* who in turn taught their skills in roping, branding, horse training, and saddle making to white and African American cowboys. About one-fourth of all cowboys were black. Although black cowboys probably experienced less discrimination than other African American laborers did on the job, off the trail they had to sit in separate sections in saloons and endured derogatory names and other mistreatment.

By the 1860s, cattle raising became increasingly profitable, as population growth boosted the demand for beef and railroads simplified the transportation of food. By 1870 drovers were herding thousands of Texas cattle northward to Kansas, Missouri, and Wyoming (see Map 17.1). At the northern terminus, the cattle were sold to northern ranches or loaded onto trains bound for Chicago and St. Louis, for slaughter and distribution to national and international markets.

The long drive gave rise to romantic lore of bellowing cattle, buckskin-clad cowboys, and smoky campfires under starry skies, but the process was not very efficient. Trekking 1,000 miles or more for two to three months made cattle sinewy and tough. Herds traveling through Indian lands and farmers' fields were sometimes shot at and later prohibited from such trespass by state laws. Ranchers adjusted by raising herds nearer to railroad routes. When ranchers discovered that crossing Texas longhorns with heavier Hereford and Angus breeds produced animals better able to survive harsh winters, cattle raising expanded northward, and proliferating herds in Kansas, Nebraska, Colorado, Wyoming, Montana, and the Dakotas crowded out already declining buffalo populations. Profits were considerable. A rancher could purchase a calf for $5, let it feed at no cost on the Plains for a few years, recapture it in a roundup, and sell it at a market price of $40 or $45.

Cattle raisers needed vast pastures to graze their herds while incurring as little expense as possible. Thus

### The Open Range

they often bought a few acres bordering a stream and turned their herds loose on adjacent public domain that no one wanted because it lacked water access. By this method, called open-range ranching, a cattle raiser could utilize thousands of acres by owning only a hundred or so. Neighboring ranchers often formed associations and allowed herds to graze together. Owners identified their cattle by burning a brand into each animal's hide. Each ranch had its own brand— a shorthand method for labeling movable property. But as

▲ A group of cowboys prepare for a roundup. Note the presence of African Americans, who, along with Mexicans, made up one-fourth of all cowboys. Though they rarely became trail bosses or ranch owners, black cowboys enjoyed an independence on the trails that was unavailable to them on tenant farms and city streets. *(Nebraska State Historical Society)*

demand for beef kept rising and as ranchers and capital flowed into the Great Plains, cattle began to overrun the range, and other groups' interests began challenging ranchers over use of the land.

Sheepherders from California and New Mexico were also using the public domain, sparking territorial clashes. Ranchers complained that sheep ruined grassland by eating down to the roots and that cattle refused to graze where sheep had been. Occasionally ranchers and sheepherders resorted to armed conflict rather than settle disagreements in court, where a judge might discover that both were using public land illegally.

More important, however, the advancing farming frontier was generating new demands for land. Devising a way to organize property resulted in an unheralded but highly significant change in land management. The problem was fencing. Lacking sufficient timber and stone for traditional fencing, western settlers could not easily define and protect their property. Tensions flared when farmers accused cattle raisers of allowing their herds to trespass on cropland and when herders in turn charged that farmers should fence their property against grazing animals. But ranchers and farmers alike lacked an economical means of enclosing their herds and fields.

The solution was barbed wire. Invented in 1873 by Joseph F. Glidden, a DeKalb, Illinois, farmer, this fencing consisted of wires held in place by sharp spurs twisted around them.

### Barbed Wire

Mass-produced by the Washburn and Moen Manufacturing Company of Worcester, Massachusetts—80.5 million pounds worth in 1880 alone—barbed wire provided a cheap and durable means of enclosure. It opened the Plains to homesteaders by enabling them to protect their farms from grazing cattle. It also ended open-range ranching and made roundups unnecessary, because it enabled large-scale ranchers to enclose their herds within massive stretches of private property. In addition, the development of the round silo for storing and making feed (silage) enabled cattle raisers to feed their herds without grazing them on vast stretches of land.

By 1890 big businesses were taking over the cattle industry and applying scientific methods of breeding and feeding. Corporations also used technology to squeeze larger returns out of meatpacking. Like buffalo, all parts of a cow had uses.

### Ranching as Big Business

Only about half of it consisted of salable meat. Meatpackers' largest profits came from

▲ Bordered by the product it was promoting, this advertisement conveyed the message that railroads and farmers could protect their property from each other by utilizing a new type of fencing. *(Elwood House Museum, DeKalb, Illinois)*

livestock by-products: hides for leather, blood for fertilizer, hooves for glue, fat for candles and soap, and the rest for sausages. But cattle processing also had harmful environmental impact. What meatpackers and leather tanners could not sell was dumped into rivers and streams. By the late nineteenth century, the Chicago River, which flowed past the city's mammoth processing plants, created such a powerful stench that nearby residents became sick in the summer.

Open-range ranching made beef a staple of the American diet and created a few fortunes, but its features could not survive the spurs of barbed wire and the rush of history. During the 1880s, overgrazing destroyed nourishing grass supplies on the Plains, and the brutal winter of 1886–1887 destroyed 90 percent of some herds and drove small ranchers out of business. By 1890, large-scale ranchers owned or leased the land they used, though some illegal fencing persisted. Cowboys formed labor organizations and participated in strikes for higher pay. The myth of the cowboy's freedom and individualism lived on, but ranching, like mining and farming, quickly became a corporate business.

# *Legacy* FOR A PEOPLE AND A NATION

## The Myth of the Cowboy

The image of the cowboy has been one of America's most distinctive icons. Yet its legacy reveals much about how the nation's culture has transformed an ordinary phenomenon into a myth. The actual American cowboys, whose heyday lasted only twenty-five years, about 1865–1890, were poorly paid, poorly fed, poorly dressed, illiterate young men who sometimes stole cattle from their employers. They were, as one Wyoming newspaper called them, "rough men with shaggy hair and wild staring eyes in butternut trousers stuffed into great rough boots." From a total of about 35,000 cowboys, 25 percent were black and another 15 percent were Mexican, Indians, and Chinese, all of whom their employers treated even more unfairly than they did white cowboys. Working at dirty jobs and often unemployed, some white and nonwhite cowboys joined unions and went on strike for job security and better wages. Mostly, however, cowboys got drunk more often than (as the myth suggests) they engaged in gunfights, enforced the law, or defended a woman's honor.

Yet the apparently independent, highly masculine, outdoor existence that cowboys led fueled a romantic notion that they somehow embodied the true American. Buffalo Bill Cody was one of the first to create this image by featuring in his Wild West shows a cattle herder named Buck Taylor, whom Cody glamorized as "King of the Cowboys." Shortly thereafter, fiction writers and artists began depicting cowboys as valiant characters. A best-selling novel, *The Virginian* (1902) by Owen Wister, about a Wyoming cowboy, helped reinforce the image of a rugged, self-reliant individualist who took the law into his own hands, and thereafter myriad films, radio, and television programs turned what once was a common laborer into a hero. A new "King of the Cowboys," Roy Rogers, who acted in hundreds of movies and TV shows between 1938 and 1964, was just one of many media characters who enlarged the myth, aided by the rise of the cowboy theme in country and western music. Gone was the ill-fitting, makeshift clothing of the past, now replaced by fancy boots, huge belt buckles, Stetson hats, and blue jeans, all of which became popular American fashion, worn at home and exported abroad.

Equally important, the disreputable, low-life reality was replaced by a no-nonsense lawman battling evil. President Ronald Reagan, a Californian, embellished his image by wearing western clothing and being photographed on horseback. And President George W. Bush, a Texan, stirred patriotism by assuming the role of a "good cowboy" after September 11, 2001, while opponents of his Iraq invasion criticized America's "bad cowboy" tactics of recklessly using violence to achieve a quick solution. The cowboy myth has consequently left a legacy not only of images but also of actions.

## SUMMARY

The reality of history revealed that both Frederick Jackson Turner's image of the West as the home of democratic spirit and Buffalo Bill's depiction of the West as the battlefield of the white man's victory were incomplete at best. Interaction between people and the environment proved to be far more intricate than either understood.

The landscape of the American West exerted lasting influence, through both its dominance and its fragility, on the complex mix of people who built communities there. Indians, the original inhabitants, had used, and sometimes abused, the land to support subsistence cultures that included trade and war as well as hunting and farming. Living mostly in small groups, they depended on delicate resources, such as buffalo herds and salmon runs. When they came into contact with commerce-minded, migratory European-Americans, their resistance to the market economy, diseases, and violence that whites brought into the West failed.

Mexicans, Chinese, African Americans, and Anglos discovered a reciprocal relationship between human activities and the nonhuman world which they had not always anticipated. Miners, timber cutters, farmers, and builders extracted raw minerals to supply eastern factories, used irrigation and mechanization to bring forth agricultural abundance from the land, filled pastures with cattle and sheep to expand food sources, and constructed railroads to tie the nation together. In doing so, they transformed half of the continent within a few decades. But the environment also exerted its own power over humans, through its climate, its insects and predators, its undesirable plant growth, and its impenetrable hazards and barriers to human movement and agriculture.

The West's settlers, moreover, employed force, violence, and greed that sustained discrimination within a multiracial society; left many farmers feeling cheated and betrayed; provoked contests over use of water and pastures; and sacrificed environmental balance for market profits. The region's raw materials and agricultural products improved living standards and hastened the industrial progress of the Machine Age, but not without human and environmental costs.

## SUGGESTIONS FOR FURTHER READING

William Cronon, *Nature's Metropolis: Chicago and the Great West* (1991)

Albert L. Hurtado and Peter Iverson, *Major Problems in American Indian History: Documents and Essays*, 2d ed. (2001)

Karl Jacoby, *Crimes Against Nature: Squatters, Poachers, Thieves and the Hidden History of American Conservation* (2001)

Patricia Nelson Limerick, *The Legacy of Conquest: The Unbroken Past of the American West* (1987)

Eugene P. Moehring, *Urbanism and Empire in the Far West, 1840–1890* (2004)

Alan Trachtenberg, *The Incorporation of America: Culture and Society in the Gilded Age* (1982)

Robert M. Utley, *The Indian Frontier of the American West, 1846–1890* (1984)

Richard White, *"It's Your Misfortune and None of My Own": A New History of the American* (1991)

*For a more extensive list for further reading, go to* college.hmco.com/pic/norton8e.

# The Machine Age
# 1877-1920

*I*n 1911 iron molders at the Watertown Arsenal, a government weapons factory near Boston, went on strike after a fellow worker, Joseph Cooney, was fired. Cooney had objected when an efficiency expert timed his work with a stopwatch, and the molders feared that such a time study was the first step in management's imposition of new standards on their labor. Iron molders' union president John Frey explained, "The workman believes when he goes on strike that he is defending his job." Frey meant that the molders felt a property right to their labor, that a job was not something that could be changed or removed from them without their consent.

The army officers who ran the factory believed differently. They thought that they owned the molders' labor and that the output was "not much more than one-half what it should be." To increase production, they hired Dwight Merrick, an expert in a new field called "scientific management," to time workers and suggest ways to speed their performance.

The day Merrick began his study, a molder named Perkins secretly timed the same task that Merrick did. Merrick reported that the job should take twenty-four minutes; Perkins found that to do the job right required fifty minutes. Merrick concluded that the workers were wasting time and materials in making molds; Perkins maintained that the molders knew more about making molds than Merrick did. That evening, the molders met to discuss how they should respond to the discrepancy between Merrick's report and their own sense of their job. Joseph Cooney argued that they should not submit to the system of scientific management, and the workers drew up a petition expressing their views. When Cooney confronted Merrick the next day, the molders were ready to walk out.

◄ Building parts for mowing machines at the McCormick farm implements factory, these workers are engaged in mechanized, mass production. Machines, standardized parts, and assembly-line production transformed American industrialization, the status of labor, and the availability of consumer goods. *(Navistar Archives)*

## CHRONOLOGY

**1869** ■ Knights of Labor founded

**1873–78** ■ Economy declines

**1876** ■ Bonsack invents machine for rolling cigarettes

**1877** ■ Widespread railroad strikes protest wage cuts

**1878** ■ Edison Electric Light Company founded

**1879** ■ George's *Poverty and Progress* argues for taxing unearned wealth

**1881** ■ First federal trademark law begins spread of brand names

**1882** ■ Standard Oil Trust founded

**1884–85** ■ Economy declines

**1886** ■ Haymarket riot in Chicago protests police brutality against labor demonstrations
■ American Federation of Labor (AFL) founded

**1890** ■ Sherman Anti-Trust Act outlaws "combinations in restraint of trade"

**1892** ■ Homestead (Pennsylvania) steelworkers strike against Carnegie Steel Company

**1893–97** ■ Economic depression causes high unemployment and business failures

**1894** ■ Workers of Pullman Palace Car Company strike

**1895** ■ *U.S. v. E. C. Knight Co.* limits Congress's power to regulate manufacturing

**1896** ■ *Holden v. Harcy* upholds law regulating miners' working hours

**1903** ■ Women's Trade Union League (WTUL) founded

**1905** ■ *Lochner v. New York* overturns law limiting bakery workers' working hours and limits labor protection laws
■ Industrial Workers of the World (IWW) founded

**1908** ■ *Muller v. Oregon* upholds law limiting women to ten-hour workday
■ First Ford Model T built

**1911** ■ Triangle Shirtwaist Company fire in New York City leaves 146 workers dead

**1913** ■ Ford begins moving assembly-line production

**1919** ■ Telephone operators strike in New England

Eventually, molders and their bosses at the Watertown Arsenal compromised and settled the strike, but this incident reveals one of the important consequences of the industrialization that was making countless new products available in the late 1800s. Four themes characterized the era. First, inventors and manufacturers harnessed technology in ways never before imagined. Second, the new economic order had a profound impact on production and labor. To increase production and maximize use of machines, factory owners divided work routines into minute, repetitive tasks and organized them according to the dictates of the clock. Workers (employees) like the Watertown molders, who had long thought of themselves as valued for their skills, now struggled to avoid becoming slaves to machines. Third, a new consumer society took shape as goods that had once been accessible to a few became available to many. Products such as canned foods and machine-made clothing, which had hardly existed before the Civil War, became common by the turn of the century. Finally, in their quest for growth and profits, corporation owners (employers) amassed great power. Defenders of the new system devised theories to justify it, while critics and laborers tried to combat what they thought were abuses of power.

Industrialization is a complex process whose chief feature is production of goods by machine rather than by hand. In the mid-nineteenth century, an industrial revolution had swept through parts of the United States, and the mechanization that characterized it powered a second round in the late 1800s and early 1900s. Three technological developments characterized this new process: electricity, the internal-combustion engine, and new applications in the use of chemicals. These technologies followed from earlier industrialization. Electricity provided a needed alternative to steam engines, which had reached their peak of utility. The demand for transportation to supplement railroads spurred progress in automobile manufacture. And the textile industry's experiments with dyes, bleaches, and cleaning agents advanced chemical research.

Until the late nineteenth century, the United States was just another developing nation. In 1860 only one-fourth of the American labor force worked in manufacturing and transportation; by 1900 over half did so. As the twentieth century dawned, the United States had become

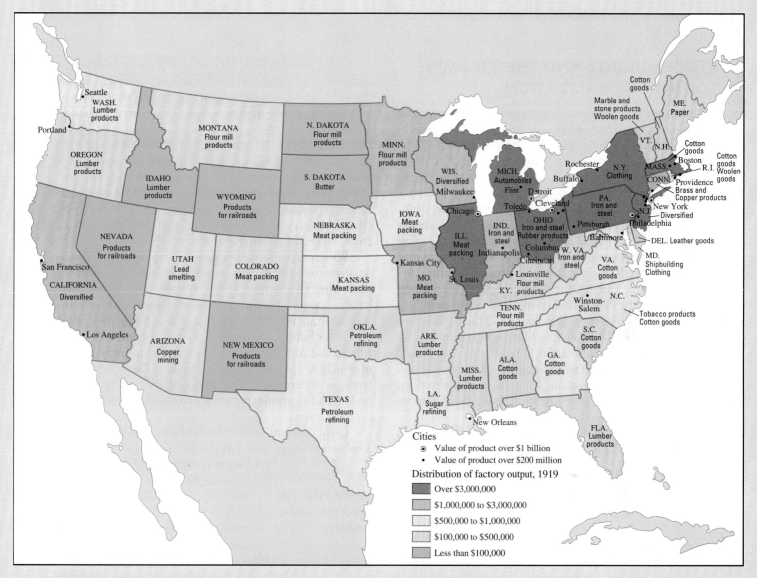

**Map 18.1    Industrial Production, 1919**

By the early twentieth century, each state could boast at least one kind of industrial production. Although the value of goods produced was still highest in the Northeast, states such as Minnesota and California had impressive dollar values of outputs.

(Source: *Data from U.S. Bureau of the Census,* Fourteenth Census of the United States, 1920, *Vol. IX, Manufacturing* [Washington, D.C.: U.S. Government Printing Office, 1921].)

not only the world's largest producer of raw materials and food, but also the most productive industrial nation (see Map 18.1). Between 1877 and 1920, migrants from farms and abroad swelled the industrial work force (see Chapter 19), but labor-saving machines, more than people, boosted productivity. Innovations in business organization and marketing also fueled the drive for profits.

These developments had momentous effects on standards of living and everyday life. The accomplishments of industrialization provided a complementary episode to the extraction of natural resources and the expansion of agriculture (see Chapter 17). Together, these processes combined people, the environment, and technology in a mix that gave rise to both constructive and destructive forces.

- How did mechanization affect the lives of average workers and the makeup of the labor force?

- In what ways did technological innovation alter the American standard of living?

- What ideas did some Americans use to justify industrialization, and how did others criticize it?

## TECHNOLOGY AND THE TRIUMPH OF INDUSTRIALIZATION

While some people pursued opportunity in the American West, others sought new ways of doing things with technology. Thomas Edison was one such person. In 1876 he and his associates opened an "invention factory" in Menlo Park, New Jersey, where they intended to turn out "a minor invention every ten days and a big thing every six months or so." If Americans wanted new products, Edison believed, they had to organize and work purposefully to bring about progress. His attitude reflected the spirit that enlivened American inventiveness, which in turn propelled industrialization in the late nineteenth century. Activity at the U.S. Patent Office, created by the Constitution to "promote the Progress of science and useful Arts," reflects this spirit. Between 1790 and 1860 the government granted a total of 36,000 patents. In the next seventy-year span, between 1860 and 1930, it registered 1.5 million. Inventions often sprang from a marriage between technology and business organization. The harnessing of electricity, internal combustion, and industrial chemistry illustrates how this marriage worked.

Most of Edison's more than one thousand inventions used electricity to transmit light, sound, and images. His biggest "big thing" project began in 1878 when he embarked on a search for a cheap, efficient means of indoor lighting. After tedious experiments, Edison perfected an incandescent bulb that used tungsten to prevent the filament from burning up when electrical current passed through it. At the same time, his Edison Electric Light Company devised a system of power generation and distribution that could provide electricity conveniently to a large number of customers. To market his ideas, Edison acted as his own publicist. During the 1880 Christmas season he illuminated Menlo Park, and in 1882 he built a power plant that lighted eighty-five buildings on New York's Wall Street. A *New York Times* reporter marveled that working in his office at night now "seemed almost like writing in daylight."

**Birth of the Electrical Industry**

Edison's system of direct current could transmit electric power only a mile or two, because it lost voltage the farther it was transmitted. George Westinghouse, an inventor from Schenectady, New York, who had previously created an air brake for railroad cars, solved the problem. Westinghouse purchased European patent rights to generators that used alternating current and to transformers that reduced high-voltage power to lower voltage levels, thus making long-distance transmission more efficient.

Other entrepreneurs utilized new business practices to market Edison's and Westinghouse's technological breakthroughs. Samuel Insull, Edison's private secretary, organized Edison power plants across the country, amassing an electric utility empire. In the late 1880s and early 1890s, financiers Henry Villard and J. P. Morgan bought up patents in electric lighting and merged small equipment-manufacturing companies into the General Electric Company. Equally important, General Electric and Westinghouse Electric encouraged practical applications of electricity by establishing research laboratories that paid scientists to create electrical products for everyday use.

While corporations organized company labs, individual inventors continued to work independently and tried, sometimes successfully and sometimes not, to sell their handiwork and patents to manufacturers. One such inventor, Granville T. Woods, an engineer sometimes called "the black Edison," patented thirty-five devices vital to electronics and communications. Among his inventions, most of which he sold to companies such as General Electric, were an automatic circuit breaker, an electromagnetic brake, and instruments to aid communications between railroad trains.

Early innovations in the technology of the internal-combustion engine took place in Europe. In 1885 a German engineer, Gottlieb Daimler, built a lightweight engine driven by vaporized gasoline. This development inspired one of America's most visionary manufacturers, Henry Ford. In the 1890s, Ford, an electrical engineer in Detroit's Edison Company, experimented in his spare time with using Daimler's engine to power a vehicle. George Selden, a Rochester, New York, lawyer, had already been tinkering with such technology, but Ford applied organizational genius to this invention and spawned a massive industry.

**Henry Ford and the Automobile Industry**

Like Edison, Ford had a scheme as well as a product. In 1909 he declared, "I am going to democratize the automobile. When I'm through, everybody will be able to afford one, and about everyone will have one." Ford proposed to reach this goal by mass-producing thousands of identical cars in exactly the same way. Adapting the methods of the meatpacking and metalworking industries, Ford engineers set up assembly lines that drastically reduced the time and cost of producing autos. Instead of performing numerous tasks, each worker was assigned only one task, performed repeatedly, using the same specialized machine. In this way, workers assembled the entire car as it passed by them on a conveyor belt.

## The Atlantic Cable

During the late nineteenth century, as American manufacturers expanded their markets overseas, their ability to communicate with customers and investors improved immeasurably as a result of a telegraph cable laid beneath the Atlantic Ocean. The telegraph was an American invention, and Cyrus Field, the man who thought up the idea to lay a cable across the ocean, was an American. Yet most of the engineers who worked on the Atlantic cable, as well as most of the capitalists involved in the venture, were British. In 1851 a British company laid the first successful undersea telegraph cable from Dover, England, to Calais, France, proving that an insulated wire could carry signals underwater. The effectiveness of this venture, which connected the Reuters news service to the European continent and allowed French investors to receive instantaneous messages from the London Stock Exchange, inspired British and American businessmen to attempt a larger project across the Atlantic.

The first attempts to build a transatlantic cable failed, but in 1866 a British ship, funded by British investors, successfully laid a telegraph wire that operated without interruption. The project was designed by cooperative efforts of American and British electrical engineers. Thereafter, England and the United States grew more closely linked in their diplomatic relations, and citizens of both nations developed greater concern for each other as a result of their ability to receive international news more quickly. When American president James Garfield was assassinated in 1881, the news traveled almost instantly to Great Britain, and Britons mourned the death more profusely than they had mourned the passing of Abraham Lincoln, whose death was not known in England until eleven days after it had occurred, because transatlantic messages at that time traveled by steamship.

Some people lamented the stresses that near-instant international communications now created. One observer remarked that the telegraph tended "to make every person in a hurry, and I do not believe that with our business it is very desirable that it should be so." But financially savvy individuals experienced welcome benefits as a result of the cable's link. Rapid availability of stock quotes boomed the businesses of the New York and London stock exchanges, much to investors' delight. Newspaper readers enjoyed reading about events on the other side of the ocean the next day, instead of a week after they had occurred. And the success of the Atlantic cable inspired similar ventures in the Mediterranean Sea, the Indian Ocean, and, eventually, across the Pacific. By 1902 underwater cables circled the globe, and the age of global telecommunications had begun.

▲ Laid by British ships across the ocean in 1866, the Atlantic cable linked the United States with England and continental Europe so that telegraph communications could be sent and received much more swiftly than ever before. Now Europeans and Americans could exchange news about politics, business, and military movements almost instantly, whereas previously such information could take a week or more to travel from one country to another. *(Library of Congress)*

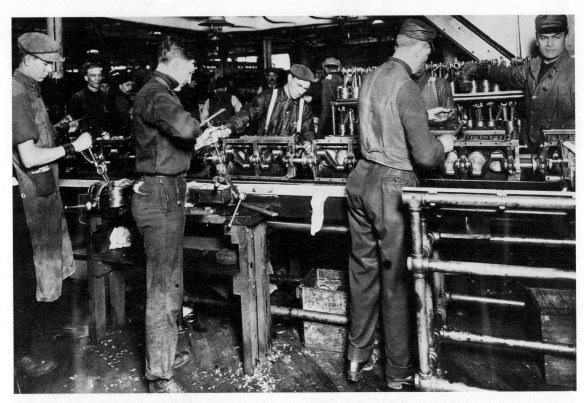

▲ The assembly line broke the production process down into simple tasks that individual workers could efficiently repeat hour after hour. Here, assembly-line workers at the Ford plant in Highland Park, Michigan, outside Detroit, are installing pistons in engines of the Model T around 1914.

*(Henry Ford Museum and Greenfield Village)*

In 1913 the Ford Motor Company's first full assembly line began operation in Highland Park outside Detroit, Michigan, and the next year, Ford sold 248,000 cars. Soon, other manufacturers entered the field. Rising automobile output created more jobs, higher earnings, and greater profits in such companies, but also in related industries, such as oil, paint, rubber, and glass, which in turn necessitated increased extraction of resources from the West and abroad. Moreover, assembly-line production in these and many other industries would not have been possible without precision machine tools to create standardized parts. Advances in grinding and cutting technology in this era made production processes accurate to one-thousandth of an inch.

By 1914 a Ford car cost $490, about one-fourth of the price a decade earlier. Yet even $490 was too expensive for many workers, who earned at best $2 a day. That year, however, Ford tried to spur productivity, prevent high labor turnover, head off unionization, and better enable his workers to buy the cars they produced by offering them the Five-Dollar-Day plan—a combination of wages and profit sharing.

The du Pont family did for the chemical industry what Edison and Ford did for the electrical and automobile industries. The du Ponts began manufacturing gunpowder in Delaware in the early 1800s. In 1902, fearing antitrust prosecution for the company's near monopoly of the American explosives industry, three cousins, Alfred, Coleman, and Pierre, took over E. I. du Pont de Nemours and Company, and broadened production into fertilizers, dyes, and other chemical products. In 1911 du Pont scientists and engineers working in the nation's first corporate research laboratory adapted cellulose to the production of such consumer goods as photographic film, lacquer, textile fibers, and plastics. In 1914 Pierre du Pont invested $25 million in fledgling automobile manufacturer General Motors, helping that company rise to compete with Ford. The du Pont company also pi-

### The Du Ponts and the Chemical Industry

▲ Tobacco production was one southern industry that traditionally hired African American laborers. This scene from a Richmond tobacco factory around 1880 shows women and children preparing leaves for curing by tearing off the stems. *(Library of Congress)*

oneered methods of management, accounting, and reinvestment of earnings, all of which contributed to efficient production, better recordkeeping, and higher profits.

The South's major staple crops, tobacco and cotton, drew industry to the region after the Civil War, and other forms of production grew as well. Before the 1870s, Americans used tobacco mainly for snuff, cigars, and chewing. But in 1876 James Bonsack, an eighteen-year-old Virginian, invented a machine for rolling cigarettes. In 1885 James B. Duke, owner of a North Carolina tobacco company, licensed Bonsack's machine and began mass-production. Like Edison and Ford, Duke marketed what he manufactured. Sales soared when he began enticing consumers with free samples, trading cards, and billboard ads. By 1900 his American Tobacco Company was a global business, dominating sales in England and Japan as well

### Technology and Southern Industry

as the United States. Duke's and other cigarette factories employed black and white workers (including women), though in separate locations of the plant.

New technology helped relocate the textile industry to the South, as electricity made New England's water-powered mills obsolete. Factories with electric looms were more efficient, because they needed fewer workers with fewer skills, and electric lighting expanded the hours of production. Investors built new plants in southern communities, where a cheap labor force was available. By 1900 the South had more than four hundred textile mills, with a total of 4 million spindles. Women and children who worked in these mills earned 50 cents a day for twelve or more hours of work—about half the wages that northern workers received. Most mills refused to hire black workers except as janitors. Many companies built villages around their mills, where they controlled housing, stores, schools, and churches. Inside these towns, owners banned criticism of the company and squelched attempts at union organization.

Northern and European as well as the region's own investors financed other southern industries. During the 1880s, northern capitalists developed southern iron and steel manufacturing, much of it in the boom city of Birmingham, Alabama. Between 1890 and 1900, northern lumber syndicates moved into the pine forests of the Gulf states, boosting production 500 percent. Southern wood production not only advanced the construction industry but also prompted the relocation of furniture and paper production from the North to the South.

Encouraged by industrial expansion, boosters heralded the emergence of a New South. Challenging the power of the planter class, a business class of manufacturers, merchants, and financiers were making southern cities the nerve centers of a new economic order (see Chapter 19). These promoters believed that the South should put the military defeat of the Civil War behind it—though never forget the heroism of Confederate soldiers—and emulate the North's economic growth. Henry Grady, editor of the *Atlanta Constitution* and a passionate advocate of southern progress, proclaimed, "We have sowed towns and cities in the place of theories, and put business in place of politics. We have challenged your spinners in Massachusetts and your iron-makers in Pennsylvania. . . . We have fallen in love with work."

In all regions, the timing of technological innovation varied from one industry to another, but machines broadly altered the economy and everyday life. Telephones and typewriters made face-to-face communication less important and facilitated correspondence and recordkeeping in growing insurance, banking, and advertising firms. Electric sewing machines made mass-produced clothing available to almost everyone. Refrigeration changed dietary habits by enabling the preservation and shipment of meat, fruit, vegetables, and dairy products. Cash registers and adding machines revamped accounting and created new clerical jobs. At the same time, American universities established programs in engineering, enabling manufacturers such as Edison and the du Ponts to hire new graduates in chemistry and physics.

Profits resulted from higher production at lower costs. Small crafts, such as cabinet making and metalworking, persisted, but as technological innovations made large-scale production more economical, owners replaced small factories with larger ones. Between 1850 and 1900, average capital investment in a manufacturing firm increased by 250 percent. Only large companies could afford to buy

### Consequences of Technology

▲ Taken at the historic moment of liftoff, this photograph shows the first airplane flight at Kitty Hawk, North Carolina, on December 17, 1903. With Orville Wright lying at the controls and brother Wilbur standing nearby, the plane was airborne only twelve seconds and traveled 120 feet. Even so, the flight marked the beginning of one of the twentieth century's most influential industries.

*(Library of Congress)*

complex machines and operate them at full capacity. And large companies could best take advantage of discounts for shipping products in bulk and for buying raw materials in quantity. Economists call such advantages economies of scale.

Profitability depended as much on how production was arranged as on the machines in use. Where once shop-floor workers such as the Watertown molders controlled the methods and timing of production, by the 1890s engineers and managers with specialized, "scientific" knowledge had assumed this responsibility. They planned every task to increase output. Through standardization, they reduced the need for worker skills and judgment, boosting profits at the expense of worker independence.

The most influential advocate of efficient production was Frederick W. Taylor. As foreman and engineer for the Midvale Steel Company in the 1880s, Taylor concluded that the best way a company could reduce fixed costs and increase profits was to apply systematic studies of "how quickly the various kinds of work . . . ought to be done." The "ought" in Taylor's formulation signified producing more for lower cost per unit, usually by eliminating unnecessary workers. Similarly, "how quickly" meant that time and money were equivalent. He called his scheme "scientific management."

### Frederick W. Taylor and Efficiency

In 1898 Taylor took his stopwatch to the Bethlehem Steel Company to illustrate how his principles worked. His experiments, he explained, required studying workers and devising "a series of motions which can be made quickest and best." Applying this technique to the shoveling of ore, Taylor designed fifteen kinds of shovels and prescribed the proper motions for using each one, thereby reducing a crew of 600 men to 140. Soon other companies, including the Watertown Arsenal, began applying Taylor's theories to their production lines.

As a result of Taylor's writings and experiments, time, as much as quality, became the measure of acceptable work, and management accumulated knowledge of and power over the ways of doing things. As integral elements of the assembly line, which divided work into specific time-determined tasks, employees such as the Watertown molders feared that they were becoming another kind of interchangeable part.

## MECHANIZATION AND THE CHANGING STATUS OF LABOR

By 1900, the status of labor had shifted dramatically in just a single generation. Technological innovation and

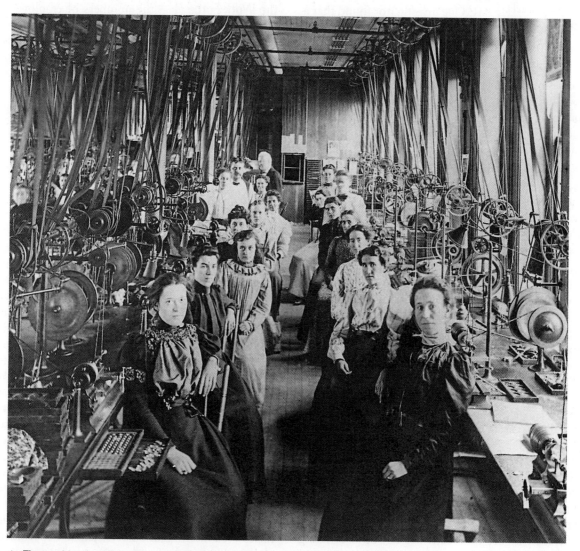

▲ The combination of machines and workers still required meticulous hand-work in some industries. Often women with nimble fingers could find jobs in industries such as jewelry and watch-making where, as at this room at the Elgin National Watch Company, they could swiftly manipulate tiny production processes. *(Chicago Historical Society)*

assembly-line production created new jobs, but because most machines were labor saving, fewer workers could produce more in less time. Moreover, workers could no longer accurately be termed producers, as farmers and craftsmen had traditionally thought of themselves. The working class now consisted mainly of employees—people who worked not on their own but when someone hired them. Producers had been paid in accordance with the quality of what they produced; employees received wages for time spent on the job.

By subdividing manufacturing into small tasks, mass production required workers to repeat the same standardized operation all day every day. One investigator found that a worker became

## Mass Production

a mere machine. . . . Take the proposition of a man operating a machine to nail on 40 to 60 cases of heels in a day. That is 2,400 pairs, 4,800 shoes in a day. One not accustomed to it would wonder how a man could pick up and lay down 4,800 shoes in a day, to say nothing of putting them . . . into a machine. . . . That is the driving method of the manufacture of shoes under these minute subdivisions.

Assembly lines and scientific management also deprived employees of their independence. Workers could no longer decide when to begin and end the workday, when to rest, and what tools and techniques to use. The clock regulated them. As a Massachusetts factory laborer testified in 1879, "During working hours the men are not allowed to speak to each other, though working close together, on pain of instant discharge. Men are hired to watch and patrol the shop." And employees now were surrounded by others who labored at the same rate for the same pay, regardless of the quality of their effort.

Workers affected by these changes, such as the Watertown iron molders, struggled to retain autonomy and self-respect in the face of employers' ever-increasing power. Artisans such as glass workers and coopers (barrel makers), caught in the transition from hand labor to machine production, fought to preserve their work pace and customs— say, by appointing a fellow worker to read a newspaper aloud while they worked. When immigrants went to work in factories, they tried to persuade foremen to hire their relatives and friends, thus preserving on-the-job family and village ties. Off the job, workers gathered in saloons and parks for such leisure-time activities as social drinking and holiday celebrations, ignoring employers' attempts to control their social lives as well.

Employers, concerned with efficiency, wanted certain standards of behavior upheld. Ford Motor Company required workers to satisfy the company's behavior code before becoming eligible for a part of the Five-Dollar-Day plan. To increase worker incentives, some employers established piecework rates, paying laborers an amount per item produced rather than an hourly wage. These efforts to increase productivity and maximize use of machines were intended to make workers perform like the machines they operated.

As machines and assembly lines reduced the need for skilled workers, employers found that they could cut labor costs by hiring women and children, and paying them low wages. Between 1880 and 1900, the numbers of employed women soared from 2.6 million to 8.6 million. At the same time, their occupational patterns underwent striking changes (see Figure 18.1). The proportion of women in domestic service (maids, cooks, laundresses)—the most common and lowest-paid form of female employment—dropped as jobs opened in other sectors. In manufacturing, women usually held menial positions in textile mills and food-processing plants that paid as little as $1.56 a week for seventy hours of labor. (Unskilled men received $7 to $10 for a similar workweek.) Although the number of female factory hands tripled between 1880 and 1900, the proportion of women workers in these jobs remained about the same.

## Restructuring of the Work Force

General expansion of the clerical and retail sectors, however, greatly boosted the numbers and percentages of women who were typists, bookkeepers, and sales clerks. Previously, men with accounting and letter-writing skills had dominated sales and office positions. New inventions, such as the typewriter, cash register, and adding machine, simplified these tasks, and employers replaced males with lower-paid females, many of whom had taken courses in typing and shorthand, and were looking for the better pay and conditions that clerical jobs offered compared with factory and domestic work. By 1920, women filled nearly half of all clerical jobs; in 1880 only 4 percent had been women. An official of a sugar company observed in 1919 that "all the bookkeeping of this company . . . is done by three girls and three bookkeeping machines . . . one operator takes the place of three men." Although poorly paid, women were attracted to sales jobs because of the respectability, pleasant surroundings, and contact with affluent customers that such positions offered. Nevertheless, sex discrimination persisted. In department stores, male cashiers took in cash and made change; women seldom were given responsibility for billing or for counting money. Women held some low-level supervisory positions, but males dominated the managerial ranks.

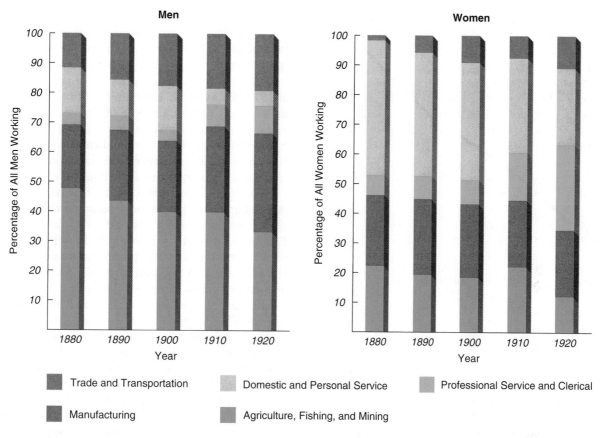

**Figure 18.1    Distribution of Occupational Categories Among Employed Men and Women, 1880–1920**

The changing lengths of the bar segments of each part of this graph represent trends in male and female employment. Over the forty years covered by this graph, the agriculture, fishing, and mining segment for men and the domestic service segment for women declined the most, whereas notable increases occurred in manufacturing for men and professional services (especially store clerks and teachers) for women.

(Source: *U.S. Bureau of the Census,* Census of the United States, 1880, 1890, 1900, 1910, 1920 *[Washington, D.C.: U.S. Government Printing Office].)*

Although most children who worked toiled on their parents' farms, the number in nonagricultural occupations tripled between 1870 and 1900. In 1890 over 18 percent of all children between ages ten and fifteen were gainfully employed (see Figure 18.2). Textile and shoe factories in particular employed young workers. Mechanization created numerous light tasks, such as running errands and helping machine operators, which children could handle at a fraction of adult wages. Conditions were especially hard for child laborers in the South, where growing numbers of textile mills needed unskilled hands. Mill owners induced white sharecroppers and tenant farmers, who desperately needed extra income, to bind their children over to factories at miserably low wages.

Several states, especially in the Northeast, passed laws specifying minimum ages and maximum workday hours for child labor. But large companies could evade regulations because such statutes regulated only firms operating within state borders, not those engaged in interstate commerce. Enforcing age requirements proved difficult because many parents, needing income from child labor, lied about their children's ages, and employers rarely asked. After 1900, state laws and automation, along with compulsory school attendance laws, began to

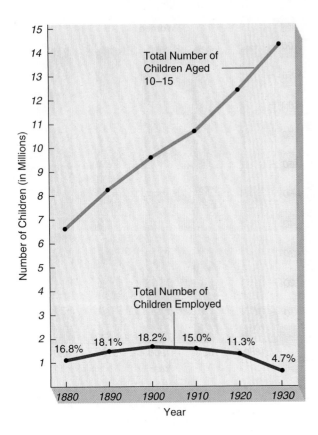

**Figure 18.2   Children in the Labor Force, 1880–1930**

The percentage of children in the labor force peaked around the turn of the century. Thereafter, the passage of state laws requiring children to attend school until age fourteen and limiting the ages at which children could be employed caused child labor to decline.

(Source: *Data from* The Statistical History of the United States from Colonial Times to the Present *[Stamford, Conn.: Fairfield Publishers, 1965].*)

reduce the number of children employed in manufacturing, and Progressive era reformers sought federal legislation to restrict child labor (see Chapter 21). Still, many children continued to work at street trades—shining shoes and peddling newspapers and other merchandise—and as helpers in stores. The poorest children also scavenged city streets for pieces of coal and wood, discarded clothing and furniture, and other items that their families could use.

For all workers, industrial labor was highly dangerous. Repetitive tasks using high-speed machinery dulled concen-

## Industrial Accidents

tration, and the slightest mistake could cause serious injury. Industrial accidents rose steadily before 1920, killing or maiming hundreds of thousands of people each year. In 1913, for example, even after factory owners had installed safety devices, some 25,000 people died in industrial mishaps, and 1 million were injured. For those with mangled limbs, infected cuts, and chronic illnesses, there was no disability insurance to replace lost income, and families stricken by such misfortunes suffered acutely.

Sensational disasters, such as explosions and mine cave-ins, aroused outcries for better safety regulations. The most notorious tragedy was a fire at New York City's Triangle Shirtwaist Company in 1911, which killed 146 workers, most of them teenage immigrant women trapped in locked workrooms. Despite public clamor, prevailing free-market views hampered passage of legislation that would regulate working conditions, and employers denied responsibility for employees' well-being. As one railroad manager declared, "The regular compensation of employees covers all risk or liability to accident. If an employee is disabled by sickness or any other cause, the right to claim compensation is not recognized."

To justify their treatment of workers, employers asserted the principle of "freedom of contract." The relation-

## Freedom of Contract

ship between an employee and an employer, according to this principle, resembled one between a customer and a seller. Like the price of an item for sale, wages and working conditions were the result of a free market in which laws of supply and demand prevailed. In addition, employers asserted, workers entered into a contract with bosses, either explicit or assumed, in which they "sold" their labor. If a worker did not like the contract's provisions, such as the wages and hours, the worker was free to decline and seek another job elsewhere, just as the customer was free to buy a product somewhere else. In practice, however, employers used supply and demand to set wages as low as laborers would accept, causing workers to conclude that the system trapped them. A factory worker told Congress in 1879, "The market is glutted, and we have seasons of dullness; advantage is taken of men's wants, and the pay is cut down; our tasks are increased, and if we remonstrate, we are told our places can be filled. I work harder now than when my pay was twice as high."

Reformers and union leaders lobbied Congress for laws to improve working conditions, but the Supreme Court,

▲ As textile mills often employed young children, so too did the food-processing industry. In 1913, Rosie, age seven, worked full time at the Varn & Platt Canning Company, in Bluffton, South Carolina. She started at 4 a.m. every day and did not go to school. *(Library of Congress)*

## Court Rulings on Labor Reform

agreeing with business interests, limited the scope of such legislation by narrowly defining which jobs were dangerous and which workers needed protection. In *Holden v. Hardy* (1896), the Court upheld a law regulating miners' working hours, concluding that an overly long workday would increase the threat of injury. In *Lochner v. New York* (1905), however, the Court voided a law limiting bakery workers to a sixty-hour week and ten-hour day. Offsetting the argument that states had authority to protect workers' health and safety, the Court ruled that baking was not a dangerous enough occupation to justify restricting workers' right to sell their labor freely. Such restriction, according to the Court, violated the Fourteenth Amendment's guar-

antee that no state could "deprive any person of life, liberty, or property without due process of law."

In *Muller v. Oregon* (1908), the Court used a different rationale to uphold a law limiting women in laundries to a ten-hour workday. In this case the Court set aside its *Lochner* argument that a state could not interfere with an individual's right of contract, asserting instead that a woman's well-being "becomes an object of public interest and care in order to preserve the strength and vigor of the race." The case represented a victory for reform groups such as the Consumers' League, which had sought government regulation of women's hours and working conditions. As a result of the *Muller* decision, however, labor laws effectively barred women from occupations, such as in printing and transportation, that

On March 25, 1911, the worst factory ▶
fire in U.S. history occurred at the Triangle
Shirtwaist Company, which occupied the
top three floors of a building in New York
City. Fed by piles of fabric, the fire spread
quickly, killing 146 of the 500 young women,
mostly Jewish immigrants, employed in the
factory. Many of the victims, lined up at the
morgue in this scene, were trapped inside
rooms locked by their employer; others
plunged to their death out of the upper-
story windows.

*(Juanita Hadwin Collector. Triangle Fire Lantern Slides,
Kheel Center, Cornell University, Ithaca, NY 14853-3901)*

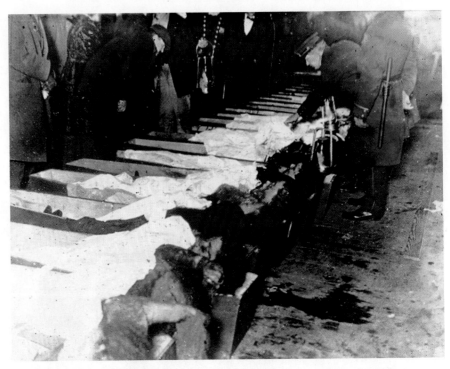

required heavy lifting, long hours, or
night work, further confining women
to low-paying, dead-end jobs.

## LABOR VIOLENCE
## AND THE UNION MOVEMENT

Workers adjusted to mechanization as best they could.
Some people submitted to the demands of the factory, machine, and time clock. Some tried to blend old ways of
working into the new system. Others turned to resistance.
Individuals challenged the system by ignoring management's orders, skipping work, or quitting. But also, anxiety over the loss of independence and a desire for better
wages, hours, and working conditions drew disgruntled
workers into unions. Organized labor was not new in the
late nineteenth century. Trade unions for skilled workers in
crafts such as printing and iron molding dated from the
early 1800s, but their influence was limited. The National
Labor Union, founded in 1866, claimed 640,000 members
from a variety of industries, but it collapsed in 1873 when it
failed to convince Congress to legislate a shorter workday.

In the economic slump that followed the Panic of
1873, railroad managers cut wages, increased workloads,
and laid off workers, especially
those who had joined unions. Such
actions drove workers to strike and
riot. The year 1877 marked a crisis.
In July, unionized railroad workers
organized a series of strikes to protest wage cuts. Venting
pent-up anger, rioters attacked railroad property from Pennsylvania and West Virginia to the Midwest, Texas, and

**Railroad Strikes
of 1877**

California, derailing trains and burning rail yards. State
militia companies, organized and commanded by employers, broke up picket lines and fired into threatening crowds.
In several communities, factory workers, wives, and merchants aided the strikers, while railroads enlisted strikebreakers to replace union men.

The worst violence occurred in Pittsburgh, where on
July 21 state troops bayoneted and fired on rock-throwing
demonstrators, killing ten and wounding many more. Infuriated, the mob drove the troops into a railroad roundhouse and set fires that destroyed 39 buildings, 104 engines,
and 1,245 freight and passenger cars. The next day, the
troops shot their way out of the roundhouse and killed
twenty more citizens before fleeing the city. After more than
a month of unprecedented violence, President Rutherford B. Hayes sent in federal soldiers—the first significant use of the army to quell labor unrest. Throughout
the strike, emotions ran high. A Pennsylvania militiaman,
ordered out to break the 1877 strike, recalled, "I talked to
all the strikers I could get my hands on, and I could find
but one spirit and one purpose among them—that they
were justified in resorting to any means to break down
the power of the corporations."

Although they sometimes spoke for all laborers, railroad workers had struck in 1877 in their own interest.

## Knights of Labor

About the same time, however, an organization called the Knights of Labor tried to attract a broad base of laborers. Founded in 1869 by Philadelphia garment cutters, the Knights began recruiting other workers in the 1870s. In 1879 Terence V. Powderly, a machinist and mayor of Scranton, Pennsylvania, was elected grand master. Under his forceful guidance, Knights membership grew rapidly, peaking at 730,000 in 1886. In contrast to most craft unions, Knights welcomed unskilled and semiskilled workers, including women, immigrants, and African Americans (but not Chinese laborers).

The Knights tried to avert the bleak future that they believed industrialism portended by building an alliance that offered an alternative to profit-oriented industrial capitalism. They intended to eliminate conflict between labor and management by establishing a cooperative society in which laborers, not capitalists, owned factories, mines, and railroads. The goal, argued Powderly, was to "eventually make every man his own master—every man his own employer." This view had its drawbacks. The cooperative idea, attractive in the abstract, was unattainable because employers held the economic leverage and could outcompete laborers who might try to establish their own businesses. Strikes offered one means of achieving immediate goals, but Powderly and other Knights leaders argued that strikes tended to divert attention from the long-term goal of a cooperative society and that workers tended to lose more by striking than they won.

Some Knights, however, did support militant action. In 1886 the Knights demanded higher wages and union recognition from railroads in the Southwest. Railroad magnate Jay Gould refused to negotiate, and a strike began in Texas and spread to Kansas, Missouri, and Arkansas. As violence increased, Powderly met with Gould and called off the strike, hoping for a settlement. But Gould again rejected concessions, and the Knights gave in. Militant craft unions began to desert the Knights, upset by Powderly's compromise and confident that they could attain more on their own.

After the Haymarket riot (see below), Knights membership dwindled, although the union and its cooperative vision survived in a few small towns, where it made a brief attempt to unite with Populists in the 1890s (see Chapter 20). The special interests of craft unions replaced the Knights' broad-based but often vague appeal, and dreams of labor unity faded.

## Haymarket Riot

At the same time that Knights went on strike in the Southwest, workers both inside and outside of formal labor organizations generated mass strikes in favor of an eight-hour workday. On May 1, 1886, in Chicago, some 100,000 workers turned out for the largest labor demonstration in the country's history. Their numbers included anarchists who believed in using violence to replace all government with voluntary cooperation. Chicago police, fearing that European radicals were transplanting a tradition of violence to the United States, mobilized to prevent disorder, especially among striking workers at the huge McCormick reaper plant. The day passed calmly, but two days later, police stormed an area near the factory and broke up a battle between striking unionists and nonunion strikebreakers. Police shot and killed two unionists and wounded several others.

The next evening, laborers rallied at Haymarket Square near downtown Chicago, to protest police brutality. As a

▲ The Haymarket riot of 1886 was one of the most violent incidents of labor unrest in the late nineteenth century. This drawing, from *Frank Leslie's Illustrated Newspaper,* shows workers fleeing while police beat demonstrators with nightsticks. As this clash was occurring, a bomb, allegedly set off by anarchists, exploded, killing both police and workers. *(Library of Congress)*

police company approached, a bomb exploded, killing seven and injuring sixty-seven. In reaction, authorities made mass arrests of anarchists and unionists. Eventually a court convicted eight anarchists of the bombing, though evidence of their guilt was questionable. Four were executed, and one committed suicide in prison. The remaining three received pardons in 1893 from Illinois governor John P. Altgeld, who believed they had been victims of the jurors' "malicious ferocity." Denounced by capitalists as a friend of anarchy, Altgeld found that his act of conscience ruined his political career.

The Haymarket bombing, like the 1877 railroad strikes, drew attention to labor's growing discontent and heightened fear of radicalism. The participation of anarchists and socialists, many of them foreign-born, created a feeling that forces of law and order must act swiftly to prevent social turmoil. To protect their interests, private Chicago donors helped to establish a military base just outside the city. Elsewhere, governments strengthened police forces and armories. Employer associations, coalitions of manufacturers in the same industry, countered labor militancy by circulating blacklists of union activists whom they would not employ and by hiring private detectives to guard company property and suppress strikes.

**American Federation of Labor**

The American Federation of Labor (AFL), founded in 1886, emerged from the upheavals of that year as the major workers' organization. An alliance of national craft unions, the AFL had about 140,000 members, most of them skilled workers. Led by Samuel Gompers, former head of the Cigar Makers' Union, the AFL avoided the Knights' and anarchists' idealism to press for concrete goals: higher wages, shorter hours, and the right to bargain collectively. Born in London to German Jewish parents, Gompers developed his commitment to unionism from interactions with émigré socialists, but he was more of a pragmatist than a radical. In contrast to the Knights, Gompers and the AFL accepted capitalism and worked to improve conditions within it.

AFL member unions retained autonomy in their own areas of skill but tried to develop a general policy that would suit all members. The national organization required constituent unions to hire organizers to expand membership, and it collected dues for a fund to aid members on strike. The AFL avoided party politics, adhering instead to Gompers's dictum of supporting labor's friends and opposing its enemies, regardless of party.

AFL membership grew to 1 million by 1901 and 2.5 million by 1917, when it consisted of 111 national unions and 27,000 locals. But because member unions organized by craft rather than by workplace, they had little interest in recruiting unskilled workers. Nor did they recruit women. Of 6.3 million employed women in 1910, fewer than 2 percent belonged to unions. Male unionists often rationalized women's exclusion by insisting that women should not be employed. According to one labor leader, "Woman is not qualified for the conditions of wage labor. . . . The mental and physical makeup of woman is in revolt against wage service. She is competing with the man who is her father or husband or is to become her husband." Mostly, unionists worried that, because women were paid less, men's wages would be lowered or they would lose jobs if women invaded the workplace. Moreover, male workers, accustomed to sex segregation in employment, could not imagine working side by side with women.

Organized labor also excluded most immigrant and African American workers. Many white workers feared that such groups would depress wages, but long-standing nativism and racism also influenced union policies. Only a few trade unions in which foreign-born craftsmen were leaders welcomed immigrants. Blacks were prominent in the coal miners' union and were partially unionized in such trades as construction, barbering, and dock work, which employed large numbers of African American workers. But they could belong only to segregated local unions in the South, and the majority of northern AFL unions had exclusion policies. Long-held prejudices were reinforced when blacks and immigrants, eager for any work they could get, were hired as strikebreakers to replace striking whites.

**Homestead Strike**

The AFL and the labor movement suffered a series of setbacks in the early 1890s, when once again labor violence stirred public fears. In July 1892 the AFL-affiliated Amalgamated Association of Iron and Steelworkers refused to accept pay cuts and went on strike in Homestead, Pennsylvania. In response, Henry C. Frick, president of the Carnegie Steel Company, closed the plant. Shortly thereafter, Frick hired three hundred guards from the Pinkerton Detective Agency to protect the factory and floated them in by barge under cover of darkness. Lying in wait on the shore of the Monongahela River, angry workers attacked and routed the Pinkertons. State troops intervened, and after five months the strikers gave in. By then public opinion had turned against the union, after a young anarchist who was not a striker attempted to assassinate Frick.

In 1894 workers at the Pullman Palace (railroad passenger) Car Company walked out in protest over ex-

**Pullman Strike**

ploitative policies at the company town near Chicago. The paternalistic owner, George Pullman, provided everything for the twelve thousand residents of the so-called model town named after him. His company controlled all land and buildings, the school, the bank, and the water and gas systems. It paid wages, fixed rents, and spied on disgruntled employees. As one laborer grumbled, "We are born in a Pullman house, fed from the Pullman shop, taught in the Pullman school, catechized in the Pullman church, and when we die we shall be buried in the Pullman cemetery and go to the Pullman hell."

One thing Pullman would not do was negotiate with workers. When hard times hit in 1893, Pullman tried to protect profits and stock dividends by cutting wages 25 to 40 percent while holding firm on rents and prices in the town. Hard-pressed workers sent a committee to Pullman to protest his policies. He reacted by firing three committee members. Enraged workers, most of them from the American Railway Union, called a strike; Pullman retaliated by closing the factory. The union, led by the charismatic Eugene V. Debs, voted to aid strikers by refusing to handle any Pullman cars attached to any trains anywhere. Pullman rejected arbitration. The railroad owners' association then enlisted aid from U.S. Attorney General Richard Olney, a former railroad lawyer, who obtained a court injunction to prevent the union from "obstructing the railways and holding up the mails." President Grover Cleveland ordered federal troops to Chicago, ostensibly to protect rail-carried mail, but in reality to crush the strike. Within a month strikers gave in, and Debs went to prison for defying the court injunction. The Supreme Court upheld Debs's six-month sentence on grounds that the federal government could legally remove obstacles to interstate commerce.

In the West, Colorado miners engaged in several bitter struggles and violent strikes. In 1905 they helped form

**IWW**

a new, radical labor organization, the Industrial Workers of the World (IWW). Unlike the AFL but like the Knights of Labor, the IWW strove to unite all laborers of all races who were excluded from craft unions. Its motto was "An injury to one is an injury to all," and its goal was "One Big Union." But the "Wobblies," as IWW members were known, exceeded the tactics of the Knights by espousing violence and sabotage.

Embracing the rhetoric of class conflict—"The final aim is revolution," according to IWW creed—and an ideology of socialism, Wobblies believed workers should seize and run the nation's industries. Leaders such as Mary "Mother" Jones, an Illinois coalfield union organizer; Elizabeth Gurley Flynn, a fiery orator known as the "Joan of Arc of the labor movement"; Italian radical Carlo Tresca; Swedish-born organizer and songwriter Joe Hill; and William D. (Big Bill) Haywood, the brawny, one-eyed founder of the Western Federation of Miners, headed a series of strife-torn strikes. Demonstrations erupted in western lumber and mining camps, in the steel town of McKees Rocks, Pennsylvania (1907), and in the textile mills of Lawrence, Massachusetts (1912). Although the Wobblies' anticapitalist goals and aggressive tactics attracted considerable publicity, IWW membership probably never exceeded 150,000. The organization collapsed during the First World War when federal prosecution sent many of its leaders to jail and local police forces violently harassed IWW members.

Despite their general exclusion from unions, some women employees did organize and fight employers as strenuously as men did. The "Up-

**Women Unionists**

rising of the 20,000" in New York City, a 1909 strike by male and female immigrant members of the International Ladies' Garment Workers' Union (ILGWU), was one of the country's largest strikes to that time. Women were also prominent in the 1912 Lawrence, Massachusetts, textile workers' "Bread and Roses" strike. Female trade-union membership swelled during the 1910s, but men monopolized national leadership, even in industries with large female work forces, such as garment manufacturing, textiles, and boots and shoes.

Women, however, did dominate one union: the Telephone Operators' Department of the International Brotherhood of Electrical Workers. Organized in Montana and San Francisco early in the twentieth century, the union spread throughout the Bell system, the nation's monopolistic telephone company and single largest employer of women. To promote solidarity among their mostly young female members, union leaders organized dances, excursions, and bazaars. They also sponsored educational programs to enhance members' leadership skills. The union focused mainly on workplace issues. Intent on developing pride and independence among telephone operators, the union resisted scientific management techniques and tightening of supervision. In 1919 several militant union branches paralyzed the phone service of five New England states, but the union collapsed after a failed strike, again in New England, in 1923.

A key organization seeking to promote interests of laboring women was the Women's Trade Union League

▲ In 1919 telephone operators, mostly female, went out on strike and shut down phone service throughout New England. The male-dominated leadership of the International Brotherhood of Electrical Workers, to which the operators belonged, opposed the strike, but the women refused to back down and eventually achieved several of their demands against the New England Telephone Company. *(Corbis-Bettmann)*

(WTUL), founded in 1903 and patterned after a similar organization in England. The WTUL sought workplace protection legislation and reduced hours for female workers, sponsored educational activities, and campaigned for woman suffrage. It helped telephone operators organize their union, and in 1909 it supported the ILGWU's massive strike against New York City sweatshops. Initially the union's highest offices were held by middle-class women who sympathized with female wage laborers, but control shifted in the 1910s to forceful working-class leaders, notably Agnes Nestor, a glove maker; Rose Schneiderman, a cap maker; and Mary Anderson, a shoe worker. The WTUL advocated opening apprenticeship programs to women so they could enter skilled trades and training female workers to assume leadership roles. It served as a vital link between the labor and women's movements into the 1920s.

The dramatic labor struggles in the half-century following the Civil War make it easy to forget that only a

## The Experience of Wage Work

small fraction of American wage workers belonged to unions. In 1900 about 1 million out of a total of 27.6 million workers were unionized. By 1920 union membership had grown to 5 million, still only 13 percent of the work force. Unionization was strong in construction trades, transportation, communications, and, to a lesser extent, manufacturing. For many workers, getting a job and keeping it took priority over bargaining for higher wages and shorter hours. Job instability and the seasonal nature of work seriously hindered union-organizing efforts. Few companies employed a full work force year-round; most employers hired during peak seasons and laid workers off during slack periods. The 1880 census showed that in some communities 30 percent of adult males had been jobless at some time during the previous year. Moreover, union organizers took no interest in large segments of the industrial labor force and intentionally barred others.

The millions of men, women, and children who were not unionized tried in their own ways to cope with the pressures of the machine age. Increasing numbers, both native-born and immigrant, joined fraternal societies, such as the Polish Roman Catholic Union, the African American Colored Brotherhood and Sisterhood of Honor, and the Jewish B'nai B'rith. For small monthly or yearly contributions these organizations, widespread by the early twentieth century, provided members with life insurance, sickness benefits, and burial costs.

For most American workers, then, the machine age had mixed results. Industrial wages, though rarely generous, rose between 1877 and 1914, boosting purchasing power and creating a mass market for standardized goods. Yet in 1900 most employees worked sixty hours a week at wages that averaged 20 cents an hour for skilled work and 10 cents an hour for unskilled. And workers found that, even as their wages rose, living costs increased even faster.

## STANDARDS OF LIVING

Some Americans, like the Watertown molders, distrusted a system that treated them like machines, but few could resist the experts' claims that efficiency and mechanization were improving everyday life. The expansion of railroad, postal, and telephone service drew even isolated communities into the orbit of a consumer society. American ingenuity combined with mass production and mass marketing to make available myriad goods that previously had not existed or had been the exclusive property of the wealthy. As a result, Americans were better fed, better clothed, and better housed than ever before. The new material well-being, symbolized by canned foods, ready-made clothing, and home appliances, had a dual effect. It blended Americans of differing status into consumer communities defined not by place of residence but by possessions, and it accentuated differences between those who could afford goods and services and those who could not.

If a society's affluence is measured by how it converts luxuries into commonplace articles, the United States was

**Commonplace Luxuries**

indeed becoming affluent in the years between 1880 and 1920. In 1880 smokers rolled their own cigarettes; only wealthy women could afford silk stockings; only residents of Florida, Texas, and California could enjoy fresh oranges; and people made candy and soap at home. By 1899 manufactured goods and perishable foodstuffs had become increasingly available. That year Americans bought 2 billion machine-produced cigarettes and 151,000 pairs of silk stockings, consumed oranges at the rate of 100

crates for every 1,000 people, and spent averages of $1.08 per person on store-bought candy and 63 cents per person on soap. By 1921 the transformation had advanced further. Americans smoked 43 billion cigarettes that year (403 per person), bought 217 million pairs of silk stockings, ate 248 crates of oranges per 1,000 people, and spent $1.66 per person on confectionery goods and $1.40 on soap.

What people can afford obviously depends on their resources and incomes. Data for the period show that incomes rose broadly. At the top of society, the expanding economy spawned massive fortunes and created a new industrial elite. An 1891 magazine article estimated that 120 Americans were worth at least $10 million ($250 million in current dollars). By 1920 the richest 5 percent of the population received almost one-fourth of all earned income. Incomes also rose among the middle class. For example, average pay for clerical workers rose 36 percent between 1890 and 1910 (see Table 18.1). At the turn of the century, employees of the federal executive branch averaged $1,072 a year, and college professors, $1,100 (around $25,000 in modern dollars)—not handsome sums, but much more than manual workers received. With such salaries, the middle class, whose numbers were increasing as a result of new job opportunities, could afford relatively comfortable housing. A six- or seven-room house cost around $3,000 to buy or build (about $65,000 in current

| TABLE 18.1 | American Living Standards, 1890–1910 | |
|---|---|---|
| | **1890** | **1910** |
| **Income and Earnings** | | |
| Annual income | | |
|   Clerical worker | $848 | $1,156 |
|   Public school teacher | 256 | 492 |
|   Industrial worker | 486 | 630 |
|   Farm laborer | 233 | 336 |
| Hourly wage | | |
|   Soft-coal miner | 0.18[a] | 0.21 |
|   Iron worker | 0.17[a] | 0.23 |
|   Shoe worker | 0.14[a] | 0.19 |
|   Paper worker | 0.12[a] | 0.17 |
| **Labor Statistics** | | |
| Number of people in labor force | 28.5 mil. | 41.7 mil.[b] |
| Average workweek in manufacturing | 60 hrs. | 51 hrs. |

[a]1892
[b]1920

dollars) and from $15 to $20 per month ($400 to $500 in current dollars) to rent.

Although hourly wages for industrial employees increased, workers had to expend a disproportionate amount of income on necessities. On average, annual wages of factory laborers rose about 30 percent, from $486 in 1890 (about $12,000 in modern dollars) to $630 in 1910 (about $15,500 in current dollars). In industries with large female work forces, such as shoe and paper manufacturing, hourly pay rates remained lower than in male-dominated industries, such as coal mining and iron production. Regional variations were also wide. Nevertheless, as Table 18.1 shows, most wages moved upward. Income for farm laborers followed the same trend, though wages remained relatively low because farm workers usually received free room and board.

Wage increases mean little, however, if living costs rise as fast or faster. That is what happened. In few working-class occupations did incomes rise as fast as prices. The weekly cost of living for a typical wage earner's family of four rose over 47 percent between 1889 and 1913. In other words, a combination of housing, food, and other goods that cost $68 in 1889 increased, after a slight dip in the mid-1890s, to $100 by 1913.

**Cost of Living**

How, then, could working-class Americans afford machine-age goods and services? Many could not. The daughter of a textile worker, recalling her school days, described how "some of the kids would bring bars of chocolate, others an orange. . . . I suppose they were richer than a family like ours. My father used to buy a bag of candy and a bag of peanuts every payday. . . . And that's all we'd have until the next payday." Another woman explained how her family coped with high prices and low wages: "My mother made our clothes. People then wore old clothes. My mother would rip them out and make them over."

Still, a family could raise its income and partake modestly in consumer society by sending children and women into the labor market (see pages 506–508). In a household whose main breadwinner made $600 a year, wages of other family members might lift total family income to $800 or $900. Many families also rented rooms to boarders and lodgers, a practice that could yield up to $200 a year. These means of increasing family income enabled people to purchase important services. Between 1889 and 1901, working-class families markedly increased expenditures for life insurance and funeral policies, as well as for new leisure activities (see Chapter 19). Workers

**Supplements to Family Income**

were thus able to improve their living standard, but not without sacrifices.

More than ever, American working people lived within a highly developed money economy. Between 1890 and 1920, the labor force increased by 50 percent, from 28 million workers to 42 million. These figures, however, are misleading: in general, they represent a change in the nature of work as much as an increase in the number of available jobs. In the rural households that predominated in the nineteenth century, women and children performed tasks crucial to a family's daily existence—cooking, cleaning, planting, and harvesting—but these jobs seldom appeared in employment figures because they earned no wages. As the nation industrialized and the agricultural sector's share of national income declined, paid employment became more common. Jobs in urban industries and commerce were easier to define and easier to count. The proportion of Americans who worked—whether in fields, households, factories, or offices—probably did not increase markedly. Most Americans, male and female, had always worked. What was new was the increase in paid employment, making purchases of consumer goods and services more affordable.

Science and technology eased some of life's struggles, and their impact on living standards strengthened after 1900. Medical advances, better diets, and improved housing sharply reduced death rates and extended life. Between 1900 and 1920, life expectancy rose by fully six years, and the death rate dropped by 24 percent. Notable declines occurred in deaths from typhoid, diphtheria, influenza (except for a harsh pandemic in 1918 and 1919), tuberculosis, and intestinal ailments—diseases that had been scourges of earlier generations. There were, however, significantly more deaths from cancer, diabetes, and heart disease, afflictions of an aging population and of new environmental factors, such as smoke and chemical pollution. Americans also found more ways to kill one another: although suicide rates remained stable, homicides and automobile-related deaths—effects of a fast-paced urban society—increased dramatically.

**Higher Life Expectancy**

Not only were amenities and luxuries more available than in the previous half-century, means to upward mobility seemed more accessible as well. Although inequities that had pervaded earlier eras remained in place, and race, gender, religion, and ethnicity still affected access to opportunity, education increasingly became the key to success. Public education, aided by construction of new schools and passage of laws that required children to stay in school to age fourteen, equipped young people to achieve a living standard higher than their parents'. Between 1890 and 1922, the number of students enrolled in public high schools rose dramatically, though by today's standards graduation rates among young people were low—16.3 percent in 1920, up from 3.5 percent in 1890. The creation of managerial and sales jobs in service industries helped to counter the downward mobility that resulted when mechanization pushed skilled workers out of their crafts. And the resulting goods of mass production meant that even workers found life more convenient.

At the vanguard of a revolution in lifestyles stood the toilet. The chain-pull, washdown water closet, invented in

### Flush Toilets and Other Innovations

England around 1870, reached the United States in the 1880s. Shortly after 1900, the flush toilet appeared; thanks to mass production of enamel-coated metal fixtures, it became common in American homes and buildings. The toilet, cheap and easy to install, brought about a shift in habits and attitudes. Before 1880 only luxury hotels and wealthy families had private indoor bathrooms. By the 1890s the germ theory of disease was raising fears about carelessly disposed human waste as a source of infection and water contamination. Much more rapidly than Europeans did, Americans combined a desire for cleanliness with an urge for convenience and began installing modern toilets in middle-class urban houses. By the 1920s, they were prevalent in many working-class homes, too. Bodily functions took on an unpleasant image, and the home bathroom became a place of utmost privacy. Edward and Clarence Scott, who manufactured white tissue in perforated rolls, provided Americans a more convenient form of toilet tissue than the rough paper they had previously used. At the same time, toilets and private bathtubs gave Americans new ways to use—and waste—water. Plumbing advances belonged to a broader democratization of convenience that accompanied mass production and consumerism.

The tin can also altered lifestyles. Before the mid-nineteenth century, Americans typically ate only foods that were in season. Drying, smoking, and salting could preserve meat for a short time, but the availability of fresh meat and milk was limited; there was no way to prevent spoilage. A French inventor developed the cooking-and-sealing process of canning around 1810, and in the 1850s an American man named Gail Borden devised a means of condensing and preserving milk. Sales of canned goods and condensed milk increased during the 1860s, but processing some foods was difficult, and cans had to be made by hand. In the 1880s, technology solved production problems. Inventors fashioned machines to peel fruits and veg-

▲ The modern bathroom, with sink, tub, and flush toilet, marked an unheralded but noteworthy feature of American living standards. It improved habits of personal hygiene, increased household water consumption, altered patterns of waste disposal, and occupied a new and private realm of domestic space.
*(Picture Research Consultants and Archives)*

etables and to process salmon, as well as stamping and soldering machines to mass-produce cans from tin plate. Now, even people remote from markets, like sailors and cowboys, could readily consume tomatoes, milk, oysters, and other alternatives to previously monotonous diets. Housewives preserved their own fruits and vegetables, "putting up" foods in sealed glass jars.

Other trends and inventions broadened Americans' diets. Growing urban populations created demands that encouraged fruit and vegetable farmers to raise more produce. Railroad refrigerator cars enabled growers and meatpackers to ship perishables greater distances and to preserve them for longer periods. By the 1890s, northern city dwellers could enjoy southern and western strawberries, grapes, and tomatoes for several months of the year. Home iceboxes enabled middle-class families to store perishables. An easy means of producing ice commercially was invented in the 1870s, and by 1900 the nation had two thousand ice plants, most of which made home deliveries.

Availability of new foods also inspired health advocates to reform American diets. In the 1870s, John H.

### Dietary Reform

Kellogg, nutritionist and manager of the Western Health Reform Institute in Battle Creek, Michigan, began serving patients health foods, including peanut butter and wheat flakes. Several years later, his brother, William K. Kellogg, invented corn flakes, and another nutritionist, Charles W. Post, introduced Grape-Nuts, revolutionizing breakfast by replacing eggs, potatoes, and meat with ready-to-eat cereal, which supposedly was healthier. Like Edison and Ford, Post believed in the power of advertising, and he personally wrote ads for his products. His company became one of fastest growing in the country.

Other developments affected the ways people prepared and consumed food. Just before the First World War, scientists discovered the dietetic value of vitamins A and B (C and D were discovered later). Growing numbers of published cookbooks and the opening of cooking schools reflected heightened interest in food and its possibilities for health and enjoyment. Home gardens in urban backyards also became easier to tend, aided by the Burpee Company, founded in Philadelphia in 1876, which mailed flower and vegetable seeds to gardeners who bought them through mail-order catalogues—just as they bought goods from Sears, Roebuck.

As in the past, the poorest people still consumed cheap foods, heavy in starches and carbohydrates. Southern textile workers, for example, ate corn mush and fatback (the strip of meat from a hog's back) almost every day. Poor urban families seldom could afford meat. Now, though, many of them could purchase previously unavailable fruits, vegetables, and dairy products. Workers had to spend a high percentage of their income on food—almost half of a breadwinner's wages—but they never suffered the severe malnutrition that plagued other developing nations.

Just as cans and iceboxes made many foods more common, the sewing machine and standardized sizes sparked a revolution in clothing. The sew-

### Ready-Made Clothing

ing machine, invented in Europe but refined in the mid-nineteenth century by Americans Elias Howe Jr. and Isaac M. Singer, came into

▲ Using color, large-scale scenes, and fanciful images, manufacturers of consumer goods advertised their products to a public eager to buy. This ad from the W. K. Kellogg Company, maker of breakfast foods, shows the increasingly common practice of using an attractive young woman to capture attention.
*(Picture Research Consultants & Archives)*

use in clothing and shoe manufacture. Demand for uniforms during the Civil War boosted the ready-made (as opposed to custom-made) clothing industry, and by 1890 annual retail sales of machine-made garments reached $1.5 billion. Mass production enabled manufacturers to turn out good-quality apparel at relatively low cost and to standardize sizes to fit different body shapes. By 1900 only the poorest families could not afford "ready-to-wear" clothes. Tailors and seamstresses were relegated to repair work. Many women continued to make clothing at home, to save money or as a hobby, but commercial dress patterns intended for use with a sewing machine simplified home production of apparel and injected another form of standardization into everyday life.

Mass-produced garments altered clothing styles and tastes. Restrictive Victorian designs still dominated female fashion, but women were abandoning the most burdensome features. As women's participation in work and leisure activities became more active, dress designers placed greater emphasis on comfort. In the 1890s, long sleeves

classes would have owned two suits: one for Sundays and special occasions, and one for everyday wear. After 1900, however, manufacturers began producing inexpensive garments from fabrics of different weights and for different seasons. Men replaced derbies with felt hats, and stiff collars and cuffs with soft ones; somber, dark-blue serge gave way to lighter shades and more intricate weaves. Workingmen still needed durable, inexpensive overalls, shirts, and shoes. But even for males of modest means, clothing was becoming something to be bought instead of made and remade at home.

and skirt hemlines receded, and high-boned collars disappeared. Women began wearing tailored blouses called shirtwaists, manufactured by such companies as the Triangle Shirtwaist Factory. Designers used less fabric; by the 1920s a dress required three yards of material instead of ten. Petite prevailed as the ideal: the most desirable waist measurement was eighteen to twenty inches, and corsets were big sellers. In the early 1900s, long hair tied up behind the neck was the most popular style. By the First World War, when many women worked in hospitals and factories, shorter and less hindering hairstyles had become acceptable.

Men's clothes, too, became lightweight and stylish. Before 1900, men in the middle and well-off working

Department stores and chain stores helped to create and serve this new consumerism. Between 1865 and

## Department and Chain Stores

1900, Macy's Department Store in New York, Wanamaker's in Philadelphia, Marshall Field in Chicago, and Rich's in Atlanta became urban landmarks. Previously, working classes bought goods in stores with limited inventories, and wealthier people patronized fancy shops; prices, quality of goods, and social custom discouraged each from shopping at the other's establishments. Now, department stores, with their open displays of clothing, housewares, and furniture—all available in large quantities to anyone with the purchase price—caused a merchandising revolution. They offered not only variety but also home deliveries, exchange policies, and charge accounts.

Meanwhile, the Great Atlantic Tea Company, founded in 1859, became the first grocery chain. Renamed the Great Atlantic & Pacific Tea Company in 1869 (and known as A&P), the firm's stores bought in volume and sold to the public at low prices. By 1915 there were eighteen hundred A&P stores, and twelve thousand more were built over the next ten years. Other chains, such as Woolworth's dime stores, which sold inexpensive personal items and novelties, grew rapidly during the same period.

A society of scarcity does not need advertising: when demand exceeds supply, producers have no trouble selling what they market. But in a society

### Advertising

of rising abundance, such as industrial America, supply frequently outstrips demand, necessitating a means to increase and create demand. Advertising assumed this function. In 1865 retailers spent about $9.5 million on advertising; that sum reached $95 million by 1900 and nearly $500 million by 1919.

In the late nineteenth century, companies that mass-produced consumer goods hired advertisers to create "consumption communities," bodies of consumers loyal to a particular brand name. In 1881 Congress passed a trademark law enabling producers to register and protect brand names. Thousands of companies registered products as varied as Hires Root Beer, Uneeda Biscuits, and Carter's Little Liver Pills. Advertising agencies—a service pioneered by N. W. Ayer & Son of Philadelphia—in turn offered expert advice to firms that wished to cultivate brand loyalty. Newspapers served as the prime instrument for advertising. In the mid-nineteenth century, publishers began to pursue higher revenues by selling more ad space. Wanamaker's placed the first full-page ad in 1879, and advertisers began using large print and including elaborate illustrations of products. Such attention-getting techniques transformed advertising into news. More than ever before, people read newspapers to find out what was for sale as well as what was happening.

Outdoor billboards and electrical signs rivaled newspapers as important selling devices. Billboards on city buildings, in railroad stations, and alongside roads promoted such products as Gillette razors, Kodak cameras, Wrigley chewing gum, and Budweiser beer. In the mid-1890s, electric lights made billboards more dynamic and appealing. Commercial districts sparkled under what one observer called "a medium of motion, of action, of *life*, of *light*, of compulsory attraction." The flashing electrical signs on New York City's Broadway—including a forty-

▲ Advertising, which developed into a powerful medium in the late nineteenth century, used explicit and implicit domestic images to reinforce a wife's role as homemaker. This ad implies that a devoted wife lovingly assumes such tasks as sewing and mending clothing, guided into her role by a strong and superior husband.

*(Library of Congress)*

five-foot Heinz pickle in green bulbs and dazzling theater marquees—gave the street its label "the Great White Way." Soon, "talking" signs were installed, with words moving along signboards providing news as well as advertising copy in a multitude of colors. Americans now had an enticing variety of inducements to consume.

## THE CORPORATE CONSOLIDATION MOVEMENT

Neither new products nor new marketing techniques could mask unsettling factors in the American economy. The huge capital investment needed for new technology meant that factories had to operate at near capacity to recover costs. But the more manufacturers produced, the more they had to sell. To sell more and outdo competitors, they had to advertise and reduce prices. To increase profits and compensate for advertising costs and low prices, they further expanded production and often reduced wages. To expand, they borrowed money. And to repay loans, they had to produce and sell even more. This spiraling process strangled small firms that could not keep pace and thrust workers into constant uncertainty. The same cycle affected commerce, banking, and transportation as well.

In this environment, optimism could dissolve at the hint that debtors could not meet their obligations. Economic downturns occurred with painful regularity—1873, 1884, 1893. Business leaders disagreed on what caused economic strains. Some blamed overproduction; others pointed to underconsumption; still others blamed lax credit and investment practices. Whatever the explanation, businesspeople began seeking ways to combat the uncertainty of boom-and-bust business cycles. Many adopted centralized forms of business organization, notably corporations, pools, trusts, and holding companies.

Unlike laborers, industrialists never questioned the capitalist system. They sought new ways to build on the base that had supported economic growth since the early 1800s, when states revised incorporation laws to encourage commerce and industry.

### Rise of Corporations

Under such laws, almost anyone could start a company and raise money by selling stock to investors. Stockholders shared in profits without personal risk, because laws limited their liability for company debts to the amount of their own investment; the rest of their wealth was protected should the company fail. Nor did investors need to concern themselves with a firm's day-to-day operation; responsibility for company administration rested with its managers.

Corporations proved to be the best instruments to raise capital for industrial expansion, and by 1900 two-thirds of all goods manufactured in the United States were produced by corporate firms such as General Electric and the American Tobacco Company. Corporations won judicial protection in the 1880s and 1890s when the Supreme Court ruled that they, like individuals, are protected by the Fourteenth Amendment. In other words, states could not deny corporations equal protection under the law and could not deprive them of rights or property without due process of law. Such rulings insulated corporations from government interference in their operations.

To combat downward swings of the business cycle, corporation managers sought stability in new and larger forms of economic concentration. Between the late 1880s and early 1900s, an epidemic of business consolidation swept the country, re-

### Pools

sulting in massive conglomerates that have since dominated the nation's economy. At first such alliances were tentative and informal, consisting mainly of cooperative agreements among firms that manufactured the same product or offered the same service. Through these arrangements, called pools, competing companies tried to control the market by agreeing how much each should produce and by sharing profits. Used by railroads (to divide up traffic), steel producers, and whiskey distillers, pools depended on their members' honesty. Such "gentlemen's agreements" worked during good times when there was enough business for all; but during slow periods, desire for profits often tempted pool members to secretly reduce prices or sell more than the agreed quota. The Interstate Commerce Act of 1887 outlawed pools among railroads (see page 567), but by then the pool's usefulness was already fading.

John D. Rockefeller, founder of Standard Oil, disliked pools, calling them weak and undependable. In 1879 one of his lawyers, Samuel Dodd, devised a more stable means of dominating the market. Because state laws prohibited one corporation from holding stock in another corporation, Dodd suggested utilizing an old device called a trust, a legal arrangement whereby a responsible individual would manage the financial affairs of a person unwilling or unable to handle them alone. Dodd reasoned that one company could control an industry by luring or forcing stockholders of smaller companies in that industry to yield control of their stock "in trust" to the larger company's board of trustees. This device allowed Rockefeller to achieve horizontal integration—the acquisition of similar companies—of the profitable petroleum industry in 1882 by combining his corporation with other refineries that he bought up.

### Trusts and Holding Companies

In 1888 New Jersey adopted laws allowing corporations chartered there to own property in other states and to own stock in other corporations. (Trusts provided for trusteeship, not ownership.) This liberalization facilitated creation of the holding company, which owned a partial or complete interest in other companies. Holding companies could in turn merge all their holdings' assets (buildings, equipment, inventory, and cash) as well as their management. Under this arrangement, Rockefeller's holding company merged forty formerly independent operations into Standard Oil of New Jersey. By 1898 Standard Oil refined 84 percent of all oil produced in the nation, controlled most pipelines, and engaged in natural-gas production and ownership of oil-producing properties.

Standard Oil's expansion into operations besides refining exemplified a new form of economic combination. To

▲ Believing that Rockefeller's Standard Oil monopoly was exercising dangerous power, this political cartoonist depicts the trust as a greedy octopus whose sprawling tentacles already ensnare Congress, state legislatures, and the taxpayer, and are reaching for the White House.

*(Library of Congress)*

dominate their markets, many holding companies sought control over all aspects of the industry, including raw-materials extraction, product manufacture, and distribution. A model of such vertical integration, which fused related businesses under unified management, was Gustavus Swift's Chicago meat-processing operation. During the 1880s, Swift invested in livestock, slaughterhouses, refrigerator cars, and marketing to ensure profits from the sale of beef at prices he could control. With their widespread operations, both Swift & Company and Standard Oil extended the economic tentacles of single companies to all regions of the nation.

Mergers provided answers to industry's search for order and profits. Between 1889 and 1903, some three hundred combinations were formed, most of them trusts and holding companies. The most spectacular was U.S. Steel Corporation, financed by J. P. Morgan in 1901. This enterprise, made up of iron-ore properties, freight carriers, wire mills, and other firms, was capitalized at over $1.4 billion (more than $35 billion in current money). Other mammoth combinations included Amalgamated Copper Company,

American Sugar Refining Company, and U.S. Rubber Company. In 1896 fewer than a dozen corporations were worth over $10 million; by 1903 three hundred were worth that much, and seventeen had assets exceeding $100 million. At the same time, these huge companies ruthlessly put thousands of small firms out of business.

The merger movement created a new species of businessman, one whose vocation was financial organizing rather than producing a particular good. Shrewd investors sought opportunities for combination, formed a holding company, then persuaded producers to sell their firms to the new company. These financiers raised money by selling stock and borrowing from banks. Their attention ranged widely. W. H. Moore organized the American Tin Plate Company, Diamond Match Company, and National Biscuit Company, and he acquired control of the Rock Island Railroad. Elbert H. Gary similarly participated in consolidation of the barbed-wire industry and of U.S. Steel. Investment bankers such as J. P. Morgan and Jacob Schiff piloted the merger move-

**Financiers**

ment, inspiring awe with their financial power and organizational skills.

Growth of corporations turned stock and bond exchanges into hubs of activity. In 1886 trading on the New York Stock Exchange passed 1 million shares a day. By 1914 the number of industrial stocks traded reached 511, compared with 145 in 1869. Between 1870 and 1900, foreign investment in American companies rose from $1.5 billion to $3.5 billion, as the country's economy assumed the image of a safe and lucrative investment. Assets of savings banks, concentrated in the Northeast and on the West Coast, rose by 700 percent between 1875 and 1897. States loosened regulations to enable banks to invest in railroads and industrial enterprises. Commercial banks, insurance companies, and corporations also invested heavily. As one journal, exaggerating the optimism of capitalists, proclaimed, "Nearly the whole country (including the typical widow and orphan) is interested in the stock market."

## THE GOSPEL OF WEALTH AND ITS CRITICS

Business leaders used corporate consolidation to minimize competition. To justify their tactics, they invoked the doctrine of Social Darwinism. Developed by British philosopher Herbert Spencer and preached in the United States by Yale professor William Graham Sumner, Social Darwinism loosely grafted Charles Darwin's theory of survival of the fittest onto laissez faire, the doctrine that government should not interfere in private economic matters. Social Darwinists reasoned that, in a free-market economy, wealth would flow naturally to those most capable of handling it. Acquisition and possession of property were thus sacred and deserved rights. Civilization depended on this system, explained Sumner. "If we do not like the survival of the fittest," he wrote, "we have only one possible alternative, and that is survival of the unfittest." In this view, large corporations represented the natural accumulation of economic power by those best suited for wielding it.

Social Darwinists reasoned, too, that wealth carried moral responsibilities to provide for those less fortunate or less capable. Steel baron Andrew Carnegie asserted what he called "the Gospel of Wealth," meaning that he and other industrialists were guardians of society's wealth and as such had a duty to serve society in humane ways. Over his lifetime, Carnegie donated more than $350 million to libraries, schools, peace initiatives, and the arts. Such philanthropy, however, also implied a right for benefactors such as Rockefeller and Carnegie to define what was

good and necessary for society; it did not translate into paying workers decent wages.

Like western entrepreneurs who lauded rugged individualism while seeking public subsidies in their mining, transportation, and agricultural businesses, leaders in the corporate consolidation movement extolled initiative and independence but also pressed for government assistance. They denounced efforts to legislate maximum working hours or to regulate factory conditions as interference with natural economic laws, but they lobbied forcefully for public subsidies, loans, and tax relief to encourage business growth. Grants to railroads (see Chapter 17) were one form of such assistance. Tariffs, which benefited American products by placing import taxes on imported products, were another. Since the inception of tariffs in the early nineteenth century, industrialists argued that tariff protection encouraged the development of new products and new enterprises. But tariffs also forced consumers to pay artificially high prices for many goods (see page 568).

**Government Assistance to Business**

While defenders such as Carnegie and Rockefeller insisted that trusts and other forms of big business were a natural and efficient outcome of economic development, critics charged that these methods were unnatural because they stifled opportunity and originated from greed. Such charges, emanating from farmers, workers, and intellectuals, reflected an ardent fear of monopoly—the domination of an economic activity (such as oil refining) by one powerful company (such as Standard Oil). Those who feared monopoly believed that large corporations fixed prices, exploited workers by cutting wages, destroyed opportunity by crushing small businesses, and threatened democracy by corrupting politicians—all of which was not only unnatural but immoral.

**Dissenting Voices**

Critics believed they knew a better, more ethical path to progress. For example, by the mid-1880s, a number of intellectuals began to challenge Social Darwinism and laissez-faire economics. Sociologist Lester Ward, in his book *Dynamic Sociology* (1883), argued that human control of nature, not natural law, accounted for civilization's advance. A system that guaranteed survival only to the fittest was wasteful and brutal; instead, Ward reasoned, cooperative activity fostered by government intervention was more just. Economists Richard Ely, John R. Commons, and Edward Bemis agreed that natural forces should be harnessed for the public good. They denounced the laissez-faire system for its "unsound morals" and praised the positive assistance that government could offer to ordinary people.

Whereas academics endorsed intervention in the natural economic order, writers such as Henry George and Edward Bellamy questioned why the United States had to have so many poor people while a few became fabulously wealthy. Henry George was a San Francisco printer with only a seventh-grade education but an avid reader of economic theory. Alarmed at the existence of abject poverty among working people like himself, he came to believe that inequality stemmed from the ability of a few to profit from rising land values. George argued that such profits made landowners rich from ever-higher rents charged by them because of increased demand for living and working space, especially in cities. Unlike wages paid to workers, wealth from landowning was created without any productive effort. To prevent profiteering, George proposed to replace all taxes with a "single tax" on the "unearned increment"—the rise in property values caused by increased market demand rather than by owners' improvements. George's scheme, argued forcefully in *Progress and Poverty* (1879), had great popular appeal and almost won him the mayoralty of New York City in 1886.

Unlike George, who accepted private ownership, novelist Edward Bellamy believed that competitive capitalism promoted waste. Instead, he proposed a state in which government owned the means of production. Bellamy outlined his dream in *Looking Backward* (1888). The novel, which sold over a million copies, depicted Boston in the year 2000 as a peaceful community where everyone had a job and a council of benevolent elders managed the economy according to scientific principles. Although ordinary people could not vote in this utopia, Bellamy tried to convince readers that a "principle of fraternal cooperation" could replace vicious competition and wasteful monopoly. His vision, which he called "Nationalism," sparked formation of Nationalist clubs across the country and kindled popular appeals for political reform, social welfare measures, and government ownership of railroads and utilities.

Few people supported the universal government ownership envisioned by Bellamy, but several states took steps to prohibit monopolies and regulate business. By 1900 twenty-seven states had laws forbidding pools, and fifteen had constitutional provisions outlawing trusts. Most were agricultural states in the South and West that were responding to antimonopolistic pressure from farm organizations (see Chapter 20). But state governments lacked the staff and judicial support for an effective attack on big business, and corporations found ways to evade restrictions. Only national legislation, it seemed, could work.

## Antitrust Legislation

Congress moved hesitantly toward such legislation but in 1890 passed the Sherman Anti-Trust Act. Introduced by Senator John Sherman of Ohio, the law made illegal "every contract, combination in the form of trust or otherwise, or conspiracy in the restraint of trade." Those found guilty of violating the law faced fines and jail terms, and those wronged by illegal combinations could sue for triple damages. However, the law was left purposely vague, watered down when it was rewritten by pro-business eastern senators. It did not clearly define "restraint of trade" and consigned interpretation of its provisions to the courts, which at the time were allies of business.

Judges used the law's vagueness to blur distinctions between reasonable and unreasonable restraints of trade. When in 1895 the federal government prosecuted the so-called Sugar Trust for owning 98 percent of the nation's sugar-refining capacity, eight of nine Supreme Court justices ruled in *U.S. v. E. C. Knight Co.* that control of manufacturing did not necessarily mean control of trade. According to the Court, the Constitution empowered Congress to regulate interstate commerce, but manufacturing (which in the *Knight* case took place entirely within the state of Pennsylvania) did not fall under congressional control.

Between 1890 and 1900, the federal government prosecuted only eighteen cases under the Sherman Anti-Trust Act. The most successful involved railroads directly involved in interstate commerce. Ironically, the act equipped the government with a tool for breaking up labor unions: courts that did not consider monopolistic production a restraint on trade willingly applied antitrust provisions to boycotts encouraged by striking unions.

# *Legacy* FOR A PEOPLE AND A NATION

## Technology of Recorded Sound

Today's widespread markets for iPods and digital recorders derive from a combination of technology, chemistry, and human resourcefulness that came together in the late nineteenth century. In 1877, even before he invented the light bulb, Thomas Edison devised a way to preserve and reproduce his own voice by storing it on indentations made in tin foil. At first, Edison intended his "speaking machine" to help businesses store dictation and replace undependable secretaries. But in 1878 he was stirred by a rivalry with Alexander Graham Bell, inventor of the telephone who also was working on a device that reproduced sounds, to invent a phonograph that played recorded music. By the 1890s, entrepreneurs were charging audiences admission to hear recorded sounds from these machines.

By 1901, companies such as the Columbia Phonograph Company and Victor Talking Machine Company began to produce machines that played music recorded on cylinders molded from a chemical wax compound more durable than the metal cylinders that Edison had used. Over the next ten years, various inventors improved the phonograph so that it played back sound from a stylus (needle) vibrating in grooves of a shellac disc. These developments increased the playing time of records from two minutes to four.

Phonograph records now replaced sheet music as the most popular medium of popular music, but soon another technological wonder, radio, rose to prominence and helped boost record sales. The popularity of the radio could not have been possible without another feat of electronic acoustic technology: the microphone. The microphone achieved better sound quality over previously used megaphones by picking up sound from a performance and turning it into electrical currents that were transmitted via radio wire from the microphone to a radio station, which then broadcast the sound. As phonograph prices declined and sound quality improved, more records became available.

The invention in 1938 of the idler wheel, which enabled a phonograph turntable to spin a disk at the exact speed necessary for the stylus to pick up the sound accurately, brought an important advance. Shortly thereafter, more significant inventions in sound recording, such as the magnetic tape recorder, allowed for more manipulation of sound in the recording studio than ever before. Tape and slower-speed turntables lengthened play time, and in 1963 Philips, a Dutch electronics firm, introduced the compact audio cassette. Two decades later, Philips joined with the Japanese corporation Sony to adapt digital laser discs, which an American had invented to store video images, to store music by transforming sound into sequences of numbers. The compact disc (CD) was born, and from there it was a short step for the Apple Computer Company to create the iPod, which stored CD-quality music on an internal hard drive.

## SUMMARY

Mechanization and new inventions thrust the United States, once just a developing country, into the vanguard of industrial nations. By the early twentieth century, American industrial output surpassed that of Great Britain, France, and Germany combined. Industrial growth transformed the national economy and freed the United States from dependence on European capital and manufactured goods. Imports and foreign investments still flowed into the United States. But by 1900, factories, stores, and banks were converting America from a debtor agricultural nation into an industrial, financial, and exporting power. In addition, developments in electrical power, internal-combustion engines, and chemistry immeasurably altered daily life at home and abroad.

But in industry, as in farming and mining, massive size and aggressive consolidation engulfed the individual, changing the nature of work from individual activity undertaken by skilled producers to mass production undertaken by wage earners. Laborers fought to retain control of their work and struggled to organize unions that could meet their needs. The outpouring of products created a mass society based on consumerism and dominated by technology and the communications media.

The problems of enforcing the Sherman Anti-Trust Act reflected the uneven distribution of power. Corporations consolidated to control resources, production, and politics. Laborers and reformers had numbers and ideas but lacked influence. They benefited from material gains that technology and mass production provided, but they accused businesses of acquiring too much influence and profiting at their expense. In factories and homes, some people celebrated the economic transformation, while others struggled with the dilemma of industrialism: whether the new accumulations of wealth would undermine the ideal of a republic based on republicanism, democracy, and equality.

The march of industrial expansion proved almost impossible to stop, however, because so many people, powerful and ordinary, were benefiting from it. Moreover, the waves of newcomers pouring into the nation's cities were increasingly furnishing both workers and consumers for America's expanding productive capacity. The dynamo of American vitality now rested in its urban centers.

## SUGGESTIONS FOR FURTHER READING

Edward L. Ayers, *The Promise of the New South: Life After Reconstruction* (1992)

Ileen A. DeVault, *United Apart: Gender and the Rise of Craft Unionism* (2004)

Steven J. Diner, *A Very Different Age: Americans of the Progressive Era* (1998)

John F. Kasson, *Civilizing the Machine: Technology and Republican Values in America, 1776–1900* (1976)

Alice Kessler-Harris, *Out to Work: A History of Wage-Earning Women in the United States* (2003)

T. J. Jackson Lears and Richard W. Fox, eds., *The Culture of Consumption: Critical Essays in American History, 1880–1980* (1983)

David Montgomery, *The Fall of the House of Labor: The Workplace, the State and American Labor Activism, 1865–1925* (1987)

Jeffrey Sklansky, *The Soul's Economy: Market Society and Selfhood in American Thought, 1820–1920* (2002)

*For a more extensive list for further reading, go to* college.hmco.com/pic/norton8e.

# The Vitality and
# Turmoil of Urban Life
## *1877-1920*

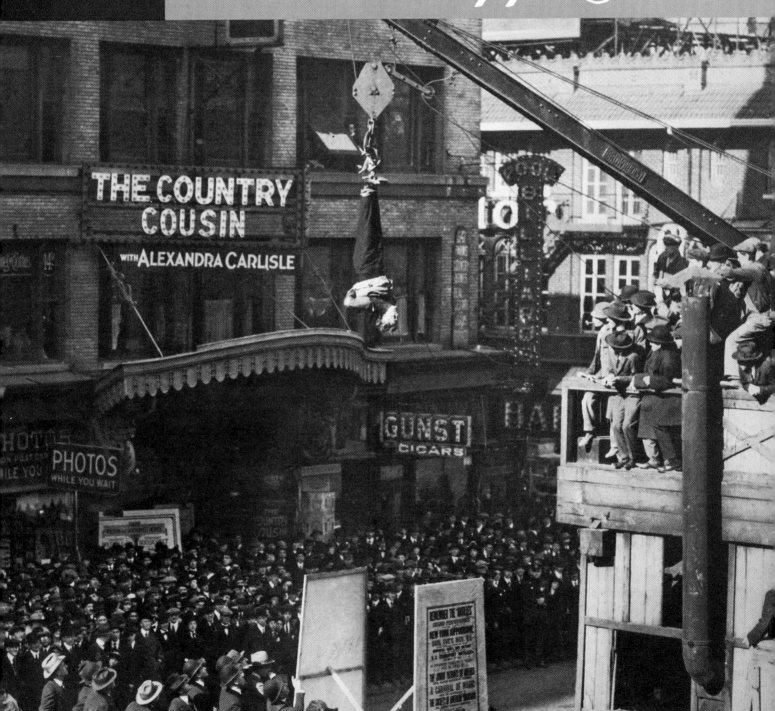

Crowds on the street gasped as they looked upward. There he was! A man, tightly bound in a straitjacket, hanging by his heels high above New York's Times Square. Suddenly, he began wriggling wildly. In seconds he was free, spreading his arms in an upside-down bow. Harry Houdini, the most celebrated showman of the early twentieth century, had escaped. As he had done so many times before, Houdini had fed the public taste for suspense, courage, and entertainment with a death-defying feat.

Harry Houdini's life epitomized both the symbol and the reality of escape from hardship and injustice. Born as Erich Weiss in Hungary in 1874, he and his family emigrated to the United States in 1878. After Erich's father lost his job as a rabbi, the family moved again, this time to seek opportunity in New York City, where they first lived in a boarding house. Erich and his father found work in a necktie factory, but when Erich's father died in 1892, the young man decided to escape factory work and become an entertainer. After a few lackluster years as a magician, Erich discovered his true talent as an illusionist and escape artist. He changed his name, remaking himself into Harry Houdini, after a French magician named Houdin, and became one of America's most enthralling performers.

By the early 1900s, "The Great Houdini" was a featured act in vaudeville, a new form of urban entertainment. His specialty was escaping from elaborate and dangerous confinements: ropes, manacles, padlocked crates, and jail cells. Like Thomas Edison and Henry Ford, Houdini not only accomplished something but also was a skillful self-publicist, advertising his act with myriad posters and leaflets. Around 1913 Houdini introduced his

◄ "Houdini's Escape Act." High above Broadway and 46th Street in New York City, Harry Houdini, the world-famous immigrant-American escape artist, hangs upside down while bound in a straitjacket. Crowds watch breathlessly, wondering whether or how he will free himself. New people, bustling cities, mass entertainment, and the quest for freedom symbolized by Houdini's act characterized American society at the end of the nineteenth century and beginning of the twentieth.

*(Bettmann/Corbis)*

## CHRONOLOGY

1867 ■ First law regulating tenements passes in New York State

1870 ■ One-fourth of Americans live in cities

1876 ■ National League of Professional Baseball Clubs founded

1880s ■ "New" immigrants from eastern and southern Europe begin to arrive in large numbers

1883 ■ Brooklyn Bridge completed
     ■ Pulitzer buys *New York World,* creating major publication for yellow journalism

1885 ■ Safety bicycle invented

1886 ■ First settlement house opens in New York City

1889 ■ Edison invents motion picture and viewing device

1890s ■ Electric trolleys replace horse-drawn mass transit

1893 ■ Columbian Exposition opens in Chicago

1895 ■ Hearst buys *New York Journal,* which becomes another popular yellow-journalism newspaper

1898 ■ Race riot erupts in Wilmington, North Carolina

1900–10 ■ Immigration reaches peak
       ■ Vaudeville rises to popularity

1903 ■ Boston beats Pittsburgh in baseball's first World Series

1905 ■ Intercollegiate Athletic Association, forerunner of National Intercollegiate Athletic Association (NCAA) is formed, restructuring rules of football

1915 ■ Griffith directs *Birth of a Nation,* one of first major technically sophisticated movies

1919 ■ Race riot erupts in East St. Louis, Illinois

1920 ■ Majority (51.4 percent) of Americans live in cities

famous "Chinese water torture cell" escape, in which he extracted himself from being bound and suspended upside down in a water-filled, locked glass-and-steel cabinet. Houdini succeeded in these escapes not only by manipulating his five-foot-five frame in unusual ways but also by concealing picks and keys, sometimes regurgitating them

while he twisted and stretched. Although he constantly defied death in his act, Houdini could not escape the abdominal infection that took his life in 1926.

He became extraordinarily successful, both in the United States and in Europe, but Houdini initially followed a path taken by many people at the end of the nineteenth century and the beginning of the twentieth. The Weiss family were immigrants who fled poverty and tried to remake themselves in a burgeoning American city where life was not easy for them and for countless other newcomers. They faced daunting challenges of where to live, where to work, how to deal with a cash-based economy, how to preserve their ethnic consciousness amid bigotry, how to achieve independence and respectability. And, like Houdini, they somehow needed to use escape and remaking as means to succeed. These challenges made cities places of hope, frustration, achievement, and conflict, where clanging trolleys, smoky air, crowded streets, and a jumble of languages saturated the senses.

Cities had influenced the nation's history since its inception, serving as marketplaces and forums that amassed people, resources, and ideas, but not until the 1880s did the United States begin to become a fully urban nation. The technological innovations and industrialization of the late nineteenth century sparked widespread economic and geographical expansion which funneled millions of people into cities. By 1920 a milestone of urbanization was passed: that year's census showed that, for the first time, a majority of Americans (51.4 percent) lived in cities (settlements with more than 2,500 people). This new fact of national life was as symbolically significant as the Census Bureau's announcement in 1890 that the frontier had disappeared.

Cities were filled with new kinds of consumerism, commercial amusement, and politics. Urban dwellers patronized dance halls, theatrical performances, vaudeville, movies, and sporting events in record numbers. By idolizing Houdini, sports heroes, and movie celebrities, or by benefiting from the largesse of a political boss, ordinary working- and middle-class people could experience the feeling that individuals could free themselves from the constraints of an emerging technological and urban society. But at the same time, poverty and discrimination haunted the lives of countless urban dwellers, combining opportunities of the era with the persistence of inequality and prejudice. Whatever people's personal experiences, cities had become central to American life, and the ways people built cities and adjusted to the urban environment have shaped modern American society.

- What were the most important factors contributing to the urban growth of the period 1877–1920?
- How did immigrants adjust to and reshape their adopted homeland?
- How did industrialization and urbanization affect patterns of family life and leisure time?

## GROWTH OF THE MODERN CITY

Although their initial functions had been commercial, cities became the main arenas for industrial growth in the late nineteenth century. As centers of labor, transportation, and communication, cities supplied everything factories needed. Capital accumulated by urban mercantile enterprises fed industrial investment. City dwellers also acted as consumers for myriad new products. Thus urban growth and industrialization wound together in a mutually advantageous spiral. The further industrialization advanced, the more opportunities it created for jobs and investment. Increased opportunities in turn drew more people to cities; as workers and as consumers, they fueled yet more industrialization. Urban growth in modern America was a dynamic process involving all groups of Americans, including those already settled and new arrivals from Europe and Asia.

Most cities housed a variety of industrial enterprises, but product specialization became common. Mass pro-

**Industrial Development**

duction of clothing concentrated in New York City, the shoe industry in Philadelphia, and textiles in New England cities such as Lowell. Other cities created goods derived from surrounding agricultural regions: flour in Minneapolis, cottonseed oil in Memphis, beef and pork in Chicago. Still others processed natural resources: gold and copper in Denver, fish and lumber in Seattle, coal and iron in Pittsburgh and Birmingham, oil in Houston and Los Angeles. Such activities increased cities' magnetic attraction for people in search of steady employment.

At the same time, the compact city of the early nineteenth century, where residences mingled among shops, factories, and warehouses, burst open. From Boston to

Los Angeles, the built environment sprawled several miles beyond the original settlement. No longer did walking distance determine a city's size. No longer did different social groups live close together. Instead, cities subdivided into distinct districts: working-class neighborhoods, commercial strips, downtown, and a ring of suburbs. Two forces were responsible for this new arrangement. One, mass transportation, was centrifugal, propelling people and enterprises outward. The other, economic change, was centripetal, drawing human and material resources inward.

Mass transportation moved people faster and farther. By the 1870s, horse-drawn vehicles began sharing city streets with motor-driven conveyances. At first, commuter railroads carried commuters to and from outlying communities, but soon mechanical vehicles were moving people from one part of the city to another. In the 1880s, cable cars (carriages that moved by clamping onto a moving underground wire) started operating in Chicago, San Francisco, and other cities. Then, in the 1890s, electric-powered streetcars began replacing horse cars and cable cars. Designed in Montgomery, Alabama, and Richmond, Virginia, electric trolleys spread to nearly every large American city. In a few cities, companies raised track onto trestles, enabling "elevated" vehicles to travel above jammed downtown streets. In Boston, New York, and Philadelphia, transit firms dug underground subway tunnels, also to avoid traffic congestion. Because "els" were extremely expensive to construct, they appeared only in the few cities where companies could amass necessary capital and where there were enough riders to ensure profits.

Another form of mass transit, the electric interurban railway, linked nearby cities. Usually built over shorter distances than steam railroads, interurbans operated between cities with growing suburban populations and furthered urban development by making outlying regions attractive for home buyers and businesses. The extensive Pacific Electric Railway network in Southern California, for example, facilitated travel and economic progress in that region.

Mass transit launched urban dwellers into remote neighborhoods and created a commuting public. The resulting urban sprawl benefited the urban public unevenly and was essentially unplanned. Streetcar lines serviced mainly districts that promised the most riders—those whose fares would increase company revenues. Working-class families, who needed

**Mechanization of Mass Transportation**

**Urban Sprawl**

▲ Electric trolley cars and other forms of mass transit enabled middle-class people such as these women and men to reside on the urban outskirts and ride into the city center for work, shopping, and entertainment.    *(Library of Congress)*

every cent, found streetcars unaffordable. But those of the growing middle class who could afford the fare— usually 5 cents a ride—could escape to quiet, tree-lined neighborhoods on the outskirts, live in bungalows with their own yards, and commute to the inner city for work, shopping, and entertainment. A home several miles from downtown was inconvenient, but benefits outweighed costs. As one suburbanite wrote in 1902, "It may be a little more difficult for us to attend the opera, but the robin in my elm tree struck a higher note and a sweeter one yesterday than any prima donna ever reached."

Streetcars, els, and subways altered commercial as well as residential patterns. When consumers moved outward, businesses followed, locating at trolley-line intersections and near elevated-railway stations. Branches of department stores and banks joined groceries, theaters, taverns, and shops to create neighborhood shopping centers, forerunners of today's suburban malls. Meanwhile, the urban core became a work zone, where tall buildings loomed over streets clogged with people, horses, and vehicles. Districts such as Chicago's Loop and New Orleans's Canal Street employed thousands in commerce and finance.

Between 1870 and 1920, the number of Americans living in cities increased from 10 million to 54 million.

**Population Growth**

During this period, the number of cities with more than 100,000 people swelled from fifteen to sixty-eight; the number with more than 500,000 rose from two to twelve (see Map 19.1). These figures, dramatic in themselves, represent millions of stories of dreams and frustration, coping and confusion, success and failure.

American urban growth derived not from natural increase (excess of births over deaths) but through the annexation of bordering land and people, and mostly by net migration (excess of in-migrants over out-migrants). Every city grew territorially. The most notable enlargement occurred in 1898, when New York City, which previously consisted of only Manhattan and the Bronx, merged with Brooklyn, Staten Island, and part of Queens, and doubled from 1.5 million to 3 million people. Elsewhere, central cities gobbled up miles of surrounding area. Suburbs often desired annexation for the schools, water, fire protection, and sewer systems that cities could

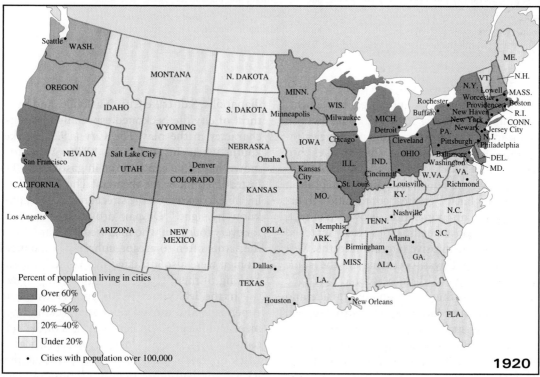

## Map 19.1    Urbanization, 1880 and 1920

In 1880 the vast majority of states were still heavily rural. By 1920 only a few had less than 20 percent of their population living in cities.

▲ Along with mass-produced consumer goods, such as clothing and appliances, Sears, Roebuck and Company marketed architectural plans for middle-class suburban housing. This drawing, taken from the Sears catalogue for 1911, illustrates the kind of housing developed on the urban outskirts in the early twentieth century. *(Sears, Roebuck and Company)*

provide. Sometimes annexation preceded settlement, adding vacant land where new residents could live. In the 1880s, Chicago, Minneapolis, and Los Angeles incorporated hundreds of undeveloped square miles into their borders.

In-migration from the countryside and immigration from abroad made by far the greatest contribution to urban population growth. In fact, movement to cities nearly matched the massive migration to the West that was occurring at the same time. Urban newcomers arrived from two major sources: the American countryside and Europe. Asia, Canada, and Latin America also supplied immigrants, though in smaller numbers.

**Urban In-Migration**

Despite land rushes in the West, rural populations declined as urban populations burgeoned. Low crop prices and high debts dashed white farmers' hopes and drove them toward opportunities that cities seemed to offer. These migrants filled major cities, such as Detroit, Chicago, and San Francisco, but also secondary cities, such as In-

dianapolis, Salt Lake City, Nashville, and San Diego. The thrill of city life beckoned especially to young people. A character in the play *The City* (1920) spoke for many youths when she exclaimed, "Who wants to smell new-mown hay, if he can breathe in gasoline on Fifth Avenue instead! Think of the theaters! The crowds! Think of being able to go out on the street and see someone you didn't know by sight!" Despair drove farm boys to cities, but for every four men who migrated cityward, five women did the same, often to escape unhappy home life. But young women were also attracted by the independence—the remaking of themselves—that urban employment offered.

In the 1880s and 1890s, thousands of rural African Americans also moved cityward, seeking better employment and fleeing crop liens, ravages of the boll weevil on cotton crops, racial violence, and political oppression. Black migration accelerated after 1915, but thirty-two cities already had more than ten thousand black residents by 1900. African American populations rose in southern cities, such as Baltimore, Atlanta, and Birmingham, but northern places, such as New York, Cleveland, and Chicago, also received thousands of black migrants. These newcomers resembled other migrants in their rural backgrounds and economic motivations, but they differed in several important ways. Because few factories would employ African Americans, most found jobs in the service sector—cleaning, cooking, and driving—rather than in industrial trades. Also, because most service openings were traditionally female jobs, black women outnumbered black men in cities such as New York, Baltimore, and New Orleans. In the South, blacks migrating from the countryside became an important source of unskilled labor in the region's growing cities. By 1900, almost 40 percent of the total population of both Atlanta, Georgia, and Charlotte, North Carolina, was black.

In the West, many Hispanics, once a predominantly rural population, also moved into cities. They took unskilled construction jobs previously held by Chinese laborers who had been driven from Southern California cities, and in some Texas cities, native Mexicans (called *Tejanos*) held the majority of all unskilled jobs. In Los Angeles and other cities, Hispanic males often left home for long periods to take temporary agricultural jobs, leaving behind female heads of household.

Even more newcomers were foreign immigrants who had fled villages and cities in Europe, Asia, Canada, and Latin America for the United

### Foreign Immigration

States. Many never intended to stay; they wanted only to make enough money to return home and live in greater comfort and security. For every hundred foreigners who entered the country, around thirty ultimately left. Still, like Houdini and his family, most of the 26 million immigrants who arrived between 1870 and 1920 remained, and the great majority settled in cities, where they helped reshape American culture.

Immigration to the United States was part of a worldwide movement pushing people away from traditional

### The New Immigration

means of support and pulling them toward better opportunities. Population pressures, land redistribution, and industrialization induced millions of peasants, small landowners, and craftsmen to leave Europe and Asia for Canada, Australia, Brazil, and Argentina, as well as the United States. Religious persecution, too, particularly the merciless pogroms and military conscription that Jews suffered in eastern Europe, forced people to escape across the Atlantic. Migration has always characterized human history, but in the late nineteenth century, technological advances in communications and transportation spread news of opportunities and made travel cheaper, quicker, and safer.

▲ The Caribbean as well as Europe sent immigrants to the United States. Hopeful that they were leaving their homeland of Guadeloupe for a better life, these women were perhaps unprepared for the disadvantages they faced as blacks, foreigners, and women.

*(William Williams Papers, Manuscripts & Archives Division, The New York Public Library)*

Immigrants from northern and western Europe had long made the United States their main destination, but after 1880 economic and demographic changes propelled a second wave of immigrants from other regions. People from Ireland, England, and Germany continued to arrive, but increased numbers came from eastern and southern Europe, plus smaller bands from Canada, Mexico, and Japan (see Map 19.2 and Figure 19.1). Between 1900 and 1909, when the new wave peaked, two-thirds of immigrants came from Italy, Austria-Hungary, and Russia. By 1910 arrivals from Mexico outnumbered arrivals from Ireland, and numerous Japanese had moved to the West Coast and Hawai'i. Foreign-born blacks, chiefly from the West Indies, also came. (See website for the nationalities of immigrants.)

Many long-settled Americans feared those whom they called "new immigrants," whose folk customs, Catholic and Jewish faiths, and poverty made them seem more

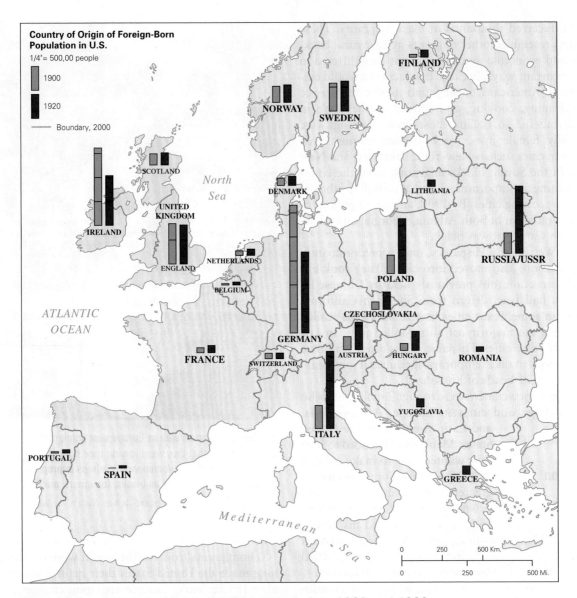

**Country of Origin of Foreign-Born Population in U.S.**

1/4" = 500,00 people

1900

1920

—— Boundary, 2000

## Map 19.2   Sources of European-Born Population, 1900 and 1920

In just a few decades, the proportion of European immigrants to the United States who came from northern and western Europe decreased (Ireland and Germany) or remained relatively stable (England and Scandinavia), while the proportion from eastern and southern Europe increased dramatically.

*(Source: Data from U.S. Census Bureau, "Historical Census Statistics on the Foreign-Born Population of the United States: 1850–1990," February 1999, http://www.census.gov/population [accessed February 12, 2000].)*

alien than previous newcomers. Unlike earlier groups from Great Britain and Ireland, new immigrants did not speak English, and more than half worked in low-skill occupations. Yet old and new immigrants closely resembled each other in their strategies for coping. The majority of both groups hailed from societies that made family the focus of all undertakings. As in the case of Erich Weiss's family, whether and when to emigrate was decided in light of family needs, and family bonds remained tight after immigrants reached America. New arrivals usually knew

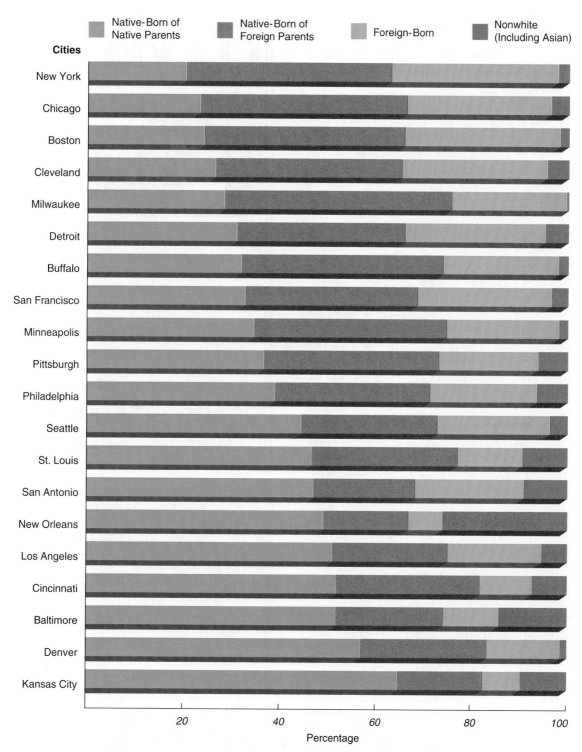

**Figure 19.1    Composition of Population, Selected Cities, 1920**

Immigration and migration made native-born whites of native-born parents minorities in almost every major city by the early twentieth century. Moreover, foreign-born residents and native-born whites of foreign parents (combining the purple and green segments of a line) constituted absolute majorities in numerous places.

where they wanted to go and how to get there, because they received aid from relatives who had already immigrated. Workers often helped kin obtain jobs, and family members pooled resources to maintain, if not improve, their standard of living.

Once they arrived, in-migrants and immigrants rarely stayed put. Each year millions of families packed up and moved elsewhere. Some moved to another neighborhood; others left town. Thus the Weiss family stayed in Appleton, Wisconsin, for only a few years before moving to New York City. A railroad ticket to another city cost only a few dollars, and many had little to lose by moving. Transience affected every region, every city. From Boston to San Francisco, from Minneapolis to San Antonio, more than half the families residing in a city at any one time were gone ten years later. Even within a city, it was not uncommon for a family to live at three or more different addresses over a ten- or fifteen-year period. Overall, one in every three or four families moved each year (today the rate is one in five). Population turnover affected almost every neighborhood, every ethnic and occupational group.

## Geographic and Social Mobility

Migration offered an escape to improved opportunity; remaking oneself occupationally offered another. An advance up the social scale through better jobs was available mostly to white males. Thousands of businesses were needed to supply goods and services to burgeoning urban populations, and as corporations grew and centralized operations, they required new managerial personnel. Capital for a large business was hard to amass, but an aspiring merchant could open a saloon or shop for a few hundred dollars. Knowledge of accounting could qualify one for white-collar jobs with higher incomes than manual labor. Thus nonmanual jobs and the higher social status and income that tended to accompany them were attainable.

Such advancement occurred often. To be sure, only a very few could accumulate large fortunes. The vast majority of the era's wealthiest businessmen began their careers with distinct advantages: American birth, Protestant religion, superior education, and relatively affluent parents. Yet considerable movement occurred along the road from poverty to moderate success, from manual to nonmanual work. Personal successes such as those of Meyer Grossman, a Russian immigrant to Omaha, Nebraska, who worked as a teamster before saving enough to open a successful furniture store, were common.

Rates of upward occupational mobility were slow but steady between 1870 and 1920. In fast-growing cities

▲ Those who wished to Americanize immigrants believed that public schools could provide the best setting for assimilation. This 1917 poster from the Cleveland Board of Education and the Cleveland Americanization Committee used the languages most common to the new immigrants—Slovene, Italian, Polish, Hungarian, and Yiddish—as well as English, to invite newcomers to free classes where they could learn "the language of America" and "citizenship."

*(National Park Service Collection, Ellis Island Immigration Museum. Photo: Chermayeff & Geismar/ MetaForm)*

such as Atlanta, Los Angeles, and Omaha, approximately one in five white manual workers rose to white-collar or owner's positions within ten years—provided they stayed in the city that long. In older cities such as Boston and Philadelphia, upward mobility averaged closer to one in six workers in ten years. Some men slipped from a higher to a lower rung on the occupational ladder, but rates of upward movement usually doubled those of downward movement. Although patterns were not consistent, immigrants generally experienced less upward and more downward mobility than did the native-born. Still, regardless of birthplace, the chances for a white male to rise occupationally over the course of his career or to hold a higher-status job than his father were relatively good.

What constitutes a better job, however, depends on one's definition of improvement. Many immigrant artisans, such as a German carpenter or an Italian shoemaker, considered an accountant's job unmanly. People with traditions of pride in working with their hands neither desired nonmanual jobs nor encouraged their children to seek them. As one Italian tailor explained, "I learned the tailoring business in the old country. Over here, in America, I never have trouble finding a job because I know my business from the other side [Italy]. . . . I want that my oldest boy learn my trade because I tell him that you could always make at least enough for the family."

Business ownership, moreover, entailed risks. Failure rates were high among saloon owners and other small proprietors in working-class neighborhoods, because the low incomes of their customers made profits uncertain. Many manual workers sought security rather than mobility, preferring a steady wage to the risks of ownership. A Sicilian who lived in Bridgeport, Connecticut, observed that "the people that come here they afraid to get in business because they don't know how that business goes. In Italy these people don't know much about these things because most of them work on farms or in [their] trade."

Many women held paying jobs and, like men, migrated within and between cities, but they often moved with fathers or husbands whose economic standing usually defined their social position. Women could improve their status by marrying men with wealth or potential, but other avenues were mostly closed to them. Laws limited what women could inherit; educational institutions blocked their training in such professions as medicine and law; and prevailing assumptions attributed higher aptitude for manual skills and business to men than to women. For African Americans, American Indians, Mexican Americans, and Asian Americans, opportunities were even scarcer. Assigned to the lowest-paying occupations by prejudice, they could make few gains.

In addition to advancing occupationally, a person might achieve social mobility by acquiring property, such as building or buying a house. But home ownership was not easy to achieve. Banks and savings-and-loan institutions had strict lending practices, and mortgage loans carried high interest rates and short repayment periods. Thus renting, even of single-family houses, was common, especially in big cities. Nevertheless, many families were able to amass savings, which they could use as down payments on property. Ownership rates varied regionally—higher in western cities, lower in eastern cities—but 36 percent of all urban American families owned their homes in 1900, the highest homeownership rate of any western nation except for Denmark, Norway, and Sweden.

Many who migrated, particularly unskilled workers, did not improve their status; they simply floated from one low-paying job to another. Others could not maintain their Old World occupations; Erich Weiss's father had to accept manual labor employment because he could not continue being a rabbi. Still others, however, did find greener pastures. Studies of Boston, Omaha, Atlanta, and other cities show that most men who rose occupationally or acquired property had migrated from somewhere else. Thus, although cities frustrated the hopes of some, they offered opportunities to others. The possibilities for upward mobility seemed to temper people's dissatisfaction with the tensions and frustrations of city life. For every story of rags to riches, there were a multitude of small triumphs mixed with dashed hopes and discrimination. Although the gap between the very rich and the very poor widened, for those in between, the expanding economies of American cities created room.

## URBAN NEIGHBORHOODS

Despite the constant turnover that made them dynamic places, American cities were characterized by collections of subcommunities where people, most of whom had migrated from somewhere else, coped with daily challenges to their cultures. Rather than yield completely to pressures to assimilate, migrants and immigrants interacted with the urban environment in a complex way that enabled them to retain their identity while also altering both their own outlook and the social structure of cities themselves.

In their new surroundings—where the English language was a struggle, where the clock regulated their workday, and where housing and employment were uncertain—immigrants first anchored their lives to the root they knew best: their culture. Old World customs persisted in immigrant districts of Italians from the same province, Japanese from the same island district, and Russian Jews from the same *shtetl*. Newcomers re-created mutual aid societies they had known in their homeland. For example, in western cities Japanese transferred *ken* societies, which organized social celebrations and relief services, and Chinese used loan associations, called *whey*,

**Cultural Retention and Change**

which raised money to help members acquire businesses. Chinese also transplanted village associations called *fongs,* which rented apartments to homeless members; *kung saw,* assistance organizations of people with the same family name regardless of what part of China they came from; and *tongs,* secret societies designed to aid people but which often acted as gangs that extorted protection money from businesses. Southern Italians transplanted the system whereby a *padrone* (boss) found jobs for unskilled workers by negotiating with—and receiving a payoff from—an employer. People practiced religion as they always had, held traditional feasts and pageants, married within their group, and pursued long-standing feuds with people from rival villages.

In large cities, such as Chicago, Philadelphia, and Detroit, European immigrants initially clustered in inner-city neighborhoods where low-skill jobs and cheap housing were most available. These districts often were multi-ethnic, places historians have called "urban borderlands," where a diversity of people, identities, and lifestyles coexisted. To be sure, members of the same group often tried to exclude outsiders from their neighborhood space and institutions, but even within districts identified with a certain group, such as Little Italy, Jewtown, Polonia, or Greektown, rapid mobility constantly undermined residential homogeneity, as former inhabitants dispersed to other neighborhoods and new inhabitants moved in. Often a particular area was inhabited by several ethnic groups, while the local businesses and institutions, such as bakeries, butcher shops, churches, and club headquarters—which usually were operated by and for one ethnic group—gave a neighborhood its identity.

## Urban Borderlands

For first- and second-generation immigrants, their neighborhoods acted as havens until individuals were ready to cross from the borderland into the majority society. But borderland experiences often dissolved, sometimes in a generation, sometimes in just a few years. The expansion of mass transportation and outward movement of factories enabled people to move to other neighborhoods, where they interspersed with families of their own socioeconomic class but not necessarily of their own ethnicity. European immigrants did encounter prejudice, such as the exclusion of Jews from certain neighborhoods, professions, and clubs, or the inability of Italians to break into urban politics, but discrimination rarely was systematic or complete. For people of color, however—African Americans, Asians, and Mexicans—the borderlands kept a more persistent character which, because of discrimination, became less multiethnic over time.

Although the small numbers of African Americans who inhabited American cities in the eighteenth and early nineteenth centuries may have lived near or interspersed with whites, by the late nineteenth century rigid racial discrimination forced them into relatively permanent, highly segregated ghettos. By 1920 in Chicago, Detroit, Cleveland, and other cities where tens of thousands of blacks now lived, two-thirds or more of the total African American population inhabited only 10 percent of the residential area. Within their neighborhoods, African Americans, like other urban dwellers, nurtured cultural institutions that helped them cope with city life: shops, schools, clubs, theaters, dance halls, newspapers, and saloons. Churches, particularly those of the Baptist and African Methodist Episcopal (AME) branches of Protestantism, were especially influential. Pittsburgh blacks boasted twenty-eight such churches in the early 1900s. Membership in Cincinnati's black Baptist churches doubled between 1870 and 1900. In Louisville, blacks pooled their resources and built their own theological institute. In virtually all cities, black religious activity not only dominated local life but also represented cooperation across class lines.

## Racial Segregation and Violence

In most cities, the only way blacks could relieve the pressures of crowding that resulted from increasing migration was to expand residential borders into surrounding, previously white neighborhoods, a process that often resulted in harassment and attacks by white residents whose intolerant attitudes were intensified by fears that black neighbors would cause property values to decline. Moreover, the increased presence of African Americans in cities, North and South, as well as their competition with whites for housing, jobs, and political influence, sparked a series of race riots. In 1898 white citizens of Wilmington, North Carolina, resenting African Americans' involvement in local government and incensed by an editorial in an African American newspaper accusing white women of loose sexual behavior, rioted and killed dozens of blacks. In the fury's wake, white supremacists overthrew the city government, expelling black and white officeholders, and instituted restrictions to prevent blacks from voting. In Atlanta in 1906, newspaper accounts alleging attacks by black men on white women provoked an outburst of shooting and killing that left twelve blacks dead and seventy injured. An influx of unskilled black strikebreakers into East St. Louis, Illinois, heightened racial tensions in 1917. Rumors that blacks were arming themselves for an attack on whites resulted in numerous attacks by white mobs on black neighborhoods. On July 1, blacks fired back at a car whose occupants they believed

▲ Although Chinese immigrants, like other immigrants, struggled to succeed in American society, they often faced severe discrimination because of their different lifestyle. As this photo of a San Francisco grocery shows, Chinese looked, dressed, and ate differently than did white Americans. Occasionally, they suffered from racist violence that caused them to fear not only for their personal safety but also for the safety of establishments such as this one that might suffer damage from resentful mobs. *(The Bancroft Library, University of California)*

had shot into their homes and mistakenly killed two policemen riding in the car. The next day, a full-scale riot erupted which ended only after nine whites and thirty-nine blacks had been killed and over three hundred buildings destroyed.

Asians also encountered discrimination and an isolated residential experience. Although Chinese immigrants often preferred to live apart from Anglos, in Chinatowns of San Francisco, Los Angeles, and New York City, where they created their own business, government, and social institutions, Anglos also made every effort to keep them separated. In San Francisco, anti-Chinese hostility was fomented by Denis Kearney, an Irish immigrant who blamed Chinese for unemployment in California in the late 1870s. Using the slogan "The Chinese must go," Kearney and his followers intimidated employers into refusing to hire Chinese, and drove hundreds of Asians out of the city. San Francisco's government prohibited Chinese laundries (which were social centers as well as commercial establishments) from locating in white neighborhoods and banned the wearing of queues, the traditional Chinese hair braid. In 1882 Congress passed the Chinese Exclusion Act, which suspended immigration of Chinese laborers and prohibited naturalization of those Chinese already residing in the United States. And in 1892 Congress approved the Geary Act, which extended immigration restriction and required Chinese Americans to carry certificates of residence issued by the Treasury Department. A San Francisco–based organization called the Chinese Six Companies fought the law, but in 1893 the U.S. Supreme Court upheld the Geary Act in *Fong Yue Ting v. United States.* Japanese immigrants, called Issei, most of whom settled in or near Los Angeles, were prevented by law from becoming American citizens and, like the Chinese, developed communities with their own economic and residential character.

Mexicans in southwestern cities experienced somewhat more complex residential patterns. In places such as

||||||||||||||||||||||||||||||||||

**Mexican Barrios**

Los Angeles, Santa Barbara, and Tucson, Mexicans had been the original inhabitants, and Anglos were migrants who overtook the city, pushing Mexicans into adjoining areas. Here, Mexicans became increasingly isolated in residential and commercial districts called barrios. Frequently, real-estate covenants, by which property owners pledged not to sell homes to Mexicans (or to African Americans, or to Jews), kept Mexican families confined in barrios of Los Angeles, Albuquerque, and San Antonio. These areas tended to be located away from central-city multiethnic borderlands housing European immigrants. To a considerable extent, then, racial bias, more than any other factor, made urban experiences of African Americans, Asians, and Mexicans unique and hindered their opportunities to remake their lives.

Virtually everywhere immigrants lived, Old World culture mingled with New World realities. On one hand,

||||||||||||||||||||||||||||||||||

**Cultural Adaptation**

people often found their local identities eclipsed by national identities. Although many foreigners identified themselves by their village or region of birth, native-born Americans simplified by categorizing them by nationality. People from County Cork and County Limerick, for example, were merged into Irish; those from Schleswig and Württemberg into Germans; those from Calabria and Campobasso into Italians. Immigrant institutions, such as newspapers and churches, found they had to appeal to the entire nationality in order to survive.

Moreover, the diversity of American cities prompted foreigners to modify their attitudes and habits. With so many people interacting on streets and in workplaces, few newcomers could avoid contact with groups different from themselves, and few could prevent such contacts from altering old ways of life. Although many immigrants tried to preserve their native language, English, taught in schools and needed on the job, soon penetrated nearly every community. Foreigners fashioned garments in homeland styles but had to use American rather than traditional fabrics. Italians went to American doctors but still carried traditional amulets to ward off evil spirits. Unavailability of Asian vegetables and spices forced Chinese American cooks to improvise by using local ingredients in a new dish they called "chop suey." Music especially revealed adaptations. Polka bands entertained at Polish social gatherings, but their repertoires blended American and Polish folk music Mexican ballads acquired new

themes that described adventures of border crossing and hardships of labor in the United States.

The influx of so many immigrants between 1870 and 1920 transformed the United States from a basically Protestant nation into a diverse collection of Protestants, Catholics, Orthodox Christians, Jews, Buddhists, and Muslims. Newcomers from Italy, Hungary, Polish lands, and Slovakia joined Irish and Germans to boost the proportion of Catholics in many cities. In Buffalo, Cleveland, Chicago, and Milwaukee, Catholic immigrants and their offspring approached a majority of the population. Catholic Mexicans constituted over half of the population of El Paso. German and Russian immigrants gave New York City one of the largest Jewish populations in the world.

Partly in response to Protestant charges that their religions prevented them from assimilating, many Catholics and Jews tried to accommodate their faiths to the new environment. Catholic and Jewish leaders from earlier immigrant groups supported liberalizing trends—use of English in services, the phasing out of such Old World rituals as saints' feasts, and a preference for public over religious schools. As long as new immigrants continued to arrive, however, these trends met stiff resistance. Catholics, for example, supported parochial schools and occasionally campaigned for public funding for them. In some cases, Catholic children's attendance at parochial schools prevented public schools from becoming even more crowded than they already were.

Newcomers usually held onto familiar religious practices, whether the folk Catholicism of southern Italy or the Orthodox Judaism of eastern Europe. Because Catholic parishes served distinct geographic areas, immigrants wanted parish priests of their own "kind," in spite of church attempts to make American Catholicism more uniform. Bishops acceded to pressures from predominantly Polish congregations for Polish rather than German-born priests. Eastern European Jews, convinced that Reform Judaism sacrificed too much to American ways, established the Conservative branch, which retained traditional ritual though it abolished the segregation of women in synagogues and allowed English prayers. But, in addition, the tendency of second-generation Catholics and Jews to marry coreligionists of other ethnic groups—an Italian Catholic marrying a Polish Catholic, for example—kept religious identity strong while undercutting ethnic identity.

Each of the three major migrant groups that peopled American cities—native-born whites, foreigners of various races, and native-born blacks—created the pluralism of modern American culture. The country's cultural diversity prevented domination by a single racial or ethnic majority. The cities nurtured rich cultural variety: American folk music and literature, Italian and Mexican cuisine, Irish comedy, Yiddish theater, African American jazz and dance, and much more. Newcomers in the late nineteenth century changed their environment as much as they were changed by it.

## LIVING CONDITIONS IN THE INNER CITY

Although filled with inhabitants rich in varied cultures, the central sections of American cities also seemed to harbor every affliction that plagues modern society: poverty, disease, crime, and the tensions that occur when large numbers of people live close together. City dwellers coped as best they could, and technology, private enterprise, and public authority achieved some remarkable successes. But many of their problems still await solution.

One of the most persistent shortcomings—the scarcity of adequate housing—has its origins in nineteenth-

### Inner-City Housing

century urban development. In spite of massive construction in the 1880s and early 1900s, population growth outpaced housing supplies. Lack of inexpensive living quarters especially afflicted working-class families who, because of low wages, had to rent their homes. As cities grew, landlords took advantage of shortages in inexpensive rental housing by splitting up existing buildings to house more people, constructing multiple-unit tenements, and hiking rents. Low-income families adapted to high costs and short supply by sharing space and expenses. It became common in many cities for a one-family apartment to be occupied by two or three families, or by a single family plus several boarders.

The result was unprecedented crowding. In 1890 New York City's immigrant-packed Lower East Side averaged 702 people per acre, one of the highest population densities in the world. Inner districts had distinctive physical appearances in different cities: six- to eight-story

▲ Inner-city dwellers used not only indoor space as efficiently as possible, but also what little outdoor space was available to them. Scores of families living in this cramped block of six-story tenements in New York strung clotheslines behind the buildings. Notice that there is virtually no space between buildings, so only rooms at the front and back received daylight and fresh air.

*(Library of Congress)*

barracks-like buildings in New York; dilapidated row houses in Baltimore and Philadelphia; converted slave quarters in Charleston and New Orleans; and crumbling two- and three-story frame houses in Seattle and San Francisco. But everywhere crowding was common.

Inside these structures, conditions were harsh. The largest rooms were barely ten feet wide, and interior rooms either lacked windows or opened onto narrow shafts that bred vermin and rotten odors. Describing such a duct, one immigrant housekeeper revealed, "It's damp down there, and the families, they throw out garbage and dirty papers and the insides of chickens, and other unmentionable filth. . . . I just vomited when I first cleaned up the air shaft." Few buildings had indoor plumbing; residents had to use privies (outdoor toilets) in the back yard or basement. Often, the only source of heat was dangerous, polluting coal-burning stoves.

**Housing Reform**

Housing problems sparked widespread reform campaigns. New York State took the lead by passing laws in 1867, 1879, and 1901 that established light, ventilation, and safety codes for new tenement buildings. These and similar measures in other states could not remedy ills of existing buildings, but they did impose minimal obligations on landlords. A few reformers, such as journalist Jacob Riis and humanitarian Lawrence Veiller, advocated housing low-income families in "model tenements," with more spacious rooms and better facilities. Model tenements, however, required landlords to accept lower profits, a sacrifice few were willing to make. Both reformers and public officials opposed government financing of better housing, fearing that such a step would undermine private enterprise. Still, housing codes and regulatory commissions strengthened the power of local government to oversee construction.

**New Home Technology**

Eventually, technology brought about important changes in home life. Advanced systems of central heating (furnaces), artificial lighting, and indoor plumbing created more comfort, first for middle-class households and later for most others. Whereas formerly families had bought coal or chopped wood for cooking and heating, made candles for light, and hauled water for bathing, their homes and apartments increasingly connected to outside pipes and wires for gas, electricity, and water. Central heat and artificial light made it possible for residents to enjoy a steady, comfortable temperature and to turn night into day, while indoor plumbing removed the unpleasant experiences of the outhouse. Moreover, these utilities helped create new attitudes about privacy among those who could afford the technology. Middle-class bedrooms and bathrooms became private retreats. Even children could have their own bedrooms, complete with individualized decoration.

Scientific and technological advances eventually enabled city dwellers and the entire nation to live in greater safety. By the 1880s, doctors had begun to accept the theory that microorganisms (germs) cause disease. In response, cities established more efficient systems of water purification and sewage disposal. Although disease and death rates remained higher in cities than in the countryside, and tuberculosis and other respiratory ills continued to plague inner-city districts, public health regulations as applied to water purity, sewage disposal, and food quality helped to control such dread diseases as cholera, typhoid fever, and diphtheria.

Meanwhile, street paving, modernized firefighting equipment, and electric street lighting spread rapidly across urban America. Steel-frame construction, which supports a building with a metal skeleton rather than with masonry walls, made possible the erection of skyscrapers—and thus more efficient vertical use of scarce and costly urban land. Electric elevators and steam-heating systems serviced these buildings. Steel-cable suspension bridges, developed by John A. Roebling and epitomized by his Brooklyn Bridge (completed in 1883), replaced ferry boats and linked metropolitan sections more closely.

**Poverty Relief**

None of these improvements, however, lightened the burden of poverty. The urban economy, though generally expanding, advanced erratically. Employment, especially for unskilled workers in manufacturing and construction, rose and fell with business cycles and changing seasons. An ever-increasing number of families lived on the margins of survival.

Since colonial days Americans have disagreed about how much responsibility the public should assume for poor relief. According to traditional beliefs, still widespread at the beginning of the twentieth century, anyone could escape poverty through hard work and clean living; indigence existed only because some people were morally weaker than others. Such reasoning bred fear that aid to poor people would encourage paupers to rely on public support rather than their own efforts. As business cycles fluctuated and poverty increased, this attitude hardened, and city governments discontinued direct grants of food, fuel, and clothing to needy families. Instead, cities provided relief in return for work on public projects and sent special cases to state-run almshouses, orphanages, and homes for the blind, deaf, and mentally ill.

Efforts to rationalize relief fostered some changes in attitude. Between 1877 and 1892, philanthropists in ninety-two cities formed Charity Organization Societies, an attempt to make social welfare (like business) more efficient by merging disparate charity groups into coordinated units. Believing poverty to be caused by personal defects, such as alcoholism and laziness, members of these organizations spent most of their time visiting poor families and encouraging them to be thriftier and more virtuous. These visits were also intended to identify the "deserving" poor.

Close observation of the poor, however, prompted some humanitarians to conclude that people's environments, not their shortcomings, caused poverty and that society ought to shoulder greater responsibility for improving social conditions. These reformers had faith that they could reduce poverty by improving housing, education, sanitation, and job opportunities rather than by admonishing the poor to be more moral. This attitude fueled campaigns for building codes, factory regulations, and public health measures in the Progressive era of the early twentieth century (see Chapter 21). Still, most middle- and upper-class Americans continued to endorse the creed that in a society of abundance only the unfit were poor and that poverty relief should be tolerated but never encouraged. As one charity worker put it, relief "should be surrounded by circumstances that shall . . . repel every one . . . from accepting it."

Crime and disorder, as much as crowding and poverty, nurtured fears that cities, especially their slums,

## Crime and Violence

threatened the nation. The more cities grew, it seemed, the more they shook with violence. While homicide rates declined in industrialized nations such as England and Germany, those in America rose alarmingly: 25 murders per million people in 1881; 107 per million in 1898. In addition, innumerable disruptions, ranging from domestic violence to muggings to gang fights, made cities scenes of constant turbulence. Pickpockets, swindlers, and burglars roamed every city. Urban outlaws, such as Rufus Minor, acquired as much notoriety as western desperadoes. Short, stocky, and bald, Minor resembled a shy clerk, but one police chief labeled him "one of the smartest bank sneaks in America." Minor often grew a beard before holding up a bank, then shaved afterward to avoid identification by eyewitnesses. Minor was implicated in bank heists in New York City, Cleveland, Detroit, Providence, Philadelphia, Albany, Boston, and Baltimore—all between 1878 and 1882.

Despite fears, however, urban crime and violence may simply have become more conspicuous and sensational rather than more prevalent. To be sure, concentrations of wealth and the mingling of different peoples provided opportunities for larceny, vice, and assault. But urban lawlessness and brutality probably did not exceed that of backwoods mining camps and southern plantations. Nativists were quick to blame immigrants for urban crime, but the law-breaking population included native-born Americans as well as foreigners. One investigation of jails in 1900 concluded that "we have ourselves evolved as cruel and cunning criminals as any that Europe may have foisted upon us."

## MANAGING THE CITY

Those concerned with managing cities faced daunting challenges in the late nineteenth century. Burgeoning populations, business expansion, and technological change created urgent needs for sewers, police and fire protection, schools, parks, and other services. Such needs strained municipal resources beyond their capacities, and city governments were poorly organized to handle them. In addition to a mayor and a city council, governmental responsibilities typically were scattered among independent boards that administered health regulations, public works, poverty relief, and other functions. Philadelphia at one time had thirty such boards. State governments also often interfered in local matters, appointing board members and limiting cities' abilities to levy taxes and borrow money.

Finding sources of clean water and a way to dispose of waste became increasingly pressing challenges. In the

## Water Supply and Sewage Disposal

early nineteenth century, urban households used privies to dispose of human excrement, and factories dumped untreated sewage into rivers, lakes, and bays. By the late nineteenth century, most cities had replaced private water companies with public water supplies, but these services did not guarantee pure water. The installation of sewer systems and flush toilets, plus use of water as a coolant in factories, overwhelmed waterways, contaminating drinking-water sources and sending pollution to communities downstream. The stench of rivers was often unbearable, and pollution bred disease. Memphis and New York experienced severe yellow-fever epidemics in the 1870s and 1880s, and typhoid fever threatened many cities. By 1900, the Passaic River in northern New Jersey, once a popular recreation and fishing site, had been ruined by discharge from the cities along its banks.

Acceptance in the 1880s of the germ theory of disease prompted city health officials to take steps to reduce chances that human waste and other pollutants would endanger water supplies, but the task proved difficult. Some states passed laws prohibiting discharge of raw sewage into rivers and streams, and a few cities began the expensive process of chemically treating sewage. Gradually,

This scene, captured by a Philadelphia ▶ photographer sent to record the extent of trash that was littering city streets and sidewalks, illustrates the problems of disposal confronting inner-city, immigrant neighborhoods and the necessity for some form of public service to remove the refuse. Seemingly oblivious to the debris, the residents pose for the photographer.

(Philadelphia City Archives, Department of Records)

water managers installed mechanical filters, and cities, led by Jersey City, began purifying water supplies by adding chlorine. These efforts dramatically reduced death rates from typhoid fever.

But waste disposal remained a thorny problem. Experts in 1900 estimated that every New Yorker generated annually some 160 pounds of garbage (food and bones); 1,200 pounds of ashes (from stoves and furnaces); and 100 pounds of rubbish (shoes, furniture, and other discarded items). Europeans of that era produced about half as much trash. Solid waste dumped from factories and businesses included tons of scrap metal, as well as wood. In addition, each of the estimated 3.5 million horses in American cities in 1900 daily dropped about 20 pounds of manure and a gallon of urine that rain washed into nearby water sources. When horses died, the disposal of their carcasses brought more environmental problems. In past eras, excrement, trash, and dead animals could be dismissed as nuisances; by the twentieth century they had become health and safety hazards.

Citizens' groups, led by women's organizations, began discussing these dilemmas in the 1880s, and by the turn of the century urban governments began to hire sanitary engi-

**Urban Engineers**

neers, such as New York's George Waring, to design efficient systems to collect garbage and dispose of it in incinerators and landfills. Engineers also were solving other urban problems and making cities more livable. Street lighting, bridge and street construction, fire protection, and other vital services required technological creativity, and in addressing these issues, the American engineering profession developed new systems and standards of worldwide significance. Elected officials came to depend on the expertise of engineers, who seemed best qualified to supervise a city's expansion. In-

sulated within bureaucratic agencies away from tumultuous party politics, engineers generally carried out their responsibilities efficiently and made some of the most lasting contributions to urban management.

After the mid-nineteenth century, urban dwellers increasingly depended on professional police to protect life and property, but law enforcement

**Law Enforcement**

became complicated and controversial, as various urban groups differed in their views of the law and how it should be enforced. Ethnic and racial minorities were more likely to be arrested than those with economic or political influence. And police officers applied the law less harshly to members of their own ethnic groups and to people with power or those who bought exemptions with bribes.

As law enforcers, police, often poorly trained and prone to corruption, were caught between demands for swift and severe action on the one hand and for leniency on the other. As urban society diversified, some people clamored for police crackdowns on saloons, gambling halls, and houses of prostitution; at the same time, others who profited from and patronized such customer-oriented criminal establishments favored loose law enforcement. Achieving balance between the idealistic intentions of criminal law and people's desire for individual freedom grew increasingly difficult, and it has remained so to this day.

Out of the apparent confusion surrounding urban management arose political machines, organizations whose

▲ "Big Tim" Sullivan, a New York City ward boss, rewarded "repeat voters" with a new pair of shoes. Sullivan once explained, "When you've voted 'em with their whiskers on, you take 'em to a barber and scrape off the chin fringe. Then you vote 'em again. . . . Then to a barber again, off comes the sides and you vote 'em a third time with the mustache. . . . [Then] clean off the mustache and vote 'em plain face. That makes every one of 'em for four votes." *(Library of Congress)*

## Political Machines

main goals were the rewards—money, influence, and prestige—of getting and keeping power. Machine politicians routinely used fraud and bribery to further their ends. But they also provided relief, security, and services to the crowds of newcomers who voted for them and kept them in power. By meeting people's needs, machine politicians accomplished things that other agencies had been unable or unwilling to attempt.

Machines bred leaders, called bosses, who built power bases among urban working classes and especially among new immigrant voters. Most bosses knew their constituents' needs firsthand; they had immigrant backgrounds and had grown up in the inner city. Bosses held power because they tended to problems of everyday life. Martin Lomasney, boss of Boston's South End, explained, "There's got to be in every ward somebody that any bloke can come to—no matter what he's done—and get help. Help, you understand, none of your law and justice, but help." In return for votes, bosses provided jobs, built parks and bathhouses, distributed food and clothing to the needy, and

helped when someone ran afoul of the law. New York's "Big Tim" Sullivan, for example, gave out free shoes and sponsored annual picnics. Such personalized service cultivated mass attachment to the boss; never before had public leaders assumed such responsibility for people in need. Bosses, moreover, made politics a full-time profession. They attended weddings and wakes, joined clubs, and held open houses in saloons where neighborhood folk could speak to them personally. According to George Washington Plunkitt, a neighborhood boss in New York City, "As a rule [the boss] has no business or occupation other than politics. He plays politics every day and night in the year and his headquarters bears the inscription, 'Never closed.'"

To finance their activities and election campaigns, bosses exchanged favors for votes and money. Power over local government enabled machines to control the awarding of public contracts, the granting of utility and streetcar franchises, and the distribution of city jobs. Recipients of city business and jobs were expected to repay the machine with a portion of their profits or salaries and to cast supporting votes on election day. Critics called this process graft; bosses called it gratitude.

Bosses such as Philadelphia's "Duke" Vare, Kansas City's Tom Pendergast, and New York's Richard Croker lived like kings, though their official incomes were slim. Yet machines were rarely as dictatorial or corrupt as critics charged. Rather, several machines, like businesses, evolved into tightly structured operations, such as New York's Tammany Hall organization (named after a society that originally began as a patriotic and fraternal club), which wedded public accomplishments with personal gain. The system rested on a popular base and was held together by loyalty and service. A few bosses had no permanent organization; they were freelance opportunists who bargained for power, sometimes winning and sometimes losing. But most machines were coalitions of smaller organizations that derived power directly from inner-city neighborhoods. Bosses also could boast major achievements. Aided by engineers, machine-led governments constructed the urban infrastructure—public buildings, sewer systems, schools, bridges, and mass-transit lines—and expanded urban services—police, firefighting, and health departments.

Machine politics, however, was rarely neutral or fair. Racial minorities and new immigrant groups, such as Italians and Poles, received only token jobs and nominal favors, if any. And bribes and kickbacks made machine projects and services costly to taxpayers. Cities could not ordinarily raise enough revenue for their construction projects from taxes and fees, so they financed expansion with loans from the public in the form of municipal bonds. Critics of bosses charged that these loans were inflated or unnecessary. Necessary or not, municipal bonds caused public debts to soar, and taxes had to be raised to repay their interest and principal. In addition, payoffs from gambling, prostitution, and illicit liquor traffic often became important sources of machine revenue. But in an age of economic individualism, bosses were no more guilty of discrimination and self-interest than were business leaders who exploited workers, spoiled the environment, and manipulated government in pursuit of profits. Sometimes humane and sometimes criminal, bosses acted as brokers between various sectors of urban society and an uncertain world.

While bosses were consolidating their power, others were trying to destroy them. Many middle- and upper-class Americans feared that immigrant-based political machines menaced democracy and that unsavory alliances between bosses and businesses wasted municipal finances. Anxious over the poverty, crowding, and disorder that accompanied city growth, and convinced that urban services were making taxes too

## Civic Reform

high, civic reformers organized to install more responsible leaders at the helm of government. Civic reform arose in part from the industrial system's emphasis on eliminating inefficiency. Business-minded reformers believed government should run like a company. The way to achieve this goal, they concluded, was to elect officials who would hold down expenses and prevent corruption.

To implement business principles in government, civic reformers supported structural changes, such as city-manager and commission forms of government, which would place administration in the hands of experts rather than politicians, and nonpartisan citywide rather than neighborhood-based election of officials. Armed with such strategies, reformers believed they could cleanse city government of party politics and weaken bosses' power bases. They rarely realized, however, that bosses succeeded because they used government to meet people's needs. Reformers noticed only the waste and dishonesty that machines bred.

A few reform mayors moved beyond structural changes to address social problems. Hazen S. Pingree of Detroit, Samuel "Golden Rule" Jones of Toledo, and Tom Johnson of Cleveland worked to provide jobs to poor people, reduce charges by transit and utility companies, and promote governmental responsibility for the welfare of all citizens. They also supported public ownership of gas, electric, and telephone companies, a quasi-socialist reform that alienated their business allies. But Pingree, Jones, and Johnson were exceptions. Civic reformers could not match the bosses' political savvy; they achieved some successes but rarely held office for very long.

## Social Reform

A different type of reform arose outside politics. Driven to improve as well as manage society, social reformers—mostly young and middle class—embarked on campaigns to investigate and solve urban problems. Housing reformers pressed local governments for building codes to ensure safety in tenements. Educational reformers sought to use public schools as a means of preparing immigrant children for citizenship by teaching them American values. Health reformers tried to improve medical care for those who could not afford it.

Perhaps the most ambitious urban reform movement was the settlement house, a place located in inner-city neighborhoods and established mostly by young, middle-class women who hoped to bridge the gulf between social classes by living among and directly helping immigrants and poor people. The first American settlement, patterned after London's Toynbee Hall, opened in New York City in 1886, and others quickly followed, including Hull

House, founded in Chicago in 1889. To help immigrants adapt to American urban life, settlements offered vocational classes, lessons in English, and childcare, and they sponsored programs to improve nutrition and housing.

As settlement-house workers such as Jane Addams and Florence Kelley of Chicago and Lillian Wald of New York broadened their scope to fight for school nurses, factory safety codes, and public playgrounds, they became reform leaders in cities and in the nation. Their efforts to involve national and local governments in the solution of social problems made them key contributors to the Progressive era, when a reform spirit swept the nation (see Chapter 21). Moreover, settlement-house programs created new professional opportunities for women in social work, public health, and child welfare. These professions enabled female reformers to build a dominion of influence over social policy independent of male-dominated professions and to make valuable contributions to national as well as inner-city life.

Like much in American life, however, settlement houses were segregated. White female reformers lobbied for government programs to aid mostly white immigrant and native-born working classes. Black women reformers, excluded from white settlements, raised funds from private donors and focused on helping members of their own race. African American women were especially active in founding schools, old-age homes, and hospitals, but they also worked for racial advancement and protection of black women from sexual exploitation. Their ranks included Jane Hunter, who founded a home for unmarried black working women in Cleveland in 1911 and inspired the establishment of similar homes in other cities, and Modjeska Simkins, who worked to overcome health problems among blacks in South Carolina.

While female activists tried to assist people in need and revive neighborhoods, a group of male reformers or-

**The City Beautiful Movement**

ganized the City Beautiful movement to improve cities' physical organization. Inspired by the Columbian Exposition of 1893, a dazzling world's fair built on Chicago's South Side, architects and planners, led by architect Daniel Burnham, urged the construction of civic centers, parks, and boulevards that would make cities economically efficient as well as beautiful. "Make no little plans," Burnham urged. "Make big plans; aim high in hope and work." This attitude spawned beautification projects in Chicago, San Francisco, and Washington, D.C., in the early 1900s. Yet most big plans existed mostly as big dreams. Neither government nor private businesses could finance large-scale projects, and planners disagreed among themselves

and with social reformers over whether beautification would truly solve urban problems.

Regardless of their focus, urban reformers wanted to save cities, not abandon them. They believed they could improve urban life by achieving cooperation among all citizens. They often failed to realize, however, that cities were places of great diversity and that different people held very different views about what reform actually meant. To civic reformers, appointing government workers on the basis of civil service exams rather than party loyalty meant progress, but to working-class men, civil service signified reduced employment opportunities. Moral reformers believed that restricting the sale of alcoholic beverages would prevent working-class breadwinners from squandering wages and ruining their health, but immigrants saw such crusades as interference in their private lives. Planners saw new streets and buildings as modern necessities, but such structures often displaced the poor. Well-meaning humanitarians criticized immigrant mothers for the way they shopped, dressed, did housework, and raised children, without regard for these mothers' inability to afford products that the consumer economy created. Thus urban reform merged idealism with naiveté and insensitivity.

## FAMILY LIFE

Although the vast majority of Americans lived within families, this basic social institution suffered strain during the era of urbanization and industrialization. New institutions—schools, social clubs, political organizations, unions—increasingly competed with the family to provide nurture, education, and security. Clergy and journalists warned that the growing separation between home and work, rising divorce rates, the entrance of women into the work force, and loss of parental control over children spelled peril for home and family. Yet the family retained its fundamental role as a cushion in a hard, uncertain world.

Throughout modern western history, most people have lived in two overlapping social units: household

**Family and Household Structures**

and family. A household is a group of people, related or unrelated, who share the same residence. A family is a group related by kinship, some members of which typically live together. In the late nineteenth and early twentieth centuries, different patterns characterized the two institutions.

Until the present, when high divorce rates and relatively late age at first marriage have increased the percentage of one-person households, most American households (75 to 80 percent) have consisted of nuclear families—usually a married couple, with or without children. About 15 to 20 percent of households consisted of extended families—usually a married couple, their children, and one or more relatives, such as parents of the husband or wife, adult siblings, aunts, uncles, or other kin. About 5 percent of households consisted of people living alone. Despite slight variations, this pattern held fairly constant among ethnic, racial, and socioeconomic groups.

Several factors explain this pattern. Because immigrants tended to be young, the American population as a whole was young. In 1880 the median age was under twenty-one, and by 1920 it was still only twenty-five. (Median age at present is above thirty-five.) Moreover, in 1900 the death rate among people aged forty-five to sixty-four was double what it is today. As a result, there were few elderly people: only 4 percent of the population was sixty-five or older, compared with almost 13 percent today. Thus few families could form extended three-generation households, and fewer children than today had living grandparents. Migration split up many families, and the ideal of a home of one's own encouraged nuclear household organization.

The average size of nuclear families also changed over time. Most of Europe and North America experienced falling birth rates in the nineteenth century. The decline in the United States began early in the 1800s and accelerated toward the end of the century. In 1880 the birth rate was 40 live births per 1,000 people; by 1900 it had dropped to 32; by 1920, to 28. Although fertility was higher among black, immigrant, and rural women than among white native-born urban females, birth rates of all groups fell.

### Declining Birth Rates

Several factors explain this decline. First, as the United States became more urbanized, the economic value of children lessened. On farms, where young children worked at home or in the fields, each child born represented an addition to the family labor force. In the wage-based urban economy, children could not contribute significantly to the family income for many years, and a new child represented a draw on family income. Second, infant mortality fell as diet and medical care improved, and families did not have to bear many children to ensure that some would survive.

Perhaps most importantly, as economic trends changed, attitudes toward children changed. No matter what the era, parents always cherished their children. But as American society industrialized and urbanized, the idea of a child as a pure, innocent being who not only needed shelter from society's corruptions but who also could provide parents with emotional rewards spread, first among the middle class and gradually to the working class as well. A mother's investment of care and attention could be more focused and effective if she had fewer rather than more children. Such an attitude seems to have stimulated decisions by parents to limit family size—either by abstaining from sex during the wife's fertile period or by using contraception. Families with six or eight children became rare; three or four became more usual. Birth-control technology—diaphragms and condoms—had been utilized for centuries, but in this era new materials made devices more convenient and dependable. Use of rubber rather than animal membranes for condoms after 1869 inspired British playwright and philosopher George Bernard Shaw to exclaim that new birth-control devices were "the greatest invention of the nineteenth century."

Although the family remained resilient and adaptable, notable changes began to occur in individual life patterns. Before the late nineteenth century, stages of life were less distinct than they are today, and generations blended together with relatively little differentiation. Childhood, for instance, had been regarded as a period during which young people prepared for adulthood by gradually assuming more roles and responsibilities. Subdivisions of youth—toddlers, schoolchildren, teenagers, and the like—were not recognized or defined. Because married couples had more children over a longer time span than is common today, active parenthood occupied most of adult life. Older children might begin parenting even before reaching adulthood by caring for younger siblings. And because relatively few people lived to advanced age or left work voluntarily, and because old-age homes were rare, older people were not isolated from other age groups. By the late nineteenth century, however, decreasing birth rates shortened the period of parental responsibility, so more middle-aged couples experienced an "empty nest" when all their children had grown up and left home. Longer life expectancy and a tendency by employers to force aged workers to retire separated the old from the young.

### Stages of Life

New patterns of childhood also emerged. The separation of home and work, especially prevalent in cities, meant that children were less likely than previously to be involved in producing income for the family. To be sure, youngsters in working-class families still helped out—working in factories, scavenging streets for scraps of wood and coal, and peddling newspapers and other goods—but generally youngsters had more time for other activities. As states passed compulsory school attendance laws in the

▲ As cities grew and became increasingly congested, children in immigrant and working-class neighborhoods used streets and sidewalks as play sites. Activities of youngsters such as these, playing unsupervised in front of a Polish saloon, prompted adults to create playgrounds, clubs, and other places where they could protect children's safety and innocence and where they could ensure that play would be orderly and obedient. *(Chicago Historical Society)*

1870s and 1880s, education occupied more of children's daily time than ever before, keeping them in school nine months of the year until they were teenagers and strengthening peer rather than family influence over their behavior. Also, in keeping with the scientific spirit of the era, physicians and psychologists began studying children in order to help shape them into moral, productive adults. Researchers such as G. Stanley Hall and Luther H. Gulick advocated that teachers and parents should match education and play activities to the needs that children had at different stages of their development. Anxious that children be protected from city streets, "child-saving" advocates asserted that adult-supervised playgrounds should be established to give children alternatives to dangerous activities.

Although marriage rates were high, large numbers of city dwellers were unmarried, largely because many people waited to wed until they were in their late twenties. In 1890 almost 42 percent of adult American men and 37 percent of women were single, almost twice as high as the figures for 1960 but slightly lower than they are today. About half of all single people still lived in their parents' household, though they led independent working and social lives, but many others inhabited boarding houses or rooms in the homes of strangers. Mostly young, these men and women constituted a separate subculture that helped support institutions such as dance halls, saloons, cafés, and the Young Men's Christian Association (YMCA) and Young Women's Christian Association (YWCA).

## The Unmarried

Some unmarried people were part of the homosexual populations that especially thrived in large cities such as New York, San Francisco, and Boston. Although numbers are difficult to estimate, gay men had their own subculture of clubs, restaurants, coffeehouses, theaters, and support networks. A number of same-sex couples, especially women, formed lasting marital-type relationships, sometimes called "Boston marriages." People in this subculture were categorized more by how they acted—men acting like women, women acting like men—than by who their sexual partners were. The term *homosexual* was not used. Men who dressed and acted like women were called "fairies," and men who displayed masculine traits could be termed "normal" even though they might have sexual relations with fairies. Gay women remained even more hidden, and a lesbian subculture of clubs and commercial establishments did not develop until the 1920s. The gay world, then, was a complex one that included a variety of relationships and institutions.

## Boarding and Lodging

In every city, large numbers of young people—and some older people—lived as boarders and lodgers. (Boarders usually received meals along with a room; lodgers only rented a room.) Boarding houses and lodging hotels were common, but families also commonly took in boarders to occupy rooms vacated by grown children and to get additional income. By 1900 as many as 50 percent of city residents, including Erich Weiss's family, had lived either as, or with, boarders at some point during their lifetime. Housing reformers charged that boarding and lodging caused overcrowding and loss of privacy. Yet the practice was highly useful. For people on the move, boarding or lodging was a transitional stage, providing a quasi-family environment until they set up their own households. Especially in communities where economic hardship or rapid growth made housing expensive or scarce, newlyweds sometimes lived temporarily with one spouse's parents. Families also took in widowed parents or unmarried siblings who otherwise would have lived alone.

At a time when welfare agencies were scarce, the family was the institution to which people could turn in times of need. Even when relatives did not live together, they often resided nearby and aided one another with childcare, meals, advice, and consolation. They also obtained jobs for each other. Factory foremen who had responsibility for hiring often recruited new workers recommended by their employees. According to one new arrival, "After two days my brother took me to the shop he was working in and his boss saw me and he gave me the job."

**Functions of Kinship**

But obligations of kinship were not always welcome. Immigrant families pressured last-born female children to stay at home to care for aging parents, a practice that stifled opportunities for education, marriage, and independence. As an aging Italian American father confessed, "One of our daughters is an old maid [and] causes plenty of troubles. . . . it may be my fault because I always wished her to remain at home and not to marry for she was of great financial help." Tensions also developed between generations, such as when immigrant parents and American-born children clashed over the abandonment of Old World ways or over the amount of wages that employed children should contribute to the household. Nevertheless, for better or worse, kinship provided people a means of coping with stresses caused by urban-industrial society. Social and economic change did not sever family ties.

Thus, by 1900, family life and functions were both changing and holding firm. New institutions were assuming tasks formerly performed by the family, and people's roles in school, in the family, on the job, and in the community came to be determined by age more than by any other characteristic. Schools made education a community responsibility. Employment agencies, personnel offices, and labor unions were taking responsibility for employee recruitment and job security. Age-based peer groups exerted greater influence over people's values and activities. Migration and divorce seemed to be splitting families apart. Yet, in the face of these pressures, the family adjusted by expanding and contracting to meet temporary needs, and kinship remained a dependable though not always appreciated institution.

An emphasis on family togetherness became especially visible at holiday celebrations. Middle-class moralists helped make Thanksgiving, Christmas, and Easter special times for family reunion and child-centered activities, and female relatives made special efforts to cook and decorate the home. Birthdays, too, took on an increasingly festive quality, both as an important family occasion and as a milestone for measuring the age-related norms that accompanied intensified consciousness of life stages. In 1914 President Woodrow Wilson signed a proclamation designating the second Sunday in May as Mother's Day, capping a six-year campaign by Anna Jarvis, a schoolteacher who believed grown children too often neglected their mothers. Ethnic and racial groups made efforts to fit national celebrations to their cultures, using holidays as occasions for preparing special ethnic foods and engaging in special ceremonies. For many, holiday celebrations were a testimony to the vitality of family life. "As I grew up, living conditions were a bit crowded," one woman reminisced, "but no one minded because we were a family . . . thankful we all lived together."

**Holiday Celebrations**

## THE NEW LEISURE AND MASS CULTURE

On December 2, 1889, as hundreds of workers paraded through Worcester, Massachusetts, in support of shorter working hours, a group of carpenters hoisted a banner proclaiming "Eight Hours for Work, Eight Hours for Rest, Eight Hours for What We Will." That last phrase was significant, for it laid claim to a special segment of daily life that belonged to the individual. Increasingly, among all urban social classes, leisure activities, doing "what we will," filled this time segment.

American inventors had long tried to create labor-saving devices, but not until the late 1800s did technology become truly timesaving. Mechanization and assembly-line production cut the average workweek in manufacturing from sixty-six hours in 1860 to sixty in 1890 and forty-seven in 1920. These reductions meant shorter workdays and freer weekends. White-collar employees spent eight to ten hours a day on the job and often worked only half a day or not at all on weekends. Laborers in steel mills and sweatshops still endured twelve- or fourteen-hour shifts and had no time or energy for leisure. But as the economy shifted from one of scarcity and production to one of sur-

**Increase in Leisure Time**

SHOOTING THE CHUTES, CONEY ISLAND, N. Y.

▲ Amusement centers such as Luna Park at Coney Island in New York City, became common and appealing features of the new leisure culture. One of the most popular Coney Island attractions was a ride called Shooting the Chutes, which resembled modern-day giant water slides. In 1904 Luna Park staged an outrageous stunt of an elephant sliding down the chute. The creature survived, apparently unfazed. *(Picture Research Consultants and Archives)*

plus and consumption, more Americans began to engage in a variety of recreations, and a substantial segment of the economy provided for—and profited from—leisure. By 1900 many Americans were enmeshed in the business of play.

Amusement became an organized, commercial activity, as the introduction of games, toys, and musical instruments for indoor family entertainment expanded. Improvements in printing and paper production, and the rise of manufacturers such as Milton Bradley and Parker Brothers, increased the popularity of board games. Significantly, the content of board games shifted from moral lessons to topics involving transportation, finance, and sports. Middle-class families were also buying mass-produced pianos and sheet music which made the singing of popular songs a common form of home entertainment. The vanguard of new leisure pursuits, however, was sports. Formerly a fashionable indulgence of elites, organized sports became a favored pastime of all classes, attracting countless participants and spectators. Even those who could not

play or watch got involved by reading about sports in the newspapers.

The most popular sport was baseball. Derived from older bat, ball, and base-circling games, baseball was formalized in 1845 by the Knickerbocker Club of New York, which standardized the rules of play. By 1860 at least fifty baseball clubs existed, and youths played informal games on city lots and rural fields across the nation. In 1869 a professional club, the Cincinnati Red Stockings, went on a national tour, and other teams followed suit. The National League of Professional Baseball Clubs, founded in 1876, gave the sport a stable, businesslike structure. Not all athletes benefited, however; as early as 1867 a "color line" excluded black players from professional teams. Nevertheless, by the 1880s professional baseball was big business. In 1903 the National League and the competing American League (formed in 1901) began a World Series between their championship teams, entrenching baseball as the

## Baseball

# Japanese Baseball

aseball, the "American pastime," was one of the new leisure-time pursuits that Americans took with them into different parts of the world. The Shanghai Base Ball Club was founded by Americans in China in 1863, but few Chinese paid much attention to the sport, largely because the Imperial Court denounced the game as spiritually corrupting. However, when Horace Wilson, an American teacher, taught the rules of baseball to his Japanese students around 1870, the game received an enthusiastic reception as a reinforcement of traditional virtues. In fact, baseball quickly became so much a part of Japanese culture that one Japanese writer commented, "Baseball is perfect for us. If the Americans hadn't invented it, we probably would have."

During the 1870s, scores of Japanese high schools and colleges sponsored organized baseball, and in 1883 Hiroshi Hiraoka, a railroad engineer who had studied in Boston, founded the first official local team, the Shimbashi Athletic Club Athletics. Fans displayed wild devotion to this and similar teams as they developed over the next several years.

Before Americans introduced baseball to Japan, the Japanese had no team sports and no predilection for recreational athletics. Once they learned about baseball, they found that the idea of a team sport fit their culture very well. But the Japanese had difficulty applying the American concept of leisure to the game. For them, baseball was serious business, involving hard and often brutal training. Practices at Ichiko, one of Japan's two great high school baseball teams in the late nineteenth century, were dubbed "Bloody Urine" because many players passed blood after a day of drilling. There was a spiritual quality as well, linked to Buddhist values. According to one Japanese coach, "The purpose of [baseball] training is not health but the forging of the soul, and a strong soul is only born from strong practice. . . . Student baseball must be the baseball of self-discipline, or trying to attain the truth, just as in Zen Buddhism." This attitude prompted the Japanese to consider baseball as a new method to pursue the spirit of Bushido, the way of the samurai.

When Americans played baseball in Japan, the Japanese found them to be strong and talented but lacking in discipline and respect. Americans insulted the Japanese by refusing to remove their hats and bow when they stepped up to bat. An international dispute occurred in 1891 when William Imbrie, an American professor at Tokyo's Meijo University, arrived late for a game. Finding the gate locked, he climbed over the fence in order to enter the field. The fence, however, had sacred meaning, and Japanese fans attacked Imbrie for his sacrilege. Imbrie suffered facial injuries, prompting the American embassy to lodge a formal complaint. Americans assumed that their game would encourage Japanese to become like westerners, but the Japanese transformed the American pastime into an expression of team spirit, discipline, and nationalism that was uniquely Japanese.

▲ Replete with bats, gloves, and uniforms, this Japanese baseball team of 1890 very much resembles its American counterpart of that era. The Japanese adopted baseball soon after Americans became involved in their country but also added their cultural qualities to the game. *(Japanese Baseball Hall of Fame)*

national pastime. The Boston Red Sox beat the Pittsburgh Pirates in that first series.

Baseball appealed mostly to men. But croquet, which also swept the nation, attracted both sexes. Middle- and

### Croquet and Cycling

upper-class people held croquet parties and outfitted wickets with candles for night contests. In an era when the departure of paid work from the home had separated men's from women's spheres, croquet increased opportunities for social contact between the sexes.

Meanwhile, cycling achieved a popularity rivaling that of baseball, especially after 1885, when the cumbersome velocipede, with its huge front wheel and tall seat, gave way to safety bicycles with pneumatic tires and wheels of identical size. By 1900 Americans owned 10 million bicycles, and clubs such as the League of American Wheelmen were petitioning state governments to build more paved roads. African American cyclists were allowed to compete as professionals, unlike baseball. One black rider, Major Taylor, won fame in Europe and the United States between 1892 and 1910. Like croquet, cycling brought men and women together, combining opportunities for exercise and courtship. Moreover, the bicycle played an influential role in freeing women from the constraints of Victorian fashions. In order to ride the dropped-frame female models, women had to wear divided skirts and simple undergarments. As the 1900 census declared, "Few articles . . . have created so great a revolution in social conditions as the bicycle."

American football, as an intercollegiate competition, attracted mostly players and spectators wealthy enough

### Football

to have access to higher education. By the late nineteenth century, however, the game was appealing to a broader audience. The 1893 Princeton-Yale game drew fifty thousand spectators, and informal games were played in yards and playgrounds throughout the country. Soon, however, football became a national scandal because of its violence and use of "tramp athletes," nonstudents whom colleges hired to help their teams win. Critics accused football of mirroring undesirable features of American society. An editor of *The Nation* charged in 1890 that "the spirit of the American Youth, as of the American man, is to win, to 'get there,' by fair means or foul; and the lack of moral scruple which pervades the struggles of the business world meets with temptations equally irresistible in the miniature contests of the football field."

The scandals climaxed in 1905, when 18 players died from game-related injuries and 159 were seriously injured.

President Theodore Roosevelt, a strong advocate of athletics, convened a White House conference to discuss ways to eliminate brutality and foul play. The gathering founded the Intercollegiate Athletic Association (renamed the National College Athletic Association in 1910) to police college sports. In 1906 the association altered the game to make it less violent and more open. New rules outlawed "flying-wedge" rushes, extended from five to ten yards the distance needed to earn a first down, legalized the forward pass, and tightened player eligibility requirements.

As more women enrolled in college, they pursued physical activities besides croquet and cycling. Believing that intellectual success required active and healthy bodies, college women participated in such sports as rowing, track, and swimming. Eventually women made basketball their most popular intercollegiate sport. Invented in 1891 as a winter sport for men, basketball received women's rules (which limited dribbling and running, and encouraged passing) from Senda Berenson of Smith College.

Three branches of American show business—popular drama, musical comedy, and vaudeville—matured with

### Show Business

the growth of cities. New theatrical performances offered audiences escape into melodrama, adventure, and comedy. Plots were simple, heroes and villains recognizable. For urban people unfamiliar with the frontier, popular plays made the mythical Wild West and Old South come alive through stories of Davy Crockett, Buffalo Bill, and the Civil War. Virtue and honor always triumphed in melodramas such as *Uncle Tom's Cabin* and *The Old Homestead*, reinforcing faith that, in an uncertain and disillusioning world, goodness would prevail.

Musical comedies entertained audiences with song, humor, and dance. The American musical derived from lavishly costumed operettas common in Europe. The introduction of American themes (often involving ethnic groups), folksy humor, and catchy tunes in the late nineteenth century helped these shows spawn the nation's most popular songs and entertainers. George M. Cohan, a singer, dancer, and songwriter born into an Irish family of entertainers, became master of American musical comedy after the turn of the century. Drawing on patriotism and traditional values in songs such as "Yankee Doodle Boy" and "You're a Grand Old Flag," Cohan helped bolster morale during the First World War. Comic opera, too, became popular. Initially, American comic operas imitated European musicals, but by the early 1900s composers such as Victor Herbert were writing for American audiences.

Vaudeville was probably the most popular mass entertainment in early-twentieth-century America because

▲ Joe Weber and Lew Fields were one of the most popular comic teams in vaudeville. They and similar comedians used fast-paced dialogue to entertain audiences with routines like this one: *Doctor:* Do you have insurance? *Patient:* I ain't got one nickel insurance. *Doctor:* If you die, what will your wife bury you with? *Patient:* With pleasure. *(Corbis-Bettmann)*

its variety offered something for everyone. Shows, whose acts followed a fixed schedule just like trains and factory production, included jugglers, magicians, puppeteers, acrobats, comedians, singers, dancers, and specialty acts like Houdini's escapes. Around 1900, the number of vaudeville theaters and troupes skyrocketed, and big-time operators such as Tony Pastor (who gave Houdini his first vaudeville job) and the partnership of Benjamin Keith and Edward Albee consolidated theaters and acts under their management in the same manner that other businessmen were consolidating factory production. Marcus Loew, an owner of theaters that attracted working-class audiences, was known as "the Henry Ford of show business." Producer Florenz Ziegfeld brilliantly packaged shows in a stylish format—the Ziegfeld Follies—and gave the nation a new model of femininity, the Ziegfeld Girl, whose graceful dancing and alluring costumes suggested a haunting sensuality.

Show business provided economic and social mobility to female, African American, and immigrant performers, but it also encouraged stereotyping and exploitation.

### Opportunities for Women and Minorities

Comic opera diva Lillian Russell, vaudeville singer-comedienne Fanny Brice, and burlesque queen Eva Tanguay attracted intensely loyal fans, commanded handsome fees, and won respect for their talents. In contrast to the demure Victorian female, they conveyed an image of pluck and independence. There was something both shocking and confident about Eva Tanguay when she moved energetically around the stage singing earthy songs like "It's All Been Done Before but Not the Way I Do It" and "I Don't Care." But lesser female performers and showgirls (called "soubrettes") were often exploited by male promoters and theater owners, many of whom wanted only to profit by titillating the public with the sight of scantily clad women.

Before the 1890s, the chief form of commercial entertainment that employed African American performers had been the minstrel show, but vaudeville opened new opportunities to them. As stage settings shifted from the plantation to the city, music shifted from sentimental folk tunes to the syncopated rhythms of ragtime. Pandering to the prejudices of white audiences, composers ridiculed blacks, and black performers were forced to portray demeaning characters. In songs such as "He's Just a Little Nigger, But He's Mine All Mine" and "You May Be a Hawaiian on Old Broadway, But You're Just Another Nigger to Me," blacks were degraded on stage much as they were in society. Burt Williams, a talented black comedian and dancer who had graduated from high school at a time when most whites did not, achieved success by wearing blackface (black makeup) and playing stereotypical roles of a smiling fool and dandy, but was tormented by the humiliation he had to suffer.

An ethnic flavor gave much of American mass entertainment its uniqueness. Like Houdini, many performers were immigrants, and their stage acts reflected their experiences. Vaudeville in particular utilized ethnic humor and exaggerated dialects. Skits and songs were fast-paced, replicating the tempo of factories, offices, and the streets. Performances reinforced ethnic stereotypes, but such distortions were more self-conscious and sympathetic than those directed at blacks. Ethnic humor often involved everyday difficulties that immigrants faced. A typical scene involving Italians, for example, highlighted a character's uncertain grasp of English, which caused him to confuse *diploma* with *the plumber* and *pallbearer* with *polar bear*. Other scenes included gags about dealing with modern society. Thus, when a stage doctor required ten dollars for his advice, the patient responded, "Ten dollars is too much. Here's two dollars. Take it, that's *my* advice." Such scenes allowed audiences to laugh with, rather than at, foibles of the human condition.

Shortly after 1900, live entertainment began to yield to a more accessible form of commercial amusement: motion pictures. Perfected by Thomas Edison in the 1880s, movies began as slot-machine peepshows in arcades and billiard parlors. Eventually, images of speeding trains, acrobats, and belly dancers were projected onto a screen so that large audiences could view them, and a new medium was born. Producers, many of them from Jewish immigrant backgrounds, soon discovered that a film could tell a story in exciting ways and, like vaudeville performers, catered to viewers' desires. Using themes of patriotism and working-class experience, early filmmakers helped shift American culture away from its more straitlaced Victorian values to a more cosmopolitan outlook.

### Movies

As they expanded from minutes to hours in length, movies presented controversial social messages as well as innovative technology and styles of expression. For example, the film *Birth of a Nation* (1915), by the creative director D. W. Griffith, was a stunning epic film about the Civil War and Reconstruction, but it also fanned racial prejudice by depicting African Americans as threats to white moral values. The National Association for the Advancement of Colored People (NAACP), formed in 1909, led organized protests against it. But the film's ground-breaking techniques—close-ups, fade-outs, and battle scenes—heightened the drama.

Technology and entrepreneurship also made news a mass consumer product. Using high-speed printing presses, cheaply produced paper, and profits from growing advertisement revenues, shrewd publishers created a medium that made people crave news and ads just as they craved amusements. City life and increased leisure time seemed to nurture a fascination with the sensational, and from the 1880s onward popular urban newspapers increasingly whetted that appetite.

Joseph Pulitzer, a Hungarian immigrant who bought the *New York World* in 1883, pioneered journalism by making news a mass commodity. Believing that newspapers should be "dedicated to the cause of the people," Pulitzer filled the *World* with stories of disasters, crimes, and scandals. Screaming headlines, set in large, bold type like that used for advertisements, attracted readers. Pulitzer's journalists not only

### Yellow Journalism

▲ Dick Merriwell and his brother, Frank, were fictional heroes of hundreds of stories written in the early 1900s by Burt Standish (the pen name used by Gilbert Patten). In a series of adventures, mostly involving sports, these popular character models used their physical skills, valor, and moral virtue to lead by example, accomplish the impossible, and influence others to behave in an upstanding way.

*(Collection of Picture Research Consultants, Inc.)*

reported news but also sought it out and created it. *World* reporter Nellie Bly (real name, Elizabeth Cochrane), for example, faked her way into a mental asylum and wrote a brazen exposé of the sordid conditions she found. Other reporters staged stunts and hunted down heart-rending human-interest stories. Pulitzer also popularized comics, and the yellow ink in which they were printed gave rise to the term *yellow journalism* as a synonym for sensationalism.

Pulitzer's strategy was immensely successful. In one year the *World*'s circulation increased from 20,000 to 100,000, and by the late 1890s it reached 1 million. Other publishers, such as William Randolph Hearst, who bought the *New York Journal* in 1895 and started an empire of mass-circulation newspapers, adopted Pulitzer's techniques. Pulitzer, Hearst, and their rivals boosted circulation further by making sports and women's news a mass commodity. Newspapers had previously reported sporting events, but yellow-journalism papers gave such stories greater prominence by printing separate, expanded sports pages. Sports news re-created a game's drama through narrative and statistics, and promoted sports as a leisure-time attraction. To capture female readers, newspapers also added special sections devoted to household tips, fashion, etiquette, and club news.

By the early twentieth century, mass-circulation magazines overshadowed the expensive elitist journals of earlier eras. Publications such as

**Other Mass-Market Publications**

*McClure's, Saturday Evening Post,* and *Ladies' Home Journal* offered human-interest stories, muckraking exposés (see page 594), titillating fiction, photographs, colorful covers, and eye-catching ads to a growing mass market. Meanwhile, the total number of published books more than quadrupled between 1880 and 1917. Rising consumption of news and books reflected growing literacy. Between 1870 and 1920, the proportion of Americans over age ten who could not read or write fell from 20 percent to 6 percent.

Other forms of communication also expanded. In 1891 there was less than 1 telephone for every 100 people in the United States; by 1901 the number had grown to 2.1, and by 1921 it swelled to 12.6. In 1900 Americans used 4 billion postage stamps; in 1922 they bought 14.3 billion. The term *community* took on new dimensions, as people used the media, mail, and telephone to extend their horizons far beyond their immediate locality.

More than ever before, people in different parts of the country knew about and discussed the same news event, whether it was a sensational murder, a sex scandal, or the fortunes of a particular entertainer or athlete. America was becoming a mass society where the same products, the same technology, and the same information dominated everyday life, regardless of region.

American mass culture, perhaps more than any other factor, represented democracy, because influences flowed upward from the experiences and desires of ordinary people as much as, if not more than, they were imposed from above by the rich and powerful. The popularity of sports, the themes depicted in movies and on stage, and the content of everyday publications reveal not only that Americans in the urban-industrial era had time to patronize leisure-time activities but also that savvy entrepreneurs understood that what they produced needed to meet the needs of the new consumers. At the same time, producers helped people adapt by providing lessons about new social and economic conditions and by making some of the disruptive factors more tolerable through drama and humor. The major exception was the portrayal and treatment of African Americans with a viciousness that did not diminish as entertainment expanded.

To some extent, then, the cities' new amusements and media had a homogenizing influence, allowing ethnic and social groups to share common experiences. Parks, ball fields, vaudeville shows, movies, and the feature sections of newspapers and magazines were nonsectarian and apolitical. Yet different consumer groups adapted them to their own cultural needs. Immigrant groups, for example, often used parks and amusement areas as sites for special ethnic gatherings. To the dismay of reformers who hoped that public recreation and holidays would assimilate newcomers and teach them habits of restraint, immigrants converted picnics and Fourth of July celebrations into occasions for boisterous drinking and sometimes violent behavior. Young working-class men and women resisted parents' and moralists' warnings, and frequented urban dance halls, where they explored forms of courtship and sexual behavior free from adult oversight. And children often used streets and rooftops to create their own entertainment rather than participate in adult-supervised games in parks and playgrounds. Thus, as Americans learned to play, their leisure—like their work and politics—expressed, and was shaped by, the pluralistic forces that thrived in urban life.

# *Legacy* FOR A PEOPLE AND A NATION

## Ethnic Food

Today, an American might eat a bagel for breakfast, a gyro sandwich for lunch, and wonton soup, shrimp creole, and rice pilaf for dinner, followed by chocolate mousse and espresso. An evening snack might consist of nachos and lager beer. These items, each identified with a different ethnic group, serve as tasty reminders that immigrants have made influential and lasting contributions to the nation's culinary culture. The American diet also represents one of the few genuine ways that the multicultural nation has served as a melting pot.

The American taste for ethnic food has a complicated history. Since the nineteenth century, the food business has offered immigrant entrepreneurs lucrative opportunities, many of which involved products unrelated to their own ethnic background. The industry is replete with success stories linked to names such as Hector Boiardi (Chef Boyardee), William Gebhardt (Eagle Brand chili and tamales), Jeno Paulucci (Chun King), and Alphonse Biardot (Franco-American), all of whom immigrated to the United States in the late nineteenth or early twentieth century. But Americans have also supported unheralded local immigrant merchants and restaurateurs who have offered special and regional fare—German, Chinese, Italian, Tex-Mex, "soul food," or Thai—in every era.

Unlike the strife that occurred over housing, jobs, schools, and politics when different nationalities and racial groups collided, the evolution of American eating habits has been peaceful. Occasionally criticisms developed, such as when dietitians and reformers in the early twentieth century charged that Mexican immigrants were harming their digestion by overusing tomatoes and peppers, and that the rich foods of eastern European Jews made them overly emotional and less capable of assimilating. But relatively conflict-free sharing and borrowing have characterized American food ways far more than "food fights" and intolerance. The sensory pleasure of eating has always overridden cultural loyalty, and mass marketers have been quick to capitalize.

As each wave of immigrants has entered the nation— and especially as these newcomers have occupied the cities, where cross-cultural contact has been inevitable— food has given them certain ways of becoming American, of finding some form of group acceptance, while also giving them a means of confirming their identity. At the same time, those who already thought of themselves as Americans have willingly made the newcomers' gastronomic legacy a part of the existing culture and a part of themselves.

## SUMMARY

People and technology made the late nineteenth and early twentieth centuries the "age of the city." Flocking cityward, migrants already in America and those coming from foreign parts remade themselves, like Houdini, and remade the urban environment as well. Although they may have escaped their places of residence, they also brought with them cultures that in turn enriched American culture. They also found new escape in new and expanded forms of mass leisure and entertainment. Cities were dynamic places, where everyday life brought new challenges, where politics and reform took on new meanings, and where family life reflected both change and continuity.

Although their governments and neighborhoods may have seemed chaotic, American cities experienced an "unheralded triumph" by the early 1900s. Amid corruption and political conflict, engineers modernized sewer, water, and lighting services, and urban governments made cities safer by expanding professional police and fire departments. When native inventiveness met the traditions of European, African, and Asian cultures, a new kind of society emerged. This society seldom functioned smoothly; there really was no coherent urban community, only a collection of subcommunities. The jumble of social classes, ethnic and racial groups, political and professional organizations, sometimes lived in harmony, sometimes not. Generally, cities managed to thrive because of, rather than in spite of, their diverse fragments.

Optimists had envisioned the American nation as a melting pot, where various nationalities would fuse into a unified people. Instead, many ethnic groups proved unmeltable, preferring—and sometimes forced—to pursue their own ways of acting, and racial minorities got burned on the bottom of the pot. As a result of immigration and urbanization, the United States became a pluralistic society in which cultural influences moved in both directions: imposed from above by people with power and influence, and adopted from below through the traditions and tastes brought to cities by disparate peoples. When the desire to retain one culture met with the need to fit in, often the results were compound identifications: Irish American, Italian American, Polish American, and the like.

By 1920, immigrants and their offspring outnumbered the native-born in many cities, and the national economy depended on these new workers and consumers. Migrants and immigrants transformed the United States into an urban nation. They gave American culture its rich and varied texture just by living their lives but also, like Harry Houdini, by changing the course of entertainment and consumerism, and they laid the foundations for the liberalism that would characterize American politics in the twentieth century.

## SUGGESTIONS FOR FURTHER READING

John Bodnar, *The Transplanted: A History of Immigrants in Urban America* (1985)

Howard P. Chudacoff and Judith E. Smith, *The Evolution of American Urban Society*, 6th ed. (2005)

John D'Emilio and Estelle Freedman, *Intimate Matters: A History of Sexuality in America* (1988)

Nancy Foner and George M. Frederickson, eds., *Not Just Black and White: Historical and Contemporary Perspectives on Immigration, Race, and Ethnicity in the United States* (2004)

Kenneth T. Jackson, *The Crabgrass Frontier: The Suburbanization of the United States* (1985)

Matthew Frye Jacobson, *Whiteness of a Different Color: European Immigrants and the Alchemy of Race* (1998)

Erika Lee, *At America's Gates: Chinese Immigration During the Exclusion Era, 1882–1943* (2003)

Martin V. Melosi, *The Sanitary City: Urban Infrastructure in America from Colonial Times to the Present* (2000)

Robyn Muncy, *Creating a Female Dominion in American Reform, 1890–1935* (1991)

Kathy Peiss, *Cheap Amusements: Working Women and Leisure in Turn-of-the-Century New York* (1986)

*For a more extensive list for further reading, go to* college.hmco.com/pic/norton8e.

# Gilded Age Politics

## *1877-1900*

𝒮 he had a sharp tongue and a combative spirit. Known to friends as the "People's Joan of Arc" and to enemies as the "Kansas Pythoness," Mary Elizabeth Lease was such an electrifying orator that, according to one observer, "she could recite the multiplication table and set a crowd hooting and harrahing at her will." Born in 1853 in Pennsylvania, she lived most of her adult life in Kansas. Married at age twenty, she bore five children but somehow found time to study law while she took in washing, pinning her notes above her washtub.

In 1885 Mary became the first woman admitted to the Kansas bar and began an activist career. Joining the Woman's Christian Temperance Union and an organization called the Farmers' Alliance, she served as spokesperson for the new Populist party and made more than 160 speeches in 1890 on behalf of downtrodden rural folk and laboring people. She later ran for the U.S. Senate and campaigned for Populist presidential candidate James B. Weaver. Lease unleashed powerful language in support of her causes, which ranged beyond Populism to prohibition, woman suffrage, and birth control. She once proclaimed, "This is a nation of inconsistencies. . . . We fought England for our liberty and put chains on four million blacks. We wiped out slavery and [then] by our tariff laws and national banks began a system of white wage slavery worse than the first." Although she denied ever making the oft-quoted suggestion that Kansas farmers should "raise less corn and more hell," she admitted that it "was a good bit of advice."

Mary Lease's turbulent career paralleled an eventful era, one that can be characterized by three themes: special interest ascendancy, legislative accomplishment, and political

◀ Politics in the late nineteenth century was a major community activity. In an age before movies, television, shopping malls, and widespread professional sports, forceful orators, such as Socialist Party leader Eugene V. Debs, shown speaking in a railroad yard, attracted large audiences for speeches that sometimes lasted for hours. *(Brown Brothers)*

## CHRONOLOGY

**1873** ■ Congress ends coinage of silver dollars

**1873–78** ■ Economic hard times hit

**1877** ■ Georgia passes poll tax, disfranchising most African Americans

**1878** ■ Bland-Allison Act requires Treasury to buy between $2 and $4 million in silver each month

**1881** ■ Garfield assassinated; Arthur assumes presidency

**1883** ■ Pendleton Civil Service Act introduces merit system
■ Supreme Court strikes down 1883 Civil Rights Act

**1886** ■ *Wabash* case declares that only Congress can limit interstate commerce rates

**1887** ■ Farmers' Alliances form
■ Interstate Commerce Commission begins regulating rates and practices of interstate shipping

**1890** ■ McKinley Tariff raises tariff rates
■ Sherman Silver Purchase Act commits Treasury to buying 4.5 million ounces of silver each month
■ "Mississippi Plan" uses poll taxes and literacy tests to prevent African Americans from voting
■ National Woman Suffrage Association formed

**1890s** ■ Jim Crow laws, discriminating against African Americans in legal treatment and public accommodations, passed by southern states

**1892** ■ Populist convention in Omaha draws up reform platform

**1893** ■ Sherman Silver Purchase Act repealed

**1893–97** ■ Major economic depression hits United States

**1894** ■ Wilson-Gorman Tariff passes
■ Coxey's Army marches on Washington, D.C.

**1896** ■ *Plessy v. Ferguson* establishes separate-but-equal doctrine

**1898** ■ Louisiana implements "grandfather clause," restricting voting by African Americans

**1899** ■ *Cummings v. County Board of Education* applies separate-but-equal doctrine to schools

exclusion. Her fiery speeches voiced the growing dissatisfaction with the ways in which powerful private interests—manufacturers, railroad managers, bankers, and wealthy men in general—were exercising greed through large corporations and political power. The era's obsession with riches seemed so widespread that, when Mark Twain and Charles Dudley Warner satirized America as a land of shallow money grubbers in their novel *The Gilded Age* (1874), the name stuck. Ever since, historians have used the expression "Gilded Age" to characterize the late nineteenth century.

At the same time, Lease's rhetoric obscured economic and political accomplishments at both national and state levels. Between 1877 and 1900, large corporations and allies of big business influenced politics and government as much as they shaped everyday life. Yet, in spite of partisan and regional rivalries, Congress achieved legislative landmarks in railroad regulation, tariff and currency reform, civil service, and other important issues. Meanwhile, the judiciary countered reform by supporting big business and defending property rights against state and federal regulation. The presidency was occupied by honest, respectable men who, though not as exceptional as Washington, Jefferson, or Lincoln, attempted to assert their authority and independence. Amid these trends, exclusion prevented the majority of Americans—including women, southern blacks, Indians, uneducated whites, and unnaturalized immigrants—from voting and from access to the tools of democracy. This exclusion deeply concerned Mary Elizabeth Lease and many others.

Until the 1890s, a stable party system and a balance of power among geographic sections kept politics in a delicate equilibrium. Then, in the 1890s, rural discontent rumbled through the West and South, and a deep economic depression bared flaws in the industrial system. Mary Lease and others like her helped awaken rural masses with her fiery rhetoric. A presidential campaign in 1896 stirred Americans as they had not been stirred for a generation. A new party arose, old parties split, sectional unity dissolved, and fundamental disputes about the nation's future climaxed. The nation emerged from the turbulent 1890s with new economic configurations and new political alignments.

- What were the functions of government in the Gilded Age, and how did they change?
- How did policies of exclusion and discrimination make their mark on the political culture of the age?
- How did the economic climate give rise to the Populist movement?

# THE NATURE OF PARTY POLITICS

At no other time in the nation's history was public interest in elections more avid than between 1870 and 1896. Consistently, around 80 percent of eligible voters (white and black males in the North, somewhat lower rates among mostly white males in the South) cast ballots in local, state, and national elections. (Under 50 percent typically do so today.) Politics served as a form of recreation, more popular than baseball or circuses. Actual voting provided only the final step in a process that included parades, picnics, and speeches. As one observer remarked, "What the theatre is to the French, or the bull fight . . . to the Spanish . . . [election campaigns] and the ballot box are to our people."

In recent times, more voters have considered themselves independents than have identified with one political

**Cultural-Political Alignments**

party or another. But in the Gilded Age, party loyalty was often vigorous and emotional. With some exceptions, people who opposed government interference in matters of personal liberty identified with the Democratic Party; those who believed government could be an agent of reform identified with the Republican Party. Democrats included foreign-born and second-generation Catholics and Jews, who followed rituals and sacraments to guide personal behavior and prove one's faith in God. Republicans consisted mostly of native-born Protestants, who believed that salvation was best achieved by purging the world of evil and that legislation could protect people from sin. Democrats would restrict government power. Republicans believed in direct government action.

There was also a geographic dimension to these divisions. Well into the 1880s, northern Republicans capitalized on bitter memories of the Civil War by "waving the bloody shirt" at northern and southern Democrats. As one Republican orator scolded in 1876, "Every man that tried to destroy this nation was a Democrat. . . . Soldiers, every scar you have on your heroic bodies was given you by a Democrat." Democrats in the north tended to focus more on urban and economic issues, but southern Democratic

candidates waved a different bloody shirt, calling Republicans traitors to white supremacy and states' rights.

At state and local levels, partisan politicians often battled over how much government should control people's lives. The most contentious issues were use of leisure time and celebration of Sunday, the Lord's day. Protestant Republicans tried to keep the Sabbath holy through legislation that prohibited bars, stores, and commercial amusements from being open on Sundays. Immigrant Democrats, accustomed to feasting and playing after church, fought saloon closings and other restrictions on the only day they had free from work. Similar splits developed over public versus parochial schools and over prohibition versus unrestricted availability of liquor.

These issues made politics a personal as well as a community activity. In an era before media celebrities occupied public attention, people formed strong loyalties to individual politicians, loyalties that often overlooked crassness and corruption. James G. Blaine—Maine's flamboyant and powerful Republican congressman, senator, presidential aspirant, and two-time secretary of state—typified this appeal. Followers called him the "Plumed Knight," composed songs and organized parades in his honor, and sat mesmerized by his long speeches, while disregarding his corrupt alliances with businessmen and his animosity toward laborers and farmers.

Allegiances to national parties and candidates were so evenly divided that no faction gained control for any sustained period of time. Between 1877 and 1897, Republicans held the presidency for three terms, Democrats for two. Rarely did the same party control both the presidency and Congress simultaneously. From 1876 through 1892, presidential elections were extremely close. The outcome often hinged on the vote in a few populous northern states—Connecticut, New York, New Jersey, Ohio, Indiana, and Illinois. Both parties tried to gain advantages by nominating presidential and vice-presidential candidates from these states (and also by committing vote fraud on their candidates' behalf).

Factional quarrels split both the Republican and the Democratic Party. Among Republicans, New York's pomp-

**Party Factions**

ous senator Roscoe Conkling led one faction, known as "Stalwarts." A physical fitness devotee labeled "the finest torso in public life," Conkling worked the spoils system to win government jobs for his supporters. The Stalwarts' rivals were the "Half Breeds," led by James G. Blaine, who pursued influence as blatantly as Conkling did. On the sidelines stood more idealistic Republicans, or "Mugwumps" (supposedly an

Indian term meaning "mug on one side of the fence, wump on the other"). Mugwumps, such as Senator Carl Schurz of Missouri, scorned the political roguishness that tainted Republican leaders and believed that only righteous, educated men like themselves should govern. Republican allies of big business supported the use of gold as the standard for currency, whereas those from mining regions favored silver. Meanwhile, Democrats subdivided into white-supremacist southerners, immigrant-stock and working-class supporters of urban political machines, business-oriented advocates of low tariffs and the gold standard, and debtor-oriented advocates of free silver. Like Republicans, Democrats avidly pursued the spoils of office.

In each state, one party usually dominated, and within that party a few men typically held dictatorial sway. Often the state "boss" was a senator who parlayed his state power into national influence and command over federal jobs. (Until the Seventeenth Amendment to the Constitution was ratified in 1913, state legislatures elected U.S. senators.) Besides Conkling and Blaine, the senatorial ranks included Thomas C. Platt of New York, Nelson W. Aldrich of Rhode Island, Mark A. Hanna of Ohio, Matthew S. Quay of Pennsylvania, and William Mahone of Virginia. These men exercised their power brazenly. Quay once responded to an inquiry about using secret information from a Senate investigation to profit from an investment in the American Sugar Refining Company by pronouncing, "I do not feel that there is anything in my connection with the Senate to interfere with my buying or selling stock when I please, and I propose to do so in the future."

## ISSUES OF LEGISLATION

In Congress, the issues of sectional controversies, patronage abuses, railroad regulation, tariffs, and currency provoked heated debates, and several times partisan discord was so fierce that it prevented passage of legislation. From the end of the Civil War into the 1880s, Congress spent much time discussing soldiers' pensions. The Grand Army of the Republic, an organization of 400,000 Union Army veterans, allied with the Republican Party and cajoled Congress into providing generous pensions for former Union soldiers and their widows. Many pensions were deserved: Union troops had been poorly paid, and thousands of wives had been widowed. But for some veterans, the war's emotional memories furnished an opportunity to profit at public expense. Although the Union Army spent $2 billion to fight the Civil War, pensions to veterans ultimately cost $8 billion, one of the largest welfare commitments the federal government has ever made. By 1900 soldiers' pensions

accounted for roughly 40 percent of the federal budget. Confederate veterans received none of this money, though some southern states funded small pensions and built old-age homes for ex-soldiers.

Few politicians dared oppose pensions, but some attempted to dismantle the spoils system. During the Civil War, the federal government had expanded considerably, and the practice of awarding government jobs to the party faithful (regardless of their qualifications), which had taken root before the Civil War, flourished afterward. As the postal service, diplomatic corps, and other government agencies expanded, so did the public payroll. Between 1865 and 1891, the number of federal jobs tripled, from 53,000 to 166,000. Elected officials scrambled to control these jobs as a means to benefit themselves and their party. In return for comparatively short hours and high pay, appointees to federal positions pledged votes and a portion of their earnings to their patrons.

### Civil Service Reform

Shocked by such corruption, especially after the revelation of scandals in the Grant administration, some reformers began advocating appointments and promotions based on merit—civil service—rather than on political connections. Support for change accelerated in 1881 with formation of the National Civil Service Reform League, led by editors E. L. Godkin and George W. Curtis. That year, the assassination of President James Garfield by a distraught job seeker hastened the drive for reform. The Pendleton Civil Service Act, passed by Congress in 1882 and signed by President Chester Arthur in 1883, created the Civil Service Commission to oversee competitive examinations for government positions. The act gave the commission jurisdiction over only 10 percent of federal jobs, though the president could expand the list. Because the Constitution barred Congress from interfering in state affairs, civil service at state and local levels developed in a more haphazard manner. Nevertheless, the Pendleton Act marked a beginning and provided a model for further reform.

Veterans' pensions and civil service reform were not the main issues of the Gilded Age, however. Rather, economic policy occupied congressional concerns more than ever before. Railroads particularly provoked controversy. As rail networks spread, so did competition. In their quest for customers, railroad lines reduced rates to outmaneuver rivals, but rate wars hurt profits, and inconsistent freight charges angered shippers and farmers. On noncompetitive routes, railroads often boosted charges as high as possible to compensate for unprofitably low rates on competitive routes, making pricing disproportionate to distance. Charges on short-distance shipments served by only one

▲ The patronage system—the practice of rewarding political supporters with jobs and favors—reached such extent during the Gilded Age that critics likened it to the stock exchange where traders clamored to be heard. President James A. Garfield is shown on a pedestal in the center of this cartoon surrounded by pleading job-seekers while on the left, Senator Thomas C. Platt, Republican leader from New York State, is handcuffed to a man handing "orders from the boss" to Vice President Chester A. Arthur. The Pendleton Civil Service Act of 1883 was intended to replace patronage by making federal appointments based on merit rather than on political connections.

*(Library of Congress)*

line could exceed those on long-distance shipments served by competing lines. Railroads also played favorites, reducing rates to large shippers and offering free passenger passes to preferred customers and politicians.

Such favoritism stirred farmers, small merchants, and reform politicians to demand rate regulation. Their efforts succeeded first at the state level. By 1880 fourteen states had established commissions to limit freight and storage charges of state-chartered lines. Using corrupt lobbyists and a variety of pressure tactics, railroads fought these measures, arguing that the Fourteenth Amendment to the Constitution guaranteed them freedom to acquire and use property without government restraint. But in 1877, in *Munn v. Illinois*, the Supreme Court upheld the principle of state regulation, declaring that grain warehouses owned by railroads acted in the public interest and

### Railroad Regulation

therefore must submit to regulation for "the common good."

State legislatures, however, could not regulate interstate lines, a limitation affirmed by the Supreme Court in the *Wabash* case of 1886, in which the Court declared that only Congress could limit rates involving interstate commerce. Reformers thereupon demanded action by the federal government. With support from some businessmen who believed that they, like farmers, were suffering from discriminatory rates, Congress passed the Interstate Commerce Act in 1887. The law prohibited pools, rebates, and long-haul/short-haul rate discrimination, and it created the Interstate Commerce Commission (ICC), the nation's first regulatory agency, to investigate railroad rate making, issue cease-and-desist orders against illegal practices, and seek court aid to enforce compliance. The legislation's weak provisions for enforcement, however, left railroads room for evasion, and federal judges chipped away at ICC powers. In the *Maximum Freight Rate* case (1897), the Supreme Court ruled that the ICC lacked power to set rates, and in the *Alabama Midlands* case (1897), the Court overturned prohibitions against long-haul/short-haul discrimination. Even so, the principle of regulation, though weakened, remained in force.

The economic issue of tariffs carried strong political implications. From 1789 onward, Congress had created tariffs, which levied duties (taxes) on imported goods, to protect American manufactures and agricultural products from European competition. But tariffs quickly became a tool by which special interests could enhance their profits. By the 1880s these interests had succeeded in obtaining tariffs on more than four thousand items. A few economists and farmers argued for free trade, but most politicians insisted that tariffs were a necessary form of government assistance to support industry and preserve jobs.

## Tariff Policy

The Republican Party put protective tariffs at the core of its political agenda to support economic growth. Democrats complained that tariffs made prices artificially high by keeping out less expensive foreign goods, thereby benefiting domestic manufacturers while hurting farmers whose crops were not protected and consumers who had to buy manufactured goods. For example, a yard of flannel produced abroad might cost 10 cents, but an 8-cent import duty raised the price paid by American consumers to 18 cents. An American manufacturer of a similar yard of flannel, also costing 10 cents, could charge 17 cents, underselling foreign competition by 1 cent yet still pocketing a 7-cent profit.

During the Gilded Age, revenues from tariffs and other levies created a surplus in the federal budget. Most Republicans liked the idea that the government was earning more than it spent and hoped to keep the extra money as a Treasury reserve or to spend it on projects such as harbor improvements, which would aid commerce. Democrats, however, asserted that the federal government should not be a profit-making operation. They acknowledged a need for protection of some manufactured goods and raw materials, but they favored lower tariff duties to encourage foreign trade and to reduce the Treasury surplus.

Manufacturers and their congressional allies firmly controlled tariff policy. The McKinley Tariff of 1890 boosted already-high rates by another 4 percent. When House Democrats supported by President Grover Cleveland passed a bill to trim tariffs in 1894, Senate Republicans, aided by southern Democrats eager to protect their region's infant industries, particularly textiles and steel,

added six hundred amendments restoring most cuts (the Wilson-Gorman Tariff). In 1897 the Dingley Tariff raised rates further. Attacks on duties, though unsuccessful, made tariffs a symbol of privileged business in the public mind and a continuing target for reformers.

## Monetary Policy

Monetary policy inflamed even stronger emotions than tariffs did. When increased industrial and agricultural production caused prices to fall after the Civil War, debtors and creditors had opposing reactions. Farmers suffered because the prices they received for crops were dropping, but because high demand for a relatively limited supply of money in circulation raised interest rates on loans, it was costly for them to borrow funds to pay mortgages and other debts. They favored schemes like the coinage of silver to increase the amount of currency in circulation. An expanded money supply, they reasoned, would reduce interest rates, making their debts less burdensome. Small businessmen, also in need of loans, agreed with farmers. Large merchants, manufacturers, and bankers favored a more stable, limited money supply backed only by gold. They feared that the value of currency not backed by gold would fluctuate; the resulting uncertainty would threaten investors' confidence in the U.S. economy.

Arguments over the quantity and quality of money, however, transcended economics. Creditor-debtor tension translated into class divisions between haves—those with easy access to money—and have-nots—those who had problems borrowing. The debate also reflected sectional cleavages: western silver-mining areas and agricultural regions of the South and West against the more conservative industrial Northeast. And the issue carried moral, almost religious, overtones. Some Americans believed that the beauty, rarity, and durability of gold gave it magical potency. Others believed the gold standard for currency was too limiting; sustained prosperity, they insisted, demanded new attitudes.

By the 1870s, the currency controversy boiled down to which precious metal should be used to back national paper money (dollar bills): gold or silver? Previously, the government had bought both gold and silver, setting a ratio that made a gold dollar worth sixteen times more than a silver dollar. In theory, a person holding a specific sum of dollar bills could exchange them for one ounce of gold or sixteen ounces of silver. Mining discoveries after the gold rush of 1848, however, increased the gold supply and lowered its market price relative to that of silver. Consequently, silver dollars disappeared from circulation—because of their inflated value relative to gold, owners

▲ Taking advantage of the new fad of bicycling (see Chapter 19), a cartoonist in an 1886 issue of the humor magazine *Puck* illustrates the controversy over silver coinage. Depicting two uncoordinated wheels, one a silver coin and the other a gold coin, the illustration conveys the message of how hard it was to proceed with conflicting kinds of currency. *(Private Collection)*

hoarded them—and in 1873 Congress officially stopped coining silver dollars. European governments also stopped buying silver, and the United States and many of its trading partners unofficially adopted the gold standard, meaning that their currency was backed chiefly by gold.

But within a few years, new mines in the American West began to flood the market with silver, and its price dropped. Because gold now was relatively less plentiful, worth more than sixteen times the value of silver (the ratio reached twenty to one by 1890), it became worthwhile for people to spend rather than hoard silver dollars. Silver producers wanted the government to resume buying silver at the old sixteen-to-one ratio, which amounted to a subsidy because they could sell silver to the government above its market price. Debtors, hurt by the economic hard times of 1873–1878, saw silver as a means of expanding the cur-

rency supply. They joined silver producers to press for resumption of silver coinage at the old sixteen-to-one ratio.

With both parties split into silver and gold factions, Congress first tried to compromise. The Bland-Allison Act (1878) authorized the Treasury to buy between $2 million and $4 million worth of silver each month, and the Sherman Silver Purchase Act (1890) increased the government's monthly silver purchase by specifying weight (4.5 million ounces) rather than dollars. Neither measure satisfied the different interest groups. Creditors wanted the government to stop buying silver, whereas for debtors, the legislation failed to expand the money supply satisfactorily and did not erase the impression that the government favored creditors' interests. The issue would become even more emotional during the presidential election of 1896 (see pages 584–587).

Members of Congress dealt with such thorny issues as civil service, railroad regulation, and monetary policy under

### Legislative Accomplishments

difficult conditions in the Gilded Age. Senators and representatives earned small salaries and usually had the financial burden of maintaining two residences: one in their home district and one in Washington. Weather in the nation's capital was sweltering in summer, muddy and icy in winter. Most members of Congress had no private office space, only a desk. They worked long hours responding to constituents' requests, wrote their own speeches, and paid for staff out of their own pocket. Yet, though corruption and greed tainted several, most politicians were principled and dedicated. They managed to deal with important issues and pass some significant legislation.

## TENTATIVE PRESIDENTS

Operating under the cloud of Andrew Johnson's impeachment, Grant's scandals, and doubts about the legitimacy of the 1876 election (see Chapter 16), American presidents between 1877 and 1900 moved gingerly to restore authority to their office. Proper and honest, Presidents Rutherford Hayes (1877–1881), James Garfield (1881), Chester Arthur (1881–1885), Grover Cleveland (1885–1889 and 1893–1897), Benjamin Harrison (1889–1893), and William McKinley (1897–1901) tried to act as legislative as well as administrative leaders. Like other politicians, they used symbols. Hayes served lemonade at the White House to emphasize that he, unlike his predecessor Ulysses Grant, was no hard drinker. McKinley set aside his cigar in public so photographers would not catch him setting a bad example for youth. More important, each president made cautious attempts to initiate legislation and use vetoes to guide national policy.

Rutherford B. Hayes had been a Union general and an Ohio congressman and governor before his disputed election to the presidency, an event that prompted opponents to label him "Rutherfraud." Although his party expected him to serve business interests, Hayes played a quiet role as conciliator. He emphasized national harmony over sectional rivalry and opposed racial violence. He tried to overhaul the spoils system by appointing civil service reformer Carl Schurz to his cabinet and by battling New York's patronage king, Senator Conkling. (He fired Conkling's protégé, Chester Arthur, from the post of New York customs house collector.) Though averse to using government power to aid the oppressed, Hayes believed society should not ignore the needs of the American Chinese and Indians, and after retiring from the presidency he worked to aid former slaves.

## Hayes, Garfield, and Arthur

When Hayes declined to run for reelection in 1880, Republicans nominated another Ohio congressman and Civil War hero, James A. Garfield, who defeated Democrat Winfield Scott Hancock, also a Civil War hero, by just 40,000 votes out of 9 million cast. By winning the pivotal states of New York and Indiana, however, Garfield carried the electoral college by a comfortable margin, 214 to 155. A solemn and cautious man, Garfield spent most of his brief presidency trying to secure an independent position among party potentates. He hoped to reduce the tariff and develop economic relations with Latin America, and he pleased civil service reformers by rebuffing Conkling's patronage demands. But his chance to make lasting contributions ended in July 1881 when Charles Guiteau shot him in a Washington railroad station. Garfield lingered for seventy-nine days while doctors tried vainly to remove a bullet lodged in his back, but he succumbed to infection and died September 19.

Garfield's successor was Vice President Chester A. Arthur, the New York spoilsman whom Hayes had fired in 1878. Republicans had nominated Arthur for vice president only to help Garfield win New York State's electoral votes. Although his elevation to the presidency made reformers shudder, Arthur became a dignified and temperate executive. He signed the Pendleton Civil Service Act, urged Congress to modify outdated tariff rates, and supported federal regulation of railroads. He wielded the veto aggressively, killing several bills that excessively benefited railroads and corporations. But congressional partisans frustrated his plans for reducing the tariff and strengthening the navy. Arthur wanted to run for president in 1884 but lost the nomination to James G. Blaine at the Republican national convention.

To oppose Blaine, Democrats named New York's governor, Grover Cleveland, a bachelor who had tainted his reputation when he fathered an out-of-wedlock son—a fact he admitted during the campaign. Both parties focused on the sordid. (Alluding to Cleveland's son, Republicans chided him with catcalls of "Ma! Ma! Where's my pa?" to which Democrats replied, "Gone to the White House, Ha! Ha! Ha!") Distaste for Blaine prompted some Mugwump Republicans to desert their party for Cleveland. On election day, Cleveland beat Blaine by only 29,000 popular votes; his tiny margin of 1,149 votes in New York gave him that state's 36 electoral votes, enough for a 219-to-182 victory in the electoral college. Cleveland may have won New York thanks to last-minute remarks of a Protestant minister, who equated Democrats with "rum, Romanism, and rebellion." Democrats eagerly publicized the slur among New York's large Irish-Catholic population, urging voters to protest by supporting Cleveland.

## Cleveland and Harrison

Cleveland, the first Democratic president since James Buchanan (1857–1861), tried to exert vigorous leadership. He expanded civil service, vetoed hundreds of private pension bills, and urged Congress to cut tariff duties. When advisers warned that his stand might weaken his chances for reelection, the president retorted, "What is the use of being elected or reelected, unless you stand for something?" But the Mills tariff bill of 1888, passed by the House in response to Cleveland's wishes, died in the Senate. When Democrats renominated Cleveland for the presidency in 1888, businessmen in the party convinced him to moderate his attacks on high tariffs.

Republicans in 1888 nominated Benjamin Harrison, former senator from Indiana and grandson of President William Henry Harrison (1841). During the campaign, some Republicans manipulated a British diplomat into stating that Cleveland's reelection would be good for England. Irish Democrats, who hated England's colonial rule over Ireland, took offense, as intended, and Cleveland's campaign was weakened. Perhaps more beneficial to Harrison were the bribery and multiple voting that helped him win Indiana by 2,300 votes and New York by 14,000. (Democrats also indulged in such cheating, but Republicans proved more successful at it.) Those states' electoral votes ensured Harrison's victory. Although Cleveland outpolled Harrison by 90,000 popular votes, Harrison carried the electoral college by 233 to 168.

The first president since 1875 whose party had majorities in both houses of Congress, Harrison used a variety

▲ During the Gilded Age, political events provided opportunity for elaborate spectacle, and office-holders occupied the limelight as major celebrities. A presidential inauguration, such as that of Rutherford B. Hayes, though perhaps no less lavish than one of the current era, functioned as a public festival at a time when mass entertainment was far less prevalent than in recent times. During a political campaign a candidate's supporters wore colorful emblems, such as the brooch pictured in the corner, reminding voters of Hayes's Civil War record.

*(Left: National Archives; Right: Collection of Janice L. and David J. Frent)*

of methods, ranging from threats of vetoes to informal dinners and consultations with politicians, to influence the course of legislation. Partly in response, the Congress of 1889–1891 passed 517 bills, 200 more than the average passed by Congresses between 1875 and 1889. Harrison showed support for civil service by appointing reformer Theodore Roosevelt as civil service commissioner, but neither the president nor Congress could resist pressures from special interests, especially those waving the bloody shirt. Harrison signed the Dependents' Pension Act, which provided pensions for Union veterans who had suffered war-related disabilities and granted aid to their widows and children. The bill doubled the number of welfare recipients from 490,000 to 966,000.

The Pension Act and other appropriations in 1890 pushed the federal budget past $1 billion for the first time in the nation's history. Democrats blamed the "Billion-Dollar Congress" on spendthrift Republicans. Voters reacted by unseating seventy-eight Republicans in the congressional elections of 1890. Seeking to capitalize on voter unrest, Democrats nominated Grover Cleveland to run against Harrison in 1892. This time Cleveland attracted large contributions from business and beat Harrison by 370,000 popular votes (3 percent of the total), easily winning the electoral vote.

In office again, Cleveland addressed problems of currency, tariffs, and labor unrest, but his actions reflected a narrow orientation toward business and bespoke political weakness. During his campaign Cleveland had promised sweeping tariff reform, but he made little effort to line up support in the Senate, where protectionists undercut efforts to reduce rates. And when 120,000 boycotting railroad workers paralyzed commerce in the Pullman strike of 1894, Cleveland bowed to requests from railroad managers and Attorney General Richard Olney (a former railroad lawyer) to send in troops. In spite of Cleveland's attempts at initiative, major events—particularly economic downturn and agrarian ferment—shoved him from the limelight.

## DISCRIMINATION, DISFRANCHISEMENT, AND RESPONSES

Although speechmakers often spoke of freedom and opportunity during the Gilded Age, policies of discrimination and exclusion continued to haunt more than half of the nation's population. Just as before the Civil War, issues of race shaped politics in the South, home to the vast majority of African Americans. Southern white farmers and workers, facing economic insecurity, feared that newly enfranchised African American men would challenge whatever political and social superiority (real and imagined) they enjoyed. Wealthy landowners and merchants fanned these fears, using them to divide the races and to distract poor whites from protesting their own economic subjugation. Even some white feminists, such as Susan B. Anthony, opposed voting and other rights for blacks on the grounds that white women deserved such rights before black men did.

The abolition of slavery altered the legal status of African Americans, but it did not markedly improve their economic opportunities. In 1880, 90 percent of all southern blacks depended for a living on farming or personal and domestic service—the same occupations they had held as slaves. Discrimination was rampant. Some communities considered themselves "sundown towns," places where only whites were allowed on the streets at night. The New South, moreover, proved to be as violent for blacks as the Old South had been. Between 1889 and 1909, more than seventeen hundred African Americans were lynched in the South. Most lynching victims were accused of assault—rarely proved—on a white woman. These acts of terror occurred often, but by no means exclusively, in sparsely populated districts where whites felt threatened by an in-

**Violence Against African Americans**

▲ In the years after Reconstruction, lynchings of African American men occurred with increasing frequency, chiefly in sparsely populated areas where whites looked on strangers, especially black strangers, with fear and suspicion.

*(© R. P. Kingston/Index Stock Imagery, Picture Cube Division)*

flux of migrant blacks who had no friends, black or white, to vouch for them.

Blacks did not suffer such violence silently, however. The most notable activist at this time was Ida B. Wells, a Memphis schoolteacher. In 1884, when she was twenty-two years old, Wells was forcibly removed from a railroad car when she refused to give up her seat to a white man. The incident sparked her career as a forceful and tireless spokesperson against white supremacy and violence. In 1889 Wells became a partner of a Memphis newspaper, the *Free Speech and Headlight,* in which she published attacks against white injustice, especially in the case of three black grocers lynched in 1892 after defending themselves against whites who had attacked them. Wells wrote an editorial urging local blacks to migrate to the West. She herself was forced to flee to England to escape threats against her life. But she soon returned and lived in Chicago, where she wrote *A Red Record* (1895), which tabulated statistics on racial lynchings and served as a foundation for further protest campaigns.

With slavery abolished, white supremacists fashioned new ways to keep blacks in an inferior position. Southern leaders, eager to reassert authority over people whom they believed to be inferior, instituted measures to prevent blacks from voting and to segregate them legally from whites. The end of Reconstruction had not stopped blacks from voting and holding office. Despite threats and intimidation, blacks still formed the backbone of the southern Republican Party and won numerous elective positions. In North Carolina, for example, eleven African Americans served in the state Senate and forty-three in the House between 1877 and 1890. In reaction, white politicians sought to impose restrictions that would disfranchise blacks; that is, deprive them of their right to vote. Beginning with Tennessee in 1889 and Arkansas in 1892, southern states levied taxes of $1 to $2 on all citizens wishing to vote. These poll taxes proved prohibitive to most blacks, who were so poor and deeply in debt that they rarely had cash for any purpose. Other schemes disfranchised blacks who could not read.

### Disfranchisement

Disfranchisement was accomplished in other devious ways. The Supreme Court determined in *U.S. v. Reese* (1876) that Congress had no control over local and state elections other than the explicit provisions of the Fifteenth Amendment, which prohibits states from denying the vote "on account of race, color, or previous condition of servitude." State legislatures found ways to exclude black voters without mentioning race, color, or servitude. For instance, an 1890 state constitutional convention established the "Mississippi Plan," requiring all voters to pay a poll tax eight months before each election, present the tax receipt at election time, and prove that they could read and interpret the state constitution. Registration officials applied stiffer standards to blacks than to whites, even declaring black college graduates ineligible on grounds of illiteracy. In 1898 Louisiana enacted the first "grandfather clause," which established literacy and property qualifications for voting but exempted sons and grandsons of those eligible to vote before 1867. Other southern states initiated similar measures.

Such restrictions proved highly effective. In South Carolina, for example, 70 percent of eligible blacks voted in the 1880 presidential election; by 1896 the rate had dropped to 11 percent. By the 1900s African Americans had effectively lost political rights in the South. More importantly, because voting is often considered a common right of citizenship, disfranchisement stripped African American men of their social standing as U.S. citizens. Disfranchisement also affected poor whites, few of whom could meet poll tax, property, and literacy requirements. Thus the total number of eligible voters in Mississippi shrank from 257,000 in 1876 to 77,000 in 1892.

Racial discrimination also stiffened in areas beyond voting, as existing customs of racial separation were expanded. In a series of cases during the 1870s, the Supreme Court opened the door to discrimination by ruling that the Fourteenth Amendment protected citizens' rights only against infringement by state governments. The amendment, according to the Court, lacked authority over what individuals or organizations might do. If blacks wanted legal protection from discriminatory behavior by individuals or companies, the Court said, they must seek it from state laws because under the Tenth Amendment states retained all powers not specifically assigned to Congress. These rulings climaxed in 1883 when, in the *Civil Rights* cases, the Court struck down the 1875 Civil Rights Act, which prohibited segregation in public facilities, such as streetcars, theaters, and parks. Again the Court declared that the federal government could not regulate private behavior in matters of race relations. Thus railroads, such as the Chesapeake & Ohio Railroad, which had forced Ida B. Wells out of her seat, could maintain discriminatory policies.

### Legal Segregation

At the state level, segregation could legally occur on a "separate-but-equal" basis, as upheld by the Supreme Court in the case of *Plessy v. Ferguson* (1896). This case began in 1892 when a New Orleans organization of prominent African Americans chose Homer Plessy, a dark-skinned creole who was only one-eighth black (but still considered black by Louisiana law), as a volunteer to violate a state law by sitting in a whites-only railroad car. As expected, Plessy was arrested, and the appeal of his conviction reached the U.S. Supreme Court in 1896. Hopes for justice faded when the Court affirmed that a state law providing for separate facilities for the two races was reasonable because it preserved "public peace and good order." Writing for the Court, Associate Justice Billings Brown said that legislation could not overcome prejudice. "If the two races are to meet upon terms of social equality," he wrote, "it must be the result of . . . a voluntary consent of individuals." Thus, in the court's mind, a law separating the races did not necessarily "destroy the legal equality of the races." Although the ruling did not use the phrase "separate but equal," it made legal separate facilities for black and white people as long as they were equal.

In 1899 the Court applied the separate-but-equal doctrine to schools in *Cummins v. County Board of Education*, legalizing school segregation until it was overturned by *Brown v. Board of Education* in 1954.

Segregation laws—known as Jim Crow laws—multiplied throughout the South, confronting African Americans with daily reminders of inferior status. State and local statutes, most of which were passed in the 1890s, restricted blacks to the rear of streetcars, to separate public drinking fountains and toilets, and to separate sections of hospitals and cemeteries. A Birmingham, Alabama, ordinance required that the races be "distinctly separated . . . by well defined physical barriers" in "any room, hall, theatre, picture house, auditorium, yard, court, ballpark, or other indoor or outdoor place." Mobile, Alabama, passed a curfew requiring blacks to be off the streets by 10 p.m., and Atlanta mandated separate Bibles for the swearing-in of black witnesses in court.

African American women and men challenged prejudice in several ways. Some organized boycotts of segregated streetcars and discriminatory businesses; others considered moving to Africa. Still others promoted "Negro enterprise." In 1898, for example, Atlanta University professor John Hope called on blacks to become their own employers and supported formation of Negro Business Men's Leagues. In the optimistic days following Reconstruction, a number of blacks used higher education as a means of elevating their status. In all-black teachers' colleges, young men and women sought opportunities for themselves and their race. Education also seemed to present a way to foster interracial cooperation. But the white supremacy campaigns that Jim Crow laws reflected taught southern blacks that they would have to negotiate in a biracial, rather than an interracial, society.

While disfranchisement pushed African American men, who in contrast to women had previously been able to vote, out of public life, African American women used traditional roles as mothers, educators, and moral guardians to uplift the race and seek better services for black communities. Their efforts signified a kind of political activity that was more subtle than voting—though they also did fight for the vote. They successfully lobbied governments in the South for cleaner city streets, better public health, expanded charity services, and vocational education. In these efforts, black women found ways to join with white women in campaigns to negotiate with the white

### African American Activism

▲ Livingstone College in North Carolina was one of several institutions of higher learning established by and for African Americans in the late nineteenth century. With a curriculum that emphasized training for educational and religious work in the South and in Africa, these colleges were coeducational, operating on the belief that both men and women could have public roles.

*(Courtesy of Heritage Hall, Livingstone College, Salisbury, North Carolina)*

male power structure to achieve their goals. In many instances, however, white women sympathized with men in support of white-supremacist campaigns.

In the North, white women contended head-on with male power structures. Their goal was the vote; their successes in reaching this goal were

## Woman Suffrage

limited. Prior to 1870, each state determined voting qualifications. The Fifteenth Amendment, ratified that year, forbade states to deny the vote "on account of race, color or previous condition" but omitted any reference to sex. For the next twenty years, two organizations, the National Woman Suffrage Association (NWSA) and the American Woman Suffrage Association (AWSA), crusaded for female suffrage. The NWSA, led by Elizabeth Cady Stanton and Susan B. Anthony, advocated women's rights in courts and workplaces as well as at the ballot box. The AWSA, led by former abolitionists Lucy Stone and Thomas Wentworth Higginson, focused more narrowly on suffrage. Congress failed to heed either group. Anthony's effort to get a constitutional amendment for woman suffrage never received support. On the few occasions when a bill for the amendment reached the Senate floor, senators voted it down, claiming that suffrage would interfere with women's family obligations. While the NWSA fought for suffrage on the national level, the AWSA worked to amend state constitutions. (The groups merged in 1890 to form the National American Woman Suffrage Associa-

tion.) Although these campaigns succeeded only slightly, they helped train a corps of female leaders in political organizing and public speaking.

Women did win partial victories. Between 1870 and 1910, eleven states (mostly in the West) legalized limited woman suffrage. By 1890 nineteen states allowed women to vote on school issues, and three granted suffrage on tax and bond issues. The right to vote in national elections awaited a later generation, but the activities of women like Mary Lease, Ida B. Wells, Susan B. Anthony, and Lucy Stone proved that women did not have to vote to be politically active.

## AGRARIAN UNREST AND POPULISM

While voting and racial segregation concerned those suffering from political exclusion, economic inequities sparked a mass movement that would shake American society. Despite rapid industrialization and urbanization in the late nineteenth century, the United States remained an agrarian society. In 1890, 64 percent of the total population lived in rural areas, many of which seethed under economic pressures and were primed for protest. The expression of farmers' discontent—a mixture of strident rhetoric, nostalgic dreams, and hard-headed egalitarianism—began in Grange organizations in the early 1870s. It accelerated when Farmers' Alliances formed in Texas in the late 1870s and spread across the Cotton Belt and Great Plains in the 1880s. The Alliance movement flourished chiefly in areas where tenancy, debt, weather, and insects endangered struggling farmers. Once under way, the agrarian rebellion inspired visions of a cooperative and democratic society.

HOW WOMEN'S SUFFRAGE WILL INCREASE THE POWER OF THE WARD HEELER.

◄ This anti–woman suffrage cartoon implies that, if women were to be allowed to vote, the inferior types among them— in this case, ugly, slovenly immigrants— would outweigh and outvote their more distinguished sisters. The artist, drawing for *Judge* magazine in 1894, was not only expressing anti-female and anti-immigrant views but also using a fear that female voters would only entrench corrupt politicians.

*(William L. Clements Library)*

Southern agriculture, unlike that of the Midwest, did not benefit much from mechanization (see Chapter 17).

## Sharecropping and Tenant Farming in the South

Tobacco and cotton, the principal southern crops, required constant hoeing and weeding by hand. Tobacco required careful harvesting, because the leaves matured at different rates and because the stems were too fragile for machines. Also, mechanical devices were not precise enough to pick cotton. Thus, in former plantation areas after the Civil War, southern agriculture remained labor-intensive, and labor-lords, who had once utilized slaves, were replaced by landlords, who employed sharecroppers and tenant farmers.

Sharecropping and tenant farming—meaning that farmers rented their land rather than owned it—entangled millions of black and white southerners in webs of debt and humiliation, at whose center loomed the crop lien. Most farmers, too poor to have ready cash, borrowed in order to buy necessities. They could offer as collateral only what they could grow. A farmer in need of supplies dealt with a "furnishing merchant," who would exchange supplies for a lien, or legal claim, on the farmer's forthcoming crop. After the crop was harvested and brought to market, the merchant collected his debt by claiming the portion of the crop that would repay the loan. All too often, however, the debt exceeded the crop's value. The farmer could pay off only part of the debt to the merchant but still needed food and supplies for the coming year. The only way he could get these supplies was to sink deeper into debt by reborrowing and giving the merchant a lien on his next crop.

Merchants frequently took advantage of indebted farmers' powerlessness by inflating prices and charging excessive interest on the advances farmers received. Suppose, for example, that a cash-poor farmer renting some land needed a 20-cent bag of seed or a 20-cent piece of cloth. The furnishing merchant would sell him the goods on credit but would boost the price to 28 cents. At year's end, that 28-cent loan would have accumulated interest of 50 percent or more, raising the farmer's debt to 42 cents—more than double the item's original cost. The farmer, having pledged more than his crop's worth against scores of such debts, fell behind in payments and never recovered. If he fell too far behind, he could be evicted.

In the southern backcountry, which in antebellum times had been characterized by small, family-owned farms, few slaves, and diversified agriculture, the crop-lien problem was compounded by other economic changes. New spending habits of backcountry farmers illustrate these changes. In 1884 Jephta Dickson, who farmed land in the northern Georgia hills, bought $55.90 worth of flour, potatoes, peas, meat, corn, and syrup from merchants. Such expenditures would have been rare before the Civil War, when farmers grew almost all the food they needed. But after the war, yeomen like Dickson shifted to commercial farming; in the South that meant raising cotton. This move to the market economy came about for two reasons: constant debt forced farmers to grow crops that would bring in cash, and railroads enabled them to transport cotton to market more easily than before. As backcountry yeomen devoted more acres to cotton, they raised less of what they needed on a daily basis and found themselves more frequently at the mercy of merchants.

In the Midwest, as growers cultivated more land, as mechanization boosted productivity, and as foreign competition increased, supplies of agricultural products exceeded national and worldwide demand. Consequently, prices for staple crops dropped steadily. A bushel of wheat that sold for $1.45 in 1866 brought only 80 cents in the mid-1880s and 49 cents by the mid-1890s. Meanwhile, transportation and storage fees remained high relative to other prices. Expenses for seed, fertilizer, manufactured goods, taxes, and mortgage interest trapped many farm families in stressful and sometimes desperate circumstances. In order to buy necessities and pay bills, farmers had to produce more. But the spiral wound ever more tightly: the more farmers produced, the lower crop prices dropped (see Figure 20.1).

## Hardship in the Midwest and West

The West suffered from special hardships. In Colorado, absentee capitalists seized control of access to transportation and water, and concentration of technology in the hands of large mining companies pushed out small firms. Charges of monopolistic behavior by railroads echoed among farmers, miners, and stockmen in Wyoming and Montana. In California, Washington, and Oregon, wheat and fruit growers found their opportunities blocked by railroads' control of transportation and storage rates.

Even before they felt the full impact of these developments, farmers began to organize. With aid from Oliver H. Kelley, a clerk in the Department of Agriculture, farmers in almost every state during the 1860s and 1870s founded a network of local organizations called Granges, dedicated to improving economic and social conditions. By 1875 the national Grange had twenty thousand branches and a million members. Like voluntary organizations throughout the country,

## Grange Movement

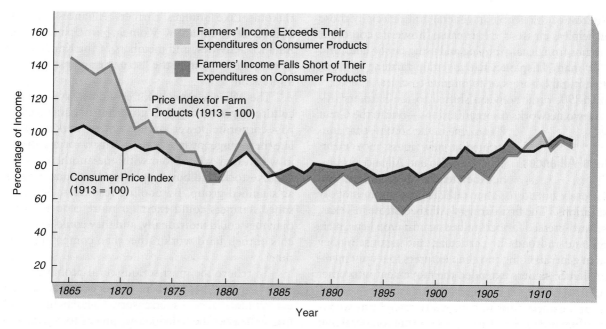

**Figure 20.1    Consumer Prices and Farm Product Prices, 1865–1913**

Until the late 1870s, in spite of falling farm prices, farmers were able to receive from their crops more income than they spent on consumer goods. But beginning in the mid-1880s, consumer prices leveled off and then rose, while prices for farm products continued to drop. As a result, farmers found it increasingly difficult to afford consumer goods, a problem that plagued them well into the twentieth century.

Granges had constitutions, elected officers, and membership oaths. Strongest in the Midwest and South, Granges sponsored meetings and educational events to relieve the loneliness of farm life. Family-oriented local Granges welcomed women's participation.

As membership flourished, Granges turned to economic and political action. Many Grange members joined the Greenback Labor Party, formed in 1876 to advocate expanding the money supply by keeping "greenbacks"—the paper money created by the government during the Civil War to help pay costs—in circulation. Local Grange branches formed cooperative associations to buy supplies and to market crops and livestock. In a few instances, Grangers operated farm-implement factories and insurance companies. Most enterprises failed, however, because farmers lacked capital for large-scale buying and because competition from large manufacturers and dealers undercut them. For example, the mail-order firm Montgomery Ward could furnish rural customers with cheaper products more conveniently than could Granges.

Despite their efforts, Granges declined in the late 1870s. They achieved some political successes, convincing states to establish agricultural colleges, electing sympathetic legislators, and pressing state legislatures for so-called Granger laws to regulate transportation and storage rates. But these ventures faltered when, in the *Wabash* case of 1886, the U.S. Supreme Court overturned Granger laws by denying states the power to regulate railroad rates. Granges disavowed party politics and thus would not challenge the power of business interests within the two major parties. After a brief assertion of economic and political influence, Granges again became farmers' social clubs.

In the Southwest, migrations of English-speaking ranchers into pastureland used communally by Mexican farmers and villagers sparked another kind of agrarian protest. In

**The White Hats**

the late 1880s, a group calling itself Las Gorras Blancas, or the White Hats, struggled to control lands that their Mexican ancestors had once held. They harassed Anglo ranchers and destroyed fences that Anglos had erected on public land. Sounding like the Grangers and Knights of Labor before them and the Populists after them, the White Hats proclaimed in 1889, "Our purpose is to protect the rights and interest of the people in general and especially those of the helpless classes." Their cause, however, could not halt Anglos from legally buying and using public land, and by 1900 many Hispanics had given up farming to work as agricultural laborers or to migrate to cities.

By 1890, rural activism shifted to the Farmers' Alliances, two networks of organizations—one in the Great Plains, one in the South—that constituted a new mass movement. (The West also had Alliance groups, but they tended to be smaller and more closely linked to labor radicals and antimonopoly organizations.) The first Farmers' Alliances arose in Texas, where hard-pressed farmers rallied against crop liens, merchants, and railroads in particular, and against money power in general. Using traveling lecturers to recruit members, Alliance leaders extended the movement into other southern states. By 1889 the southern Alliance boasted 2 million members, and a separate Colored Farmers' National Alliance claimed 1 million black members. A similar movement arose in the Plains, which in the late 1880s organized 2 million members in Kansas, Nebraska, and the

## Farmers' Alliances

Dakotas. Like Granges, Farmers' Alliances tried to foster feelings of community. Women participated actively in Alliance activities, and members of the Knights of Labor were invited to join in the "struggle against monopolistic oppression."

The Alliance remedy for economic woes combined a culture of generosity with government assistance. To bypass corporate power and to control markets, Alliances, like the Grange, proposed that farmers form cooperatives, in which they would join with one another to sell crops and livestock, and buy supplies and manufactured goods, as a unified group. By pooling resources, Alliances reasoned, farmers could exert far more economic pressure than they could individually, and they could share the benefits of their hard work rather than competing with each other.

To relieve the most serious rural problem, shortages of cash and credit, Alliances put forward a system of government aid called a subtreasury. The plan had two parts. One called for the federal government to construct warehouses where farmers could store nonperishable crops while awaiting higher market prices; the government

▲ Exhibited at the Chicago World's Fair of 1893, this cabin was the site of the first Farmers' Alliance meeting in Lampasas County, Texas. Using recruiters, rallies, and meetings replete with slogans like "We Are All Mortgaged But Our Votes," the organization voiced the grievances of rural America and laid the groundwork for formation of the Populist party in the 1890s. *(Private Collection)*

would then loan farmers Treasury notes amounting to 80 percent of the market price that the stored crops would bring. Farmers could use these notes as money to pay debts and make purchases. Once the stored crops were sold, farmers would repay the loans plus small interest and storage fees. This provision would enable farmers to avoid the exploitative crop-lien system.

The subtreasury plan's second part would provide low-interest government loans to farmers who wanted to buy land. These loans, along with the Treasury notes loaned to farmers who temporarily stored crops in government warehouses, would inject cash into the economy and encourage the kind of inflation that advocates hoped would raise crop prices without raising other prices. If the government subsidized business through tariffs and land grants, reasoned Alliance members, why should it not help farmers earn a decent living, too?

If all Farmers' Alliances had been able to unite politically, they could have been a formidable force; but racial and sectional differences and personality clashes thwarted early attempts at merging. Racial barriers weakened Alliance voter strength because, as noted earlier, southern white Democrats had succeeded in creating voting restrictions that prevented African Americans from becoming a political force. In addition, raw racism impeded acceptance of blacks by white Alliances. Some southern leaders, such as Georgia's Senator Tom Watson, tried to unite distressed black and white farmers, realizing that both races suffered from similar burdens. But poor white farmers could not forgo their prejudices. Many came from families that had once owned slaves; they considered African Americans an inferior people and took comfort in the belief that there always would be people worse off than they were. At an 1889 meeting in St. Louis, white southerners rejected uniting with northern Alliances because such a merger would have ended secret Alliance activities and whites-only membership rules.

## Problems in Achieving Alliance Unity

Differences on regional issues also prevented unity. Northern Alliances declined to merge with southerners, fearing domination by more experienced southern leaders. Northern farmers also favored protective tariffs to keep out foreign grain, whereas white southerners wanted low tariffs to hold down costs of imported manufactured goods. Northern and southern Alliances agreed on some issues, however: both favored government regulation of railroads, equitable taxation, currency reform, an end to alleged election frauds that perpetuated special interests in office, and prohibition of landownership by foreign investors.

In spite of their initial divisions, growing membership and rising confidence drew Alliances into politics. By 1890, farmers had elected several officeholders sympathetic to their cause, especially in the South, where Alliances controlled four governorships, eight state legislatures, and forty-seven seats in Congress (forty-four in the House, three in the Senate). In the Midwest, Alliance candidates often ran on third-party tickets, such as the Greenback Party, and achieved some success in Kansas, Nebraska, and the Dakotas. Leaders crisscrossed the country organizing meetings to recruit support for a new party. During the summer of 1890, the Kansas Alliance held a "convention of the people" and nominated candidates who swept the state's fall elections. Formation of this People's, or Populist, Party gave a title to Alliance political activism. (Populism, derived from *populus*, the Latin word for "people," is the political doctrine that asserts the rights and powers of common people in their struggle against the privileged elite.) The Alliance election successes in 1890 energized efforts to unite Alliance groups into a single Populist party. By 1892, southern Alliance members were ready to leave the Democratic Party and join northern counterparts in summoning a People's Party convention to draft a platform and nominate a presidential candidate. The gathering met in Omaha, Nebraska, on July 4.

## Rise of Populism

The new party's platform was a sweeping reform document, reflecting its goals of moral regeneration, political democracy, and antimonopolism. Its preamble charged that the nation had been "brought to the verge of moral, political, and material ruin. Corruption dominates the ballot box, the legislatures, the Congress, and . . . even the [courts]." Charging that inequality (between white classes) threatened to splinter society, the platform declared, "The fruits of the toil of millions are boldly stolen to build up colossal fortunes for a few," and that "wealth belongs to him that creates it." The document addressed three central sources of rural unrest: transportation, land, and money. Frustrated with weak state and federal regulation, Populists demanded government ownership of railroad and telegraph lines. They urged the federal government to reclaim all land owned for speculative purposes by railroads and foreigners. The monetary plank called on the government to expand the currency by making more money available for farm loans and by restoring free and unlimited coinage of silver. Other planks advocated a graduated income tax, postal savings banks, direct election of U.S. senators, and a shorter workday. As its presidential candidate, the party nominated James B. Weaver of Iowa, a former

## Russian Populism

Before American Populism arose late in the nineteenth century, a different form of populism took shape in another largely rural country: Russia. Whereas American Populism emerged from the Alliance organizations of farmers, Russian populism was the creation of intellectuals who wanted to educate peasants to agitate for social and economic freedom.

Propelled by reforms imposed by Czar Alexander II, Russian society had begun to modernize in the mid-nineteenth century. Government administration and the judiciary were reformed, town governments were given control of local taxation, and education became more widespread. Perhaps most importantly, in 1861 Alexander signed an Edict of Emancipation, freeing Russian serfs (slaves attached to specific lands) and granting them compensation to buy land from their landlords. The reforms were slow to take hold, however, prompting some young, educated Russians, called nihilists because they opposed the czar and feudalism, to press for more radical reforms, including socialism. The reformers became known as *narodniki,* or populists, from *narod,* the Russian term for "peasant."

*Narodniki* envisioned a society of self-governing village communes, somewhat like the cooperatives proposed by American Farmers' Alliances, and in the 1870s they visited Russian villages attempting to educate peasants to their ideas. One of their leaders, Peter Lavrov, believed that intellectuals needed to narrow the gap between themselves and the people, and help the masses improve their lives. This message, however, included a more radical tone than the American Populists' campaign for democracy, because Russian populists believed that only a social revolution, an uprising against the czar, could realize their goals. When Alexander instituted repressive policies against the *narodniki* in the late 1870s, many of them turned to terrorism, a move that resulted in the assassination of Alexander II in 1881.

Russian populism failed in different ways than American Populism. Russian peasants were not receptive to the intervention of educated young people, and many peasants remained tied to tradition and could not abandon their loyalty to the czar. Government arrests and imprisonments after Alexander's assassination discouraged populists' efforts, and the movement declined. Nevertheless, just as many of the aims of American Populists were adopted by reformers after the turn of the century, the ideas of Russian populism became the cornerstone of the Russian Revolution of 1917 and of Soviet social and political ideology that followed.

Russian peasants, like American tenant farmers and owners of small landholdings, suffered from poverty and pressures of the expanded market economy. The plight of struggling Russian farm families stirred up empathy from young populist intellectuals, who adopted radical solutions that did not capture as much political fervor among farmers as American populism did. *(Bettmann/Corbis)*

Union general and supporter of an expanded money supply, who already had run for the presidency when he was the Greenback Party's candidate in 1880.

The Populist campaign featured dynamic personalities and rousing rhetoric. The Kansas plains rumbled with speeches not only by Mary Lease

## Populist Spokespeople

but also by "Sockless Jerry" Simpson, an unschooled but canny rural reformer who got his nickname after he ridiculed silk-stockinged wealthy people, causing a reporter to muse that Simpson probably wore no stockings at all. The South produced equally dynamic leaders, such as Texas's Charles W. Macune, Georgia's Tom Watson, and North Carolina's Leonidas Polk. Colorado's governor, Davis "Bloody Bridles" Waite, attacked mine owners with prolabor and antimonopoly rhetoric. Texas's Governor James Hogg battled railroads and other corporations. Minnesota's Ignatius Donnelly, pseudoscientist and writer of apocalyptic novels, became chief visionary of the northern plains and penned the Omaha platform's thunderous language. The campaign also attracted opportunists, such as one-eyed, sharp-tongued "Pitchfork Ben" Tillman of South Carolina, who were not genuine Populists but used agrarian fervor for their own political ends.

In the 1892 presidential election, Populist candidate James Weaver garnered 8 percent of the popular vote, majorities in four states, and twenty-two electoral votes. Not since 1856 had a third party done so well in its first national effort. Nevertheless, the party faced a dilemma of whether to stand by its principles at all costs or compromise in order to gain power. The election had been successful for Populists only in the West. The vote-rich Northeast ignored Weaver, and Alabama was the only southern state that gave Populists as much as one-third of its votes.

Still, Populism gave rural dwellers in the South and West faith in a future of cooperation and democracy. Although Populists were flawed egalitarians—they mistrusted blacks and foreigners—they sought change in order to fulfill their version of American ideals. Amid hardship and desperation, millions of people came to believe that a cooperative democracy in which government would ensure equal opportunity could overcome corporate power. A banner draped above the stage at the Omaha convention captured the movement's spirit: "We do not ask for sympathy or pity. We ask for justice." With this goal in mind, Populists looked ahead to the presidential election of 1896 with hope.

## THE DEPRESSION AND PROTESTS OF THE 1890s

Before that election took place, however, the nation suffered a major economic disruption. In 1893, shortly before Grover Cleveland's second presidency began, the Philadelphia & Reading Railroad, once a thriving and profitable line, went bankrupt. Like other railroads, it had borrowed heavily to lay track and build stations and bridges. But overexpansion cut into profits, and ultimately the company was unable to pay its debts.

The same problem beset manufacturers. For example, output at McCormick farm machinery factories was nine times greater in 1893 than in 1879, but revenues had only tripled. To compensate, the company bought more equipment and squeezed more work out of fewer laborers. This strategy, however, increased debt and unemployment. Jobless workers found themselves in the same plight as employers: they could not pay their bills. Banks suffered, too, when their customers defaulted. The failure of the National Cordage Company in May 1893 sparked a chain reaction of business and bank closings. By year's end,

▲ Mary Elizabeth Lease (1850–1933) was one of the founders of the Populist party in Kansas. Tall and intense, she had a deep, almost hypnotic voice which made her an effective publicist for the farmers' cause. She gave a seconding speech to the presidential nomination of James B. Weaver in 1892.

*(The Kansas State Historical Society, Topeka, Kansas)*

five hundred banks and sixteen hundred businesses had failed. An adviser warned President Cleveland, "We are on the eve of a very dark night." He was right. Between 1893 and 1897, the nation suffered a devastating economic depression.

Personal hardship followed business collapse; nearly 20 percent of the labor force was jobless for a significant time during the depression. Falling demand caused prices to drop between 1892 and 1895, but layoffs and wage cuts more than offset declining living costs. Many people could not afford basic necessities. The New York police estimated that twenty thousand homeless and jobless people roamed the city's streets. Surveying the impact on Boston, Henry Adams wrote, "Men died like flies under the strain, and Boston grew suddenly old, haggard, and thin."

As the depression deepened, the currency dilemma reached a crisis. The Sherman Silver Purchase Act of 1890 had committed the government to use Treasury notes (silver certificates) to buy 4.5 million ounces of silver each month. Recipients could redeem these certificates for gold, at the ratio of one ounce of gold for every sixteen ounces' worth of silver. But a western mining boom made silver more plentiful, causing its market value relative to gold to fall and prompting holders of Sherman silver notes and greenback currency issued during the Civil War to cash in their notes in exchange for more valuable gold. As a result, the nation's gold reserve dwindled, falling below $100 million in early 1893.

**Continuing Currency Problems**

The $100 million level had psychological importance. If investors believed that the country's gold reserve was disappearing, they would lose confidence in America's economic stability and refrain from investing. British capitalists, for example, owned some $4 billion in American stocks and bonds. If dollars were to depreciate because there was too little gold to back them up, the British would stop investing in American economic growth. In fact, the lower the gold reserve dropped, the more people rushed to redeem their money—to get gold before it disappeared. Panic spread, causing more bankruptcies and unemployment.

Vowing to protect the gold reserve, President Cleveland called a special session of Congress to repeal the Sherman Silver Purchase Act. Repeal passed in late 1893, but the run on gold continued through 1894. In early 1895, reserves fell to $41 million. In desperation, Cleveland accepted an offer of 3.5 million ounces of gold in return for $65 million worth of federal bonds from a banking syndicate led by financier J. P. Morgan. When

the bankers resold the bonds to the public, they made a $2 million profit. Cleveland claimed that he had saved the reserves, but discontented farmers, workers, silver miners, and even some of Cleveland's Democratic allies saw only humiliation in the president's deal with big businessmen. "When Judas betrayed Christ," charged Senator Tillman, "his heart was not blacker than this scoundrel, Cleveland, in betraying the [Democratic Party]."

Few people knew what the president was privately enduring. At about the time Cleveland called Congress into special session, doctors discovered a tumor on his palate that required immediate removal. Fearful that publicity of his illness would hasten the run on gold, and intent on preventing Vice President Adlai E. Stevenson, a silver supporter, from gaining influence, Cleveland kept his condition a secret. He announced that he was going sailing, and doctors removed his cancerous upper left jaw while the yacht floated outside New York City. Outfitted with a rubber jaw, Cleveland resumed a full schedule five days later, hiding terrible pain to dispel rumors that he was seriously ill. He eventually recovered, but those who knew of his surgery believed it had sapped his vitality.

The deal between Cleveland and Morgan did not end the depression. After improving slightly in 1895, the economy plunged again. Farm income, declining since 1887, continued to slide; factories closed; banks that remained open restricted withdrawals. The tight money supply depressed housing construction, drying up jobs and reducing immigration. Cities like Detroit encouraged citizens to cultivate "potato patches" on vacant land to help alleviate food shortages. Each night, urban police stations filled up with homeless persons who had no place to stay.

The depression ultimately ran its course. In the final years of the century, gold discoveries in Alaska, good harvests, and industrial growth brought relief. But the downturn hastened the crumbling of the old economic system and the emergence of a new one. The American economy had expanded well beyond local and sectional bases; the fate of a large business in one part of the country had repercussions elsewhere. When farmers in the West fell into debt and lost purchasing power, their depressed condition in turn affected the economic health of railroads, farm-implement manufacturers, and banks in other regions. Moreover, the trend toward corporate consolidation that characterized the new business system had tempted many companies that had expanded too rapidly. When contraction occurred, as it did in 1893, their reckless

**Consequences of the Depression**

debts dragged them down, and they pulled other industries with them.

At the same time, a new global marketplace was emerging, forcing American farmers to contend not only with discriminatory transportation rates and falling crop prices at home, but also with Canadian and Russian wheat growers, Argentine cattle ranchers, Indian and Egyptian cotton manufacturers, and Australian wool producers. More than ever before, the condition of one country's economy affected the economies of other countries. In addition, the glutted domestic market persuaded American businessmen to seek new markets abroad (see Chapter 22).

The depression exposed fundamental tensions in the industrial system. Technological and organizational

### Depression-Era Protests

changes had been widening the gap between employees and employers for half a century, and an upsurge of dissent emerged from this gap. The era of labor protest began with the railroad strikes of 1877. The vehemence of those strikes, and the support they drew from working-class people, raised fears that the United States would experience a popular uprising like one in France in 1871, which had briefly overturned the government and introduced communist principles. The Haymarket riot of 1886, a general strike in New Orleans in 1891, and a prolonged strike at the Carnegie Homestead Steel plant in 1892 heightened anxieties. In the West, embittered workers also rebelled. In 1892 violence erupted at a silver mine in Coeur d'Alene, Idaho. Angered by wage cuts and a lockout, striking miners seized the mine and battled federal troops sent to subdue them.

To many middle- and upper-class people, it seemed as if worker protests portended an economic and political explosion. In 1894, the year the economy plunged into depression, there were over thirteen hundred strikes and countless riots. Contrary to accusations of business leaders, few protesters were anarchists or communists come from Europe to sabotage American democracy. Rather, the disaffected included thousands of men and women who believed that in a democracy their voices should be heard.

Small numbers of socialists participated in these and other confrontations. Some socialists believed that work-

### Socialists

ers should control factories and businesses; others supported government ownership. All socialists, however, opposed the private enterprise of capitalism. Their ideas derived from the writings of Karl Marx (1818–1883), the German philosopher and father of communism, who contended that who-

ever controls the means of production determines how well people live. Marx wrote that industrial capitalism generates profits by paying workers less than the value of their labor and that mechanization and mass production alienate workers from their labor. Thus, Marx contended, capitalists and laborers engage in an inescapable conflict over how much workers will benefit from their efforts. According to Marx, only by abolishing the return on capital—profits—could labor receive its true value, an outcome possible only if workers owned the means of production. Marx predicted that workers worldwide would become so discontented that they would revolt and seize factories, farms, banks, and transportation lines. This revolution would establish a socialist order of justice and equality. Marx's vision appealed to some workers, including many who did not consider themselves socialists, because it promised independence and abundance. It appealed to some intellectuals as well, because it promised to end class conflict and crass materialism.

In America, socialism suffered from disagreement over how to achieve Marx's vision. Much of the movement consisted of ideas brought in by immigrants, first from Germany but also by Russian Jews, Italians, Hungarians, and Poles. Although American socialism splintered into small groups, one of its main factions was the Socialist Labor Party, led by Daniel DeLeon, a fiery editor and lawyer born in Curacao and educated in Germany, who criticized American labor organizations like the AFL as too conservative. Yet, as he and other socialist leaders argued fine points of doctrine, they ignored workers' everyday needs and thus failed to attract the mass of laborers. Nor could they rebut the clergy and business leaders who celebrated opportunity, self-improvement, and consumerism. Social mobility and the philosophy of individualism also undermined socialist aims. Workers hoped that they or their children would benefit through education and acquisition of property or by becoming their own boss; most American workers sought individual advancement rather than the betterment of all.

As the nineteenth century closed, however, American socialism generated a new and inspiring leader. Indiana-

### Eugene V. Debs

born Eugene V. Debs headed the newly formed American Railway Union which had carried out the 1894 strike against the Pullman Company. Jailed for defying the injunction against striking rail workers, Debs read works of Karl Marx in prison. Once released, he flirted briefly with Populism, then became the leading spokesman for American socialism, combining visionary Marxism with Jeffersonian and Populist antimonopolism. Debs captivated audiences with passionate eloquence and indignant attacks on the free-enterprise system. "Many of you think you are competing," he would lecture. "Against whom? Against Rockefeller? About as I would if I had a wheelbarrow and competed with the Santa Fe [railroad] from here to Kansas City." By 1900 the group soon to be called the Socialist Party of America was uniting around Debs. It would make its presence felt more forcefully in the new century.

In 1894, however, not Debs but rather a quiet businessman named Jacob Coxey from Massillon, Ohio, captured public attention with his act

**Coxey's Army**

of protest. Coxey had a vision. He was convinced that, to aid debtors, the government should issue $500 million of "legal tender" paper money and make low-interest loans to local governments, which would in turn use the funds to pay the unemployed to build roads and other public works. He planned to publicize his scheme by leading a march from Massillon to Washington, D.C., gathering a "petition in boots" of unemployed workers along the way. Coxey even christened his newborn son Legal Tender and proposed that his teenage daughter lead the procession on a white horse.

Coxey's army, about 200 strong, left in March 1894. Moving across Ohio into Pennsylvania, the marchers received food and housing in depressed industrial towns and rural villages, and they attracted additional recruits. Elsewhere, a dozen similar processions from places such as Seattle, San Francisco, and Los Angeles also began the trek eastward. Sore feet prompted some marchers to commandeer trains, but most marches were peaceful and law-abiding.

Coxey's band of 500, including women and children, entered Washington on April 30. The next day (May Day, the anniversary of the Haymarket violence), the group, armed with "war clubs of peace," advanced to the Capitol. When Coxey and a few others vaulted the wall surrounding the Capitol grounds, mounted police moved in and routed the demonstrators. Coxey tried to speak from the Capitol steps, but police dragged him away. As arrests and clubbings continued, Coxey's dream of a demonstration of 400,000 jobless workers dissolved. Like the strikes, the first people's march on Washington yielded to police muscle.

Unlike socialists, who wished to replace the capitalist system, Coxey's troops merely wanted more jobs and better living standards. Today, in an age of union contracts, regulation of business, and government-sponsored unemployment relief, their goals do not appear radical. The brutal reactions of officials, however, reveal how threatening

dissenters like Coxey and Debs seemed to defenders of the existing social order.

## THE SILVER CRUSADE AND THE ELECTION OF 1896

Amid the tumult of social protest and economic depression, it appeared that the presidential election of 1896 would be pivotal. Debates over money and power were climaxing, Democrats and Republicans continued their battle over control of Congress and the presidency, and the Populists stood at the center of the political whirlwind. The key question was whether or not voters would abandon old party loyalties for the Populist party.

The Populist crusade against "money power" settled on the issue of silver, which many people saw as a simple

**Free Silver**

solution to the nation's complex ills. To them, free coinage of silver symbolized an end to special privileges for the rich and the return of

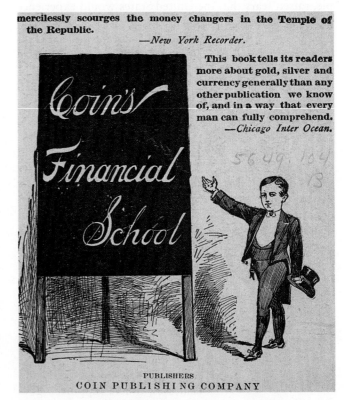

mercilessly scourges the money changers in the Temple of the Republic.
—*New York Recorder*.

This book tells its readers more about gold, silver and currency generally than any other publication we know of, and in a way that every man can fully comprehend.
—*Chicago Inter Ocean*.

PUBLISHERS
COIN PUBLISHING COMPANY

▲ Published in 1894, *Coin's Financial School* by William H. Harvey expressed the position of free silver in simple language and illustrations. Written in the form of lectures on the money question given by "Professor Coin," Harvey's book had enormous appeal to distressed farmers. *(Trustees of the Boston Public Library)*

government to the people, because it would lift the common people out of debt, increase the amount of cash in circulation, and reduce interest rates. Populists made free coinage of silver their political battle cry.

As the election of 1896 approached, Populists had to decide how to translate their few previous electoral victories into larger success. Should they join with sympathetic factions of the major parties, thus risking a loss of identity, or should they remain an independent third party and settle for minor wins at best? Except in mining areas of the Rocky Mountain states, where free coinage of silver had strong support, Republicans were unlikely allies because their support for the gold standard and their big-business orientation represented what Populists opposed.

In the North and West, alliance with Democrats was more plausible. There, the Democratic Party retained vestiges of antimonopoly ideology and sympathy for a looser currency system, though "gold Democrats," such as President Cleveland and Senator David Hill of New York, held powerful influence. Populists assumed they shared common interests with Democratic urban workers, who they believed suffered the same oppression that beset farmers. In the South, Alliances had previously supported Democratic candidates, but the failure of these candidates to carry out their promises once in office caused southern farmers to feel betrayed. Whichever option they chose, fusion (alliance with Democrats) or independence, Populists ensured that the election campaign of 1896 would be the most issue oriented since 1860.

As they prepared to nominate their presidential candidate, both parties were divided internally. Republicans

### Republican Nomination of McKinley

were guided by Ohio industrialist Marcus A. Hanna, who for a year had been maneuvering to win the nomination for Ohio's governor, William McKinley. By the time the party convened in St. Louis, Hanna had corralled enough delegates to succeed. "He had advertised McKinley," quipped Theodore Roosevelt, "as if he were a patent medicine." The Republicans' only distress

THE LOCKOUT IS ENDED; HE HOLDS THE KEY.

▲ During the 1896 presidential campaign, Republicans depicted their candidate, William McKinley, as holding the key to prosperity for both the working man and the white-collar laborer, shown here raising their hats to the candidate. Republicans successfully made this economic theme, rather than the silver crusade of McKinley's unsuccessful opponent, William Jennings Bryan, the difference in the election's outcome. *(Collection of David J. and Janice L. Frent)*

occurred when they adopted a moderate platform supporting the gold standard, rejecting a prosilver stance proposed by Colorado senator Henry M. Teller. Teller, who had been among the party's founders forty years earlier, walked out of the convention in tears, taking a small group of silver Republicans with him.

At the Democratic convention, prosilver delegates wearing silver badges and waving silver banners paraded through the Chicago Amphitheatre. Observing their tumultuous demonstrations, one delegate wrote, "For the first time I can understand the scenes of the French Revolution!" A *New York World* reporter remarked that "all the silverites need is a Moses." They found one in William Jennings Bryan.

Bryan arrived at the Democratic convention as a member of a contested Nebraska delegation. A former

||||||||||||||||||||||||||||||

### William Jennings Bryan

congressman whose support for coinage of silver had annoyed President Cleveland, Bryan found the depression's impact on midwestern farmers distressing. Shortly after the convention seated Bryan and his colleagues instead of a competing faction that supported the gold standard, Bryan joined the party's resolutions committee and helped write a platform calling for unlimited coinage of silver. When the committee presented the platform to the full convention, Bryan rose to speak on its behalf. His now-famous closing words ignited the delegates.

> Having behind us the producing masses of this nation and the world, supported by the commercial interests, the laboring interests, and the toilers everywhere, we will answer [the wealthy classes'] demand for a gold standard by saying to them: You shall not press down upon the brow of labor this crown of thorns, you shall not crucify mankind upon a cross of gold.

The speech could not have been better timed. Delegates who backed Bryan for president now began enlisting support. It took five ballots to win the nomination, but the magnetic "Boy Orator" proved irresistible. In accepting the silverite goals of southerners and westerners, and repudiating Cleveland's policies in its platform, the Democratic Party became more attractive to discontented farmers. But, like the Republicans, it, too, alienated a minority wing. Some gold Democrats withdrew and nominated their own candidate.

Bryan's nomination presented the Populist party convention meeting in St. Louis with a dilemma. Should Populists join Democrats in support of Bryan, or should they nominate their own candidate? Tom Watson, who opposed fusion with Democrats, warned that "the Demo-

▲ William Jennings Bryan (1860–1925) posed for this photograph in 1896, when he first ran for president at the age of thirty-six. Bryan's emotional speeches turned agrarian unrest and the issue of free silver into a moral crusade.   *(Library of Congress)*

cratic idea of fusion [is] that we play Jonah while they play whale." Others reasoned that supporting a separate candidate would split the anti-McKinley vote and guarantee a Republican victory. In the end the convention compromised, first naming Watson as its vice-presidential nominee to preserve party identity (Democrats had nominated Maine shipping magnate Arthur Sewall for vice president) and then nominating Bryan for president.

The campaign, as Kansas journalist William Allen White observed, "took the form of religious frenzy . . . as the crusaders of the revolution rode home, praising the people's will as though it were God's will and cursing wealth for its iniquity." Bryan preached that "every great economic question is in reality a great moral question." Republicans countered Bryan's attacks on privilege by predicting chaos if he won. While Bryan raced around the country giving twenty speeches a day, Hanna invited thousands of people to McKinley's home in Canton, Ohio, where the candidate plied them with homilies on moderation and prosperity, promising something for everyone. In an appeal to working-class voters, Republicans stressed the new jobs that a protective tariff would create.

The election results revealed that the political standoff had finally ended. McKinley, symbol of urban and

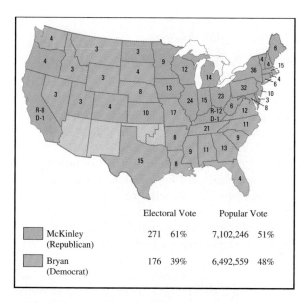

**Map 20.1    Presidential Election, 1896**

| | Electoral Vote | | Popular Vote | |
|---|---|---|---|---|
| McKinley (Republican) | 271 | 61% | 7,102,246 | 51% |
| Bryan (Democrat) | 176 | 39% | 6,492,559 | 48% |

William Jennings Bryan had strong voter support in the South and West, but the numerically superior industrial states, plus California, created majorities for William McKinley.

### Election Results

corporate ascendancy, beat Bryan by 600,000 popular votes and won in the electoral college by 271 to 176 (see Map 20.1). It was the most lopsided presidential election since 1872.

Bryan worked hard to rally the nation, but obsession with silver prevented Populists from building the urban-rural coalition that would have expanded their political appeal. The silver issue diverted voters from focusing on broader reforms of cooperation and government aid deriving from the Alliance movement and the 1892 Omaha platform. Urban workers, who might have benefited from Populist goals, feared that silver coinage would shrink the value of their wages. Labor leaders, such as the AFL's Samuel Gompers, though partly sympathetic, would not commit themselves fully because they viewed farmers as businessmen, not workers. And socialists like Daniel DeLeon denounced Populists as "retrograde" because they, unlike socialists, believed in free enterprise. Thus the Populist crusade collapsed. Although Populists and fusion candidates won a few state and congressional elections, the Bryan-Watson ticket of the Populist party polled only 222,600 votes nationwide.

As president, McKinley reinforced his support of business by signing the Gold Standard Act (1900), requiring

### The McKinley Presidency

that all paper money be backed by gold. A seasoned and personable politician, McKinley was best known for crafting protective tariffs; as a congressman, he had guided passage of record-high tariff rates in 1890. He accordingly supported the Dingley Tariff of 1897, which raised duties even higher. Domestic tensions subsided as prosperity returned. A believer in opening new markets abroad to sustain profits at home, McKinley encouraged imperialistic ventures in Latin America and the Pacific. Good times and victory in the Spanish-American War enabled him to beat Bryan again in 1900.

## SUMMARY

Politicians during the Gilded Age succeeded in making many modest, and some major, accomplishments. Guided by well-meaning, generally competent people, much of what occurred in statehouses, the halls of Congress, and the White House prepared the nation for the twentieth century. Laws encouraging economic growth with some principles of regulation, measures expanding government agencies while reducing crass patronage, and federal intervention in trade and currency issues all evolved during the 1870s and 1880s.

True to Mary Lease's characterization, the United States remained a "nation of inconsistencies." Those who supported disfranchisement of African Americans and continued discrimination against both blacks and women still polluted politics. People in power, often representing special-interest groups, could not tolerate radical views like those expressed by socialists, Coxey, or Populists, but many of the ideas raised by these groups continued to find supporters as the new century dawned.

The 1896 election realigned national politics. The Republican Party, founded in the 1850s amid a crusade against slavery and benefiting from northern victory in the Civil War, became the majority party by emphasizing government aid to business, expanding its social base among the urban middle class, and playing down its moralism. The Democratic Party miscalculated on the silver issue but held its traditional support in the South and in urban political machines. At the national level, however, loyalties lacked the potency they once had. Suspicion of party politics increased, and voter participation rates declined. The Populists tried to energize a third-party movement, but their success was fleeting. A new kind

# *Legacy* FOR A PEOPLE AND A NATION

## Interpreting a Fairy Tale

*T*he Wizard of Oz, one of the most popular movies of all time, began as a work of juvenile literature penned by journalist L. Frank Baum in 1900. Originally titled *The Wonderful Wizard of Oz,* the story used memorable characters to create a fun-filled and adventurous quest.

Although children have viewed the tale and film as a fantasy, adults have been tempted to seek hidden meanings. In 1964 one scholar, Henry M. Littlefield, published an article in which he asserted that Baum really intended to write a Populist parable about the conditions of overburdened farmers and laborers. The characters in *The Wonderful Wizard,* Littlefield opined, supported his theory. Dorothy symbolized the well-intentioned common person; the Scarecrow, the struggling farmer; the Tin Man, the industrial worker. Hoping for a better life, these friends, along with the Cowardly Lion (William Jennings Bryan with a loud roar but little power), followed a yellow brick road (the gold standard) that led nowhere. The Emerald City that they find is presided over by a wizard, who rules from behind a screen. A typical politician, the wizard tries to be all things to all people, but Dorothy reveals him as a fraud. Dorothy is able to leave this muddled society and return to her simple Kansas farm family of Aunt Em and Uncle Henry by using her magical silver slippers (representing coinage of silver, though the movie made them red).

Subsequent theorists, though sometimes qualifying Littlefield, identified additional symbols, such as Oz being the abbreviation for ounces (oz.), the chief measurement of gold. The Wicked Witch of the East—who, Baum wrote, kept the little people (Munchkins) "in bondage, . . . making them slaves for her night and day"—could be seen as representing the force of industrial capitalism. Baum's story, seen in film by most Americans, became a tool for explaining Populism to students, and by the 1970s its apparent message had strong appeal to critics of "the Establishment."

But then investigators began to take another look and to offer different conclusions. In 1983 historian William R. Leach asserted that Baum's tale actually was a celebration of urban consumer culture. Its language exalted the opulence of Emerald City, which to Leach resembled the "White City" of the Chicago World's Fair of 1893, and Dorothy's upbeat nature symbolized the optimism of the industrial era. Moreover, Baum's career supported this new interpretation. Before he was a writer, he had designed display windows and was involved in theater—activities that gave him an appreciation of modern urban life.

Rather than confusion, the real legacy of *The Wonderful Wizard of Oz* has been its ability to provoke differing interpretations. What matters is that Baum's fairy tale, the first truly American work of this sort, has bequeathed to the present so many fascinating images about the diversity and contradictions of American culture.

of politics was brewing, one in which technical experts and scientific organization would attempt to supplant the backroom deals and favoritism that had characterized the previous age.

Although the silver issue faded, by 1920 many Populist goals had been incorporated by the major parties, including regulation of railroads, banks, and utilities; shorter workdays; a variant of the subtreasury plan; a graduated income tax; and direct election of senators. These reforms succeeded because a variety of groups united behind them. Immigration, urbanization, and industrialization had transformed the United States into a pluralistic society in which compromise among interest groups had become a political fact of life. As the Gilded Age ended, business was still in the ascendancy, and large segments of the population were still excluded from political and economic opportunity. But the winds of dissent and reform had begun to blow more strongly.

## SUGGESTIONS FOR FURTHER READING

Edward L. Ayers, *The Promise of the New South: Life After Reconstruction* (1992)

Nancy Cohen, *The Reconstruction of American Liberalism, 1865–1914* (2002)

Glenda Elizabeth Gilmore, *Gender and Jim Crow: Women and the Politics of White Supremacy in North Carolina, 1896–1920* (1996)

Steven Hahn, *A Nation Under Our Feet: Black Political Struggles in the Rural South, from Slavery to the Great Migration* (2003)

Michael Kazin, *The Populist Persuasion: An American History* (1995)

Jean V. Matthews, *The Rise of the New Woman: The Women's Movement in America, 1875–1930* (2003)

Nick Salvatore, *Eugene V. Debs: Citizen and Socialist* (1992)

# CHAPTER 21

# The Progressive Era
*1895-1920*

H

hat Ben Lindsey saw made him furious. As a young Colorado lawyer in the 1890s, he had been asked by a judge to defend two boys, about twelve years old, accused of burglary. The boys had already been imprisoned for sixty days without a trial and did not understand what the word *burglary* meant, let alone how the justice system worked. When he went to visit them in jail, Lindsey found the youngsters playing poker with two older cellmates, one a safe cracker and the other a horse thief. Lindsey asked the warden how many other boys were in the jail. "Oh, quite a number" was the answer. Outraged that "good-natured" children were housed with hardened criminals, Lindsey later wrote, "Here were two boys, neither of them serious enemies of society, who were about to be convicted of burglary and have felony records for the rest of their lives. . . . I had made up my mind to smash the system that meant so much injustice to youth."

In 1901 Lindsey ran for county judge and began a long career fighting on behalf of juvenile protection. He spoke and wrote extensively about protecting children from criminal prosecution, exploitative labor practices, and the burdens of poverty. He and his wife, Henrietta, worked ceaselessly to spread the idea of a separate juvenile court system and to aid families whose children they thought might be at risk of becoming criminals. They wrote reform laws that were adopted by many states and foreign countries. The Lindseys' efforts to abolish injustice showed both genuine compassion and middle-class bias, and they occupied a part of a broader movement aimed at finding solutions to the social and economic problems of modern American society.

During the 1890s, economic depression, labor violence, political upheaval, and foreign entanglements shook the nation. Technology had fulfilled many promises, but great

◀ Judge Ben Lindsey (1869–1943) of Denver was a Progressive reformer who worked for children's legal protection. Like many reformers of his era, Lindsey had an earnest faith in the ability of humankind to build a better world. *(Library of Congress)*

591

## CHRONOLOGY

1895 ■ Booker T. Washington gives Atlanta Compromise speech
     ■ National Association of Colored Women founded

1898 ■ *Holden v. Hardy* upholds limits on miners' working hours

1901 ■ McKinley assassinated; T. Roosevelt assumes presidency

1904 ■ *Northern Securities* case dissolves railroad trust

1905 ■ *Lochner v. New York* removes limits on bakers' working hours
     ■ NCAA founded

1906 ■ Hepburn Act tightens ICC control over railroads
     ■ Meat Inspection Act passed
     ■ Pure Food and Drug Act Passed

1908 ■ *Muller v. Oregon* upholds limits on women's working hours

1909 ■ NAACP founded

1910 ■ Mann-Elkins Act reinforces ICC powers
     ■ White Slave Traffic Act (Mann Act) prohibits transportation of women for "immoral purposes"
     ■ Taft fires Pinchot

1911 ■ Society of American Indians founded

1913 ■ Sixteenth Amendment ratified, legalizing income tax
     ■ Seventeenth Amendment ratified, providing for direct election of senators
     ■ Underwood Tariff institutes income tax
     ■ Federal Reserve Act establishes central banking system

1914 ■ Federal Trade Commission created to investigate unfair trade practices
     ■ Clayton Anti-Trust Act outlaws monopolistic business practices
     ■ Adamson Act mandates eight-hour workday for railroad workers

1919 ■ Eighteenth Amendment ratified, establishing prohibition of alcoholic beverages

1920 ■ Nineteenth Amendment ratified, giving women the vote in federal elections

numbers of Americans continued to suffer from poverty and disease. Business and politics seemed out of control. Some critics regarded industrialists as monsters who controlled markets and prices for the sole purpose of maximizing profits. Others believed government was corroded by bosses who enriched themselves through politics. Still others felt that the needs of the laboring classes were being overlooked. Tensions created by urbanization and industrialization seemed to be fragmenting society into conflicting interest groups.

By 1900, however, the previous decade's political tumult had calmed, and economic depression seemed to be over. The nation emerged victorious from a war against Spain (see Chapter 22), and a new era of dynamic political leaders, such as Theodore Roosevelt and Woodrow Wilson, was dawning. A sense of renewal served both to intensify anxiety over continuing problems and to raise hopes that somehow these problems could be fixed and democracy could be reconciled with capitalism.

From these circumstances there emerged a complex and many-sided reform campaign. By the 1910s, reformers from both Republican and Democratic Parties were calling themselves Progressives; in 1912 they formed a political party by that name to embody their principles. Historians have uniformly used the term *Progressivism* to refer to the era's spirit, while disagreeing over its meaning and over which groups and individuals actually were Progressive. Nonetheless, the era between 1895 and 1920 included a series of movements, each aiming in one way or another to renovate or restore American society, values, and institutions by imposing change from above and by exercising influence from below.

The reform impulse had many sources. Industrial capitalism had created awesome technology, unprecedented productivity, and a cornucopia of consumer goods. But it had also brought harmful overproduction, domineering monopolies, labor strife, and the destruction of natural resources. Burgeoning cities facilitated the amassing and distribution of goods, services, and cultural amenities; they also bred poverty, disease, and crime. The influx of immigrants and the rise of a new class of managers and professionals reconfigured the social order. And the depression of the 1890s forced leading citizens to realize what working people already knew: the central promise of American life was not being kept; equality of opportunity was elusive.

These problems galvanized members of both the middle class and the working class to work toward change, though in differing ways. Middle-class reformers organized their ideas and actions around three goals. First, they sought to end abuses of power. Attacks on privilege, monopoly, and corruption were not new; Jacksonian reformers of the 1830s and 1840s, as well as Populists of the 1890s, belonged to the same tradition. Progressives, however, broadened the offensive. Trustbusting, consumers' rights, and good government became compelling political issues.

Second, Progressives like Ben Lindsey wished to supplant corrupt power with humane institutions, such as schools, courts, and medical clinics. Though eager to protect individual rights, they abandoned individualistic notions that hard work and good character automatically ensured success, and that the poor had only themselves to blame for their plight. Instead, Progressives acknowledged that society had responsibility and power to improve individual lives, and they believed that government, acting for society at large, must intervene in social and economic affairs to protect the common good and elevate public interest above self-interest. Their revolt against fixed categories of thought challenged entrenched views on women's roles, race relations, education, legal and scientific thought, and morality.

Third, Progressives wanted to apply scientific principles and efficient management to economic, social, and political institutions. Their aim was to establish bureaus of experts who would end wasteful competition and promote social and economic order. Science and the scientific method—planning, control, and predictability—were their central values. Just as corporations applied scientific management techniques to achieve economic efficiency, Progressives advocated expertise and planning to achieve social and political efficiency.

Another kind of reform arose from the everyday needs and problems of urban working classes. Reformers representing the interests of this group sometimes allied with others interested in broad social welfare and sometimes worked on their own to promote greater public responsibility for the health, safety, and security of families and workers at risk in the new urban industrial world.

Befitting their name, Progressives had faith in the ability of humankind to create a better world. They voiced such phrases as "humanity's universal growth" and "the upward spiral of human development." Rising incomes, new educational opportunities, and increased availability of goods and services created an aura of confidence that social improvement would follow. Judge Ben Lindsey of Denver, who spearheaded reform in the treatment of juvenile delinquents, expressed the Progressive creed when he wrote, "In the end the people are bound to do the right thing, no matter how much they fail at times."

- What were the major characteristics of Progressivism?
- In what ways did Progressive reform succeed, and in what ways did it fail?
- How did women and racial minorities challenge previous ways of thinking about American society?

## THE VARIED PROGRESSIVE IMPULSE

Progressive reformers addressed vexing issues that had surfaced in the previous half-century, but they did so in a new political climate. After the heated election of 1896, party loyalties eroded and voter turnout declined. In northern states, voter participation in presidential elections dropped from the 1880s' levels of 80 percent of the eligible electorate to less than 60 percent. In southern states, where poll taxes and literacy tests excluded most African Americans and many poor whites from the polls, it fell below 30 percent. Parties and elections, it seemed, were losing influence over government policies. At the same time, new interest groups, which championed their own special causes, gained influence.

Many formerly local organizations that had formed to shape public policy in a specific area became nationwide after 1890. These organizations in-

**National Associations and Foreign Influences**

cluded professional associations, such as the American Bar Association; women's organizations, such as the National American Woman Suffrage Association; issue-oriented groups, such as the National Consumers League; civic-minded clubs, such as the National Municipal League; and minority-group associations, such as the National Negro Business League and the Society of American Indians. Because they usually acted independently of established political parties, such groups made politics more fragmented and issue focused than in earlier eras.

American reformers also adapted foreign models and ideas. A variety of proposals traveled across the Atlantic; some were introduced by Americans who had been exposed to reforms while studying in England, France, and Germany; others, by foreigners visiting the United States. (Europeans also learned from Americans, but the balance of the idea flow tilted toward the United States.) Americans copied from England such ideas as the settlement house, in which reformers went to live among and aid the urban poor, and workers' compensation for victims of industrial accidents. Other reforms, such as old-age insurance, subsidized workers' housing, city planning, and rural reconstruction, originated abroad and were adopted or modified in America.

Issues and methods arising from a new age distinguished Progressive reform from the preceding Populist movement. Although goals of the rural-based Populists—moral regeneration, political democracy, and antimonopolism—continued after the movement faded, the Progressive quest for social justice, labor laws, educational and legal reform, and government streamlining had a largely urban bent. Utilizing advances in mail, telephone, and telegraph communications, urban reformers could exchange information and coordinate efforts more easily than rural reformers could.

Progressive goals—ending abuse of power, protecting the welfare of all classes, reforming social institutions, and promoting bureaucratic and scientific efficiency—existed in all levels of society. But a new middle class of men and women in professions of law, medicine, engineering, social service, religion, teaching, and business formed an important vanguard of reform. Offended by inefficiency and immorality in business, government, and human relations, these people determined to apply the rational techniques that they had learned in their professions to problems of the larger society. They also believed that they could create a unified society by transforming immigrants and Indians—"Americanizing" them through education and other means—to conform to middle-class customs and ideals.

## The New Middle Class and Muckrakers

Indignation motivated many middle-class reformers to seek an end to abuses of power. Their views were voiced by journalists whom Theodore Roosevelt dubbed muckrakers (after a character in the Puritan allegory *Pilgrim's Progress,* who, rather than looking heavenward at beauty, looked downward and raked the muck to find what was wrong with life). Muckrakers fed public tastes for scandal and sensation by exposing social, economic, and political wrongs. Their investigative articles in *McClure's, Cosmo-*

*politan,* and other popular magazines attacked adulterated foods, fraudulent insurance, prostitution, and political corruption. Lincoln Steffens's articles in *McClure's,* later published as *The Shame of the Cities* (1904), epitomized muckraking style. Steffens hoped his exposés of bosses' misrule would inspire mass outrage and, ultimately, reform. Other well-known muckraking works included Upton Sinclair's *The Jungle* (1906), a novel that disclosed outrages of the meatpacking industry; Ida M. Tarbell's disparaging history of Standard Oil (first published in *McClure's,* 1902–1904); Burton J. Hendrick's *Story of Life Insurance* (1907); and David Graham Phillips's *Treason of the Senate* (1906).

To improve politics, these Progressives advocated nonpartisan elections to prevent fraud and bribery bred by party loyalties. They also promoted direct primaries, in which all voters could participate, instead of party caucuses, in which only insiders had influence. To make officeholders more responsible, they urged adoption of the initiative, which permitted voters to propose new laws; the referendum, which enabled voters to accept or reject a law (Oregon was first to introduce these measures); and the recall, which allowed voters to remove offending officials and judges from office. The goal, like that of the business-consolidation movement, was efficiency: middle-class Progressives would reclaim government by replacing the boss system with accountable managers chosen by a responsible electorate.

The Progressive spirit also stirred some male business leaders and wealthy females. Executives like Alexander Cassatt of the Pennsylvania Railroad supported some government regulation and political reforms to protect their interests from more radical reformers. Others, like E. A. Filene, founder of a Boston department store, and Tom Johnson, a Cleveland streetcar magnate, were humanitarians who worked unselfishly for social justice. Business-dominated organizations like the Municipal Voters League and the U.S. Chamber of Commerce thought that running schools, hospitals, and local government like efficient businesses would help stabilize society. Elite women led organizations like the Young Women's Christian Association (YWCA), which aided unmarried working women, and they joined middle- and working-class women in the Woman's Christian Temperance Union (WCTU), the largest women's organization of its time, which supported numerous causes besides abstinence from drinking.

## Upper-Class Reformers

Vital elements of what became modern American liberalism derived from working-class urban experiences.

## Workers' Compensation

During the Progressive era, the volume and extent of industrial accidents attracted considerable attention from muckraking journalists and academic researchers. At the dawn of the twentieth century, accident rates on American railroads and in American mines and factories far exceeded those in Great Britain and Germany, the other two major industrial nations. In 1911 one study concluded that the accident rate in the nation's industries "equals the average yearly casualties of the American Civil War, plus all of those of the Philippine War, plus all of those of the Russo-Japanese War." The United States was, said one reformer, creating an "army of cripples." Prevailing American legal theory protected employers from liability and prevented workers from recovering medical costs and lost income when injured on the job. Progressives challenged that theory and proposed that employers, guided by government, should shoulder the obligation.

The principle that employers should be legally responsible for compensating victims of industrial accidents emerged most strongly in Germany and Britain. In 1884 the German government began requiring employers and wage earners to contribute to quasi-public funds that could be used to provide for those injured at work. In England, an 1897 law compelled employers to create some form of payment through contributions to an insurance company or from their own funds. Shortly thereafter, variations appeared in Denmark, France, and Italy. But not until 1907 did the reform find influential support in the United States. That year, President Theodore Roosevelt began advocating employers' liability legislation. The next year, two different Progressive organizations, the social reform–minded Russell Sage Foundation and the business-oriented National Civic Foundation, took up the cause.

Most American Progressives favored the German system because it operated more under government administration than the British method and because it encouraged industrial safety. But states, rather than the federal government, assumed responsibility for the exact form of a program. By 1911, Ohio and Washington had state-administered insurance funds into which employers made contributions, and between 1911 and 1913, twenty other states enacted some form of workers' compensation laws. Private insurance companies, however, strongly opposed state monopolies on compensation insurance, and by 1919, though employers were still required to make contributions, the majority of workers' compensation funds were in the hands of private firms. American legislators, propelled by Progressive arguments, had borrowed an insurance system from abroad but applied their own imprint of private enterprise.

### A SUCCESSFUL WORKMAN

This man who lost an arm in an industrial accident in Cleveland, invented a good substitute arm, wears it at work, and uses it in earning his living. He has made good by his own unaided efforts. The average man, however, needs a lift in the way of training.

▲ In the early twentieth century, industrial accidents continued to kill and maim thousands of workers. Without insurance to support them when they were disabled, some employees created aids to enable them to continue on the job. This man, who lost an arm in a factory mishap, invented his own artificial limb. Other victims of misfortune, however, were not so handy and could receive compensation only if their state or their employer adopted the European model and instituted a workers' insurance program. *(Library of Congress)*

## Working-Class Reformers

By 1900 many urban workers were pressing for government intervention to ensure safety and security. They advocated such "bread-and-butter reforms" as safe factories, shorter workdays, workers' compensation, protection of child and women laborers, better housing, health safeguards, and a more equitable tax structure. Politicians like Senator Robert F. Wagner of New York and Governor Edward F. Dunne of Illinois worked to alleviate hardships that resulted from urban-industrial growth. They trained in the trenches of machine politics, and their constituents were the same people who supported political bosses, supposedly the enemies of reform. Yet bossism was not necessarily at odds with humanitarianism. When "Big Tim" Sullivan, an influential boss in New York City's Tammany Hall political machine, was asked why he supported a shorter workday for women, he explained, "I had seen me sister go out to work when she was only fourteen and I know we ought to help these gals by giving 'em a law which will prevent 'em from being broken down while they're still young." Reformers who represented working-class interests did not subscribe to all reforms. As protectors of individual liberty, they opposed reforms such as prohibition, Sunday closing laws, civil service, and nonpartisan elections, which conflicted with their constituents' interests. On the other hand, they joined with other reformers to pass laws aiding labor and promoting social welfare.

## The Social Gospel

Much of Progressive reform rested on religious underpinnings. The distresses of modern society especially sparked new thoughts about how to fortify social relations with moral principles. In particular, a movement known as the Social Gospel, led by Protestant ministers Walter Rauschenbusch, Washington Gladden, and Charles Sheldon, would counter competitive capitalism by interjecting Christian churches into practical, worldly matters, such as arbitrating industrial harmony and improving the environment of the poor. Believing that service to fellow humans provided the way to securing individual salvation and to creating God's kingdom on earth, Social Gospelers actively participated in social reform and governed their lives by asking, "What would Jesus do?" Other Progressives had more secular influences. Ben Lindsey's battle for juvenile justice, for example, derived in part from the democratic ideals of Populism.

Those who believed in service to all people tried to "Americanize" immigrants and Indians by expanding their educational, economic, and cultural opportunities. But at times, by imposing their own values on people of different cultures, they undermined their efforts to help. Catholic and Jewish immigrants, for example, sometimes rejected the Protestant creed and Americanization efforts of Social Gospelers, settlement-house workers, and other reformers. Working-class families, too, often resented middle-class reformers' interference in their prerogative to raise their children according to their own beliefs.

Some disillusioned people wanted a different society altogether. A blend of immigrant intellectuals, industrial workers, Populists, miners, and women's rights activists, they turned to socialism. Taking a cue from European counterparts, especially in Germany, England, and France, where the government sponsored such socialist goals as low-cost housing, workers' compensation, old-age pensions, public ownership of municipal services, and labor reform, they advocated that similar measures be adopted in the United States. By 1912, the Socialist Party of America, a merger of several groups and founded in 1901, claimed 150,000 members, and the socialist newspaper *Appeal to Reason* achieved the largest circulation—700,000 subscribers—of any weekly newspaper in the country. But American socialism had difficulty sustaining widespread acceptance. Although some AFL unions supported socialist goals and candidates, many unions opposed a reform like social insurance because it would increase taxes on members' wages. Moreover, private real-estate interests opposed any government intervention in housing, and manufacturers blacklisted militant socialist laborers.

## Socialists

In politics, many socialists united behind Eugene V. Debs, the American Railway Union organizer who drew nearly 100,000 votes as the Socialist presidential candidate in the 1900 presidential election. A spellbinding orator who was able to appeal to urban immigrants and western farmers alike, Debs won 400,000 votes in 1904 and polled 900,000 in 1912, at the pinnacle of his and his party's career. Although Debs and other Socialist leaders, such as Victor Berger of Wisconsin, the first Socialist to be elected to the U.S. Congress, and New York's Morris Hillquit, did not always agree on tactics, they made compelling overtures to reform-minded people. Some Progressives joined the Socialist Party, but most Progressives had too much at stake in capitalism to want to overthrow it. Municipal ownership of public utilities represented their limit of drastic change. In Wisconsin, where Progressivism was most advanced, reformers refused to ally with Berger's more radical group. California Progressives temporarily allied with conservatives to prevent Socialists from gaining power in Los Angeles. And few

▲ Although their objectives sometimes differed from those of middle-class Progressive reformers, socialists also became a more active force in the early twentieth century. Socialist parades on May Day, like this one in 1910, were meant to express the solidarity of all working people. *(Library of Congress)*

Progressives objected when Debs was jailed in 1918 for giving an antiwar speech.

In some ways, Progressive reform in the South resembled that in other regions. Essentially urban and middle class in nature, it included the same goals of railroad and utility regulation, factory safety, pure food and drug legislation, and moral reform as existed in the North. The South pioneered some political reforms; the direct primary originated in North Carolina; the city-commission plan arose in Galveston, Texas; and the city-manager plan began in Staunton, Virginia. Progressive governors, such as Braxton Bragg Comer of Alabama and Hoke Smith of Georgia, introduced business regulation, educational expansion, and other reforms that duplicated actions taken by northern counterparts.

### Southern and Western Progressivism

In the West, several politicians championed humanitarianism and regulation, putting the region at the forefront of the campaign to expand functions of federal and state governments. Nevada's Progressive Senator Francis Newlands advocated national planning and federal control of water resources. In California, Governor Hiram Johnson fought for direct primaries, regulation of child and women's labor, workers' compensation, a pure food and drug act, and educational reform. Montana's Senator Thomas J. Walsh fought against corruption and for woman suffrage.

Southern and western women, white and black, made notable contributions to Progressive causes, just as they did in the North and the East. In western states, women could vote on state and local matters, so that they could participate directly in political reform. But the more effective women's reform efforts in both regions took place outside of politics, and their projects remained racially distinct. White women crusaded against child labor, founded social service organizations, and challenged unfair wage rates. African American women, using a nonpolitical guise as homemakers and religious leaders—roles that whites found more acceptable than political activism—served their communities by acting as advocates for street cleaning, better education, and health reforms.

It would be a mistake to assume that a Progressive spirit captivated all of American society between 1895 and

## Opponents of Progressivism

1920. Large numbers of people, heavily represented in Congress, disliked government interference in economic affairs and found no fault with existing power structures. Defenders of free enterprise opposed regulatory measures out of fear that government programs undermined the initiative and competition that they believed were basic to a free-market system. "Old-guard" Republicans, such as Senator Nelson W. Aldrich of Rhode Island and House Speaker Joseph Cannon of Illinois, championed this ideology. Outside of Washington, D.C., tycoons like J. P. Morgan and John D. Rockefeller insisted that progress would result only from maintaining the profit incentive and an unfettered economy.

Moreover, prominent Progressives were not "progressive" in every respect. Their attempts to Americanize immigrants reflected prejudice as well as naiveté. As governor, Hiram Johnson promoted discrimination against Japanese Americans, and whether Progressive or not, most southern governors, such as Smith, Comer, Charles B. Aycock of North Carolina, and James K. Vardaman of Mississippi, rested their power on appeals to white supremacy. In the South, the exclusion of blacks from voting through poll taxes, literacy requirements, and other means meant that electoral reforms affected only whites—and then only white men with enough cash and schooling to satisfy voting prerequisites. Settlement houses in northern cities kept blacks and whites apart in separate programs and buildings.

Progressive reformers generally occupied the center of the ideological spectrum. Moderate, socially aware, sometimes contradictory, they believed on one hand that laissez faire was obsolete and on the other that a radical departure from free enterprise was dangerous. Like Thomas Jefferson, they expressed faith in the conscience and will of the people; like Alexander Hamilton, they desired a strong central government to act in the interest of conscience. Their goals were both idealistic and realistic. As minister-reformer Walter Rauschenbusch wrote, "We shall demand perfection and never expect to get it."

## GOVERNMENT AND LEGISLATIVE REFORM

Mistrust of tyranny had traditionally prompted Americans to believe that democratic government should be small, should interfere in private affairs only in unique circumstances, and should withdraw when balance had been restored. But in the late 1800s this viewpoint weakened when problems resulting from economic change seemed to overwhelm individual effort. Corporations pursued government aid and protection for their enterprises. Discontented farmers sought government regulation of railroads and other monopolistic businesses. And city dwellers, accustomed to favors performed by political machines, came to expect government to act on their behalf. Before 1900, state governments had been concerned largely with railroads and economic growth; the federal government had focused primarily on tariffs and the currency. But after 1900, issues of regulation, both economic and social, demanded attention. More than in the past, public opinion, roused by muckraking media, influenced change.

Middle-class Progressive reformers rejected the laissez-faire principle of government. Increasingly aware that a simple, inflexible government was inadequate in a complex industrial age, they reasoned that public authority needed to counteract inefficiency and exploitation. But before activists could effectively use such power, they would have to reclaim government from politicians whose greed they believed had soiled the democratic system. Thus eliminating corruption from government was one central thrust of Progressive activity.

## Restructuring Government

Prior to the Progressive era, reformers had attacked corruption in cities by trying to regulate government through such structural reforms as civil service, nonpartisan elections, and close scrutiny of public expenditures. After 1900, campaigns to make cities run more efficiently resulted in city-manager and commission forms of government, in which urban officials were chosen for professional expertise rather than for political connections. But reforming city management was not sufficient to realize the improvements reformers sought, and they turned their attention to state and federal governments for support.

At the state level, faith in a reform-minded executive prompted Progressives to support a number of skillful and charismatic governors. In the West, California's Hiram Johnson, who attacked business and political corruption, was an example of such a governor. With Johnson's inspiration, California passed laws regulating utilities and child labor, as well as workers' compensation for state employees. In the South, Georgia's Hoke Smith achieved railroad regulation, juvenile courts, and better-funded public education—though he also supported voting restrictions that disfranchised blacks.

Wisconsin's Robert M. La Follette was one of the most dynamic Progressive governors. A small-town lawyer, La Follette rose through the state Republican Party to become

▲ Robert M. La Follette (1855–1925) was one of the most dynamic of Progressive politicians. As governor of Wisconsin, he sponsored a program of political reform and business regulation known as the Wisconsin Plan. In 1906 he entered the U.S. Senate and continued to champion Progressive reform. The National Progressive Republican League, which La Follette founded in 1911, became the core of the Progressive Party. *(State Historical Society of Wisconsin)*

governor in 1900. In office, he initiated a multipronged reform program, including direct primaries, more equitable taxes, and regulation of railroads. He also appointed commissions staffed by experts, who supplied him with data that he used in speeches to arouse support for his policies. After three terms as governor, La Follette became a U.S. senator and carried his ideals into national politics. "Battling Bob" displayed a rare ability to approach reform scientifically while still exciting people with moving rhetoric. His goal, he proclaimed, was "not to 'smash' corporations, but to drive them out of politics, and then to treat them exactly the same as other people are treated."

Crusades against corrupt politics made the system more democratic. By 1916 all but three states had direct primaries, and many had adopted the initiative, referendum, and recall. Political reformers achieved a major goal in 1913 with adoption of the Seventeenth Amendment to the Constitution, which provided for direct election of U.S. senators, replacing election by state legislatures. Such measures, however, did not always achieve the desired ends. Party bosses, better organized and more experienced than reformers, were still able to control elections, and special-interest groups spent large sums to influence the voting. Moreover, courts usually aided rather than reined in entrenched power.

State laws resulting from Progressive efforts to improve labor conditions had more effect than did political reforms, because middle-class and working-class reformers could agree on the need for them. At the instigation of middle-class/working-class coalitions, many states enacted factory inspection laws, and by 1916 nearly two-thirds of the states required compensation for victims of industrial accidents. An alliance of labor and humanitarian groups induced some legislatures to grant aid to mothers with dependent children. Under pressure from the National Child Labor Committee, nearly every state set a minimum age for employment (varying from twelve to sixteen) and limited the hours that employers could make children work. Labor laws did not work perfectly, however. They seldom provided for the close inspection of factories that enforcement required. And families that needed extra income evaded child labor restrictions by falsifying their children's ages to employers.

Several middle- and working-class groups also united behind measures that restricted working hours for women and that aided retirees. After the Supreme Court, in *Muller v. Oregon*, upheld Oregon's ten-hour limit in 1908, more states passed laws protecting female workers. Meanwhile, in 1914 efforts of the American Association for Old Age Security showed signs of success when Arizona established old-age pensions. Judges struck down the law, but demand for pensions continued, and in the 1920s many states enacted laws to provide for needy elderly people.

Opening up government and protecting women and children brought together reform coalitions. But when an issue involved regulating behavior, such as drinking habits and sexual conduct, differences emerged. One group of reformers used both morality and social control as a basis for their agenda. For example, the Anti-Saloon League, formed in 1893, intensified the long-standing campaign against drunkenness and its costs to society. This organization allied with the

**Labor Reform**

**Prohibition**

Woman's Christian Temperance Union (founded in 1874) to publicize alcoholism's role in causing liver disease and other health problems. The League was especially successful in shifting attention from the immorality of drunkenness to using law enforcement to break the alleged link between the drinking that saloons encouraged and the accidents, poverty, and poor productivity that were consequences of drinking.

Against the wishes of many working-class residents who valued individual freedom, the war on saloons prompted many states and localities to restrict liquor consumption. By 1900 almost one-fourth of the nation's population lived in "dry" communities (which prohibited the sale of liquor). But consumption of alcohol increased after 1900 as a result of the influx of immigrants whose cultures included social drinking, convincing prohibitionists that a nationwide ban was the best solution. They enlisted support from such notables as Supreme Court Justice Louis D. Brandeis and former president William Howard Taft, and in 1918 Congress passed the Eighteenth Amendment (ratified in 1919 and implemented in 1920), outlawing the manufacture, sale, and transportation of intoxicating liquors. Not all prohibitionists were Progressive reformers, and not all Progressives were prohibitionists. Nevertheless, the Eighteenth Amendment can be seen as an expression of the Progressive goal to protect family and workplace through reform legislation.

Moral outrage erupted when muckraking journalists charged that international gangs were kidnapping young women and forcing them into pros-

||||||||||||||||||||||||||||||||

**Controlling
Prostitution**

titution, a practice called white slavery. Accusations were exaggerated, but they alarmed some moralists who falsely perceived a link between immigration and prostitution, and who feared that prostitutes were producing genetically inferior children. Although some women voluntarily entered "the profession" because it offered much higher income than any other form of work available to them and other women occasionally performed sexual favors in return for male gifts, those fearful about the social consequences of prostitution prodded governments to investigate and pass corrective legislation. The Chicago Vice Commission, for example, undertook a "scientific" survey of dance halls and illicit sex, and published its findings as *The Social Evil in Chicago* in 1911. The report concluded that poverty, gullibility, and desperation drove women into prostitution.

Such investigations found rising numbers of prostitutes but failed to prove that criminal organizations deliberately lured women into "the trade." Reformers nonetheless believed they could attack prostitution by punishing both those who promoted it and those who practiced it. In 1910 Congress passed the White Slave Traffic Act (Mann Act), prohibiting interstate and international transportation of a woman for immoral purposes. By 1915 nearly every state had outlawed brothels and solicitation of sex. Such laws ostensibly protected young women from exploitation, but in reality they failed to address the more serious problem of sexual violence that women suffered at the hands of family members, presumed friends, and employers.

Like prohibition, the Mann Act reflected growing sentiment that government could improve behavior by restricting it. Middle-class reformers believed that the source of evil was neither original sin nor human nature but the social environment. If evil was created by human will, it followed that it could be eradicated by human effort. Intervention in the form of laws could help create a heaven on earth. The new working classes, however, resented such meddling as unwarranted attempts to control them. Thus, when Chicagoans voted on a referendum to make their city dry shortly before the Eighteenth Amendment was passed, three-fourths of the city's immigrant voters opposed it, and the measure went down to defeat.

## NEW IDEAS IN SOCIAL INSTITUTIONS

In addition to legislative paths, reform impulses opened new vistas in the ways social institutions were organized. Preoccupation with efficiency and scientific management infiltrated the realms of education, law, religion, and the social sciences. Darwin's theory of evolution had challenged traditional beliefs in a God-created world; immigration had created complex social diversity; and technology had made old habits of production obsolete. Thoughtful people in several professions grappled with how to respond to the new era yet preserve what was best from the past.

Changing attitudes about childhood and new patterns of school attendance altered approaches to education.

||||||||||||||||||||||||||||||||

**John Dewey
and Progressive
Education**

As late as 1870, when families needed children at home to do farm work, Americans attended school for an average of only a few months a year for four years. By 1900, however, the urban-industrial economy and its expanding middle class had helped to create a more widespread appreciation of children's innocence and advanced the goal of sheltering youngsters from the dangers of society by channeling them toward a protected physical and emotional growth. Those concerned about children's development believed that youngsters required particular forms of education and other activity appropriate to a child's biological and cultural development.

Thus schools shared with, and even replaced, the home as the best environment for promoting children's development. Educators argued that schooling produced better adult citizens and workers. In the 1870s and 1880s, states passed laws that required children to attend school to age fourteen, and swelling populations of immigrant and migrant children jammed schoolrooms. Meanwhile, the number of public high schools grew from five hundred in 1870 to ten thousand in 1910. By 1900 educational reformers, such as psychologist G. Stanley Hall and philosopher John Dewey, asserted that schools needed to prepare children for a modern world. They insisted that personal development should be the focus of the curriculum and the school the center of the community.

Progressive education, based on Dewey's *The School and Society* (1899) and *Democracy and Education* (1916), was a uniquely American phenomenon. Dewey believed that learning should involve real-life problems and that children should be taught to use intelligence and ingenuity as instruments for controlling their environments. From kindergarten through high school, Dewey asserted, children needed to learn through direct experience, not by rote memorization. Dewey and his wife, Alice, put these ideas into practice in their own Laboratory School located at the University of Chicago.

A more practical curriculum became the driving principle behind reform in higher education as well. Previously, the purpose of American colleges and universities had resembled that of European counterparts: to train a select few for careers in law, medicine, and religion. But in the late 1800s, institutions of higher learning multiplied as states eager to establish their own universities used federal funds from the Morrill Acts of 1862 and 1890 to establish new schools. The number of private institutions also expanded. Between 1870 and 1910, the total of American colleges and universities grew from 563 to nearly 1,000. Curricula expanded as educators sought to make learning more appealing and to keep pace with technological and social changes. Harvard University, under President Charles W. Eliot, pioneered in substituting electives for required courses and experimenting with new teaching methods. The University of Wisconsin

## Growth of Colleges and Universities

▲ These members of the University of Michigan's Class of 1892 represent the student body of a publicly funded college in the late nineteenth century. With their varied curricula, inclusion of women, and increasing enrollments, such schools transformed American higher education in the Progressive era. *(University of Michigan)*

▲ "Business Education at the National Cash Register Company." John H. Patterson, founder of the National Cash Register Company, innovated educational reform of a different sort by promoting the training of salesmen. A social progressive who believed in providing his factories with good light and ventilation, Patterson also pioneered the use of flip charts, seen in this photograph, as means of representing business conditions and of educating his employees. Many of the most forward-looking business executives of the early twentieth century had worked for and learned from Patterson. *(NCR Archive at Dayton History)*

and other state universities achieved distinction in new areas of study, such as political science, economics, and sociology. Many schools, private and public, considered athletics vital to a student's growth, and men's intercollegiate sports became a permanent feature of student life as well as a source of school pride.

Southern states, in keeping with separate-but-equal policies, created segregated land-grant colleges for blacks in addition to institutions for whites. Aided by land-grant funds, such schools as Alabama Agricultural and Mechanical University (A&M), South Carolina State University, and the A&M College for the Colored Race (North Carolina) opened their doors. Separate was a more accurate

description of these institutions than equal. African Americans continued to suffer from inferior educational opportunities. Nevertheless, African American men and women found intellectual stimulation in all-black colleges and hoped to use their education to promote the uplifting of their race.

As higher education expanded, so did female enrollments. Between 1890 and 1910, the number of women in colleges and universities swelled from 56,000 to 140,000. Of these, 106,000 attended coeducational institutions (mostly state universities); the rest enrolled in women's colleges, such as Wellesley and Barnard. By 1920, 283,000 women attended college, accounting for 47 percent of total enrollment. But discrimination lingered in admissions and curriculum policies. Women were encouraged (indeed, they usually sought) to take home economics and education courses rather than science and mathematics, and most medical schools, including Harvard and Yale, refused to admit women or imposed stringent quotas. Separate women's medical schools, such as the Women's Medical College of Philadelphia and Women's Medical College of Chicago, trained numerous female physicians, but most of these schools were absorbed or put out of business by larger institutions dominated by men.

American educators justifiably congratulated themselves for increasing enrollments and making instruction more meaningful. By 1920, 78 percent of children between ages five and seventeen were enrolled in public schools; another 8 percent attended private and parochial schools. These figures represented a huge increase over 1870 attendance rates. There were 600,000 college and graduate students in 1920, compared with only 52,000 in 1870. Yet few people looked beyond the numbers to assess how well schools were doing their job. Critical analysis seldom tested the faith that schools could promote equality as well as personal growth and responsible citizenship.

The legal profession also embraced new emphases on experience and scientific principles. Harvard law professor

**Progressive Legal Thought**

Roscoe Pound and Oliver Wendell Holmes Jr., associate justice of the Supreme Court between 1902 and 1932, led the attack on the traditional view of law as universal and unchanging. "The life of the law," wrote Holmes, sounding like Dewey, "has not been logic; it has been experience." The opinion that law should reflect society's needs challenged the practice of invoking inflexible legal precedents which often obstructed social legislation. Louis D. Brandeis, a lawyer who later joined Holmes on the Supreme Court, insisted that judges' opinions be based on scientifically gathered information about social realities. Using this approach, Brandeis collected extensive data on harmful effects of long working hours to convince the Supreme Court, in *Muller v. Oregon* (1908), to uphold Oregon's ten-hour limit to women's workday.

New legal thinking provoked some resistance. Judges raised on laissez-faire economics and strict interpretation of the Constitution overturned laws that Progressives thought necessary for effective reform. Thus, despite Holmes's forceful dissent, in 1905 the Supreme Court, in *Lochner v. New York,* revoked a New York law limiting bakers' working hours. In this and similar cases, the Court's majority argued that the Fourteenth Amendment protected an individual's right to make contracts without

government interference. Judges weakened other federal regulations by invoking the Tenth Amendment, which prohibited the federal government from interfering in matters reserved to the states.

Courts did uphold some regulatory measures, particularly those intended to safeguard life and limb. A string of decisions, beginning with *Holden v. Hardy* (1898), in which the Supreme Court sustained a Utah law regulating working hours for miners, confirmed the use of state police power to protect health, safety, and morals. Judges also affirmed federal police power and Congress's authority over interstate commerce by upholding federal legislation, such as the Pure Food and Drug Act, the Meat Inspection Act, and the Mann Act. In these instances citizens' welfare took precedence over the Tenth Amendment.

But the concept of general welfare often conflicted with the concept of equal rights when local majorities imposed their will on minorities. Even if one agreed that laws should address society's needs, whose needs should prevail? The United States was (and remains) a mixed nation; gender, race, religion, and ethnicity deeply influenced law. In many localities a native-born Protestant majority imposed Bible reading in public schools (offending Catholics and Jews), required businesses to close on Sundays, limited women's rights, restricted religious practices of Mormons and other groups, prohibited interracial marriage, and enforced racial segregation. Justice Holmes asserted that laws should be made for "people of fundamentally differing views," but fitting such laws to a nation of so many different interest groups has sparked debates that continue to this day.

Social science—the study of society and its institutions—experienced changes similar to those affecting education and law. In economics, a

**Social Science**

group of scholars used statistics to argue that laws governing economic relationships were not timeless. Instead, they claimed, theory should reflect prevailing social conditions. Richard T. Ely of Johns Hopkins University and the University of Wisconsin, for example, argued that poverty and impersonality resulting from industrialization required intervention by "the united efforts of Church, state, and science." Similarly, a new breed of sociologists led by Lester Ward, Albion Small, and Edward A. Ross agreed, adding that citizens should actively work to cure social ills rather than passively wait for problems to solve themselves.

Meanwhile, historians Frederick Jackson Turner, Charles A. Beard, and Vernon L. Parrington examined the past to explain present American society. Beard, like other Progressives, believed that the Constitution was a flexible document amenable to growth and change, not a sacred code imposed by wise forefathers. His *Economic Interpretation of the Constitution* (1913) argued that a group of merchants and business-oriented lawyers created the Constitution to defend private property. If the Constitution had served special interests in one age, it could be changed to serve broader interests in another age.

In the field of public health, organizations such as the National Consumers League (NCL) joined physicians and social scientists to bring about some of the most far-reaching Progressive reforms. Founded by Florence Kelley in 1899, the NCL pursued activities including protection of female and child laborers, and elimination of potential health hazards. After aiding in the success of *Muller v. Oregon,* the organization became active in sponsoring court cases on behalf of women workers and joined reform lawyers Louis Brandeis and Felix Frankfurter in support of these cases. Local branches united with women's clubs to advance consumer protection measures, such as the licensing of food vendors and inspection of dairies. They also urged city governments to fund neighborhood clinics that provided health education and medical care to the poor.

The Social Gospel served as a response to Social Darwinism, the application of biological natural selection and survival of the fittest to human interactions. But another movement

**Eugenics**

that flourished during the Progressive era, eugenics, sought to apply Darwinian principles to society in a more intrusive way. The brainchild of Francis Galton, an English statistician and cousin of Charles Darwin, eugenics was more of a social philosophy than a science. It rested on the belief that human character and habits could be inherited. If good traits could be inherited, so could bad traits, such as criminality, insanity, and feeblemindedness. Just as some Progressives believed that society had an obligation to intervene and erase poverty and injustice, eugenicists believed that society had an obligation to prevent the reproduction of the mentally defective and the criminally inclined, by preventing such people from marrying and, in extreme cases, by sterilizing them. Inevitably such ideas targeted immigrants and people of color. Supported by such American notables as Alexander Graham Bell, Margaret Sanger, and W. E. B. Du Bois, eugenics was discredited, especially after it became a linchpin of Nazi racial policies, but modern genetic engineering has evolved from some of the eugenics legacy.

Some reformers endorsed eugenics, but others saw immigration restriction as a more acceptable way of controlling the composition of American society. Both a eugenicist and a Progressive (in his ideas about conservation),

Madison Grant's *The Passing of the Great Race* (1916) strongly bolstered theories that immigrants from southern and eastern Europe threatened to weaken American society because they were inferior mentally and morally to earlier Nordic immigrants. Such ideas prompted many people, including some Progressives, to conclude that new laws should curtail the influx of Poles, Italians, Jews, and other eastern and southern Europeans, as well as Asians. Efforts to limit immigration reached fruition in the 1920s, when restrictive legislation drastically closed the door to "new" immigrants.

Thus a new breed of men and women pressed for political reform and institutional change in the two decades before the First World War. Concerned middle-class professionals, confident that new ways of thinking could bring about progress, and representatives of working classes, who experienced social problems first-hand, these people helped broaden government's role to meet the needs of a mature industrial society. But their questioning of prevailing assumptions also unsettled conventional attitudes toward race and gender.

## CHALLENGES TO RACIAL AND SEXUAL DISCRIMINATION

The white male reformers of the Progressive era dealt primarily with issues of politics and institutions, and in so doing ignored issues directly affecting former slaves, non-white immigrants, Indians, and women. Yet activists within these groups caught the Progressive spirit, challenged entrenched ideas and customs, and made strides toward their own advancement. Their efforts, however, posed a dilemma. Should women and nonwhites aim to imitate white men, with white men's values as well as their rights? Or was there something unique about racial and sexual cultures that they should preserve at the risk of sacrificing broader gains? Both groups fluctuated between attraction to and rejection of the culture that excluded them.

In 1900 nine-tenths of African Americans lived in the South, where repressive Jim Crow laws had multiplied in the 1880s and 1890s (see page 574). Denied legal and voting rights, and officially segregated in almost all walks of life, southern blacks faced constant exclusion. In 1910 only 8,000 out of 970,000 high-school-age blacks in the South were enrolled in high schools. And blacks met with relentless violence from lynching and countless acts of intimidation. In response, many African Americans moved northward in the 1880s, accelerating their migration after 1900. The conditions they found in places like Chicago,

**Continued Discrimination for African Americans**

Cleveland, and Detroit represented relative improvement over rural sharecropping, but job discrimination, inferior schools, and segregated housing still prevailed.

African American leaders differed sharply over how—and whether—to pursue assimilation in their new environments. In the wake of emancipation, ex-slave Frederick Douglass urged "ultimate assimilation through self-assertion, and on no other terms." Others favored separation from white society and supported emigration to Africa or the establishment of all-black communities in Oklahoma Territory and Kansas. Others advocated militancy, believing, as one writer stated, "Our people must die to be saved and in dying must take as many along with them as it is possible to do with the aid of firearms and all other weapons."

Most blacks could neither escape nor conquer white society. They sought other routes to economic and social improvement. Self-help, a strategy articulated by educator Booker T. Washington, offered one popular alternative. Born into slavery in Virginia in 1856, Washington obtained an education and in 1881

## Booker T. Washington and Self-Help

founded Tuskegee Institute, an all-black vocational school, in Alabama. There he developed a philosophy that blacks' best hopes for assimilation lay in at least temporarily accommodating to whites. Rather than fighting for political rights, Washington counseled African Americans to work hard, acquire property, and prove they were worthy of respect. Washington voiced his views in a speech at the Atlanta Exposition in 1895. "Dignify and glorify common labor," he urged, in what became known as the Atlanta Compromise. "Agitation of questions of racial equality is the extremest folly." Envisioning a society where blacks and whites would remain apart but share similar goals, Washington observed that "in all things that are purely social we can be as separate as the fingers, yet one as the hand in all matters essential to mutual progress."

Whites welcomed Washington's accommodation policy because it advised patience and reminded black people to stay in their place. Because he said what they wanted to hear, white businesspeople, reformers, and politicians chose to regard Washington as representing all African Americans. Yet though Washington endorsed a separate-but-equal policy, he projected a subtle racial pride that would find more direct expression in black nationalism

▲ Booker T. Washington's Tuskegee Institute helped train young African Americans in useful crafts, such as shoemaking and shoe repair, as illustrated here. At the same time, however, Washington's intentions and the Tuskegee curriculum reinforced what many whites wanted to believe: that blacks were unfit for anything except manual labor. *(Tuskegee University Library)*

in the twentieth century, when some African Americans would advocate control of their own businesses and schools. Washington never argued that blacks were inferior to whites; rather, he asserted that they could enhance their dignity through self-improvement.

Some blacks, however, concluded that Washington endorsed second-class citizenship. His southern-based philosophy did not appeal to educated northern African Americans like newspaper editors William Monroe Trotter and T. Thomas Fortune. In 1905 a group of "anti-Bookerites" convened near Niagara Falls and pledged militant pursuit of such rights as unrestricted voting, economic opportunity, integration, and equality before the law. Representing the Niagara movement was W. E. B. Du Bois, an outspoken critic of the Atlanta Compromise.

## W. E. B. Du Bois and the "Talented Tenth"

A New Englander and the first black to receive a Ph.D. degree from Harvard, Du Bois was both a Progressive and a member of the black elite. He held an undergraduate degree from all-black Fisk University and studied in Germany, where he learned about scientific investigation. While a faculty member at Atlanta University, Du Bois compiled fact-filled sociological studies of black urban life and wrote poetically in support of civil rights. He treated Washington politely but could not accept accommodation. "The way for a people to gain their reasonable rights," Du Bois asserted, "is not by voluntarily throwing them away." Instead, blacks must agitate for what was rightfully theirs. Du Bois believed that an intellectual vanguard of cultured, educated blacks, the "Talented Tenth," could use their skill to pursue racial equality. In 1909 he joined with white liberals who also were discontented with Washington's accommodationism to form the National Association for the Advancement of Colored People (NAACP). The organization aimed to end racial discrimination, prevent lynching, and obtain voting rights through legal redress in the courts. By 1914 the NAACP had fifty branch offices and six thousand members.

Within the NAACP and in other ways, African Americans struggled with questions about identity and their place in white society. Du Bois voiced this dilemma poignantly, observing that "one ever feels his twoness—an American, a Negro, two souls, two thoughts, two unreconciled strivings, two warring ideals in one dark body." Somehow blacks had to reconcile that "twoness" by combining racial pride with national identity. As Du Bois wrote in 1903, a black "would not Africanize America, for America has too much to teach the world and Africa. He would not bleach his Negro soul in a flood of white Americanism, for he knows that Negro blood has a message for the world. He simply wishes to make it possible for a man to be both a Negro and an American." That simple wish would haunt the nation for decades to come.

The dilemma of identity vexed American Indians, but it had an added tribal dimension. Since the 1880s, most Native American reformers had belonged to white-led organizations.

## Society of American Indians

In 1911, however, some middle-class Indians formed their own association, the Society of American Indians (SAI), to work for better education, civil rights, and healthcare. It also sponsored "American Indian Days" to cultivate pride and offset the images of savage peoples promulgated in Wild West shows.

The SAI's emphasis on racial pride, however, was squeezed between pressures for assimilation on one side and tribal allegiance on the other. Its small membership did not fully represent the diverse and unconnected Indian nations, and its attempt to establish a unifying governing body fizzled. Some tribal governments no longer existed to select representatives, and most SAI members simply promoted their self-interest. At the same time, the goal of achieving acceptance in white society proved elusive. Individual hard work was not enough to overcome white prejudice and condescension, and attempts to redress grievances through legal action faltered for lack of funds. Ultimately, the SAI had little effect on poverty-stricken Indians who seldom knew that the organization even existed. Torn by internal disputes, the association folded in the early 1920s.

Challenges to established social assumptions also raised questions of identity among women. The ensuing quandaries resembled those faced by racial minorities: What tactics should women use to achieve rights? What should be women's role in society? Should they try to achieve equality within a male-dominated society? Or should they assert particular female qualities to create a new place for themselves within society?

## "The Woman Movement"

The answers that women found involved a subtle but important shift in their politics. Before 1910, crusaders for women's rights referred to themselves as "the woman movement." This label applied to middle-class women who strived to move beyond the household into higher education and paid professions. Like African American and Indian leaders, women argued that legal and voting rights were indispensable to such moves. They based their claims on the theory that women's special, even superior, traits as guardians of family and morality would humanize all of society. Settlement-house founder Jane Addams, for example, endorsed woman suffrage by asking, "If women have in any sense been responsible for the gentler side of life which softens and blurs some of its harsher conditions, may not they have a duty to perform in our American cities?"

Women's clubs represented a unique dimension of the woman movement. Originating as literary and educational

### Women's Clubs

organizations, women's clubs began taking stands on public affairs in the late nineteenth century. Because female activists were generally barred from holding public office (except in a few western states), they asserted traditional female responsibilities for home and family as the rationale for reforming society through an enterprise that historians have called social housekeeping. Rather than advocate reforms like trustbusting and direct primaries, female reformers worked for factory inspection, regulation of children's and women's labor, improved housing and education, and consumer protection.

Such efforts were not confined to white women. Mostly excluded from white women's clubs, African American women had their own club movement, including the Colored Women's Federation, which sought to establish a training school for "colored girls." Founded in 1895, the National Association of Colored Women was the nation's first African American social service organization; it concentrated on establishing nurseries, kindergartens, and retirement homes. Black women also developed reform organizations within Black Baptist and African Methodist Episcopal churches.

Around 1910 some of those concerned with women's place in society began using the term *feminism* to represent their ideas. Whereas the

### Feminism

woman movement spoke generally of moral purity and duty to society, feminists emphasized women's rights and self-development as key to economic and sexual independence. Charlotte Perkins Gilman, a major figure in the movement, denounced Victorian notions of womanhood and articulated feminist goals in her numerous writings. Her book *Women and Economics* (1898), for example, declared that domesticity and female innocence were obsolete ,and attacked men's monopoly on economic opportunity. Arguing that paid employees should handle domestic chores, such as cooking, cleaning, and childcare, Gilman asserted that modern women must have access to and take jobs in industry and the professions.

Feminists also supported a single standard of behavior for men and women, and several feminists joined the birth-

▲ The rise of the settlement-house movement and of the Visiting Nurse Association provided young middle-class women with opportunities to aid inner-city working-class neighborhoods and formed the basis of the social work profession. Here a group of visiting nurses prepares to apply their medical training to the disadvantaged.

*(Corbis-Bettmann)*

### Margaret Sanger's Crusade

control movement led by Margaret Sanger. A former visiting nurse who believed in women's rights to sexual pleasure and to determine when to have a child, Sanger helped reverse state and federal "Comstock laws"—named after a nineteenth-century New York moral reformer—which had banned publication and distribution of information about sex and contraception. Although Sanger later gained acceptance, her speeches and actions initially aroused opposition from those who saw birth control as a threat to family and morality. Sanger persevered and in 1921 formed the American Birth Control League, enlisting physicians and social workers to convince judges to allow distribution of birth-control information. Most states still prohibited the sale of contraceptives, but Sanger succeeded in introducing the issue into public debate.

**Map 21.1    Woman Suffrage Before 1920**

Before Congress passed and the states ratified the Nineteenth Amendment, woman suffrage already existed, but mainly in the West. Several midwestern states allowed women to vote only in presidential elections, but legislatures in the South and Northeast generally refused such rights until forced to do so by constitutional amendment.

||||||||||||||||||||||||||||

## Woman Suffrage

During the Progressive era, a generation of feminists, represented by Harriot Stanton Blatch, daughter of nineteenth-century suffragist Elizabeth Cady Stanton, carried on women's battle for the vote. Blatch had broad experience in the campaign to obtain the vote for women, having accompanied her mother on speaking tours at home and abroad, and participated in the British women's suffrage movement. In America, Blatch's chief goal was improvement of women's working conditions. She joined the Women's Trade Union League and tried hard to recruit working women into the movement by founding the Equality League of Self Supporting Women in 1907. Declaring that every woman worked, whether she performed paid labor or unpaid housework, Blatch believed that all women's efforts contributed to society's betterment. In her view, achievement rather than wealth and refinement was the best criterion for public status. Thus women should exercise the vote,

not to enhance the power of elites, but to promote and protect women's economic roles.

By the early twentieth century, suffragists had achieved some successes. Nine states, all in the West, allowed women to vote in state and local elections by 1912, and women continued to press for national suffrage (see Map 21.1). Their tactics ranged from moderate but persistent letter-writing and publications of the National American Woman Suffrage Association, led by Carrie Chapman Catt, to spirited meetings and militant marches of the National Woman's Party, led by Alice Paul and Harriot Stanton Blatch. All these activities heightened public awareness. More decisive, however, was women's service during the First World War as factory laborers, medical volunteers, and municipal workers. By convincing legislators that women could shoulder public responsibilities, women's wartime contributions gave final impetus to passage of the national suffrage amendment (the Nineteenth) in 1920.

In spite of these accomplishments, the activities of women's clubs, feminists, and suffragists failed to create an interest group united or powerful enough to overcome men's political, economic, and social control. During the Progressive era, the resolve and energy of leaders like Blatch, Paul, and Catt helped clarify issues that concerned women and finally won women the right to vote, but that victory was only a step, not a conclusion. Discrimination in employment, education, and the law continued to shadow women for decades to come. As feminist Crystal Eastman observed in the aftermath of the suffrage crusade: "Men are saying perhaps, 'Thank God, this everlasting women's fight is over!' But women, if I know them, are saying, 'Now at last we can begin.' . . . Now they can say what they are really after, in common with all the rest of the struggling world, is freedom."

## THEODORE ROOSEVELT AND THE REVIVAL OF THE PRESIDENCY

The Progressive era's theme of reform in politics, institutions, and social relations drew attention to government, especially the federal government, as the foremost agent of change. Although the federal government had notable accomplishments during the preceding Gilded Age, its role had been mainly to support rather than to control economic expansion, as when it transferred western public lands and resources to private ownership. Then, in September 1901, the political climate suddenly shifted. The assassination of President William McKinley by anarchist Leon Czolgosz vaulted Theodore Roosevelt, the young vice president (he was forty-two), into the White House. As governor of New York, Roosevelt had angered state Republican bosses by showing sympathy for regulatory legislation, so they rid themselves of him by pushing him into national politics. Little did they anticipate that they provided the steppingstone for the nation's most forceful president since Lincoln, one who bestowed the office with much of its twentieth-century character.

**Theodore Roosevelt**

As a youth Roosevelt suffered from asthma and nearsightedness. Driven throughout his life by an obsession to overcome his physical limitations, he exerted what he and his contemporaries called "manliness," meaning a zest for action and display of courage in a "strenuous life." In his teens he became an expert marksman and horseman, and later competed on Harvard's boxing and wrestling teams. In the 1880s he went to live on a Dakota ranch, where he roped cattle and brawled with cowboys. Descended from a Dutch aristocratic family, Roosevelt had the wealth to indulge in such pursuits. But he also inherited a sense of civic responsibility which guided him into a career in public service. He served three terms in the New York State Assembly, sat on the federal Civil Service Commission, served as New York City's police commissioner, and was assistant secretary of the navy. In these offices Roosevelt earned a reputation as a combative, politically crafty leader. In 1898 he thrust himself into the Spanish-American War by organizing a

◀ Theodore Roosevelt (1858–1919) liked to think of himself as a great outdoorsman. He loved most the rugged countryside and believed that he and his country should serve as examples of "manliness."

*(California Museum of Photography, University of California)*

volunteer cavalry brigade, called the Rough Riders, to fight in Cuba. Although his dramatic act had little impact on the war's outcome, it excited public imagination and made him a media hero.

When he assumed the presidency, Roosevelt carried his youthful exuberance into the White House. (A British diplomat once quipped, "You must always remember that the president is about 6.") Considering himself a Progressive, he concurred with his allies that a small, uninvolved government would not suffice in the industrial era. Instead, economic progress necessitated a government powerful enough to guide national affairs broadly. "A simple and poor society," he observed, "can exist as a democracy on the basis of sheer individualism. But a rich and complex society cannot so exist." Especially in economic matters, he wanted the government to act as an umpire, deciding when big business was good and when it was bad. But his brash patriotism and dislike of qualities that he considered effeminate also recalled earlier eras of unbridled expansion, when raw power prevailed in social and economic affairs.

The federal regulation of business that characterized twentieth-century American history began with Roosevelt's presidency. Roosevelt

### Regulation of Trusts

turned his attention first to big corporations, where consolidation had created massive, monopolistic trusts. Although labeled a trustbuster, Roosevelt actually considered business consolidation an efficient means to achieve material progress. He believed in distinguishing between good and bad trusts, and preventing bad ones from manipulating markets. Thus he instructed the Justice Department to use antitrust laws to prosecute railroad, meatpacking, and oil trusts, which he believed unscrupulously exploited the public. Roosevelt's policy triumphed in 1904 when the Supreme Court, convinced by the government's arguments, ordered the breakup of Northern Securities Company, the huge railroad combination created by J. P. Morgan and his business allies. Roosevelt chose, however, not to attack other trusts, such as U.S. Steel, another of Morgan's creations.

When prosecution of Northern Securities began, Morgan reportedly collared Roosevelt and offered, "If we have done anything wrong, send your man to my man and they can fix it up." The president refused but was more sympathetic to cooperation between business and government than his rebuff might suggest. Rather than prosecute at every turn, he urged the Bureau of Corporations (part of the newly created Department of Labor and Commerce) to

assist companies in merging and expanding. Through investigation and consultation, the administration cajoled businesses to regulate themselves; corporations often cooperated because government regulation helped them operate more efficiently and reduced overproduction.

Roosevelt also supported regulatory legislation, especially after his resounding electoral victory in 1904, in which he won votes from Progressives and businesspeople alike. After a year of wrangling with railroads and their political allies, Roosevelt persuaded Congress to pass the Hepburn Act (1906), which strengthened the Interstate Commerce Commission (ICC) by giving it greater authority to set railroad freight rates and extending that authority over ferries, express companies, storage facilities, and oil pipelines. In the Elkins Act of 1903, Congress had already allowed the ICC to levy heavy fines against railroads and their customers involved in rebates on published shipping rates. The Hepburn Act still allowed courts to overturn ICC decisions, but, in a break from previous laws, it required shippers to prove they were not in violation of regulations, rather than making the government demonstrate violations.

Knowing that the political process made it difficult to achieve full business regulation, Roosevelt showed willingness to compromise on legislation

### Pure Food and Drug Laws

to ensure the purity of food and drugs. For decades reformers had been urging government regulation of processed meat and patent medicines. Public outrage at fraud and adulteration flared in 1906 when Upton Sinclair published *The Jungle*, a fictionalized exposé of Chicago meatpacking plants. Sinclair, a socialist whose objective was to improve working conditions, shocked public sensibilities with his vivid descriptions.

> There would be meat stored in great piles in rooms; and the water from the leaky roofs would drip over it, and thousands of rats would race about on it. It was too dark in these storage places to see well, but a man could run his hand over these piles of meat and sweep off handfuls of dried dung of rats. These rats were a nuisance, and the packers would put poisoned bread out for them; they would die, and then rats, bread, and meat would go into the hoppers together.

After reading the novel, Roosevelt ordered an investigation. Finding Sinclair's descriptions accurate, he supported the Meat Inspection Act, which passed Congress in 1906. Like the Hepburn Act, this law reinforced the principle of government regulation, requiring that government agents monitor the quality of processed meat. But as

▲ Makers of unregulated patent medicines advertised that their products had exorbitant abilities to cure almost any ailment and remedy any unwanted physical condition. Loring's Fat-Ten-U tablets and Loring's Corpula were two such products. The Pure Food and Drug Act of 1906 did not ban these items but tried to prevent manufacturers from making unsubstantiated claims. *(© Bettmann/Corbis)*

were companies required to provide date-of-processing information on canned meats. Most large meatpackers welcomed the legislation anyway, because it helped them force out smaller competitors and restored foreign confidence in American meat products.

The Pure Food and Drug Act (1906) not only prohibited dangerously adulterated foods but also addressed abuses in the patent medicine industry. Makers of tonics and pills had long been making undue claims about their products' effects and liberally using alcohol and narcotics as ingredients. Ads in popular publications, like one for a "Brain Stimulator and Nerve Tonic" in the Sears, Roebuck catalogue, made wildly exaggerated claims. Although the law did not ban such products, it required that labels list the ingredients—a goal consistent with Progressive confidence that if people knew the truth they would make wiser purchases.

Roosevelt's approach to labor resembled his compromises with business over matters of regulation. When the United Mine Workers struck against Pennsylvania coal-mine owners in 1902 over an eight-hour workday and higher pay, the president employed Progressive tactics of investigation and arbitration. Owners, however, stubbornly refused to recognize the union or to arbitrate grievances. As winter approached and fuel shortages threatened, Roosevelt roused public opinion. He threatened to use federal troops to reopen the mines, thus forcing management to accept arbitration of the dispute by a special commission. The commission decided in favor of higher wages and reduced hours. It also required management to deal with grievance committees elected by the miners, but, in a compromise with management, it did not mandate recognition of the union. The decision, according to Roosevelt, provided a "square deal" for all. The settlement also embodied Roosevelt's belief that the president or his representatives should determine which labor demands were legitimate and which were not. In Roosevelt's mind there were good and bad labor organizations (socialists, for example, were bad), just as there were good and bad business combinations.

Although he angered southern congressmen by inviting Booker T. Washington to the White House to discuss

## Race Relations

racial matters, Roosevelt believed in white superiority and was neutral toward blacks only when it helped him politically. An incident in 1906 illustrates this belief. That year, the army transferred a battalion of African American soldiers from Nebraska to Brownsville, Texas. Anglo and Mexican residents resented their presence and banned them from

part of a compromise with meatpackers and their congressional allies, the bill provided that the government, rather than the meatpackers, had to finance inspections, and meatpackers could appeal adverse decisions in court. Nor

parks and businesses. They also protested unsuccessfully to Washington. On August 14, a battle between blacks and whites broke out, and a white man was killed. Brownsville residents blamed the soldiers, but when army investigators asked the troops to identify who had participated in the riot, none of the soldiers cooperated. As a result, however, Roosevelt discharged 167 black soldiers without a hearing or trial, and prevented them from receiving their pay and pensions even though there was no evidence against them. Black leaders were outraged. Roosevelt, hoping that blacks would support Republican candidates in the 1906 elections, had stalled before doing anything. But after the elections, he signed the discharge papers and offered no support when a bill was introduced in the Senate to allow the soldiers to reenlist.

Roosevelt combined the Progressive impulse for efficiency with his love for the outdoors to make lasting contributions to modern resource conservation. Government involvement in this endeavor, especially the establishment of national parks, had begun in the late nineteenth century. Roosevelt advanced the movement by favoring *conservation* over *preservation*. Thus he not only exercised presidential power to protect such natural wonders as the Olympic Peninsula in Washington and the Grand Canyon in Arizona, as well as such human marvels as the native cliff dwellings in Colorado and Arizona, by declaring them national monuments, but also backed a policy of "wise use" of forests, waterways, and other resources in order to conserve them for future generations. Previously, the government had transferred ownership and control of natural resources on federal land to the states and to private interests. Roosevelt, however, believed the most efficient way to use and conserve resources would be for the federal government to retain management over lands that remained in the public domain.

**Conservation**

Roosevelt exerted federal authority over resources in several ways. He created five national parks and fifty-one national bird reservations. He protected waterpower sites from sale to private interests and charged permit fees for users who wanted to produce hydroelectricity. He also supported the Newlands Reclamation Act of 1902, which controlled sale of irrigated federal land in the West (see page 483), and in 1908 he brought the nation's governors to the White House to discuss the efficient use of resources. During his presidency, Roosevelt tripled the number and acreage of national forests, identified a score of national monuments, and supported conservationist Gifford Pinchot in creating the U.S. Forest Service.

As chief forester of the United States and principal advocate of the "wise use" policy, Pinchot promoted scientific management of the nation's woodlands. He obtained Roosevelt's support for transferring management of the national forests from the Interior Department to his bureau in the Agriculture Department, arguing that forests were crops grown on "tree farms." Under his guidance, the Forest Service charged fees for grazing livestock within the national forests, supervised bidding for the cutting of timber, and hired university-trained foresters as federal employees.

**Gifford Pinchot**

Pinchot and Roosevelt did not seek to lock up—preserve—resources permanently; rather, they wanted to guarantee—conserve—their efficient use and make those who profited from using public lands pay the government for that use. Although antigovernment, pro-development attitudes still prevailed in the West, many of those involved in natural-resource exploitation welcomed such a policy because, like regulation of food and drugs, it enabled them to have better control over products, such as when Roosevelt and Pinchot encouraged large lumber companies to engage in reforestation. As a result of new federal policies, the West and its resources fell under the Progressive spell of management.

In 1907 economic crisis forced Roosevelt to compromise his principles and work more closely with big business. That year a financial panic caused by reckless speculation forced some New York banks to close in order to prevent frightened depositors from withdrawing money. J. P. Morgan helped stem the panic by persuading financiers to stop dumping their stocks. In return for Morgan's aid, Roosevelt approved a deal allowing U.S. Steel to absorb the Tennessee Iron and Coal Company—a deal at odds with Roosevelt's trustbusting aims.

**Panic of 1907**

But during his last year in office, Roosevelt retreated from the Republican Party's traditional friendliness to big business. He lashed out at irresponsible "malefactors of great wealth" and supported stronger business regulation and heavier taxation of the rich. Having promised that he would not seek reelection, Roosevelt backed his friend, Secretary of War William Howard Taft, for the Republican nomination in 1908, hoping that Taft would continue his initiatives. Democrats nominated William Jennings Bryan for the third time, but the "Great Commoner" lost again. Aided by Roosevelt, who still enjoyed great popularity, Taft won by 1.25 million popular votes and a 2-to-1 margin in the electoral college.

Early in 1909, Roosevelt traveled to Africa to shoot game, leaving Taft to face political problems that Roosevelt had managed to postpone.

## Taft Administration

Foremost was the tariff; rates had risen to excessive levels. Honoring Taft's pledge to cut rates, the House passed a bill sponsored by Representative Sereno E. Payne that provided for numerous reductions. Protectionists in the Senate prepared, as in the past, to amend the bill and revise rates upward. But Senate Progressives, led by La Follette, attacked the tariff for benefiting special interests, trapping Taft between reformers who claimed to be preserving Roosevelt's antitrust campaign and protectionists who still dominated the Republican Party. In the end, Senator Aldrich restored many of the cuts the Payne bill had made, and Taft—who believed the bill had some positive provisions and understood that extreme cuts were not politically possible—signed what became known as the Payne-Aldrich Tariff (1909). In the eyes of Progressives, Taft had failed the test of filling Roosevelt's shoes.

Progressive and conservative wings of the Republican Party openly split. Soon after the tariff controversy, a group of insurgents in the House, led by Nebraska's George Norris, challenged Speaker "Uncle Joe" Cannon of Illinois, whose power over committee assignments and the scheduling of debates could make or break a piece of legislation. Taft first supported, then abandoned, the insurgents, who nevertheless managed to liberalize procedures by enlarging the influential Rules Committee and removing selection of its members from Cannon's control. In 1910 Taft also angered conservationists by firing Gifford Pinchot, who had protested Secretary of the Interior Richard A. Ballinger's plans to sell Alaskan coal lands and to reduce federal supervision of western waterpower sites, both of which were intended to aid private development.

In reality Taft was as sympathetic to reform as Roosevelt was. He prosecuted more trusts than Roosevelt, expanded national forest reserves, signed the Mann-Elkins Act (1910), which bolstered regulatory powers of the ICC, and supported such labor reforms as shorter work hours and mine safety legislation. The Sixteenth Amendment, which legalized the federal income tax as a permanent part of federal power, and the Seventeenth Amendment, which provided for direct election of U.S. senators, were initiated during Taft's presidency (and ratified in 1913). Like Roosevelt, Taft compromised with big business, but unlike Roosevelt, he lacked the ability to manipulate the public with spirited rhetoric. Roosevelt had expanded presidential power and infused the presidency with vitality.

"I believe in a strong executive," he once asserted. "I believe in power." Taft, by contrast, believed in the strict restraint of law. He had been a successful lawyer and judge, and returned to the bench as chief justice of the United States between 1921 and 1930. His caution and unwillingness to offend disappointed those accustomed to Roosevelt's magnetism.

In 1910, when Roosevelt returned from Africa, he found his party torn and tormented. Reformers, angered by Taft's apparent insensitivity to their causes, formed the National Progressive Republican League and rallied behind Robert La Follette

## Candidates in 1912

for president in 1912, though many hoped Roosevelt would run. Another wing of the party remained loyal to Taft. Disappointed by Taft's performance (particularly his firing of Pinchot), Roosevelt began to speak out. He filled speeches with references to "the welfare of the people" and stronger regulation of business. When La Follette became ill early in 1912, Roosevelt, proclaiming himself fit as a "bull moose," threw his hat into the ring for the Republican presidential nomination.

Taft's supporters controlled the Republican convention and nominated him for a second term. In protest, Roosevelt's supporters bolted the convention to form a third party—the Progressive, or Bull Moose, Party—and nominated the fifty-three-year-old former president. Meanwhile, Democrats took forty-six ballots to select their candidate, New Jersey's Progressive governor Woodrow Wilson. Socialists, by now an organized and growing party, again nominated Eugene V. Debs. The ensuing campaign exposed voters to the most thorough debate on the nature of the American system since 1896.

Central to Theodore Roosevelt's campaign as the Progressive Party's nominee was a scheme called the New Nationalism, a term coined by reform editor Herbert Croly. The

## New Nationalism Versus New Freedom

New Nationalism envisioned an era of national unity in which government would coordinate and regulate economic activity. Echoing his statements in the last years of his presidency, Roosevelt asserted that he would establish regulatory commissions of experts who would protect citizens' interests and ensure wise use of economic power. "The effort at prohibiting all combinations has substantially failed," he claimed. "The way out lies . . . in completely controlling them."

Wilson offered a more idealistic proposal, the "New Freedom," based on ideas of Progressive lawyer Louis Brandeis. Wilson argued that concentrated economic

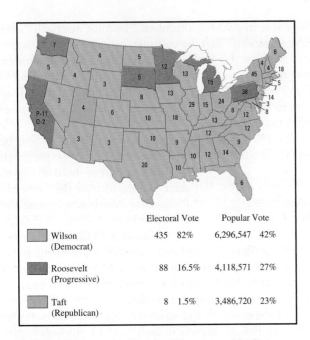

| | Electoral Vote | | Popular Vote | |
|---|---|---|---|---|
| Wilson (Democrat) | 435 | 82% | 6,296,547 | 42% |
| Roosevelt (Progressive) | 88 | 16.5% | 4,118,571 | 27% |
| Taft (Republican) | 8 | 1.5% | 3,486,720 | 23% |

**Map 21.2    Presidential Election, 1912**

Although he had only a minority of the popular votes, Woodrow Wilson captured so many states that he achieved an easy victory in the electoral college.

the popular vote was inconclusive. The victorious Wilson won just 42 percent, though he did capture 435 out of 531 electoral votes (see Map 21.2). Roosevelt received 27 percent of the popular vote. Taft finished third, polling 23 percent of the popular vote and only 8 electoral votes. Debs won 6 percent of the total but no electoral votes. One major outcome was evident, however; three-quarters of the electorate supported some alternative to the view of restrained government that Taft represented. Thus Wilson could proclaim on inauguration day in 1913, "The Nation has been deeply stirred by a solemn passion. . . . The feelings with which we face this new age of right and opportunity sweep across our heartstrings like some air out of God's own presence, where justice and mercy are reconciled and the judge and the brother are one."

## WOODROW WILSON AND THE EXTENSION OF PROGRESSIVE REFORM

The public fondly called Roosevelt "Teddy" and "TR," but Thomas Woodrow Wilson was too aloof ever

**Woodrow Wilson**

to be nicknamed "Woody" or "WW." Born in Virginia in 1856 and raised in the South, Wilson was the son of a Presbyterian minister. He earned a B.A. degree at Princeton University, studied law at the University of Virginia, received a Ph.D. degree from Johns Hopkins University, and became a professor of history, jurisprudence, and political economy. Between 1885 and 1908, he published several respected books on American history and government.

Wilson's manner reflected his background. He exuded none of Roosevelt's brashness, yet he was a superb orator who could inspire intense loyalty with religious imagery and eloquent expressions of American ideals. Wilson's convictions led him early into reform. In 1902 he became president of Princeton and upset tradition with curricular reforms and battles against the university's aristocratic elements. But his racist leanings showed themselves when he refused to admit blacks to the college. In 1910 New Jersey's Democrats, eager for respectability, nominated Wilson for governor. After winning the election, Wilson repudiated the party bosses and promoted Progressive legislation. A poor administrator, he often lost his temper and stubbornly refused to compromise. His accomplishments nevertheless attracted national attention and won him the Democratic nomination for president in 1912.

power threatened individual liberty and that monopolies should be broken up so that the marketplace could become genuinely open. But he would not restore laissez faire. Like Roosevelt, Wilson would enhance government authority to protect and regulate. "Freedom today," he declared, "is something more than being let alone. Without the watchful . . . resolute interference of the government, there can be no fair play between individuals and such powerful institutions as the trust." Wilson stopped short, however, of advocating the cooperation between business and government inherent in Roosevelt's New Nationalism.

Roosevelt and Wilson stood closer together than their rhetoric implied. Despite his faith in experts as regulators, Roosevelt's belief in individual freedom was as strong as Wilson's. And Wilson was not completely hostile to concentrated economic power. Both men supported equality of opportunity (chiefly for white males), conservation of natural resources, fair wages, and social betterment for all. Neither would hesitate to expand government activity through strong personal leadership and bureaucratic reform.

Amid passionate moral pronouncements from Roosevelt and Wilson, as well as a hard-hitting critique from Debs and a low-key defense of conservatism from Taft,

As president, Wilson found it necessary to blend New Freedom competition with New Nationalism regulation;

EXECVTRIX
AVGVSTA
      MINERVA
LVMINARIA!

SALVE
  O WOODRECINA
ATHENA
      PROLETARIA!
PRINCETONIENSIS
      POPVLIOVE
DEA
  TVTORLARIA
          !

▲ Depicted here as a stern Roman consul, Woodrow Wilson was a former professor (his university background is represented here by the scholarly owl at his side) who as president used a stubborn moralism to guide the nation toward his ideals.

*(Picture Research Consultants & Archives)*

## Wilson's Policy on Business Regulation

in so doing, he set the direction of future federal economic policy. The corporate merger movement had made restoration of open competition impossible. Wilson could only try to prevent abuses by expanding government's regulatory powers. He thus supported congressional passage in 1914 of the Clayton Anti-Trust Act and a bill creating the Federal Trade Commission (FTC). The Clayton Act corrected deficiencies of the Sherman Anti-Trust Act of 1890 by outlawing such corporate practices as price discrimination (lowering prices in some regions but not in others) and interlocking directorates (management of two or more competing companies by the same executives). The act also aided labor by exempting unions from its anticombination provision, thereby making peaceful strikes, boycotts, and picketing less vulnerable to government interference. The FTC could investigate companies and issue cease-and-desist orders against unfair practices. Accused companies could appeal FTC orders in court; nevertheless, the FTC represented another step toward consumer protection.

Wilson expanded banking regulation with the Federal Reserve Act (1913), which established the nation's first central banking system since 1836, when the Second Bank of the United States expired. To break the power that banking syndicates like that of J. P. Morgan held over the money supply, the act created twelve district banks to hold reserves of member banks throughout the nation. The district banks, supervised by the Federal Reserve Board, would lend money to member banks at a low interest rate called the discount rate. By adjusting this rate (and thus the amount a bank could afford to borrow), district banks could increase or decrease the amount of money in circulation. In other words, in response to the nation's currency needs, the Federal Reserve Board could loosen or tighten credit, making interest rates fairer, especially for small borrowers.

Wilson and Congress attempted to restore competition in commerce with the Underwood Tariff of 1913. By the

## Tariff and Tax Reform

1910s, prices for some consumer goods had become unnaturally high because tariffs discouraged the importation of cheaper foreign materials and manufactured goods. By reducing or eliminating certain tariff rates, the Underwood Tariff encouraged imports. To replace revenues lost because of tariff reductions, the act levied a graduated income tax on U.S. residents—an option made possible when the Sixteenth Amendment was ratified earlier that year. The tax was tame by today's standards. Incomes under $4,000 were exempt; thus almost all factory workers and farmers escaped taxation. Individuals and corporations earning between $4,000 and $20,000 had to pay a 1 percent tax; thereafter rates rose gradually to a maximum of 6 percent on earnings over $500,000.

The outbreak of the First World War (see Chapter 23) and the approaching presidential election campaign prompted Wilson to support stronger reforms in 1916. To aid farmers, the president backed the Federal Farm Loan Act. This measure created twelve federally supported banks (not to be confused with Federal Reserve banks), which could lend money at moderate interest to farmers who belonged to credit institutions—a watered-down version of the subtreasury plan that Populists had proposed a generation earlier (see pages 578–579). To forestall railroad strikes that might disrupt transportation at a time of national emergency, Wilson in 1916 also pushed passage of the Adamson Act, which mandated eight-hour workdays and time-and-a-half overtime pay for railroad laborers. He pleased Progressives by appointing Brandeis, the "people's advocate," to the Supreme Court, though an

# *Legacy* FOR A PEOPLE AND A NATION

## Margaret Sanger, Planned Parenthood, and the Birth-Control Controversy

Some reforms of the Progressive era illustrate how earnest intentions to help can become tangled in divisive issues of morality. Such is the legacy of birth-control advocate Margaret Sanger. In 1912 Sanger began writing a column on sex education in the *New York Call* entitled "What Every Girl Should Know." Almost immediately, strict moralists accused her of writing obscene literature because she publicly discussed venereal disease and contraception. The issue of limiting family size, however, became her passion, and she began counseling poor women on New York's Lower East Side about how to avoid the pain of frequent childbirth, miscarriage, and bungled abortion. In 1914 Sanger published the first issue of *The Woman Rebel,* a monthly newspaper that advocated a woman's right to practice birth control. Indicted for distributing obscenity through the mails, she fled to England. There she joined a set of radicals and gave speeches on behalf of family planning and a woman's need to enjoy sexual fulfillment without fear of pregnancy.

Returning to the United States, Sanger opened the country's first birth-control clinic in Brooklyn in 1916. She was arrested, but when a court exempted physicians from a law prohibiting dissemination of contraceptive information, she set up a doctor-run clinic in 1923. Staffed by female doctors and social workers, the Birth Control Clinical Research Bureau acted as a model for other clinics. Sanger also organized the American Birth Control League (1921) and tried to win support from medical and social reformers, including some from the eugenics movement, for legalized birth control. Eventually, her radical views caused her to fall out with some of her allies, and she resigned from the American Birth Control League in 1928.

The movement continued, however, and in 1938 the American Birth Control League and the Birth Control Clinical Research Bureau merged to form the Birth Control Federation of America, renamed the Planned Parenthood Federation of America (PPFA) in 1942. The organization's name defined its mission to strengthen the family and stabilize society with the help of governmental support, rather than to focus more directly on the feminist issue of whether or not a woman should have the right of voluntary motherhood. Throughout the 1940s, the PPFA emphasized family planning through making contraceptives more accessible. In 1970 it began receiving funds under a federal program to provide family-planning services.

In the 1960s, the emergence of new feminist agitation for women's rights and rising concerns about overpopulation moved issues of birth control and abortion into an arena of passionate controversy. Although the PPFA had initially dissociated itself from abortion as a means of family planning, the debate between a woman's "choice" and a fetus's "right to life" drew the organization into the fray, especially after 1973, when the Supreme Court validated women's right to an abortion in *Roe v. Wade.* The national PPFA and its local branches fought legislative and court attempts to make abortions illegal, and in 1989 it helped organize a women's march on Washington for equality and abortion rights. At the same time, some Latino and African American groups attacked the PPFA's stance, charging that legalized abortion was a kind of eugenics program meant to reduce births among nonwhite races.

Because of the PPFA's involvement in abortion politics, several of its clinics have been targets of picketing and even violence by those who believe abortion to be immoral. The PPFA now operates nearly nine hundred health centers providing medical services and education nationwide, and has fulfilled Margaret Sanger's dream of legalized contraception and family planning. But, as with other reforms dealing with issues of morality and individual rights, birth control has left a legacy to a people and a nation of disagreement over whose rights and whose morality should prevail.

anti-Semitic backlash almost blocked Senate approval of the Court's first Jewish justice. In addition, Wilson pleased social reformers by backing laws that regulated child labor and provided workers' compensation for federal employees who suffered work-related injuries or illness.

Amid his reforms, however, Wilson never overcame his racism. Although in 1918 he tried to appoint W. E. B. Du Bois as an army officer to help keep race relations calm (Du Bois, age fifty, failed the physical.). Wilson fired several black federal officials, and his administration preserved racial separation in restrooms, restaurants, and government office buildings. Wilson responded to protesting blacks that "segregation is not a humiliation but a benefit, and ought to be so regarded by you gentlemen." When the pathbreaking but inflammatory film about the Civil War and Reconstruction, *The Birth of a Nation* was released in 1915, Wilson allowed a showing at the White House, though he subsequently prohibited it during the First World War.

In selecting a candidate to oppose Wilson in the presidential election of 1916, Republicans snubbed Theodore Roosevelt in favor of Charles Evans Hughes, Supreme Court justice and former reform governor of New York. Aware of public anxiety over

**Election of 1916**

the world war raging in Europe since 1914, Wilson ran on a platform of neutrality and Progressivism, using the campaign slogan "He Kept Us Out of War." Hughes advocated greater military preparedness, but Wilson's peace platform resonated with the voters. The election outcome was close. Wilson received 9.1 million votes to Hughes's 8.5 million and barely won in the electoral college, 277 to 254. The Socialist candidate drew only 600,000 votes, down from 901,000 in 1912, largely because Wilson's reforms had won over some Socialists and because the ailing Eugene Debs was no longer the party's standard-bearer.

During Wilson's second term, U.S. involvement in the First World War increased government regulation of the economy. Mobilization and war, he came to believe, required greater coordination of production and cooperation between the public and private sectors. The War Industries Board exemplified this cooperation: private businesses regulated by the board submitted to its control on condition that their profit motives would continue to be satisfied. After the war, Wilson's administration dropped most cooperative and regulatory measures, including farm price supports, guarantees of collective bargaining, and high taxes. This retreat from regulation, prompted in part by the election of a Republican Congress in 1918, stimulated a new era of business ascendancy in the 1920s.

## SUMMARY

By 1920 a quarter-century of reform had wrought momentous changes. Government, economy, and society as they had existed in the nineteenth century were gone forever. In their efforts to achieve goals of ending abuses of power, reforming institutions, and applying scientific and efficient management, Progressives established the principle of public intervention to ensure fairness, health, and safety. Concern over poverty and injustice reached new heights. But reformers could not sustain their efforts indefinitely. Although Progressive values lingered after the First World War, a mass-consumer society began to refocus people's attention away from reform to materialism.

Multiple and sometimes contradictory goals characterized the Progressive era. By no means was there a single Progressive movement. Programs on the national level ranged from Roosevelt's faith in big government as a coordinator of big business to Wilson's promise to dissolve economic concentrations and legislate open competition. At state and local levels, reformers pursued causes as varied as neighborhood improvement, government reorganization, public ownership of utilities, and betterment of work-

ing conditions. National associations coordinated efforts on specific issues, but reformers with different goals often worked at cross-purposes. New consciousness about identity confronted women and African Americans, and although women made some inroads into public life, both groups still found themselves in confined social positions and dependent on their own resolve in their quest for dignity and recognition.

In spite of their successes, the failure of many Progressive initiatives indicates the strength of the opposition, as well as weaknesses within the reform movements themselves. As issues such as Americanization, eugenics, prohibition, education, and general moral uplift illustrate, social reform often merged into social control—attempts to impose one group's values on all of society and to regulate behavior of immigrant and nonwhite racial groups. In political matters, courts asserted constitutional and liberty-of-contract doctrines in striking down key Progressive legislation, notably the federal law prohibiting child labor. In states and cities, adoption of the initiative, referendum, and recall did not encourage greater participation in government as had been hoped; those mechanisms either were seldom used or became tools of special interests. Federal regulatory agencies rarely had enough resources for thorough investigations; they had to depend on information from the very companies they policed. Progressives thus failed in many respects to redistribute power. In 1920, as in 1900, government remained under the influence of business, a state of affairs that many people in power considered quite satisfactory.

Yet the reform movements that characterized the Progressive era reshaped the national outlook. Trustbusting, however faulty, made industrialists more sensitive to public opinion, and insurgents in Congress partially diluted the power of dictatorial politicians. Progressive legislation equipped government with tools to protect consumers against price fixing and dangerous products. Social reformers relieved some ills of urban and industrial life. And, perhaps most important, Progressives challenged old ways of thinking. Although the questions they raised about the quality of American life remained unresolved, Progressives made the nation acutely aware of its principles and promises.

## SUGGESTIONS FOR FURTHER READING

Francis L. Broderick, *Progressivism at Risk: Electing a President in 1912* (1989)

Nancy F. Cott, *The Grounding of Modern Feminism* (1987)

Steven J. Diner, *A Very Different Age: Americans of the Progressive Era* (1998)

Glenda Gilmore, *Who Were the Progressives?* (2002)

Hugh D. Hindman, *Child Labor: An American History* (2002)

Alice Kessler-Harris, *Out to Work: A History of Wage-Earning Women in the United States,* 20th anniversary ed. (2003)

Michael McGerr, *A Fierce Discontent: The Rise and Fall of the Progressive Movement in America, 1870–1920* (2003)

Patricia A. Schecter, *Ida B. Wells and American Reform, 1880–1930* (2001)

David Tyack, *Seeking Common Ground: Public Schools in a Diverse Society* (2003)

*For a more extensive list for further reading, go to* college.hmco.com/pic/norton8e.

# The Quest for Empire *1865-1914*

evil!" they shouted at Lottie Moon. "Foreign devil!" The Southern Baptist missionary, half a world away from home, braced herself against the cries of the Chinese "rabble" whom she had been determined to convert to Christianity. On that day in the 1880s, she walked "steadily and persistently" through the throng of hecklers, silently vowing to win their acceptance and then their souls.

Born in 1840 in Virginia and educated at what is now Hollins College, Charlotte Diggs Moon volunteered in 1873 for "woman's work" in northern China. There she taught and proselytized, largely among women and children, because women seldom preached to men and men were forbidden to preach to women. This compassionate, pious, and courageous single woman, "putting love into action," worked in China until her death in 1912.

In the 1870s and 1880s, Lottie Moon (Mu Ladi, or 幕拉第) made bold and sometimes dangerous evangelizing trips to isolated Chinese hamlets. "O! The torture of human eyes upon you; scanning every feature, every look, every gesture!" Curious peasant women pinched her, pulled on her skirts, and purred, "How white her hand is!" They peppered her with questions: "How old are you?" "Where do you get money to live on?" Speaking in Chinese, Lottie held high a picture book of Jesus Christ's birth and crucifixion, drawing the crowd's attention to the "foreign doctrine" that she hoped would displace Confucianism, Buddhism, and Taoism.

In the 1890s, a "storm of persecution" directed against foreigners swept China. Because missionaries were upending traditional ways and authority, they became hated targets. One missionary conceded that, in "believing Jesus," girls and women alarmed men who worried that "disobedient wives and daughters" would no longer "worship the idols when told." In the village of Shaling in early 1890, Lottie Moon's Christian converts were beaten and the "foreign devils" ordered to move out. Fearing for her life, she had to flee.

◄ The missionary Lottie Moon (1840–1912) in 1901 with English-language students in Japan, during her refuge from the Boxer Rebellion in China.

*(Virginia Baptist Historical Society & University Archives)*

## CHRONOLOGY

**1861–69** ■ Seward sets expansionist course

**1867** ■ United States acquires Alaska and Midway

**1876** ■ Pro-U.S. Díaz begins thirty-four-year rule in Mexico

**1878** ■ United States gains naval rights in Samoa

**1885** ■ Strong's *Our Country* celebrates Anglo-Saxon destiny of dominance

**1887** ■ United States gains naval rights to Pearl Harbor, Hawai'i

■ McKinley Tariff hurts Hawaiian sugar exports

**1893** ■ Economic crisis leads to business failures and mass unemployment

■ Pro-U.S. interests stage successful coup against Queen Lili'uokalani of Hawai'i

**1895** ■ Cuban revolution against Spain begins

■ Japan defeats China in war, annexes Korea and Formosa (Taiwan)

**1898** ■ United States formally annexes Hawai'i

■ U.S. battleship *Maine* blows up in Havana harbor

■ United States defeats Spain in Spanish-American War

**1899** ■ Treaty of Paris enlarges U.S. empire

■ United Fruit Company forms and becomes influential in Central America

■ Philippine insurrection breaks out, led by Emilio Aguinaldo

**1901** ■ McKinley assassinated; Theodore Roosevelt becomes president

**1903** ■ Panama grants canal rights to United States

■ Platt Amendment subjugates Cuba

**1904** ■ Roosevelt Corollary declares United States a hemispheric "police power"

**1905** ■ Portsmouth Conference ends Russo-Japanese War

**1906** ■ San Francisco School Board segregates Asian schoolchildren

■ United States invades Cuba to quell revolt

**1907** ■ "Great White Fleet" makes world tour

**1910** ■ Mexican revolution threatens U.S. interests

**1914** ■ U.S. troops invade Mexico

■ First World War begins

■ Panama Canal opens

For several months in 1900, during the violent Boxer Rebellion, she had to leave China altogether, as a multinational force (including U.S. troops) intervened to save foreign missionaries, diplomats, and merchants.

Lottie Moon and thousands of other missionaries managed to convert to Christianity only a very small minority of the Chinese people. Although she, like other missionaries, probably never shed the western view that she represented a superior religion and culture, she seldom wavered in her affection for the Chinese people and in her devotion to the foreign missionary project—in her "rejoicing to suffer." In frequent letters and articles directed to a U.S. audience, she lobbied to recruit "a band of ardent, enthusiastic, and experienced Christian women," to stir up "a mighty wave of enthusiasm for Woman's Work for Woman." To this day, the Lottie Moon Christmas Offering in Southern Baptist churches raises millions of dollars for missions abroad.

Like so many other Americans who went overseas in the late nineteenth and early twentieth centuries, Lottie Moon helped spread American culture and influence abroad. In this complex process, other peoples sometimes adopted and sometimes rejected American ways. At the same time, American participants in this cultural expansion and the cultural collisions that it generated became transformed. Lottie Moon, for example, strove to understand the Chinese people and to learn their language. She assumed their dress and abandoned such derogatory phrases as "heathen Chinese" and "great unwashed." She reminded other, less sensitive missionaries that the Chinese rightfully took pride in their own ancient history and thus had no reason to "gape in astonishment at Western civilization."

Lottie Moon also changed—again, in her own words—from "a timid self-distrustful girl into a brave self-reliant woman." As she questioned the Chinese confinement of women, most conspicuous in arranged marriages, foot binding, and sexual segregation, she advanced women's rights. She understood that she could not convert Chinese women unless they had the freedom to listen to her appeals. Bucking the gender ideology of the times, she also uneasily rose to challenge the male domination of America's religious missions. When the Southern Baptist Foreign Mission Board denied woman missionaries the right to vote in meetings, she resigned in protest. The board soon reversed itself.

In later decades, critics labeled the activities of Lottie Moon and other missionaries "cultural imperialism," accusing them of seeking to subvert indigenous traditions and of sparking destructive cultural clashes. Defenders of missionary work, on the other hand, have celebrated their efforts to break down cultural barriers and to bring the world's peoples closer together. Either way, Lottie Moon's story illustrates how Americans in the late nineteenth century interacted with the world in diverse ways, how through their experiences the categories "domestic" and "foreign" came to intersect, and how they expanded abroad not only to seek land, trade, investments, and strategic bases, but also to promote American culture, including the Christian faith.

Between the Civil War and the First World War, an expansionist United States joined the ranks of the great world powers. Before the Civil War, Americans had repeatedly extended the frontier: they bought Louisiana; annexed Florida, Oregon, and Texas; pushed Indians out of the path of white migration westward; seized California and other western areas from Mexico; and acquired southern parts of present-day Arizona and New Mexico from Mexico (the Gadsden Purchase). Americans had also developed a lucrative foreign trade with most of the world and promoted American culture wherever they traveled. They rekindled their expansionist course after the Civil War, building, managing, and protecting an overseas empire.

It was an age of empire. By the 1870s, most of Europe's powers were carving up Africa and large parts of Asia and Oceania for themselves. By 1900 the powers had conquered more than 10 million square miles (one-fifth of the earth's land), and 150 million people. As the century turned, France, Russia, and Germany were spending heavily on modern steel navies, challenging an overextended Great Britain. In Asia, meanwhile, a rapidly modernizing Japan expanded at the expense of both China and Russia.

Engineering advances altered the world's political geography through the Suez Canal (1869), the British Trans-Indian railroad (1870), and the Russian Trans-Siberian Railway (1904), while steamships, machine guns, telegraphs, and malaria drugs greatly facilitated the im-

perialists' task. Simultaneously, the optimistic spirit that had characterized European political discourse in the 1850s and 1860s gave way to a brooding pessimism and a sense of impending warfare informed by notions of racial conflict and survival of the fittest.

This transformation of world politics did not escape notice by observant Americans; some argued that the United States risked being "left behind" if it failed to join the scramble for territory and markets. Republican senator Henry Cabot Lodge of Massachusetts, claiming that the "great nations" were seizing "the waste areas of the world," advised that "the United States must not fall out of the line of march," because "civilization and the advancement of the [Anglo-Saxon] race" were at stake. Such thinking helped fuel Americans' desire in the years after the Civil War to exert their influence beyond the continental United States, to reach for more space, more land, more markets, more cultural penetration, and more power.

By 1900 the United States had emerged as a great power with particular clout in Latin America, especially as Spain declined and Britain disengaged from the Western Hemisphere. In the Pacific, the new U.S. empire included Hawai'i, American Samoa, and the Philippines. Theodore Roosevelt, who in the 1890s was a leading spokesman for the imperialist cause, would, as president in the decade that followed, seek to consolidate this newfound power.

Most Americans applauded expansionism—the outward movement of goods, ships, dollars, people, and ideas—as a traditional feature of their nation's history. But many became uneasy whenever expansionism gave way to imperialism—the imposition of control over other peoples, undermining their sovereignty and usurping their freedom to make their own decisions. Abroad, native nationalists, commercial competitors, and other imperial nations tried to block the spread of U.S. influence.

- What accounts for the increased importance of foreign policy concerns in American politics in the closing years of the nineteenth century?

- What key arguments were made by American anti-imperialists?

- How did late-nineteenth-century imperialism transform the United States?

▲ As one expression of the theme of economic expansion, this poster, advertising the Uncle Sam stove manufactured in New York by the Abendroth Bros. company, announces that food links the United States with the rest of the world. Although the foods on the long list are international—potatoes from Ireland and macaroni from Italy, for example—the message here is that the United States itself is "feeding the world." The turkey being removed from the oven seems to be the only uniquely American offering, but many of the items on the list were also produced in the United States. The poster was issued in 1876, which explains the image of the Centennial building in Philadelphia and the patriotic red, white, and blue colors. *(© Collection of The New York Historical Society)*

## IMPERIAL DREAMS

Foreign policy assumed a new importance for Americans in the closing years of the nineteenth century. For much of the Gilded Age, they had been preoccupied by internal matters, such as industrialization, the construction of the railroads, and the settlement of the West. Over time, however, increasing numbers of political and business leaders began to look outward, and to advocate a more activist approach to world affairs. The motives of these expansionists were complex and varied, but all of them emphasized the supposed benefits of such an approach to the country's domestic health.

That proponents of overseas expansion stressed the benefits that would accrue at home should come as no surprise, for foreign policy has always sprung from the domestic setting of a nation—its needs and moods, ideology and culture. The leaders who guided America's expansionist foreign relations were the same ones who guided the economic development of the machine age, forged the transcontinental railroad, built America's bustling cities and giant corporations, and shaped a mass culture. They unabashedly espoused the idea that the United States was an exceptional nation, so different from and superior to others because of its Anglo-Saxon heritage and its God-favored and prosperous history.

Exceptionalism was but one in an intertwined set of ideas that figured prominently in the American march toward empire. Nationalism, capitalism, Social Darwinism, and a paternalistic attitude toward foreigners influenced American leaders as well. "They are children and we are men in these deep matters of government," future president Woodrow Wilson announced in 1898. The very words he chose reveal the gender and age bias of American attitudes. Where these attitudes intersected with foreign cultures, there came not only adoption but rejection, not only imitation but clash, as Lottie Moon learned.

It would take time for most Americans to grasp the changes under way. "The people" may influence domestic

### Foreign Policy Elite

policy directly, but the making of foreign policy is usually dominated by what scholars have labeled the "foreign policy elite"— opinion leaders in politics, journalism, business, agriculture, religion, education, and the military. In the post–Civil War era, this small group, whom Secretary of State Walter Q. Gresham called "the thoughtful men of the country," expressed the opinions that counted. Better read and better traveled than most Americans, more cosmopolitan in outlook, and politically active, they believed that U.S. prosperity and security depended on the exertion of U.S. influence abroad. Increasingly in the late nineteenth century, and especially in the 1890s, the expansionist-minded elite urged both formal and informal imperialism. Ambitious and clannish, the imperialists often met in Washington, D.C., at the homes of historian Henry Adams and of writer and diplomat John Hay (who became secretary of state in 1898) or at the Metropolitan Club. They talked about building a bigger navy and digging a canal across Panama, Central America, or Mexico; establishing colonies; and selling surpluses abroad. Theodore Roosevelt, appointed assistant secretary of the navy in 1897, was among them; so were Senator Henry Cabot Lodge, who joined the Foreign Relations Committee in 1896, and corporate lawyer Elihu Root, who later would serve as both secretary of war and secretary of state. Such well-positioned luminaries kept up the drumbeat for empire.

These American leaders believed that selling, buying, and investing in foreign marketplaces were important to the United States. Why? One reason was profits from foreign sales. "It is my dream," declared the governor of Georgia in 1878, to see "in every valley . . . a cotton factory to convert the raw material of the neighborhood into fabrics which shall warm the limbs of Japanese and Chinese." Fear also helped make the case for foreign trade, as foreign commerce might serve as a safety valve to relieve overproduction, unemployment, economic depression, and the social tension that arose from them. The nation's farms and factories produced more than Americans could consume, all the more so during the 1890s' depression. Surpluses had to be exported, the economist David A. Wells warned, or "we are certain to be smothered in our own grease." Economic ties also permitted political influence to be exerted abroad and helped spread the American way of life, especially capitalism, creating a world more hospitable to Americans. In an era when the most powerful nations in the world were also the greatest traders, vigorous foreign economic expansion symbolized national stature.

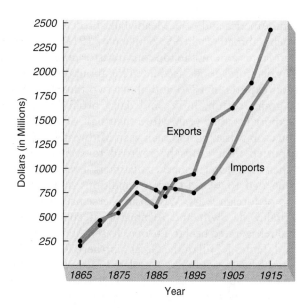

**Figure 22.1    U.S. Trade Expansion, 1865–1914**

This figure illustrates two key characteristics of U.S. foreign trade: first, that the United States began in the 1870s to enjoy a favorable balance of trade (exporting more than it imported), and second, that U.S. exports expanded tremendously, making the United States one of the world's economic giants.

(Source: *Thomas G. Paterson, J. Garry Clifford, and Kenneth J. Hagan, American Foreign Relations: A History, 5th ed. Copyright © 2000 by Houghton Mifflin Company. Used by permission of Houghton Mifflin Company.*)

### Foreign Trade Expansion

Although most business leaders remained focused on the domestic marketplace, foreign trade figured prominently in the tremendous economic growth of the United States after the Civil War. Foreign commerce in turn stimulated the building of a larger protective navy, the professionalization of the foreign service, calls for more colonies, and a more interventionist foreign policy. In 1865 U.S. exports totaled $234 million; by 1900 they had climbed to $1.5 billion (see Figure 22.1). By 1914, at the outbreak of the First World War, exports had reached $2.5 billion, prompting some Europeans to protest an American "invasion" of goods. In 1874 the United States reversed its historically unfavorable balance of trade (importing more than it exported) and began to enjoy a long-term favorable balance (exporting more than it imported)—though the balance of payments remained in the red. Most of America's products went to Britain, continental Europe, and Canada, but increasing amounts flowed to new markets in Latin America and Asia. Meanwhile, direct American investments abroad reached $3.5 billion by 1914, placing the United States among the top four investor countries.

Agricultural goods accounted for about three-fourths of total exports in 1870 and about two-thirds in 1900, with grain, cotton, meat, and dairy products topping the export list that year. More than half of the annual cotton crop was exported each year. Midwestern farmers transported their crops by railroad to seaboard cities and then on to foreign markets. Farmers' livelihoods thus became tied to world-market conditions and the outcomes of foreign wars. Wisconsin cheesemakers shipped to Britain; the Swift and Armour meat companies exported refrigerated beef to Europe. To sell American grain abroad, James J. Hill of the Great Northern Railroad distributed wheat cookbooks translated into several Asian languages.

In 1913, when the United States outranked both Great Britain and Germany in manufacturing production (see Figure 22.2), manufactured goods led U.S. exports for the first time. Substantial proportions of America's steel, copper, and petroleum were sold abroad, making many workers in those industries dependent on American exports. George Westinghouse marketed his air brakes in Europe; almost as many Singer sewing machines were exported as were sold at home; and Cyrus McCormick's "reaper kings" harvested the wheat of Russian fields.

In promoting the expansion of U.S. influence overseas, many officials championed a nationalism based on

## Race Thinking and the Male Ethos

notions of American supremacy. Some, echoing the articulations of European imperialists (who had their own conceptions of national supremacy), found justification for expansionism in racist theories then permeating western thought and politics. For decades, the western scientific establishment had classified humankind by race, and students of physical anthropology drew on phrenology and physiognomy—the analysis of skull size and shape, and the comparison of facial features—to produce a hierarchy of superior and inferior races. One well-known French researcher, for example, claimed that blacks represented a "female race" and "like the woman, the black is deprived of political and scientific intelligence; he has never created a great state . . . he has never accomplished anything in industrial mechanics. But on the other hand he has great virtues of sentiment. Like women he also likes jewelry, dancing, and singing."

The language of U.S. leaders was also weighted with words like *manliness* and *weakling*. Member of Congress, son-in-law of Senator Lodge, and Spanish-American War veteran Augustus P. Gardner extolled the "arena of lust and blood, where true men are to be found." The warrior and president Theodore Roosevelt viewed people of color (or "darkeys," as he called them) as effeminate weaklings who lacked the ability to govern themselves and could not cope with world politics. Americans regularly debased Latin Americans as half-breeds needing close supervision,

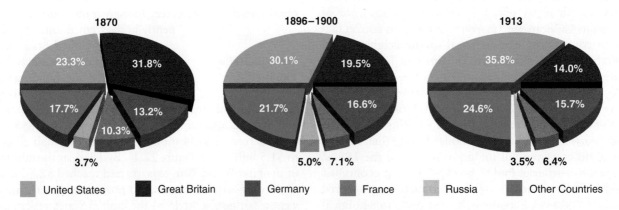

**Figure 22.2   The Rise of U.S. Economic Power in the World**
These pie charts showing percentage shares of world manufacturing production for the major nations of the world demonstrate that the United States came to surpass Great Britain in this significant economic measurement of power.

*(Source: League of Nations data presented in Aaron L. Friedberg, The Weary Titan: Britain and the Experience of Relative Decline, 1895–1905 [Princeton, N.J.: Princeton University Press, 1988], p. 26.)*

## National Geographic

On a winter day in early 1888, thirty-three members of the elite Cosmos Club in Washington, D.C., convened around a mahogany table to consider "the advisability of organizing a society for the increase and diffusion of geographical knowledge." The result was the National Geographic Society, destined to become the largest non-profit scientific and educational institution in the world.

At the heart of the enterprise would be a magazine designed to win broad support for the society. *National Geographic Magazine* (later simply *National Geographic*) appeared for the first time in October 1888. Early issues were brief, technical, and visually bland, and sales lagged. In 1898, however, Alexander Graham Bell became president of the society and made two key changes: he shifted emphasis from newsstand sales to society membership, reasoning correctly that armchair travelers would flock to join a distinguished fellowship, and he appointed a talented new editor, Gilbert H. Grosvenor, age twenty-three. Grosvenor commissioned articles of general interest and, in an unprecedented move, filled eleven pages of one issue with photographs.

These and other early photos showed people stiffly posed in their native costumes, displayed as anthropological specimens. But they caused a sensation. By 1908 pictures occupied 50 percent of the magazine's space. In 1910 the first color photographs appeared, in a twenty-four-page spread on Korea and China—at that time the largest collection of color photographs ever published in a single issue of any magazine. In later years, *National Geographic* would have several other photographic firsts, including the first natural-color photos of Arctic life and the undersea world.

The society also used membership dues to sponsor expeditions, such as the 1909 journey to the North Pole by Robert Peary and Matthew Henson and, later, Jacques Cousteau's many oceanic explorations and Jane Goodall's up-close observations of wild chimpanzees. The tales of these adventures then appeared in the magazine's pages, along with stunning photographs. By the end of Grosvenor's tenure as editor, in 1954, circulation had grown to more than 2 million.

Grosvenor's winning formula included less-admirable elements. His editors pressured photographers to provide "pictures of pretty girls" to the point at which, as one photographer recalled, "hundreds of bare-breasted women, all from poorer countries, were published at a time of booming subscription rates." Editors also developed a well-earned reputation for avoiding controversial issues and presenting a rosy view of the world. An article about Berlin published just before the start of World War II, for example, contained no criticism of the Nazi regime and no mention of its persecution of Jews. Recent years have seen the magazine take on more newsworthy items—AIDS, stem cell research, Hurricane Katrina, global warming—but in measured, generally nonpolitical tones.

Throughout, the society has continued to expand its reach, moving into the production of books, atlases, globes, and television documentaries. Targeting overseas readers, the society in 1995 launched a Japanese-language edition and subsequently added twenty-five other foreign editions. *National Geographic*, after a century of linking Americans to faraway places, now went in the other direction, connecting readers in many of those locales to the United States.

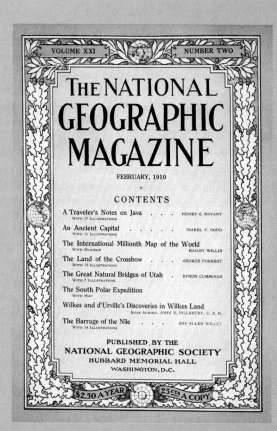

▲ *National Geographic* had already gone through five different cover formats when Robert Weir Crouch, an English-born Canadian decorative artist came up with a design that cemented the magazine's visual identity. Singular and immediately recognizable, the oak-and-laurel frame on the cover of the February 1910 issue would remain largely unchanged for nearly half a century, though the buff-colored border would be replaced with a golden one.

*(National Geographic Society Image Collection)*

distressed damsels begging for manly rescue, or children requiring tutelage. The gendered imagery prevalent in U.S. foreign relations joined race thinking to place women, people of color, and nations weaker than the United States in the low ranks of the hierarchy of power and, hence, in a necessarily dependent status justifying U.S. dominance.

Reverend Josiah Strong's popular and influential *Our Country* (1885) celebrated an Anglo-Saxon race destined to lead others. "As America goes, so goes the world," he declared. A few years later, he wrote that "to be a Christian and an Anglo-Saxon and an American . . . is to stand at the very mountaintop of privilege." Social Darwinists saw Americans as a superior people certain to overcome all competition. Secretary of State Thomas F. Bayard (1885–1889) applauded the "overflow of our population and capital" into Mexico to "saturate those regions with Americanism." But, he added, "we do not want them" until "they are fit."

Race thinking—popularized in magazine photos and cartoons, world's fairs, postcards, school textbooks, museums, and political orations—reinforced notions of American greatness, influenced the way U.S. leaders dealt with other peoples, and obviated the need to think about the subtle textures of other societies. The magazine *National Geographic,* which published its first issue in 1888, chronicled with photographs America's new overseas involvements in Asia and the Pacific. Even when smiling faces predominated in these shots, the image portrayed was that of strange, exotic, premodern peoples who had not become "Western." Fairs also put so-called uncivilized people of color on display in the "freak" or "midway" section. Dog-eating Filipinos aroused particular comment at the 1904 St. Louis World's Fair. Such racism downgraded diplomacy and justified domination and war, because self-proclaimed superiors do not negotiate with people ranked as inferiors.

The same thinking permeated attitudes toward immigrants, whose entry into the United States was first restricted in these years. Although the Burlingame Treaty (1868) had provided for free immigration between the United States and China, riots against Chinese immigrants erupted again and again in the American West—in Los Angeles (1871), San Francisco (1877), Denver (1880), and Seattle (1886). A new treaty in 1880 permitted Congress to suspend Chinese immigration to the United States, and it did so two years later. A violent incident occurred in Rock Springs, Wyoming, in 1885, when white coal miners and railway workers rioted and massacred at least twenty-five Chinese.

In 1906 the San Francisco School Board, reflecting the anti-Asian bias of many West Coast Americans, or-

dered the segregation of all Chinese, Koreans, and Japanese in special schools. Tokyo protested the discrimination against its citizens. The following year, President Roosevelt quieted the crisis by striking a "gentleman's agreement" with Tokyo restricting the inflow of Japanese immigrants; San Francisco then rescinded its segregation order. Relations with Tokyo were jolted again in 1913 when the California legislature denied Japanese residents the right to own property in the state.

With a mixture of self-interest and idealism typical of American thinking on foreign policy, expansionists believed that empire benefited both Americans and those who came under their control. When the United States intervened in other lands or lectured weaker states, Americans claimed that in remaking foreign societies they were extending liberty and prosperity to less fortunate people. William Howard Taft, as civil governor of the Philippines (1901–1904), described the United States' mission

### The "Civilizing" Impulse

▲ Missionaries Charles and Anna Hartwell, brother and sister, travel in 1901 on their "gospel boat," working out of the Fuzhou mission in China. *(ABCFM Picture Collection: Individuals, Woodhull, Kate C., Courtesy Houghton Library, Harvard College Library)*

in its new colony as lifting Filipinos up "to a point of civilization" that will make them "call the name of the United States blessed." Later, after becoming secretary of war (1904–1908), Taft said about the Chinese that "the more civilized they become . . . the wealthier they become, and the better market they become for us." "The world is to be Christianized and civilized," declared Reverend Josiah Strong. "And what is the process of civilizing but the creating of more and higher wants."

Missionaries dispatched to Africa and Asia, like Lottie Moon, helped spur the transfer of American culture and power abroad—"the peaceful conquest of the world," as Reverend Frederick Gates put it. One organization, the Student Volunteers for Foreign Missions, began in the 1880s on college campuses and by 1914 had placed some 6,000 missionaries abroad. In 1915 a total of 10,000 American missionaries worked overseas. In China by 1915, more than 2,500 American Protestant missionaries—most of them female—labored to preach the gospel, teach school, and administer medical care.

## AMBITIONS AND STRATEGIES

The U.S. empire grew gradually, sometimes haltingly, as American leaders defined guiding principles and built institutions to support overseas ambitions. William H. Seward, one of its chief architects, argued relentlessly for extension of the American frontier as senator from New York (1849–1861) and secretary of state (1861–1869). "There is not in the history of the Roman Empire an ambition for aggrandizement so marked as that which characterizes the American people," he once said. Seward envisioned a large, coordinated U.S. empire encompassing Canada, the Caribbean, Cuba, Central America, Mexico, Hawai'i, Iceland, Greenland, and the Pacific islands. This empire would be built not by war but by a natural process of gravitation toward the United States. Commerce would hurry the process, as would a canal across Central America, a transcontinental American railroad to link up with Asian markets, and a telegraph system to speed communications.

Most of Seward's grandiose plans did not reach fruition in his own day. In 1867, for example, he signed a treaty with Denmark to buy the Danish West Indies (Virgin Islands), but his domestic political foes in the Senate and a hurricane that wrecked St. Thomas scuttled his effort. The Virgin Islanders, who had voted for annexation, had to wait until 1917 for official U.S. status. Also doomed to failure was Seward's scheme with unscrupulous Dominican Republic leaders to gain a Caribbean naval base at Samaná Bay. The stench of corruption rising over this unsavory deal-making wafted into the Ulysses S. Grant administration and foiled Grant's initiative in 1870 to buy the entire island nation. The Senate rejected annexation.

**Seward's Quest for Empire**

Anti-imperialism, not just politics, blocked Seward. Anti-imperialists, such as Senator Carl Schurz and E. L. Godkin, editor of the magazine *The Nation*, argued that the country already had enough unsettled land and that creating a showcase of democracy and prosperity at home would best persuade other peoples to adopt American institutions and principles. Some anti-imperialists, sharing

◄ Beginning in the late nineteenth century, Standard Oil (the forerunner of Exxon Mobil Corporation) sent agents to China to persuade the Chinese to use American-made kerosene in their lamps and cooking stoves. To promote sales, the American entrepreneurs gave away small lamps, which the Chinese called *Mei Foo* (Beautiful Companion). One agent who popularized the lamp was William P. Coltman, shown here with Chinese business associates.

*(Exxon Mobil Corporation)*

the racism of the times, opposed the annexation of territory populated by dark-skinned people.

Seward did enjoy some successes. In 1866, citing the Monroe Doctrine (see page 242), he sent troops to the border with Mexico and demanded that France abandon its puppet regime there. Also facing angry Mexican nationalists, Napoleon III abandoned the Maximilian monarchy that he had installed by force three years earlier. In 1867 Seward paid Russia $7.2 million for the 591,000 square miles of Alaska—land twice the size of Texas. Some critics lampooned "Seward's Icebox," but the secretary of state extolled the Russian territory's rich natural resources, and the Senate voted overwhelmingly for the treaty. That same year, Seward laid claim to the Midway Islands (two small islands and a coral atoll northwest of Hawai'i) in the Pacific Ocean.

Seward realized his dream of a world knit together by a giant communications system. In 1866, through the persevering efforts of financier Cyrus Field, an underwater transatlantic cable linked European and American telegraph networks. Backed by J. P. Morgan's capital, communications pioneer James A. Scrymser strung telegraph lines to Latin America, entering Chile in 1890. In 1903 a submarine cable reached across the Pacific to the Philippines; three years later, it extended to Japan and China. Information about markets, crises, and war flowed steadily and quickly. Wire telegraphy—like radio (wireless telegraphy) later—shrank the globe. Nellie Bly, a reporter for the *New York World,* accented the impact of new technology in 1890 when she completed a well-publicized trip around the world in seventy-two days. Drawn closer to one another through improved communications and transportation, nations found that faraway events had more and more impact on their prosperity and security. Because of the communications revolution, "every nation elbows other nations to-day," observed Amherst College professor Edwin Grosvenor in 1898.

**International Communications**

More and more, American diplomats found that they could enter negotiations with their European counterparts on roughly equal terms—a sure sign that the United States had arrived on the international stage. Seward's successor Hamilton Fish (1869–1887), for example, achieved a diplomatic victory in resolving the knotty problem of the *Alabama* claims. The *Alabama* and other vessels built in Great Britain for the Confederacy during the Civil War had preyed on Union shipping. Senator Charles Sumner demanded that Britain pay $2 billion in damages or cede Canada to the United States, but Fish favored negotiations. In 1871 Britain and America signed the Washington Treaty, whereby the British apologized and agreed to the creation of a tribunal which later awarded the United States $15.5 million.

Washington officials also confronted European powers in a contest over Samoa, a group of beautiful South Pacific islands located 4,000 miles from San Francisco on the trade route to Australia. In 1878 the United States gained exclusive right to a coaling station at Samoa's coveted port of Pago Pago. Eyeing the same prize, Britain and Germany began to cultivate ties with Samoan leaders. Year by year tensions grew, as the powers dispatched warships to Samoa and aggravated factionalism among Samoa's chiefs. War seemed possible. At the eleventh hour, however, Britain, Germany, and the United States met in Berlin in 1889 and, without consulting the Samoans, devised a three-part protectorate that limited Samoa's independence. Ten years later, the three powers partitioned Samoa: the United States received Pago Pago through annexation of part of the islands (now called American Samoa and administered by the U.S. Department of the Interior); Germany took what is today independent Western Samoa; and Britain, for renouncing its claims to Samoa, obtained the Gilbert Islands and Solomon Islands.

With eyes on all parts of the world, even on Africa, where U.S. interests were minimal, ardent expansionists embraced navalism—the campaign to build an imperial navy. Calling attention to the naval buildup by the European powers, notably Germany, they argued for a bigger, modernized navy, adding the "blue water" command of the seas to its traditional role of "brown water" coastline defense and riverine operations. Captain Alfred Thayer Mahan became a major popularizer for this "New Navy." Because foreign trade was vital to the United States, he argued, the nation required an efficient navy to protect its shipping; in turn, a navy required colonies for bases. "Whether they will or no," Mahan wrote, "Americans must now begin to look outward. The growing production of the country demands it." Mahan's lectures at the Naval War College in Newport, Rhode Island, where he served as president, were published as *The Influence of Sea Power upon History* (1890). This book sat on every serious expansionist's shelf, and foreign leaders turned its pages. Theodore Roosevelt and Henry Cabot Lodge eagerly consulted Mahan, sharing his belief in the links between trade, navy, and colonies, and his growing alarm over "the aggressive military spirit" of Germany.

**Alfred T. Mahan and Navalism**

Moving toward naval modernization, Congress in 1883 authorized construction of the first steel-hulled warships. American factories went to work to produce steam engines, high-velocity shells, powerful guns, and precision instruments. The navy shifted from sail power to steam and from wood construction to steel. Often named for states and cities to kindle patriotism and local support for naval expansion, New Navy ships, such as the *Maine, Oregon,* and *Boston,* thrust the United States into naval prominence, especially during crises in the 1890s.

## CRISES IN THE 1890s: HAWAI'I, VENEZUELA, AND CUBA

In the depression-plagued 1890s, crises in Hawai'i and Cuba gave expansionist Americans opportunities to act on their zealous arguments for what Senator Lodge called a "large policy." Belief that the frontier at home had closed accentuated the expansionist case. In 1893 historian Frederick Jackson Turner postulated that an ever-expanding continental frontier had shaped the American character. That "frontier has gone," Turner pronounced, "and with its going has closed the first period of American history." He did not explicitly say that a new frontier had to be found overseas in order to sustain the American way of life, but he did claim that "American energy will continually demand a wider field for its exercise."

Hawai'i, the Pacific Ocean archipelago of eight major islands located 2,000 miles from the West Coast

**Annexation of Hawai'i**

of the United States, emerged as a new frontier for Americans. The Hawaiian Islands had long commanded American attention— commercial, missionary religious, naval, and diplomatic. Wide-eyed U.S. expansionists envisioned ships sailing from the eastern seaboard through a Central American canal to Hawai'i and then on to the fabled China market. By 1881 Secretary of State James Blaine had already declared the Hawaiian Islands "essentially a part of the American system." By 1890 Americans owned about three-quarters of Hawai'i's wealth and subordinated its economy to that of the United States through sugar exports that entered the U.S. marketplace duty-free.

In Hawai'i's multiracial society, Chinese and Japanese nationals far outnumbered Americans, who represented a mere 2.1 percent of the population. Prominent Americans on the islands—lawyers, businessmen, and sugar planters, many of them the sons of missionaries— organized secret clubs and military units to contest the royal government. In 1887 they forced the king to accept a constitution that granted foreigners the right to vote and shifted decision-making authority from the monarchy to the legislature. The same year, Hawai'i granted the United States naval rights to Pearl Harbor. Many native

▲ Queen Lili'uokalani (1838–1917), ousted from her throne in 1893 by wealthy revolutionaries, vigorously protested in her autobiography and diary, as well as in interviews, the U.S. annexation of Hawai'i in 1898. For years she defended Hawaiian nationalism and emphasized that American officials in 1893 had conspired with Sanford B. Dole and others to overthrow the native monarchy.
*(Courtesy of the Lili'uokalani Trust)*

Hawaiians (53 percent of the population in 1890) believed that the *haole* (foreigners)—especially Americans—were taking their country from them.

The McKinley Tariff of 1890 created an economic crisis for Hawai'i that further undermined the native government. The tariff eliminated the duty-free status of Hawaiian sugar exports in the United States. Suffering declining sugar prices and profits, the American island elite pressed for annexation of the islands by the United States so that their sugar would be classified as domestic rather than foreign. When Princess Lili'uokalani assumed the throne in 1891, she sought to roll back the political power of the *haole.* The next year, the white oligarchy— questioning her moral rectitude, fearing Hawaiian nationalism, and reeling from the McKinley Tariff—formed the subversive Annexation Club.

The annexationists struck in January 1893 in collusion with John L. Stevens, the chief American diplomat in Hawai'i, who dispatched troops from the USS *Boston* to occupy Honolulu. The queen, arrested and confined, surrendered. However, rather than yield to the new provisional regime, headed by Sanford B. Dole, son of missionaries and a prominent attorney, she relinquished authority to the U.S. government. Up went the American flag. "The Hawaiian pear is now fully ripe and this is the golden hour to pluck it," a triumphant Stevens informed Washington. Against the queen's protests as well as those of Japan, President Benjamin Harrison hurriedly sent an annexation treaty to the Senate.

Sensing foul play, incoming President Grover Cleveland ordered an investigation, which confirmed a conspiracy by the economic elite in league with Stevens and noted that most Hawaiians opposed annexation. Down came the American flag. But when Hawai'i gained renewed attention as a strategic and commercial way station to Asia and the Philippines during the Spanish-American War, President William McKinley maneuvered annexation through Congress on July 7, 1898, by means of a majority vote (the Newlands Resolution) rather than by a treaty, which would have required a two-thirds count. Under the Organic Act of June 1900, the people of Hawai'i became U.S. citizens with the right to vote in local elections and to send a nonvoting delegate to Congress. Statehood for Hawai'i came in 1959.

The Venezuelan crisis of 1895 also saw the United States in an expansive mood. For decades Venezuela and Great Britain had quarreled over the border between Venezuela and British Guiana. The disputed territory contained rich gold deposits and the mouth of the Orinoco River, a commercial gateway to northern South America. Venezuela asked for U.S. help. President Cleveland decided that the "mean and hoggish" British had to be warned away. In July 1895, Secretary of State Richard Olney brashly lectured the British that the Monroe Doctrine prohibited European powers from denying self-government to nations in the Western Hemisphere. He aimed his spread-eagle words at an international audience, proclaiming the United States "a civilized state" whose "fiat is law" in the Americas. The United States, he declared, is "master of the situation and practically invulnerable as against any or all other powers." The British, seeking international friends to counter intensifying competition from Germany, quietly retreated from the crisis. In 1896 an Anglo-American arbitration board divided the disputed territory between Britain and Venezuela. The Venezuelans were barely consulted. Thus the United States displayed a trait common to imperialists: disregard for the rights and sensibilities of small nations.

**Venezuelan Boundary Dispute**

In 1895 came another crisis forced by U.S. policy, this one in Cuba. From 1868 to 1878 the Cubans had battled Spain for their independence. Slavery was abolished but independence denied. While the Cuban economy suffered depression, repressive Spanish rule continued. Insurgents committed to *Cuba libre* waited for another chance, and José Martí, one of the heroes of Cuban history, collected money, arms, and men in the United States.

American financial support of the Cuban cause was but one of the many ways the lives of Americans and Cubans intersected. Their cultures, for example, melded. Cubans of all classes had settled in Baltimore, New York, Boston, and Philadelphia. Prominent Cubans on the island had sent their children to schools in the United States. When Cuban expatriates returned home, many came in American clothes, spoke English, had American names, played baseball, and had jettisoned Catholicism for Protestant denominations. Struggling with competing identities, Cubans admired American culture but resented U.S. economic hegemony (predominance).

**Revolution in Cuba**

The Cuban and U.S. economies were also intertwined. American investments of $50 million, mostly in sugar plantations, dominated the Caribbean island. More than 90 percent of Cuba's sugar was exported to the United States, and most island imports came from the United States. Havana's famed cigar factories relocated to Key West and Tampa to evade protectionist U.S. tariff laws. Martí, however, feared that "economic union means political union," for "the nation that buys, commands" and "the nation that sells, serves." Watch out, he warned, for a U.S. "conquering policy" that reduced Latin American countries to "dependencies."

Martí's fears were prophetic. In 1894 the Wilson-Gorman Tariff imposed a duty on Cuban sugar, which had been entering the United States duty-free under the McKinley Tariff. The Cuban economy, highly dependent on exports, plunged into deep crisis, hastening the island's revolution against Spain and its further incorporation into "the American system."

In 1895, from American soil, Martí launched a revolution against Spain that mounted in human and material costs. Rebels burned sugar-cane fields and razed mills, conducting an economic war and using guerrilla tactics to avoid head-on clashes with Spanish soldiers. "It is necessary to burn the hive to disperse the swarm," explained insurgent leader Máximo Gomez. U.S. investments went up in smoke, and Cuban-American trade dwindled. To separate the insurgents from their supporters among the Cuban people, Spanish general Valeriano Weyler instituted a policy of "reconcentration." Some 300,000 Cubans were

◀ On July 1, 1898, U.S. troops stormed Spanish positions on San Juan Hill near Santiago, Cuba. Both sides suffered heavy casualties. A *Harper's* magazine correspondent reported a "ghastly" scene of hundreds killed and thousands wounded. The American painter William Glackens (1870–1938) put to canvas what he saw. Because Santiago surrendered on July 17, propelling the United States to victory in the war, and because Rough Rider Theodore Roosevelt fought at San Juan Hill and later gave a self-congratulatory account of the experience, the human toll has often gone unnoticed.

*(The Wadsworth Atheneum Museum of Art, Hartford, Connecticut. Gift of Henry E. Schnakenberg.)*

herded into fortified towns and camps, where hunger, starvation, and disease led to tens of thousands of deaths. As reports of atrocity and destruction became headline news in the American yellow press, Americans increasingly sympathized with the insurrectionists. In late 1897, a new government in Madrid modified reconcentration and promised some autonomy for Cuba, but the insurgents continued to gain ground.

President William McKinley had come to office as an imperialist who advocated foreign bases for the New

### Sinking of the *Maine*

Navy, the export of surplus production, and U.S. supremacy in the Western Hemisphere. Vexed by the turmoil in Cuba, he came to believe that Spain should give up its colony. At one point he explored the purchase of Cuba by the United States for $300 million. Events in early 1898 caused McKinley to lose faith in Madrid's ability to bring peace to Cuba. In January, when antireform pro-Spanish loyalists and army personnel rioted in Havana, Washington ordered the battleship *Maine* to Havana harbor to demonstrate U.S. concern and to protect American citizens.

On February 15 an explosion ripped the *Maine,* killing 266 of 354 American officers and crew. Just a week earlier, William Randolph Hearst's inflammatory *New York Journal* had published a stolen private letter written by the Spanish minister in Washington, Enrique Dupuy de Lôme, who belittled McKinley as "weak and a bidder for the admiration of the crowd" and suggested that Spain would fight on. Congress soon complied unanimously with McKinley's request for $50 million in defense funds. The naval board investigating the *Maine* disaster then reported that a mine had caused the explosion. Vengeful Americans blamed Spain. (Later, official and unofficial studies attributed the sinking to an accidental internal explosion, most likely caused by spontaneous combustion of inadequately ventilated coal bunkers.)

The impact of these events narrowed McKinley's diplomatic options. Though reluctant to go to war, he decided

### McKinley's Ultimatum and War Decision

to send Spain an ultimatum. In late March, the United States insisted that Spain accept an armistice, end reconcentration altogether, and designate McKinley as arbiter. Madrid made concessions. It abolished reconcentration and rejected, then accepted, an armistice. The weary president hesitated, but he would no longer tolerate chronic disorder just 90 miles off the U.S. coast. On April 11, McKinley asked Congress for authorization to use force "to secure a full and final termination of hostilities between . . . Spain and . . . Cuba, and to secure in the island the establishment of a stable government, capable of maintaining order." American intervention, he said, meant "hostile constraint upon both the parties to the contest."

McKinley listed the reasons for war: the "cause of humanity"; the protection of American life and property; the "very serious injury to the commerce, trade, and business of our people"; and, referring to the destruction of the *Maine,* the "constant menace to our peace." At the end of his message, McKinley mentioned Spain's recent concessions but made little of them. He did not mention another possible motivation: de Lôme's depiction of him as "weak," a charge also leveled by Assistant Secretary of the Navy Theodore Roosevelt. On April 19, Congress declared Cuba free and independent, and directed the president to use force to remove Spanish authority from the island. The legislators also passed the Teller Amendment, which disclaimed any U.S. intention to annex Cuba or control the island except to ensure its "pacification" (by which they meant the suppression of any actively hostile elements of the population). McKinley beat back a congressional amendment to recognize the rebel government. Believing that the Cubans were not ready for self-government, he argued that they needed a period of American tutoring.

## THE SPANISH-AMERICAN WAR AND THE DEBATE OVER EMPIRE

Diplomacy had failed. By the time the Spanish concessions were on the table, events had already pushed the antagonists to the brink. Washington might have been more patient, and Madrid might have faced the fact that its once-grand empire had disintegrated. Still, prospects for compromise appeared dim, because the advancing Cuban insurgents would settle for nothing less than full independence, and no Spanish

government could have given up and remained in office. Nor did the United States welcome a truly independent Cuban government that might attempt to reduce U.S. interests. As historian Louis A. Pérez Jr. has argued, McKinley's decision for war may have been "directed as much against Cuban independence as it was against Spanish sovereignty." Thus came a war some have titled (awkwardly, but accurately) the "Spanish-American-Cuban-Filipino War" so as to represent all the major participants and identify where the war was fought and whose interests were most at stake.

The motives of Americans who favored war were mixed and complex. McKinley's April message expressed a humanitarian impulse to stop the bloodletting, a concern for commerce and property, and the psychological need to end the nightmarish anxiety once and for all. Republican politicians advised McKinley that their party would lose the upcoming congressional elections unless he solved the Cuba question. Many businesspeople, who had been hesitant before the crisis of early 1898, joined many farmers in the belief that ejecting Spain from Cuba would open new markets for surplus production.

**Motives for War**

Inveterate imperialists saw the war as an opportunity to fulfill expansionist dreams, while conservatives, alarmed

Like soldiers in all wars at all times, ▶ those in the Spanish-American War were keen to receive news from home. Here two unidentified soldiers sit on the ground in front of their tent reading their mail. *(Kansas State Historical Society)*

▲ The Spanish fleet in the Caribbean was commanded by Admiral Pascual Cervera y Topete. His squadron entered Santiago Bay, Cuba, May 19, 1898, where it was immediately blockaded by Admiral William T. Sampson's fleet. On July 3 Cervera, following orders from Madrid, tried a heroic but unsuccessful escape from the U.S. blockade. This painting by Henry Reuterdahl depicts the destruction of the squadron. Cervera survived and became a prisoner of war.

*(From* The Story of the Spanish-American War of 1898 *as told by W. Newphew King, Lieutenant U.S.N.)*

by Populism and violent labor strikes, welcomed war as a national unifier. One senator commented that "internal discord" was disappearing in the "fervent heat of patriotism." Sensationalism also figured in the march to war, with the yellow press exaggerating stories of Spanish misdeeds. Theodore Roosevelt and others too young to remember the bloody Civil War looked on war as adventure and used masculine rhetoric to trumpet the call to arms.

More than 263,000 regulars and volunteers served in the army and another 25,000 in the navy during the war. Most of them never left the United States. The typical volunteer was young (early twenties), white, unmarried, native-born, and working class. Many were southerners, a fact that helped the cause of reconciliation following the bitter divisions of the Civil War era. Deaths numbered 5,462—but only 379 in combat. The rest fell to yellow fever and typhoid, and most died in the United States, especially in camps in Tennessee, Virginia, and Florida, where in July and August a typhoid epidemic devastated the ranks. About 10,000 African American troops, assigned to segregated regiments, found no relief from racism and Jim Crow, even though black troops played a key role in the victorious battle for Santiago de Cuba. For all, food, sanitary conditions, and medical care were bad.

Still, Roosevelt could hardly contain himself. Although his Rough Riders, a motley unit of Ivy Leaguers and cowboys, proved undisciplined and often ineffective, they nonetheless received good press largely because of Roosevelt's self-serving publicity efforts.

To the surprise of most Americans, the first war news actually came from faraway Asia, from the Spanish colony of the Philippine Islands. Here, too, Madrid faced a rebellion from Filipinos seeking independence. On May 1, 1898, Commodore George Dewey's New Navy ship *Olympia* led an American squadron into Manila Bay and wrecked the outgunned Spanish fleet. Dewey and his sailors had been on alert in Hong Kong since February, when he received orders from imperial-minded Washington to attack the islands if war broke out. Manila ranked with Pearl Harbor and Pago Pago as a choice harbor, and the Philippines sat significantly on the way to China and its potentially huge market.

**Dewey in the Philippines**

Facing Americans and rebels in both Cuba and the Philippines, Spanish resistance collapsed rapidly. U.S. ships blockaded Cuban ports to prevent Spain from resupplying its army, which suffered hunger and disease because

Cuban insurgents had cut off supplies from the country-side. American troops saw their first ground-war action on June 22, the day several thousand of them landed near Santiago de Cuba and laid siege to the city. On July 3, U.S. warships sank the Spanish Caribbean squadron in Santiago harbor. American forces then assaulted the Spanish colony of Puerto Rico to obtain another Caribbean base for the navy and a strategic site to help protect a Central American canal. Losing on all fronts, Madrid sued for peace.

On August 12, Spain and the United States signed an armistice to end the war. In Paris, in December 1898,

**Treaty of Paris**

American and Spanish negotiators agreed on the peace terms: independence for Cuba from Spain; cession of the Philippines, Puerto Rico, and the Pacific island of Guam to the United States; and American payment of $20 million to Spain for the territories. The U.S. empire now stretched deep into Asia, and the annexation of Wake Island (1898), Hawai'i (1898), and Samoa (1899) gave American traders, missionaries, and naval promoters other steppingstones to China.

During the war with Spain, the *Washington Post* detected "a new appetite, a yearning to show our strength. . . . The taste of empire is in the mouth of the people." But as the nation debated the Treaty of Paris, anti-imperialists such as author Mark Twain, Nebraska politician William Jennings Bryan, intellectual William Graham Sumner, reformer Jane Addams, industrialist Andrew Carnegie, and Senator George Hoar of Massachusetts argued vigorously against annexation of the Philippines. They were disturbed that a war to free Cuba had led to empire, and they stimulated a momentous debate over the fundamental course in American foreign policy.

Imperial control could be imposed either formally (by military occupation, annexation, or colonialism) or

**Anti-Imperialist Arguments**

informally (by economic domination, political manipulation, or the threat of intervention). Anti-imperialist ire focused mostly on the formal kind of imperial control, involving an overseas territorial empire comprised of people of color living far from the mainland. Some critics appealed to principle, citing the Declaration of Independence and the Constitution: the conquest of people against their wills violated the right of self-determination. Philosopher William James charged that the United States was throwing away its special place among nations; it was, he warned, about to "puke up its heritage."

Other anti-imperialists feared that the American character was being corrupted by imperialist zeal. Jane Ad-

dams, seeing children play war games in the streets of Chicago, pointed out that they were not freeing Cubans but rather slaying Spaniards. Hoping to build a distinct foreign policy constituency out of networks of women's clubs and organizations, prominent women like Addams championed peace and an end to imperial conquest.

Some anti-imperialists protested that the United States was practicing a double standard—"offering liberty to the Cubans with one hand, cramming liberty down the throats of the Filipinos with the other, but with both feet planted upon the neck of the negro," as an African American politician from Massachusetts put it. Still other anti-imperialists warned that annexing people of color would undermine Anglo-Saxon purity and supremacy at home.

For Samuel Gompers and other anti-imperialist labor leaders, the issue was jobs: they worried that what Gompers called the "half-breeds and semi-barbaric people" of the new colonies would undercut American labor. Might not the new colonials be imported as cheap contract labor to drive down the wages of American workers? Would not exploitation of the weak abroad become contagious and lead to further exploitation of the weak at home? Would not an overseas empire drain interest and resources from pressing domestic problems, delaying reform?

The anti-imperialists entered the debate with many handicaps and never launched an effective campaign. Although they organized the Anti-Imperialist League in November 1898, they differed so profoundly on domestic issues that they found it difficult to speak with one voice on a foreign question. They also appeared inconsistent: Gompers favored the war but not the postwar annexations; Carnegie would accept colonies if they were not acquired by force; Hoar voted for annexation of Hawai'i but not of the Philippines; Bryan backed the Treaty of Paris but only, he said, to hurry the process toward Philippine independence. Finally, possession of the Philippines was an established fact, very hard to undo.

The imperialists answered their critics with appeals to patriotism, destiny, and commerce. They sketched a scenario of American greatness: mer-

**Imperialist Arguments**

chant ships plying the waters to boundless Asian markets; naval vessels cruising the Pacific to protect American interests; missionaries uplifting inferior peoples. It was America's duty, they insisted, quoting a then-popular Rudyard Kipling poem, to "take up the white man's burden." Furthermore, Filipino insurgents were beginning to resist U.S. rule, and it seemed cowardly to pull out under fire. Germany and Japan, two powerful international competitors, were nosing around the Philippines, apparently ready to seize them if the United States' grip loosened. National honor dictated that Americans keep what they had shed blood to take. Republican Senator Albert Beveridge of Indiana asked, "Shall [history] say that, called by events to captain and command the proudest, ablest, purest race of history in history's noblest work, we declined that great commission?"

In February 1899, by a 57-to-27 vote (just 1 more than the necessary two-thirds majority), the Senate passed the Treaty of Paris, ending the war with Spain. Most Republicans voted yes and most Democrats no. An amendment promising independence as soon as the Filipinos formed a stable government lost by only the tie-breaking ballot of the vice president. Democratic presidential candidate Bryan carried the anti-imperialist case into the election of 1900, warning that repudiation of self-government in the Philippines would weaken the principle at home. But the victorious McKinley refused to apologize for American imperialism, asserting that his policies had served the nation's interests.

## ASIAN ENCOUNTERS: WAR IN THE PHILIPPINES, DIPLOMACY IN CHINA

As McKinley knew, however, the Philippine crisis was far from over. He said he intended to "uplift and civilize" the Filipinos, but they denied that they needed U.S. help. Emilio Aguinaldo, the Philippine nationalist leader who had been battling the Spanish for years, believed that American officials had promised independence for his country. But after the victory over Spain, U.S. officers ordered Aguinaldo out of Manila and isolated him from decisions affecting his nation. In early 1899, feeling betrayed by the Treaty of Paris, he proclaimed an independent Philippine Republic and took up arms. U.S. officials soon set their jaws against the rebellion.

In a war fought viciously by both sides, American soldiers burned crops and villages and tortured captives,

||||||||||||||||||||||||||||||||

**Philippine Insurrection and Pacification**

while Filipino forces staged hit-and-run ambushes that were often brutally effective. Like guerrillas in many later wars, they would strike suddenly and ferociously, and then melt into the jungle or friendly villages. Americans spoke of the "savage" Filipino; one soldier declared that the Philippines "won't be pacified until the niggers [Filipinos] are killed off like the Indians." U.S. troops introduced a variant of the Spanish reconcentration policy—in the province of Batangas, for instance, U.S. troops forced residents to live in designated zones in an effort to separate the insurgents from local support-

ers. Disaster followed. Poor sanitation, starvation, and malaria and cholera killed several thousand people. Outside the secure areas, Americans destroyed food supplies to starve out the rebels. At least one-quarter of the population of Batangas died or fled.

Before the Philippine insurrection was suppressed in 1902, some 20,000 Filipinos had died in combat, and as many as 600,000 had succumbed to starvation and disease. More than 4,000 Americans lay dead. Resistance to U.S. rule, however, did not disappear. The fiercely independent, vehemently anti-Christian, and often violent Muslim Filipinos of Moro Province refused to knuckle under. The U.S. military ordered them to submit or be exterminated. In 1906 the Moros finally met defeat; 600 of them, including many women and children, were slaughtered at the Battle of Bud Dajo. As General Leonard Wood, the Moro provincial governor, wrote the president, "Work of this kind has its disagreeable side."

U.S. officials, with a stern military hand, soon tried to Americanize the Philippines. Architect Daniel Burnham, leader of the City Beautiful movement, planned modern Manila. U.S. authorities instituted a new educational system, with English as the main language of instruction. Thousands of young American educators, many of them motivated by idealism, were recruited to teach in the new schools. The Philippine economy grew while it was an American satellite, and a sedition act silenced critics of U.S. authority by sending them to prison. In 1916 the Jones Act vaguely promised independence once the Philippines established a "stable government." The United States finally ended its rule in 1946 during an intense period of decolonization after the Second World War.

In China, McKinley opted for an approach that emphasized negotiations, with greater success. Outsiders

||||||||||||||||||||||||||||||||

**China and the Open Door Policy**

had been pecking away at China since the 1840s, but the Japanese onslaught intensified the international scramble. Taking advantage of the Qing (Manchu) dynasty's weakness, the major imperial powers carved out spheres of influence (regions over which the outside powers claimed political control and exclusive commercial privileges): Germany in Shandong; Russia in Manchuria; France in Yunnan and Hainan; Britain in Kowloon and Hong Kong. Then, in 1895, the same year as the outbreak of the Cuban revolution, Japan claimed victory over China in a short war and assumed control of Formosa and Korea as well as parts of China proper (see Map 22.1). American religious and business leaders petitioned Washington to halt the dismemberment of China before they were closed out.

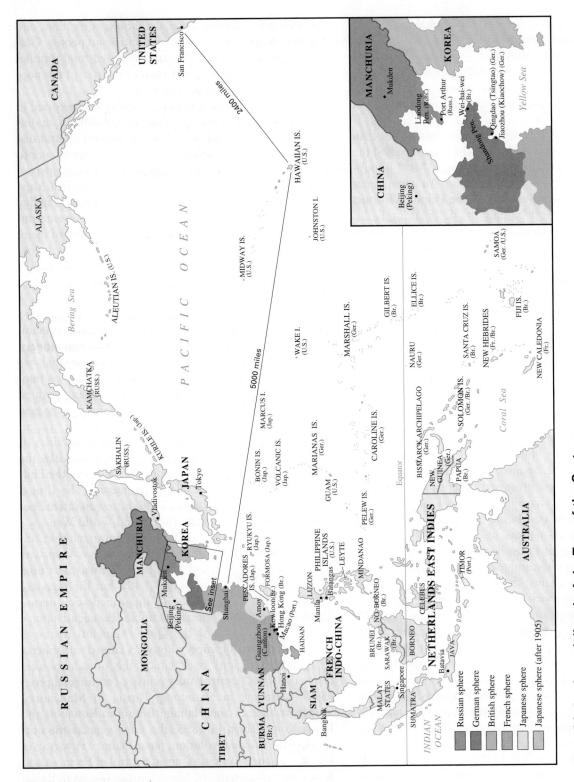

**Map 22.1    Imperialism in Asia: Turn of the Century**

China and the Pacific region had become imperialist hunting grounds by the turn of the century. The European powers and Japan controlled more areas than the United States, which nonetheless participated in the imperial race by annexing the Philippines, Wake, Guam, Hawai'i, and Samoa; announcing the Open Door policy; and expanding trade. As the spheres of influence in China demonstrate, that besieged nation succumbed to outsiders despite the Open Door policy.

Secretary of State John Hay knew that the United States could not force the imperial powers out of China, but he was determined to protect American commerce and missionaries like Lottie Moon. He knew that missionaries had become targets of Chinese nationalist anger and that American oil and textile companies had been disappointed in the results of their investments in the country. Thus, in September 1899, Hay sent the nations with spheres of influence in China a note asking them to respect the principle of equal trade opportunity—an Open Door. The recipients sent evasive replies, privately complaining that the United States was seeking, for free, the trade rights in China that they had gained at considerable military and administrative cost.

The next year, a Chinese secret society called the Boxers (so named in the western press because some members were martial artists) incited riots that killed foreigners, including missionaries, and laid siege to the foreign legations in Beijing. The Boxers sought ultimately to expel all foreigners from China. The United States, applauded by American merchants and missionaries alike, joined the other imperial powers in sending troops to lift the siege. Hay also sent a second Open Door note in July, which instructed other nations to preserve China's territorial integrity and to honor "equal and impartial trade." Hay's protests notwithstanding, China continued for years to be fertile soil for foreign exploitation, especially by the Japanese.

Although Hay's foray into Asian politics settled little, the Open Door policy became a cornerstone of U.S. diplomacy. The "open door" had actually been a long-standing American principle, for as a trading nation the United States opposed barriers to international commerce and demanded equal access to foreign markets. After 1900, however, when the United States began to emerge as the premier world trader, the Open Door policy became an instrument first to pry open markets and then to dominate them, not just in China but throughout the world. The Open Door also developed as an ideology with several tenets: first, that America's domestic well-being required exports; second, that foreign trade would suffer interruption unless the United States intervened abroad to implant American principles and keep markets open; and third, that the closing of any area to American products, citizens, or ideas threatened the survival of the United States itself.

## TR's World

Theodore Roosevelt played an important role in shaping U.S. foreign policy in the McKinley administration. As as-sistant secretary of the navy (1897–1898), as a Spanish-American War hero, and then as vice president in McKinley's second term, Roosevelt worked tirelessly to make the United States a key member of the great power club. He had long had a fascination with power and its uses. He also relished hunting and killing. After an argument with a girlfriend in his youth, he vented his anger by shooting a neighbor's dog. When he killed his first buffalo in the West, he danced crazily around the carcass as his Indian guide watched in amazement. Roosevelt justified the slaughtering of American Indians, if necessary, and took his Rough Riders to Cuba, desperate to get in on the fighting. He was not disappointed. "Did I tell you," he wrote Henry Cabot Lodge afterward, "that I killed a Spaniard with my own hands?"

Like many other Americans of his day, Roosevelt took for granted the superiority of Protestant Anglo-American culture, and he believed in the importance of using American power to shape world affairs (a conviction he summarized by citing the West African proverb "Speak softly and carry a big stick, and you will go far"). In TR's world there were "civilized" and "uncivilized" nations; the former, primarily white and Anglo-Saxon or Teutonic, had a right and a duty to intervene in the affairs of the latter (generally nonwhite, Latin, or Slavic, and therefore "backward") to preserve order and stability. If violent means had to be used to accomplish this task, so be it.

Roosevelt's love of the good fight caused many to rue his ascension to the presidency after McKinley's assassination in September 1901. But there was more to this "cowboy" than mere bluster; he was also an astute analyst of foreign policy and world affairs. TR understood that American power, though growing year by year, remained limited, and that in many parts of the world the United States would have to rely on diplomacy and nonmilitary means to achieve satisfactory outcomes. It would have to work in concert with other powers.

**Presidential Authority**

Roosevelt sought to centralize foreign policy in the White House. The president had to take charge of foreign relations, he believed, in the same way he took the lead in formulating domestic priorities of reorganization and reform. Congress was too large and unwieldy. As for public opinion, it was, Roosevelt said, "the voice of the devil, or what is still worse, the voice of the fool." This conviction that the executive branch should be supreme in foreign policy was to be shared by most presidents who followed TR in office, down to the present day.

With this bald assertion of presidential and national power, Roosevelt stepped onto the international stage. His

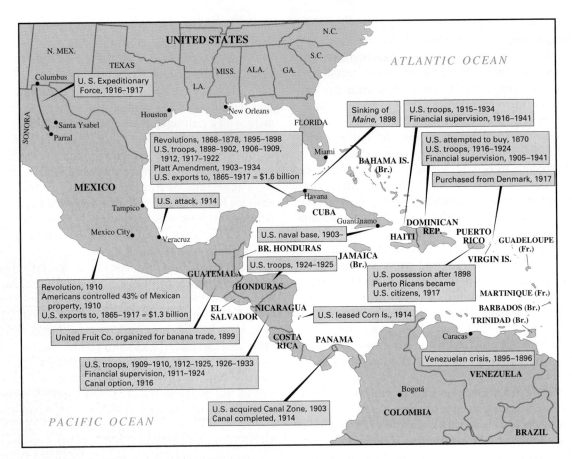

**Map 22.2    U.S. Hegemony in the Caribbean and Latin America**

Through many interventions, territorial acquisitions, and robust economic expansion, the United States became the predominant power in Latin America in the early twentieth century. The United States often backed up the Roosevelt Corollary's declaration of a "police power" by dispatching troops to Caribbean nations, where they met nationalist opposition.

first efforts were focused on Latin America, where U.S. economic and strategic interests and power towered (see Map 22.2), and on Europe, where repeated political and military disputes persuaded Americans to develop friendlier relations with Great Britain while avoiding entrapment in the continent's troubles, many of which Americans blamed on Germany.

As U.S. economic interests expanded in Latin America, so did U.S. political influence. Exports to Latin America, which exceeded $50 million in the 1870s, had risen to more than $120 million when Roosevelt became president in 1901, and then reached $300 million in 1914. Investments by U.S. citizens in Latin America climbed to a commanding $1.26 billion in 1914. In 1899 two large banana importers had merged to form the

United Fruit Company. United Fruit owned much of the land in Central America (more than a million acres in 1913), as well as the railroad and steamship lines, and the firm became an influential economic and political force in the region. The company worked to eradicate yellow fever and malaria at the same time that it manipulated Central American politics, partly by bankrolling favored officeholders.

After the destructive war in Cuba, U.S. citizens and corporations continued to dominate the island's economy,

## Cuba and the Platt Amendment

controlling the sugar, mining, tobacco, and utilities industries, and most of the rural lands. Private U.S. investments in Cuba grew from $50 million before the revolution to $220 million by 1913, and U.S. exports to the island rose from $26 million in 1900 to $196 million in 1917. The Teller Amendment outlawed the annexation of Cuba, but officials in Washington soon used the document's call for "pacification" to justify U.S. control. American troops remained there until 1902.

Favoring the "better classes," U.S. authorities restricted voting rights largely to propertied Cuban males, excluding two-thirds of adult men and all women. American officials also forced the Cubans to append to their constitution a frank avowal of U.S. hegemony known as the Platt Amendment. This statement prohibited Cuba from making a treaty with another nation that might impair its independence; in practice, this meant that all treaties had to have U.S. approval. Most important, another Platt Amendment provision granted the United States "the right to intervene" to preserve the island's independence and to maintain domestic order. The amendment also required Cuba to lease a naval base to the United States (at Guantánamo Bay, still under U.S. jurisdiction today). Formalized in a 1903 treaty, the amendment governed Cuban-American relations until 1934. "There is, of course, little or no independence left Cuba under the Platt Amendment," General Wood, military governor of the island until 1902, told President Roosevelt.

The Cubans, like the Filipinos, chafed under U.S. mastery. Widespread demonstrations protested the Platt Amendment, and a rebellion against the Cuban government in 1906 prompted Roosevelt to order another invasion of Cuba. The marines stayed until 1909, returned briefly in 1912, and occupied the island again from 1917 to 1922. All the while, U.S. officials helped to develop a transportation system, expand the public school system, found a national army, and increase sugar production. When Dr. Walter Reed's experiments, based on the theory of the Cuban physician Carlos Juan Finlay, proved that mosquitoes transmitted yellow fever, sanitary engineers controlled the insect and eradicated the disease.

Puerto Rico, the Caribbean island taken as a spoil of war in the Treaty of Paris, also developed under U.S. tutelage. Although no Puerto Rican sat at the negotiating table for that treaty, the Puerto Rican elite at first welcomed the United States as an improvement over Spain. But disillusionment soon set in. The condescending U.S. military governor, General Guy V. Henry, regarded Puerto Ricans as naughty, ill-educated children who needed "kindergarten instruction in controlling themselves without allowing them too much liberty." Some residents warned against the "Yankee peril"; others applauded the "Yankee model" and futilely anticipated statehood.

▲ In a suit and hat, President Theodore Roosevelt occupies the controls of a ninety-five-ton power shovel at a Panama Canal worksite. Roosevelt's November 1906 trip to inspect the massive project was the first time a sitting president left the United States.

*(AP/Wide World)*

Panama, meanwhile, became the site of a bold U.S. expansionist venture. In 1869 the world had marveled at the completion of the Suez Canal, a waterway in Northeast Africa that greatly facilitated travel between the Indian Ocean and Mediterranean Sea, and enhanced the power of the British Empire. Surely that feat could be duplicated in the Western Hemisphere, possibly in Panama, a province of Colombia. One expansionist, U.S. navy captain Robert W. Shufeldt, predicted that a new canal would convert "the Gulf of Mexico into an American lake." Business interests joined

**Panama Canal**

politicians, diplomats, and navy officers in insisting that the United States control such an interoceanic canal.

To construct such a canal, however, the United States had to overcome daunting obstacles. The Clayton-Bulwer Treaty with Britain (1850) had provided for joint control of a canal. The British, recognizing their diminishing influence in the region and cultivating friendship with the United States as a counterweight to Germany, stepped aside in the Hay-Pauncefote Treaty (1901) to permit a solely U.S.-run canal. When Colombia hesitated to meet Washington's terms, Roosevelt encouraged Panamanian rebels to declare independence and ordered American warships to the isthmus to back them.

In 1903 the new Panama awarded the United States a canal zone and long-term rights to its control. The treaty also guaranteed Panama its independence. (In 1922 the United States paid Colombia $25 million in "conscience money" but did not apologize.) The completion of the Panama Canal in 1914 marked a major technological achievement. During the canal's first year of operation, more than one thousand merchant ships squeezed through its locks.

As for the rest of the Caribbean, Theodore Roosevelt resisted challenges to U.S. hegemony. Worried that Latin American nations' defaults on debts owed to European banks were provoking European intervention (England, Germany, and Italy sent warships to Venezuela in 1902), the president in 1904 issued the Roosevelt Corollary to the Monroe Doctrine. He warned Latin Americans to stabilize their politics and finances. "Chronic wrongdoing," the corollary lectured, might require "intervention by some civilized nation," and "in flagrant cases of such wrongdoing or impotence," the United States would have to assume the role of "an international police power." Laced with presumptions of superiority, Roosevelt's declaration provided the rationale for frequent U.S. interventions in Latin America.

**Roosevelt Corollary**

From 1900 to 1917, U.S. presidents ordered American troops to Cuba, Panama, Nicaragua, the Dominican Republic, Mexico, and Haiti to quell civil wars, thwart challenges to U.S. influence, gain ports and bases, and forestall European meddling (see Map 22.2). U.S. authorities ran elections, trained national guards that became politically powerful, and renegotiated foreign debts, shifting them to U.S. banks. They also took over customs houses to control tariff revenues and government budgets (as in the Dominican Republic, from 1905 to 1941).

U.S. officials focused particular attention on Mexico, where long-time dictator Porfirio Díaz (1876–1910)

▲ Francisco "Pancho" Villa presented himself as a selfless Mexican patriot. Americans living along the border thought otherwise, particularly after Villa's forces murdered more than 30 U.S. civilians. American troops pursued Villa more than 300 hundred miles into Mexico but never caught him. *(John O. Hardman Collection)*

**U.S.-Mexican Relations**

aggressively recruited foreign investors through tax incentives and land grants. American capitalists came to own Mexico's railroads and mines, and invested heavily in petroleum and banking. By the early 1890s, the United States dominated Mexico's foreign trade. By 1910 Americans controlled 43 percent of Mexican property and produced more than half of the country's oil; in the state of Sonora, 186 of 208 mining companies were American owned. The Mexican revolutionaries who ousted Díaz in 1910, like nationalists elsewhere in Latin America, set out to reclaim their nation's sovereignty by ending their economic dependency on the United States.

The revolution descended into a bloody civil war with strong anti-Yankee overtones, and the Mexican government intended to nationalize extensive American-owned properties. Washington leaders worked to thwart this aim, with President Woodrow Wilson twice ordering troops onto Mexican soil: once in 1914, at Veracruz, to avenge a slight to the U.S. uniform and flag, and to overthrow the nationalistic government of President Victoriano Huerta, who was also trying to import German weapons; and again in 1916, in northern Mexico, where General John J. "Black Jack" Pershing spent months pursuing Pancho Villa after the Mexican rebel had raided an American border town. Having failed to capture Villa and facing another nationalistic government led by Venustiano Carranza, U.S. forces departed in January 1917.

As the United States reaffirmed the Monroe Doctrine against European expansion in the hemisphere and demonstrated the power to enforce it, European nations reluctantly honored U.S. hegemony in Latin America. In turn, the United States held to its tradition of standing outside European embroilments. The balance of power in Europe was precarious, and seldom did an American president involve the United States directly. Theodore Roosevelt did help settle a Franco-German clash over Morocco by mediating a settlement at Algeciras, Spain (1906). But the president drew American criticism for entangling the United States in a European problem. Americans endorsed the ultimately futile Hague peace conferences (1899 and 1907) and negotiated various arbitration treaties, but on the whole stayed outside the European arena, except to profit from extensive trade with it.

In East Asia, though, both Roosevelt and his successor, William Howard Taft, took an activist approach.

### Peacemaking in East Asia

Both sought to preserve the Open Door and to contain Japan's rising power in the region. Many race-minded Japanese interpreted the U.S. advance into the Pacific as an attempt by whites to gain ascendancy over Asians. Japanese leaders nonetheless urged their citizens to go to America to study it as a model for industrializing and achieving world power. Although some Americans proudly proclaimed the Japanese the "Yankees of the East," the United States gradually had to make concessions to Japan to protect the vulnerable Philippines and to sustain the Open Door policy. Japan continued to plant interests in China and then smashed the Russians in the Russo-Japanese War (1904–1905). President Roosevelt mediated the negotiations at the Portsmouth Conference in New Hampshire and won the Nobel Peace Prize for this effort to preserve a balance of power in Asia and shrink Japan's "big head."

In 1905, in the Taft-Katsura Agreement, the United States conceded Japanese hegemony over Korea in return for Japan's pledge not to undermine the U.S. position in the Philippines. Three years later, in the Root-Takahira Agreement, Washington recognized Japan's interests in Manchuria, whereas Japan again pledged the security of the Pacific possessions held by the United States and endorsed the Open Door in China. Roosevelt also built up American naval power to deter the Japanese; in late 1907 he sent on a world tour the navy's "Great White Fleet" (so named because the ships were painted white for the voyage). Duly impressed, the Japanese began to build a bigger navy of their own.

President Taft, for his part, thought he might counter Japanese advances in Asia through dollar diplomacy—

### Dollar Diplomacy

the use of private funds to serve American diplomatic goals and garner profits for American financiers, and at the same time bring reform to less-developed countries. In this case, Taft induced American bankers to join an international consortium to build a railway in China. Taft's venture, however, seemed only to embolden Japan to solidify and extend its holdings in China, where internal discord continued after the nationalist revolution of 1911 overthrew the Qing dynasty.

In 1914, when the First World War broke out in Europe, Japan seized Shandong and some Pacific islands from the Germans. In 1915 Japan issued its Twenty-One Demands, virtually insisting on hegemony over all of China. The Chinese door was being slammed shut, but the United States lacked adequate countervailing power in Asia to block Japan's imperial thrusts. A new president, Woodrow Wilson, worried about how the "white race" could blunt the rise of "the yellow race."

British officials in London shared this concern, though their attention was focused primarily on rising tensions in Europe. A special feature of American-European relations in the TR-Taft years was the

### Anglo-American Rapprochement

flowering of an Anglo-American cooperation that had been growing throughout the late nineteenth century. One outcome of the intense German-British rivalry and the rise of the United States to world power was London's quest for friendship with Washington. Already prepared by racial ideas of Anglo-Saxon kinship, a common language, and respect for representative government and private-property rights, Americans appreciated British support in the 1898 war and the Hay-Pauncefote Treaty, and London's virtual endorsement of the Roosevelt Corollary and withdrawal of British warships from the Caribbean. As Mark Twain said of the two imperialist powers, "We are kin in sin."

British-American trade and U.S. investment in Britain also secured ties. By 1914 more than 140 American companies operated in Britain, including H. J. Heinz's processed foods and F. W. Woolworth's "penny markets." Many Britons decried an Americanization of British culture. One journalist complained that a Briton "wakes in the morning at the sound of an American alarm clock; rises from his New England sheets, and shaves with . . . a Yankee safety razor. He . . . slips his Waterbury watch into his pocket [and] catches an electric train made in New York. . . . At his office . . . he sits on a Nebraskan swivel chair, before a Michigan roll-top desk." Such exaggerated fears and the always prickly character of the Anglo-American relationship, however, gave way to cooperation in world affairs, most evident in 1917 when the United States threw its weapons and soldiers into the First World War on the British side against Germany.

# *Legacy* FOR A PEOPLE AND A NATION

## Guantánamo Bay

our hundred miles from Miami, near the southeastern corner of Cuba, sits U.S. Naval Base Guantánamo Bay. It is the oldest American base outside the United States, and the only one located in a country with which Washington does not have an open political relationship. The United States has occupied the base for more than a century, since the aftermath of the Spanish-American War, leasing it from Cuba for $4,085 per year (originally $2,000 in gold coins).

From an early point, Cuban leaders expressed dissatisfaction with the deal, and in the aftermath of Fidel Castro's communist takeover in 1959, Guantánamo was a source of constant tension between the two countries. Castro called the 45-square-mile base "a dagger pointed at Cuba's heart" and over the years has pointedly refused to cash the rent checks. He did cash the very first check, though, and Washington has used that fact to argue that his government accepts the terms of the lease.

Since late 2001 "Gitmo," as the base is known to U.S. service members, has contained a detainment camp for persons alleged to be militant combatants captured in Afghanistan and, later, Iraq and elsewhere. The first group of twenty detainees arrived in January 2002, after a twenty-hour flight from Afghanistan. By the end of 2005, the number exceeded five hundred, from more than forty countries. The George W. Bush administration called the detainees "unlawful enemy combatants" rather than "prisoners of war" but promised early on to abide by the Geneva accords governing prisoners of war. But soon there were allegations of abuse and complaints that holding detainees without trial, charges, or any prospect of release was cruel and unlawful. Some detainees committed suicide. For many critics the camp became an international symbol of American heavy-handedness, and even some administration allies said that the controversy surrounding the camp was severely hurting America's image abroad.

In June 2006, the U.S. Supreme Court ruled that President Bush had overstepped his power in setting up the procedures for the Guantánamo detainees without specific authority from Congress. The Court further said that the procedures violated both the Uniform Code of Military Justice and the Geneva accords. Bush responded by saying publicly that he would like to close the Guantánamo camp but that some prisoners were just too "darned dangerous" to release or return to their home governments. The question for a people and a nation thus remained: how would the United States balance its security needs with its commitment to due process and the rule of law?

## SUMMARY

In the years from the Civil War to the First World War, expansionism and imperialism elevated the United States to world power status. By 1914 Americans held extensive economic, strategic, and political interests in a world made smaller by modern technology. The victory over Spain in 1898 was but the most dramatic moment in the long process. The outward reach of U.S. foreign policy from Seward to Wilson sparked opposition from domestic critics, other imperialist nations, and foreign nationalists, but expansionists prevailed, and the trend toward empire endured.

From Asia to Latin America, economic and strategic needs and ideology motivated and justified expansion and empire. The belief that the United States needed foreign markets to absorb surplus production in order to save the domestic economy joined missionary zeal in reforming other societies through the promotion of American products and culture. Notions of racial and male supremacy and appeals to national greatness also fed the appetite for foreign adventure and commitments. The greatly augmented navy became a primary means for satisfying American ideas and wants.

Revealing the great diversity of America's intersection with the world, missionaries like Moon in China, generals like Wood in Cuba, companies like Singer in Africa and Heinz in Britain, and politicians like Taft in the Philippines carried American ways, ideas, guns, and goods abroad to a mixed reception. The conspicuous declarations of Olney, Hay, Roosevelt, and other leaders became the guiding texts for U.S. principles and behavior in world affairs. A world power with far-flung interests to protect, the United States had to face a tough test of its self-proclaimed greatness and reconsider its political isolation from Europe when a world war broke out in August 1914.

## SUGGESTIONS FOR FURTHER READING

Robert L. Beisner, *Twelve Against Empire: The Anti-Imperialists, 1898–1900* (1968)

Kristin L. Hoganson, *Fighting for American Manhood: How Gender Politics Provoked the Spanish-American and Philippine-American Wars* (1998)

Michael H. Hunt, *Ideology and U.S. Foreign Policy* (1987)

Paul A. Kramer, *The Blood of Government: Race, Empire, the United States, and the Philippines* (2006)

Walter LaFeber, *The American Search for Opportunity, 1865–1913* (1993)

Brian M. Linn, *The Philippine War, 1899–1902* (2000)

Eric T. Love, *Race over Empire: Racism and U.S. Imperialism, 1865–1900* (2004)

Stuart Creighton Miller, *"Benevolent Assimilation": The American Conquest of the Philippines, 1899–1903* (1982)

John Offner, *An Unwanted War: The Diplomacy of the United States and Spain over Cuba, 1895–1898* (1992)

Louis A. Perez Jr., *The War of 1898: The United States and Cuba in History and Historiography* (1998)

*For a more extensive list for further reading, go to* college.hmco.com/pic/norton8e.

# Americans in the
# Great War *1914-1920*

ENLIST

On May 7, 1915, Secretary of State William Jennings Bryan was having lunch with several cabinet members at the Shoreham Hotel in Washington when he received a bulletin: the luxurious British ocean liner *Lusitania* had been sunk, apparently by a German submarine. He rushed to his office, and at 3:06 p.m. came the confirmation from London: "THE LUSITANIA WAS TORPEDOED OFF THE IRISH COAST AND SANK IN HALF AN HOUR. NO NEWS YET OF PASSENGERS." In fact, 1,198 people had perished, including 128 Americans. The giant vessel had taken, not half an hour, but just eighteen minutes to go down. Bryan was deeply distraught but not altogether surprised. The European powers were at war, and he had feared precisely this kind of calamity. Britain had imposed a naval blockade on Germany, and the Germans had responded by launching submarine warfare against Allied shipping. Berlin authorities had proclaimed the North Atlantic a danger zone, and German submarines had already sunk numerous British and Allied ships. As a passenger liner, the *Lusitania* was supposed to be spared, but German officials had placed notices in U.S. newspapers warning that Americans who traveled on British or Allied ships did so at their own risk; passenger liners suspected of carrying munitions or other contraband were subject to attack. For weeks Bryan had urged President Woodrow Wilson to stop Americans from booking passage on British ships; Wilson had refused.

That evening Bryan mused to his wife, "I wonder if that ship carried munitions of war. . . . If she did carry them, it puts a different phase on the whole matter! England has been using our citizens to protect her ammunition!" The *Lusitania*, it soon emerged, *was* carrying munitions, and Bryan set about urging a restrained U.S. response. Desperate to

◀ This poster by Fred Spear, published in Boston not long after the *Lusitania* sinking, captured the anger Americans felt at the loss of 128 of their fellow citizens, among them women and children. Nearly two years before U.S. entry in the war, posters like this one urged Americans to enlist as preparation for the day when they must surely confront the German enemy.

*(Library of Congress)*

## CHRONOLOGY

1914 ■ First World War begins in Europe

1915 ■ Germans sink *Lusitania* off coast of Ireland

1916 ■ After torpedoing the *Sussex,* Germany pledges not to attack merchant ships without warning
■ National Defense Act expands military

1917 ■ Germany declares unrestricted submarine warfare
■ Russian Revolution ousts the czar; Bolsheviks later take power
■ United States enters First World War
■ Selective Service Act creates draft
■ Espionage Act limits First Amendment rights
■ Race riot breaks out in East St. Louis, Illinois

1918 ■ Wilson announces Fourteen Points for new world order
■ Sedition Act further limits free speech
■ U.S. troops at Château-Thierry help blunt German offensive
■ U.S. troops intervene in Russia against Bolsheviks
■ Spanish flu pandemic kills 20 million worldwide
■ Armistice ends First World War

1919 ■ Paris Peace Conference punishes Germany and launches League of Nations
■ May Day bombings help instigate Red Scare
■ American Legion organizes for veterans' benefits and antiradicalism
■ Wilson suffers stroke after speaking tour
■ Senate rejects Treaty of Versailles and U.S. membership in League of Nations
■ *Schenck v. U.S.* upholds Espionage Act

1920 ■ Palmer Raids round up suspected radicals

protest note to Berlin, calling on the German government to end its submarine warfare.

For the next several weeks, as Bryan continued to press his case, he sensed his growing isolation within the administration. When in early June Wilson made it clear that he would not ban Americans from travel on belligerent ships and that he intended to send a second protest note to Germany, Bryan resigned. Privately, Wilson called Bryan a "strange man" who suffered from a "singular sort of moral blindness."

The division between the president and his secretary of state reflected divisions within the American populace over Europe's war. The split could be seen in the reaction to Bryan's resignation. Eastern newspapers charged him with "unspeakable treachery" and of stabbing the country in the back. But in the Midwest and South, Bryan was accorded respect, and he won praise from pacifists and German American groups for his "act of courage." A few weeks later, speaking to a capacity crowd of fifteen thousand at Madison Square Garden (another fifty thousand had been turned away), Bryan was loudly applauded when he warned against "war with any of the belligerent nations." Although many Americans felt, like President Wilson, that honor was more important than peace, others joined Bryan in thinking that some sacrifice of neutral rights was reasonable if the country could thereby stay out of the fighting. The debate would continue up until U.S. entry into the war in 1917, and the tensions would still ripple thereafter.

Like most Americans, Bryan had been stunned by the outbreak of the Great War (as it quickly became known) in 1914. For years the United States had participated in the international competition for colonies, markets, and weapons supremacy. But full-scale war seemed unthinkable. The new machine guns, howitzers, submarines, and dreadnoughts were such awesome death engines that leaders surely would not use them. When they did, lamented one social reformer, "civilization is all gone, and barbarism comes."

For almost three years President Wilson kept America out of the war. During this time, he sought to protect U.S. trade interests and improve the nation's military posture. He lectured the belligerents to rediscover their humanity and to respect international law. But American

keep the United States out of the war, he urged Wilson to couple his condemnation of the German action with an equally tough note to Britain protesting its blockade and to ban Americans from traveling on belligerent ships. Wilson hesitated. Others, including former president Theodore Roosevelt, called the sinking "an act of piracy" and pressed for war. Wilson did not want war, but neither did he accept Bryan's argument that the British and German violations should be treated the same. He sent a strong

property, lives, and neutrality fell victim to British and German naval warfare. When, two years after the *Lusitania* went down, the president finally asked Congress for a declaration of war, he did so with his characteristic crusading zeal. America entered the battle not just to win the war but to reform the postwar world: to "make the world safe for democracy."

A year and a half later, the Great War would be over. It exacted a terrible cost on Europe, for a whole generation of young men was cut down—some 10 million soldiers perished. Europeans looked at their gigantic cemeteries and could scarcely believe what had happened. They experienced an acute spiritual loss in the destruction of ideals, confidence, and goodwill. Economically, too, the damage was immense. Most portentous of all for the future of the twentieth century, the Great War toppled four empires of the Old World—German, Austro-Hungarian, Russian, and Ottoman Turkish—and left two others, British and French, drastically weakened.

For the United States the human and material cost was comparatively small, yet Americans could rightly claim to have helped tip the scales in favor of the Allies with their infusion of war materiel and troops, as well as their extension of loans and food supplies. The war years also witnessed a massive international transfer of wealth from Europe across the Atlantic, as the United States went from being the world's largest debtor nation to being its largest creditor nation. The conflict marked the United States' coming of age as a world power. In these and other respects the Great War was a great triumph for Americans.

In other ways, though, World War I was a difficult, painful experience. It accentuated and intensified social divisions. Racial tensions accompanied the northward migration of southern blacks, and pacifists and German Americans were harassed. The federal government, eager to stimulate patriotism, trampled on civil liberties to silence critics. And following a communist revolution in Russia, a Red Scare in America repressed radicals and tarnished America's reputation as a democratic society. After the war, groups that sought to consolidate wartime gains vied with those that wanted to restore the prewar status quo. Although reformers continued to devote themselves to issues like prohibition and woman suffrage, the war experience helped splinter the Progressive movement. Jane Addams

sadly remarked that "the spirit of fighting burns away all those impulses . . . which foster the will to justice."

Abroad, Americans who had marched to battle as if on a crusade grew disillusioned with the peace process. They recoiled from the spectacle of the victors squabbling over the spoils, and they chided Wilson for failing to deliver the "peace without victory" that he had promised. As in the 1790s, the 1840s, and the 1890s, Americans once again engaged in a searching national debate about the fundamentals of their foreign policy. After negotiating the Treaty of Versailles at Paris following World War I, the president urged U.S. membership in the new League of Nations, which he promoted as a vehicle for reforming world politics. The Senate rejected his appeal (the League nonetheless organized without U.S. membership), because many Americans feared that the League might threaten the U.S. empire and entangle Americans in Europe's problems.

- Why did the United States try to remain neutral and then enter the European war in 1917?
- How was American society changed by the war?
- What were the main elements of Woodrow Wilson's postwar vision, and why did he fail to realize them?

## PRECARIOUS NEUTRALITY

The war that erupted in August 1914 grew from years of European competition over trade, colonies, allies, and armaments. Two powerful alliance systems had formed: the Triple Alliance of Germany, Austria-Hungary, and Italy, and the Triple Entente of Britain, France, and Russia. All had imperial holdings and ambitions for more, but Germany seemed particularly bold, as it rivaled Great Britain for world leadership. Many Americans saw Germany as a threat to U.S. interests in the Western Hemisphere and viewed Germans as an excessively militaristic people who embraced autocracy and spurned democracy.

Strategists said that Europe enjoyed a balance of power, but crises in the Balkan countries of southeastern

**Outbreak of the First World War**

Europe triggered a chain of events that shattered the "balance." Slavic nationalists sought to enlarge Serbia, an independent Slavic nation, by annexing regions such as Bosnia, then a province of the Austro-Hungarian Empire (see Map 23.1). On June 28, 1914, Archduke Franz Ferdinand, heir to the Austro-Hungarian throne, was assassinated by a

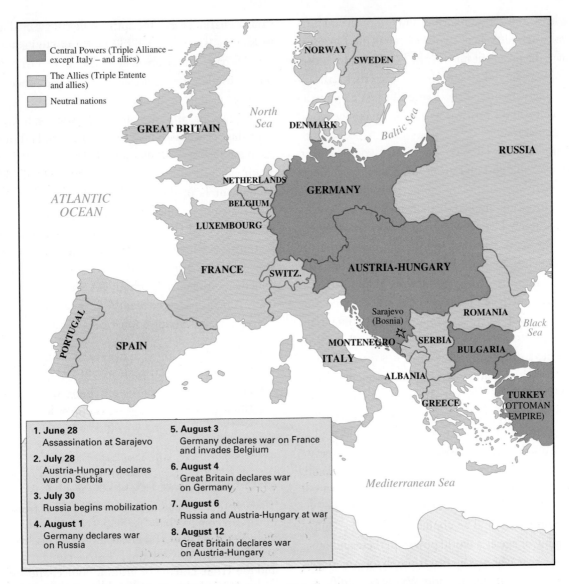

**Central Powers** (Triple Alliance – except Italy – and allies)

**The Allies** (Triple Entente and allies)

**Neutral nations**

1. **June 28**
Assassination at Sarajevo

2. **July 28**
Austria-Hungary declares war on Serbia

3. **July 30**
Russia begins mobilization

4. **August 1**
Germany declares war on Russia

5. **August 3**
Germany declares war on France and invades Belgium

6. **August 4**
Great Britain declares war on Germany

7. **August 6**
Russia and Austria-Hungary at war

8. **August 12**
Great Britain declares war on Austria-Hungary

**Map 23.1    Europe Goes to War, Summer 1914**

Bound by alliances and stirred by turmoil in the Balkans, where Serbs repeatedly upended peace, the nations of Europe descended into war in the summer of 1914. Step by step a Balkan crisis escalated into the "Great War."

Serbian nationalist while on a state visit to Sarajevo, the capital of Bosnia. Alarmed by the prospect of an engorged Serbia on its border, Austria-Hungary consulted its Triple Alliance partner Germany, which urged toughness. When Serbia called on its Slavic friend Russia for help, Russia in turn looked for backing from its ally France. In late July, Austria-Hungary declared war against Serbia. Russia then began to mobilize its armies.

Germany—having goaded Austria-Hungary toward war and believing war inevitable—struck first, declaring war against Russia on August 1 and against France two days later. Britain hesitated, but when German forces slashed into neutral Belgium to get at France, London declared war against Germany on August 4. Eventually Turkey (the Ottoman Empire) joined Germany and Austria-Hungary as the Central Powers, and Italy (switching sides) and Japan teamed up with Britain, France, and Russia as the Allies. Japan took advantage of the European war to seize Shandong, Germany's area of influence in China.

President Wilson at first sought to distance America from the conflagration by issuing a proclamation of neutrality—the traditional U.S. policy toward European wars. He also asked Americans to refrain from taking sides, to exhibit "the dignity of self-control." In private, the president said, "We definitely have to be neutral, since otherwise our mixed populations would wage war on each other." The United States, he fervently hoped, would stand apart as a sane, civilized nation in a deranged international system.

Wilson's lofty appeal for American neutrality and unity at home collided with several realities. First, ethnic groups in the United States did take sides. Many German Americans and anti-British Irish Americans (Ireland was then trying to break free from British rule) cheered for the Central Powers. Americans of British and French ancestry, and others with roots in Allied nations, tended to champion the Allied cause. Germany's attack on Belgium confirmed in many people's minds that Germany had become the archetype of unbridled militarism.

**Taking Sides**

The pro-Allied sympathies of Wilson's administration also weakened the U.S. neutrality proclamation. Honoring Anglo-American rapprochement, Wilson shared the conviction with British leaders that a German victory would destroy free enterprise and government by law. If Germany won the war, he prophesied, "it would change the course of our civilization and make the United States a military nation." Several of Wilson's chief advisers and diplomats—his assistant, Colonel Edward House; ambassador to London Walter Hines Page; and Robert Lansing, a counselor in the State Department who later became secretary of state—held similar anti-German views which often translated into pro-Allied policies.

U.S. economic links with the Allies also rendered neutrality difficult, if not impossible. England had long been one of the nation's best customers. Now the British flooded America with new orders, especially for arms. Sales to the Allies helped pull the American economy out of its recession. Between 1914 and 1916, American exports to England and France grew 365 percent, from $753 million to $2.75 billion. In the same period, however, largely because of Britain's naval blockade, exports to Germany dropped by more than 90 percent, from $345 million to only $29 million. Loans to Britain and France from private American banks—totaling $2.3 billion during the neutrality period—financed much of U.S. trade with the Allies. Germany received only $27 million in the same period. The Wilson administration, which at first frowned on these transactions, came to see them as necessary to the economic health of the United States.

From Germany's perspective, the links between the American economy and the Allies meant that the United States had become the Allied arsenal and bank. Americans, however, faced a dilemma: cutting their economic ties with Britain would constitute a nonneutral act in favor of Germany. Under international law, Britain—which controlled the seas—could buy both contraband (war-related goods) and noncontraband from neutrals. It was Germany's responsibility, not America's, to stop such trade in ways that international law prescribed—that is, by an effective blockade of the enemy's territory, by the seizure of contraband from neutral (American) ships, or by the confiscation of goods from belligerent (British) ships. Germans, of course, judged the huge U.S. trade with the Allies an act of nonneutrality that had to be stopped.

The president and his aides believed, finally, that Wilsonian principles stood a better chance of international acceptance if Britain, rather than the Central Powers, sat astride the postwar world. "Wilsonianism," the cluster of ideas that Wilson espoused, consisted of traditional American principles (such as democracy and the Open Door) and a conviction that the United States was a beacon of freedom to the world. Only the United States could lead the convulsed world into a new, peaceful era of unobstructed commerce, free-market capitalism, democratic politics, and open diplomacy. American Progressivism, it seemed, was to be projected onto the world.

**Wilsonianism**

"America had the infinite privilege of fulfilling her destiny and saving the world," Wilson claimed. Empires had to be dismantled to honor the principle of self-determination. Armaments had to be reduced. Critics charged that Wilson often violated his own credos in his eagerness to force them on others—as his military interventions in Mexico in 1914, Haiti in 1915, and the Dominican Republic in 1916 testified. All agreed, though, that such ideals served American commercial purposes; in this way idealism and self-interest were married.

To say that American neutrality was never a real possibility given ethnic loyalties, economic ties, and Wilsonian preferences is not to say that Wilson sought to enter the war. He emphatically wanted to keep the United States out. Time and again, he tried to mediate the crisis to prevent one power from crushing another. In early 1917, the president remarked that "we are the only one of the great white nations that is free from war today, and it would be a crime against civilization for us to go in." But go in the United States finally did. Why?

The short answer is that Americans got caught in the Allied–Central Power crossfire. British naval policy aimed

||||||||||||||||||||||||||||||||

**Violations of Neutral Rights**

to sever neutral trade with Germany in order to cripple the German economy. The British, "ruling the waves and waiving the rules," declared a blockade of water entrances to Germany and mined the North Sea. They also harassed neutral shipping by seizing cargoes and defining a broad list of contraband (including foodstuffs) that they prohibited neutrals from shipping to Germany. American commerce with Germany dwindled rapidly. Furthermore, to counter German submarines, the British flouted international law by arming their merchant ships and flying neutral (sometimes American) flags. Wilson frequently protested British violations of neutral rights, pointing out that neutrals had the right to sell and ship noncontraband goods to belligerents without interference. But London often deftly defused Washington's criticism by paying for confiscated cargoes, and German provocations made British behavior appear less offensive by comparison.

Unable to win the war on land and determined to lift the blockade and halt American-Allied commerce, Germany looked for victory at sea by using submarines. In February 1915, Berlin declared a war zone around the British Isles, warned neutral vessels to stay out so as not to be attacked by mistake, and advised passengers from neutral nations to stay off Allied ships. President Wilson

informed Germany that the United States would hold it to "strict accountability" for any losses of American life and property.

Wilson was interpreting international law in the strictest possible sense. The law that an attacker had to warn a passenger or merchant ship before attacking, so that passengers and crew could disembark safely into lifeboats, predated the submarine. The Germans thought the slender, frail, and sluggish *Unterseebooten* (U-boats) should not be expected to surface to warn ships, for surfacing would cancel out the U-boats' advantage of surprise and leave them vulnerable to attack. Berlin protested that Wilson was denying it the one weapon that could break the British economic stranglehold, disrupt the Allies' substantial connection with U.S. producers and bankers, and win the war. To all concerned—British, Germans, and Americans—naval warfare became a matter of life and death.

## THE DECISION FOR WAR

Ultimately, it was the war at sea that doomed the prospects for U.S. neutrality. In the early months of 1915, German U-boats sank ship after ship, most notably the British liner *Lusitania* on May 7. In mid-August, after a lull following Germany's promise to refrain from attacking passenger liners, another British vessel, the *Arabic*, was sunk off Ireland. Three Americans died. The Germans

Initially underestimated as a ▶ weapon, the German U-boat proved to be frighteningly effective against Allied ships. At the beginning of the war, Germany had about twenty operational submarines in its High Seas Fleet, but officials moved swiftly to speed up production. This photograph shows a German U-boat under construction in 1914.

*(Bibliothek für Zeitgeschichte, Stuttgart)*

quickly pledged that an unarmed passenger ship would never again be attacked without warning. But the sinking of the *Arabic* fueled debate over American passengers on belligerent vessels. Echoing Bryan's plea from the previous spring (see the chapter-opening vignette), critics asked: why not require Americans to sail on American craft? From August 1914 to March 1917, after all, only 3 Americans died on an American ship (the tanker *Gulflight*, sunk by a German U-boat in May 1915), whereas about 190 were killed on belligerent ships.

In March 1916, a U-boat attack on the *Sussex*, a French vessel crossing the English Channel, took the United States a step closer to war.

## Peace Advocates

Four Americans were injured on that ship, which the U-boat commander mistook for a minelayer. Stop the marauding submarines, Wilson lectured Berlin, or the United States will sever diplomatic relations. Again the Germans retreated, pledging not to attack merchant vessels without warning. At about the same time, U.S. relations with Britain soured. The British crushing of the Easter Rebellion in Ireland and further British restriction of U.S. trade with the Central Powers aroused American anger.

As the United States became more entangled in the Great War, many Americans urged Wilson to keep the nation out. In early 1915, Jane Addams, Carrie Chapman Catt, and other suffragists helped found the Woman's Peace Party, the U.S. section of the Women's International League for Peace and Freedom. "The mother half of humanity," claimed women peace advocates, had a special role as "the guardians of life." Later that same year, some pacifist Progressives—including Oswald Garrison Villard, Paul Kellogg, and Lillian Wald—organized an antiwar coalition, the American Union Against Militarism. The businessman Andrew Carnegie, who in 1910 had established the Carnegie Endowment for International Peace, helped finance peace groups. So did Henry Ford, who in late 1915 traveled on a "peace ship" to Europe to propagandize for a negotiated settlement. Socialists like Eugene Debs added their voices to the peace movement.

Antiwar advocates emphasized several points: that war drained a nation of its youth, resources, and reform impulse; that it fostered repression at home; that it violated Christian morality; and that wartime business barons reaped huge profits at the expense of the people. Militarism and conscription, Addams pointed out, were what millions of immigrants had left behind in Europe. Were they now—in the United States—to be forced into the decadent system they had escaped? Although the peace movement was splintered—some wanted to keep the United States out of the conflict but did not endorse the pacifists' claim that intervention could never be justified—it carried political and intellectual weight that Wilson could not ignore, and it articulated several ideas that he shared. In fact, he campaigned on a peace platform in the 1916 presidential election. After his triumph, Wilson futilely labored once again to bring the belligerents to the conference table. In early 1917 he advised them to temper their acquisitive war aims, appealing for "peace without victory."

In Germany, Wilson's overture went unheeded. Since August 1916, leaders in Berlin had debated whether to resume the unrestricted U-boat campaign.

## Unrestricted Submarine Warfare

Opponents feared a break with the United States, but proponents claimed there was no choice. Only through an all-out attack on Britain's supply shipping, they argued, could Germany win the war before the British blockade and trench warfare in France had exhausted Germany's ability to keep fighting. If the U-boats could sink 600,000 tons of Allied shipping per month, the German admiralty estimated, Britain would be brought to the brink of starvation. True, the United States might enter the war, but that was a risk worth taking. Victory might be achieved before U.S. troops could be ferried across the Atlantic in sizable numbers. It proved a winning argument. In early February 1917, Germany launched unrestricted submarine warfare. All warships and merchant vessels—belligerent or neutral—would be attacked if sighted in the declared war zone. Wilson quickly broke diplomatic relations with Berlin.

This German challenge to American neutral rights and economic interests was soon followed by a German threat to U.S. security. In late February, British intelligence intercepted and passed to U.S. officials a telegram addressed to the German minister in Mexico from German foreign secretary Arthur Zimmermann. Its message: If Mexico joined a military alliance against the United States, Germany would help Mexico recover the territories it had lost in 1848, including several western states. Zimmermann hoped to "set new enemies on America's neck—enemies which give them plenty to take care of over there."

The Zimmermann telegram stiffened Wilson's resolve. Even though Mexico City rejected Germany's offer, the Wilson administration judged Zimmermann's telegram "a conspiracy against this country." Mexico still might let German agents use Mexican soil to propagandize against the United States, if not sabotage American properties. The prospect of a German-Mexican collaboration helped turn the tide of opinion in the American Southwest, where antiwar sentiment had been strong.

Soon afterward, Wilson asked Congress for "armed neutrality" to defend American lives and commerce. He requested authority to arm American merchant ships and to "employ any other instrumentalities or methods that may be necessary." In the midst of the debate, Wilson released Zimmermann's telegram to the press. Americans were outraged. Still, antiwar senators Robert M. La Follette and George Norris, among others, saw the armed-ship bill as a blank check for the president to move the country to war, and they filibustered it to death. Wilson proceeded to arm America's commercial vessels anyway. The action came too late to prevent the sinking of several American ships. War cries echoed across the nation. In late March, an agonized Wilson called Congress into special session.

On April 2, 1917, the president stepped before a hushed Congress. Solemnly he accused the Germans of "warfare against mankind." Pas-

||||||||||||||||||||||||||||||||||||

## War Message and War Declaration

sionately and eloquently, Wilson enumerated U.S. grievances: Germany's violation of freedom of the seas, disruption of commerce, interference with Mexico, and breach of human rights by killing innocent Americans. The "Prussian autocracy" had to be punished by "the democracies." Russia was now among the latter, he was pleased to report, because the Russian Revolution had ousted the czar just weeks before. Congress declared war against Germany on April 6 by a vote of 373 to 50 in the House and 82 to 6 in the Senate. (This vote was for war against Germany only; a declaration of war against Austria-Hungary came several months later, on December 7.) Montana's Jeannette Rankin, the first woman ever to sit in Congress, cast a ringing no vote. "Peace is a woman's job," she declared, "because men have a natural fear of being classed as cowards if they oppose war" and because mothers should protect their children from death-dealing weapons.

For principle, for morality, for honor, for commerce, for security, for reform—for all of these reasons, Wilson took the United States into the Great War. The submarine was certainly the culprit that drew a reluctant president and nation into the maelstrom. Yet critics did not attribute the U.S. descent into war to the U-boat alone. They emphasized Wilson's rigid definition of international law, which did not accommodate the submarine's tactics. They faulted his contention that Americans should be entitled to travel anywhere, even on a belligerent ship loaded with contraband. They criticized his policies as nonneutral. But they lost the debate. Most Americans came to accept Wilson's view that the Germans had to be checked to ensure an open, orderly world in which U.S. principles and interests would be safe.

▲ Jeannette Rankin (1880–1973) of Montana was the first woman to sit in the House of Representatives (elected in 1916) and the only member of Congress to vote against U.S. entry into both world wars (in 1917 and 1941). A lifelong pacifist, she led a march in Washington, D.C.—at age eighty-seven—against U.S. participation in the Vietnam War. *(Brown Brothers)*

America went to war to reform world politics, not to destroy Germany. Wilson once claimed that the United States was "pure air blowing in world politics, destroying illusions and cleaning places of morbid miasmic gasses." By early 1917 the president concluded that America would not be able to claim a seat at the postwar peace conference unless it became a combatant. At the peace conference, Wilson intended to promote the principles he thought essential to a stable world order, to advance democracy and the Open Door, and to outlaw revolution and aggression. Wilson tried to preserve part of his country's status as a neutral by designating the United States an "Associated" power rather than a full-fledged Allied nation, but this was akin to a hope of being only partly pregnant.

## WINNING THE WAR

Even before the U.S. declaration of war, the Wilson administration—encouraged by such groups as the National

Security League and the Navy League, and by mounting public outrage against Germany's submarine warfare—had been strengthening the military under the banner of "preparedness." When the pacifist song "I Didn't Raise My Boy to Be a Soldier" became popular, preparedness proponents retorted, "I Didn't Raise My Boy to Be a Coward." The National Defense Act of 1916 provided for increases in the army and National Guard, and for summer training camps modeled on the one in Plattsburgh, New York, where a slice of America's social and economic elite had trained in 1915 as "citizen-soldiers." The Navy Act of 1916 started the largest naval expansion in American history.

To raise an army after the declaration of war, Congress in May 1917 passed the Selective Service Act, re-

### The Draft and the Soldier

quiring all males between the ages of twenty-one and thirty (later changed to eighteen and forty-five) to register. National service, proponents believed, would not only prepare the nation for battle but also instill patriotism and respect for order, democracy, and personal sacrifice. Critics feared it would lead to the militarization of American life.

On June 5, 1917, more than 9.5 million men signed up for the "great national lottery." By war's end, 24 million men had been registered by local draft boards. Of this number, 4.8 million had served in the armed forces, 2 million of that number in France. Among them were hundreds of thousands who had volunteered before December 1917, when the government prohibited enlistment because the military judged voluntarism too inefficient (many volunteers were more useful in civilian factories than in the army) and too competitive (enlistees got to choose the service they wanted, thus setting off recruiting wars). Millions of laborers received deferments from military duty because they worked in war industries or had dependents.

The typical soldier was a draftee in his early to midtwenties, white, single, American-born, and poorly educated (most had not attended high school, and perhaps 30 percent could not read or write). Tens of thousands of women enlisted in the army Nurse Corps, served as "hello girls" (volunteer bilingual telephone operators) in the army Signal Corps, and became clerks in the navy and Marine Corps. On college campuses, 150,000 students joined the Student Army Training Corps or similar navy and marine units. At officer training camps, the army turned out "ninety-day wonders."

Some 400,000 African Americans also served in the military. Although many southern politicians feared arming African Americans, the army drafted them into segre-

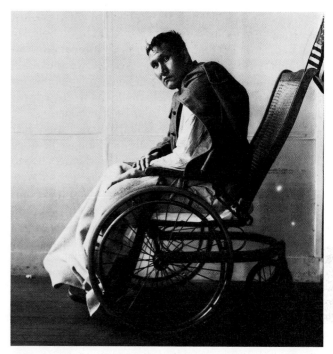

▲ Some fifteen thousand Native Americans served in the military in World War I. Most of them were enlistees who sought escape from restrictive Indian schools and lives of poverty, opportunities to develop new skills, and chances to prove their patriotism. This photo shows Fast Fred Horse, a Rosebud Sioux, as he recuperates in a New York hospital after suffering injury and paralysis during the Meuse-Argonne campaign of fall 1918. Unlike African Americans, Native Americans were not assigned to segregated units during the war. Native Americans participated in all major battles against German forces and suffered a high casualty rate in large part because they served as scouts, messengers, and snipers.

*(William Hammond Mathers Museum, Indiana University)*

gated units, where they were assigned to menial labor and endured crude abuse and miserable conditions. Ultimately more than 40,000 blacks would see combat in Europe, however, and several black units served with distinction in various divisions of the French army. The all-black 369th Infantry Regiment, for example, spent more time in the trenches—191 days—and received more medals than any other American outfit. The French government awarded the entire regiment the Croix de Guerre.

Although French officers had their share of racial prejudice and often treated the soldiers from their own African colonies poorly, black Americans serving with the French reported a degree of respect and cooperation generally lacking in the American army. They also spoke of getting a much warmer reception from French civilians than they were used to in the United States. The irony was not lost on African American leaders, such as W. E. B. Du Bois. Du Bois had endorsed the support of the National Association for the Advancement of Colored People (NAACP) for the war and echoed its call for blacks to volunteer for the fight so that they might help make the world safe for democracy and help blur the color lines at home.

Not everyone eligible for military service was eager to sign up, however. Approximately 3 million men evaded draft registration. Some were arrested, and others fled to Mexico or Canada, but most stayed at home and were never discovered. Another 338,000 men who had registered and been summoned by their draft boards failed to show up for induction. According to arrest records, most of these "deserters" and the more numerous "evaders" were lower-income agricultural and industrial laborers. Some simply felt overwhelmed by the government bureaucracy and stayed away; others were members of minority or ethnic groups who felt alienated. Although nearly 65,000 draftees initially applied for conscientious-objector status (refusing to bear arms for religious or pacifist reasons), some changed their minds or, like so many others, failed preinduction examinations. Quakers and Mennonites were numerous among the 4,000 inductees actually classified as conscientious objectors (COs). They did not have it easy. General Leonard Wood called COs "enemies of the Republic," and the military harassed them. COs who refused noncombat service, such as in the medical corps, faced imprisonment.

The U.S. troops who shipped out to France would do their fighting under American command. General John J. Pershing, head of the American Expeditionary Forces (AEF), insisted that his "sturdy rookies" remain a separate, independent army. He was not about to turn over his "doughboys" (so termed, apparently, because the large buttons on American uniforms in the 1860s resembled a deep-fried bread of that name) to Allied commanders, who had become wedded to unimaginative and deadly trench warfare, producing a military stalemate and ghastly casualties on the western front. Since the fall of 1914, zigzag trenches fronted by

## Trench Warfare

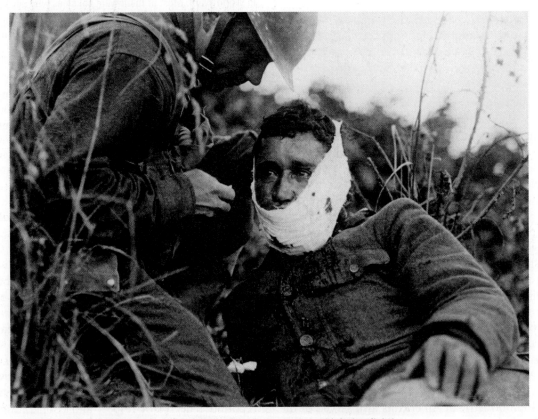

▲ A U.S. soldier of Company K, 110th Infantry Regiment, receives aid during fighting at Verennes, France. *(National Archives)*

barbed wire and mines stretched across France. Between the muddy, stinking trenches lay "no man's land," denuded by artillery fire. When ordered out, soldiers would charge enemy trenches. If machine gun fire did not greet them, poison gas might.

First used by the Germans in April 1915, chlorine gas stimulated overproduction of fluid in the lungs, leading to death by drowning. One British officer tending to troops who had been gassed reported that "quite 200 men passed through my hands. . . . Some died with me, others on the way down. . . . I had to argue with many of them as to whether they were dead or not." Gas in a variety of forms (mustard and phosgene, in addition to chlorine) would continue in use throughout the war, sometimes blistering, sometimes incapacitating, often killing.

The extent of the dying in the trench warfare is hard to comprehend. At the Battle of the Somme in 1916, the British and French suffered 600,000 dead or wounded to earn only 125 square miles; the Germans lost 400,000 men. At Verdun that same year, 336,000 Germans perished, and at Passchendaele in 1917 more than 370,000 British men died to gain about 40 miles of mud and barbed wire. Ambassador Page grew sickened by what Europe had become—"a bankrupt slaughter-house inhabited by unmated women."

The first American units landed in France on June 26, 1917, marched in a Fourth of July parade in Paris, and

## Shell Shock

then moved by train toward the front. They soon learned about the horrors caused by advanced weaponry. Some suffered shell shock, a form of mental illness also known as war psychosis. Symptoms included a fixed, empty stare; violent tremors; paralyzed limbs; listlessness; jabbering and screaming; and haunting dreams. The illness could strike anyone; even those soldiers who appeared most manly and courageous cracked after days of incessant shelling and inescapable human carnage. "There was a limit to human endurance," one lieutenant explained. Providing some relief were Red Cross canteens, staffed by women volunteers, which gave soldiers way stations in a strange land and offered haircuts, food, and recreation. Some ten thousand Red Cross nurses also cared for the young warriors, while the American Library Association distributed 10 million books and magazines.

In Paris, where forty large houses of prostitution thrived, it became commonplace to hear that the British were drunkards, the French were whoremongers, and the Americans were both. Venereal disease became a serious problem. French prime minister Georges Clemenceau offered licensed, inspected prostitutes in "special houses" to the American army. When the generous Gallic offer reached Washington, Secretary of War Newton Baker gasped, "For God's sake . . . don't show this to the President or he'll stop the war." By war's end, about 15 percent of America's soldiers had contracted venereal disease, costing the army $50 million and 7 million days of active duty. Periodic inspections, chemical prophylactic treatments, and the threat of court-martial for infected soldiers kept the problem from being even greater.

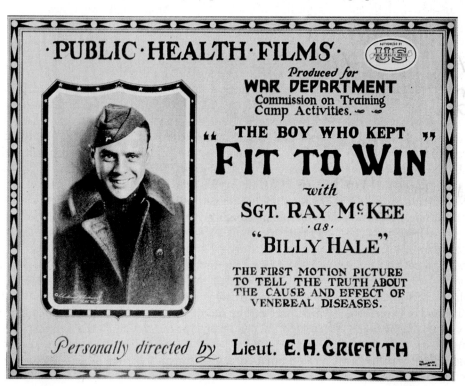

◀ During the First World War, the War Department promoted a film to combat sexually transmitted diseases. After the war, the New York State Board of Censors declared the film obscene.

*(Social Welfare History Archives Center, University of Minnesota)*

The experience of being in Europe enlarged what for many American draftees had been a circumscribed world.

### American Units in France

Soldiers filled their diaries and letters with descriptions of the local customs and "ancient" architecture, and noted how the grimy and war-torn French countryside bore little resemblance to the groomed landscapes they had seen in paintings. Some felt both admiration for the spirit of endurance they saw in the populace and irritation that the locals were not more grateful for the Americans' arrival. "Life in France for the American soldier meant marching in the dirt and mud, living in cellars in filth, being wet and cold and fighting," the chief of staff of the Fourth Division remarked. "He had come to help France in the hour of distress and he was glad he came but these French people did not seem to appreciate him at all."

The influx of American men and materiel—and the morale blow they delivered to the Central Powers—decided the outcome of the First World War. With both sides exhausted, the Americans tipped the balance toward the Allies. It took time, though, for the weight of the American military machine to make itself felt. From an early point, the U.S. Navy battled submarines and escorted troop carriers, and pilots in the U.S. Air Service, flying mostly British and French aircraft, saw limited action, mostly against German ground troops and transport. American "aces" like Eddie Rickenbacker took on their German counterparts in aerial "dogfights" and became heroes, as much in France as in their own country. But only ground troops could make a decisive difference, and American units actually did not engage in much combat until after the lull in the fighting during the harsh winter of 1917–1918.

By then, the military and diplomatic situation had changed dramatically, because of an event that was arguably the most important political

### The Bolshevik Revolution

development of the twentieth century: the Bolshevik Revolution in Russia. In November 1917, the liberal-democratic government of Aleksander Kerensky, which had led the country since the czar's abdication early in the year, was overthrown by radical socialists led by V. I. Lenin. Lenin seized power vowing to change world politics and end imperial rivalries on terms that challenged Woodrow Wilson's. Lenin saw the war as signaling the impending end of capitalism and looked for a global revolution, carried out by workers, that would sweep away the "imperialist order." For western leaders, the prospect of Bolshevik-style revolutions

spreading worldwide was too frightening to contemplate. The ascendancy of the world's laboring classes working in unity would destroy governments everywhere.

In the weeks following their takeover, the Bolsheviks attempted to embarrass the capitalist governments and incite world revolution by publishing several secret agreements among the Allies for dividing up the colonies and other territories of the Central Powers in the event of an Allied victory. Veteran watchers of world affairs found nothing particularly shocking in the documents, and Wilson had known of them, but the disclosures belied the noble rhetoric of Allied war aims. Wilson confided to Colonel House that he really wanted to tell the Bolsheviks to "go to hell," but he accepted the colonel's argument that he would have to address Lenin's claims that there was little to distinguish the two warring sides and that socialism represented the future.

The result was the Fourteen Points, unveiled in January 1918, in which Wilson reaffirmed America's commit-

### Fourteen Points

ment to an international system governed by laws and renounced territorial gains as a legitimate war aim. The first five points called for diplomacy "in the public view," freedom of the seas, lower tariffs, reductions in armaments, and the decolonization of empires. The next eight points specified the evacuation of foreign troops from Russia, Belgium, and France, and appealed for self-determination for nationalities in Europe, such as the Poles. For Wilson, the fourteenth point was the most important—the mechanism for achieving all the others: "a general association of nations" or League of Nations.

Wilson's appeal did not impress Lenin, who called for an immediate end to the fighting, the eradication of colonialism, and self-determination for all peoples. Lenin also made a separate peace with Germany—the Treaty of Brest-Litovsk, signed on March 3, 1918. The deal erased centuries of Russian expansion, as Poland, Finland, and the Baltic states were taken from Russia and Ukraine was granted independence. One of Lenin's motives was to allow Russian troops loyal to the Bolsheviks to return home to fight anti-Bolshevik forces, who had launched a civil war to oust the new government.

The emerging feud between Lenin and Wilson contained the seeds of the superpower confrontation that would dominate the international system after 1945. Both men rejected the old diplomacy which they claimed had created the conditions for the current war; both insisted on the need for a new world order. Although each professed adherence to democratic principles, they defined democracy differently. For Lenin, it meant workers everywhere seizing control from the owners of capital and establishing worker-led governments. For Wilson, it meant independent governments operating within capitalist systems and according to republican political practices.

In March 1918, with German troops released from the Russian front and transferred to France, the Germans

|||||||||||||||||||||||||||||||||||||

## Americans in Battle

launched a major offensive. By May they had pushed to within 50 miles of Paris. Late that month, troops of the U.S. First Division helped blunt the German advance at Cantigny (see Map 23.2). In June the Third Division and French forces held positions along the Marne River at

Château-Thierry, and the Second Division soon attacked the Germans in the Belleau Wood. American soldiers won the battle after three weeks of fighting, but thousands died or were wounded after they made almost sacrificial frontal assaults against German machine guns.

Allied victory in the Second Battle of the Marne in July 1918 stemmed all German advances. In September, French and American forces took St. Mihiel in a ferocious battle in which American gunners fired 100,000 rounds of phosgene gas shells. Then the Allies began their massive Meuse-Argonne offensive. More than 1 million Americans joined British and French troops in weeks of fierce combat; some 26,000 Americans died before the Allies claimed the Argonne Forest on October 10. For Germany—its

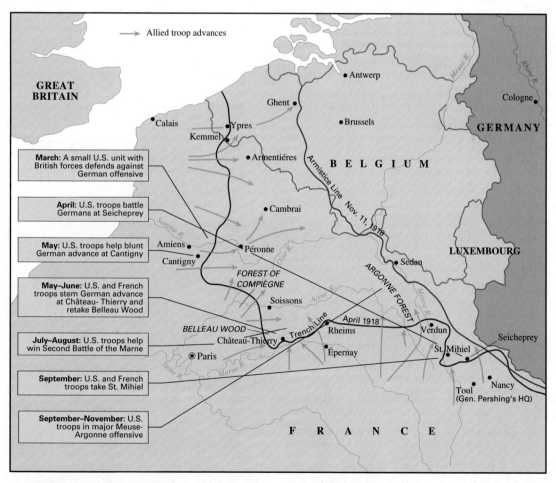

**Map 23.2    American Troops at the Western Front, 1918**

America's 2 million troops in France met German forces head-on, ensuring the defeat of the Central Powers in 1918.

# The Influenza Pandemic of 1918

*I*n the summer and fall of 1918, as World War I neared its end, a terrible plague swept the earth. It was a massive outbreak of influenza, and it would kill more than twice as many as the Great War itself—somewhere between 25 and 40 million people. In the United States, 675,000 people died.

The first cases were identified in midwestern military camps in early March. Soldiers complained of flulike symptoms—headache, sore throat, fever—and many did not recover. At Fort Riley, Kansas, 48 men died. But with the war effort in full swing, few in government or the press took notice. Soldiers shipped out to Europe in large numbers (84,000 in March), some unknowingly carrying the virus in their lungs. The illness appeared on the western front in April. By the end of June, an estimated 8 million Spaniards were infected, thereby giving the disease its name, the Spanish flu.

In August, after a midsummer lull, a second, deadlier form of the influenza began spreading. This time, the epidemic erupted simultaneously in three cities on three continents: Freetown, Sierra Leone, in Africa; Brest, France, the port of entry for many American soldiers; and Boston, Massachusetts. In September, the disease swept down the East Coast to New York, Philadelphia, and beyond. That month, 12,000 Americans died.

It was a flu like no other. People could be healthy at the start of the weekend and dead by the end of it. Some experienced a rapid accumulation of fluid in the lungs and would quite literally drown. Others died more slowly, of secondary infections with bacterial pneumonia. Mortality rates were highest for twenty- to twenty-nine-year-olds—the same group dying in huge numbers in the trenches.

In October, the epidemic hit full force. It spread to Japan, India, Africa, and Latin America. In the United States, 200,000 perished. There was a nationwide shortage of caskets and gravediggers, and funerals were limited to fifteen minutes. Bodies were left in gutters or on front porches, to be picked up by trucks that drove the streets. Stores were forbidden to hold sales; schools and cinemas closed. Army surgeon general Victor Vaughan made a frightening calculation: "If the epidemic continues its mathematical rate of acceleration, civilization could easily disappear from the face of the earth within a few weeks."

Then, suddenly, in November, for reasons still unclear, the epidemic eased, though the dying continued into 1919. In England and Wales, the final toll was 200,000. Samoa lost a quarter of its population, while in India the epidemic may have claimed a staggering 20 million. It was, in historian Roy Porter's words, "the greatest single demographic shock mankind has ever experienced."

World War I had helped spread the disease, but so had technological improvements that in previous decades facilitated global travel. The world was a smaller, more intimate place, often for good but sometimes for ill. Americans, accustomed to thinking that two great oceans could isolate them, were reminded that they were immutably linked to humankind.

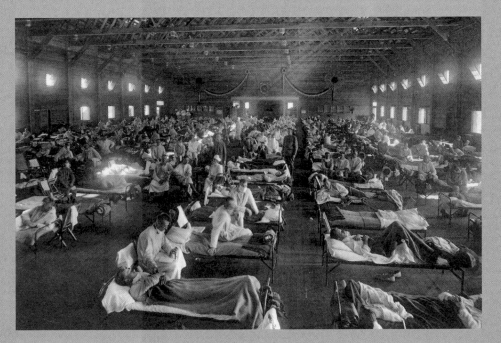

The influenza pandemic of 1918 ▶ perhaps started in earnest here, at Camp Funston, Kansas, in the spring of that year. Soldiers were struck with a debilitating illness they called "knock me down fever."

*(National Museum of Health & Medicine, Armed Forces Institute of Pathology)*

ground and submarine war stymied, its troops and cities mutinous, its allies Turkey and Austria dropping out, its Kaiser abdicated, and facing the prospect of endless American troop reinforcements—peace became imperative. The Germans accepted a punishing armistice that took effect on the morning of November 11, 1918, at the eleventh hour of the eleventh day of the eleventh month.

The cost of the war is impossible to compute, but the scale is clear enough: the belligerents counted 10 million soldiers and 6.6 million civil-

|||||||||||||||||||||||||||||||||

**Casualties**

ians dead and 21.3 million people wounded. Fifty-three thousand American soldiers died in battle, and another 62,000 died from disease. Many of the latter died from the virulent strain of influenza that ravaged the world in late 1918 and would ultimately claim more victims than the Great War itself. The economic damage was colossal as well, helping to account for the widespread starvation Europe experienced in the winter of 1918–1919. Economic output on the continent dwindled, and transport over any distance was in some countries virtually nonexistent. "We are at the dead season of our fortunes," wrote one British observer. "Never in the lifetime of men now living has the universal element in the soul of man burnt so dimly."

The German, Austro-Hungarian, Ottoman, and Russian empires were no more, themselves casualties of the conflagration. For a time it appeared the Bolshevik Revolution might spread westward, as communist uprisings shook Germany and parts of central Europe. Even before the armistice, revolutionaries temporarily took power in the German cities of Bremen, Hamburg, and Lübeck. In Hungary, a government actually held power for several months, while Austria was racked by left-wing demonstrations. In Moscow, meanwhile, the new Soviet state sought to consolidate its power. "We are sitting upon an open powder magazine," Colonel House worried, "and some day a spark may ignite it."

## MOBILIZING THE HOME FRONT

It is not an army that we must shape and train for war," declared President Wilson, "it is a nation." The United States was a belligerent for only nineteen months, but the war had a tremendous impact at home. The federal government moved swiftly to expand its power over the economy to meet war needs and intervened in American life as never before. The vastly enlarged Washington bureaucracy managed the economy, labor force, military, public opinion, and more. Federal expenditures increased tremen-

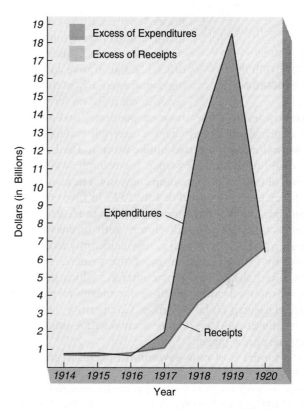

**Figure 23.1    The Federal Budget, 1914–1920**
During the First World War, the federal government spent more money than it received from increased taxes. It borrowed from banks or sold bonds through Liberty Loan drives. To meet the mounting costs of the war, in other words, the federal government had to resort to deficit spending. Expenditures topped receipts by more than $13 billion in 1919. Given this wartime fiscal pattern, moreover, the U.S. federal debt rose from $1 billion in 1914 to $25 billion in 1919.    *(Source: U.S. Department of Commerce, Historical Statistics of the United States: Colonial Times to 1957 [Washington, D.C.: Bureau of the Census, 1960], p. 711.)*

dously as the government spent more than $760 million a month from April 1917 to August 1919. As tax revenues lagged behind, the administration resorted to deficit spending (see Figure 23.1). The total cost of the war was difficult to calculate, because future generations would have to pay veterans' benefits and interest on loans. To Progressives of the New Nationalist persuasion, the wartime expansion and centralization of government power were welcome. To others, these changes seemed excessive, leading to concentrated, hence dangerous, federal power.

The federal government and private business became partners during the war. So-called dollar-a-year executives

||||||||||||||||||||||||||||||

**Business-
Government
Cooperation**

flocked to the nation's capital from major companies, retaining their corporate salaries while serving in official administrative and consulting capacities. Early in the war, the government relied on several industrial committees for advice on purchases and prices. But evidence of self-interested businesspeople cashing in on the national interest aroused public protest. The head of the aluminum advisory committee, for example, was also president of the largest aluminum company. The assorted committees were disbanded in July 1917 in favor of a single manager, the War Industries Board. But the federal government continued to work closely with business through trade associations, which grew significantly to two thousand by 1920. The government also suspended antitrust laws and signed cost-plus contracts, which guaranteed companies a healthy profit and a means to pay higher wages to head off labor strikes. Competitive bidding was virtually abandoned. Under such wartime practices, big business grew bigger.

Hundreds of new government agencies, staffed primarily by businesspeople, placed controls on the economy in order to shift the nation's resources to the Allies, the AEF, and war-related production. The Food Administration, led by engineer and investor Herbert Hoover, launched voluntary programs to increase production and conserve food—Americans were urged to grow "victory gardens" and to eat meatless and wheatless meals—but it also set prices and regulated distribution. The Railroad Administration took over the railway industry. The Fuel Administration controlled coal supplies and rationed gasoline. When strikes threatened the telephone and telegraph companies, the federal government seized and ran them.

The largest of the superagencies was the War Industries Board (WIB), headed by financier Bernard Baruch. At one point, this Wall Streeter told Henry Ford frankly that he would dispatch the military to seize his plants if the automaker did not accept WIB limits on car production. Ford relented. Although the WIB seemed all-powerful, in reality it had to conciliate competing interest groups and compromise with the business executives whose advice it so valued. Designed as a clearing-house for coordinating the national economy, the WIB made purchases, allocated supplies, and fixed prices at levels that business requested. The WIB also ordered the standardization of goods to save materials and streamline production. The varieties of automobile tires, for example, were reduced from 287 to 3.

The performance of the mobilized economy was mixed, but it delivered enough men and materiel to

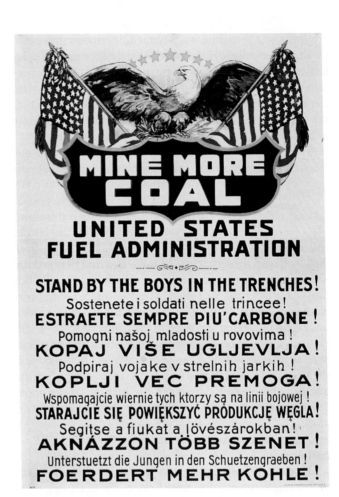

▲ During the First World War, the U.S. Fuel Administration promoted economic mobilization at home in this poster printed in several languages.

*(National Park Service Collection, Ellis Island Immigration Museum. Photo Chermayeff and Geismar MetaForm)*

||||||||||||||||||||||||||||||||

**Economic
Performance**

France to ensure the defeat of the Central Powers. About one-quarter of all American production was diverted to war needs. As farmers enjoyed boom years of higher prices, they put more acreage into production and mechanized as never before. From 1915 to 1920 the number of tractors in American fields jumped tenfold. Gross farm income for the period from 1914 to 1919 increased more than 230 percent. Although manufacturing output leveled off in 1918, some industries realized substantial growth because of wartime demand. Steel reached a peak production of 45 million tons in 1917, twice the prewar figure. As U.S. soldiers popularized American brands in Europe, tobacconists profited from a huge increase in cigarette sales:

from 26 billion cigarettes in 1916 to 48 billion in 1918. Overall, the gross national product in 1920 stood 237 percent higher than in 1914.

The rush to complete massive assignments caused mistakes to be made. Weapons deliveries fell short of demand; the bloated bureaucracy of the War Shipping Board failed to build enough ships. In the severe winter of 1917–1918, millions of Americans could not get coal. Coal companies held back on production to raise prices; railroads did not have enough coal cars; and harbors froze, closing out coal barges. People died from pneumonia and freezing. A Brooklyn man went out in the morning to forage for coal and returned to find his two-month-old daughter frozen to death in her crib.

To help pay its wartime bills, the government dramatically increased taxes. The Revenue Act in 1916 started the process by raising the surtax on high incomes and corporate profits, imposing a federal tax on large estates, and significantly increasing the tax on munitions manufacturers. Still, the government financed only one-third of the war through taxes. The other two-thirds came from loans, including Liberty bonds sold to the American people through aggressive campaigns. The War Revenue Act of 1917 provided for a more steeply graduated personal income tax, a corporate income tax, an excess-profits tax, and increased excise taxes on alcoholic beverages, tobacco, and luxury items.

Although these taxes did curb excessive corporate profiteering, there were loopholes. Sometimes companies inflated costs to conceal profits or paid high salaries and bonuses to their executives. Four officers of Bethlehem Steel, for example, divided bonuses of $2.3 million in 1917 and $2.1 million the next year. Corporate net earnings for 1913 totaled $4 billion; in 1917 they reached $7 billion; and in 1918, after the tax bite and the war's end, they still stood at $4.5 billion. Profits and patriotism went hand in hand in America's war experience. The abrupt cancellation of billions of dollars' worth of contracts at the end of the war, however, caused a brief economic downturn, a short boom, and then an intense decline (see Chapter 24).

For American workers, the full-employment wartime economy increased earnings and gave many of them time-and-a-half pay for overtime work. With the higher cost of living, however, workers saw minimal improvement in their economic standing.

## Labor Shortage

Turnover rates were high as workers switched jobs for higher pay and better conditions. Some employers sought to overcome labor shortages by expanding welfare and social programs, and by establishing personnel departments—"specialized human nature engineers to keep its human machinery frictionless," as General Electric explained.

To meet the labor crisis, the Department of Labor's U.S. Employment Service matched laborers with job vacancies, especially attracting workers from the South and Midwest to war industries in the East. The department also temporarily relaxed the literacy-test and head-tax provisions of immigration law to attract farm labor, miners, and railroad workers from Mexico. Because the labor crisis also generated a housing crisis as workers crammed into cities, the U.S. Housing Corporation and Emergency Fleet Corporation, following British example, built row houses in Newport News, Virginia, and Eddystone, Pennsylvania.

The tight wartime labor market had another consequence: new work opportunities for women. In Connecticut, a special motion picture, *Mr. and Mrs. Hines of Stamford Do Their Bit,* appealed to housewives' patriotism, urging them to take factory jobs. Although the total number of women in the work force increased slightly, the real story was that many changed jobs, sometimes moving into formerly male domains. Some white women left domestic service for factories, shifted from clerking in department stores to stenography and typing, or departed textile mills for employment in firearms plants. At least 20 percent of all workers in the wartime electrical-machinery, airplane, and food industries were women. Some 100,000 women worked in the railroad industry. As white women took advantage of these new opportunities, black women took some of their places in domestic service and in textile factories. For the first time, department stores employed black women as elevator operators and cafeteria waitresses. Most working women were single and remained concentrated in sex-segregated occupations, serving as typists, nurses, teachers, and domestic servants.

Women also participated in the war effort in other ways. As volunteers, they made clothing for refugees and soldiers, served at Red Cross facilities, and taught French to nurses assigned to the war zone. Many worked for the Women's Committee of the Council of National Defense, whose leaders included Ida Tarbell and Carrie Chapman Catt. A vast network of state, county, and town volunteer organizations, the council publicized government mobilization programs, encouraged home gardens, sponsored drives to sell Liberty bonds, and continued the push for social welfare reforms. This patriotic work won praise from men and improved the prospects for passage of the Nineteenth Amendment granting woman suffrage. "We have made partners of women in this war," Wilson said as he endorsed woman suffrage in 1918. "Shall we admit

▲ Stella Young (1896–1989), a Canadian-born woman from Chelsea, Massachusetts, became widely known as the "Doughnut Girl" because of her service during the First World War with the American branch of the Salvation Army, an international organization devoted to social work. She arrived in France in March 1918 and worked in emergency canteens near the battle front, providing U.S. troops with coffee, cocoa, sandwiches, doughnuts, pie, and fruit. Stella Young became famous when this picture of her wearing a khaki uniform and a "doughboy" steel helmet was widely circulated as a postcard. A piece of sheet music was even written about her. She served again in World War II. Chelsea named a city square in her honor in 1968.

*(Picture Research Consultants & Archives)*

them only to a partnership of suffering and sacrifice . . . and not to a partnership of privilege and right?"

Among African Americans, war mobilization wrought significant change as southern blacks undertook a great migration to northern cities to work in railroad yards, packing houses, steel mills, shipyards, and coal mines. Between 1910 and 1920, Cleveland's black population swelled by more than 300 percent, Detroit's by more than 600 percent, and Chicago's by 150 percent. Much of the increase

occurred between 1916 and 1919. All told, about a half-million African Americans uprooted themselves to move to the North. Families sometimes pooled savings to send one member; others sold their household goods to pay for the journey. Most of the migrants were males—young (in their early twenties), unmarried, and skilled or semiskilled. Wartime jobs in the North provided an escape from low wages, sharecropping, tenancy, crop liens, debt peonage, lynchings, and political disfranchisement. To a friend back in Mississippi, one African American wrote: "I just begin to feel like a man. . . . I don't have to humble to no one. I have registered. Will vote the next election."

To keep factories running smoothly, Wilson instituted the National War Labor Board (NWLB) in early 1918.

**National War Labor Board**

The NWLB discouraged strikes and lockouts and urged management to negotiate with existing unions. In July, after the Western Union Company fired eight hundred union members for trying to organize the firm's workers and then defied an NWLB request to reinstate the employees, the president nationalized the telegraph lines and put the laborers back to work. That month, too, the NWLB directed General Electric to raise wages and stop discriminating against metal trades union members in Schenectady, New York. On the other hand, in September the NWLB ordered striking Bridgeport, Connecticut, machinists back to munitions factories, threatening to revoke their draft exemptions (granted earlier because they worked in an "essential" industry).

Many labor leaders hoped the war would offer opportunities for recognition and better pay through partnership with government. Samuel Gompers threw the AFL's loyalty to the Wilson administration, promising to deter strikes. He and other moderate labor leaders accepted appointments to federal agencies. The antiwar Socialist Party blasted the AFL for becoming a "fifth wheel on [the] capitalist war chariot," but union membership climbed from roughly 2.5 million in 1916 to more than 4 million in 1919.

The AFL, however, could not curb strikes by the radical Industrial Workers of the World (IWW, also known as "Wobblies") or rebellious AFL locals, especially those controlled by labor activists and socialists. In the nineteen war months, more than six thousand strikes expressed workers' demands for a "living wage" and improved working conditions (many called for an eight-hour workday). Exploiting Wilsonian wartime rhetoric, workers and their unions also sought to create "industrial democracy," a more representative workplace with a role for labor in determining job categories and content, and with workplace representation through shop committees. By 1920, in defiance of the national AFL, labor parties had sprung up in twenty-three states.

## CIVIL LIBERTIES UNDER CHALLENGE

Gompers's backing of the call to arms meant a great deal to Wilson and his advisers, and they noted with satisfaction that most newspapers, religious leaders, and public officials were similarly supportive. They were less certain, however, about the attitudes of ordinary Americans. "Woe be to the man that seeks to stand in our way in this day of high resolution," the president warned. An official and unofficial campaign soon began to silence dissenters who questioned Wilson's decision for war or who protested the draft. In the end, the Wilson administration compiled one of the worst civil liberties records in American history.

The targets of governmental and quasi-vigilante repression were the hundreds of thousands of Americans and aliens who refused to support the war: pacifists from all walks of life, conscientious objectors, socialists, radical labor groups, the debt-ridden tenant farmers of Oklahoma who staged the Green Corn Rebellion against the draft, the Non-Partisan League, reformers like Robert La Follette and Jane Addams, and countless others. In the wartime process of debating the question of the right to speak freely in a democracy, the concept of "civil liberties" emerged for the first time in American history as a major public policy issue (see "Legacy for a People and a Nation," page 674).

The centerpiece of the administration's campaign to win support for the war was the Committee on Public Information (CPI), formed in April 1917 and headed by Progressive journalist George Creel. Employing some of the nation's most talented writers and scholars, the CPI used propaganda to shape and mobilize public opinion. Pamphlets and films demonized the Germans, and CPI "Four-Minute Men" spoke at movie theaters, schools, and churches to pump up a patriotic mood. Encouraged by the CPI to promote American participation in the war, film companies and their trade association, the National Association of the Motion Picture Industry, produced documentaries, newsreels, and anti-German movies, such as *The Kaiser, the Beast of Berlin* (1918) and *To Hell with the Kaiser* (1918).

The committee also urged the press to practice "self-censorship" and encouraged people to spy on their neighbors. Ultrapatriotic groups, such as the Sedition Slammers

**The Committee on Public Information**

▲ A member of the Eighth Regiment of the Illinois National Guard with his family, circa 1918. Originally organized as a volunteer regiment during the Spanish-American War in 1898, the Eighth Regiment achieved its greatest fame during World War I. The only regiment to be entirely commanded by blacks and headquartered at the only black armory in the U.S., the "Fighting 8th" served with distinction in France, with 143 of its members losing their lives.

*(Chicago Historical Society)*

and the American Defense Society, used vigilantism. A German American miner in Illinois was wrapped in a flag and lynched. In Hilger, Montana, citizens burned history texts that mentioned Germany. By the end of the war, sixteen states had banned the teaching of the German language. To avoid trouble, the Kaiser-Kuhn grocery in St. Louis changed its name to Pioneer Grocery. Germantown, Nebraska, became Garland, and the townspeople in Berlin, Iowa, henceforth hailed from Lincoln. The German shepherd became the Alsatian shepherd.

Because towns had Liberty Loan quotas to fill, they sometimes bullied "slackers" into purchasing bonds. Nativist advocates of "100% Americanism" exploited the emotional atmosphere to exhort immigrants to throw off their Old World cultures. Companies offered English language and naturalization classes in their factories, and refused jobs and promotions to those who did not make adequate strides toward learning English. Even labor's

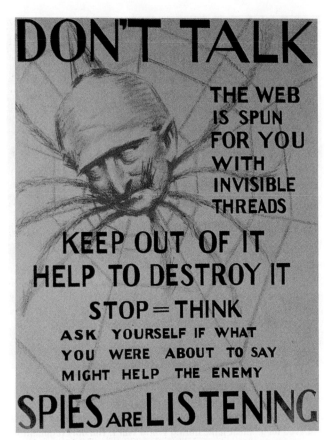

▲ Through its concerted propaganda effort, the Committee on Public Information helped sell to the American people U.S. participation in the First World War. In this 1917 poster, the committee also warned against German spies, perhaps even German American spies, who might pick up secrets from unsuspecting citizens. *(Private Collection)*

drive for compulsory health insurance, which before the war had gained advocates in several states, including New York and California, became victimized by the poisoned war atmosphere. Many physicians and insurance companies had for years denounced health insurance as "socialistic"; after the United States entered the war, they discredited it as "Made in Germany."

Even institutions that had long prided themselves on tolerance became contaminated by the spirit of coercion. Wellesley College economics professor Emily Greene Balch was fired for her pacifist views (she won the Nobel Peace Prize in 1946). Three Columbia University students were apprehended in mid-1917 for circulating an antiwar petition. Columbia also fired Professor J. M. Cattell, a distinguished psychologist, for his antiwar stand. His colleague Charles Beard, a historian with a prowar perspective, resigned in protest, stating, "If we have to suppress every-

thing we don't like to hear, this country is resting on a pretty wobbly basis." In a number of states, local school boards dismissed teachers who questioned the war.

The Wilson administration also guided through an obliging Congress the Espionage Act (1917) and the Sedition Act (1918). The first statute forbade "false statements" designed to impede the draft or promote military insubordination, and it banned from the mails materials considered treasonous. The Sedition Act made it unlawful to obstruct the sale of war bonds and to use "disloyal, profane, scurrilous, or abusive" language to describe the government, the Constitution, the flag, or the military uniform. These loosely worded laws gave the government wide latitude to crack down on critics. More than two thousand people were prosecuted under the acts, and many others were intimidated into silence.

**Espionage and Sedition Acts**

Progressives and conservatives alike used the war emergency to throttle the Industrial Workers of the World and the Socialist Party. Government agents raided IWW meetings, and the army marched into western mining and lumber regions to put down IWW strikes. By the end of the war, most of the union's leaders were in jail. In summer 1918, with a government stenographer present, Socialist Party leader Eugene V. Debs delivered a spirited oration extolling socialism and freedom of speech—including the freedom to criticize the Wilson administration for taking America into the war. Federal agents arrested him. Debs told the court what many dissenters—and, later, many jurists and scholars—thought of the Espionage Act: it was "a despotic enactment in flagrant conflict with democratic principles and with the spirit of free institutions." Handed a ten-year sentence, Debs remained in prison until late 1921, when he received a pardon.

The Supreme Court endorsed such convictions. In *Schenck v. U.S.* (1919), the Court unanimously upheld the conviction of a Socialist Party member who had mailed pamphlets urging resistance to the draft. In time of war, Justice Oliver Wendell Holmes wrote, the First Amendment could be restricted: "Free speech would not protect a man falsely shouting 'fire' in a theater and causing panic." If, according to Holmes, words "are of such a nature as to create a clear and present danger that they will bring about the substantial evils that Congress has a right to prevent," free speech could be limited.

## RED SCARE, RED SUMMER

The line between wartime suppression of dissent and the postwar Red Scare is not easily drawn. In the name of patriotism, both harassed suspected internal enemies and deprived them of their constitutional rights; both had government sanction. Together they stabbed at the Bill of Rights and wounded radicalism in America. Yet in at least two respects the phenomena were different. Whereas in wartime the main fear had been of subversion, after the armistice it was revolution; and whereas in 1917 the target had often been German Americans, in 1919 it was frequently organized labor. The Russian Revolution and the communist uprisings elsewhere in Europe alarmed many Americans, and the fears grew when in 1919 the Soviet leadership announced the formation of the Communist International (or Comintern), whose purpose was to export revolution throughout the world. Terrified conservatives responded by looking for pro-Bolshevik sympathizers (or "Reds," from the red flag used by communists) in the United States, especially in immigrant groups and labor unions.

Labor union leaders emerged out of the war determined to secure higher wages for workers, to meet rising prices, and to retain wartime bargaining rights. Employers instead rescinded benefits they had been forced to grant to labor during the war, including recognition of unions. The result was a rash of labor strikes in 1919, which sparked the Red Scare. All told, more than 3,300 strikes involving 4 million laborers jolted the nation that year, including the Seattle general strike in January. On May 1, a day of celebration for workers around the world, bombs were sent through the mails to prominent Americans. Most of the devices were intercepted and dismantled, but police never captured the conspirators. Most people assumed, not unreasonably, that anarchists and others bent on the destruction of the American way of life were responsible. Next came the Boston police strike in September. Some sniffed a Bolshevik conspiracy, but others thought it ridiculous to label Boston's Irish American, Catholic cops "radicals." The conservative governor of Massachusetts, Calvin Coolidge, gained national attention by proclaiming that nobody had the right to strike against the public safety. State guardsmen soon replaced the striking policemen.

## Labor Strikes

Unrest in the steel industry in September stirred more ominous fears. Many steelworkers worked twelve hours a day, seven days a week, and lived in squalid housing. They looked to local steel unions, organized by the National Committee for Organizing Iron and Steel Workers, to help them improve their lives. When postwar unemployment in the industry climbed and the U.S. Steel Corporation refused to meet with committee representatives, some 350,000 workers walked off the job, demanding the right to collective bargaining, a shorter workday, and a living wage. The steel barons hired strikebreakers and sent agents to club strikers. Worried about both the 1919 strikes and Bolshevism, President Wilson warned against "the poison of disorder" and the "poison of revolt." But in the case of steel, the companies won; the strike collapsed in early 1920.

One of the leaders of the steel strike was William Z. Foster, a former IWW member and militant labor organizer who later joined the Communist Party. His presence in a labor movement seeking bread-and-butter goals permitted political and business leaders to dismiss the steel strike as a foreign threat orchestrated by American radicals. There was in fact no conspiracy, and the American left was badly splintered. Two defectors from the Socialist Party, John Reed and Benjamin Gitlow, founded the Communist Labor Party in 1919. The rival Communist Party of the United States of America, composed largely of aliens, was launched the same year. Neither party commanded many followers—their combined membership probably did not exceed 70,000—and in 1919 the harassed Socialist Party could muster no more than 30,000 members.

Although divisiveness among radicals actually signified weakness, both Progressives and conservatives interpreted the advent of the new parties as strengthening the radical menace. That is certainly how the American Legion saw the question. Organized in May 1919 to lobby for veterans' benefits, the Legion soon preached an antiradicalism that fueled the Red Scare. By 1920, 843,000 Legion members, mostly middle- and upper-class, had become stalwarts of an impassioned Americanism that demanded conformity.

## American Legion

Wilson's attorney general, A. Mitchell Palmer, also insisted that Americans think alike. A Progressive reformer, Quaker, and ambitious politician, Palmer declared that "revolution" was "eating its way into the homes of the American workmen, licking the altars of the churches, leaping into the belfry of the school bell." Palmer appointed J. Edgar Hoover to head the Radical Division of the Department of Justice. The zealous Hoover compiled index cards bearing the names of allegedly radical individuals and organizations. During 1919, agents jailed IWW members, and Palmer saw to it that 249 alien radicals, including the outspoken anarchist Emma Goldman, were deported to Russia.

Again, state and local governments took their cue from the Wilson administration. States passed peacetime sedition acts under which hundreds of people were arrested. Vigilante groups and mobs flourished once again, their numbers swelled by returning veterans. In November 1919, in Centralia, Washington, American Legionnaires broke from a parade to storm the IWW hall. Several were wounded. A number of Wobblies were soon arrested, and one of them, an ex-soldier, was taken from jail by a mob, then beaten, castrated, and shot. The New York State legislature expelled five duly elected Socialist Party members in early 1920.

The Red Scare reached a climax in January 1920 in the Palmer Raids. J. Edgar Hoover planned and directed the operation; government agents in thirty-three cities broke into meeting halls and homes without search warrants. More than four thousand people were jailed and denied counsel. In Boston some four hundred people were kept in detainment on bitterly cold Deer Island; two died of pneumonia, one leaped to his death, and another went insane. Because of court rulings and the courageous efforts of Assistant Secretary of Labor Louis Post, who deliberately held up paperwork, most of the arrestees were released, although in 1920–1921 nearly six hundred aliens were deported.

**Palmer Raids**

Palmer's disregard for elementary civil liberties drew criticism, with many charging that his tactics violated the Constitution. Many of the arrested "communists" had committed no crimes. When Palmer called for a peacetime sedition act, he alarmed both liberal and conservative leaders. His dire prediction that pro-Soviet radicals would incite violence on May Day 1920 proved mistaken—not a single disturbance occurred anywhere in the country. Palmer, who had taken to calling himself the "Fighting Quaker," was jeered as the "Quaking Fighter."

Palmer also blamed communists for the racial violence that gripped the nation in these years. Here again, the charge was baseless. African Americans realized well before the end of the war that their participation did little to change discriminatory white attitudes. Segregation remained social custom. The Ku Klux Klan was reviving, and racist films like D. W. Griffith's *The Birth of a Nation* (1915) fed prejudice with its celebration of the Klan and its demeaning depiction of blacks. Lynching statistics exposed the wide gap between wartime declarations of humanity and the American practice of inhumanity at home: between 1914 and 1920, 382 blacks were lynched, some of them in military uniform.

**Racial Unrest**

Northern whites who resented "the Negro invasion" vented their anger in riots, as in East St. Louis, Illinois, in July 1917. The next month, in Houston, where African American soldiers faced white harassment and refused to obey segregation laws, whites and blacks exchanged gunfire. Seventeen whites and two African Americans died, and the army sentenced thirteen black soldiers to death and forty-one to life imprisonment for mutiny. During the bloody "Red Summer" of 1919 (so named by black author James Weldon Johnson for the blood that was spilled), race riots rocked two dozen cities and towns. The worst violence occurred in Chicago, a favorite destination for migrating blacks. In the very hot days of July 1919, a black youth swimming at a segregated white beach was hit by a thrown rock and drowned. Rumors spread, tempers flared, and soon blacks and whites were battling each other. Stabbings, burnings, and shootings went on for days until state police restored some calm. Thirty-eight people died, twenty-three African Americans and fifteen whites.

By the time of this tragedy, a disillusioned W. E. B. Du Bois had already concluded that black support for the war had not diminished whites' adherence to inequality and segregation. That spring he vowed a struggle: "We return. We return from fighting. We return fighting." Or, as poet Claude McKay put it after the Chicago riot in a poem he titled "If We Must Die,"

Like men we'll face the murderous cowardly pack.
Pressed to the wall, dying, but fighting back.

The exhortations of Du Bois and McKay reflected a newfound militancy among black veterans and in the growing black communities of the North. Editorials in African American newspapers subjected white politicians, including the president, to increasingly harsh criticism and at the same time implored readers to embrace their own prowess and beauty: "The black man is a power of great potentiality upon whom consciousness of his own strength is about to dawn." The NAACP stepped up its campaign for civil rights and equality, vowing in 1919 to publicize the terrors of the lynch law and to seek legislation to stop "Judge Lynch." Other blacks, doubting the potential for equality, turned instead to a charismatic Jamaican immigrant named Marcus Garvey (see page 685), who called on African Americans to abandon their hopes for integration and to seek a separate black nation.

**Black Militancy**

The crackdown on laborers and radicals, and the resurgence of racism in 1919, dashed wartime hopes. Although the passage of the Nineteenth Amendment in 1920, guaranteeing women the right to vote, showed that reform could happen, it was the exception to the rule. Unemployment, inflation, racial conflict, labor upheaval, a campaign against free speech—all inspired disillusionment in the immediate postwar years.

◀ An African American is confronted by state militia members during the race riots in Chicago in 1919. The troops were called in after Mayor Bill Thompson determined that the city police could not restore order.

*(Chicago Historical Society photo by Jun Fujita)*

## THE DEFEAT OF PEACE

President Wilson seemed focused on confronting the threat of radicalism more abroad than at home. Throughout the final months of the war he fretted about the Soviet takeover in Russia, and he watched with apprehension the communist uprisings in various parts of central Europe. Months earlier, in mid-1918, Wilson had revealed his ardent anti-Bolshevism when he ordered five thousand American troops to northern Russia and ten thousand more to Siberia, where they joined other Allied contingents in fighting what was now a Russian civil war. They fought on the side of the "Whites" (various counterrevolutionary forces) against the "Reds" (the Bolsheviks). Wilson did not consult Congress. He said the military expeditions would guard Allied supplies and Russian railroads from German seizure, and would also rescue a group of Czechs who wished to return home to fight the Germans.

Worried that the Japanese were building influence in Siberia and closing the Open Door, Wilson also hoped to deter Japan from further advances in Asia. Mostly, though, he wanted to smash the infant Bolshevik government, a challenge to his new world order. Thus he backed an economic blockade of Russia, sent arms to anti-Bolshevik forces, and refused to recognize Lenin's government. The United States also secretly passed military information to anti-Bolshevik forces and used food relief to shore up opponents of the Soviets in the Baltic region. Later, at the Paris Peace Conference, representatives of the new Soviet government were denied a seat. U.S. troops did not leave Russia until spring 1920, after the Bolsheviks had demonstrated their staying power. The actions by Wilson and other Allied leaders in 1918–1920 generated powerful feelings of resentment and suspicion among many Russians.

Wilson faced a monumental task in securing a postwar settlement. When he departed for the Paris Peace Conference in December 1918, he faced obstacles erected by his political enemies, by the Allies, and by himself. Some observers suggested that a cocky Wilson underestimated his task. During the 1918 congressional elections, Wilson committed the blunder of suggesting that patriotism required the election of a Democratic Congress; Republicans had a field day blasting the president for questioning their love of country. The GOP gained control of both houses, signaling trouble for Wilson in two ways. First, a peace treaty would have to be submitted for approval to a potentially hostile Senate. Second, the election results at home diminished Wilson's stature in the eyes of foreign leaders. Wilson aggravated his political problems by not naming a senator to his advisory American Peace Commission. He also refused to take any prominent Republicans with him to Paris or to consult with the Senate Foreign Relations

Committee before the conference. It did not help that the president denounced his critics as "blind and little provincial people."

Wilson was greeted with huge and adoring crowds in Paris, London, and Rome. Behind closed doors, however, the leaders of these countries—Georges Clemenceau of France, David Lloyd George of Britain, and Vittorio Orlando of Italy (with Wilson, the Big Four)—became formidable adversaries. Clemenceau mused, "God gave man the Ten Commandments, and he broke every one. Wilson has given us Fourteen Points. We shall see." After four years of horrible war, the Allies were not about to be cheated out of the fruits of victory. Wilson could wax lyrical about a "peace without victory," but the late-arriving Americans had not suffered the way the peoples of France and Great Britain had suffered. Germany would have to pay, and pay big, for the calamity it had caused.

At the conference, held at the ornate palace of Versailles, the Big Four tried to work out an agreement, mostly behind closed doors. Critics

**Paris Peace Conference**

quickly pointed out that Wilson had immediately abandoned the first of his Fourteen Points: diplomacy "in the public view." The victors demanded that Germany (which had not been invited to the proceedings) pay a huge reparations bill. Wilson instead called for a small indemnity, fearing that a resentful and economically hobbled Germany might turn to Bolshevism or disrupt the postwar community in some other way. Unable to moderate the Allied position, the president reluctantly gave way, agreeing to a clause blaming the war on the Germans and to the creation of a commission to determine the amount of reparations (later set at $33 billion). Wilson acknowledged that the peace terms were "hard," but he also came to believe that "the German people must be made to hate war."

As for the breaking up of empires and the principle of self-determination, Wilson could deliver on only some of his goals. To the crushing disappointment of much of the world's nonwhite majority, the imperial system emerged largely unscathed, as the conferees created a League-administered "mandate" system which placed former German and Turkish colonies under the control of other imperial nations. Japan gained authority over Germany's colonies in the Pacific, while France and Britain obtained parts of the Middle East—the French obtained what became Lebanon and Syria, while the British received the three former Ottoman provinces that became Iraq. Britain also secured Palestine, on the condition that it uphold its wartime promise to promote "the establishment in Palestine of a national home for the Jewish people" without prejudice to "the civil and religious rights of existing non-Jewish communities"—the so-called Balfour Declaration of 1917.

In other arrangements, Japan replaced Germany as the imperial overlord of China's Shandong Peninsula, and France was permitted occupation rights in Germany's Rhineland. Elsewhere in Europe, Wilson's prescriptions fared better. Out of Austria-Hungary and Russia came the newly independent states of Austria, Hungary, Yugoslavia, Czechoslovakia, and Poland. Wilson and his colleagues also built a *cordon sanitaire* (buffer zone) of new westward-looking nations (Finland, Estonia, Latvia, and Lithuania) around Russia, to quarantine the Bolshevik contagion (see Map 23.3).

Wilson worked hardest on the charter for the League of Nations, the centerpiece of his plans for the postwar world. He envisioned the League

**League of Nations and Article 10**

as having power over all disputes among states, including those that did not arise from the peace agreement; as such, it could transform international relations. Even so, the great powers would have preponderant say: the organization would have an influential council of five permanent members and elected delegates from smaller states, an assembly of all members, and a World Court.

Wilson identified Article 10 as the "kingpin" of the League covenant: "The Members of the League undertake to respect and preserve as against external aggression the territorial integrity and existing political independence of all Members of the League. In case of any such aggression or in case of any threat or danger of such aggression the Council shall advise upon the means by which this obligation shall be fulfilled." This collective-security provision, along with the entire League charter, became part of the peace treaty because Wilson insisted that there could be no future peace with Germany without a league to oversee it.

German representatives at first refused to sign the punitive treaty but submitted in June 1919. They gave up 13 percent of Germany's territory, 10 percent of its population, all of its colonies, and a huge portion of its national wealth. Many people wondered how the League could function in the poisoned postwar atmosphere of humiliation and revenge. But Wilson waxed euphoric: "The stage is set, the destiny disclosed. It has come about by no plan of our conceiving, but by the hand of God."

Critics in the United States were not so sure. In March 1919, thirty-nine senators (enough to deny the

**Map 23.3  Europe Transformed by War and Peace**
After President Wilson and the other conferees at the Paris Peace Conference negotiated the Treaty of Versailles, empires were broken up. In eastern Europe in particular, new nations emerged.

**Critics of the Treaty**

treaty the necessary two-thirds vote) had signed a petition stating that the League's structure did not adequately protect U.S. interests. Wilson denounced his critics as "pygmy" minds, but he persuaded the peace conference to exempt the Monroe Doctrine and domestic matters from League jurisdiction. Having made these concessions to senatorial advice, Wilson would budge no more. Compromises with other nations had been necessary to keep the conference going, he insisted, and the League would rectify wrongs. Could his critics not see that membership in the League would give the United States "leadership in the world"?

By summer, criticism intensified: Wilson had bastardized his own principles. He had conceded Shandong to Japan. He had personally killed a provision affirming the racial equality of all peoples. The treaty did not mention freedom of the seas, and tariffs were not reduced. Reparations on Germany promised to be punishing. Senator La Follette and other critics on the left protested that the League would perpetuate empire. Conservative critics feared that the League would limit American freedom of action in world affairs, stymie U.S. expansion, and intrude on domestic questions. And Article 10 raised serious questions: Would the United States be *obligated* to use armed force to ensure collective security? And what about colonial rebellions, such as in Ireland or India? Would the League feel compelled to crush them? "Were a League of Nations in existence in the days when George Washington fought and won," an Irish American editor wrote, "we would still be an English colony."

Henry Cabot Lodge of Massachusetts led the Senate opposition to the League. A Harvard-educated Ph.D. and partisan Republican who also had an intense personal dislike of Wilson, Lodge packed the Foreign Relations Committee with critics and prolonged public hearings. He introduced several reservations to the treaty, the most important of which held that Congress had to approve any obligation under Article 10.

In September 1919 Wilson embarked on a speaking tour of the United States. Growing more exhausted every day, he dismissed his antagonists as "contemptible quitters." Provoked by Irish American and German American hecklers, he lashed out in Red Scare terms: "Any man who carries a hyphen about him carries a dagger which he is ready to plunge into the vitals of the Republic." While doubts about Article 10 multiplied, Wilson tried to highlight neglected features of the League charter—such as the arbitration of disputes and an international conference to abolish child labor. In Colorado, a day after delivering another passionate speech, the president awoke to nausea and uncontrollable facial twitching. "I just feel as if I am going to pieces," he said. A few days later, he suffered a massive stroke that paralyzed his left side. He became peevish and even more stubborn, increasingly unable to conduct presidential business. More and more, his wife Edith had to select issues for his attention and delegate other matters to his cabinet heads. Advised to placate Lodge and other "Reservationist" senatorial critics so the Versailles treaty would have a chance of being approved by Congress, Wilson rejected "dishonorable compromise." From Senate Democrats he demanded utter loyalty—a vote against all reservations.

▲ In October 1919 President Woodrow Wilson (1856–1924) receives assistance after his massive stroke, which made it difficult for him to maintain his train of thought and manage government affairs. Historians continue to debate the influence of Wilson's poor health on the president's losing battle for U.S. membership in the League of Nations. *(Library of Congress)*

Twice in November the Senate rejected the Treaty of Versailles and thus U.S. membership in the League. In the

### Senate Rejection of the Treaty and League

first vote, Democrats joined sixteen "Irreconcilables," mostly Republicans who opposed any treaty whatsoever, to defeat the treaty with reservations (39 for and 55 against). In the second vote, Republicans and Irreconcilables turned down the treaty without reservations (38 for and 53 against). In March 1920 the Senate again voted; this time, a majority (49 for and 35 against) favored the treaty with reservations, but the tally fell short of the two-thirds needed. Had Wilson permitted Democrats to compromise—to accept reservations—he could have achieved his fervent goal of membership in the League, which, despite the U.S. absence, came into being.

At the core of the debate lay a basic issue in American foreign policy: whether the United States would endorse collective security or continue to travel the more solitary path articulated in George Washington's Farewell Address and in the Monroe Doctrine. In a world dominated by imperialist states unwilling to subordinate their strategic ambitions to an international organization, Americans preferred their traditional nonalignment and freedom of choice over binding commitments to collective action. That is why so many of Wilson's critics targeted Article 10. Wilson countered that this argument amounted to embracing the status quo—the European imperialist states are selfish, so the United States should be, too. Acceptance of Article 10 and membership in the League promised something better, he believed, for the United States and for the world; it promised collective security in place of the frail protection of alliances and the instability of a balance of power.

In the end, World War I did not make the world safe for democracy. Wilson failed to create a new world order

### An Unsafe World

through reform. Still, the United States emerged from the First World War an even greater world power. By 1920 the United States had become the world's leading economic power, producing 40 percent of its coal, 70 percent of its petroleum, and half of its pig iron. It also rose to first rank in world trade. American companies took advantage of the war to nudge the Germans and British out of foreign markets, especially in Latin America. Meanwhile, the United States shifted from being a debtor to being a creditor nation, becoming the world's leading banker.

After the disappointment of Versailles, appeals for arms control accelerated, and the peace movement revitalized. At the same time, the military became better armed and more professional. The Reserve Officers Training Corps (ROTC) became permanent; military "colleges" provided upper-echelon training; and the Army Industrial College, founded in 1924, pursued business-military cooperation in the area of logistics and planning. The National Research Council, created in 1916 with government money and Carnegie and Rockefeller funds, continued after the war as an alliance of scientists and businesspeople engaged in research relating to national defense. Tanks, quick-firing guns, armor-piercing explosives, and oxygen masks for high-altitude-flying pilots were just some of the technological advances that emerged from the First World War.

The international system born in these years was unstable and fragmented. Espousing decolonization and taking to heart the Wilsonian principle of self-determination, nationalist leaders active during the First World War, such as Ho Chi Minh of Indochina and Mohandas K. Gandhi of India, vowed to achieve independence for their peoples. Communism became a disruptive force in world politics, and the Soviets bore a grudge against those invaders who had tried to thwart their revolution. The new states in central and eastern Europe proved weak, dependent on outsiders for security. Germans bitterly resented the harsh peace settlement, and German war debts and reparations problems dogged international order for many years. As it entered the 1920s, the international system that Woodrow Wilson had vowed to reform was fraught with unresolved problems.

# *Legacy* FOR A PEOPLE AND A NATION

## Freedom of Speech and the ACLU

Although freedom of speech is enshrined in the U.S. Constitution, for more than a century after the nation's founding the concept had little standing in American jurisprudence. Before World War I, those with radical views often met with harsh treatment for exercising what today would be termed their freedom of speech. During the war, however, the Wilson administration's suppression of dissidents led some Americans to reformulate the traditional definition of allowable speech. Two key figures in this movement were Roger Baldwin, a conscientious objector, and woman suffrage activist Crystal Eastman. Baldwin and Eastman were among the first to advance the idea that the content of political speech could be separated from the identity of the speaker and that patriotic Americans could—indeed should—defend the right of others to express political beliefs abhorrent to their own. After working during the war to defend the rights of conscientious objectors, Baldwin and Eastman—joined by activists such as Jane Addams, Helen Keller, and Norman Thomas—formed the American Civil Liberties Union (ACLU).

Since 1920 the ACLU, which today has some 300,000 members in three hundred chapters nationwide, has aimed to protect the basic civil liberties of all Americans and to extend them to those to whom they have traditionally been denied. The organization has been involved in almost every major civil liberties case contested in U.S. courts, among them the John Scopes "monkey trial" (1925), concerning the teaching of evolution at a Tennessee school, and the landmark *Brown v. Board of Education* case (1954) which ended federal tolerance of racial segregation. More recently, the ACLU was involved in a 1997 case in which the Supreme Court decided that the 1996 Communications Act banning "indecent speech" violated First Amendment rights.

Conservatives have long criticized the ACLU for its opposition to official prayers in public schools and its support of the legality of abortion, as well as for what they see as its selectivity in deciding whose freedom of speech to defend. Backers of the organization counter that it has also defended those on the right, such as Oliver North, a key figure in the Iran-contra scandal of the 1980s.

Either way, the principle of free speech is today broadly accepted by Americans, so much so that even ACLU bashers take it for granted. Membership has risen sharply since the terrorist attacks on September 11, 2001, due to concern among some people that government policies have eroded privacy and legal protections, not only for Americans but also for foreign detainees at the Guantánamo Bay detention facility. Ironically, the Wilson administration's crackdown on dissent produced an expanded commitment to freedom of speech for a people and a nation.

## SUMMARY

At the close of the First World War, historian Albert Bushnell Hart observed that "it is easy to see that the United States is a new country." Actually, America came out of the war an unsettled mix of the old and the new. The war years marked the emergence of the United States as a world power, and Americans could take justifiable pride in the contribution they had made to the Allied victory. At the same time, the war exposed deep divisions among Americans: white versus black, nativist versus immigrant, capital versus labor, men versus women, radical versus Progressive and conservative, pacifist versus interventionist, nationalist versus internationalist. It is little wonder that Americans—having experienced race riots, labor strikes, disputes over civil liberties, and the League fight—wanted to escape into what President Warren G. Harding called "normalcy."

During the war, the federal government intervened in the economy and influenced people's everyday lives as never before. Centralization of control in Washington, D.C., and mobilization of the home front served as models for the future. Although the Wilson administration shunned reconstruction or reconversion plans (war housing projects, for example, were sold to private investors) and quickly dismantled the many government agencies, the World War I experience of the activist state served as guidance for 1930s reformers battling the Great Depression (see Chapter 25). The partnership of government and business in managing the wartime economy advanced the development of a mass society through the standardization of products and the promotion of efficiency. Wilsonian wartime policies also nourished the concentration of corporate ownership through the suspension of antitrust laws. Business power dominated the next decade. American labor, by contrast, entered lean years, although new labor management practices, including corporate welfare programs, survived.

Although the disillusionment evident after Versailles did not cause the United States to adopt a policy of isolationist withdrawal (see Chapter 26), skepticism about America's ability to right wrongs abroad marked the postwar American mood. The war was grimy and ugly, far less glorious than Wilson's lofty rhetoric had suggested. People recoiled from photographs of shell-shocked faces and of bodies dangling from barbed wire. American soldiers, tired of idealism, craved the latest baseball scores and their regular jobs. Those Progressives who had believed that entry into the war would deliver the millennium later marveled at their naiveté. Many lost their enthusiasm for crusades, and many others turned away in disgust from the bickering of the victors. Some felt betrayed. Journalist William Allen White angrily wrote to a friend that the Allies "have—those damned vultures—taken the heart out of the peace, taken the joy out of the great enterprise of the war, and have made it a sordid malicious miserable thing like all the other wars in the world."

By 1920 Woodrow Wilson's idealism seemed to many Americans to be a spent force, both at home and abroad. Aware of their country's newfound status as a leading world power, they were unsure what this reality meant for the nation, or for their individual lives. With a mixed legacy from the Great War, and a sense of uneasiness, the country entered the new era of the 1920s.

## SUGGESTIONS FOR FURTHER READING

John Milton Cooper Jr., *Breaking the Heart of the World: Woodrow Wilson and the Fight for the League of Nations* (2001)

David S. Foglesong, *America's Secret War Against Bolshevism* (1995)

James B. Grossman, *Land of Hope: Chicago, Black Southerners, and the Great Migration* (1989)

Michael Kazin, *A Godly Hero: The Life of William Jennings Bryan* (2006)

Jennifer D. Keene, *Doughboys, the Great War, and the Remaking of America* (2001)

David M. Kennedy, *Over Here: The Home Front in the First World War* (1980)

Thomas J. Knock, *To End All Wars: Woodrow Wilson and the Quest for a New World Order* (1992)

Margaret MacMillan, *Paris 1919: Six Months That Changed the World* (2002)

John A. Thompson, *Woodrow Wilson* (2002)

Robert H. Zieger, *America's Great War: World War I and the American Experience* (2000)

*For a more extensive list for further reading, go to* college.hmco.com/pic/norton8e.

# The New Era

## *1920-1929*

$\mathcal{B}$eth and Robert Gordon were not very compatible marriage partners. Beth was frumpy and demanding; Robert liked to party. One evening at a nightclub, he met Sally Clark, who liked to party, too. They danced, and when Robert came home, Beth smelled perfume on his suit. The spouses argued, and shortly they divorced. It was not long, however, before Robert found that Sally's appeal had worn off; he missed Beth's intellect and wisdom. Meanwhile, Beth concluded that she needed to change her dowdy image. She bought new clothes and makeup, turning herself into a glamorous beauty. By coincidence, Beth and Robert visited the same summer resort and rekindled their romance. When Robert was injured in an accident, Beth took him home and nursed him back to health, much to Sally's disappointment. In the end, as Beth and Robert remarried, Sally accepted her loss of Robert philosophically, concluding with the wry remark "The only good thing about marriage, anyway, is the alimony."

The experiences of Beth, Robert, and Sally make up the plot of the 1920 motion picture *Why Change Your Wife?*—one of dozens of films directed by Cecil B. DeMille. DeMille succeeded by giving audiences what they wanted to see and what they fantasized about doing. Beth, Robert, and Sally dressed stylishly, went out dancing, listened to phonograph records, rode in cars, and visited resorts. Although DeMille's films and others of the 1920s usually ended by reinforcing marriage, ruling out premarital sex, and supporting the work ethic, they also exuded a new morality. Female lead characters were not mothers tied to the home; both male and female characters shed old-style values for the pursuit of luxury, fun, and the trappings of sexual freedom, just as the actors and actresses themselves, such as Gloria Swanson and Thomas Meighan, the stars of *Why Change Your Wife?* were doing in

◀ Dressed in stylish fashions and indulging in some flirtatious banter, Thomas Meighan and Gloria Swanson, stars of Cecil B. DeMille's romantic comedy *Why Change Your Wife?* represent ways that movies and movie personalities gave the public images, sometimes accurate but often exaggerated, of new social mores in the 1920s. *(Copyright © Courtesy Everett Collection)*

## CHRONOLOGY

1920 ■ Volstead Act implements prohibition
(Eighteenth Amendment)
■ Nineteenth Amendment ratified, legalizing
vote for women in federal elections
■ Harding elected president
■ KDKA transmits first commercial radio
broadcast

1920–21 ■ Postwar deflation and depression

1921 ■ Federal Highway Act funds national highway
system
■ Emergency Quota Act establishes immigration
quotas
■ Sacco and Vanzetti convicted
■ Sheppard-Towner Act allots funds to states to
set up maternity and pediatric clinics

1922 ■ Economic recovery raises standards of living
■ *Coronado Coal Company v. United Mine
Workers* rules that strikes may be illegal actions
in restraint of trade
■ *Bailey v. Drexel Furniture Company* voids
restrictions on child labor
■ Federal government ends strikes by railroad
shop workers and miners
■ Fordney-McCumber Tariff raises rates on
imports

1923 ■ Harding dies; Coolidge assumes presidency
■ *Adkins v. Children's Hospital* overturns a
minimum wage law affecting women

1923–24 ■ Government scandals (Teapot Dome)
exposed

1924 ■ Snyder Act grants citizenship to all Indians
not previously citizens
■ National Origins Act revises immigration quotas
■ Coolidge elected president

1925 ■ Scopes trial highlights battle between religious
fundamentalists and modernists

1927 ■ Lindbergh pilots solo transatlantic flight
■ Ruth hits sixty home runs
■ *The Jazz Singer*, first movie with sound, released

1928 ■ Stock market soars
■ Hoover elected president

1929 ■ Stock market crashes; Great Depression begins

their off-screen lives. In this way, *Why Change Your Wife?* was a harbinger, though an inexact one, of a new era.

During the 1920s, consumerism flourished, represented by the products, entertainment, and leisure that film characters and the stars who played them enjoyed. Although poverty beset small farmers, workers in declining industries, and nonwhites in inner cities, most other people enjoyed a high standard of living relative to that of previous generations. Spurred by advertising and installment buying, Americans eagerly acquired radios, automobiles, real estate, and stocks. As in the Gilded Age, the federal government maintained a favorable climate for business. And, in contrast to the Progressive era, few people worried about abuses of private power. Yet state and local governments, extending the reach of public authority, undertook important reforms.

It was an era in which people of all types embraced new technology while trying to preserve values they had long understood. New forms of leisure activity coincided with creativity in the arts and notable advances in science and technology. Changes in work habits, family responsibilities, and healthcare fostered new uses of time and new attitudes about behavior, including encouragements to "think young." While material bounty and expanded consumerism touched the lives of many people, others continued to endure hardship and exclusion. Winds of change also stirred up waves of resistance from those who held tight to traditional beliefs, and cultural divisions came to affect politics. Thus the decade was both appealing and unsettling, prompting enthusiasm and rejection.

An unseen storm lurked on the horizon, however. The glitter of consumer culture that dominated DeMille's films and their audiences' everyday lives blinded Americans to rising debt and uneven prosperity. Just before the decade closed, a devastating depression brought the era to a brutal close.

- How did developments in technology and the workplace stimulate social change during the 1920s?
- What were the benefits and costs of consumerism, and how did people deal with challenges to old-time values?
- What caused the stock market crash and the ensuing deep depression that signaled the end of the era?

# BIG BUSINESS TRIUMPHANT

The 1920s began with a jolting economic decline. Shortly after the First World War ended, industrial output dropped as wartime orders dried up. As European agriculture recovered from war, American exports contracted and farm incomes plunged. In the West, railroads and the mining industry suffered. When demobilized soldiers flooded the work force, unemployment, around 2 percent in 1919, passed 12 percent in 1921. Layoffs spread through New England as textile companies abandoned outdated factories for the convenient raw materials and cheap labor of the South. The consequence of all these patterns was that consumer spending dwindled, causing more contraction and joblessness.

Aided by electric energy, a recovery began in 1922 and continued unevenly until 1929. Electric motors enabled

**New Economic Expansion**

manufacturers to replace steam engines and to produce old and new goods more cheaply and efficiently. Using new metal alloys, such as aluminum, and synthetic materials, such as rayon, producers could turn out an expanded array of consumer goods, including refrigerators, toasters, vacuum cleaners, and clothing. In addition, most urban households now had electric service, enabling them to utilize the new appliances. The growing economy gave Americans more spending money for these products, as well as for restaurants, beauty salons, and movie theaters. But, more important, installment, or time-payment, plans ("A dollar down and a dollar forever," one critic quipped) drove the new consumerism. Of 3.5 million automobiles sold in 1923, some 80 percent were bought on credit.

Economic expansion in the 1920s brought a continuation of the corporate consolidation that had created trusts and holding companies in the late nineteenth century. Although Progressive era trustbusting had achieved some regulation of big business, it had not eliminated oligopoly, the control of an entire industry by one or a few large firms. A few sprawling companies, such as U.S. Steel and General Electric, dominated basic industries, and oligopolies controlled much of marketing, distribution, and finance as well.

Business and professional organizations that had arisen around 1900 also expanded in the 1920s. Retailers

**Associations and "New Lobbying"**

and manufacturers formed trade associations to swap information and coordinate planning. Farm bureaus promoted scientific agriculture and tried to stabilize markets.

Lawyers, engineers, and social scientists expanded their professional societies. These special-interest groups participated in what is called the "new lobbying." In a complex society in which government was playing an increasingly influential role, hundreds of organizations sought to convince federal and state legislators to support their interests. One Washington, D.C., observer contended that "lobbyists were so thick they were constantly falling over one another."

Government policies helped business thrive, and legislators depended on lobbyists' expertise in making decisions. Prodded by lobbyists, Congress cut taxes on corporations and wealthy individuals in 1921, and passed the Fordney-McCumber Tariff Act (1922) to raise tariff rates. Presidents Warren G. Harding, Calvin Coolidge, and Herbert Hoover appointed cabinet officers who were favorable toward business. Regulatory agencies, such as the Federal Trade Commission and the Interstate Commerce Commission, monitored company activities but, under the influence of lobbyists, cooperated with corporations more than they regulated them.

The Supreme Court, led by Chief Justice William Howard Taft, the former president whom Harding nominated to the Court in 1921, protected business and private property as aggressively as in the Gilded Age, and abandoned its Progressive era antitrust stance. Key decisions sheltered business from government regulation and hindered organized labor's ability to achieve its ends through strikes and legislation. In *Coronado Coal Company v. United Mine Workers* (1922), Taft ruled that a striking union, like a trust, could be prosecuted for illegal restraint of trade, yet in *Maple Floor Association v. U.S.* (1929), the Court decided that trade associations that distributed anti-union information were not acting in restraint of trade. The Court also voided the federal law restricting child labor (*Bailey v. Drexel Furniture Company*, 1922), because it infringed on state power, and overturned a minimum wage law affecting women, because it infringed on liberty of contract (*Adkins v. Children's Hospital*, 1923).

Organized labor suffered other setbacks during the 1920s. Fearful of communism allegedly brought into the

**Setbacks for Organized Labor**

country by radical immigrants, public opinion turned against workers who disrupted everyday life with strikes. Perpetuating tactics used during the Red Scare of 1919, the Harding administration in 1922 obtained a sweeping court injunction to quash a strike by 400,000 railroad shop workers. The same year, the Justice Department helped end a nationwide strike by 650,000 miners. Courts at both the state and federal level issued injunctions to prevent strikes and permitted businesses to sue unions for damages suffered because of labor actions.

Meanwhile, corporations fought unions in several ways. To prevent labor organization, employers imposed yellow-dog contracts which, as a condition of employment, compelled an employee to agree not to join a union. Companies also countered the appeal of unions by offering pensions, profit sharing, and company-sponsored picnics and sporting events—a policy known as welfare capitalism. State legislators aided employers by prohibiting closed shops (workplaces where unions required that all employees be members of their labor organization) and permitting open shops (in which employers could hire nonunion employees). As a result of court action, welfare capitalism, and ineffective leadership, union membership fell from 5.1 million in 1920 to 3.6 million in 1929.

Agriculture was one sector of the national economy that languished during the 1920s. Pressed into competition with growers in other countries and trying to increase productivity by investing in new machines, such as harvesters and tractors, American farmers found themselves further beset by hardship. Irrigation and mechanization had created "factories in the fields," making large-scale farming so efficient that fewer farmers could produce more crops than ever before. As a result, crop prices plunged, big agribusinesses took over, and small landholders and tenants could not make a living. Shortly after the end of the First World War, for example, the price that farmers could get for cotton dropped by two-thirds, and that for hogs and cattle fell by half. Foreign competition made matters worse. Incomes of small farmers (but not agribusinesses) plummeted, and debts rose.

**Languishing Agriculture**

## POLITICS AND GOVERNMENT

A series of Republican presidents extended Theodore Roosevelt's notion of government-business cooperation, but they made government a compliant coordinator rather than the active manager Roosevelt had advocated. A symbol of government's goodwill toward business was President Warren G. Harding, elected in 1920 when the populace no longer desired national or international crusades. Democrats had nominated Ohio's Governor James M. Cox, who supported Woodrow Wilson's fading hope for U.S. membership in the League of Nations. But Cox and running mate Franklin D. Roosevelt, governor of New York, failed to excite voters. Harding, who kept his position on the League vague, captured 16 million popular votes to 9 million for Cox. (The total vote in the 1920 presidential election was 36 percent higher than in 1916, reflecting participation of women voters for the first time.)

A popular small-town newspaperman and senator from Ohio, Harding appointed some capable assistants who helped promote business growth, notably Secretary of State Charles Evans Hughes, Secretary of Commerce Herbert Hoover, Secretary of the Treasury Andrew Mellon, and Secretary of Agriculture Henry C. Wallace. Harding also backed some reforms. His administration helped streamline federal spending with the Budget and Accounting Act of 1921 (which created the Bureau of the Budget), supported antilynching legislation (rejected by Congress), and approved bills assisting farm cooperatives and liberalizing farm credit.

Harding, however, had personal weaknesses. As a senator, he had an extramarital liaison with the wife of an Ohio merchant. In 1917 he began a relationship with Nan Britton, who was thirty-one years his junior. A daughter was born from the affair in 1919, and Britton reputedly continued to visit Harding in the White House after he became president. Unlike Grover Cleveland, Harding never acknowledged his illegitimate offspring.

**Scandals of the Harding Administration**

Of more consequence than his sexual escapades, Harding appointed cronies who saw office holding as an invitation to personal gain. Charles Forbes, head of the Veterans Bureau, went to federal prison, convicted of fraud and bribery in connection with government contracts. Attorney General Harry Daugherty resigned after being implicated in a kickback scheme involving bootleggers of illegal liquor; he escaped prosecution by refusing to testify against himself. Most notoriously, a congressional inquiry in 1923 and 1924 revealed that Secretary of the Interior Albert Fall had accepted bribes to lease government property to private oil companies. For his role in the affair—called the Teapot Dome scandal after a Wyoming oil reserve that he handed to the Mammoth Oil Company—Fall was fined $100,000 and spent a year in jail, the first cabinet member ever to be so disgraced.

By mid-1923, Harding had become disillusioned. Amid rumors of mismanagement and crime, he told a journalist, "My God, this is a hell of a job. I have no trouble with my enemies. . . . But my friends, my God-damned friends . . . they're the ones that keep me walking the floor nights." On a speaking tour that summer, Harding became ill and died in San Francisco on August 2. Although his death preceded revelation of the Teapot Dome scandal, some people speculated that, to avoid im-

◄ **President Calvin Coolidge liked to hobnob with business leaders but also display his Vermont background. He is shown here at his home in Plymouth, Vermont, in 1925, holding a bucket of maple syrup and sitting with Harvey Firestone (of the tire company) on his right, Henry Ford on his left, and Thomas Edison on Ford's left.**

*(Calvin Coolidge Memorial Room, Forbes Library, Northampton, MA)*

peachment, Harding committed suicide or was poisoned by his wife. Most evidence, however, points to death from natural causes, probably heart disease. Regardless, Harding was widely mourned. A warm, dignified-looking man who relished a good joke and an evening of poker, he seemed suited to a nation recovering from world war and domestic hard times.

Vice President Calvin Coolidge, who now became president, was far less outgoing than his predecessor. Nicknamed "Silent Cal," he once observed that he seldom spoke to people who interviewed him because when he did, "it winds them up for twenty minutes more." As governor of Massachusetts, Coolidge had attracted national attention in 1919 when he used the national guard to end a strike by Boston policemen, an action that won him business support and the vice-presidential nomination in 1920.

Coolidge's presidency coincided with and assisted business prosperity. Respectful of private enterprise and

||||||||||||||||||||||||||||||||

**Coolidge Prosperity**

aided by Andrew Mellon, who was retained as treasury secretary, Coolidge's administration reduced federal debt, lowered income-tax rates (especially for the wealthy), and began construction of a national highway system. But Coolidge refused to apply government power to assist struggling farmers. Responding to farmers' complaints of falling prices, Congress twice passed bills to establish government-backed price supports for staple crops (the McNary-Haugen bills of 1927 and 1928). Resembling the subtreasury scheme that Farmers' Alliances had advocated in the 1890s, these bills proposed to establish a system whereby the government would buy surplus farm products and either hold them until prices rose or sell them abroad. Farmers argued that they deserved as much government protection as manufacturers got. Coolidge, however, vetoed the measures both times as improper government interference in the market economy.

"Coolidge prosperity" was the decisive issue in the 1924 presidential election. Both major parties ran candidates who favored private initiative over government intervention. Republicans nominated Coolidge with little dissent. At their national convention, Democrats first debated whether to denounce the revived Ku Klux Klan, voting 542 to 541 against condemnation. They then endured 103 ballots, deadlocked between southern prohibitionists, who supported former treasury secretary William G. McAdoo, and antiprohibition easterners, who backed New York's governor, Alfred E. Smith. They finally compromised on John W. Davis, a New York corporate lawyer.

Remnants of the Progressive movement, along with farm, labor, and socialist groups, formed a new Progressive Party and nominated Robert M. La Follette, the aging Wisconsin reformer. The new party stressed issues of the previous two decades: public ownership of railroads and power plants, conservation of natural resources, aid to farmers, rights for organized labor, and regulation of business. The electorate, however, endorsed Coolidge prosperity. Coolidge beat Davis by 15.7 million to 8.4 million popular votes, and 382 to 136 electoral votes. La Follette finished third, receiving 4.8 million popular votes and 13 electoral votes.

In Congress and the presidency, the urgency for political and economic reform that had moved the generation of Progressive reformers faded in the 1920s. Much reform, however, occurred at state and local levels. Following initiatives begun before the First World War, thirty-four states instituted or expanded workers' compensation laws and public welfare programs in the 1920s. In cities, social workers strived for better housing and poverty relief. By 1926 every major city and many smaller ones had planning and zoning commissions to harness physical growth to the common good. As a result of their efforts, a new generation of reformers who later influenced national affairs acquired valuable experience in the nation's statehouses, city halls, and universities.

### Extensions of Progressive Reform

Some reformers were disturbed by the federal government's generally apathetic Indian policy. Organizations such as the Indian Rights Association, the Indian Defense Association, and the General Federation of Women's Clubs worked to obtain justice and social services, including better education and return of tribal lands. But most Americans perceived Indians as no longer a threat to whites' ambitions and expected them to assimilate like other minorities. Such assumption overlooked important drawbacks. Severalty, the federal policy created by the Dawes Act of 1887, allotting land to individuals rather than to tribes, failed to make Indians self-supporting. Indian farmers had to suffer poor soil, lack of irrigation, scarce medical care, and cattle thieves. Deeply attached to their land, they showed little inclination to move to cities. Whites still hoped to convert native peoples into "productive" citizens, but in a way that ignored indigenous cultures. Reformers were especially critical of Indian women, who refused to adopt middle-class homemaking habits and balked at sending their children to boarding schools.

### Indian Affairs and Politics

Meanwhile, the federal government struggled to clarify Indians' citizenship status. The Dawes Act had conferred citizenship on all Indians who accepted land allotments, but not on those who remained on reservations. Also, the government retained control over Indians that it did not exercise over others. For example, because of alleged drunkenness on reservations, federal law prevented the sale of liquor to Indians even before ratification of prohibition. After several court challenges, Congress finally passed an Indian Citizenship Act (Snyder Act) in 1924, granting full citizenship to all Indians who previously had not received it. In addition, President Hoover reinforced the intent of this measure by stating that citizenship was the best means for Indians to assimilate.

Even after achieving suffrage in 1920 with ratification of the Nineteenth Amendment, politically active women remained excluded from local and national power structures. But, like business associations, their voluntary organizations used tactics that advanced modern pressure-group politics. Whether the issue was birth control, peace, education, Indian affairs, or opposition to lynching, women in these associations lobbied legislators to support their causes. For example, the League of Women Voters, reorganized out of the National Woman Suffrage Association, encouraged women to run for office and actively lobbied for laws to improve conditions for employed women, the mentally ill, and the urban poor.

### Women and Politics

In 1921 action by women's groups persuaded Congress to pass the Sheppard-Towner Act, which allotted funds to states to create maternity and pediatric clinics as means of reducing infant mortality. (The measure ended in 1929, when Congress, under pressure from private physicians, canceled funding.) The Cable Act of 1922 reversed the law under which an American woman who married a foreigner assumed her husband's citizenship, allowing such a woman to retain U.S. citizenship. At the state level, too, women achieved rights, such as the ability to serve on juries.

As new voters, however, women faced daunting tasks in achieving their goals and overcoming internal differences. Women in the National Association of Colored Women, for example, fought for the rights of minority women and men without support from either the National Woman's Party or the newly organized League of Women Voters. Some groups, such as the National Woman's Party, pressed for an equal rights amendment to ensure women's equality with men under the law. But such activity alienated the National Consumers League, the Women's Trade Union League, the League of Women Voters, and other organizations that supported special protective legislation to limit hours and improve conditions for employed women. But, like men, women of all types sought participation in the new era's consumerism.

## A CONSUMER SOCIETY

The consumerism depicted in *Why Change Your Wife?* reflected important economic changes affecting the nation.

| TABLE 24.1 | Consumerism in the 1920s |
|---|---|
| **1900** | |
| 2 bicycles | $ 70.00 |
| Wringer and washboard | 5.00 |
| Brushes and brooms | 5.00 |
| Sewing machine (mechanical) | 25.00 |
| TOTAL | $ 105.00 |
| **1928** | |
| Automobile | $ 700.00 |
| Radio | 75.00 |
| Phonograph | 50.00 |
| Washing machine | 150.00 |
| Vacuum cleaner | 50.00 |
| Sewing machine (electric) | 60.00 |
| Other electrical equipment | 25.00 |
| Telephone (per year) | 35.00 |
| TOTAL | $1,145.00 |

*Source:* From an article in *Survey Magazine* in 1928 reprinted in *Another Part of the Twenties,* by Paul Carter. Copyright 1977 by Columbia University Press. Reprinted with permission of the publisher.

Between 1919 and 1929, the gross national product—the total value of all goods and services produced in the United States—swelled by 40 percent. Wages and salaries also grew (though not as drastically), while the cost of living remained relatively stable. People had more purchasing power, and they spent as Americans had never spent before (see Table 24.1). Technology's benefits reached more people than ever before. By 1929, two-thirds of all Americans lived in dwellings that had electricity, compared with one-sixth in 1912. In 1929 one-fourth of all families owned vacuum cleaners, and one-fifth had toasters. Many could afford these goods as well as radios, beauty products, and movie tickets, because more than one family member earned wages or because the breadwinner took a second job. Nevertheless, new products and services were available to more than just the rich, especially to people of other classes living in cities. For example, indoor plumbing and electricity became more common in private residences, and canned foods and ready-made clothes were more affordable.

The automobile stood as vanguard of the era's material wonders. During the 1920s, automobile registrations soared from 8 million to 23 million, and by 1929 there was one car on the road for every five Americans. Mass production and competition made cars affordable even to some working-class families. A Ford Model T cost less than $300, and a Chevrolet sold for $700 by 1926—

**Effects of the Automobile**

when factory workers earned about $1,300 a year and clerical workers about $2,300. Used cars cost less. At those prices, people could consider the car a necessity rather than a luxury. "There is no such thing as a 'pleasure automobile,'" proclaimed one newspaper ad in 1925. "You might as well talk of 'pleasure fresh air,' or of 'pleasure beef steak.' . . . The automobile increases length of life, increases happiness, represents above all other achievements the progress and the civilization of our age."

Cars altered American life as much as railroads had seventy-five years earlier. Those who could afford autos acquired a new "riding habit" and abandoned crowded, inconvenient streetcars. Streets became cleaner as autos replaced the horses that had dumped tons of manure every day. Women who learned to drive achieved newfound independence, taking touring trips with female friends, conquering muddy roads, and making repairs when their vehicles broke down. Families created "homes on wheels," packing food and camping equipment to "get away from it all." By 1927 most autos were enclosed (they previously had open tops), offering young people new private space for courtship and sex. A vast choice of models (there were 108 automobile manufacturers in 1923) and colors allowed owners to express personal tastes. Most important, the car was the ultimate social equalizer. As one writer observed in 1924, "It is hard to convince Steve Popovich, or Antonio Branca, or plain John Smith that he is being ground into the dust by Capital when at will he may drive the same highways, view the same scenery, and get as much enjoyment from his trip as the modern Midas."

Americans' passion for driving necessitated extensive road construction and abundant fuel supplies. Since the late 1800s, farmers and bicyclists had been lobbying for improved roads. After the First World War, motorists joined the campaign, and in the 1920s government aid made "automobility" truly feasible. In 1921 Congress passed the Federal Highway Act, providing funds for state roads, and in 1923 the Bureau of Public Roads planned a national highway system. Roadbuilding in turn inspired such technological developments as mechanized road graders and concrete mixers. The oil-refining industry, which produced gasoline, became vast and powerful. In 1920 the United States produced about 65 percent of the world's oil. Automobiles also forced public officials to pay more attention to safety and traffic control. General Electric Company produced the first timed stop-and-go traffic light in 1924.

Advertising, an essential component of consumerism, acquired new prominence. By 1929 more money was spent

▲ During the 1920s, the desire to own an automobile spread to members of all classes, races, and ethnic groups. Low prices and available credit enabled this family from Beaumont, Texas, to own a "touring car." *(Tyrrell Historical Library)*

## Advertising

on advertising automobiles and other goods and services than on all types of formal education. Blending psychological theory with practical cynicism, advertising theorists confidently asserted that any person's tastes could be manipulated, and marketers developed new techniques to achieve their ends. For example, cosmetics manufacturers like Max Factor, Helena Rubenstein, and African American entrepreneur Madame C. J. Walker used movie stars and beauty advice in magazines to induce women to buy their products. Other advertisers hired baseball star Babe Ruth and football's Red Grange to endorse food and sporting goods.

## Radio

Radio became one of consumer society's most influential advertising and entertainment media. By 1929 over 10 million families owned radios, and Americans spent $850 million a year on radio equipment. In the early 1920s, Congress decided that broadcasting should be a private enterprise, not a tax-supported public service as in Great Britain. As a result,

American radio programming consisted mainly of entertainment rather than educational content, because entertainment attracted larger audiences and therefore higher profits from advertisers. Station KDKA in Pittsburgh, owned by Westinghouse Electric Company, pioneered commercial radio in 1920, broadcasting results of the 1920 presidential election. Then, in 1922, an AT&T-run station in New York City broadcast recurring advertisements—"commercials"—for a Long Island real estate developer. Other stations began airing commercials; by the end of 1922 there were 508 such stations. In 1929 the National Broadcasting Company began to assemble a network of stations and soon was charging advertisers $10,000 to sponsor an hour-long show.

Like automobiles, radio transformed American society. In 1924 the presidential nominating conventions of both political parties were the first to be broadcast, enabling candidates and issues to reach more Americans simultaneously than ever before. And, as a result of its mass marketing and standardized programming, radio had the effect of blurring ethnic boundaries and creating—at least in one way—a homogeneous "American" culture, an effect

# VICTROLA
REG. U. S. PAT. OFF.

**All you need to enjoy the world's best music—a Victrola and Victor Records**

Victor Talking Machine Co., Camden, N. J.

"HIS MASTER'S VOICE"

▲ The spread of electric service to households gave families access to new forms of entertainment, such as recorded music. The Victrola Talking Machine Company, with its trademark of a little fox terrier looking into the horn of a gramophone, became one of the world's most recognized advertisers, even after it was purchased by RCA in 1929. *(Picture Research Consultants & Archives)*

that television and other mass media expanded throughout the twentieth century.

## CITIES, MIGRANTS, AND SUBURBS

Consumerism signified not merely an economically mature nation but also an urbanized one. The 1920 federal census revealed that, for the first time, a majority of Americans lived in urban areas (defined as places with 2,500 or more people); the city had become the focus of national experience. In addition to growth in metropolises like Chicago and New York, manufacturing and services helped propel expansion in dozens of regional centers. Industries like steel, oil, and auto production energized Birmingham, Houston, and Detroit; services and retail trades boosted expansion in Seattle, Atlanta, and Minneapolis. Explosive

growth also occurred in warm-climate cities—notably Miami and San Diego—where promises of comfort and profit attracted thousands of real estate speculators.

As cities grew, the agrarian way of life waned. During the 1920s, 6 million Americans left their farms for the city. Young farm people who felt stifled when they compared their existence with the flashy openness of urban life moved to regional centers like Kansas City and Indianapolis or to the West. Between 1920 and 1930, California's population increased 67 percent, and California became a highly urbanized state while retaining its status as a leader in agricultural production. Meanwhile, streams of rural southerners moved to that region's industrial cities or rode railroads northward to Chicago and Cleveland.

African Americans, in what has come to be called the Great Migration, made up a sizable portion of people on the move during the 1920s. Pushed from cotton farming by a boll weevil plague and lured by industrial jobs, 1.5 million blacks moved, doubling the African American populations of New York, Chicago, Detroit, and Houston. Black communities were also growing in Los Angeles, San Francisco, and San Diego. In cities, however, racial biases blocked opportunity. Forced by low wages and discrimination to seek the cheapest housing, black newcomers squeezed into low-rent ghettos like Chicago's South Side, New York's Harlem, and Los Angeles's Central Avenue. On the West Coast, however, black home ownership rates were higher than in the Northeast and Midwest. Many, for example, took advantage of Los Angeles's "bungalow boom," in which they could purchase a small, one-story house for as little as $900. But unlike white migrants, who were free to move out of the inner city when they could afford to, blacks everywhere found better neighborhoods closed to them. They could either crowd further into already densely populated black neighborhoods or spill into nearby white neighborhoods, a process that sparked resistance and violence. Fears of such "invasion" prompted neighborhood associations to adopt restrictive covenants, whereby white homeowners pledged not to sell or rent property to blacks.

**African American Migration**

In response to discrimination, threats, and violence, thousands of urban blacks joined movements that glorified racial independence. The most influential of these black nationalist groups was the Universal Negro Improvement Association (UNIA), headquartered in Harlem and led by Marcus Garvey, a Jamaican immigrant who believed blacks should separate

**Marcus Garvey**

from corrupt white society. Proclaiming, "I am the equal of any white man," Garvey spread his message with mass meetings and parades. He also promoted black-owned businesses that would manufacture and sell products to black consumers, and he incorporated the Negro Factories Corporation to finance such companies. Garvey's newspaper, *Negro World*, preached black independence, and he founded the Black Star steamship line to transport manufactured goods and raw materials among black businesses in North America, the Caribbean, and Africa.

The UNIA declined in the mid-1920s after mismanagement forced dissolution of the Negro Factories Corporation, and Garvey was deported for mail fraud involving the bankrupt Black Star line. He had been charged with trying to sell stock in the company by advertising a ship that it did not own. His prosecution, however, was politically motivated. Middle-class black leaders, such as W. E. B. Du Bois, and several clergymen opposed the UNIA, fearing that its extremism would undermine their efforts and influence. The U.S. Bureau of Investigation had been mon-

itoring Garvey's radical activities since 1919, and in 1923 eight prominent blacks petitioned the attorney general to deport Garvey. Du Bois also had been incensed when word leaked out in 1922 that Garvey had met secretly with the leader of the Ku Klux Klan. Nevertheless, for several years the UNIA attracted a large following (contemporaries estimated 500,000; Garvey claimed 6 million), especially in the cities, and Garvey's speeches instilled in many African Americans a heightened sense of racial pride.

The newest immigrants to urban America came from Mexico and Puerto Rico, where, as in rural North America, declining fortunes pushed people off the land. During the 1910s, Anglo farmers' associations encouraged Mexican immigration as a source of cheap agricultural labor, and by the 1920s Mexican migrants constituted three-fourths of farm labor in the American West. Growers treated Mexican laborers as slaves, paying them extremely low wages. Resembling other new

### Newcomers from Mexico and Puerto Rico

▲ Over half a million Mexicans immigrated to the United States during the 1920s. Many of them traveled in families and worked together in the fields and orchards of California and other western states. This family is shown pitting apricots in Los Angeles County in 1924.

*(Seaver Center for Western History Research, Natural History Museum of Los Angeles County)*

## Pan American Airways

*a*ir transportation and airmail service between the United States and Latin America began in the 1920s, but establishing the connections was not easy at first, because of anti-American hostility in the region. In 1926 the U.S. government, fearful that German aircraft might drop bombs on the Panama Canal if the United States were ever again to go to war with Germany, signed a treaty with Panama giving American airplanes exclusive rights to operate in Panamanian airports. But America's hero of the air, Charles Lindbergh (see pages 698–699), and a formerly obscure pilot, Juan Trippe, played key roles in changing sentiments and expanding American air service to other parts of Latin America.

Trippe dreamed of creating an international airline. With help from his father-in-law, a banking partner of J. P. Morgan, he established Pan American Airways (informally known as Pan Am) in 1927, invested in modern airplane technology, and won a contract to carry mail between Florida and Cuba. In December of that year, still basking in fame from his transatlantic heroics, Lindbergh flew to Mexico and used his charm to persuade the Mexicans to accept airline links to the United States. The next year, Lindbergh joined Pan Am and began flying company planes to destinations in Central and South America. Welcomed wildly everywhere he landed, Lindbergh helped Trippe initiate mail and passenger service to Panama, Mexico, and other Latin American countries in 1929. Trippe advertised to wealthy Americans the opportunity to escape prohibition and enjoy Caribbean beaches by taking Pan Am flights to Havana and beyond, and he offered in-flight meals to travelers.

Needing landing facilities in order to operate, Pan Am built some of the airports that became essential connections between Latin America and the rest of the world. Trippe's employees created aerial maps that provided navigational aids for many years. Pan Am not only linked Latin America more closely with the United States but also helped unite parts of Latin America that had previously been divided by impenetrable mountain ranges. Yet Pan Am was also willing to resort to almost any tactic to build an airport and to start service. Thus it cooperated with unsavory dictators, engaged in bribery, and violated human rights, in one case helping Bolivian police to corral local Indians behind barbed wire for several days in order to clear land for a new airport.

Still, Pan Am both enabled Americans (mostly the wealthy) to travel abroad more conveniently and brought more foreigners to the United States. In 1942 one of its aircraft became the first to fly around the world. In the 1940s, the company began offering flights to Europe and Africa, and in 1950 changed its name to Pan American World Air-ways to emphasize its global character. Until its demise in 1991, Pan Am provided a leading link between the United States and the rest of the world.

▲ Providing air transport connections to the Caribbean, Central America, and South America, Pan American Airways established the first major passenger and cargo links between the United States and other nations. By the early 1930s, flights were so numerous that the timetable announced in this illustration consisted of twelve pages. *(The Pan American Heritage Web Site)*

▲ Wide highways, cheap land, and affordable housing allowed automobile commuters to move to the urban periphery. In this photo, young women wearing 1920s flapper-style outfits celebrate the phenomenal growth of Culver City, outside Los Angeles. Notice the strong presence of the motor car. *(Security Pacific National Bank Collection, Los Angeles Public Library)*

immigrant groups, Mexican newcomers generally lacked resources and skills, and men outnumbered women. Although some achieved middle-class status as shopkeepers and professionals, most crowded into low-rent districts in growing cities like Denver, San Antonio, Los Angeles, and Tucson, where they suffered poor sanitation, poor police protection, and poor schools. Both rural and urban Mexicans moved back and forth between their homeland and the United States, seeking available jobs and creating a way of life that Mexicans called *sin fronteras*—without borders.

The 1920s also witnessed an influx of Puerto Ricans to the mainland. Puerto Rico had been a U.S. possession since 1898, and its natives were granted U.S. citizenship in 1916. As a shift in the island's economy from sugar to coffee production created a labor surplus, Puerto Ricans moved to New York and other cities, attracted by contracts from employers seeking cheap labor. In the cities, they created *barrios* (communities) and found jobs in fac-

tories, hotels, restaurants, and domestic service. Puerto Ricans maintained traditional customs and developed businesses—*bodegas* (grocery stores), cafés, boarding houses—and social organizations to help them adapt to American society. As with Mexicans, educated Puerto Rican elites—doctors, lawyers, business owners—became community leaders.

As urbanization peaked, suburban growth accelerated. Although towns had sprouted around major cities since the nation's earliest years, prosperity and automobile transportation in the 1920s made suburbs more accessible to those wishing to flee congested urban neighborhoods. Between 1920 and 1930, suburbs of Chicago (such as Oak Park and Evanston), Cleveland (Shaker Heights), and Los Angeles (Burbank and Inglewood) grew five to ten times faster than did the nearby central cities. They sparked an outburst of home construction; Los Angeles builders alone

**Growth of Suburbs**

erected 250,000 homes for auto-owning suburbanites. Although some suburbs, such as Highland Park (near Detroit) and East Chicago, were industrial satellites, most were middle- and upper-class bedroom communities.

Increasingly, suburbs resisted annexation to core cities. Suburbanites wanted to escape big-city crime, grime, and taxes, and they fought to preserve control over their own police, schools, and water and gas services. Particularly in the Northeast and Midwest, the suburbs' fierce independence choked off expansion by the central cities and prevented them from access to the resources and tax bases of wealthier suburban residents. Suburban expansion had other costs, too, as automobiles and the dispersal of population spread the environmental problems of city life—trash, pollution, noise—across the entire metropolitan area.

Together, cities and suburbs fostered the mass culture that gave the decade its character. Most of the consumers who jammed shops, movie houses, and sporting arenas, and who embraced fads like crossword puzzles and miniature golf, lived in or around cities. These were the places where people defied older morals by patronizing speakeasies (illegal saloons during prohibition), wearing outlandish clothes, and dancing to jazz. Yet the ideal of small-town society survived. While millions thronged cityward, Americans reminisced about the simplicity of a world gone by, however mythical that world might have been. This was the dilemma the modern nation faced: how does one anchor oneself in a world of rampant materialism and rapid social change?

## NEW RHYTHMS OF EVERYDAY LIFE

Amid changes to modern consumer society, Americans developed new patterns of everyday life. One pattern involved uses of time. People increasingly split their day into distinct time compartments: work, family, and leisure. For many, time on the job shrank as mechanization and higher productivity enabled employers to shorten the workweek for many industrial laborers from six days to five and a half. White-collar employees often worked a forty-hour week, enjoyed a full weekend off, and received annual vacations as a standard job benefit.

Family time is hard to measure, but certain trends are clear. Family size decreased between 1920 and 1930 as birth control became more widely practiced. Among American women who married in the 1870s and 1880s, well over half who survived to age fifty had five or more children; of their counterparts who married in the 1920s, however, just 20 percent had five or more children. Lower birth rates and longer life expectancy meant that adults were devoting a smaller portion of their lives to raising children and having more time for nonfamily activities. Meanwhile, the divorce rate rose. In 1920 there was 1 divorce for every 7.5 marriages; by 1929 the national ratio was 1 in 6, and in many cities it was 2 in 7.

At home, housewives still worked long hours cleaning, cooking, and raising children, but machines now lightened some of their tasks and enabled them to use time differently than their forebears had. Especially in middle-class households, electric irons and washing machines simplified some chores. Gas- and oil-powered central heating and hot-water heaters eliminated the hauling of wood, coal, and water, the upkeep of a kitchen fire, and the removal of ashes.

**Household Management**

Even as technology and economic change made some tasks simpler, they also created new demands on a mother's time. Daughters of working-class families stayed in school longer, and alternative forms of employment caused a shortage of domestic servants, with the result that the pool of those who helped housewives with cleaning, cooking, and childcare shrank. In addition, the availability of washing machines, hot water, vacuum cleaners, and commercial soap put greater pressure on housewives to keep everything clean. Advertisers of these products tried to make women feel guilty for not devoting enough attention to cleaning the home. No longer a producer of food and clothing, as her ancestors had been, a housewife instead became the chief shopper, responsible for making sure her family spent money wisely. And the automobile made the wife a family's chief chauffeur. One survey found that urban housewives spent on average seven and one-half hours per week driving to shop and to transport children.

New emphasis on nutrition added a scientific dimension to housewives' responsibilities. With the discovery of vitamins between 1915 and 1930, nutritionists began advocating consumption of certain foods to prevent illness. Giant companies scrambled to advertise their products as filled with vitamins and minerals beneficial to growth and health. Producers of milk, canned fruits and vegetables, and other foods exploited the vitamin craze with claims that were hard to dispute because little was known about these invisible, tasteless ingredients. Welch's Grape Juice, for example, avoided mentioning the excess sugars in its product when it advertised that it was "Rich in Health Values" and "the laxative properties you cannot do without." Even chocolate candy manufacturers plugged their bars as vitamin packed.

**Health and Life Expectancy**

# Your Children ___
___ is their food safe?

YOU, as a conscientious mother, buy the best food for your children, prepare it with scrupulous care and cook it correctly. Yet, in spite of all, you may be giving your children food which is not wholesome—possibly dangerous!

For even the best food becomes unsafe to eat unless it is *kept* at the proper degree of cold, which medical authorities agree should be 50 degrees or less—always. Above that temperature, bacteria multiply, food is contaminated—becomes a menace to health.

There is only one way to be sure that your children's food is fresh and healthful—correct refrigeration. There is one refrigerator that assures you of scientifically perfect refrigeration at all times—the General Electric. Faithfully, quietly, day and night, it maintains a

temperature safely below the danger point—50 degrees.

The General Electric is ideal for the home. Its simple mechanism which you never need to oil, is mounted on top

*The price of this new all-steel refrigerator—the small-family model—is now*
**$215** AT THE FACTORY

of the cabinet and hermetically sealed in a steel casing. It has a simple and accessible temperature control, makes a generous supply of ice cubes, creates no radio interference. It has the only all-steel, warp-proof cabinet—easily cleaned, sanitary.

Your dealer will be glad to explain the spaced payment plan, which makes it so easy to own this faithful watchman of the family health. Let him help you select the particular model that fits your needs. If there is not a dealer near you, write Electric Refrigeration Dept., General Electric Co., Hanna Building, Cleveland, Ohio, for booklet Q-9.

*An unmatched record*
*There are now more than 300,000 homes enjoying the comfort and protection of General Electric Refrigerators—and not one of the owners has ever had to pay a single dollar for repairs or service.*

# GENERAL ⓖⓔ ELECTRIC
## ALL-STEEL REFRIGERATOR

▲ While electric appliances gave mothers and housewives more convenient ways to carry out their roles, producers tried to sell their products by creating guilt among women who were concerned about their families' safety. Here, the General Electric Company warns a mother that she needs a GE refrigerator if she is to be "conscientious" and "scrupulous" about giving her children wholesome and healthy food. *(Picture Research Consultants & Archives)*

Better diets and improved hygiene made Americans generally healthier. Life expectancy at birth increased from fifty-four to sixty years between 1920 and 1930, and infant mortality decreased by two-thirds. Public sanitation and research in bacteriology combined to reduce risks of life-threatening diseases, such as tuberculosis and diphtheria. But medical progress did not benefit all groups equally; race and class mattered in health trends as they did in everything else. Rates of infant mortality were 50 to 100 percent higher among nonwhites than among whites, and tuberculosis in inner-city slums remained alarmingly

common. Moreover, fatalities from car accidents rose 150 percent, and deaths from heart disease and cancer— diseases of old age—increased 15 percent. Nevertheless, Americans in general were living longer: the total population over age sixty-five grew 35 percent between 1920 and 1930, while the rest of the population increased only 15 percent.

As the numbers of elderly increased, their worsening economic status stirred interest in pensions and other forms of old-age assistance. Industrialism put premiums on youth and agility, pushing older people into poverty from forced retirement and reduced income. Recognizing the needs of aging citizens, most European countries established state-supported pension systems in the early 1900s. Many Americans, however, believed that individuals should prepare for old age by saving in their youth; pensions, they felt, smacked of socialism. As late as 1923, the Pennsylvania Chamber of Commerce labeled old-age assistance "un-American and socialistic . . . an entering wedge of communistic propaganda."

## Older Americans and Retirement

Yet conditions were alarming. Most inmates in state poorhouses were older people, and almost one-third of Americans age sixty-five and older depended financially on someone else. Few employers, including the federal government, provided for retired employees. Noting that the government fed retired horses until they died, one postal worker complained, "For the purpose of drawing a pension, it would have been better had I been a horse than a human being." Resistance to pension plans finally broke at the state level in the 1920s. Led by physician Isaac Max Rubinow and journalist Abraham Epstein, reformers persuaded voluntary associations, labor unions, and legislators to endorse old-age assistance through pensions, insurance, and retirement homes. By 1933 almost every state provided at least minimal support to needy elderly people, and a path had been opened for a national program of old-age insurance.

## Social Values

As Americans encountered new influences in their time away from work and family, altered habits and values were inevitable. Aided by new fabrics and chemical dyes, clothes became a means of self-expression as women and men wore more casual and gaily colored styles than their parents would have considered. The line between acceptable and inappropriate behavior blurred as smoking, drinking, and frankness about sex became fashionable. Birth control gained a large following in respectable circles. Newspapers, magazines, motion pictures, and popular songs (such as "Hot Lips" and

"Burning Kisses") made certain that Americans did not suffer from "sex starvation." A typical movie ad promised "brilliant men, beautiful jazz babies, champagne baths, midnight revels, petting parties in the purple dawn, all ending in one terrific smashing climax that makes you gasp."

Other trends weakened inherited customs. Because state child-labor laws and compulsory-attendance rules kept children in school longer than ever before, peer groups rather than parents played an influential role in socializing youngsters. In earlier eras, different age groups had often shared the same activities: children interacted with adults in fields and kitchens, and young apprentices toiled in workshops beside journeymen and craftsmen. Now, graded school classes, sports, and clubs constantly brought together children of the same age, separating them from the company and influence of adults. Meanwhile, parents tended to rely less on traditions of childcare and more on experts who wrote manuals on how best to raise children.

Furthermore, the ways that young males and females interacted with each other underwent fundamental changes. Between 1890 and the mid-1920s, ritualized middle- and upper-class courtship, consisting of men's formally "calling on" women and of chaperoned social engagements, faded in favor of "dating," without adult supervision, in which a man "asked out" a woman and, usually, spent money on her. The more liberal practice arose from new freedoms and opportunities of urban life, and spread from the working class to the middle and upper classes. Employed unmarried young people, living away from family restraints, were eager to go on dates to new commercial amusements, such as movies and nightclubs, and when automobiles became the major mode of transportation, as they did in the 1920s, they made dating even more extensive. A woman's job, however, seldom provided sufficient income for her to afford these entertainments, but she could enjoy them if a man "treated" and escorted her. Companionship, romance, and, at times, sexual exploitation accompanied the practice, especially when a woman was expected to give sexual favors in return for being treated. A date thus ironically weakened a woman's prerogative at the same time that it expanded her opportunities. Under the courtship system, a woman had control over who could "call" on her and who could not. But once she entered a system in which a man's money enabled her to fulfill her desire for entertainment and independence, a young woman might find herself faced with difficult moral choices.

The practice of dating burgeoned because, after the First World War, women continued to stream into the labor force. By 1930, 10.8 million women held paying jobs, an increase of 2 million since war's end. Although the proportion of women working in agriculture shrank, proportions in categories of urban jobs grew or held steady (see Figure 24.1). The sex segregation that had long characterized workplaces persisted; most women took jobs that men seldom sought and vice versa. Thus, over 1 million women held jobs as teachers and nurses. In the clerical

## Women in the Work Force

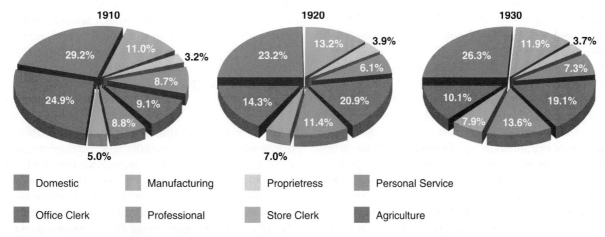

**Figure 24.1    Changing Dimensions of Paid Female Labor, 1910–1930**

These charts reveal the extraordinary growth in clerical and professional occupations among employed women and the accompanying decline in agricultural labor in the early twentieth century. Notice that manufacturing employment peaked in 1920 and that domestic service fluctuated as white immigrant women began to move out of these jobs and were replaced by women of color.

▲ The expansion of service-sector jobs and new technology opened new opportunities for women in the 1920s. This telephone operator handled scores of phone calls and monitored a huge switchboard at the same time. Her dress and jewelry contrasted with the simpler styles worn by factory women, who had to be more careful in working with dangerous machines. *(George Eastman House)*

category, some 2.2 million women were typists, book-keepers, and filing clerks, a tenfold increase since 1920. Another 736,000 were store clerks, and growing numbers could be found in the personal service category as wait-resses and hairdressers. Although almost 2 million women worked in manufacturing, their numbers grew very little over the decade. Wherever women were employed, their wages seldom exceeded half of those paid to men.

Although women worked outside the home for a va-riety of reasons, their families' economic needs were para-mount. The consumerism of the 1920s tempted working-class and middle-class families to satisfy their wants and needs by living beyond their means or by expanding their income with women's wages. In previous eras, most people whose earnings supplemented those of the primary bread-winner had been young and single. Even though the vast majority of married women did not hold paying jobs (only 12 percent were employed in 1930), married women as a

proportion of the work force rose by 30 percent during the 1920s, and the number of employed married women swelled from 1.9 million to 3.1 million. These figures omit countless widowed, divorced, and abandoned women who held jobs and who, like married women, often had chil-dren to support.

The proportion of nonwhite women in paid labor was double that of white women. Often they entered the

**Employment of Minority Women**

workforce because their husbands were unemployed or underem-ployed. The majority of employed African American women held do-mestic jobs doing cooking, clean-ing, and laundry. The few who held factory jobs, such as in cigarette factories and meatpacking plants, performed the least desirable, lowest-paying tasks. Some opportuni-ties opened for educated black women in social work, teaching, and nursing, but these women also faced dis-crimination and low incomes. More than white mothers, employed black mothers called on a family network of grandmothers and aunts to help with childcare.

Economic necessity also drew thousands of other minority women into the labor force. Mexican women increasingly entered into wage labor, although their tradi-tion resisted female employment. Exact figures are difficult to uncover, but it is certain that many Mexican women in the Southwest worked as domestic servants, operatives in garment factories, and agricultural laborers. Next to black women, Japanese American women were the most likely to hold paying jobs. They, too, worked as field hands and domestics, jobs in which they encountered racial bias and low pay.

Employed or not, some women remade the image of femininity. In contrast to the heavy, floor-length dresses

**Alternative Images of Femininity**

and long hair of previous genera-tions, the short skirts and bobbed hair of the 1920s "flapper" symbol-ized new independence and sex-ual freedom. Although few women lived the flapper life, the look became fashionable among office workers and store clerks as well as college coeds. As Cecil B. DeMille's movies showed, chaste models of fe-male behavior were eclipsed by movie temptresses, such as Clara Bow, known as the "It Girl," and Gloria Swanson, notorious for torrid love affairs on and off the screen. Many women were asserting a new social equality with men. One observer described "the new woman" as in-triguingly independent.

> She takes a man's point of view as her mother never could. . . . She will never make you a hatband or knit

you a necktie, but she'll drive you from the station . . . in her own little sports car. She'll don knickers and go skiing with you, . . . she'll dive as well as you, perhaps better, she'll dance as long as you care to, and she'll take everything you say the way you mean it.

The era's openness regarding sexuality also enabled the underground homosexual culture to surface a little more than in previous eras. In nontraditional city neighborhoods, such as New York's Greenwich Village and Harlem, cheap rents and an apparent tolerance for alternate lifestyles attracted gay men and lesbians, who patronized dance halls, speakeasies, cafés, and other gathering places. Establishments that catered to a gay clientele remained targets for police raids, however, demonstrating that gays and lesbians could not expect acceptance from the rest of society.

**Gay and Lesbian Culture**

These trends represented a break with the more restrained culture of the nineteenth century. But social change rarely proceeds smoothly. As the decade wore on, various groups mobilized to defend older values.

## LINES OF DEFENSE

Early in 1920, the leader of a newly formed organization, using a tactic adopted by modern businesses, hired two public relations experts to recruit members. The experts, Edward Clarke and Elizabeth Tyler, canvassed communities in the South, Southwest, and Midwest, where they found countless people eager to pay a $10 membership fee and $6 for a white uniform. Clarke and Tyler pocketed $2.50 from each membership they sold. Their success helped build the organization to 5 million members and four thousand chapters by 1923.

No ordinary civic club like the Lions or Kiwanis, this was the Ku Klux Klan, a revived version of the hooded order that had terrorized southern communities after the Civil War. More than its predecessor, the new KKK vowed to protect female purity as well as racial and ethnic purity. As one pamphlet distributed by Clarke and Tyler declared, "Every criminal, every gambler, every thug, every libertine, every girl ruiner, every home wrecker, every wife beater, every dope peddler, every moonshiner, every white slaver, every Rome-controlled newspaper, every black spider—is fighting the Klan. Think it over, which side are you on?"

**Ku Klux Klan**

Reconstituted in 1915 by William J. Simmons, an Atlanta, Georgia, evangelist and insurance salesman, the Klan adopted the hoods, intimidating tactics, and mystical terminology of its forerunner (its leader was the Imperial Wizard; its book of rituals, the Kloran). But Klan of the early 1920s had broader objectives than the old. It fanned outward from the Deep South and for a time wielded political power in places as diverse as Oregon, where Portland's mayor was a Klan member, and Indiana, where Klansmen held the governorship and several seats in the legislature. Its membership included many from the urban middle class who were fearful of losing social and economic gains achieved from postwar prosperity and nervous about a new youth culture that seemed to be eluding family control. It included a women's adjunct, Women of the Ku Klux Klan, consisting of an estimated half-million members.

One phrase summed up Klan goals: "Native, white, Protestant supremacy." Native meant no immigration, no "mongrelization" of American culture. According to Imperial Wizard Hiram Wesley Evans, white supremacy was a matter of survival. "The world," he warned, "has been so made so that each race must fight for its life, must conquer, accept slavery, or die. The Klansman believes the whites will not become slaves, and he does not intend to die before his time." Evans praised Protestantism for promoting "unhampered individual development," and he accused the Catholic Church of discouraging assimilation and enslaving people to priests and a foreign pope.

Using threatening assemblies, violence, and political and economic pressure, the Klan menaced many communities in the early 1920s. Klansmen meted out vigilante justice to suspected bootleggers, wife beaters, and adulterers; forced schools to stop teaching the theory of evolution; campaigned against Catholic and Jewish political candidates; pledged members not to buy from merchants who did not share their views; and fueled racial tensions against Mexicans in Texas border cities. Although men firmly controlled Klan activities, women not only joined male members in efforts to promote native white Protestantism but also, with male approval, worked for moral reform and enforcement of prohibition. Because the KKK vowed to protect the "virtue" of women, housewives and other women sometimes appealed to the Klan for help in punishing abusive, immoral, or irresponsible husbands and fathers when legal authorities would not intervene. Rather than an arrest and trial, the Klan's method of justice was a flogging.

By 1925, however, the Invisible Empire was weakening, as scandal undermined its moral base. In 1925 Indiana grand dragon David Stephenson was convicted of second-degree murder after he kidnapped and raped a woman who later died either from taking poison or from infection

▲ When Nicola Sacco and Bartolomeo Vanzetti were convicted of murder and robbery in 1921, people who believed that the men's anarchist political beliefs had caused the judge and jury to be overly biased tried to raise money for court appeals. Contributors received buttons to wear in support of the two Italian immigrants. Efforts by sympathizers, both in the U.S. and abroad, failed, however, and Sacco and Vanzetti were executed in August of 1927. *(© Bettmann/Corbis)*

caused by bites on her body. More generally, the Klan's negative, exclusive brand of patriotism and purity could not compete in a pluralistic society.

The KKK had no monopoly on bigotry in the 1920s; intolerance pervaded American society. Nativists had urged an end to free immigration since the 1880s. They charged that Catholic and Jewish immigrants clogged city slums, flouted community norms, and stubbornly embraced alien religious and political beliefs. Fear of immigrant radicals also fueled a dramatic trial in 1921, when two Italian anarchists, Nicola Sacco and Bartolomeo Vanzetti, were convicted of murdering a paymaster and guard in Braintree, Massachusetts. Evidence for their guilt was flimsy, but Judge Webster Thayer openly sided with the prosecution, privately calling the defendants "anarchistic bastards."

Guided by such sentiments, the movement to restrict immigration gathered support. Labor leaders warned that floods of alien workers would depress wages and raise unemployment. Business executives, who formerly had opposed restrictions

**Immigration Quotas**

because they desired cheap immigrant laborers, changed their minds, having realized that they could keep wages low by mechanizing. Even some humanitarian reformers supported restriction as a means of reducing poverty and easing assimilation. Drawing support from such groups, Congress reversed previous policy and, in the Emergency Quota Act of 1921, set yearly immigration allocations for each nationality. Reflecting preference for Anglo-Saxon Protestant immigrants and prejudice against Catholics and Jews from southern and eastern Europe, Congress stipulated that annual immigration of a given nationality could not exceed 3 percent of the number of immigrants from that nation residing in the United States in 1910. The act thereby discriminated against immigrants from southern and eastern Europe, whose numbers were small in 1910 relative to those from northern Europe.

The Quota Act was a temporary measure, and in 1924 Congress replaced it with the National Origins Act. This law limited annual immigration to 150,000 people and set quotas at 2 percent of each nationality residing in the United States in 1890, except for Asians, who were banned completely. (Chinese had been excluded by legislation in 1882.) The act further restricted southern and eastern Europeans, because even fewer of those groups lived in the United States in 1890 than in 1910. The law did, however, allow wives and children of U.S. citizens to enter as nonquota immigrants. In 1927 a revised National Origins Act apportioned new quotas to begin in 1929. It retained the annual limit of 150,000 but redefined quotas to be distributed among European countries in proportion to the "national-origins" (country of birth or descent) of American inhabitants in 1920. People coming from the Western Hemisphere did not fall under the quotas (except for those whom the Labor Department defined as potential paupers), and soon they became the largest immigrant groups (see Figure 24.2).

Whereas nativists tried to establish ethnic and racial purity, the pursuit of spiritual purity stirred religious fundamentalists. Millions of Americans sought certainty and salvation from what they perceived as the irreverence of a materialistic, hedonistic society by following evangelical denominations of Protestantism that interpreted the Bible literally. Resolutely believing that God's miracles created the world and its living creatures, they condemned the theory of evolution as heresy, and argued that wherever fundamentalists constituted a majority of a community, as they did in many places, they should be able to determine what would be taught in schools. Their enemies were "modernists," who used reasoning from social sciences, such

**Fundamentalism**

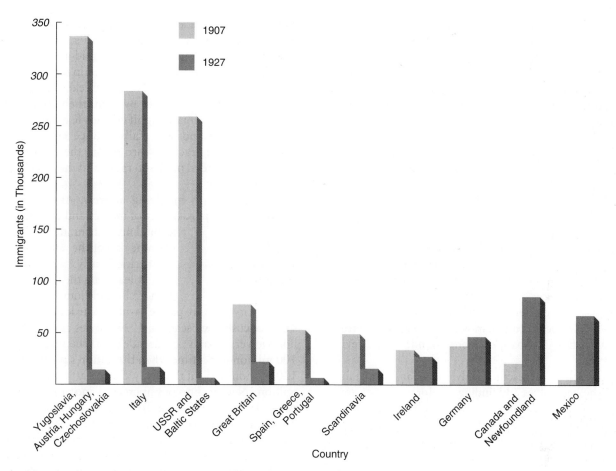

**Figure 24.2    Sources of Immigration, 1907 and 1927**
Immigration peaked in 1907 and 1908, when newcomers from southern and eastern Europe poured into the United States. After immigration restriction laws were passed in the 1920s, the greatest number of immigrants came from the Western Hemisphere (Canada and Mexico), which was exempted from the quotas, and the number coming from eastern and southern Europe shrank.

as psychology and anthropology, to interpret behavior. To modernists, God was important to the study of culture and history, but science was responsible for advancing knowledge.

In 1925 Christian fundamentalism clashed with modernism in a celebrated case in Dayton, Tennessee.

||||||||||||||||||||||||||||||||||
**Scopes Trial**

Early that year, the state legislature had passed a law forbidding public school instructors from teaching the theory that humans had evolved from lower forms of life rather than having descended from Adam and Eve. Shortly thereafter, high-school teacher John Thomas Scopes volunteered to serve in a test case and was arrested for violating the law. Scopes's trial that summer became a headline event. William Jennings Bryan, former secretary of state and three-time presiden-

tial candidate, argued for the prosecution, and a team of civil liberties lawyers headed by Clarence Darrow represented Scopes. News correspondents crowded into town, and radio stations broadcast the trial.

Although Scopes was convicted—clearly he had broken the law—modernists claimed victory. The testimony, they believed, showed fundamentalism to be illogical. The trial's climax was Bryan's taking the witness stand as an expert on the Bible. Responding to Darrow's probing, Bryan asserted that Eve really had been created from Adam's rib, that the Tower of Babel was responsible for the diversity of languages, and that Jonah had actually been swallowed by a big fish. Spectators in Dayton cheered Bryan for his testimony, but the liberal press mocked him and his allies. Nevertheless, fundamentalists were not discouraged. For example, the Southern Baptist Convention, the fastest-growing Protestant sect, continued to attract members and, along with other fundamentalist groups, pressured school boards to stop teaching about evolution. Advocates for what they believed to be basic values of family and conduct, these churches created an independent subculture, with their own schools, camps, radio ministries, and missionary societies.

Religious fervor spread wherever people struggling with economic insecurity became nervous about modernism's attack on old-time religion.

**Religious Revivalism**

Cities housed countless Pentecostal churches, which attracted blacks and whites who were swayed by their pageantry and depiction of a personal Savior. Using modern advertising techniques and elaborately staged broadcasts on radio, magnetic "revivalist" preachers, such as the flamboyant Aimee Semple McPherson of Los Angeles, former baseball player Billy Sunday who preached on nationwide travels, and Father Divine, an African American who amassed an interracial following from his base on Long Island, stirred revivalist fervor.

Revivalism represented only one means of sustaining old-fashioned values and finding comfort in a fast-moving consumer society. Millions who did not belong to the KKK firmly believed that nonwhites and immigrants were inferior people who imperiled national welfare. Clergy and teachers of all faiths condemned dancing, new dress styles, and sex in movies and in parked cars. Many urban dwellers supported prohibition, believing that eliminating the temptation of drink would help win the battle against poverty, vice, and corruption. Yet even while mourning a lost past, most Americans sincerely sought some kind of balance as they tried to adjust to the modern order in one way or another. Few refrained from listening to the radio and seeing movies like *Why Change Your Wife?*—activities that proved less corrupting than critics feared. More than ever, Americans sought fellowship in civic organizations, such as Rotary, Elks, and women's clubs. Perhaps most important, more people were finding release in recreation and new uses of leisure time.

## THE AGE OF PLAY

Americans in the 1920s embraced commercial entertainment as never before. In 1919 they spent $2.5 billion on leisure activities; by 1929 such expenditures topped $4.3 billion, a figure not again equaled until after the Second World War. Spectator amusements—movies, music, and sports—accounted for 21 percent of the 1929 total; the rest involved participatory recreation, such as games, hobbies,

and travel. Entrepreneurs responded quickly to an appetite for fads and spectacles. Early in the 1920s, mahjong, a Chinese tile game, was the craze. In the mid-1920s, devotees popularized crossword puzzles, printed in mass-circulation newspapers and magazines. Next, funseekers adopted miniature golf as their new fad. By 1930 the nation boasted thirty thousand miniature golf courses featuring tiny castles, windmills, and waterfalls. Dance crazes like the Charleston were practiced throughout the country, aided by live and recorded music on radio and the growing popularity of jazz.

In addition to indulging actively, Americans were avid spectators, particularly of movies and sports. In total capital investment, motion pictures became one of the nation's leading industries. Nearly every community had at least one theater, whether a hundred-seat Bijou on Main Street or a big-city "picture palace" with ornate lobbies and thousands of cushioned seats. In 1922 movies attracted 40 million viewers weekly; by decade's end the number neared 100 million—at a time when the nation's population was 120 million and total weekly church attendance was 60 million. New technology increased movies' appeal. Between 1922 and 1927, the Technicolor Corporation developed a means of producing movies in color. This process, along with the introduction of sound in *The Jazz Singer* in 1927, made movies even more exciting and realistic.

**Movies and Sports**

Responding to tastes of mass audiences, the movie industry produced escapist entertainment. Although DeMille's romantic comedies like *Why Change Your Wife?* were entertaining, his most popular films—*The Ten Commandments* (1923) and *The King of Kings* (1927)—were biblical. Lurid dramas like *Souls for Sale* (1923) and *A Woman Who Sinned* (1924) also drew big audiences, as did slapstick comedies starring Harold Lloyd and Charlie Chaplin. Movie content was tame by current standards, however. In 1927 producers, bowing to pressure from legislators and religious leaders, instituted self-censorship, forbidding nudity, rough language, and plots that did not end with justice and morality triumphant. Movies also reproduced social prejudices. Although white actresses and actors played roles as glamour queens and action heroes, what few black actors there were had to take roles as maids and butlers.

Spectator sports also boomed. Each year millions packed stadiums and parks to cheer athletic events. In an age when technology and mass production had robbed experiences and objects of their uniqueness, sports provided some of the unpredictability and drama that people craved. Newspapers and radio magnified this tension, feed-

▲ Excluded from playing in white-dominated professional baseball, African Americans organized their own teams and leagues. The Indianapolis ABCs, named after the American Brewing Company, was one of the more successful teams in the Negro National League during the 1920s, and featured some of the best black baseball players of the era, including Oscar Charleston, Elwood "Bingo" DeMoss, and "Cannonball" Dick Redding. *(National Baseball Hall of Fame, Cooperstown, NY)*

ing sports news to an eager public and glorifying events with such dramatic narrative that sports promoters did not need to buy advertising.

Baseball's drawn-out suspense, variety of plays, and potential for keeping statistics attracted a huge following. After the "Black Sox scandal" of 1919, when eight members of the Chicago White Sox were banned from the game for allegedly throwing the World Series to the Cincinnati Reds (even though a jury acquitted them), baseball regained respectability by transforming itself. Discovering that home runs excited fans, the leagues redesigned the ball to make it livelier. Game attendance skyrocketed. A record 300,000 people attended the six-game 1921 World Series between the New York Giants and New York Yankees. Millions gathered regularly to watch local teams, and even more listened to professional games on the radio. Although African American ballplayers were prohibited from playing in the major leagues, they formed their own teams, and in 1920 the first successful Negro League was founded in Kansas City, Missouri, with Andrew "Rube" Foster as its president. The league consisted of eight teams from places such as Chicago, Kansas City, and Indianapolis, and several rival leagues were formed in the following years.

Sports, movies, and the news created a galaxy of heroes. As technology and mass society made the individual less significant, people clung to heroic personalities as a means of identifying with the unique. Athletes like Bill Tilden in tennis, Gertrude Ederle in swimming (in 1926 she became the first woman to swim across the English Channel), and Bobby Jones in golf were household words. The power and action of boxing, football, and baseball produced the most popular sports heroes. Heavyweight champion Jack Dempsey, the "Manassa (Colorado) Mauler," attracted the first of several million-dollar gates in his fight with French boxer Georges Carpentier in 1921. Harold "Red" Grange, running back for the University of Illinois football team, thrilled fans and sportswriters with his speed and agility.

## Sports Heroes

▲ Standing beside his plane, the "Spirit of St. Louis," shortly before takeoff on his solo trans-atlantic flight, young Charles Lindbergh exhibits the self-reliance and determination that made him one of the most revered heroes of the 1920s. Lindbergh's feat signified a blend of new technology with old-fashioned individual effort. *(Picture Research Consultants & Archives)*.

Baseball's foremost hero was George Herman "Babe" Ruth, who began his career as a pitcher but found he could use his prodigious strength to better advantage hitting home runs. Ruth hit twenty-nine homers in 1919, fifty-four in 1920 (the year the Boston Red Sox traded him to the New York Yankees), fifty-nine in 1921, and sixty in 1927—each year a record. His talent and boyish grin endeared him to millions. Known for overindulgence in food, drink, and sex, he charmed fans into forgiving his excesses by appearing at public events and visiting hospitalized children.

Beyond sports, Americans also fulfilled their yearning for romance and adventure through movie idols. The films and personal lives of Douglas Fairbanks, Gloria Swanson, and Charlie Chaplin were discussed in parlors and pool halls across the country. One of the decade's most adored movie personalities was Rudolph Valentino, whose suave manner made women swoon and men imitate his pomaded hairdo and slick sideburns. Valentino's image exploited the era's sexual liberalism and flirtation with wickedness. In his most famous film, Valentino played a

## Movie Stars and Public Heroes

passionate sheik who carried away beautiful women to his tent, combining the roles of abductor and seducer. When he died at thirty-one of complications from ulcers and appendicitis, the press turned his funeral into a public extravaganza. Mourners lined up for a mile to file past his coffin.

The era's most celebrated hero, however, was Charles A. Lindbergh, an indomitable aviator who in May 1927 flew a plane solo from New York to Paris. The flight seized the attention of practically every American, as newspaper and telegraph reports followed Lindbergh's progress. After the pilot landed successfully, President Coolidge dispatched a warship to bring "Lucky Lindy" back home. Celebrants sent Lindbergh 55,000 telegrams and dropped 1,800 tons of shredded paper on him during a triumphant homecoming parade. Among countless prizes, Lindbergh received the Distinguished Flying Cross and the Congressional Medal of Honor. Promoters offered him millions of dollars to tour the world and $700,000 for a movie contract. Through it all, Lindbergh, nicknamed "The Lone Eagle," remained dignified, even aloof. Although his flight and its aftermath symbolized the new combination of technology and mass culture of the 1920s, Lindbergh himself epitomized individual achievement, self-reliance, and courage—old-fashioned values that attracted public allegiance amid the media frenzy.

In their quest for fun and self-expression, some Americans became lawbreakers by refusing to give up drinking. The Eighteenth Amend-

### Prohibition

ment (1919), which prohibited the manufacture, sale, and transportation of alcoholic beverages, and the federal law that implemented it (the Volstead Act of 1920) worked well at first. Per capita consumption of liquor dropped, as did arrests for drunkenness, and the price of illegal booze rose above what average workers could afford. But federal and state authorities for the most part refrained from enforcing the new law. In 1922 Congress gave the Prohibition Bureau only three thousand employees and less than $7 million for nationwide enforcement, and by 1927 most state budgets omitted funds to enforce prohibition.

After 1925 the so-called noble experiment of prohibition broke down as thousands of people made their own wine and gin illegally, and bootleg importers along the country's borders and shorelines easily evaded the few patrols that attempted to intercept them. Moreover, drinking, like gambling and prostitution, was a business with willing customers, and criminal organizations quickly capitalized on public demand. The most notorious of such mobs belonged to Al Capone, a burly tough who seized control of illegal liquor and vice in Chicago, maintaining power over politicians and the vice business through intimidation, bribery, and violence. But Capone contended, in a statement revealing of the era, "Prohibition is a business. All I do is supply a public demand." Americans wanted their liquor and beer, and until 1931, when a federal court convicted and imprisoned him for income-tax evasion (the only charge for which authorities could obtain hard evidence), Capone supplied them. Reflecting on the contradictions inherent in prohibition, columnist Walter Lippmann wrote in 1931, "The high level of lawlessness is maintained by the fact that Americans desire to do so many things which they also desire to prohibit."

## CULTURAL CURRENTS

Along with the consumerism of the 1920s, hardship and crassness spawned unease, and intellectuals like Lippmann were quick to point to the era's hypocrisies. Serious writers and artists felt at odds with society, and their rejection of materialism and conformity was both biting and bitter.

Several writers from the so-called Lost Generation, including novelist Ernest Hemingway and poets Ezra Pound and T. S. Eliot, abandoned

### Literature of Alienation

the United States for Europe. Others, like novelists William Faulkner and Sinclair Lewis, remained in America but, like the expatriates, expressed disillusionment with the materialism that they witnessed. F. Scott Fitzgerald's novels *This Side of Paradise* (1920) and *The Great Gatsby* (1925); Lewis's *Babbitt* (1922), *Arrowsmith* (1925), and *Elmer Gantry* (1927); and Eugene O'Neill's plays scorned Americans' preoccupation with money. Edith Wharton explored the clash of old and new moralities in novels such as *The Age of Innocence* (1920). Ellen Glasgow, one of the South's leading literary figures, lamented the trend toward impersonality in *Barren Ground* (1925). John Dos Passos's *Three Soldiers* (1921) and Hemingway's *A Farewell to Arms* (1929) interwove antiwar sentiment with critiques of the emptiness in modern relationships.

Discontent quite different from that of white authors inspired a new generation of African American artists.

### Harlem Renaissance

Middle-class, educated, and proud of their African heritage, black writers rejected white culture and exalted the militantly assertive "New Negro." Most of them lived in New York's Harlem; in this "Negro Mecca," black intellectuals and artists, aided by a few white patrons, celebrated black culture during what became known as the Harlem Renaissance.

The popular 1921 musical comedy *Shuffle Along* is often credited with launching the Harlem Renaissance. The musical showcased talented African American artists, such as lyricist Noble Sissle, composer Eubie Blake, and singers Florence Mills, Josephine Baker, and Mabel Mercer. Harlem in the 1920s also fostered a number of gifted writers, among them poets Langston Hughes, Countee Cullen, and Claude McKay; novelists Zora Neale Hurston, Jessie Fauset, and Jean Toomer; and essayist Alain Locke. The movement also included such visual artists as painter Aaron Douglas and sculptress Augusta Savage. Lesser-known writers from other parts of the country also flourished during the decade. They included novelist Sutton E. Griggs of Houston and Memphis, and journalist and historian Drusilla Dunjee Houston from Oklahoma.

These artists and intellectuals grappled with notions of identity. Though cherishing their African heritage and the black folk culture of the slave South, they realized that blacks had to come to terms with themselves as free Americans. Thus Alain Locke urged that the New Negro should become "a collaborator and participant in American civilization." But Langston Hughes wrote, "We younger

This painting by African American artist Archibald Motley represented the "Ash-Can" style, which considered no subject too undignified to paint, as well as the sensual relationship between jazz music and dancing in African American culture.

*(Collection of Archie Motley and Valerie Gerrard Browne. Photo courtesy of The Art Institute of Chicago)*

Negro artists who create now intend to express our individual dark-skinned selves without fear or shame. If white people are pleased, we are glad. If they are not, it doesn't matter. We know we are beautiful."

### Jazz

The Jazz Age, as the 1920s is sometimes called, owes its name to the music of black culture. Evolving from African and black American folk music, early jazz communicated exuberance, humor, and autonomy that African Americans seldom experienced in their public and political lives. With its emotional rhythms and improvisation, jazz blurred the distinction between composer and performer and created intimacy between performer and audience. As African Americans moved northward and westward, jazz traveled with them; they created centers of their music in Kansas City, Chicago, and San Diego. Urban dance halls and nightclubs, some of which included interracial audiences of blacks, whites, Latinos, and Asians, featured gifted jazz performers like trumpeter Louis Armstrong, trombonist Kid Ory, and blues singer Bessie Smith, who enjoyed wide fame thanks to phonograph records and radio. Music recorded by black artists and aimed at black consumers (sometimes called "race records") gave African Americans a place in commercial culture. More important, jazz endowed America with its own distinctive art form.

In many ways the 1920s were the most creative years the nation had yet experienced. Painters such as Georgia O'Keeffe, Aaron Douglas, and John Marin forged a uniquely American style of visual art. Composer Henry Cowell pioneered electronic music, and Aaron Copland built orchestral works around native folk motifs. George Gershwin blended jazz rhythms, classical forms, and folk melodies in serious works (*Rhapsody in Blue,* 1924, and Piano Concerto in F, 1925), musical dramas (*Funny Face,* 1927), and hit tunes, such as "The Man I Love." In architecture, skyscrapers, including the art deco Chrysler Building of New York designed by William van Allen, drew worldwide attention to American forms. At the beginning of the decade, essayist Harold Stearns had complained that "the most . . . pathetic fact in the social life of America today is emotional and aesthetic starvation." By 1929 that contention had been disproved.

## THE ELECTION OF 1928 AND THE END OF THE NEW ERA

Intellectuals' uneasiness about materialism seldom affected the confident rhetoric of politics. Herbert Hoover voiced that confidence when he accepted the Republican nomination for president in 1928. "We in America today," Hoover boasted, "are nearer to the final triumph over poverty than ever before in the history of any land. . . . We have not yet reached the goal, but, given a chance to go forward with the policies of the last eight years, we shall soon, with the help of God, be in sight of the day when poverty will be banished from this nation."

Hoover was an apt Republican candidate in 1928 (Coolidge chose not to seek reelection) because he fused

||||||||||||||||||||||||||||||||||||
**Herbert Hoover**

the traditional value of individual hard work with modern emphasis on corporate action. A Quaker from Iowa, orphaned at age ten, Hoover worked his way through Stanford University and became a wealthy mining engineer. During and after the First World War, he distinguished himself as U.S. food administrator and head of food relief for Europe.

As secretary of commerce under Harding and Coolidge, Hoover promoted what has been called "associationalism." Recognizing the extent to which nationwide associations dominated commerce and industry, Hoover wanted to stimulate cooperation between business and government. He took every opportunity to make the Commerce Department a center for the promotion of business, encouraging the formation of trade associations, holding conferences, and issuing reports, all aimed at improving productivity and profits. His active leadership prompted one observer to quip that Hoover was "Secretary of Commerce and assistant secretary of everything else."

As their candidate, Democrats in 1928 chose New York's governor Alfred E. Smith, whose background

||||||||||||||||||||||||||||||||||||
**Al Smith**

contrasted sharply with Hoover's. Hoover had rural, native-born, Protestant, and business roots, and had never run for public office. Smith was an urbane, gregarious politician of Irish stock with a career embedded in New York City's Tammany Hall political machine. His relish for the give-and-take of city streets is apparent in his response to a heckler during the campaign. When the heckler shouted, "Tell them all you know, Al. It won't take long!" Smith unflinchingly retorted, "I'll tell them all we both know, and it won't take any longer!"

Smith was the first Roman Catholic to run for president on a major party ticket. His religion enhanced his appeal among urban ethnics, who were voting in increasing numbers, but intense anti-Catholic sentiments lost him southern and rural votes. Smith had compiled a strong record on Progressive reform and civil rights during his governorship, but his campaign failed to build a coalition of farmers and city dwellers because he stressed issues unlikely to unite these groups, particularly his opposition to prohibition.

Smith waged a spirited campaign, directly confronting anti-Catholic critics, but Hoover, who emphasized national prosperity under Republican administrations, won the popular vote by 21 million to 15 million and the electoral vote by 444 to 87. Smith's candidacy nevertheless had beneficial effects on the Democratic Party. By luring millions of foreign-stock voters to the polls, he carried the nation's twelve largest cities, which formerly had given majorities to Republican candidates. For the next forty years, the Democratic Party solidified this urban base, which in conjunction with its traditional strength in the South made the party a formidable force in national elections.

At his inaugural Hoover proclaimed a New Day, "bright with hope." His cabinet, composed mostly of busi-

||||||||||||||||||||||||||||||||||||
**Hoover's Administration**

nessmen committed to the existing order, included six millionaires. To the lower ranks of government Hoover appointed young professionals who agreed with him that a scientific approach could solve national problems. If Hoover was optimistic, so were most Americans. The belief was widespread that success resulted from individual effort and that unemployment and poverty suggested personal weakness. Prevailing opinion also held that fluctuations of the business cycle were natural and therefore not to be tampered with by government.

This trust dissolved on October 24, 1929, later known as Black Thursday, when stock market prices suddenly

||||||||||||||||||||||||||||||||||||
**Stock Market Crash**

plunged, wiping out $10 billion in value (worth around $100 billion today). Panic selling set in. Prices of many stocks hit record lows; some sellers could find no buyers. Stunned crowds gathered outside the frantic New York Stock Exchange. At noon, leading bankers met at the headquarters of J. P. Morgan and Company. To restore faith, they put up $20 million and ceremoniously began buying stocks. The mood brightened, and some stocks rallied. The bankers, it seemed, had saved the day.

But as news of Black Thursday spread, frightened investors decided to sell stocks rather than risk further losses. On Black Tuesday, October 29, prices plummeted again. Hoover, who had never approved of what he called "the fever of speculation," assured Americans that "the crisis will be over in sixty days." Three months later, he still believed that "the worst is over without a doubt." He shared the popular assumptions that the stock market's ills could be quarantined and that the economy was strong enough to endure until the market righted itself. Instead, the crash ultimately helped to unleash a devastating worldwide depression.

In hindsight, it is easy to see that the depression began long before the stock market crash. Prosperity in the 1920s was not as widespread as optimists believed. Agriculture

▲ As the stock market tumbled on October 24, 1929, a crowd of concerned investors gathered outside the New York Stock Exchange on Wall Street, unprepared for an unprecedented economic decline that would send the country into a tailspin for the next decade. *(Corbis-Bettmann)*

had been languishing for decades, and many areas, especially in the South, had been excluded from the new bounty of consumer society. Racial minorities suffered from economic as well as social discrimination in both urban and rural settings. Industries such as mining and textiles failed to sustain profits throughout most of the decade, and even the high-flying automotive and household goods industries had been stagnant since 1926. The fever of speculation that concerned Hoover had included rash investment in California and Florida real estate, as well as in the stock market, and had masked much of what was unhealthy in the national economy.

More generally, the economic weakness that underlay the Great Depression had several interrelated causes.

**Declining Demand**

One was declining demand. Since mid-1928, demand for new housing had faltered, leading to declining sales of building materials and unemployment among construction workers. Growth industries, such as automobiles and electric appliances, had been able to expand as long as consumers bought their products. Expansion, however, could not continue unabated. When demand leveled off, factory owners had to cut back production and their workforce. Retailers had amassed large inventories that were going unsold, and in turn they started ordering less from manufacturers. Farm prices continued to sag, leaving farmers with less income to purchase new machinery and goods. As wages and employment fell, families could not afford things they needed and wanted. Thus by 1929 a sizable population of under-consumers was causing serious repercussions.

Underconsumption also resulted from widening divisions in income distribution. As the rich grew richer, middle- and lower-income Americans made modest gains at best. Although average per capita disposable income (income after taxes) rose about 9 percent between 1920 and 1929, income of the wealthiest 1 percent rose 75 percent, accounting for most of the increase. Much of this increase was put into stock market investments, not consumer goods.

Furthermore, in their eagerness to boost profits, many businesses overloaded themselves with debt. To obtain

### Corporate Debt and Stock Market Speculation

loans, they misrepresented their assets in ways that hid their inability to repay if forced to do so. Such practices, overlooked by lending agencies, put the nation's banking system on precarious footing. When one part of the edifice collapsed, the entire structure crumbled.

Risky stock market speculation also precipitated the depression. Individuals and corporations had bought millions of stock shares on margin, meaning that they invested by placing a down payment of only a fraction of a stock's actual price and then used stocks they had bought, but not fully paid for, as collateral for more stock purchases. When stock prices stopped rising, people tried to minimize losses by selling holdings they had bought on margin. But numerous investors selling at the same time caused prices to drop. As stock values collapsed, brokers demanded full payment for stocks bought on margin. Investors attempted to comply by withdrawing savings from banks or selling stocks at a loss for whatever they could get. Cash-short bankers pressured businesses to pay back their loans, tightening the vise further. The more obligations went unmet, the more the system tottered. Inevitably, banks and investment companies collapsed.

International economic conditions also contributed to the depression. During the First World War and postwar

### International Economic Troubles

reconstruction, Americans loaned billions of dollars to European nations. By the late 1920s, however, American investors were keeping their money at home, investing instead in the stock market. Europeans, unable to borrow more funds and unable to sell goods in the American market because of high tariffs, began to buy less from the United States. Moreover, the Allied nations depended on German war reparations to pay their own war debts to the United States, and the German government depended on American bank loans to pay those reparations. When the crash choked off American loans, the Germans could not meet obligations to the Allies, and in turn the Allies were unable to pay war debts to the United States. The western economy ground to a halt.

Federal policies also underlay the crisis. The government refrained from regulating speculation and only

### Failure of Federal Policies

occasionally scolded bankers and businesspeople. In keeping with government support of business expansion, the Federal Reserve Board pursued easy credit policies before the crash, charging low discount rates (interest rates on its loans to member banks) even though such loans were financing the speculative mania.

Partly because of optimism and partly because of the relatively unsophisticated state of economic analysis, neither experts nor people on the street realized what really had happened in 1929. Conventional wisdom, based on experiences from previous depressions, held that little could be done to correct economic problems; they simply had to run their course. So in 1929 people waited for the tailspin to ease, never realizing that the "new era" had come to an end and that the economy, politics, and society would have to be rebuilt.

# *Legacy* FOR A PEOPLE AND A NATION

## Intercollegiate Athletics

In 1924 scandals of brutality, academic fraud, and illegal payments to recruits prompted the Carnegie Foundation for the Advancement of Higher Education to undertake a five-year investigation of college sports. Its 1929 report condemned coaches and alumni supporters for violating the amateur code and recommended the abolition of varsity football. The report had minimal effect, however. As the career of Red Grange illustrated, football had become immensely popular during the 1920s, and scores of colleges and universities built stadiums and arenas to attract spectators, bolster alumni allegiance, enhance revenues, and promote school spirit.

For most of the twentieth century and into the twenty-first, big-time intercollegiate athletics, with professional coaches and highly recruited student athletes, ranked as one of the nation's major commercial entertainments. At the same time, American institutions have struggled to reconcile conflicts between the commercialism of athletic competition on one hand and the academic mission and the ideal of athletic amateurism on the other. No other country developed as extensive a link between high-caliber competitive athletics and higher education as the United States. Supposedly, cultivation of the mind is the objective of higher education. But the economic potential of college sports coupled with expanding athletic departments—including administrators, staffs, and tutors, as well as coaches and trainers—has created programs that compete with and sometimes overshadow the academic mission of the institutions that sponsor intercollegiate athletics.

Since the 1920s, recruiting scandals, academic fraud, and felonious behavior have sparked controversy in college sports. In 1952, after revelations of point-shaving (fixing the outcome) of basketball games involving several colleges in New York City and elsewhere, the American Council on Education undertook a study of college sports similar to that of the Carnegie Foundation a generation earlier. Its recommendations, including the elimination of football bowl games, went largely unheeded. In 1991 further abuses, especially in academics, prompted the Knight Foundation Commission on Intercollegiate Athletics to conduct a study that urged college presidents to take the lead in reforming intercollegiate athletics. Few significant changes resulted, even after a follow-up study in 2001. The most sweeping reforms followed court rulings in the 1990s, mandating under Title IX of the Educational Amendments Act of 1972 that women's sports be treated equally with men's sports. Enforcement, however, provoked a backlash that resulted in suggested changes to prevent men's teams from being cut in order to satisfy Title IX requirements. In recent years, the National College Athletic Association (NCAA) has initiated efforts to regulate academic standards in college athletics in addition to its voluminous rules on recruitment and amateurism, but its success depends on cooperation from member institutions. As long as millions of dollars are involved and sports remain a vital component of college as well as national culture, the system established in the 1920s shows the ability to withstand most pressures for change.

## SUMMARY

Two critical events, the end of the First World War and the beginning of the Great Depression, marked the boundaries of the 1920s. In the war's aftermath, traditional customs and values weakened as women and men sought new forms of self-expression and gratification. A host of new effects from modern science and technology—automobiles, such conveniences as electric appliances, and broadened exposure from mass media, such as radio—touched the lives of rich and poor alike. Sports and movies made entertainment more accessible. Moreover, the decade's freewheeling consumerism enabled ordinary Americans to emulate wealthier people not only by purchasing more but also by trying to get rich through stock market speculation. The depression that set in following the stock market crash stifled these habits, at least for a while.

Beneath the "new era" lurked two important phenomena rooted in previous eras. One was the continued prejudice and ethnic tensions that had long tainted the American dream. As prohibitionists, Klansmen, and immigration restrictionists made their voices heard, they encouraged discrimination against racial minorities and slurs against supposedly inferior ethnic groups. Meanwhile, the distinguishing forces of twentieth-century life—technological change, bureaucratization, mass culture, and growth of the middle class—accelerated, making the decade truly "new." Both phenomena would recur as major themes in the nation's history for the rest of the twentieth century.

## SUGGESTIONS FOR FURTHER READING

Lynn Dumenil, *The Modern Temper: American Culture and Society in the 1920s* (1995)

James R. Grossman, *Land of Hope: Chicago, Black Southerners, and the Great Migration* (1989)

Maury Klein, *Rainbow's End: The Crash of 1929* (2003)

Roland Marchand, *Advertising the American Dream: Making Way for Modernity, 1920–1940* (1985)

David Montgomery, *The Fall of the House of Labor: The Workplace, the State, and American Activism, 1865–1925* (1987)

Mae M. Ngai, *Impossible Subjects: Illegal Aliens and the Making of Modern America* (2004)

George Sanchez, *Becoming Mexican American: Ethnicity, Culture and Identity in Chicano Los Angeles, 1900–1945* (1993)

Susan Thistle, *From Marriage to the Market: The Transformation of Women's Lives and Work* (2006)

Michael Miller Topp, *The Sacco and Vanzetti Case: A Brief History With Documents* (2005)

*For a more extensive list for further reading, go to* college.hmco.com/pic/norton8e.

# The Great Depression and the New Deal *1929-1941*

I n 1931 the rain stopped in the Great Plains. Montana and North Dakota became as arid as the Sonora Desert. Temperatures reached 115 degrees in Iowa. The soil baked. Farmers watched rich black dirt turn to
gray dust.

Then the winds began to blow. Farmers had stripped the Plains of
native grasses in the 1920s, using tractors to put millions of acres of new
land into production. Now, with nothing to hold the earth, it began to
blow away. The dust storms began in 1934—and worsened in 1935. Dust
obscured the noonday sun; some days it was pitch black at noon. Cattle,
blinded by blowing grit, ran in circles until they died. A seven-year-old
boy in Smith Center, Kansas, suffocated in a dust drift. Boiling clouds of
dust filled the skies in parts of Kansas, Colorado, Oklahoma, Texas, and
New Mexico—the Dust Bowl.

In late 1937, on a farm near Stigler, Oklahoma, Marvin Montgomery
counted up his assets: $53 and a car—a 1929 Hudson he had just bought.
"The drought and such as that, it just got so hard," he said later. "I decided it would help me to change countries." So, on December 29, 1937,
Montgomery and his wife and four children—along with their furniture, bedding, pots,
and pans—squeezed into the Hudson. "I had that old car loaded to the full capacity,"
Montgomery told a congressional committee conducting hearings in a migratory labor
camp in 1940, "on top, the sides, and everywhere else." Traveling west on Route 66, the
Montgomerys headed for California.

They were not alone. At least a third of farms in the Dust Bowl were abandoned in
the 1930s, and many families made the westward trek, lured by circulars and newspaper
advertisements promising work in the fields of California. Some 300,000 people migrated

◀ This 1939 photograph, titled "Mother and Children on the Road," was taken in Tule Lake,
California, by Farm Security Administration photographer Dorothea Lange. The FSA used photos
like this one to build public support for New Deal programs to assist migrant workers and the
rural poor. *(Library of Congress)*

## CHRONOLOGY

**1929** ■ Stock market crash (October); Great Depression begins

**1930** ■ Hawley-Smoot Tariff raises rates on imports

**1931** ■ "Scottsboro Boys" arrested in Alabama

**1932** ■ Banks fail throughout nation
■ Bonus Army marches on Washington
■ Hoover's Reconstruction Finance Corporation tries to stabilize banks, insurance companies, railroads
■ Roosevelt elected president

**1933** ■ 13 million Americans unemployed
■ "First Hundred Days" of Roosevelt administration offer major legislation for economic recovery and poor relief
■ National bank holiday halts run on banks
■ Agricultural Adjustment Act (AAA) encourages decreased farm production
■ National Industrial Recovery Act (NIRA) attempts to spur industrial growth
■ Tennessee Valley Authority (TVA) established

**1934** ■ Long starts Share Our Wealth Society
■ Townsend proposes old-age pension plan
■ Indian Reorganization (Wheeler-Howard) Act restores lands to tribal ownership

**1935** ■ National Labor Relations (Wagner) Act guarantees workers' right to unionize
■ Social Security Act establishes insurance for the aged, the unemployed, and needy children
■ Works Progress Administration (WPA) creates jobs in public works projects
■ Revenue (Wealth Tax) Act raises taxes on business and the wealthy

**1936** ■ 9 million Americans unemployed
■ United Auto Workers win sit-down strike against General Motors

**1937** ■ Roosevelt's court-packing plan fails
■ Memorial Day massacre of striking steelworkers
■ "Roosevelt recession" begins

**1938** ■ 10.4 million Americans unemployed
■ 80 million movie tickets sold each week

**1939** ■ Marian Anderson performs at Lincoln Memorial
■ Social Security amendments add benefits for spouses and widows

to California in the 1930s. Most of these were not displaced and poverty-stricken farm families like the Montgomerys; many were white-collar workers seeking better opportunities in California's cities. It was the plight of families like the Montgomerys, however, captured in federal government–sponsored Farm Security Administration (FSA) photographs and immortalized in John Steinbeck's bestselling 1938 novel *The Grapes of Wrath*, that came to represent the human suffering of the Great Depression.

The Montgomerys' trip was not easy. The family ran out of money somewhere in Arizona and worked in the cotton fields there for five weeks before they moved on. Once in California, "I hoed beets some; hoed some cotton, and I picked some spuds," Montgomery reported, but wages were low, and migrant families found little welcome. As they took over the agricultural labor formerly done by Mexicans and Mexican Americans, they learned that, by doing fieldwork, they had forfeited their "whiteness" in the eyes of many rural Californians. "Negroes and 'Okies' upstairs," read a sign in a San Joaquin valley movie theater.

Most migrants to rural California lived in squalid makeshift camps, but the Montgomerys were lucky. They got space in housing provided for farm workers by the Farm Security Administration. The FSA camp at Shafter in Kern County had 240 tents and 40 small houses. For nine months the Montgomery family of six lived in a fourteen-by-sixteen-foot tent, which rented for 10 cents a day plus four hours of volunteer labor a month. Then they proudly moved into an FSA house, "with water, lights, and everything, yes sir; and a little garden spot furnished." Montgomery, homesick for the farm, told the congressional committee that he hoped to return to Oklahoma, but his seventeen-year-old son, Harvey, saw a different future. "I like California," he said. "I would rather stay out here." And soon there were plentiful employment opportunities in California, not only for Harvey Montgomery but for many other newcomers, in aircraft factories and shipyards mobilizing for the Second World War.

The Montgomerys' experience shows the human costs of the Great Depression, but statistics are necessary to give a sense of its magnitude. In the 1930s, as nations worldwide plunged into depression, the United States confronted a crisis of enormous proportions. Between 1929 and 1933, the gross national product was cut in half. Corporate profits fell from $10 billion to $1 billion; 100,000 businesses shut their doors altogether. As businesses failed or cut back, they laid off workers. Every day, thousands of men and women lost their jobs. Four million workers were unemployed in January 1930; by November the number had jumped to 6 million. When President Herbert Hoover left office in 1933, 13 million workers—about one-fourth of the labor force—were idle, and millions more had only part-time work. There was no national safety net: no welfare system, no unemployment compensation, no Social Security. And, as banks failed by the thousands, with no federally guaranteed deposit insurance, families' savings simply disappeared.

Herbert Hoover, who had been elected president in the prosperity and optimism of the late 1920s, looked first to private enterprise for solutions. By the end of his term, he had extended the federal government's role in managing an economic crisis further than any of his predecessors. Still, the economy had not improved, and, as the depression deepened, the mood of the country became increasingly desperate. The economic catastrophe exacerbated existing racial and class tensions, and law and order seemed to be breaking down. In Germany, the international economic crisis propelled Adolf Hitler to power. Although America's leaders did not really expect the United States to turn to fascism, they also knew that the German people had not anticipated Hitler's rise either. By late 1932 the depression seemed more than just "hard times." Many feared it was a crisis of capitalism, even of democracy itself.

In 1932 voters turned Hoover out of office, replacing him with a man who promised a New Deal and projected hope in a time of despair. Franklin Delano Roosevelt seemed willing to experiment, and although his scatter-shot approach did not end the economic depression (only the massive mobilization for World War II did that), New Deal programs did alleviate suffering. For the first time, the federal government assumed responsibility for the nation's economy and the welfare of its citizens. New federal agencies regulated a financial system badly in need of reform; Franklin Roosevelt's administration gave legitimacy to labor unions and collective bargaining. Social Security guaranteed assistance to many of America's elderly citizens and to others who could not support themselves. In the process, the federal government strengthened its power in relation to states and local authorities.

As it transformed the role and power of the federal government, however, the New Deal maintained America's existing economic and social systems. Although some Americans saw the depression crisis as an opportunity for major economic change—even revolution—Roosevelt's goal was to save capitalism. New Deal programs increased federal government regulation of the economy, but they did not fundamentally alter the existing capitalist system or the distribution of wealth. And, despite pressure (even within his own administration) to attack the social system that denied equality to African Americans, Roosevelt never directly challenged legal segregation in the South—in part because he relied on the votes of southern white Democrats to pass New Deal legislation.

Despite its limits, the New Deal preserved America's democratic experiment through a time of uncertainty and crisis. By the end of the decade, the widening force of world war shifted America's focus from domestic to foreign policy. But the changes set in motion by the New Deal continued to transform the United States for decades to come.

- How did economic hard times during the 1930s affect Americans, and what differences were there in the experiences of specific groups and regions?
- How and why did the power of the federal government expand during the Great Depression?
- What were the successes and the failures of the New Deal?

## HOOVER AND HARD TIMES, 1929–1933

By the early 1930s, as the depression continued to deepen, tens of millions of Americans were desperately poor. In the cities, hungry men and women lined up at soup kitchens. People survived on potatoes, crackers, or dandelion greens; some scratched through garbage cans for bits of food. In West Virginia and Kentucky, hunger was so widespread—and resources so limited—that the American Friends Service Committee distributed food only to those who were at least 10 percent below the normal weight for their height. In November 1932, *The Nation* told its readers that one-sixth of the American population risked starvation over the coming winter. Social workers in New York reported there was "no food at all" in the homes of many of the city's black children. In Albany, New York, a ten-year-old girl died of starvation in her elementary school classroom.

Families, unable to pay rent, were evicted. The new homeless poured into shantytowns, called "Hoovervilles" in ironic tribute to the formerly popular president. Over a million men took to the road or the rails in desperate search of any sort of work. Teenage boys and girls (the latter called "sisters of the road") also left destitute families to strike out on their own. With uncertain futures, many young couples delayed marriage; the average age at marriage rose by more than two years during the 1930s. Married people put off having children, and in 1933 the birth rate sank below replacement rates. (Contraceptive sales, with condoms costing at least $1 per dozen, did not fall during the depression.) More than 25 percent of women who were between the ages of twenty and thirty during the Great Depression never had children.

Farmers were hit especially hard by the economic crisis. The agricultural sector, which employed almost one-quarter of American workers, had never shared in the good times of the 1920s. But as urbanites cut back on spending and foreign competitors dumped agricultural surpluses into the global market, farm prices hit rock bottom. Farmers tried to compensate for lower prices by producing more, thus adding to the surplus and depressing prices even further. By 1932, a bushel of wheat that cost North Dakota farmers 77 cents to produce brought only 33 cents. Throughout the nation, cash-strapped farmers could not pay their property taxes or mortgages. Banks, facing their own ruin, foreclosed. In Mississippi, it was reported in 1932, on a single day in April approximately one-fourth of all the farmland in the state was being auctioned off to meet debts. By the middle of the decade, the ecological crisis of the Dust Bowl would drive thousands of farmers from their land.

Unlike farmers, America's industrial workers had seen a slow but steady rise in their standard of living during the 1920s. In 1929 almost every urban American who wanted a job had one, and workers' spending on consumer goods had bolstered the nation's economic growth. But as Americans had less money to spend, sales of manufactured goods plummeted and factories closed—more than seventy thousand had gone out of business by 1933. As car sales

### Farmers and Industrial Workers

dropped from 4.5 million in 1929 to 1 million in 1933, Ford laid off more than two-thirds of its Detroit workers. The remaining workers at U.S. Steel, America's first billion-dollar corporation, were put on "short hours"; the huge steel company had no full-time workers in 1933. Almost one-quarter of industrial workers were unemployed, and those who managed to hang onto a job saw the average wage fall by almost one-third.

For workers on the lowest rungs of the employment ladder, the depression was a crushing blow. In the South, where opportunities were already most limited for African Americans, jobs that many white men had considered below their dignity before the depression—street cleaner, bellhop, garbage collector—seemed suddenly desirable. In 1930 a short-lived fascist-style organization, the Black Shirts, recruited 40,000 members with the slogan "No Jobs for Niggers Until Every White Man Has a Job!" Northern blacks did not fare much better. As industry cut production, African Americans were the first fired. An Urban League survey of 106 cities found black unemployment rates averaged 30 to 60 percent higher than rates for whites. By 1932, African American unemployment reached almost 50 percent.

### Marginal Workers

Mexican Americans and Mexican nationals trying to make a living in the American Southwest also felt the twin impacts of economic depression and racism. Their wages on California farms fell from a miserable 35 cents an hour in 1929 to a cruel 14 cents an hour by 1932. Throughout the Southwest, Anglo-Americans claimed that foreign workers were stealing their jobs. Campaigns against "foreigners" hurt not only Mexican immigrants but also American citizens of Hispanic background whose families had lived in the Southwest for centuries, long before the land belonged to the United States. In 1931 the Labor Department announced plans to deport illegal immigrants to free jobs for American citizens. This policy fell hardest on people of Mexican origin. Even those who had immigrated legally often lacked full documentation. Officials often ignored the fact that children born in the United States were U.S. citizens. The U.S. government officially deported 82,000 Mexicans between 1929 and 1935, but a much larger number—almost half a million people—repatriated to Mexico during the 1930s. Some left voluntarily, but many were coerced or tricked into believing they had no choice.

Even before the economic crisis, women of all classes and races were barred from many jobs and were paid significantly less than men. As the economy worsened, discrimination increased. Most Americans already believed

◀ As hard times grew worse, families were evicted from their houses or apartments. In desperation, many moved into shantytowns—called Hoovervilles, after the now-unpopular president—on the outskirts of the nation's cities. These shacks, photographed in October 1931, are in Seattle's Hooverville. Despite the squalor of the surroundings, someone has done laundry and hung it to dry in the sun.

*(University of Washington Libraries, Seattle, Washington).*

that men should be breadwinners and women homemakers. With widespread male unemployment, it was easy to believe that women who worked took jobs from men. In fact, men laid off from U.S. Steel would not likely have been hired as elementary school teachers, secretaries, "salesgirls," or maids. Nonetheless, when a 1936 Gallup poll asked whether wives should work if their husbands had jobs, 82 percent of the respondents (including 75 percent of the women) answered no. Such beliefs translated into policy. Of fifteen hundred urban school systems surveyed in 1930 and 1931, 77 percent refused to hire married women as teachers, and 63 percent fired female teachers who married while employed.

The depression had a mixed impact on women workers. At first, women lost jobs more quickly than men. Women in low-wage manufacturing jobs were laid off before male employees, who were presumed to be supporting families. Hard times hit domestic workers especially hard, as middle-class families economized by dispensing with household help. Almost one-quarter of women in domestic service—a high percentage of them African American—were unemployed by January 1931. And, as jobs disappeared, women of color lost even these poorly paid positions to white women who were newly willing to do domestic labor. Despite discrimination and a poor economy, however, the number of women working outside the home rose during the 1930s. "Women's

jobs," such as teaching, clerical work, and switchboard operating, were not hit as hard as "men's jobs" in heavy industry, and women—including married women who previously did not work for wages—increasingly sought employment to keep their families afloat during hard times. Still, by 1940 only 15.2 percent of married women worked outside the home.

Although unemployment rates climbed to 25 percent, most Americans did not lose their homes or their jobs during the depression. Professional and white-collar workers did not fare as badly as industrial workers and farmers. Many middle-class families, however, while never hungry or homeless, "made do" with less. "Use it up, wear it out, make it do, or do without," the saying went, and middle-class women cut back on household expenses by canning food or making their own clothes. Newspapers offered imaginative suggestions for cooking cheap cuts of meat ("Liverburgers") or for using "extenders," cheap ingredients to make food go further ("Cracker-Stuffed Cabbage"). Although most families' incomes fell, the impact was cushioned by the falling cost of consumer goods, especially food. In early 1933, for example, a café in Omaha offered a ten-course meal, complete with a rose for ladies and a cigar for gentlemen, for 60 cents.

As housewives scrambled to make do, men who could no longer provide well for their families often blamed themselves for their "failures." But even for the relatively affluent, the psychological impact of the depression was

## Middle-Class Workers and Families

5 ways to use
ARMOUR'S FIXED FLAVOR STAR HAM
LEFTOVERS

ARMOUR HIGHEST QUALITY FOODS
"BETTER BUY ARMOUR'S AND BE SURE"

▲ As the economic depression deepened, Americans had less money to spend, even on necessities, and manufacturers of consumer goods struggled to sell their products and stay in business. In this 1932 *Ladies' Home Journal* advertisement, Armour Foods tried to convince housewives who were making do with less that it was economical— "often as low as 10¢ a serving"—to purchase a whole ham instead of cheaper cuts of meat. *(Picture Research Consultants & Archives)*

inescapable. The human toll of the depression was visible everywhere, and no one took economic security for granted any more. Suffering was never equal, but all Americans had to contend with years of uncertainty and with fears about the future of their family and their nation.

Although Herbert Hoover, "the Great Engineer," had a reputation as a problem solver, the economic crisis

## Hoover's Limited Solutions

was not easily solved, and no one, including Hoover, really knew what to do. Experts and leaders disagreed about the causes of the depression, and they disagreed about the proper course of action as well. Many prominent business leaders believed that financial panics and depressions, no matter how painful, were part of a natural and ultimately beneficial "business cycle." Economic depressions, according to this theory, brought down inflated

prices and cleared the way for real economic growth. As one banker told a Senate committee investigating the rising unemployment rates, "You are always going to have, once in so many years, difficulties in business, times that are prosperous and times that are not prosperous. There is no commission or any brain in the world that can prevent it."

Herbert Hoover disagreed. "The economic fatalist," he said, "believes that these crises are inevitable. . . . I would remind these pessimists that exactly the same thing was once said of typhoid, cholera, and smallpox." Hoover had great faith in "associationalism": business and professional organizations, coordinated by the federal government, working together to solve the nation's problems. The federal government's role was limited to gathering information and serving as a clearing-house for ideas and plans that state and local governments, along with private industry, could then choose—voluntarily—to implement.

While many Americans thought that Hoover was doing nothing to fight the economic downturn, in truth he stretched his core beliefs about the proper role of government to their limit. He tried voluntarism, exhortation, and limited government intervention. First, he sought voluntary pledges from hundreds of business groups to keep wages stable and renew economic investment. But when individual businessmen looked at their own bottom lines, few could live up to those promises.

As unemployment climbed, Hoover continued to encourage voluntary responses to mounting need, creating the President's Organization on Unemployment Relief (POUR) to generate private contributions to aid the destitute. Although 1932 saw record charitable contributions, they were nowhere near adequate. By mid-1932 one-quarter of New York's private charities, funds exhausted, had closed their doors. Atlanta's Central Relief Committee could provide only $1.30 per family per week to those seeking help. State and city officials found their treasuries drying up, too. Hoover, however, held firm. "It is not the function of the government to relieve individuals of their responsibilities to their neighbors," he insisted.

Hoover feared that government "relief" would destroy the spirit of self-reliance among the poor. Thus he authorized federal funds to feed the drought-stricken livestock of Arkansas farmers but rejected a smaller grant to provide food for impoverished farm families. Many Americans were becoming angry at Hoover's seeming insensitivity. When Hoover, trying to restore confidence to the increasingly anxious nation, said, "What this country needs is a good big laugh. . . . If someone could get off a good joke every ten days, I think our troubles would be over," the resulting jokes were not exactly what he had in mind.

"Business is improving," one man tells another. "Is Hoover dead?" asks his companion. In the two short years since his election, Hoover had become the most hated man in America.

Hoover eventually endorsed limited federal action to combat the economic crisis, but it was much too little. Federal public works projects, such as the Grand Coulee Dam in Washington, created some jobs. The Federal Farm Board, established under the Agricultural Marketing Act of 1929, supported crop prices by lending money to cooperatives to buy crops and keep them off the market. But the board soon ran short of money, and unsold surpluses jammed warehouses.

Hoover also signed into law the Hawley-Smoot Tariff (1930), which was meant to support American farmers and manufacturers by raising import duties on foreign goods to a staggering 40 percent. Instead it hampered international trade as other nations created their own protective tariffs. And, as other nations sold fewer goods to the United States, they had less money to repay their U.S. debts or buy American products. Fearing the collapse of the international monetary system, Hoover in 1931 announced a moratorium on the payment of First World War debts and reparations.

In January 1932, the administration took its most forceful action. The Reconstruction Finance Corporation (RFC) provided federal loans to banks, insurance companies, and railroads, an action Hoover hoped would shore up those industries and halt the disinvestment in the American economy. New York mayor Fiorello La Guardia called this provision of taxpayers' dollars to private industry "a millionaire's dole." But with the RFC Hoover had compromised his ideological principles. This was direct government intervention, not "voluntarism." If he would support direct assistance to private industries, why not direct relief to the millions of unemployed?

More and more Americans had begun to ask that question. Although most met the crisis with bewilderment or quiet despair, social unrest and violence began to surface as the depression deepened. In scattered incidents, farmers and unemployed workers took direct action against what they saw as the causes of their plight. Others lashed out in anger, scapegoating those even weaker than themselves. Increasing violence raised the specter of popular revolt, and Chicago mayor Anton Cermak told Congress that if the federal government did not send his citizens aid, it would have to send troops instead.

### Protest and Social Unrest

Throughout the nation, tens of thousands of farmers took the law into their own hands. Angry crowds forced auctioneers to accept just a few dollars for foreclosed property, and then returned it to the original owners. Farmers also tried to stop produce from reaching the market. In August 1932, a new group, the Farmers' Holiday Association, encouraged farmers to take a "holiday"—to hold back agricultural products as a way to limit supply and drive prices up. In the Midwest, farmers barricaded roads with spiked logs and telegraph poles to stop other farmers' trucks, and then dumped the contents in roadside ditches. In Iowa, strikers shot four other farmers who tried to run a roadblock.

In the cities, too, protest grew. The most militant actions came from Unemployed Councils, local groups similar to unions for unemployed workers that were created and led by Communist Party members. Communist leaders believed that the depression demonstrated capitalism's failure and offered an opportunity for revolution. Few of the quarter-million Americans who joined the local Unemployed Councils sought revolution, but they did demand action. "Fight, Don't Starve," read banners in a Chicago demonstration. Demonstrations often turned ugly. When three thousand members of Detroit Unemployment Councils marched on Ford's River Rouge plant in 1932, Ford security guards opened fire on the crowd, killing four men and wounding fifty. Battles between protesters and police broke out in cities from the East Coast to the West Coast but rarely were covered as national news.

As social unrest spread, so, too, did racial violence. Vigilante committees offered bounties in an attempt to force African American workers off the Illinois Central Railroad's payroll: $25 for maiming and $100 for killing black workers. Ten men were murdered and at least seven more wounded. With the worsening economy, the Ku Klux Klan reemerged, and at least 140 attempted lynchings were recorded between January 1930 and February 1933. In most cases local authorities were able to prevent the lynchings, but white mobs tortured, hanged, and mutilated thirty-eight black men during the early years of the Great Depression. Racial violence was not restricted to the South; lynchings took place in Pennsylvania, Minnesota, Colorado, and Ohio as well.

### Bonus Army

The worst public confrontation shook the nation in the summer of 1932. More than fifteen thousand unemployed World War I veterans and their families converged on the nation's capital as Congress debated a bill authorizing immediate payment of cash "bonuses" that veterans had been scheduled to receive in 1945. Calling themselves the Bonus Expeditionary Force, or Bonus Army, they set up a sprawling "Hooverville" shantytown in Anacostia Flats, just across

In the summer of 1932, unemployed ▶ veterans of the First World War gathered in Washington, D.C. to demand payment of their soldiers' bonuses. After Congress rejected the appeal of the "Bonus Army," some refused to leave and President Hoover sent U.S. Army troops to force them out. Here, police battle Bonus Marchers in July 1932.

*(National Archives)*

the river from the Capitol. Concerned about the impact on the federal budget, President Hoover opposed the bonus bill, and after much debate the Senate voted it down. "We were heroes in 1917, but we're bums today," one veteran shouted after the Senate vote.

Most of the Bonus Marchers left Washington after this defeat, but several thousand stayed on. Some were simply destitute, with nowhere to go; others stayed to press their case. The president called them "insurrectionists" and set a deadline for their departure. On July 28, Hoover sent in the U.S. Army, led by General Douglas MacArthur. Four infantry companies, four troops of cavalry, a machine gun squadron, and six tanks converged on the veterans and their families. What followed shocked the nation. Men and women were chased down by horsemen; children were tear-gassed; shacks were set afire. The next day, newspapers carried photographs of U.S. troops attacking their own citizens. Hoover was unrepentant, insisting in a campaign speech, "Thank God we still have a government that knows how to deal with a mob."

While desperation-driven social unrest raised fears of revolution, some saw an even greater danger in the growing disillusionment with democracy itself. As the depression worsened, the appeal of a strong leader—someone who would take decisive action, unencumbered by constitutionally mandated checks and balances—grew. In early 1933, media magnate William Randolph Hearst released the film *Gabriel over the White House*, in which a political hack of a president is possessed by the archangel Gabriel and, divinely inspired, assumes dictatorial powers to end the misery of the Great Depression. More significantly, in February 1933 the U.S. Senate passed a resolution calling for newly elected president Franklin D. Roosevelt to as-

sume "unlimited power." The rise to power of Hitler and his National Socialist Party in depression-ravaged Germany was an obvious parallel, adding to the sense of crisis that would come to a head in early 1933.

## FRANKLIN D. ROOSEVELT AND THE LAUNCHING OF THE NEW DEAL

In the presidential campaign of 1932, voters were presented with a clear choice. In the face of the Great Depression, incumbent Herbert Hoover held to a platform of limited federal intervention. Democratic challenger Franklin Delano Roosevelt insisted that the federal government had to play a much greater role. He supported direct relief payments for the unemployed, declaring that such governmental aid was not charity, but instead "a matter of social duty." He pledged "a new deal for the American people." During the campaign, he was never very explicit about the outlines of his New Deal. His most concrete proposals, in fact, were sometimes contradictory (in a nation without national news media, this was less a problem than it would be today). But all understood that he had committed to use the power of the federal government to combat the economic crisis that was paralyzing the nation. Voters chose Roosevelt over Hoover overwhelmingly: Roosevelt's 22.8 million popular votes far outdistanced Hoover's 15.8 million (see Map 25.1). Third-party Socialist candidate Norman Thomas drew nearly 1 million votes.

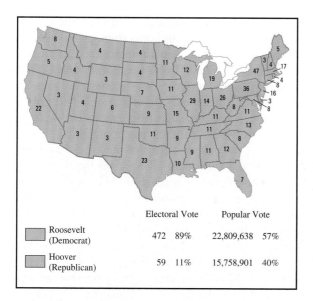

**Map 25.1    Presidential Election, 1932**
One factor above all decided the 1932 presidential election: the Great Depression. Roosevelt won 42 states and Hoover 6.

|  | Electoral Vote | | Popular Vote | |
|---|---|---|---|---|
| Roosevelt (Democrat) | 472 | 89% | 22,809,638 | 57% |
| Hoover (Republican) | 59 | 11% | 15,758,901 | 40% |

▲ In November 1930, Franklin D. Roosevelt (1882–1945) read the good news. Reelected governor of New York by 735,000 votes, he immediately became a leading contender for the Democratic presidential nomination. Notice Roosevelt's leg braces, rarely shown because of an unwritten agreement by photographers to shoot him from the waist up. *(© Bettmann/Corbis)*

Franklin Roosevelt, the twentieth-century president most beloved by America's "common people," had been born into a world of old money and upper-class privilege. The talented son of a politically prominent family, he seemed destined for political success. After graduating from Harvard College and Columbia Law School, he had married Eleanor Roosevelt, Theodore Roosevelt's niece and his own fifth cousin, once removed. He served in the New York State legislature, was appointed assistant secretary of the navy by Woodrow Wilson, and, at the age of thirty-eight, ran for vice president in 1920 on the Democratic Party's losing ticket.

Then, in 1921, Roosevelt was stricken with polio. For two years he was bedridden, fighting one of the most feared diseases of the early twentieth century. He lost the use of his legs but gained, according to his wife Eleanor, a new strength of character that would serve him well as he reached out to depression-scarred America. As Roosevelt explained it, "If you had spent two years in bed trying to wiggle your big toe, after that anything would seem easy." By 1928 Roosevelt was sufficiently recovered to run for—and win—the governorship of New York, and then to accept the Democratic Party's presidential nomination in 1932.

Elected in November 1932, Roosevelt would not take office until March 4, 1933. (The Twentieth Amendment to the Constitution—the so-called Lame Duck Amendment, ratified in 1933—shifted all future inaugurations to January 20.) In this long interregnum, the American banking system reached the verge of collapse.

The origins of the banking crisis lay in the flush years of World War I and the 1920s, when American banks made countless risky loans. After real-estate and stock market bubbles burst in 1929 and agricultural prices collapsed, many of these loans went bad. As a result, many banks lacked sufficient funds to cover their customers' deposits. Fearful of losing their savings in a bank collapse, depositors pulled money out of banks and put it into gold or under mattresses. "Bank runs," in which crowds of angry, frightened customers lined up to demand their money, became a common sight in economically ravaged towns throughout the nation.

## Banking Crisis

By the 1932 election, the bank crisis was escalating rapidly. Hoover, the lame-duck president, refused to take action without Roosevelt's support, while Roosevelt called Hoover's request for support "cheeky" and refused to endorse actions he could not control. Meanwhile, the situation worsened. By Roosevelt's inauguration on March 4, every state in the Union had either suspended banking operations or restricted depositors' access to their money. The new president understood that this was more than a test of his administration. The total collapse of the U.S. banking system would threaten the nation's survival.

Roosevelt (who reportedly saw the film *Gabriel over the White House* several times before his inauguration) used his inaugural address to promise the American people decisive action. Standing in a cold rain on the Capitol steps, he vowed to face the crisis "frankly and boldly." The lines we best remember from his speech are words of comfort: "Let me assert my firm belief," the new president told the thousands gathered on the Capitol grounds and the millions gathered around their radios, "that the only thing we have to fear is fear itself—nameless, unreasoning, unjustified terror." But the only loud cheers that day came when Roosevelt invoked "the analogue of war," asserting that, if need be, "I shall ask the Congress for the one remaining instrument to meet the crisis—broad Executive power to wage a war against the emergency, as great as the power that would be given to me if we were in fact invaded by a foreign foe."

The next day Roosevelt, using powers legally granted by the World War I Trading with the Enemy Act, closed the nation's banks for a four-day "holiday" and summoned Congress to an emergency session. He immediately introduced the Emergency Banking Relief Bill, which was passed sight unseen by unanimous House vote, approved

73 to 7 in the Senate, and signed into law the same day. This bill provided federal authority to reopen solvent banks and reorganize the rest, and authorized federal money to shore up private banks. In his inaugural address, Roosevelt had attacked "unscrupulous money changers," and many critics of the failed banking system had hoped he planned to remove the banks from private hands. Instead, as one North Dakota congressman complained, "the President drove the money changers out of the Capitol on March 4th and they were all back on the 9th." Roosevelt's banking policy was much like Hoover's—a fundamentally conservative approach that upheld the status quo.

The banking bill could save the U.S. banking system only if Americans were confident enough to deposit money in the reopened banks. So Roosevelt, in the first of his radio "Fireside Chats," asked the support of the American people. "We have provided the machinery to restore our financial system," he said. "It is up to you to support and make it work." The next morning, when the banks opened their doors, people lined up—but this time, most waited to deposit money. It was an enormous triumph for the new president. It also demonstrated that Roosevelt, though unafraid to take bold action, was not as radical as some wished or as others feared.

During the ninety-nine-day-long special session of Congress, dubbed by journalists "The First Hundred Days," the federal government took on dramatically new roles.

## First Hundred Days

Roosevelt, aided by a group of advisers—lawyers, university professors, and social workers, who were collectively nicknamed "the Brain Trust"—and by the enormously capable First Lady, set out to revive the American economy. These "New Dealers" had no single, coherent plan, and Roosevelt's economic policies fluctuated between attempts to balance the budget and massive deficit spending (spending more than is taken in in taxes and borrowing the difference). But with a strong mandate for action and the support of a Democrat-controlled Congress, the new administration produced a flood of legislation. The first priority was economic recovery. Two basic strategies emerged during the First Hundred Days. New Dealers experimented with national economic planning, and they created a range of "relief" programs to help those in need.

At the heart of the New Deal experiment in planning were the National Industrial Recovery Act (NIRA) and the Agricultural Adjustment Act (AAA). The NIRA was based on the belief that "destructive competition" had worsened industry's economic woes. Skirting antitrust

## National Industrial Recovery Act

regulation, the NIRA authorized competing businesses to cooperate in crafting industrywide codes. Thus automobile manufacturers, for example, would cooperate to limit production, establish industrywide prices, and set workers' wages. Competition among manufacturers would no longer drive down prices and wages. With wages and prices stabilized, the theory went, consumer spending would increase, thus allowing industries to rehire workers. Significantly, Section 7(a) guaranteed industrial workers the right to "organize and bargain collectively"—in other words, to unionize.

Individual businesses' participation in this program, administered by the National Recovery Administration (NRA), was voluntary—with one catch. Businesses that adhered to the industrywide codes could display the Blue Eagle, the NRA symbol; the government urged consumers to boycott businesses that did not fly the Blue Eagle. This voluntary program, though larger in scale than any previous government–private sector cooperation, was not very different from Hoover-era "associationalism."

From the beginning, the NRA faced serious problems. As small-business owners had feared, big business easily dominated the NRA-mandated cartels. NRA staff lacked the training and experience to stand up to the representatives of corporate America. The twenty-six-year-old NRA staffer who oversaw the creation of the petroleum industry code was "helped" by twenty highly paid oil industry lawyers. The majority of the 541 codes eventually approved by the NRA reflected the interests of major corporations, not small-business owners, labor, or consumers. Most fundamentally, the NRA did not deliver economic recovery. In 1935 the Supreme Court put an end to the fragile, floundering system. Using an old-fashioned (what Roosevelt called a "horse-and-buggy") definition of interstate commerce, the Supreme Court found that the NRA extended federal power past its constitutional bounds.

The Agricultural Adjustment Act (AAA) had a more enduring effect on the United States. Establishing a national system of crop controls, the

||||||||||||||||||||||||||||||||||

**Agricultural Adjustment Act**

AAA offered subsidies to farmers who agreed to limit production of specific crops. (Overproduction drove crop prices down.) The subsidies, funded by taxing the processors of agricultural goods, were meant to give farmers the same purchasing power they had had during the prosperous period before World War I. But to reduce production in 1933, the nation's farmers agreed to destroy 8.5 million piglets and to plow under crops in the fields. Although limiting production did raise agricultural prices, millions of hungry Amer-

▲ Under the Agricultural Adjustment Act, farmers received government payments for not planting crops or for destroying crops they had already planted. Some farmers, however, needed help of a different kind. The Resettlement Administration, established by executive order in 1935, was authorized to resettle destitute farm families from areas of soil erosion, flooding, and stream pollution to homestead communities. This poster was done by Ben Shahn. *(Library of Congress)*

icans found it difficult to understand the economic theory behind this waste of food.

Government crop subsidies had unintended consequences: they were a disaster for tenant farmers and sharecroppers. Despite government hopes to the contrary, as landlords cut production they turned tenant farmers off their land. In the South the number of sharecropper farms dropped by almost one-third between 1930 and 1940. The result was a homeless population of dispossessed Americans—many of them African American—heading to cities and towns throughout the nation. But the subsidies did help many. In the depression-ravaged Dakotas, for example, government payments accounted for almost three-quarters of the total farm income for 1934.

In 1936 the Supreme Court found that the AAA, like the NRA, was unconstitutional. But the AAA (unlike the NRA) was too popular with its constituency, American farmers, to disappear. The legislation was rewritten to meet the Supreme Court's objections, and farm subsidies continue into the twenty-first century.

With millions of Americans in desperate poverty, Roosevelt also moved quickly to implement poor relief: $3 billion in federal dollars were allocated in 1935. New Dealers, however—like many other Americans—disapproved of direct relief payments. "Give a man a dole and you save his body and destroy his spirit; give him a job and pay him an assured

**Relief Programs**

wage and you save both the body and the spirit," wrote Harry Hopkins, Roosevelt's trusted adviser and head of the president's major relief agency, the Federal Emergency Relief Administration (FERA). Thus New Deal programs emphasized "work relief." By January 1934, the Civil Works Administration had hired 4 million people, most earning $15 a week. And the Civilian Conservation Corps (CCC) paid unmarried young men (young women were not eligible) $1 a day to do hard outdoor labor: building dams and reservoirs, creating trails in national parks. The program was segregated by race but brought together young men from very different backgrounds. By 1942 the CCC had employed 2.5 million men, including 80,000 Native Americans who worked on western Indian reservations.

Work relief programs rarely addressed the needs of poor women. Mothers of young children were usually classified as "unemployable" and were offered relief instead of

---

**TABLE 25.1   New Deal Achievements**

| Year | Labor | Agriculture and Environment | Business and Industrial Recovery | Relief | Reform |
|------|-------|------------------------------|-----------------------------------|--------|--------|
| 1933 | Section 7(a) of NIRA | Agricultural Adjustment Act<br><br>Farm Credit Act | Emergency Banking Relief Act<br><br>Economy Act<br><br>Beer-Wine Revenue Act<br><br>Banking Act of 1933 (guaranteed deposits)<br><br>National Industrial Recovery Act | Civilian Conservation Corps<br><br>Federal Emergency Relief Act<br><br>Home Owners Refinancing Act<br><br>Public Works Administration<br><br>Civil Works Administration | TVA<br><br>Federal Securities Act |
| 1934 | National Labor Relations Board | Taylor Grazing Act | | | Securities Exchange Act |
| 1935 | National Labor Relations (Wagner) Act | Resettlement Administration<br><br>Rural Electrification Administration | | Works Progress Administration<br><br>National Youth Administration | Social Security Act<br><br>Public Utility Holding Company Act<br><br>Revenue Act (wealth tax) |
| 1937 | | Farm Security Administration | | National Housing Act | |
| 1938 | Fair Labor Standards Act | Agricultural Adjustment Act of 1938 | | | |

*Source*: Adapted from Charles Sellers, Henry May, and Neil R. McMillen, *A Synopsis of American History,* 6th ed. Copyright © 1985 by Houghton Mifflin Company. Reprinted by permission.

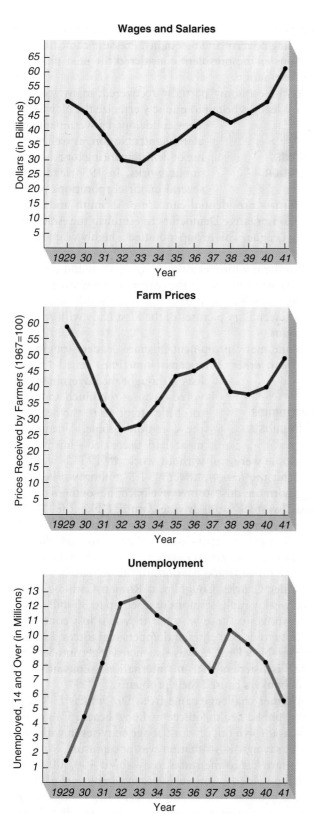

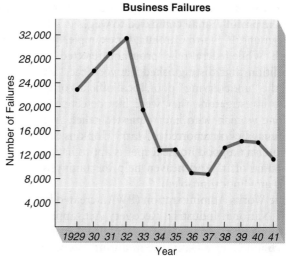

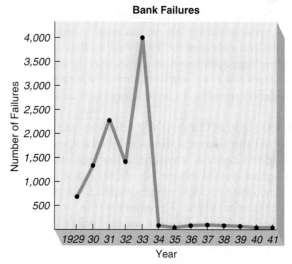

**Figure 25.1    The Economy Before and After the New Deal, 1929–1941**

The New Deal reduced bank closings, business failures, and unemployment, and it increased farm prices, wages, and salaries. Some of the nation's most persistent economic problems, however, did not disappear until the advent of the Second World War.

jobs. But, as historian Linda Gordon explains, "mother's-aid" grants were pitifully small compared to wages in federal works programs. In North Carolina, for example, they were one-sixth. While federal relief programs rejected the poor-law tradition that distinguished between the "deserving" and the "undeserving" poor, local officials often did not. "The investigators, they were like detectives," complained one woman who had requested relief. And journalist Lorena Hickok reported to Harry Hopkins that "a woman who isn't a good housekeeper is apt to have a pretty rough time of it. And heaven help the family in which there is any 'moral problem'."

The Public Works Administration (PWA), created by Title II of the National Industrial Recovery Act, appropriated $3.3 billion for public works in 1933. PWA workers built the Grand Coulee Dam (begun during Hoover's administration) and the Triborough Bridge in New York City, as well as hundreds of public buildings. But the PWA's main purpose was to pump federal money into the economy. As federal revenues for 1932 had totaled only $1.9 billion, this huge appropriation shows that the Roosevelt administration was willing to use the controversial technique of deficit spending in an attempt to stimulate the economy.

The special session of Congress adjourned on June 16, 1933. In just over three months, Roosevelt had delivered fifteen messages to Congress proposing major legislation, and Congress had passed fifteen significant laws (see Table 25.1). The United States had rebounded from near collapse. As columnist Walter Lippmann wrote, at the time of Roosevelt's inauguration the country was a collection of "disorderly panic-stricken mobs and factions. In the hundred days from March to June we became again an organized nation confident of our power to provide for our own security and to control our own destiny." Throughout the remainder of 1933 and the spring and summer of 1934, more New Deal bills became law. And as New Deal programs were implemented, unemployment fell steadily from 13 million in 1933 to 9 million in 1936. Farm prices rose, along with wages and salaries, and business failures abated (see Figure 25.1).

## POLITICAL PRESSURE AND THE SECOND NEW DEAL

Roosevelt's New Deal had enjoyed unprecedented popular and congressional support, but that would not last. The seeming unity of the First Hundred Days masked deep divides within the nation, and once the immediate crisis was averted, the struggle over solutions began in earnest. As some tried to stop the expansion of government power, others pushed for increased governmental action to combat continuing poverty and inequality. Pressure came from all directions as the president considered the next phase of New Deal action.

As the economy partially recovered, many wealthy business leaders began to publicly criticize the New Deal.

**Business Opposition**

They condemned government regulation and taxation, as well as the use of deficit financing for relief and public works. In 1934 leaders of several major corporations joined with former presidential candidate Al Smith and disaffected conservative Democrats to establish the American Liberty League. This group mounted a highly visible campaign against New Deal "radicalism." In an attempt to turn southern whites against the New Deal and so splinter the Democratic Party, the Liberty League also secretly channeled funds to a racist group in the South, which circulated incendiary pictures of the First Lady with African Americans.

While many prominent business leaders fought the New Deal, other Americans (sometimes called "populists") thought the government favored business too much and paid too little attention to the needs of the common people. Unemployment had decreased—but 9 million people were still without work. In 1934 a wave of strikes hit the nation, affecting 1.5 million workers. In 1935 enormous dust storms enveloped the southern plains, killing livestock and driving families like the Montgomerys from their land. Millions of Americans still suffered. As their dissatisfaction mounted, so, too, did the appeal of various demagogues, who played to the prejudices and unreasoning passions of the people.

**Demagogues and Populists**

Father Charles Coughlin, a Roman Catholic priest whose weekly radio sermons reached up to 30 million listeners, spoke to those who felt they had lost control of their lives to distant elites and impersonal forces. Increasingly anti–New Deal, he was also increasingly anti-Semitic, telling his listeners that an international conspiracy of Jewish bankers caused their problems.

Another challenge came from Dr. Francis E. Townsend, a public health officer in Long Beach, California, who was thrown out of work at age sixty-seven with only $100 in savings. His situation was not unusual. With social welfare left to the states, only about 400,000 of the 6.6 million elderly Americans received any sort of state-supplied pension. And as employment and savings disappeared with the depression, many older people fell into desperate poverty. Townsend proposed that Americans over the age of sixty should receive a government pension of $200 a month, financed by a new "transaction" (sales) tax. In fact, Townsend's plan was fiscally impossible (almost three-quarters of working Americans earned $200 a month or less) and profoundly regressive (because sales tax rates are the same for everyone, they take a larger share of income from those who earn least). Thus Townsend actually sought a massive transfer of income from the working poor to the nonworking elderly. Nonetheless, 20 million Americans, or 1 in 5 adults—concerned about the plight of the elderly and not about details of funding—signed petitions supporting this plan.

Then there was Huey Long, perhaps the most successful populist demagogue in American history. Long was elected governor of Louisiana in 1928 with the slogan "Every Man a King, But No One Wears a Crown." As a U.S. senator, Long initially supported the New Deal but soon decided that Roosevelt had fallen captive to big business. Long countered in 1934 with the Share Our Wealth Society, advocating the seizure (by taxation) of all income exceeding $1 million a year and of wealth in excess of $5 million per family. From these funds, the government would provide each American family an annual income of $2,000 and a one-time homestead allowance of $5,000. (Long's plan was fiscally impossible but definitely not regressive.) By mid-1935 Long's movement claimed 7 million members, and few doubted that he aspired to the presidency. But Long was killed by a bodyguard's bullet during an assassination attempt in September 1935.

The political left also gained ground as hard times continued. Socialists and communists alike criticized the New Deal for trying to save capitalism instead of working to lessen the inequality of power and wealth in American society. In California, muckraker and socialist Upton Sinclair won the Democratic gubernatorial nomination in 1934 with the slogan "End Poverty in California." That year in Wisconsin, the left-wing Progressive Party provided seven of the state's ten representatives to Congress, as voters reelected Robert La Follette to the Senate and gave his brother Philip the state governorship. Even the U.S. Communist Party found new support as it campaigned for social welfare and relief. Changing its strategy to disclaim any intention of overthrowing the U.S. government, the party proclaimed that "Communism Is Twentieth Century Americanism" and began to cooperate with left-wing labor unions, student groups, and writers' organizations in a "Popular Front" against fascism abroad and racism at home. In the late 1920s, attempting to appeal to African Americans, it established the League of Struggle for Negro Rights to fight lynching, and from 1931 on provided critical legal and financial support to the "Scottsboro Boys," who were falsely accused of raping two white women in Alabama (see page 733). As one black worker who became a communist organizer in Alabama explained, the Communist Party "fought selflessly and tirelessly to undo the wrongs perpetrated upon my race. Here was no dilly-dallying, no pussyfooting on the question of

### Left-Wing Critics

◀ In the 1930s, Senator Huey Long (center) had a mass following and presidential ambitions. But he was assassinated in 1935, the evening this photograph was taken. When Long was shot, he fell into the arms of James O'Connor (left), a political crony. Louisiana governor O. K. Allen (right) seized a pistol and dashed into the corridor in pursuit of the murderer, shouting, "If there's shooting, I want to be in on it." *(Wide World Photos, Inc.)*

full equality of the Negro people." In 1938, at its high point for the decade, the party had 55,000 members.

It was not only external critics who pushed Roosevelt to focus on social justice. His administration—largely

## Shaping the Second New Deal

due to Eleanor Roosevelt's influence—included many progressive activists. Frances Perkins, America's first woman cabinet member, came from a social work background, as did Roosevelt's close adviser Harold Ickes. A group of women social reformers who coalesced around the First Lady became important figures in government and in the Democratic Party. And African Americans had an unprecedented voice in this White House. By 1936 at least fifty black Americans held relatively important positions in New Deal agencies and cabinet-level departments. Journalists called these officials—who met on Friday evenings at the home of Mary McLeod Bethune, a distinguished educator who served as Director of Negro Affairs for the National Youth Administration—the "black cabinet." Finally, Eleanor Roosevelt herself worked tirelessly to put social justice issues at the center of the New Deal agenda.

As Roosevelt faced the election of 1936, he understood that he had to appeal to Americans who had seemingly contradictory desires. Those who had been hit hard by the depression looked to the New Deal for help and for social justice. If that help was not forthcoming, Roosevelt would lose their support. Other Americans—not the poorest, but those with a tenuous hold on the middle class—were afraid of the continued chaos and disorder. They wanted security and stability. Still others, with more to lose, were frightened by the populist promises of people like Long and Coughlin. They wanted the New Deal to preserve American capitalism. With these lessons in mind, Roosevelt took the initiative once more.

During the period historians call the Second New Deal, Roosevelt introduced a range of progressive programs aimed at providing, as he said in a 1935 address to Congress, "greater security for the average man than he has ever known before in the history of America." The first triumph of the Second New Deal was an innocuous-sounding but momentous law that Roosevelt called "the Big Bill." The Emergency Relief Appropriation Act provided $4 billion in new deficit spending, primarily to create massive public works programs for the jobless. It also established the Resettlement Administration, which resettled destitute families and organized rural homestead communities and suburban greenbelt towns for low-income workers; the Rural Electrification Administration, which brought electricity to isolated rural areas; and the National Youth Administration, which sponsored work-relief programs for young adults and part-time jobs for students.

The largest and best-known program funded by the Emergency Relief Appropriation Act was the Works Prog-

## Works Progress Administration

ress Administration (WPA), later renamed the Work Projects Administration. The WPA employed more than 8.5 million people who built 650,000 miles of highways and roads, and 125,000 public buildings, as well as bridges, reservoirs, irrigation systems, sewage treatment plants, parks, playgrounds, and swimming pools

Mary McLeod Bethune, pictured here ▶ with her friend and supporter Eleanor Roosevelt, became the first African American woman to head a federal agency as director of the Division of Negro Affairs for the National Youth Administration.

*(© Bettmann/Corbis)*

▲ In 1930, 90 percent of American farms did not have electricity. This 1936 cover from *Fortune* magazine celebrates the work of the Rural Electrification Administration, which brought power to some of America's most remote regions. *(Fortune magazine, March 1936)*

throughout the nation. Many WPA projects helped local communities: WPA workers built or renovated schools and hospitals, operated nurseries for preschool children, and taught 1.5 million adults to read and write.

The WPA also employed artists, musicians, writers, and actors for a wide range of cultural programs. The WPA's Federal Theater Project brought vaudeville, circuses, and theater, including African American and Yiddish plays, to cities and towns across the country. Its Arts Project hired painters and sculptors to teach their crafts in rural schools, and commissioned artists to decorate post office walls with murals depicting ordinary life in America past and present. The Federal Music Project employed 15,000 musicians in government-sponsored orchestras and collected folk songs from around the nation. Perhaps the most ambitious of the New Deal's cultural programs was the WPA's Federal Writers' Project (FWP), which hired talented authors, such as John Steinbeck and Richard Wright. FWP writers created guidebooks for every state and territory, and they wrote about the plain people of the United States. More than 2,000 elderly men and women who

had been freed from slavery by the Civil War told their stories to FWP writers, who collected these "slave narratives"; life stories of sharecroppers and textile workers were published as *These Are Our Lives* (1939). These and other WPA arts projects were controversial, for many of the WPA artists, musicians, actors, and writers sympathized with the political struggles of workers and farmers. Critics assailed them as left-wing propaganda, and in fact some of these artists were communists. However, the goal of this "Popular Front" culture was not to overthrow the government, but to recover a tradition of American radicalism through remembering, and celebrating artistically, the lives and labor of America's plain folk.

Big Bill programs and agencies were part of a short-term "emergency" strategy meant to address the immediate needs of the nation. Roosevelt's long-term strategy centered around the second major piece of Second New Deal legislation, the Social Security Act. The Social Security Act created, for the first time, a federal system to provide for the social welfare of American citizens. Its key provision was a federal pension system in which eligible workers paid mandatory Social Security taxes on their wages and their employers contributed an equivalent amount; these workers then received federal retirement benefits. The Social Security Act also created several welfare programs, including a cooperative federal-state system of unemployment compensation and Aid to Dependent Children (later renamed Aid to Families with Dependent Children, AFDC) for needy children in families without fathers present. Over the course of the twentieth century, benefits provided through the Social Security system would save tens of millions of Americans, especially the elderly, from poverty and despair.

**Social Security Act**

Compared with the national systems of social security already in place in most western European nations, the U.S. Social Security system was fairly conservative. First, the government did not pay for old-age benefits; workers and their bosses did. Second, the tax was regressive in that the more workers earned, the less they were taxed proportionally. Finally, the law did not cover agricultural labor, domestic service, and "casual labor not in the course of the employer's trade or business" (for example, janitorial work at a hospital). Thus a disproportionately high number of people of color, who worked as farm laborers, as domestic servants, and in service jobs in hospitals and restaurants, received no benefits. The act also excluded public-sector employees, so that many teachers, nurses, librarians, and social workers, the majority of whom were women, went uncovered. (Although the original Social Security Act provided no retirement benefits for

▲ The Works Progress Administration commissioned twenty-six artists to create a mural depicting scenes of life in modern California for San Francisco's Coit Tower, which had been completed in 1933. "The Woman with Cala Lilies," a detail from the large fresco that filled the lobby, was painted by Maxine Albro. *(Coit Tower, San Francisco)*

spouses or widows of covered workers, Congress added these benefits in 1939.) Despite these limitations, the Social Security Act was a highly significant development. With its passage, the federal government took some responsibility for the economic security of the aged, the temporarily unemployed, dependent children, and people with disabilities.

As the election of 1936 approached, Roosevelt adopted the populist language of his critics. He made scathing attacks on big business. Denouncing "entrenched greed" and the "unjust concentration of wealth and power," he proposed that government should "cut the

||||||||||||||||||||||||||||||

**Roosevelt's Populist Strategies**

giants down to size" through antitrust suits and heavy corporate taxes. He also supported the Wealth Tax Act, which some critics saw as the president's attempt to "steal Huey Long's thunder." The tax act helped achieve a slight redistribution of income by raising the income taxes of the wealthy (see Figure 25.2). It also imposed a new tax on business profits and increased taxes on inheritances, large gifts, and profits from the sale of property.

In November 1936, Roosevelt won the presidency by a landslide, defeating Republican nominee Governor Alf Landon of Kansas by a margin of 27.8 to 16.7 million votes. The Democrats also won huge majorities in the House and Senate. The Democratic victory was so overwhelming that some worried the two-party system might collapse. In fact, Roosevelt and the Democrats had forged a powerful "New Deal coalition." This new alliance pulled together groups from very different backgrounds and with different interests: the urban working class (especially immigrants from southern and eastern Europe and their sons and daughters), organized labor, the eleven states of the Confederacy (the "Solid South"), and northern blacks. By this time, the African American population in northern cities was large enough to constitute voting blocks, and New Deal benefits drew them away from the Republican Party, which they had long supported as the party of Lincoln. This New Deal coalition gave the Democratic Party dominance in the two-party system and ensured that Democrats would occupy the White House for most of the next thirty years.

## LABOR

During the worst years of the depression, American workers continued to organize and to struggle for the rights of labor. Management, however, resisted unionization vigorously. Many employers refused to recognize unions, and some hired armed thugs to intimidate workers. One business publication declared that "a few hundred funerals will have a quieting influence." As employers refused to negotiate with union representatives, workers walked off the job. Employers tried to replace striking workers with strikebreakers—and workers tried to keep the strikebreakers from crossing their picket lines. The situation often turned violent. Local police or National Guard troops frequently intervened on the side of management, smashing workers' picket lines. As strikes spread throughout the nation, violence erupted in the steel, automobile, and textile industries, among lumber workers in the Pacific Northwest, and among teamsters in the Midwest. In 1934 police met a longshoremen's strike with violence on the

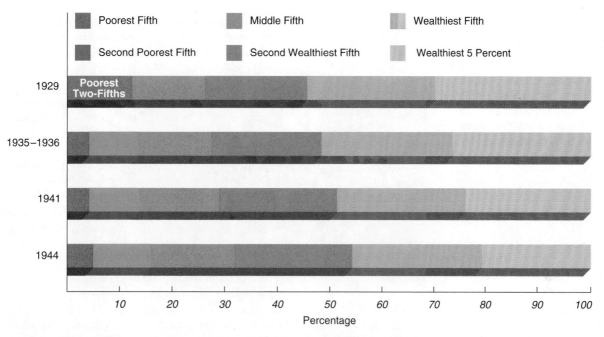

**Figure 25.2    Distribution of Total Family Income Among the American People, 1929–1944 (percentage)**

Although the New Deal provided economic relief to the American people, it did not, as its critics so often charged, significantly redistribute income downward from the rich to the poor.

*(Source: Adapted from U.S. Bureau of the Census,* Historical Statistics of the United States, Colonial Times to 1970, *2 parts [Washington, D.C.: U.S. Government Printing Office, 1975], Part 1, p. 301.)*

docks of San Francisco; 2 union members were killed, and workers' anger spread to other industries. Eventually 130,000 workers joined the general strike.

Workers pushed the Roosevelt administration for support, which came in the 1935 National Labor Relations (Wagner) Act. This act guaranteed workers the right to organize unions and to bargain collectively. It outlawed "unfair labor practices," such as firing workers who joined unions, prohibited management from sponsoring company unions, and required employers to bargain with labor's elected union representatives to set wages, hours, and working conditions. Critical for its success, the Wagner Act created a mechanism for enforcement: the National Labor Relations Board (NLRB). Although labor-management conflict continued, by the end of the decade the NLRB played a key role in mediating disputes. With federal protection, union membership grew. Organizers in the coalfields told miners that "President Roosevelt wants you to join the union," and join they

did—along with workers in dozens of industries. In 1929 union membership stood at 3.6 million; in mid-1938 it surpassed 7 million.

The Wagner Act further alienated business leaders from the New Deal. "No Obedience," proclaimed an editorial in a leading business magazine. The business-sponsored Liberty League insisted—incorrectly—that the Supreme Court would soon find the Wagner Act unconstitutional.

Conflict existed not only between labor and management, but also within the labor movement itself. The

||||||||||||||||||||||||||||||||||

**Rivalry Between Craft and Industrial Unions**

rapid growth and increasing militancy of the movement exacerbated an existing division between "craft" and "industrial" unions in the United States. Craft unions represented labor's elite: the skilled workers in a particular trade, such as carpentry. Industrial unions represented all the workers, skilled and

During the 1937 sit-down strike by ▶ automobile workers in Flint, Michigan, a women's "emergency brigade" of wives, mothers, daughters, sisters, and sweethearts demonstrated daily at the plant. When the police tried to force the men out of Chevrolet Plant No. 9 by filling it with teargas, the women used these clubs to smash the plant's windows and let in fresh air.

*(AP Images)*

unskilled, in a given industry, such as automobile manufacture. In the 1930s, it was the industrial unions that had grown dramatically.

Craft unions dominated the American Federation of Labor, the powerful umbrella organization for specific unions. Most AFL leaders offered little support for industrial organizing. Many looked down on the industrial workers, disproportionately immigrants from southern and eastern Europe—"the rubbish at labor's door," in the words of the Teamsters' president. Skilled workers had economic interests different from those of the great mass of unskilled workers, and more conservative craft unionists were often alarmed at what they saw as the radicalism of industrial unions.

In 1935 the industrial unionists made their move. John L. Lewis, head of the United Mine Workers and the nation's most prominent labor leader, resigned as vice president of the AFL. He and other industrial unionists created the Committee for Industrial Organization (CIO); the AFL responded by suspending all CIO unions. In 1938 the slightly renamed Congress of Industrial Organizations had 3.7 million members, slightly more than the AFL's 3.4 million. Unlike the AFL, the CIO included women and people of color in its membership. Union membership gave these "marginal" workers greater employment security and the benefits of collective bargaining.

The most decisive labor conflict of the decade came in late 1936, when the United Auto Workers (UAW), an industrial union, demanded recognition from General Motors (GM), Chrysler, and Ford. When GM refused, UAW organizers responded with a relatively new tactic: a "sit-down strike." On De-

**Sit-Down Strikes**

cember 30, 1936, workers at the Fisher Body plant in Flint, Michigan, went on strike *inside* the Fisher One factory. They refused to leave the building, thus immobilizing a key part of the GM production system. GM tried to force the workers out by turning off the heat. When police attempted to take back the plant, strikers hurled steel bolts, coffee mugs, and bottles. The police tried tear gas. Strikers turned the plant's water hoses on the police.

As the sit-down strike spread to adjacent plants, auto production plummeted. General Motors obtained a court order to evacuate the plant, but the strikers stood firm, risking imprisonment and fines. In a critical decision, Michigan's governor refused to send in the National Guard to clear workers from the buildings. After forty-four days, the UAW triumphed. GM agreed to recognize the union, and Chrysler quickly followed. Ford held out until 1941.

On the heels of this triumph, however, came a grim reminder of the costs of labor's struggle. On Memorial Day 1937, a group of picnicking workers and their families marched toward the Republic Steel plant in Chicago, intending to show support for strikers on a picket line in front of the plant. Police blocked their route and ordered them to disperse. One of the marchers threw something at the police, and the police attacked. Ten men were killed,

**Memorial Day Massacre**

seven of them shot in the back. Thirty marchers were wounded, including woman and three children. Many Americans, fed up with labor strife and violence, showed little sympathy for the workers. The antilabor *Chicago Tribune* blamed the marchers and praised police for repelling "a trained military unit of a revolutionary body."

At great cost, organized labor made great gains during the 1930s. Gradually violence receded, as the National Labor Relations Board proved effective in mediating disputes. And unionized workers—about 23 percent of the nonagricultural work force—saw their standard of living rise. By 1941 the average steelworker could afford to buy a new coat for himself and his wife every six years and, every other year, a pair of shoes for each of his children.

## FEDERAL POWER AND THE NATIONALIZATION OF CULTURE

In the 1930s, national culture, politics, and policies played an increasingly important role in the lives of Americans from different regions, classes, and ethnic backgrounds, as the reach of the national mass media grew and the power of the federal government expanded. This happened in large part because the power of the federal government expanded. During the decade-long economic crisis, political power moved from the state and local level to the White House and Congress. Individual Americans, in new ways, found their lives bound up with the federal government. In 1930, with the single exception of the post office, Americans had little direct contact with the federal government. By the end of the 1930s, almost 35 percent of the population had received some sort of federal government benefit, whether crop subsidies through the federal AAA or a WPA job or relief payments through FERA. As political analyst Michael Barone argues, "The New Deal changed American life by changing the relationship between Americans and their government." Americans in the 1930s began to look to the federal government to play a major and active role in the life of the nation.

The New Deal changed the American West more than any other region, as federally sponsored construction of dams and other public works projects reshaped the region's economy and environment. During the 1930s, the federal Bureau of Reclamation, an obscure agency created by the Newlands Reclamation Act of 1902 to provide irrigation for small farms and ranches, expanded its mandate dramatically to build large multipurpose dams that controlled entire river systems. The Central Valley Project dammed the Sacramento River and its tributaries. The

|||||||||||||||||||||||||||||||||

**New Deal in the West**

Boulder Dam (later renamed for Herbert Hoover) harnessed the Colorado River, providing water to southern California municipalities and using hydroelectric power to produce electricity for Los Angeles and southern Arizona. The water from these dams opened new areas to agriculture and allowed western cities to expand; the cheap electricity they produced attracted industry to the region. Large factory farms consolidated their hold in the region with water from these massive projects, which were paid for by taxpayers across the nation and by regional consumers of municipal water and electricity. These federally managed projects also gave the federal government an unprecedented role in the West. Especially after the completion of Washington State's Grand Coulee Dam in 1941, the federal government controlled both a great deal of water and hydroelectric power in the region. And in the West, control of water meant control over the region's future.

The federal government also brought millions of acres of western land under its control in the 1930s. Attempting to combat the environmental disaster of the Dust Bowl and to keep crop and livestock prices from falling further, federal programs worked to limit agricultural production. To reduce pressure on the land from overgrazing, the federal government bought 8 million cattle from farmers in a six-month period in 1934–1935 and transported the healthy cattle out of the region. In 1934 the Taylor Grazing Act imposed new restrictions on ranchers' use of public lands for grazing stock. Federal stock reduction programs probably saved the western cattle industry, but they destroyed the traditional economy of the Navajos by forcing them to reduce the size of their sheep herds on their federally protected reservation lands. The large farms and ranches of the West benefited immensely from federal subsidies and crop supports through the AAA, but such programs also increased federal government control in the region. As western historian Richard White argues, by the end of the 1930s, "federal bureaucracies were quite literally remaking the American West."

New federal activism extended to the West's people as well. Over the past several decades, federal policy toward Native Americans, especially those on western Indian reservations, had been disastrous. The Bureau of Indian Affairs (BIA) was riddled with corruption; in its attempts to "assimilate" Native Americans, it had separated children from their parents, suppressed native languages, and outlawed tribal religious practices. Such BIA-enforced assimilation was not successful. Division of tribal lands had failed to promote individual land ownership—almost half of those living on reservations in 1933

|||||||||||||||||||||||||||||||||

**New Deal for Native Americans**

As the commissioner of Indian affairs, ▶ John Collier *(right)* reversed long-standing U.S. policy, insisting that "the cultural history of Indians is in all respects to be considered equal to that of any non-Indian group." However, some of the reforms he introduced were at odds with traditional practices, as in the case of the Hopis, whose tradition of independent villages did not fit the model of centralized tribal control mandated by the Indian Reorganization Act. Here, Hopi leaders Loma Haftowa *(left)* and Chaf Towa *(middle)* join Collier at the opening ceremonies for the new Department of the Interior building in Washington, D.C. *(Wide World Photos, Inc.)*

owned no land. In the early 1930s, Native Americans were the poorest group in the nation, plagued by epidemics and malnutrition, with an infant mortality rate twice that of white Americans.

In 1933 Roosevelt named one of the BIA's most vocal critics to head the agency. John Collier, founder of the American Indian Defense Agency, meant to completely reverse the course of America's Indian policy, and his initiatives had many positive results. The Indian Reorganization Act (1934) went a long way toward ending the forced assimilation of native peoples and restoring Indian lands to tribal ownership. It also gave federal recognition to tribal governments. Indian tribes had regained their status as semisovereign nations, guaranteed "internal sovereignty" in all matters not specifically limited by acts of Congress.

Not all Indian peoples supported the IRA. Some saw it as a "back-to-the-blanket" measure based on romantic notions of "authentic" Indian culture. The tribal government structure specified by the IRA was culturally alien—and quite perplexing—to tribes such as the Papagos, whose language had no word for "representative." The Navajo nation also refused to ratify the IRA; in a terrible case of bad timing, the vote took place during the federally mandated destruction of Navajo sheep herds. Eventually, however, 181 tribes organized under the IRA. Collier had succeeded in reversing some of the destructive policies of the past, and the IRA laid the groundwork for future economic development and limited political autonomy among native peoples.

New Dealers did not set out to transform the American West, but they did intend to transform the American

## New Deal in the South

South. Well before the Great Depression, the South was mired in widespread and debilitating poverty. In 1929 the South's per capita income of $365 per year was less than half of the West's $921. More than half of the region's farm families were tenants or sharecroppers with no land of their own. "Sickness, misery, and unnecessary death," in the words of a contemporary study, plagued the southern poor. Almost 15 percent of South Carolina's people could not read or write.

Roosevelt, who sought a cure for his polio in the pools of Warm Springs, Georgia, had seen southern poverty firsthand and understood its human costs. But in describing the South as "the Nation's No. 1 economic problem" in 1938, he was referring to the economic theory that underlay many New Deal programs. As long as its people were too poor to participate in the nation's mass consumer economy, the South would be a drag on national economic recovery.

The largest federal intervention in the South was the Tennessee Valley Authority (TVA), authorized by Congress during Roosevelt's First Hundred Days. The TVA was created to develop a water and hydroelectric power project similar to the multipurpose dams of the West; dams would not only control flooding but also produce electric power for the region (see Map 25.2). However, confronted with the poverty and hopelessness of the Ten-

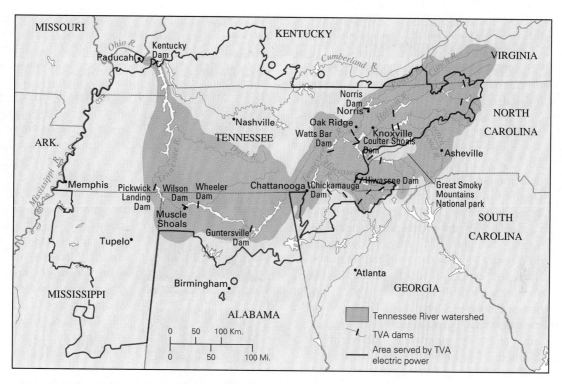

**Map 25.2    The Tennessee Valley Authority**
To control flooding and generate electricity, the Tennessee Valley Authority constructed dams
along the Tennessee River and its tributaries from Paducah, Kentucky, to Knoxville, Tennessee.

nessee River Valley region (which included parts of Virginia, North Carolina, Tennessee, Georgia, Alabama, Mississippi, and Kentucky), the TVA quickly extended its focus. Through the TVA, the federal government promoted economic development, helped bring electricity to rural areas, restored fields worn out from overuse, and fought the curse of malaria.

Although it benefited many poor southerners, over time the TVA proved to be a monumental environmental disaster. TVA strip mining caused soil erosion. Its coal-burning generators released sulfur oxides, which combined with water vapor to produce acid rain. Above all, the TVA degraded the water by dumping untreated sewage, toxic chemicals, and metal pollutants from strip mining into streams and rivers.

During the 1930s, the Roosevelt administration faced a very difficult political situation in the South. The southern senators whose support Roosevelt so desperately needed benefited from the flow of federal dollars to their states. But they were also suspicious of federal intervention and determined to preserve states' rights. Especially when federal action threatened the South's racial hier-

archy, they resisted passionately. As the nation's poorest and least educated region, the South would not easily be integrated into the national culture and economy. But New Deal programs began that process and in so doing improved the lives of at least some of the region's people.

It was not only federal government programs that broke down regional boundaries and fostered national connections during the 1930s. The national mass medium of radio helped millions survive hard times, and America's national popular culture played a critical role in the life of Americans throughout the 1930s.

## Mass Media and Popular Culture

The sound of the radio filled the days and nights of the depression era. Manufacturers rushed to produce cheaper models, and by 1937 Americans were buying radios at the rate of twenty-eight a minute. By the end of the decade, 27.5 million households owned radios, and families listened on average five hours a day. Roosevelt understood the importance of the radio in American life, going directly to the American people with radio "Fireside Chats" throughout his presidency. Americans, in fact,

## The 1936 Olympic Games

The 1936 Olympic Games that were scheduled to take place in Berlin, under the Nazi regime, created a dilemma for the United States and other nations. Should they go to Berlin? Would participation in the Nazi-orchestrated spectacle lend credence to Hitler's regime? Or would victories won by other nations undermine Hitler's claims about the superiority of Germany's "Aryan race"?

Although the modern Olympic Games had been founded in 1896 with high hopes that they might help unite the nations of the world in peace and understanding, international politics were never far from the surface. Germany had been excluded from the 1920 and 1924 games following its aggression and defeat in World War I, and the International Olympic Committee's choice (in 1931) of Berlin for the XI Olympiad was intended to welcome Germany back into the world community. However, with Hitler's rise to power in 1933, Germany determined to use the games as propaganda for the Nazi state and to demonstrate the superiority of its pure "Aryan" athletes. Soon thereafter, campaigns to boycott the Berlin Olympics emerged in several nations, including Great Britain, Sweden, France, Czechoslovakia, and the United States.

The American people were divided over the question of a boycott. Some U.S. Jewish groups led campaigns against U.S. participation in Berlin, while others took no public position, concerned that their actions might lead to increased anti-Semitic violence within Germany. Jewish athletes made individual decisions about whether or not to boycott the Olympics. But the debate over the Berlin Olympics revealed pockets of American anti-Semitism. The president of the American Olympic Committee, Avery Brundage, attributed the boycott movement to a "conspiracy" of Jews and communists, and instructed American athletes not to get involved in the "present Jew-Nazi altercation." African Americans, overwhelmingly, opposed boycotting the games.

Well aware of Hitler's attitudes toward "mongrel" peoples, many looked forward to demonstrating on the tracks and fields of Berlin just how wrong Hitler's notions of Aryan superiority were. Some also pointed out the hypocrisy of American officials who criticized Germany while ignoring U.S. discrimination against black athletes.

In the end, the United States sent 312 athletes to Berlin; 18 were African American. These athletes won 14 medals, almost one-quarter of the U.S. total of 56. Track and field star Jesse Owens came home with 4 gold medals. Jewish athletes won 13 medals in the 1936 Olympics; one of those athletes was American. But German athletes won 89 medals to U.S. athletes' 56, and despite the initial controversy, the XI Olympiad was a public relations triumph for Germany. The *New York Times*, impressed by the spectacle of the games and the hospitality of the Germans, proclaimed that the XI Olympiad had put Germany "back in the fold of nations."

The idealistic vision of nations linked together through peaceful athletic competition hit a low point at the 1936 Olympics. The 1940 Olympic Games, scheduled for Tokyo, were cancelled because of the escalating world war.

The eleventh summer Olympic Games in Berlin were carefully crafted as propaganda for the Nazi state. And the spectacle of the 1936 games, as represented in this poster, was impressive. But on the athletic fields, Nazi claims of Aryan superiority were challenged by athletes such as African American Jesse Owens, who is shown breaking the Olympic record in the 200-meter race.

*(Above: © Leonard de Selva/Corbis;*
*Right: © Corbis-Bettmann)*

put him eleventh in a ranking of America's top "radio personalities" in 1938.

The radio offered Americans many things. In a time of uncertainty, radio gave citizens immediate access—as never before—to the political news of the day and to the actual voices of their elected leaders. During hard times, radio offered escape: for children, the adventures of *Flash Gordon* and *Jack Armstrong, The All-American Boy;* for housewives, new soap operas, such as *The Romance of Helen Trent* and *Young Widder Brown.* Entire families gathered to listen to the comedy of ex-vaudevillians George Burns and Gracie Allen, and Jack Benny.

Radio also gave people a chance to participate—however vicariously—in events they could never have experienced before: listeners were carried to New York City for performances of the Metropolitan Opera on Saturday afternoons; to the Moana Hotel on the beach at Waikiki through the live broadcast of *Hawaii Calls;* to major league baseball games (begun by the St. Louis Cardinals in 1935) in distant cities. Millions shared the horror of the kidnapping of aviator Charles Lindbergh's son in 1932; black Americans in the urban North and rural South shared the triumphs of African American boxer Joe Louis ("the Brown Bomber"). Radio lessened the isolation of individuals and communities. It helped create a more homogeneous mass culture, as children throughout the nation acted out the same stories they had learned from the radio, but by offering a set of shared experiences, it also lessened the gulfs among Americans from different regions and class backgrounds.

The shared popular culture of 1930s America also centered on Hollywood movies. The film industry suffered in the initial years of the depression—almost one-third of all movie theaters closed, and ticket prices fell from 30 cents to 20 cents—but it rebounded after 1933. In a nation of fewer than 130 million people, between 80 and 90 million movie tickets were sold each week by the mid-1930s. Film's power to influence American attitudes was clearly demonstrated when sales of undershirts plummeted after Clark Gable took off his shirt to reveal a bare chest in *It Happened One Night.* As the depression continued, many Americans sought escape from grim realities at the movies. Comedies were especially popular, from the slapstick of the Marx Brothers to the sophisticated banter of *My Man Godfrey* or *It Happened One Night.* However, the appeal of upbeat movies was in the context of economic hard times. The song "Who's Afraid of the Big Bad Wolf?" from Disney's *Three Little Pigs,* was a big hit in 1933—as the economy hit bottom.

Yet as a cycle of gangster movies (including *Little Caesar* and *Scarface*) drew crowds in the early 1930s, many Americans worried about the effect of such films.

▲ *King Kong* broke all box-office records in 1933, as Americans flocked to see the giant ape fighting off airplanes from the top of New York's new Empire State Building—the tallest building in the world. *(Granger Collection)*

Crime seemed to be glamorized, no matter that the gangster hero always met death or destruction. Faced with a boycott organized by the Roman Catholic Legion of Decency, in 1934 the film industry established a production code that would determine what American film audiences saw—and did not see—for decades. "The vulgar, the cheap, and the tawdry is out," pledged the head of the Production Code Administration. "There is no room on the screen at any time for pictures which offend against common decency."

Finally, in an unintended consequence, federal policies intended to channel jobs to male heads of households strengthened the power of national popular culture. During Roosevelt's first two years in office, 1.5 million youths lost jobs; many young people who would have gone to work at the age of fourteen in better times decided to stay in school. By the end of the decade, three-quarters of American youth went to high school—up from one-half in 1920—and graduation rates doubled. School was free, classrooms were warm, and education seemed to promise a better future. The exuberant, fad-driven peer cultures that had developed in 1920s high schools and colleges were no more, but consumer-oriented youth culture had not died out. And as more young people went to high school, more participated in that national youth culture. Increasingly, young people listened to the same music. More than ever before, they adopted the same styles of clothing, of dance, of speech. Paradoxically, the hard times of the depression did not destroy youth culture; instead, they caused youth culture to spread more widely among America's young.

## THE LIMITS OF THE NEW DEAL

Roosevelt began his second term with great optimism and a strong mandate for reform. Almost immediately, however, the president's own actions undermined his New Deal agenda. Labor strife and racial issues divided the American people. As fascism spread in Europe, the world inched toward war, and domestic initiatives lost ground to foreign affairs and defense. By the end of 1938, New Deal reform had ground to a halt, but it had already had a profound impact on the United States.

Following his landslide electoral victory in 1936, Roosevelt set out to safeguard his progressive agenda. The

**Court-Packing Plan**

greatest danger he saw was from the U.S. Supreme Court. In ruling unconstitutional both the National Industrial Recovery Act (in 1935) and the Agricultural Adjustment Act (in 1936), the Court rejected not only specific provisions of hastily drafted New Deal legislation but also the expansion of presidential and federal power such legislation entailed. Only three of the nine justices were consistently sympathetic to New Deal "emergency" measures, and Roosevelt was convinced the Court would invalidate most of the Second New Deal legislation. Citing the advanced age and heavy workload of the nine justices, he asked Congress for authority to appoint up to six new justices to the Supreme Court. But in an era that had seen the rise to power of Hitler, Mussolini, and Stalin, many Americans saw Roosevelt's plan as an attack on constitutional government. Even those sympathetic to the New Deal worried about politicizing the Court. "Assuming, which is not at all impossible," wrote prominent journalist William Allen White, "a reactionary president, as charming, as eloquent and as irresistible as Roosevelt, with power to change the court, and we should be in the

devil's own fix." Congress rebelled, and Roosevelt experienced his first major congressional defeat.

The episode had a final, ironic twist. During the long public debate over court packing, the ideological center of the Supreme Court shifted. Key swing-vote justices began to vote in favor of liberal, pro–New Deal rulings. In short order the Court upheld both the Wagner Act (*NLRB v. Jones & Laughlin Steel Corp.*), ruling that Congress's power to regulate interstate commerce also involved the power to regulate the production of goods for interstate commerce, and the Social Security Act. Moreover, a new judicial pension program encouraged older judges to retire, and the president appointed seven new associate justices in the next four years, including such notables as Hugo Black, Felix Frankfurter, and William O. Douglas. In the end, Roosevelt got what he wanted from the Supreme Court, but the court-packing plan damaged his political credibility.

Another New Deal setback was the renewed economic recession of 1937–1939, sometimes called the Roosevelt

**Roosevelt Recession**

recession. Despite his use of deficit spending, Roosevelt had never abandoned his commitment to a balanced budget. In 1937, confident that the depression had largely been cured, he began to cut back government spending. At the same time, the Federal Reserve Board, concerned about a 3.6 percent inflation rate, tightened credit. The two actions sent the economy into a tailspin: unemployment climbed from 7.7 million in 1937 to 10.4 million in 1938. Soon Roosevelt resumed deficit financing.

The New Deal was in trouble in 1937 and 1938, and New Dealers struggled over the direction of liberal reform. Some urged vigorous trustbusting; others advocated the resurrection of national economic planning as it had existed under the National Recovery Administration. But in the end Roosevelt rejected these alternatives and chose deficit financing as a means of stimulating consumer demand and creating jobs. And in 1939, with conflict over the world war that had begun in Europe commanding more and more of the nation's attention, the New Deal came to an end. Roosevelt sacrificed further domestic reforms in return for conservative support for his programs of military rearmament and preparedness.

No president had ever served more than two terms, and many Americans speculated about whether Franklin

**Election of 1940**

Roosevelt would run for a third term in 1940. Roosevelt seemed undecided until that spring, when Adolf Hitler's military advances in Europe apparently convinced him to stay on. Roosevelt

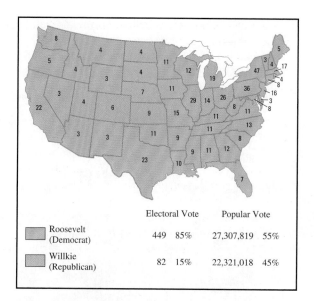

**Map 25.3  Presidential Election, 1940**

Roosevelt won an unprecedented third term in the 1940 presidential election. He did not repeat his landslide 1936 victory, in which he won all but two states. But he did capture 38 states in 1940 to Republican Wendell Willkie's 10.

headed off the predictable attacks from his opponent, Republican Wendell Willkie, by expanding military and naval contracts and thus reducing unemployment. Roosevelt also promised Americans, "Your boys are not going to be sent into any foreign wars."

Roosevelt did not win this election in a landslide, as he had in 1936 (see Map 25.3). But the New Deal coalition held. Once again Roosevelt won in the cities, supported by blue-collar workers, ethnic Americans, and African Americans. He also carried every state in the South. Although New Deal reform was over at home, Roosevelt was still riding a wave of public approval.

While the New Deal directly touched the lives of a great many Americans, not all benefited equally. More

### Race and the Limits of the New Deal

than anything else, differences were based on race. The New Deal fell short of equality for people of color for two major reasons.

First was the relationship between local and national power. National programs were implemented at the local level, and where local custom conflicted with national intent, as in the South and West, local custom won. In the South, African Americans received lower relief payments than whites and were paid lower wages in WPA jobs. The situation was similar in the Southwest. In Tucson, Arizona,

for example, Federal Emergency Relief Agency officials divided applicants into four groups—Anglos, Mexican Americans, Mexican immigrants, and Indians—and allocated relief payments in descending order.

Such discriminatory practices were rooted not only in racism but also in the economic interests of whites/Anglos. The majority of African American and Mexican American workers were paid so poorly that they *earned* less than impoverished whites got for "relief." Why would these workers take low-paying private jobs if government relief or government work programs provided more income? Local communities understood that federal programs threatened a political, social, and economic system based on racial hierarchies.

The case of the Scottsboro Boys illustrates the power of racism in the conflict between local and national power in 1930s America. One night in March 1931, a fight broke out between groups of young black and white "hobos" on a Southern Railroad freight train as it passed through Alabama. The black youths won the fight and tossed the whites off the train. Not long afterward, a posse stopped the train, arrested the black youths, and threw them in the Scottsboro, Alabama, jail. The posse also discovered two white women "riding the rails," who claimed that the young men had raped them. Word spread, and the youths were barely saved from a lynch mob. Medical evidence later showed that the women were lying. But within two weeks, eight of the so-called Scottsboro Boys were convicted of rape by all-white juries and sentenced to death. The ninth, a boy of thirteen, was saved from the death penalty by one vote. The case—so clearly a product of southern racism—became a cause célèbre, both in the nation and, through the efforts of the Communist Party, around the world.

The Supreme Court intervened, ruling that Alabama deprived black defendants of equal protection under the law by systematically excluding African Americans from juries and that the defendants had been denied counsel. Alabama, however, staged new trials. Five of the young men were convicted (four would be paroled by 1950, and one escaped from prison). Despite federal action through the Supreme Court, Alabama prevailed. Southern resistance to federal intervention, centered around issues of race, would not yield easily to federal power.

Second, the gains made by people of color under the New Deal were limited by the political realities of southern resistance. Roosevelt needed the support of southern Democrats to pass his legislative program, and they were willing to hold him hostage over race. For example, in 1938 southern Democrats blocked an antilynching bill with a six-week-long filibuster in the Senate. Roosevelt

Marchers in Washington ▶ (January 1, 1934) demand freedom for the "Scottsboro Boys," who were falsely accused and convicted of raping two white women in Alabama, and call on President Roosevelt for "Equal Rights for Negroes." The case of the Scottsboro Boys came to symbolize not only the racism and violence of the Jim Crow South, but also the discriminatory policies and practices that harmed African Americans throughout the nation. *(© Corbis/Bettmann)*

refused to use his political capital to break the filibuster and pass the bill. Politically, he had much to lose and little to gain. He knew that blacks would not desert the Democratic Party, but without southern senators, his legislative agenda was dead. Roosevelt wanted all Americans to enjoy the benefits of democracy, but he had no strong commitment to the cause of civil rights. As the NAACP's Roy Wilkins put it, "Mr. Roosevelt was no friend of the Negro. He wasn't an enemy, but he wasn't a friend."

Why, then, did African Americans support Roosevelt and the New Deal? Because, despite discriminatory policies, the New Deal helped African Americans. By the end of the 1930s, almost one-third of African American households survived on income from a WPA job. African Americans held some significant positions in the Roosevelt administration. Finally, there was the First Lady. When the acclaimed black contralto Marian Anderson was barred from performing in Washington's Constitution Hall by its owners, the Daughters of the American Revolution, Eleanor Roosevelt arranged for Anderson to sing at the Lincoln Memorial on Easter Sunday 1939. Such public commitment to racial equality was enormously important to African American citizens.

Despite widespread support for Roosevelt and the New Deal, many African Americans were well aware of the limits of New Deal reform. Some concluded that they

### African American Support

could depend only on themselves and organized self-help and direct-action movements. In 1934 black tenant farmers and sharecroppers joined with poor whites to form the Southern Tenant Farmers' Union. In the North, the militant Harlem Tenants League fought rent increases and evictions, and African American consumers began to boycott white merchants who refused to hire blacks as clerks. Their slogan was "Don't Buy Where You Can't Work." And the Brotherhood of Sleeping Car Porters, under the astute leadership of A. Philip Randolph, fought for the rights of black workers. Such actions, along with the limited benefits of New Deal programs, helped to improve the lives of black Americans during the 1930s.

Any analysis of the New Deal must begin with Franklin Delano Roosevelt himself. Assessments of Roosevelt varied widely during his presidency: he was passionately hated, and just as passionately loved. Roosevelt personified the presidency for the American people. When he spoke directly to Americans in his Fireside Chats, hundreds of thousands wrote to him, sharing their problems, asking for his help, offering their advice.

### An Assessment of the New Deal

▲ Robert Abbott, owner of the African American newspaper *The Chicago Defender*, and newspaper employees prepare to hand out food so needy families could celebrate Thanksgiving in 1931. *The Chicago Defender* was a strong voice for African Americans, and Abbott chronicled the devastating effects of the depression on the nation's black citizens. *(The Chicago Defender)*

Eleanor Roosevelt, the nation's First Lady, played a crucial and unprecedented role in the Roosevelt administration. As First Lady, she worked tirelessly for social justice and human rights, bringing reformers, trade unionists, and advocates for the rights of women and African Americans to the White House. Described by some as the conscience of the New Deal, she took public positions—especially on African American civil rights—far more progressive than those of her husband's administration. In some ways she served as a lightning rod, deflecting conservative criticism from her husband to herself. But her public stances also cemented the allegiance of other groups, African Americans in particular, to the New Deal.

Most historians and political scientists consider Franklin Roosevelt a truly great president, citing his courage and buoyant self-confidence, his willingness to experiment, and his capacity to inspire the nation during the most somber days of the depression. Some, who see the New Deal as a squandered opportunity for true political and economic change, charge that Roosevelt lacked vision and courage. They judge Roosevelt by goals that were not his own: Roosevelt was a pragmatist whose goal was to preserve the

system. But even scholars who criticize Roosevelt's performance agree that he transformed the presidency. "Only Washington, who made the office, and Jackson, who remade it, did more than Roosevelt to raise it to its present condition of strength, dignity, and independence," claims political scientist Clinton Rossiter. Some find this transformation troubling, tracing the roots of "the imperial presidency" to the Roosevelt administration.

During his more than twelve years in office, Roosevelt strengthened not only the presidency but also the federal government. In the past, the federal government had exercised little control over the economy. Through New Deal programs, the government greatly added to its regulatory responsibilities, including overseeing the nation's financial systems. For the first time the federal government assumed a responsibility to offer relief to the jobless and the needy, and for the first time it used deficit spending to stimulate the economy. Millions of Americans benefited from government programs that are still operating today. The New Deal laid the foundation of the Social Security system on which subsequent presidential administrations would build.

New Deal programs pumped money into the economy and saved millions of Americans from hunger and misery. However, as late as 1939, more than 10 million men and women were still jobless, and the nation's unemployment rate stood at 19 percent. In the end it was not the New Deal, but massive government spending during the Second World War that brought full economic recovery. In 1941, as a result of mobilization for war, unemployment declined to 10 percent, and in 1944, at the height of the war, only 1 percent of the labor force was jobless. World War II, not the New Deal, would reinvigorate the American economy.

# *Legacy* FOR A PEOPLE AND A NATION

## Social Security

The New Deal's Social Security system has created a more secure and enjoyable old age for millions of Americans who might otherwise have lived in poverty. Although Social Security initially excluded some of America's neediest citizens, such as farm and domestic workers, amendments to the law have expanded eligibility. Today, almost 99 percent of American workers are covered by Social Security. Social Security has dramatically reduced the poverty rate among the nation's elderly, and payments provide critical support for the disabled and dependent children.

Despite its successes, today's Social Security system faces an uncertain future. Its troubles are due in part to decisions made during the 1930s. President Franklin Roosevelt did not want Social Security to be confused with poor relief. Therefore, he rejected the European model of government-funded pensions and instead created a system financed by payments from workers and their employers—a system based on individual accounts. This system, however, presented a short-term problem. If benefits came from their own contributions, workers who began receiving Social Security payments in 1940 would have received less than $1 a month. Therefore, Social Security payments from current workers paid the benefits of those already retired.

Over the years, this system of financing has become increasingly unstable, as an ever larger pool of retirees has to be supported by those currently in the work force. People are living longer. In 1935, when the system was created, average life expectancy was lower than sixty-five years, the age one could begin to collect benefits. Today, on average, American men live almost sixteen years past the retirement age of sixty-five, and women come close to twenty years past retirement age. In 1935 there were 16 current workers paying into the system for each person receiving retirement benefits. In 2000 there were fewer than 3.5 workers per retiree. Almost 77 million baby boomers born in the 1940s, 1950s, and 1960s will retire in the first decades of the twenty-first century. Unless the system is reformed, many argue, the retirement of the baby-boom cohort could even bankrupt the system

While the stock market was rising rapidly during the 1990s, some proposed that, because Social Security paid only a fraction of what individuals might have earned by investing their Social Security tax payments in the stock market, Americans be allowed to do just that. Some opponents declared this proposal too risky; others simply pointed to the structure of Social Security retirement. If current workers kept their money to invest, where would benefits for current retirees come from? The stock market's huge decline in the first years of the twenty-first century (and the losses sustained by private pension funds) slowed the push for privatization, and President George W. Bush's privatization initiative gained little congressional support. But, with the oldest baby boomers beginning to retire, questions about the future of the Social Security system will become increasingly important in the years to come.

## SUMMARY

In the 1930s, a major economic crisis threatened the future of the nation. By 1933 almost one-quarter of America's workers were unemployed. Millions of people did not have enough to eat or adequate places to live. Herbert Hoover, elected president in 1928, believed that government should play only a limited role in managing and regulating the nation's economy. He tried to solve the nation's economic problems through a voluntary partnership of businesses and the federal government known as associationalism. In the 1932 presidential election, voters turned to the candidate who promised them a "New Deal." President Franklin Delano Roosevelt acted decisively to stabilize America's capitalist system and then worked to ameliorate its harshest impacts on the nation's people.

The New Deal was a liberal reform program that developed within the parameters of America's capitalist and democratic system. Most fundamentally, it expanded the role and power of the federal government. Because of New Deal reforms, banks, utilities, stock markets, farms, and most businesses operated in accord with rules set by the federal government. The federal government guaranteed workers' right to join unions without fear of employer reprisals, and federal law required employers to negotiate with workers' unions to set wages, hours, and working conditions. Many unemployed workers, elderly and disabled Americans, and dependent children were protected by a national welfare system administered through the federal government. And the president, through the power of the mass media and his own charisma, became an important presence in the lives of ordinary Americans.

The New Deal faced challenges from many directions. As the depression wore on, populist demagogues blamed scapegoats or offered overly simple explanations for the plight of the American people. Business leaders attacked the New Deal for its new regulation of business and its support of organized labor. As the federal government expanded its role throughout the nation, tensions between national and local authority sometimes flared up, and differences in regional ways of life and in social and economic structures presented challenges to national policymakers. Both the West and the South were transformed by federal government action, but citizens of both regions were suspicious of federal intervention, and white southerners strongly resisted any attempt to challenge the racial system of Jim Crow. The political realities of a fragile New Deal coalition and strong opposition shaped—and limited—New Deal programs of the 1930s and the social welfare systems with which Americans still live today.

It was the economic boom created by America's entry into World War II, not the New Deal, that ended the Great Depression. However, New Deal programs helped many of America's people live better, more secure lives. And the New Deal fundamentally changed the way that the U.S. government would deal with future economic downturns and with the needs of its citizens in good times and in bad.

## SUGGESTIONS FOR FURTHER READING

Anthony J. Badger, *The New Deal: The Depression Years, 1933–1940* (1989)

Alan Brinkley, *The End of Reform: New Deal Liberalism in Recession and War* (1995)

Alan Brinkley, *Voices of Protest: Huey Long, Father Coughlin, and the Great Depression* (1982)

Lizabeth Cohen, *Making a New Deal: Industrial Workers in Chicago* (1990)

Blanche Wiesen Cook, *Eleanor Roosevelt*, Vols. 1 and 2 (1992, 1999)

Sidney Fine, *Sitdown: The General Motors Strike of 1936–37* (1969)

James E. Goodman, *Stories of Scottsboro* (1994)

David M. Kennedy, *Freedom from Fear: The American People in Depression and War* (1999)

Robert McElvaine, The *Great Depression: America, 1929–1941* (1984)

Donald Worster, *Dust Bowl: The Southern Plains in the 1930s* (2004)

*For a more extensive list for further reading, go to* college.hmco.com/pic/norton8e.

# The United States in a Troubled World *1920-1941*

In 1921 the Rockefeller Foundation declared war on the mosquito in Latin America. As the carrier of yellow fever, the biting insect *Aedes aegypti* transmitted a deadly virus that caused severe headaches, vomiting, jaundice (yellow skin), and, for many, death. With clearance from the U.S. Department of State, the foundation dedicated several million dollars for projects to control yellow fever in Latin America, beginning with Mexico. Learning from the pioneering work of Carlos Juan Finlay of Cuba, Oswaldo Cruz of Brazil, and U.S. Army surgeon Walter Reed, scientists sought to destroy the mosquito in its larval stage, before it became an egg-laying adult.

Nothing less than U.S. dominance in the hemisphere seemed at stake. U.S. diplomats, military officers, and business executives agreed with foundation officials that the disease threatened public health, which in turn disturbed political and economic order. When outbreaks occurred, ports were closed and quarantined, disrupting trade and immigration. The infection struck down American officials, merchants, investors, and soldiers stationed abroad. Workers became incapacitated, reducing productivity. Throughout Latin America, insufficient official attention to yellow-fever epidemics stirred public discontent against regimes the United States supported. When the Panama Canal opened its gates to ships from around the world in 1914, some leaders feared that the death-dealing disease would spread, even reinfecting the United States, which had suffered its last epidemic in 1905.

In Veracruz, a Mexican province of significant U.S. economic activity, where American troops had invaded in 1914, a yellow-fever outbreak in 1920 killed 235 people. The next year, gradually overcoming strong local anti-U.S. feelings, Rockefeller personnel

◀ Officials of the Brazilian Federal Health Service, in cooperation with the Rockefeller Foundation, spray houses in Bahía to control mosquitoes during a campaign in the 1920s to battle yellow fever.

*(Courtesy of the Rockefeller Archive Center)*

## CHRONOLOGY

**1921–22** ■ Washington Conference limits naval arms
  ■ Rockefeller Foundation begins battle against yellow fever in Latin America

**1922** ■ Mussolini comes to power in Italy

**1924** ■ Dawes Plan eases German reparations

**1928** ■ Kellogg-Briand Pact outlaws war

**1929** ■ Great Depression begins
  ■ Young Plan reduces German reparations

**1930** ■ Hawley-Smoot Tariff raises duties

**1931** ■ Japan seizes Manchuria

**1933** ■ Adolf Hitler becomes chancellor of Germany
  ■ United States extends diplomatic recognition to Soviet Union
  ■ United States announces Good Neighbor policy for Latin America

**1934** ■ Fulgencio Batista comes to power in Cuba

**1935** ■ Italy invades Ethiopia
  ■ Congress passes first Neutrality Act

**1936** ■ Germany reoccupies Rhineland
  ■ Spanish Civil War breaks out

**1937** ■ Sino-Japanese War breaks out
  ■ Roosevelt makes "quarantine speech" against aggressors

**1938** ■ Mexico nationalizes American-owned oil companies
  ■ Munich Conference grants part of Czechoslovakia to Germany

**1939** ■ Germany and Soviet Union sign nonaggression pact
  ■ Germany invades Poland; Second World War begins

**1940** ■ Germany invades Denmark, Norway, Belgium, the Netherlands, and France
  ■ Selective Training and Service Act starts first U.S. peacetime draft

**1941** ■ Lend-Lease Act gives aid to Allies
  ■ Germany attacks Soviet Union
  ■ United States freezes Japanese assets
  ■ Roosevelt and Churchill sign Atlantic Charter
  ■ Japanese flotilla attacks Pearl Harbor, Hawai'i; United States enters Second World War

painstakingly inspected breeding places in houses and deposited larvae-eating fish in public waterworks. In 1924 La Fundación Rockefeller declared yellow fever eradicated in Mexico. Elsewhere in Latin America, the foundation's antimosquito campaign proved successful in maritime and urban areas but less so in rural and jungle regions. Rockefeller Foundation efforts in the 1920s and 1930s also carried political effects: strengthening central governments by providing a national public health infrastructure and helping diminish anti-U.S. sentiment in a region known for virulent anti-Yankeeism.

The Rockefeller Foundation's drive to eradicate the mosquito offers insights into Americans' fervent but futile effort to build a stable international order after the First World War. The United States did not cut itself off from international affairs, despite the tag "isolationist" which is sometimes still applied to U.S. foreign relations during the interwar decades. Americans remained very active in world affairs in the 1920s and 1930s—from gunboats on Chinese rivers, to negotiations in European financial centers, to marine occupations in Haiti and Nicaragua, to oil wells in the Middle East, to campaigns against diseases in Africa and Latin America. President Wilson had it right when he said after the First World War that the United States had "become a determining factor in the history of mankind, and after you have become a determining factor you cannot remain isolated, whether you want to or not."

Even so, a majority of Americans came out of World War I deeply suspicious of foreign entanglements, of using collective action to address the world's ills. The most apt description of interwar U.S. foreign policy is "independent internationalism." In other words, the United States was active on a global scale but retained its independence of action, its traditional unilateralism. Notwithstanding the nation's far-flung overseas projects—colonies, spheres of influence, naval bases, investments, trade, missionary activity, humanitarian projects—many Americans did think of themselves as isolationists, by which they meant that they wanted no part of Europe's political squabbles, military alliances and interventions, or the League of Nations, which might drag them unwillingly into war. More internationalist-minded Americans—a group that included most senior officials—were equally desirous of staying out of any future European war but were more willing than isolationists to work to shape the world to their liking.

Such a world would be peaceful and stable, the better to facilitate American prosperity and security. In the interwar years, American diplomats increasingly sought to exercise the power of the United States through conferences, humanitarian programs, cultural penetration ("Americanization"), moral lectures and calls for peace, nonrecognition of disapproved regimes, arms control, and economic and financial ties under the Open Door principle. In Latin America, for example, U.S. leaders downgraded military interventions to fashion a Good Neighbor policy.

But a stable world order proved elusive. Some nations schemed to disrupt it, and severe economic problems undercut it. Public health projects saved countless lives but could not address the low living standards and staggering poverty of dependent peoples around the globe. The debts and reparations bills left over from the First World War bedeviled the 1920s, and the Great Depression of the 1930s shattered world trade and finance. The depression threatened America's prominence in international markets; it also spawned totalitarianism and political extremism, militarism, and war in Europe and Asia. As Nazi Germany marched toward world war, the United States tried to protect itself from the conflict by adopting a policy of neutrality. At the same time, the United States sought to defend its interests in Asia against Japanese aggression by invoking the Open Door policy.

In the late 1930s, and especially after the outbreak of European war in September 1939, many Americans came to agree with President Franklin D. Roosevelt that Germany and Japan imperiled the U.S. national interest because they were building exclusive, self-sufficient spheres of influence based on military power and economic domination. Roosevelt first pushed for American military preparedness and then for the abandonment of neutrality in favor of aiding Britain and France. A German victory in Europe, he reasoned, would undermine western political principles, destroy traditional economic ties, threaten U.S. influence in the Western Hemisphere, and place at the pinnacle of European power a fanatical man— Adolf Hitler—whose ambitions and barbarities seemed limitless.

At the same time, Japan seemed determined to dismember America's Asian friend China, to destroy the Open Door principle by creating a closed economic sphere in Asia, and to endanger a U.S. colony—the Philippines. To deter Japanese expansion in the Pacific, the United States ultimately cut off supplies of vital American products, such as oil. But economic warfare only intensified antagonisms. Japan's surprise attack on Pearl Harbor, Hawai'i, in December 1941 finally brought the United States into the Second World War.

- Why and by what means did Americans try to facilitate a stable world order in the interwar period?
- How did the Roosevelt administration respond to the growing Nazi German threat in the second half of the 1930s?
- Why did the United States enter World War II?

## SEARCHING FOR PEACE AND ORDER IN THE 1920S

The First World War left Europe in a shambles. Between 1914 and 1921, Europe suffered tens of millions of casualties from world war, civil wars, massacres, epidemics, and famine. Germany and France both lost 10 percent of their workers. Crops, livestock, factories, trains, forests, bridges—little was spared. The American Relief Administration and private charities delivered food to needy Europeans, including Russians wracked by famine in 1921 and 1922. Americans hoped not only to feed desperate Europeans but also to dampen any appeal political radicalism might have for them. As Secretary of State Charles Evans Hughes put it in the early 1920s, "There will be no permanent peace unless economic satisfactions are enjoyed." Hughes and other leaders expected American economic expansion to promote international stability—that is, out of economic prosperity would spring a world free from ideological extremes, revolution, arms races, aggression, and war.

Collective security, as envisioned by Woodrow Wilson (see page 670), elicited far less enthusiasm among Hughes and other Republican leaders. Senator Henry Cabot Lodge gloated in 1920 that "we have destroyed Mr. Wilson's League of Nations and . . . we have torn up Wilsonism by the roots." Not quite. The Geneva-headquartered League of Nations, envisioned as a peacemaker, did prove feeble, not just because the United States did not join, but also because members failed to utilize the new organization to settle important disputes. Still, starting in the mid-1920s, American officials participated discreetly in League meetings on public health, prostitution, drug and arms trafficking, counterfeiting of currency, and other questions. American jurists served on the Permanent Court of International Justice (World Court), though the United States also refused to join that League body. The Rockefeller Foundation, meanwhile, donated $100,000 a year to the League to support its work in public health.

Wilson's legacy was felt in other ways as well. In the United States, peace societies worked for international stability, many of them keeping alive the Wilsonian preference for a world body. During the interwar years, peace groups, such as the Fellowship of Reconciliation and the National Council for Prevention of War, drew widespread public support. Women peace advocates gravitated to several of their own organizations because they lacked influence in the male-dominated groups and because of the popular assumption that women—as life givers and nurturing mothers—had a unique aversion to violence and war. Carrie Chapman Catt's moderate National Conference on the Cure and Cause of War, formed in 1924, and the more radical U.S. section of the Women's International League for Peace and Freedom (WILPF), organized in 1915 under the leadership of Jane Addams and Emily Greene Balch, became the largest women's peace groups. When Addams won the Nobel Peace Prize in 1931, she transferred her award money to the League of Nations.

**Peace Groups**

Most peace groups pointed to the carnage of the First World War and the futility of war as a solution to international problems, but they differed over strategies to ensure world order. Some urged cooperation with the League of Nations and the World Court. Others championed the arbitration of disputes, disarmament and arms reduction, the outlawing of war, and strict neutrality during wars. The WILPF called for an end to U.S. economic imperialism, which, the organization claimed, compelled the United States to intervene militarily in Latin America to protect U.S. business interests. The Women's Peace Union (organized in 1921) lobbied for a constitutional amendment to require a national referendum on a declaration of war. The Carnegie Endowment for International Peace (founded in 1910) promoted peace education through publications. Quakers, YMCA officials, and Social Gospel clergy in 1917 created the American Friends Service Committee to identify pacifist alternatives to warmaking. All in all, peaceseekers believed that their various reform activities could and must deliver a world without war.

▲ The Women's Peace Union (WPU) distributed this flier in the 1920s to remind Americans of the human costs of the First World War. One of many peace societies active in the interwar years, the WPU lobbied for a constitutional amendment requiring a national referendum on a declaration of war. In the 1930s, Representative Louis Ludlow (Democrat from Indiana) worked to pass such a measure in Congress, but he failed.

*(Schwimmer-Lloyd Collection, Freida Langer Lazarus Papers. The New York Public Library, Astor, Lenox, and Tilden Foundations)*

Peace advocates influenced Warren G. Harding's administration to convene the Washington Naval Conference of November 1921–February 1922. Delegates from Britain, Japan, France, Italy, China, Portugal, Belgium, and the Netherlands joined a U.S. team led by Secretary of State Charles Evans Hughes to discuss limits on naval armaments. Britain, the United States, and Japan were fac-

**Washington Naval Conference**

▲ French foreign minister Aristide Briand (1862–1932) *(left)* and U.S. secretary of state Charles Evans Hughes (1862–1948) join other diplomats at the Washington Naval Conference of 1921–1922, where they negotiated a naval arms control agreement. Years later, Briand helped craft the Kellogg-Briand Pact outlawing war. A graduate of Brown University and Columbia Law School, Hughes also served on the Supreme Court at two different times: 1910–1916 (associate justice) and 1930–1941 (chief justice). Conservative and reserved (Theodore Roosevelt called him "the bearded iceberg"), Hughes argued that the United States must be internationalist, leading the world to respect law and order. *(National Archives)*

ing a naval arms race whose huge military spending endangered economic rehabilitation. American leaders also worried that an expansionist Japan, with the world's third largest navy, would overtake the United States, ranked second behind Britain.

Hughes opened the conference by making a stunning announcement: he proposed to achieve real disarmament by offering to scrap thirty major U.S. ships, totaling 846,000 tons. He then turned to the shocked British and Japanese delegations and urged them to do away with somewhat smaller amounts. The final limit, Hughes declared, should be 500,000 tons each for the Americans and the British; 300,000 tons for the Japanese; and 175,000 tons each for the French and the Italians (that is, a ratio of

5:3:1.75). These totals were agreed to in the Five-Power Treaty, which also set a ten-year moratorium on the construction of capital ships (battleships and aircraft carriers). The governments also pledged not to build new fortifications in their Pacific possessions (such as the Philippines).

Next, the Nine-Power Treaty reaffirmed the Open Door in China, recognizing Chinese sovereignty. Finally, in the Four-Power Treaty, the United States, Britain, Japan, and France agreed to respect one another's Pacific possessions. The three treaties did not limit submarines, destroyers, or cruisers, nor did they provide enforcement powers for the Open Door declaration. Still, the conference was a major achievement for Hughes. He achieved genuine arms limitation and at the same time improved America's strategic position vis-à-vis Japan in the Pacific.

Peace advocates also welcomed the Locarno Pact of 1925, a set of agreements among European nations that sought to reduce tensions between Germany and France, and the Kellogg-Briand Pact of 1928. In the latter document, named for its chief promoters, U.S. secretary of state Frank B. Kellogg and French premier Aristide Briand, sixty-two nations agreed to "condemn recourse to war for the solution of international controversies, and renounce it as an instrument of national policy." The accord passed the Senate 85 to 1, but many lawmakers considered it little more than a statement of moral preference because it lacked enforcement provisions. Although weak—skeptics called it a mere "international kiss"—the Kellogg-Briand Pact reflected popular opinion that war was barbaric and wasteful, and the agreement stimulated serious public discussion of peace and war. But arms limitations, peace pacts, and efforts by peace groups and international institutions all failed to muzzle the dogs of war, which fed on the economic troubles that upended world order.

**Kellogg-Briand Pact**

## THE WORLD ECONOMY, CULTURAL EXPANSION, AND GREAT DEPRESSION

While Europe struggled to recover from the ravages of the First World War, the international economy wobbled and then, in the early 1930s, collapsed. The Great Depression set off a political chain reaction that carried the world to war. Cordell Hull, secretary of state under President Franklin D. Roosevelt from 1933 to 1944, often pointed out that political extremism and militarism sprang from maimed economies. "We cannot have a peaceful

John D. Rockefeller Jr. (1874–1960) *(second from right)* traveled to China in 1921 for the dedication of the Peking Union Medical College, a project of the Rockefeller Foundation, the philanthropic organization founded in 1913 by oil industrialist John D. Rockefeller Sr. At the center of this photograph is Xu Shi Chang (1855–1939), China's president.

*(Courtesy of the Rockefeller Archive Center)*

world," he warned, "until we rebuild the international economic structure." Hull proved right.

For leaders like Hughes and Hull, who believed that economic expansion by the United States would stabilize world politics, America's prominent position in the international economy seemed opportune. Because of World War I, the United States became a creditor nation and the financial capital of the world (see Figure 26.1). From 1914 to 1930, private investments abroad grew fivefold, to more than $17 billion. By the late 1920s, the United States produced nearly half of the world's industrial goods and ranked first among exporters ($5.2 billion worth of shipments in 1929). For example, General Electric invested heavily in Germany, American companies began to exploit Venezuela's rich petroleum resources, and U.S. firms began to challenge British control of oil resources in the Middle East. Britain and Germany lost ground to American businesses in Latin America, where Standard Oil operated in eight nations and where the United Fruit Company became a huge landowner.

America's economic prominence facilitated the export of American culture. Hollywood movies saturated the global market and stimulated interest in American ways and products. In Britain, where American silent and talkie films dominated, one woman from a mining town recalled seeing on the screen "all these marvelous [American] film stars. Everything was bright. I just wanted to go there and be like them." Although some foreigners warned against Americanization, others aped American mass-production

## Economic and Cultural Expansion

methods and emphasis on efficiency and modernization. Coca-Cola opened a bottling plant in Essen, Germany; Ford built an automobile assembly plant in Cologne; and General Motors built one for trucks near Berlin. German writer Hans Joachim claimed that this cultural adoption might help deliver a peaceful, democratic world because "our interest in elevators, radio towers, and jazz was . . . an attitude that wanted to convert the flame thrower into a vacuum cleaner."

Germans marveled at Henry Ford's economic success and industrial techniques ("Fordismus"), buying out copies of his translated autobiography, *My Life and Work* (1922). In the 1930s, Nazi leader Adolf Hitler sent German car designers to Detroit before he launched the Volkswagen. Further advertising the American capitalist model were the Phelps-Stokes Fund, exporting to black Africa Booker T. Washington's Tuskegee philosophy of education, and the Rockefeller Foundation, battling diseases in Latin America and Africa, supporting colleges to train doctors in Lebanon and China, and funding medical research and nurses' training in Europe.

The U.S. government assisted this cultural and economic expansion. The Webb-Pomerene Act (1918) excluded from antitrust prosecution those combinations set up for export trade; the Edge Act (1919) permitted American banks to open foreign-branch banks; and the overseas offices of the Department of Commerce gathered and disseminated valuable market information. The federal

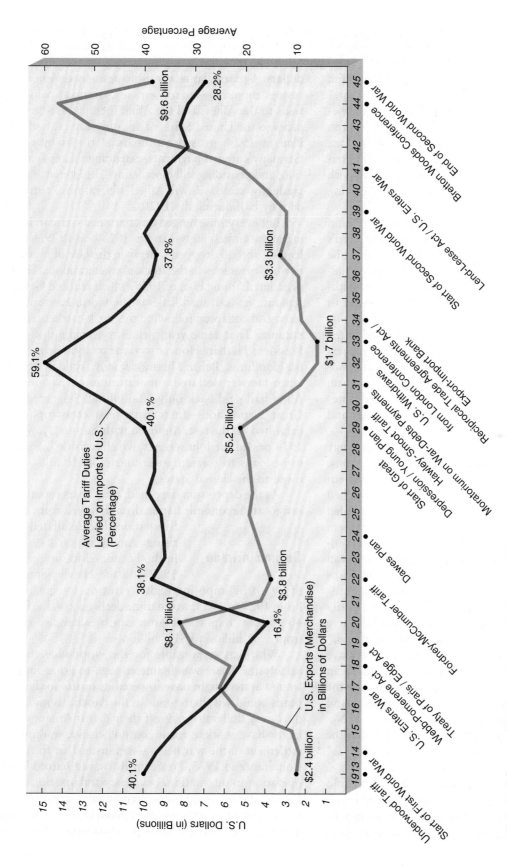

**Figure 26.1    The United States in the World Economy**

In the 1920s and 1930s, global depression and war scuttled the United States' hope for a stable economic order. This graph suggests, moreover, that high American tariffs meant lower exports, further impeding world trade. The Reciprocal Trade Agreements program initiated in the early 1930s was designed to ease tariff wars with other nations.

(Source: U.S. Bureau of the Census, Historical Statistics of the United States, Colonial Times to 1970 (Washington, D.C., 1975).)

government also stimulated foreign loans by American investors, discouraging those that might be used for military purposes. "In these days of competition," an American diplomat explained, "capital, trade, agriculture, labor, and statecraft all go hand in hand if a country is to profit." U.S. government support for the expansion of the telecommunications industry helped International Telegraph and Telephone (IT&T), Radio Corporation of America (RCA), and the Associated Press (AP) become international giants by 1930. The U.S. Navy's cooperation with Juan Trippe's Pan American Airways helped its "flying boats" reach Asia.

Europeans watched American economic expansion with wariness. Even as they snapped up copies of Ford's autobiography, many old-world elites worried that the populist consumerism that he and other U.S. industrialists championed portended social upheaval and the withering of established habits. As a result, the prospect of mass consumerism became a politically charged class issue. When the French Popular Front government in the 1930s sought to raise the purchasing power of workers through wage increases and a shorter workweek, the notion was condemned by conservatives for its radicalism and revolutionary spirit—a spirit that in the United States had generated a consumption-led boom in goods and services in the 1920s.

Some Europeans also branded the United States stingy for its handling of World War I debts and reparations.

**War Debts and German Reparations**

Twenty-eight nations became entangled in the web of inter-Allied government debts, which totaled $26.5 billion ($9.6 billion of them owed to the U.S. government). Europeans owed private American creditors another $3 billion. Europeans urged Americans to erase the government debts as a magnanimous contribution to the war effort. During the war, they angrily charged, Europe had bled while America profited. "There is only one way we could be worse with the Europeans," remarked the humorist Will Rogers, "and that is to have helped them out in two wars instead of one." American leaders insisted on repayment, some pointing out that the victorious European nations had gained vast territory and resources as war spoils. Senator George Norris of Nebraska, emphasizing domestic priorities, declared that the United States could build highways in "every county seat" if only the Europeans would pay their debts.

The debts question became linked to Germany's $33 billion reparations bill—an amount some believed Germany had the capacity but not the willingness to pay. In any case, hobbled by inflation and economic disorder, Ger-

many began to default on its payments. To keep the nation afloat and to forestall the radicalism that might thrive on economic troubles, American bankers loaned millions of dollars. A triangular relationship developed: American investors' money flowed to Germany, Germany paid reparations to the Allies, and the Allies then paid some of their debts to the United States. The American-crafted Dawes Plan of 1924 greased the financial tracks by reducing Germany's annual payments, extending the repayment period, and providing still more loans. The United States also gradually scaled down Allied obligations, cutting the debt by half during the 1920s.

But everything hinged on continued German borrowing in the United States, and in 1928 and 1929 American lending abroad dropped sharply in the face of more lucrative opportunities in the stock market at home. The U.S.-negotiated Young Plan of 1929, which reduced Germany's reparations, salvaged little as the world economy sputtered and collapsed following the stock market crash that autumn. That same year, Britain rejected an offer from President Herbert Hoover to trade its total debt for British Honduras (Belize), Bermuda, and Trinidad. By 1931, when Hoover declared a moratorium on payments, the Allies had paid back only $2.6 billion. Staggered by the Great Depression—an international catastrophe—they defaulted on the rest. Annoyed with Europe, Congress in 1934 passed the Johnson Act, which forbade U.S. government loans to foreign governments in default on debts owed to the United States.

As the depression deepened, tariff wars revealed a reinvigorated economic nationalism. By 1932 some twenty-five nations had retaliated against rising American tariffs (created in the Fordney-McCumber Act of 1922 and the Hawley-Smoot Act of 1930) by imposing higher rates on foreign imports. From 1929 to 1933, world trade declined in value by some 40 percent. Exports of American merchandise slumped from $5.2 billion to $1.7 billion.

**Decline in Trade**

Who was responsible for the worldwide economic cataclysm? There was blame enough to go around. The United States might have lowered its tariffs so that Europeans could sell their goods in the American market and thus earn dollars to pay off their debts. Americans also might have worked for a comprehensive, multinational settlement of the war debts issue. Instead, at the London Conference in 1933, President Roosevelt barred U.S. cooperation in international currency stabilization. Vengeful Europeans might have trimmed Germany's huge indemnity. The Germans might have borrowed less from abroad and taxed themselves more. The Soviets might have agreed to pay rather than repudiate Russia's $4 billion debt.

For Secretary of State Hull, finding a way out of the crisis depended on reviving world trade. Increased trade, he insisted, would not only help the United States pull itself out of the economic doldrums but also boost the chances for global peace. Calling the protective tariff the "king of evils," he successfully pressed Congress to pass the Reciprocal Trade Agreements Act in 1934. This important legislation empowered the president to reduce U.S. tariffs by as much as 50 percent through special agreements with foreign countries. The central feature of the act was the most-favored-nation principle, whereby the United States was entitled to the lowest tariff rate set by any nation with which it had an agreement. If, for example, Belgium and the United States granted each other most-favored-nation status, and Belgium then negotiated an agreement with Germany that reduced the Belgian tariff on German typewriters, American typewriters would receive the same low rate.

In 1934 Hull also helped create the Export-Import Bank, a government agency that provided loans to foreigners for the purchase of American goods. The bank stimulated trade and became a diplomatic weapon, allowing the United States to exact concessions through the approval or denial of loans. But in the short term, Hull's ambitious programs—examples of America's independent internationalism—brought only mixed results.

Economic imperatives also lay behind another major policy decision in these years: the move by the Roosevelt

### U.S. Recognition of the Soviet Union

administration to extend diplomatic recognition to the Soviet Union. Throughout the 1920s the Republicans had refused to open diplomatic relations with the Soviet government, which had failed to pay $600 million for confiscated American-owned property and had repudiated preexisting Russian debts. To many Americans, the communists ranked as godless, radical malcontents bent on destroying the American way of life through world revolution. Nonetheless, in the late 1920s American businesses, such as General Electric and International Harvester, entered the Soviet marketplace, and Henry Ford signed a contract to build an automobile plant there. By 1930 the Soviet Union had become the largest buyer of American farm and industrial equipment.

Upon entering the White House, Roosevelt concluded that nonrecognition had failed to alter the Soviet system, and he speculated that closer Soviet-American relations might help the economy and also deter Japanese expansion. In 1933 Roosevelt granted U.S. diplomatic recogni-

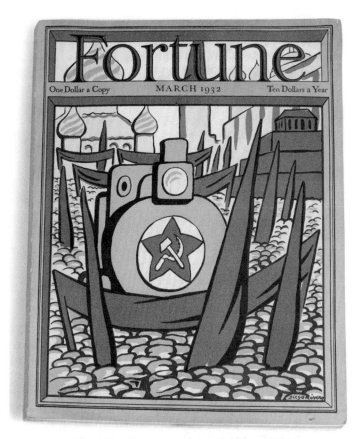

▲ In the early 1930s, treatments of the Soviet Union in the American press were generally mild and polite. The March 1932 issue of Henry Luce's *Fortune* magazine, appearing a year before the U.S. government extended recognition to the Soviet Union, featured this cover illustration by Diego Rivera and a special thirty-page section entitled "Russia, Russia, Russia." One appendix explicated the teachings of Karl Marx, while another listed dozens of U.S. businesses that had sold more than $1 million worth of goods to the Soviet Union in 1930, among them Ford, Westinghouse, Caterpillar, John Deere, American Express, and RCA. *(The Michael Barson Collection/Past Perfect)*

tion to the Soviet Union in return for Soviet agreement to discuss the debts question, to forgo subversive activities in the United States, and to grant Americans in the Soviet Union religious freedom and legal rights.

## U.S. DOMINANCE IN LATIN AMERICA

One of the assumptions behind Hughes's Washington Treaty system of 1921–1922 was that certain powers would be responsible for maintaining order in their regions—Japan in East Asia, for example, and the United States in Latin America. Through the Platt Amendment,

Among the U.S. companies with large holdings in Latin America in the interwar period was F. W. McLaughlin & Co. of Chicago. Here, workers on a private company wharf in Santos, Brazil, prepare to load coffee for shipment to the United States.

*(© Curt Teich Postcard Archives, Lake County Museum)*

PRIVATE WHARF, W. F. McLAUGHLIN & CO., SANTOS, BRAZIL.

the Roosevelt Corollary, the Panama Canal, military intervention, and economic preeminence the United States had thrown an imperial net over Latin America in the early twentieth century. U.S. dominance in the hemisphere grew apace after the First World War. A prominent State Department officer patronizingly remarked that Latin Americans were incapable of political progress because of their "low racial quality." They were, however, "very easy people to deal with if properly managed."

And managed they were. American-made schools, roads, telephones, and irrigation systems dotted Caribbean and Central American nations. American "money doctors" in Colombia and Peru helped reform tariff and tax laws, and invited U.S. companies to build public works. Washington forced private high-interest loans on the Dominican Republic and Haiti as ways to wield influence there. In El Salvador, Honduras, and Costa Rica, the State Department pressed governments to silence anti-imperialist intellectuals. For a time, Republican administrations curtailed U.S. military intervention in the hemisphere, withdrawing troops from the Dominican Republic (1924) and Nicaragua (1925) that had been committed in the previous decade. But the marines returned to Nicaragua in 1926 to end fighting between conservative and liberal Nicaraguans and to protect American property. In Haiti, the U.S. troop commitment made under Woodrow Wilson in 1915 lasted until 1934, with the soldiers there to keep pro-Washington governments in power. All the while, U.S. authorities maintained Puerto Rico as a colony (see Map 26.1).

By 1929 direct American investments in Latin America (excluding bonds and securities) totaled $3.5 billion, and U.S. exports dominated the trade of the area. Country after country experienced the repercussions of U.S. economic and political decisions.

**American Economic Muscle**

For example, the price that Americans set for Chilean copper determined the health of Chile's economy. North American oil executives bribed Venezuelan politicians for tax breaks.

Latin American nationalists protested that their resources were being drained away as profits for U.S. companies, leaving too many nations in a disadvantageous position. A distinguished Argentine writer, Manuel Ugarte, asserted that the United States had become a new Rome, which annexed wealth rather than territory, and that unapologetic Americans believed they were bringing not only material improvements but also the blessings of liberty to Latin American neighbors.

Criticism of U.S. imperialism in the region mounted in the interwar years. In 1928, at the Havana Inter-American conference, U.S. officials unsuccessfully tried to kill a resolution stating that "no state has a right to intervene in the internal affairs of another." Two years later, a prominent Chilean newspaper warned that the American "Colossus" had "financial might" without "equal in history" and that its aim was "Americas for the Americans— of the North." In the United States, Senator William Borah of Idaho urged that Latin Americans be granted the right of self-determination, letting them decide their own futures. Business leaders feared that Latin American nationalists would direct their anti-Yankee feelings against American-owned property. Some Americans also became troubled by the double standard that prevailed. Hoover's secretary of state, Henry L. Stimson, acknowledged the problem in 1932 when he was protesting Japanese incursions in China: "If we landed a single soldier among those South Americans now . . . it would put me absolutely in the wrong in China, where Japan has done all

**Map 26.1   The United States and Latin America Between the Wars**

The United States often intervened in other nations to maintain its hegemonic power in Latin America, where nationalists resented outside meddling in their sovereign affairs. The Good Neighbor policy decreased U.S. military interventions, but U.S. economic interests remained strong in the hemisphere.

this monstrous work under the guise of protecting her nationals with a landing force."

Renouncing unpopular military intervention, the United States shifted to other methods to maintain its influence in Latin America: Pan-Americanism (a concept dating back some fifty years, which aimed to bring about closer ties between North and South America); support for strong local leaders; the training of national guards; economic and cultural penetration; Export-Import Bank loans; financial supervision; and political subversion. Although this general approach predated his presidency, Franklin Roosevelt gave it a name in 1933: the Good Neighbor policy. It meant that the United States would be less blatant in its domination—less willing to defend exploitative business practices, less eager to launch military expeditions, and less reluctant to consult with Latin Americans.

### Good Neighbor Policy

"Give them a share," Roosevelt said, as he took several measures to show he meant business. Most notably, he ordered home the U.S. military forces that had been stationed in Haiti (since 1915) and Nicaragua (since 1912, with a hiatus in 1925–1926), and he restored some sovereignty to Panama and increased that nation's income from the canal. Such acts greatly enhanced Roosevelt's popularity in Latin America, and his image was further boosted when, in a series of pan-American conferences, he joined in pledging that no nation in the hemisphere would intervene in the "internal or external affairs" of any other.

Here Roosevelt promised more than he was prepared to deliver. His administration continued to support and bolster dictators in the region, believing that they would promote stability and preserve U.S. economic interests. ("He may be an S.O.B.," Roosevelt supposedly remarked of the Dominican Republic's ruthless leader Rafael Leonidas Trujillo, "but he is our S.O.B.") And, when a revolution brought a radical government to power in Cuba in 1933, FDR proved unwilling to let the matter be. Although he refrained from sending U.S. ground troops to Cuba, he instructed the American ambassador in Havana to work with conservative Cubans to replace the new government with a regime more friendly to U.S. interests. With Washington's support, army sergeant Fulgencio Batista took power in 1934.

During the Batista era, which lasted until Fidel Castro dethroned Batista in 1959, Cuba attracted and protected U.S. investments while it aligned itself with U.S. foreign policy goals. In return, the United States provided military aid and Export-Import Bank loans, abrogated the unpopular Platt Amendment, and gave Cuban sugar a favored position in the U.S. market. Cuba became further incorporated into the North American consumer culture, and American tourists flocked to Havana's nightlife of rum, rhumba, prostitution, and gambling. Nationalistic Cubans protested that their nation had become a mere extension—a dependency—of the United States.

In Mexico, Roosevelt again showed a level of restraint that his predecessors had lacked. Since Woodrow Wilson sent troops to Mexico in 1914 and again in 1916, U.S.-Mexican relations had endured several difficult periods as the two governments wrangled over the rights of U.S. economic interests. Still, throughout the post–World War I period the United States stood as Mexico's chief trading partner, accounting for 61 percent of Mexico's imports and taking 52 percent of its exports in 1934. That year, however, a new government under Lázaro Cárdenas pledged "Mexico for the Mexicans" and promptly strengthened trade unions so they could strike against foreign corporations.

### Clash with Mexican Nationalism

In 1937 workers struck foreign oil companies for higher wages and recognition, but the companies, including Standard Oil, rejected union appeals, hoping to send a message across the hemisphere that economic nationalism could never succeed. In a statement of economic independence the following year, the Cárdenas government boldly expropriated the property of all foreign-owned petroleum companies, calculating that the approaching war in Europe would restrain the United States from attacking Mexico. The United States countered by reducing purchases of Mexican silver and promoting a multinational business boycott against the nation. But Roosevelt rejected appeals from some business leaders that he intervene militarily and instead decided to compromise, in part because he feared that the Mexicans would increase oil sales to Germany and Japan. Negotiations were long and difficult, but in 1942 an agreement was reached whereby the United States conceded that Mexico owned its raw materials and could treat them as it saw fit, and Mexico compensated the companies for their lost property.

All in all, then, under Roosevelt the Good Neighbor policy can be said to have gone a considerable distance toward living up to its name—or at least the United States was now a Markedly Better Neighbor. Even as it remained the dominant power in the hemisphere, its newfound restraint created hopes among Latin Americans that a new era had dawned. Yet the more sober-minded nationalists in the region knew that Washington might be acting differently were it not for the deepening tensions in Europe and

◄ Ambassador Josephus Daniels (1862–1948) *(second from left)* and Mexican president Lázaro Cárdenas (1895–1970) *(second from right)* enjoy a cordial moment during the often stormy relations between the United States and Mexico in the 1930s. When Cárdenas attempted to regain control of his nation's oil resources from multinational corporations through expropriation, Daniels defended him as a "New Dealer" seeking to improve his country's living standards. Accepting Daniels's description and calling Cárdenas "one of the few Latin leaders who was actually preaching and trying to practice democracy," President Roosevelt compromised with Mexico in 1941.

*(Library of Congress)*

Asia. These threats created a sense that all the nations in the Western Hemisphere should stand together.

## THE COURSE TO WAR IN EUROPE

The main threat came from a revitalized Germany. On March 5, 1933, one day after the inauguration of Franklin Roosevelt, Germany's parliament granted dictatorial powers to the new chancellor, Adolf Hitler, leader of the Nazi Party. The act marked the culmination of a stunning rise to power for Hitler, whose Nazis very likely would have remained a fringe party had the Great Depression not hit Germany with such force. Production plummeted 40 percent, and unemployment ballooned to 6 million, meaning that two workers out of five did not have jobs. Together with a disintegrating banking system, which robbed millions of their savings, as well as widespread resentment among Germans over the Versailles peace settlement, the plummeting employment figures brought mass discontent to the country. While the communists preached a workers' revolution, German business executives and property owners threw their support to Hitler and the Nazis, many of them believing they could manipulate him once he had thwarted the communists. They were wrong.

Like Benito Mussolini, who had gained control of Italy in 1922, Hitler was a fascist. Fascism (called Nazism, or National Socialism, in Germany) was a collection of ideas and prejudices that celebrated supremacy of the state over the individual; of dictatorship over

democracy; of authoritarianism over freedom of speech; of a regulated, state-oriented economy over a free-market economy; and of militarism and war over peace. The Nazis vowed not only to revive German economic and military strength but also to cripple communism and "purify" the German "race" by destroying Jews and other people, such as homosexuals and Gypsies, whom Hitler disparaged as inferiors. The Nuremberg Laws of 1935 stripped Jews of citizenship and outlawed intermarriage with Germans. Teachers, doctors, and other professionals could not practice their craft, and half of all German Jews were without work.

Determined to get Germany out from under the Versailles treaty system, Hitler withdrew Germany from the League of Nations, ended reparations payments, and began to rearm. While secretly laying plans for the conquest of neighboring states, he watched admiringly as Mussolini's troops invaded the African nation of Ethiopia in 1935. The next year Hitler ordered his own goose-stepping troopers into the Rhineland, an area that the Versailles treaty had demilitarized. When Germany's timid neighbor France did not resist this act, Hitler crowed, "The world belongs to the man with guts!"

**German Aggression Under Hitler**

Soon the aggressors joined hands. In 1936 Italy and Germany formed an alliance called the Rome-Berlin Axis. Shortly thereafter, Germany and Japan united against the Soviet Union in the Anti-Comintern Pact. To these events Britain and France responded with a policy of appeasement, hoping to curb Hitler's expansionist appetite by permitting him a few territorial nibbles. The policy of appeasing Hitler, though not altogether unreasonable in terms of what could be known at the time, proved disastrous, for the hate-filled German leader continually raised his demands.

Hitler also made his presence felt in Spain, where a civil war broke out in 1936. Beginning in July, the Loyalists defended Spain's elected republican government against Francisco Franco's fascist movement. The U.S. government was officially neutral, but about three thousand American volunteers, known as the Abraham Lincoln Battalion of the "International Brigades," joined the fight on the side of the Loyalist republicans, which also had the backing of the Soviet Union. Many American Catholics, meanwhile, believed Franco would promote social stability and therefore should be supported, a view also held by some State Department officials. Hitler and Mussolini sent military aid to Franco, who won in 1939, tightening the grip of fascism on the European continent.

Early in 1938, Hitler once again tested the limits of European tolerance when he sent soldiers into Austria to annex the nation of his birth. Then, in September, he seized the largely German-speaking Sudeten region of Czechoslovakia. Appeasement reached its apex that month when France and Britain, without consulting the Czechs, agreed at Munich to allow Hitler this territorial bite, in exchange for a pledge that he would not take more. British prime minister Neville Chamberlain returned home to proclaim "peace in our time," confident that Hitler was satiated. In March 1939 Hitler swallowed the rest of Czechoslovakia (see Map 26.3).

Americans had watched this buildup of tension in Europe with apprehension. Many sought to distance themselves from the tumult by embracing isolationism, whose key elements were abhorrence of war and fervent opposition to U.S. alliances with other nations. Americans had learned powerful negative lessons from the First World War: that war damages reform movements, undermines civil liberties, dangerously expands federal and presidential power, disrupts the economy, and accentuates racial and class tensions. A 1937 Gallup poll found that nearly two-thirds of the respondents thought U.S. participation in World War I had been a mistake.

**Isolationist Views in the United States**

Conservative isolationists feared higher taxes and increased executive power if the nation went to war again. Liberal isolationists worried that domestic problems might go unresolved as the nation spent more on the military. Many isolationists predicted that, in attempting to spread democracy abroad or to police the world, Americans would lose their freedoms at home. The vast majority of isolationists opposed fascism and condemned aggression, but they did not think the United States should have to do what Europeans themselves refused to do: block Hitler. Isolationist sentiment was strongest in the Midwest and among anti-British ethnic groups, especially Americans of German or Irish descent, but it was a nationwide phenomenon that cut across socioeconomic, ethnic, party, and sectional lines, and it attracted a majority of the American people.

Some isolationists charged that corporate "merchants of death" had promoted war and were assisting the aggressors. A congressional committee headed by Senator Gerald P. Nye held hearings from 1934 to 1936 on the role of business and financiers in the U.S. decision to enter the First World War. The Nye committee did not prove that American munitions makers had dragged the nation into that war, but it did uncover evidence that corporations practicing "rotten commercialism" had bribed foreign politicians to bolster arms sales in the 1920s and 1930s, and had lobbied against arms control.

**Nye Committee Hearings**

Isolationists grew suspicious of American business ties with Nazi Germany and fascist Italy which might endanger U.S. neutrality. Twenty-six of the top one hundred American corporations, including DuPont, Standard Oil, and General Motors, had contractual agreements in 1937 with German firms. And after Italy attacked Ethiopia in 1935, American petroleum, copper, scrap iron, and steel exports to Italy increased substantially, despite Roosevelt's call for a moral embargo on such commerce. A Dow Chemical official stated, "We do not inquire into the uses of the products. We are interested in selling them." Not all American executives thought this way. The Wall Street law firm of Sullivan and Cromwell, for example, severed lucrative ties with Germany to protest the Nazi persecution of Jews.

Reflecting the popular desire for distance from Europe's disputes, Roosevelt signed a series of neutrality acts. Congress sought to protect the nation by outlawing the kinds of contacts that had compromised U.S. neutrality during World War I. The Neutrality Act of 1935 prohibited arms shipments to either side in a war, once the president had declared the existence of belligerency. Roosevelt had wanted the authority to name the aggressor and apply an arms embargo against it alone, but Congress would not grant the president such discretionary power. The Neutrality Act of 1936 forbade loans to belligerents. After a joint resolution in 1937 declared the United States neutral in the Spanish Civil War, Roosevelt embargoed arms shipments to both sides. The Neutrality Act of 1937 introduced the cash-and-carry principle: warring nations wishing to trade with the United States would have to pay cash for their nonmilitary purchases and carry the goods from U.S. ports in their own ships. The act also forbade Americans from traveling on the ships of belligerent nations.

President Roosevelt shared isolationist views in the early 1930s. Although prior to World War I he was an

## Roosevelt's Evolving Views

expansionist and interventionist like his older cousin Theodore, during the interwar period FDR talked less about preparedness and more about disarmament and the horrors of war, less about policing the world and more about handling problems at home. In a passionate speech delivered in August 1936 at Chautauqua, New York, Roosevelt expressed prevailing isolationist opinion and made a pitch for the pacifist vote in the upcoming election: "I have seen war. . . . I have seen blood running from the wounded. I have seen men coughing out their gassed lungs. . . . I have seen the agony of mothers and wives. I hate war." The United States, he promised, would remain unentangled in the European conflict. During the crisis over Czechoslovakia in 1938, Roosevelt endorsed appeasement and greeted the Munich accord with a "universal sense of relief."

All the while, Roosevelt grew troubled by the arrogant behavior of Germany, Italy, and Japan—aggressors that he tagged the "three bandit nations." He condemned the Nazi persecution of the Jews and Japan's expansionist actions in East Asia. Privately he chastised the British and French for failing to collar Hitler. Yet he himself also moved cautiously in confronting the German leader. In November 1938, Hitler launched *Kristallnacht* (or "Crystal Night," so named for the shattered glass that littered the streets after the attack on Jewish synagogues, businesses, and homes) and sent tens of thousands of Jews to concentration camps. Roosevelt expressed his shock, recalled the U.S. ambassador to Germany, and allowed 15,000 refugees on visitor permits to remain longer in the United States. But he would not do more, such as break trade relations with Hitler or push Congress to loosen tough immigration laws enacted in the 1920s. Congress, for its part, rejected all measures, including a bill to admit 20,000 children under the age of fourteen. Motivated by economic concerns and widespread anti-Semitism, more than 80 percent of Americans supported Congress's decision to uphold immigration restrictions.

Even the tragic voyage of the *St. Louis* did not change government policy. The vessel left Hamburg in mid-1939 carrying 930 desperate Jewish refugees who lacked proper immigration documents. Denied entry to Havana, the *St. Louis* headed for Miami, where Coast Guard cutters prevented it from docking. The ship was forced to return to Europe. Some of those refugees took shelter in countries that later were overrun by Hitler's legions. "The cruise of the *St. Louis,*" wrote the *New York Times,* "cries to high heaven of man's inhumanity to man."

Quietly, though, Roosevelt had begun moving to ready the country for war. In early 1938 he successfully pressured the House of Representatives to defeat a constitutional amendment proposed by Indiana Democrat Louis Ludlow to require a majority vote in a national referendum before a congressional declaration of war could go into effect (unless the United States were attacked). Later that year, in the wake of the Munich crisis, Roosevelt asked Congress for funds to build up the air force, which he believed essential to deter aggression. In January 1939 the president secretly decided to sell bombers to France, saying privately that "our frontier is on the Rhine." Although

▲ German leader Adolf Hitler (1889–1945) is surrounded in this propagandistic painting by images that came to symbolize hate, genocide, and war: Nazi flags with emblems of the swastika, the iron cross on the dictator's pocket, Nazi troops in loyal salute. The anti-Semitic Hitler denounced the United States as a "Jewish rubbish heap" of "inferiority and decadence" that was "incapable of conducting war." *(U.S. Army Center of Military History)*

President Franklin D. Roosevelt ▶ relaxes with his favorite hobby, stamp collecting, from which he said he learned history and geography. During World War II he once showed British prime minister Winston Churchill a stamp from "one of your colonies." Churchill asked, "Which one?" Roosevelt replied, "One of your last. . . . You won't have them much longer, you know."

*(Franklin D. Roosevelt Library)*

the more than five hundred combat planes delivered to France did not deter war, French orders spurred growth of the U.S. aircraft industry.

For Roosevelt and for other Western leaders, Hitler's swallowing of the whole of Czechoslovakia in March 1939 proved a turning point, forcing them to face a stark new reality. Until now, they had been able to explain away Hitler's actions by saying he was only trying to reunite German-speaking peoples. That argument no longer worked. Leaders in Paris and London realized that, if the German leader was to be stopped, it would have to be by force. When Hitler began eyeing his neighbor Poland, London and Paris announced they would stand by the Poles. Undaunted, Berlin signed a nonaggression pact with Moscow in August 1939. Soviet leader Joseph Stalin believed that the West's appeasement of Hitler had left him no choice but to cut a deal with Berlin. But Stalin also coveted territory: a top-secret protocol attached to the pact carved eastern Europe into German and Soviet zones, and permitted the Soviets to grab the eastern half of Poland and the three Baltic states of Lithuania, Estonia, and Latvia, formerly part of the Russian Empire.

In the early morning hours of September 1, German tank columns rolled into Poland. German fighting planes covered the advance, thereby launching a new type of warfare, the *blitzkrieg* (lightning war)— highly mobile land forces and armor combined with tactical aircraft. Within forty-eight hours, Britain and France responded by declaring war on Ger-

**Poland and the Outbreak of World War II**

many. "It's come at last," Franklin Roosevelt murmured. "God help us all."

When Europe descended into the abyss of war in September 1939, Roosevelt declared neutrality and pressed for repeal of the arms embargo. Isolationist senator Arthur Vandenberg of Michigan roared back that the United States could not be "an arsenal for one belligerent without becoming a target for the other." After much debate, however, Congress in November lifted the embargo on contraband and approved cash-and-carry exports of arms. Using "methods short of war," Roosevelt thus began to aid the Allies. Hitler sneered that a "half Judaized . . . half Negrified" United States was "incapable of conducting war."

## JAPAN, CHINA, AND A NEW ORDER IN ASIA

While Europe succumbed to political turmoil and war, Asia suffered the aggressive march of Japan. The United States had interests at stake in Asia: the Philippines and Pacific islands, religious missions, trade and investments, and the Open Door in China. In traditional missionary fashion, Americans also believed that they were China's special friend and protector. "With God's help," Senator Kenneth Wherry of Nebraska once proclaimed, "we will lift Shanghai up and up, ever up, until it is just like Kansas City." Pearl Buck's bestselling novel *The Good Earth* (1931), made into a widely distributed film six years later, countered prevailing images of the very different—and thus deviant—"heathen Chinee" by representing the Chinese as noble, persevering peasants. The daughter of Presbyterian missionaries, Buck helped shift negative American images of China to positive ones. By contrast, the aggressive Japan loomed as a threat to American attitudes and interests. The Tokyo government seemed bent on subjugating China and unhinging the Open Door doctrine of equal trade and investment opportunity.

The Chinese themselves were uneasy about the U.S. presence in Asia. Like the Japanese, they wished to reduce the influence of westerners. The Chinese Revolution of 1911 still rumbled in the 1920s, as antiforeign riots damaged American property and imperiled American missionaries. Chinese nationalists criticized Americans for the imperialist practice of extraterritoriality (the exemption from Chinese legal jurisdiction of foreigners accused of crimes), and they demanded an end to this affront to Chinese sovereignty.

In the late 1920s, civil war broke out in China when Jiang Jieshi (Chiang Kai-shek) ousted Mao Zedong and

**Jiang Jieshi**

his communist followers from the ruling Guomindang Party. Americans applauded this display of anti-Bolshevism and Jiang's conversion to Christianity in 1930. Jiang's new wife, Soong Meiling, also won their hearts. American-educated, Madame Jiang spoke flawless English, dressed in western fashion, and cultivated ties with prominent Americans. Warming to Jiang, U.S. officials abandoned one imperial vestige by signing a treaty in 1928 restoring control of tariffs to the Chinese. U.S. gunboats and marines still remained in China to protect American citizens and property.

The Japanese grew increasingly suspicious of U.S. ties with China. In the early twentieth century, Japanese-American relations steadily deteriorated as Japan gained influence in Manchuria, Shandong, and Korea. The Japanese sought not only to oust western imperialists from Asia but also to dominate Asian territories that produced the raw materials that their import-dependent island nation required. The Japanese also resented the discriminatory immigration law of 1924, which excluded them from emigrating to the United States and declared they were "aliens ineligible to citizenship." Secretary Hughes urged Congress not to pass the act; when it rejected his counsel, he sadly called the law "a lasting injury" to Japanese-American relations. Despite the Washington Conference treaties, naval competition continued, and there was also rivalry in the commercial arena. In the United States the

importation of inexpensive Japanese goods, especially textiles, spawned "Buy America" campaigns and boycotts.

Relations further soured in 1931 after the Japanese military seized Manchuria from China (see Map 26.2), weakened by civil war and unable

**Manchurian Crisis**

to resist. Larger than Texas, Manchuria served Japan both as a buffer against the Soviets and as a vital source of coal, iron, timber, and food. More than half of Japan's foreign investments rested in Manchuria. "We are seeking room that will let us breathe," said a

▲ After the outbreak of the Sino-Japanese War (termed the "China Incident" by Japan) in 1937, Japanese postcard publishers churned out large numbers of postcards showing the newly conquered territories, or weaponry, or scenes of army life. Soldiers would send the postcards back to family members in Japan. This image appeared on the cover of a packet of eight postcards in the late 1930s. The text reads, "China Incident Postcard—Fourth Set."

*(Eric Politzer/Curt Teich Postcard Archives, Lake County Museum)*

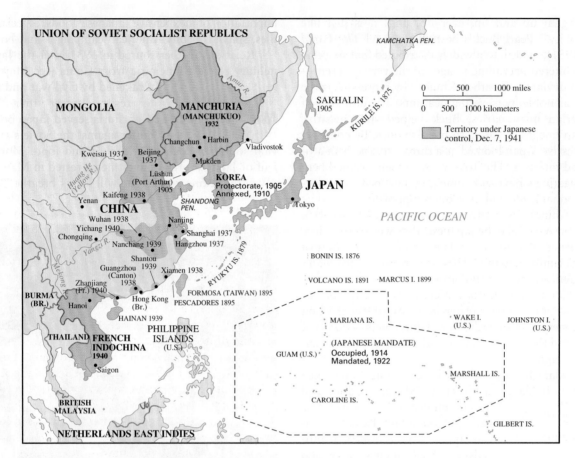

**Map 26.2   Japanese Expansion Before Pearl Harbor**

The Japanese quest for predominance began at the turn of the century and intensified in the 1930s.
China suffered the most at the hands of Tokyo's military. Vulnerable U.S. possessions in Asia and
the Pacific proved no obstacle to Japan's ambitions for a Greater East Asia Co-Prosperity Sphere.

Japanese politician, arguing that his heavily populated island nation (65 million people in an area slightly smaller
than California) needed to expand in order to survive.
Although the seizure of Manchuria violated the Nine-
Power Treaty and the Kellogg-Briand Pact, the United
States did not have the power to compel Japanese withdrawal, and the League of Nations did little but condemn
the Tokyo government. The American response came as a
moral lecture known as the Stimson Doctrine: the United
States would not recognize any impairment of China's sovereignty or of the Open Door policy, Secretary Stimson
declared in 1932. He himself later described his policy as
largely "bluff."

Japan continued to pressure China. In mid-1937,
owing to Japanese provocation, the Sino-Japanese War
erupted. Japanese forces seized Beijing and cities along
the coast. The gruesome bombing of Shanghai intensified

anti-Japanese sentiment in the United States. Senator
Norris, an isolationist who moved further away from isolationism with each Japanese thrust, condemned the Japanese as "disgraceful, ignoble, barbarous, and cruel, even
beyond the power of language to describe." In an effort to
help China by permitting it to buy American arms, Roosevelt refused to declare the existence of war, thus avoiding activation of the Neutrality Acts.

In a speech denouncing the aggressors on October 5,
1937, the president called for a "quarantine" to curb the
"epidemic of world lawlessness."
People who thought Washington
had been too gentle with Japan
cheered. Isolationists warned that
the president was edging toward
war. On December 12, Japanese
aircraft sank the American gunboat *Panay,* an escort for

**Roosevelt's
Quarantine
Speech**

Standard Oil Company tankers on the Yangtze River. Two American sailors died during the attack. Roosevelt was much relieved when Tokyo apologized and offered to pay for damages.

Japan's declaration of a "New Order" in Asia, in the words of one American official, "banged, barred, and bolted" the Open Door. Alarmed, the Roosevelt administration during the late 1930s gave loans and sold military equipment to Jiang's Chinese government. Secretary Hull declared a moral embargo on the shipment of airplanes to Japan. Meanwhile, the U.S. Navy continued to grow, aided by a billion-dollar congressional appropriation in 1938. In mid-1939 the United States abrogated its trade treaty with Tokyo, yet Americans continued to ship oil, cotton, and machinery to Japan. The administration hesitated to initiate economic sanctions because such pressure might spark a Japanese-American war at a time when Germany posed a more serious threat and the United States was unprepared for war. When war broke out in Europe in the late summer of 1939, Japanese-American relations were stalemated.

## U.S. ENTRY INTO WORLD WAR II

A stalemate was just fine with many Americans if it served to keep the United States out of war. But how long could the country stay out? Roosevelt remarked in 1939 that the United States could not "draw a line of defense around this country and live completely and solely to ourselves." Thomas Jefferson had tried that with his 1807 embargo— "the damned thing didn't work," and "we got into the War of 1812." America, the president insisted, could not insulate itself from world war. Polls showed that Americans strongly favored the Allies and that most supported aid to Britain and France, but the great majority emphatically wanted the United States to remain at peace. Troubled by this conflicting advice—oppose Hitler, aid the Allies, but stay out of the war—the president gradually moved the nation from neutrality to undeclared war against Germany and then, after the Japanese attack on Pearl Harbor, to full-scale war itself.

Because the stakes were so high, Americans vigorously debated the direction of their foreign policy from 1939 through 1941. Unprecedented numbers of Americans spoke out on foreign affairs and joined organizations that addressed the issues. Spine-chilling events and the widespread use of radio, the nation's chief source of news, helped stimulate this high level of public interest. So did ethnic affiliations with the various belligerents and victims of aggression. The American Legion, the League of Women Voters, labor unions, and local chapters of the Committee to Defend America by Aiding the Allies and of the isolationist America First Committee (both organized in 1940) provided outlets for citizen participation in the national debate. African American churches organized anti-Italian boycotts to protest Mussolini's pummeling of Ethiopia.

In March 1940, the Soviet Union invaded Finland. In April, Germany conquered Denmark and Norway (see Map 26.3). "The small countries are smashed up, one by one, like matchwood," sighed Winston Churchill, who became Britain's prime minister on May 10, 1940, the day Germany attacked Belgium, the Netherlands, and France. German divisions ultimately pushed French and British forces back to the English Channel. At Dunkirk, France, between May 26 and June 6, more

your BRITAIN · fight for it now

ISSUED BY A·B·C·A

◀ Guns, tanks, and bombs were the principal weapons of the war, but there were other, subtler forms of warfare as well. Words, posters, and films waged a constant battle for the hearts and minds of the citizenry of each belligerent nation just as surely as military weapons engaged the enemy. This scene of the South Downs in England sought to arouse feelings for an idealized pastoral Britain.

*(Frank Newbould)*

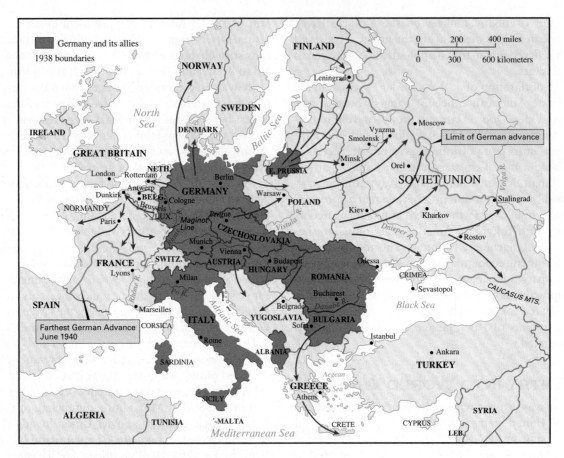

**Map 26.3    The German Advance**

Hitler's drive to dominate Europe pushed German troops deep into France and the Soviet Union. Great Britain took a beating but held on with the help of American economic and military aid before the United States itself entered the Second World War in late 1941.

than 300,000 Allied soldiers frantically escaped to Britain on a flotilla of small boats. The Germans occupied Paris a week later. A new French government located in the town of Vichy decided to collaborate with the conquering Nazis and, on June 22, surrendered France to Berlin. With France knocked out of the war, the German Luftwaffe (air force) launched massive bombing raids against Great Britain in preparation for a full-scale invasion. Stunned Americans asked whether Washington or New York could be the Luftwaffe's next target.

Alarmed by the swift defeat of one European nation after another, Americans gradually shed their isolationist sentiment. Some liberals left the isolationist fold; it became more and more the province of conservatives. Emotions ran high. Roosevelt called the isolationists "ostriches" and

charged that some were pro-Nazi subversives. Assuring Americans that New Deal reforms would not have to be sacrificed to achieve military preparedness, the president began to aid the beleaguered Allies to prevent the fall of Britain. In May 1940 he ordered the sale of old surplus military equipment to Britain and France. In July he cultivated bipartisan support by naming Republicans Henry L. Stimson and Frank Knox, ardent backers of aid to the Allies, secretaries of war and the navy, respectively. In September, by executive agreement, the president traded fifty over-age American destroyers for leases to eight British military bases, including Newfoundland, Bermuda, and Jamaica.

Two weeks later, Roosevelt signed into law the hotly debated and narrowly passed Selective Training and

## Radio News

*I*n radio's early years, stations broadcast little news. Network executives believed their job was to entertain Americans and that current affairs should be left to newspapers. Yet radio could do something that no previous medium of communication could do: it could report not merely what had happened, but what was happening as it happened.

Franklin Roosevelt was among the first to grasp radio's potential in this regard. As governor of New York, he occasionally went on the air, and after becoming president, he commenced his Fireside Chats. With a voice perfectly suited to the medium, he reassured Americans suffering through the depression that, although current conditions were grim, the government was working hard to help them. So successful were these broadcasts that, in the words of one journalist, "The President has only to look toward a radio to bring Congress to terms."

Across the Atlantic, another leader also understood well the power of radio. Adolf Hitler determined early that he would use German radio to carry speeches directly to the people. His message: Germany had been wronged by enemies abroad and by Marxists and Jews at home. But the Nazis under Hitler's direction would lead the country back to its former greatness. As "Sieg Heil!" thundered over the airwaves, millions of Germans came to see Hitler as their salvation.

In 1938, as events in Europe reached a crisis, American radio networks increased their news coverage. When Hitler annexed Austria in March, NBC and CBS broke into scheduled programs to deliver news bulletins. Then, on the evening of Saturday, March 13, CBS went its rival one better by broadcasting the first international news roundup, a half-hour show featuring live reports on the annexation from the major capitals of Europe. A new era in American radio was born. In the words of author Joseph Persico, what made the broadcast revolutionary "was the listener's sensation of being on the scene" in far-off Europe.

When leaders from France and Britain met with Hitler in Munich later that year, millions of Americans listened with rapt attention to live radio updates. Correspondents soon became well known, none more so than Edward R. Murrow of CBS. During the Nazi air blitz of London in 1940–1941, Murrow's rich, understated, nicotine-scorched voice kept Americans spellbound. "This—is London," he would begin each broadcast, then proceed to give graphic accounts that tried, as he put it, to "report suffering to people [Americans] who have not suffered."

Murrow was resolutely pro-Allies, and there is little doubt his reports strengthened the interventionist voices in Washington by emphasizing Winston Churchill's greatness and England's bravery. More than that, though, radio reports from Europe made Americans feel more closely linked than before to people living thousands of miles and an ocean away. As American writer Archibald MacLeish said of Murrow's broadcasts, "Without rhetoric, without dramatics, without more emotion than needed be, you destroyed the superstition of distance and of time."

▲ Edward R. Murrow at his typewriter in wartime London.
*(Library of Congress)*

|||||||||||||||||||||||||||||||

**First Peacetime
Military Draft**

Service Act, the first peacetime military draft in American history. The act called for the registration of all men between the ages of twenty-one and thirty-five. Soon more than 16 million men had signed up, and draft notices began to be delivered. Meanwhile, Roosevelt won reelection in November 1940 with promises of peace: "Your boys are not going to be sent into any foreign wars." Republican candidate Wendell Willkie, who in the emerging spirit of bipartisanship had not made an issue of foreign policy, snapped, "That hypocritical son of a bitch! This is going to beat me!" And it did.

Roosevelt claimed that the United States could stay out of the war by enabling the British to win. The United States, he said, must become the "great arsenal of democracy." In January 1941, Congress debated the president's Lend-Lease bill. Because Britain was broke, the president explained, the United States should lend rather than sell weapons, much as a neighbor lends a garden hose to fight a fire. Most lawmakers needed little persuasion. In March 1941, with pro-British sentiment running high, the House passed the Lend-Lease Act by 317 votes to 71; the Senate followed with a 60-to-31 tally. The initial appropriation was $7 billion, but by the end of the war the amount had reached $50 billion, more than $31 billion of it for Britain.

To ensure the safe delivery of Lend-Lease goods, Roosevelt ordered the U.S. Navy to patrol halfway across the Atlantic, and he sent American troops to Greenland. In July, arguing that Iceland was also essential to the defense of the Western Hemisphere, the president dispatched marines there. He also sent Lend-Lease aid to the Soviet Union, which Hitler had attacked in June (thereby shattering the 1939 Nazi-Soviet nonaggression pact). If the Soviets could hold off two hundred German divisions in the east, Roosevelt calculated, Britain would gain some breathing time. Churchill, who had long thundered against communists, now applauded aid to the Soviets: "If Hitler invaded Hell, I would make at least a favorable reference to the Devil in the House of Commons."

In August 1941, Churchill and Roosevelt met for four days on a British battleship off the coast of New-

|||||||||||||||||||||||||||||||

**Atlantic Charter**

foundland. They got along well, trading naval stories and enjoying the fact that Churchill was half American (his mother was from New York). The two leaders issued the Atlantic Charter, a set of war aims reminiscent of Wilsonianism: collective security, disarmament, self-determination, economic cooperation, and freedom of the seas. Churchill later recalled

that the president told him in Newfoundland that he could not ask Congress for a declaration of war against Germany, but "he would wage war" and "become more and more provocative."

Within days, German and American ships came into direct contact in the Atlantic. On September 4, a German submarine launched torpedoes at (but did not hit) the American destroyer *Greer.* Henceforth, Roosevelt said, the U.S. Navy would have authority to fire first when under threat. He also announced a policy that he already had promised Churchill in private: American warships would convoy British merchant ships across the ocean. Thus the United States entered into an undeclared naval war with Germany. When in early October a German submarine torpedoed the U.S. destroyer *Kearny* off the coast of Iceland, the president announced that "the shooting has started. And history has recorded who fired the first shot." Later that month, when the destroyer *Reuben James* went down with the loss of more than one hundred American lives, Congress scrapped the cash-and-carry policy and further revised the Neutrality Acts to permit transport of munitions to Britain on armed American merchant ships. The United States was edging very close to being a belligerent.

It seems ironic, therefore, that the Second World War came to the United States by way of Asia. Roosevelt had

|||||||||||||||||||||||||||||||

**U.S. Demands
on Japan**

wanted to avoid war with Japan in order to concentrate American resources on the defeat of Germany. In September 1940, after Germany, Italy, and Japan had signed the Tripartite Pact (to form the Axis powers), Roosevelt slapped an embargo on shipments of aviation fuel and scrap metal to Japan. Because the president believed the Japanese would consider a cutoff of oil a life-or-death matter, he did not embargo that vital commodity. But after Japanese troops occupied French Indochina in July 1941, Washington froze Japanese assets in the United States, virtually ending trade (including oil) with Japan. "The oil gauge and the clock stood side by side" for Japan, wrote one observer.

Tokyo recommended a summit meeting between President Roosevelt and Prime Minister Prince Konoye, but the United States rejected the idea. American officials insisted that the Japanese first agree to respect China's sovereignty and territorial integrity, and to honor the Open Door policy—in short, to get out of China. According to polls taken in fall 1941, the American people seemed willing to risk war with Japan to thwart further aggression. For Roosevelt, Europe still claimed first priority, but he supported Secretary Hull's hard-line policy against Japan's pursuit of the Greater East Asia Co-Prosperity Sphere—

▲ President Franklin D. Roosevelt *(left)* and British prime minister Winston Churchill (1874–1965) confer on board a ship near Newfoundland during their summit meeting of August 1941. During the conference, they signed the Atlantic Charter. On his return to Great Britain, Churchill told his advisers that Roosevelt had promised to "wage war" against Germany and do "everything" to "force an incident." *(Franklin D. Roosevelt Library)*

the name Tokyo gave to the vast Asian region it intended to dominate.

Roosevelt told his advisers to string out ongoing Japanese-American talks to gain time—time to fortify the Philippines and check the fascists in Europe. By breaking the Japanese diplomatic code and deciphering intercepted messages through Operation MAGIC, American officials learned that Tokyo's patience with diplomacy was fast dissipating. In late November, the Japanese rejected American demands that they withdraw from Indochina. An intercepted message that American experts decoded on December 3 instructed the Japanese embassy in Washington to burn codes and destroy cipher machines—a step suggesting that war was coming.

The Japanese plotted a daring raid on Pearl Harbor in Hawai'i. An armada of sixty Japanese ships, with a core of six carriers bearing 360 airplanes, crossed 3,000 miles of the Pacific Ocean. To avoid detection, every ship maintained radio silence. In the early morning of December 7, some 230 miles northwest of Honolulu, the carriers unleashed their planes, each stamped with a red sun representing the Japanese flag. They swept down on the unsuspecting American naval base and nearby airfields, dropping torpedoes and bombs and strafing buildings.

The battleship USS *Arizona* fell victim to a Japanese bomb that ignited explosives below deck, killing more

## Surprise Attack on Pearl Harbor

▲ The stricken USS *West Virginia* was one of eight battleships caught in the surprise Japanese attack at Pearl Harbor, Hawaiʻi, on December 7, 1941. In this photograph, sailors on a launch attempt to rescue a crew member from the water as oil burns around the sinking ship. *(U.S. Army)*

than 1,000 sailors. The USS *Nevada* tried to escape the inferno by heading out to sea, but a second wave of aerial attackers struck the ship. Altogether the invaders sank or damaged eight battleships and many smaller vessels, and smashed more than 160 aircraft on the ground. Huddled in an air-raid shelter, sixteen-year-old Mary Ann Ramsey watched the injured come in "with filthy black oil covering shredded flesh. With the first sailor, so horribly burned, personal fear left me; he brought me the full tragedy of the day." A total of 2,403 died; 1,178 were wounded. By chance, three aircraft carriers at sea escaped the disaster. The Pearl Harbor tragedy, from the perspective of the war's

outcome, amounted to a military inconvenience more than a disaster.

How could the stunning attack on Pearl Harbor have happened? After all, American cryptanalysts had broken the Japanese diplomatic code. Although the intercepted Japanese messages told policymakers that war lay ahead, the intercepts never revealed naval or military plans and never mentioned Pearl Harbor specifically. Roosevelt did not, as some critics charged, conspire to leave the fleet vulnerable to attack so that the United States could enter the

**Explaining Pearl Harbor**

Second World War through the "back door" of Asia. The base at Pearl Harbor was not on red alert because a message sent from Washington warning of the imminence of war had been too casually transmitted by a slow method and had arrived too late. Base commanders were too relaxed, believing Hawai'i too far from Japan to be a target for all-out attack. Like Roosevelt's advisers, they expected an assault on British Malaya, Thailand, or the Philippines (see Map 26.2). The Pearl Harbor calamity stemmed from mistakes and insufficient information, not from conspiracy.

On December 8, referring to the previous day as "a date which will live in infamy," Roosevelt asked Congress for a declaration of war against Japan. He noted that the Japanese had also, almost simultaneously, attacked Malaya, Hong Kong, Guam, the Philippines, Wake, and Midway, and he expressed the prevailing sense of revenge when he vowed that Americans would never forget "the character of the onslaught against us." A unanimous vote in the Senate and a 388-to-1 vote in the House thrust America into war. Representative Jeannette Rankin of Montana voted no, repeating her vote against entry into the First World War. Britain declared war on Japan, but the Soviet Union did not. Three days later, Germany and Italy, honoring the Tripartite Pact they had signed with Japan in September 1940, declared war against the United States. "Hitler's fate was sealed," Churchill later wrote. "Mussolini's fate was sealed. As for the Japanese, they would be ground to powder. . . . I went to bed and slept the sleep of the saved and thankful."

A fundamental clash of systems explains why war came. Germany and Japan preferred a world divided into closed spheres of influence. The United States sought a liberal capitalist world order in which all nations enjoyed freedom of trade and investment. American principles manifested respect for human rights; fascists in Europe and militarists in Asia defiantly trampled such rights. The United States prided itself on its democratic system; Germany and Japan embraced authoritarian regimes backed by the military. When the United States protested against German and Japanese expansion, Berlin and Tokyo charged that Washington was applying a double standard, conveniently ignoring its own sphere of influence in Latin America and its own history of military and economic aggrandizement. Americans rejected such comparisons and claimed that their expansionism had benefited not just themselves but the rest of the world. So many incompatible objectives and outlooks obstructed diplomacy and made war likely.

Likely, but perhaps not inevitable. At least with respect to the Japanese, there is the tantalizing question of whether a more flexible American negotiating posture in the fall of 1941 might have averted a U.S.-Japanese war. Privately, after all, American planners admitted that they were largely powerless to affect Japan's moves in China; they further conceded among themselves that any Japanese withdrawal from China would take many months to carry out. So why the public insistence that Japan had to get out, and get out now? Why not assent, grudgingly, to the Japanese presence in China and also reopen at least limited trade with the Tokyo government, in order to forestall further Japanese expansion in Southeast Asia? Such a policy would have delayed any showdown with Japan, allowed continued concentration on the European war, and also given Washington more time to rearm. Writes historian David M. Kennedy, "Whether under those circumstances a Japanese-American war might have been avoided altogether is among the weightiest of might-have-beens, with implications for the nature and timing of America's struggle against Hitler and for the shape of postwar Europe as well as Asia." It was not to be, though, and the United States now prepared to wage war in two theaters half a world apart.

**Avoidable War?**

## *Legacy* FOR A PEOPLE AND A NATION

### Presidential Deception of the Public

Before U-652 launched two torpedoes at the *Greer,* heading for Iceland on September 4, 1941, the U.S. destroyer had stalked the German submarine for hours. Twice the *Greer* signaled the U-boat's location to British patrol bombers, one of which dropped depth charges on the submarine. After the torpedo attack, which missed its mark, the *Greer* also released depth charges. But when President Roosevelt described the encounter in a dramatic radio Fireside Chat on September 11, he declared that the German submarine, without warning, had fired the first shot, and he protested German "piracy" as a violation of the principle of freedom of the seas.

Roosevelt misled the American people about the events of September 4. The incident had little to do with freedom of the seas—a principle relating to neutral merchant ships, not to U.S. warships operating in a war zone. Roosevelt's words amounted to a call to arms, yet he never asked Congress for a declaration of war against Germany. The president believed that he had to deceive Americans in order to move them toward noble positions that they would ultimately see as necessary. The practice worked: polls showed that most Americans approved Roosevelt's shoot-on-sight policy following the *Greer* incident.

Over time, however, questions were raised—even by those who agreed that Germany had to be stopped. Crit-ics have seen in Roosevelt's methods a danger to the democratic process, which cannot work in an environment of dishonesty and a usurping of congressional powers. In the 1960s, during the Vietnam War, Senator J. William Fulbright of Arkansas recalled the *Greer* incident: "FDR's deviousness in a good cause made it easier for LBJ to practice the same kind of deviousness in a bad cause." In the mid-1980s, Reagan administration officials consciously and publicly lied about U.S. arms sales to Iran and about covert aid to Nicaraguan rebels, and after the March 2003 U.S. invasion of Iraq, there were charges that President George W. Bush and his aides did the same in claiming that Iraq had weapons of mass destruction and that its leader, Saddam Hussein, intended to use them. Bush, critics charged, had used "weapons of mass deception" to justify the invasion of Iraq.

Following Roosevelt, presidents have found it easier to exaggerate, distort, withhold, or even lie about the facts of foreign relations in order to shape a public opinion favorable to their policies. One result: the growth of the "imperial presidency"—the president's grabbing of power from Congress and use of questionable means to reach his objectives. The practice of deception—for an end the president calls noble—was one of Roosevelt's legacies for a people and a nation.

## SUMMARY

In the 1920s and 1930s, Americans proved unable to create a peaceful and prosperous world order. The Washington Conference treaties failed to curb a naval arms race or to protect China, and both the Dawes Plan and the Kellogg-Briand Pact proved ineffective. Philanthropic activities fell short of need, and the process of cultural Americanization provided no panacea. In the era of the Great Depression, U.S. trade policies, shifting from protectionist tariffs to reciprocal trade agreements, only minimally improved U.S. or international commerce. Recognition of the Soviet Union barely improved relations. Most ominous of all, the aggressors Germany and Japan ignored repeated U.S. protests, from the Stimson Doctrine onward; as the 1930s progressed, the United States became more entangled in the crises in Europe and Asia. Even where American power and policies seemed to work to satisfy Good Neighbor goals—in Latin America—nationalist resentments simmered and Mexico challenged U.S. dominance.

During the late 1930s and early 1940s, President Roosevelt hesitantly but steadily moved the United States from neutrality to aid for the Allies, to belligerency, and finally to a declaration of war after the attack on Pearl Harbor. Congress gradually revised and retired the Neutrality Acts in the face of growing danger and receding isolationism. Independent internationalism and economic and nonmilitary means to peace gave way to alliance building and war.

The Second World War offered yet another opportunity for Americans to set things right in the world. As publisher Henry Luce wrote in *American Century* (1941), the United States must "exert upon the world the full impact of our influence, for such purposes as we see fit and by such means as we see fit." As they had so many times before, Americans flocked to the colors. Isolationists joined the president in spirited calls for victory. "We are going to win the war, and we are going to win the peace that follows," Roosevelt predicted.

## SUGGESTIONS FOR FURTHER READING

Patrick Cohrs, *The Unfinished Peace After World War I: America, Britain and the Stabilization of Europe, 1919–1932* (2006)

Frank Costigliola, *Awkward Dominion: American Political, Economic, and Cultural Relations with Europe* (1984)

Robert Dallek, *Franklin D. Roosevelt and American Foreign Policy* (1995)

Justus D. Doenecke, *Storm on the Horizon: The Challenge to American Intervention, 1939–1941* (2000)

Akira Iriye, *The Origins of the Second World War in Asia and the Pacific* (1987)

David M. Kennedy, *Freedom from Fear: The American People in Depression and War, 1929–1945* (1999)

Walter LaFeber, *Inevitable Revolutions: The United States in Central America*, 2d and extended ed. (1993)

Fredrick B. Pike, *FDR's Good Neighbor Policy* (1995)

Emily S. Rosenberg, *Spreading the American Dream: American Economic and Cultural Expansion, 1890–1945* (1982)

Linda A. Schott, *Reconstructing Women's Thoughts: The Women's International League for Peace and Freedom Before World War II* (1997)

*For a more extensive list for further reading, go to* college.hmco.com/pic/norton8e.

# The Second World War at Home and Abroad

## 1941-1945

illiam Dean Wilson was only sixteen in 1942 when U.S. Marine Corps recruiters came to Shiprock, New Mexico, where he was a student at the Navajo boarding school, but he was eager to fight the war. Five years too young to be drafted and a year too young to volunteer for the marines, he lied about his age. His parents did not want him to drop out of school and go to war, but he removed the note reading, "Parents will not consent" from his recruiting file and was inducted into the Marine Corps.

Despite his youth, Wilson was recruited for one of the most important projects of the war. Battles were won or lost because nations broke the codes in which their enemies transmitted messages. The marines sought to use a code based on Diné, the Navajo language, which is extremely complex because of its syntax and tonal qualities. In 1942 it did not exist in written form, and there were fewer than thirty non-Navajos in the world—none of them Japanese—who could understand it. Unlike written ciphers, this code promised to be unbreakable.

Wilson and his fellow Navajo recruits trained as radio operators and helped devise a basic code. Navajo words represented the first letter of their English translations; thus *wol-la-chee* ("ant") stood for the letter *A*. Each also memorized a special dictionary of Navajo words that represented 413 basic military terms and concepts. *Dah-he-tih-hi* ("hummingbird") meant fighter plane; *ne-he-mah,* "our mother," was the United States; *beh-na-ali-tsosie,* "slant-eye," stood for Japan.

By the time Wilson's seventeenth birthday arrived, he was fighting in the Pacific. Beginning with the Battle of Guadalcanal, he and others from the corps of 420 code talkers

◄ Navajo "code talkers," who were U.S. Marines, were among the first assault forces to land on Pacific beaches. Dodging enemy fire, they set up radio equipment and transmitted vital information to headquarters, including enemy sightings and targets for American shelling. The Japanese never broke the special Navajo code. The artist is Colonel C. H. Waterhouse, U.S. Marine Corps (retired).

*(U.S. Marine Corps Art Collection/Colonel C. H. Waterhouse)*

## CHRONOLOGY

**1941** ■ Japan attacks Pearl Harbor
■ United States enters World War II

**1942** ■ War Production Board created to oversee conversion to military production
■ Allies losing war in Pacific to Japan; U.S. victory at Battle of Midway in June is turning point
■ Office of Price Administration creates rationing system for food and consumer goods
■ United States pursues "Europe First" war policy; Allies reject Stalin's demands for a second front and invade North Africa
■ West Coast Japanese Americans relocated to internment camps
■ Manhattan Project set up to create atomic bomb
■ Congress of Racial Equality established

**1943** ■ Soviet army defeats German troops at Stalingrad
■ Congress passes War Labor Disputes (Smith-Connally) Act following coal miners' strike
■ "Zoot suit riots" in Los Angeles; race riots break out in Detroit, Harlem, and other cities
■ Allies invade Italy
■ Roosevelt, Churchill, and Stalin meet at Teheran Conference

**1944** ■ Allied troops land at Normandy on D-Day, June 6
■ Roosevelt elected to fourth term as president
■ United States retakes Philippines

**1945** ■ Roosevelt, Stalin, and Churchill meet at Yalta Conference
■ British and U.S. forces firebomb Dresden, Germany
■ Battles of Iwo Jima and Okinawa result in heavy Japanese and American losses
■ Roosevelt dies; Truman becomes president
■ Germany surrenders; Allied forces liberate Nazi death camps
■ Potsdam Conference calls for Japan's "unconditional surrender"
■ United States uses atomic bombs on Hiroshima and Nagasaki
■ Japan surrenders

took part in every assault the marines conducted in the Pacific from 1942 to 1945. Usually, two code talkers were assigned to a battalion, one going ashore with the assault forces and the other remaining on ship to receive messages. Often under hostile fire, code talkers set up their radio equipment and began transmitting, reporting sightings of enemy forces and directing shelling by American detachments. Their work required great courage, and it paid off. "Were it not for the Navajos," declared Major Howard Conner, Fifth Marine Division signal officer, "the Marines would never have taken Iwo Jima. The entire operation was directed by Navajo code. . . . I had six Navajo radio sets operating around the clock. In that period alone they sent and received over eight hundred messages without an error."

As it did for millions of other American fighting men and women, wartime service changed the Navajo code talkers' lives, broadening their horizons and often deepening their ambitions. Many became community leaders. William Dean Wilson, for example, became a tribal judge. From "the service," recalled Raymond Nakai, a navy veteran who became chairman of the Navajo nation, "the Navajo got a glimpse of what the rest of the world is doing." But in 1945 most Navajo war veterans were happy to return to their homes and traditional culture. And, in accordance with Navajo ritual, the returning veterans participated in purification ceremonies to dispel the ghosts of the battlefield and invoke blessings for the future.

The Second World War marked a turning point in the lives of millions of Americans, as well as in the history of the United States. Most deeply affected were those who fought the war, on the beaches and battlefields, in the skies and at sea. For forty-five months Americans fought abroad to subdue the German, Italian, and Japanese aggressors. Although the war began badly for the United States, by mid-1942 the Allies had halted the Axis powers' advance. In June 1944, American troops, together with Canadian, British, and Free French units, launched a massive invasion across the English Channel, landing at Normandy and pushing into Germany by the following spring. Battered by merciless bombing raids, leaderless after Adolf Hitler's suicide, and pressed by a Soviet advance from the east, the Nazis capitulated in May 1945.

In the Pacific, Americans drove Japanese forces back, island by island, toward Japan. America's devastating conventional bombing of Japanese cities, followed by the atomic bombs that demolished Hiroshima and Nagasaki in August 1945, led to the surrender of Japan. Throughout the war, the "Grand Alliance"—Britain, the Soviet Union, and the United States—stuck together to defeat Germany. But they disagreed about how best to fight the war and had profound differences over how to shape the postwar world. Prospects for postwar international cooperation seemed bleak, and the advent of the atomic age frightened everyone.

The war was fought far from the United States, but it had a major impact on American society. America's leaders sought to fight the war on the "production front" as well as on the battlefield and committed the United States to become the "arsenal of democracy," producing vast quantities of arms for the war against the Axis. All sectors of the economy—industry, finance, agriculture, labor—were mobilized. America's big businesses got even bigger, as did its central government, labor unions, and farms. The federal government had the monumental task of coordinating activity in these spheres, as well as in two new ones: higher education and science.

During the war, nearly one of every ten Americans moved permanently to another state. Most headed for war-production centers, especially cities in the North and on the West Coast. Japanese Americans moved, too, but involuntarily, as they were rounded up by the army and placed in internment camps. And while the war offered new economic and political opportunities for African Americans, encouraging them to demand their full rights as citizens, competition for jobs and housing created the conditions for an epidemic of race riots. For women, the war offered new job opportunities in the armed forces and in war industries.

On the home front, the American people united behind the war effort, collecting scrap iron, rubber, and newspapers for recycling, and planting "victory gardens." Although commodities such as food and gasoline were rationed, the war had brought prosperity back to the United States. At war's end, although many Americans grieved for loved ones lost in battle and worried about the stability of the emerging postwar order, the United States had unprecedented power and unmatched prosperity among the world's nations.

- What military, diplomatic, and social factors influenced decisions about how to fight the Second World War?
- Was the generation of Americans that fought World War II "the greatest generation"?
- How did World War II transform the United States?

## THE UNITED STATES AT WAR

As Japanese bombs fell in the U.S. territory of Hawai'i, American antiwar sentiment evaporated. Franklin Roosevelt summoned the nation to war with Japan on December 8, proclaiming that "the American people in their righteous might will win through to absolute victory." When Germany formally declared war on the United States three days later, America joined British and Soviet Allied nations in the ongoing war against the Axis powers of Japan, Germany, and Italy. The American public's shift from caution—even isolationism—to fervent support for war was sudden and dramatic. Some former critics of intervention, seeking a persuasive explanation, turned to the popular children's story *Ferdinand the Bull*. Ferdinand, though huge and powerful, just liked to "sit and smell the flowers"—until the day he was stung by a bee. It was a comforting tale, but inaccurate. As the world went to war, the United States had not been, like Ferdinand, just "smell[ing] the flowers." America's embargo of shipments to Japan and refusal to accept Japan's expansionist policies had brought the two nations to the brink of war, and the United States was deeply involved in an undeclared naval war with Germany well before Japan's attack on Pearl Harbor. By December 1941, Roosevelt had long since instituted an unprecedented peacetime draft, created war mobilization agencies, and commissioned war plans for simultaneous struggle in Europe and the Pacific. America's entry into World War II was not a surprise.

Nonetheless, the nation was not ready for war. Throughout the 1930s, military funding had been a low priority. In September 1939 (when Hitler invaded Poland and began the Second World War), the U.S. Army ranked forty-fifth in size among the world's armies and could fully equip only one-third of its 227,000 men. A peacetime draft instituted in 1940 expanded the U.S.

**A Nation Unprepared**

▲ "MEN MAKE THE NAVY," proclaims this U.S. Navy recruiting booklet, which encourages men to enlist by highlighting the good pay, food, and shipmates, as well as the possibility of "fighting action." One hundred thousand women also responded to the navy's recruiting efforts by joining the WAVES. *(Private Collection)*

military to 2 million men, but Roosevelt's 1941 survey of war preparedness, the "Victory Plan," estimated that the United States could not be ready to fight before June 1943.

In December 1941, U.S. victory must have seemed unlikely. In Europe, the Allies were losing the war (see Map 26.3). Hitler had claimed Austria, Czechoslovakia, Poland, the Netherlands, Denmark, and Norway. Romania was lost, then Greece and Bulgaria. France had fallen in 1940. Britain fought on, but German planes rained bombs on London. More than 3 million soldiers under German command had penetrated deep into the Soviet Union and

Africa. German U-boats controlled the Atlantic from the Arctic to the Caribbean. Within months of America's entry into the war, German submarines sank 216 vessels—some so close to American shores that people could see the glow of burning ships.

In the Pacific, the war was largely America's to fight. The Soviets had not declared war on Japan, and although British troops protected Great Britain's Asian colonies, there were too few to make much difference. By late spring of 1942 Japan had captured most of the European colonial possessions in Southeast Asia: the Dutch East Indies (Indonesia), French Indochina (Vietnam), and the British colonies of Malaya, Burma, Western New Guinea, Hong Kong, and Singapore. In the American Philippines, the struggle went on longer, but also in vain. The Japanese attacked the Philippines hours after their success at Pearl Harbor and, finding the entire force of B-17 bombers sitting on the airfields, destroyed U.S. air capability in the region. American and Filipino troops retreated to the Bataan Peninsula, hoping to hold the main island, Luzon, but Japanese forces were superior. In March 1942, under orders from Roosevelt, General Douglas MacArthur, the commander of U.S. forces in the Far East, departed the Philippines for Australia, proclaiming, "I shall return."

Left behind were almost eighty thousand American and Filipino troops. Starving and weakened by disease, they held on for almost another month before surrendering. Those who survived long enough to surrender faced worse horror. The Japanese troops, lacking supplies themselves, were unprepared to deal with such a large number of prisoners, and most believed the prisoners had forfeited honorable treatment by surrendering. In what came to be known as the Bataan Death March, the Japanese force-marched their captives to prison camps 80 miles away. Guards denied the prisoners food and water, and bayoneted or beat to death those who fell behind. As many as ten thousand Filipinos and six hundred Americans died on the march. Filipino civilians suffered horribly. Tens of thousands of refugees and prisoners of war died under Japanese occupation.

As losses mounted, the United States began to strike back. On April 18, sixteen American B-25s appeared in the skies over Japan. The Doolittle raid (named after the mission's leader) did little harm to Japan, but it had an enormous psychological impact on Japanese leaders. The image of American bombers over Japan's home islands pushed Japanese commander Yamamoto to bold action. Instead of consolidating control close to home, Yamamoto concluded, Japan must move quickly to lure the weak-

**War in the Pacific**

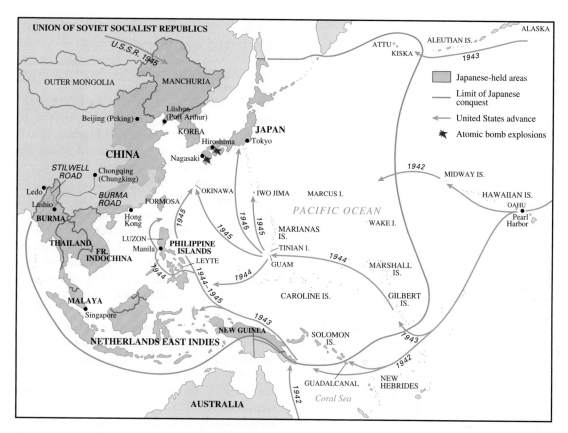

## Map 27.1    The Pacific War

The strategy of the United States was to "island-hop"—from Hawai'i in 1942 to Iwo Jima and Okinawa in 1945. Naval battles were also decisive, notably the Battles of the Coral Sea and Midway in 1942. The war in the Pacific ended with Japan's surrender on August 15, 1945 (V-J Day).

*(Source: Thomas G. Paterson, J. Garry Clifford, Kenneth J. Hagan,* American Foreign Policy: A History, *Vol. 2, 3d revised ed. Copyright © 1991 by D. C. Heath and Company. Used by permission of Houghton Mifflin Company.)*

ened United States into a "decisive battle." The target was Midway—two tiny islands about 1,000 miles northwest of Honolulu, where the U.S. Navy had a base. If Japan could take Midway—not implausible, given Japan's string of victories—it would have a secure defensive perimeter far from the home islands (see Map 27.1). By using Guam, the Philippines, and perhaps even Australia as hostages, Japan believed, it could negotiate a favorable peace agreement with the United States.

General Yamamoto did not know that America's MAGIC code-breaking machines could decipher Japanese messages. This time, surprise was on the side of the United States, as the Japanese fleet found the U.S. Navy and its carrier-based dive bombers lying in wait. The Battle of Midway in June 1942 was a turning point in the Pacific war. Japanese strategists had hoped that the United

States, discouraged by Japan's early victories, would withdraw and leave Japan to control the Pacific. That outcome was no longer a possibility. Now Japan was on the defensive.

Despite the importance of these early Pacific battles, America's war strategy was "Europe First." Germany,

### "Europe First" Strategy

American war planners recognized, was a greater danger to the United States than Japan. If Germany conquered the Soviet Union, they believed, it might directly threaten the United States. Roosevelt also feared that the Soviet Union, suffering almost unimaginable losses as its military battled Hitler's invading army, might pursue a separate peace with Germany and so undo the Allied coalition. Therefore, the United States would work first with Britain and the USSR to defeat Germany, then deal with an isolated Japan.

British prime minister Winston Churchill and Soviet premier Joseph Stalin disagreed vehemently, however, over how to wage the war against Germany. By late 1941, before the fierce Russian winter stalled their onslaught, German troops had nearly reached Moscow and Leningrad (present-day St. Petersburg) and had slashed deeply into Ukraine, taking Kiev. Over a million Soviet soldiers had died defending their country. Stalin pressed for British and American troops to attack Germany from the west, through France, to draw German troops away from the Soviet front. Roosevelt believed "with heart and *mind*" that Stalin was right and promised to open a "second front" to Germany's west before the end of 1942. Churchill, however, blocked this plan. He had not forgotten Stalin's nonaggression pact with Hitler (see page 754). More fundamentally, in large part because of experience with the agonies of prolonged trench warfare in World War I, British military commanders did not want a large-scale invasion of Europe. Churchill wanted to win control of the North Atlantic shipping lanes first and promoted air attacks on Germany. He also pushed for a smaller, safer attack on Axis positions in North Africa; halting the Germans there would protect British imperial possessions in the Mediterranean and the oil-rich Middle East.

Against his advisers' advice, Roosevelt accepted Churchill's plan. The U.S. military was not yet ready for a major campaign, and Roosevelt needed to show the American public some success in the European war. Thus, instead of coming to the rescue of the USSR, the British and Americans made a joint landing in North Africa in November 1942. American troops, facing relatively light resistance, won quick victories in Algeria and Morocco. In Egypt, the British confronted General Erwin Rommel and his Afrika Korps in a struggle for control of the Suez Canal and the Middle East oil fields. Rommel's army, trapped between British and American troops, surrendered after six months. And in Russia, against all odds, the Soviet army hung on, fighting block by block for control of Stalingrad in the deadly cold, to defeat the German Sixth Army in early 1943. Stalingrad, like Midway, was a major turning point in the war. By the spring of 1943, Germany, like Japan, was on the defensive. But relations among the Allies remained precarious. The Soviet Union had lost 1.1 million men in the Battle of Stalingrad. The United States and Britain, however, continued to resist Stalin's demand that they immediately open a second front. The death toll, already in the millions, continued to mount.

## THE PRODUCTION FRONT AND AMERICAN WORKERS

In late December 1940—almost a year before the United States entered the war—Franklin Roosevelt pledged that America would serve as the world's "great arsenal of democracy," making the machines that would win the war for the Allies. After Pearl Harbor, U.S. strategy remained much the same. The United States would prevail through a "crushing superiority of equipment," Roosevelt told Congress. Although the war would be fought on the battlefields of Europe and the Pacific, the nation's strategic advantage lay on the "production front" at home.

Goals for military production were staggering. In 1940, with war looming, American factories had built only 3,807 airplanes. Following Pearl Harbor, Roosevelt asked for 60,000 aircraft in 1942 and double that number in 1943. Plans called for the manufacture of 16 million tons of shipping and 120,000 tanks. The military needed supplies to train and equip a force that would grow to almost 16 million men. Thus, for the duration of the war, military production took precedence over the manufacture of civilian goods. Automobile plants built tanks and airplanes instead of cars; dress factories sewed military uniforms. The War Production Board, established by Roosevelt in early 1942, had the enormous task of allocating resources and coordinating production among thousands of independent factories.

During the war, American businesses overwhelmingly cooperated with government war-production plans.

**Businesses, Universities, and the War Effort**

Patriotism was one reason, but generous incentives were another. Major American industries had at first resisted government pressure to shift to military production. In 1940, as the United States produced armaments for the Allies, the American economy began to recover from the depression. Rising consumer spending built industrial confidence. Auto manufacturers, for example, expected to sell 4 million cars in 1941, a more than 25 percent increase over 1939. The massive retooling necessary to produce planes or tanks instead of cars would be enormously expensive and leave manufacturers totally dependent on a single client—the federal government. Moreover, many major industrialists, such as General Motors head Alfred Sloan, remained suspicious of Roosevelt and what they saw as his antibusiness policies.

Government, however, met business more than halfway. The federal government paid for expensive retooling and factory expansions; it guaranteed profits by allowing

GM
GENERAL MOTORS

PRODUCING MORE FOR VICTORY

*Folks*

"UNITED WE STAND"

JULY, 1942
VOL. 5    NO. 7

Dayton Presents Arms for Victory
Pageant "Plowshares"...Pages 2-5

▲ Unprepared to fight a war of such magnitude, the U.S. government turned to the nation's largest and most efficient corporations to produce the planes and ships and guns that would make America the "great arsenal of democracy," and General Motors received 8 percent of the value of all government war contracts. With no new cars to sell, GM continued to advertise in national magazines, proclaiming "Victory Is Our Business." Pictured here is GM's in-house magazine for employees, reminding these "production soldiers" of the importance of their work.

*(Courtesy, Collection of Peter Kreitler/General Motors)*

guarantee rapid, efficient production. From mid-1940 through September 1944 the government awarded contracts totaling $175 billion, with about two-thirds going to the top hundred corporations. General Motors alone received 8 percent of the total. This approach made sense for a nation that wanted enormous quantities of war goods manufactured in the shortest possible time; most small businesses just did not have the necessary capacity. However, wartime government contracts further consolidated American manufacturing in the hands of a few giant corporations.

Wartime needs also created a new relationship between science and the U.S. military. Millions of dollars went to fund research programs at America's largest universities: $117 million to Massachusetts Institute of Technology alone. Such federally sponsored research programs developed new technologies of warfare, such as vastly improved radar systems and the proximity fuse. The most important government-sponsored scientific research program was the Manhattan Project, a $2 billion secret effort to build an atomic bomb. Roosevelt had been convinced by scientists fleeing the Nazis in 1939 that Germany was working to create an atomic weapon, and he resolved to beat them at their own efforts. The Manhattan Project achieved the world's first sustained nuclear chain reaction in 1942 at the University of Chicago, and in 1943 the federal government set up a secret community for atomic scientists and their families at Los Alamos, New Mexico. In this remote, sparsely populated, and beautiful setting, some of America's most talented scientists worked with Jewish refugees from Nazi Germany to develop the weapon that would change the world.

**Manhattan Project**

America's new defense factories, running around the clock, required millions of workers. At first workers were plentiful: 9 million Americans were still unemployed in 1940 when war mobilization began, and 3 million remained without work in December 1941. But during the war, the armed forces took almost 16 million men out of the potential civilian labor pool, forcing industry to look elsewhere for workers. Women, African Americans, Mexican Americans, poor whites from the isolated mountain hollows of Appalachia and the tenant farms of the Deep South—all streamed into jobs in defense plants.

**New Opportunities for Workers**

In some cases, federal action eased their path. In 1941, as the federal government poured billions of dollars into war industries, many industries refused to hire

corporations to charge the government for production costs plus a fixed profit; it created generous tax write-offs and exemptions from antitrust laws. War mobilization did not require America's businesses to sacrifice profits. Instead, corporations doubled their net profits between 1939 and 1943. As Secretary of War Henry Stimson explained, when a "capitalist country" goes to war, it must "let business make money out of the process or business won't work."

Most military contracts went to America's largest corporations, which had the facilities and experience to

African Americans. "The Negro will be considered only as janitors and other similar capacities," one executive notified black applicants. A. Philip Randolph, head of the Brotherhood of Sleeping Car Porters, proposed a march on Washington, D.C., to demand equal access to defense industry jobs. Roosevelt, fearing that the march might provoke race riots and also that communists might infiltrate the movement, offered the March on Washington movement a deal. In exchange for canceling the march, the president issued Executive Order No. 8802, which prohibited discrimination in war industries and government jobs. The Fair Employment Practices Committee (FEPC) was established to ensure that its provisions were respected. Although enforcement was uneven, hundreds of thousands of black Americans migrated from the South to the industrial cities of the North and West on the strength of this official guarantee of job equality.

Mexican workers also filled wartime jobs in the United States. Although the U.S. government had deported Mexicans as unemployment rose during the Great Depression, about 200,000 Mexican farm workers, or *braceros,* were offered short-term contracts to fill agricultural jobs left vacant as Americans sought well-paid war work. Mexican and Mexican American workers alike faced discrimination and segregation, but they seized the economic opportunities newly available to them. In 1941 not a single Mexican American worked in the Los Angeles shipyards; by 1944, 17,000 were employed there.

Early in the war production boom, employers insisted that women were not suited for industrial jobs. But

### Women at Work

as labor shortages began to threaten the war effort, employers did an about-face. "Almost overnight," said Mary Anderson, head of the Women's Bureau of the Department of Labor, "women were reclassified by industrialists from a marginal to a basic labor supply for munitions making." Posters and billboards urged women to "Do the Job HE Left Behind." The government's War Manpower Commission glorified the invented worker "Rosie the Riveter," who was featured on posters, in magazines, and in the recruiting jingle "Rosie's got a boyfriend, Charlie / Charlie, he's a marine / Rosie is protecting Charlie / Working overtime on the riveting machine."

Rosie the Riveter was an inspiring image, but she did not accurately represent women in the American work force. Only 16 percent of women workers held jobs in defense plants, and only 4.4 percent of "skilled" jobs (such as riveting) were held by women. Nonetheless, during the war years, more than 6 million women entered the labor force, and the number of working women increased by 57 percent. More than 400,000 African American women left domestic service for higher-paying industrial jobs, often with union benefits. Seven million women moved to war-production areas, such as southern California, home of both shipyards and aircraft factories. And the majority of women workers who did not hold war-production jobs—whether they took traditional "women's jobs" as clerical workers or filled traditionally male jobs as bus drivers or even "lumberjills," as men left for military service or better-paid factory jobs—kept the American economy going and freed other workers for the demanding work in war-production plants.

Workers in defense plants were often expected to work ten days for every day off or to accept difficult night shifts. Recognizing the importance of keeping people on the job, both businesses and the federal government provided workers new forms of support. The West Coast Kaiser shipyards offered not only high pay, but also childcare, subsidized housing, and healthcare: the Kaiser Permanente Medical Care Program, a forerunner of the health maintenance organization (HMO), supplied medical care to workers for a weekly payroll deduction of 50 cents. The federal government also funded childcare centers and before- and after-school programs. At its peak, 130,000 preschoolers and 320,000 school-age children were enrolled in federally sponsored childcare.

Because industrial production was key to America's war strategy, the federal government attempted to make

### Organized Labor During Wartime

sure that labor strikes, so common in the 1930s, would not interrupt production. Less than a week after Pearl Harbor, a White House labor-management conference agreed to a no-strike/no-lockout pledge. In 1942 Roosevelt created the National War Labor Board (NWLB) to settle labor disputes. The NWLB forged a temporary compromise between labor union demands for a "closed shop," in which only union members could work, and management's desire for "open" shops. Workers could not be required to join a union, but unions could enroll as many members as possible. Between 1940 and 1945, union membership ballooned from 8.5 million to 14.75 million.

However, the government did not hesitate to restrict union power if it threatened war production. When coal miners in the United Mine Workers union went on strike in 1943, following an attempt by the NWLB to limit wage increases to a cost-of-living adjustment, lack of coal halted railroads and shut down steel mills. Few Americans supported this strike. An air force pilot said, "I'd just as soon shoot down one of those strikers as shoot

◀ War production plans called for defense factories to build 120,000 new aircraft in 1943. Here, women workers take on "men's jobs" at Vultee Aircraft Corporation, using riveting guns and bucking bars to build the center section of wings for training planes. *(© Corbis)*

440-foot-long cargo ships that transported the tanks and guns and bullets overseas—from 355 to 56 days. (As a publicity stunt, Kaiser's Richmond shipyard, near San Francisco, built one Liberty ship in 4 days, 15 hours, and 26 minutes.) The ships were not well made; welded hulls sometimes split in rough seas, and one ship foundered while still docked at the pier. However, as the United States struggled to produce cargo ships faster than German U-boats could sink them, speed of production was more important than quality.

A visitor to the Willow Run plant described "the roar of the machinery, the special din of the riveting gun absolutely deafening nearby, the throbbing crash of the giant metal presses . . . the far-reaching line of half-born skyships growing wings under swarms of workers." His words reveal the might of American industry but also offer a glimpse of the experience of workers, who did dirty, repetitive, and physically exhausting work day after day "for the duration." Although American propaganda during the war badly overstated the contributions of well-paid war workers as being equal to those of men in combat, the American production front played a critical role in winning the war.

## LIFE ON THE HOME FRONT

The United States was the only major combatant in World War II that did not experience warfare directly (Hawai'i was a U.S. territory and the Philippines a U.S. possession, but neither was part of the nation proper). Americans worried about loved ones fighting in distant places; they grieved over the loss of sons and brothers and fathers and husbands and friends. Their lives were disrupted. But the United States, protected by two oceans

down Japs—they're doing as much to lose the war for us." As antilabor sentiment grew, Congress passed the War Labor Disputes (Smith-Connally) Act. This act gave the president authority to seize and operate any strike-bound plant deemed necessary to the national security, but it also contained broad, punitive provisions that created criminal penalties for leading strikes and tried to constrain union power by prohibiting contributions to political campaigns during time of war.

For close to four years, American factories operated twenty-four hours a day, seven days a week, fighting the war on the production front.

### Success on the Production Front

Between 1940 and 1945, American factories turned out roughly 300,000 airplanes; 102,000 armored vehicles; 77,000 ships; 20 million small arms; 40 billion bullets; and 6 million tons of bombs. By war's end, the United States was producing 40 percent of the world's weaponry. This amazing feat depended on transforming formerly skilled work in industries like shipbuilding into an assembly-line process of mass production. Henry Ford, now seventy-eight years old, created a massive bomber plant on farmland along Willow Run Creek not far from Detroit. Willow Run's assembly lines, almost a mile long, turned out B-24 Liberator bombers at the rate of one an hour. On the West Coast, William Kaiser used mass-production techniques to cut construction time for Liberty ships—the huge,

from its enemies, was spared the war that other nations experienced. Bombs did not fall on American cities; invading armies did not burn and rape and kill. Instead, war mobilization ended the Great Depression and brought prosperity. American civilians experienced the paradox of good times amid global conflagration.

Although the war was distant, it was a constant presence in the lives of Americans on "the home front."

## Supporting the War Effort

Civilians supported the war effort in many ways, though Americans were never so unified or committed to shared sacrifice as the images of "the greatest generation" that were widespread in popular history and popular culture in the early twenty-first century suggest. During the war, however, families planted 20 million "victory gardens" to free up food supplies for the armed forces. Housewives saved fat from cooking and returned it to butchers, for cooking fat yielded glycerin to make black powder used in shells or bullets. Children collected scrap metal, aware that the iron in one old shovel blade was enough for four hand grenades and that every tin can helped make a tank or Liberty ship.

Many consumer goods were rationed or unavailable. To save wool for military use, the War Production Board basically redesigned men's suits, narrowing lapels, shortening jackets, and dispensing with vests and pant cuffs. Bathing suits, the WPB specified, must shrink by 10 percent. When silk and nylon were diverted from stockings to parachutes, women used makeup on their legs and drew in the "stocking" seam with eyebrow pencil. The Office of Price Administration (OPA), created by Congress in 1942, established a nationwide rationing system for such consumer goods as sugar, coffee, and gasoline. By early 1943, the OPA had instituted a point system for rationing food. Feeding a family required complex calculations. Every citizen—regardless of age—received two ration books each month. Blue stamps were for canned fruits and vegetables; red for meat, fish, and dairy. To buy a pound of meat, for example, consumers had to pay its cost in dollars and in points. With only 48 blue points and 64 red points per person per month, in September 1944 a small bottle of ketchup "cost" 20 blue points, while "creamery butter" cost 20 red points and sirloin steak 13 red points a pound. Pork shoulder, however, required only dollars. Sugar was tightly rationed, and people saved for months to make a birthday cake or holiday dessert. A black market existed, but most Americans understood that sugar produced alcohol for weapons manufacture and meat went to feed "our boys" overseas.

Despite near-unanimous support for the war, government leaders worried that, over time, public willingness

▲ In the days following the attack on Pearl Harbor, the Japanese were often pictured as subhuman—buck-toothed, nearsighted rodents and other vermin. Racial stereotyping would affect how both the Americans and the Japanese waged war. The Americans badly underestimated the Japanese, leaving themselves open for the surprise attack on Pearl Harbor and American forces in the Philippines. And the Japanese, believing Americans were barbarians who lacked a sense of honor, mistakenly expected that the United States would withdraw from East Asia once confronted with Japanese power and determination. *(Collier's, December 12, 1942)*

## Propaganda and Popular Culture

to sacrifice might lag. In 1942 Roosevelt created the Office of War Information (OWI), which took charge of domestic propaganda and hired Hollywood filmmakers and New York copywriters to sell the war at home. OWI posters exhorted Americans to save and sacrifice, and reminded them to watch what they said, for "loose lips sink ships."

Popular culture also reinforced wartime messages. A *Saturday Evening Post* advertisement for vacuum cleaners (unavailable for the duration) urged women war workers to fight "for freedom and all that means to women everywhere. You're fighting for a little house of your own, and a husband to meet every night at the door. You're fighting for the right to bring up your children without the shadow of fear." Popular songs urged Americans to "Remember December 7th" or to "Accentuate the Positive." Others made fun of America's enemies ("You're a sap, Mr. Jap / You make a Yankee cranky / You're a sap, Mr. Jap / Uncle Sam is gonna spanky") or, like "Cleanin' My Rifle (and Dreamin' of You)," dealt with the hardship of wartime separation.

Movies drew 90 million viewers a week in 1944—out of a total population of 132 million. Hollywood sought to meet Eleanor Roosevelt's challenge to "Keep 'em laughing." *A WAVE, a WAC, and a Marine* promised "no battle scenes, no message, just barrels of fun and jive to make you happy you're alive." Others, such as *Bataan* or *Wake Island*, portrayed actual—if sanitized—events in the war. Even at the most frivolous comedies, however, the war was always present. Theaters held "plasma premieres," offering free admission to those who donated a half-pint of blood to the Red Cross. Audiences rose to sing "The Star Spangled Banner," then watched newsreels featuring carefully censored footage of recent combat before the feature film began. On D-Day, June 6, 1944, as Allied troops landed at Normandy, theater managers across the nation led audiences in the Lord's Prayer or the Twenty-third Psalm ("The Lord is my shepherd . . ."). It was in movie theaters that Americans saw the horror of Nazi death camps in May 1945. The Universal newsreel narrator ordered audiences, "Don't turn away. Look."

The war demanded sacrifices from Americans, but it also rewarded them with new highs in personal income.

### Wartime Prosperity

Between 1939 and the end of the war, per capita income rose from $691 to $1,515. Wages and salaries increased more than 135 percent from 1940 to 1945. OPA-administered price controls kept inflation down so that wage increases did not disappear to higher costs. And with little to buy, savings rose.

Fighting World War II cost the United States approximately $304 billion (more than $3 trillion in today's dollars). Instead of financing the war primarily through taxation, the government relied on deficit spending, borrowing money in the form of war bonds sold to patriotic citizens and financial institutions. The national debt skyrocketed, from $49 billion in 1941 to $259 billion in 1945 (and was not paid off until 1970). However, wartime revenue acts increased the number of Americans paying personal income tax from 4 million to 42.6 million—at rates ranging from 6 to 94 percent—and introduced a new system in which employers "withheld" taxes from employee paychecks. For the first time, individual Americans paid more in taxes than corporations.

Despite hardships and fears, the war offered home-front Americans new opportunities, and millions of Americans took them. More than 15 million civilians moved during the war (see Map 27.2). More than half moved to another state, and half that number moved to another region. Seven hundred thousand black Americans left the South during the war years; in 1943, ten thousand black migrants poured into Los Angeles every month. People who had never traveled farther than the next county found themselves on the other side of the country—or of the world. People moved for defense jobs or to be close to loved ones at stateside military postings. Southerners moved north, northerners moved south, and 1.5 million people moved to California.

### A Nation in Motion

The rapid influx of war workers to major cities and small towns strained community resources. Migrants crowded into substandard housing—even woodsheds, tents, or cellars—and into trailer parks without adequate sanitary facilities. Disease spread: scabies and ringworm, polio, tuberculosis. Many long-term residents found the newcomers—especially the unmarried male war workers—a rough bunch. In the small town of Lawrence, Kansas, civic leaders bragged of the economic boost a new war plant gave the town but fretted over the appearance of bars, "dirty windowed dispensaries" that sold alcohol to the war workers.

In and around Detroit, where car factories now produced tanks and planes, established residents called war workers freshly arrived from southern Appalachia "hillbillies" and "white trash." A new joke circulated: "How many states are there in the Union? Forty-five. Tennessee and Kentucky moved to Michigan, and Michigan went to hell." Many of these migrants knew little about urban life. One young man from rural Tennessee, unfamiliar with traffic lights and street signs, navigated by counting the number of trees between his home and the war plant where he worked. Some Appalachian "trailer-ites" appalled their neighbors by building outdoor privies or burying garbage in their yards.

As people from different backgrounds confronted one another under difficult conditions, tensions rose. Widespread racism made things worse. In 1943 almost 250 racial conflicts exploded in forty-seven cities. Outright racial warfare bloodied the streets of Detroit in June. White mobs, undeterred by police, roamed the city attacking blacks. Blacks hurled rocks at police and dragged white passengers off streetcars. At

### Racial Conflicts

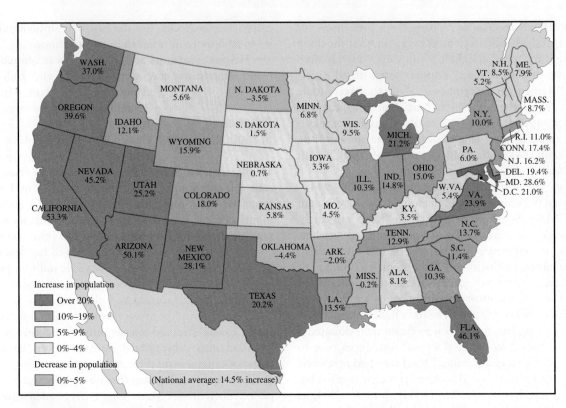

**Map 27.2   A Nation on the Move, 1940–1950**

American migration during the 1940s was the largest on record to that time. The farm population dropped dramatically as men, women, and children moved to war-production areas and to army and navy bases, particularly on the West Coast. Well over 30 million Americans (civilian and military) migrated during the war. Many returned to their rural homes after the war, but 12 million migrants stayed in their new locations. Notice the population increases on the West Coast, as well as in the Southwest and Florida.

the end of thirty hours of rioting, twenty-five blacks and nine whites lay dead. Surveying the damage, an elderly black woman said, "There ain't no North anymore. Everything now is South."

The heightened racial and ethnic tensions of wartime also led to riots in Los Angeles in 1943. Young Mexican American gang members, or *pachucos*, had adopted the zoot suit: a long jacket with wide padded shoulders, loose pants "pegged" below the knee, a wide-brimmed hat, and dangling watch chain. With cloth rationed, wearing pants requiring five yards of fabric was a political statement, and some young men wore the zoot suit as a purposeful rejection of wartime ideals of service and sacrifice. Although in fact a high percentage of Mexican Americans served in the armed forces, many white servicemen believed otherwise. Racial tensions were not far from the surface in overcrowded L.A., and rumors that *pachucos*

had attacked white sailors quickly led to violence. For four days, mobs of white men—mainly soldiers and sailors—roamed the streets attacking zoot-suiters and stripping them of their clothes. The city of Los Angeles outlawed zoot suits and arrested men who wore them. The "zoot suit riots" ended only when naval personnel were removed from the city.

The dislocations of war also had profound impacts on the nation's families. Despite policies that exempted married men and fathers from the draft during most of the war, almost 3 million families were broken up. Young children grew up not knowing their father. The divorce rate of 16 per 1,000 marriages in 1940 almost doubled to 27 per 1,000 in 1944. At the same time, hundreds of thousands of men and women were getting married.

### Families in Wartime

▲ Members of the Vega family pose for the camera in uniforms of the Marine Corps, National Guard, and U.S. Navy.

*(Los Angeles Public Library)*

The number of marriages rose from 73 per 1,000 unmarried women in 1939 to 93 in 1942. Some couples scrambled to get married before the man was sent overseas; others sought military deferments. The birth rate climbed as well: 2.4 million babies were born in 1939 and 3.1 million in 1943. Many were "goodbye babies," conceived to guarantee the continuation of the family if the father died in war.

On college campuses, some virtually stripped of male students, women complained, along with the song lyrics, "There is no available male." But other young women found an abundance of male company, sparking concern about wartime threats to sexual morality. *Youth in Crisis,* a 1943 newsreel, featured a girl with "experience far beyond her age" necking with a soldier on the street. These "victory girls" or "cuddle bunnies" were said to support the war effort by giving their all to men in uniform. Many young men and women, caught up in the emotional intensity of war, behaved as they never would in peacetime.

Often that meant hasty marriages to virtual strangers, especially if a baby was on the way. Taboos against unwed motherhood remained strong, however, and babies born outside marriage increased only from 0.7 percent to 1 percent of all births. Wartime mobility also increased opportunities for young men and women to explore sexual attraction to members of the same sex, and gay communities grew in such cities as San Francisco.

In many ways, the war reinforced traditional gender roles that had been weakened during the depression, when many men lost the role of breadwinner. Now men defended their nation while women "kept the home fires burning." Some women took "men's jobs," but those few who did so from patriotism rather than need understood their work to be "for the duration"—the home-front equivalent to men's wartime military service. Even so, women who worked were frequently blamed for neglecting their children and creating an "epidemic" of juvenile delinquency—evidenced by the "victory girl." Nonetheless, millions of women took on new responsibilities in wartime, whether on the factory floor or within their family. Many husbands returned to find that the lives of their wives and children seemed complete without them, and some women realized how much they had enjoyed their greater freedom and independence.

## THE LIMITS OF AMERICAN IDEALS

During the war, the U.S. government worked hard to explain to its citizens the reasons for their sacrifices. In 1941 Roosevelt had pledged America to defend "four essential human freedoms"—freedom of speech, freedom of religion, freedom from want, and freedom from fear—and government-sponsored films contrasted democracy and totalitarianism, freedom and fascism, equality and oppression.

Despite such confident proclamations, as America fought the totalitarian regimes of the Axis powers, the nation confronted questions with no easy answers: What limits on civil liberties were justified in the interest of national security? How freely could information flow to the nation's citizens without revealing military secrets to the enemy and costing American lives? How could the United States protect itself against the threat of spies or saboteurs, especially from German, Italian, or Japanese citizens living in the United States? And what about America's ongoing domestic problems—particularly the problem of race? Could the nation address its own citizens' demands for reform as it fought the war against the Axis? The answers to these questions often revealed tensions between the nation's democratic ideals and its wartime practices.

## War Brides

During and immediately after World War II, more than 60,000 American servicemen married women from other nations, both those the United States had fought alongside and those it had fought against. The U.S. government promised these servicemen that it would deliver their wives and babies to their doorstep, free of charge.

The U.S. Army's "Operation War Bride," which would eventually transport more than 70,000 women and children, began in Britain in early 1946. The first group of war brides—455 British women and their 132 children—arrived in the United States on February 4, 1946. As the former World War II transport *Argentina* sailed into New York harbor in the predawn darkness, the Statue of Liberty was specially illuminated to greet them. Women who had sung, "There'll Always Be an England" as they set sail from Southampton, England, gathered on the deck to attempt "The Star-Spangled Banner." These women, many of them teenagers, had left their homes and families behind to join their new husbands in a strange land. Mrs. Edna Olds Butler, "nearly seventeen," practiced a southern accent in hopes that her new in-laws in Roanoke Rapids, North Carolina, would be able to understand her. Two young British women had married African American soldiers, and one carried with her a letter from her husband promising that she would be the "white queen of Atlanta."

War brides fanned out to every state of the Union. Women from war-destroyed cities were impressed by the material abundance of American society and pleased by the warm welcome they received. But America's racial prejudice shocked Shanghai native Helen Chia Wong, wife of Staff Sgt. Albert Wong of the Fourteenth Air Force Service Command, when she and her husband were turned away from a house by a rental agent with the explanation "The neighbors wouldn't like it." The file of one young woman who sought passage back to England showed another kind of distress. An American official recorded that she was "too shocked to bring her baby up on the black tracks of a West Virginia [coal] mining town as against her own home in English countryside of rose-covered fences." It was not always easy, but most of the war brides settled into their new families and communities, becoming part of their new nation and helping to forge an intimate link between America and other nations of the world.

▲ The army's "Operation War Bride" (sometimes called "Operation Mother-in-Law" or "the Diaper Run") began in Britain in early 1946. Employing eleven former World War II troopships, including the *Queen Mary,* the U.S. government relocated the wives and babies of U.S. servicemen from dozens of nations to the United States. These English war brides, with babies their fathers have not yet seen, are waiting to be reunited with their husbands in Massachusetts, Missouri, and Iowa. *(© Bettmann/Corbis)*

For the most part, America handled the issue of civil liberties well. American leaders embraced a "strategy of truth," declaring that citizens of a democratic nation required a truthful accounting of the war's progress. However, the government closely controlled information about military matters. Censorship was serious business, as even seemingly unimportant details might tip off enemies about troop movements or invasion plans. Government-created propaganda sometimes dehumanized the enemy. Nonetheless, the American government resorted to hate mongering much less frequently than during the First World War.

More complex was the question of how to handle dissent and how to guard against the possibility that enemy agents were operating within the nation's borders. The Alien Registration (Smith) Act, passed in 1940, made it unlawful to advocate the overthrow of the U.S. government by force or violence, or to join any organization that did so. After Pearl Harbor, the government used this authority to take thousands of Germans, Italians, and other Europeans into custody as suspected spies and potential traitors. During the war, the government interned 14,426 Europeans in Enemy Alien Camps. Fearing subversion, the government also prohibited ten thousand Italian Americans from living or working in restricted zones along the California coast, including San Francisco and Monterey Bay.

In March 1942, Roosevelt ordered that all 112,000 foreign-born Japanese and Japanese Americans living in California, Oregon, and the state of Washington (the vast majority of the mainland population) be removed from the West Coast to "relocation centers" for the duration of the war. Each of the Italian and German nationals interned by the U.S. government faced specific, individual charges. That was not the case for Japanese nationals and Japanese Americans. They were imprisoned as a group, under suspicion solely because they were of Japanese descent.

### Internment of Japanese Americans

American anger at Japan's "sneak attack" on Pearl Harbor fueled the calls for internment, as did fears that West Coast cities might yet come under enemy attack. Long-standing racism was evident, as the chief of the Western Defense Command warned, "The Japanese race is an enemy race." Finally, people in economic competition with Japanese Americans strongly supported internment. Although Japanese nationals were forbidden to gain U.S. citizenship or own property, American-born Nissei (second generation) and Sansei (third generation), all U.S. citizens, were increasingly successful in business and agriculture. The relocation order forced Japanese Americans

▲ In February 1942 President Franklin D. Roosevelt ordered that all Japanese resident aliens and Japanese Americans living on the West Coast—about 110,000 people—be confined in remote "internment camps." Residents were not allowed to take photographs, but many tried to illustrate their experiences. This watercolor, "First Impressions of Manzanar," shows internees' constant struggle against the harsh desert climate, with its high winds, swirling dust, and extreme temperatures. Manzanar War Relocation Camp was located in California, at the foot of the Sierra Nevadas. The eight guard towers that surrounded the camp were manned by military police with submachine guns.

*(Gift of Tango Takamura, Department of Special Collections Charles E. Young Research Library, UCLA)*

to sell property valued at $500 million for a fraction of its worth. West Coast Japanese Americans also lost their positions in the truck-garden, floral, and fishing industries.

The internees were sent to flood-damaged lands at Relocation, Arkansas; to the intermountain terrain of Wyoming and the desert of western Arizona; and to other arid and desolate spots in the West. The camps were bleak and demoralizing. Behind barbed wire stood tarpapered wooden barracks where entire families lived in a single room furnished only with cots, blankets, and a bare light bulb. Toilets and dining and bathing facilities were communal; privacy was almost nonexistent. In such difficult circumstances, people nonetheless attempted to sustain community life, setting up schools for the children and clubs for adults.

Betrayed by their government, almost 6,000 internees renounced U.S. citizenship and demanded to be sent to Japan. Some sought legal remedy, but the Supreme Court upheld the government's action in *Korematsu v. U.S.* (1944). Still others sought to demonstrate their loyalty. The all–Japanese American 442nd Regimental Combat Team, drawn heavily from young men in internment camps, was the most decorated unit of its size. Suffering heavy casualties in Italy and France, members of the 442nd were awarded a Congressional Medal of Honor, 47 Distinguished Service Crosses, 350 Silver Stars, and more than 3,600 Purple Hearts. In 1988 Congress issued a public apology and largely symbolic payment of $20,000 to each of the 60,000 surviving Japanese American internees.

As America mobilized for war, some African American leaders attempted to force the nation to confront the

### African Americans and "Double V"

uncomfortable parallels between the racist doctrines of the Nazis and the persistence of Jim Crow segregation in the United States. Proclaiming a "Double V" campaign (victory at home and abroad), groups such as the National Association for the Advancement of Colored People (NAACP) hoped to "persuade, embarrass, compel and shame our government and our nation . . . into a more enlightened attitude toward a tenth of its people." Membership in civil rights organizations soared. The NAACP, 50,000 strong in 1940, had 450,000 members by 1946. And in 1942 civil rights activists, influenced by the philosophy of India's Mohandas Gandhi, founded the Congress of Racial Equality (CORE), which stressed "nonviolent direct action" and staged sit-ins to desegregate restaurants and movie theaters in Chicago and Washington, D.C.

Military service was a key issue for African Americans, who understood the traditional link between the duty to defend one's country and the rights of full citizenship. But the U.S. military remained segregated by race and strongly resisted efforts to use black units as combat troops. As late as 1943, less than 6 percent of the armed forces were African American, compared with more than 10 percent of the population. The marines at first refused to accept African Americans at all, and the navy approximated segregation by assigning black men to service positions in which they would rarely interact with nonblacks as equals or superiors.

Why did the United States fight a war for democracy with a segregated military? The U.S. military understood

### A Segregated Military

that its sole priority was to stop the Axis and win the war, and the federal government and War Department decided that the midst of world war was no time to try to integrate the armed forces. The majority of Americans (approximately 89 percent of Americans were white) opposed integration, many of them vehemently. As a sign of how deeply racist beliefs penetrated the United States, the Red Cross segregated blood plasma during the war.

▲ During World War II, for the first time, the War Department sanctioned the training and use of African American pilots. These members of the 99th Pursuit Squadron—known as "Tuskegee Airmen" because they trained at Alabama's all-black Tuskegee Institute—joined combat over North Africa in June 1943. Like most African American units in the racially segregated armed forces, the men of the 99th Pursuit Squadron were under the command of white officers. *(National Archives)*

In most southern states, racial segregation was not simply custom; it was the law. Integration of military installations and training camps, the majority of which were in the South, would have provoked a crisis as federal power contradicted state law. Pointing to outbreaks of racial violence in southern training camps as evidence, government and military officials argued that wartime integration would almost certainly provoke even more racial violence, create disorder within the military, and hinder America's war effort. Such resistance might have been short-term, but the War Department did not take that chance. Justifying its decision, the War Department argued that it could not "act outside the law, nor contrary to the will of the majority of the citizens of the Nation." General George C. Marshall, Army Chief of Staff, proclaimed that it was not the job of the army to "solve a social problem that has perplexed the American people throughout the history of this nation. . . . The army is not a sociological laboratory." Hopes for racial justice, so long deferred, were another casualty of the war.

Despite such discrimination, many African Americans stood up for their rights. Lt. Jackie Robinson refused to move to the back of the bus while training at the army's Camp Hood, Texas, in 1944—and faced court-martial, even though military regulations forbade racial discrimination on military vehicles, regardless of local law or custom. Black sailors disobeyed orders to return to work after surviving an explosion that destroyed two ships, killed 320 men, and shattered windows 35 miles away—an explosion caused by the navy practice of assigning men who were completely untrained in handling high explosives to load bombs from the munitions depot at Port Chicago, near San Francisco, onto Liberty ships. When they were court-martialed for mutiny, future Supreme Court justice and chief counsel for the NAACP Thurgood Marshall asked why only black sailors did this work. He proclaimed, "This is not fifty men on trial for mutiny. This is the Navy on trial for its whole vicious policy toward Negroes."

As the war wore on, African American servicemen did fight on the front lines, and fought well. The Marine Corps commandant in the Pacific proclaimed that "Negro Ma-

rines are no longer on trial. They are Marines, period." The "Tuskegee Airmen," pilots trained at the Tuskegee Institute in Alabama, saw heroic service in all-black units, such as the Ninety-ninth Pursuit Squadron, which won eighty Distinguished Flying Crosses. After the war, African Americans—as some white Americans had feared—called on their wartime service to claim the full rights of citizenship. Black men and women shared fully in the benefits offered to veterans under the GI Bill (see page 827). African Americans' wartime experiences were mixed, but the war was a turning point in the movement for equal rights.

## America and the Holocaust

America's inaction in the face of what we now call the Holocaust is a tragic failure, though the consequences are clearer in retrospect than they were at the time. As the United States turned away refugees on the *St. Louis* (page 753) in early 1939 and refused to relax its immigration quotas to admit European Jews and others fleeing Hitler's Germany, almost no one foresaw that the future would bring death camps like Auschwitz or Treblinka. Americans knew they were turning away people fleeing dire persecution, and while anti-Semitism played a significant role in that decision, it was not unusual to refuse those seeking refuge, especially in the midst of a major economic crisis that seemed to be worsening.

As early as 1942, American newspapers reported the "mass slaughter" of Jews and other "undesirables" (Gypsies, homosexuals, the physically and mentally handicapped) under Hitler. Many Americans, having been taken in by manufactured atrocity tales during World War I,

◀ Millions of civilians were starved, gassed, machine gunned, or worked to death by their Nazi jailers during the war. Here, U.S. Army troops force Nazi Party members to exhume the bodies of two hundred Russian officers and others who were shot by the SS near Wuelfel, while the residents of Hannover watch. Allied troops often compelled local townspeople to watch exhumations of mass graves, attempting to make them confront the atrocities that many insisted they never knew were happening.

*(United States Holocaust Memorial Museum)*

wrongly discounted these stories. But Roosevelt knew about the existence of Nazi death camps capable of killing up to two thousand people an hour using the gas Zyklon-B.

In 1943 British and American representatives met in Bermuda to discuss the situation but took no concrete action. Many Allied officials, though horrified, saw Hitler's "Final Solution" as just one part of a larger, worldwide holocaust in which tens of millions were dying. Appalled by the reluctance to act, Secretary of the Treasury Henry Morgenthau Jr. charged that the State Department's foot dragging made the United States an accessory to murder. "The matter of rescuing the Jews from extermination is a trust too great to remain in the hands of men who are indifferent, callous, and perhaps even hostile," he wrote bitterly in 1944. Later that year, stirred by Morgenthau's well-documented plea, Roosevelt created the War Refugee Board, which set up refugee camps in Europe and played a crucial role in saving 200,000 Jews from death. But, lamented one American official, "by that time it was too damned late to do too much." By war's end, the Nazis had systematically murdered almost 11 million people.

## LIFE IN THE MILITARY

More than 15 million men and approximately 350,000 women served in the U.S. armed forces during World War II. Eighteen percent of American families had a father, son, or brother in the armed forces. Some of these men (and all of the women) volunteered, eager to defend their nation. But most who served—more than 10 million— were draftees. By presidential order, the military stopped accepting volunteers in December 1942. Faced with the challenge of filling a broad range of military positions while maintaining war production and the civilian economy, the Selective Service system and the new War Manpower Commission attempted to centralize control over the allocation of manpower. Their efforts were often defeated as tensions between local and national control remained strong throughout the war. Most Americans, however, believed that the draft operated fairly. Compared with the Civil War and the Vietnam War, the draft reached broadly and mostly equitably through the American population during World War II.

The Selective Service Act did allow deferments, but they did not disproportionately benefit the well-to-do.

||||||||||||||||||||||||||||||||||||

**Selective Service**

Almost 10,000 Princeton students or alumni served—as did all 4 of Franklin and Eleanor Roosevelt's sons—while throughout the nation judges offered minor criminal offenders the choice of the military or jail. The small number of college deferments was more than balanced by deferments for a long list of "critical occupations," including not only war industry workers but also almost 2 million agricultural workers. Most exemptions from military service were for men deemed physically or mentally unqualified to serve. Army physicians discovered what a toll the depression had taken on the nation's youth as draftees arrived with rotted teeth and deteriorated eyesight—signs of malnutrition. Army dentists pulled 15 million teeth and fitted men with dentures; optometrists prescribed 2.5 million pairs of glasses. Hundreds of thousands of men with venereal diseases were cured by sulfa drugs, developed in 1942. Military examiners also found evidence of the impact of racism and poverty. Half of African American draftees had no schooling beyond the sixth grade, and up to one-third were functionally illiterate. Forty-six percent of African Americans and almost one-third of European-Americans called for the draft were classified "4-F"—unfit for service.

Nonetheless, almost 12 percent of America's total population served in the military. Regiments were created rapidly, throwing together men from very different backgrounds. Regional differences were profound, and northerners and southerners often—literally—could not understand one another. Ethnic differences complicated things further. Although African Americans and Japanese Americans served in their own separate units, Hispanics, Native Americans, and Chinese Americans served in "white" units. Furthermore, the differences among "whites"—the "Italian" kid from Brooklyn and the one from rural Mississippi (or rural Montana)—were profound. The result was often tension, but many Americans became less prejudiced and less provincial as they served with men unlike themselves.

Although military service was widespread, the burdens of combat were not equally shared. Although women served their nation honorably and often courageously, women's roles in the U.S. military were much more restricted than in the British or Soviet militaries, where women served as anti-aircraft gunners and in other combat-related positions. U.S. women served as nurses, in communications offices, and as typists or cooks. The recruiting slogan for the WACs (Women's Army Corps) was "Release a Man for Combat." However, most men in the armed forces never saw combat either; one-quarter never left the United States. The United States had the lowest "teeth-to-tail" ratio of any of the combatants, with each combat soldier backed up by eight or more support personnel. Japan's ratio was

||||||||||||||||||||||||||||||||

**Fighting the War**

close to one to one. One-third of U.S. military personnel served in clerical positions, with well-educated men most likely to be slotted into noncombat positions. African Americans, though assigned dirty and dangerous tasks, were largely kept from combat service. In World War II, lower-class, less-educated white men bore the brunt of the fighting.

For those who fought, combat in World War II was as horrible as anything humans have experienced. Home-front audiences for the war films Hollywood churned out saw men die bravely, shot cleanly through the heart and comforted by their buddies in their last moments. What men experienced was carnage. Less than 10 percent of casualties were caused by bullets. Most men were killed or wounded by mortars, bombs, or grenades. Seventy-five thousand American men remained missing in action at the end of the war, blown into fragments of flesh too small to identify. Combat meant days and weeks of unrelenting rain in malarial jungles, sliding down a mud-slicked hill to land in a pile of putrid corpses. It meant drowning in the waters of the frigid North Atlantic amid burning wreckage of a torpedoed ship. It meant using flamethrowers that burned at 2,000 degrees Fahrenheit on other human beings. It meant being violently ill on a landing craft steering through floating body parts of those who had attempted the landing first, knowing that if you tripped you would likely drown under the sixty-eight-pound weight of your pack, and that if you made it ashore you would likely be blown apart by artillery shells. Service was "for the duration" of the war. Only death, serious injury, or victory offered release. In this hard world, men fought to victory.

In forty-five months of war, close to 300,000 American servicemen died in combat. Almost 1 million American troops were wounded, half of them seriously. Medical advances, such as the development of penicillin and the use of blood plasma to prevent shock, helped wounded men survive—but many never fully recovered from those wounds. Between 20 and 30 percent of combat casualties were psychoneurotic, as men were pushed past the limits of endurance. The federal government strictly censored images of American combat deaths for most of the war, consigning them to a secret file known as "the chamber of horrors." Americans at home rarely understood what combat had been like, and many men, upon return, never talked about their experiences in the war.

## WINNING THE WAR

Axis hopes for victory depended on a short war. Leaders in Germany and Japan knew that, if the United States

had time to fully mobilize, flooding the theaters of war with armaments and reinforcing Allied troops with fresh, trained men, the war was lost. However, powerful factions in the Japanese military and German leadership believed that the United States would concede if it met with early, decisive defeats. As Hitler, blinded by racial arrogance, had stated shortly after declaring war on the United States, "I don't see much future for the Americans. . . . It's a decayed country. . . . American society [is] half Judaized, and the other half Negrified. How can one expect a State like that to hold together." By mid-1942 the Axis powers understood that they had underestimated not only American resolve but also the willingness of other Allies to sacrifice unimaginable numbers of their citizens to stop the Axis advance (see Map 27.3). The chance of an Axis victory grew increasingly slim as the months passed, but though the outcome was virtually certain after spring 1943, two years of bloody fighting lay ahead.

As the war continued, the Allies concentrated on defeating the aggressors, but their suspicions of one another undermined cooperation. The Soviets continued to press Britain and the United States to open a second front to the west of Germany and so draw German troops away from the USSR. The United States and Britain, however, continued to delay. Stalin was not mollified by the massive "thousand-bomber" raids on Germany begun by Britain's Royal Air Force in 1942, nor by the Allied invasion of Italy in the summer of 1943. With the alliance badly strained, Roosevelt sought reconciliation through personal diplomacy. The three Allied leaders met in Teheran, Iran, in December 1943. Stalin dismissed Churchill's repetitive justifications for further delaying a second front that would draw German troops away from the Soviet Union. Roosevelt had had enough, too; he also rejected Churchill's proposal for another peripheral attack, this time through the Balkans to Vienna. The three finally agreed to launch Operation Overlord—the cross-Channel invasion of France—in early 1944. And the Soviet Union promised to aid the Allies against Japan once Germany was defeated.

**Tensions Among the Allies**

The second front opened in the dark morning hours of June 6, 1944: D-Day. In the largest amphibious landing in history, more than 140,000 Allied troops under the command of American general Dwight D. Eisenhower scrambled ashore at Normandy, France. Thousands of ships ferried the men within one hundred yards of the sandy beaches. Landing craft and soldiers immediately encountered the enemy; they triggered mines and were pinned down by fire from

**War in Europe**

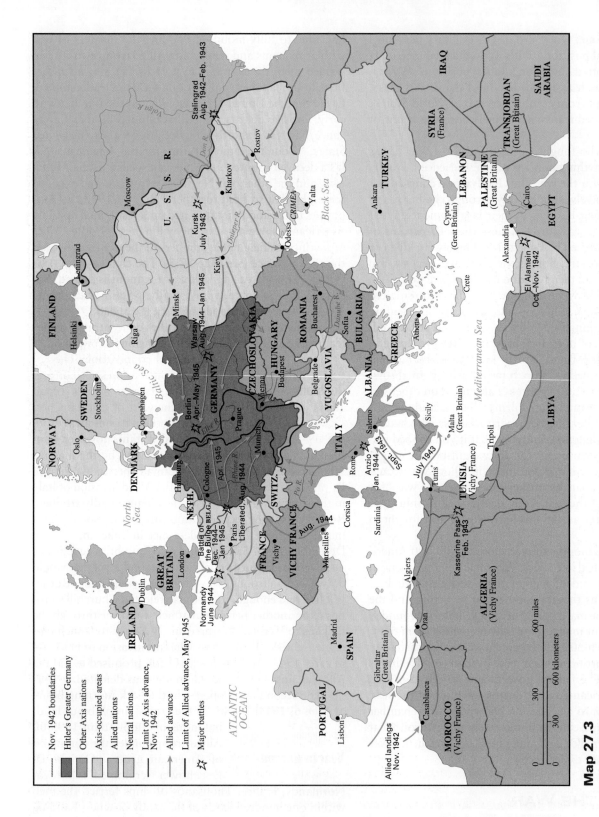

**Map 27.3**

**The Allies on the Offensive in Europe, 1942–1945**

The United States pursued a "Europe First" policy: first defeat Germany, then focus on Japan. American military efforts began in North Africa in late 1942 and ended in Germany in 1945 on May 8 (V-E Day).

▲ U.S. troops land at Normandy during the D-Day invasion on June 6, 1944. Men drowned as they lost their footing in the rough surf and were pulled under by the weight of their 68-pound packs; others were torn by artillery or machine gun fire from German gun batteries on the cliffs that rose steeply from the beaches. About 2500 Allied troops died in the D-Day invasion. Together, Allied and German troops suffered more than 450,000 casualties (killed, missing, or wounded) during the Battle of Normandy, which lasted until the end of August. *(Robert Capa/Magnum Photos, Inc.)*

cliffside pillboxes. Meanwhile, 15,500 Allied airborne troops, along with thousands of dummies meant to confuse the German defense, dropped from aircraft. Although heavy aerial and naval bombardment and the clandestine work of saboteurs had softened the German defenses, the fighting was ferocious.

By the end of June 11, 170,000 more Allied troops were fighting in France. They spread across the countryside, liberating France and Belgium by the end of August. Almost 54,000 Allied troops died in that struggle, and up to 20,000 French civilians were killed, most by Allied bombing. In September the Allies pushed into Germany. German armored divisions counterattacked in Belgium's Ardennes Forest in December, hoping to push on to

Antwerp to halt the flow of Allied supplies through that Belgian port. After weeks of heavy fighting in what has come to be called the Battle of the Bulge—because of a "bulge" 60 miles deep and 40 miles wide where German troops had pushed back the Allied line—the Allies gained control in late January 1945.

By that point, "strategic" bombing (though not nearly as precise as was publicly claimed) had destroyed Germany's war-production capacity and devastated its economy. In early 1945, the British and Americans began "morale" bombing, killing tens of thousands of civilians in aerial attacks on Berlin and then Dresden. Meanwhile, battle-hardened Soviet troops marched through Poland and cut a path to Berlin. American forces crossed the

Rhine River in March 1945 and captured the heavily industrial Ruhr valley. Several units peeled off to enter Austria and Czechoslovakia, where they met up with Soviet soldiers.

Even as Allied forces faced the last, desperate resistance from German troops in the Battle of the Bulge, Allied leaders began planning the peace. In early 1945, Franklin Roosevelt, by this time very ill, called for a summit meeting to discuss a host of political questions— including what to do with Germany. The three Allied leaders met at Yalta, in the Russian Crimea, in February 1945. Each had definite goals for the shape of the postwar world. Britain, its formerly powerful empire now vulnerable and shrinking, sought to protect its colonial possessions and to limit Soviet power. The Soviet Union, with 21 million dead, wanted Germany to pay reparations to fund its massive rebuilding effort. The Soviets hoped to expand their sphere of influence throughout eastern Europe and to guarantee their national security; Germany, Stalin insisted, must be permanently weakened. Two German invasions in a quarter-century were more than enough.

**Yalta Conference**

The United States, like the other powers, hoped to expand its influence and to control the peace. To that end, Roosevelt lobbied for the United Nations Organization, approved in principle the previous year at Dumbarton Oaks in Washington, D.C., through which the United States hoped to exercise influence. The lessons of World War I also shaped American proposals; seeking long-term peace and stability, the United States hoped to avoid the debts-reparations fiasco that had plagued Europe after the First World War. U.S. goals included self-determination for liberated peoples; gradual and orderly decolonization; and management of world affairs by what Roosevelt had once called the Four Policemen: the Soviet Union, Great Britain, the United States, and China. (Roosevelt hoped China might help stabilize Asia after the war; the United States abolished the Chinese Exclusion Act in 1943 in an attempt to consolidate ties between the two nations.) The United States was also determined to limit Soviet influence in the postwar world. Obviously, there was much about which to disagree.

Military positions at the time of the Yalta conference helped shape the negotiations. Soviet troops occupied eastern European nations that they had liberated, including Poland, where Moscow had installed a pro-Soviet regime despite a British-supported Polish government-in-exile in London. With Soviet troops in place in eastern Europe, Britain and the United States were limited in what they could negotiate regarding these lands. As for Germany, the Big Three agreed that some eastern German territory would be transferred to Poland and the remainder divided into four zones—the fourth zone to be administered by France, which Britain had pressed to be included in plans for postwar control of Germany, so as to reduce the Soviet zone from one-third to one-quarter. Berlin, within the Soviet zone, would also be divided among the four victors. Yalta marked the high point of the Grand Alliance; in the tradition of diplomatic give-

The three Allied leaders—Winston ▶ Churchill, Franklin D. Roosevelt, and Joseph Stalin—met at Yalta in February 1945. Having been president for twelve years, Roosevelt showed signs of age and fatigue. Two months later, he died of a massive cerebral hemorrhage. *(Franklin D. Roosevelt Library)*

and-take, each of the Allies came away with something it wanted. In exchange for U.S. promises to support Soviet claims on territory lost to Japan in the Russo-Japanese War of 1904–1905, Stalin agreed to sign a treaty of friendship with Jiang Jieshi (Chiang Kai-shek), America's ally in China, rather than with the communist Mao Zedong (Mao Tse-tung), and to declare war on Japan two or three months after Hitler's defeat.

Franklin D. Roosevelt, reelected to an unprecedented fourth term in November 1944, did not live to see the war's end. He died on April 12, and Vice President Harry S. Truman became president and commander-in-chief. Truman, a senator from Missouri who had replaced former vice president Henry Wallace as Roosevelt's running mate in 1944, was inexperienced in foreign policy. He was not even informed about the top-secret atomic weapons project until after he became president. The day after Roosevelt's death, Truman sought out old friends, Democrats and Republicans, in Congress, to ask their help in this "terrible job." Shortly afterward, he told reporters, "Boys, if you ever pray, pray for me now. I don't know whether you fellows ever had a load of hay fall on you, but when they told me yesterday what had happened, I felt like the moon, the stars, and all the planets had fallen on me." Eighteen days into Truman's presidency, Adolf Hitler killed him-

### Harry Truman

self in a bunker in bomb-ravaged Berlin. On May 8 Germany surrendered.

As the great powers jockeyed for influence after Germany's surrender, the Grand Alliance began to crumble. At the Potsdam Conference in mid-July, Truman—a novice at international diplomacy—was less patient with the Soviets than Roosevelt had been. And Truman learned during the conference that a test of the new atomic weapon had been successful. The United States, possessing such a weapon, no longer needed the Soviet Union's help in fighting the Pacific war. Roosevelt had secretly promised Stalin territory from Japan's wartime holdings in exchange for help in defeating Japan; the bomb made those concessions unnecessary. The Allies did agree that Japan must surrender unconditionally. But with the defeat of Hitler and the end of the European war, the wartime bonds between the Allies were strained to breaking.

In the Pacific, the war continued. Since halting the Japanese advance in the Battle of Midway in June 1942, American strategy had been to "island-hop" toward Japan, skipping the most strongly fortified islands whenever possible and taking the weaker ones, aiming to strand the Japanese armies on their island outposts. To cut off supplies being shipped from Japan's home islands, Americans also targeted the Japanese merchant marine. Allied and Japanese forces fought savagely for control of tiny specks of land scattered throughout the Pacific. By 1944, Allied troops—from the United States, Britain,

### War in the Pacific

◀ On Okinawa, a wounded GI prays while awaiting evacuation to a field hospital. Medical advances, such as the discovery of penicillin and the use of glucose saline solution to replace lost blood, greatly improved the survival rate for those wounded in combat. But where combat was especially horrific, as it was on Okinawa, psychiatric casualties might outnumber combat deaths three to one.

*(W. Eugene Smith/Timepix/Getty Images)*

Australia, and New Zealand—had secured the Solomon, Gilbert, Marshall, and Mariana Islands. General Douglas MacArthur landed at Leyte to retake the Philippines for the United States in October 1944.

In February 1945, while the Big Three were meeting at Yalta, U.S. and Japanese troops battled for Iwo Jima, an island less than 5 miles long, located about 700 miles south of Tokyo. Twenty-one thousand Japanese defenders occupied the island's high ground. Hidden in a network of caves, trenches, and underground tunnels, they were protected from the aerial bombardment that U.S. forces used to clear the way for an amphibious landing. The stark volcanic island offered no cover, and marines were slaughtered as they came ashore. For twenty days, U.S. forces fought their way, yard by yard, up Mount Suribachi, the highest and most heavily fortified point on Iwo Jima. The struggle for Iwo Jima cost the lives of 6,821 Americans and more than 20,000 Japanese—some of whom committed suicide rather than surrender. Only 200 Japanese survived.

A month later, American troops landed on Okinawa, an island in the Ryukyus chain at the southern tip of Japan, from which Allied forces planned to invade the main Japanese islands. Fighting raged for two months; death was everywhere. The monsoon rains began in May, turning battlefields into seas of mud filled with decaying corpses. The supporting fleet endured waves of mass kamikaze (suicide) attacks, in which Japanese pilots intentionally crashed bomb-laden planes into American ships. Almost 5,000 seamen perished in these attacks. On Okinawa, 7,374 American soldiers and marines died in battle. Almost the entire Japanese garrison of 100,000 was killed. More than one-quarter of Okinawa's people, or approximately 80,000 civilians, perished as the two powers struggled over their island.

Even with American forces entrenched just 350 miles from Japan's main islands, Japanese leaders still refused to admit defeat. A powerful military faction was determined to avoid the humiliation of an unconditional surrender and to preserve the emperor's sovereignty. They hung on even while American bombers leveled their cities. On the night of March 9, 1945, 333 American B-29 Superfortresses dropped a mixture of explosives and incendiary devices on a 4-by-3-mile area of Tokyo. Attempting to demonstrate the strategic value of airpower, they created a firestorm, a blaze so fierce that it sucked all the oxygen from the air, creating hurricane-force winds and growing so hot it could melt concrete and steel. Almost 100,000 people were incinerated, suffocated, or boiled to death in canals where

**Bombing of Japan**

they had taken refuge from the fire. Over the following five months, American bombers attacked sixty-six Japanese cities, leaving 8 million people homeless, killing almost 900,000.

Japan, at the same time, was attempting to bomb the U.S. mainland. Thousands of bomb-bearing high-altitude balloons, constructed out of rice paper and potato-flour paste by schoolgirls, were launched into the jet stream. Those that did reach the United States fell on unpopulated areas, occasionally starting forest fires. The only mainland U.S. casualties in the war were five children and an adult on a Sunday school picnic in Oregon who accidentally detonated a balloon bomb that they found in the underbrush. As General Yamamoto had realized at the war's beginning, American resources would far outlast Japan's.

Early in the summer of 1945, Japan began to send out peace feelers through the Soviets. Japan was not, however, willing to accept the "unconditional surrender" terms on which the Allied leaders had agreed at Potsdam, and Truman and his advisers chose not to pursue a negotiated peace. By this time, U.S. troops were mobilizing for an invasion of the Japanese home islands. The experiences of Iwo Jima and Okinawa weighed heavily in the planning; Japanese troops had fought on, well past any hope of victory, and death tolls for Japanese and American troops alike had been enormous. News of the success of the Manhattan Project offered another option, and President Truman took it. Using atomic bombs on Japan, Truman believed, would end the war quickly and save American lives.

Historians still debate Truman's decision to use the atomic bomb. Why would he not negotiate surrender terms? Was Japan on the verge of an unconditional surrender, as some argue? Or was the antisurrender faction of Japanese military leaders strong enough to prevail? Truman knew the bomb could give the United States both real and psychological power in negotiating the peace; how much did his desire to demonstrate the bomb's power to the Soviet Union, or to prevent the Soviets from playing a major role in the last stages of the Pacific war, influence his decision? Did racism or a desire for retaliation play a role? How large were the projected casualty figures for invasion on which Truman based his decision, and were they accurate? No matter the answers to these ongoing debates, bombing (whether conventional or atomic) fit the established U.S. strategy of using machines rather than men whenever possible.

The decision to use the bomb did not seem as momentous to Truman as it does in retrospect. The moral line had already been crossed, as the move to wholesale bombing of civilian populations continued throughout the war: The

▲ This scorched watch, found in the rubble at Hiroshima, stopped at the time of the blast—8:16. The shock waves and fires caused by the atomic bomb leveled great expanses of the city. Radiation released by the bomb caused lingering deaths for thousands who survived the explosion. The photo of Hiroshima shown above was taken eight months after the attack.    *(Watch: John Launois/Black Star; Hiroshima: U.S. Air Force)*

Japanese had bombed the Chinese city of Shanghai in 1937. Germans had "terror-bombed" Warsaw, Rotterdam, and London. British and American bombers had purposely created firestorms in German cities; on a single night in February 1945, 225,000 people perished in the bombing of Dresden. The American bombing of Japanese cities—accomplished with conventional weapons—had already killed close to a million people and destroyed 56 square miles of Tokyo alone. What distinguished the atomic bombs from conventional bombs was their power and their efficiency—not that they killed huge numbers of innocent civilians in unspeakably awful ways.

On July 26, 1945, the Allies delivered an ultimatum to Japan: promising that the Japanese people would not be "enslaved," the Potsdam Declaration called for the Japanese to surrender unconditionally or face "prompt and utter destruction." Tokyo radio announced that the government would respond with *mokusatsu* (literally, "kill with silence," or ignore the ultimatum). On August 6, 1945, a B-29 bomber named after the pilot's mother, the

*Enola Gay*, dropped an atomic bomb above the city of Hiroshima. A flash of dazzling light shot across the sky; then a huge, purplish mushroom cloud boiled forty thousand feet into the atmosphere. Much of the city was leveled by the blast. The bomb ignited a firestorm, and thousands who survived the initial blast burned to death. Approximately 130,000 people were killed. Tens of thousands more would suffer the effects of radiation poisoning.

American planes continued their devastating conventional bombing. On August 8, the Soviet Union declared war on Japan. On August 9, a second American atomic bomb fell on Nagasaki, killing at least 60,000 people. Five days later, on August 14, Japan surrendered. Recent histories argue that the Soviet declaration of war played a much more significant role in Japan's decision to surrender than America's use of atomic weapons. In the end, the Allies promised that the Japanese emperor could remain as the nation's titular head. Formal surrender ceremonies were held September 2 aboard the battleship *Missouri* in Tokyo Bay. The Second World War was over.

# *Legacy* FOR A PEOPLE AND A NATION

## Nuclear Proliferation

Virtually from the moment of the Hiroshima and Nagasaki atomic bombings, American strategists grappled with the problem of erecting barriers to membership in the "nuclear club." The early focus was on the Soviet Union. How long, analysts wondered, before Stalin gets the bomb? On September 23, 1949, came the answer, as President Truman informed a shocked American public that the Soviets had successfully tested an atomic device.

In the years thereafter, membership in the nuclear club grew, through a combination of huge national investments, espionage, and a black market of willing western suppliers of needed raw materials and technologies. There were successful detonations by Great Britain (1952), France (1960), China (1964), India (1974), and Pakistan (1998). Israel crossed the nuclear weapon threshold on the eve of the 1967 Six-Day War but to this day has always refused to confirm or deny that it has the bomb. More recently, creditable reports indicate that North Korea has a small nuclear arsenal and that Iran is working to get one.

If this is a sizable number of nuclear states, it is far fewer than experts predicted in the 1960s. "If three nations made nuclear weapons in the 1970s," one senior British analyst warned then, "ten might do so in the 1980s and thirty in the 1990s." It did not happen, and the main reason is that the 5 existing nuclear powers committed themselves in the mid-1960s—for a complex set of self-interested reasons—to promoting nonproliferation. Subsequently, the rate of proliferation steadily declined; all told, 22 of 31 states that started down the nuclear path changed course and renounced the bomb. By late 2006, the Treaty on the Non-Proliferation of Nuclear Weapons (NPT), enacted on July 1, 1968, had 187 signatories and was widely hailed as one of the great international agreements of the post-1945 era.

Skeptics took a different view. They noted that 3 states outside the NPT (Israel, India, and Pakistan) became nuclear powers, and they charged the "original five" with hypocrisy, for doing everything possible to prevent others from obtaining nuclear arms while keeping large stockpiles for themselves. With the world in 2007 awash in some 27,000 nuclear weapons (97 percent belonging to the United States and Russia), critics feared a new kind of proliferation, in which a terrorist group or other nonstate actor got its hands on one or more bombs. In that nightmare scenario, they warned, the de facto post-Nagasaki international moratorium on the use of nuclear weapons would soon be—literally—blown away.

## SUMMARY

Hitler once prophesied, "We may be destroyed, but if we are, we shall drag a world with us—a world in flames." In that, at least, Hitler was right. World War II devastated much of the globe. In Asia and in Europe, ghostlike people wandered through rubble, searching desperately for food. One out of nine people in the Soviet Union had perished: a total of at least 21 million civilian and military war dead. The Chinese calculated their war losses at 10 million; the Germans and Austrians at 6 million; the Japanese at 2.5 million. Up to 1 million died of famine in Japanese-controlled Indochina. Almost 11 million people had been systematically murdered in Nazi death camps. Across the globe, the Second World War killed at least 55 million people.

Waging war required the cooperation of Allied nations with very different goals and interests. Tensions among them remained high throughout the war, as the United States and Britain resisted Stalin's demands that they open a second front to draw German soldiers away from the Soviet Union. The United States, meanwhile, was fighting a brutal war in the Pacific, pushing Japanese forces back toward their home islands. By the time Japan surrendered in August 1945, the strains between the Soviet Union and its English-speaking Allies made postwar peace and stability unlikely.

American men and machines were a critical part of the Allied war effort. Although Americans did not join in the perfect unity and shared sacrifice suggested by current descriptions of "the greatest generation," American servicemen covered the globe, from the Arctic to the tropics. And on the home front, Americans worked around the clock to make the weapons that would win the war. Although they made sacrifices during the war—including almost 300,000 who gave their lives—many Americans found that the war had changed their lives for the better. Mobilization for war ended the Great Depression, reducing unemployment practically to zero. War jobs demanded workers, and Americans moved in huge numbers to war-production centers. The influx of workers strained the resources of existing communities and sometimes led to social friction and even violence. But many Americans— African Americans, Mexican Americans, women, poor whites from the South—found new opportunities for employment in well-paid war jobs.

The federal government, in order to manage the nation's war efforts, became a stronger presence in the lives of individual Americans—regulating business and employment; overseeing military conscription, training, and deployment; and even controlling what people could buy to eat or to wear. The Second World War was a powerful engine of social change.

Americans emerged from World War II fully confident that theirs was the greatest country in the world. It was certainly the most powerful. At war's end, only the United States had the capital and economic resources to spur international recovery; only the United States was more prosperous and more secure than when war began. In the coming struggle to fashion a new world out of the ashes of the old, soon to be called the Cold War, the United States held a commanding position. For better or worse—and clearly there were elements of each—the Second World War was a turning point in the nation's history.

## SUGGESTIONS FOR FURTHER READING

Michael C. C. Adams, *The Best War Ever: America and World War II* (1993)

Roger Daniels, *Prisoners Without Trial: Japanese Americans in World War II* (1993)

Tsuyoshi Hasegawa, *Racing the Enemy: Stalin, Truman, and the Surrender of Japan* (2005)

David M. Kennedy, *Freedom from Fear: The American People in Depression and War, 1929–1945* (1999)

Warren F. Kimball, *Forged in War: Roosevelt, Churchill, and the Second World War* (1997)

Nelson Lichtenstein, *Labor's War at Home: The CIO in World War II* (1983)

Gerald F. Linderman, *The World Within War: America's Combat Experience in World War II* (1997)

Leisa Meyers, *Creating G.I. Jane: Sexuality and Power in the Women's Army Corps During World War II* (1996)

George Roeder, Jr., *The Censored War: American Visual Experience During World War II* (1993)

Ronald Takaki, *Double Victory: A Multicultural History of America in World War II* (2000)

For a more extensive list for further reading, go to college.hmco.com/pic/norton8e.

# The Cold War and American Globalism *1945-1961*

O n July 16, 1945, the "Deer" Team leader parachuted into northern Vietnam, near Kimlung, a village in a valley of rice paddies. Colonel Allison Thomas could not know that the end of the Second World War was just weeks away, but he and the other five members of his Office of Strategic Services (OSS) unit knew their mission: to work with the Vietminh, a nationalist Vietnamese organization, to sabotage Japanese forces that in March had seized Vietnam from France. After disentangling himself from the banyan tree into which his parachute had slammed him, Thomas spoke a "few flowery sentences" to two hundred Vietminh soldiers assembled near a banner proclaiming, "Welcome to Our American Friends." Ho Chi Minh, head of the Vietminh, ill but speaking in good English, cordially greeted the OSS team and offered supper. The next day Ho denounced the French but remarked that "we welcome 10 million Americans." "Forget the Communist Bogy," Thomas radioed OSS headquarters in China.

A communist who had worked for decades to win his nation's independence from France, Ho joined the French Communist Party after World War I and sought to use it as a vehicle for Vietnamese independence. For the next two decades, living in China, the Soviet Union, and elsewhere, he patiently planned and fought to free his nation from French colonialism. During World War II, Ho's Vietminh warriors harassed both French and Japanese forces and rescued downed American pilots. In March 1945 Ho met with U.S. officials in China, where he read the *Encyclopaedia Americana* and *Time* magazine at an Office of War Information facility. Receiving no aid from his ideological allies in the Soviet Union, Ho hoped that the United States would favor his nation's long quest for liberation from colonialism.

Other OSS personnel soon parachuted into Kimlung, including a male nurse who diagnosed Ho's ailments as malaria and dysentery. Quinine and sulfa drugs restored his

◀ The Vietnamese nationalist Ho Chi Minh (1890–1969) meets with OSS "Deer" Team members in 1945. On the far left is Ho's military aide Vo Nguyen Giap. *(Private Collection)*

## CHRONOLOGY

**1945** ■ Roosevelt dies; Truman becomes president
■ Atomic bombings of Japan

**1946** ■ Kennan's "long telegram" criticizes USSR
■ Vietnamese war against France erupts

**1947** ■ Truman Doctrine seeks aid for Greece and Turkey
■ Marshall offers Europe economic assistance
■ National Security Act reorganizes government

**1948** ■ Communists take power in Czechoslovakia
■ Truman recognizes Israel
■ United States organizes Berlin airlift

**1949** ■ NATO founded as anti-Soviet alliance
■ Soviet Union explodes atomic bomb
■ Mao's communists win power in China

**1950** ■ NSC-68 recommends major military buildup
■ Korean War starts in June; China enters in fall

**1951** ■ United States signs Mutual Security Treaty with Japan

**1953** ■ Eisenhower becomes president
■ Stalin dies
■ United States helps restore shah to power in Iran
■ Korean War ends

**1954** ■ Geneva accords partition Vietnam
■ CIA-led coup overthrows Arbenz in Guatemala

**1955** ■ Soviets create Warsaw Pact

**1956** ■ Soviets crush uprising in Hungary
■ Suez crisis sparks war in Middle East

**1957** ■ Soviets fire first ICBM and launch *Sputnik*

**1958** ■ U.S. troops land in Lebanon
■ Berlin crisis

**1959** ■ Castro ousts Batista in Cuba

**1960** ■ Eighteen African colonies become independent
■ Vietcong organized in South Vietnam

eigners' presence as a sign of U.S. anticolonial and anti-Japanese sentiments. In early August the Deer Team began to give Vietminh soldiers weapons training. During many conversations with the OSS members, Ho said he hoped young Vietnamese could study in the United States and that American technicians could help build an independent Vietnam. Citing history, Ho remarked that "your statesmen make eloquent speeches about . . . self-determination. We are self-determined. Why not help us? Am I any different from . . . your George Washington?"

A second OSS unit, the "Mercy" Team, headed by Captain Archimedes Patti, arrived in the city of Hanoi on August 22. When Patti met Ho—"this wisp of a man," as Patti put it—the Vietminh leader applauded America's assistance and called for future "collaboration." But, unbeknownst to these OSS members, who believed that President Franklin D. Roosevelt's general sympathy for eventual Vietnamese independence remained U.S. policy, the new Truman administration in Washington had decided to let France decide the fate of Vietnam. That change in policy explains why Ho never received answers to the several letters and telegrams he sent to Washington—the first dated August 30, 1945.

On September 2, 1945, amid great fanfare in Hanoi, with OSS personnel present, an emotional Ho Chi Minh read his declaration of independence for the Democratic Republic of Vietnam: "All men are created equal; they are endowed by their Creator with certain unalienable Rights; among these are Life, Liberty, and the pursuit of Happiness." Having borrowed from the internationally renowned American document of 1776, Ho then itemized Vietnamese grievances against France. At one point in the ceremonies, two American P-38 aircraft swooped down over the square. Many in the crowd cheered, interpreting the flyby as U.S. endorsement of Vietnamese independence. Actually, the pilots had no orders to make a political statement; they just wanted to see what was happening.

By early autumn both OSS teams had departed Vietnam. In a last meeting with Captain Patti, Ho expressed his sadness that the United States had armed the French to reestablish their colonial rule in Vietnam. Sure, Ho said, U.S. officials in Washington judged him a "Moscow puppet" because he was a communist. But Ho claimed that he drew inspiration from the American struggle for inde-

health, but Ho remained frail. As a sign of friendship, the Americans in Vietnam named Ho "OSS Agent 19." Everywhere the Americans went, impoverished villagers thanked them with gifts of food and clothing, despite the devastating famine of 1944–1945 in which at least a million Vietnamese died. The villagers interpreted the for-

pendence and that he was foremost "a free agent," a nationalist. If necessary, Ho insisted, the Vietnamese would go it alone, with or without American or Soviet help. And they did—first against the French and eventually against more than half a million U.S. troops in what became America's longest war. How different world history would have been had President Harry S Truman responded favorably to Ho Chi Minh's last letter to Washington, dated February 16, 1946, which asked the United States "as guardians and champions of World Justice to take a decisive step in support of our independence."

Because Ho Chi Minh and many of his nationalist followers had declared themselves communists, U.S. leaders rejected their appeal. Endorsing the containment doctrine to draw the line against communism everywhere, American presidents from Truman to George H. W. Bush believed that a ruthless Soviet Union was directing a worldwide communist conspiracy against peace, free-market capitalism, and political democracy. Soviet leaders from Joseph Stalin to Mikhail Gorbachev protested that a militarized, economically aggressive United States sought nothing less than world domination. This protracted contest between the United States and the Soviet Union acquired the name Cold War.

The primary feature of world affairs for more than four decades, the Cold War was fundamentally a bipolar contest between the United States and the Soviet Union over spheres of influence and world power. Decisions made in Washington and Moscow dominated world politics as the capitalist "West" squared off against the communist "East." The contest dominated international relations and eventually took the lives of millions, cost trillions of dollars, spawned doomsday fears, and destabilized one nation after another. On occasion the two superpowers negotiated at summit conferences and signed agreements to temper their dangerous arms race; at other times they went to the brink of war and armed allies to fight vicious Third World conflicts. Sometimes these allies had their own ideas and ambitions, and they often proved adept at resisting pressure applied on them by one or both of the superpowers. Over time, American and Soviet leaders came to realize that, notwithstanding the immense military might at their disposal, their power to effect change was in key respects limited.

Vietnam was part of the Third World, a general term for those nations that during the Cold War era wore neither the "West" (the "First World") nor the "East" (the "Second World") label. Sometimes called "developing countries," Third World nations were on the whole nonwhite, nonindustrialized, and located in the southern half of the globe—in Asia, Africa, the Middle East, and Latin America. Many had been colonies of European nations or Japan, and they were vulnerable to the Cold War rivalry that intruded on them. U.S. leaders often interpreted their anticolonialism, political instability, and restrictions on foreign-owned property as Soviet or communist inspired, or capable of being exploited by Moscow—in short, as Cold War matters rather than as expressions of profound indigenous nationalism. As an example, Vietnam became one among many sites where Cold War fears and Third World aspirations intersected, prompting American intervention. Such intervention bespoke a globalist foreign policy, meaning that U.S. officials now regarded the entire world as the appropriate sphere for America's influence.

Critics in the United States challenged the architects of the Cold War, questioning their exaggerations of threats from abroad, meddlesome interventions in the Third World, and expensive militarization of foreign policy. But when leaders like Truman described the Cold War in extremist terms as a life-and-death struggle against a monstrous enemy, legitimate criticism became suspect and dissenters were discredited. Critics' searching questions about America's global, interventionist foreign policy and its reliance on nuclear weapons were drowned out by charges that dissenters were "soft on communism," if not un-American. Decision makers in the United States successfully cultivated a Cold War consensus that stifled debate and shaped the mindset of generations of Americans.

- Why did relations between the Soviet Union and the United States turn hostile soon after their victory in World War II?
- When and why did the Cold War expand from a struggle over the future of Europe and central Asia to one encompassing virtually the entire globe?
- By what means did the Truman and Eisenhower administrations seek to expand America's global influence in the late 1940s and the 1950s?

THE BIG THREE
One job done.

PONY EDITION
SPECIALLY PRINTED
FOR AIR TRANSPORT
•
Editorial content
unchanged from
the regular
edition

▲ The wartime Grand Alliance of the United States, Britain, and the Soviet Union was never without tension, but it succeeded in producing a victory over the Axis powers. This cover of *Time* magazine from May 14, 1945, celebrates the defeat of Nazi Germany. It was a high point in Soviet-American relations, but it would not last.

*(Time Life Pictures/Time Life Picture Collection/Getty Images)*

## FROM ALLIES TO ADVERSARIES

The Second World War had a deeply unsettling effect on the international system. At its end, Germany was in ruins. Great Britain was badly overstrained and exhausted; France, having endured five years of Nazi occupation, was rent by internal division. Italy also emerged drastically weakened, and, in Asia, Japan was decimated and under occupation, and China was headed toward a renewed civil war. Throughout Europe and Asia, factories, transportation, and communications links had been reduced to rubble. Agricultural production plummeted,

and displaced persons wandered about in search of food and family. How would the devastated economic world be pieced back together? The United States and the Soviet Union, though allies in the war, offered very different answers and models. The collapse of Germany and Japan, moreover, had created power vacuums that drew the two major powers into collision as they sought influence in countries where the Axis aggressors had once held sway. And the political turmoil that many nations experienced after the war also spurred Soviet-American competition. For example, in Greece and China, where civil wars raged between leftists and conservative regimes, the two powers supported different sides.

The international system also experienced instability because empires were disintegrating, creating the new Third World. Financial constraints and nationalist rebellions forced the imperial states to set their colonies free. Britain exited India (and Pakistan) in 1947 and Burma and Sri Lanka (Ceylon) in 1948. The Philippines gained independence from the United States in 1946. After four years of battling nationalists in Indonesia, the Dutch left in 1949. In the Middle East, Lebanon (1943), Syria (1946), and Jordan (1946) gained independence, while in Palestine British officials faced growing pressure from Zionists intent on creating a Jewish homeland and from Arab leaders opposed to the prospect. In Iraq, too, nationalist agitation increased against the British-installed government. Washington and Moscow paid close attention to this anticolonial ferment, seeing these new or emerging Third World states as potential allies that might provide military bases, resources, and markets. Not all new nations were willing to play along; some chose nonalignment in the Cold War. "We do not intend to be the playthings of others," declared India's leader, Jawaharlal Nehru.

### Decolonization

Driven by different ideologies and different economic and strategic needs in this volatile international climate, the United States and the Soviet Union assessed their most pressing tasks in very different terms. The Soviets, though committed to seeking ultimate victory over the capitalist countries, were most concerned about preventing another invasion of their homeland. It was a homeland much less secure than the United States, for reasons both geographic and historical. Its land mass was huge—three times as large as that of the United States—but it had only 10,000 miles of seacoast, much of which was under ice for a large part of the year. Russian leaders both before and after the revolution

### Stalin's Aims

had made increased maritime access a chief foreign policy aim.

What is more, the geographical frontiers of the USSR were hard to defend. Siberia, vital for its mineral resources, lay 6,000 miles east of Moscow and was vulnerable to encroachment by Japan and China. In the west, the border with Poland had generated violent clashes ever since World War I, and eastern Europe had been the launching pad for Hitler's invasion in 1941: the resulting war cost the lives of at least 21 million Russians and caused massive physical destruction. Henceforth, Soviet leaders determined, they could have no dangers along their western borders.

Overall, however, Soviet territorial objectives were limited. Although many Americans were quick to compare Stalin to Hitler, Stalin did not have the Nazi leader's grandiose plans for world hegemony. In general, his aims resembled those of the czars before him: he wanted to push the USSR's borders to include the Baltic states of Estonia, Latvia, and Lithuania, as well as the eastern part of prewar Poland. Fearful of a revived Germany, he sought to ensure pro-Soviet governments in eastern Europe. To the south, Stalin wanted to have a presence in northern Iran, and he pressed the Turks to grant him naval bases and free access out of the Black Sea. Economically, the Soviet government promoted economic independence more than trade with other countries; suspicious of their European neighbors, they did not promote rapid rebuilding of the war-ravaged economies of the region or, more generally, expanded world trade.

The leadership in the United States, by contrast, came out of the war extremely confident about the immediate security of the country's borders. Separated from the other world powers by two vast oceans, the American home base had been virtually immune from attack during the fighting—only an occasional shell from a submarine or a hostile balloon reached the shores of the continental United States. American casualties were fewer than those of any of the other major combatants—hugely so in comparison with the Soviet Union. With its fixed capital intact, its resources more plentiful than ever, and in lone possession of the atomic bomb, the United States was the strongest power in the world at war's end.

## U.S. Economic and Strategic Needs

Yet this was no time for complacency, Washington officials reminded one another. Some other power—almost certainly the USSR—could take advantage of the political and economic instability in war-torn Europe and Asia, and eventually seize control of these areas, with dire implications for America's physical and economic security. To prevent this eventuality, officials in Washington sought forward bases overseas, in order to keep an airborne enemy at bay. To further enhance U.S. security, American planners, in direct contrast to their Soviet counterparts, sought the quick reconstruction of nations—including the former enemies Germany and Japan—and a world economy based on free trade. Such a system, they reasoned, was essential to preserve America's economic well-being.

The Soviets, on the other hand, refused to join the new World Bank and International Monetary Fund (IMF), created at the July 1944 Bretton Woods Conference by forty-four nations to stabilize trade and finance. They held that the United States dominated both institutions and used them to promote private investment and open international commerce, which Moscow saw as capitalist tools of exploitation. With the United States as its largest donor, the World Bank opened its doors in 1945 and began to make loans to help members finance reconstruction projects; the IMF, also heavily backed by the United States, helped members meet their balance-of-payments problems through currency loans.

The personalities of the two countries' leaders also mattered. Joseph Stalin, though hostile to the western powers and capable of utter ruthlessness against his own people (his periodic purges since the 1930s had taken the lives of millions), had no wish for an immediate war. With the huge Russian losses in World War II, he was all too aware of his country's weakness vis-à-vis the United States. For a time at least, he appears to have believed he could achieve his aspirations peacefully, through continued cooperation with the Americans and the British. Over the long term, though, he envisaged more conflict. Stalin believed that Germany and Japan would rise again to threaten the USSR, probably by the 1960s, and his suspicion of the other capitalist powers knew no bounds. Many have concluded that Stalin was clinically paranoid: the first to do so, a leading Russian neuropathologist in 1927, died a few days later! As historian David Reynolds has noted, this paranoia, coupled with Stalin's xenophobia (fear of anything foreign) and his Marxist-Leninist ideology, created in the Soviet leader a mental map of "them" versus "us" that decisively influenced his approach to world affairs.

## Stalin and Truman

Harry Truman had none of Stalin's capacity for deception or ruthlessness, but to a lesser degree he, too, was prone to a "them" versus "us" world-view. Truman often glossed over nuances, ambiguities, and counterevidence; he preferred the simple answer stated in either/or terms. As

Winston Churchill, who admired Truman's decisiveness, once observed, the president "takes no notice of delicate ground, he just plants his foot firmly on it." Truman constantly exaggerated, as when he declared in his undelivered farewell address that he had "knocked the socks off the communists" in Korea. Shortly after Roosevelt's death in early 1945, Truman met the Soviet commissar of foreign affairs, V. M. Molotov, at the White House. When the president sharply protested that the Soviets were not fulfilling the Yalta agreement on Poland, Molotov stormed out. Truman had self-consciously developed what he called his "tough method," and he bragged after the encounter that "I gave it to him straight 'one-two to the jaw.'" Truman's display of toughness became a trademark of American Cold War diplomacy.

At what point did the Cold War actually begin? No precise start date can be given. The origins must be thought

### The Beginning of the Cold War

of as a process, one that arguably began in 1917 with the Bolshevik Revolution and the western powers' hostile response, but in a more meaningful sense began in mid-1945, as World War II drew to a close. By the spring of 1947, certainly, the struggle had begun.

One of the first Soviet-American clashes came in Poland in 1945, when the Soviets refused to allow the Polish government-in-exile in London to be a part of the communist government that Moscow sponsored. The Soviets also snuffed out civil liberties in the former Nazi satellite of Romania, justifying their actions by pointing to what they claimed was an equivalent U.S. manipulation of Italy. Moscow initially allowed free elections in Hungary and Czechoslovakia, but as the Cold War accelerated and U.S. influence in Europe expanded, the Soviets encouraged communist coups in Hungary (1947) and Czechoslovakia (1948). Yugoslavia stood as a unique case: its independent communist government, led by Josip Broz Tito, successfully broke with Stalin in 1948.

To defend their actions, Moscow officials pointed out that the United States was reviving their traditional enemy, Germany. Twice in the lifetime of Soviet leaders Germany had wrought enormous suffering on Russia, and Stalin and his associates were determined to prevent a third occurrence. The Soviets also protested that the United States was meddling in eastern Europe. They cited clandestine American meetings with anti-Soviet groups, repeated calls for elections likely to produce anti-Soviet regimes, and the use of loans to gain political influence (financial diplomacy). Moscow charged that the United States was pursuing a double standard—intervening in the affairs of eastern Europe but demanding that the Soviet Union stay

out of Latin America and Asia. Americans called for free elections in the Soviet sphere, Moscow noted, but not in the U.S. sphere in Latin America, where several military dictatorships ruled.

The atomic bomb also divided the two major powers. The Soviets believed that the United States was practicing

### Atomic Diplomacy

"atomic diplomacy"—maintaining a nuclear monopoly to scare the Soviets into diplomatic concessions. Secretary of State James F. Byrnes thought that the atomic bomb gave the United States bargaining power and could serve as a deterrent to Soviet expansion, but Secretary of War Henry L. Stimson thought otherwise in 1945. If Americans continued to have "this weapon rather ostentatiously on our hip," he warned Truman, the Soviets' "suspicions and their distrust of our purposes and motives will increase."

In this atmosphere of suspicion and distrust, Truman refused to turn over the weapon to an international control authority. In 1946 he backed the Baruch Plan, named after its author, financier Bernard Baruch. Largely a propaganda ploy, this proposal provided for U.S. abandonment of its atomic monopoly only after the world's fissionable materials were brought under the authority of an international agency. The Soviets retorted that this plan would require them to shut down their atomic-bomb development project while the United States continued its own. Washington and Moscow soon became locked in an expensive and frightening nuclear arms race.

By the middle of 1946, the wartime Grand Alliance was but a fading memory; that year, Soviets and Americans clashed on every front. When the United States turned down a Soviet request for a reconstruction loan but gave a loan to Britain, Moscow upbraided Washington for using its dollars to manipulate foreign governments. The two Cold War powers also backed different groups in Iran, where the United States helped bring the pro-West shah to the throne. Unable to agree on the unification of Germany, the former allies built up their zones independently.

After Stalin gave a speech in February 1946 that depicted the world as threatened by capitalist acquisitiveness,

### Warnings from Kennan and Churchill

the American chargé d'affaires in Moscow, George F. Kennan, sent a pessimistic "long telegram" to Washington. Kennan asserted that Soviet fanaticism made even a temporary understanding impossible. His widely circulated report fed a growing belief among American officials that only toughness would work with the Soviets. The following month, Winston Churchill de-

▲ On March 5, 1946, former British prime minister Winston S. Churchill (1874–1965) delivered a speech, which he intended for a worldwide audience, at Westminster College in Fulton, Missouri. President Harry S Truman *(right)* had encouraged Churchill *(seated)* to speak on two themes: the need to block Soviet expansion and the need to form an Anglo-American partnership. Always eloquent and provocative, Churchill denounced the Soviets for drawing an "iron curtain" across eastern Europe. This speech became one of the landmark statements of the Cold War. *(Harry S. Truman Library)*

livered a stirring speech in Fulton, Missouri. The former British prime minister warned that a Soviet-erected "iron curtain" had cut off eastern European countries from the West. With an approving Truman sitting on the stage, Churchill called for Anglo-American partnership to resist the new menace.

The growing Soviet-American tensions had major implications for the functioning of the United Nations. The delegates who gathered in San Francisco in April 1945 to sign the U.N. charter had agreed on an organization that would include a General Assembly of all member states, as well as a smaller Security Council which would take the lead on issues of peace and security. Five great powers were given permanent seats on the council—the United States, the Soviet Union, Great Britain, China, and France.

These permanent members could not prohibit discussion of any issue, but they could exercise a veto against any proposed action. To be effective on the major issues of war and peace, therefore, the U.N. needed great-power cooperation of the type that had existed in wartime but was a distant memory by mid-1946. Of the fifty-one founding states, twenty-two came from the Americas and another fifteen from Europe, which in effect gave the United States a large majority in the assembly. In retaliation, Moscow began to exercise its veto in the Security Council.

Some high-level U.S. officials were dismayed by the administration's harsh anti-Soviet posture. Secretary of Commerce Henry A. Wallace, who had been Roosevelt's vice president before Truman, charged that Truman's get-tough policy was substituting atomic and economic coercion for diplomacy. Wallace told a Madison Square Garden audience in September 1946 that "'getting tough' never brought anything real and lasting—whether for schoolyard bullies or businessmen or world powers. The tougher we get, the tougher the Russians will get." Truman soon fired Wallace from the cabinet, blasting him privately as "a real Commy and a dangerous man" and boasting that he, Truman, had now "run the crackpots out of the Democratic Party."

East-West tensions escalated further in early 1947, when the British requested American help in Greece to

|||||||||||||||||||||||||||||||||||||||||

**Truman Doctrine**

defend their conservative client-government (a government dependent on the economic or military support of a more powerful country) in a civil war against leftists. In his March 12, 1947, speech to Congress, Truman requested $400 million in aid to Greece and Turkey. He had a selling job to do. The Republican Eightieth Congress wanted less, not more, spending; many of its members had little respect for the Democratic president whose administration the voters had repudiated in the 1946 elections by giving the GOP ("Grand Old Party," the Republican Party) majorities in both houses of Congress. Republican senator Arthur Vandenberg of Michigan, a bipartisan leader who backed Truman's request, bluntly told the president that he would have to "scare hell out of the American people" to gain congressional approval.

With that advice in mind, the president delivered a speech laced with alarmist language intended to stake out the American role in the postwar world. Truman claimed that communism, feeding on economic dislocations, imperiled the world. "If Greece should fall under the control of an armed minority," he gravely concluded in an early version of the domino theory (see page 812), "the effect upon its neighbor, Turkey, would be immediate and serious.

Confusion and disorder might well spread throughout the entire Middle East." Truman articulated what became known as the Truman Doctrine: "I believe that it must be the policy of the United States to support free peoples who are resisting attempted subjugation by armed minorities or by outside pressures."

Critics correctly pointed out that the Soviet Union was little involved in the Greek civil war, that the communists in Greece were more pro-Tito than pro-Stalin, and that the resistance movement had noncommunist as well as communist members. Nor was the Soviet Union threatening Turkey at the time. Others suggested that such aid should be channeled through the United Nations. Truman countered that, should communists gain control of Greece, they might open the door to Soviet power in the Mediterranean. After much debate, the Senate approved Truman's request by 67 to 23 votes. Using U.S. dollars and military advisers, the Greek government defeated the insurgents in 1949, and Turkey became a staunch U.S. ally on the Soviets' border.

In the months after Truman's speech, the term *Cold War* slipped into the lexicon as a description of the Soviet-American relationship. Less than two years had passed since the glorious victory over the Axis powers, and the two Grand Alliance members now found themselves locked in a tense struggle for world dominance. It would last almost half a century. Could the confrontation have been avoided? Not altogether, it seems clear. Even before World War II had ended, perceptive observers anticipated that the United States and the USSR would seek to fill the power vacuum that would exist after the armistice, and that friction would result. The two countries had a history of hostility and tension, and both were militarily powerful. Most of all, the two nations were divided by sharply differing political economies with widely divergent needs and by a deep ideological chasm. Some kind of confrontation was destined to occur.

It is far less clear that the conflict had to result in a Cold War. The "cold peace" that had prevailed from the revolution in 1917 through World War II could conceivably have been maintained into the postwar years as well. Neither side's leadership wanted war. Both hoped—at least in the initial months—that a spirit of cooperation could be maintained. The Cold War resulted from decisions by individual human beings who might well have chosen differently, who might have done more, for example, to maintain diplomatic dialogue, to seek negotiated solutions to complex international problems. For decades,

**Inevitable Cold War?**

many Americans would wonder if the high price they were paying for victory in the superpower confrontation was necessary.

## CONTAINMENT IN ACTION

Having committed themselves to countering Soviet and communist expansion, the Truman team had to figure out just how to fight the Cold War. The policy they chose, containment, was in place before the term was coined. George Kennan, having moved from the U.S. embassy in Moscow to the State Department in Washington, published an influential statement of the containment doctrine. Writing as "Mr. X" in the July 1947 issue of the magazine *Foreign Affairs*, Kennan advocated a "policy of firm containment, designed to confront the Russians with unalterable counterforce at every point where they show signs of encroaching upon the interests of a peaceful and stable world." Such counterforce, Kennan argued, would check Soviet expansion and eventually foster a "mellowing" of Soviet behavior. Along with the Truman Doctrine, Kennan's "X" article became a key manifesto of Cold War policy.

The veteran journalist Walter Lippmann took issue with the containment doctrine in his slim but powerful book *The Cold War* (1947), calling it a "strategic monstrosity" that failed to distinguish between areas vital and peripheral to U.S. security. If American leaders defined every place on earth as strategically important, Lippmann reasoned, the nation's patience and resources soon would be drained. Nor did Lippmann share Truman's conviction that the Soviet Union was plotting to take over the world. The president, he asserted, put too little emphasis on diplomacy. Ironically, Kennan himself agreed with much of Lippmann's critique, and he soon began to distance himself from the doctrine he had helped to create.

**Lippmann's Critique**

Invoking the containment doctrine, the United States in 1947 and 1948 began to build an international economic and defensive network to protect American prosperity and security, and to advance U.S. hegemony. In western Europe, the region of primary concern, American diplomats pursued a range of objectives, including economic reconstruction and fostering a political environment friendly to the United States. They sought the ouster of communists from governments, as occurred in 1947 in France and Italy, and blockage of "third force" or neutralist tendencies. To maintain political stability in key capitals, U.S. officials worked to keep the decolonization of

▲ Under official postwar relief and recovery programs, including the Marshall Plan, the United States shipped billions of dollars' worth of food and equipment to western European nations struggling to overcome the destruction of the Second World War. Private efforts, such as this one in 1950, also succeeded. The people of Jersey City, New Jersey, sent this snowplow to the mountainous village of Capracotta, Italy. *(Corbis-Bettmann)*.

European empires orderly. In Germany, they advocated the unification of the western zones. At the same time, American culture—consumer goods, music, consumption ethic, and production techniques—permeated European societies. Some Europeans resisted Americanization, but transatlantic ties strengthened.

The first instrument designed to achieve U.S. goals in western Europe was the Marshall Plan. European nations, still reeling economically and unstable politically, lacked the dollars to buy vital American-made goods. Americans, who had already spent billions of dollars on European relief and recovery by 1947, remembered all too well the troubles of the 1930s: global depression, political extremism, and war born of economic discontent. Such cataclysms could not be allowed to happen again; communism must not replace fascism. Western Europe, said one State Department diplomat, was "the keystone in the arch which supports the kind of a world which we have to have in order to conduct our lives."

**Marshall Plan**

In June 1947, Secretary of State George C. Marshall announced that the United States would finance a massive European recovery program. Launched in 1948, the Marshall Plan sent $12.4 billion to western Europe before the program ended in 1951 (see Map 28.1). To stimulate business at home, the legislation required that Europeans spend the foreign-aid dollars in the United States on American-made products. The Marshall Plan proved a mixed success; some scholars today even argue that Europe could have revived without it. The program caused inflation, failed to solve a balance-of-payments problem, took only tentative steps toward economic integration, and further divided Europe between "East" and "West." But the program spurred impressive western European industrial production and investment, and started the region toward self-sustaining economic growth. From the American perspective, moreover, the plan succeeded because it helped contain communism.

To streamline the administration of U.S. defense, Truman worked with Congress on the National Security

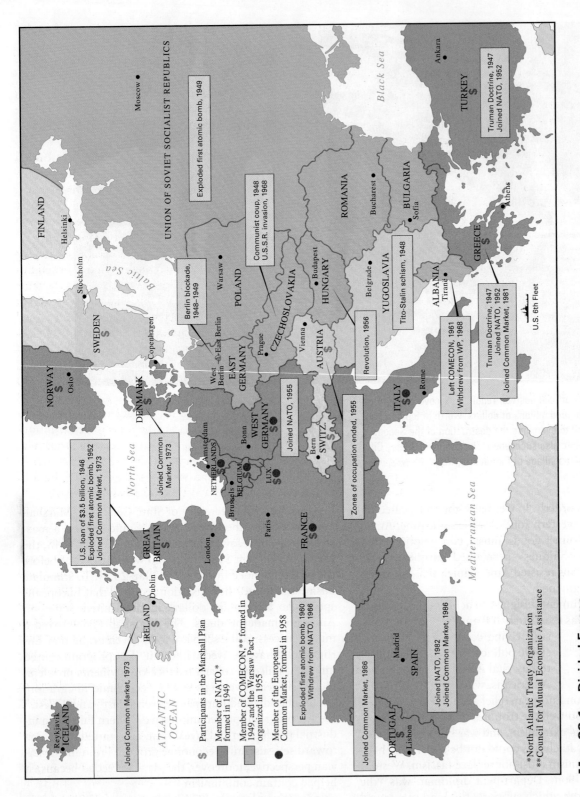

## Map 28.1   Divided Europe

After the Second World War, Europe broke into two competing camps. When the United States launched the Marshall Plan in 1948, the Soviet Union countered with its own economic plan the following year. When the United States created NATO in 1949, the Soviet Union answered with the Warsaw Pact 1955. On the whole, these two camps held firm until the late 1980s.

*North Atlantic Treaty Organization
**Council for Mutual Economic Assistance

## National Security Act

Act of July 1947. The act created the Office of Secretary of Defense (which became the Department of Defense two years later) to oversee all branches of the armed services, the National Security Council (NSC) of high-level officials to advise the president, and the Central Intelligence Agency (CIA) to conduct spy operations and information gathering overseas. By the early 1950s the CIA had become a significant element in national security policy and had expanded its functions to include covert (secret) operations aimed at overthrowing unfriendly foreign leaders and, as a high-ranking American official put it, a "Department of Dirty Tricks" to stir up economic trouble in "the camp of the enemy." Taken together, the components of the National Security Act gave the president increased powers with which to conduct foreign policy.

In the wake of the Marshall Plan and the National Security Act, Stalin hardened his Cold War posture. He forbade communist satellite governments in eastern Europe to accept Marshall Plan aid and ordered communist parties in western Europe to work to thwart the plan. He also created the Cominform, an organization designed to coordinate communist activities around the world. It was a classic example of what historian Herbert Butterfield called the "security dilemma": whereas American planners saw the Marshall Plan as helping their European friends achieve security against a potential Soviet threat, in Stalin's mind it raised anew the specter of capitalist penetration. He responded by tightening his grip on eastern Europe—most notably, he engineered a coup in Czechoslovakia in February 1948 that ensured full Soviet control of the country—which in turn created more anxiety in the United States. In this way the U.S.-Soviet relationship became a downward spiral that seemed to gain in velocity with each passing month.

The German problem remained especially intractable. In June 1948, the Americans, French, and British

## Berlin Blockade and Airlift

agreed to fuse their German zones, including their three sectors of Berlin. They sought to integrate West Germany (the Federal Republic of Germany) into the western European economy, complete with a reformed German currency. Fearing a resurgent Germany tied to the American Cold War camp, the Soviets cut off western land access to the jointly occupied city of Berlin, located well inside the Soviet zone. In response to this bold move, President Truman ordered a massive airlift of food, fuel, and other supplies to Berlin. Their spoiling effort blunted, the Sovi-

ets finally lifted the blockade in May 1949 and founded the German Democratic Republic, or East Germany.

The successful airlift was a big victory for Harry Truman, and it may have saved his political career: he surprised pundits by narrowly defeating Republican Thomas E. Dewey in the presidential election that occurred in the middle of the crisis in November 1948. Safely elected, Truman took the major step of formalizing what was already in essence a military alliance among the United States, Canada, and the nations of western Europe. In April 1949, twelve nations signed a mutual defense treaty, agreeing that an attack on any one of them would be considered an attack on all, and establishing the North Atlantic Treaty Organization (NATO; see Map 28.1).

The treaty aroused considerable domestic debate, for not since 1778 had the United States entered a formal European military alliance, and some critics, such as Senator Robert A. Taft, Republican of Ohio, claimed that NATO would provoke rather than deter war. Other critics argued that the Soviet threat was political, not military. Administration officials themselves did not anticipate a Soviet military thrust against western Europe, but they responded that, should the Soviets ever probe westward, NATO would function as a "tripwire," bringing the full force of the United States to bear on the Soviet Union. Truman officials also hoped that NATO would keep western Europeans from embracing communism or even neutralism in the Cold War. The Senate ratified the treaty by 82 votes to 13, and the United States soon began to spend billions of dollars under the Mutual Defense Assistance Act.

By the summer of 1949, Truman and his advisers were basking in the successes of their foreign policy. Containment was working splendidly, they and many outside observers had concluded. West Germany was on the road to recovery. The Berlin blockade had been defeated, and NATO had been formed. In western Europe, the threat posed by communist parties seemed lessened. True, there was trouble in China, where the communists under Mao Zedong were winning that country's civil war. But that struggle would likely wax and wane for years or even decades to come, and besides, Truman could not be held responsible for events there. Just possibly, some dared to think, Harry Truman was on his way to winning the Cold War.

Then, suddenly, in late September, came the "twin shocks," two momentous developments that made Amer-

## Twin Shocks

icans feel in even greater danger than ever before—two decades later, they were still dealing with the reverberations. First, an American

▲ Richard Edes Harrison's illustration of the Soviet Union's detonation of an atomic bomb appeared in the October 1949 issue of *Life* magazine. A leading journalist-cartographer of the mid-twentieth century, Harrison was known for incorporating a global perspective in his work. Here he uses a single cloud of smoke to suggest the potentially far-reaching effects of an isolated bomb explosion. *(Library of Congress)*

reconnaissance aircraft detected unusually high radioactivity in the atmosphere. The news stunned U.S. officials: the Soviets had exploded an atomic device. With the American nuclear monopoly erased, western Europe seemed more vulnerable. At the same time, the communists in China completed their conquest—the end came more quickly than many expected. Now the world's largest and most populous countries were ruled by communists, and one of them had the atomic bomb. The bipartisan foreign policy of 1945–1948 broke down, as Republicans, bitter over Truman's reelection, declared that traitors in America must have given Stalin the bomb and allowed China to be "lost."

Rejecting calls by Kennan and others for high-level negotiations, Truman in early 1950 gave the go-ahead to begin production of a hydrogen bomb, the "Super," and ordered his national security team to undertake a thorough review of policy. Kennan bemoaned the militarization of the Cold War and was replaced at the State Department by Paul Nitze. The National Security Council delivered to the president in April 1950 a significant top-secret document tagged NSC-68. Predicting continued tension with

expansionistic communists all over the world and describing "a shrinking world of polarized power," the report, whose primary author was Nitze, appealed for a much enlarged military budget and the mobilization of public opinion to support such an increase. The Cold War was about to become a vastly more expensive, more far-reaching affair.

## THE COLD WAR IN ASIA

Although Europe was the principal battleground in the early Cold War, Asia gradually became ensnared in the conflict as well. Indeed, it was in Asia that the consequences of an expansive containment doctrine would exact its heaviest price on the United States, in the form of large-scale and bloody wars in Korea and Vietnam. Though always less important to both superpowers than Europe, Asia would be the continent where the Cold War most often turned hot.

From the start, Japan was crucial to U.S. strategy. Much to Stalin's dismay, the United States monopolized Japan's reconstruction through a military occupation directed by General Douglas MacArthur, who envisioned turning the Pacific Ocean into "an Anglo-Saxon lake." Truman did not like "Mr. Prima Donna, Brass Hat" MacArthur, but the general initiated "a democratic revolution from above," as the Japanese called it, that reflected Washington's wishes. MacArthur wrote a democratic constitution, gave women voting rights, revitalized the economy, and destroyed the nation's weapons. U.S. authorities also helped Americanize Japan through censorship; films that hinted at criticism of the United States (for the destruction of Hiroshima, for example) or that depicted traditional Japanese customs, such as suicide, arranged marriages, and swordplay, were banned. In 1951 the United States and Japan signed a separate peace that restored Japan's sovereignty and ended the occupation. A Mutual Security Treaty that year provided for the stationing of U.S. forces on Japanese soil, including a base on Okinawa.

The administration had less success in China. The United States had long backed the Nationalists of Jiang Jieshi (Chiang Kai-shek) against Mao Zedong's communists. But after the Second World War, Generalissimo Jiang became an unreliable partner who rejected U.S. advice. His government had become corrupt, inefficient, and out of touch with discontented peasants, whom the communists enlisted with promises of land reform. Jiang also subverted American efforts to negotiate a cease-fire and a coalition government.

**Chinese Civil War**

◀ Mao Zedong was a military theoretician who also involved himself in day-to-day military decision making. He was responsible for, or at least approved, all of the major strategic moves the communists made on their way to power. This image shows him applauding soldiers and other supporters on Tiananmen Square in Beijing.

*(Sovfoto/Eastfoto)*

"We picked a bad horse," Truman admitted, privately denouncing the Nationalists as "grafters and crooks." Still, seeing Jiang as the only alternative to Mao, Truman backed him to the end.

American officials divided on the question of whether Mao was a puppet of the Soviet Union. Some considered him an Asian Tito—communist but independent—but most believed him to be part of an international communist movement that might give the Soviets a springboard into Asia. Thus, when the Chinese communists made secret overtures to the United States to begin diplomatic talks in 1945 and again in 1949, American officials rebuffed them. Mao decided to "lean" to the Soviet side in the Cold War. Because China always maintained a fierce independence that rankled the Soviets, before long a Sino-Soviet schism opened. Indeed, Mao deeply resented the Soviets' refusal to aid the communists during the civil war.

Then came Mao's victory in September 1949. Jiang fled to the island of Formosa (Taiwan), and in Beijing (formerly Peking) Mao proclaimed the People's Republic of China (PRC). Truman hesitated to extend diplomatic recognition to the new government, even after the British prime minister asked him, "Are we to cut ourselves off from all contact with one-sixth of the inhabitants of the world?" U.S. officials became alarmed by the 1950 Sino-Soviet treaty of friendship and by the harassment of Americans and their property in China. Truman also chose nonrecognition because a vocal group of Republican critics, the so-called China lobby, was winning headlines by asking the question "Who lost China?" The publisher

Henry Luce, Senator William Knowland of California, and Representative Walter Judd of Minnesota pinned Jiang's defeat on Truman. The president stoutly answered that the self-defeating Jiang, despite billions of dollars in American aid, had proven a poor instrument of the containment doctrine. The administration nonetheless took the politically safe route and rejected recognition. (Not until 1979 did official Sino-American relations resume.)

Mao's victory in China drew urgent American attention to Indochina, the southeast Asian peninsula that had been held by France for the better part of a century. The Japanese had wrested control over Indochina during World War II, but even then Vietnamese nationalists dedicated to independence grew in strength. One leading nationalist, Ho Chi Minh, hoped to use Japan's defeat to assert Vietnamese independence, and he asked for U.S. support. American officials had few kind things to say about French colonial policy, and many were pessimistic that France could achieve a military solution to the conflict. Nevertheless, they rejected Ho's appeals in favor of a restoration of French rule, mostly to ensure France's cooperation in the emerging Soviet-American confrontation. Paris warned that American support of the Vietnamese independence movement would alienate French public opinion and strengthen the French Communist Party, perhaps even drive France into the arms of the USSR. In addition, the Truman administration was wary of Ho Chi Minh's communist politics. Ho, the State Department declared, was an "agent of international communism" who, it was assumed, would assist Soviet and, after 1949, Chinese expansionism. Overlooking the native roots of the nationalist rebellion

## Vietnam's Quest for Independence

against French colonialism, and the tenacious Vietnamese resistance to foreign intruders, Washington officials interpreted events in Indochina through a Cold War lens.

Even so, when war between the Vietminh and France broke out in 1946, the United States initially took a hands-off approach. But when Jiang's regime collapsed in China three years later, the Truman administration made two crucial decisions—both of them in early 1950, before the Korean War. First, in February, Washington recognized the French puppet government of Bao Dai, a playboy and former emperor who had collaborated with the French and Japanese. In the eyes of many Vietnamese, the United States thus became in essence a colonial power, an ally of the hated French. Second, in May, the administration agreed to send weapons and other assistance to sustain the French in Indochina. From 1945 to 1954, the United States gave $2 billion of the $5 billion that France spent to keep Vietnam within its empire—to no avail (see Chapters 30 and 31). How Vietnam ultimately became the site of America's longest war, and how the world's most powerful nation failed to subdue a peasant people who suffered enormous losses, is one of the most remarkable and tragic stories of modern history.

## THE KOREAN WAR

Before Vietnam, however, the United States would fight another large-scale military conflict, in Korea. In the early morning of June 25, 1950, a large military force of the Democratic People's Republic of Korea (North Korea) moved across the 38th parallel into the Republic of Korea (South Korea). Colonized by Japan since 1910, Korea had been divided in two by the victorious powers after Japan's defeat in 1945. Although the Soviets had armed the North and the Americans had armed the South (U.S. aid had reached $100 million a year), the Korean War began as a civil war. Virtually from the moment of the division, the two parts had been skirmishing along their supposedly temporary border while antigovernment (and anti-U.S.) guerrilla fighting flared in the South.

Both the North's communist leader, Kim Il Sung, and the South's president, Syngman Rhee, sought to reunify their nation. Kim's military in particular gained strength when tens of thousands of battle-tested Koreans returned home in 1949 after serving in Mao's army. Displaying the Cold War mentality of the time, however, President Truman claimed that the Soviets had masterminded the North Korean attack. "Communism was acting in Korea just as Hitler, Mussolini, and the Japanese had acted," he said, recalling Axis aggression.

Actually, Kim had to press a doubting Joseph Stalin,

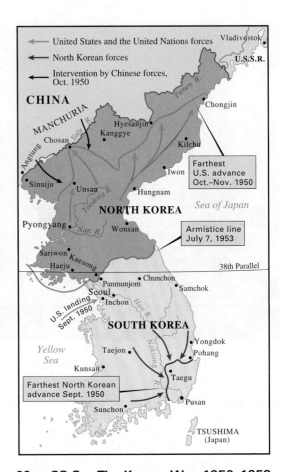

**Map 28.2   The Korean War, 1950–1953**

Beginning as a civil war between North and South, this war became international when the United States, under the auspices of the United Nations, and the People's Republic of China intervened with their military forces.

*(Source: Adapted from Thomas G. Paterson, J. Garry Clifford, and Kenneth J. Hagan,* American Foreign Relations: A History, *vol. 2, 5th ed. Copyright © 2000 by Houghton Mifflin Company.)*

who only reluctantly approved the attack after Kim predicted an easy, early victory and after Mao backed Kim. Whatever Stalin's reasoning, his support for Kim's venture remained lukewarm. When the U.N. Security Council voted to defend South Korea against the invasion from north, the Soviet representative was not even present to veto the resolution, because the Soviets were boycotting the United Nations to protest its refusal to grant membership to the People's Republic of China. During the war, Moscow gave limited aid to North Korea and China, which grew angry at Stalin for reneging on promised Soviet airpower. Stalin, all too aware of his strategic inferiority vis-à-vis the United States, did not want to be dragged into a costly war.

▲ Chinese soldiers guard marching American prisoners of the Korean War during the cold winter of 1950. *(Xinhua, New China News Agency)*

The president first ordered General Douglas Mac-Arthur to send arms and troops to South Korea. He did

### U.S. Forces Intervene

not seek congressional approval—he and his aides feared that lawmakers would initiate a lengthy debate—and thereby set the precedent of waging war on executive authority alone. Worried that Mao might use the occasion to take Formosa, Truman also directed the Seventh Fleet to patrol the waters between the Chinese mainland and Jiang's sanctuary on Formosa, thus inserting the United States again into Chinese politics. After the Security Council voted to assist South Korea, MacArthur became commander of U.N. forces in Korea. Sixteen nations contributed troops to the U.N. command, but 40 percent were South Korean and about 50 percent American. In the war's early weeks, North Korean tanks and superior firepower sent the South Korean army into chaotic retreat. The first American soldiers, taking heavy casualties, could not stop the North Korean advance. Within weeks, the South Kore-

ans and Americans had been pushed into the tiny Pusan perimeter at the tip of South Korea (see Map 28.2).

General MacArthur planned a daring operation: an amphibious landing at heavily fortified Inchon, several hundred miles behind North Korean lines. After U.S. guns and bombs pounded Inchon, marines sprinted ashore on September 15, 1950. The operation was a brilliant success, and the troops soon liberated the South Korean capital of Seoul and pushed the North Koreans back to the 38th parallel. Even before Inchon, Truman had redefined the U.S. war goal, changing it from the containment of North Korea to the reunification of Korea by force. Communism not only would be stopped; it would be rolled back.

In September, Truman authorized U.N. forces to cross the 38th parallel. These troops drove deep into

### Chinese Entry into the War

North Korea, and American aircraft began strikes against bridges on the Yalu River, the border between North Korea and China. The Chinese watched warily, fearing that the Americans would next stab at the People's Republic. Mao publicly warned that China could not permit the bombing of its transportation links with Korea and would not accept the annihilation of North Korea itself. MacArthur shrugged off the warnings, and Washington officials agreed with the strong-willed general, drawing further confidence from the fact that, as MacArthur had predicted, the Soviets were not preparing for war.

MacArthur was right about the Soviets, but wrong about the Chinese. Mao, concluding that the "Americans would run more rampant" unless stopped, on October 25 sent Chinese soldiers into the war near the Yalu. Perhaps to lure American forces into a trap or to signal willingness to begin negotiations, they pulled back after a brief and successful offensive against South Korean troops. Then, after MacArthur sent the U.S. Eighth Army northward, tens of thousands of Chinese troops counterattacked on November 26, surprising American forces and driving them pell-mell southward. One U.S. officer termed it "a sight that hasn't been seen for hundreds of years: the men of a whole United States Army fleeing from a battlefield, abandoning their wounded, running for their lives."

By early 1951 the front had stabilized around the 38th parallel. A stalemate set in. Both Washington and Moscow welcomed negotiations, but MacArthur had other ideas.

### Truman's Firing of MacArthur

The theatrical general recklessly called for an attack on China and for Jiang's return to the mainland. Now was the time, he insisted, to smash communism by destroying its Asian flank. Denouncing the concept of limited war (war without nuclear weapons, confined to one place), MacArthur hinted that the president was practicing appeasement. In April, backed by the Joint Chiefs of Staff (the heads of the various armed services), Truman fired MacArthur. The general, who had not set foot in the United States for more than a decade, returned home a hero, with ticker-tape parades and cheers on the lecture circuit. Truman's popularity sagged, but he weathered scattered demands for his impeachment.

Armistice talks began in July 1951, but the fighting and dying went on for two more years. The most contentious point in the negotiations was the fate of prisoners of war (POWs). Defying the Geneva Prisoners of War Convention (1949), U.S. officials announced that only those North Korean and Chinese POWs who wished to go home would be returned. Responding to the American statement that there would be no forced repatriation, the North Koreans denounced forced retention. Both sides undertook "reeducation" or "brainwashing" programs to persuade POWs to resist repatriation.

As the POW issue stalled negotiations, U.S. officials made deliberately vague public statements about using atomic weapons in Korea. American bombers obliterated dams (whose rushing waters then destroyed rice fields), factories, airfields, and bridges in North Korea. Casualties on all sides mounted. Not until July 1953 was an armistice signed. Stalin's death in March and the advent of new leaders in both Moscow and Washington helped ease the way to a settlement that all sides welcomed. The combatants agreed to hand over the POW question to a special panel of neutral nations, which later gave prisoners their choice of staying or leaving. (In the end, 70,000 of about 100,000 North Korean and 5,600 of 20,700 Chinese POWs elected to return home; 21 American and 325 South Korean POWs of some 11,000 decided to stay in North Korea.) The North Korean–South Korean borderline was set near the 38th parallel, the prewar boundary, and a demilitarized zone was created between the two Koreas.

### Peace Agreement

American casualties totaled 54,246 dead and 103,284 wounded. Close to 5 million Asians died in the war: 2 million North Korean civilians and 500,000 soldiers; 1 million South Korean civilians and 100,000 soldiers; and at least 1 million Chinese soldiers—ranking Korea as one of the costliest wars of the twentieth century.

The Korean War carried major domestic political consequences. The failure to achieve victory and the public's impatience with a stalemated war undoubtedly helped to elect Republican Dwight Eisenhower to the presidency in 1952, as the former general promised to "go to Korea" to end the war. The powers of the presidency grew as Congress repeatedly deferred to Truman. The president had never asked Congress for a declaration of war, believing that, as commander-in-chief, he had the authority to send troops wherever he wished. He saw no need to consult Congress—except when he wanted the $69.5 billion Korean War bill paid. In addition, the war, which occurred in the midst of the "who lost China?" debate, inflamed antileftist politics in the United States. Republican lawmakers, including Wisconsin senator Joseph McCarthy, accused Truman and Secretary of State Dean Acheson of being "soft on communism" in failing first to prevent, and then to go all-out to win, the war; their verbal attacks strengthened the administration's determination to take an uncompromising position in the negotiations.

### Consequences of the War

The impact on foreign policy was even greater. The Sino-American hostility generated by the war ensured that there would be no U.S. reconciliation with the Beijing government and that South Korea and Formosa would become major recipients of American foreign aid. The alliance with Japan strengthened as the island's economy boomed after filling large procurement orders from the United States. Australia and New Zealand joined the United States in a mutual defense agreement, the ANZUS Treaty (1951). The U.S. Army sent four divisions to Europe, and the administration initiated plans to rearm West Germany. The Korean War also persuaded Truman to do what he had been unwilling to do before the outbreak of hostilities—approve NSC-68. Indeed, the military budget shot up from $14 billion in 1949 to $44 billion in 1953; it remained between $35 billion and $44 billion a year throughout the 1950s. The Soviet Union sought to match this military buildup, and the result was a major arms race between the two nations. In sum, Truman's legacy was a highly militarized U.S. foreign policy active on a global scale.

## UNRELENTING COLD WAR

The new foreign policy team of President Eisenhower and Secretary of State John Foster Dulles largely sustained Truman's Cold War policies. Both brought abundant experience in foreign affairs to their posts. Eisenhower had lived and traveled in Europe, Asia, and Latin America and, as a general during the Second World War, had ne-

gotiated with world leaders. After the war, he had served as army chief of staff and NATO supreme commander. Dulles had been closely involved with U.S. diplomacy since the first decade of the century. "Foster has been studying to be secretary of state since he was five years old," Eisenhower observed. He relied heavily on Dulles to be his emissary abroad. The secretary of state spent so much time traveling to world capitals that critics exclaimed, "Don't do something, Foster, just stand there!"

Eisenhower and Dulles accepted the Cold War consensus about the threat of communism and the need for

**Eisenhower and Dulles**

global vigilance. Although Democrats promoted an image of Eisenhower as a bumbling, passive, aging hero, deferring most foreign policy matters to Dulles, the president in fact commanded the policymaking process and on occasion tamed the more hawkish proposals of Dulles and Vice President Richard Nixon. Even so, the secretary of state's influence was considerable. Few Cold Warriors rivaled Dulles's impassioned anticommunism, often expressed in biblical terms. A graduate of Princeton and George Washington Universities, Dulles had assisted Woodrow Wilson at Versailles and later became a senior partner in a prestigious Wall Street law firm and an officer of the Federal Council of Churches. Though polished and articulate, Dulles impressed people as arrogant, stubborn, and hectoring—and averse to compromise, an essential ingredient in successful diplomacy. Behind closed doors Dulles could show a different side, one considerably more flexible and pragmatic, but there is little evidence that he saw much utility in negotiations, at least where communists were involved. His assertion that neutrality was an "immoral and shortsighted conception" did not sit well with Third World leaders, who resented being told they had to choose between East and West.

◀ President Eisenhower *(left)* confers with Secretary of State John Foster Dulles (1888–1959), known for his strong anticommunism and his often self-righteous, lecturing style. Dulles once remarked that the United States "is almost the only country strong enough and powerful enough to be moral." *(© Bettmann/Corbis)*

Like the president, Dulles conceded much to the anticommunist McCarthyites, who claimed that the State Department was infested with communists (see pages 835–836). The State Department's chief security officer, a McCarthy follower, targeted homosexuals and other "incompatibles," and made few distinctions between New Dealers and communists. Dulles thus forced many talented officers out of the Foreign Service with unsubstantiated charges that they were disloyal. Among them were Asia specialists whose expertise was thus denied to the American leaders who were steadily expanding the U.S. presence on that continent. "The wrong done," the journalist Theodore A. White wrote, "was to poke out the eyes and ears of the State Department on Asian affairs, to blind American foreign policy."

Dulles said that he considered containment too defensive a stance toward communism. He called instead

**"Massive Retaliation"**

for "liberation," although he never explained precisely how the countries of eastern Europe could be freed from Soviet control. "Massive retaliation" was the administration's plan for the nuclear obliteration of the Soviet state or its assumed client, the People's Republic of China, if either one took aggressive actions. Eisenhower said that it "simply means the ability to blow hell out of them in a hurry if they start anything." The ability of the United States to make such a threat was thought to provide "deterrence," the prevention of hostile Soviet behavior.

In their "New Look" for the American military, Eisenhower and Dulles emphasized airpower and nuclear weaponry. The president's preference for heavy weapons stemmed in part from his desire to trim the federal budget ("more bang for the buck," as the saying went). Galvanized by the successful test of the world's first hydrogen bomb in November 1952, Eisenhower oversaw a massive stockpiling of nuclear weapons—from 1,200 at the start of his presidency to 22,229 at the end. Backed by its huge military arsenal, the United States could practice "brinkmanship": not backing down in a crisis, even if it meant taking the nation to the brink of war. Eisenhower also popularized the "domino theory": that small, weak, neighboring nations would fall to communism like a row of dominoes if they were not propped up by the United States.

Eisenhower increasingly utilized the Central Intelligence Agency as an instrument of foreign policy. Headed by Allen Dulles, brother of the sec-

**CIA as Foreign Policy Instrument**

retary of state, the CIA put foreign leaders (such as King Hussein of Jordan) on its payroll; subsidized foreign labor unions, newspapers, and political parties (such as the conservative Liberal Democratic Party of Japan); planted false stories in newspapers through its "disinformation" projects; and trained foreign military officers in counterrevolutionary methods. It hired American journalists and professors; secretly funded the National Student Association to spur contacts with foreign student leaders; used business executives as "fronts"; and conducted experiments on unsuspecting Americans to determine the effects of "mind control" drugs (the MKULTRA program). The CIA also launched covert operations (including assassination schemes) to subvert or destroy governments in the Third World. The CIA helped overthrow the governments of Iran (1953) and Guatemala (1954) but failed in attempts to topple regimes in Indonesia (1958) and Cuba (1961).

The CIA and other components of the American intelligence community followed the principle of plausible deniability: covert operations should be conducted in such a way, and the decisions that launched them concealed so well, that the president could deny any knowledge of them. Thus President Eisenhower disavowed any U.S. role in Guatemala, even though he had ordered the operation. He and his successor, John F. Kennedy, also denied that they had instructed the CIA to assassinate Cuba's Fidel Castro, whose regime after 1959 became stridently anti-American.

It did not take leaders in Moscow long to become aware of Eisenhower's expanded use of covert action, as

**Nuclear Buildup**

well as his stockpiling of nuclear weapons. They increased their own intelligence activity and tested their first H-bomb in 1953. Four years later, they shocked Americans by firing the world's first intercontinental ballistic missile (ICBM) and then propelling the satellite *Sputnik* into orbit in outer space. Americans felt more vulnerable to air attack and inferior in rocket technology, even though in 1957 the United States had 2,460 strategic weapons and a nuclear stockpile of 5,543, compared with the Soviet Union's 102 and 650. As President Eisenhower said, "If we were to release our nuclear stockpile on the Soviet Union, the main danger would arise not from retaliation but from fallout in the earth's atmosphere." The administration enlarged its fleet of long-range bombers (B-52s) and deployed intermediate-range missiles in Europe, targeted against the Soviet Union. At the end of 1960 the United States began adding Polaris missile–bearing submarines to its navy. To foster future technological advancement, the National Aeronautics and Space Administration (NASA) was created in 1958.

Overall, though, Eisenhower sought to avoid any kind of military confrontation with the Soviet Union and China;

## The People-to-People Campaign

Not long after the start of the Cold War, U.S. officials determined that the Soviet-American confrontation was as much psychological and ideological as military and economic. One result was the People-to-People campaign, a state-private venture initiated by the United States Information Agency (USIA) in 1956, which aimed to win the "hearts and minds" of people around the world. In this program, American propaganda experts sought to channel the energies of ordinary Americans, businesses, civic organizations, labor groups, and women's clubs to promote confidence abroad in the basic goodness of the American people and, by extension, their government. In addition, the campaign was designed to raise morale at home by giving Americans a sense of personal participation in the Cold War struggle. The People-to-People campaign, one USIA pamphlet said, made "every man an ambassador."

Campaign activities resembled the home-front mobilization efforts of World War II. If, during the war, Americans were exhorted by the Office of War Information to purchase war bonds, now they were told that $30 could send a ninety-nine-volume portable library of American books to schools and libraries overseas. Publishers donated magazines and books for free distribution to foreign countries—*Woman's Day,* for example, volunteered six thousand copies of the magazine per month. People-to-People committees organized sister-city affiliations and "pen-pal" letter exchanges, hosted exchange students, and organized traveling "People-to-People delegations" representing their various communities. The travelers were urged to behave like goodwill ambassadors when abroad and to "help overcome any feeling that America is a land that thinks money can buy everything." They were to "appreciate [foreigners'] manners and customs, not to insist on imitations of the American way of doing things."

To extol everyday life in the United States, Camp Fire Girls in more than three thousand communities took photographs on the theme "This is our home. This is how we live. These are my People." The photographs, assembled in albums, were sent to girls in Latin America, Africa, Asia, and the Middle East. The Hobbies Committee, meanwhile, connected people with interests in radio, photography, coins, stamps, and horticulture. One group represented dog owners, in the belief that "dogs make good ambassadors and are capable of hurdling the barriers of language and ideologies in the quest for peace."

Just what effect the People-to-People campaign had on foreign images of the United States is hard to say. The persistence to this day of the widespread impression that Americans are a provincial, materialistic people suggests that skepticism is in order. But alongside this negative image is a more positive one that sees Americans as admirably open, friendly, optimistic, and pragmatic; if the campaign did not erase the former impression, it may have helped foster the latter. Whatever role the People-to-People campaign played in the larger Cold War struggle, it certainly achieved one of its chief objectives: to link ordinary Americans more closely to people in other parts of the world.

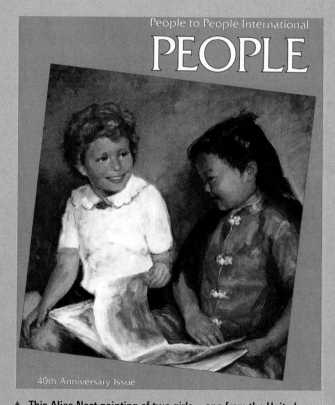

▲ This Alice Nast painting of two girls—one from the United States and one from Taiwan—was commissioned by the Kansas City chapter of People to People and the Kansas City/Tainan Sister City Committee. The painting was presented to the mayor of Tainan in September 1994, prior to the 11th Worldwide Conference of the People-to-People International. *(People to People)*

notwithstanding Dulles's tough talk of "liberation" and "massive retaliation," the administration was content to follow Truman's lead and emphasize the *containment* of communism. Eisenhower rejected opportunities to use nuclear weapons, and he proved more reluctant than many other Cold War presidents to send American soldiers into battle. He preferred to fight the Soviets at the level of propaganda. Convinced that the struggle against Moscow would in large measure be decided in the arena of international public opinion, he wanted to win the "hearts and minds" of people overseas. The "People-to-People" campaign, launched in 1956, sought to use ordinary Americans and nongovernmental organizations to enhance the international image of the United States and its people.

Likewise, American cultural exchanges and participation in trade fairs in the Eisenhower years were used to create a favorable atmosphere abroad for U.S. political, economic, and military policies. Sometimes the propaganda war was waged on the Soviets' own turf. In 1959 Vice President Richard Nixon traveled to Moscow to open an American products fair. In the display of a modern American kitchen, part of a model six-room ranch-style house, Nixon extolled capitalist consumerism, while Soviet premier Nikita Khrushchev, Stalin's successor, touted the merits of communism. The encounter became famous as the "kitchen debate."

Eisenhower showed his restraint in 1956 when turmoil rocked parts of eastern Europe. In February, Khrushchev called for "peaceful coexistence"

**Rebellion in Hungary**

between capitalists and communists, denounced Stalin, and suggested that Moscow would tolerate different brands of communism. Revolts against Soviet power promptly erupted in Poland and Hungary, testing Khrushchev's new permissiveness. After a new Hungarian government in 1956 announced its withdrawal from the Warsaw Pact (the Soviet military alliance formed in 1955 with communist countries of eastern Europe), Soviet troops and tanks battled students and workers in the streets of Budapest and crushed the rebellion.

Although the Eisenhower administration's propaganda had been encouraging liberation efforts, U.S. officials found themselves unable to aid the rebels without igniting a world war. They stood by, promising only to welcome Hungarian immigrants in greater numbers than American quota laws allowed. Even so, the West could have reaped some propaganda advantage from this display of Soviet brute force had not British, French, and Israeli troops—U.S. allies—invaded Egypt during the Suez crisis just before the Soviets smashed the Hungarian uprising (see page 820).

Hardly had the turmoil subsided when the divided city of Berlin once again became a Cold War flash point. The Soviets railed against the placement in West Germany of American bombers capable of carrying nuclear warheads, and they complained that West Berlin had become an escape route for disaffected East Germans. In 1958 Khrushchev announced that the Soviet Union would recognize East German control of all of Berlin unless the United States and its allies began talks on German reunification and rearmament. The United States refused to give up its hold on West Berlin or to break West German ties with NATO. Khrushchev backed away from his ultimatum but promised to press the issue again.

Khrushchev hoped to do just that at a summit meeting planned for Paris in mid-1960. But two weeks before the conference, on May 1, a U-2

**U-2 Incident**

spy plane carrying high-powered cameras crashed 1,200 miles inside the Soviet Union. Moscow claimed credit for shooting down the plane, which the Soviets put on display along with Francis Gary Powers, the captured CIA pilot, and the pictures he had been snapping of Soviet military sites. Khrushchev demanded an apology for the U.S. violation of Soviet airspace. When Washington refused, the Soviets walked out of the Paris summit—"a graveyard of lost opportunities," as a Soviet official put it.

While sparring over Europe, both sides kept a wary eye on the People's Republic of China, which denounced the Soviet call for peaceful coexistence. Despite evidence of a widening Sino-Soviet split, most American officials still treated communism as a monolithic world movement. The isolation separating Beijing and Washington stymied communication and made continued conflict between China and the United States likely. In 1954, in a dispute over Jinmen (Quemoy) and Mazu (Matsu), two tiny islands off the Chinese coast, the United States and the People's Republic of China lurched toward the brink. Taiwan's Jiang Jieshi used these islands as bases from which to raid the mainland. Communist China's guns bombarded the islands in 1954. Thinking that U.S. credibility was at stake, Eisenhower decided to defend the outposts; he even hinted that he might use nuclear weapons. Why massive retaliation over such an insignificant issue? "Let's keep the Reds guessing," advised John Foster Dulles. "But what if they guessed wrong?" critics replied.

In early 1955, Congress passed the Formosa Resolution, authorizing the president to deploy American forces

**Formosa Resolution**

to defend Formosa and adjoining islands. In so doing, Congress formally surrendered to the president what it had informally given up at the time of the Korea decision in

1950: the constitutional power to declare war. Although the crisis passed in April 1955, war loomed again in 1958 over Jinmen and Mazu. But this time, after Washington strongly cautioned him not to use force against the mainland, Jiang withdrew some troops from the islands. China then relaxed its bombardments. One consequence accelerated the arms race: Eisenhower's nuclear threats persuaded the Chinese that they, too, needed nuclear arms. In 1964 China exploded its first nuclear bomb.

## THE STRUGGLE FOR THE THIRD WORLD

Like Truman before him and all Cold War presidents after him, Eisenhower worried most about the fate of western Europe. Over time, however, his administration focused more and more attention on the threat of communist expansion in Africa, Asia, Latin America, and the Middle East. In much of the Third World, the process of decolonization that began during the First World War accelerated after the Second World War, when the economically wracked imperial countries proved incapable of resisting their colonies' demands for freedom. A cavalcade of new nations cast off their colonial bonds (see Map 28.3). In 1960 alone, eighteen new African nations did so. From 1943 to 1994, a total of 125 countries became independent (the figure includes the former Soviet republics that departed the USSR in 1991). The emergence of so many new states in the 1940s and after, and the instability associated with the transfer of authority, shook the foundations of the international system. Power was redistributed, creating "near chaos," said one U.S. government report. In the traditional U.S. sphere of influence, Latin America, nationalists once again challenged Washington's dominance.

By the late 1940s, when Cold War lines were drawn fairly tightly in Europe, Soviet-American rivalry shifted increasingly to the Third World.

**Interests in the Third World**

Much was at stake. The new nations could buy American goods and technology, supply strategic raw materials, and invite investments (more than one-third of America's private foreign investments were in Third World countries in 1959). And they could build cultural ties with the United States. Both great powers, moreover, looked to these new states for votes in the United Nations and sought sites within their borders for military and intelligence bases. But, often poor and unstable—and rife with tribal, ethnic, and class rivalries—many new nations sought to end the economic, military, and cultural hegemony of the West. Many learned to play off the two superpowers against each other to garner more aid and arms. U.S. interventions—military and

otherwise—in the Third World, American leaders believed, became necessary to impress Moscow with Washington's might and to resolve and counter the nationalism and radical anticapitalist social change that threatened American strategic and economic interests.

To thwart nationalist, radical, and communist challenges, the United States directed massive resources—foreign aid, propaganda, development projects—toward the Third World. By 1961 more than 90 percent of U.S. foreign aid was going to developing nations. Washington also allied with native elites and with undemocratic but anticommunist regimes, meddled in civil wars, and unleashed CIA covert operations. These American interventions often generated resentment among the local populace. When some of the larger Third World states—notably India, Ghana, Egypt, and Indonesia—refused to take sides in the Cold War, Secretary of State Dulles declared that neutralism was a step on the road to communism. Both he and Eisenhower insisted that every nation should take a side in the life-and-death Cold War struggle.

American leaders argued that technologically "backward" Third World countries needed western-induced capitalist development and modernization in order to enjoy economic growth, social harmony, and political moderation. Often these U.S. officials also ascribed stereotyped race-, age-, and gender-based characteristics to Third World peoples, seeing them as dependent, emotional, and irrational, and therefore dependent on the fatherly tutelage of the United States. Cubans, CIA director Allen Dulles told the National Security Council in early 1959, "had to be treated more or less like children. They had to be led rather than rebuffed. If they were rebuffed, like children, they were capable of almost anything."

At other times American officials used gendered language, suggesting that Third World countries were weak women—passive and servile, unable to resist the menacing appeals of communists and neutralists. In speaking of India, for example—a neutralist nation that Americans deemed effeminate and submissive—Eisenhower condescendingly described it as a place where "emotion rather than reason seems to dictate policy."

Race attitudes and segregation practices in the United States especially influenced U.S. relations with Third World countries.

**Racism and Segregation as U.S. Handicaps**

In 1955 G. L. Mehta, the Indian ambassador to the United States, was refused service in the whites-only section of a restaurant at Houston International Airport. The insult stung deeply, as did many similar indignities experienced by other Third World diplomats. Fearing damaged relations with India, a large nation whose allegiance the United States sought in the

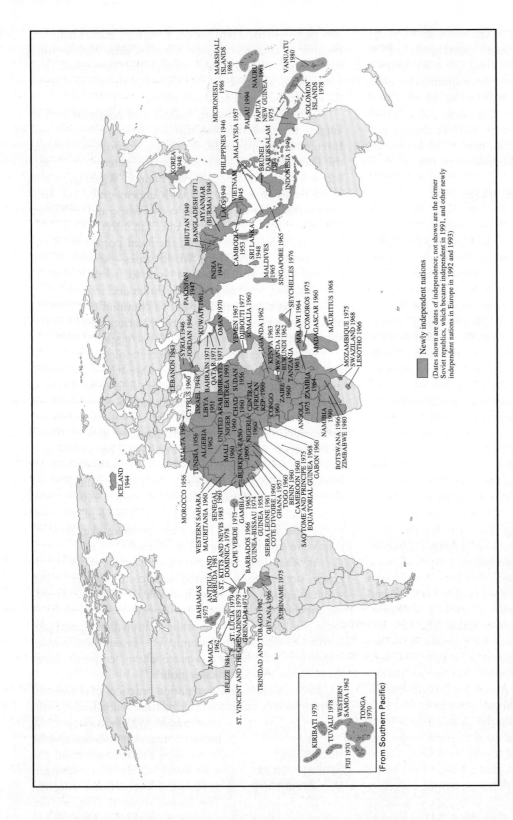

**Map 28.3   The Rise of the Third World: Newly Independent Nations Since 1943**

Accelerated by the Second World War, decolonization liberated many peoples from imperial rule. New nations emerged in the postwar international system dominated by the Cold War rivalry of the United States and the Soviet Union. Many newly independent states became targets of great-power intrigue but chose nonalignment in the Cold War.

Cold War, John Foster Dulles apologized to Mehta. The secretary thought racial segregation in the United States was a "major international hazard," spoiling American efforts to win friends in Third World countries and giving the Soviets a propaganda advantage. American practices and ideals did not align.

Thus, when the U.S. attorney general appealed to the Supreme Court to strike down segregation in public schools, he underlined that the humiliation of dark-skinned diplomats "furnished grist for the Communist propaganda mills." When the Court announced its *Brown* decision in 1954 (see page 838), the government quickly broadcast news of the desegregation order around the world in thirty-five languages on its Voice of America overseas radio network. But the problem did not go away. For example, after the 1957 Little Rock crisis (see page 840), Dulles remarked that racial bigotry was "ruining our foreign policy. The effect of this in Asia and Africa will be worse for us than Hungary was for the Russians." Still, when an office of the Department of State decided to counter Soviet propaganda by creating for the 1958 World's Fair in Brussels an exhibit titled "The Unfinished Work"—on race relations in the United States and strides taken toward desegregation—southern conservatives kicked up such a furor that the Eisenhower administration closed the display.

American hostility toward revolution also obstructed the quest for influence in the Third World. In the twentieth century, the United States openly opposed revolutions in Mexico, China, Russia, Cuba, Vietnam, Nicaragua, and Iran, among other nations. Americans celebrated the Spirit of '76 but grew intolerant of revolutionary disorder because many Third World revolutions arose against America's Cold War allies and threatened American investments, markets, and military bases. Preferring, like most other great powers in history, to maintain the status quo, the United States usually supported its European allies or the conservative, propertied classes in the Third World. In 1960, for example, when forty-three African and Asian states sponsored a U.N. resolution endorsing decolonization, the United States abstained from the vote.

Yet the American approach also had its element of idealism. Believing that Third World peoples craved modernization and that the American economic model of private enterprise and cooperation among business, labor, and government was best for them, American policymakers launched various "development" projects. Such projects held out the promise of sustained economic growth, prosperity, and stability, which the benefactors hoped would undermine radicalism. In the 1950s, the Carnegie, Ford, and Rockefeller Foundations worked with the U.S. Agency for International Development (AID) to sponsor a Green Revolution, a dramatic increase in agricultural production—for example, by the use of hybrid seeds. The Rockefeller Foundation supported foreign universities' efforts to train national leaders committed to nonradical development; from 1958 to 1969 the philanthropic agency spent $25 million in Nigeria. Before Dean Rusk became secretary of state in 1961, he served as president of the Rockefeller Foundation.

To persuade Third World peoples to abandon radical doctrines and neutralism, American

### Development and Modernization

◀ In the 1950s, these specially outfitted jeeps (equipped with projectors, screens, and films) served America's overseas information program in what the State Department called "isolated areas." Believing that social modernization and economic progress would counter leftist and communist ideas, U.S. propaganda officials dispatched these "mobile motion picture units" to such places as rural Mexico, seeking to reach people with films on U.S. sports, music, health, and agriculture. *(National Archives)*

leaders, often in cooperation with the business-sponsored Advertising Council, directed propaganda at developing nations. The United States Information Agency (USIA), founded in 1953, used films, radio broadcasts, the magazine *Free World,* exhibitions, exchange programs, and libraries (in 162 cities worldwide by 1961) to trumpet the theme of "People's Capitalism." Citing America's economic success—contrasted with "slave-labor" conditions in the Soviet Union—the message showcased well-paid American workers, political democracy, and religious freedom. To counter ugly pictures of segregation and white attacks on African Americans and civil rights activists in the South, the USIA applauded success stories of individual African Americans, such as boxers Floyd Patterson and Sugar Ray Robinson. In 1960 alone, some 13.8 million people visited U.S. pavilions abroad, including 1 million at the consumer-products exhibit "Tradeways to Peace and Prosperity" in Damascus, Syria.

Undoubtedly the American way of life had appeal for some Third World peoples. They, too, wanted to enjoy American consumer goods, rock music, economic status, and educational opportunities. Hollywood movies offered enticing glimpses of middle-class materialism, and American films dominated many overseas markets. Blue jeans, advertising billboards, and soft drinks flooded foreign societies. But if foreigners often envied Americans, they also resented them for having so much and wasting so much, while poorer peoples went without. The popular American novel *The Ugly American* (1958) spotlighted the "golden ghettoes" where American diplomats lived in compounds separated from their poorer surroundings by high walls. The people of many countries, moreover, resented the ample profits that U.S. corporations extracted from them. Americans often received blame for the persistent poverty of the developing world, even though the leaders of those nations made decisions that hindered their own progress, such as pouring millions of dollars into their militaries while their people needed food. Nonetheless, anti-American resentments could be measured in the late 1950s in attacks on USIA libraries in Calcutta, India; Beirut, Lebanon; and Bogotá, Colombia.

When the more benign techniques of containment—aid, trade, cultural relations—proved insufficient to get Third World nations to line up on the American side in the Cold War, the Eisenhower administration often showed a willingness to press harder, by covert or overt means. Guatemala was an early test case. In 1951 leftist Jacobo Arbenz Guzmán was elected president of Guatemala, a poor country whose largest landowner was the American-

### Intervention in Guatemala

owned United Fruit Company. United Fruit was an economic power throughout Latin America, where it owned 3 million acres of land and operated railroads, ports, ships, and telecommunications facilities. To fulfill his promise of land reform, Arbenz expropriated United Fruit's uncultivated land and offered compensation. The company dismissed the offer and charged that Arbenz posed a communist threat—a charge that CIA officials had already floated because Arbenz employed some communists in his government. The CIA began a secret plot to overthrow Arbenz. He turned to Moscow for military aid, thus reinforcing American suspicions. The CIA airlifted arms into Guatemala, dropping them at United Fruit facilities, and in mid-1954, CIA-supported Guatemalans struck from Honduras. U.S. planes bombed the capital city, and the invaders drove Arbenz from power. The new pro-American regime returned United Fruit's land, but an ensuing civil war staggered the Central American nation for decades.

Eisenhower also watched with apprehension as turmoil gripped Cuba in the late 1950s. In early 1959, Fidel Castro's rebels, or *barbudos* ("bearded ones"), driven by profound anti-American nationalism, ousted Fulgencio Batista, a longtime U.S. ally who had welcomed North American investors, U.S. military advisers, and tourists to the Caribbean island. Batista's corrupt, dictatorial regime had helped turn Havana into a haven for gambling and prostitution run by organized crime. Cubans had resented U.S. domination ever since the early twentieth century, when the Platt Amendment had compromised their independence. Curbing U.S. influence became a rallying cry of the Cuban revolution, all the more so after the CIA conspired secretly but futilely to block Castro's rise to power in 1958. From the start Castro sought to roll back the influence of American business, which had invested some $1 billion on the island, and to break the U.S. grasp on Cuban trade.

### The Cuban Revolution and Fidel Castro

Castro's increasing authoritarianism, anti-Yankee declarations, and growing popularity in the hemisphere alarmed Washington. In early 1960, after Cuba signed a trade treaty with the Soviet Union, Eisenhower ordered the CIA to organize an invasion force of Cuban exiles to overthrow the Castro government. The agency also began to plot an assassination of the Cuban leader. When the president drastically cut U.S. purchases of Cuban sugar, Castro seized all North American–owned companies that had not yet been nationalized. Threatened by U.S. decisions designed to bring him and his revolution down, Castro appealed to the Soviet Union, which offered loans

and expanded trade. Just before leaving office in early 1961, Eisenhower broke diplomatic relations with Cuba and advised president-elect John F. Kennedy to advance plans for the invasion, which came—and failed—in early 1961 (see page 862).

In the Middle East, meanwhile, the Eisenhower administration confronted challenges posed by ongoing tensions between Arabs and Jews, and by nationalist leaders in Iran and Egypt (see Map 33.2). Prior to the end of World War II, only France and Britain among the great powers had been much concerned with this region of the world; they had effectively dominated the area during the prior three decades. But the dissolution of empires and the rise of Cold War tensions drew Washington into the region, as did the deepening tensions in British-held Palestine. From 1945 to 1947, Britain tried to enlist U.S. officials in the effort to find a solution to the vexing question of how to split Palestine between the Arabs and Jews who lived there. The Truman administration rejected London's solicitations, and the British, despairing at the violence between Arabs and Jews and at the rising number of British deaths, in 1947 turned the issue over to the United Nations, which voted to partition Palestine into separate Arab and Jewish states. Arab leaders opposed the decision, but in May 1948 Jewish leaders announced the creation of Israel.

The United States, which had lobbied hard to secure the U.N. vote, extended recognition to the new state mere minutes after the act of foundation. A moral conviction

### Arab-Israeli Conflict

that Jews deserved a homeland after the suffering of the Holocaust, and that Zionism was a worthy movement that would create a democratic Israel, influenced Truman's decision, as did the belief that Jewish votes might swing some states to the Democrats in the 1948 election. These beliefs trumped some senior officials' concerns that Arab oil producers might turn against the United States and that close Soviet-Israeli ties could turn Israel into a pro-Soviet bastion in the Middle East. The Soviet Union did promptly recognize the new nation, but Israeli leaders kept Moscow at arm's length, in part because they had more pressing concerns. Palestinian Arabs, displaced from land they considered theirs, joined with Israel's Arab neighbors to make immediate war on the new state. The Israelis stopped the offensive in bloody fighting over the next six months until a U.N.-backed truce was called.

In the years thereafter, American policy in the Middle East centered on ensuring Israel's survival and cementing ties with Arab oil producers. U.S. oil holdings were extensive: American companies produced about half of the region's petroleum in the 1950s. Eisenhower consequently sought to avoid actions that might alienate Arab states, such as drawing too close to Israel, and he cultivated close relations with oil-rich Iran. Its ruling shah had granted American oil companies a 40 percent interest in a new petroleum consortium in return for CIA help in the successful overthrow, in 1953, of his rival, Mohammed Mossadegh, who had attempted to nationalize foreign oil interests. Nor was it only about petroleum: Iran's position on the Soviet border made the shah a particularly valuable friend.

American officials faced a more formidable foe in Egypt, in the form of Gamal Abdul Nasser, a towering figure in a pan-Arabic movement to reduce western interests in the Middle East. Nasser vowed to expel the British from the Suez Canal and the Israelis from Palestine. The United States wished neither to anger the Arabs, for fear of losing valuable oil supplies, nor to alienate its ally Israel, which was supported at home by politically active American Jews. But when Nasser declared neutrality in the Cold War, Dulles lost patience.

In 1956 the United States abruptly reneged on its offer to Egypt to help finance the Aswan Dam, a project to provide inexpensive electricity and water for thirsty Nile valley farmland. Secretary Dulles's blunt economic pressure backfired, for Nasser responded by nationalizing the British-owned Suez Canal, intending to use its profits to build the dam. At a mass rally in Alexandria, Nasser expressed the profound nationalism typical of Third World peoples shedding an imperial past: "Tonight our Egyptian canal will be run by Egyptians. Egyptians!" Fully 75 percent of western Europe's oil came from the Middle East, most of it transported through the Suez Canal. Fearing an interruption in this vital trade, the British and French conspired with Israel to bring down Nasser. On October 29, 1956, the Israelis invaded Suez, joined two days later by British and French forces.

**Suez Crisis**

Eisenhower fumed. America's allies had not consulted him, and the attack had shifted attention from Soviet intervention in Hungary. The president also feared that the invasion would cause Nasser to seek help from the Soviets, inviting them into the Middle East. Eisenhower sternly demanded that London, Paris, and Tel Aviv pull their troops out, and they did. Egypt took possession of the canal, the Soviets built the Aswan Dam, and Nasser became a hero to Third World peoples. French and British influence in the region declined sharply. To counter Nasser, the United States determined to "build up" as an "Arab rival" the conservative King Ibn Saud of Saudi Arabia. Although the monarch renewed America's lease of an air base, few Arabs respected the notoriously corrupt Saud.

Washington officials worried that a "vacuum" existed in the Middle East—and that the Soviets might fill it. Nasserites insisted that there was no vacuum but rather a growing Arab nationalism that provided the best defense against communism. In an effort to improve the deteriorating western position in the Middle East and to protect American interests there, the president proclaimed the Eisenhower Doctrine in 1957. The United States would intervene in the Middle East, he declared, if any government threatened by a communist takeover asked for help.

**Eisenhower Doctrine**

In 1958 fourteen thousand American troops scrambled ashore in Lebanon to quell an internal political dispute that Washington feared might be exploited by pro-Nasser groups or communists. Concentrating the troops in the area of Beirut, Eisenhower said their mission was "not primarily to fight" but merely to show the flag. The restrained use of U.S. military power served to defuse the crisis, as Lebanese officials agreed to work for a peaceful transition to a new leadership. In Dulles's view, the intervention also served to "reassure many small nations that they could call on us in a time of crisis."

Cold War concerns also drove Eisenhower's policy toward Vietnam, where nationalists battled the French for independence. Despite a substantial U.S. aid program initiated under Truman, the French lost steadily to the Vietminh. Finally, in early 1954, Ho's forces surrounded the French fortress at Dienbienphu in northwest Vietnam (see Map 30.2). Although some of Eisenhower's advisers recommended a massive American air strike against Vietminh positions, perhaps even using tactical atomic weapons, the president moved cautiously. The United States had been advising and bankrolling the French, but it had not committed its own forces to the war. If American airpower did not save the French, would ground troops be required next, and in hostile terrain? As one high-level doubter remarked, "One cannot go over Niagara Falls in a barrel only slightly."

Worrying aloud about a communist victory, Eisenhower pressed the British to help form a coalition to address the Indochinese crisis, but they refused. At home, influential members of Congress—including Lyndon Baines Johnson of Texas, who as president would wage large-scale war in Vietnam—told Eisenhower they wanted "no more Koreas" and warned him against any U.S. military commitment, especially in the absence of cooperation from America's allies. Some felt very uneasy about supporting colonialism. The issue became moot on May 7, when the weary French defenders at Dienbienphu surrendered.

Peace talks, already under way in Geneva, brought Cold War and nationalist contenders together—the United States, the Soviet Union, Britain, the People's Republic of China, Laos, Cambodia, and the competing Vietnamese regimes of Bao Dai and Ho Chi Minh. John Foster Dulles, a reluctant participant, feared the communists would get the better of any agreement, yet in the end the Vietminh received less than their dominant military position suggested they should. The 1954 Geneva accords, signed by France and Ho's Democratic Republic of Vietnam, temporarily divided Vietnam at the 17th parallel;

**Geneva Accords on Vietnam**

Eisenhower refused, fearing that the popular Vietminh leader would win. From 1955 to 1961, the Diem government received more than $1 billion in American aid, most of it military. American advisers organized and trained Diem's army, and American agriculturalists worked to improve crops. Diem's Saigon regime became dependent on the United States for its very existence, and the culture of South Vietnam became increasingly Americanized.

Ho's government was confined to the North, Bao Dai's to the South. Only after pressure from the Chinese and the Soviets, who feared U.S. intervention in Vietnam without an agreement, did Ho's government agree to this compromise. The 17th parallel was meant to serve as a military truce line, not a national boundary; the country was scheduled to be reunified after national elections in 1956. Meanwhile, neither North nor South was to join a military alliance or permit foreign military bases on its soil.

Confident that the Geneva agreements ultimately would mean communist victory, the United States from an early point set about trying to undermine them. Soon after the conference, a CIA team entered Vietnam and undertook secret operations against the North, including commando raids across the 17th parallel. In the South, the United States helped Ngo Dinh Diem push Bao Dai aside and inaugurate the Republic of Vietnam. A Catholic in a Buddhist nation, Diem was a dedicated nationalist and anticommunist, but he had little mass support. He staged a fraudulent election in South Vietnam that gave him 99 percent of the vote (in Saigon he received 200,000 more votes than there were registered voters). When Ho and some in the world community pressed for national elections in keeping with the Geneva agreements, Diem and

## National Liberation Front

Diem proved a difficult ally. He acted dictatorially, abolishing village elections and appointing to public office people beholden to him. He threw dissenters in jail and shut down newspapers that criticized his regime. When U.S. officials periodically urged him to implement meaningful land reform, he blithely ignored them. Noncommunists and communists alike began to strike back at Diem's repressive government. In Hanoi, Ho's government initially focused on solidifying its control on the North, but in the late 1950s it began to send aid to southern insurgents, who embarked on a program of terror, assassinating hundreds of Diem's village officials. In late 1960, southern communists, acting at the direction of Hanoi, organized the National Liberation Front (NLF), known as the Vietcong. The Vietcong in turn attracted other anti-Diem groups in the South. And the Eisenhower administration, all too aware of Diem's shortcomings and his unwillingness to follow American advice, continued to affirm its commitment to the preservation of an independent, noncommunist South Vietnam.

# *Legacy* FOR A PEOPLE AND A NATION

## The National Security State

To build a cathedral, someone has observed, you first need a religion, and a religion needs inspiring texts that command authority. For decades, America's Cold War religion has been national security; its texts, the Truman Doctrine, the "X" article, and NSC-68; and its cathedral, the national security state. The word *state* in this case means "civil government." During the Cold War, embracing preparedness for total war, the U.S. government essentially transformed itself into a huge military headquarters that interlocked with corporations and universities. Preaching the doctrine of national security, moreover, members of Congress strove to gain lucrative defense contracts for their districts.

Overseen by the president and his advisory body, the National Security Council, the national security state has had as its core what the National Security Act of 1947 called the National Military Establishment; in 1949 it became the Department of Defense. This department ranks as a leading employer; its payroll by 2007 included 1.4 million people on active duty and almost 600,000 civilian personnel, giving it more employees than Exxon-Mobil, Ford, General Motors, and GE combined. Almost 700,000 of these troops and civilians served overseas, in 177 countries covering every time zone. Although spending for national defense declined in the years after the end of the Cold War, it never fell below $290 billion. In the aftermath of the 9/11 terrorist attacks and the invasion of Iraq, the military budget rose again, reaching $439 billion in 2007. That figure represents the approximate size of the entire economy of Poland and the Netherlands, and equals the combined military spending of the twenty-five countries with the next-largest defense budgets. Nor does that sum include tens of billions of dollars in supplementary funds allocated by Congress to pay for operations in Afghanistan and Iraq.

Joining the Department of Defense as instruments of national security policy were the Joint Chiefs of Staff, the Central Intelligence Agency, and dozens more government bodies. The focus of all these entities was on finding the best means to combat real and potential threats from foreign governments. But what about threats from within? The terrorist attacks of September 2001 made starkly clear that enemies existed who, while perhaps beholden to a foreign entity—it need not be a government—launched their attacks from inside the nation's borders. Accordingly, in 2002 President George W. Bush proposed the creation of a Department of Homeland Security, which would have 170,000 employees and would include all or part of twenty-two agencies, including the Coast Guard, the Customs Service, the Federal Emergency Management Administration (FEMA), and the Internal Revenue Service. It would involve the biggest overhaul of the federal bureaucracy since the Department of Defense was created, and it signified a more expansive notion of national security. By 2006, the number of DHS employees had risen to 190,000.

In 1961 President Eisenhower warned against a "military-industrial complex," while others feared a "garrison state" or a "warfare state." Despite the warnings, by the start of the twenty-first century, the national security state remained vigorous, a lasting legacy of the early Cold War period for a people and a nation.

## SUMMARY

The United States emerged from the Second World War as the preeminent world power. Confident in the nation's immediate physical security, Washington officials nevertheless worried that the unstable international system, an unfriendly Soviet Union, and the decolonizing Third World could upset American plans for the postwar peace. Locked with the Soviet Union in a "Cold War," U.S. leaders marshaled their nation's superior resources to influence and cajole other countries. Foreign economic aid, atomic diplomacy, military alliances, client states, covert operations, interventions, propaganda, cultural infiltration—these and more became the instruments for waging the Cold War, a war that began as a conflict over the future of Europe but soon spread to encompass the globe.

America's claim to international leadership was welcomed by many in western Europe and elsewhere who feared Stalin's intentions and those of his successors in the Soviet Union. The reconstruction of former enemies Japan and (West) Germany helped those nations recover swiftly and become staunch members of the western alliance. But U.S. policy also sparked resistance. Communist countries condemned financial and atomic diplomacy, while Third World nations, many of them newly independent, sought to undermine America's European allies and sometimes identified the United States as an imperial coconspirator. On occasion even America's allies bristled at a United States that boldly proclaimed itself economic master and global policeman, and haughtily touted its hegemonic status.

At home, liberal and radical critics protested that Presidents Truman and Eisenhower exaggerated the communist threat, wasting U.S. assets on immoral foreign ventures; crippled legitimate nationalist aspirations; and displayed racial bias. Still, these presidents and their successors held firm to the mission of creating a nonradical, capitalist, free-trade international order in the mold of domestic America. Determined to contain Soviet expansion, fearful of domestic charges of being "soft on communism," they worked to enlarge the U.S. sphere of influence and shape the world. In their years of nurturing allies and applying the containment doctrine worldwide, Truman and Eisenhower held the line—against the Soviet Union and the People's Republic of China, and against nonalignment, communism, nationalism, and revolution everywhere. One consequence was a dramatic increase in presidential power in the realm of foreign affairs—what the historian Arthur M. Schlesinger Jr. called "the Imperial Presidency"—as Congress ceded constitutional power.

Putting itself at odds with many in the Third World, the United States usually stood with its European allies to slow decolonization and to preach evolution rather than revolution. The globalist perspective of the United States prompted Americans to interpret many troubles in the developing world as Cold War conflicts, inspired if not directed by Soviet-backed communists. The intensity of the Cold War obscured for Americans the indigenous roots of most Third World troubles, as the wars in Korea and Vietnam attested. Nor could the United States abide developing nations' drive for economic independence— for gaining control of their own raw materials and economies. Deeply intertwined in the global economy as importer, exporter, and investor, the United States read challenges from this "periphery" as threats to the American standard of living and a way of life characterized by private enterprise. The Third World, in short, challenged U.S. strategic power by forming a third force in the Cold War, and it challenged American economic power by seeking a new economic order of shared interests. Overall, the rise of the Third World introduced new actors to the world stage, challenging the bipolarity of the international system and diffusing power.

All the while, the threat of nuclear war unsettled Americans and foreigners alike. In the film *Godzilla* (1956), a prehistoric monster, revived by atomic bomb tests, rampages through Tokyo. Stanley Kramer's popular but disturbing movie *On the Beach* (1959), based on Nevil Shute's bestselling 1957 novel, depicts a nuclear holocaust in which the last humans on earth choose to swallow government-issued poison tablets so that they can die before H-bomb radiation sickness kills them. Such doomsday or Armageddon attitudes contrasted sharply with official U.S. government assurances that Americans would survive a nuclear war. In *On the Beach*, a dying wife asks her husband, "Couldn't anyone have stopped it?" His answer: "Some kinds of silliness you just can't stop." Eisenhower did not halt it, even though he told Khrushchev in 1959 that "we really should come to some sort of agreement in order to stop this fruitless, really wasteful rivalry."

## SUGGESTIONS FOR FURTHER READING

Campbell Craig, *Destroying the Village: Eisenhower and Thermonuclear War* (1998)

Nick Cullather, *Secret History: The CIA's Classified Account of Its Operations in Guatemala, 1952–1954* (1999)

Mary L. Dudziak, *Cold War Civil Rights: Race and the Image of American Democracy* (2000)

John Lewis Gaddis, *Strategies of Containment*, 2nd ed. (2005)

Walter LaFeber, *America, Russia, and the Cold War, 1945–2006*, 10th ed. (2006)

Douglas Little, *American Orientalism: The United States and the Middle East Since 1945* (2002)

Fredrik Logevall, *The Origins of the Vietnam War* (2001)

Robert J. McMahon, *The Limits of Empire: The United States and Southeast Asia Since World War II* (1999)

Geoffrey Roberts, *Stalin's Wars: From World War to Cold War, 1939–1953* (2007)

Marc Trachtenberg, *A Constructed Peace: The Making of the European Settlement, 1945–1963* (1999)

*For a more extensive list for further reading, go to* college.hmco.com/pic/norton8e.

CHAPTER

29

# America at
# Midcentury
## *1945-1960*

𝓔venings after supper, when the hot, sticky heat of the Georgia summer days had started to ebb, most of the families on Nancy Circle went out for a walk. The parents stood chatting, watching the children play swing-the-statue or hide-and-seek.

In 1959 the twenty houses on Nancy Circle were just a couple of years old. Some lots still looked raw, but in that climate grass grew quickly, and the few remaining vacant lots were covered over with kudzu. The small houses stood on land that had once belonged to the Cherokees, in a development carved from the old Campbell plantation, not far from the site where, during the Civil War, Confederate troops had made their final attempt to prevent General William Tecumseh Sherman's Union Army from launching its attack on Atlanta. Slaves had picked cotton there a century before, but no African Americans lived in the suburban homes. Sometimes an elderly black man came by on a mule cart, selling vegetables.

Nancy Circle was part of a new suburban development in Smyrna, Georgia, just northwest of Atlanta, but few of the people who lived there worked in the city. Most, instead, traveled the other direction, to the massive Lockheed Georgia airplane plant that had been created, in large part, by Cold War defense spending. This suburb was born of the union of Cold War and baby boom: families with small children lived there. With three small bedrooms, two baths, a kitchen, a combined living-dining room, and a garage for about $17,000, the houses on Nancy Circle were ones that young families could afford.

On Nancy Circle, children ran in and out of each other's houses, and women gathered to drink coffee and gossip in the morning. The men left early for work. There were several aerospace engineers, three career military men (one of whom was rumored to be

◄ A four-year-old boy stares at military aircraft, the real version of the toy he holds in his hand. The Cold War growth of defense industry plants, such as Lockheed Georgia near Atlanta, meant that many children grew up in suburbs shaken by sonic booms from military aircraft being tested overhead. *(© Bettmann/Corbis)*

## CHRONOLOGY

1945 ■ World War II ends

1946 ■ Marriage and birth rates skyrocket
■ More than 1 million veterans enroll in colleges under GI Bill
■ More than 5 million U.S. workers go on strike

1947 ■ Taft-Hartley Act limits power of unions
■ Truman orders loyalty investigation of 3 million government employees
■ Mass-production techniques used to build Levittown houses

1948 ■ Truman issues executive order desegregating armed forces and federal government
■ Truman elected president

1949 ■ Soviet Union explodes atomic bomb

1950 ■ Korean War begins
■ McCarthy alleges communists in government
■ "Treaty of Detroit" creates model for new labor-management relations

1951 ■ Race riots in Cicero, Illinois, as white residents oppose residential integration

1952 ■ Eisenhower elected president

1953 ■ Korean War ends
■ Congress adopts termination policy for Native American tribes
■ Rosenbergs executed as atomic spies

1954 ■ *Brown v. Board of Education* decision reverses "separate but equal" doctrine
■ Senate condemns McCarthy

1955 ■ Montgomery bus boycott begins

1956 ■ Highway Act launches interstate highway system
■ Eisenhower reelected
■ Elvis Presley appears on *Ed Sullivan Show*

1957 ■ King elected first president of Southern Christian Leadership Conference
■ School desegregation crisis in Little Rock, Arkansas
■ Congress passes Civil Rights Act
■ Soviet Union launches *Sputnik*

1958 ■ Congress passes National Defense Education Act

1959 ■ Alaska and Hawai'i become forty-ninth and fiftieth states

in military intelligence), an auto mechanic, and a musician. Only two women held paid jobs. One had almost-grown children and taught second grade; the other was divorced and worked as a secretary. She dyed her hair blonde and drove a convertible. People were suspicious of her but liked her sister, born with dwarfism, who had left her job in a North Carolina textile mill to move to Nancy Circle and help care for her nephew. Two war brides—one Japanese and one German—lived in the neighborhood. The Japanese woman spoke little English, and people worried that she was unhappy. The German woman taught the girls in the neighborhood to do Swedish embroidery and to crochet.

The people who lived on Nancy Circle read national magazines that criticized the homogeneity and conformity of suburban life, but it didn't feel that way to them. On this single street, people from deep Appalachia or the small farms of south Georgia lived side by side with people who had grown up in crowded city apartments or dilapidated boarding houses; a Pennsylvania Dutch family brought Southern Baptist neighbors to join the new Lutheran church they'd helped found; and women who'd done graduate work baked Christmas cookies with women who had not finished high school. These new suburbanites were creating for themselves a new world and a new middle-class culture. They had grown up with the Great Depression and world war; now, on this suburban street, they believed they had found good lives.

Of all the major nations in the world, only the United States had emerged from World War II stronger and more prosperous than when the war began. Europe and Asia had been devastated, but America's farms and cities and factories were intact. U.S. production capacity had increased during the war, and despite social tensions and inequalities, the fight against fascism gave Americans a unity of purpose. Victory seemed to confirm their struggles. But sixteen years of depression and war shadowed the U.S. victory, and memories of these experiences would continue to shape the choices Americans made in their private lives, their domestic policies, and their relations with the world.

In the postwar era, the actions of the federal government and the choices made by individual Americans began a profound reconfiguration of American society. Postwar social policies that sent millions of veterans to college on the GI Bill, linked the nation with high-speed interstate highways, fostered the growth of suburbs and the Sunbelt, and disrupted regional isolation helped to create a national middle-class culture that encompassed an unprecedented majority of the nation's citizens. Countless individual decisions—to go to college, to marry young, to have a large family, to move to the suburbs, to start a business—were made possible by these federal initiatives. The cumulative weight of these individual decisions would change the meanings of class and ethnicity in American society. Americans in the postwar era defined a new American Dream—one that centered on the family, on a new level of material comfort and consumption, and on a shared sense of belonging to a common culture. Elite cultural critics roundly denounced this ideal of suburban comfort as "conformism," but many Americans found satisfaction in this new way of life.

Almost one-quarter of the American people did not share in the postwar prosperity—but they were ever less visible to the middle-class majority. Rural poverty continued, and inner cities became increasingly impoverished as more-affluent Americans moved to the suburbs and new migrants—poor black and white southerners, new immigrants from Mexico and Puerto Rico, and Native Americans resettled by the federal government from tribal lands—arrived.

As class and ethnicity became less important in suburbia, race continued to divide the American people. African Americans faced racism and discrimination throughout the nation, but the war had been a turning point in the struggle for equal rights. During this period, African Americans increasingly took direct action, and in 1955 the year-long Montgomery bus boycott launched the modern civil rights movement. Their initiatives led to important federal actions to protect the civil rights of black Americans, including the Supreme Court's school desegregation decision in *Brown v. Board of Education*.

After the dramatic accomplishments of the New Deal, the national politics of the postwar era were circumscribed. Truman pledged to expand the New Deal but was stymied by a conservative Congress. General Dwight D. Eisenhower, elected in 1952 as the first Republican president in twenty years, offered a solid Republican platform,

seeking—though rarely attaining—a balanced budget, reduced taxes, and lower levels of government spending. Both men focused primarily on the foreign policy challenges of the Cold War. The most significant domestic political ferment, in fact, was a byproduct of the Cold War: a ferocious anticommunism that narrowed the boundaries of acceptable dissent.

The economic boom that began with the end of the war lasted twenty-five years, bringing new prosperity to the American people. Although fears—of nuclear war, of returning hard times—lingered, prosperity bred complacency by the late 1950s. At decade's end, people sought satisfaction in their families and in the consumer pleasures newly available to so many.

- How did the Cold War affect American society and politics?
- How did federal government actions following World War II change the nation?
- During the 1950s, many people began to think of their country as a middle-class nation. Were they correct?

## SHAPING POSTWAR AMERICA

As Americans celebrated the end of World War II and mourned those who would never return, many feared the challenges that lay ahead. It seemed almost inevitable that the economy would plunge back into depression—and in the immediate aftermath of the war, unemployment rose and a wave of strikes rocked the nation. But economists who made dire predictions were wrong. In the postwar years the American economy flourished, and Americans' standard of living improved. And the GI Bill and other new federal programs created opportunities for Americans that changed the nation in fundamental ways.

As the end of the war approached and the American war machine slowed, factories began to lay off workers.

**Postwar Economic Uncertainty**

At Ford Motor Company's massive Willow Run plant outside Detroit, where nine thousand Liberator bombers had been produced, most workers were let go in the spring of 1945. Ten days after the victory over Japan, 1.8 million people nationwide received pink slips, and 640,000 filed for unemployment compensation. More than 15 million GIs awaited demobilization; how were they to be absorbed into the shrinking job base?

Anticipating a postwar crisis, the federal government planned for demobilization even while some of the war's most difficult battles lay ahead. In the spring of 1944—a year before V-E Day—Congress unanimously passed the Servicemen's Readjustment Act, known as the GI Bill of Rights. The GI Bill showed the nation's gratitude to the men who fought. But it also attempted to keep the flood of demobilized veterans (almost all of them male) from swamping the U.S. economy: year-long unemployment benefits allowed veterans to be absorbed gradually into civilian employment, and higher-education benefits were designed to keep men in college and out of the job market. In winter 1945, congressional Democrats introduced a national Full Employment Act guaranteeing work to all who were able and willing, through public-sector employment if necessary. By the time conservatives in Congress had finished with the bill and Truman signed it into law in early 1946, key provisions regarding guaranteed work had virtually disappeared. But the act did reaffirm the federal government's responsibility for managing the economy and created a Council of Economic Advisers to help the president prevent economic downturns.

Conversion to a peacetime economy hit workers hard, especially as the end of wartime price controls sent inflation skyrocketing. Workers had ac-

### Postwar Strikes and the Taft-Hartley Act

cepted wartime limits on wages, but they would not stand by as unemployment threatened and their paychecks were eaten away. More than 5 million workers walked off the job in the year following Japan's surrender. Unions shut down the coal, automobile, steel, and electric industries, and halted railroad and maritime transportation. The strikes were so disruptive that Americans began hoarding food and gasoline.

By spring 1946, Americans were losing patience with the strikes and with the Democratic administration, which they saw as partly responsible. When unions threatened a national railway strike, President Truman made a dramatic appearance before a joint session of Congress. If strikers in an industry deemed vital to national security refused a presidential order to return to work, he announced, he would ask Congress to immediately draft into the armed forces "all workers who are on strike against their government." The Democratic Party, Truman made clear, would not offer unlimited support to organized labor.

Making the most of public anger at the strikes, in 1947 a group of pro-business Republicans and their conservative Democratic allies worked to restrict the power of labor unions. The Taft-Hartley Act permitted states to enact right-to-work laws that outlawed "closed shops," in which all workers were required to join the union if a majority of their number favored a union shop. The law also mandated an eighty-day cooling-off period before unions initiated strikes that imperiled national security. These restrictions limited unions' ability to expand their membership, especially in the South and West, where states passed right-to-work laws. Although Truman had used the power of the presidency to avert a national railroad strike, he did not want to see union power so limited. But Congress passed the Taft-Hartley Act over Truman's veto.

Despite widespread fears, economic depression did not return. The first year of adjustment to a peacetime

### Economic Growth

economy was difficult, but the economy recovered quickly, fueled by consumer spending. Although Americans had brought home steady paychecks during the war, there was little on which to spend them. No new cars, for example, had been built since 1942. Americans had saved their money for four years—and when new cars and appliances appeared at war's end, they were ready to buy. Companies like General Motors, which flouted conventional wisdom about a coming depression and expanded its operations just after the war, found millions of eager buyers. And because most other factories around the world were in ruins, U.S. corporations expanded their global dominance. America's leading corporations rode this postwar boom, increasing dramatically in size. Many created huge conglomerates. International Telegraph and Telephone (IT&T), for instance, bought up companies in several fields, including suburban development, insurance, and hotels. In keeping with the thrust of America's postwar boom, the country's ten largest corporations were in automobiles (GM, Ford, Chrysler); oil (Standard Oil of New Jersey, Mobil, Texaco); and electronics and communications (GE, IBM, IT&T, AT&T).

In the agricultural sector, new machines, such as mechanical cotton, tobacco, and grape pickers, and crop-dusting planes, revolutionized farming, and the increased use of fertilizers and pesticides raised the total value of farm output from $24.6 billion in 1945 to $38.4 billion in 1961. At the same time, the productivity of farm labor tripled. Large investors were drawn to agriculture by its increased profitability, and the average size of farms increased from 195 to 306 acres.

Economic growth was also fueled by government programs, such as the GI Bill, which pumped money into the economy. By 1949, veterans had received close to $4 billion in unemployment compensation. But the GI Bill did more than help forestall economic collapse. It offered veterans low-interest loans to buy a house or start a business, and—perhaps most significantly—stipends to cover college or technical school tuition and living expenses. As individ-

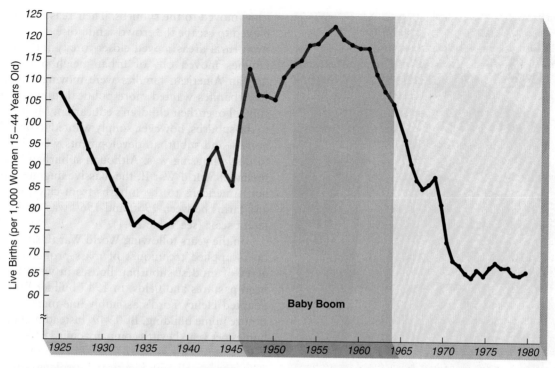

**Figure 29.1    Birth Rate, 1945–1964**

The birth rate began to rise in 1942 and 1943, but it skyrocketed during the postwar years beginning in 1946, reaching its peak in 1957. From 1954 to 1964, the United States recorded more than 4 million births every year.

*(Source: Adapted from U.S. Bureau of the Census,* Historical Statistics of the United States, Colonial Times to 1970, *Bicentennial Edition [Washington, D.C.: U.S. Government Printing Office, 1975], p. 49.)*

uals grasped these opportunities, they changed their own lives and the shape of American society.

Before the war, higher education was for the affluent; only about 7.5 percent of young Americans went to college. With GI benefits, almost half of America's returning veterans sought some form of higher education. The resulting increase in the number of well-educated or technically trained workers benefited the American economy. And although University of Chicago president Robert Maynard Hutchins protested that the GI Bill would turn universities into "educational hobo jungles," the flood of students and federal dollars into the nation's colleges and universities created a golden age for higher education.

Education obtained through the GI Bill created social mobility: children of barely literate menial laborers became white-collar professionals. And postwar universities, like the military, brought together people from vastly different backgrounds. The GI Bill fostered the emergence of a national middle-class culture, for as colleges exposed people to new ideas and to new experiences, their students tended to become less provincial, less rooted in ethnic or regional cultures.

During the Great Depression, young people had delayed marriage, and America's birth rate had plummeted.

**Baby Boom**

Marriage and birth rates began to rise as war brought economic recovery. But the end of the war brought a boom. In 1946 the U.S. marriage rate was higher than that of any record-keeping nation (except Hungary) in the history of the twentieth century. The birth rate soared, reversing the downward trend of the past 150 years. "Take the 3,548,000 babies born in 1950," wrote Sylvia F. Porter in her syndicated newspaper column. "Bundle them into a batch, bounce them all over the bountiful land that is America. What do you get?" Porter's answer: "Boom. The biggest, boomiest boom ever known in history. Just imagine how much these extra people, these new markets, will absorb—in food, clothing, in gadgets, in housing, in services. Our factories must expand just to keep pace." Although the baby boom peaked in 1957, more than 4 million babies were born every year until 1965 (see Figure 29.1). As this vast cohort grew older, it had successive impacts on housing, nursery schools, grade schools, and high schools, fads and

▲ Housing was so tight in the years following World War II that many young couples had to move in with one set of their parents—or accept some unusual housing options. Former marine lieutenant Willard Pedrick and his family made their home in a Quonset hut on the campus of Northwestern University in Evanston, Illinois, where Pedrick was an associate professor in the economics department.

*(© Bettmann/Corbis)*

popular music, colleges and universities, the job market, and retirement funds, including Social Security.

Where were all these baby-boom families to live? Scarcely any new housing had been built since the 1920s. Almost 2 million families were doubled up with relatives in 1948; 50,000 people were living in Quonset huts, and in Chicago housing was so tight that 250 used trolley cars were sold as homes.

A combination of market forces, government actions, and individual decisions solved the housing crisis and, in so doing, changed the way large numbers of Americans lived.

**Suburbanization**

In the postwar years, white Americans moved to the suburbs. Their reasons varied. Some moved to escape the crowds and noise of the city. People from rural areas moved closer to city jobs. Some white families moved out of urban neighborhoods because African American families were moving in. Many new suburbanites wanted more political influence and more control over their children's education. Most who moved to the suburbs, however, simply wanted to own their own home—and suburban developments were where the affordable housing was. Although suburban development predated World War II, the massive migration of 18 million Americans to the suburbs from cities, small towns, and farms between 1950 and 1960 was on a wholly different scale (see Table 29.1).

In the years following World War II, suburban developers applied techniques of mass production to create acres of modest suburban houses in what had recently been pastures and fields. In 1947 builder William Levitt adapted Henry Ford's assembly-line methods to revolutionize home building. By 1949, instead of 4 or 5 custom homes per year, Levitt's company built 180 houses a week. They were very basic—four and a half rooms on a 60-by-100-foot lot, all with identical floorplans—the Model Ts of houses. But the same floorplan could be disguised by four different exteriors, and by rotating seven paint colors Levitt guaranteed that only 1 in every 28 houses would be identical. In the Levittown on Long Island, a tree was planted every 28 feet (two and a half trees per house). The basic house, appliances included, sold for $7,990. Other homebuilders quickly adopted Levitt's techniques.

Suburban development could never have happened on such a large scale, however, without federal policies that encouraged it. Federal Housing Administration (FHA) mortgage insurance made low-interest GI mortgages and loans possible. New highways also promoted suburban development. Congress authorized construction of a 37,000-mile chain of highways in 1947 and in 1956 passed the Highway Act to create a 42,500-mile interstate highway system. Intended to facilitate commerce and rapid mobilization of the military in case of a threat to national security, these highways also allowed workers to live farther and farther from their jobs in central cities.

Postwar federal programs did not benefit all Americans equally. First, federal policies often assisted men at the expense of women. The federal

**Inequality in Benefits**

Selective Service Act guaranteed veterans (overwhelmingly men) priority in postwar employment over the war workers who had replaced them. As industry laid off civilian workers to make room for veterans, women lost their jobs at a rate 75 percent

| TABLE 29.1 | Geographic Distribution of the U.S. Population, 1930–1970 (in percentages) | | |
| --- | --- | --- | --- |
| Year | Central Cities | Suburbs | Rural Areas and Small Towns |
| 1930 | 31.8 | 18.0 | 50.2 |
| 1940 | 31.6 | 19.5 | 48.9 |
| 1950 | 32.3 | 23.8 | 43.9 |
| 1960 | 32.6 | 30.7 | 36.7 |
| 1970 | 31.4 | 37.6 | 31.0 |

*Source:* Adapted from U.S. Bureau of the Census, *Decennial Censuses, 1930–1970* (Washington, D.C.: U.S. Government Printing Office).

higher than men. Many women stayed in the work force but were pushed into less well-paying jobs. Universities made room for veterans on the GI Bill by excluding qualified women students; a much smaller percentage of college degrees went to women after the war than before.

Inequities were also based on race. Like European American veterans, African American, Native American, Mexican American, and Asian American veterans received educational benefits and hiring preference in civil service jobs following the war. But war workers from these groups were among the first laid off as factories made room for white, male veterans. Federal housing policies also exacerbated racial inequality. Federal loan officers and bankers often labeled African American or racially mixed neighborhoods "high risk" for lending, denying mortgages to members of racial minorities regardless of individual creditworthiness. This practice, called "redlining" because such neighborhoods were outlined in red on lenders' maps, kept African Americans and many Hispanics from buying into the great economic explosion of the postwar era. White families who bought homes with federally guaranteed mortgages saw their small investments grow dramatically over the years. Discriminatory policies denied most African Americans and other people of color that opportunity.

## DOMESTIC POLITICS IN THE COLD WAR ERA

Although the major social and economic transformations of the postwar era were due in great part to federal policies and programs, domestic politics were not at the forefront of American life. Foreign affairs were usually paramount, as Democratic president Harry Truman and Republican president Dwight D. Eisenhower both faced significant challenges in the expanding Cold War. Domestically, Truman attempted to build on the New Deal's liberal agenda, while Eisenhower called for balanced budgets and business-friendly policies. But neither administration approached the level of political and legislative activism of the 1930s New Deal.

Harry Truman, the plain-spoken former haberdasher from Missouri, had never expected to be president. In 1944, when Franklin Roosevelt asked him to join the Democratic ticket as the vice-presidential candidate, he almost refused. Roosevelt, the master politician, played hardball. "If he wants to break up the Democratic Party in the middle of the war, that's his responsibility," the president said flatly. "Oh shit," said Truman, "if that's the situation, I'll have to say yes." But the president, with his hands full as America entered its fourth year of war, had little time for his new vice president and left Truman in the dark about everything from the Manhattan Project to plans for postwar domestic policy. When Roosevelt died, suddenly, in April 1945, Truman was unprepared to take his place.

### Harry S Truman and Postwar Liberalism

Truman stepped forward, however, placing a sign on his desk that proclaimed, "The Buck Stops Here." Most of Truman's presidency focused on foreign relations, as he led the nation through the last months of World War II and into the new Cold War with the Soviet Union. Domestically, he oversaw the process of reconversion from war to peace and attempted to keep a liberal agenda—the legacy of Roosevelt's New Deal—alive.

In his 1944 State of the Union address, President Roosevelt had offered Americans a "Second Bill of Rights": the right to employment, healthcare, education, food, and housing. This declaration of government responsibility for the welfare of the nation and its citizens was the cornerstone of postwar liberalism. Truman's legislative program sought to maintain the federal government's active role in guaranteeing social welfare, promoting social justice,

▲ A large crowd gathered to hear President Truman in 1948, as he campaigned in Harlem. African American voters were an increasingly important political force in the postwar era, and Truman was the first presidential candidate to go to Harlem seeking support. Truman had political reasons for appealing to black voters, but he also felt a moral obligation to support their struggle for civil rights. *(Left: Chicago Historical Society; Right: Collection of Janice L. and David J. Frent)*

managing the economy, and regulating the power of business corporations. Truman proposed an increase in the minimum wage and national housing legislation offering loans for mortgages, and he supported the Full Employment Act. To pay for his proposed social welfare programs, Truman gambled that full employment would generate sufficient tax revenue and that consumer spending would fuel economic growth.

The gamble on economic growth paid off, but Truman quickly learned the limits of his political influence. The conservative coalition of Republicans and southern Democrats that had stalled Roosevelt's New Deal legislation in the late 1930s was even less inclined to support Truman. Congress gutted the Full Employment Act, refused to raise the minimum wage, and passed the antiunion Taft-Hartley Act over Truman's veto. With powerful congressional opposition, Truman had little chance of major legislative accomplishments. But his inexperience contributed to the political impasse. "To err is Truman," people began to joke. As Truman presided over

the rocky transition from wartime to peacetime economy, he had to deal with massive inflation (briefly hitting 35 percent), shortages of consumer goods, and a wave of postwar strikes that slowed production of eagerly awaited consumer goods and drove prices up further. Truman's approval rating plunged from 87 percent in late 1945 to 32 percent in 1946.

By 1948 it seemed that Republicans would win the White House in November. A confident Republican Party nominated Thomas Dewey, the man Roosevelt had defeated in 1944, as its presidential candidate.

**1948 Election**

The Republicans were counting on schisms in the Democratic Party to give them victory. Two years before, Truman had fired Henry A. Wallace, the only remaining New Dealer in the cabinet, for publicly criticizing U.S. foreign policy. In 1948 Wallace ran for president on the Progressive Party ticket, advocating friendly relations with the Soviet Union, racial desegregation, and nationalization of basic industries. A fourth party, the Dixiecrats (States' Rights Democratic Party), was organized by white southerners who walked out of the 1948 Democratic convention when it adopted a pro-civil rights plank; they nominated the fiercely segregationist governor Strom Thurmond of South Carolina. If Wallace's candidacy did not destroy Truman's chances, experts said, the Dixiecrats certainly would.

Truman, however, refused to give up. He resorted to red-baiting, denouncing "Henry Wallace and his communists" at every opportunity. Most important, he directly appealed to the burgeoning population of African American voters in northern cities, becoming the first presidential candidate to campaign in Harlem. In the end, Truman prevailed. The Progressive and Dixiecrat Parties attracted far fewer voters than had been predicted; most Democrats saw Truman—in contrast to Thurmond or Wallace—as an appealing moderate. African American voters made the difference, giving Truman the electoral votes of key northern states. Roosevelt's New Deal coalition—African Americans, union members, northern urban voters, and most southern whites—had endured.

Truman began his new term brimming with confidence. It was time, he believed, for government to fulfill its responsibility to provide economic security for the poor and the elderly. As he worked on his 1949 State of the Union message, he penciled in his intentions: "I expect to give every segment of our population a fair deal." Truman, unlike Roosevelt, pushed forward legislation to support the civil rights of African Americans, including the antilynching bill that Roosevelt had given only lukewarm support. He proposed a national health insurance program and federal aid for education. Once again, however, little of Truman's legislative agenda came to fruition. A filibuster by southern conservatives in Congress destroyed his civil rights legislation; the American Medical Association denounced his health insurance plan as "socialized medicine"; and the Roman Catholic Church opposed aid to education because it would not include parochial schools.

**Truman's Fair Deal**

When the postwar peace proved short-lived and Truman ordered troops to Korea in June 1950, there was much grumbling among Americans as the nation again mobilized for war. People remembered the shortages of the last war and stocked up on sugar, coffee, and canned goods. Fueled by panic buying, inflation began to rise. Many reservists and national guardsmen resented being called to active duty. An unpopular war and charges of influence peddling by some of Truman's cronies pushed the president's public approval rating to an all-time low of 23 percent in 1951, where it stayed for a year.

"It's Time for a Change" was the Republican presidential campaign slogan in 1952, and voters agreed, especially when the Republican candidate was General Dwight D. Eisenhower. Americans hoped that the immensely popular World War II hero could end the Korean War. And Eisenhower appealed to moderates in both parties (in fact, the Democrats had tried to recruit him as their presidential candidate).

**Eisenhower's Dynamic Conservatism**

With a Republican in the White House for the first time in twenty years, conservatives hoped to roll back such New Deal liberal programs as the mandatory Social Security system. Eisenhower, however, had no such intention, in part because it was politically almost impossible to dismantle New Deal and Fair Deal programs without harming a great many Americans. Eisenhower, as a moderate Republican, adopted an approach that he called "dynamic conservatism": being "conservative when it comes to money and liberal when it comes to human beings." On the liberal side, in 1954 Eisenhower signed into law amendments to the Social Security Act that raised benefits and added 7.5 million workers, mostly self-employed farmers, to the Social Security rolls. The Eisenhower administration also increased government funding for education—though increases were motivated by Cold War fears, not liberal principles. When the Soviet Union launched *Sputnik,* the first earth-orbiting satellite, in 1957 (and America's first launch exploded seconds after liftoff), improving science and technology education became an issue of national security. Congress responded in 1958 with the National Defense Education Act (NDEA), which funded enrichment of elementary and high-school programs in mathematics, foreign languages, and the sciences, and offered fellowships and loans to college students. This attempt to win the "battle of brainpower" increased the educational opportunities available to young Americans.

Overall, however, Eisenhower's was unabashedly "an Administration representing business and industry," as Interior Secretary Douglas McKay acknowledged. The Eisenhower administration's tax reform bill raised business depreciation allowances, and the Atomic Energy Act of 1954 granted private companies the right to own reactors and nuclear materials to produce electricity. Eisenhower also tried to reduce the federal budget. In fact, he balanced only three of his eight budgets, turning to deficit spending to cushion the impact of three recessions (in 1953–1954, 1957–1958,

**Growth of the Military-Industrial Complex**

and 1960–1961) and to fund the tremendous cost of America's global activities. In 1959 federal expenditures climbed to $92 billion, about half of which went to the military, much of that for developing new weapons.

Just before leaving office in early 1961, at the end of his second term, Eisenhower went on national radio and television to deliver his farewell address to the nation. Because of the Cold War, he observed, the United States had begun to maintain a large standing army—3.5 million men. And ever greater percentages of the nation's budget went to developing and building weapons of war. Condemning the new "conjunction of an immense military establishment and a large arms industry," Eisenhower warned, "The total influence—economic, political, even spiritual—is felt in every city, every statehouse, every office of the federal government" and threatened the nation's democratic process. Eisenhower, the former five-star general and war hero, urged Americans to "guard against . . . the military-industrial complex."

During Eisenhower's presidency, both liberal Democrats and moderate Republicans seemed satisfied to be occupying what historian Arthur M. Schlesinger Jr. called "the vital center." And with the Cold War between the United States and the Soviet Union portrayed as a battle between good and evil, a struggle for the future of the world, criticism of American society seemed suspect—even unpatriotic. British journalist Godfrey Hodgson described this time as an era of "consensus," when Americans were "confident to the verge of complacency about the perfectibility of American society, anxious to the point of paranoia about the threat of communism."

## COLD WAR FEARS AND ANTICOMMUNISM

International relations had a profound influence on America's domestic politics in the years following World War II. Americans were frightened by the Cold War tensions between the United States and the Soviet Union—and there were legitimate reasons for fear. Reasonable fears, however, spilled over into anticommunist demagoguery and witch hunts. Fear allowed the trampling of civil liberties, the suppression of dissent, and the persecution of thousands of innocent Americans.

Anticommunism was not new in American society. A Red Scare had swept the nation following the Russian Revolution of 1917, and opponents of America's labor movement had used charges of communism to block unionization through the 1930s. Many saw the Soviet Union's virtual takeover of eastern Europe in the late 1940s as an alarming parallel to Nazi Germany's takeover of neighboring states. People remembered the failure of "appeasement" at Munich and worried that the United States was "too soft" in its policy toward the Soviet Union.

In addition, top U.S. government officials knew that the Soviet Union was spying on the United States (the United States also had spies within the Soviet Union). A top-secret project, code-named "Venona," decrypted almost three thousand Soviet telegraphic cables that proved Soviet spies had infiltrated U.S. government agencies and nuclear programs. Intelligence officials resolved to prosecute Soviet spies, but they kept their evidence from the American public so that the Soviets would not realize their codes had been compromised.

### Espionage and Nuclear Fears

Fear of nuclear war also contributed to American anticommunism. For four years, the United States alone possessed what seemed the ultimate weapon, but in 1949 the Soviet Union exploded its own atomic device. President Truman, initiating a national atomic civil defense program shortly thereafter, told Americans, "I cannot tell you when or where the attack will come or that it will come at all. I can only remind you that we must be ready when it does come." Children practiced "duck-and-cover" positions in their school classrooms, learning how to shield their faces from the atomic flash and flying debris in the event of an attack. *Life* magazine featured backyard fallout shelters. As the stakes of the global struggle increased, Americans worried that the United States was newly vulnerable to attack on its own soil.

### Politics of Anticommunism

At the height of the Cold War, American leaders, including Presidents Truman and Eisenhower, did not always draw a sufficient line between prudent attempts to prevent Soviet spies from infiltrating important government agencies and anticommunist scare-mongering for political gain. Truman purposely invoked "the communist threat" to gain support for aid to Greece and Turkey in 1947. Republican politicians "red-baited" Democratic opponents, eventually targeting the Truman administration as a whole. In 1947 President Truman ordered investigations into the loyalty of more than 3 million U.S. government employees. As anticommunist hysteria grew, the government began discharging people deemed "security risks," among them alcoholics, homosexuals, and debtors thought susceptible to blackmail. In most cases there was no evidence of disloyalty.

Leading the anticommunist crusade was the House Un-American Activities Committee (popularly known as HUAC). Created in 1938 to investigate "subversive and

un-American propaganda," the viciously anti–New Deal committee had lost credibility then by charging that film stars—including eight-year-old Shirley Temple—were dupes of the Communist Party. In 1947, in a shameless publicity-grabbing tactic, HUAC attacked Hollywood again, using Federal Bureau of Investigation (FBI) files and the testimony of people like Screen Actors Guild president Ronald Reagan (who was also a secret informant for the FBI, complete with code name). Members of a group of screenwriters and directors known as the "Hollywood Ten" were sent to prison for contempt of Congress when they refused to "name names" of suspected communists for HUAC. At least a dozen other Hollywood figures committed suicide. Studios panicked and blacklisted hundreds of actors, screenwriters, directors, even makeup artists, who were suspected of communist affiliations. With no evidence of wrongdoing, these men and women had their careers—and sometimes their lives—ruined.

University professors became targets of the growing "witch hunt" in 1949, when HUAC demanded lists of

### McCarthyism and the Growing "Witch Hunt"

the textbooks used in courses at eighty-one universities. When the board of regents at the University of California, Berkeley, instituted a loyalty oath for faculty, firing twenty-six who resisted on principle, protests from faculty members across the nation forced

the regents to back down. But many professors, afraid of the reach of HUAC, began to downplay controversial material in their courses. In the labor movement, the CIO expelled eleven unions, with more than 900,000 members, for alleged communist domination. The red panic reached its nadir in February 1950, when a relatively obscure U.S. senator came before an audience in Wheeling, West Virginia, to charge that the U.S. State Department was "thoroughly infested with Communists." Republican senator Joseph R. McCarthy of Wisconsin was not an especially credible source. He made charges and then retracted them, claiming first that there were 205 communists in the State Department, then 57, then 81. He had a severe drinking problem; downing a water glass full of Scotch in a single gulp, he would follow it with a quarter-pound stick of butter, hoping to counteract the effects of the liquor. He had a record of dishonesty as a lawyer and judge in his hometown of Appleton, Wisconsin. But McCarthy crystallized the anxieties many felt as they faced a new and difficult era in American life, and the anticommunist excesses of this era came to be known as McCarthyism.

With HUAC and McCarthy on the attack, Americans began pointing accusing fingers at one another. The anticommunist crusade was embraced by labor union officials, religious leaders, and the media, as well as by politicians. A bootblack at the Pentagon was questioned by the FBI seventy times because he had given $10 during the 1930s to a defense fund for the Scottsboro Boys, who had been represented by an attorney from the Communist Party.

THE WEEKLY NEWSMAGAZINE

SENATOR McCARTHY
Opportunity keeps knocking.

▲ In 1954 Senator Joseph R. McCarthy, surrounded by his own newspaper headlines, adorns the cover of *Time* magazine. His downfall came later that year, during the televised Army-McCarthy hearings. McCarthy's wild accusations and abusive treatment of witnesses disgusted millions of viewers. *(© 1954 Time Inc.)*

Women in New York who lobbied for the continuation of wartime daycare programs were denounced as communists by the *New York World Telegram*. "Reds, phonies, and 'parlor pinks,'" in Truman's words, seemed to lurk everywhere.

In such a climate, most public figures found it too risky to stand up against McCarthyist tactics. And most Democrats did support the domestic Cold War and its anticommunist actions. In 1950, with bipartisan support, Congress passed the Internal Security (McCarran) Act, which required members of "Communist-front" organizations to register with the government and prohibited them from holding government jobs or traveling abroad. In 1954 the Senate unanimously passed the Communist Control Act (there were two dissenting votes in the

## Anticommunism in Congress

House), which effectively made membership in the Communist Party illegal. Its chief sponsor, Democratic senator Hubert H. Humphrey of Minnesota, told his colleagues just before he cast his vote, "We have closed all of the doors. The rats will not get out of the trap."

The anticommunist fervor was fueled by spectacular and controversial trials of Americans accused of passing secrets to the Soviet Union. In 1948 Congressman Richard Nixon of California, a member of HUAC, was propelled onto the national stage when he accused former State Department official Alger Hiss of espionage. In 1950 Hiss was convicted of lying about his contacts with Soviet agents. That same year, Ethel and Julius Rosenberg were arrested for passing atomic secrets to the Soviets; they were found guilty of treason and executed in 1953. For decades, many historians believed that the Rosenbergs were primarily victims of a witch hunt. In fact, there was strong evidence of Julius Rosenberg's guilt in cables decrypted by the Venona Project (as well as evidence that Ethel Rosenberg was less involved than had been charged), but this evidence was not presented at their trial for reasons of national security. The cables remained top secret until 1995, when a Clinton administration initiative opened the files to historians.

Some of the worst excesses of Cold War anticommunism waned when Senator McCarthy was discredited on national television in 1954. McCarthy himself was a master at using the press, making sensational accusations—front-page material—just before reporters' deadlines.

## Waning of the Red Scare

When the evidence did not pan out or McCarthy's charges proved untrue, retractions appeared in the back pages of the newspapers. Even journalists who knew McCarthy was unreliable continued to report his charges. Sensational stories sell papers, and McCarthy became a celebrity.

But McCarthy badly misunderstood the power of television. His crucial mistake was taking on the U.S. Army in front of millions of television viewers. At issue was the senator's wild accusation that the army was shielding and promoting communists; he cited the case of one army dentist. The so-called Army-McCarthy hearings, held by a Senate subcommittee in 1954, became a showcase for the senator's abusive treatment of witnesses. McCarthy, apparently drunk, alternately ranted and slurred his words. Finally, after he maligned a young lawyer who was not even involved in the hearings, army counsel Joseph Welch protested, "Have you no sense of decency, sir?" The gallery erupted in applause, and McCarthy's career as a witch-hunter was over. In December 1954, the Senate voted to "condemn" McCarthy for sullying the dignity of the Senate. He remained a senator, but exhaustion and alcohol took their toll, and he died in 1957 at the age of forty-eight. With McCarthy discredited, the most virulent strand of anticommunism had run its course. However, the use of fear tactics for political gain, and the narrowing of American freedoms and liberties, were chilling domestic legacies of the Cold War.

## THE STRUGGLE FOR CIVIL RIGHTS

The Cold War—at home and abroad—also shaped African American struggles for social justice and the nation's responses to them. As the Soviet Union was quick to point out, the United States could hardly pose as the leader of the free world or condemn the denial of human rights in eastern Europe and the Soviet Union if it practiced segregation at home. Nor could the United States convince new African and Asian nations of its dedication to human rights if African Americans were subjected to segregation, discrimination, disfranchisement, and racial violence. Some African American leaders, in fact, understood their struggle for equal rights in the United States as part of a larger, international movement. To win the support of nonaligned nations, the United States would have to live up to its own ideals. At the same time, many Americans viewed social criticism of any kind as a Soviet-inspired attempt to weaken the United States in the ongoing Cold War. The Federal Bureau of Investigation and local law enforcement agencies commonly used such anticommunist fears to justify attacks on civil rights activists. In this heated environment, African Americans struggled to seize the political initiative.

Americans had seen the Second World War as a struggle for democracy and against hatred. African Americans who had helped win the war were determined that their lives in postwar America would be better because of their sacrifices. Moreover, politicians like Harry Truman were beginning to pay attention to black aspirations, especially as black voters in some urban-industrial states began to strongly influence the political balance of power.

**Growing Black Political Power**

President Truman had compelling political reasons for supporting African American civil rights. But he also felt a moral obligation to do something, for he genuinely believed it was only fair that every American, regardless of race, should enjoy the full rights of citizenship. Truman was disturbed by a resurgence of racial terrorism, as a revived Ku Klux Klan was burning crosses and murdering blacks who sought civil rights and racial justice in

▲ Jackie Robinson cracked the color line in major league baseball when he joined the Brooklyn Dodgers for the 1947 season. Sliding safely into third base, Robinson displays the aggressive style that won him rookie-of-the-year honors. He was later elected to the Baseball Hall of Fame. *(Hy Peskin, Life Magazine © Time Inc.)*

the aftermath of World War II. But what really horrified Truman was the report that police in Aiken, South Carolina, had gouged out the eyes of a black sergeant just three hours after he had been discharged from the army. Several weeks after this atrocity, in December 1946, Truman signed an executive order establishing the President's Committee on Civil Rights. The committee's report, *To Secure These Rights,* would become the civil rights movement agenda for the next twenty years. It called for antilynching and antisegregation legislation, and for laws guaranteeing voting rights and equal employment opportunity. For the first time since Reconstruction, a president had acknowledged the federal government's responsibility to protect blacks and to strive for racial equality.

Truman took this responsibility seriously, and in 1948 he issued two executive orders declaring an end to racial discrimination in the federal government. One proclaimed a policy of "fair employment throughout the federal establishment" and created the Employment Board of the Civil Service Commission to hear charges of discrimination. The other ordered the racial desegregation of the armed forces and appointed a committee to oversee this process. Despite strong opposition to desegregation within the military, segregated units were being phased out by the beginning of the Korean War.

Such actions were possible in part because of changing social attitudes and experiences in postwar America. A new and visible black middle class was emerging, composed of college-educated activists, war veterans, and union workers. White awareness of social injustice had been increased by Gunnar Myrdal's social science study *An American Dilemma* (1944) and by Richard Wright's novel *Native Son* (1940) and autobiography *Black Boy* (1945). Blacks and whites also worked together in CIO unions and service organizations, such as the National Council of Churches. In 1947 a black baseball player, Jackie Robinson, broke the major league color barrier and electrified Brooklyn Dodgers fans with his spectacular hitting and base running.

African Americans were successfully challenging racial discrimination in the courts. In 1939 the NAACP had established its Legal Defense and Educational Fund under Thurgood Marshall. By the 1940s, Marshall (who in 1967 would become the first African American Supreme Court justice) and his colleagues carried forward the plan devised by Charles Hamilton Houston to destroy the separate-but-equal doctrine established in *Plessy v. Ferguson* (1896) by insisting on its literal interpretation. In higher education, the NAACP calculated, the cost of true equality in racially separate schools would be prohibitive. "You can't build a cyclotron for one student," the president of the University of Oklahoma acknowledged. As a result of NAACP lawsuits, African American students won admission to professional and graduate schools at several formerly segregated state universities. The NAACP also won major victories through the Supreme Court in *Smith v. Allwright* (1944), which outlawed the whites-only primaries held by the Democratic Party in some southern states; *Morgan v. Virginia* (1946), which struck down segregation in interstate bus transportation; and *Shelley v. Kraemer* (1948), in which the Court held that racially restrictive covenants (private agreements among white homeowners not to sell to blacks) could not legally be enforced.

Even so, segregation was still standard practice in the 1950s, and blacks continued to suffer disfranchisement, job discrimination, and violence, including the 1951 bombing murder of the Florida state director of the NAACP and his wife. But in 1954 the NAACP won a historic victory that stunned the white South and energized African Americans to challenge segregation on several fronts. *Brown v. Board of Education of Topeka*, which Thurgood

### Supreme Court Victories and School Desegregation

Marshall argued before the high court, incorporated school desegregation cases from several states. The Court's unanimous decision was written by Chief Justice Earl Warren, who, as California's attorney general, had pushed for the internment of Japanese Americans during World War II and had come to regret that action. The Court concluded that "in the field of public education the doctrine of 'separate but equal' has no place. Separate educational facilities are inherently unequal." But the ruling that overturned *Plessy v. Ferguson* did not demand immediate compliance. A year later, the Court finally ordered school desegregation, but only "with all deliberate speed."

By the mid-1950s, African Americans were increasingly engaged in a grassroots struggle for civil rights, and that struggle, through news reporting and television, attracted the attention of the nation. In 1955 Rosa Parks, a department store seamstress and long-time NAACP activist, was arrested when she refused to give up her seat to a white man on a public bus in Montgomery, Alabama. Her arrest gave local black women's organizations and civil rights groups a cause around which to organize a boycott of the city's bus system. They selected Martin Luther King Jr., a recently ordained minister who had just arrived in Montgomery, as their leader. King launched the boycott with a moving speech, declaring, "If we are wrong, the Constitution is wrong. If we are wrong, God Almighty is wrong. If we are wrong, Jesus of Nazareth was merely a utopian dreamer. . . . If we are wrong, justice is a lie."

### Montgomery Bus Boycott

Martin Luther King Jr. was a twenty-six-year-old Baptist minister with a recent Ph.D. from Boston University. Committed to the transforming potential of Christian love and schooled in the teachings of India's leader Mohandas K. Gandhi, King believed in nonviolent protest and civil disobedience. By refusing to obey unjust and racist laws, he hoped to focus the nation's attention on the immorality of Jim Crow. King persisted in this struggle even as opponents bombed his house and he was jailed for "conspiring" to boycott.

During the year-long Montgomery bus boycott, blacks young and old rallied in their churches, sang hymns, and prayed that the nation would awaken to the evils of segregation and racial discrimination. They maintained their boycott through heavy rains and the steamy heat of summer, often walking miles a day. One elderly black woman, offered a ride to work by a white reporter, told him, "No, my feets is tired, but my soul is rested." With the bus company near bankruptcy and downtown merchants suffering from declining sales, city officials adopted ha-

▲ For leading the movement to gain equality for blacks riding city buses in Montgomery, Alabama, Martin Luther King Jr. (1929–1968) and other African Americans, including twenty-three other ministers, were indicted by an all-white jury for violating an old law banning boycotts. In late March 1956, King was convicted and fined $500. A crowd of well-wishers cheered a smiling King (here with his wife, Coretta) outside the courthouse, where King proudly declared, "The protest goes on!" King's arrest and conviction made the bus boycott front-page news across America.

*(© Bettmann/Corbis)*

rassment tactics to bring an end to the boycott. But the black people of Montgomery persevered. Thirteen months after the boycott began, the Supreme Court declared Alabama's bus segregation laws unconstitutional.

As the civil rights movement won significant victories, white reactions varied. Some communities in border states like Kansas and Maryland quietly implemented the school desegregation order, and many southern moderates advocated a gradual rollback of segregation. But others urged defiance. The Klan experienced another resurgence, and white violence against blacks increased. In August 1955, Emmett Till, a fourteen-year-old from Chicago, was murdered by white men in Mississippi who took offense at the way he spoke to a white woman. Business and professional people created White Citizens' Councils for the express purpose of resisting the school desegregation order. Known familiarly as "uptown Ku Klux Klans," the councils brought their economic power to bear against black civil rights activists. In keeping with the program of "massive resis-

## White Resistance

tance" proposed by Virginia's U.S. senator, Harry F. Byrd Sr., they pushed through state laws that provided private-school tuition for white children who left public schools to avoid integration and, in Virginia, refused state funding to integrated schools. When FBI director J. Edgar Hoover briefed President Eisenhower on southern racial tensions in 1956, he warned of communist influences among the civil rights activists and even suggested that, if the Citizens' Councils did not worsen the racial situation, their actions might "control the rising tension."

White resistance to civil rights also gained strength in large northern cities. Chicago's African American population had increased from 275,000 in 1940 to 800,000 in 1960. These newcomers found good jobs in industry, and their increased numbers gave them political power. But they faced racism and segregation in the North as well. In 1951 in Cicero, a town adjoining Chicago, several thousand whites who were determined to keep blacks from moving into their neighborhood provoked a race riot. So racially divided was Chicago that the U.S. Commission on Civil Rights in 1959 described it as "the most residentially segregated city in the nation." Detroit and other northern cities were not far behind. And because children attended neighborhood schools, education in the North was in fact often segregated as well, though not by law, as it had been in the South.

Unlike Truman, President Eisenhower wanted to avoid dealing with civil rights, preferring gradual and voluntary change in race relations over executive orders and court mandates.

||||||||||||||||||||||||||||||||||

**Federal Authority and States' Rights**

Although the president disapproved of racial segregation, he objected to "compulsory federal law," believing instead that race relations would improve "only if [desegregation] starts locally." He also feared that the ugly public confrontations likely to follow rapid desegregation would jeopardize Republican inroads in the South. Thus Eisenhower did not state forthrightly that the federal government would enforce the *Brown* decision as the nation's law. In short, instead of leading, he spoke ambiguously and thereby tacitly encouraged white resistance. In 1956, 101 congressmen and senators from eleven southern states, all Democrats, issued "The Southern Manifesto." This document condemned the *Brown* decision as an "unwarranted exercise of power by the Court" which violated the principle of states' rights and commended those states that sought to "resist forced integration by any lawful means."

Events in Little Rock, Arkansas, forced the president to stop sidestepping the issue. In September 1957, Arkansas governor Orval E. Faubus defied a court-supported desegregation plan for Little Rock's Central High School. Faubus went on television the night before school began and told Arkansans that "blood would run in the streets" if black students tried to enter the high school the next day. He deployed 250 Arkansas National Guard troops to block their entrance. Eight black teenagers tried to enter Central High on the second day of school but were turned away by the National Guard. The ninth, separated from the others, was surrounded by jeering whites and narrowly escaped the mob with the help of a sympathetic white woman.

The "Little Rock Nine" entered Central High for the first time more than two weeks after school began, after a federal judge intervened. An angry crowd surrounded the school, and television broadcast the scene to the nation and the world. Eisenhower, fearing violence and angry at what he saw as Faubus's attempt to provoke a crisis, nationalized the Arkansas National Guard (placing it under federal, not state, control) and dispatched 1,000 army paratroopers to Little Rock. Troops guarded the students

for the rest of the year. Eisenhower's use of federal power in Little Rock was a critical step in America's struggle over racial equality, for he had directly confronted the conflict between federal authority and states' rights. However, state power triumphed the following year, when Faubus closed all public high schools in Little Rock rather than desegregate them.

Nonetheless, federal action continued. In 1957 Congress passed the first Civil Rights Act since Reconstruction, creating the United States Commission on Civil Rights to investigate systemic discrimination, such as in voting. Although this measure, like a voting rights act passed three years later, was not fully effective, it was another federal recognition of the centrality of civil rights. Most important, however, was the growing strength of a new, grassroots civil rights activism. In 1957 Martin Luther King Jr. became the first president of the Southern Christian Leadership Conference (SCLC), organized to coordinate civil rights activities. With the success in Montgomery and the gains won through the Supreme Court and the Truman administration, African Americans were poised to launch a major national movement for civil rights in the years to come.

## CREATING A MIDDLE-CLASS NATION

Even as African Americans encountered massive resistance in their struggles for civil rights during the 1950s, in other ways the United States was becoming a more inclusive society. More Americans than ever before participated in a broad middle-class and suburban culture, and divisions among Americans based on class, ethnicity, religion, and regional identity became less important. National prosperity offered ever greater numbers of Americans material comfort and economic security through entrance into an economic middle class. Old European ethnic identities were fading, as an ever smaller percentage of America's people were first- or second-generation immigrants.

In the new suburbs, people from different backgrounds worked together to create communities and build schools, churches, and other institutions. Middle-class Americans, like those on Nancy Circle, increasingly looked to powerful national media rather than to regional or ethnic traditions for advice on matters ranging from how to celebrate Thanksgiving to what car to buy to how to raise children. New opportunities for consumption—whether the fads of a powerful teenage culture or the suburban ranch-style house—also tied Americans from different backgrounds together. In the postwar years, a new middle-class way of life was transforming the United States.

During the 1950s, sustained economic growth created unprecedented levels of prosperity and economic security for a broad range of America's people (see Figure 29.2). Several factors contributed to the economic boom. In great part it was driven by consumer spending. Americans eagerly bought consumer goods that had not been available during the war, and industries expanded production to meet consumer demand. Government spending also played an important role. As the Cold War deepened, the government poured money into defense industries, creating jobs and stimulating the economy.

## Prosperity for More Americans

Cold War military and aerospace spending changed American society and culture in unintended ways. The professional middle class grew because the government's weapons development and space programs required highly educated scientists, engineers, and other white-collar workers. And as universities received billions of dollars to fund such research, universities expanded, playing a variety of new roles in American life. The results of such government-funded research were not limited to military applications or the space race; the transistor, invented during the 1950s, made possible both the computer revolution and the transistor radio, which was critically important to 1950s youth culture.

A new era of labor relations also helped bring economic prosperity to more Americans. By 1950, labor and management created a new, more stable relationship. In peaceful negotiations, the United Auto Workers (UAW) and General Motors led the way for other corporations in providing workers with health insurance, pension plans, and guaranteed cost-of-living adjustments, or COLAs, to

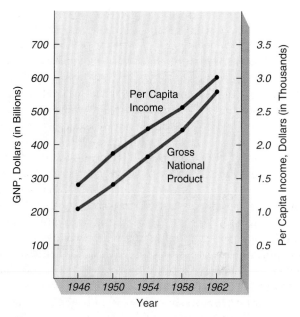

**Figure 29.2    Gross National Product and Per Capita Income, 1946–1962**

Both gross national product and per capita income soared during the economic boom from 1946 to 1962.

*(Source: Adapted from U.S. Bureau of the Census,* Historical Statistics of the United States, Colonial Times to 1970, *Bicentennial Edition [Washington, D.C.: U.S. Government Printing Office, 1975], p. 224.)*

Bernard Levey, a truck supervisor, stands with his family in front of their new home in Levittown, PA. This house, with four and a half rooms, sold for under $8,000.

*(Bernard Hoffman//Time Life Pictures/Getty Images)*

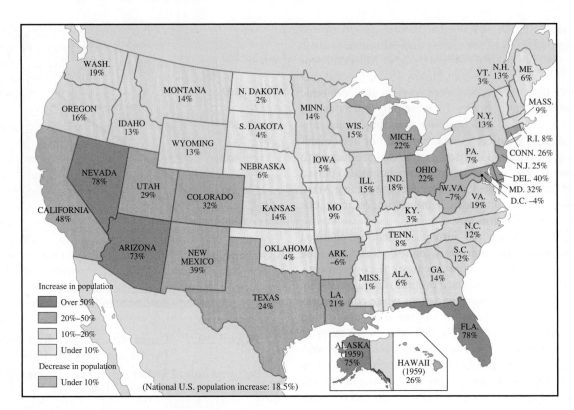

**Map 29.1   Rise of the Sunbelt, 1950–1960**
The years after the Second World War saw a continuation of the migration of Americans to the Sunbelt states of the Southwest and the West Coast.

protect wages from inflation. The 1950 agreement that *Fortune* magazine called "The Treaty of Detroit" gave GM's workers a five-year contract, with regular wage increases tied to corporate productivity. This was a turning point for the labor movement. In exchange for wages and benefits, organized labor gave up its demands for greater control in corporate affairs. And with wage increases tied to corporate productivity, labor cast its lot with management: workplace stability and efficiency, not strikes, would bring higher wages. During the 1950s, wages and benefits often rivaled those of college-educated professionals and propelled union families into the ranks of the economic middle class.

Just as labor agreements helped create prosperity for union members and their families, government policies helped bring the nation's poorest region into the American economic mainstream. In the 1930s, Roosevelt had called the South "the nation's No. 1 economic problem."

### Sunbelt and Economic Growth

During World War II, new defense industry plants and military training camps channeled federal money to the region, stimulating economic growth. In the postwar era, huge levels of defense spending, especially for the nation's aerospace industry, continued to shift economic development from the Northeast and Midwest to the South and Southwest—the Sunbelt (see Map 29.1). Government actions—including generous tax breaks for oil companies, siting of military bases, and awarding of defense and aerospace contracts—were crucial to the region's new prosperity.

The Sunbelt's spectacular growth was also due to agribusiness, the oil industry, real-estate development, and recreation. Sunbelt states aggressively—and successfully—sought foreign investment. Industry was drawn to the South by right-to-work laws, which outlawed closed shops, and by low taxes and low heating bills. The development of air conditioning was also crucial, for it made bearable even the hottest summer days. Houston, Phoenix, Los Angeles, San Diego, Dallas, and Miami all boomed; the population of Houston, a center of the aerospace industry and also of oil and petrochemical production, more than tripled between 1940 and 1960. California absorbed no less than one-fifth of the nation's entire population increase in the 1950s. By 1963 it was the most populous state in the Union.

By the 1950s, it seemed that America was becoming a middle-class nation. Unionized blue-collar workers gained

## A New Middle-Class Culture

middle-class incomes, and veterans with GI Bill college educations swelled the growing managerial and professional class. In 1956, for the first time, the United States had more white-collar than blue-collar workers, and in 1957 there were 61 percent more salaried middle-class workers than just a decade earlier. Also for the first time, a majority of families—60 percent—had incomes in the middle-class range (approximately $3,000 to $9,000 a year in the mid-1950s).

However, middle-class identity was not simply a matter of economics. Half of teenagers whose fathers did unskilled menial labor or whose mothers had only a sixth-grade education, a major 1952 survey discovered, believed their family was "middle class" (not working class or lower class). Paradoxically, the strength of unions in the postwar era contributed to a decline in working-class identity: as large numbers of blue-collar workers participated fully in the suburban middle-class culture, the lines separating working class and middle class seemed less important. Increasingly, a family's standard of living mattered more than what sort of work made the standard of living possible. People of color did not share equally in America's postwar prosperity and were usually invisible in American representations of "the good life." However, many middle-income African Americans, Latinos, and Asian Americans did participate in the broad middle-class culture.

The emergence of a national middle-class culture was possible in part because America's population was more

## Whiteness and National Culture

homogeneous in the 1950s than before or since. In the nineteenth and early twentieth centuries, the United States had restricted or prohibited immigration from Asia, Africa, and Latin America while accepting millions of Europeans to America's shores. This large-scale European immigration had been shut off in the 1920s, so that by 1960 only 5.7 percent of Americans were foreign-born (compared with approximately 15 percent in 1910 and 12.4 percent in 2005). In 1950, 88 percent of Americans were of European

ancestry (compared with 69 percent in 2000); 10 percent of the population was African American; 2 percent was Hispanic; and Native Americans and Asian Americans each accounted for about one-fifth of 1 percent. But almost all European-Americans were at least a generation removed from immigration. Instead of "Italians" or "Russians" or "Jews," they were increasingly likely to describe themselves as "white." In 1959 the addition of two new states, Alaska and Hawai'i, brought more people of native, Asian, or Pacific origin to the U.S. population.

Although the new suburbs were peopled mostly by white families, these suburbs were usually more diverse than the communities from which their residents had come. America's small towns and urban ethnic enclaves were quite homogeneous and usually intolerant of difference and of challenges to traditional ways. In the suburbs, people from different backgrounds came together: migrants from the city and the country; from different regions of the nation, different ethnic cultures, and different religious backgrounds. It was in the suburbs, paradoxically, that many people encountered different customs and beliefs. But as they joined with neighbors to forge new communities, the new suburbanites frequently adopted the norms of the developing national middle class. They traded the provincial homogeneity of specific ethnic or regional cultures for a new sort of homogeneity: a national middle-class culture.

Because many white Americans were new to the middle class, they were uncertain about what behaviors were proper and expected of them. They

## Television

found instruction, in part, in the national mass media. Women's magazines helped housewives replace the ethnic and regional dishes with which they had grown up with "American" recipes created from national brandname products—such as casseroles made with Campbell's Cream of Mushroom soup. Television also fostered America's shared national culture and taught Americans how to be middle class. Although television sets cost about $300—the equivalent of $2,000 today—almost half of American homes had TVs by 1953. Television ownership rose to 90 percent by 1960, when more American households had a television set than a washing machine or an electric iron.

On television, suburban families like the Andersons (*Father Knows Best*) and the Cleavers (*Leave It to Beaver*) ate dinner at a properly set dining room table. The mothers were always well groomed; June Cleaver did housework in a carefully ironed dress. When children faced moral dilemmas, parents gently but firmly guided them toward correct decisions. Every crisis was resolved through paternal wisdom—and a little humor. In these families, no one ever yelled or hit. These popular family situation comedies portrayed and reinforced the suburban middle-class ideal that so many American families sought.

The "middle-classness" of television programming was due in part to the economics of the television industry. Advertising paid for television programming, and the corporations that bought advertising did not want to offend potential consumers. Thus, although African American musician Nat King Cole drew millions of viewers to his NBC television show, it never found a sponsor. National corporations were afraid that being linked to a black performer like Cole would hurt their sales among whites—especially in the South. Because African Americans made up only about 10 percent of the population and many had little disposable income, they had little power in this economics-driven system. The *Nat King Cole Show* was canceled within a year; it was a decade before the networks again tried to anchor a show around a black performer.

Television's reach extended beyond the suburbs. People from the inner cities and from isolated rural areas also watched family sitcoms or laughed at the antics of Milton Berle and Lucille Ball. With only network television available— ABC, CBS, and NBC (and, until 1956, DuMont)—at any one time 70 percent or more of all viewers might be watching the same popular program. (In the early twenty-first century the most popular shows might attract 12 percent of the viewing audience.) Television gave Americans a shared set of experiences; it also helped create a more homogeneous, white-focused, middle-class culture.

Linked by a shared national culture, Americans also found common ground in a new abundance of consumer goods. After decades of scarcity, Americans had what seemed a dazzling array of consumer goods from which to choose, and they embraced them with unmatched exuberance. Even the most utilitarian objects got two-tone paint jobs or rocket-ship details; there was an optimism and vulgar joy in the popularity of turquoise refrigerators, furniture shaped like boomerangs, and cars designed to resemble fighter jets. In this consumer society, people used consumer choices to express their personal identity and to claim status within the broad boundaries of the middle class. Cars more than anything else embodied the consumer fantasies and exuberance of newly prosperous Americans. Expensive Cadillacs were the first to develop tail fins, and fins soon soared from midrange Chevys, Fords, and Plymouths as well. Americans spent $65 billion on automobiles in 1955—a figure equivalent to almost 20 percent of the gross national product. To pay for all those cars—and for suburban houses with modern appliances—America's consumer debt rose from $5.7 billion in 1945 to $58 billion in 1961.

## Consumer Culture

Admiral's "Up-Side-Down" refrigerator boasted a full-size freezer that would hold up to 120 pounds of frozen food, making life easier for the modern housewife. It also captured the new consumer exuberance: even the inside of this refrigerator is colorful!

*(Picture Research Consultants & Archives)*

In the same years, Americans turned in unprecedented numbers to organized religion. Membership (primarily in mainline Christian churches) doubled between the end of World War II and the beginning of the 1960s. The uncertainties of the nuclear age likely contributed to the resurgence of religion, and some Americans may have sought spiritual consolation in the wake of the immensely destructive world war. The increasingly important national mass media played a role, as preachers like Billy Graham created national congregations from television audiences, preaching a message that combined the promise of salvation with Cold War patriotism. But along with religious teachings, local churches and synagogues offered new suburbanites a sense of community. They welcomed newcomers, celebrated life's rituals, and supported the sick and the bereaved who were often far from their extended families and old communities. It is difficult to measure the depth of religious belief in postwar America, but church fellowship halls were near the center of the new postwar middle-class culture.

**Religion**

## MEN, WOMEN, AND YOUTH AT MIDCENTURY

Most of all, Americans pursued "the good life" and sought refuge from the tensions of the Cold War world through their homes and families. Having survived the Great Depression and a world war, many sought fulfillment in private life rather than public engagement; they saw their commitment to home and family as an expression of faith in the future. However, despite the real satisfactions that many Americans found in family life, both men and women found their life choices limited by powerful social pressures to conform to narrowly defined gender roles.

During the 1950s, few Americans remained single, and most people married very young. By 1959, almost half of American brides had yet to reach their nineteenth birthday; their husbands were usually only a year or so older. This trend toward early marriage was endorsed by experts and approved by most parents, in part as a way to prevent premarital sex. As Americans accepted psychotherapeutic insights in the years following the war, they worried not only that premarital sex might leave the young woman pregnant or ruin her "reputation," but also that the experience could so damage her psychologically that she could never adjust to "normal" marital relations. One popular women's magazine argued, "When two people

**Marriage and Families**

are ready for sexual intercourse at the fully human level they are ready for marriage. . . . Not to do so is moral cowardice. And society has no right to stand in their way."

Many young couples—still teenagers—found autonomy and freedom from parental authority by marrying and setting up their own household. Most newlyweds quickly had babies—an average of three—completing their family while still in their twenties. Birth control (condoms and diaphragms) was widely available and widely used, for most couples planned the size of their family. But almost all married couples, regardless of race or class, wanted a large family. Two children were the American ideal in 1940; by 1960, most couples wanted four. And though many families looked nothing like television's June, Ward, Wally, and Beaver Cleaver, 88 percent of children under eighteen lived with two parents (in 2000, the figure was 69 percent). Fewer children were born outside marriage then; only 3.9 percent of births were to unmarried women in 1950 (compared with more than one-third of births in 2000). Divorce rates were also lower. As late as 1960, there were only 9 divorces per 1,000 married couples.

In these 1950s families, men and women usually took distinct and different roles, with male breadwinners and female homemakers. This division of labor, contemporary commentators insisted, was based on the timeless and essential differences between the sexes. In fact, the economic and social structure and the cultural values of postwar American society largely determined what choices were available to American men and women.

**Gender Roles in 1950s Families**

During the 1950s, it was possible for many families to live in modest middle-class comfort on one (male) salary. There were strong incentives for women to stay at home, especially while children were young. Good childcare was rarely available, and fewer families lived close to the grandparents or other relatives who had traditionally helped with the children. A new cohort of childcare experts, including Dr. Spock, whose 1946 *Baby and Child Care* sold millions of copies, insisted that a mother's full-time attention was necessary for her children's well-being. Because of hiring discrimination, women who could afford to stay home often did not find the jobs available to them attractive enough to justify a double shift, with paid employment simply added to their responsibilities for cooking and housework. Many women thus chose to devote their considerable energies to family life. America's schools and religious institutions also benefited immensely from their volunteer labor.

A great number of women, however, found that their lives did not completely match the ideal of 1950s family

## Women and Work

life. Suburban domesticity left many women feeling isolated, cut off from the larger world of experiences that their husbands still inhabited. The popular belief that one should find complete emotional satisfaction in private life put unrealistic pressures on marriages and family relationships. And finally, despite near-universal celebration of women's domestic roles, many women found themselves managing both job and family responsibilities (see Figure 29.3). Twice as many women were employed in 1960 as in 1940, including 39 percent of women with children between the ages of six and seventeen. A majority of these women worked part-time for some specific family goal: a new car; college tuition for the children. They did not see these jobs as violating their primary role as housewife; these jobs were in service to the family, not a means to independence from it.

Whether she worked to supplement a middle-class income, to feed her children, or to support herself, however, a woman faced discrimination in the world of work. Want ads were divided into "Help Wanted—Male" and "Help Wanted—Female" categories. Female full-time workers earned, on average, just 60 percent of what male full-time workers were paid and were restricted to less well-paid "female" fields, as maids, secretaries, teachers, and nurses. Women with exceptional talent or ambition often found their aspirations blocked. A popular book, *Modern Woman: The Lost Sex,* explained that ambitious women and "feminists" suffered from "penis envy." Textbooks for college psychology and sociology courses warned women not to "compete" with men; magazine articles described "career women" as a "third sex." Medical schools commonly limited the admission of women to 5 percent of each class. In 1960 less than 4 percent of lawyers and judges were female. When future Supreme Court Justice Ruth Bader Ginsburg graduated at the top of her Columbia Law School class in 1959, she could not find a job.

While academics and mass media critics alike stressed the importance of "proper" female roles, they devoted equal attention to the plight of the American male. American men

## "Crisis of Masculinity"

faced a "crisis of masculinity," proclaimed the nation's mass-circulation magazines, quoting an array of psychological experts. In a bestselling book, sociologist William H. Whyte explained that postwar corporate employees had become "organization men," succeeding through cooperation and conformity, not through individual initiative and risk. Women, too, were blamed for men's crisis: women's "natural" desire for security and comfort, experts insisted, was stifling men's

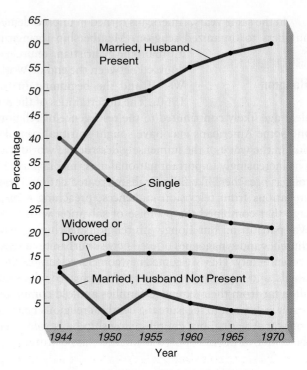

**Figure 29.3   Marital Distribution of the Female Labor Force, 1944–1970**

The composition of the female labor force changed dramatically from 1944 to 1970. In 1944, 41 percent of women in the labor force were single; in 1970, only 22 percent were single. During the same years, the percentage of the female labor force who had a husband in the home jumped from 34 to 59. The percentage who were widowed or divorced remained about the same from 1944 to 1970.

(Source: Adapted from U.S. Bureau of the Census, Historical Statistics of the United States, Colonial Times to 1970, Bicentennial Edition [Washington, D.C.: U.S. Government Printing Office, 1975], p. 133.)

natural instinct for adventure. Some even linked concerns about masculinity to the Cold War, arguing that, unless America's men recovered masculinity diminished by white-collar work or a suburban, family-centered existence, the nation's future was at risk. At the same time, however, men who did not conform to current standards of male responsibility—husband, father, breadwinner—were forcefully condemned, sometimes in the same magazines that preached the crisis of masculinity. One influential book advocated mandatory psychotherapy for men who reached thirty without having married; such single men were open to charges of "emotional immaturity" or "latent homosexuality."

Sexuality was complicated terrain in postwar America. Only heterosexual intercourse within marriage was

## Sexuality

deemed socially acceptable, and consequences for sexual misconduct could be severe. Women who became pregnant outside marriage were often ostracized by friends and family, and expelled from schools or colleges. Homosexuality was grounds for dismissal from a job, expulsion from college, even jail. At the same time, a great many Americans were breaking the sexual rules of the era. In his major works on human sexuality, *Sexual Behavior in the Human Male* (1948) and *Sexual Behavior in the Human Female* (1953), Dr. Alfred Kinsey, director of the Institute for Sex Research at Indiana University, informed Americans that, despite the fact that more than 80 percent of his female sample disapproved of premarital sex on "moral grounds," half of these women had had premarital sex. He also reported that at least 37 percent of American men had had "some homosexual experience." Americans made bestsellers of Kinsey's dry, quantitative studies—as many rushed to condemn him. One congressman charged Kinsey with "hurling the insult of the century against our mothers, wives, daughters and sisters"; the *Chicago Tribune* called him a "menace to society." Although Kinsey's population samples did not provide a completely accurate picture of American sexual behavior, his findings made many Americans aware that they were not alone in breaking certain rules.

Another challenge to the sexual rules of 1950s America came from Hugh Hefner, who launched *Playboy* magazine in 1953. Within three years, the magazine had a circulation of 1 million. Hefner saw *Playboy* as an attack on America's "ferocious anti-sexuality [and] dark antieroticism" and his nude "playmates" as a means for men to combat what he considered the increasingly "blurred distinctions between the sexes" in a family-centered suburban culture.

## Youth Culture

As children grew up in relative stability and prosperity, a distinctive "youth culture" developed. Youth culture was really a set of subcultures; the culture of white, middle-class, suburban youth was not the same as that of black, urban teens or even of the white working class. Youth culture was, however, distinct from the culture of adults. Its customs and rituals were created within peer groups and shaped by national media—teen magazines, movies, radio, advertising, music—targeted toward this huge potential audience.

The sheer numbers of "baby boom" youth made them a force in American society. People sometimes described the baby-boom generation as "a pig in a python," and as this group moved from childhood to youth, communities successively built elementary schools, junior high schools, and high schools. America's corporations quickly learned the power of youth, as children's fads launched multimillion-dollar industries. Slinky, selling for a dollar, began loping down people's stairs in 1947; Mr. Potato Head—probably the first toy advertised on television—had $4 million in sales in 1952. In the mid-1950s, when Walt Disney's television show *Disneyland* featured Davy Crockett, "King of the Wild Frontier," every child in America (and more than a few adults) just *had* to have a coonskin cap. When the price of raccoon fur skyrocketed from 25 cents to $8 a pound, many children had to make do with a Davy Crockett lunchbox or toothbrush instead. As these baby-boom children grew up, their buying power shaped American popular culture.

By 1960, America's 18 million teenagers were spending $10 billion a year. Seventy-two percent of movie tickets in the 1950s were sold to teenagers, and Hollywood catered to this audience with a flood of teen films, ranging from forgettable B-movies like *The Cool and the Crazy* and *Senior Prom* to controversial and influential movies, such as James Dean's *Rebel Without a Cause*. Adults worried that teens would be drawn to romantic images of delinquency in *Rebel Without a Cause*, and teenage boys did copy Dean's rebellious look. The film, however, blamed parents for teenage confusion, drawing heavily on popular psychological theories about sexuality and the "crisis of masculinity." "What can you do when you have to be a man?" James Dean's character implored his father.

Movies helped shape teen fads and fashions, but nothing defined youth culture as much as its music. Young Americans were electrified by the driving energy and beat of Bill Haley and the Comets, Chuck Berry, Little Richard, and Buddy Holly. Elvis Presley's 1956 appearance on TV's *Ed Sullivan Show* touched off a frenzy of teen adulation—and a flood of letters from parents scandalized by his "gyrations." As one reviewer noted, "When Presley executes his bumps and grinds, it must be remembered that even the 12-year-old's curiosity may be overstimulated." Although few white musicians acknowledged the debt, the roots of rock 'n' roll lay in African American rhythm and blues. The raw energy and sometimes sexually suggestive lyrics of early rock music faded as the music industry sought white performers, like Pat Boone, to do blander, more acceptable "cover" versions of music by black artists.

The distinct youth culture that developed in the 1950s made many adults uneasy. Parents worried that the common practice of "going steady" made it more likely that teens would "go too far" sexually. Juvenile delinquency was a major concern. Crime rates for young people had, in fact, risen dramatically in the years following World

# Barbie

arbie, the "all-American doll," is—like many Americans—an immigrant. Although Barbie was introduced in 1959 by the American toy company Mattel, her origins lie in Germany, where she went by the name Lilli.

As many mothers at the time suspected, noting the new doll's figure (equivalent to 39-21-31 in human proportions), Barbie's background was not completely respectable. The German Lilli doll was a toy for adult men, not little girls. She was based on a character that cartoonist Reinhard Beuthien drew to fill some empty space in the June 24, 1952, edition of the German tabloid *Das Bild*. The cartoon was meant to appear just once, but Lilli was so popular that she became a regular feature. Soon Lilli appeared in three-dimensional form as *Bild* Lilli, an eleven-and-a-half-inch-tall blonde doll—with the figure Barbie would make famous. Dressed in a variety of sexy outfits, Lilli was sold in tobacco shops and bars as a "novelty gift" for men.

Lilli came to America with Ruth Handler, one of the founders and codirectors of the Mattel toy company. In a time when girls were given baby dolls, Handler imagined a grown-up doll that girls could dress as they did their paper dolls. When she glimpsed Lilli while on vacation in Europe, Handler bought three—and gave one to her daughter Barbara, after whom Lilli would be renamed. Mattel bought the rights to Lilli (the doll and the cartoon, which Mattel quietly retired) and unveiled Barbie in March 1959. Despite mothers' hesitations about buying a doll that looked like Barbie, within the year Mattel had sold 351,000 Barbies at $3 each (or about $17 in 2000 dollars). The billionth Barbie was sold in 1997.

Within the United States, Barbie has been controversial—at least among adults. Some have worried that Barbie's wildly unrealistic figure fosters girls' dissatisfaction with their own body—a serious problem in a culture plagued with eating disorders. Others claim that, despite Barbie's 1980s "Girls Can Do

Anything" makeover, Barbie represents a model of empty-headed femininity, focused on endless consumption. And many have criticized the ways in which blonde, blue-eyed Barbie failed to represent the diversity of America's people, especially as Mattel's early attempts at racial and ethnic diversity (such as "Colored Francie," introduced in 1967) created dolls with the same Caucasian features as the original Barbie, except with darker skin coloring and hair.

In recent years, Barbie has played a role in important international issues. In 2002 international labor-rights groups called for a boycott of Barbie. They cited studies showing that half of all Barbies are made by exploited young women workers in mainland China: of the $10 retail cost of an average Barbie, Chinese factories receive only 35 cents per doll to pay for all their costs, including labor. Barbie has also played a role in international relations. Saudi Arabia banned sales of Barbie in 2003, arguing that her skimpy outfits and the values she represents are not suitable for a Muslim nation. And a poll found that, following the beginning of the United States' war in Iraq, people in other nations said they were less likely to buy Barbie because she was so closely identified with America.

Even so, the eleven-and-a-half-inch doll remains popular throughout the world, sold in more than 150 countries. Today, the average American girl has ten Barbies—and the typical German girl owns five. Over the years, for better or worse, Barbie has continued to link the United States and the rest of the world.

► Before Barbie became an American child's toy, she was "Lilli," a German sex symbol. Mattel transformed the doll into a wholesome American teenager with a new wardrobe to match.

*(Spielzeug Museum, Munich).*

▲ Elvis Presley "gyrates" during a live performance in 1956. Many adults were horrified ("sexhibitionist," *Time* magazine sneered), but Elvis was selling $75,000 worth of records a day in April 1956.

*(Picture Research Consultants & Archives)*

War II, but that was partly because there were so many young people, and they were under greater scrutiny than before. Much juvenile delinquency consisted of "status" crimes—curfew violations, sexual experimentation, underage drinking—activities that were criminal because of the person's age, not because of the action itself. Congress held extensive hearings on juvenile delinquency, with experts testifying to the corrupting power of youth-

oriented popular culture, comic books in particular. In 1955 *Life* magazine reported, "Some American parents, without quite knowing what it is their kids are up to, are worried that it's something they shouldn't be." Most youthful behavior, however—from going steady to fads in music and dress—fit squarely into the consumer culture that youth shared with their parents. "Rebellious youth" rarely questioned the logic of postwar American culture.

Despite the growing reach and power of this middle-class culture, there were pockets of cultural dissent. Beat

**Challenges to Middle-Class Culture**

(a word that suggested both "down and out" and "beatific") writers rejected both middle-class social decorum and contemporary literary conventions. Jack Kerouac, author of *On The Road*, traced his inspiration to "weariness with all forms of the modern industrial state." The Beat Generation embraced spontaneity in their art, in their lives sought freedom from the demands of everyday life, and enjoyed a more open sexuality and drug use. Perhaps the most significant beat work was Allen Ginsberg's angry, incantational poem "Howl" (1956), the subject of an obscenity trial whose verdict opened American publishing to a much broader range of works. The mainstream press made fun of the beats, dubbing them and their followers "beatniks" (after *Sputnik*, suggesting their un-Americanness). Although they attracted little attention in the 1950s, they laid the groundwork for the 1960s counterculture.

## THE LIMITS OF THE MIDDLE-CLASS NATION

During the 1950s, America's popular culture and mass media celebrated the opportunities available to the nation's people. At the same time, a host of influential critics rushed to condemn the new middle-class culture as a wasteland of conformity, homogeneity, and ugly consumerism.

These critics were not lone figures crying out in the wilderness. Americans, obsessed with self-criticism even

**Critics of Conformity**

as most participated wholeheartedly in the celebratory "consensus" culture of their age, rushed to buy books like John Keats's *The Crack in the Picture Window* (1957), which portrayed three families—the "Drones," the "Amiables," and the "Fecunds"—who lived in identical suburban tract houses "vomited" up by developers and sacrificed their remaining individuality in the quest for consumer goods. Some of the most popular fiction of the postwar era, such as J. D. Salinger's *The Catcher in the*

During the Second World War, DDT was used to protect American troops from bug-borne diseases and was hailed as a miracle insecticide. The use of DDT spread in postwar America, but little attention was paid to its often-fatal consequences for birds, mammals, and fish. In 1945, even as children ran alongside, this truck sprayed DDT as part of a mosquito-control program at New York's Jones Beach State Park.

*(© Bettmann/Corbis)*

*Rye* and Norman Mailer's *The Naked and the Dead,* was profoundly critical of American society. Americans even made bestsellers of difficult academic works, such as David Riesman's *The Lonely Crowd* (1950) and William H. Whyte's *The Organization Man* (1955), both of which criticized the rise of conformity in American life. Versions of these critiques also appeared in mass-circulation magazines like *Ladies' Home Journal* and *Reader's Digest.* Steeped in such cultural criticism, many Americans even understood *Invasion of the Body Snatchers*—a 1956 film in which zombielike aliens grown in huge pods gradually replace a town's human inhabitants—as criticism of suburban conformity and the bland homogeneity of postwar culture.

Most of these critics were attempting to understand large-scale and significant changes in American society. Americans were contending with some loss of autonomy in work as large corporations replaced smaller businesses; they experienced the homogenizing force of mass production and a national consumer culture; they saw distinctions among ethnic groups and even among socioeconomic classes decline in importance. Many wanted to understand these social dislocations better. Critics of the new culture, however, were often elitist and antidemocratic. Many saw only bland conformity and sterility in the emerging middle-class suburban culture and so missed something important. Identical houses did not produce identical souls; instead, inexpensive suburban housing gave healthier, and perhaps happier, lives to millions who had grown up in dank, dark tenements or ramshackle farmhouses without indoor plumbing. In retrospect, however, other criticisms are obvious.

First, the new consumer culture encouraged wasteful habits and harmed the environment. *Business Week* noted

## Environmental Degradation

during the 1950s that corporations need not rely on "planned obsolescence," purposely designing a product to wear out so that consumers would have to replace it. Americans replaced products because they were "out of date," not because they did not work, and automakers, encouraging the trend, revamped designs every year. New and inexpensive plastic products and detergents made consumers' lives easier—but were not biodegradable. And America's new consumer society used an ever larger share of the world's resources. By the 1960s, the United States, with only 5 percent of the world's population, consumed more than one-third of its goods and services.

The rapid economic growth that made the middle-class consumer culture possible exacted environmental costs. Steel mills, coal-powered generators, and internal-combustion car engines burning lead-based gasoline polluted the atmosphere and imperiled people's health. As suburbanites commuted greater distances to their jobs, and neighborhoods were built without public transportation or shopping within walking distance of people's homes, Americans relied on private automobiles, consuming the nonrenewable resources of oil and gasoline, and filling cities and suburbs with smog. Vast quantities of water were diverted from lakes and rivers to meet the needs of America's burgeoning Sunbelt cities, including the swimming pools and golf courses that dotted parched Arizona and southern California.

Defense contractors and farmers were among the country's worst polluters. Refuse from nuclear weapons facilities at Hanford, Washington, and at Colorado's

Rocky Flats arsenal poisoned soil and water resources for years. Agriculture began employing massive amounts of pesticides and other chemicals. DDT, a chemical used on Pacific islands during the war to kill mosquitoes and lice, was used widely in the United States from 1945 until after 1962, when wildlife biologist Rachel Carson specifically indicted DDT for the deaths of mammals, birds, and fish in her bestselling book *Silent Spring*.

In the midst of prosperity, few understood the consequences of the economic transformation taking place. The nation was moving toward a postindustrial economy in which providing goods and services to consumers was more important than producing goods. Therefore, though union members prospered during the 1950s, union membership grew slowly—because most new jobs were being created not in heavy industries that hired blue-collar workers but in the union-resistant white-collar service trades. Technological advances increased productivity, as automated electronic processes replaced slower mechanical ones—but they pushed people out of relatively well paid blue-collar jobs into the growing and less well-paid service sector.

Largely oblivious to the environmental degradation and work-sector shifts that accompanied economic growth and consumerism, the new middle-class culture also largely ignored

## Continuing Racism

those who did not belong to its ranks. Race remained a major dividing line in American society, even as fewer Americans were excluded because of ethnic identity. Racial discrimination stood unchallenged in most of 1950s America. Suburbs, both North and South, were almost always racially segregated. Many white Americans had little or no contact in their daily lives with people of different races—not only because of residential segregation but also because the relatively small populations of nonwhite Americans were not dispersed equally throughout the nation. In 1960 there were 68 people of Chinese descent and 519 African Americans living in Vermont; 181 Native Americans lived in West Virginia; and Mississippi had just 178 Japanese American residents. Most white Americans in the 1950s—especially those outside the South, where there was a large African American population—gave little thought to race. They did not think of the emerging middle-class culture as "white," but as "American," marginalizing people of color in image as in reality (see Map 29.2).

The new middle-class culture was also indifferent to the plight of the poor. In an age of abundance, more than one in five Americans lived in poverty. One-fifth of the poor were people of color, including almost half of the nation's

**1950**

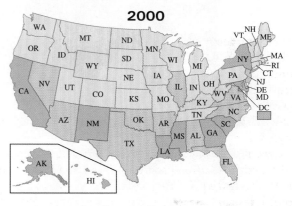

**2000**

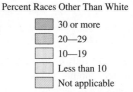

Percent Races Other Than White

- 30 or more
- 20—29
- 10—19
- Less than 10
- Not applicable

**Map 29.2    Racial Composition of the United States, 1950 and 2000**

Compared with present-day America, most states were fairly racially homogeneous in 1950. The exception was the Deep South, where most African Americans still lived.

(Source: Adapted from "Demographic Trends in the Twentieth Century," U.S. Census Bureau; www.census.gov/population/www/censusdata /hiscendata.html.)

African American population and more than half of all Native Americans. Two-thirds of the poor lived in households headed by a person with an eighth-grade education or less, one-fourth in households headed by a single woman. More than one-third of the poor were under age eighteen; one-fourth were over age sixty-five. Social Security payments helped the elderly, but many retirees were not yet covered, and medical costs drove many older

▲ A volunteer from the Community Service Organization (CSO) registers a Mexican American mother and daughter as part of a massive voter registration drive in postwar Los Angeles. Women played a critical role in the CSO, which was founded in 1947 to address Mexican American civil rights issues, including education and labor, in East Los Angeles.

*(Los Angeles Daily News Collection, Department of Special Collections, University Research Library, UCLA)*

According to the 1960 census, over a half-million Mexican Americans had migrated to the barrios of the Los Angeles–Long Beach area since 1940. And New York City's Puerto Rican population exploded from 70,000 in 1940 to 613,000 in 1960.

All of these newcomers to the cities came seeking better lives and greater opportunities. Because of the strong economy and low unemployment rate, many did gain a higher standard of living. But discrimination limited their advances, and they endured crowded and decrepit housing and poor schools. In addition, the federal programs that helped middle-class Americans sometimes made the lives of the poor worse. For example, the National Housing Act of 1949, passed to make available "a decent home . . . for every American family," provided for "urban redevelopment." Redevelopment meant slum clearance. Many poor people lost what housing they had as entire neighborhoods were leveled and replaced with luxury high-rise buildings, parking lots, and even highways.

Rural poverty was a long-standing problem in America, but the growth of large agribusinesses pushed more tenant farmers and owners of small farms off the land. From 1945 to 1961 the nation's farm population declined from 24.4 million to 14.8 million. When the harvesting of cotton in the South was mechanized in the 1940s and 1950s, more than 4 million people were displaced. Southern tobacco growers dismissed their tenant farmers, bought tractors to plow the land, and hired migratory workers to harvest the crops. Many of these displaced farmers traded southern rural poverty for northern urban poverty. And in the West and Southwest, Mexican citizens continued to serve as cheap migrant labor under the *bracero* program. Almost 1 million Mexican workers came legally to the United States in 1959; many more were undocumented workers. Entire families labored, enduring conditions little better than in the Great Depression.

Native Americans were America's poorest people, with an average annual income barely half that of the poverty level. Conditions for native peoples were made worse by a federal policy implemented during the Eisenhower administration: termination. Termination reversed the Indian Reorganization Act of 1934, allowing Indians to terminate their tribal status and so remove reservation lands from federal protection that prohibited their sale. Sixty-one tribes were terminated between 1954 and 1960. Termination could take place only with a tribe's agreement, but pressure was sometimes intense—especially when reservation land was rich in natural resources. The Klamaths of Oregon, for example, lived on a reservation rich in ponderosa pine, which lumber interests coveted. Enticed by cash payments, almost four-fifths of the Klamaths ac-

Americans into poverty. Few of these people had much reason for hope.

As millions of Americans (most of them white) were settling in the suburbs, the poor were ever more concentrated in the inner cities. African American migrants from the South were joined by poor whites from the southern Appalachians, many of whom moved to Chicago, Cincinnati, Baltimore, and Detroit. Meanwhile, Latin Americans were arriving in growing numbers from Mexico, the Dominican Republic, Colombia, Ecuador, and Cuba.

## Poverty in an Age of Abundance

◄ After the war, American Indians lost sacred land to both big corporations and the federal government. In 1948 George Gillette *(left)*, chairman of the Fort Berthold, North Dakota, Indian Tribal Council, covers his face and weeps as Secretary of the Interior J. A. Krug signs a contract buying 155,000 acres of tribal land for a reservoir. *(Wide World Photos, Inc.)*

cepted termination and voted to sell their shares of the forest land. With termination, their way of life collapsed. Many Indians left reservation land for the city, joining the influx of other poor Americans seeking jobs and new lives. By the time termination was halted in the 1960s, observers compared the situation of Native Americans to the devastation their forebears had endured in the nineteenth century. Like most of the poor, these Americans were invisible to the growing middle class in the suburbs.

Overall, Americans who had lived through the devastation of the Great Depression and World War II enjoyed the relative prosperity and economic security of the postwar era. But those who had made it to the comfortable middle class often ignored the plight of those left behind. It would be their children—the generation of the baby boom, many reared in suburban comfort—who would see racism, poverty, and the self-satisfaction of postwar suburban culture as a failure of American ideals.

## SUMMARY

As the experiences of economic depression and world war receded, Americans worked to create good lives for themselves and their families. People married and had children in record numbers. Millions of veterans used the GI Bill to attend college, buy homes, and start businesses. Although American leaders feared that the nation would lapse back into economic depression after wartime government spending ended, consumer spending brought economic growth. The sustained economic growth of the postwar era lifted a majority of Americans into an expanding middle class.

The Cold War presidencies of Truman and Eisenhower focused on international relations and a global struggle against communism, rather than on domestic politics. Within the United States, Cold War fears provoked an extreme anticommunism that stifled political dissent and diminished Americans' civil liberties and freedoms.

The continuing African American struggle for civil rights drew national attention during the Montgomery bus boycott, reminding whites that not all Americans enjoyed equality. African Americans won important victories in

# *Legacy* FOR A PEOPLE AND A NATION

## The Pledge of Allegiance

The Pledge of Allegiance that Americans recite in school classrooms and sports stadiums throughout the nation today was shaped by America's Cold War struggle against the Soviet Union. Congress added the phrase "under God" to the existing pledge in 1954, as part of an attempt to emphasize the difference between the god-fearing United States and the "godless communists" of the Soviet Union.

The Pledge of Allegiance was not always an important part of American public life. The original version was written in 1892 by Francis Bellamy, editor of *The Youth's Companion,* to commemorate the four hundredth anniversary of Columbus's arrival in North America. On October 11, 1892, more than 11 million schoolchildren recited the words "I pledge allegiance to my flag and the Republic for which it stands; one nation indivisible, with liberty and justice for all." In 1942 Congress officially adopted a revised version of this pledge as an act of wartime patriotism. The Supreme Court ruled in 1943, however, that schoolchildren could not be forced to say the "Pledge to the Flag."

During the Cold War years, the pledge became more and more important as a way to demonstrate loyalty to the United States. Cold War fears lent force to a campaign by the Knights of Columbus, a Catholic men's service organization, to include "under God" in the pledge. Supporting the bill, President Eisenhower proclaimed that

*in this way we are reaffirming the transcendence of religious faith in America's heritage and future; in this way we shall constantly strengthen those spiritual weapons which forever will be our country's most powerful resource in peace and war. From this day forward, the millions of our schoolchildren will daily proclaim in every city and town, every village and every rural schoolhouse, the dedication of our nation and our people to the Almighty.*

Some Americans, citing the doctrine of separation of church and state, have protested the inclusion of "under God" in the nation's pledge. In June 2002, the Ninth District Court (covering California and eight other western states) touched off a major controversy by ruling that the 1954 version of the pledge was unconstitutional because it conveyed a "state endorsement" of a religious belief. Questions about the proper role of religion in American life are sure to remain controversial, a legacy for a people and a nation as America's people become even more diverse in the twenty-first century.

the Supreme Court, including the landmark decision in *Brown v. Board of Education,* and both Truman and Eisenhower used federal power to guarantee the rights of black Americans. With these victories, a national civil rights movement began to coalesce, and racial tensions within the nation increased.

Despite continued racial divisions, the United States became in many ways a more inclusive nation in the 1950s, as a majority of Americans participated in a national, consumer-oriented, middle-class culture. This culture largely ignored the poverty that remained in the nation's cities and rural areas, and contributed to rapidly increasing economic degradation. But for the growing number of middle-class Americans who, for the first time, lived in modest material comfort, the American dream seemed a reality.

# SUGGESTIONS FOR FURTHER READING

Taylor Branch, *Parting the Waters: America in the King Years, 1954–1963* (1988)

Lizabeth Cohen, *A Consumer's Republic: The Politics of Mass Consumption in Postwar America* (2003)

Stephanie Coontz, *The Way We Never Were: American Families and the Nostalgia Trap* (1992)

Mary Dudziak, *Cold War Civil Rights: Race and the Image of American Democracy* (2000)

James Gregory, *The Southern Diaspora: How the Great Migrations of Black and White Southerners Transformed the Nation* (2007)

Thomas Hine, *Populuxe* (1986)

Grace Palladino, *Teenagers* (1996)

James T. Patterson, *Grand Expectations: The United States, 1945–1974* (1996)

Ellen W. Schrecker, *Many Are the Crimes: McCarthyism in America* (1998)

Thomas J. Sugrue, *The Origins of the Urban Crisis: Race and Inequality in Postwar Detroit* (1996)

*For a more extensive list for further reading, go to* college.hmco.com/pic/norton8e.

# The Tumultuous Sixties *1960-1968*

It was late at night, and Ezell Blair had a big exam the next day. But there he was with his friends in the dormitory, talking—as they so often did—about injustice, and discrimination, and about living in a nation that proclaimed equality for all but denied full citizenship to some of its people because of the color of their skin. They were complaining about all the do-nothing adults, condemning pretty much the entire black community of Greensboro—and not for the first time—when Franklin McCain said, as if he meant it, "It's time to fish or cut bait." And Joe McNeil said, "Yes, we're a bunch of hypocrites. Come on, let's do it. Let's do it tomorrow." McCain's roommate, David Richmond, agreed. Blair hesitated. "I was thinking about my grades," he said later, just "trying to deal with that architecture and engineering course I was taking."

But Blair was outvoted. The next day, February 1, 1960, after their classes at North Carolina Agricultural and Technical College were over, the four freshmen walked into town. At the F. W. Woolworth's on South Elm Street, one of the most profitable stores in the national chain, each bought a few small things, mostly school supplies. Then, nervously, they sat down on the vinyl-covered stools at the lunch counter and tried to order coffee. These young men—seventeen and eighteen years old—were prepared to be arrested, even physically attacked. But nothing happened. The counter help ignored them as long as possible; they never got their coffee. When one worker finally reminded them, "We don't serve colored here," the four made their point: they had already been served just a few feet away when they made their purchases. Why not at the lunch counter? An elderly white woman came up to the boys and told them

◀ When four freshmen from North Carolina Agricultural and Technical College sat down and tried to order coffee at the whites-only Woolworth's lunch counter in Greensboro, North Carolina, they did not know if they would be met with arrest or even violence. This photograph is from the second day of the sit-in, when the young men were joined by classmates. Two of the original four, Joseph McNeil and Franklin McCain, are on the left. *(© Corbis-Bettmann)*

how proud she was of them. "We got so much courage and so much pride" from that "little old lady," McCain said later. But still nothing happened. The store closed; the manager turned out the lights. After sitting in near darkness for about forty-five minutes, the four men who had begun the sit-in movement got up and walked from the store.

The next day they returned, but they were not alone. Twenty fellow students joined the sit-in. By February 3, sixty-three of the sixty-five seats were taken. On February 4, students from other colleges arrived, and the sit-in spread to the S. H. Kress store across the street. By February 7, there were sit-ins in Winston-Salem; by February 8, in Charlotte; on February 9, sit-ins began in Raleigh. By the third week in February, students were picketing Woolworth's stores in the North, and at lunch counters throughout the South, well-dressed young men and women sat, politely asking to be served. On July 26, 1960, they won. F. W. Woolworth's ended segregation, not only in Greensboro but in all its stores.

When these four college freshmen sat down at the Woolworth's lunch counter in Greensboro, they signaled the beginning of a decade of public activism rarely matched in American history. During the 1960s, millions of Americans—many of them young people—took to the streets. Some marched for civil rights or against the war in Vietnam; others lashed out in anger over the circumstances of their lives. Passion over the events of the day revitalized democracy—and threatened to tear the nation apart.

John F. Kennedy, the nation's youngest president, told Americans as he took office in 1961, "The torch has been passed to a new generation." Despite his inspirational language, Kennedy had only modest success implementing his domestic agenda. As he began his third year as president, pushed by the bravery of civil rights activists and the intransigence of their white opponents, Kennedy began to offer more active support for civil rights and to propose more ambitious domestic policies. But Kennedy was assassinated in November 1963. His death seemed, to many, the end of an era of hope.

Lyndon Johnson, Kennedy's successor, called on the memory of the martyred president to launch an ambitious program of civil rights and other liberal legislation. Johnson meant to use the power of the federal government to eliminate poverty and to guarantee equal rights to all America's people. He called his vision the Great Society.

Despite liberal triumphs in Washington, D.C., and real gains by the African American civil rights movement, social tensions escalated during the mid-1960s. A revitalized conservative movement emerged, and Franklin Roosevelt's old New Deal coalition fractured as white southerners abandoned the Democratic Party. Many African Americans, especially in the North, were angry that poverty and racial discrimination persisted despite the passage of landmark civil rights laws, and their discontent exploded during the "long, hot summers" of the mid-1960s. White youth culture, which seemed intent on rejecting everything an older generation had worked for, created a division that Americans came to call "the generation gap."

Developments overseas also contributed to a growing national instability. After the Cuban missile crisis of 1962 brought the Soviet Union and the United States close to nuclear disaster, President John F. Kennedy and Soviet leader Nikita Khrushchev moved to reduce bilateral tensions in 1963, with the result that Cold War pressures in Europe lessened appreciably. In the rest of the world, however, the superpowers continued their frantic competition. Throughout the 1960s, the United States used a variety of approaches—including foreign aid, CIA covert actions, military assaults, cultural penetration, economic sanctions, and diplomacy—in its attempts to win the Cold War, draw unaligned nations into its orbit, and defuse revolutionary nationalism. In Vietnam, Kennedy chose to expand U.S. involvement significantly. Johnson "Americanized" the war, increasing U.S. troops to more than half a million in 1968.

By 1968 the war in Vietnam had divided the American people and undermined Johnson's Great Society. With the assassinations of Martin Luther King Jr. and Robert Kennedy—two of America's brightest leaders—that spring, with cities in flames, and with tanks in the streets of Chicago in August, the fate of the nation seemed to hang in the balance.

- What were the successes and failures of American liberalism in the 1960s?
- Why did the United States expand its participation in the war in Vietnam and continue in the war so long?
- By 1968, many believed the fate of the nation hung in the balance. What did they think was at stake? What divided Americans, and how did they express their differences?

## KENNEDY AND THE COLD WAR

President John F. Kennedy was, as writer Norman Mailer observed, "our leading man." Young, handsome, and vigorous, the new chief executive was the first president born in the twentieth century. Kennedy had a genuinely inquiring mind, and as a patron of the arts he brought wit and sophistication to the White House. He was born to wealth and politics: his Irish American grandfather had been mayor of Boston, and his millionaire father, Joseph P. Kennedy, had served as ambassador to Great Britain. In 1946 the young Kennedy, having returned from the Second World War a naval hero (the boat he commanded had been rammed and sunk by a Japanese destroyer in 1943, and Kennedy had saved his crew), continued the family tradition by campaigning to represent Boston in the U.S. House of Representatives. He won easily, served three terms in the House, and in 1952 was elected to the Senate.

As a Democrat, Kennedy inherited the New Deal commitment to America's social welfare system. He generally cast liberal votes in line with the pro-labor sentiments of his low-income, blue-collar constituents. But he avoided controversial issues, such as civil rights and the censure of Joseph McCarthy. Kennedy won a Pulitzer Prize for his *Profiles in Courage* (1956), a study of politicians who had acted on principle, but he shaded the truth when he claimed sole authorship of the book, which had been written largely by aide Theodore Sorensen (though based on more than one hundred pages of notes dictated by Kennedy). In foreign policy, Senator Kennedy endorsed the Cold War policy of containment, and his interest in world affairs deepened as the 1950s progressed. His record as a legislator was not impressive, but he enjoyed an enthusiastic following, especially after his landslide reelection to the Senate in 1958.

Kennedy and his handlers worked hard to cultivate an image of him as a happy and healthy family man. To some

**John Fitzgerald Kennedy**

▲ Many Americans were enchanted with the youthful and photo-genic Kennedys. Here the president and his family pose outside the Palm Beach, Florida, home of the president's father after a private Easter Service, April 14, 1963. *(AP Images)*

*not as perf as seen by public*

War II. After the war, Kennedy was diagnosed with Addison's disease, an adrenalin deficiency that required daily injections of cortisone in order to be contained. At the time, the disease was thought to be terminal; though Kennedy survived, he was often in acute pain. As president he would require plenty of bed rest and frequent therapeutic swims in the White House pool.

Kennedy's rhetoric and style captured the imagination of many Americans. Yet his election victory over Republican Richard Nixon in 1960 was extraordinarily narrow—118,000 votes out of nearly 69 million cast. Kennedy achieved only mixed success in the South, but he ran well in the Northeast and Midwest. His Roman Catholic faith hurt him in some states, where voters feared he would take direction from the pope, but helped in states with large Catholic populations. As the sitting vice president, Nixon was saddled with the handicaps of incumbency; he had to answer for sagging economic figures and the Soviet downing of a U-2 spy plane. Nixon also looked disagreeable on TV; in televised debates against the telegenic Kennedy, he looked alternately nervous and surly, and the camera made him appear unshaven. Perhaps worse, Eisenhower gave Nixon only a tepid endorsement. Asked to list Nixon's significant decisions as vice president, Eisenhower replied, "If you give me a week, I might think of one."

**Election of 1960**

In a departure from the Eisenhower administration's staid, conservative image, the new president surrounded himself with mostly young advisers of intellectual verve, who proclaimed that they had fresh ideas for invigorating the nation; writer David Halberstam called them "the best and the brightest." Secretary of Defense Robert McNamara (age forty-four) had been an assistant professor at Harvard at twenty-four and later the whiz-kid president of the Ford Motor Company. Kennedy's special assistant for national security affairs, McGeorge Bundy (age forty-one) had become a Harvard dean at thirty-four with only a bachelor's degree. Secretary of State Dean Rusk, the old man in the group at fifty-two, had been a Rhodes scholar in his youth. Kennedy himself was only forty-three, and his brother Robert, the attorney general, was thirty-five.

It was no accident that most of these "best and brightest" operated in the realm of foreign policy. From the start, Kennedy gave top priority to waging the Cold War. In the campaign he had criticized Eisenhower's foreign policy as unimaginative, accusing him of missing chances to reduce the threat of nuclear war with the Soviet Union and of weakening America's standing in the Third World. Kennedy and his advisers exuded confidence that they would change things. As national security adviser Mc-

extent it was a ruse. He was a chronic womanizer, and his liaisons continued even after he married Jacqueline Bouvier in 1953. Nor was he the picture of physical vitality that his war-hero status and youthful handsomeness seemed to project. As a child he had almost died of scarlet fever, and he spent large portions of his early years in bed, suffering from one ailment after another. He developed severe back problems, made worse by his fighting experience in World

George Bundy put it, "The United States is the engine of mankind, and the rest of the world is the caboose." Kennedy's inaugural address suggested no halfway measures: "Let every nation know that we shall pay any price, bear any burden, meet any hardship, support any friend, oppose any foe to assure the survival and the success of liberty."

In reality, Kennedy in office would not be prepared to pay any price or bear any burden in the struggle against communism. He came to understand, sooner than many of his advisers, that there were limits to American power abroad; overall he showed himself to be cautious and pragmatic in foreign policy. More than his predecessor, he proved willing to initiate dialogue with the Soviets, sometimes using his brother Robert as a secret back channel to Moscow. Yet Kennedy also sought victory in the Cold War. After Soviet leader Nikita Khrushchev endorsed "wars of national liberation," such as the one in Vietnam, Kennedy called for "peaceful revolution" based on the concept of nation building. The administration set out to help developing nations through the early stages of nationhood with aid programs aimed at improving agriculture, transportation, and communications. Kennedy thus oversaw the creation of the multibillion-dollar Alliance for Progress in 1961 to spur economic development in Latin America. In the same year he also created the Peace Corps, dispatching thousands of American teachers, agricultural specialists, and health workers, many of them right out of college, to assist authorities in developing nations.

## Nation Building in the Third World

Cynics then and later dismissed the Alliance and the Peace Corps as Cold War tools by which Kennedy sought to counter anti-Americanism and defeat communism in the developing world. The programs did have those aims, but both were also born of genuine humanitarianism. The Peace Corps in particular embodied both the idealistic, can-do spirit of the 1960s and Americans' long pursuit of moral leadership in the world. "More than any other entity," historian Elizabeth Cobbs Hoffman has written, "the Peace Corps broached an age-old dilemma of U.S. foreign policy: how to reconcile the imperatives and temptations of power politics with the ideals of freedom and self-determination for all nations."

It was one thing to broach the dilemma, and quite another to resolve it. Kennedy and his aides considered themselves to be supportive of social revolution in the Third World, but they could not imagine the legitimacy of communist involvement in any such uprising, or that developing countries might wish to be neutral in the East-West struggle. In addition to largely benevolent programs like the Peace Corps, therefore, the administration also relied on the more insidious concept of counterinsurgency to defeat revolutionaries who challenged pro-American Third World governments. American military and technical advisers trained native troops and police forces to quell unrest.

Nation building and counterinsurgency encountered numerous problems. The Alliance for Progress was only partly successful; infant mortality rates improved, but Latin American economies registered unimpressive growth rates, and class divisions continued to widen, exacerbating political unrest. Americans assumed that the U.S. model of capitalism and representative government could be transferred successfully to foreign cultures. But although many foreign peoples welcomed U.S. economic assistance and craved American material culture, they resented meddling by outsiders. And because aid was usually funneled through a self-interested elite, it often failed to reach the very poor. To people who preferred the relatively quick solutions of a managed economy, moreover, the American emphasis on private enterprise seemed inappropriate.

Nor did the new president have success in relations with the Soviet Union. A summit meeting with Soviet leader Nikita Khrushchev in Vienna in June 1961 went poorly, with the two leaders disagreeing over the preconditions for peace and stability in the world. Consequently, the administration's first year witnessed little movement on controlling the nuclear arms race or even on getting a superpower ban on testing nuclear weapons in the atmosphere or underground. The latter objective mattered a great deal to Kennedy, who saw a test ban as a prerequisite to preventing additional nations from getting the terrifying weapon. Instead, both superpowers continued testing and accelerated their arms production. In 1961 the U.S. military budget shot up 15 percent; by mid-1964, U.S. nuclear weapons had increased by 150 percent. Government advice to citizens to build fallout shelters in their backyards intensified public fear of devastating war.

## Soviet-American Tensions

If war occurred, many believed it would be over the persistent problem of Berlin. In mid-1961 Khrushchev ratcheted up the tension by demanding an end to western occupation of West Berlin and a reunification of East and West Germany. Kennedy replied that the United States would stand by its commitment to West Berlin and West Germany. In August the Soviets, at the urging of the East German regime, erected a concrete and barbed-wire barricade across the divided city to halt the exodus of East Germans into the more prosperous and politically free West Berlin. The Berlin Wall inspired protests throughout the noncommunist world, but Kennedy privately sighed that "a wall is a hell of a lot better than a war." The ugly barrier shut off the flow of refugees, and the crisis passed.

Yet Kennedy knew that Khrushchev would continue to press for advantage in various parts of the globe. The president was particularly rankled by the growing Soviet assistance to the Cuban government of Fidel Castro. Kennedy once acknowledged that most American allies thought the United States had a "fixation" with Cuba; whether true of the country as a whole, he himself certainly did. The Eisenhower administration had contested the Cuban revolution and bequeathed to the Kennedy administration a partially developed CIA plan to overthrow Fidel Castro: CIA-trained Cuban exiles would land and secure a beachhead; the Cuban people would rise up against Castro and welcome a new government brought in from the United States.

## Bay of Pigs Invasion

Kennedy approved the plan, and the attack took place on April 17, 1961, as twelve hundred exiles landed at the swampy Bay of Pigs in Cuba. But no discontented Cubans were there to greet them, only troops loyal to the Castro government. The invaders were quickly surrounded and captured. Kennedy had tried to keep the U.S. participation in the operation hidden—for this reason he refused to provide air cover for the attackers—but the CIA's role swiftly became public. Anti-American sentiment shot up throughout Latin America. Castro, concluding that the United States would not take defeat well and might launch another invasion, looked even more toward the Soviet Union for a military and economic lifeline.

Embarrassed by the Bay of Pigs fiasco, Kennedy vowed to bring Castro down. The CIA soon hatched a project called Operation Mongoose to disrupt the island's trade, support raids on Cuba from Miami, and plot to kill Castro. The agency's assassination schemes included providing Castro with cigars laced with explosives and deadly poison, and an attempt to harpoon him while he was snorkeling at a Caribbean resort. The United States also tightened its economic blockade and undertook military maneuvers in the Caribbean. The Joint Chiefs of Staff sketched plans to spark a rebellion in Cuba that would be followed by an invasion of U.S. troops. "If I had been in Moscow or Havana at that time," defense secretary Robert McNamara later remarked, "I would have believed the Americans were preparing for an invasion."

▲ The October 29 meeting of the "ExComm," or Executive Committee (the only meeting photographed). To President Kennedy's immediate right is Secretary of State Dean Rusk; to his left, in front of the Presidential Seal on the wall, is Secretary of Defense Robert McNamara. Presidential adviser Theodore Sorensen *(near side, third from right)* later wrote, "I saw first-hand how brutally physical and mental fatigue can numb the good sense as well as the senses of normally articulate men." *(John F. Kennedy Library)*

McNamara knew whereof he spoke, for both Castro and Khrushchev believed an invasion was coming. This

## Cuban Missile Crisis

was one reason for the Soviet leader's risky decision in 1962 to secretly deploy nuclear missiles in Cuba: he hoped the presence of such weapons on the island would deter any attack. But Khrushchev also had other motives. Installing atomic weaponry in Cuba would instantly improve the Soviet position in the nuclear balance of power, he believed, and might also force Kennedy to resolve the German problem once and for all. Khrushchev still wanted to oust the West from Berlin, and he also worried that Washington might provide West Germany with nuclear weapons. What better way to prevent such a move than to put Soviet missiles just 90 miles off the coast of Florida? With Castro's support, Khrushchev moved to install the weapons. The world soon faced brinkmanship at its most frightening.

In mid-October 1962, a U-2 plane flying over Cuba photographed the missile sites. The president immediately organized a special Executive Committee (ExComm) of advisers to find a way to force the missiles and their nuclear warheads out of Cuba. Options that the ExComm considered ranged from full-scale invasion to limited bombing to quiet diplomacy. McNamara proposed the formula that the president ultimately accepted: a naval quarantine of Cuba.

Kennedy addressed the nation on television on October 22 and demanded that the Soviets retreat. U.S. warships began crisscrossing the Caribbean, while B-52s with nuclear bombs took to the skies. Khrushchev replied that the missiles would be withdrawn if the United States pledged never to attack Cuba. And he added that American Jupiter missiles aimed at the Soviet Union must be removed from Turkey. Edgy advisers predicted war, and for several days the world teetered on the brink of disaster. Then, on October 28, came a compromise. The United States promised not to invade Cuba, secretly pledging to withdraw the Jupiters from Turkey in exchange for the withdrawal of Soviet offensive forces from Cuba. Fearing accidents or some provocative action by Castro that might start a "real fire," Khrushchev decided to settle without consulting the Cubans. The missiles were removed from the island.

Many observers then and later called it Kennedy's finest hour. Tapes of the ExComm meetings recorded during the crisis reveal a deeply engaged, calmly authoritative commander-in-chief, committed to removing the missiles peacefully if possible. Critics claim that Kennedy helped cause the crisis in the first place with his anti-Cuban projects; some contend that quiet diplomacy could have

achieved the same result, without the extraordinary tension. Other skeptics assert that Kennedy rejected a diplomatic solution because he feared the Republicans would ride the missiles to victory in the upcoming midterm elections. Still, it cannot be denied that the president handled the crisis skillfully, exercising both restraint and flexibility. At this most tense moment of the Cold War, Kennedy had proven equal to the task.

The Cuban missile crisis was a watershed in the Soviet-American relationship. Both Kennedy and Khrushchev acted with greater prudence in its aftermath, taking determined steps toward improved bilateral relations. Much of the hostility drained out of the relationship. In June 1963 Kennedy spoke in conciliatory terms during a commencement address at American University, urging cautious Soviet-American steps toward disarmament. In August the adversaries signed a treaty banning nuclear tests in the atmosphere, the oceans, and outer space. They also installed a coded wire-telegraph "hot line" staffed around the clock by translators and technicians, to allow near-instant communication between the capitals. Both sides refrained from further confrontation in Berlin.

Individually these steps were small, but together they reversed the trend of the previous years and began to build much-needed mutual trust. One could even argue that, by the autumn of 1963, the Cold War in Europe was drawing to a close. Both sides, it seemed, were prepared to accept the status quo of a divided continent and a fortified border. At the same time, though, the arms race continued and in some respects accelerated, and the superpower competition in the Third World showed little sign of cooling down.

## MARCHING FOR FREEDOM

From the beginning of his presidency, John Kennedy believed that the Cold War was the most important issue facing the American people. But in the early 1960s, young civil rights activists seized the national stage and demanded that the force of the federal government be mobilized behind them. They won victories in their struggle for racial justice, but their gains were paid for in blood.

The Woolworth's lunch counter sit-in begun by the four freshmen from North Carolina A&T marked a turning point in the African American struggle for civil rights. In 1960, six years after the *Brown* decision had declared "separate but equal" unconstitutional, only 10 percent of southern public schools had begun desegregation. Fewer than one in four adult black Americans in the South had access to the voting booth, and water fountains in public places were still labeled "White Only" and "Colored Only." But one year after the young men had sat down at the all-white lunch counter in Greensboro, more than seventy thousand Americans—most of them college students—had participated in the sit-in movement. City by city, they challenged Jim Crow segregation at lunch counters in the South and protested at the northern branches of national chains that practiced segregation in their southern stores.

The young people who created the Student Nonviolent Coordinating Committee (SNCC) in the spring of 1960 to help coordinate the sit-in movement were, like Martin Luther King Jr., committed to nonviolence. In the years to come, SNCC stalwarts—including lifelong activist Diane Nash; future NAACP chair Julian Bond; future Washington, D.C., mayor Marion Barry; and future member of the U.S. House of Representatives John Lewis—would risk their lives in the struggle for social justice.

On May 4, 1961, thirteen members of the Congress of Racial Equality (CORE), a nonviolent civil rights organization formed during World War II, purchased bus tickets in Washington, D.C., for a 1,500-mile trip through the South to New Orleans. This racially integrated group, calling themselves Freedom Riders, meant to demonstrate that, despite Supreme Court rulings ordering the desegregation of interstate buses and bus stations, Jim Crow still ruled in the South. These men and women knew they were risking their lives, and some suffered injuries from which they never recovered. One bus was firebombed outside Anniston, Alabama. Riders were badly beaten in Birmingham. In Montgomery, after reinforcements replaced the injured, a mob of more than a thousand whites attacked riders on another bus with baseball bats and steel bars. Police were nowhere to be seen; Montgomery's police commissioner declared, "We have no intention of standing guard for a bunch of troublemakers coming into our city."

News of the violent attacks made headlines around the world. In the Soviet Union, commentators pointed out the "savage nature of American freedom and democracy." One southern business leader, in Tokyo to promote Birmingham as a site for international business development, saw Japanese interest evaporate when photographs of the Birmingham attacks appeared in Tokyo newspapers.

In America, the violence—reported by the national news media—forced many to confront the reality of racial discrimination and hatred in their nation. Middle- and upper-class white southerners had participated in the "massive resistance" to integration following the *Brown* decision, and many white southerners, even racial moderates, remained highly suspicious of interference by the "Yankee" federal government almost a century after the Civil War. The Freedom Rides made some think differently. The *Atlanta Journal* editorialized: "[I]t is time for the decent people . . . to muzzle the jackals." The national and international outcry pushed a reluctant President Kennedy to act. In a direct challenge to southern doctrines of states' rights, Kennedy sent federal marshals to Alabama to safeguard the Freedom Riders and their supporters. At the same time, bowing to white southern pressure, he allowed the Freedom Riders to be arrested in Mississippi.

While some activists pursued these "direct action" tactics, others worked to build black political power in the South. Beginning in 1961, thousands of SNCC volunteers, many of them high school and college students, risked their lives walking the dusty back roads of Mississippi and Georgia, encouraging African Americans to register to vote. Some SNCC volunteers were white, and some were from the North, but many were black southerners, and many were from low-income families. These volunteers understood from experience how racism, powerlessness, and poverty intersected in the lives of African Americans.

President Kennedy was generally sympathetic—though not terribly committed—to the civil rights movement, and he realized that racial oppression hurt the United States in the Cold War struggle for international opinion. However, like Franklin D. Roosevelt, he also understood that, if he alienated conservative southern Democrats in Congress, his legislative programs would founder. Thus he appointed five die-hard segregationists to the federal bench in the Deep South and delayed issuing an executive order forbidding segregation in federally subsidized housing (a pledge made in the 1960 campaign) until late 1962. Furthermore, he allowed FBI director J. Edgar Hoover to harass Martin Luther King and other civil rights leaders, using wiretaps and surveillance to gather personal information and circulating rumors of communist connections and of personal improprieties in efforts to discredit their leadership.

But grassroots civil rights activism—and the violence of white mobs—relentlessly forced Kennedy's hand. In September 1962, the president ordered 500 U.S. marshals to protect James Meredith, the first African American student to attend the University of Mississippi. In response, thousands of whites attacked the marshals with guns, gasoline bombs, bricks, and pipes. The mob killed two men and seriously wounded 160 federal marshals. The marshals

## Freedom Rides and Voter Registration

## Kennedy and Civil Rights

did not back down, nor did James Meredith. He broke the color line at "Ole Miss."

In 1961 the Freedom Riders had captured the attention of the nation and the larger Cold War world, and forced the hand of the president.

## Birmingham and the Children's Crusade

Martin Luther King Jr., having risen through the Montgomery bus boycott to leadership in the movement, understood the implications of these events. He and his allies, still committed to principles of nonviolence, concluded that the only way to move to the next stage of the struggle for civil rights was to provoke a crisis that would attract national and international attention, and create pressure for further change. King and his Southern Christian Leadership Conference (SCLC) began to plan a 1963 campaign in the most violently racist city in America: Birmingham, Alabama. Fully aware that their nonviolent protests would draw violent response, they called their plan Project C—for "confrontation." King wanted all Americans to see the racist hate and violence that marred their nation.

Through most of April 1963, nonviolent protests in Birmingham led to hundreds of arrests. Then, on May 2, in a highly controversial action, King and the parents of Birmingham raised the stakes. They put children, some as young as six, on the front lines of protest. As about a thousand black children marched for civil rights, police commissioner Eugene "Bull" Connor ordered his police to train "monitor" water guns—powerful enough to strip bark from a tree at 100 feet—on them. The water guns mowed the children down, and then police loosed attack dogs. It was all captured on television, as the nation watched in horror. President Kennedy, once again, was pushed into action. He demanded that Birmingham's white business and political elite negotiate a settlement. Under pressure, they agreed. The Birmingham movement had won a concrete victory. Even more, activists had pushed civil rights to the fore of President Kennedy's political agenda.

The Kennedy administration also confronted the defiant governor of Alabama, George C. Wallace. On June 11,

## "Segregation Forever!"

Wallace fulfilled a promise to "bar the schoolhouse door" himself to prevent the desegregation of the University of Alabama. Hearing echoes of Wallace's January 1963 inaugural pledge "Segregation now, segregation tomorrow, segregation forever!" and facing a nation rocked by hundreds of civil rights protests, many of them met with white mob violence, Kennedy committed the power of the federal government to guarantee racial justice—even over the opposition of individual states. The next evening, June 12,

in a televised address, Kennedy told the American people, "Now the time has come for this nation to fulfill its promise." A few hours later, thirty-seven-year-old civil rights leader Medgar Evers was murdered—in front of his children—in his driveway in Jackson, Mississippi. The next week, the president asked Congress to pass a comprehensive civil rights bill that would end legal discrimination on the basis of race in the entire United States.

On August 28, 1963, a quarter-million Americans gathered in the steamy heat on the Washington Mall.

## March on Washington

They came from all over America to show Congress their support for Kennedy's civil rights bill; many also wanted federal action to guarantee work opportunities. Behind the scenes, organizers from the major civil rights groups—SCLC, CORE, SNCC, the NAACP, the Urban League, and A. Philip Randolph's Brotherhood of Sleeping Car Porters—grappled with growing tensions within the movement. SNCC activists saw Kennedy's proposed legislation as too little, too late, and wanted radical action. King and other older leaders counseled the virtues of moderation. The movement was beginning to splinter.

Those divisions were not completely hidden. SNCC's John Lewis told the assembled crowd that SNCC members had come to the march "with a great sense of misgiving" and asked, "Where is the political party that will make it unnecessary to march on Washington?" What most Americans saw, however, was a celebration of unity. Black and white celebrities joined hands; folk singers sang songs of freedom. Television networks cut away from afternoon soap operas as Martin Luther King Jr., in southern-preacher cadences, prophesied a day when "all God's children, black men and white men, Jews and Gentiles, Protestants and Catholics, will be able to join hands and sing in the words of the old Negro spiritual, 'Free at last! Free at last! Thank God Almighty, we are free at last!'" The 1963 March on Washington for Jobs and Freedom was a moment of triumph, powerfully demonstrating to the nation the determination of its African American citizens to secure equality and justice. But the struggle was far from over. Just days later, white supremacists bombed the Sixteenth Street Baptist Church in Birmingham, killing four black girls.

In the face of violence, the struggle for racial justice continued. During the summer of 1964, more than one

## Freedom Summer

thousand white students joined the voter mobilization project in Mississippi. These workers formed Freedom Schools, teaching literacy

A historic moment for the civil ▶ rights movement was the March on Washington of August 28, 1963. The Reverend Martin Luther King Jr. *(center)* joined a quarter-million black people and white people in their march for racial equality. Addressing civil rights supporters, and the nation, from the steps of the Lincoln Memorial, King delivered his "I Have a Dream" speech.

*(R. W. Kelley,* Life *magazine © Time, Inc.)*

and constitutional rights, and helped organize the Mississippi Freedom Democratic Party as an alternative to the regular, white-only Democratic Party. Key SNCC organizers also believed that large numbers of white volunteers would focus national attention on Mississippi repression and violence. Not all went smoothly: local black activists were sometimes frustrated when well-educated white volunteers stepped into decision-making roles, and tensions over interracial sexual relationships complicated an already difficult situation. Far worse, project workers were arrested over a thousand times and were shot at, bombed, and beaten. On June 21, local black activist James Cheney and two white volunteers, Michael Schwerner and Andrew Goodman, were murdered by a Klan mob. Four days later, before their bodies had been found, Walter Cronkite told the nightly news audience that all of America was watching Mississippi. CBS played footage of black and white workers holding hands, singing "We Shall Overcome." That summer, black and white activists risked their lives together, challenging the racial caste system of the Deep South.

## LIBERALISM AND THE GREAT SOCIETY

By 1963, with civil rights at the top of his domestic agenda, Kennedy seemed to be taking a new path. Campaigning in 1960, he had promised to lead Americans into a "New Frontier," a society in which the federal government would work to eradicate poverty, restore the nation's cities, guarantee healthcare to the elderly, and provide decent schools for all America's children. But few of Kennedy's domestic initiatives were passed into law, in part because Kennedy

did not use his political capital to support them. Lacking a popular mandate in the 1960 election, fearful of alienating southern Democrats in Congress, and without a strong vision of domestic reform, Kennedy let his administration's social policy agenda languish.

Instead, Kennedy focused on less controversial attempts to fine-tune the American economy, believing that continued economic growth and prosperity would solve America's social problems. Kennedy's vision was perhaps best realized in America's space program. As the Soviets drew ahead in the Cold War space race, Kennedy vowed in 1961 to put a man on the moon before decade's end. With billions in new funding, the National Aeronautics and Space Administration (NASA) began the Apollo program. And in February 1962, astronaut John Glenn orbited the earth in the space capsule *Friendship 7*.

The nation would not learn what sort of president John Kennedy might have become. On November 22, 1963, Kennedy visited Texas, the home state of his vice president, Lyndon Johnson. In Dallas, riding with his wife, Jackie, in an open-top limousine, Kennedy was cheered by thousands of people lining the motorcade's route. Suddenly shots rang out. The president crumpled, shot in the head. Tears ran down the cheeks of CBS anchorman Walter Cronkite as he told the nation their president was dead. The word spread quickly, in whispered messages to classroom teachers, by somber announcements in facto-

**Kennedy Assassination**

ries and offices, through the stunned faces of people on the street.

That same day police captured a suspect: Lee Harvey Oswald, a former U.S. marine (dishonorably discharged) who had once attempted to gain Soviet citizenship. Just two days later, in full view of millions of TV viewers, Oswald himself was shot dead by shady nightclub owner Jack Ruby. Americans, already in shock, were baffled. What was Ruby's motive? Was he silencing Oswald to prevent him from implicating others? The seven-member Warren Commission, headed by U.S. Supreme Court Chief Justice Earl Warren, concluded that Oswald had acted alone. But debates still rage over whether Oswald was a lone assassin or part of a larger conspiracy.

For four days the tragedy played uninterrupted on American television. Millions of Americans watched their president's funeral: the brave young widow behind a black veil; a riderless horse; three-year-old "John-John" saluting his father's casket. In one awful moment in Dallas, the reality of the Kennedy presidency had been transformed into myth, the man into martyr. People would remember Kennedy less for any specific accomplishment than for his youthful enthusiasm, his inspirational rhetoric, and the romance he brought to American political life. In a peculiar way, he accomplished more in death than in life. In the postassassination atmosphere of grief and remorse, Lyndon Johnson, sworn in as president aboard *Air Force One*, invoked Kennedy's memory to push through the most ambitious program of legislation since the New Deal.

The new president was a big and passionate man, different from his predecessor in almost every respect. While

## Johnson and the Great Society

Kennedy had been raised to wealth and privilege and was educated at Harvard, Johnson had grown up in modest circumstances in the Texas hill country and was graduated from Southwest Texas State Teachers' College. He was as earthy as Kennedy was elegant, prone to colorful curses and willing to use his physical size to his advantage. Advisers and aides reported that he expected them to follow him into the bathroom and conduct business while he showered or used the toilet. But Johnson had been in

▲ Poverty in America was not only an urban problem, and President Johnson visited poverty-stricken areas throughout the nation during the summer of 1964. Here he talks with the Marlow family of Rocky Mount, North Carolina, on the steps of their farmhouse. *(© Bettmann/Corbis)*

national politics most of his adult life. He filled an empty congressional seat from Texas in 1937, and as Senate majority leader from 1954 to 1960, he had learned how to manipulate people and wield power to achieve his ends. Now, as president, he used these political skills in an attempt to unite and reassure the nation. "Let us here highly resolve," he told a joint session of Congress five days after the assassination, "that John Fitzgerald Kennedy did not live—or die—in vain."

Johnson, a liberal in the style of Franklin D. Roosevelt, believed that the federal government must work actively to improve the lives of Americans. In a 1964 commencement address at the University of Michigan, he described his vision of a nation built on "abundance and liberty for all . . . demand[ing] an end to poverty and racial injustice . . . where every child can find knowledge to enrich his mind and to enlarge his talents . . . where every man can renew contact with nature . . . where men are more concerned with the quality of their goals than the quantity of their goods." Johnson called this vision "The Great Society."

Johnson made civil rights his top legislative priority, and in July he signed into law the Civil Rights Act of 1964. This legislation ended *legal*

### Civil Rights Act

discrimination on the basis of race, color, religion, national origin, in federal programs, voting, employment, and public accommodation; sex discrimination in employment was also banned. The original bill did not include sex discrimination; that provision was introduced by a southern congressman who hoped it would engender so much opposition that the bill as a whole would fail. However, when a bipartisan group of women members of the House of Representatives took up the cause, the bill was passed—with sex as a protected category. Significantly, the Civil Rights Act of 1964 created mechanisms for enforcement, giving the government authority to withhold federal funds from public agencies or federal contractors that discriminated and establishing the Equal Employment Opportunity Commission (EEOC) to investigate and judge claims of job discrimination. However, the EEOC paid little attention to sex discrimination, and in response, in 1966 supporters of women's equality formed the National Organization for Women (NOW). It would be one element in a broad movement for women's rights and equality that would take off in the next decade (see page 895).

Many Americans did not believe that it was the federal government's job to end racial discrimination or to fight poverty. Many white southerners, especially, resented federal intervention in what they considered local customs.

And throughout the nation, millions of conservative Americans believed that since the New Deal the federal government had been overstepping its constitutional boundaries. They sought a return to local control and states' rights in the face of growing federal power. In the 1964 election, this conservative vision was championed by the Republican candidate, Arizona senator Barry Goldwater.

Goldwater had not only voted against the 1964 Civil Rights Act; he also opposed the national Social Security

### Election of 1964

system. Like many conservatives, he believed that individual *liberty*, not equality, was the most important American value. Goldwater also believed that the United States needed a more powerful national military to fight communism; in campaign speeches he suggested that the United States should use tactical nuclear weapons against its enemies. "Extremism in the defense of liberty is no vice," he told delegates at the 1964 Republican National Convention.

Goldwater's campaign slogan, "In your heart you know he's right," was turned against him by Lyndon Johnson supporters: "In your heart you know he's right . . . far right," one punned. Another version warned of Goldwater's willingness to use nuclear weapons: "In your heart you know he might." Johnson campaigned on his record, with an unemployment rate under 4 percent and economic growth at better than 6 percent. But he knew that his support of civil rights had broken apart the New Deal coalition. Shortly after signing the Civil Rights Act of 1964, he told an aide, "I think we just delivered the south to the Republican Party for my lifetime and yours."

The tension between Johnson's support of civil rights and his need for southern Democratic support came to a head at the 1964 Democratic National Convention. Two delegations h[ad] [arrived from] [Mississippi seeki]ng to be seated. [The first] [w]as exclusively [white, the Democratic] Party (MFDP[)] [reprsent]nt a state in whi[ch] [bla]ce disenfranchis[ed] [a]ic tives from s[outh] walkout if the[y] gate Fannie L[ou Hamer] convention's [credentials] Freedom Part[y] Johnson tried had no interes[t] way for no tw[o] walked out.

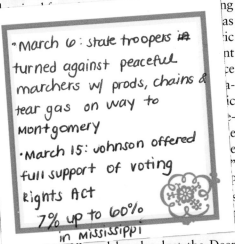

- March 6: state troopers turned against peaceful marchers w/ prods, chains & tear gas on way to Montgomery
- March 15: Johnson offered full support of voting Rights Act 7% up to 60% in Mississippi

Johnson lost the MFDP, and he also lost the Deep South—the first Democrat since the Civil War to do so. Yet

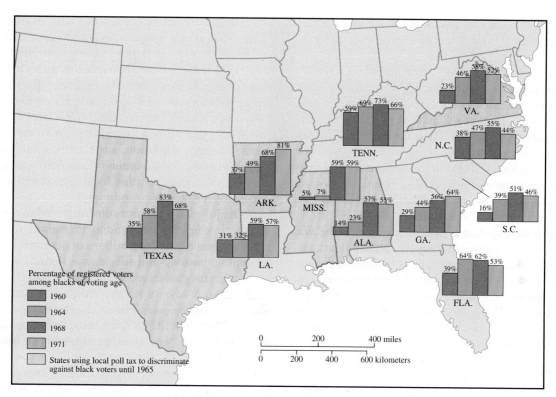

**Map 30.1    African American Voting Rights, 1960–1971**

After passage of the 1965 Voting Rights Act, African American registration skyrocketed in Mississippi and Alabama, and rose substantially in other southern states.

*(Source: Harold W. Stanley,* Voter Mobilization and the Politics of Race: The South and Universal Suffrage, 1952–1984. *Praeger Publishers, p. 97. Copyright © 1987 by Greenwood Publishing Group. Reproduced with permission of Greenwood Publishing Group, Inc., Westport, CT.)*

he won the election by a landslide, and American voters also gave him the most liberal Congress in American history. With the mandate provided by a record 61.1 percent of the popular vote, Johnson launched his Great Society. Congress responded to Johnson's election with the most sweeping reform legislation since 1935.

Civil rights remained a critical issue. In late 1964, the SCLC put voting rights at the top of its agenda. Martin Luther King Jr. and other leaders turned to Selma, Alabama—a town with a history of vicious response to civil rights protest—seeking another public confrontation that would mobilize national support and federal action. That confrontation came on March 6, when state troopers turned electric cattle prods, chains, and tear gas against peaceful marchers as they crossed the Edmund Pettus Bridge on the way to Montgomery. On March 15, the president addressed Congress and the nation, offering full support for a second monumental civil rights bill, the Voting

Rights Act. This act outlawed practices that had prevented most black citizens in the Deep South from voting and provided for federal oversight of elections in districts where there was evidence of past discrimination (see Map 30.1). Within two years, the percentage of African Americans registered to vote in Mississippi jumped from 7 percent to almost 60 percent. Black elected officials became increasingly common in southern states over the following decade.

Seeking to improve the quality of American life, the Johnson administration established new student loan and grant programs to help low- and moderate-income Americans attend college, and created the National Endowment for the Arts and the National Endowment for the Humanities. The Immigration Act of 1965 ended the racially based quotas that had shaped American immigration

**Improving American Life**

policy for decades. And Johnson supported important consumer protection legislation, including the 1966 National Traffic and Motor Vehicle Safety Act, which was inspired by Ralph Nader's exposé of the automobile industry, *Unsafe at Any Speed* (1965).

Environmentalists found an ally in the Johnson administration as well. First Lady Claudia Alta Taylor Johnson (known to all as "Lady Bird") successfully pushed for legislation to restrict the billboards and junkyards that had sprung up along the nation's new interstate highway system. Johnson signed "preservation" legislation to protect America's remaining wilderness and supported laws addressing environmental pollution.

At the heart of Johnson's Great Society was the War on Poverty. Johnson and other liberals believed that, in a time of great economic affluence, the nation had the resources for programs that could end "poverty, ignorance and hunger as intractable, permanent features of American society." Beginning in 1964, the Johnson administration passed more than a score of major legislative acts meant to do so (see Table 30.1).

**War on Poverty**

Johnson's goal, in his words, was "to offer the forgotten fifth of our people opportunity, not doles." Thus many new laws focused on increasing opportunity. Billions of federal dollars were channeled to municipalities and school districts to improve opportunities for the poverty-stricken, from preschoolers (Head Start) to high schoolers (Upward Bound) to young adults (Job Corps). The Model Cities program offered federal funds to upgrade employment, housing, education, and health in targeted urban neighborhoods, and Community Action Programs involved poor Americans in creating local grassroots antipoverty programs for their own communities.

The Johnson administration also tried to ensure basic economic safeguards, expanding the existing Food Stamp program and earmarking billions of dollars for constructing public housing and subsidizing rents. Two new federal programs guaranteed healthcare for specific groups of Americans: Medicare for those sixty-five and older, and Medicaid for the poor. Finally, Aid to Families with Dependent Children (AFDC), the basic welfare program created during the New Deal, expanded both benefits and eligibility.

| **TABLE 30.1**   Great Society Achievements, 1964–1966 | | | |
|---|---|---|---|
| | **1964** | **1965** | **1966** |
| **Civil Rights** | Civil Rights Act<br>Equal Employment Commission<br>Twenty-fourth Amendment | Voting Rights Act | |
| **War on Poverty** | Economic Opportunity Act<br>Office of Economic Opportunity<br>Job Corps<br>Legal Services for the Poor<br>VISTA | | Model Cities |
| **Education** | | Elementary and Secondary<br>  Education Act<br>Head Start<br>Upward Bound | |
| **Environment** | | Water Quality Act<br>Air Quality Act | Clean Water<br>  Restoration Act |
| **New Government Agencies** | | Department of Housing and<br>  Urban Development<br>National Endowments for the<br>  Arts and Humanities | Department of<br>Transportation |
| **Other** | | Medicare and Medicaid<br>Immigration and Nationality Act | |

The Great Society of the mid-1960s saw the biggest burst of reform legislation since the New Deal of the 1930s.

▲ This three-year-old Hispanic girl learns to read in a Head Start program. One of several programs established by the 1964 Economic Opportunity Act, Head Start prepared preschoolers from low-income families for grade school. *(E. Crews/The Image Works)*

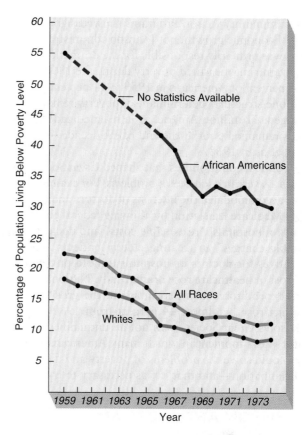

**Figure 30.1    Poverty in America for Whites, African Americans, and All Races, 1959–1974**

Because of rising levels of economic prosperity, combined with the impact of Great Society programs, the percentage of Americans living in poverty in 1974 was half as high as in 1959. African Americans still were far more likely than white Americans to be poor. In 1959 more than half of all blacks (55.1 percent) were poor; in 1974 the figure remained high (30.3 percent). The government did not record data on African American poverty for the years 1960 through 1965.

The War on Poverty was controversial from its beginnings. Leftists believed that the government was doing too little to change fundamental structural inequality. Conservatives argued that Great Society programs created dependency among America's poor. Policy analysts noted that specific programs were ill conceived and badly implemented. Even supporters acknowledged that programs were vastly underfunded and marred by political compromises. Responding to criticisms, Joseph Califano, one of the "generals" in the War on Poverty, claimed, "Whatever historians of the Great Society say twenty years later, they must admit we tried, and I believe they will conclude that America is a better place because we did."

Decades later, most historians judge the War on Poverty a mixed success. War on Poverty programs improved the quality of housing, healthcare, and nutrition available to the nation's poor. Between 1965 and 1970, federal spending for Social Security, healthcare, welfare, and education more than doubled, and the trend continued into the next decade. By 1975, for instance, the number of eligible Americans receiving food stamps had increased from 600,000 (in 1965) to 17 million. Poverty among the elderly fell from about 40 percent in 1960 to 16 percent in 1974, due largely to increased Social Security benefits and to Medicare. The War on Poverty undoubtedly improved the quality of life for many low-income Americans (see Figure 30.1).

But War on Poverty programs less successfully addressed the root causes of poverty. Neither the Job Corps nor Community Action Programs showed significant results. Economic growth, not Johnson administration policies, was primarily responsible for the dramatic decrease in government-measured poverty during the 1960s—from 22.4 percent of Americans in 1959 to 11 percent in 1973. And one structural determinant of poverty remained unchanged: 11 million Americans in female-headed households remained poor at the end of the decade—the same number as in 1963.

Political compromises that shaped Great Society programs also created long-term problems. For example, Congress accommodated the interests of doctors and hospitals in its Medicare legislation by allowing federal reimbursements of hospitals' "reasonable costs" and doctors' "reasonable charges" in treating elderly patients. With no incentives for doctors or hospitals to hold prices down, the cost of healthcare rose dramatically. National healthcare expenditures as a percentage of the gross national product rose by almost 44 percent from 1960 to 1971. Johnson's Great Society was not an unqualified success, but it was a moment in which many Americans believed they could solve the problems of poverty and disease and discrimination—and that it was necessary to try.

## JOHNSON AND VIETNAM

Johnson's domestic ambitions were threatened from an early point by turmoil overseas. In foreign policy, he held firmly to ideas about U.S. superiority and the menace of communism. He saw the world in simple, bipolar terms—them against us—and he saw a lot of "them." But, mostly, he preferred not to see the world beyond America's shores at all. International affairs had never much interested him, and he had little appreciation for foreign cultures. Once, on a visit to Thailand while vice president, he flew into a rage when an aide gently advised him that the Thai people recoil from physical contact with strangers. Dammit, Johnson exploded, he shook hands with people everywhere, and they loved it. At the Taj Mahal in India, Johnson tested the monument's echo with a Texas cowboy yell. And on a trip to Senegal he ordered that an American bed, a special showerhead, and cases of Cutty Sark be sent along with him. "Foreigners," Johnson quipped early in his administration, only half-jokingly, "are not like the folks I am used to."

Yet Johnson knew from the start that foreign policy, especially regarding Vietnam, would demand a good deal of his attention. Since the late 1950s, hostilities in Vietnam had increased, as Ho Chi Minh's North assisted the Vietcong guerrillas in the South to advance the reunification of the country under a communist government. President Kennedy had stepped up aid dollars to the Diem regime in Saigon, increased the airdropping of raiding teams into North Vietnam, and launched crop destruction by herbicides to starve the Vietcong and expose their hiding places. Kennedy also strengthened the U.S. military presence in South Vietnam, to the point that by 1963 more than sixteen thousand military advisers were in the country, some authorized to take part in combat alongside the U.S.-equipped Army of the Republic of Vietnam (ARVN).

Meanwhile, opposition to Diem's repressive regime increased, and not just by communists. Peasants objected to programs that removed them from their villages for their own safety, and Buddhist monks, protesting the Roman Catholic Diem's religious persecution, poured gasoline over their robes and ignited themselves in the streets of Saigon. Although Diem was personally honest, he countenanced corruption in his government and concentrated power in the hands of family and friends. He jailed critics to silence them. Eventually U.S. officials, with Kennedy's approval, encouraged ambitious South Vietnamese generals to remove Diem. On November 1, 1963, the generals struck, murdering Diem. Just a few weeks later, Kennedy himself was assassinated.

The timing of Kennedy's murder ensured that Vietnam would be the most controversial aspect of his legacy. Just what would have happened in Southeast Asia had Kennedy returned from Texas alive can never be known, of course, and the speculation is made more difficult by his contradictory record on the conflict. He expanded U.S. involvement and approved a coup against Diem, but despite the urgings of top advisers he refused to commit American ground forces to the struggle. Over time he became increasingly skeptical about South Vietnam's prospects and hinted that he would end the American commitment after winning reelection in 1964. Some authors have gone further and argued that he was ending U.S. involvement even at the time of his death, but the evidence for this claim is thin. More likely, Kennedy arrived in Dallas that fateful day still uncertain about how to solve the Vietnam problem, postponing the truly difficult choices until later.

Lyndon Johnson viewed his Vietnam options through the lens of the impending 1964 election. He wanted to do nothing that could complicate his aim of winning the presidency in his own right, and that meant keeping Vietnam on the back burner. Yet Johnson also sought victory, or at least that he would not lose the war, which in practice amounted to the same thing. As a result, throughout 1964 the administration secretly laid

**Kennedy's Legacy in Vietnam**

**Tonkin Gulf Incident and Resolution**

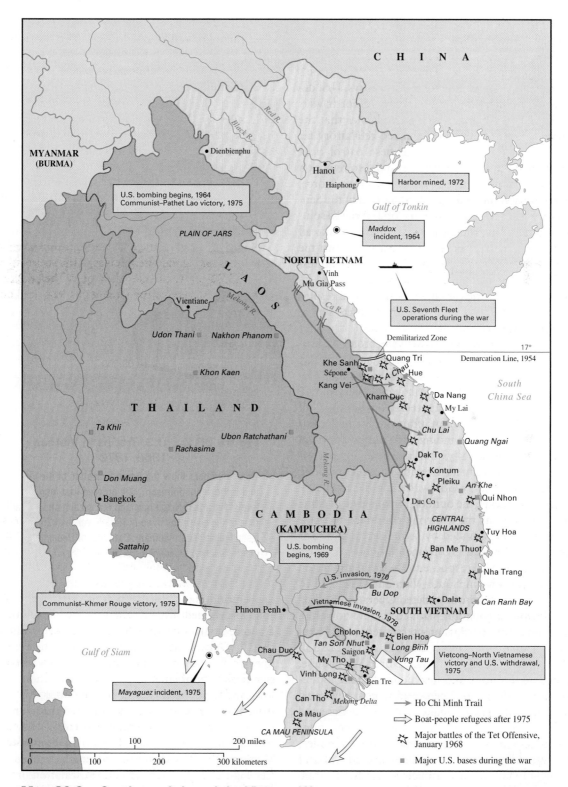

**Map 30.2   Southeast Asia and the Vietnam War**

To prevent communists from coming to power in Vietnam, Cambodia, and Laos in the 1960s, the United States intervened massively in Southeast Asia. The interventions failed, and the remaining American troops made a hasty exit from Vietnam in 1975, when the victorious Vietcong and North Vietnamese took Saigon and renamed it Ho Chi Minh City.

plans to expand the war to North Vietnam and never seriously considered negotiating a settlement.

In early August 1964, an incident in the Gulf of Tonkin, off the coast of North Vietnam, drew Johnson's involvement (see Map 30.2). Twice in three days, U.S. destroyers reported coming under attack from North Vietnamese patrol boats. Despite a lack of evidence that the second attack occurred, Johnson ordered retaliatory air strikes against selected North Vietnamese patrol boat bases and an oil depot. He also directed aides to rework a long-existing congressional resolution on the use of force. By a vote of 416 to 0 in the House and 88 to 2 in the Senate, Congress quickly passed the Gulf of Tonkin Resolution, which gave the president the authority to "take all necessary measures to repel any armed attack against the forces of the United States and to prevent further aggression." In so doing, Congress essentially surrendered its warmaking powers to the executive branch. The resolution, Secretary of Defense McNamara later noted, served "to open the floodgates."

President Johnson, delighted with the broad authority the resolution gave him, used a different metaphor. "Like grandma's nightshirt," he quipped, "it covered everything." He also appreciated what the Gulf of Tonkin affair did for his political standing—his public approval ratings went up dramatically, and his show of force effectively removed Vietnam as a campaign issue for GOP presidential nominee Barry Goldwater. On the ground in South Vietnam, however, the outlook remained grim in the final weeks of 1964, as the Vietcong continued to make gains. U.S. officials responded by laying secret plans for an escalation of American involvement.

### Decision for Escalation

In February 1965, in response to Vietcong attacks on American installations in South Vietnam which killed thirty-two Americans, Johnson ordered Operation Rolling Thunder, a bombing program planned the previous fall, which continued, more or less uninterrupted, until October 1968. Then, on March 8, the first U.S. combat battalions came ashore near Danang. The North Vietnamese, however, would not give up. They hid in shelters and rebuilt roads and bridges with a perseverance that frustrated and awed American decision makers. They also increased infiltration into the South. In Saigon, meanwhile, coups and countercoups by self-serving military leaders undermined U.S. efforts to turn the war effort around. "I don't think we ought to take this government seriously," Ambassador Henry Cabot Lodge told a White House meeting. "There is simply no one who can do anything."

In July 1965, Johnson convened a series of high-level discussions about U.S. policy in the war. Although these

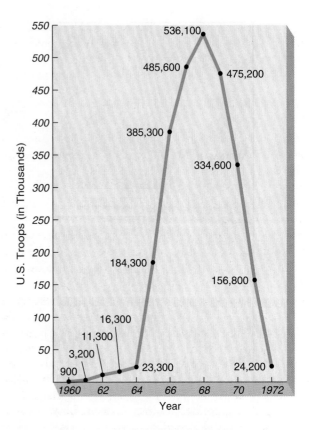

**Figure 30.2   U.S. Troops in Vietnam, 1960–1972**

These numbers show the Americanization of the Vietnam War under President Johnson, who ordered vast increases in troop levels. President Nixon reversed the escalation, so that by the time of the cease-fire in early 1973 fewer than 25,000 American troops remained in Vietnam. Data are for December 31 of each year. *(Source: U.S. Department of Defense.)*

deliberations had about them the character of a charade—Johnson wanted history to record that he agonized over a choice he had in fact already made—they did confirm that the American commitment would be more or less open-ended. On July 28, Johnson publicly announced a significant troop increase, disclosing that others would follow. By the end of 1965, more than 180,000 U.S. ground troops were in South Vietnam. In 1966 the figure climbed to 385,000. In 1967 alone, U.S. warplanes flew 108,000 sorties and dropped 226,000 tons of bombs on North Vietnam. In 1968 U.S. troop strength reached 536,100 (see Figure 30.2). Each American escalation brought not victory, but a new North Vietnamese escalation. The Soviet Union and China responded to the stepped-up U.S. involvement by increasing their material assistance to the Hanoi government.

The initiation of Rolling Thunder and the U.S. troop commitment "Americanized" the war. What could have been seen as a civil war between North and South, or a war of national reunification, was now clearly an American war against the communist Hanoi government. This "Americanization" of the war in Vietnam came despite deep misgivings on the part of influential and informed voices at home and abroad. In the key months of decision, Democratic leaders in the Senate, major newspapers such as the *New York Times* and the *Wall Street Journal,* and prominent columnists like Walter Lippmann warned against deepening involvement. So did some within the administration, including Vice President Hubert H. Humphrey and Undersecretary of State George W. Ball. Abroad, virtually all of America's allies—including France, Britain, Canada, and Japan—cautioned against escalation and urged a political settlement, on the grounds that no military solution favorable to the United States was possible. Remarkably, top U.S. officials themselves shared this deep pessimism. Most of them knew that the odds of success were small. They certainly hoped that the new measures would cause Hanoi to end the insurgency in the South, but it cannot be said they were confident.

## Opposition to Americanization

Why, then, did America's leaders choose war? At stake was "credibility." They feared that, if the United States failed to prevail in Vietnam, friends and foes around the world would find American power less credible. The Soviets and Chinese would be emboldened to challenge U.S. interests elsewhere in the world, and allied governments might conclude that they could not depend on Washington. For at least some key players, too, including the president himself, domestic political credibility and personal credibility were also on the line. Johnson worried that failure in Vietnam would harm his domestic agenda; even more, he feared the personal humiliation that he imagined would inevitably accompany a defeat— and for him, a negotiated withdrawal constituted defeat. As for the stated objective of helping a South Vietnamese ally repulse external aggression, that, too, figured into the equation, but not as much as it would have had the Saigon government—racked with infighting among senior leaders and possessing little popular support—done more to assist in its own defense.

Even as Johnson Americanized the Vietnam War, he sought to keep the publicity surrounding the action as low as possible. Thus he rejected the Joint Chiefs' view that U.S. reserve forces should be mobilized and a national emergency declared. This decision not to call up reserve

## American Soldiers in Vietnam

units had a momentous impact on the makeup of the American fighting force sent to Vietnam. It forced the military establishment to rely more heavily on the draft, which in turn meant that Vietnam became a young man's war—the average age of soldiers was twenty-two, as compared with twenty-six in World War II. It also became a war of the poor and the working class. Through the years of heavy escalation (1965–1968), college students could get deferments, as could teachers and engineers. (In 1969 the draft was changed so that some students were called up through a lottery system.) The poorest and least educated young men were less likely to be able to avoid the draft and also more likely to volunteer. The armed services recruited hard in poor communities, many of them heavily African American and Latino, advertising the military as an avenue of training and advancement; very often, the pitch worked. Once in uniform, those with fewer skills were far more likely to see combat, and hence to die.

Infantrymen on maneuvers carried heavy rucksacks into thick jungle growth, where every step was precarious. Booby traps and land mines were a constant threat. Insects swarmed, and leeches sucked at weary bodies. Boots and human skin rotted from the rains, which alternated with withering suns. "It was as if the sun and the land itself were in league with the Vietcong," recalled marine officer Philip Caputo in *A Rumor of War* (1977), "wearing us down, driving us mad, killing us." The enemy, meanwhile, was hard to find, often burrowed into elaborate underground tunnels or melded into the population, where any Vietnamese might be a Vietcong.

The American forces fought well, and their entry into the conflict in 1965 helped stave off a South Vietnamese defeat. In that sense, Americanization achieved its most immediate and basic objective. But if the stepped-up fighting that year demonstrated to Hanoi leaders that the war would not swiftly be won, it also showed the same thing to their counterparts in Washington. As the North Vietnamese matched each American escalation with one of their own, the war became a stalemate. The U.S. commander, General William Westmoreland, proved mistaken in his belief that a strategy of attrition represented the key to victory—the enemy had a seemingly endless supply of recruits to throw into battle. Under Westmoreland's strategy, the measure of success became the "body count"—that is, the number of North Vietnamese and Vietcong corpses found after battle. From the start, the counts were subject to manipulation by officers eager to convince superiors of the success of an operation. Worse, the American reliance on massive military and other technology—including carpet bombing, napalm (jellied gasoline), and crop defoliants that destroyed entire forests—alienated many South Vietnamese and brought new recruits to the Vietcong.

▲ **Wounded American soldiers after a battle in Vietnam.** *(Larry Burrows/*Life *magazine © Time Warner, Inc.)*

Increasingly, Americans divided into those who supported the war and those who did not. As television coverage brought the war—its body counts and body bags, its burned villages and weeping refugees—into homes every night, the number of opponents grew. On college campuses, professors and students organized debates and lectures on American policy. Sometimes going around the clock, these intense public discussions became a form of protest, called "teach-ins" after the sit-ins of the civil rights movement. The big campus and street demonstrations were still to come, but pacifist groups, such as the American Friends Service Committee and the Women's International League for Peace and Freedom, organized early protests.

## Divisions at Home

In early 1966 Senator William Fulbright held televised public hearings on whether the national interest was being served by pursuing the war. What exactly was the threat? senators asked. To the surprise of some, George F. Kennan testified that his containment doctrine was meant for Europe, not the volatile environment of Southeast Asia. America's "preoccupation" with Vietnam, Kennan asserted, was undermining its global obligations. Whether many minds were changed by the Fulbright hear-

ings is hard to say, but they constituted the first in-depth national discussion of the U.S. commitment in Vietnam. They provoked Americans to think about the conflict and the nation's role in it. No longer could anyone doubt that there were deep divisions on Vietnam among public officials, or that two of them, Lyndon Johnson and William Fulbright, had broken completely over the war.

Defense secretary Robert McNamara, who despite private misgivings championed the Americanization of the war in 1965, became increasingly troubled by the killing and destructiveness of the bombing. Already in November 1965 he expressed skepticism that victory could ever be achieved, and in the months thereafter he agonized over how the United States looked in the eyes of the world. American credibility, far from being protected by the staunch commitment to the war, was suffering grievous damage, McNamara feared. "The picture of the world's greatest superpower killing or seriously injuring 1,000 noncombatants a week, while trying to pound a tiny backward nation into submission on an issue whose merits are hotly disputed, is not a pretty one," he told Johnson in mid-1967.

But Johnson was in no mood to listen or reconsider. Determined to prevail in Vietnam, he dug in, snapping at

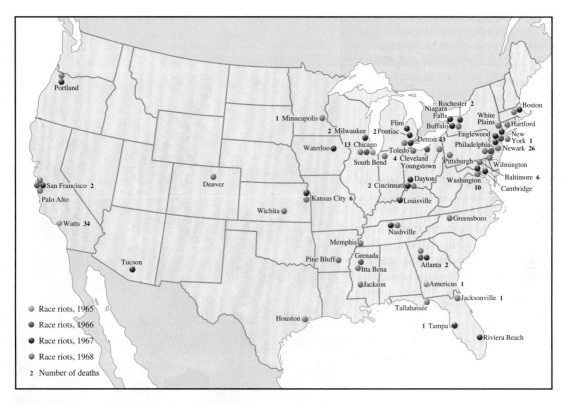

**Map 30.3    Race Riots, 1965–1968**
The first major race riot of the 1960s exploded in the Los Angeles neighborhood of Watts in 1965.
The bloodiest riots of 1967 were in Newark, New Jersey, and Detroit. Scores of riots erupted in
the aftermath of Martin Luther King Jr.'s assassination in 1968.

"those little shits on the campuses." Although on occasion he halted the bombing to encourage Ho Chi Minh to negotiate (on America's terms), and to disarm critics, such pauses often were accompanied by increases in American troop strength. And the United States sometimes resumed or accelerated the bombing just when a diplomatic breakthrough seemed possible. Hanoi demanded a complete suspension of bombing raids before sitting down at the conference table. And Ho could not accept American terms, which amounted to abandonment of his lifelong dream of an independent, unified Vietnam.

## A NATION DIVIDED

As Johnson struggled to overcome an implacable foe in Vietnam, his liberal vision of a Great Society faced challenges at home. The divisions among Americans over policy in Vietnam were only one fissure in a society that was fracturing along many different lines: black and white, youth and age, radical and conservative.

Even as the civil rights movement was winning important victories in the mid-1960s, many African Ameri-

### Urban Unrest

cans had given up on the promise of liberal reform. In 1964, shortly after President Johnson signed the landmark Civil Rights Act, racial violence erupted in northern cities. Angry residents of Harlem took to the streets after a white police officer shot a black teenager. The following summer, in the predominantly black Watts section of Los Angeles, crowds burned, looted, and battled police for five days and nights. The riot, which began when a white police officer attempted to arrest a black resident on suspicion of drunken driving, left thirty-four dead and more than one thousand injured. In July 1967, twenty-six people were killed in street battles between African Americans and police and army troops in Newark, New Jersey. A week later, in Detroit, forty-three died as 3 square miles of the city went up in flames. In 1967 alone, there were 167 violent outbreaks in 128 cities (see Map 30.3).

The "long, hot summers" of urban unrest in the 1960s differed from almost all previous race riots. Past riots were typically started by whites. Here, black residents exploded in anger and frustration over the conditions of their

During award ceremonies at the 1968 Olympic Games in Mexico City, American sprinters Tommie Smith *(center)* and John Carlos *(right)* extend gloved hands skyward to protest racial inequality and express Black Power. In retaliation, Olympic officials suspended Smith and Carlos. *(Wide World Photos, Inc.)*

lives. They looted and burned stores, most of them white-owned. But in the process they devastated their own neighborhoods.

In 1968 the National Advisory Commission on Civil Disorders, chaired by Governor Otto Kerner of Illinois, warned that America was "moving towards two societies, one white, one black—separate and unequal," and blamed white racism for the riots. "What white Americans have never fully understood—but what the Negro can never forget—is that white society is deeply implicated in the ghetto. White institutions created it, white institutions maintain it, and white society condones it," concluded the Kerner Commission. Some white Americans rejected this interpretation. Others, shocked at what appeared to be senseless violence, wondered why African Americans were venting their frustration so destructively just when they were making real progress in the civil rights struggle.

The answer stemmed in part from regional differences. The civil rights movement had focused mostly on fighting *legal* disenfranchisement and discrimination in the South. But northern African Americans also suffered racial discrimination. Increasingly concentrated in the deteriorating ghettos of inner cities, most northern African Americans lived in societies as segregated as any in the Deep South. They faced discrimination in housing, in the availability of credit and mortgages, and in employment. The median income of northern blacks was little more than half that of northern whites, and their unemployment rate was twice as high. Many northern blacks had given up on the civil rights movement, and few believed that Great Society liberalism would solve their plight.

In this climate, a new voice urged blacks to seize their freedom "by any means necessary." Malcolm X, a onetime pimp and street hustler who had converted while in prison to the Nation of Islam faith, offered African Americans a new di-

## Black Power

rection of leadership. Members of the Nation of Islam, commonly known as Black Muslims, espoused black pride and separatism from white society. Their faith, combining elements of traditional Islam with a belief that whites were subhuman "devils" whose race would soon be destroyed, also emphasized the importance of sobriety, thrift, and social responsibility. By the early 1960s, Malcolm X had become the Black Muslims' chief spokesperson, and his advice was straightforward: "If someone puts a hand on you, send him to the cemetery." But Malcolm X was murdered in early 1965 by members of the Nation of Islam who believed he had betrayed their cause by breaking with the Black Muslims to start his own, more racially tolerant organization. In death, Malcolm X became a powerful symbol of black defiance and self-respect.

A year after Malcolm X's death, Stokely Carmichael, SNCC chairman, denounced "the betrayal of black dreams by white America." To be truly free from white oppression, Carmichael proclaimed, blacks had to "stand up and take over"—to elect black candidates, to organize their own schools, to control their own institutions, to embrace "Black Power." That year, SNCC expelled its white members and repudiated both nonviolence and integration. CORE followed suit in 1967.

The best known black radicals of the era were the Black Panthers, an organization formed in Oakland, California, in 1966. Blending black separatism and revolutionary communism, the Panthers dedicated themselves to destroying both capitalism and "the military arm of our oppressors," the police in the ghettos. In direct contrast to earlier, nonviolent civil rights protesters, who had worn suits and ties or dresses to demonstrate their respectability, male Panthers dressed in commando gear, carried weapons, and talked about killing "pigs"—and did kill eleven officers by 1970. Police responded in kind; most infamously, Chicago police murdered local Panther leader Fred Hampton in his bed. However, the group also worked to improve life in their neighborhoods by instituting free breakfast and healthcare programs for ghetto children, offering courses in African American history, and demanding jobs and decent housing for the poor. The Panthers' platform attracted many young African Americans, while their public embrace of violence frightened many whites. Radicalism, however, was not limited to black nationalist groups. Before the end of the decade, a vocal minority of America's young would join in calls for revolution.

By the mid-1960s, 41 percent of the American population was under the age of twenty. These young people

### Youth and Politics

spent more time in the world of peer culture than had any previous generation, as three-quarters of them graduated from high school (up from one-fifth in the 1920s) and almost half of them went to college (up from 16 percent in 1940). As this large baby-boom generation came of age, many young people took seriously the idea that they must provide democratic leadership for their nation. Black college students had begun the sit-in movement, infusing new life into the struggle for African American civil rights. Some white college students—from both political left and right—also committed themselves to changing the system.

In the fall of 1960, a group of conservative college students came together at the family estate of William F. Buckley in Sharon, Connecticut, to create Young Americans for Freedom (YAF). Their manifesto, the "Sharon Statement," endorsed Cold War anticommunism and a vision of limited government power directly opposed to New Deal liberalism and its heritage. "In this time of moral and political crises," they wrote, "it is the responsibility of the youth of America to affirm certain eternal truths. . . . [F]oremost among the transcendent values is the individual's use of his God-given free will." The YAF planned to capture the Republican Party and move it to the political right; Goldwater's selection as the Republican candidate for president in 1964 demonstrated their early success.

At the other end of the political spectrum, an emerging "New Left" soon joined conservative youth in rejecting liberalism. Whereas conservatives believed that liberalism's activist government encroached on individual liberty, these young Americans believed that liberalism was not enough, that it could never offer true democracy and equality to all America's people. At a meeting in Port Huron, Michigan, in 1962, founding members of Students for a Democratic Society (SDS) proclaimed, "We are people of this generation, bred in at least modest comfort, housed now in the universities, looking uncomfortably to the world we inherit." Their "Port Huron Statement" condemned racism, poverty in the midst of plenty, and the Cold War. Calling for "participatory democracy," SDS sought to wrest power from the corporations, the military, and the politicians and return it to "the people."

The first indication of the new power of activist white youth came at the University of California, Berkeley. In the fall of 1964, the univer-

### Free Speech Movement

sity administration banned political activity—including recruiting volunteers for civil rights work in Mississippi—from its traditional place along a university-owned sidewalk bordering the campus. When the administration called police to arrest a CORE worker who defied the order, some four thousand students surrounded the police car. Berkeley graduate student and Mississippi Freedom Summer veteran Mario Savio ignited the movement, telling students, "You've got to put your bodies upon the levers . . . [and] you've got to indicate to the people who run it, to the people who own it, that unless you're free, the machine will be prevented from working at all."

Student political groups, left and right, came together to create the Free Speech Movement (FSM). The FSM did win back the right to political speech, but not before state police had arrested almost eight hundred student protesters. Berkeley students took two lessons from the Free Speech Movement. Many saw the administration's actions as a failure of America's democratic promises, and they were radicalized by the experience. But the victory of the FSM also demonstrated to students their potential power. By the end of the decade, the activism born at Berkeley would spread to hundreds of college and university campuses (see Map 30.4).

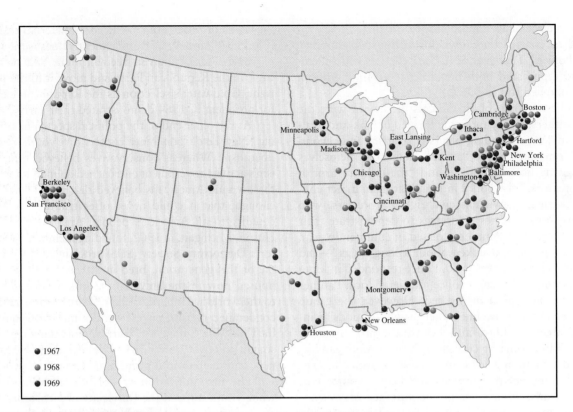

**Map 30.4    Disturbances on College and University Campuses, 1967–1969**

Students on campuses from coast to coast protested against the Vietnam War. Some protests were peaceful; others erupted into violent confrontations between protesters and police or the National Guard.

## Student Activism

Many student protesters in the 1960s sought greater control over their lives as students, demanding more relevant class offerings, more freedom in selecting their courses of study, and a greater voice in the running of universities. A major target of protest was the doctrine of in loco parentis, which until the late 1960s put universities legally "in the place of parents" to their students, allowing control over student behavior that went well beyond the laws of the land. The impact of in loco parentis fell heaviest on women, who were subject to strict curfew regulations called parietals, while men had no such rules. Protesters demanded an end to discrimination on the basis of sex, but rejected in loco parentis for other reasons as well. A group at the University of Kansas demanded that the administration explain how its statement that "college students are assumed to have maturity of judgment necessary for adult responsibility" squared with the minute regulation of students' nonacademic lives. One young man complained that "a

high school dropout selling cabbage in a supermarket" had more rights and freedoms than successful university students. Increasingly, students insisted they should be allowed the full rights and responsibilities of citizens in a democratic society.

It was the war in Vietnam, however, that mobilized a nationwide student movement. Believing that it was the democratic responsibility of citizens to learn about and speak out on issues of vital national importance, university students and faculty held "teach-ins" about U.S. involvement in Vietnam as the war escalated in 1965. Students for a Democratic Society sponsored the first major antiwar march that year, drawing twenty thousand protesters to Washington, D.C. Local SDS chapters grew steadily as opposition to the war increased. On campuses throughout the nation, students adopted tactics developed in the civil rights movement, picketing ROTC buildings and protesting military research and recruiting done on

## Youth and the War in Vietnam

◀ Hundreds of thousands of young people came together for the Woodstock Music and Art Fair in August 1969. In its coverage, *Time* magazine warned adults that "the children of the welfare state and the atom bomb do indeed march to the beat of a different drummer, as well as to the tune of an electric guitarist," but the local sheriff called them "the nicest bunch of kids I've ever dealt with." *(Pictorial Press)*

their campuses. However, despite the visibility of campus antiwar protests, most students did not yet oppose the war: in 1967, only 30 percent of male college students declared themselves "doves" on Vietnam, while 67 percent proclaimed themselves "hawks." And many young men were, in fact, in Vietnam fighting the war. But as the war continued to escalate, an increasing number of America's youth came to distrust the government that turned a deaf ear to their protests, as well as the university administrations that seemed more a source of arbitrary authority than of democratic education.

But the large baby-boom generation would change the nation's culture more than its politics. Although many young people protested the war and marched for social justice, most did not. The sixties' "youth culture" was never homogeneous. Fraternity and sorority life stayed strong on most campuses, even as radicalism flourished. And although there was some crossover, black, white, and Latino youth had different cultural styles: different music, different clothes, even different versions of a youth dialect often incomprehensible to adults. Nonetheless, as potential consumers, young people as a group exercised tremendous cultural authority. Their music and their styles drove Amer-

## Youth Culture and the Counterculture

ican popular culture in the late 1960s.

The most unifying element of youth culture was the importance placed on music. The Beatles had electrified American teenagers—73 million viewers watched their first television appearance on the *Ed Sullivan Show* in 1964. Bob Dylan promised revolutionary answers in "Blowin' in the Wind"; Janis Joplin brought the sexual power of the blues to white youth; James Brown and Aretha Franklin proclaimed black pride; and the psychedelic rock of Jefferson Airplane and the Grateful Dead—along with hallucinogenic drugs—redefined reality. That new reality took brief form in the Woodstock Festival in upstate New York in 1969, as more than 400,000 people reveled in the music and in a world of their own making, living in rain and mud for four days without shelter and without violence.

Some young people hoped to turn youth rebellion into something more than a consumer-based lifestyle, rejecting what they saw as hypocritical middle-class values. They attempted to craft an alternative way of life, or counterculture, liberated from competitive materialism and celebrating the legitimacy of pleasure. "Sex, drugs, and rock 'n' roll" became a mantra of sorts, offering these "hippies," or "freaks," a path to a new consciousness. Many did the hard work of creating communes and intentional communities, whether in cities or in hidden stretches of rural America. Although the New Left criticized the counterculture as apolitical, many freaks did envision revolutionary change. As John Sinclair, manager of the rock band MC5, explained, mind-blowing experiences with sex, drugs, or

# The British Invasion

The British invasion began in earnest on February 7, 1964. London and Paris had already fallen, reported *Life* magazine, and New York was soon to follow. Three thousand screaming American teenagers were waiting when Pan Am's *Yankee Clipper* touched down at Kennedy Airport with four British "moptops" aboard. "I Want to Hold Your Hand" was already at the top of the U.S. charts, and the Beatles' conquest of America was quick. Seventy-three million people—the largest television audience in history—watched them on the *Ed Sullivan Show* the following Sunday night.

Although the Beatles led the invasion, they did not conquer America alone. The Rolling Stones' first U.S. hit single also came in 1964. The Dave Clark Five appeared on *Ed Sullivan* eighteen times. And there was a whole list of others, some now forgotten, some not: Freddie and the Dreamers, Herman's Hermits, the Animals, the Yardbirds, the Hollies, the Kinks, Gerry and the Pacemakers, Chad and Jeremy, Petula Clark.

The British invasion was, at least in part, the triumphal return of American music, part of a transatlantic exchange that reinvigorated both nations. American rock 'n' roll had lost much of its early energy by the early 1960s, and in England, the London-centered popular music industry was pumping out a highly produced, saccharine version of American pop. But other forms of American music had made their way across the Atlantic, often carried by travelers through port cities like Liverpool, where the Beatles were born. By the late 1950s, young musicians in England's provincial cities were listening to the music of African American bluesmen Muddy Waters and Howlin' Wolf; they were playing cover versions of the early rock 'n' roll of Buddy Holly and Chuck Berry; and they were experimenting with skiffle, a sort of jazz- and blues-influenced folk music played mostly with improvised instruments. None of this music had a large popular audience in the United States, where *Billboard* magazine's number one hit for 1960 was Percy Faith's "Theme from *A Summer Place*" (a movie starring Sandra Dee and Troy Donahue), and the Singing Nun was at the top of the charts just before the Beatles arrived.

Young British musicians, including John Lennon, Eric Clapton, and Mick Jagger, re-created American musical forms and reinvented rock 'n' roll. By the mid-1960s, the Beatles and the other bands of the British invasion were at the heart of a youth culture that transcended the boundaries of nations. This music not only connected Britain and America but also reached across the Atlantic and the Pacific to link America's youth with young people throughout the world.

The Beatles perform on the *Ed Sullivan Show* in February 1964. Although Britain's Queen Mother thought the Beatles "young, fresh, and vital," American parents were appalled when the "long" Beatles haircut swept the nation.

*(AP/Wide World Photos, Inc.)*

music were far more likely to change young people's minds than earnest speeches: "Rather than go up there and make some speech about our moral commitment in Vietnam, you just make 'em so freaky they'd never want to go into the army in the first place."

The nascent counterculture had first burst on the national consciousness during the summer of 1967, when tens of thousands of young people poured into the Haight-Ashbury district of San Francisco, the heart of America's psychedelic culture, for the "summer of love." As an older generation of "straight" (or Establishment) Americans watched with horror, white youth came to look—and act—more and more like the counterculture. Coats and ties disappeared, as did stockings—and bras. Young men grew long hair, and parents throughout the nation complained, "You can't tell the boys from the girls." Millions used marijuana or hallucinogenic drugs, read underground newspapers, and thought of themselves as alienated from "straight" culture even though they were attending high school or college and not completely "dropping out" of the Establishment.

Some of the most lasting cultural changes involved attitudes about sex. The mass media were fascinated with "free love," and some people did embrace a truly promiscuous sexuality. More important, however, premarital sex no longer destroyed a woman's "reputation." The birth-control pill, distributed since 1960 and widely available to single women by the late 1960s, greatly lessened the risk of unplanned pregnancy, and venereal diseases were easily cured by a basic course of antibiotics. The number of couples living together—"without benefit of matrimony," as the phrase went at the time—increased 900 percent from 1960 to 1970; many young people no longer tried to hide the fact that they were sexually active. Still, 68 percent of American adults disapproved of premarital sex in 1969.

Adults were baffled and often angered by the behavior of youth. A generation that had grown up in the hard decades of depression and war, many of whom saw middle-class respectability as crucial to success and stability, just did not understand. How could young people put such promising futures at risk by having sex without marriage, taking drugs, or opposing the American government over the war in Vietnam?

# 1968

By the beginning of 1968, it seemed that the nation was coming apart. Divided over the war in Vietnam, frustrated by the slow pace of social change or angry over the racial violence that wracked America's cities, Americans looked for solutions as the nation faced the most serious domestic crisis of the postwar era.

The year opened with a major attack in Vietnam. On January 31, 1968, the first day of the Vietnamese New Year (Tet), Vietcong and North Vietnamese forces struck all across South Vietnam, capturing provincial capitals (see Map 30.2). During the carefully planned offensive, the Saigon airport, the presidential palace, and the ARVN headquarters came under attack. Even the American embassy compound in the city was penetrated by Vietcong soldiers, who occupied its courtyard for six hours. U.S. and South Vietnamese units eventually regained much of the ground they had lost, inflicting heavy casualties and devastating numerous villages.

**The Tet Offensive**

Although the Tet Offensive did not achieve the resounding battlefield victory that Hanoi strategists had hoped for, the heavy fighting called into question American military leaders' confident predictions in earlier months that the war would soon be won. Had not the Vietcong and North Vietnamese demonstrated that they could strike when and where they wished? If America's airpower, dollars, and half a million troops could not now defeat the Vietcong, could they ever do so? Had the American public been deceived? In February, the highly respected CBS television anchorman Walter Cronkite went to Vietnam to find out. The military brass in Saigon assured him that "we had the enemy just where we wanted him." The newsman recalled, "Tell that to the Marines, I thought—the Marines in the body bags on that helicopter."

Top presidential advisers sounded notes of despair. Clark Clifford, who had succeeded Robert McNamara as secretary of defense, told Johnson that the war—"a sinkhole"—could not be won, even with the 206,000 additional soldiers requested by Westmoreland. Aware that the nation was suffering a financial crisis prompted by rampant deficit spending to sustain the war and other global commitments, they knew that taking the initiative in Vietnam would cost billions more, further derail the budget, panic foreign owners of dollars, and wreck the economy. Clifford heard from his associates in the business community; "These men now feel we are in a hopeless bog," he told the president. To "maintain public support for the war without the support of these men" was impossible.

**Johnson's Exit**

Controversy over the war split the Democratic Party, just as a presidential election loomed in November. Senator Eugene McCarthy of Minnesota and Robert F. Kennedy (now a senator from New York), both strong opponents of Johnson's war

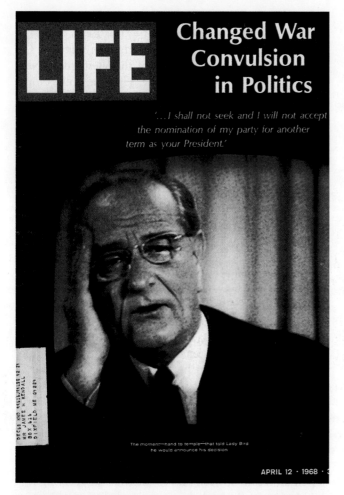

LIFE

### Changed War Convulsion in Politics

*'...I shall not seek and I will not accept the nomination of my party for another term as your President.'*

The moment—hand to temple—that told Lady Bird he would announce his decision

APRIL 12 · 1968 ·

▲ *Life* magazine captures the moment when President Lyndon Johnson, in a televised address, told the nation he would not seek another term as president of the United States. Johnson's face shows the toll taken by his years in the White House, as the war in Vietnam gradually destroyed his presidency and divided the nation.

*(Time Life Pictures/Time Life Picture Collection/Getty Images)*

policies, forcefully challenged the president in early primaries. Strained by exhausting sessions with skeptical advisers, troubled by the economic implications of escalation, and sensing that more resources would not bring victory, Johnson changed course. During a March 31 television address he announced a halt to most of the bombing, asked Hanoi to begin negotiations, and stunned his listeners by withdrawing from the presidential race. He had become a casualty of the war, his presidency doomed by a seemingly interminable struggle 10,000 miles from Washington. Peace talks began in May in Paris, but the war ground on.

Less than a week after Johnson's shocking announcement, Martin Luther King Jr. was murdered in Memphis, where he had traveled to support striking sanitation workers. It is still not clear why James Earl Ray, a white forty-year-old drifter and petty criminal, shot King—or whether he acted alone or as part of a conspiracy. By 1968 King, the senior statesman of the civil rights movement, had become an outspoken critic of the Vietnam War and of American capitalism. Although some Americans hated what he stood for, he was widely respected and honored. Most Americans mourned his death, even as black rage and grief exploded into riots in 130 cities. Once again, ghetto neighborhoods burned; thirty-four blacks and five whites died. The violence provoked a backlash from whites—primarily urban, working-class people who were tired of violence and quickly losing whatever sympathy they might have had for black Americans' increasingly radical demands. In Chicago, Mayor Richard Daley ordered police to shoot rioters.

An already shaken nation watched in disbelief as another leader fell to violence only two months later. Antiwar Democratic presidential candidate Robert Kennedy was shot and killed as he celebrated his victory in the California primary. His assassin, Sirhan Sirhan, an Arab nationalist, targeted Kennedy because of his support for Israel.

Violence erupted again in August at the Democratic National Convention in Chicago. Thousands of protesters converged on the city: students who'd gone "Clean for Gene,"

### Chicago Democratic National Convention

*" clean for Gene" - campaign for antiwar candidate Eugene McCarthy*

from the anarch Life" to counter antiwar groups Mayor Daley, re convention, assi hour shifts and h zookas, rifles, an attacked peacefu whole world is w swinging police i and Americans gathered around their television sets, despairing over the future of their nation.

Although American eyes were focused on the clashes in Chicago, upheavals burst forth around the world that

▲ A military truck with civilians waving Czech flags drives past a Soviet truck in Prague on August 21, 1968, shortly after Warsaw Pact troops invaded Czechoslovakia. More than one hundred people were killed in the clashes, and several Prague Spring leaders, including Alexander Dubček, were arrested and taken to Moscow. Dubček's attempts to create "socialism with a human face" are often seen as historical and ideological forerunners to Mikhail Gorbachev's reform policies in the 1980s in the Soviet Union.    *(Hulton Archive/Getty Images)*

## Global Protest

spring and summer. In France, university students protested both rigid academic policies and the Vietnam War. They received support from French workers, who occupied their factories and paralyzed public transport; the turmoil contributed to the collapse of Charles de Gaulle's government the following year. In Italy, Germany, England, Ireland, Sweden, Canada, Mexico, Chile, Japan, and South Korea, students also protested—sometimes violently—against universities, governments, and the Vietnam War. In Czechoslovakia, hundreds of thousands of demonstrators flooded the streets of Prague, demanding democracy and an end to repression by the Soviet-controlled government. This so-called Prague Spring developed into a full-scale national rebellion before being crushed by Soviet tanks.

Why so many uprisings occurred in so many places simultaneously is not altogether clear. Sheer numbers had an impact. The postwar baby boom experienced by many nations produced by the late 1960s a huge mass of teenagers and young adults, many of whom had grown up in relative prosperity, with high expectations for the future. The expanded reach of global media also mattered. Technological advances allowed the nearly instantaneous transmittal of televised images around the world, so protests in one country could readily inspire similar actions in others. Although the worldwide demonstrations might have occurred even without the Vietnam War, television news footage showing the wealthiest and most industrialized nation carpet-bombing a poor and developing one—whose leader was the charismatic revolutionary Ho Chi Minh—surely helped fuel the agitation.

## Nixon's Election

The presidential election of 1968, coming at the end of such a difficult year, did little to heal the nation. Democratic nominee Hubert Humphrey, Johnson's vice president, seemed a continuation of the old politics. Republican candidate

Richard Nixon, no newcomer to the political scene, called for "law and order"—a phrase some understood as racist code words—to appeal to those who were angry about racial violence and tired of social unrest. Promising to "bring us together," he reached out to those he called "the great, quite forgotten majority—the nonshouters and the non-demonstrators, the millions who ask principally to go their own way in decency and dignity." On Vietnam, Nixon vowed he would "end the war and win the peace." Governor George Wallace of Alabama, who only five years before had vowed, "Segregation forever!" and who proposed using nuclear weapons on Vietnam, ran as a third-party candidate. Wallace carried five southern states, drawing almost 14 percent of the popular vote, and Nixon was elected president with the slimmest of margins (see Map 30.5). Divisions among Americans deepened.

Yet on Christmas Eve 1968—in a step toward fulfilling the pledge John Kennedy had made at the opening of a tumultuous decade—*Apollo 8* entered lunar orbit. Looking down on a troubled world, the astronauts broadcast photographs of the earth seen from space, a fragile blue orb floating in darkness. As people around the world listened, the astronauts read aloud the opening passages of Genesis, "In the beginning, God created the heaven and the earth . . . and God saw that it was good," and many listeners found themselves in tears.

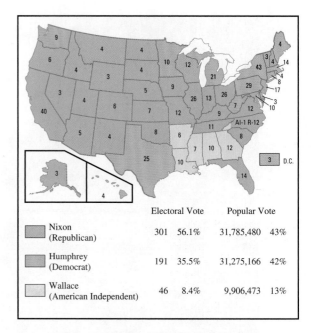

| | Electoral Vote | | Popular Vote | |
|---|---|---|---|---|
| Nixon (Republican) | 301 | 56.1% | 31,785,480 | 43% |
| Humphrey (Democrat) | 191 | 35.5% | 31,275,166 | 42% |
| Wallace (American Independent) | 46 | 8.4% | 9,906,473 | 13% |

**Map 30.5    Presidential Election, 1968**

The popular vote was almost evenly split between Richard M. Nixon and Hubert Humphrey, but Nixon won 31 states to Humphrey's 14 and triumphed easily in electoral votes. George Wallace, the American Independent Party candidate, won 5 states in the Deep South.

## SUMMARY

The 1960s began with high hopes for a more democratic America. Civil rights volunteers, often risking their lives, carried the quest for racial equality to all parts of the nation. Gradually, the nation's leaders put their support behind the movement, and the 1964 Civil Rights Act and the 1965 Voting Rights Act were major landmarks in the quest for a more just society. America was shaken by the assassination of President John Kennedy in 1963, but under President Johnson, the liberal vision of government power used to create a better life for the nation's citizens reached new heights, as a flood of legislation was enacted in hopes of creating a Great Society.

But throughout this period, the nation was troubled by threats to its stability. The Cold War between the United States and the USSR grew in size and scope during the 1960s. The world came close to nuclear war in the 1962 Cuban missile crisis. Cold War geopolitics led the United States to become more and more involved in the ongoing war in Vietnam. Determined not to let Vietnam "fall" to communists, the United States sent military forces to prevent the victory of communist Vietnamese nationalists led by Ho Chi Minh in that nation's civil war. By 1968 there were more than half a million American ground troops in Vietnam. America's war in Vietnam divided the country, undermined Great Society domestic programs, and destroyed the presidency of Lyndon Johnson.

Despite real gains in civil rights and in attempts to promote justice and end poverty, divisions among Americans deepened. Many African Americans turned away from the civil rights movement, seeking more immediate change in their lives. Poor African American neighborhoods burned as riots spread through the nation. Integrationists and civil rights advocates fought both separatist Black Power militants and white segregationists. Vocal young people—and some of their elders—questioned whether democracy truly existed in the United States. Large numbers of the nation's

## *Legacy* FOR A PEOPLE AND A NATION

### The Immigration Act of 1965

When President Johnson signed the 1965 Immigration Act in a ceremony at the foot of the Statue of Liberty, he stated, "This bill that we sign today is not a revolutionary bill. It does not affect the lives of millions. It will not reshape the structure of our daily lives, or really add importantly to our wealth and power." Johnson believed that the act was important in an era of struggle over the role of race in American society because it "repair[ed] a very deep and painful flaw in the fabric of American justice" by ending national-origins quotas that all but excluded "Polynesians, orientals, and Negroes" (as Hawai'i's senator Hiram Fong pointed out in 1963). Nevertheless, the president and his advisers saw it as primarily symbolic. They were wrong. This relatively obscure act may have had greater long-term impact on Americans' lives than any other piece of Great Society legislation.

The 1965 Immigration Act ended blatant discrimination against potential immigrants from Asia, Africa, and various Third World nations by substituting Eastern and Western Hemispheric "caps" for national quotas and establishing a policy of family reunification that allowed immediate relatives of U.S. citizens to immigrate to the United States regardless of numerical ceilings on immigration. The architects of the Immigration Act did not expect the scale or the sources of immigration to change, but world events decreed otherwise. Political instability, including wars in southeast Asia and civil conflict in Latin America and Africa, along with rapidly growing population in many of the world's poorer nations, created a large pool of potential immigrants who were drawn by the continuing prosperity of the United States. Immigration rates skyrocketed.

By the 1990s, immigration accounted for almost 60 percent of America's population growth. By 2000, more Americans were foreign-born than at any time since the 1930s—and their numbers continued to grow. No longer were most immigrants from western Europe. The majorities came from Mexico, the Philippines, Vietnam, China, the Dominican Republic, Korea, India, the former USSR, Jamaica, and Iran.

More than two-thirds of the new immigrants settled in six states—New York, California, Florida, New Jersey, Illinois, and Texas—but many found their way to parts of America that had previously been much more homogeneous. By the late twentieth century, Spanish-language signs appeared in South Carolina, and Hmong farmers from the mountains of southeast Asia offered their produce at the farmers' market in Missoula, Montana. The legacy of the 1965 Immigration Act was unintended but profound: the people and the nation are today much more diverse than they otherwise would have been.

white youth embraced another form of rebellion, claiming membership in a "counterculture" that rejected white middle-class respectability. With great passion, Americans struggled over the future of their nation.

1968 was a year of crisis, of assassinations and violence in the streets. The decade that had started with such promise was moving toward its end in fierce political polarization.

## SUGGESTIONS FOR FURTHER READING

Beth Bailey, *Sex in the Heartland* (1999)

David Farber, *Chicago '68* (1988)

Lawrence Freedman, *Kennedy's Wars: Berlin, Cuba, Laos, and Vietnam* (2000)

George C. Herring, *LBJ and Vietnam: A Different Kind of War* (1994)

Michael Kazin and Maurice Isserman, *America Divided: The Civil War of the 1960s* (1999)

Fredrik Logevall, *Choosing War: The Lost Chance for Peace and the Escalation of War in Vietnam* (1999)

Lisa McGirr, *Suburban Warriors: The Origins of the New American Right* (2001)

Charles Payne, *I've Got the Light of Freedom: The Organizing Tradition and the Mississippi Freedom Struggle* (1995)

*For a more extensive list for further reading, go to* college.hmco.com/pic/norton8e.

# Continuing Divisions and New Limits
## *1969-1980*

n 1969 Daniel Ellsberg was a thirty-eight-year-old former aide to Assistant Secretary of Defense John McNaughton. At the Pentagon Ellsberg had worked on a top-secret study of U.S. decision making in Vietnam requested by Secretary of Defense Robert S. McNamara. When he left office following the election of Richard Nixon, Ellsberg gained access to a copy of the study being stored at the Rand Corporation, where he intended to resume his pregovernment career as a researcher. He spent the next six months poring over the forty-seven volumes and seven thousand pages that made up what would come to be called the Pentagon Papers.

Initially supportive of U.S. military intervention in Vietnam, Ellsberg had in the last years of his government career grown deeply disillusioned. A Harvard-trained Ph.D., former marine officer, and Cold Warrior with a moral fervor to preserve America's nuclear strength, he had spent nearly two years in South Vietnam, from 1965 to 1967, assessing the war's progress for his superiors in Washington. Several times he had gone on combat patrols and come under enemy fire, and he had interviewed military officials, U.S. diplomats, and Vietnamese leaders. The war, he concluded, was in multiple respects—military, political, moral—a lost enterprise.

Ellsberg was at first reluctant to act on that conviction and disassociate himself from the policy. "Like so many," he later recalled, "I put personal loyalty to the president . . . above all else." But when in 1969 it became clear that the incoming Nixon administration had no intention of ending the war, he decided on a bold course of action:

◀ Daniel Ellsberg talks to reporters on January 17, 1973, after the opening session of his trial. Behind him is codefendant Anthony Russo, Ellsberg's colleague at the Rand Corporation who had assisted in the secret photocopying of the Pentagon Papers. The government indicted Ellsberg and Russo on charges of espionage, theft, and conspiracy, but in May 1973 a federal court judge dismissed all charges against them because of improper government conduct. *(© Corbis-Bettmann)*

## CHRONOLOGY

**1969** ■ Stonewall Inn uprising begins gay liberation movement
■ *Apollo 11* Astronaut Neil Armstrong becomes first person to walk on moon's surface
■ National Chicano Liberation Youth Conference held in Denver
■ "Indians of All Tribes" occupy Alcatraz Island
■ Nixon administration begins affirmative-action plan

**1970** ■ United States invades Cambodia
■ Students at Kent State and Jackson State Universities shot by National Guard troops
■ First Earth Day celebrated
■ Environmental Protection Agency created

**1971** ■ Pentagon Papers published

**1972** ■ Nixon visits China and Soviet Union
■ CREEP stages Watergate break-in
■ Congress approves ERA and passes Title IX, which creates growth in women's athletics

**1973** ■ Peace agreement in Paris ends U.S. involvement in Vietnam
■ OPEC increases oil prices, creating U.S. energy crisis
■ *Roe v. Wade* legalizes abortion
■ Agnew resigns; Ford named vice president

**1974** ■ Nixon resigns under threat of impeachment; Ford becomes president

**1975** ■ In deepening economic recession, unemployment hits 8.5 percent
■ New York City saved from bankruptcy by federal loan guarantees
■ Congress passes Indian Self-Determination and Education Assistance Act in response to Native American activists

**1976** ■ Carter elected president

**1978** ■ *Regents of the University of California v. Bakke* outlaws quotas but upholds affirmative action
■ California voters approve Proposition 13

**1979** ■ Three Mile Island nuclear accident raises fears
■ Camp David accords signed by Israel and Egypt
■ American hostages seized in Iran
■ Soviet Union invades Afghanistan
■ Consumer debt doubles from 1975 to hit $315 billion

he would make the Pentagon Papers public, even though doing so might land him in prison. The study, he believed, showed incontrovertibly that presidents had repeatedly escalated the American commitment in Vietnam despite uniformly pessimistic estimates from their advisers—and that they had repeatedly lied to the public about what they were doing and the results achieved. Perhaps, Ellsberg thought, disclosure of this information would generate sufficient uproar to force a dramatic change in policy.

With the assistance of a Rand colleague, Ellsberg surreptitiously photocopied the entire study, then spent months pleading with antiwar senators and representatives to release it. When they refused, he went to the press. On June 13, 1971, the world first learned of the Pentagon Papers through a front-page article in the *New York Times*. Numerous other newspapers soon began publishing excerpts as well.

Ellsberg's act of leaking a top-secret study became intensely controversial, particularly with Nixon's decision to try to stop the papers' publication—among the first such efforts to muzzle the press since the American Revolution—and to discredit Ellsberg and deter other leakers through the illegal actions of a group of petty operatives. To many Americans, Ellsberg was a hero whose defiant act might at least indirectly shorten an illegitimate war. To many others, he was a publicity-seeking traitor. These divergent views reflected the deep schisms in American society during the latter stages of the Vietnam era.

The 1970s would be, for Americans, a decade of division and an age of limits. The violence and chaos of 1968 continued in Richard Nixon's first years as president. Opposition to the war in Vietnam became more extreme. As government deceptions were exposed, the American people were ever more divided over U.S. policy in Vietnam. The movements for racial equality and social justice that had flowered in the 1960s also became more radical by the early 1970s. Although some continued to work for racial integration, many activists embraced cultural nationalism, which emphasized the differences among Americans and sought separatist cultures and societies. Even the women's movement, which was the strongest social movement of the 1970s and won great victories against sex discrimination, had a polarizing effect. Opponents, many of them women, understood feminism as an attack on their chosen way of life and mobilized a conservative grassroots movement that had great political importance over the subsequent decades.

This divided America faced great challenges abroad and at home. To some of these challenges leaders responded boldly and imaginatively. Richard Nixon and his national security adviser, Henry Kissinger, understood that, in foreign affairs, America's capacity to effect change was limited. They grasped that the United States and the Soviet Union, weakened by the huge costs of their competition and challenged by other nations, faced an international system in which power had become diffused. Accordingly, even as they stubbornly and futilely pursued victory in Vietnam, Nixon and Kissinger worked to improve relations with the People's Republic of China and the Soviet Union. In an increasingly multipolar system, they reasoned, the maintenance of world order depended on stable relations among the great powers. Through the opening to China and through improved relations with the USSR, the two men helped reduce the threat of great-power war.

Ultimately, however, exposure of Richard Nixon's illegal acts in the political scandal known as "Watergate" shook the faith of Americans not already disillusioned by presidential deception over the war in Vietnam. By the time Nixon, under threat of impeachment, submitted his resignation, the American people were cynical about politics and skeptical of military and executive leaders. Neither of Nixon's successors, Gerald Ford or Jimmy Carter, though both honorable men, was able to regain the faith of the American people. Despite some domestic successes, Carter's presidency was undermined by international events beyond his control. In the Middle East—a region of increasing importance in U.S. foreign policy—Carter helped broker a peace deal between Egypt and Israel but proved powerless to end a lengthy crisis in Iran involving American hostages. Meanwhile, the Soviet invasion of Afghanistan in 1979 revived Cold War tensions.

Adding to Carter's woes was a deepening economic crisis that defied traditional remedies. Suddenly in the 1970s, middle-class Americans saw their savings disappearing to double-digit inflation and their seemingly secure jobs vanishing overnight. The economic crisis was caused in large part by changes in the global economy and international trade, made worse by the oil embargo launched by Arab members of the Organization of Petroleum Exporting Countries in 1973. Americans realized anew that they were vulnerable to decisions made in far-off lands—decisions the United States could not control.

- How did American foreign policy change as a result of involvement in Vietnam?
- Why did Americans see this era as an age of limits?
- Some historians describe the period between 1968 and 1980 as a time when many Americans lost faith—in their government, in the possibility of joining together in a society that offered equality to all, in the possibility of consensus instead of conflict. Do you agree, or were the struggles and divisions of this era similar to those of previous decades?

## THE NEW POLITICS OF IDENTITY

By the end of the 1960s, as divisions continued to deepen among the American people, movements for social justice and racial equality had become stronger, louder, and often more radical. The civil rights movement, begun in a quest for equal rights and integration, splintered, as many young African Americans turned away from the tactics of nonviolence, rejected integration in favor of separatism, and embraced a distinct African American culture. Mexican Americans and Native Americans, inspired by the civil rights movement to struggle against their own marginalization in American society, had created powerful "Brown Power" and "Red Power" movements by the early 1970s. Like young African Americans, they demanded not only equal rights but also recognition of their distinct cultures. These movements fueled the development of a new "identity politics." Advocates of identity politics believed that differences among American racial and ethnic groups were critically important. Group identity, these Americans argued, must be the basis for political action. And government and social leaders must stop imagining the American public as individuals and instead address the needs of different identity-based groups.

By 1970, most African American activists no longer sought political power and racial justice through the universalist claim of the civil rights movement that "We are all the same but for the color of our skin." Instead, they emphasized the distinctiveness of black culture and society. These ideas attracted a large following,

||||||||||||||||||||||||||||||||||||

**African American Cultural Nationalism**

▲ United Farm Workers leaders César Chávez and Dolores Huerta talk during the 1968 grape pickers' strike. The statue of the Virgin Mary, poster for presidential candidate Robert Kennedy, and photograph of Mahatma Gandhi suggest the guiding religious, political, and philosophical understandings of the movement.

*(Arthur Schatz/Time Life Pictures/Getty Images)*

even among older, less radical people. Many black Americans, powerfully disillusioned by the racism that outlasted the end of legal segregation, had come to believe that integration would mean subordination in a white-dominated society that had no respect for their history and cultural traditions.

In the early 1970s, though mainstream groups like the NAACP continued to seek political and social equal-ity through the nation's courts and ballot boxes, many African Americans (like the white youth of the counter-culture) looked to culture rather than to narrow political action for social change. Rejecting current European American standards of beauty, young people let their hair grow into "naturals" and "Afros"; they claimed the power of black "soul." Seeking strength in their own histories and cultural heritages, black college students and young faculty members fought successfully to create black studies departments in American universities. African traditions were reclaimed—or sometimes created. The new holiday Kwanzaa, created in 1966 by Maulana Karenga, professor of black studies at California State University, Long Beach, offered celebration of a shared African heritage. Many African Americans found a new pride in their history and culture; the most radical activists gave up on the notion of a larger "American" culture altogether.

In 1970 the nation's 9 million Mexican Americans (4.3 percent of America's total population) were heavily con-centrated in the Southwest and California. Although these Americans were officially classified as white by the federal government—all Hispanics were counted as white in the federal census—discrimination in hiring, pay, housing, schools, and the courts was com-monplace. In cities, poor Mexican Americans lived in run-down barrios. In rural areas, poverty was widespread. Almost half of Mexican Americans were functionally illit-erate, and even among the young, high school drop-out rates were astronomical: in 1974, only 21 percent of Mex-ican American males graduated high school. Although growing numbers of Mexican Americans were middle class, almost one-quarter of Mexican American families remained below the poverty level in the 1970s. Especially dire was the plight of migrant farm workers.

The national Mexican American movement for social justice began with these migrant workers. From 1965 through 1970, labor organizers César Chávez and Dolores Huerta led migrant workers, the majority of whom were of Mexican ancestry, in a strike (*huelga*) against large grape growers in California's San Joaquin Valley. Chávez and the AFL-CIO–affiliated United Farm Workers (UFW) drew national attention to the working conditions of migrant laborers. Grape growers paid workers as little as 10 cents an hour (the minimum wage in 1965 was $1.25) and often lodged them in squalid housing without running water or indoor toilets. A national consumer boycott of table grapes brought the growers to the bargaining table, and in 1970 the UFW won its fight for better wages and working

## Mexican American Activism

conditions. The UFW's roots in the Mexican and Mexican American communities were critical to its success. The union resembled nineteenth-century Mexican *mutualistas,* or cooperative associations, as much as it did a traditional American labor union. Its members founded cooperative groceries, a Spanish-language newspaper, and a theater group; they called on the Virgin de Guadalupe for assistance in their struggle.

During the same period, more radical struggles were also beginning. In northern New Mexico, Reies Tijerina

||||||||||||||||||||||||||||||||||

### Chicano Movement

created the Alianza Federal de Mercedes (Federal Alliance of Grants) to fight for the return of land that the organization claimed belonged to local *hispano* villagers, whose ancestors had occupied the territory before it was claimed by the United States, under the 1848 Treaty of Guadalupe Hidalgo. In Denver, former boxer Rudolfo "Corky" Gonzáles drew Mexican American youth to his "Crusade for Justice"; more than one thousand young people gathered there for the National Chicano Liberation Youth Conference in 1969. They adopted a manifesto, *El Plan Espiritual de Aztlán,* which condemned the "brutal 'Gringo' invasion of our territories" and declared "the Independence of our . . . Nation."

These young activists called for the liberation of "La Raza" (from *La Raza de Bronze,* "the brown people") from the oppressive force of American society and culture, not for equal rights through integration. They also rejected a hyphenated "Mexican-American" identity. The "Mexican American," they explained in *El Plan Espiritual de Aztlán,* "lacks respect for his culture and ethnic heritage . . . [and] seeks assimilation as a way out of his 'degraded' social status." These young people called themselves "Chicanos" or "Chicanas"—a term drawn from barrio slang and associated with *pachucos,* the hip, rebellious, and sometimes criminal young men who symbolized much of what "respectable" Mexican Americans despised.

Many middle-class Mexican Americans and members of the older generations never embraced the term *Chicano* or the separatist, cultural nationalist agenda of *el movimiento.* Throughout the 1970s, however, younger activists continued to seek "Brown Power" based on a separate and distinct Chicano/Chicana culture. They succeeded in introducing Chicano studies into local high school and college curricula and in creating a strong and unifying sense of cultural identity for Mexican American youth. Some activists made clear political gains as well, founding La Raza Unida (RUP), a Southwest-based political party that registered tens of thousands of voters and won several lo-

▲ Calling their movement "Red Power," these American Indian activists dance in 1969 while "reclaiming" Alcatraz Island in San Francisco Bay. Arguing that an 1868 Sioux treaty entitled them to possession of unused federal lands, the group occupied the island until mid-1971. *(Ralph Crane,* Life *magazine © Time, Inc.)*

cal elections. The Chicano movement was never as influential nationally as the African American civil rights movement or the Black Power movement. However, it effectively challenged discrimination on the local level and created a basis for political action as the Mexican American (and broader Latino) population of the United States grew dramatically over the following decades.

Between 1968 and 1975, Native American activists forced American society to hear their demands and to re-

||||||||||||||||||||||||||||||||||

### Native American Activism

form U.S. government policies toward native peoples. Like African Americans and Mexican Americans, young Native American activists were greatly influenced by cultural nationalist beliefs. Many young activists, seeking a return to the "old ways," joined with "traditionalists" among their elders to challenge tribal leaders who advocated assimilation and cooperation with federal agencies.

In November 1969 a small group of activists, calling themselves "Indians of All Tribes," occupied Alcatraz Island in San Francisco Bay, demanding that the land be returned to native peoples for an Indian cultural center. The protest, which lasted nineteen months and eventually involved more than four hundred people from fifty different tribes, marked the consolidation of a "pan-Indian" approach to activism. Before Alcatraz, protests tended to be reservation based and concerned with specific local issues. Many of the Alcatraz activists were urban Indians, products in part of government policies that led Native Americans to leave reservations and seek jobs in the nation's cities. They were interested in claiming a shared "Indian" identity that transcended tribal differences. Although the protesters did not succeed in reclaiming Alcatraz Island, they drew national attention to their struggle and inspired the growing "Red Power" movement. In 1972 members of the radical American Indian Movement occupied a Bureau of Indian Affairs office in Washington, D.C., and then in 1973 a trading post at Wounded Knee, South Dakota, where U.S. Army troops had massacred three hundred Sioux men, women, and children in 1890.

At the same time, more moderate activists, working through such pan-tribal organizations as the National Congress of American Indians and the Native American Rights Fund, lobbied Congress for greater rights and resources to govern themselves and to strengthen their tribal cultures. In response to those demands, Congress and the federal courts returned millions of acres of land to tribal ownership, and in 1975 Congress passed the Indian Self-Determination and Education Assistance Act. Despite these successes, conditions for most Native Americans remained grim during the 1970s and 1980s: American Indians had a higher rate of tuberculosis, alcoholism, and suicide than any other group. Nine of ten lived in substandard housing, and unemployment rates for Indians were almost 40 percent.

As activists from various groups made all Americans increasingly aware of discrimination and inequality, policymakers struggled to frame remedies. As early as 1965, President Johnson had acknowledged the limits of civil rights legislation. "You do not take a person who, for years, has been hobbled by chains and liberate him, bring him up to the starting line of a race and then say, 'you are free to compete with all the others,'" Johnson told an audience at Howard University, "and still justly believe that you have been completely fair." In this speech, Johnson called for "not just

**Affirmative Action**

legal equality . . . but equality as a fact and equality as a result." Here Johnson joined his belief that the federal government must help *individuals* attain the skills necessary to compete in American society to a new concept: equality could be measured by *group* outcomes or results.

Practical issues also contributed to the shift in emphasis from individual opportunity to group outcomes. The 1964 Civil Rights Act had outlawed discrimination but seemingly had stipulated that action could be taken only when an employer "intentionally engaged" in discrimination against an individual. This individual, case-by-case approach to equal rights created a nightmare for the Equal Employment Opportunity Commission (EEOC). The tens of thousands of cases filed suggested a pervasive pattern of racial and sexual discrimination in American education and employment, but each required proof of "intentional" actions against an individual. Some people were beginning to argue that it was possible, instead, to prove discrimination by "results"—by the relative number of African Americans or women, for example, an employer had hired or promoted.

In 1969 the Nixon administration implemented the first major government affirmative-action program to promote "equality of results." The Philadelphia Plan (so called because it targeted government contracts in that city) required businesses contracting with the federal government to show (in the words of President Nixon) "affirmative action to meet the goals of increasing minority employment" and set specific numerical "goals," or quotas, for employers. Affirmative action for women and members of racial and ethnic minorities was soon required by all major government contracts, and many large corporations and educational institutions began their own programs.

Supporters saw affirmative action as a remedy for the lasting effects of past discrimination. Critics (some of whom were supporters of racial and sexual equality) argued that attempts to create proportional representation for women and minorities meant discrimination against other individuals who had not created past discrimination, and that group-based remedies violated the principle that individuals should be judged on their own merits. As affirmative-action programs began to have an impact in hiring and university admissions, bringing members of underrepresented groups into college classrooms, law firms, schoolrooms, construction companies, police stations, and firehouses nationwide, a deepening recession made jobs scarce. Thus increasing the number of minorities and women hired often meant reducing the number of white men. White working-class men were most adversely affected by the policy, and many resented it.

# THE WOMEN'S MOVEMENT AND GAY LIBERATION

During the 1950s, even as more and more women joined the paid work force and participated in the political life of the nation, American society and culture emphasized women's private roles as wives and mothers. The women's movement that had won American women the vote in the 1920s had all but disappeared. But during the 1960s, a "second wave" of the American women's movement emerged, and by the 1970s mainstream and radical activists waged a multifront battle for "women's liberation."

In 1963, the surprise popularity of Betty Friedan's *The Feminine Mystique* signaled that there was ample fuel for a revived women's movement. Writing as a housewife and mother (though she had a long history of political activism as well), Friedan described "the problem with no name," the dissatisfaction of educated, middle-class wives and mothers like herself, who—looking at their nice homes and families—wondered guiltily if that was all there was to life. This "problem" was not new; the vague sense of dissatisfaction plaguing housewives had been a staple topic for women's magazines in the 1950s. But Friedan, instead of blaming individual women for failing to adapt to women's proper role, blamed the role itself and the society that created it.

The organized, liberal wing of the women's movement emerged in 1966, with the founding of the National Organization for Women (NOW).

## Liberal and Radical Feminism

NOW, made up primarily of educated, professional women, was a traditional lobbying group; its goal was to pressure the EEOC to enforce the 1964 Civil Rights Act. Racial discrimination was the EEOC's focus, and discrimination on the basis of sex was such a low priority that the topic could be treated as a joke. When a reporter asked EEOC chair Franklin Roosevelt Jr., "What about sex?" Roosevelt laughed, "Don't get me started. I'm all for it." Women who faced workplace discrimination were not amused by such comments, and by 1970, NOW had one hundred chapters with more than three thousand members nationwide.

Another strand of the women's movement developed from the nation's increasingly radical movements for social change and justice. Many women, as they worked for civil rights or against the war in Vietnam, found themselves treated as second-class citizens—making coffee, not policy. As they analyzed inequality in America's social and political structure, these young women began to discuss their own oppression, and the oppression of all women, in American society. In 1968 a group of women gathered outside the Miss America Pageant in Atlantic City to protest the "degrading mindless-boob girlie symbol" represented by the beauty pageant. Although nothing was burned, the pejorative 1970s term for feminists, "bra-burners," came from this event, in which women threw items of "enslavement" (girdles, high heels, curlers, and bras) into a "Freedom Trashcan."

The feminism embraced by these young activists and others who challenged women's oppression was never a single, coherent set of beliefs. Some argued that the world should be governed by peaceful, noncompetitive values, which they believed were intrinsically female; others claimed that society imposed gender roles and that there were no innate differences between men and women. Most radical feminists, however, practiced what they called "personal politics." They believed, as feminist author Charlotte Bunch explained, that "there is no private domain of a person's life that is not political, and there is no political issue that is not ultimately personal." Some of these young women began to meet in "consciousness-raising" groups to discuss how, in their personal, everyday lives, women were subordinated by men and by a patriarchal society. In the early 1970s, women throughout the nation came together, in suburban kitchens, college dorm rooms, and churches or synagogues, to create their own consciousness-raising groups, exploring topics such as power relationships in romance and marriage, sexuality, abortion, healthcare, work, and family.

During the 1970s, the diverse groups that made up the women's movement claimed significant achievements.

## Accomplishments of the Women's Movement

Feminists worked for reforms that touched all aspects of American life: the right of a married woman to obtain credit in her own name; the right of an unmarried woman to obtain birth control; the right of women to serve on juries; the end of sex-segregated help wanted ads. They sought to change attitudes about rape and procedures for dealing with rape victims, such as the claim by a psychiatrist at the University of Kansas student health center in 1970: "A woman sometimes plays a big part in provoking her attacker by . . . her overall attitude and appearance." But by the end of the decade, activists working on the state and local level had established rape crisis centers, educated local police and hospital officials about procedures for protecting survivors of rape, and even changed laws.

As most of the medical establishment paid little attention to women's desires to understand—and take control of—their own sexual and reproductive health, the Boston Women's Health Collective published *Our Bodies,*

▲ On August 26, 1977, supporters of the Equal Rights Amendment (ERA) march down Pennsylvania Avenue following a ceremony in the White House Rose Garden that had proclaimed it "Women's Equality Day." The ERA initially had broad support from both Democrats and Republicans, but was ratified by only thirty-five of the necessary thirty-eight states.   *(AP Images)*

*Ourselves* in 1971 (the original edition sold more than 3 million copies). And women who sought the right to safe and legal abortions won a major victory in 1973 when the Supreme Court, in a 7-to-2 decision on *Roe v. Wade,* ruled that privacy rights protected a woman's choice to end a pregnancy.

NOW and many other women's organizations worked together to promote an Equal Rights Amendment that would end all discriminatory treatment on the basis of sex, the same amendment first proposed by the National Woman's Party in the 1920s. On March 22, 1972, Congress approved the amendment, stating simply that "equality of rights under the law shall not be denied or abridged by the United States or by any State on account of sex." By the end of the year, 22 states (of the 38 necessary to amend the Constitution) had ratified the ERA. Also in 1972, Congress passed Title IX of the Higher Education Act, which prevented federal funds from going to any college or university that discriminated against women. As a result, universities began to channel money to women's athletics, and women's participation in sports boomed.

Women's applications to graduate programs also boomed. In 1970 only 8.4 percent of medical school graduates and 5.4 percent of law school graduates were women. By 1979, 23 percent of the graduating class of America's medical schools was female, and 28.5 percent of new lawyers were women. During the 1970s, women greatly increased their roles in religious organizations, including the Church of Christ, the Unitarian and Episcopalian churches, and Reform and Conservative Judaism. Some denominations began to ordain women. Colleges and universities established women's studies departments, and by 1980 more than thirty thousand college courses focused on the study of women or gender relations.

The women's movement encompassed a broad range of women, but it was met by powerful opposition, much of it from women. Many women believed that middle-class feminists did not understand the realities of their world. They had no desire to be "equal" if that meant giving up traditional gender roles in marriage

## Opposition to the Women's Movement

or going out to work at low-wage, physically exhausting jobs. African American women and Latinas, many of whom had been active in movements for the liberation of their peoples and some of whom had helped create second-wave feminism, often came to regard feminism as a "white" movement that ignored their cultural traditions and needs; some believed that the women's movement diverted time and energy away from the fight for racial equality.

Organized opposition to feminism came primarily from conservative, often religiously motivated men and women. As one conservative Christian writer claimed, "The Bible clearly states that the wife is to submit to her husband's leadership . . . just as she would to Christ her Lord." Such beliefs, along with fears about changing gender roles and expectations, fueled the STOP-ERA movement led by Phyllis Schlafly, a lawyer and prominent conservative political activist. Schlafly argued that ERA supporters were "a bunch of bitter women seeking a constitutional cure for their personal problems." She attacked the women's movement as "a total assault on the role of the American woman as wife and mother, and on the family as the basic unit of society." Schlafly and her supporters argued that the ERA would foster federal intervention in personal life, decriminalize rape, force Americans to use unisex toilets, and make women subject to the military draft.

Many women saw feminism as an attack on the choices they had made and felt that by opposing the ERA they were defending their traditional roles. In fighting the ERA, tens of thousands of women became politically experienced; they fed a growing grassroots conservative movement that would come into its own in the 1980s. And by the mid-1970s, the STOP-ERA movement had stalled the Equal Rights Amendment. Despite Congress's extension of the ratification deadline, the amendment would fall three states short of ratification and expire in 1982.

In the early 1970s, gay men and lesbians faced widespread discrimination. Consensual sexual intercourse between people of the same sex was illegal in almost every state, and until 1973 homosexuality was labeled a mental disorder by the American Psychiatric Association. Homosexual couples did not receive partnership benefits, such as health insurance; they could not marry or adopt children. The issue of gay and lesbian rights divided even progressive organizations: in 1970 the New York City chapter of NOW expelled its lesbian officers. As open racism declined, gay men and women remained targets of discrimination in

**Gay Liberation**

hiring and endured public ridicule, harassment, and physical attacks.

Gay men and lesbians, unlike most members of racial minorities, could conceal the identity that made them vulnerable to discrimination and harassment. Remaining "in the closet" offered individuals some protection, but that option also made it very difficult to organize a political movement. There were small "homophile" organizations, such as the Mattachine Society (named for the Société Mattachine, a medieval musical organization whose members performed in masks, to evoke the "masked" lives of gay Americans) and the Daughters of Bilitis (after a work of love poems between women), which had worked for gay rights since the 1950s. But the symbolic beginning of the gay liberation movement came on June 28, 1969, when New York City police raided the Stonewall Inn, a gay bar in Greenwich Village, for violating the New York City law that made it illegal for more than three homosexual patrons to occupy a bar at the same time. That night, for the first time, patrons stood up to the police. As word spread through New York's gay community, hundreds more joined the confrontation. The next morning, New Yorkers found a new slogan spray-painted on neighborhood walls: "Gay Power."

Inspired by the Stonewall riot, some men and women worked openly and militantly for gay rights. They focused on a dual agenda: legal equality and the promotion of Gay Pride. In a version of the identity politics adopted by racial and ethnic communities, some rejected the notion of fitting into straight (heterosexual) culture and helped create distinctive gay communities. "Look out, straights," wrote gay liberation activist Martha Shelley in 1970. "We're gonna make our own revolution." By 1973, there were about eight hundred gay organizations in the United States. Centered in big cities and on college campuses, most organizations tried to create supportive environments for gay men and lesbians to come "out of the closet." Once "out," they could use their numbers ("We are everywhere" was a popular slogan) to push for political reform, such as nondiscrimination statutes similar to those that protected women and racial minority groups. By the end of the decade, gay men and lesbians were a public political force in cities including New York, Miami, and San Francisco, and played an increasingly visible role in the social and political life of the nation.

## THE END IN VIETNAM

Of all the divisions in American politics and society at the end of the 1960s, none was as pervasive as that over the war in Vietnam. "I'm not going to end up like LBJ,"

Richard Nixon vowed after winning the 1968 presidential election, recalling that the war had destroyed Johnson's political career. "I'm going to stop that war. Fast." But he did not. He understood that the conflict was generating deep divisions at home and hurting the nation's image abroad, yet—like officials in the Johnson administration—he feared that a precipitous withdrawal would harm American credibility on the world stage. Anxious to get American troops out of Vietnam, Nixon was at the same time no less committed than his predecessors to preserving an independent, noncommunist South Vietnam. To accomplish these aims, he set upon a policy that at once contracted and expanded the war.

A centerpiece of Nixon's policy was "Vietnamization"—the building up of South Vietnamese forces to re-

### Invasion of Cambodia

place U.S. forces. Nixon hoped that such a policy would quiet domestic opposition and also advance the peace talks under way in Paris since May 1968. Accordingly, the president began to withdraw American troops from Vietnam, decreasing their number from 543,000 in the spring of 1969 to 156,800 by the end of 1971, and to 60,000 by the fall of 1972. Vietnamization did help limit domestic dissent, but it did nothing to end the stalemate in the Paris negotiations. Even as he embarked on this troop withdrawal, therefore, Nixon intensified the bombing of North Vietnam and enemy supply depots in neighboring Cambodia, hoping to pound Hanoi into concessions (see Map 30.2 on page 873).

The bombing of neutral Cambodia commenced in March 1969. Over the next fourteen months, B-52 pilots flew 3,600 missions and dropped over 100,000 tons of bombs on that country. At first the administration went to great lengths to keep the bombing campaign secret. When the North Vietnamese refused to buckle, Nixon turned up the heat: in April 1970 South Vietnamese and U.S. forces invaded Cambodia in search of arms depots and North Vietnamese army sanctuaries. The president announced publicly that he would not allow "the world's most powerful nation" to act "like a pitiful, helpless giant."

Instantly, the antiwar movement rose up, as students on about 450 college campuses went out on strike and hun-

### Protests and Counter-demonstrations

dreds of thousands of demonstrators gathered in various cities to protest the administration's policies. The crisis atmosphere intensified further on May 4, when National Guardsmen in Ohio fired into a crowd of fleeing students at Kent State University, killing 4 young people and wounding 11. Ten days later,

police and state highway patrolmen armed with automatic weapons blasted a women's dormitory at Jackson State, a historically black university in Mississippi, killing 2 students and wounding 9 others. The police claimed they had been shot at, but no evidence of sniping could be found. In Congress, where opposition to the war had been building over the previous months, Nixon's widening of the war sparked outrage, and in June the Senate terminated the Tonkin Gulf Resolution of 1964. After two months, U.S. troops withdrew from Cambodia, having accomplished little.

Americans still, however, remained divided on the war. Although a majority told pollsters they thought the original American troop commitment to Vietnam to have been a mistake, 50 percent said they believed Nixon's claim that the Cambodia invasion would shorten the war. Angered by the sight of demonstrating college students, many voiced support for the president and the war effort. In Washington, an "Honor America Day" program attracted more than 200,000 people who heard Billy Graham and Bob Hope laud administration policy. Nevertheless, though Nixon welcomed these expressions of support, the tumult over the invasion served to reduce his options on the war. Henceforth, solid majorities could be expected to oppose any new missions for U.S. ground troops in Southeast Asia.

Nixon's troubles at home mounted in June 1971, when the *New York Times* began to publish the Pentagon Papers, the top-secret official study of U.S. decisions in the Vietnam War. Nixon secured an injunction to prevent publication, but the Supreme Court overturned the order. Americans learned from this study that political and military leaders frequently had lied to the public about their aims and strategies in Southeast Asia.

Equally troubling, to both opponents and supporters of the war, was the growing evidence of decay within the

### Morale Problems in Military

armed forces. Morale and discipline among troops had been on the decline even before Nixon took office, and there were growing reports of drug addiction, desertion, racial discord, even the murder of unpopular officers by enlisted men (a practice called "fragging"). Stories of atrocities committed by U.S. troops also began to make their way home. The court-martial and conviction in 1971 of Lieutenant William Calley, who was charged with overseeing the killing of more than three hundred unarmed South Vietnamese civilians in the hamlet of My Lai in 1968, got particular attention. An army photographer captured the horror in graphic pictures. For many, the massacre signified the dehumanizing impact of the war on those who fought it.

▲ Aftermath of the My Lai massacre, March 16, 1968, photographed by U.S. Army photographer Ronald Haeberle of the 11th Infantry Brigade, Americal Division. *(Ron Haeberle/Life magazine © Time Inc.)*

The Nixon administration, meanwhile, stepped up its efforts to pressure Hanoi into a settlement. Johnson had lacked the will to "go to the brink," Nixon told Kissinger, "I have the will in spades." When the North Vietnamese launched a major offensive across the border into South Vietnam in March 1972, Nixon responded with a massive aerial onslaught against North Vietnam. In December 1972, after an apparent peace agreement collapsed when the South Vietnamese refused to moderate their position, the United States launched a massive air strike on the North—the so-called Christmas bombing.

**Paris Peace Accords**

A diplomatic agreement was, however, close. Months earlier, Kissinger and his North Vietnamese counterpart in the negotiations, Le Duc Tho, had resolved many of the outstanding issues. Most notably, Kissinger agreed that North Vietnamese troops could remain in the South after the settlement, while Tho abandoned Hanoi's insistence that the Saigon government of Nguyen Van Thieu be removed. Nixon had instructed Kissinger to make concessions because the president was eager to improve relations with the Soviet Union and China, to win back the allegiance of America's allies, and to restore stability at home. On January 27, 1973, Kissinger and Le Duc Tho signed a cease-fire agreement in Paris, and Nixon compelled a reluctant Thieu to accept it by threatening to cut off U.S. aid while at the same time promising to defend the South if the North violated the agreement. In the accord, the United States promised to withdraw all of its troops within sixty days. North Vietnamese troops would be allowed to stay in South Vietnam, and a coalition government that included the Vietcong eventually would be formed in the South.

The United States pulled its troops out of Vietnam, leaving behind some military advisers. Soon, both North and South violated the cease-fire, and full-scale war erupted once more. The feeble South Vietnamese government, despite holding a clear superiority in the number of tanks and combat-ready troops, could not hold out. Just before its surrender, hundreds of Americans and Vietnamese who had worked for them were hastily evacuated from Saigon. On April 29, 1975, the South Vietnamese government collapsed, and Vietnam was reunified under a communist government based in Hanoi. Shortly thereafter, Saigon was renamed Ho Chi Minh City for the persevering patriot who had died in 1969.

The overall costs of the war were immense. More than 58,000 Americans and between 1.5 and 2 million Vietnamese had died. Civilian deaths in Cambodia and Laos numbered in the hundreds of thousands. The war cost the United States at least $170 billion, and billions more would be paid out in veterans' benefits. The vast sums spent on the war became unavailable for investment in domestic programs. Instead, the nation suffered inflation and retreat from reform, as well as political schism and abuses of executive power. The war also delayed accommodation with the Soviet Union and the People's Republic of China, fueled friction with allies, and alienated Third World nations.

**Costs of the Vietnam War**

In 1975 communists assumed control and formed repressive governments in Vietnam, Cambodia, and Laos, but beyond Indochina the domino effect once predicted by U.S. officials never occurred. Acute hunger afflicted the people of those devastated lands. Soon refugees—"boat people"—crowded aboard unsafe vessels in an attempt to escape their battered homelands. Many emigrated to the United States, where they were received with mixed feelings by Americans reluctant to be reminded of defeat in Asia. But many Americans faced the fact that the United States, which had relentlessly bombed, burned, and defoliated once-rich agricultural lands, bore considerable responsibility for the plight of the southeast Asian peoples.

Americans seemed both angry and confused about the nation's war experience. As historian William Appleman Williams observed, for the first time Americans had had their overseas sphere of influence pushed back, violently, and they were suffering from a serious case of "empire shock." Hawkish observers claimed that America's failure in Vietnam undermined the nation's credibility and tempted enemies to exploit opportunities at the expense of U.S. interests. They pointed to a "Vietnam syndrome"—a resulting American suspicion of foreign entanglements—which they feared would inhibit the future exercise of U.S. power. America lost in Vietnam, they asserted, because Americans had lost their guts at home.

**Debate over the Lessons of Vietnam**

Dovish analysts drew different conclusions, denying that the military had suffered undue restrictions. Some blamed the war on an imperial presidency that had permitted strong-willed men to act without restraint and on a weak Congress that had conceded too much power to the executive branch. Make the president adhere to the checks-and-balances system—make him go to Congress for a declaration of war—these critics counseled, and America

▲ Dedicated in 1993 in Washington, D.C., the Vietnam Women's Memorial honors the several thousand military women who served in Vietnam, many of them as nurses who volunteered for duty. One nurse, Judy Marron, remembered treating wounded soldiers round the clock: "There were days when the stress and strain and blood and guts almost had to equal the frontlines." This bronze sculpture, by Glenna Goodacre, stands near the long wall on which are etched the names of Americans who died in Vietnam. *(Brad Markel/Liaison Agency)*

would become less interventionist. This view found expression in the War Powers Act of 1973, which sought to limit the president's warmaking freedom. Henceforth, Congress would have to approve any commitment of U.S. forces to combat action lasting more than sixty days. In the same year, the draft (which had been shifted to a lottery system in 1969), came to an end; the U.S. military would henceforth be a volunteer army.

Public discussion of the lessons of the Vietnam War was also stimulated by veterans' calls for help in dealing with posttraumatic stress disorder, which afflicted thousands of the 2.8 million Vietnam veterans. Once home, they suffered nightmares and extreme nervousness. Doctors reported that the disorder stemmed primarily from the soldiers' having seen so many

**Vietnam Veterans**

children, women, and elderly people killed. Some GIs inadvertently killed these people; some killed them vengefully and later felt guilt. Other veterans heightened public awareness of the war by publicizing their deteriorating health from the effects of the defoliant Agent Orange and other herbicides they had handled or were accidentally sprayed with in Vietnam. The Vietnam Veterans Memorial, erected in Washington, D.C., in 1982, has kept the issue alive, as have many oral history projects of veterans conducted by school and college students in classes to this day.

## NIXON, KISSINGER, AND THE WORLD

Even as Nixon and Kissinger tried to achieve victory in Vietnam, they understood that the United States had overreached in the 1960s with a military commitment that had caused massive bloodshed, deep domestic divisions, and economic dislocation. The difficulties of the war signified to them that American power was limited and, in relative terms, in decline. This reality necessitated a new approach to the Cold War, and both moved quickly to reorient American policy. In particular, they believed the United States had to adapt to a new, multipolar international system; no longer could that system be defined simply by the Soviet-American rivalry. Western Europe was becoming a major player in its own right, as was Japan. The Middle East loomed increasingly large, due in large part to America's growing dependence on oil from the region. Above all, Americans had to come to grips with the reality of China by rethinking the policy of hostile isolation followed since the communist takeover in 1949.

They were an unlikely duo—the reclusive, ambitious Californian, born of Quaker parents, and the sociable, dynamic Jewish intellectual who had fled Nazi Germany as a child. Nixon, ten years older, was more or less a career politician, while Kissinger had made his name as a Harvard professor and foreign policy consultant. Whereas Nixon was a staunch Republican, Kissinger would have been quite prepared to join Hubert Humphrey's administration had the Democrat prevailed in the election. What the two men had in common was a tendency toward paranoia about rivals and a capacity to think in large conceptual terms about America's place in the world.

In July 1969 Nixon and Kissinger acknowledged the limits of American power and resources when they announced the Nixon Doctrine. The United States, they said, would continue to provide economic aid to allies in Asia and elsewhere, but these allies should no longer count on American troops. It was

**Nixon Doctrine**

an admission that Washington could no longer afford to sustain its many overseas commitments and therefore would have to rely more on regional allies—including, it turned out, many authoritarian regimes—to maintain an anticommunist world order. Although Nixon did not say so, his doctrine amounted to a partial retreat from the 1947 Truman Doctrine, with its promise to support noncommunist governments facing internal or external threats to their existence.

If the Nixon Doctrine was one pillar of the new foreign policy, the other was détente: measured cooperation with the Soviets through negotiations within a general environment of rivalry, drawn from the French word for "relaxation." Détente's

**Détente**

primary purpose, like that of the containment doctrine it resembled, was to check Soviet expansion and limit the Soviet arms buildup, though now that goal would be accomplished through diplomacy and mutual concessions. The second part of the strategy sought to curb revolution and radicalism in the Third World so as to quash threats to American interests. More specifically, the Cold War and limited wars like that in Vietnam were costing too much; expanded trade with friendlier Soviets and Chinese might reduce the huge U.S. balance-of-payments deficit. And improving relations with both communist giants, at a time when Sino-Soviet tensions were increasing, might exacerbate feuding between the two, weakening communism.

The Soviet Union's leadership had its own reasons for wanting détente. The Cold War was a drain on its resources, too, and by the late 1960s defense needs and consumer demands were increasingly at odds. Improved ties with Washington would also allow the USSR to focus more on its increasingly fractious relations with China and might generate serious progress on outstanding European issues, including the status of Germany and Berlin. Some ideologues in the Moscow leadership remained deeply suspicious of cozying up to the American capitalists, but they did not prevail over advocates of change. Thus in May 1972 the United States and the USSR agreed in the ABM Treaty (officially the Treaty on the Limitation of Anti-Ballistic Missile Systems) to slow the costly arms race by limiting the construction and deployment of intercontinental ballistic missiles and antiballistic missile defenses.

While cultivating détente with the Soviet Union, the United States took dramatic steps to end more than two decades of Sino-American hostility. The Chinese welcomed the change because they wanted to spur trade and hoped that friendlier Sino-American relations would make their onetime ally and now enemy, the Soviet Union, more cautious. Nixon reasoned

**Opening to China**

▲ "This was the week that changed the world," Richard Nixon said of his visit to China in February 1972. Many historians agree and consider the China opening Nixon's greatest achievement as president. When he and wife Pat visited the Great Wall the president reportedly remarked: "This is a great wall." *(Chicago Historical Society)*

the same way: "We're using the Chinese thaw to get the Russians shook." In early 1972 Nixon made a historic trip to "Red China," where he and the venerable Chinese leaders Mao Zedong and Zhou Enlai agreed to disagree on a number of issues, except one: the Soviet Union should not be permitted to make gains in Asia. Sino-American relations improved slightly, and official diplomatic recognition and the exchange of ambassadors came in 1979.

The opening to communist China and the policy of détente with the Soviet Union reflected Nixon's and Kissinger's belief in the importance of maintaining stability among the great powers. In the Third World, too, they sought stability, though there they hoped to get it not by change but by maintaining the status quo. As it happened, events in the Third World would provide the Nixon-Kissinger approach with its greatest test, and not merely because of Vietnam.

In the Middle East the situation had grown more volatile in the aftermath of the Arab-Israeli Six-Day War

## Wars in the Middle East

in 1967. In that conflict, Israel had scored victories against Egypt and Syria, seizing the Sinai Peninsula and the Gaza Strip from Egypt, the West Bank and East Jerusalem from Jordan, and the Golan Heights from Syria (see Map 33.2). Instantly, Israel's regional position was transformed, as it gained 28,000 square miles and could henceforth defend itself more easily against invading military forces. But the victory came at a price. Gaza and the West Bank were the ancestral home of hundreds of thousands of Palestinians and the more recent home of additional hundreds of thousands of Palestinian refugees from the 1948 Arab-Israeli conflict (see Chapter 28). Suddenly Israel found itself governing large numbers of people who wanted nothing more than to see Israel destroyed. When the Israelis began to establish Jewish settlements in their newly won areas, Arab resentment grew even stronger. Terrorists associated with the Palestinian Liberation Organization (PLO) made hit-

# OPEC and the 1973 Oil Embargo

*I*f one date can be said to have marked the relative decline of American power in the Cold War era and the arrival of the Arab nations of the Middle East as important players on the world stage, it would be October 20, 1973. That day, the Arab members of the Organization of Petroleum Exporting Countries (OPEC)—Saudi Arabia, Iraq, Kuwait, Libya, and Algeria—imposed a total embargo on oil shipments to the United States and to other allies of Israel. The move was in retaliation against U.S. support of Israel in the two-week-old Yom Kippur War. The embargo followed a decision by the members three days earlier to unilaterally raise oil prices, from $3.01 to $5.12 per barrel. In December, the five Arab countries, joined by Iran, raised prices again, to $11.65 per barrel, close to a fourfold increase from early October. "This decision," said National Security Adviser Henry Kissinger of the price hike, "was one of the pivotal events in the history of this century."

If Kissinger exaggerated, it was not by much. Gasoline prices surged across America, and some dealers ran low on supplies. Frustrated Americans endured endless lines at the pumps and shivered in underheated homes. Letters to newspaper editors expressed anger not merely at the Arab governments but also at the major oil companies, whose profits soared. When the embargo was lifted after five months, in April 1974, oil prices stayed high, and the aftereffects of the embargo would linger through the decade.

Like no other event could, it confirmed the extent to which Americans no longer exercised full control over their own economic destiny.

Just twenty years before, in the early 1950s, Americans had produced at home all the oil they needed. Detroit automakers had no difficulty selling ever larger gas-guzzlers with ever more outrageous tail fins. By the early 1960s, the picture had begun to change, as American factories and automobiles then were dependent on foreign sources for one out of every six barrels of oil they used. By 1972, the figure had gone up to about two out of six, or more than 30 percent. Although in absolute terms the amount was massive—U.S. motorists consumed one of every seven barrels used in the world each day—few Americans worried. Hence the shock of the embargo. As author Daniel Yergin has put it, "The shortfall struck at fundamental beliefs in the endless abundance of resources, convictions so deeply rooted in the American character and experience that a large part of the public did not even know, up until October 1973, that the United States imported any oil at all."

Although Americans resumed their wasteful ways after the embargo ended, an important change had occurred, whether people understood it or not. The United States had become a dependent nation, its economic future linked to decisions by Arab leaders half a world away.

◀ In 1976 OPEC sharply raised the price of oil a second time, prompting this editorial cartoon by Don Wright of the *Miami News*.
*(Don Wright in the* Miami News, *1976, Tribune Media Services)*

and-run raids on Jewish settlements, hijacked jetliners, and murdered Israeli athletes at the 1972 Olympic Games in Munich, West Germany. The Israelis retaliated by assassinating PLO leaders.

In October 1973, on the Jewish High Holy Day of Yom Kippur, Egypt and Syria attacked Israel. Their motives were complex, but primarily they sought revenge for the 1967 defeat. Caught by surprise, Israel reeled before launching an effective counteroffensive against Soviet-armed Egyptian forces in the Sinai. In an attempt to punish Americans for their pro-Israel stance, the Organization of Petroleum Exporting Countries (OPEC), a group of mostly Arab nations that had joined together to raise the price of oil, embargoed shipments of oil to the United States and other supporters of Israel. An energy crisis and dramatically higher oil prices rocked the nation. Soon Kissinger arranged a cease-fire in the war, but not until March 1974 did OPEC lift the oil embargo. The next year Kissinger persuaded Egypt and Israel to accept a U.N. peacekeeping force in the Sinai. But peace did not come to the region, for Palestinians and other Arabs still vowed to destroy Israel, and Israelis insisted on building more Jewish settlements in occupied lands.

In Latin America, meanwhile, the Nixon administration sought to preserve stability and to thwart radical leftist challenges to authoritarian rule. In Chile, after voters in 1970 elected a Marxist president, Salvador Allende, the CIA began secret operations to disrupt Chile and encouraged military officers to stage a coup. In 1973 a military junta ousted Allende and installed an authoritarian regime under General Augusto Pinochet. (Allende was subsequently murdered.) Washington publicly denied any role in the affair that implanted iron-fisted tyranny in Chile for two decades.

**Antiradicalism in Latin America and Africa**

In Africa as well, Washington preferred the status quo. Nixon backed the white-minority regime in Rhodesia (now Zimbabwe) and activated the CIA in a failed effort to defeat a Soviet- and Cuban-backed faction in newly independent Angola's civil war. In South Africa, Nixon tolerated the white rulers who imposed the segregationist policy of apartheid on blacks and mixed-race "coloureds" (85 percent of the population), keeping them poor, disfranchised, and ghettoized in prisonlike townships. After the leftist government came to power in Angola, however, Washington took a keener interest in the rest of Africa, building economic ties and sending arms to friendly black nations, such as Kenya and the Congo. The administration also began to distance the

United States from the white governments of Rhodesia and South Africa. America had to "prevent the radicalization of Africa," said Kissinger.

## PRESIDENTIAL POLITICS AND THE CRISIS OF LEADERSHIP

Richard Nixon took pride in his foreign policy accomplishments, but they were overshadowed by his failures at home. He betrayed the public trust and broke laws, large and small. His misconduct, combined with Americans' growing belief that their leaders had lied to them repeatedly about the war in Vietnam, shook Americans' faith in government. This new mistrust joined with conservatives' traditional suspicion of big, activist government to create a crisis of leadership and undermine liberal policies that had governed the nation since the New Deal, even in the Eisenhower era. The profound suspicion of presidential leadership and government action that enveloped the nation by the end of the Watergate hearings would limit what Gerald Ford and Jimmy Carter, Nixon's successors to the presidency, could accomplish.

Richard Nixon was one of America's most complex presidents. Brilliant, driven, politically cunning, able to address changing global realities with creativity—Nixon was also crude, prejudiced against Jews and African Americans, happy to use dirty tricks and the power of the presidency against those he considered his enemies, and driven by a sense of resentment that bordered on paranoia. Despite his tenacity and intelligence, Nixon—the son of a grocer from an agricultural region of southern California—was never accepted by the sophisticated northeastern liberal elite. (After Nixon's election, *Washingtonian* magazine joked that "cottage cheese with ketchup" had replaced elegant desserts at White House dinners.) Nixon loathed the liberal establishment, which loathed him back, and his presidency was driven by that hatred as much as by any strong philosophical commitment to conservative principles.

**Nixon's Domestic Agenda**

Nixon's domestic policy initiatives have long confused historians. Much of his agenda was liberal, expanding federal programs to improve society. The Nixon administration pioneered affirmative action. It doubled the budgets of the new National Endowment for the Humanities (NEH) and National Endowment for the Arts (NEA). Nixon supported the ERA, signed major environmental legislation, created the Occupational Safety and Health Administration (OSHA), actively attempted to manage the economy using deficit spending, and even proposed a guaranteed minimum income for all Americans.

At the same time, Nixon pursued a conservative agenda. One of his major legislative goals was "devolution," or shifting federal government authority to states and localities. He promoted revenue-sharing programs that distributed federal funds back to the states to use as they saw fit, thus appealing to those who were angry about, as they saw it, paying high taxes to support liberal "giveaway" programs for poor and minority Americans. As president, Nixon worked to equate the Republican Party with law and order and the Democrats with permissiveness, crime, drugs, radicalism, and the "hippie lifestyle." To capitalize on the backlash against the 1960s movements for social change and consolidate the support of those he called "the silent majority," Nixon fostered division, using his outspoken vice president, Spiro Agnew, to attack war protesters and critics as "naughty children," "effete . . . snobs," and "ideological eunuchs." He appointed four conservative justices to the Supreme Court: Warren Burger, Harry Blackmun, Lewis Powell Jr., and William Rehnquist.

With such a confusing record, was Nixon liberal, conservative, or simply pragmatic? Much of his "liberal" agenda was not so much liberal as it was tricky—a term commonly applied to Nixon at the time. Instead of attacking liberal programs and the entrenched government bureaucracies that administered them, he attempted to undermine them while appearing to offer support. For example, when the Nixon administration proposed a guaranteed minimum income for all Americans, including the working poor, his larger goal was to dismantle the federal welfare system and destroy its liberal bureaucracy of social workers (no longer necessary under Nixon's model). And though Nixon doubled funding for the NEA, he redirected awards from the northeastern art establishment—the "elite" that he thought of as an enemy—toward local and regional art groups that sponsored popular art forms, such as representational painting or folk music.

In addition, recognizing the possibility of attracting white southerners to the Republican Party, Nixon pursued a highly pragmatic "southern strategy." He nominated two southerners for positions on the Supreme Court—one of whom had a segregationist record—and when Congress declined to confirm either nominee, Nixon protested angrily, saying, "I understand the bitter feelings of millions of Americans who live in the South." After the Supreme Court upheld a school desegregation plan that required a North Carolina school system—still highly segregated fifteen years after the *Brown* decision—to achieve racial in-tegration by removing both black and white children from their neighborhood schools and busing them to schools elsewhere in the county (*Swann v. Charlotte-Mecklenburg*, 1971), Nixon denounced busing as a reckless and extreme remedy.

Nixon was almost sure of reelection in 1972. His Democratic opponent was George McGovern, a progressive senator from South Dakota and strong opponent of the Vietnam War. McGovern appealed to the left and essentially wrote off the middle, declaring, "I am not a centrist candidate." Alabama governor George Wallace, running on a third-party ticket, withdrew from the race after an assassination attempt left him paralyzed. The Nixon campaign, however, was taking no chances. On June 17, four months before the election, five men were caught breaking into the Democratic National Committee's offices at the Watergate apartment and office complex in Washington, D.C. The men were associated with the Committee to Re-elect the President, known as CREEP. The break-in got little attention at the time, and Nixon was swept into office in November with 60 percent of the popular vote. McGovern carried only Massachusetts and the District of Columbia. But even as Nixon triumphed, his downfall had begun.

## Enemies and Dirty Tricks

From the beginning of his presidency, Nixon was obsessed with the idea that, in a time of national turmoil, he was surrounded by enemies. He made "enemies lists," hundreds of names long, that included all black members of Congress and the presidents of most Ivy League universities. The Nixon administration worked, in the words of one of its members, to "use the available federal machinery to screw our political enemies." On Nixon's order, his aide Charles Colson (best known for his maxim "When you've got them by the balls, their hearts and minds will follow") formed a secret group called the Plumbers. Their first job was to break into the office of the psychiatrist treating Daniel Ellsberg, the former Pentagon employee who had gone public with the Pentagon Papers, looking for material to discredit him. The Plumbers expanded their "dirty tricks" operations during the 1972 presidential primaries and campaign, bugging phones, infiltrating campaign staffs, even writing and distributing anonymous letters falsely accusing Democratic candidates of sexual misconduct. They had already bugged the Democratic National Committee offices and were going back to plant more surveillance equipment when they were caught by the D.C. police at the Watergate complex.

Nixon was not directly involved in the Watergate affair. But instead of distancing himself and firing those

**Watergate Cover-up and Investigation**

responsible, he chose to cover up their connection to the break-ins. He had the CIA stop the FBI's investigation, citing reasons of national security. At this point, Nixon had obstructed justice—a felony and, under the Constitution, an impeachable crime—but he had also, it seemed, halted the investigation. However, two young, relatively unknown reporters for the *Washington Post,* Carl Bernstein and Bob Woodward, would not give up on the story. Aided by an anonymous, highly placed government official whom they code-named Deep Throat (the title of a notorious 1972 X-rated film), they began to follow a money trail that led straight to the White House. (W. Mark Felt, who was second-in-command at the FBI in the early 1970s, publicly identified himself as Watergate's Deep Throat in 2005.)

The Watergate cover-up continued to unravel under the scrutiny of both the courts and Congress. From May to August 1973, the Senate held televised public hearings on the Watergate affair. White House Counsel John Dean, fearful that he was being made the fall guy for the entire Watergate fiasco, gave damning testimony. Then, on July 13, a White House aide told the Senate Committee that Nixon regularly recorded his conversations in the Oval Office. These tape recordings were the "smoking gun" that could prove Nixon's direct involvement in the cover-up—but Nixon refused to turn the tapes over to Congress.

As Nixon and Congress fought over the tapes, Nixon faced scandals on other fronts. In October 1973, Vice

**Impeachment and Resignation**

President Spiro Agnew resigned, following charges that he had accepted bribes while governor of Maryland. Following constitutional procedures, Nixon appointed and Congress approved Michigan's Gerald Ford, the House minority leader, as Agnew's replacement. Meanwhile, Nixon's staff was increasingly concerned about his excessive drinking and seeming mental instability. Then, on October 24, 1973, the House of Representatives began impeachment proceedings against the president.

Under court order, Nixon began to release edited portions of the Oval Office tapes to Congress. Although the first tapes revealed no criminal activity, the public was shocked by Nixon's constant obscenities and racist slurs. Finally, in July 1974, the Supreme Court ruled that Nixon must release all the tapes. Despite "mysterious" erasures

▲ Resigning in disgrace as impeachment for his role in the Watergate cover-up became a certainty, Richard Nixon flashes the "V for victory" sign as he leaves the White House for the last time. *(Nixon Presidential Materials Project, National Archives and Record Administration)*

on two key tapes, the House Judiciary Committee found evidence to impeach Nixon on three grounds: obstruction of justice, abuse of power, and contempt of Congress. On August 9, 1974, facing certain impeachment and conviction, Richard Nixon became the first president of the United States to resign his office.

The Watergate scandal shook the confidence of American citizens in their government. It also prompted Congress to reevaluate the balance of power between the executive and legislative branches. Beginning in 1973, Congress passed several major bills aimed at restricting presidential power. They included not only the War Powers Act, but also the 1974 Budget and Impoundment Control Act, which made it impossible for the president to disregard congressional spending mandates.

Gerald Ford, the nation's first unelected president, faced a nation awash in cynicism. The presidency was

### Ford's Presidency

discredited. The economy was in decline. The nation's people were divided. Ford was a decent and honorable man who did his best to end what he called "the long national nightmare." In one of his first official acts as president he issued a full pardon to Richard Nixon, forestalling any attempts to bring criminal charges. Ford's approval ratings plummeted from 71 to 41 percent. Some suggested, with no evidence, that he had struck some sort of sordid deal with Nixon. Ford insisted, for decades, that he had simply acted in the interest of the nation, but shortly before his death in late 2006 he told a reporter that, though few knew it, he and Nixon had been good friends and "I didn't want to see my real friend have the stigma" of criminal charges.

Ford accomplished little domestically during his two and a half years in office. The Democrats gained a large margin in the 1974 congressional elections, and, after Watergate, Congress was willing to exercise its power. Ford almost routinely vetoed its bills—39 in one year—but Congress often overrode his veto. In addition, Ford, during the course of his brief presidency, was the object of constant mockery. In political cartoons, comedy monologues, and especially on the new hit television show *Saturday Night Live,* he was portrayed as a buffoon and a klutz. When he slipped on the steps exiting *Air Force One,* footage appeared on major newscasts. The irony of portraying Ford—who had turned down a chance to play in the National Football League in order to attend Yale Law School—as physically inept was extraordinary. But, as Ford understood, these portrayals began to give the impression that he was a "stumbler," in danger of making blunders of all kinds. Ford caught the fallout of disrespect that Nixon's actions had unleashed. No longer would respect for the office of the presidency prevent the mass media from reporting presidential slips, stumbles, frailties, or misconduct. Ford was the first president to discover how much the rules had changed.

Jimmy Carter, who was elected in 1976 by a slim margin, initially benefited from Americans' suspicion of political leadership. Carter was a

### Carter as "Outsider" President

one-term governor of Georgia, one of the new southern leaders who were committed to racial equality and integration. He had grown up in the rural Georgia town of Plains, where his family owned a peanut farm, graduated from the Naval Academy, then served as an engineer in the navy's nuclear submarine program. Carter, a deeply religious born-again Christian, made a virtue of his lack of political experience. Promising the American people, "I will never lie to you," he emphasized his distance from Washington and the political corruption of recent times.

From his inauguration, when he broke with the convention of a motorcade and walked down Pennsylvania Avenue holding hands with his wife and close adviser, Rosalynn, and their young daughter, Amy, Carter rejected the trappings of the imperial presidency and emphasized his populist, outsider appeal. But the outsider status that gained him the presidency would be one of Carter's major drawbacks as president. Though an astute policymaker, he scorned the deal making that was necessary to pass legislation in Congress.

Carter faced problems that would have challenged any leader: the economy continued to decline, energy shortages had not abated, the American people distrusted their government. More than any other American leader of the post–World War II era, Carter was willing to tell the American people things they did not want to hear. As shortages of natural gas forced schools and businesses to close during the bitterly cold winter of 1977, Carter went on television—wearing a cardigan sweater—to speak to the American people about the new era of limits and called for "sacrifice." Carter put energy conservation measures into effect at the White House and government buildings, and proposed to Congress a detailed energy plan that emphasized conservation. In the defining speech of his presidency, as the nation struggled with a sense of uncertainty and unease, Carter told Americans that the nation suffered from a crisis of the spirit. He talked about the false lures of "self-indulgence and consumption," about "paralysis and stagnation and drift." And he called for a "new commitment to the path of common purpose." But he was unable to offer practical solutions for what was then described as a national malaise.

Carter did score some noteworthy domestic accomplishments. He worked to ease burdensome government regulations without destroying consumer and worker safeguards, and created the Departments of Energy and Education. He also created environmental protections, establishing a $1.6 billion "superfund" to clean up abandoned chemical-waste sites and placing more than 100 million acres of Alaskan land under the federal government's protection as national parks, national forests, and wildlife refuges.

## ECONOMIC CRISIS

Americans' loss of confidence in their political leaders was intensified by a growing economic crisis. Since World War II, except for a few brief downturns, prosperity had been a fundamental condition of American life. A steadily rising gross national product, based largely on growing rates of productivity, had propelled large numbers of Americans into the economically comfortable middle class. Prosperity had made possible the great liberal initiatives of the 1960s and improved the lives of America's poor and elderly citizens. But in the early 1970s, that long period of economic expansion and prosperity came to an end. Almost every economic indicator drove home bad news. In 1974 alone, the gross national product dropped 2 full percentage points. Industrial production fell 9 percent. Inflation—the increase in costs of goods and services—skyrocketed, and unemployment grew.

Throughout most of the 1970s, the U.S. economy floundered in a condition that economists dubbed "stagflation": a stagnant economy characterized by high unemployment combined with out-of-control inflation (see Figure 31.1). Stagflation was almost impossible to manage with traditional economic remedies. When the federal government increased spending to stimulate the economy and so reduce unemployment, inflation grew. When the federal government tried to rein in inflation by cutting government spending or tightening the money supply, the recession deepened and unemployment rates skyrocketed.

## Stagflation and Its Causes

The causes of the economic crisis were complex. Federal management of the economy was in part to blame: President Johnson had reversed conventional economic wisdom and created inflationary pressure by insisting that the United States could have both "guns and butter," as he waged a very expensive war in Vietnam while greatly expanding domestic spending in his Great Society programs. But fundamental problems also came from America's changing role in the global economy. After World War II, with most leading industrial nations in ruins, the United States had stood alone at the pinnacle of the global economy. But the war-ravaged nations—often with major economic assistance from the United States—rebuilt their productive capacities with new, technologically advanced industrial plants. By the early 1970s, both of America's major wartime adversaries, Japan and Germany, had become major economic powers—and major competitors in global trade. In 1971, for the first time since the end of the nineteenth century, the United States imported more goods than it exported, beginning an era of American trade deficits.

American corporate actions also contributed to the growing trade imbalance. During the years of global dominance, few American companies had reinvested profits in

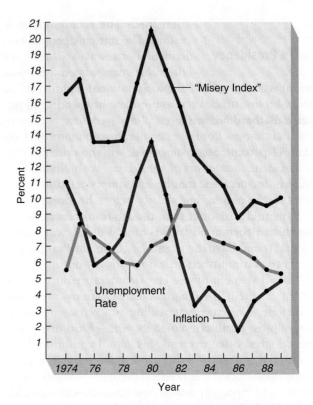

**Figure 31.1** **"Misery Index" (Unemployment Plus Inflation), 1974–1989**

Americans' economic discomfort directly determined their political behavior. When the "misery index" was high in 1976 and 1980, Americans voted for a change in presidents. When economic discomfort declined in 1984 and 1988, Ronald Reagan and George Bush were the political beneficiaries.

*(Source: Adapted from* Economic Report of the President, *1992 [Washington, D.C.: 1992], pp. 340, 365.)*

improving production techniques or educating workers. Consequently, American productivity—that is, the average output of goods per hour of labor—had begun to decline. As workers' productivity declined, however, their wages rarely did. The combination of falling productivity and high labor costs meant that American goods became more and more expensive—both for American consumers and for consumers in other nations. Even worse, without significant competition from foreign manufacturers, American companies had allowed the quality of their goods to decline. From 1966 to 1973, for example, American car and truck manufacturers had to recall almost 30 million vehicles because of serious defects.

America's global economic vulnerability was driven home by the energy crisis that began in 1973. Americans had grown up with cheap and abundant energy, and their lifestyles showed it. American passenger cars got an average of 13.4 miles per gallon in 1973, when a gallon of gas cost 38 cents (about $1.40 in 2006 dollars); neither home heating nor household appliances were designed to be energy-efficient. The country, however, depended on imported oil for almost one-third of its energy supply. When OPEC cut off oil shipments to the United States, U.S. oil prices rose 350 percent. The increases reverberated through the economy: heating costs, shipping costs, and manufacturing costs increased, and so did the cost of goods and services. Inflation jumped from 3 percent in early 1973 to 11 percent in 1974. Sales of gas-guzzling American cars plummeted as people rushed to buy energy-efficient subcompacts from Japan and Europe. American car manufacturers, stuck with machinery for producing large cars, were hit hard. GM laid off 6 percent of its domestic work force and put an even larger number on rolling unpaid leaves. As the ailing automobile industry quit buying steel, glass, and rubber, manufacturers of these goods laid off workers, too.

American political leaders tried desperately to manage the economic crisis, but their actions often exacerbated it

## Attempts to Fix the Economy

instead. As America's rising trade deficit undermined international confidence in the dollar, the Nixon administration ended the dollar's link to the gold standard; free-floating exchange rates increased the price of foreign goods in the United States and stimulated inflation. President Ford created a voluntary program, Whip Inflation Now (complete with red and white "WIN" buttons), in 1974 to encourage grassroots anti-inflation efforts. Following the tenets of monetary theory, which held that, with less money available to "chase" the supply of goods, price increases would gradually slow down, ending the inflationary spiral, Ford curbed federal spending and encouraged the Federal Reserve Board to tighten credit—and prompted the worst recession in forty years. In 1975 unemployment climbed to 8.5 percent.

Carter first attempted to bring unemployment rates down by stimulating the economy, but inflation careened out of control; he then tried to slow the economy down—and prompted a major recession during the election year of 1980. In fact, Carter's larger economic policies, including his 1978 deregulation of airline, trucking, banking, and communications industries, would eventually foster economic growth—but not soon enough. After almost a decade of decline, Americans were losing faith in the American economy and in the ability of their political leaders to manage it.

The economic crisis of the 1970s accelerated the nation's transition from an industrial to a service economy.

## Impacts of the Economic Crisis

During the 1970s, the American economy "deindustrialized." Automobile companies laid off workers. Massive steel plants shut down, leaving entire communities devastated. Other manufacturing concerns moved overseas, seeking lower labor costs and fewer government regulations. New jobs were created—27 million of them—but they were overwhelmingly in what economists called the "service sector": retail sales, restaurants, and other service providers. As heavy industries collapsed, formerly highly paid, unionized workers took jobs in the growing but not unionized service sector. These jobs—such as warehouse work or retail sales, for example—paid much lower wages and often lacked healthcare and other important benefits.

Formerly successful blue-collar workers saw their middle-class standards of life slipping away. More married women joined the work force because they had to—though some were drawn by new opportunities. Even in the best of times the economy would have been hard pressed to produce jobs for the millions of baby boomers who joined the labor market in the 1970s. Young people graduating from high school or college in the 1970s, raised with high expectations, suddenly found very limited possibilities—if they found jobs at all.

The economic crisis also helped to shift the economic and population centers of the nation. As the old industrial regions of the North and Midwest went into decline, people fled the "snow belt" or the "rust belt," speeding up the Sunbelt boom already in progress (see Map 31.1). The Sunbelt was where the jobs were. The federal government had invested heavily in the South and West during the postwar era, especially in military and defense industries, and in the infrastructures necessary for them. Never a major center for heavy manufactures, the Sunbelt was primed for the rapid growth of modern industries and services—aerospace, defense, electronics, transportation, research, banking and finance, and leisure. City and state governments competed to lure businesses and investment dollars, in part by preventing the growth of unions. Atlanta, Houston, and other southern cities marketed themselves as cosmopolitan, sophisticated, and racially tolerant; they bought sports teams and built museums.

This population shift south and west, combined with the flight of middle-class taxpayers to the suburbs, created disaster in northern and midwestern cities. New York City, close to financial collapse by late 1975, was saved only when the House and Senate Banking Committees approved federal loan guarantees. Cleveland defaulted on its debts

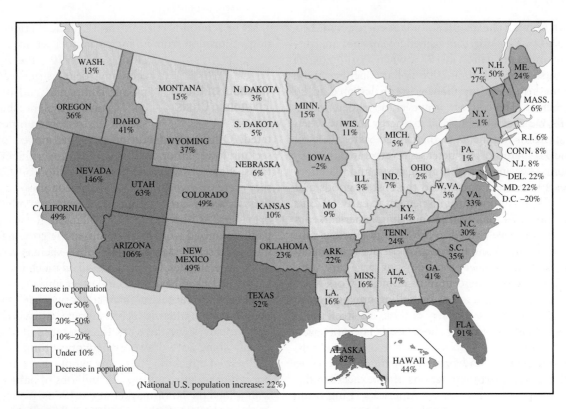

**Map 31.1    The Continued Shift to the Sunbelt in the 1970s and 1980s**

Throughout the 1970s and 1980s, Americans continued to leave economically declining areas of the North and East in pursuit of opportunity in the Sunbelt. States in the Sunbelt and in the West had the largest population increases.    *(Source: "Shift to the Sunbelt," Newsweek, September 10, 1990.)*

in 1978, the first major city to do so since Detroit declared bankruptcy in 1933.

Even as stagflation and Sunbelt growth transformed American politics, a "tax revolt" movement emerged in the rapidly growing American West. In California, inflation had driven property taxes up rapidly, hitting middle-class taxpayers hard. In this era of economic decline and post-Watergate suspicion, angry taxpayers saw government as the problem. Instead of calling for wealthy citizens and major corporations to pay a larger share of taxes, voters rebelled against taxation itself. California's Proposition 13, passed by a landslide in 1978, rolled back property taxes and restricted future increases. Within months of Proposition 13's passage, thirty-seven states cut property taxes, and twenty-eight lowered their state income-tax rates.

The impact of Proposition 13 and similar initiatives was initially cushioned by state budget surpluses, but as those surpluses turned to deficits, states cut services—

**Tax Revolts**

closing fire stations and public libraries, ending or limiting mental health services and programs for the disabled. Public schools were hit especially hard. The tax revolt movement signaled the growth of a new conservatism; voters who wanted lower taxes and smaller government would help bring Ronald Reagan to the White House in the election of 1980.

The runaway inflation of the 1970s also changed how Americans managed their money. Before this era, home mortgages and auto loans were the only kind of major debt most Americans would venture. National credit cards had become common only in the late 1960s, and few Americans—especially those who remembered the Great Depression—were willing to spend money they did not have. In the 1970s, however, thriftiness stopped making sense. Double-digit inflation rates meant double-digit declines in the purchasing power of a dollar. It was economically smarter to buy goods before their prices

**Credit and Investment**

went up—even if it meant borrowing the money. Because debt was paid off later with devalued dollars, the consumer came out ahead. In 1975 consumer debt hit a high of $167 billion; it almost doubled, to $315 billion, by 1979.

The 1970s were also the decade in which average Americans became investors rather than savers. Throughout the 1970s, because of regulations created during the Great Depression, the interest rates that banks could pay on individual savings accounts were capped. An average savings account bearing 5 percent interest actually *lost* more than 20 percent of its value from 1970 through 1980 because of inflation. That same money, invested at market rates, would have grown dramatically. Fidelity Investments, a mutual fund company, saw a business opportunity: its money market accounts combined many smaller investments to purchase large-denomination Treasury bills and certificates of deposit, thus allowing small investors to get the high interest rates normally available only to major investors. Money flooded out of passbook accounts and into money funds, and money market investments grew from $1.7 billion in 1974 to $200 billion in 1982. At the same time, deregulation of the New York Stock Exchange spawned discount brokerage houses, whose low commission rates made it affordable for middle-class investors to trade stocks.

## AN ERA OF CULTURAL TRANSFORMATION

The 1970s have been dismissed as a cultural wasteland, an era in which the nation confronted new limits without much passion or creativity. But it was during the 1970s, as Americans struggled with economic recession, governmental betrayal, and social division, that major strands of late-twentieth-century culture were developed or consolidated. The current environmental movement, the growth of technology, the rise of born-again Christianity and a "therapeutic culture," contemporary forms of sexuality and the family, and America's emphasis on diversity all have roots in this odd decade sandwiched between the political vibrancy of the 1960s and the conservatism of the 1980s.

Just as Americans were forced to confront the end of postwar prosperity, a series of ecological crises drove home the limits on natural resources and the fragility of the environment. In 1969 a major oil spill took place off the coast of Santa Barbara, California; that same year, the polluted Cuyahoga River, flowing through Cleveland, caught fire. Although the energy crisis of the 1970s was due to an oil

**Environmentalism**

▲ Celebrants of the first Earth Day, on April 22, 1970, gather in an urban park. More than 20 million Americans across the nation participated in local teach-ins, celebrations, and protests to draw attention to environmental issues. By 1990 Earth Day was celebrated globally, drawing 200 million participants from 141 countries. *(Ken Regan)*

embargo, not a scarcity of oil, it drove home the real limits of the world's supplies of oil and natural gas. In 1979 human error contributed to a nuclear accident at the Three Mile Island nuclear power plant near Harrisburg, Pennsylvania, and in 1980 President Carter declared a federal emergency at New York State's Love Canal, which had served as a dump site for a local chemical manufacturer, after it was discovered that 30 percent of local residents had suffered chromosome damage. Public activism during the 1970s produced major environmental regulations and initiatives, from the Environmental Protection Agency (EPA), created (under strong public pressure) in 1970 by the Nixon administration, to eighteen major environmental laws enacted by Congress during the decade.

When almost 20 million Americans—half of them schoolchildren—gathered in local communities to celebrate the first Earth Day on April 22, 1970, they signaled the triumph of a relatively new understanding of environmentalism. Traditional concerns about preserving "unspoiled" wilderness had joined with a new focus on "ecology," which stressed the connections between the earth and all living organisms, including humans. Central to this movement was a recognition that the earth's resources were finite and must be both conserved and protected from the consequences of human action, such as pollution. In 1971 biologist Barry Commoner insisted, "The present course of environmental degradation . . . is so serious, that, if continued, it will destroy the capability of the environment to support a reasonably civilized human society." Many of those concerned about the strain on earth's resources also identified rapid global population growth as a problem, and state public health offices frequently dispensed contraceptives as a way to stem this new "epidemic."

During these years, Americans became increasingly uneasy about the science and technology that had been

### Technology

one source of America's might. In a triumph of technology, American astronaut Neil Armstrong stepped onto the lunar surface on July 20, 1969, as people worldwide watched the grainy television transmission and heard, indistinctly, his first words— "That's one small step for a man, one giant step for mankind." But the advances that could take a man to the moon seemed unable to cope with earthbound problems of poverty, crime, pollution, and urban decay; and the failure of technological warfare to deliver victory in Vietnam came at the same time antiwar protesters were questioning the morality of using such technology. Some Americans joined a movement for "appropriate technology" and human-scale development, but the nation was profoundly dependent on complex technological systems. And it was during the 1970s that the foundation was laid for America's computer revolution. The integrated circuit was created in 1970, and by 1975 the MITS Altair 8800— operated by toggle switches that entered individual binary numbers, boasting 256 bytes of memory, and requiring about thirty hours to assemble—could be mail-ordered from Albuquerque, New Mexico.

As Americans confronted material limits, they increasingly sought spiritual fulfillment and well-being. Some

### Religion and the Therapeutic Culture

turned to religion, though not to traditional mainstream Protestantism. Methodist, Presbyterian, and Episcopalian churches all lost members during this era, while membership in evangelical and fundamentalist Christian churches grew dramatically. Protestant evangelicals, professing a personal relationship with their savior, described themselves as "born again" and emphasized the immediate, daily presence of God in their lives. Even some Catholics, such as the Mexican Americans who embraced the *cursillo* movement (a "little course" in faith), sought a more personal relationship with God. Other Americans looked to the variety of beliefs and practices described as "New Age." The New Age movement drew from and often combined versions of nonwestern spiritual and religious practices, including Zen Buddhism, yoga, and shamanism, along with insights from western psychology and a form of spiritually oriented environmentalism.

Also in the 1970s, America saw the full emergence of a "therapeutic" culture. Although some Americans were disgusted with the self-centeredness of the "Me-Decade," bestselling books by therapists and self-help gurus insisted that individual feelings offered the ultimate measure of truth; emotional honesty and self-awareness were social goods surpassing the bonds of community, friendship, or family. Self-help books with titles like *I Ain't Much Baby—But I'm All I've Got,* or *I'm OK—You're OK* (first published in 1967, it became a bestseller in the mid-1970s) made up 15 percent of all bestselling books during the decade.

One such self-help book was *The Joy of Sex* (1972), which sold 3.8 million copies in two years. Sex became

### Sexuality and the Family

much more visible in America's public culture during the 1970s, as network television loosened its regulation of sexual content. At the beginning of the 1960s, married couples in television shows were required to occupy twin beds; in the 1970s, hit television shows included *Three's Company,* a situation comedy based on the then-scandalous premise that a single man shared an apartment with two beautiful female roommates—and got away with it only by pretending to their suspicious landlord that he was gay. *Charlie's Angels,* another major television hit, capitalized on what people called the "jiggle factor," and displayed (for the time) lots of bare female flesh. A major youth fad of the era was "streaking," running naked through public places. Donna Summers's 1975 disco hit "Love to Love You Baby" contained sixteen minutes of sexual moaning. And though very few Americans participated in heterosexual orgies at New York City's Plato's Retreat, many knew about them through a *Time* magazine feature story.

Sexual behaviors had also changed. The seventies were the era of singles bars and gay bathhouses, and some Americans led sexual lives virtually unrestrained by the old rules. For most Americans, however, the major changes brought about by the "sexual revolution" were a broader public acceptance of premarital sex and a limited acceptance of homosexuality, especially among more educated Americans. More and more heterosexual young people "lived together" without marriage during the 1970s; the census bureau even coined the term *POSSLQ* ("persons of opposite sex sharing living quarters") to describe the relationship. When First Lady Betty Ford said on *60 Minutes* that she would not be surprised if her then-seventeen-year-old daughter Susan began a sexual relationship, it was clear that much had changed in the course of a decade.

Changes in sexual mores and in the roles possible for women helped to alter the shape of the American family as well. Both men and women married later than in recent decades, and American women had fewer children. By the end of the 1970s, the birth rate had dropped almost 40 percent from its 1957 peak. Almost one-quarter of young single women in 1980 said that they did not plan to have children. And a steadily rising percentage of babies were born to unmarried women, as the number of families headed by never-married women rose 400 percent during the 1970s. The divorce rate also rose, in part because states implemented "no fault" divorce, which did not require evidence of adultery, physical cruelty, abandonment, or other wrongdoing. Although families seemed less stable in the 1970s than in the previous postwar decades, Americans also developed a greater acceptance of various family forms (the blended family of television's *Brady Bunch,* for example), and many young couples sought greater equality between the sexes in romantic relationships or marriages.

The racial-justice and identity movements of the late 1960s and 1970s made all Americans more aware of differences among the nation's peoples—

**Diversity**

an awareness made stronger by the great influx of new immigrants, not from Europe but from Latin America and Asia. It was a challenge, however, to figure out how to acknowledge the new importance of "difference" in public policy. The solution developed in the 1970s was the idea of "diversity." Difference was not a problem but a strength; the nation should not seek policies to diminish differences among its peoples but should instead seek to foster the "diversity" of its schools, workplaces, and public culture.

One major move in this direction came in the 1978 Supreme Court decision *Regents of the University of California v. Bakke.* Allan Bakke, a thirty-three-year-old white man with a strong academic record, had been denied admission to the medical school of the University of California at Davis. Bakke sued, charging that he had been denied "equal protection" of the law because the medical school's affirmative-action program reserved 16 percent

of its slots for racial-minority candidates, who were held to lower standards than other applicants. The case set off furious debates nationwide over the legitimacy of affirmative action. In 1978 the Supreme Court, in a split decision, decided in favor of Bakke. Four justices argued that any race-based decision violated the Civil Rights Act of 1964; four saw affirmative-action programs as constitutionally acceptable remedies for past discrimination. The deciding vote, though for Bakke, contained an important qualification. A "diverse student body," Justice Lewis Powell wrote, is "a constitutionally permissible goal for an institution of higher education." To achieve the positive quality of "diversity," educational institutions could take race into account when making decisions about admissions.

## RENEWED COLD WAR AND MIDDLE EAST CRISIS

When Jimmy Carter took office in 1977, he asked Americans to put their "inordinate fear of Communism" behind them. With reformist zeal, Carter vowed to reduce the U.S. military presence overseas, to cut back arms sales (which had reached the unprecedented height of $10 billion per year under Nixon), and to slow the nuclear arms race. At the time, more than 400,000 American military personnel were stationed abroad, the United States had military links with ninety-two nations, and the CIA was active on every continent. Carter promised to avoid new Vietnams through an activist preventive diplomacy in the Third World and to give more attention to environmental issues as well as relations between rich and poor nations. He especially determined to improve human rights abroad—the freedom to vote, worship, travel, speak out, and get a fair trial. Like his predecessors, however, Carter identified revolutionary nationalism as a threat to America's prominent global position.

Carter spoke and acted inconsistently, in part because in the post-Vietnam years no consensus existed in foreign

**Carter's Divided Administration**

policy and in part because his advisers squabbled among themselves. One source of the problem was the stern-faced Zbigniew Brzezinski, a Polish-born political scientist who became Carter's national security adviser. An old-fashioned Cold Warrior, Brzezinski blamed foreign crises on Soviet expansionism. Carter gradually listened more to Brzezinski than to Secretary of State Cyrus Vance, an experienced public servant who advocated quiet diplomacy. Vocal neoconservative intellectuals, such as Norman Podhoretz, editor of *Commentary* magazine, and the Committee on the Present Danger, founded in 1976 by such Cold War hawks as Paul Nitze, who had composed NSC-68 in 1950, criticized Carter for any relaxation of the Cold War and demanded that he jettison détente.

Nitze got his wish. Under Carter détente deteriorated, and the Cold War deepened. But it did not happen right away. Initially, Carter maintained fairly good relations with Moscow and was able to score some foreign policy successes around the world. In Panama, where citizens longed for control over the Canal Zone, which they believed had been wrongfully taken from them in 1903, Carter reenergized negotiations that had begun after anti-American riots in Panama in 1964. The United States signed two treaties with Panama in 1977. One provided for the return of the Canal Zone to Panama in 2000, and the other guaranteed the United States the right to defend the canal after that time. With conservatives denouncing the deal as a sellout, the Senate narrowly endorsed both agreements in 1978. The majority agreed with Carter's argu-

ment that relinquishing the canal was the best way to improve U.S. relations with Latin America.

Important though it was, the Panama agreement paled next to what must be considered the crowning accomplishment of Carter's presidency: the Camp David accords, the first mediated peace treaty between Israel and an Arab nation. Through tenacious personal diplomacy at a Camp David, Maryland, meeting in September 1978 with Egyptian and Israeli leaders, the president persuaded Israel and Egypt to agree to a peace treaty, gained Israel's promise to withdraw from the Sinai Peninsula, and forged a provisional agreement that provided for continued negotiations on the future status of the Palestinian people living in the occupied territories of Jordan's West Bank and Egypt's Gaza Strip (see Map 33.2). Other Arab states denounced the agreement for not requiring Israel to relin-

**Camp David Accords**

▲ Egyptian president Anwar al-Sadat, U.S. President Jimmy Carter, and Israeli Prime Minister Menachem Begin sit together outside the White House on March 26, 1979, ready to sign the peace treaty based on the Camp David Accords of September 1978. The treaty ended the long-standing state of war between Egypt and Israel. *(© Wally McNamee/CORBIS)*

quish all occupied territories and for not guaranteeing a Palestinian homeland. But the accord at least ended warfare along one frontier in that troubled area of the world. On March 26, 1979, Israeli prime minister Menachem Begin and Egyptian president Anwar al-Sadat signed the formal treaty on the White House lawn, with a beaming Carter looking on.

Carter's moment of diplomatic triumph did not last long, for soon other foreign policy problems pressed in.

### Soviet Invasion of Afghanistan

Relations with Moscow had deteriorated, with U.S. and Soviet officials sparring over the Kremlin's reluctance to lift restrictions on Jewish emigration from the USSR, and over the Soviet decision to deploy new intermediate-range ballistic missiles aimed at western Europe. Then, in December 1979, the Soviets invaded Afghanistan. A remote, mountainous country, Afghanistan had been a source of great-power conflict because of its strategic position. In the nineteenth century it was the fulcrum of the Great Game, the contest between Britain and Russia for control of Central Asia and India. Following World War II, Afghanistan settled into a pattern of ethnic and factional squabbling; few in the West paid attention until the country spiraled into anarchy in the 1970s. In late 1979, the Red Army bludgeoned its way into Afghanistan to shore up a faltering communist government under siege by Muslim rebels. Moscow officials calculated that they could be in and out of the country before anyone really noticed, including the Americans.

To their dismay, Carter not only noticed but reacted forcefully. He suspended shipments of grain and high-technology equipment to the Soviet Union, withdrew a major new arms control treaty from Senate consideration, and initiated an international boycott of the 1980 Summer Olympics in Moscow. He also secretly authorized the CIA to distribute aid, including arms and military support, to the Mujahidin (Islamic guerillas) fighting the communist government and sanctioned military aid to their backer, Pakistan. Announcing the Carter Doctrine, the president asserted that the United States would intervene, unilaterally and militarily if necessary, should Soviet aggression threaten the petroleum-rich Persian Gulf. This string of measures represented a victory of the hawkish Brzezinski over the pro-détente Vance. Indeed, Carter seemed more ardent than Brzezinski in his denunciations of the Kremlin. He warned aides that the Soviets, unless checked, would likely attack elsewhere in the Middle East, but declassified documents confirm what critics at the time said: that the Soviet invasion was limited in scope and did not presage a push southwest to the Persian Gulf.

### Iranian Hostage Crisis

Carter's aggressive rhetoric on Afghanistan may be partly explained by the fact that he simultaneously faced a tough foreign policy test in neighboring Iran. The shah, long the recipient of American favor, had been driven from his throne by a broad coalition of Iranians, many of whom resented that their traditional ways had been dislocated by the shah's attempts at modernization. American analysts failed to perceive the volatility that this dislocation generated and were caught off guard when riots led by anti-American Muslim clerics erupted in late 1978. The shah went into exile, and in April 1979 Islamic revolutionaries, led by the Ayatollah Khomeini, an elderly cleric who denounced the United States as the stronghold of capitalism and western materialism, proclaimed a Shi'ite Islamic Republic. In November, with the exiled shah in the United States for medical treatment, mobs stormed the U.S. embassy in Teheran. They took American personnel as hostages, demanding the return of the shah to stand trial. The Iranians eventually released a few American prisoners, but fifty-two others languished under Iranian guard. They suffered solitary confinement, beatings, and terrifying mock executions.

Unable to gain the hostages' freedom through diplomatic intermediaries, Carter said that he felt "the same kind of impotence that a powerful person feels when his child is kidnapped." He took steps to isolate Iran economically, freezing Iranian assets in the United States. When the hostage takers paraded their blindfolded captives before television cameras, Americans felt taunted and humiliated. In April 1980, frustrated and at a low ebb in public opinion polls, Carter broke diplomatic relations with Iran and ordered a daring rescue mission. But the rescue effort miscarried after equipment failure in the sandy Iranian desert, and during the hasty withdrawal two aircraft collided, killing eight American soldiers. The hostages were not freed until January 1981, after Carter left office and the United States unfroze Iranian assets and promised not to intervene again in Iran's internal affairs.

The Iranian revolution, together with the rise of the Mujahidin in Afghanistan, signified the emergence of Islamic fundamentalism as a force in world affairs. Socialism and capitalism, the great answers that the two superpowers offered to the problems of modernization, had failed to solve the problems in Central Asia and the Middle East, let alone satisfy the passions and expectations they had aroused. Nor had they assuaged deeply held feelings of humiliation generated by centuries of western domination. As a result, Islamic orthodoxy found growing support for its message: that secular leaders such as Nasser in Egypt

▲ An Iranian is pictured reading a newspaper not long before mobs in Teheran stormed the American embassy and took more than fifty Americans hostage. Behind him are posters mocking U.S. President Carter and denouncing the shah. *(Picture Research Consultants & Archives)*

and the shah in Iran had taken their peoples down the wrong path, necessitating a return to conservative Islamic values and Islamic law. The Iranian revolution in particular expressed a deep and complex mixture of discontents within many Islamic societies.

U.S. officials took some consolation from the fact that Iran faced growing friction from the avowedly secular government in neighboring Iraq. Ruled by the Ba'athist Party (a secular and quasi-socialist party with branches in several Arab countries), Iraq had already won favor in Washington for its ruthless pursuit and execution of Iraqi communists. When a Ba'athist leader named Saddam Hussein took over as president of Iraq in 1979 and began threatening the Teheran government, U.S. officials were not displeased; to them, Saddam seemed likely to offset the Iranian danger in the Persian Gulf region. As border clashes between Iraqi and Iranian forces escalated in 1980, culminating in the outbreak of large-scale war in September, Washington policymakers took an officially neutral position but soon tilted toward Iraq.

### Rise of Saddam Hussein

Jimmy Carter's record in foreign affairs sparked considerable criticism from both left and right. He had earned some diplomatic successes in the Middle East, Africa, and Latin America, but the revived Cold War and the prolonged Iranian hostage crisis had hurt the administration politically. Contrary to Carter's goals, more American military personnel were stationed overseas in 1980 than in 1976; the defense budget climbed and sales of arms abroad grew to $15.3 billion in 1980. On human rights, the president proved inconsistent. He practiced a double standard by applying the human-rights test to some nations (the Soviet Union, Argentina, and Chile) but not to U.S. allies (South Korea, the shah's Iran, and the Philippines). Still, if inconsistent, Carter's human-rights policy was not unimportant: he gained the release and saved the lives of some political prisoners, and he popularized and institutionalized concern for human rights around the world. But Carter did not satisfy Americans who wanted a post-Vietnam restoration of the economic dominance and military edge that the United States once enjoyed. He lost the 1980 election to the hawkish Ronald Reagan, former Hollywood actor and governor of California.

# Legacy FOR A PEOPLE AND A NATION

## The All-Volunteer Force

On June 30, 1973, the United States ended its military draft. From that date on, the nation relied on an all-volunteer force (AVF). The draft had been in effect, with only a brief interruption in the late 1940s, since the United States had begun to mobilize in 1940 for World War II. Never before had the United States had a peacetime draft. But as the country took on new roles of global leadership after the war, and as the dark shadow of the Cold War grew, the draft became an accepted part of American life. In 1973 more than 50 million American men had been inducted into the nation's military since the end of World War II.

Richard Nixon had promised to end the draft during his presidential campaign in 1968. It was an astute political move, for the draft had become a focus for widespread protest during the failing—and increasingly unpopular—war in Vietnam. Ending the draft was not feasible during the war, but Nixon kept his promise and began planning for an all-volunteer force as soon as he took office. Many Americans supported the shift because they believed it would be more difficult for a president to send an all-volunteer military to war because he or she could not rely on a draft to compel people to fight a war they did not support.

The military, however, was not enthusiastic about Nixon's plan. The war in Vietnam had shattered morale and left much of the nation's military—particularly the army—in disarray. Public opinion of the military was at an all-time low. How were they to attract volunteers?

The army, as the largest of the four services, had to draw the largest number of volunteers. It faced a difficult task. Reform was the first step: getting rid of make-work ("chickenshit") tasks and enhancing military professionalism. The army also turned to state-of-the-art market research and advertising. Discovering that many young men were afraid they would lose their individuality in the army, the army's advertising agency launched a new campaign. Instead of the traditional poster of Uncle Sam proclaiming, "I Want You," the new volunteer army claimed, "Today's Army Wants to Join You."

The AVF had a rough beginning. The army had to recruit about 225,000 new soldiers each year (compared to about 80,000 per year in 2006) and had difficulty attracting enough capable young men and women. Within a decade, however, America's military boasted a higher rate of high school graduates and higher mental "quality" (as measured by standardized tests) than the comparable age population in the United States. During an era of relative peace, many young men and women found opportunities for education and training through military service. Military service was particularly attractive to capable but economically disadvantaged young people, a high percentage of whom were African American.

The move to a volunteer force had major legacies for the American people. The military understood that, without a draft, it would have to turn to women in order to fill the ranks. The proportion of women in the military increased from 1.9 percent in 1972 to about 15 percent currently, and the roles they were allowed to fill widened dramatically. At the same time, the nation's understanding of military service changed. No longer was it seen as an obligation of (male) citizenship. Instead, it was a voluntary choice. The implications seemed less urgent in peacetime. But in time of war, the legacy of the move to an AVF is highly charged. What does it mean when only a small number of volunteers bears the burden of warfare and most Americans never have to consider the possibility of going to war?

## SUMMARY

The 1970s were a difficult decade for Americans. From the crisis year of 1968 on, it seemed that Americans were ever more polarized—over the war in Vietnam, over the best path to racial equality and equal rights for all Americans, over the meaning of equality, and over the meaning of America itself. As many activists for social justice turned to "cultural nationalism," or group-identity politics, notions of American unity seemed a relic of the past. And though a new women's movement won great victories against sex discrimination, a powerful opposition movement arose in response.

During this era, Americans became increasingly disillusioned with politics and presidential leadership. Richard Nixon's abuses of power in the Watergate scandal and cover-up, combined with growing awareness that the administration had lied to its citizens repeatedly about America's role in Vietnam, produced a profound suspicion of government. A major economic crisis ended the post–World War II expansion that had fueled the growth of the middle class and social reform programs alike, and Americans struggled with the psychological impact of a new age of limits and with the effects of stagflation: rising unemployment rates coupled with high rates of inflation.

Overseas, a string of setbacks—defeat in Vietnam, the oil embargo, and the Iranian hostage crisis—signified the waning of American power during the 1970s. The nation seemed increasingly unable to have its own way on the world stage. Détente with the Soviet Union had flourished for a time, as both superpowers sought to adjust to the new geopolitical realities; however, by 1980 Cold War tensions were again on the rise. But if the nation's most important bilateral relationship remained that with the USSR, an important change, not always perceptible at the time, was under way: more and more, the focus of U.S. foreign policy was on the Middle East.

Plagued by political, economic, and foreign policy crises, America ended the 1970s bruised, battered, and frustrated. The age of liberalism was long over; the elements for a conservative resurgence were in place.

## SUGGESTIONS FOR FURTHER READING

Donald T. Critchlow, *Phyllis Schlafly and Grassroots Conservatism: A Woman's Crusade* (2005)

Daniel Ellsberg, *Secrets: A Memoir of Vietnam and the Pentagon Papers* (2002)

David Farber, *Taken Hostage: The Iran Hostage Crisis and America's First Encounter with Radical Islam* (2004)

Ian F. Haney-Lopez, *Racism on Trial: The Chicano Fight for Justice* (2003)

Richard Reeves, *President Nixon: Alone in the White House* (2001)

Ruth Rosen, *The World Split Open: How the Modern Women's Movement Changed America* (2000)

Hal Rothman, *The Greening of a Nation: Environmentalism in the U.S. Since 1945* (1997)

Bruce Schulman, *The Seventies: The Great Shift in American Culture, Society, and Politics* (2001)

John D. Skrentny, *The Minority Rights Revolution* (2002)

Odd Arne Westad, *The Global Cold War: Third World Interventions and the Making of Our Times* (2005)

*For a more extensive list for further reading, go to* college.hmco.com/pic/norton8e.

# Conservatism Revived *1980-1992*

It was hot and there was a lot of desert," Luisa Orellana remembered, as she described crossing the border from Mexico into the United States in the early 1980s. "All of us started running, each one with a child in our arms. My mother was praying the rosary the whole time and suddenly the sky opened up and started raining. It rained so hard we couldn't see where we were going, but it helped because the Border Patrol couldn't see us either."

Three months earlier Luisa's father had been murdered. Tanis Stanislaus Orellana had worked in El Salvador with Archbishop Óscar Romero, the most powerful critic of the ruling military dictatorship whose death squads were responsible for the murder of about thirty thousand Salvadorans between 1979 and 1981. In 1980 Romero had been assassinated—shot, publicly, as he consecrated the Eucharist during Mass. The civil war that followed lasted twelve years; an estimated 1 million Salvadorans sought refuge in other nations from the death squads and the torture, rape, and murder that had become commonplace in their own country.

Luisa's father, along with other church officials, had been targeted. After his murder, his widow took her children, including teenage Luisa, and fled their home, leaving behind almost everything they owned. They took the bus through Guatemala, crossed illegally into Mexico, and, given shelter by one church after another, made their way from Chiapas to Mexico City to Agua Prieta, on the U.S.-Mexico border.

From Agua Prieta, Luisa and her family ran for two miles through blinding rain. They crossed into Douglas, Arizona, cold, wet, hungry, and scared, seeking refuge. They were met there by members of the Sanctuary movement, Americans who believed that the U.S. government's refugee policy, which offered asylum to those who fled violent repression and the threat of death or torture, must include those who escaped the deadly

◄ Social worker Sarah Martinez assisted refugees from Central America at Los Angeles's Rescate Refugee Center during the 1980s. Martinez was also a refugee; she fled her homeland of El Salvador after a Salvadoran death squad murdered her husband, a university professor, and she was imprisoned and tortured. *(AP Images)*

## CHRONOLOGY

**1980** ■ Reagan elected president

**1981** ■ AIDS first observed in United States
  ■ Economic problems continue; prime interest rate reaches 21.5 percent
  ■ Reagan breaks air traffic controllers' strike
  ■ "Reaganomics" plan of budget and tax cuts approved by Congress

**1982** ■ Unemployment reaches 10.8 percent, highest rate since Great Depression
  ■ ERA dies after Stop-ERA campaign prevents ratification in key states

**1983** ■ Reagan introduces SDI
  ■ Terrorists kill U.S. marines in Lebanon
  ■ U.S. invasion of Grenada

**1984** ■ Reagan aids contras despite congressional ban
  ■ Economic recovery; unemployment rate drops and economy grows without inflation
  ■ Reagan reelected
  ■ Gorbachev promotes reforms in USSR

**1986** ■ Iran-contra scandal erupts

**1987** ■ Stock market drops 508 points in one day
  ■ Palestinian *intifada* begins

**1988** ■ George H. W. Bush elected president

**1989** ■ Tiananmen Square massacre in China
  ■ Berlin Wall torn down
  ■ U.S. troops invade Panama
  ■ Gulf between rich and poor at highest point since 1920s

**1990** ■ Americans with Disabilities Act passed
  ■ Communist regimes in eastern Europe collapse
  ■ Iraq invades Kuwait
  ■ South Africa begins to dismantle apartheid

**1991** ■ Persian Gulf War
  ■ USSR dissolves into independent states
  ■ United States enters recession

**1992** ■ Annual federal budget deficit reaches high of $300 billion at end of Bush presidency

The originators of the U.S. Sanctuary movement used church networks and human rights groups throughout Central America to investigate and verify the refugees' stories of rape, torture, and murder. Faced with the human toll of such violence, they believed it necessary to protect human rights and to save those they could from torture and death. Many members of the Sanctuary movement belonged to faith-based communities, although secular institutions, including public and private universities and the state of New Mexico, also participated. Some members of the movement went to prison for their work, charged with transporting or harboring fugitives.

Luisa and her family went from the sanctuary offered by Tucson churches, which were at the center of the movement, to live in the basement of a Catholic church in Spokane, Washington. In 1989 the U.S. government granted protection and work permits to the Central American refugees who had sought refuge in the United States. Luisa stayed in the state of Washington, where she became a teacher of English as a second language. When she looks back to the Sanctuary movement and the people who helped her family, she says, "They were like saints. They risked their lives to save ours."

Luisa Orellana and her family were part of the "new immigration" that began in the early 1970s and grew throughout the 1980s, as record numbers of immigrants came to the United States from Asia, Mexico, Central and South America, and the Caribbean. These immigrants came under a wide range of circumstances; many from Central America, Vietnam, the Soviet Union, and Cuba were political refugees granted asylum in the United States. The Orellanas found safety and peace in the United States, but not all immigrants—or all Americans—fared so well in the 1980s. The decade saw increasing divisions between rich and poor in America. A host of social problems—drugs, violence, homelessness, the growing AIDS epidemic—made life even more difficult for the urban poor. But for those on the other side of the economic divide, the 1980s were an era of luxury and ostentation. One of the most poignant images from the time was of a homeless man huddled just outside the Reagan White House—the two Americas, divided by a widening gulf.

The election of Ronald Reagan in 1980 began a twelve-year period of Republican rule, as Reagan was

civil wars that ravaged much of Central America in the 1980s. Officially, however, the U.S. government designated them "economic refugees" and denied them asylum.

▲ On a snowy November day, a homeless man makes his bed on park benches in Lafayette Square, across the street from the White House. This 1987 photograph symbolized the stark contrasts between dire poverty and great wealth in 1980s America. *(© Corbis-Bettmann)*

government oversight, and taxpayers paid the bill for bailouts. By the end of the Reagan-Bush era, a combination of tax cuts and massive increases in defense spending left a budget deficit five times larger than when Reagan took office.

The most dramatic events of the Reagan-Bush years were not domestic, however, but international. In the span of a decade, the Cold War intensified drastically and then ended. The key figure in the intensification was Reagan, who entered office promising to reassert America's military might and stand up to the Soviet Union, and he delivered on both counts. The key figure in ending the Cold War was Soviet leader Mikhail Gorbachev, who came to power in 1985 determined to address the USSR's long-term economic decline and needed a more amicable superpower relationship to do so. Gorbachev, though no revolutionary—he hoped to reform the Soviet system, not eradicate it—lost control of events as a wave of revolutions in eastern Europe toppled one communist regime after another. In 1991 the Soviet Union itself disappeared, and the United States found itself the world's lone superpower. The Persian Gulf War of that same year demonstrated America's unrivaled world power, and also the unprecedented importance of the Middle East in U.S. foreign policy.

- Ronald Reagan, campaigning for president in 1984, told voters, "It's morning again in America." How would Americans from different backgrounds judge the accuracy of his claim?

- What issues, beliefs, backgrounds, and economic realities divided Americans in the 1980s, and how do those divisions shape the culture and politics of contemporary America?

- Why did the Cold War intensify and then wane during the decade of the 1980s?

succeeded by his vice president, George Bush, in 1988. Reagan was a popular president who seemed to restore the confidence and optimism that had been shaken by the social, economic, and political crises of the 1970s. Throughout the 1980s, Reagan drew support from a wide variety of Americans: wealthy people who liked his pro-business economic policies; the religious New Right who sought the creation of "God's America"; white middle- and working-class Americans attracted by Reagan's charisma and his embrace of "old-fashioned" values.

Reagan supported social issues that were important to the New Right: he was anti-abortion; he embraced causes such as prayer in schools; he reversed the GOP's position in support of the Equal Rights Amendment, which would expire in 1983 after the necessary three-quarters of U.S. states failed to approve it. Most important, Reagan appointed judges to the Supreme Court and to the federal bench whose judicial rulings strengthened social-conservative agendas. Nonetheless, the Reagan administration focused primarily on the agendas of political and economic conservatives: reducing the size and power of the federal government and creating favorable conditions for business and industry. The U.S. economy recovered from the stagflation that had plagued the nation in the 1970s, and through much of the 1980s, it boomed. But corruption flourished in financial institutions freed from

## REAGAN AND THE CONSERVATIVE RESURGENCE

The 1970s had been a hard decade for Americans: defeat in Vietnam; the resignation of a president in disgrace; the energy crisis; economic "stagflation" and the Iranian hostage crisis. In the election year of 1980, President Carter's public approval rating stood at 21 percent, even lower than

Richard Nixon's during the depths of Watergate. The nation was divided and dispirited as people who had grown accustomed to seemingly endless economic growth and unquestioned world power confronted new limits at home and abroad. The time was ripe for a challenge to Carter's presidential leadership, to the Democratic Party, and to the liberal approaches that had, in the main, governed the United States since Franklin Roosevelt's New Deal.

In 1980 several conservative Republican politicians ran for the White House. Foremost among them was

### Ronald Reagan

Ronald Reagan, former movie star and two-term governor of California. In the 1940s, as president of the Screen Actors Guild in Hollywood, Reagan had been a New Deal Democrat. But in the 1950s, as a corporate spokesman for General Electric, he became increasingly conservative. In 1964 Reagan's televised speech in support of Republican presidential candidate Barry Goldwater catapulted him to the forefront of conservative politics. America, Reagan said, had come to "a time for choosing" between free enterprise and big government, between individual liberty and "the ant heap of totalitarianism."

Elected governor of California just two years later, Reagan became well known for his right-wing rhetoric: America should "level Vietnam, pave it, paint stripes on it, and make a parking lot out of it," Reagan claimed. And in 1969, when student protesters occupied "People's Park" near the University of California in Berkeley, he threatened a "bloodbath" and dispatched National Guard troops in full riot gear. Reagan was often pragmatic, however, about policy decisions. He denounced welfare but presided over reform of the state's social welfare bureaucracy. And he signed one of the nation's most liberal abortion laws.

In the 1980 election, Reagan, in stark contrast to incumbent Jimmy Carter, offered an optimistic vision for America's future. With his

### The New Conservative Coalition

Hollywood charm and strong conservative credentials, he succeeded in forging very different sorts of American conservatives into a new political coalition. Reagan built on a natural constituency of political conservatives. These strong anticommunists wanted to strengthen national defense; they also believed the federal government should play a more limited role in the nation's domestic life and wished to roll back the liberal programs begun under the New Deal in the 1930s and the Great Society in the 1960s. Reagan also reached out to less ideologically oriented economic conservatives, gaining their support by promising economic deregulation and tax policies that would benefit corporations, wealthy investors, and entrepreneurs. He

also attracted a relatively new cohort of neoconservatives, a small but influential group composed primarily of academics and intellectuals, many of them former Democrats who believed the party had lost its way after Vietnam and who rejected the old conservatism as backward looking. The neoconservatives took particular interest in foreign policy and embraced the Reagan campaign's aggressively anti-Soviet posture.

In a major accomplishment, Reagan managed to unite these political, economic, and neoconservatives with two new constituencies. He tapped into the sentiments that fueled the tax revolt movement of the 1970s, drawing voters from traditionally Democratic constituencies, such as labor unions and urban ethnic groups. Many middle- and working-class whites resented their hard-earned money's going to what they saw as tax-funded welfare for people who did not work; some had reacted angrily to government programs, such as busing children to achieve racial integration of schools, meant to combat racial inequities. Many also thought that Reagan's joke that there was nothing more frightening than finding a government official on the doorstep saying, "I'm from the government and I'm here to help," rang true. These "Reagan Democrats" found the Republican critique of tax-funded social programs and "big government" appealing, even though Reagan's proposed economic policies would benefit the wealthy at their expense.

Finally, in the largest leap, Reagan tied these groups to the religiously based New Right, an increasingly powerful movement of social conservatives. "When political conservative leaders began to . . . strike an alliance with social conservatives—the pro-life people, the anti-ERA people, the evangelical and born-again Christians, the people concerned about gay rights, prayer in the schools, sex in the movies or whatever," explained conservative fundraiser Richard Viguerie, "that's when this whole movement began to come alive."

On election day, Reagan and his running mate, George Bush, claimed victory with 51 percent of the popular vote.

### Reagan's Conservative Agenda

Jimmy Carter carried only six states. Reagan's victory in 1980 began more than a decade of Republican power in Washington: Reagan served two terms as president, followed by his vice president, George Bush, who was elected as Reagan's successor in 1988. Reagan, as much as any president since Franklin Roosevelt, defined the era over which he presided.

Reagan, as president, was not especially focused on the details of governing or the specifics of policies and programs. When outgoing president Jimmy Carter briefed him on urgent issues of foreign and domestic policy, Rea-

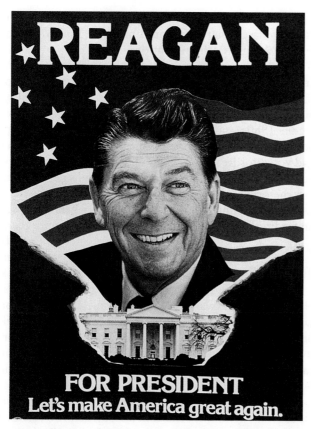

**FOR PRESIDENT**
**Let's make America great again.**

▲ Ronald Reagan, the Republican presidential candidate in 1980, campaigned for "family values," an aggressive anti-Soviet foreign and military policy, and tax cuts. He also exuded optimism and appealed to Americans' patriotism. This poster issued by the Republican National Committee included Reagan's favorite campaign slogan, "Let's make America great again." *(Collection of David J. and Janice L. Frent)*

gan listened politely but took not a single note and asked no questions. Critics argued that his lack of knowledge could prove dangerous—as when he insisted that intercontinental ballistic missiles carrying nuclear warheads could be called back once launched, or when he said that "approximately 80 percent of our air pollution stems from hydrocarbons released by vegetation."

But supporters insisted that Reagan was a great president in large part because he focused on the big picture. When he spoke to the American people, he offered what seemed to be simple truths—and he did it with the straightforwardness of a true believer and the warmth and humor of an experienced actor. Although many—even among Reagan supporters—winced at his willingness to reduce complex policy issues to simple (and often misleading) stories, Reagan was to most Americans the "Great Communicator." He won admiration for his courage after he

was seriously wounded in an assassination attempt just sixty-nine days into his presidency. Reagan quipped to doctors preparing to remove the bullet lodged near his heart, "I hope you're all Republicans."

Most important, Reagan had a clear vision for America's future. He and his advisers wanted nothing less than to roll back the liberalism of the past fifty years that had made government responsible for the health of the nation's economy and for the social welfare of its citizens. In the words of David Stockman, a Reagan appointee who headed the Office of Management and Budget, the administration meant to "create a minimalist government" and sever "the umbilical cords of dependency that run from Washington to every nook and cranny of the nation."

Reagan, like traditional conservatives, believed that America's social problems could not be solved by the federal government. But he also tapped into a broader, and less coherent, backlash against the social policies and programs of the Great Society. Many Americans who struggled to make ends meet during the economic crises of the 1970s and early 1980s resented paying taxes that, they believed, went to fund government "handouts" to people who did not work. Lasting racial tensions also fueled public resentment: Reagan fed a stereotype of welfare recipients as unwed, black, teenage mothers who kept having babies to collect larger checks. Even before he became president, Reagan played to these resentments with fabricated tales of a Chicago "welfare queen" who collected government checks under eighty different false names.

In 1981 the administration cut funding for social welfare programs by $25 billion. But "welfare" (Aid to Families with Dependent Children and food stamp programs) was a small part of the budget compared with Social Security and Medicare—social welfare programs that benefited Americans of all income levels, not just the poor. Major budget cuts for these popular, broadly based programs proved impossible. The Reagan administration did shrink the *proportion* of the federal budget devoted to social welfare programs (including Social Security and Medicare) from 28 to 22 percent by the late 1980s—but only because of a $1.2 trillion increase in defense spending.

Reagan also attacked federal environmental, health, and safety regulations that he believed reduced business profits and discouraged economic growth. Administration officials claimed that removing the stifling hand of government regulation would restore the energy and creativity of America's free-market

**Attacks on Social Welfare Programs**

**Pro-Business Policies and the Environment**

system. However, they did not so much end government's role as deploy government power to aid corporate America. The president went so far as to appoint opponents of federal regulations to head agencies charged with enforcing them—letting foxes guard the chicken coop, critics charged.

Environmentalists were appalled when Reagan appointed James Watt, a well-known antienvironmentalist, as secretary of the interior. Watt was a leader in the "Sagebrush Rebellion," which sought the return of publicly owned lands in the West, such as national forests, from federal to state control. Land control issues were complicated: the federal government controlled more than half of western lands—including 83 percent of the land in Nevada, 66 percent in Utah, and 50 percent in Wyoming—and many westerners believed that eastern policymakers did not understand the realities of western life. But states' ability to control land within their borders was not the sole issue; Watt and his group wanted to open western public lands to private businesses for logging, mining, and ranching.

Watt also dismissed the need to protect national resources and public wilderness lands for future generations, telling members of Congress during his 1981 Senate confirmation hearing, "I don't know how many generations we can count on until the Lord returns." As interior secretary, Watt allowed private corporations to acquire oil, mineral, and timber rights to federal lands for minuscule payments. He was forced to resign in 1983 after he dismissively referred to a federal advisory panel as "a black . . . a woman, two Jews, and a cripple." Even before Watt's resignation, his appointment had backfired, as his actions reenergized the nation's environmental movement and even provoked opposition from business leaders who understood that uncontrolled strip-mining and clear-cut logging of western lands could destroy lucrative tourism and recreation industries in western states.

As part of its pro-business agenda, the Reagan administration undercut organized labor's ability to negotiate wages and working conditions. Union power was already waning; labor union membership declined in the 1970s as jobs in heavy industry disappeared, and efforts to unionize the high-growth electronics and service sectors of the economy had not succeeded. Reagan's policies made hard times for unions worse. Setting the tone for his administration, in August 1981 Reagan intervened in a strike by the Professional Air Traffic Controllers Organization (PATCO). The air traffic controllers—federal employees, for whom striking was illegal—had walked out in protest over working conditions that they believed compromised the safety of American air travel. Only forty-

**Attacks on Organized Labor**

eight hours into the strike, Reagan fired the 11,350 strikers and stipulated that they could never be rehired by the Federal Aviation Administration.

With the support of an anti-union secretary of labor and appointees to the National Labor Relations Board who consistently voted for management and against labor, businesses took an increasingly hard line with labor during the 1980s, and unions failed to mount an effective opposition. Yet an estimated 44 percent of union families had voted for Reagan in 1980, drawn to his geniality, espousal of old-fashioned values, and vigorous anticommunist rhetoric.

Although much of Reagan's domestic agenda focused on traditional conservative political and economic goals, the New Right and its agenda played an increasingly important role in Reagan-era social policy. It is surprising that the strongly religious New Right was drawn to Reagan, a divorced man without strong ties to religion or, seemingly, his own children. But the non-church-going Reagan lent his support to New Right social issues: he endorsed the anti-abortion cause, and his White House issued a report supporting prayer in public schools.

**The New Right**

Reagan's judicial nominations also pleased the religious New Right. The Senate, in a bipartisan vote, refused to confirm Supreme Court nominee Robert Bork after eighty-seven hours of antagonistic hearings. Congress eventually confirmed Anthony M. Kennedy instead. Reagan also appointed Anton Scalia, who would become a key conservative force on the Court, and Sandra Day O'Connor (the first woman appointee), and elevated Nixon appointee William Rehnquist to chief justice.

All these appointments made the Court more conservative. In 1986, for example, the Supreme Court upheld a Georgia law that punished consensual anal or oral sex between men with up to twenty years in jail (*Bowers v. Hardwick*); in 1989 justices ruled that a Missouri law restricting the right to an abortion was constitutional (*Webster v. Reproductive Health Services*), thus encouraging further challenges to *Roe v. Wade*. In federal courts, Justice Department lawyers argued New Right positions on such social issues, and Reagan's 378 appointees to the federal bench usually ruled accordingly. Overall, however, the Reagan administration did not push a conservative social agenda as strongly as some members of the new Republican coalition had hoped.

## REAGANOMICS

The centerpiece of Reagan's domestic agenda was the economic program that took his name: Reaganomics. The

U.S. economy was in bad shape at the beginning of the 1980s. Stagflation had proved resistant to traditional economic remedies: when the government increased spending to stimulate a stagnant economy, inflation skyrocketed; when it cut spending or tightened the money supply to reduce inflation, the economy plunged deeper into recession, and unemployment rates jumped. Everyone agreed that something had to be done to break the cycle, but few thought that government intervention would work. Even some Democrats, such as Colorado senator Gary Hart, voiced a "nonideological skepticism about the old, Rooseveltian solutions to social problems."

Reagan offered the American people a simple answer to economic woes. Instead of focusing on the complexities of global competition, deindustrialization, and OPEC's control of oil, Reagan argued that U.S. economic problems were caused by government intrusion in the "free-market" economic system. At fault were intrusive government regulation of business and industry, expensive government social programs that offered "handouts" to nonproductive citizens, high taxes, and deficit spending—in short, government itself. The Reagan administration's economic agenda was closely tied to its larger conservative ideology of limited government: it sought to "unshackle" the free-enterprise system from government regulation and control, to slash spending on social programs, to limit government's use of taxes to redistribute income among the American people, and to balance the budget by reducing the role of the federal government.

Reagan's economic policy was based largely on supply-side economics, the theory that tax cuts (rather than government spending) will create economic growth. Econo-

**Supply-Side Economics**

mist Arthur Laffer had proposed one key concept for supply-siders, sketching his soon-to-be-famous Laffer curve on a cocktail napkin for a *Wall Street Journal* writer and President Gerald Ford's chief of staff (and the future vice president) Dick Cheney in 1974. According to Laffer's theory, at some point rising tax rates discourage people from engaging in taxable activities (such as investing their money): if profits from investments simply disappear to taxes, what is the incentive to invest? As people invest less, the economy slows. Even though tax rates remain high, the government collects less in tax revenue because the economy stalls. Cutting taxes, on the other hand, reverses the cycle and increases tax revenues.

Although economists at the time accepted the larger principle behind Laffer's curve, almost none believed that U.S. tax rates approached the point of disincentive. Even conservative economists were highly suspicious of supply-

side principles. Reagan and his staff, however—on the basis of the unproven assumption that both corporate and personal tax rates in the United States had reached a level that discouraged investment—sought a massive tax cut. They argued that American corporations and individuals would invest funds freed up by lower tax rates, producing new plants, new jobs, and new products. Economic growth would more than make up for the tax revenues lost. And as prosperity returned, the profits at the top would "trickle down" to the middle classes and even to the poor.

Reagan's economic program was most fully developed by David Stockman, head of the Office of Management and Budget. Stockman proposed a five-year plan to balance the federal budget through economic growth (created by tax cuts) and deep cuts, primarily in social programs. Congress cooperated with a three-year, $750 billion tax cut, at that point the largest ever in American history. Cutting the federal budget, however, proved more difficult. Stockman's plan for balancing the budget assumed $100 billion in cuts from government programs, including Social Security and Medicare—and Congress was not about to cut Social Security and Medicare benefits. Reagan, meanwhile, canceled out gains from domestic spending cuts by dramatically increasing annual defense spending.

Major tax cuts, big increases in defense spending, small cuts in social programs: the numbers did not add up. The annual federal budget deficit exploded—from $59 billion in 1980 to more than $100 billion in 1982 to almost $300 billion by the end of George Bush's presidency in 1992. The federal government borrowed money to make up the difference, transforming the United States from the world's largest creditor nation to its largest debtor (see Figure 32.1). The national debt grew to almost $3 trillion. Because an ever greater share of the federal budget went to pay the interest on this ballooning debt, less was available for federal programs, foreign or domestic.

Reaganomics attempted to stimulate the economy—but economic growth would not solve the persistent problem of inflation. Here the Federal Reserve Bank, an autonomous fed-

**Harsh Medicine for Inflation**

eral agency, stepped in. In 1981 the Federal Reserve Bank raised interest rates for bank loans to an unprecedented 21.5 percent, battling inflation by tightening the money supply and slowing the economy down. The nation plunged into recession. During the last three months of the year, the gross national product (GNP) fell 5 percent, and sales of cars and houses dropped sharply. With declining economic activity, unemployment soared to 8 percent, the highest level in almost six years.

By late 1982, unemployment had reached 10.8 percent, the highest rate since 1940. For African Americans,

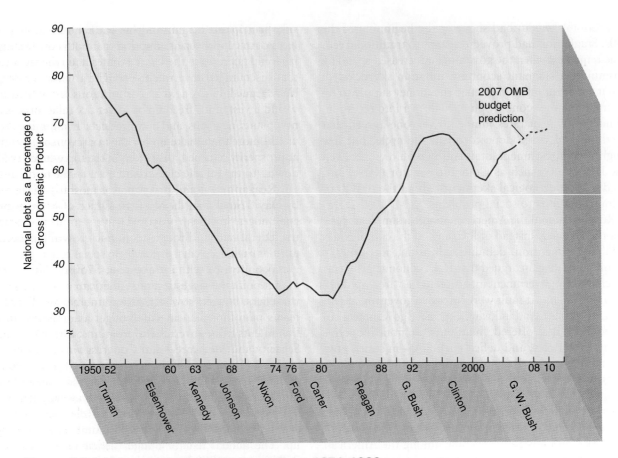

**Figure 32.1    America's Rising National Debt, 1974–1989**
America's national debt, which rose sporadically throughout the 1970s, soared to record heights during the 1980s. Under President Reagan, large defense expenditures and tax cuts caused the national debt to grow by $1.5 trillion.

*(Source: Adapted from U.S. Bureau of the Census, Statistical Abstract of the United States [Washington, D.C.: 1992], p. 315.)*

it was 20 percent. Many of the unemployed were blue-collar workers in ailing "smokestack industries," such as steel and automobiles. Reagan and his advisers promised that consumers would lift the economy out of the recession by spending their tax cuts. But as late as April 1983, unemployment still stood at 10 percent, and people were angry. Jobless steelworkers paraded through McKeesport, Pennsylvania, carrying a coffin that bore the epitaph "American Dream." Agriculture, too, was faltering and near collapse. Farmers suffered not only from falling crop prices due to overproduction, but also from floods, droughts, and burdensome debts which they had incurred at high interest rates. Many lost their property through mortgage foreclosures and farm auctions. Others filed for bankruptcy. As the recession deepened, poverty rose to its highest level since 1965.

It was harsh medicine, but the Federal Reserve Bank's plan to end stagflation worked. High interest rates helped drop inflation from 12 percent in 1980 to less than 7 percent in 1982. The economy also benefited from OPEC's 1981 decision, after eight years of engineering an artificial scarcity, to increase oil production, thus lowering prices. In 1984 the GNP rose 7 percent, the sharpest increase since 1951, and midyear unemployment fell to a four-year low of 7 percent. The economy was booming, but without sparking inflation.

By the presidential election of 1984, the recession was only a memory. Reagan got credit for the recovery, though it had little to do with his supply-side policies. In fact, the Democratic candidate, former vice president Walter Mondale, repeat-

**"Morning in America"**

▲ The 1980s savings-and-loan crisis led to the greatest collapse of U.S. financial institutions since the Great Depression. The federal bailout of S&Ls would cost American taxpayers at least $124 billion.

*(From* Newsweek, *May 21, 1990 © 1990 Newsweek, Inc. All rights reserved. Used by permission and protected by the Copyright Laws of the United States. The printing, copying, redistribution, or retransmission of the material without express written permission is prohibited.)*

edly hammered at Reagan's economic policies. Insisting that the rapidly growing budget deficit would have dire consequences for the American economy, he said (honestly, but probably not very astutely) that he would raise taxes. And he focused on themes of fairness and compassion; not all Americans, Mondale told the American public, were prospering in Reagan's America. Reagan, in contrast, proclaimed, "It's morning again in America." Television ads showed heartwarming images of American life, as an off-screen narrator told viewers, "Life is better. America is back. And people have a sense of pride they never felt they'd feel again." Reagan won in a landslide, with 59 percent of the vote. Mondale, with running mate Geraldine Ferraro—U.S. congresswoman from New York and the first woman vice-presidential candidate—carried only his home state of Minnesota.

Supply-side economics was not the only policy that transformed America's economy in the 1980s. Deregulation, begun under Jimmy Carter and expanded vastly under Reagan (the *Federal Register,* which contains all federal regulations, shrank from 87,012 pages in 1980 to 47,418 pages in 1986), created new opportunities for American business and industry. The 1978 deregulation of the airline industry lowered ticket prices both short-term and long-term; airline tickets cost almost 45 percent less in the early twenty-first century (in constant dollars) than in 1978. Deregulation of telecommunications industries created serious competition for the giant AT&T, and long-distance calling became inexpensive.

## Deregulation

The Reagan administration loosened regulation of the American banking and finance industries and purposely cut the enforcement ability of the Securities and Exchange Commission (SEC), which oversees Wall Street. In the early 1980s, Congress deregulated the nation's savings-and-loan institutions (S&Ls), organizations previously required to invest depositors' savings in thirty-year, fixed-rate mortgages secured by property within a 50-mile radius of the S&L's main office. Stagflation had already left many S&Ls insolvent, but the 1980s legislation created conditions for a collapse. By ending government oversight of investment practices, while guaranteeing to cover losses from bad S&L investments, Congress left no penalties for failure. S&Ls increasingly put depositors' money into high-risk investments and engaged in shady—even criminal—deals.

## Junk Bonds and Merger Mania

High-risk investments carried the day on Wall Street as well, as Michael Milken, a reclusive bond trader for the firm Drexel Firestone, pioneered the "junk bond" industry and created wildly lucrative investment possibilities. Milken offered financing to debt-ridden or otherwise weak corporations that could not get traditional, low-interest bank loans to fund expansion, using bond issues that paid investors high interest rates because they were high-risk (thus "junk" bonds). Many of these corporations, Milken realized, were attractive targets for takeover by other corporations or investors—who, in turn, could finance takeovers with junk bonds. Such "predators" could use the first corporation's existing debt as a tax write-off, sell off unprofitable units, and lay off employees to create a more efficient—and thus more profitable—corporation. Investors in the original junk bonds could make huge profits by selling their shares to the corporate raiders.

By the mid-1980s, it was no longer only weak corporations that were targeted for these "hostile takeovers"; hundreds of major corporations—including giants Walt Disney and Conoco—fell prey to merger mania. Profits for investors were staggering, and by 1987 Milken, the guru of junk bonds, was earning $550 million a year—about $1,046 a minute—in salary; counting investment returns, Milken's income was about $1 billion a year.

What were the results of such practices? Heightened competition and corporate downsizing often created more-efficient businesses and industries. Deregulation helped smaller and often innovative corporations challenge the virtual monopolies of giant corporations in fields like telecommunications. And through much of the 1980s, following the "Reagan recession," the American economy boomed. Although the stock market plunged 508 points on a single day in October 1987—losing 22.6 percent of its value, or almost double the percentage loss in the crash of 1929—it rebounded quickly. The high-risk boom of the 1980s did, however, have significant costs. Corporate downsizing meant layoffs for white-collar workers and management personnel, many of whom (especially those past middle age) had difficulty finding comparable positions. The wave of mergers and takeovers left American corporations as a whole more burdened by debt than before. It also helped to consolidate sectors of the economy—such as the media—under the control of an ever smaller number of players.

The high-risk, deregulated boom of the 1980s, furthermore, was rotten with corruption. By the late 1980s, insider trading scandals—in which people used "inside" information about corporations, which was not available to the general public, to make huge profits trading stocks—rocked financial markets and sent some of the most prominent figures on Wall Street to jail (albeit comfortable, "country club" jails). Savings and loans lost billions of dollars in bad investments, sometimes turning to fraud to cover them up. Scandal reached all the way to the White House: Vice President Bush's son Neil was involved in shady S&L deals. The Reagan-Bush administration's bailout of the S&L industry cost taxpayers half a trillion dollars.

## The Rich Get Richer

Finally, during the 1980s, the rich got richer, and the poor got poorer (see Figure 32.2). Merger mania and the financial market bonanza contributed, as the number of Americans reporting an annual income of $500,000 increased tenfold between 1980 and 1989. According to the Economic Policy Institute, the average compensation of a corporate executive officer increased from approximately 35 times an average worker's pay in 1978 to 71 times workers' average pay in 1989 (in 2005 the ratio

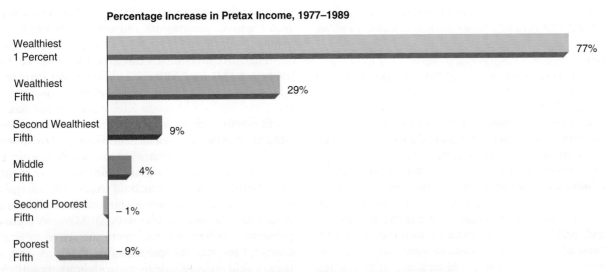

**Percentage Increase in Pretax Income, 1977–1989**

| | |
|---|---|
| Wealthiest 1 Percent | 77% |
| Wealthiest Fifth | 29% |
| Second Wealthiest Fifth | 9% |
| Middle Fifth | 4% |
| Second Poorest Fifth | – 1% |
| Poorest Fifth | – 9% |

**Figure 32.2    While the Rich Got Richer in the 1980s, the Poor Got Poorer**
Between 1977 and 1989, the richest 1 percent of American families reaped most of the gains from economic growth. In fact, the average pretax income of families in the top percentage rose 77 percent. At the same time, the typical family saw its income edge up only 4 percent. And the bottom 40 percent of families had actual declines in income.

(Source: *Data from the* New York Times, *March 5, 1992.)*

was 262 to 1). In 1987 the United States had forty-nine billionaires—up from one in 1978. While the number of very wealthy Americans grew, middle-class incomes were stagnant.

Most of the new inequality was due to Reagan's economic policies, which benefited the wealthy at the expense of middle- and lower-income Americans. Reagan's tax policies decreased the "total effective tax rates"—income taxes plus Social Security taxes—for the top 1 percent of American families by 14.4 percent. But they increased tax rates for the poorest 20 percent of families by 16 percent. By 1990, the richest 1 percent of Americans controlled 40 percent of the nation's wealth; fully 80 percent of wealth was controlled by the top 20 percent. Not since the 1920s had America seen such economic inequality.

# REAGAN AND THE WORLD

A key element in Reagan's winning strategy in the 1980 election was his forthright call for the United States to assert itself on the world stage. Though lacking a firm grasp of world issues, history, and geography—friends and associates often marveled at his ability to get even elementary facts wrong—Reagan adhered to a few core principles. One was a deep and abiding anticommunism which had dictated his world-view for decades and which formed the foundation of his presidential campaign. A second was an underlying optimism about the ability of American power and values to bring positive change in the world. Reagan liked to quote Thomas Paine of the American Revolution: "We have it in our power to begin the world over again." Yet Reagan was also a political pragmatist, particularly as time went on and his administration became mired in scandal. Together, these elements of the president's personality help explain both his aggressive anticommunist foreign policy and his willingness to respond positively in his second term to Soviet leader Mikhail Gorbachev's call for "new thinking" in world affairs.

Initially, toughness vis-à-vis Moscow was the watchword. Embracing the strident anticommunism that char-

**Soviet-American Tension**

acterized U.S. foreign policy in the early Cold War, Reagan and his advisers rejected both the détente of the Nixon years and the Carter administration's focus on extending human rights abroad. Where Nixon and Carter perceived an increasingly multipolar international system, the Reagan team reverted to a bipolar perspective defined by the Soviet-American relationship. Young neoconservatives, such as Richard Perle and Paul Wolfowitz, who held mid-level positions in the administration, provided much of

the intellectual ballast and moral fervor for this shift toward confrontation with Moscow.

In his first presidential press conference Reagan described a malevolent Soviet Union, whose leaders thought they had "the right to commit any crime, to lie, to cheat." When Poland's pro-Soviet leaders in 1981 cracked down on an independent labor organization, Solidarity, Washington responded by restricting Soviet-American trade and hurled angry words at Moscow. In March 1983, Reagan told an audience of evangelical Christians in Florida that the Soviets were "the focus of evil in the modern world . . . an evil empire." That same year, Reagan restricted commercial flights to the Soviet Union after a Soviet fighter pilot mistakenly shot down a South Korean commercial jet that had strayed some 300 miles off course into Soviet airspace. The world was shocked by the death of 269 passengers, and Reagan exploited the tragedy to score Cold War points.

A key Reagan tenet held that a substantial military buildup would thwart the Soviet threat and intimidate Moscow. Accordingly, the administration launched the largest peacetime arms buildup in American history, driving up the federal debt. In 1985, when the military budget hit $294.7 billion (a doubling since 1980), the Pentagon was spending an average of $28 million an hour. Assigning low priority to arms control talks, Reagan announced in 1983 his desire for a space-based defense shield against incoming ballistic missiles: the Strategic Defense Initiative (SDI). His critics tagged it "Star Wars" and said such a system could never be made to work scientifically—some enemy missiles would always get through the shield. Moreover, the critics warned, SDI would have the effect of elevating the arms race to dangerous new levels. But Reagan was undaunted, and in the years that followed, SDI research and development consumed tens of billions of dollars.

Because he attributed Third World disorders to Soviet intrigue, the president declared the Reagan Doctrine: the

**Reagan Doctrine**

United States would openly support anticommunist movements—"freedom fighters"—wherever they were battling the Soviets or Soviet-backed governments. In Afghanistan, the president continued Jimmy Carter's policy of providing covert assistance, through Pakistan, to the Mujahidin rebels in their war against the Soviet occupation. CIA director William J. Casey made numerous trips to Pakistan to coordinate the flow of arms and other assistance. When the Soviets stepped up the war in 1985, the Reagan administration responded by sending more high-tech weapons. Particularly important were the anti-aircraft Stinger missiles. Easily transportable and fired by a single soldier, the Stingers turned the tide in the Afghan war by making Soviet jets and helicopters vulnerable below fifteen thousand feet.

The administration also applied the Reagan Doctrine aggressively in the Caribbean and Central America. Senior officials believed that the Soviets and Castro's Cuba were fomenting disorder in the region (see Map 32.1). Accordingly, in October 1983 the president sent U.S. troops into the tiny Caribbean island of Grenada to oust a pro-Marxist government that appeared to be forging ties with Moscow and Havana. In El Salvador, he provided military and economic assistance to a military-dominated government engaged in a struggle with left-wing revolutionaries. The regime used (or could not control) right-wing death squads, from which Luisa Orellana and her family fled. By the end of the decade they had killed forty thousand dissidents and other citizens, as well as several American missionaries who had been working with landless peasants. By the end of the decade the United States had spent more than $6 billion there in a counterinsurgency war. In January 1992 the Salvadoran combatants finally negotiated a U.N.-sponsored peace.

The Reagan administration also meddled in the Nicaraguan civil war. In 1979 leftist insurgents in Nicaragua overthrew Anastasio Somoza, a

### Contra War in Nicaragua

long-time ally of the United States and member of the dictatorial family that had ruled the Central American nation since the mid-1930s. The revolutionaries called themselves Sandinistas in honor of César Augusto Sandino—who had headed the nationalistic, anti-imperialist Nicaraguan opposition against U.S. occupation in the 1930s, battled U.S. marines, and was finally assassinated by Somoza henchmen—and they denounced the tradition of U.S. imperialism in their country. When the Sandinistas aided rebels in El Salvador, bought Soviet weapons, and invited Cubans to work in Nicaragua's hospitals and schools and help reorganize the Nicaraguan army, Reagan officials charged that Nicaragua was becoming a Soviet client. In 1981 the CIA began to train, arm, and direct more than ten thousand counterrevolutionaries, known as contras, to overthrow the Nicaraguan government.

The U.S. interventions in El Salvador and Nicaragua sparked a debate much like the earlier one over Vietnam. Many Americans, including Democratic leaders in Congress, were skeptical about the communist threat to the region and warned that Nicaragua could become another Vietnam. Congress in 1984 voted to stop U.S. military aid to the contras. Secretly, the Reagan administration lined up other countries, including Saudi Arabia, Panama, and

South Korea, to funnel money and weapons to the contras, and in 1985 Reagan imposed an economic embargo against Nicaragua. The president might have opted for a diplomatic solution, but he rejected a plan proposed by Costa Rica's president Oscar Arias Sánchez in 1987 to obtain a cease-fire in Central America through negotiations and cutbacks in military aid to all rebel forces. (Arias won the 1987 Nobel Peace Prize.) Three years later, after Reagan had left office, all of the Central American presidents at last brokered a settlement; in the national election that followed, the Sandinistas lost to a U.S.-funded party. After nearly a decade of civil war, thirty thousand Nicaraguans had died, and the ravaged economy had dwindled to one of the poorest in the hemisphere.

Reagan's obsession with defeating the Sandinistas almost caused his political undoing. In November 1986 it

### Iran-Contra Scandal

became known that the president's national security adviser, John M. Poindexter, and an aide, marine lieutenant colonel Oliver North, in collusion with CIA director Casey, had covertly sold weapons to Iran as part of a largely unsuccessful attempt to win the release of several Americans being held hostage by Islamic fundamentalist groups in the Middle East. During the same period, Washington had been condemning Iran as a terrorist nation and demanding that America's allies not trade with the Islamic state. Still more damaging was the revelation that money from the Iran arms deal had been illegally diverted to a fund to aid the contras—this after Congress had unambiguously rejected providing such aid. North later admitted that he had illegally destroyed government documents and lied to Congress to keep the operation clandestine.

Although Reagan survived the scandal—it remained unclear just what he did and did not know about the operation—his presidency suffered a major blow. His personal popularity declined, and an emboldened Congress began to reassert its authority over foreign affairs. In late 1992, outgoing president George Bush pardoned several former government officials who had been convicted of lying to Congress. Critics smelled a cover-up, for Bush himself, as vice president, had participated in high-level meetings on Iran-contra deals. As for North, his conviction was overturned on a technicality. In view of its deliberate thwarting of congressional authority, the Iran-contra secret network, the scholar William LeoGrande has argued, "posed a greater threat to democracy in the United States than Nicaragua ever did."

The Iran-contra scandal also pointed to the increased importance in U.S. foreign policy of the Middle East and

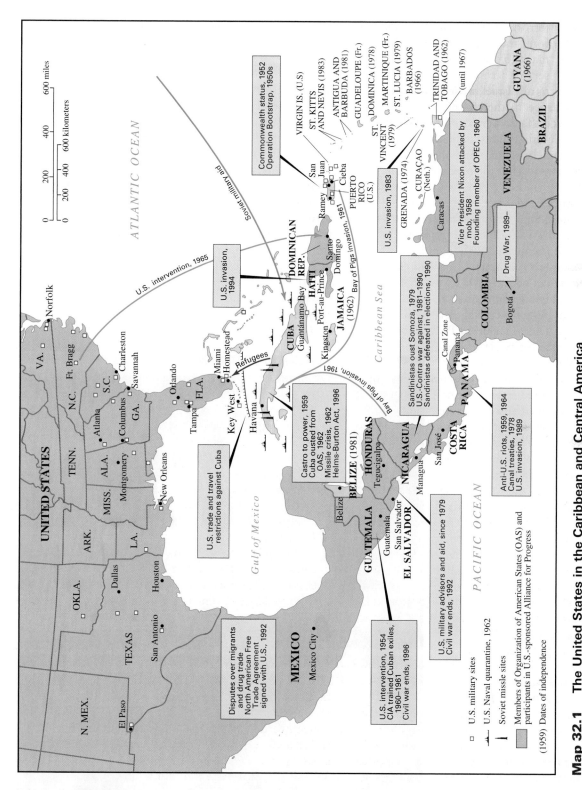

**Map 32.1  The United States in the Caribbean and Central America**

The United States has often intervened in the Caribbean and Central America. Geographical proximity, economic stakes, political disputes, security links, trade in illicit drugs, and Cuba's alliance with the Soviet Union and defiance of the United States have kept North American eyes fixed on events in the region.

## U.S. Interests in the Middle East

terrorism (see Map 33.2). As before, the United States had as its main goals in the Middle East preserving access to oil and supporting its ally Israel, while at the same time checking Soviet influence in the region. In the 1980s, though, American leaders faced new pressures, in the form of a deepened Israeli-Palestinian conflict and an anti-American and anti-Israeli Islamic fundamentalist movement that began to spread after the ouster of the shah of Iran in 1979.

The 1979 Camp David accords between Israel and Egypt had raised hopes of a lasting settlement involving self-government for the Palestinian Arabs living in the Israeli-occupied Gaza Strip and West Bank. It did not happen, as Israel and the Palestinian Liberation Organization (PLO) remained at odds. In 1982, in retaliation for Palestinian shelling of Israel from Lebanon, Israeli troops invaded Lebanon, reaching the capital, Beirut, and inflicting massive damage. The beleaguered PLO and various Lebanese factions called on Syria to contain the Israelis. Thousands of civilians died in the multifaceted conflict, and a million people became refugees. Reagan made no effort to halt the Israeli offensive, but he agreed to send U.S. marines to Lebanon to join a peacekeeping force. Soon the American troops became embroiled in a war between Christian and Muslim factions, as the latter accused the marines of helping the Christian-dominated government rather than acting as neutral peacekeepers. In October 1983, terrorist bombs demolished a barracks, killing 241 American servicemen. Four months later, Reagan recognized failure and pulled the remaining marines out.

## Terrorism

The attack on the marine barracks showed the growing danger of terrorism to the United States and other western countries. In the 1980s, numerous otherwise powerless groups, many of them associated with the Palestinian cause or with Islamic fundamentalism, relied on terrorist acts to further their political aims. Often they targeted American citizens and property, on account of Washington's support of Israel and U.S. involvement in the Lebanese civil war. Of the 690 hijackings, kidnappings, bombings, and shootings around the world in 1985, for example, 217 were against Americans. Most of these actions originated in Iran, Libya, Lebanon, and the Gaza Strip. In June 1985, for example, Shi'ite Muslim terrorists from Lebanon hijacked an American jetliner, killed one passenger, and held thirty-nine Americans hostage for seventeen days. Three years later, a Pan American passenger plane was destroyed over Scotland, probably by pro-Iranian terrorists who concealed the bomb in a cassette player.

On April 18, 1983, a car bomb placed by terrorists demolished the U.S. embassy in Beirut, Lebanon, killing 63 people, 17 of them Americans. An American soldier stands guard near the destroyed building. Then, in October of the same year, terrorist bombs leveled a military barracks, killing 241 American personnel. A few months later, President Reagan withdrew U.S. marines from a multinational peacekeeping force that had been dispatched to Lebanon to calm a war waged there by Israel against PLO and Syrian forces.

*(Bill Pierce/Sygma)*

Washington, firmly allied with Israel, continued to propose peace plans designed to persuade the Israelis to give back occupied territories and the Arabs to give up attempts to push the Jews out of the Middle East (the "land-for-peace" formula). As the peace process stalled in 1987, Palestinians living in the West Bank began an *intifada* (Arabic for "uprising") against Israeli forces. Israel refused to negotiate, but the United States decided to talk with PLO chief Yasir Arafat after he renounced terrorism and accepted Israel's right to live in peace and security. For the PLO to recognize Israel and, in effect, for the United States to recognize the PLO were major developments in the Arab-Israeli conflict, even as a lasting settlement remained elusive.

In South Africa, too, American diplomacy became more aggressive as the decade progressed. At first, the Reagan administration followed a policy of "constructive engagement"—asking the increasingly isolated government to reform its apartheid system, designed to preserve white supremacy. But many Americans demanded economic sanctions: cutting off imports from South Africa and pressuring some 350 American companies—top among them Texaco, General Motors, Ford, and Goodyear—to cease operations there. Some American cities and states passed divestment laws, withdrawing dollars (such as pension funds used to buy stock) from American companies active in South Africa. Public protest and congressional legislation forced the Reagan administration in 1986 to impose economic restrictions against South Africa. Within two years, about half of the American companies in South Africa had pulled out.

Many on the right were unhappy with the South Africa sanctions policy—they believed the main black opposition group, the African National Congress (ANC), was dominated by communists, and they doubted the efficacy of sanctions—and the more extreme among them soon found another reason to be disenchanted with Reagan. A new Soviet leader, Mikhail S. Gorbachev, had come to power, and Reagan, his own popularity declining somewhat, showed a newfound willingness to enter negotiations with the "evil empire." Gorbachev called for a friendlier superpower relationship and a new, more cooperative world system. At a 1985 Geneva summit meeting between the two men, Reagan agreed in principle with Gorbachev's contention that strategic weapons should be substantially reduced, and at a 1986 Reykjavik, Iceland, meeting they came very close to a major reduction agreement. SDI, however, stood in the way: Gorbachev insisted that the initiative be shelved, and Rea-

## Enter Gorbachev

▲ In one of several summit meetings, top Soviet leader Mikhail Gorbachev (b. 1931) and President Ronald Reagan (1911–2004) met in Moscow in May 1988 in hopes of signing a Strategic Arms Reduction Talks (START) agreement. The chemistry of warm friendship that Reagan later claimed characterized his personal relationship with Gorbachev fell short of producing cuts in dangerous strategic weapons. But their cordial interaction encouraged the diplomatic dialogue that helped end the Cold War.

*(Ronald Reagan Presidential Library)*

gan refused to part with it, despite continuing scientific objections that the plan would cost billions of dollars and never work.

But Reagan and Gorbachev got along well, despite the language barrier and their differing personalities. Reagan's penchant for telling stories rather than discussing the intricacies of policy did not trouble the detail-oriented Gorbachev. As General Colin Powell commented, though the Soviet leader was far superior to Reagan in mastery of specifics, he never exhibited even a trace of condescension. He understood that Reagan was, as Powell put it, "the embodiment of his people's down-to-earth character, practicality, and optimism." And Reagan toned down his strident anti-Soviet rhetoric, particularly as his more hawkish advisers left the administration in the late 1980s.

The turnaround in Soviet-American relations stemmed more from changes abroad than from Reagan's decisions.

||||||||||||||||||||||||||||||||||

### *Perestroika* and *Glasnost*

As Reagan said near the end of his presidency, he had been "dropped into a grand historical moment." Under the dynamic Gorbachev, a younger generation of Soviet leaders came to power in 1985. They began to modernize the highly bureaucratized, decaying economy through a reform program known as *perestroika* ("restructuring") and to liberalize the authoritarian political system through *glasnost* ("openness"). For these reforms to work, however, Soviet military expenditures had to be reduced and foreign aid decreased.

In 1987 Gorbachev and Reagan signed the Intermediate-Range Nuclear Forces (INF) Treaty banning all land-based intermediate-range nuclear missiles in Europe. Soon began the destruction of 2,800 missiles, including Soviet missiles targeted at western Europe and NATO missiles aimed at the Soviet Union. Gorbachev also unilaterally reduced his nation's armed forces, helped settle regional conflicts, and began the withdrawal of Soviet troops from Afghanistan. After more than forty chilling years, the Cold War was coming to an end.

## AMERICAN SOCIETY IN THE 1980s

As the Cold War waned, so, too, did the power of the belief in an America united by a set of shared, middle-class values. Although the ideal of shared values was never a reality, it had exercised a powerful hold in the nation's public culture from World War II well into the 1960s. By the 1980s, after years of social struggle and division, few Americans believed in the reality of that vision; many rejected it as undesirable. And though the 1980s were never as contentious and violent as the era of social protest in the 1960s and early 1970s, deep social and cultural divides existed among Americans. A newly powerful group of Christian conservatives challenged the secular culture of the American majority. A growing class of affluent, well-educated Americans seemed a society apart from the urban poor, whom sociologists and journalists began calling "the underclass." At the same time, the composition of the American population was changing dramatically, as people immigrated to the United States from more different nations than ever before.

As late as 1980, many Americans believed that the 1925 Scopes trial over the teaching of evolution had been the last gasp of fundamentalist Christianity in the United States.

||||||||||||||||||||||||||||||||||

### Growth of the Religious Right

They were wrong. Since the 1960s, America's mainline liberal Protestant churches—Episcopalian, Presbyterian, Methodist—had been losing members, while Southern Baptists and other denominations that offered the spiritual experience of being "born again" through belief in Jesus Christ and that accepted the literal truth of the Bible (fundamentalism) had grown rapidly. Fundamentalist preachers reached out to vast audiences through television: by the late 1970s, televangelist Oral Roberts was drawing an audience of 3.9 million. Close to 20 percent of Americans identified themselves as fundamentalist Christians in 1980.

Most fundamentalist Christian churches stayed out of the social and political conflicts of the 1960s and early 1970s, arguing that preaching the "pure saving gospel of Jesus Christ" was more important. But in the late 1970s—motivated by what they saw as the betrayal of God's will in an increasingly permissive American society—some influential preachers began to mobilize their flocks for political struggle. In a "Washington for Jesus" rally in 1980, fundamentalist leader Pat Robertson told crowds, "We have enough votes to run the country. . . . And when the people say, 'We've had enough,' we are going to take over." The Moral Majority, founded in 1979 by Jerry Falwell, sought to create a "Christian America," in part by supporting political candidates on the local and national levels. Falwell's defense of socially conservative "family values" and his condemnation of feminism (he called NOW the "National Order of Witches"), homosexuality, pornography, and abortion resonated with many Americans.

Throughout the 1980s, the coalition of conservative Christians known as the New Right waged campaigns against America's secular culture. Rejecting the idea associated with multiculturalism that different cultures and lifestyle choices were equally valid, the New Right worked to establish what they believed to be "God's law" as the basis for American society. Concerned Women for America, founded by Beverly LaHayes in 1979, attempted to have elementary school readers containing "unacceptable" religious beliefs (including excerpts from *The Diary of Anne Frank* and *The Wizard of Oz*) removed from school classrooms. In 1989 the American Family Association protested network television shows including *Cheers* (a popular comedy set in a Boston neighborhood bar) and *Nightline*. Fundamentalist Christian groups once again began to challenge the teaching of evolutionary theory in public schools. The Reagan administration frequently turned to James Dobson, founder of the conservative Focus on the Family organization, for policy advice. Conservative Christians also joined with Roman Catholics, Mormons, and other religious opponents of abortion in the anti-abortion or "prolife" movement, which had sprung up in the wake of the Supreme Court's 1973 decision in *Roe v. Wade*.

▲ Holding his Bible, the Reverend Jerry Falwell stands before his church in Lynchburg, Virginia, on a Sunday morning before services. An evangelical preacher whose "Old Time Gospel Hour" program reached 15 million Americans, Falwell encouraged his congregation—and the religious right in general—to show their political power in the 1980 presidential election. *(© Wally McNamee/Corbis)*

Although the New Right often found an ally in the Reagan White House, many other Americans vigorously

### "Culture Wars"

opposed a movement that they saw as preaching a doctrine of intolerance and threatening basic freedoms—including freedom of religion for those whose beliefs did not accord with the conservative Christianity of the New Right. In 1982 politically progressive television producer Norman Lear, influential former congresswoman Barbara Jordan, and other prominent figures from the fields of business, religion, politics, and entertainment founded People for the American Way to support American civil liberties and free-

doms, the separation of church and state, and the values of tolerance and diversity. The struggle between the religious right and their opponents for the future of the nation came to be known as the "culture wars."

It was not only organized groups, however, that opposed the agenda of the religious right. Many beliefs of Christian fundamentalists ran counter to the way most Americans lived—especially when it came to women's roles. The women's movement, like the civil rights movement, had brought about significant changes in American society. By the 1980s, a generation of girls had grown up expecting freedoms and opportunities that their mothers never had. Legislation such as the Civil Rights Act of 1964 and Title IX had opened both academic and athletic programs to girls and women. In 1960 there were thirty-eight male lawyers for every female lawyer in the United States; by 1983, the ratio was 5.5 to 1. By 1985, more than half of married women with children under three worked outside the home—many from economic necessity. The religious right's insistence that women's place was in the home, subordinated to her husband, contradicted not only the gains made toward sexual equality in American society but also the reality of many women's lives.

As Americans fought the "culture wars" of the 1980s, another major social divide threatened the na-

### The New Inequality

tion. A 1988 national report on race relations looked back to the 1968 Kerner Commission report to claim, "America is again becoming two separate societies," white and black. It argued that African Americans endured poverty, segregation, and crime in inner-city ghettos while most whites lived comfortably in suburban enclaves. In fact, America's separate societies of comfort and hardship were not wholly determined by race. The majority of America's poor were white, and the black middle class was strong and expanding. But people of color made up a disproportionate share of America's poor. In 1980, 33 percent of blacks and 26 percent of Latinos lived in poverty, compared with 10 percent of whites (see Figure 32.3).

Reasons for poverty varied. For people of color, the legacies of racism played a role. The changing job structure was partly responsible, as the overall number of well-paid jobs for both skilled and unskilled workers decreased, replaced by lower-paid service jobs. New York alone had 234,000 fewer blue-collar workers in 1980 than at the beginning of the 1970s. In addition, families headed by a single mother were more likely to be poor—five times more likely than families of the same race maintained by a married couple. By 1990, a high rate of unwed pregnancy and a rising divorce rate meant that about one-quarter of all

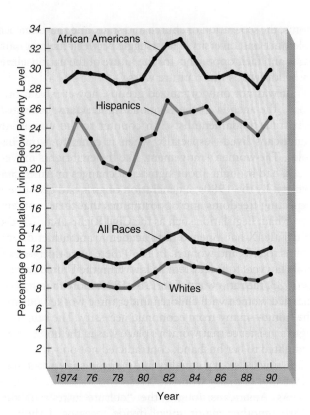

**Figure 32.3    Poverty in America by Race, 1974–1990**

Poverty in America rose in the early 1980s but subsided afterward. Many people of color, however, experienced little relief during the decade. Notice that the percentage of African Americans living below the poverty level was three times higher than that for whites. It was also much higher for Hispanics.

*(Source: Adapted from U.S. Bureau of the Census, Statistical Abstract of the United States [Washington, D.C.: 1992], p. 461.)*

children lived in a household without a father. Racial differences were significant: by 1992, 59 percent of African American children and 17 percent of white children lived in female-headed households, and almost half of black children lived in poverty.

As inequality increased, so, too, did social pathology. In impoverished and often hopeless inner-city neighborhoods, violent crime—particularly homicides and gang warfare—grew alarmingly, as did school dropout rates, crime rates, and child abuse.

**Social Crises in American Cities**

Some people tried to find escape in hard drugs, especially crack, a derivative of cocaine, which first struck New York City's poorest neighborhoods in

1985. Crack's legacy included destroyed families, abused children, and heavily armed teenage drug dealers. Gang shootouts over drugs were deadly: the toll in Los Angeles in 1987 was 387 deaths, more than half of them innocent bystanders. Shocked by the violence, many states instituted mandatory prison sentences for possessing small amounts of crack, making penalties for a gram of crack equivalent to those for 100 grams of cocaine, the drug of choice for more-affluent, white Americans during the 1980s. Such policies increased America's prison population almost fourfold from 1980 to the mid-1990s, with black and Latino youth arrested in disproportionate numbers. By 2000, young black men were more likely to have been arrested than to have graduated from a four-year college.

Rates of homelessness also grew during the 1980s, in part because of major cuts to low-income housing subsidies. Some of the homeless were impoverished families; many of the people living on the streets had problems with drugs or alcohol. About one-third of the homeless were former psychiatric patients discharged from psychiatric wards in a burst of enthusiasm for "deinstitutionalization." By 1985, 80 percent of the total number of beds in state mental hospitals had been eliminated on the premise that small neighborhood programs would be more responsive to people's needs than large state hospitals. Such local programs failed to materialize. Without adequate medical supervision and medication, many of America's mentally ill citizens wandered the streets.

Another social crisis confronting Americans in the 1980s was the global spread of acquired immune deficiency syndrome, or AIDS. Caused by the human immunodeficiency virus (HIV), which attacks cells in the immune system, AIDS leaves its victims susceptible to deadly infections and cancers. The human immunodeficiency virus itself is spread through the exchange of blood or body fluids, often through sexual intercourse or needle sharing by intravenous drug users.

**The AIDS Epidemic**

AIDS was first diagnosed in the United States in 1981. Between 1981 and 1988, of the 57,000 AIDS cases reported, nearly 32,000 resulted in death. Politicians were slow to devote resources to combating AIDS, in part because it was initially perceived as a "gay man's disease" which did not threaten other Americans. "A man reaps what he sows," declared the Reverend Jerry Falwell of the Moral Majority. AIDS, along with other sexually transmitted diseases, such as genital herpes and chlamydia, ended an era defined by penicillin and "the pill," in which sex was freed from the threat of serious disease or unwanted pregnancy.

▲ In the 1980s there was an alarming spread of sexually transmitted diseases, especially acquired immune deficiency syndrome (AIDS). Campaigns for "safe sex," such as this New York City subway ad, urged people to use condoms.

*(Reprinted with permission of Saatchi & Saatchi)*

As America confronted the spreading AIDS epidemic, as well as what seemed to be epidemics of drug addiction, violence, and urban despair, some Americans were living extraordinarily well. "Greed is all right," Wall Street financier Ivan Boesky told students at the University of California, Berkeley, the center of 1960s campus protest, and he was met with cheers and laughter. For the rich, the 1980s were an era of ostentation. New York entrepreneur Donald Trump's $29 million yacht had gold-plated bathroom fixtures. Publisher Malcolm Forbes flew eight hundred guests to Morocco for his seventieth birthday; with an honor guard of three hundred Berber horsemen and six hundred acrobats, jugglers, and belly dancers to entertain the guests, the party cost $2 million.

With Wall Street booming, just-graduated M.B.A.s were offered starting salaries of $80,000 and new graduates from top law schools the same. Nineteen eighty-four was the "Year of the Yuppie"—Young Urban Professional—proclaimed *Newsweek* magazine. *Yuppie* was a derogatory term from the beginning (as was *Buppie,* for Black Urban Professional), but it described the lives of many ambitious and successful young Americans who worked hard in demanding careers and who created an identifiable lifestyle defined by consumer goods: BMWs,

### An Era of Ostentation

Sub-Zero refrigerators, Armani suits, Häagen-Dazs ice cream. Americans in the 1980s seemed fascinated with tales of the super-rich (making *Dallas* a top-rated television show) and with Yuppie lifestyles (chronicled on the popular show *thirtysomething*). But Yuppies also represented those who got ahead without caring about those left behind. As Yuppies led the way in gentrifying urban neighborhoods, displacing poorer residents, graffiti began to appear in New York: "Die, Yuppie Scum."

The divisions affecting American society in the 1980s were complicated by the arrival of large numbers of new immigrants from regions not formerly strongly represented in the U.S. ethnic mix. Between 1970 and 1990 the United States absorbed more than 13 million new arrivals, most from Latin America and Asia. Before the immigration act reforms of 1965, Americans of Asian ancestry had made up less than 1 percent of the nation's total population; that percentage more than tripled, to almost 3 percent, by 1990.

### New Immigrants from Asia

The composition of this small slice of America's population also changed dramatically. Before 1965, the majority of Asian Americans were of Japanese ancestry (about 52 percent in 1960), followed by Chinese and Filipino. In contrast, in the 1960s and 1970s, the highest rates of immigration were from nations not previously represented in the U.S. population. There were only 603 Vietnamese residents of the United States in 1964. By 1990, the United States had absorbed almost 800,000 refugees from Indochina, casualties of the war in Vietnam and surrounding nations. Immigrants flooded in from South Korea, Thailand, India, Pakistan, Bangladesh, Indonesia, Singapore, Laos, Cambodia, and Vietnam. Japanese Americans became a much smaller portion of the Asian American population, at 15 percent surpassed by Chinese and Filipino Americans and rivaled by the Vietnamese.

Immigrants from Asia tended to be either highly skilled or unskilled. Unsettled conditions in the Philippines in the 1970s and 1980s created an exodus of well-educated Filipinos to the United States. India's economy was not able to support its abundance of well-trained physicians and healthcare workers, who increasingly found employment in the United States and elsewhere. Korea, Taiwan, and China also lost skilled and educated workers to the United States. Other immigrants from China, however, had few job skills and spoke little or no English. Large numbers of new immigrants crowded into neighborhoods like New York City's Chinatown, where women worked long hours under terrible conditions in the city's nonunion garment industry. Immigrants from southeast Asia were the most

Applicants for visas wait in line ▶ at the U.S. embassy in New Delhi, India. In 1985, 140,000 people were on the waiting list for one of 20,000 annual immigrant visas. Many poorer nations, such as India, experienced a "brain drain" of highly educated people to the United States and western Europe.

*(Sandro Tucci/Time Life Pictures/Getty Images)*

likely to be unskilled and to live in poverty in the United States, though some found opportunities for success.

But even highly educated immigrants often found their options limited. A 1983 study found that Korean immigrants or Korean Americans owned three-quarters of the approximately twelve hundred greengroceries in New York City. Though often cited as a great immigrant success story, Korean greengrocers usually had descended the professional ladder: 78 percent of them had college or professional degrees.

Although immigration from Asia was high, unprecedented rates of immigration coupled with a high birth rate made Latinos the fastest-growing group of Americans. New immigrants from Mexico joined Mexican Americans and other Spanish-surnamed Americans, many of whose families had lived in the United States for generations. In 1970 Latinos comprised 4.5 percent of the nation's population; that percentage jumped to 9 percent by 1990, when one out of three Los Angelenos and Miamians were Hispanic, as were 48 percent of the population of San Antonio and 70 percent of El Paso. Mexican Americans, concentrated in California and the Southwest, made up the majority of this population, but Puerto Ricans, Cubans, Dominicans, and other immigrants from the Caribbean also lived in the United States, clustered principally in East Coast cities.

During the 1980s, people from Guatemala and El Salvador, like Luisa Orellana, fled civil war and government violence, and many found their way to the United States. Although the U.S. government commonly refused to grant them political asylum (about 113,000 Cubans received political refugee status during the 1980s, compared with

### The Growing Latino Population

fewer than 1,400 El Salvadorans), a national Sanctuary movement of Christian churches defied the law to protect refugees from deportation back to places where they risked violence or death. Economic troubles in Mexico and throughout Central and South America also produced a flood of a different sort of refugee: undocumented workers who crossed the poorly guarded 2,000-mile border between the United States and Mexico, seeking economic opportunities. Some were sojourners, who moved back and forth across the border. A majority meant to stay. These new Americans created a new hybrid culture that became an important part of the American mosaic. "We want to be here," explained Daniel Villanueva, a TV executive in Los Angeles, "but without losing our language and our culture. They are a richness, a treasure that we don't care to lose."

The incorporation of so many newcomers into American society was not always easy, as many Americans believed new arrivals threatened their jobs and economic security, and nativist violence and simple bigotry increased. In 1982 twenty-seven-year-old Vincent Chin was beaten to death in Detroit by an unemployed auto worker and his uncle. American auto plants were losing in competition with Japanese imports, and the two men seemingly mistook the Chinese American Chin for Japanese, reportedly shouting at him, "It's because of you little [expletive deleted] that we're out of work." In New York, Philadelphia, and Los Angeles, inner-city African Americans boycotted Korean groceries. Riots broke out in Los Angeles schools between black students and newly arrived Mexicans. In Dade County, Florida, voters passed an antibilingual measure that led to the removal of Spanish-language signs on public transportation, while at the state and national level people debated initiatives declaring English the "official" language of the United States. Public school classrooms, however, struggled with practical issues: in 1992 more than one thousand school districts in the United States enrolled students from at least eight different language groups.

Concerned about the flow of illegal aliens into the United States, Congress passed the Immigration Reform and Control (Simpson-Rodino) Act in 1986. The act's purpose was to discourage illegal immigration by imposing sanctions on employers who hired undocumented workers, but it also provided amnesty to millions who had immigrated illegally before 1982. As immigration continued at a high rate into the 1990s, however, it would further transform the face of America, offering both the richness of diverse cultures and the potential for continued social conflict.

## THE END OF THE COLD WAR AND GLOBAL DISORDER

The departure of Ronald Reagan from the presidency coincided with a set of changes in world affairs that would lead in short order to the end of the Cold War and the dawn of a new international system. Reagan's vice president, George Herbert Walker Bush, would become president and oversee the transition. The scion of a Wall Street banker who had been a U.S. senator from Connecticut, Bush had attended an exclusive boarding school and then gone on to Yale. An upper-class, eastern Establishment figure of the type that was becoming increasingly rare in the Republican Party, he had the advantage over his rivals for the presidential nomination in that he had been a loyal vice president. And he possessed a formidable résumé—he had been ambassador to the United Nations, chairman of the Republican Party, special envoy to China, and director of the CIA. He had also been a war hero, flying fifty-eight combat missions in the Pacific in World War II and receiving the Distinguished Flying Cross.

Bush entered the 1988 presidential campaign trailing his Democratic opponent, Massachusetts governor Michael Dukakis, by a wide margin. Repub-

**George Herbert Walker Bush**

lican operatives turned that around by waging one of the most negative campaigns in American history. Most notoriously, the Bush camp aired a television commercial featuring a black convicted murderer, Willie Horton, who had terrorized a Maryland couple, raping the woman, while on weekend furlough—a temporary release program begun under Dukakis's Re-

publican predecessor but associated in the ad with the implication that Dukakis was "soft on crime." The Republicans also falsely suggested that Dukakis had a history of psychiatric problems. His patriotism was questioned, as was that of his wife, who was wrongly accused of having burned an American flag while protesting the Vietnam War. These personal attacks generally did not come from Bush himself, but neither did he disavow them. Dukakis, meanwhile, did not engage in personal attacks on Bush but ran an uninspired campaign. On election day, Bush won by 8 percentage points in the popular vote and received 426 electoral votes to Dukakis's 112. The Democrats, however, retained control of both houses of Congress.

From the start, Bush focused most of his attention on foreign policy, but he was by nature cautious and reactive in world affairs, much to the chagrin of neoconservatives, even in the face of huge changes in the international system. Mikhail Gorbachev's reforms in the Soviet Union were now taking on a life of their own, stimulating reforms in eastern Europe that ultimately led to revolution. In 1989 many thousands of people in East Germany, Poland, Hungary, Czechoslovakia, and Romania, longing for personal freedom, startled the world by repudiating their communist governments and staging mass protests against a despised ideology. In November 1989, Germans scaled the Berlin Wall and then tore it down; the following October, the two Germanys reunited after forty-five years of separation. By then, the other communist governments in eastern Europe had either fallen or were about to do so.

Challenges to communist rule in China met with less success. In June 1989, hundreds—perhaps thousands—of

**Pro-Democracy Movements**

unarmed students and other citizens who for weeks had been holding peaceful pro-democracy rallies in Beijing's Tiananmen Square were slaughtered by Chinese armed forces. The Bush administration, anxious to preserve influence in Beijing, did no more than denounce the action, allowing the Chinese government, whose successful economic reforms had won much admiration in the 1980s, to emphatically reject political liberalization.

Elsewhere, however, the forces of democratization proved too powerful to resist. In South Africa, a new government under F. W. de Klerk, responding to increased domestic and international pressure, began a cautious retreat from the apartheid system. In February 1990, de Klerk legalized all political parties in South Africa, including the ANC, and ordered the release of Nelson Mandela, a hero to black South Africans, after a twenty-seven-year imprisonment. Then, in a staged process lasting several years, the government repealed its apartheid laws and

▲ African National Congress (ANC) leader Nelson Mandela gestures after casting his vote at Ohlange High School hall in Inanda, on April 27, 1994, for South Africa's first all-race elections. When results were announced later in the week, Mandela had been elected South Africa's first black president. *(John Parkin/AP Images)*

opened up the vote to all citizens, regardless of color. Mandela, who became South Africa's first black president in 1994, called the transformation of his country "a small miracle."

In 1990 the Soviet Union itself began to disintegrate. First the Baltic states of Lithuania, Latvia, and Estonia declared independence from Moscow's rule. The following year, the Soviet Union itself ceased to exist, disintegrating into independent successor states—Russia, Ukraine, Tajikistan, and many others (see Map 32.2). Muscled aside by Russian reformers who thought he was moving too

### Collapse of Soviet Power

slowly toward democracy and free-market economics, Gorbachev himself lost power. The breakup of the Soviet empire, the dismantling of the Warsaw Pact (the Soviet military alliance formed in 1955 with communist countries of eastern Europe), the repudiation of communism by its own leaders, German reunification, and a significantly reduced risk of nuclear war signaled the end of the Cold War. The Soviet-American rivalry that for half a century had dominated international politics—and circumscribed domestic prospects in both countries—was over.

The United States and its allies had won. The containment policy followed by nine presidents—from Truman through Bush—had had many critics over the years, on both the left and the right, but it had succeeded on a most basic level: it had contained communism for four-plus decades without blowing up the world and without obliterating freedom at home. Two systems competed in this East-West confrontation, and that of the West had clearly triumphed—as anyone who experienced life in both a NATO country and a Warsaw Pact nation quickly realized. Next to the glitz and bustle and well-stocked store shelves of the former were the drab housing projects, polluted skies, and scarce consumer goods of the latter. Over time, the Soviet socialist economy proved less and less able to compete with the American free-market one, less and less able to cope with the demands of the Soviet and eastern European citizenry.

Yet the Soviet empire might have survived for years more had it not been for Gorbachev, one of the most influential figures of the twentieth century. His ascension to the top of the Soviet leadership was the single most important event in the final phase of the Cold War, and it is hard to imagine the far-reaching changes of the 1985–1990 period without his influence. Through a series of unexpected overtures and decisions, Gorbachev fundamentally transformed the nature of the superpower relationship in a way that could scarcely have been anticipated a few years before. Ronald Reagan's role was less central but still vitally important, not so much because of his hard-line policies in his first term as because of his later willingness to enter into serious negotiations and to treat Gorbachev more as a partner than as an adversary. George H. W. Bush, too, followed this general approach. In this way, just as personalities mattered in starting the Cold War, so they mattered in ending it.

The victory in the Cold War elicited little celebration among Americans. The struggle had exacted a heavy price in money and lives. The confrontation may never have become a hot war on a global level, but the period after 1945 nevertheless witnessed numerous bloody Cold War–related conflicts claim-

### Costs of Victory

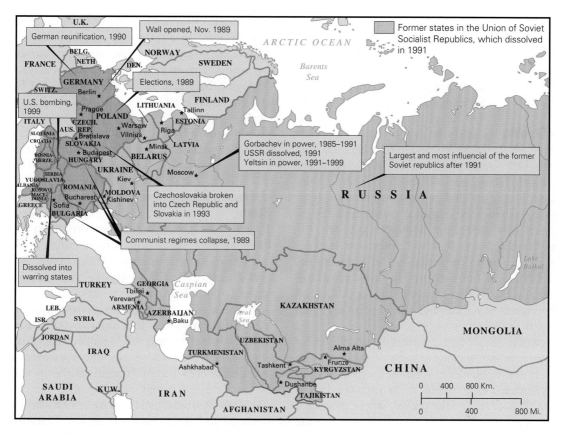

**Map 32.2    The End of the Cold War in Europe**
When Mikhail Gorbachev came to power in the Soviet Union in 1985, he initiated reforms that ultimately undermined the communist regimes in eastern Europe and East Germany, and led to the breakup of the Soviet Union itself, ensuring an end to the Cold War.

ing millions of lives. In the Vietnam War alone, between 1.5 million and 2 million people died, more than 58,000 of them Americans. Military budgets, meanwhile, had eaten up billions upon billions of dollars that could have been allocated to domestic programs. Some Americans wondered whether the steep price had been necessary, whether the communist threat had ever been as grave as officials, from the late 1940s on, had claimed.

Bush proclaimed a "new world order," but for him and his advisers the question was: what happens next? As the Cold War closed, they struggled futilely to describe the dimensions of an international system that they said would be based on democracy, free trade, and the rule of law. The administration signed important arms reduction treaties with the Soviet Union in 1991 and with the post-breakup Russia in 1993, leading to major reductions in nuclear weapons on both sides, but the United States sustained a large defense budget and continued to station large numbers of military forces overseas. As a result, Ameri-

cans were denied the "peace dividend" that they hoped would reduce taxes and free up funds to address domestic problems.

In Central America, the Bush administration cooled the zeal with which Reagan had meddled, because the interventions had largely failed, and, with the Cold War over, anticommunism seemed irrelevant. Still, like so many presidents before him, Bush showed no reluctance to intervene forcefully and unilaterally in the region to further U.S. aims. In December 1989, American troops invaded Panama to oust military leader Manuel Noriega. A long-time drug trafficker, Noriega had stayed in Washington's favor in the mid-1980s by providing logistical support for the contras in nearby Nicaragua, but in the early 1990s, exposés of his sordid record, which provoked protests in Panama, changed Bush's mind. Noriega was captured in the invasion and taken to Miami, where, in 1992, he was convicted of drug trafficking and imprisoned. Devastated Panama, meanwhile, became all the more dependent on the United States, which offered little reconstruction aid.

The strongest test of Bush's foreign policy came in the Middle East. The Iran-Iraq War had ended inconclusively in August 1988, after eight years of fighting and almost 400,000 dead. The Reagan administration had assisted the Iraqi war effort with weapons and intelligence, as had many other NATO countries. In mid-1990 Iraqi president Saddam Hussein, facing massive war debts and growing domestic discontent, invaded neighboring Kuwait, hoping thereby to enhance his regional power and his oil revenues and also shore up domestic support. He counted on Washington to look the other way. Instead, George Bush condemned the invasion and vowed to defend Kuwait. He was outraged by Hussein's act of aggression and also feared that Iraq might threaten U.S. oil supplies, not merely in Kuwait but also in petroleum-rich Saudi Arabia next door.

**Saddam Hussein's Gamble**

Within weeks, Bush had convinced virtually every important government, including most of the Arab and Islamic states, to sign on to an economic boycott of Iraq. Then, in Operation Desert Shield, Bush dispatched more than 500,000 U.S. forces to the region, where they were joined by more than 200,000 from the allies. Likening Saddam to Hitler and declaring the moment the first post-Cold War "test of our mettle," Bush rallied a deeply divided Congress to authorize "all necessary means" to oust Iraq from Kuwait (a vote of 250 to 183 in the House and 52 to 47 in the Senate). Although Bush did not invoke the 1973 War Powers Act, numerous observers saw his seeking a congressional resolution of approval as reinforcing the intent of the act. Many Americans believed that economic sanctions imposed on Iraq should be given more time to work, but Bush would not wait. "This will not be another Vietnam," the president said, by which he meant it would not be a lengthy and frustrating affair. Victory would come swiftly and cleanly.

Operation Desert Storm began on January 16, 1991, with the greatest air armada in history pummeling Iraqi targets. American cruise missiles reinforced round-the-clock bombing raids on Baghdad, Iraq's capital. It was a television war, in which CNN reporters broadcast live from a Baghdad hotel while bombs were falling in the city, and millions of Americans sat transfixed in their living rooms, eyes glued to the TV. In late February, coalition forces under General Norman Schwartzkopf launched a ground war that quickly routed the Iraqis from Kuwait. When the war ended on March 1, at least 40,000 Iraqis had been killed, while the death toll for allied troops stood at 240 (148 of them Americans). Almost one-quarter of the American dead were killed by "friendly fire"—by weapons fired by U.S. or allied troops.

**Operation Desert Storm**

Bush rejected a call from some of his advisers to take Baghdad and topple Hussein's regime. Coalition members would not have agreed to such a plan—it would go beyond the original objective of forcing Iraq out of Kuwait—and it was also not clear who in Iraq would replace the dictator. Some also warned that the drive to Baghdad could

In the Persian Gulf War of early ▶ 1991, Operation Desert Storm forced Iraqi troops out of Kuwait. Much of that nation's oil industry was destroyed by bombs and by the retreating Iraqis, who torched oil facilities as they left. Oil wells burned for months, darkening the sky over these American forces and causing environmental damage.

*(Bruno Barbey/Magnum Photos, Inc.)*

## CNN

When Ted Turner launched CNN, his Cable News Network, on June 1, 1980, few people took it seriously. CNN, with a staff of three hundred—mostly young, mostly inexperienced—operated out of the basement of a converted country club in Atlanta. Dismissed by critics as the Chicken Noodle Network, CNN was at first best known for its on-air errors, as when a cleaning woman walked onto the set and emptied anchor Bernard Shaw's trash during his live newscast. But by 1992, against all expectations, CNN was seen in more than 150 nations worldwide, and *Time* magazine named Ted Turner its "Man of the Year" for realizing media theorist Marshall McLuhan's vision of the world as a "global village" united by mass media.

Throughout the 1980s, CNN steadily built relations with local news outlets in nations throughout the world. As critical—and sometimes unanticipated—events reshaped the world, CNN reported live from Tiananmen Square and from the Berlin Wall in 1989. Millions watched as CNN reporters broadcast live from Baghdad in the early hours of the Gulf War in 1991. CNN changed not only viewers' experience of these events but diplomacy itself. When the Soviet Union wanted to denounce the 1989 U.S. invasion of Panama, officials called CNN's Moscow bureau instead of the U.S. embassy. During the Gulf War, Saddam Hussein reportedly kept televisions in his bunker tuned to CNN, and U.S. generals relied on its broadcasts to judge the effectiveness of missile attacks. In 1992 President George H. W. Bush noted, "I learn more from CNN than I do from the CIA."

Although Turner's twenty-four-hour news network had a global mission, its American origins were often apparent. During the U.S. invasion of Panama, CNN cautioned correspondents not to refer to the American military forces as "our" troops. Turner himself once sent his staff a memo insisting that anyone who used the word *foreign* instead of *international* would be fined $100. What CNN offered was not so much international news, but a global experience: people throughout the world joined in watching the major moments in contemporary history as they unfolded. America's CNN created new links among the world's people. But, as *Time* magazine noted (while praising Turner as the "Prince of the Global Village"), such connections "did not produce instantaneous brotherhood, just a slowly dawning awareness of the implications of a world transfixed by a single TV image."

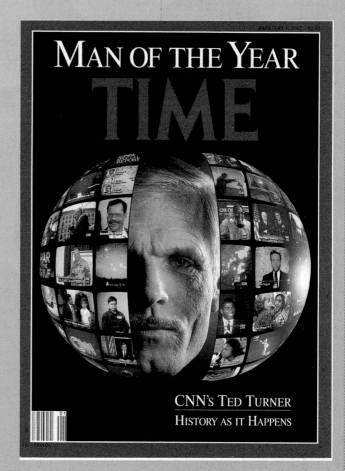

▲ "I am the right man in the right place at the right time," Ted Turner declared at the time of CNN's founding in 1980. "Not me alone, but all the people who think the world can be brought together by telecommunications." Just over a decade later Turner was rewarded for his visionary idea by being named *Time* magazine's "Man of the Year" for 1991. *(Time & Life Pictures/Getty Images)*

▲ President George Bush signs the Americans with Disabilities Act (ADA) on the White House lawn, July 26, 1990. As he lifted his pen, the president said: "Let the shameful wall of exclusion finally come tumbling down." *(© Ron Sachs/CNP/Corbis)*

bog down, subjecting U.S. forces to a costly and drawn-out campaign. So Saddam Hussein survived in power, though with his authority curtailed. The U.N. maintained an arms and economic embargo, and the Security Council issued Resolution 687, demanding that Iraq provide full disclosure of all aspects of its program to develop weapons of mass destruction and ballistic missiles with a range greater than 150 kilometers. In Resolution 688, the Security Council condemned a brutal crackdown by the Iraqi regime against Kurds in northern Iraq and Shi'ite Muslims in the south and demanded access for humanitarian groups. The United States, Britain, and France seized on Resolution 688 to create a northern "no-fly zone" prohibiting Iraqi aircraft flights. A similar no-fly zone was set up in southern Iraq in 1992 and expanded in 1996.

Although in time some would question President Bush's decision to stop short of Baghdad, initially there

## Domestic Problems

were few objections. In the wake of Desert Storm the president's popularity in the polls soared to 91 percent, beating the previous high of 89 percent set by Harry Truman in June 1945 after the surrender of Germany. Cocky White House advisers thought Bush could ride his popularity right through the 1992 election and beyond. In the afterglow of military victory it seemed a good bet, particularly as Bush could also claim achievements on the domestic front that seemed to affirm his inauguration-day pledge to lead a "kinder, gentler nation."

In 1990, for example, Bush had signed the Americans with Disabilities Act. This act, which applied to companies with twenty-five or more employees and covered 87 percent of all wage earners, banned job discrimination against those with disabilities who can, with reasonable accommodation, perform the essential tasks required by the job. It also required that "reasonable accommodations," such as wheelchair ramps, be made available to people with disabilities. Also in 1990, the president, much to the disappointment of conservatives, who opposed increased regulation, signed the Clean Air Act, which sought to reduce acid rain by limiting emissions from factories and automobiles. And in 1991, after many months of contentious debate, Bush and Congress agreed on a civil rights bill to protect against job discrimination.

Yet not long after reaching their historic highs, Bush's poll numbers started falling and kept falling, largely because of the president's ineffectual response to the weakening American economy. He was slow to grasp the implications of the heavy burden of national debt and the massive federal deficit which had been out of control for nearly a decade. When the nation entered into a full-fledged recession in the months after the Gulf War, Bush did not respond, beyond proclaiming that things were not really that bad. Echoed his treasury secretary Nicholas Brady, "I don't think it's the end of the world even if we have a recession. We'll pull out of it again. It's no big deal."

For millions of ordinary Americans, it was a big deal. Business shrank, despite low interest rates that theoretically should have encouraged investment. Real-estate prices plummeted. American products faced steadily tougher competition from products made overseas, especially in Japan and elsewhere in Asia. As unemployment climbed to 8 percent, consumer confidence sank. By late 1991, fewer than 40 percent of the American people felt comfortable with the way the country was going. Many demanded that the federal government address neglected problems, such as the rising cost of healthcare.

Bush's credibility was diminished further by confirmation hearings for Clarence Thomas, whom Bush nominated to the Supreme Court in the fall of 1991. The Bush administration hoped that those who opposed the nomination of yet another conservative to the high court might nonetheless support the addition of an African American justice. But in October, Anita Hill, an African American law professor at the University of Oklahoma, charged that Thomas had sexually harassed her when she worked for him during the early 1980s. The Judiciary Committee hearings, carried live on television, turned ugly, and some Republican members suggested that Hill was either lying or mentally ill. Thomas described himself as the "victim" of a "high-tech lynching," and African American groups were passionately divided over the Hill-Thomas testimony. However, Hill's testimony focused the nation's attention on issues of power, gender, sex, and the workplace. And the Senate's confirmation of Thomas, along with the attacks on Hill, angered many, further increasing the gender gap in American politics.

**Clarence Thomas Nomination**

As George H. W. Bush and the Republicans entered the election year of 1992, the glow of military victory in the Gulf War had faded completely.

## SUMMARY

When Ronald Reagan left the White House in 1988, succeeded by his vice president, George Bush, the *New York Times* summed up his presidency: "Ronald Reagan leaves no Vietnam War, no Watergate, no hostage crisis. But he leaves huge question marks—and much to do." George H. W. Bush met the foreign policy promises of the 1980s, as the Soviet Union collapsed and America achieved victory in the decades-long Cold War. He also led the United States into war with Iraq—a war that ended in swift and decisive victory but left Saddam Hussein in power.

During the 1980s, the United States moved from deep recession to economic prosperity. However, deep tax cuts and massive increases in defense spending created huge budget deficits, increasing the national debt from $994 billion to more than $2.9 trillion. This enormous debt would limit the options of subsequent presidential administrations. Pro-business policies, such as deregulation, created opportunities for the development of new technologies and prompted economic growth but also opened the door to corruption and fraud. Policies that benefited the wealthy at the expense of middle-class or poor Americans widened the gulf between the rich and everyone else. The social pathologies of drug addiction, crime, and violence grew, especially in the nation's most impoverished areas. The legacies of the 1980s included thousands of children born addicted to crack, who would live the rest of their lives with mental and physical impairments, and prisons that overflowed with young men.

The 1980s also saw the coalescence of the "culture wars" between fundamentalist Christians who sought to "restore" America to God and opponents who championed separation of church and state, and embraced liberal values. The nation shifted politically to the right, though the coalitions of economic and social conservatives that

*Legacy* FOR A PEOPLE AND A NATION

## The Americans with Disabilities Act

The Americans with Disabilities Act (ADA), passed by large bipartisan majorities in Congress and signed into law by President George Bush on July 26, 1990, built on the legacy of America's civil rights movement; President Bush called it "the world's first comprehensive declaration of equality for people with disabilities." But the ADA did more than prohibit discrimination against people with physical and mental disabilities. It mandated that public and private entities—including schools, stores, restaurants and hotels, libraries and other government buildings, and public transportation authorities—provide "reasonable accommodations" to allow people with disabilities to participate fully in the life of their communities and their nation.

In less than two decades, the equal-access provisions of the ADA have changed the landscape of America. Steep curbs and stairs once blocked access to wheelchair users; now ramps and lifts are common. Buses "kneel" for passengers with limited mobility; crosswalks and elevators use audible signals for the sight-impaired. At colleges and universities, qualified students (including those with learning disabilities) receive a wide range of assistance or accommodation. The National Park Service's "accessibility" program has enabled people with a whole spectrum of disabilities to travel into the Grand Canyon and on trails in many parks. Lee Page, a wheelchair user and sports fan from Virginia, described the impact of ADA standards for sports stadiums: "We were able to see over the standing spectators as the anthem was sung. I could see the flag and everything that was happening down on the field. . . . I finally felt like a part of the crowd."

At the same time that the ADA has offered greater opportunity to many Americans, regulations covering employment have generated some difficult legal questions. Which conditions are covered by the ADA? (The Supreme Court has ruled that asymptomatic HIV infection is a covered disability and carpal tunnel syndrome is not.) Employers may not discriminate against qualified people who can, with "reasonable" accommodation, perform the "essential" tasks of a job—but what is "reasonable" and what is "essential"? The specific provisions of the ADA will likely continue to be contested and redefined in the courts. But as Attorney General Janet Reno noted, as she celebrated the tenth anniversary of the ADA with a ceremony at Warm Springs, Georgia, where President Franklin Roosevelt had sought therapy for the effects of polio, the true legacy of the ADA is the determination "to find the best in everyone and to give everyone equal opportunity."

supported Reagan were fragile and did not guarantee continued Republican dominance.

Finally, during the 1980s, the face of America changed. A society that many had thought of as white and black became ever more diverse. The nation's Latino population grew in size and visibility. New immigrants from Asia arrived in large numbers; though still a small part of the population, they would play an increasingly important role in American society. During the Reagan-Bush years, America had become both more divided and more diverse. In the years to come, Americans and their leaders would struggle with the legacies of the "Reagan era."

## SUGGESTIONS FOR FURTHER READING

Elijah Anderson, *Streetwise: Race, Class, and Change in an Urban Community* (1992)

A. J. Bacevich et al., *The Gulf War of 1991 Reconsidered* (2003)

Lou Cannon, *President Reagan: The Role of a Lifetime* (2000)

Robert M. Collins, *Transforming America: Politics and Culture During the Reagan Years* (2006)

Jack F. Matlock, *Reagan and Gorbachev: How the Cold War Ended* (2004)

John Micklethwait and Adrian Wooldridge, *The Right Nation: Conservative Power in America* (2004)

James A. Morone, *Hellfire Nation: The Politics of Sin in American History* (2003)

James Patterson, *The Restless Giant: The United States from Watergate to Bush vs. Gore* (2005)

*For a more extensive list for further reading, go to* college.hmco.com/pic/norton8e.

# Into the Global Millennium
## America Since 1992

*America Since 1992*

*α* t 8:46 a.m. on that fateful Tuesday morning, Jan Demczur, a window washer, stepped into an elevator in the North Tower of the World Trade Center in New York City. The elevator started to climb, but before it reached its next landing, one of the six occupants recalled, "We felt a muted thud. The whole building shook. And the elevator swung from side to side like a pendulum." None of the occupants knew it, but American Airlines Flight 175 had just crashed into the building, at a speed of 440 miles per hour.

The elevator started plunging. Someone pushed the emergency stop button, and the descent stopped. For several minutes, nothing happened. Then a voice came over the intercom to deliver a blunt message: there had been an explosion. The line went dead, as smoke began to seep through the elevator's doors. Using the wooden handle of Demczur's squeegee, several of the men forced open the doors but discovered they were on the fiftieth floor, five hundred feet above the ground, where this elevator did not stop. In front of them was a wall.

Demczur, a Polish immigrant who once worked as a builder, saw that the wall was made of Sheetrock, a plasterboard he knew could be cut. Using the squeegee, he started to scrape the metal edge against the wall, back and forth, over and over again. When the blade broke and fell down the shaft, he used a short metal handle that he had in his bucket. It took more than an hour, but the six men took turns scraping and poking, and finally burst through to a men's bathroom. Startled firefighters guided them to a stairwell. After an agonizingly slow descent through the heavy smoke, they finally burst onto the street at 10:23 a.m. Five minutes later the tower collapsed.

It was September 11, 2001.

◄ "The Tribute of Light," dedicated to the memory of the victims of the World Trade Center terrorist attacks, lights up the sky above Lower Manhattan on March 11, 2002, the six-month anniversary of the attacks. The Brooklyn Bridge is seen in the foreground. *(Daniel P. Derella/AP/Wide World Photos, Inc.)*

## CHRONOLOGY

1992 ■ Violence erupts in Los Angeles over Rodney King verdict
■ Major economic recession
■ Clinton elected president
■ United States sends troops to Somalia

1993 ■ Congress approves North American Free Trade Agreement (NAFTA)
■ United States withdraws from Somalia

1994 ■ Contract with America helps Republicans win majorities in House and Senate
■ Genocide in Rwanda
■ U.S. intervention in Haiti

1995 ■ Domestic terrorist bombs Oklahoma City federal building
■ U.S. diplomats broker peace for Bosnia

1996 ■ Welfare reform bill places time limits on welfare payments
■ Clinton reelected

1998 ■ House votes to impeach Clinton

1999 ■ Senate acquits Clinton of impeachment charges
■ NATO bombs Serbia over Kosovo crisis
■ Antiglobalization demonstrators disrupt World Trade Organization (WTO) meeting in Seattle

2000 ■ Nation records longest economic expansion in its history
■ Supreme Court settles contested presidential election in favor of Bush

2001 ■ Economy dips into recession; period of low growth and high unemployment begins
■ Bush becomes president
■ Al Qaeda terrorists attack World Trade Center and Pentagon
■ PATRIOT Act passed by Congress
■ United States attacks Al Qaeda positions in Afghanistan, topples ruling Taliban regime

2003 ■ United States invades Iraq, ousts Saddam Hussein regime

2004 ■ Bush reelected

2005 ■ Hurricane Katrina strikes Gulf Coast

2006 ■ Iraq War continues; by end of year U.S. deaths reach three thousand
■ Democrats take both houses of Congress in midterm elections

Only later that day did Demczur learn what had happened: terrorists had hijacked four airliners and turned them into missiles. Two had been flown into the World Trade Center; one had slammed into the Pentagon in Washington, D.C.; and one had crashed in a field in rural Pennsylvania after passengers tried to wrest control of the plane from the hijackers. Both World Trade Center towers had collapsed, killing close to three thousand people, including Demczur's close friend Roko Camaj, a window washer from Albania.

It was the deadliest attack the United States had ever suffered on its soil, and it would lead to far-ranging changes in American life. But the events of the day sent shock waves well beyond the country's shores, indeed around the globe, and made starkly clear just how interconnected the world had become at the dawn of the twenty-first century. At the World Trade Center alone, nearly five hundred foreigners from more than eighty countries lost their lives. Sixty-seven Britons died, twenty-one Jamaicans, and twenty-seven Japanese. Mexico lost seventeen of its citizens; India lost thirty-four. Sixteen Canadians perished, as did fifteen Australians and seven Haitians. The tiny Caribbean nation of Trinidad and Tobago counted fifteen deaths.

The list of victims revealed the extraordinary diversity of people who inhabited New York, showing the city once again to be a melange of world cultures. According to a chaplain at "ground zero," the victims' families communicated their grief in well over a hundred languages. Many of the victims were, like Demczur and Camaj, immigrants who had come to New York to seek a better life for themselves and their families; others were there on temporary work visas. But all helped to make the World Trade Center a kind of global city within a city, where some 50,000 people worked and another 140,000 visited on any given day.

A symbol of U.S. financial power, the World Trade Center towers were also—as their very name suggested—a symbol of the globalization of world trade that had been a central phenomenon of the 1980s and 1990s. The towers housed the offices and Wall Street infrastructure of more than four hundred businesses, including some of the world's leading financial institutions—Bank of America,

Switzerland's Credit Suisse Group, Germany's Deutsche Bank, and Japan's Dai-Ichi Kangyo Bank.

*Globalization* had become one of the buzzwords of the 1990s and by most definitions went beyond trade and investment to include the web of connections—in commerce, communications, and culture—that increasingly bound the world together. The terrorists, who were tied to a radical Islamic group called Al Qaeda, sought to strike a blow at that globalization, yet their attack was also an expression of it. In other words, Al Qaeda depended on the same international technological, economic, and travel infrastructure that had fueled global integration. Cell phones, computers, intercontinental air travel—the plotters made full use of these instruments of globalization in preparing to carry out their attack, then turned four modern jetliners into lethal weapons.

Islamic militants had actually struck at the World Trade Center before, in 1993, detonating a massive bomb in the center's underground parking garage and causing significant damage. But Americans at the time paid only fleeting attention. With the demise of Soviet communism and the end of the Cold War, most were intent on focusing inward. President Bill Clinton had come into office in 1993 determined to concentrate less on foreign policy and more on such domestic issues as healthcare and deficit reduction. Convinced that advances in digital technology would fundamentally change how Americans did business at home and abroad, Clinton sought to harness the forces of globalization to America's benefit.

For a broad majority of the American people, the last decade of the century offered good times. The stock market soared, unemployment dropped, and more Americans than ever before owned their own homes. But the 1990s were also marked by violence and cultural conflict—the first multiethnic uprising in Los Angeles, domestic terrorism in Oklahoma City, shootings by students at their schools, hate crimes that shocked the nation.

These were also years of political volatility and divisions. From the first days of Clinton's presidency, conservative Republicans blocked the Democrats' legislative programs. With a conservative agenda of limited government and "family values," the GOP routed Democrats in the 1994 midterm elections. But Republicans overesti-

mated their power, alienating many voters by forcing the federal government to shut down during the winter of 1995–1996 in a standoff over the federal budget, and Clinton was reelected in 1996. However, scandal plagued the Clinton White House, and in 1999 Clinton was impeached by the House of Representatives, which alleged that he had committed perjury and obstructed justice. Clinton survived the crisis; the Senate failed to convict him, and his popularity figures remained high. But his ability to lead the nation was compromised and his presidency tarnished.

Clinton's successor, George W. Bush, successful in an extremely close and controversial election, responded to the 9/11 attacks by declaring a "war on terrorism." In so doing, he committed his administration and the nation to a complex and dangerous campaign of undefined scope and duration. Twice within eighteen months, Bush ordered U.S. forces into large-scale military action, first in Afghanistan, where Al Qaeda had its headquarters with the blessing of the ruling Taliban regime, then in Iraq to oust the government of Saddam Hussein. Both operations initially went well militarily, as the Taliban and the Iraqi government were quickly beaten. Al Qaeda, however, did not cease to be a threat, and in Afghanistan fighting eventually resumed. In Iraq, U.S. occupying forces battled a large-scale insurgency. Bush saw his high approval ratings begin to drop, and though he won reelection in 2004, his second term was undermined by continued bloodshed in Iraq and scandal at home.

- What was "The New Economy" of the 1990s, and how did it contribute to the globalization of business?
- Did the attacks of September 11, 2001 change America in fundamental ways? Explain.
- Why did the United States invade Iraq in 2003, and why did its occupying forces subsequently face a drawn-out and bloody insurgency?

## SOCIAL STRAINS AND NEW POLITICAL DIRECTIONS

Although the 1990s would be remembered as an era of relative peace and prosperity, the decade did not start that way. Stories on the evening news portrayed a divided and troubled nation. Scourges of drugs, homelessness, and crime plagued America's cities. Racial tensions had worsened; the gulf between rich and poor had grown more pronounced. The economy, slowing since 1989, had tipped into recession. Public disillusionment with political leaders ran strong, but members of an otherwise ineffective and scandal-ridden Congress had voted themselves a pay raise. As the 1992 presidential election year began, Americans were frustrated and looking for a change.

The racial tensions that troubled the nation erupted in the South Central neighborhood of Los Angeles in 1992. Like most such outbreaks of violence, there was an immediate cause. A jury (with no African American members) had acquitted four white police officers charged with beating a black man, Rodney King, who had fled a pursuing police car at speeds exceeding 110 miles per hour. A bystander's video of the beating had been played so often on CNN, the new twenty-four-hour news network, that CNN's vice president called it "wallpaper." Thus the local event became a national story, the beating a symbol of continuing racism in American society. Within hours of the verdict, fires were burning in South Central.

### Violence in Los Angeles

The roots of this violence, however, went deeper. Well-paid jobs had disappeared in the deindustrialization of the 1970s and 1980s, as Firestone, Goodyear, and Bethlehem Steel, along with more than a hundred other manufacturing and industrial plants, shut their doors. By the early 1990s, almost one-third of South Central residents lived in poverty—a rate 75 percent higher than for the city as a whole.

Tensions increased as new immigrants sought a foothold in the area—Latino immigrants from Mexico and Central America who competed with African American residents for scarce jobs; Korean immigrants establishing small businesses, such as grocery stores. Outside the legitimate economy, the 40 Crips (an African American gang) and the 18th Street gang (Latino) struggled over territory in South Central as the crack epidemic further decimated the neighborhood and the homicide rate soared. The police did not succeed in controlling gang violence, and their tactics alienated neighborhood residents. Relations between African Americans and Korean immigrants were especially strained. Many African American and Latino residents saw high prices in Korean-owned shops as exploitation and claimed that shopkeepers treated them disrespectfully, while Korean shopkeepers complained of frequent shoplifting, robberies, even beatings.

The violence in Los Angeles (what the Korean community called Sa-I-Gu, or 4/29, for the date it began) was a multiethnic uprising that left at least fifty-three people dead, some victims of random violence, some targeted because of their race or ethnicity, some killed by law enforcement, a few victims of accidents in the overwhelming chaos. Almost a billion dollars' worth of property was destroyed, including 2,300 stores owned by Koreans or Korean Americans. More than sixteen thousand people were arrested, half of them Latinos, many of them recent immigrants.

Americans were shocked by the events in L.A. They were also increasingly worried about the economy. During the Bush administration, the economy had grown slowly or not at all, the worst showing since the Great Depression of the 1930s. Some city and state governments faced bankruptcy. In 1978 California's Proposition 13—the first in a series of "tax revolts" across the nation—had cut property taxes while the population boomed, and the state government, out of money in mid-1992, paid its workers and bills in IOUs. California was not alone; thirty states were in financial trouble in the early 1990s. Many businesses, deeply burdened with debt, closed down or cut back. Factory employment was at its lowest level since the recession of 1982, and corporate downsizing meant that well-educated white-collar workers were losing jobs as well. In 1991 median household incomes hit the most severe decline since the 1973 recession; in 1992 the number of poor people in America reached the highest level since 1964.

### Economic Troubles and the 1992 Election

As economic woes continued, President George H. W. Bush's approval rating fell—down to half of its high point of 91 percent after the Persian Gulf War. Americans seized on a news story about the president's amazed reaction to a grocery store price scanner—though Bush was admiring the prototype for a new scanning mechanism at a trade fair and not encountering a supermarket scanner for the first time—as evidence that the president was out of touch with the everyday lives and problems of American citizens who had to do their own shopping. Despite the credit Bush gained for foreign policy—the end of the Cold War and the quick victory in the Gulf War—economic woes and a lack of what he once called the "vision thing" left him vulnerable in the 1992 presidential election.

Democratic nominee Bill Clinton, the governor of Arkansas, offered a profound contrast to George Bush. Clinton's campaign headquarters bore signs with the four-word reminder "It's the economy, stupid." In a town hall-format presidential debate, a woman asked how the economic troubles had affected each candidate, and Clinton moved from behind the podium to ask her, "Tell me how it's affected you again? You know people who've lost their jobs and lost their homes?" George Bush was caught on camera looking at his watch.

On election day, Americans denied George Bush a second term. Ross Perot, a Texas billionaire who claimed he would bring economic common sense to the federal government, claimed almost 20 percent of the popular vote—the highest percentage for a third-party candidate in eighty years—but did not carry a single state. Clinton and his running mate, Tennessee Senator Al Gore, with 43 percent of the popular vote, swept New England, the West Coast, and much of the industrial Midwest, even making inroads into what had become an almost solidly Republican South and drawing "Reagan Democrats" back to the fold. The American people were voting for change, and their discontent carried over to congressional elections. Democrats remained in control of both houses, but incumbents did not fare well. The 103rd Congress had 110 new representatives and 11 new senators.

Bill Clinton was one of the most paradoxical presidents in American history. A journalist described him in

## William Jefferson Clinton

a 1996 *New York Times* article as "one of the biggest, most talented, articulate, intelligent, open, colorful characters ever to inhabit the White House," while noting that Clinton "can also be an undisciplined, fumbling, obtuse, defensive, self-justifying rogue. . . . He is breathtakingly bright while capable of doing really dumb things." Clinton was a larger-than-life figure, a born politician from a small town called Hope who had wanted to be president most of his life. In college at Georgetown University in Washington, D.C., during the 1960s he had protested the Vietnam War and (like many of his generation) had maneuvered to keep himself from being sent to Vietnam. Clinton had won a Rhodes scholarship to Oxford, earned his law degree from Yale, and returned to his home state of Arkansas, where he was elected governor in 1978 at the age of thirty-two.

In 1975 Clinton had married Hillary Rodham, whom he met when they were both law students at Yale. Rodham Clinton, who made Law Review at Yale (an honor not shared by her husband), was the first First Lady to have a significant career of her own during her married life, and she spoke of balancing her commitments to her professional life with those to her husband and their daughter, Chelsea. Although Clinton boasted during the campaign that his slogan might be "Buy one, get one free," Rodham Clinton was quickly attacked by conservatives and antifeminists. After she told a hostile interviewer, "I suppose I could have stayed home and baked cookies and had teas. But what I decided to do was pursue my profession, which I entered

◀ Presidential candidate Bill Clinton campaigns in Jackson, Mississippi in 1992. Describing Clinton's campaign appearance the night before the election, a *New York Times* journalist wrote: "Bill Clinton, a middling amateur saxophonist, is playing his true instrument, the crowd." *(Ira Wyman)*

before my husband was in public life," the *New York Post* called her "a buffoon, an insult to most women."

Politically, Bill Clinton was a "new Democrat." He, along with other members of the new Democratic Leadership Council, advocated a more centrist—though still socially progressive—position for the Democratic Party. Clinton and his colleagues asked whether large government bureaucracies were still appropriate tools for addressing social problems in modern America. They emphasized private-sector economic development rather than public jobs programs, focusing on job training and other policies that they believed would promote opportunity, not dependency. They championed a global outlook in both foreign policy and economic development. Finally, they emphasized an ethic of "mutual responsibility" and "inclusiveness." Some Democrats found Clinton's policies too conservative. However, the political right attacked Clinton with a vehemence unmatched since the attacks on Franklin Roosevelt's New Deal, and the political struggles of the 1990s were exceptionally partisan and rancorous.

## A New Democrat's Promise and Pitfalls

Clinton began his presidency with a great sense of promise. "Profound and powerful forces are shaking and remaking our world," he proclaimed in his inaugural address. "Well, my fellow citizens, this is our time. Let us embrace it." Clinton plunged into an ambitious program of reform and revitalization, beginning with his goal of appointing a cabinet that "looks like America" in all its diversity. But almost immediately he ran into trouble. Republicans, determined not to allow Clinton the traditional "honeymoon" period, maneuvered him into fulfilling a campaign pledge to end the ban on gays in the military before he had secured congressional or widespread military support. Amid great public controversy, Clinton finally accepted a "don't ask, don't tell" compromise that alienated liberals and conservatives, the gay community and the military.

Clinton's major goal was to make healthcare affordable and accessible for all Americans, including the millions who had no insurance coverage. But special interests mobilized in opposition: the insurance industry worried about lost profits; the business community feared higher taxes to support the uninsured; the medical community was concerned about more regulation, lower government reimbursement rates, and reduced healthcare quality. The administration's healthcare task force, cochaired by Hillary Rodham Clinton, could not create a political coalition strong enough to defeat these forces. Within a year, the centerpiece of Clinton's fledgling presidency had failed.

With Clinton beleaguered, new-style Republicans seized the chance to challenge the new Democrat. In September 1994, shortly before the midterm congressional elections, more than three hundred Republican candidates for the House of Representatives endorsed the "Contract with America." Developed under the leadership of Georgia congressman Newt Gingrich, the "Contract" promised "the end of government that is too big, too intrusive, and too easy with the public's money [and] the beginning of a Congress that respects the values and shares the faith of the American family." It called for a balanced-budget amendment to the Constitution, reduction of the capital gains tax, a two-year limit on welfare payments (while making unmarried mothers under eighteen ineligible), and increased defense spending.

## "Republican Revolution"

In the midterm elections, the Republican Party mobilized socially conservative voters to score a major victory. Republicans took control of both houses of Congress for the first time since 1954 and made huge gains in state legislatures and governorships. Ideological passions ran high, and many Republicans believed that their ongoing attempts to weaken federal power and to dismantle the welfare state would now succeed.

The Republicans of the 104th Congress, however, miscalculated. Although many Americans applauded the idea of cutting government spending, they opposed cuts to most specific programs, including Medicare and Medicaid, education and college loans, highway construction, farm subsidies, veterans' benefits, and Social Security. Republicans made a bigger mistake when they issued President Clinton an ultimatum on the federal budget. Clinton refused to accept their terms; Republicans refused to pass a continuing resolution to provide interim funding; and the government was forced to suspend all nonessential action during the winter of 1995–1996. An angry public blamed the Republicans.

Such struggles showed Clinton's resolve, but they also led him to make compromises that moved American politics to the right. For example, he signed the 1996 Personal Responsibility and Work Opportunity Act, a welfare reform measure that eliminated the provision in the 1935 Social Security Act guaranteeing cash assistance for poor children (Aid to Families with Dependent Children). The law mandated that heads of families on welfare must find work within two years—though states could exempt up to 20 percent of recipients—and limited welfare benefits to five years

## Political Compromise and the Election of 1996

over an individual's lifetime. It also made many legal immigrants ineligible for welfare. The Telecommunications Act of 1996, signed by Clinton, reduced diversity in America's media by permitting companies to own more television and radio stations.

Clinton and Gore were reelected in 1996 (defeating Republican Bob Dole and Reform Party candidate Ross Perot), in part because Clinton stole some of the conservatives' thunder. He declared that "the era of big government is over" and invoked family values, a centerpiece of the Republican campaign. Sometimes Clinton's actions were true compromises with conservative interests; other times he attempted to reclaim issues from the conservatives, as when he redefined family values as "fighting for the family-leave law or the assault-weapons ban or . . . trying to keep tobacco out of the hands of kids." And despite scandal and gridlock and ideological chasms that divided politicians and the American people alike, Clinton's election-year promise to "build a bridge to the future" seemed plausible in a time of increasing prosperity.

## "THE NEW ECONOMY" AND GLOBALIZATION

Just how much credit Clinton deserved for the improved economic figures in mid-decade is a matter of debate. Presidents typically get too much blame when the economy struggles and too much credit when times are good. The roots of the 1990s boom were in the 1970s, when American corporations began investing in new technologies, retooling plants to become more energy-efficient, and cutting labor costs. Specifically, companies reduced the influence of organized labor by moving operations, some to the South and West, where unions were weak, and some out of the United States entirely, to countries like China and Mexico, where labor was cheap and pollution controls were lax.

Even more important than the restructuring of existing corporations was the emergence of a powerful new sector of the economy associated with digital technology. The rapid

||||||||||||||||||||||||||||||||||

**Digital Revolution**

development of what came to be called "information technology"— computers, fax machines, cell phones, and the Internet— had a huge economic impact in the 1980s and 1990s. New companies and industries sprang up, many headquartered in the "Silicon Valley" near San Francisco. By the second half of the 1990s, the Forbes list of the 400 Richest Americans featured high-tech leaders like Bill Gates of Microsoft, who became the wealthiest person in the world with worth approaching $100 billion, as his company produced the software for operating most personal

▲ Apple cofounder and CEO Steve Jobs holds an iPod digital audio player on the cover of *Newsweek* in July 2004. Developed by Apple engineers in 2001 to take advantage of the pending revolution in digital music, the iPod was launched that October, barely a month after 9/11. The initial price: $399.00. Technical refinements improved the product and lowered the price, and sales surged. As of April 2007 more than 100 million units had been sold worldwide.

*(From* Newsweek, *July 25, 2004 © 2004 Newsweek, Inc. All rights reserved. Reprinted by permission. Used by permission and protected by the Copyright Laws of the United States. The printing, copying, redistribution, or retransmission of the material without express written permission is prohibited.)*

computers. The high-tech industry had considerable spillover effects on the broader economy, generating improved productivity, new jobs, and sustained economic growth.

The heart of this technological revolution was the microprocessor. Introduced in 1970 by Intel, the microprocessor miniaturized the central processing unit of a computer, meaning that small machines could now perform calculations previously requiring large machines. In the next decades the power of these integrated circuits increased by a factor of seven thousand. Computing chores that took a week in the early 1970s took one minute by

2000; the cost of storing one megabyte of information, or enough for a 320-page book, fell from more than $5,000 in 1975 to 17 cents in 1999. The implications for business were enormous.

Analysts dubbed this technology-driven sector "The New Economy," and it would have emerged whether or not Bill Clinton had won the White House. Yet Clinton and his advisers had some responsibility for the dramatic upturn. With the U.S. budget deficit topping $500 billion, they made the politically risky move of abandoning the middle-class tax cut and making deficit reduction a top priority. White House officials rightly concluded that, if the deficit could be brought under control, interest rates would be reduced and the economy would rebound. And that is what happened. The budget deficit started to come down (by 1997 it had been erased), a development that lowered interest rates, which in turn helped boost investment. Stock prices soared to unprecedented levels, and the gross national product rose by an average of 3.5 to 4 percent annually.

Clinton perceived early on that the technology revolution would shrink the world and make it more interconnected. He was convinced that,

### Globalization of Business

with the demise of Soviet communism, capitalism was spreading around the globe—if not full-blown capitalism, at least the introduction of market forces, freer trade, and widespread deregulation.

Globalization was not a new phenomenon—it had been under way for a century—but now it had unprecedented momentum. Journalist Thomas L. Friedman asserted that the post-Cold War world was "the age of globalization," characterized by the integration of markets, finance, and technologies. U.S. officials lowered trade and investment barriers, completing the North American Free Trade Agreement (NAFTA) with Canada and Mexico in 1993, and in 1994 concluding the Uruguay Round of the General Agreement on Tariffs and Trade (GATT), which lowered tariffs significantly for the seventy member nations that accounted for about 80 percent of world trade. The administration also endorsed the creation in 1995 of the World Trade Organization (WTO), to administer and enforce agreements made at the Uruguay Round. In a sign of how important trade had become to the administration's foreign agenda, the president formed a National Economic Council to complement the National Security Council and established a "war room" in the Commerce Department to promote trade missions around the world.

Multinational corporations were the hallmark of this global economy. By 2000 there were 63,000 parent com-

▲ Protesting that the World Trade Organization (WTO) possessed the dangerous power to challenge any nation's environmental laws if the WTO deemed them barriers to trade, chanting demonstrators marched in the streets of Seattle on November 29, 1999. Critics of the WTO have claimed that sea turtles and dolphins had already been victimized by the organization. Demonstrators identified the WTO as an example of globalization gone wrong. The WTO meeting went on, but the results proved meager because nations could not agree on rules governing dumping, subsidies for farm goods, genetically altered foods, and lower tariffs on high-tech goods. *(AP Photo/Beth A. Keiser)*

panies worldwide and 690,000 foreign affiliates. Some, like Nike and Gap, Inc., subcontracted production of certain merchandise to whichever developing countries had the lowest labor costs. Such arrangements created a "new international division of labor" and generated a boom in world exports, which, at $5.4 trillion in 1998, had doubled in two decades. U.S. exports climbed steadily, reaching $680 billion in 1998, but imports rose even higher, to

$907 billion in the same year (for a trade deficit of $227 billion). Sometimes the multinationals directly affected foreign policy, as when Clinton in 1995 extended full diplomatic recognition to Vietnam partly in response to pressure from such corporations as Coca-Cola, Citigroup, General Motors, and United Airlines, which wanted to enter that emerging market.

While the administration promoted open markets, labor unions argued that free-trade agreements exacer-

### Critics of Globalization

bated the trade deficit and often exported American jobs. Average real wages for American workers declined steadily after 1973, from $320 per week to $260 by the mid-1990s, a drop that labor leaders blamed on the inability of laid-off workers in import-competing industries to find jobs at their previous pay. Other critics extended this argument to the global level, maintaining that globalization was widening the gap between rich and poor countries, creating a mass of "slave laborers" in poor countries who endured working conditions that would never be tolerated in the West. Environmentalists charged that globalization also exported pollution and toxic waste into countries unprepared to deal with them, and warned of increased loss of biodiversity and the depletion of natural resources the world over. Still other critics warned that the power of multinational corporations and the global financial markets threatened both national sovereignty and traditional cultures.

Antiglobalization fervor reached a peak in the fall of 1999, when thousands of protesters disrupted a meeting of WTO ministers in Seattle. Hundreds were arrested. In the months that followed, there were smaller but sizable protests at meetings of the International Monetary Fund (IMF), which controls international credit and exchange rates, and the World Bank, which issues funds for development projects in numerous countries. In July 2001, some fifty thousand demonstrators descended on Genoa, Italy, to protest a meeting of the IMF and World Bank. Clashes with police resulted in one death and hundreds of injuries.

Activists also targeted individual corporations, such as the Gap, Starbucks, Nike, and, especially, McDon-

### Target: McDonald's

ald's, which by 1995 was serving 30 million customers a day in some twenty thousand franchises in over one hundred countries. Critics assailed the company's slaughterhouse techniques, its alleged exploitation of low-skilled workers, and its high-fat menu, as well as its role in a global culture that they denounced as increasingly homoge-

▲ McDonald's restaurants circled the globe by the early twenty-first century, exemplifying the globalization of American culture. This Ukrainian woman in Kiev seems to enjoy both her hamburger and a conversation with the human symbol of the fast-food chain, Ronald McDonald. *(Wide World Photos, Inc.)*

neous and sterile, a so-called McWorld. Starting in 1996 and continuing for the next six years, McDonald's endured hundreds of often-violent protests, including bombings in Rome, Prague, London, Macao, Rio de Janeiro, and Jakarta.

Others decried both the violence and the underlying arguments of the antiglobalization campaigners. True, some economists acknowledged, statistics showed that global inequality had grown in recent years. But if one included quality-of-life measurements, such as literacy and health, global inequality had actually declined. In the United States, some studies found, wage and job losses for workers were caused not primarily by globalization factors, such as imports, production outsourcing, and immigration, but by technological change that made production processes more efficient and reduced the need for unskilled labor. Other researchers saw no evidence that governments' sovereignty had been seriously compromised as a result of globalization or that there was a "race to the bottom" in environmental standards. For them, the essential point was incontrovertible: poor countries that increased their economic openness enjoyed higher growth rates, and no country had prospered by turning its back on the world economy.

Others pointed out that the big franchise operations were not homogenizing global culture to the degree that critics claimed. McDonald's, they said, supposedly a prime mover of "McWorld," tailored its menu and operating practices to local tastes. And although American movies, TV programs, music, computer software, and other "intellectual property" often dominated world markets in the 1990s, foreign competition also made itself felt in America. Millions of American children were gripped by the Japanese fad game Pokemon, and if satellite television established a worldwide following for Michael Jordan and the Chicago Bulls, it did the same for soccer's David Beckham and Manchester United. An influx of foreign players added to the international appeal of both the National Basketball Association and Major League Baseball, while in the National Hockey League some 20 percent of players by the late 1990s hailed from Europe.

Yet if it was erroneous to glibly equate globalization with Americanization, it remained true that the United States occupied a uniquely powerful position on the world stage. The

### Clinton's Diplomacy

demise of the Soviet Union had created a one-superpower world, in which the United States stood far above other powers in terms of political and military as well as economic might. The "unipolar moment" was the phrase one commentator used in urging an aggressive U.S. posture. Yet in his first term Clinton was far more wary in handling the traditional aspects of foreign policy—great-power diplomacy, arms control, regional disputes—than in facilitating American cultural and trade expansion. He was deeply suspicious of foreign military involvements. The Vietnam debacle had taught him that the American public had limited patience for wars lacking clear-cut national interest, a lesson he found confirmed by George Bush's failure to gain lasting political strength from the Gulf War victory.

This mistrust of foreign interventions was cemented for Clinton by the difficulties he inherited from Bush in Somalia. In 1992 Bush had sent U.S. marines to the East African nation as part of a U.N. effort to ensure that humanitarian supplies reached starving Somalis. But in the summer of 1993, when Americans came under deadly attack from forces loyal to a local warlord, Clinton withdrew U.S. troops. And he did not intervene in Rwanda, where in 1994 the majority Hutus butchered 800,000 of the minority Tutsis in a brutal civil war.

That Somalia and Rwanda were on the policy agenda at all testified to the growing importance of humanitarian

### Balkan Crisis

concerns in post–Cold War U.S. policy. Many administration officials argued for using America's power to contain ethnic hatreds, support human rights, and promote democracy around the world. The notion faced a severe test in the Balkans, which erupted in a series of ethnic wars. Bosnian Muslims, Serbs, and Croats were soon killing one another by the tens of thousands. Clinton, critical of Europe's reluctance to act in its own backyard, talked tough against Serbian aggression and atrocities in Bosnia-Herzegovina, especially the Serbs' cruel "ethnic cleansing" of Muslims through massacres and rape camps. On occasion he ordered U.S. airpower to strike Serb positions, but he put primary emphasis on diplomacy. In late 1995, after American diplomats brokered an agreement among the belligerents for a new multiethnic state in Bosnia-Herzegovina, a fragile peace took hold.

But Yugoslav president Slobodan Milosevic did not stop the anti-Muslim and anti-Croat fervor. When Serb forces moved to violently rid Serbia's southern province of Kosovo of its majority ethnic Albanians, Clinton was pressed to intervene. Initially he was reluctant; the ghosts of Vietnam were ever present in Oval Office deliberations. But reports of Serbian atrocities against the Muslim Kosovars and a major refugee crisis generated by the Yugoslavian military action stirred world opinion and finally caused the administration to act. In 1999 NATO forces led by the United States launched a massive aerial bombardment of Serbia. Milosevic withdrew his brutal military from Kosovo, where U.S. troops joined a U.N. peacekeeping force. That same year, the International War Crimes Tribunal indicted Milosevic and his top aides for atrocities.

In the Middle East, Clinton took an active role in trying to bring the PLO and Israel together to settle their differences. In September 1993 the

### Agreements in the Middle East

PLO's Yasir Arafat and Israel's prime minister, Yitzhak Rabin, signed an agreement at the White House for Palestinian self-rule in the Gaza Strip and the West Bank's Jericho. The following year Israel signed a peace accord with Jordan, further reducing the chances of another full-scale Arab-Israeli war. Radical anti-Arafat Palestinians, however, continued to stage bloody terrorist attacks on Israelis, while extremist Israelis killed Palestinians and, in November 1995, Rabin himself. Only after American-conducted negotiations and renewed violence in the West Bank did Israel agree in early 1997 to withdraw its forces from the Palestinian city of Hebron. Thereafter the peace process alternately sagged and spurted.

▲ In spring 1999, as NATO bombing raids pounded Serbia (Yugoslavia) and Serb military positions in Kosovo to punish Serbia for killing and displacing ethnic Albanians, the number of Kosovar refugees increased dramatically. Desperate and hungry, they fled to neighboring nations. Here, in a NATO-run refugee camp outside Skopje, Macedonia, U.S. marines distribute food to some of the 850,000 forced to leave their Kosovo homes. *(Wide World Photos, Inc.)*

The same could be said of international efforts to protect the environment, which gathered pace in the 1990s. The George H. W. Bush administration had opposed many of the provisions of the 1992 Rio de Janeiro Treaty protecting the diversity of plant and animal species, on the grounds that the likely economic consequences would be too severe. For the same reason the administration had blocked efforts to draft stricter rules to reduce global warming. Clinton, urged on by Vice President Al Gore, an ardent environmentalist, took a more proactive posture. Most notably, his administration signed the 1997 Kyoto protocol, which aimed to combat emissions of carbon dioxide and other gases that most scientists believe trap heat in the atmosphere. The treaty required the United States to reduce its emissions by 2012 to 7 percent below its 1990 levels. But facing strong congressional opposition, Clinton never submitted the protocol for ratification to the Republican-controlled Senate.

Far less publicized than the Israeli-Palestinian conflict or the debate over Kyoto was the growing adminis-

## Bin Laden and Al Qaeda

tration concern about the threat to U.S. interests posed by Islamic fundamentalism. In particular, senior officials worried about the rise of Al Qaeda (Arabic for "the base"), an international terrorist network led by Osama bin Laden, which was dedicated to purging Muslim countries of what it saw as the profane influence of the West and installing fundamentalist Islamic regimes.

The son of a Yemen-born construction tycoon in Saudi Arabia, bin Laden had supported the Afghan Mujahidin in their struggle against Soviet occupation. He then founded Al Qaeda and began financing terrorist projects with the fortune he received on his father's death. U.S. officials grew steadily more concerned, particularly as it became clear that bin Laden intended to go after American targets. In 1995 a car bomb in Riyadh killed 7 people, 5 of them Americans. In 1998 simultaneous bombings at the American embassies in Kenya and Tanzania killed 224 people, including 12 Americans. In Yemen in

2000, a small boat laden with explosives hit the destroyer *USS Cole,* killing 17 American sailors. Although bin Laden was understood to have masterminded and financed these attacks, he eluded U.S. attempts to apprehend him. In 1998 Clinton approved a plan to assassinate bin Laden at an Al Qaeda camp in Afghanistan, but the attempt failed.

## PARADOXES OF PROSPERITY

Despite conflicts abroad and partisan struggles in Washington, the majority of Americans experienced the late 1990s as a time of unprecedented peace and prosperity, fueled by the dizzying rise of the stock market. The Dow Jones Industrial Average increased almost twelvefold in the last two decades of the twentieth century. Between 1991 and 1999 alone, it climbed from 3,169 to a high of 11,497 (see Figure 33.1). The booming market benefited the middle class as well as the wealthy, for the mutual funds created during the 1970s and other new investment vehicles, such as 401(k) retirement plans, had drawn a majority of

Americans into the stock market. In 1952 only 4 percent of American households owned stocks. That percentage soared to almost 60 percent by the year 2000.

At the end of the 1990s, the unemployment rate stood at 4.3 percent—the lowest peacetime rate since 1957. Plentiful jobs made it easier to implement welfare reform, and welfare rolls were cut almost in half. The standard of living rose for all income groups: both the richest 5 percent and the least well-off 20 percent of American households saw their incomes rise almost 25 percent. But as that meant an average gain of $50,000 for the top 5 percent and only $2,880 for the bottom 20 percent, the gap between rich and poor continued to grow. Still, by the end of the decade more than two-thirds of Americans were homeowners—the highest percentage in history. Differences among groups were significant but declining: 52 percent of families earning less than the median income were homeowners in 2000, as were 48 percent of people of color. Teen pregnancy began to decline. Infant mortality dropped to the lowest rate in American history. Violent crime decreased; murder rates hit a thirty-year low.

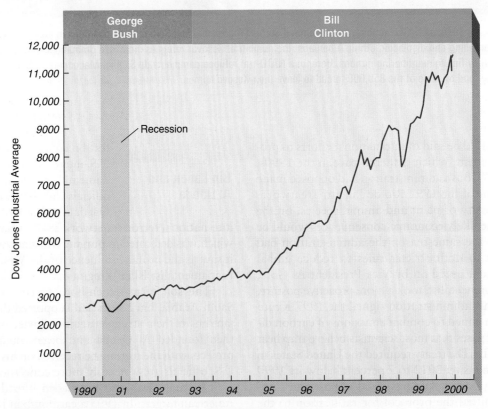

**Figure 33.1    The American Stock Market**
This graph of the Dow Jones Industrial Average, climbing steadily in the bull market of the 1990s, illustrates the great economic expansion of the decade.    *(Source: Adapted from Dow Jones & Company.)*

Despite these positive signs, there were new and unexpected crises. On April 19, 1995, 168 children, women,

### Oklahoma City Bombing

and men were killed in a powerful bomb blast that destroyed the nine-story Alfred P. Murrah Federal Building in downtown Oklahoma City. At first, many thought the bomb had come from abroad, perhaps set off by Middle Eastern terrorists. But a charred piece of truck axle located two blocks from the explosion, with the vehicle identification number still legible, proved otherwise. The bomber was Timothy McVeigh, a native-born white American and a veteran of the Persian Gulf War. He sought revenge for the deaths of members of the Branch Davidian religious sect, whom he believed the FBI had deliberately slaughtered in a standoff over firearms charges on that date two years before in Waco, Texas.

In the months that followed, reporters and government investigators discovered networks of militias, tax resisters, and various white-supremacist groups throughout the nation. These groups were united by distrust of the federal government. Many saw federal gun control laws, such as the Brady Bill, signed into law in 1993, as a dangerous usurpation of citizens' right to bear arms. Members of these groups believed that the federal government was controlled by "sinister forces," including Zionists, cultural elitists, Queen Elizabeth, and the United Nations. After McVeigh's act of domestic terrorism these groups lost members but also turned to the new Internet to spread their beliefs.

Other forms of violence also haunted America. On April 20, 1999, eighteen-year-old Eric Harris and

### Violence and Hate Crimes

seventeen-year-old Dylan Klebold opened fire on classmates and teachers at Columbine High School in Littleton, Colorado, killing thirteen before turning their guns on themselves. No clear reason why two academically successful students in a middle-class suburb would commit mass murder ever emerged. And the Columbine massacre was not an isolated event: students in Paducah, Kentucky; Springfield, Oregon; and Jonesboro, Arkansas, massacred classmates

In the late 1990s, two hate crimes shocked the nation. In 1998 James Byrd Jr., a forty-nine-year-old black man, was murdered by three white supremacists who dragged him for miles by a chain from the back of a pickup truck in Jasper, Texas. Later that year, Matthew Shepherd, a gay college student, died after being beaten unconscious and left tied to a wooden fence in freezing weather outside Laramie, Wyoming. His killers said they were "humili-

▲ On April 20, 1999, students evacuated Columbine High School in Littleton, Colorado, after two schoolmates went on a shooting rampage, killing twelve students and a teacher before killing themselves. *(Wide World Photos, Inc.)*

ated" when he flirted with them at a bar. Some argued that these murders demonstrated the strength of racism and homophobia in American society, while others saw the horror that most Americans expressed at these murders as a sign of positive change.

Throughout the Clinton years, scandals and rumors of scandal plagued the White House. The independent

### Scandal in the Clinton White House

counsel's office (independent counsels were appointed by a judicial board independent from the Justice Department to investigate possible misdeeds of high government officials) would eventually spend $72 million investigating allegations of wrongdoing by Hillary and Bill Clinton. Independent counsel Kenneth Starr, a conservative Republican and former judge, was originally charged with investigating Whitewater, a 1970s Arkansas real-estate deal in which the Clintons had invested. He turned up no evidence against the Clintons in his Whitewater investigation. However, Starr expanded the range of his investigation.

Early in Clinton's presidency, former Arkansas state employee Paula Jones had brought charges of sexual harassment against the president. Clinton denied the charges, which were eventually dropped. But when asked during questioning before a grand jury whether he had engaged in sexual relations with twenty-two-year-old White House intern Monica Lewinsky, Clinton said no. Speaking to the American people, Clinton angrily declared, "I did not have sexual relations with that woman, Miss Lewinsky." Starr, however, produced proof of the sexual relationship, including DNA evidence: a navy blue dress of Lewinsky's, stained with Clinton's semen.

In a 445-page report to Congress, Starr outlined eleven possible grounds for impeachment of the president, accusing Clinton of lying under oath, obstruction of justice, witness tampering, and abuse of power. On December 19, 1998, the House voted

**Impeachment**

on four articles of impeachment against Clinton; largely along party lines, the House passed two of the articles, one alleging that the president had committed perjury in his grand jury testimony, the other that he had obstructed justice. Clinton became only the second president—and the first in 130 years—to face a trial in the Senate, which has the constitutional responsibility to decide (by two-thirds vote) whether to remove a president from office.

But the American people did not want Clinton removed from office. Polls showed that large majorities approved of the president's job performance, even as many condemned his personal behavior. And many did not believe that his actions rose to the level of "high crimes and misdemeanors" (normally acts such as treason) required by the Constitution as grounds for impeachment. The Republican-controlled Senate, responding at least in part to popular opinion, voted against the charge of perjury 55 to 45 and, to the charge of obstructing justice, 50 to 50, thus clearing Clinton, because a two-thirds majority is required for conviction.

Clinton, of course, bears responsibility for his own actions. However, how those actions became grounds for impeachment, with the explicit sexual details contained in the Starr Report circulated by Internet around the world, is part of a larger story. Clinton was not the first president to engage in illicit sex. President John F. Kennedy had numerous and well-known sexual affairs, including one

**Political Partisanship, the Media, and Celebrity Culture**

with a nineteen-year-old intern. But after the Watergate scandals of the early 1970s, the mass media were no longer willing to turn a blind eye to presidential misconduct. The fiercely competitive twenty-four-hour news networks that began with CNN in 1980 relied on scandal, spectacle, and crisis to lure viewers. Public officials also contributed to the blurring of lines between public and private, celebrity and statesman. Clinton, for example, had appeared on MTV during his first campaign and answered a question about his preference in underwear (boxers).

The partisan political wars of the 1990s created a take-no-prisoners climate in which no politician's missteps would be overlooked. As fallout from the Clinton impeachment, both Republican Speaker of the House Newt Gingrich and his successor, Robert Livingston, resigned when faced with evidence of their own extramarital affairs. Finally, as former Clinton aide Sidney Blumenthal writes, the impeachment struggle was about more than presidential perjury and sexual infidelity. It was part of the "culture wars" that divided the American people: "a monumental battle over very large political questions about the Constitution, about cultural mores and the position of women in American society, and about the character of the American people. It was, ultimately, a struggle about the identity of the country."

Clinton's legislative accomplishments during his two terms in office were modest but included programs that made life easier for American families. The Family and Medical Leave Act guaranteed 91 million workers the right to take time off to care for ailing relatives or newborn children. The Health Insurance Portability and Accountability Act ensured that, when Americans changed jobs, they would not lose health insurance because of pre-existing medical conditions. Government became more efficient: the federal government operated with 365,000 fewer employees by the end of Clinton's term, and Vice President Gore led an initiative that eliminated sixteen thousand pages of federal regulations. Clinton created national parks and monuments that protected 3.2 million acres of American land and made unprecedented progress cleaning up toxic waste dumps throughout the nation.

**Clinton's Legislative Record**

Vice President Al Gore was the favorite in the 2000 presidential election. The son of a prominent senator from Tennessee, Gore had graduated cum laude from Harvard in 1969 and, despite his reservations about the war, had enlisted in the army and served in Vietnam. He had served six terms in Congress and in the Clinton administration had played a greater role than any vice president

**The Bush-Gore Race**

in American history. After eight years of prosperity and relative peace, he had a strong platform on which to run. Gore, however, failed to inspire voters. Earnest and highly intelligent, he appeared to many to be a well-informed policy wonk rather than a charismatic leader.

Gore's Republican opponent was best known nationally as the son of George H. W. Bush, the forty-first president of the United States. An indifferent student, George W. Bush had graduated from Yale in 1968 and pulled strings to jump ahead of a one-and-a-half-year waiting list for the Texas Air National Guard, thus avoiding service in Vietnam. After a difficult period, which included a rocky career in the oil business, at the age of forty Bush gave up alcohol and embraced Christianity. His fortunes improved while his father was president, and in 1994 he was elected to the first of two terms as governor of Texas.

As a presidential candidate, Bush made up for his limited foreign policy knowledge, often garbled syntax, and lack of interest in the intricacies of public policy with a direct, confident style that connected with many Americans. Unlike Gore, who peppered his stump speeches with statistics and programmatic initiatives, Bush spoke of his relationship with God and his commitment to conservative social values, styling himself a "compassionate conservative." Supported heavily by prominent Republicans and business leaders, Bush amassed the largest campaign war chest in history ($67 million, compared with Gore's $28 million).

Finally, in 2000, consumer rights activist Ralph Nader ran on the Green Party ticket. Condemning globalization and environmental despoilation, he attacked both Bush and Gore, calling them "Tweedledee and Tweedledum." Nader drew support from left-liberal voters who would have been more likely to vote for Gore and possibly helped tip some states to Bush.

On election day 2000, Al Gore narrowly won the popular vote (see Map 33.1). But he did not win the presidency. It all came down to Florida

## The Contested Election of 2000

(where Bush's brother Jeb was governor) and its twenty-five electoral votes. According to the initial tally, Bush narrowly edged Gore out in Florida, but by so close a margin that a recount was legally required. Charges and countercharges flew. In several heavily African American counties, tens of thousands of votes were not counted because voters failed to fully dislodge the "chads," or small perforated squares, when punching the old-fashioned paper ballots. Lawyers struggled over whether "hanging chads" (partially detached) and "pregnant chads" (punched but not detached) were sufficient signs of voter intent. In Palm Beach County, many elderly Jewish residents were confused by a poorly designed ballot. Thinking they were selecting Gore, they voted instead for the allegedly anti-Semitic Pat Buchanan. After thirty-six days of confusion, with court cases at the state and federal levels, the Supreme Court voted 5 to 4 along narrowly partisan lines to end the recount process. Florida's electoral votes—and the presidency—went to George Bush.

In the 2000 election, Gore won the West Coast, Northeast, and industrial Midwest. The South, Rocky Mountain West (except New Mexico), and heartland went to Bush. More than 90 percent of black voters selected Gore, as did 63 percent of Latinos and 55 percent of Asian Americans. Bush won 60 percent of the white vote, and, overall, 95 percent of his supporters were white. The gender gap was 12 points: 54 percent of women voted for Gore, as opposed to 42 percent of men (see Figure 33.2). And the struggles over the election outcome had further polarized the nation. As Bush waited for the January inaugural, critics and comics began referring to him as the "president-select."

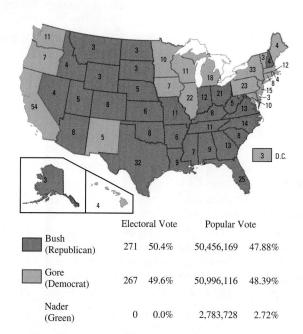

| | | Electoral Vote | | Popular Vote | |
|---|---|---|---|---|---|
| | Bush (Republican) | 271 | 50.4% | 50,456,169 | 47.88% |
| | Gore (Democrat) | 267 | 49.6% | 50,996,116 | 48.39% |
| | Nader (Green) | 0 | 0.0% | 2,783,728 | 2.72% |

### Map 33.1 Presidential Election, 2000

Democratic candidate Al Gore won the popular vote, but George W. Bush succeeded in gaining electoral victory by four votes. Among white males, Bush ran extremely well, while Gore won a majority of minority and women voters. Ralph Nader's Green Party won less than 3 percent of the national vote, but his votes in Florida may have detracted from the Gore tally, helping Bush win the critical electoral votes.

(Source: Carol Berkin et al., Making America, Third Edition. Used by permission of Houghton Mifflin Company.)

▶ Supporters of Democratic presidential candidate Al Gore and Republican candidate George Bush confront each other in front of the U.S. Supreme Court as attorneys prepare to argue the postelection legal case *Bush v. Gore.* The Supreme Court's 5-4 decision to end the Florida recount would give the presidency to George Bush.

*(© Reuters/Corbis)*

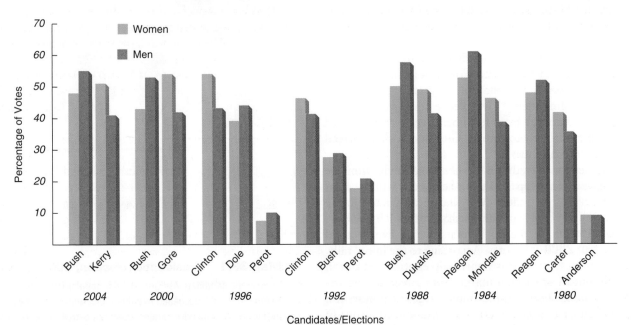

**Figure 33.2    The Gender Gap in American Presidential Elections**

The gender gap, or the difference in voting patterns between men and women, was first identified in 1980 by National Organization for Women president Eleanor Smeal and has been recognized as an important force in American politics ever since. In virtually every presidential election portrayed here, greater percentages of women (no matter their race or ethnicity, income, level of education, or marital status) than men voted for the Democratic candidate.

*(Source: Based on data from the Center for American Women and Politics.)*

# SEPTEMBER 11 AND THE WAR ON TERRORISM

In view of the close election and bitter Florida controversy, many believed that Bush would govern from the center. Some also thought that he was philosophically centrist, as his father had been, and that he had moved to the right only to ensure turnout among conservative evangelical Christians, who made up an increasingly large part of the Republican base. From the administration's first days, however, Bush governed from the right, arguably further to the right than any administration of modern times. As the head of the Heritage Foundation, a conservative Washington think tank, enthused, the new team was "more Reaganite than the Reagan administration."

The centerpiece of the Bush agenda was a massive tax cut, to be financed by the predicted budget surplus.

**Bush's Tax Plan**

"A surplus in tax revenue, after all, means that taxpayers have been overcharged," the president said. "And usually when you've been overcharged, you expect to get something back." Critics replied that a massive cut would wipe out the surplus and that the Bush plan favored the wealthy, but Bush persisted, using his party's control of Congress to push through the largest tax cut in U.S. history—$1.3 trillion. To the dismay of environmentalists, he also reiterated his campaign proposal to drill for oil in America's last wilderness, the Arctic National Wildlife Refuge, and chose a secretary of the interior with close ties to the energy industry who favored scaling back regulations protecting the environment.

In international affairs, the administration moved swiftly to chart a more unilateralist course than its predecessors. Given America's preponderant power, senior Bush officials reasoned, it did not need the help of others in the international system; accordingly they attached less importance to consultation and cooperation than had the Clinton administration. Soon after taking office, Bush announced that the United States would exit the 1972 Anti-Ballistic Missile Treaty with Russia to develop a National Missile Defense system (forbidden under the treaty) broadly similar to Reagan's "Star Wars" plan. Such a system, Bush said, would protect the United States from missile threats by potentially hostile nations, such as North Korea, Iraq, and Iran. The White House also renounced the 1997 Kyoto protocol on controlling global warming and registered opposition to a carefully negotiated protocol to strengthen the 1972 Biological and Toxin Weapons Convention. All three decisions caused consternation in Europe, as did the administration's hands-off policy toward the Israeli-Palestinian peace process.

Then came September 11. On that sunny Tuesday morning, nineteen hijackers seized control of four commercial jets that had taken off from East Coast airports. At 8:46 a.m.

**9/11**

one plane crashed into the 110-story North Tower of the World Trade Center in New York City, causing a huge explosion and fire. At 9:03 a.m., a second plane flew into the South Tower. In less than two hours, both buildings collapsed, killing thousands of office workers, firefighters, and police officers. At 9:43, the third plane crashed into the Pentagon, leaving a huge hole in its west side. The fourth plane was also headed toward Washington, but several passengers—learning of the World Trade Center attacks through cell-phone conversations—stormed the cockpit; in the scuffle that followed, the plane crashed in Somerset County, Pennsylvania, killing all aboard.

More than three thousand people died, making this the deadliest act of terrorism in history. Not since the Japanese assault on Pearl Harbor in 1941 had the United States experienced such a devastating attack on its soil. The hijackers—fifteen Saudi Arabians, two Emiratis, one Lebanese, and, leading them, an Egyptian—had ties to Al Qaeda, Osama bin Laden's radical Islamic organization. Some officials in the Clinton and Bush administrations had warned that an attack by Al Qaeda was inevitable: when Clinton's national security adviser met with his successor, Condoleezza Rice, shortly before Bush's inauguration, he told her, "You're going to spend more time during your four years on terrorism generally and Al Qaeda specifically than any issue." Broadly speaking, however, neither administration made counterterrorism a top foreign policy priority.

In an instant, counterterrorism was priority number one. President Bush decided immediately, indeed before 9/11 had become 9/12, to respond with large-scale military force. Al

**Afghanistan War**

Qaeda operated out of Afghanistan with the blessing of the ruling Taliban, a repressive Islamic fundamentalist group that had gained power in 1996 in the turmoil following the defeat of the Soviet-backed government in 1989. In early October, the United States launched a sustained bombing campaign against Taliban and Al Qaeda positions, and sent special operations forces to help a resistance organization based in northern Afghanistan. Within two months, the Taliban had been driven from power, although bin Laden as well as top Taliban leaders eluded capture.

As administration officials were quick to acknowledge, the swift military victory did not end the terrorist threat. Bush spoke of a long and difficult struggle that he called a war against evil forces, in which the nations of the world were either with the United States or against it. Some questioned whether a "war on terrorism" could ever be won in a meaningful sense, given that the foe was a nonstate actor weak in the traditional measures of power—territory and governmental power—and with little to lose. A war against such an adversary could have no definable end, observers noted, and they questioned whether Bush, by speaking in such unambiguous terms, was setting himself and the nation up for eventual failure. Most Americans, however, were ready to believe. Stunned by September 11, they experienced a renewed sense of national unity and pride. Flag sales soared, and Bush's approval ratings skyrocketed. Citizenship applications from immigrants rose dramatically.

But the new patriotism had a dark side. Just as the outbreak of the Cold War half a century earlier had

**PATRIOT Act**

brought a search for domestic traitors, the war on terrorism incorporated a hunt for potential Al Qaeda supporters at home. Congress passed the USA PATRIOT Act (Uniting and Strengthening America by Providing Appropriate Tools Required to Intercept and Obstruct Terrorism), making it easier for law enforcement to conduct searches, wiretap telephones, and obtain electronic records on individuals. Attorney General John Ashcroft approved giving FBI agents new powers to monitor the Internet, mosques, and rallies. Civil libertarians charged that the Justice Department had overstepped sensible boundaries, and some judges ruled against the tactics. Yet, according to a June 2002 Gallup poll, 80 percent of Americans were willing to give up some freedoms for security.

In surveys weeks after the attacks, 71 percent of respondents said that they felt depressed, and one-third said that they had trouble sleeping. The figures dropped thereafter, but anxiety remained. The discovery of anthrax-laden letters in several East Coast cities heightened fears about vulnerability to bioterrorism, particularly after post offices and government buildings were closed and five people died. Investigators found no evidence to connect the letters to the 9/11 hijackings, but also no good clues as to who the perpetrator might be, despite conducting more than five thousand interviews and pursuing hundreds of leads.

Yet continuity was as evident as change. People continued shopping in malls, visiting amusement parks, purchasing cars and homes. Employees still showed up for work, even in skyscrapers, and still gossiped around the lunch table. Although airline bookings dropped significantly in the early weeks (causing severe economic problems for many airlines), people still took to the skies. Some even complained about the new security measures at airports. In Washington, the partisanship that had all but disappeared after 9/11 returned, as Democrats and Republicans sparred over judicial appointments, energy policy, and the proposed new Department of Homeland Security. Approved by Congress in November 2002, the department was designed to coordinate intelligence and consolidate defenses against terrorism. Incorporating parts of eight cabinet departments and twenty-two agencies, it was the first new department since the Department of Veterans Affairs in 1989.

Economically, the months before September 11 witnessed a collapse of the so-called dot-coms, the Internet

**Economic Uncertainty**

companies that had been the darlings of Wall Street in the 1990s. In the course of 2001 some five hundred dot-coms declared bankruptcy or closed, and analysts warned of worse to come. There were other economic warning signs as well, notably a meager 0.2 percent growth rate in the nation's goods and services for the second quarter of 2001—the slowest growth in eight years. Corporate revenues were also down.

Economic concerns deepened after 9/11 with a four-day closing of Wall Street and a subsequent sharp drop in stock prices. The week after the markets reopened, the Dow Jones Industrial Average plunged 14.26 percent—the fourth largest weekly drop in percentage terms since 1900. The markets eventually rebounded, but questions remained about the economy's overall health. Such was Bush's political strength after 9/11, however, that neither this economic uncertainty nor the failure to capture Osama bin Laden and top Taliban leaders dented his popularity. In the midterm elections of 2002, the Republicans retook the Senate and added to their majority in the House.

Overseas, the president's standing was not nearly so high. Immediately after September 11, there was an outpouring of support from people

**International Responses**

everywhere. "We are all Americans now," said the French newspaper *Le Monde* the day after the attacks. Moments of silence in honor of the victims were held in many countries, and governments all over the world announced that they would cooperate with Washington in the struggle against terrorism. But within a year, attitudes had changed dramatically. Bush's bellicose stance and good-versus-evil terminology had put off many foreign observers from the start, but they initially swallowed their objections. But when the president started hinting that America might unilaterally strike Saddam Hussein's Iraq or deal forcefully with North Korea or Iran—the three countries of Bush's "axis of evil"—many allied governments registered strong objections.

▲ The attacks on 9/11 brought forth an outpouring of sympathy for the victims and their families, and for the United States generally, from people around the world. Here firefighters in Taipei, Taiwan, attend a prayer service during a global day of mourning.  *(AFP/Getty)*

At issue was not merely the prospect of an American attack on one of these countries but the underlying rationale that would accompany it. Bush and other top officials were in effect saying that the strategy of containment and deterrence that had guided U.S. foreign policy for more than fifty years was outmoded. In an age of terrorism, they maintained, the United States would not wait for a potential security threat to become real; henceforth, it would strike first. "In the world we have entered, the only path to safety is the path of action and this nation will act," Bush declared. Americans had to be "ready for preemptive action when necessary to defend our liberty and to defend our lives." Critics of the strategy, among them many world leaders, called it recklessly aggressive and contrary to international law, and they wondered what would happen if dictators around the world began claiming the same right of preemption.

## WAR AND OCCUPATION IN IRAQ

But Bush was determined, particularly on Iraq. Several of his top advisers, including Secretary of Defense Donald Rumsfeld and Vice President Dick Cheney, had wanted to oust Saddam Hussein for years, indeed since the end of the Gulf War in 1991; for them it was a piece of unfinished business. Before 9/11, however, these Iraq hawks were stymied by officials who sought in effect to maintain the Bush, Sr.–Clinton policy of keeping Saddam Hussein contained through a mix of sanctions and military coercion, such as periodic air strikes to enforce the no-fly zones in the north and south. Secretary of State Colin Powell, the first African American to hold that position and a figure of growing influence in the administration's early months, talked only of improving the sanctions policy, and National Security adviser Condoleezza Rice—the first African American and first woman to hold *that* post—made it "extremely clear" to colleagues that there would be no move to oust the Iraqi dictator militarily.

No sooner had the Twin Towers fallen, however, than President Bush began contemplating a move against Saddam. Along with Cheney and Rumsfeld, Bush saw an opportunity to fold Iraq into the larger war on terrorism—this despite the fact that counterterrorism experts saw no link between Saddam and Al Qaeda. For a time Powell succeeded in keeping the focus on Afghanistan, but little by little the thinking in the White House shifted. In November 2001 Bush ordered the Pentagon to initiate war planning for Iraq; by spring 2002 a secret consensus had been reached: Saddam Hussein would be removed by force.

In September Bush challenged the United Nations to immediately enforce its resolutions against Iraq, or the

### Why Iraq?

United States would be compelled to act on its own. In the weeks that followed, he and his aides offered sometimes-shifting reasons for getting tough with Iraq, if necessary through military action. They said that Saddam was a major threat to the United States and its allies, a leader who possessed and would use banned biological and chemical "weapons of mass destruction" (WMDs) and who actively sought to acquire nuclear weapons. They claimed, contrary to their own intelligence estimates, that he had ties to Al Qaeda and could be linked to the 9/11 attacks. They said that he brutalized his own people and generated regional instability with his tyrannous rule.

Beneath the surface lurked other motivations. Neoconservatives, enjoying influence in Washington for the first time since the Reagan years, saw in Iraq a chance to use U.S. power to reshape the region in America's image, to oppose tyranny and spread democracy. Ousting Saddam, they said, would enhance the security of Israel, America's key ally in the Middle East, and would likely start a chain reaction that would extend democracy throughout the region. White House political strategists, meanwhile, thinking in mundane but for them crucial terms, believed that a swift and decisive removal of a hated dictator would cement Republican domination in Washington and virtually assure Bush's reelection two years hence. Oil, too, entered the picture, though not quite in the way many antiwar activists assumed: for Bush and his aides, it was not so much about access to Iraqi oil as about preventing an Iraq armed with WMDs from destabilizing an oil-rich region.

Like his father in 1991, Bush claimed he did not need congressional authorization to launch military action against Iraq; also like his father, he

### Congressional Approval

nevertheless sought such backing. In early October 2002, the House of Representatives voted 296 to 133 and the Senate 77 to 23 to authorize the use of force against Iraq. The lopsided vote was misleading; many who voted in favor were unwilling to defy a president so close to a midterm election, even though they opposed military action without U.N. sanction. Vietnam veteran and Nebraska Republican senator

Chuck Hagel protested that "many of those who want to rush this country into war and think it would be quick and easy don't know anything about war." Both inside and outside Congress, critics complained that the president had not presented evidence that Saddam Hussein constituted an imminent threat or was connected to the 9/11 attacks. Bush switched to a less hawkish and unilateral stance, and in so doing gained U.N. backing: in early November, the U.N. Security Council unanimously approved Resolution 1441, imposing rigorous new arms inspections on Iraq.

Behind the scenes, though, the Security Council was deeply divided over what should happen next. In late January 2003, the weapons inspector's report castigated Iraq for failing to carry out "the disarmament that was demanded of it" but also said it was too soon to tell whether the inspections would succeed. Whereas U.S. and British officials emphasized the first point and said the time for diplomacy was up, France, Russia, and China emphasized the second point and called for more inspections. Some at the world body also warned that toppling the regime could cause an explosion of sectarian bloodshed between Iraq's Sunni Muslims and the majority Shi'ites who had suffered so grievously under the Sunni Saddam's rule. As the U.N. debate continued, and as massive antiwar demonstrations took place around the world, Bush sent about 250,000 soldiers to the region. Britain sent about 45,000 troops.

In late February, the United States floated a draft resolution to the U.N. that proposed issuing an ultimatum

### Fall of Baghdad

to Iraq, but only three of the fifteen Security Council members affirmed support. Faced with an embarrassing political defeat, Bush abandoned the resolution and all further diplomatic efforts on March 17, when he ordered Saddam Hussein to leave Iraq within forty-eight hours or face an attack. Saddam ignored the ultimatum, and on March 19 the United States and Britain launched an aerial bombardment of Baghdad and other areas. A ground invasion followed a few days later (see Map 33.2). The Iraqis initially offered stiff resistance, but soon the advancing forces gained momentum. On April 9, Baghdad fell to American troops.

The military victory was swift and decisive, the result of sixteen months of careful planning, smooth cooperation among the services, and precisely executed operations. Barely had the celebrations begun, however, before trouble started. So careful in making military preparations, senior policymakers showed scant interest in planning for postwar Iraq. The State Department's extensive studies were ignored, as Bush assigned responsibility for the postwar effort to the Pentagon. From consistently voicing the worst-case scenarios in making the case for war, top officials

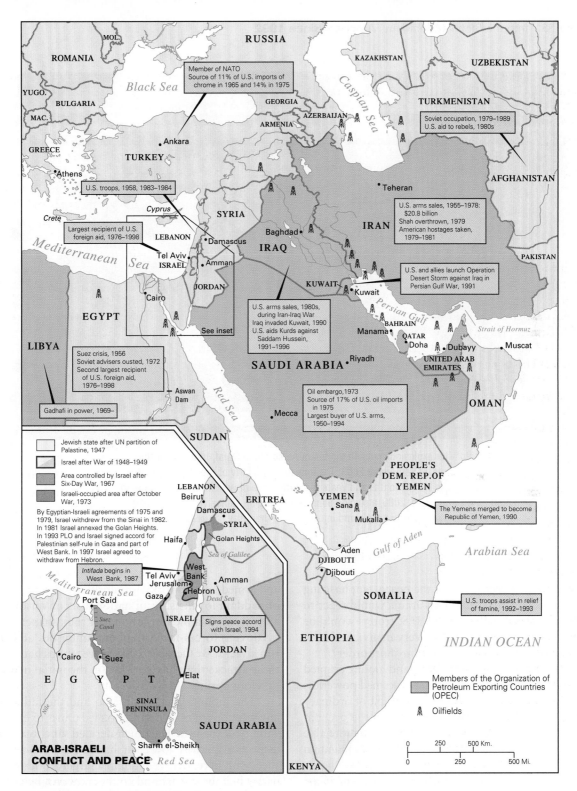

**Map 33.2  The Middle East**

Extremely volatile and often at war, the nations of the Middle East maintained precarious relations with the United States. To protect its interests, the United States extended large amounts of economic and military aid, and sold huge quantities of weapons to the area. At times, Washington ordered U.S. troops to the region. The Arab-Israeli dispute particularly upended order, although the peace process moved forward intermittently.

▲ A man cries for help after explosions outside the Imam Ali shrine in Najaf, Iraq, one of the holiest sites for Shia Muslims, in September 2003. The immediate vicinity of the shrine would be the scene of frequent attacks in the months and years thereafter, one of which caused damage to two of the minarets. On August 10, 2006, a suicide bomber wearing an explosive harness blew himself up near the shrine, killing forty people and injuring more than fifty. *(Kate Books/Polaris)*

did the opposite in preparing for the peace, emphasizing best-case outcomes regarding how Iraqis would react to "liberation" (with joy), how many U.S. troops would be required to secure the country (not very many), and how quickly a stable Iraq would emerge (in short order).

Thus, when violence, lawlessness, and looting erupted almost immediately, American planners seemed powerless to respond. The plight of ordinary Iraqis deteriorated as the occupation authority proved no more able to provide services than to maintain order. In Baghdad, electricity worked only a few hours each day, and telephone service was nonexistent. Garbage piled up in the streets, and hospitals had far too few workers to care for the influx of wounded and sick. Several decisions by the Coalition Governing Council (CPA), headed by Ambassador Paul Bremer, contributed to the lawlessness—notably Bremer's decision in May to disband the Iraqi army, which left tens of thousands of men, angry

### Insurgency

and armed, out of work. A multisided insurgency made up of Saddam loyalists, Iraqi nationalists of various stripes, and foreign Islamic revolutionaries took shape; soon, U.S. occupying forces faced frequent ambushes and hit-and-run attacks. By October 2003 more troops had died from these attacks than had perished in the initial invasion the previous spring.

The mounting chaos in Iraq and the failure to find any weapons of mass destruction led critics to question the validity of the war. The much-derided sanctions and U.N. inspections, it was now clear, had in fact been remarkably successful in rendering Saddam a largely toothless tyrant, with a hollow military and no chemical or biological weapons. Prewar claims of a "rush to war" resounded once again. Even many defenders of the invasion castigated the administration for its failure to anticipate the occupation problems and, once it learned of them, being tentative and slow-footed in responding. In the spring of 2004, graphic photos showing Iraqi detainees being abused and tortured by American guards at Abu Ghraib prison were broadcast around the world, generating international condemnation and adding fuel to the insurgency.

President Bush, facing reelection that fall, expressed disgust at the Abu Ghraib images and fended off charges that he and his top aides knew of and condoned the abuse. The White House also made much of the dissolution of the CPA in late June and the transfer of sovereignty to an interim Iraqi government—developments, it predicted, that would soon take the steam out of the insurgency. Many were skeptical, but voters that fall were prepared to give Bush the benefit of the doubt. His Democratic opponent, Senator John Kerry of Massachusetts, a Vietnam veteran who had reluctantly voted for the Iraq resolution in October 2002, had difficulty finding his campaign footing and never articulated a clear alternative strategy on the war. With the electorate deeply split, Bush won reelection with 51 percent of the popular vote to Kerry's 48 percent, and 279 electoral votes to Kerry's 252. The GOP also increased its majorities in the House and Senate.

|||||||||||||||||||||||||||||||||||
**Election of 2004**

White House aides crowed that the result validated the administration's foreign and domestic policies. Bush told the American people that he would use this "mandate" to make major changes in U.S. domestic policy. In his State of the Union address in early February 2005, Bush focused on his plan to partially privatize the Social Security system. This plan failed, as both Democratic and Republican members of Congress argued that it would not work, either economically or politically. The president did have success, however, in his efforts to reshape the Supreme Court. Conservative U.S. Circuit Court judge John Roberts was confirmed as chief justice following the death of Chief Justice William Rehnquist, and another strong conservative, Samuel Alito, became junior associate justice following the resignation of Sandra Day O'Connor. This conservative reorientation of the Supreme Court, along with the war in Iraq, are likely to be George Bush's major presidential legacies.

In the months following the 2004 election, the increasing evidence that the war in Iraq had little chance of success, by any definition, began to undermine the American people's confidence in President Bush and his administration. Growing perceptions of administrative incompetence were exacerbated when a major hurricane hit the Gulf Coast and New Orleans in late August 2005. Hurricane Katrina was the sixth most powerful Atlantic hurricane on record, with winds reaching 100 miles from its center. Katrina had fallen from force 5 (the highest rating) to force 3 by the time it slammed into New Orleans, but the high winds and storm surge destroyed the levees that kept low-lying parts of the city from being swamped by water from Lake Pontchartrain and surrounding canals. Floodwaters covered 80 percent of the city, and more than eighteen hundred people died in the storm and the floods that followed.

Tens of thousands of people who lacked the resources to evacuate the city sought shelter at the Superdome. Supplies of food and water quickly ran low, and toilets backed up; people wrapped the dead in blankets and waited for rescue. Those outside the Gulf region, watching the suffering crowd of poor, black New Orleanians stranded at the Superdome, began a soul-searching conversation about what Democratic party leader Howard Dean called the "ugly truth": that poverty remains linked to race in this nation. Quickly, however, public attention shifted to charges of administrative mismanagement and the seeming indifference of the president. "Nothing about the President's demeanor yesterday," reported the *New York Times* shortly after the hurricane, "which seemed casual to the point of carelessness—suggested that he understood the depth of the current crisis." Despite the federal government's failure to manage the crisis in New Orleans, President Bush cheered on Federal Emergency Management Association (FEMA) director Michael Brown with the words "Brownie, you're doing a heck of a job." In fact, poor planning on local, state, and federal levels compounded the human suffering caused by Katrina and made Americans wonder how well the nation was prepared, four years after the 9/11 attacks, to meet a major crisis. Many, looking at Katrina in the context of the continuing war in Iraq, questioned the competence of the Bush administration.

Internationally, too, Bush faced growing criticism, not only on account of Iraq and Abu Ghraib, but also because of his administration's continued lack of engagement in the Israeli-Palestinian dispute and what observers saw as its continuing disdain for the messy compromises of diplomacy. The White House, critics said, rightly sought to prevent North Korea and Iran from joining the nuclear club but seemed incapable of working imaginatively and multilaterally to make it happen. In Europe, where most editorial observers had hoped for a Kerry victory, Bush continued to be depicted as a gun-slinging cowboy whose moralistic rhetoric and aggressive policies threatened world peace. According to a Pew survey in June 2006, the percentage of the public expressing confidence in Bush's leadership in international affairs had fallen to 30 in Britain, 25 in Germany, 15 in France, and 7 in Spain.

|||||||||||||||||||||||||||||||||||
**America Isolated**

Iraq, though, remained the chief problem. The bill for the war now exceeded $1 billion per week and appeared certain to continue rising. In March 2005, the number of American war dead reached 1,500; that October, the figure hit 2,000; and in December 2006, it reached 3,000. The insurgents, too, suffered major casualties but showed no sign of weakening. Meanwhile, estimates of Iraqi civilian deaths since the invasion ranged by mid-2006 from a low of 60,000 to a high of 655,000. These Iraqi casualties resulted from insurgent suicide attacks and U.S. bombing of suspected insurgent hideouts, as well as from increasing sectarian violence between Sunnis and Shi'ites. In July 2006 alone, according to an authoritative tally, more than 3,400 civilians were killed, most of them from this sectarian conflict. In January 2007, the Iraq Health Ministry reported 17,310 civilian deaths over the previous six months.

The Bush administration denied that Iraq had degenerated into civil war or that the struggle had become a Vietnam-like quagmire, but it seemed to have little clue how to bring the fighting to an end. Far from helping to reduce the threat of terrorism to Americans and others, the Iraq invasion seemed only to have increased it, as the Al Qaeda presence in the country (nonexistent before the war) became pronounced and as the ongoing struggle in Afghanistan suffered comparative neglect.

In Congress and the press, calls for withdrawal from Iraq multiplied, but skeptics cautioned that disengagement would make things worse: it would cause an explosion of sectarian bloodshed and, almost certainly, a collapse of the Baghdad government. The power and regional influence of neighboring Iran would increase, and American credibility would be undermined throughout the Middle East. Some commentators instead called for a major increase in the number of U.S. forces in Iraq, but it was not clear where these troops would be found in the overstretched American military or whether they would do much good on the ground. The 2006 midterm election was at least in part a referendum on the war, and the voters made their feeling clear: 55 percent nationally voted for Democratic candidates, and the party seized control of both houses of Congress. Not a single Democratic incumbent in either house suffered defeat.

## AMERICANS IN THE FIRST DECADE OF THE NEW MILLENNIUM

At the beginning of the twenty-first century, the United States is a nation of extraordinary diversity. For much of the twentieth century, however, it had seemed that the United States was moving in the opposite direction. Very few immigrants had been allowed into the United States from the 1920s through 1965. New technologies, such as radio and television, had a homogenizing effect at first, for these mass media were dependent on reaching the broadest possible audience—a mass market. Although local and ethnic traditions persisted, more and more Americans participated in a shared mass culture. During the last third of the twentieth century, however, those homogenizing trends were reversed. Immigration reform in the mid-1960s opened American borders to large numbers of people from a wider variety of nations than ever before. New technologies—the Internet, and cable and satellite television, with their proliferation of channels—replaced mass markets with niche markets. Everything from television shows to cosmetics to cars could be targeted toward specific groups defined by age, ethnicity, class, gender, or lifestyle choices. These changes did not simply make American society more fragmented. Instead, they helped to make Americans' understandings of identity more fluid and more complex.

In the 2000 U.S. government census, for the first time Americans were allowed to identify themselves as belonging to more than one race. New census categories recognized that notions of biological "race" were problematic. Why could a white woman bear a "black" child when a black woman could not bear a white child? The change also acknowledged the growing number of Americans born to parents of different racial backgrounds, as American mixed-race and mixed-ethnicity marriages grew from less than 1 percent in 1970 to 5.4 percent at the turn of the millennium. Critics, however, worried that, because census data are used to gather information about social conditions in the United States and as a basis for allocating resources, the new "multiracial" option would reduce the visibility and clout of minority groups. Thus the federal government counted those who identified both as white and as members of a racial or ethnic minority as belonging to the minority group. Under this system, the official population of some groups increased: more Americans than ever before, for example, identified themselves as at least partly Native American. Others rejected racial and ethnic categories altogether: 20 million people identified themselves simply as "American," up more than 50 percent since 1990.

On October 17, 2006, the United States officially passed the 300 million population mark (it hit 100 million in 1915 and 200 million in 1967), and its people were increasingly diverse. During the 1990s, the population of people of color grew twelve times as fast as the white

### Race and Ethnicity in Recent America

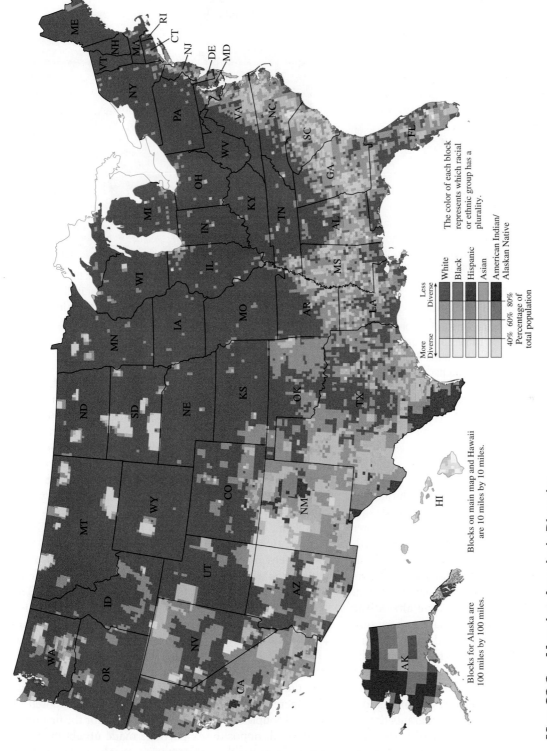

**Map 33.3   Mapping America's Diversity**

**Aggregate figures (more than 12 percent of the U.S. population was African American and about 4 percent Asian American in 2000, for example) convey America's ethnic and racial diversity. However, as this map shows, members of racial and ethnic groups are not distributed evenly throughout the nation.**

*(Source: Adapted from the New York Times National Edition, April 1, 2001, "Portrait of a Nation," p. 18. Copyright © 2001 by The New York Times Co. Reprinted with permission.)*

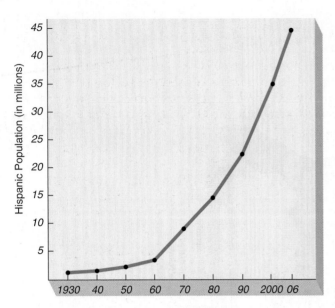

**Figure 33.3    The Growth of the
U.S. Hispanic Population**

"Hispanic" combines people from a wide variety of national origins or ancestries—including all the nations of Central and South America, Mexico, Cuba, Puerto Rico, the Dominican Republic, Spain—as well as those who identify as Californio, Tejano, Nuevo Mexicano, and Mestizo.

*(Source: Adapted from the U.S. Department of Commerce, Economics and Statistics Information, Bureau of the Census, 1993 report "We, the American . . . Hispanics"; also recent Census Bureau figures for the Hispanic population.)*

▲ This twenty-first-century American family shows the increasing complexity of racial and ethnic identities. The father is Chinese, Irish, French, German, and Swedish; the mother, Italian, Irish, and Japanese. *(Terrence Mielse/Newsweek)*

population, fueled by both immigration and birth rates. In 2003 Latinos moved past African Americans to become the second largest ethnic or racial group in the nation (after non-Hispanic whites), making the United States the fifth largest "Latino" country in world (see Figure 33.3). Immigration from Asia also remained high, and in 2006, 5 percent of the U.S. population was Asian or Asian American.

These rapid demographic changes have altered the face of America. At a Dairy Queen in the far southern suburbs of Atlanta, 6 miles from the Gone with the Wind Historical District, teenage children of immigrants from India and Pakistan serve Blizzards and Brownie Earthquakes. In the small town of Ligonier, Indiana, the formerly empty main street now boasts three Mexican restaurants and a Mexican western-wear shop; Mexican immigrants drawn in the 1990s by plentiful industrial jobs cross paths with the newest immigrants, Yemenis, some in traditional dress, and with Amish families in horse-drawn buggies.

Although many of America's schools and neighborhoods remain racially segregated and public debates about

the consequences of illegal immigration are heated, American popular culture has embraced the influences of this new multiethnic population. Economics were important: the buying power of the growing Latino population exceeded $798 billion in 2006, and average income for Asian American households topped that for all other groups. But American audiences also crossed racial and ethnic lines. Golfer Tiger Woods became a symbol of this new hybrid, multiethnic nation: of African, European, Native American, Thai, and Chinese descent, he calls himself "Cablinasian" (CAucasian-BLack-INdian-ASIAN).

Americans were divided over the meaning of other changes as well—especially the changing shape of American families (see Figure 33.4). The

**The Changing
American Family**

median age at marriage continued to rise, reaching 27.1 for men and 25.8 for women in 2006 (for women who pursued graduate degrees, the median age at first marriage was almost 30). The number of people living together without marriage also increased. In 2006, when households composed of married couples slipped below 50 percent for the first time, unmarried, opposite-sex partners made up about 5 percent of households, and same-sex couples accounted for slightly less than 1 percent. One-third of female-partner households and one-fifth of male-partner households had children, and in 2002 the American Academy of Pedi-

▲ Rescuers save a family from floodwaters in Bay St. Louis, Mississippi after Hurricane Katrina. Katrina destroyed not only New Orleans, but much of the U.S. Gulf Coast from Louisiana into Alabama. The federal government designated 90,000 square miles as disaster area. More than 1,800 people lost their lives in the storm. *(AP Photo/Ben Sklar)*

atrics endorsed adoption by gay couples. A vocal antigay movement coexisted with rising support for the legal equality of gay, lesbian, transgendered, and bisexual Americans. Although many states and private corporations extended domestic-partner benefits to gay couples, the federal Defense of Marriage Act, passed by Congress in 1996, defined marriage as "only" a union between one man and one woman, and state legislatures continue to grapple with the issue.

Early in the twenty-first century, one-third of all American children and more than two-thirds of African American children were born to unmarried women. (In Britain, the rate was 42 percent.) In the majority of married-couple families with children under eighteen, both parents held jobs. Although almost one-third of families with children had only one parent present—usually the mother—children also lived in blended families created by second marriages or moved back and forth between households of parents who had joint custody. Based on current statistical analysis, for couples who married in the mid-1990s the woman's level of education was the clearest predictor of divorce: if the woman graduated from a four-year college, the couple

had a 25 percent likelihood of divorce; if she had not, the rate jumped to 50 percent.

In 2006 the leading edge of the baby-boom generation turned 60; the median age of the American population was 36.2, up from 29.5 in 1967. Although baby boomers are not aging in the same manner as their parents and grandparents—"Sixty is the new forty," the saying goes—the large and growing proportion of older people will have a major impact on American society. As life expectancy increases, the growing number of elderly Americans will put enormous pressure on the nation's healthcare system and family structure—who will care for people as they can no longer live independently?—and strain the Social Security and Medicare systems.

Other health issues have become increasingly important as well. In a rapid change over the course of a decade, more than 65 percent of American adults are now overweight or obese—conditions linked to hypertension, cardiovascular disease, and diabetes. In 1995 no state had an adult obesity rate that hit 20 percent. By 2005, only four states were under that 20 percent marker, and Louisiana, Mississippi, and West Virginia topped 30 percent. On the

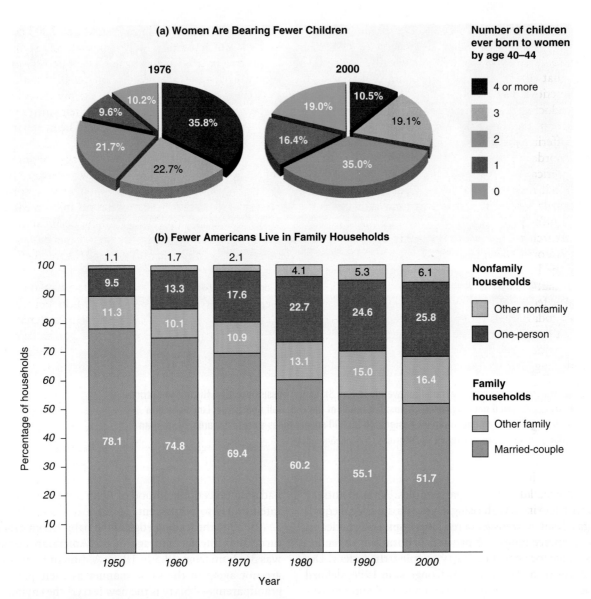

**Figure 33.4    The Changing American Family**

American households became smaller in the latter part of the twentieth century, as more people lived alone and women had, on average, fewer children.

*(Source: Adapted from U.S. Bureau of the Census, http://www.census.gov/prod/2002pubs/censr-4.pdf and http://www.census.gov/population/pop-profile/2000/chap04.pdf.)*

other hand, cigarette smoking continues a slow but steady decline. About one-fifth of American adults smoked in 2005, down from about one-third of adults in 1980. Approximately 440,000 people die each year from illness caused by smoking, and medical costs and lost productivity total about $157 billion a year. With clearer understanding of the danger of second-hand smoke, local governments have increasingly banned smoking in public spaces, including restaurants and bars.

As scientists and medical researchers continue to struggle to find cures for devastating diseases like cancer and AIDS, rapid advances in the field of biogenetics offer great new possibilities and, for many Americans, raise ethical or philosophical conundrums. During in vitro fertilizations—in which sperm and egg combine in a sterile dish and the fertilized egg or eggs

## Medicine, Science, and Religion

are then transferred to the uterus—five- or six-cell blastocytes are formed by the initial division of fertilized eggs. These blastocytes contain stem cells, unspecialized cells that can be induced to become cells with specialized functions. For example, stem cells might become insulin-producing cells of the pancreas, and thus a cure for diabetes; or they might become dopamine-producing neurons, offering therapy for Parkinson's disease, a progressive disorder of the nervous system affecting over 1 million Americans. President Bush in 2001 called embryonic stem cell research "the leading edge of a series of moral hazards," because extracting stem cells destroys the blastocyte's "potential for life," and limited federally funded research to the existing seventy-eight stem cell lines, the majority of which turned out not to be viable for research. In 2006 he vetoed a bipartisan congressional bill that expanded the number of stem cell lines available for federally funded research. Like many issues in America today, the controversy over stem cells is often treated as a conflict between religion and science. However, the majority of Americans support stem cell research, arguing that the moral good of curing diseases that devastate the lives of many men, women, and children outweighs the moral good of preserving the potential life of blastocytes.

At the same time, many Americans see a fundamental conflict between religious belief and scientific study. Fundamentalist Christians have struggled to prevent the teaching of evolution in the nation's science classes or to introduce parallel instruction of biblical "creationism" or theories of "intelligent design," which hold that an intelligent creator lies behind the development of life on earth. The percentage of Americans who accept the scientific evidence for evolution is lower than that in any other major nation in the world, with the sole exception of Turkey.

The twentieth century had seen more momentous change than any previous century—change that brought enormous benefits to human beings, change that threatened the

### Century of Change

very existence of the human species. Research in the physical and biological sciences had provided insight into the structure of matter and of the universe. Technology—the application of science—had made startling advances that benefited Americans in nearly every aspect of life: better health, more wealth, more mobility, less drudgery, greater access to information.

Through these advances, Americans at the start of the new century were more connected to the rest of humankind than ever before. This interconnection was perhaps the most powerful product of globalization. A

commodities trader in Chicago in March 2003 could send an e-mail to her fiancé in Tokyo while she spoke on the phone to a trader in Frankfurt and kept one eye on CNN's real-time coverage of the air war over Baghdad; within a minute or two she could receive a reply from her fiancé saying that he missed her, too. If she felt sufficiently lovesick, she could board an airplane and be in Japan the following day.

The world had shrunk to the size of an airplane ticket. In 1955, 51 million people a year traveled by plane. By the turn of the century, 1.6 billion were airborne every year, and 530 million—or about 1.5 million each day—crossed international borders. This permeability of national boundaries brought many benefits, as did the integration of markets and the global spread of information that occurred alongside it.

But there was a flip side to this growing connectivity, which even advocates of globalization perceived. The

### Globalization and World Health

rapid increase in international air travel was a particularly potent force for the dissemination of global disease, as flying made it possible for people to reach the other side of the world in far less time than the incubation period for many ailments. In early 2003, a respiratory illness known as severe acute respiratory syndrome (SARS) emerged in China and threatened to spread rapidly across the globe. Thirteen labs in ten countries worked day and night to map the genome, whereupon efforts to devise a diagnostic test for the virus began. SARS did not develop into a worldwide epidemic, but health authorities were put on notice: international cooperation would be essential to combat the health threats intensified by globalization and the rapidity of world travel.

Environmental degradation also created major global health threats. In 2003 the World Health Organization (WHO) estimated that nearly one-quarter of the global burden of disease and injury was related to environmental disruption and decline. For example, some 90 percent of diarrheal diseases (such as cholera), which were killing 3 million people a year, resulted from contaminated water. WHO also pointed to globalization and environmental disruption as contributing to the fact that, in the final two decades of the twentieth century, more than thirty infectious diseases were identified in humans for the first time—including AIDS, Ebola virus, hantavirus, and hepatitis C and E. Environmentalists, meanwhile, insisted that the growing interaction of national economies was having a deleterious impact on the ecosystem through climate change, ozone depletion, hazardous waste, and damage to fisheries.

# The Global AIDS Epidemic

IDS, first reported in the United States in 1981, has become a global epidemic. Researchers now believe that the first infection with HIV, the human immunodeficiency virus that causes AIDS, may have appeared in West Africa around 1930. HIV/AIDS began spreading rapidly in the late 1970s, in part as a byproduct of globalization. Increasingly commonplace international travel allowed for sexual transmission of HIV between populations; the international heroin trade that grew in the 1970s stimulated intravenous drug use, another means of transmission; and the international circulation of blood for transfusions in medical procedures also contributed to the virus's spread. In 2003 the World Health Organization estimated that 58 million people worldwide were living with HIV/AIDS and that 23 million had died from the disease.

Globally, AIDS claims 350 lives per hour, and though altered behavior and new drug therapies have slowed the progress of the disease in North America and western Europe, infection and death rates continue to grow rapidly in sub-Saharan Africa, Thailand, eastern Europe and the former Soviet Union, and Latin America, especially the Caribbean. In the African nation of Malawi, 1 in 6 adults is HIV-positive, and the nation expects to lose almost one-quarter of its work force to AIDS in the next decade. Half of current teenagers in the hardest-hit African nations will eventually die of AIDS; more than 14 million children across the globe have been orphaned by the disease.

The human suffering is staggering. However, U.S. worries about the global spread of AIDS are not based solely on humanitarian concerns. In 2000 the U.S. National Intelligence Council concluded that AIDS and other new and reemerging infectious diseases must be treated as threats to the health of U.S. citizens and to global security, stating, "These diseases will endanger U.S. citizens at home and abroad, threaten U.S. armed forces deployed overseas, and exacerbate social and political instability in key countries and regions in which the United States has significant interests." In nations already facing shortages of food and clean water, and riven by war and ethnic conflict, AIDS has further undermined both individual and governmental ability to cope with crisis; political instability and social disorder result.

In 2002 U.N. secretary general Kofi Annan estimated that between $7 billion and $10 billion are needed each year to combat the spread of AIDS—and of tuberculosis and malaria, both of which have reemerged as major threats to world health. President Bush called for major increases in U.S. spending to combat AIDS internationally, but many believe the United States must take more responsibility for combating the epidemic. In the era of globalization, diseases do not stop at borders or respect wealth and power. The links between Americans and the rest of the world's peoples cannot be denied.

▲ Activists protest outside Parliament in Cape Town, South Africa, calling on South African president Thabo Mbeki to make the struggle against AIDS a national priority. An estimated 20 percent of South Africans between the ages of fifteen and forty-nine are HIV-positive.

*(AP/Wide World Photos, Inc.)*

▲ Melinda and Bill Gates hold babies as they visit the Manhica Research Center in Mozambique in 2003. The Center was one of the recipients of a $168 million grant for malaria research funded by the Bill and Melinda Gates Foundation. Bill and Melinda Gates co-chair the foundation, whose mission is to "reduce inequities and improve lives around the world." It is active in all fifty U.S. states and one hundred other nations; in 2006 it made grants of more than one and a half billion dollars.  *(© Naashon Zalk/Corbis)*

But if the interaction between national economies and the rapid increase in person-to-person contacts were responsible for many health and other problems, they also were essential in mobilizing the world to find solutions. Whereas it took centuries to identify the cause of cholera and two years to identify the virus that causes AIDS, in the case of SARS, thirteen labs in ten countries put everything else aside and in a matter of weeks determined that the coronavirus was responsible. Within a month, laboratories from Vancouver to Atlanta to Singapore had mapped the genome, whereupon efforts to devise a diagnostic test for the virus began. Thus, although the disease spread internationally with unprecedented speed, so did the response. Speed of communication allowed for a coordinated international effort at finding the cause

## International Response to Disease

of SARS and also allowed individual countries, including the United States, to adopt measures that succeeded, in the early months at least, in keeping the epidemic out.

Even in the interconnected world of the new millennium, then, national borders still mattered. There were limits to their permeability. In the wake of 9/11, indeed, the process of integration was to some degree reversed. To prevent future terrorist attacks, the United States and other countries imposed tighter security measures on air travelers, imported goods, immigration, and information flows. Some economists predicted these measures would stall the global movement toward integration of markets; in the short term they certainly did, but the long-term outlook was less clear. Trade and investment shrank in 2001, but they were falling before September 11 as a result of economic slowdowns in the world's biggest economies, including the United States, Europe, and Japan.

| TABLE 33.1 | U.S. Military Personnel on Active Duty in Foreign Countries, 2005[1] | | |
|---|---|---|---|
| **Region/Country[2]** | **Personnel** | **Region/Country[2]** | **Personnel** |
| **United States and Territories** | | Thailand | 116 |
| Continental U.S. | 894, 921 | **North Africa, Near East, and South Asia** | |
| Alaska | 18,980 | Bahrain | 1,482 |
| Hawai'i | 33,816 | Diego Garcia | 773 |
| Guam | 2, 931 | Egypt | 424 |
| Puerto Rico | 211 | Iraq | 207,000 |
| **Europe** | | Israel | 43 |
| Belgium* | 1,388 | Oman | 36 |
| Bosnia and Herzegovina | 261 | Pakistan | 195 |
| France* | 56 | Qatar | 387 |
| Germany* | 66,000 | Saudi Arabia | 269 |
| Greece* | 431 | United Arab Emirates | 72 |
| Greenland* | 144 | **Sub-Saharan Africa** | |
| Iceland* | 1,257 | Kenya | 32 |
| Italy* | 11,428 | South Africa | 33 |
| Macedonia | 40 | **Western Hemisphere** | |
| Netherlands* | 579 | Brazil | 39 |
| Norway* | 74 | Canada | 145 |
| Portugal* | 990 | Chile | 29 |
| Russia | 44 | Colombia | 96 |
| Serbia (includes Kosovo) | 1,909 | Cuba (Guantánamo) | 950 |
| Spain* | 1,634 | Honduras | 416 |
| Turkey* | 1,738 | Peru | 36 |
| United Kingdom* | 10,536 | Venezuela | 21 |
| **East Asia and Pacific** | | **Total foreign countries[2]** | **271,381** |
| Australia | 140 | **Ashore** | **247,341** |
| China (includes Hong Kong) | 71 | **Afloat** | **24,040** |
| Japan | 35,050 | **Total worldwide[2]** | **1,605,414** |
| Korea, Rep. of | 29,982 | **Ashore** | **1,249,616** |
| Philippines | 44 | **Afloat** | **128,398** |
| Singapore | 159 | | |

*NATO countries
[1]Only countries with 35 or more U.S. military personnel are listed.
[2]Includes all regions/countries, not simply those listed.

*Source:* U.S. Department of Defense, Defense Manpower Data Center.

Moreover, the falloff in international economic activity in the months after the attacks was not massive.

In military and diplomatic terms, though, 9/11 made a deep and lasting impression. The attacks that day brought home what Americans had only dimly perceived before then: that globalization had shrunk the natural buffers that distance and two oceans provided the United States.

## Confronting Terrorism

Al Qaeda, it was clear, had used the increasingly open, integrated, globalized world to give itself new power and reach. It had shown that small cells of terrorists could become true transnational threats—thriving around the world without any single state sponsor or home base. According to American intelligence, Al Qaeda operated in more than ninety countries—including the United States.

How would one go about vanquishing such a foe? Was a decisive victory even possible? These remained open questions five years after the World Trade Center collapsed. Unchallenged militarily and seeing no rival great power, the United States felt few constraints about intervening in Afghanistan and then Iraq, but the problems in Iraq showed that it could take scant comfort from this superiority. It continued to spend colossal sums on its military, more indeed than the rest of the world combined. (Including the supplemental appropriations for Iraq and Afghanistan, the Pentagon in 2006 spent more than $500 billion, or roughly $60 million dollars per hour.) America had taken on military commitments all over the globe, from the Balkans and Iraq to Afghanistan and Korea (see Table 33.1). Its armed forces looked colossal, but its obligations looked even larger.

*Legacy* FOR A PEOPLE AND A NATION

## The Internet

"oogle it"—the phrase, essentially unknown before the new century, had within its first years become a household expression like "Xerox it" or "FedEx it." Google was the hugely popular Internet search engine that had gone from obscurity in the mid-1990s to a point where it responded, more or less instantly, to 200 million queries per day from around the world—almost 40 percent of all Internet search requests.

Google's phenomenal rise was one sign among many of how the Internet had become, by the early years of the twenty-first century, an ordinary, expected part of many Americans' daily lives. For younger people in particular, the Internet was something to be taken for granted, like refrigerators, microwaves, stereos, and televisions.

Yet the widespread use of the Internet was a recent phenomenon, even though its history went back some four decades. In the mid-1960s, the U.S. military's Advanced Research Projects Agency (ARPA) hoped to create a communications network for government and university researchers spread out across the nation. In 1969 the first portions of the experimental system, called ARPANET, went online at UCLA; the University of California, Santa Barbara; Stanford Research Institute; and the University of Utah. By 1971, twenty-three computers were connected, and gradually the numbers grew, reaching close to a thousand by 1984. This system, which by the late 1980s had been renamed the Internet, transmitted only words, but in 1990 computer scientists developed the World Wide Web, which used the Internet to send graphic and multimedia information as well. Then in 1993 the first commercial "browser" to aid navigation through the Web hit the market. It was followed in 1994 and 1995 by two superior browsers: Netscape and Internet Explorer. The prospect of millions of computers connected worldwide had become a reality.

By early 2007, there were more than a billion Internet users worldwide, including 200 million Americans. Thanks to technological advances and to the new forms of "broadband" access that provided high-speed connections, these users could do an astonishing array of things online. They could send and receive e-mail, join online discussion groups, read newspapers, book vacations, download movies and music, purchase everything from books to private jets, even do their banking—all through a small computer in their home. For the American people in the new globally connected millennium, there could be no more fitting legacy of the twentieth century than the Internet.

## SUMMARY

The 1990s were, for most Americans, good times. A digitized revolution in communications and information—as fundamental as the revolution brought about by electricity and the combustion engine a century earlier, or the steam engine a century before that—was generating prosperity and transforming life in America and around the globe. The longest economic expansion in American history—from 1991 to 2001—meant that most Americans who wanted jobs had them, that the stock market boomed, that the nation had a budget surplus instead of a deficit, and that more Americans than ever before owned their own homes. And America was not only prosperous; it was powerful. With the Soviet Union gone and no other formidable rival on the horizon, the United States stood as the world's lone superpower, its economic and military power daunting to friend and foe alike.

Yet, although America seemed at the apex of power and prosperity, unsettling events troubled the nation. Localized and ethnic conflicts in the Balkans, the Middle East, Central Asia, and Africa crowded the international agenda, as did human rights and the natural environment. At home, high-profile acts of violence—the domestic terrorist attack in Oklahoma City in 1995; a rash of school shootings—captured headlines, even as the crime rate dropped. And scandal further undermined the faith of Americans in their government, as President Bill Clinton was impeached by the House of Representatives.

Just minutes before midnight on December 31, 1999, President Clinton called on the American people not to fear the future, but to "welcome it, create it, and embrace it." The challenges of the future would be greater than Americans imagined as they welcomed the new millennium that night. In 2000 the contested presidential election was decided by the Supreme Court in a partisan 5-to-4 vote; in 2001 the ten-year economic expansion came to an end.

Then, on September 11 of that year, radical Islamic terrorists attacked the World Trade Center and the Pentagon, killing thousands and altering many aspects of American life. The new president, George W. Bush, declared a "war on terrorism," one with both foreign and domestic components. While U.S. air and ground forces went after targets in Afghanistan, Congress moved to create the Department of Homeland Security and passed the PATRIOT Act, expanding the federal government's powers of surveillance. In March 2003, Bush took the nation into war in Iraq, not expecting what followed: a full-fledged insurgency by disaffected Iraqis against U.S. occupying forces and sectarian violence between Sunnis and Shi'ites. To counter a troubled economy, Bush pushed through tax cuts each of his first three years in office, something no wartime president had ever done.

The world that Americans found in the first years of the twenty-first century was much different from the one they had looked forward to with confidence and high hopes as they celebrated the coming of the new millennium on New Year's Eve 1999. The horror of the terror attacks of September 11, 2001, shook America to its core. Throughout the nation, people declared that life would never again be the same. And it was not, not for those who had lost loved ones that day or for a people now forcibly aware of the powerful and inescapable links that bind their nation to the rest of the world's nations and peoples. But, as Americans attempted to cope with the aftermath of 9/11, crafting new foreign and domestic policies, the resilience of the American people was clear. For Americans continued to struggle over these plans and policies, over the direction of their nation, with the passion and commitment that keeps democracy alive.

## SUGGESTIONS FOR FURTHER READING

Daniel Benjamin and Steven Simon, *The Sacred Age of Terror* (2002)

Barbara Ehrenreich, *Nickled and Dimed: On (Not) Getting by in America* (2002)

David Halberstam, *War in a Time of Peace: Bush, Clinton, and the Generals* (2001)

John F. Harris, *The Survivor: Bill Clinton in the White House* (2005)

Jennifer L. Hochschild, *Facing up to the American Dream: Race, Class, and the Soul of the Nation* (1995)

James Mann, *Rise of the Vulcans: The History of Bush's War Cabinet* (2004)

Alejandro Portes and Reuben G. Rumbaut, *Immigrant America: A Portrait*, 3d ed. (2006)

Thomas E. Ricks, *Fiasco: The American Military Adventure in Iraq* (2006)

Joseph E. Stiglitz, *Globalization and Its Discontents* (2002)

*For a more extensive list for further reading, go to* college.hmco.com/pic/norton8e.

# Declaration of Independence in Congress, July 4, 1776

When, in the course of human events, it becomes necessary for one people to dissolve the political bonds which have connected them with another, and to assume, among the powers of the earth, the separate and equal station to which the laws of nature and of nature's God entitle them, a decent respect to the opinions of mankind requires that they should declare the causes which impel them to the separation.

We hold these truths to be self-evident: That all men are created equal; that they are endowed by their Creator with certain unalienable rights; that among these are life, liberty, and the pursuit of happiness; that, to secure these rights, governments are instituted among men, deriving their just powers from the consent of the governed; that whenever any form of government becomes destructive of these ends, it is the right of the people to alter or to abolish it, and to institute new government, laying its foundation on such principles, and organizing its powers in such form, as to them shall seem most likely to effect their safety and happiness. Prudence, indeed, will dictate that governments long established should not be changed for light and transient causes; and accordingly all experience hath shown that mankind are more disposed to suffer, while evils are sufferable, than to right themselves by abolishing the forms to which they are accustomed. But when a long train of abuses and usurpations, pursuing invariably the same object, evinces a design to reduce them under absolute despotism, it is their right, it is their duty, to throw off such government, and to provide new guards for their future security. Such has been the patient sufferance of these colonies; and such is now the necessity which constrains them to alter their former systems of government. The history of the present King of Great Britain is a history of repeated injuries and usurpations, all having in direct object the establishment of an absolute tyranny over these states. To prove this, let facts be submitted to a candid world.

He has refused his assent to laws, the most wholesome and necessary for the public good.

He has forbidden his governors to pass laws of immediate and pressing importance, unless suspended in their operation till his assent should be obtained; and, when so suspended, he has utterly neglected to attend to them.

He has refused to pass other laws for the accommodation of large districts of people, unless those people would relinquish the right of representation in the legislature, a right inestimable to them, and formidable to tyrants only.

He has called together legislative bodies at places unusual, uncomfortable, and distant from the depository of their public records, for the sole purpose of fatiguing them into compliance with his measures.

He has dissolved representative houses repeatedly, for opposing, with manly firmness, his invasions on the rights of the people.

He has refused for a long time, after such dissolutions, to cause others to be elected; whereby the legislative powers, incapable of annihilation, have returned to the people at large for their exercise; the state remaining, in the mean time, exposed to all the dangers of invasions from without and convulsions within.

He has endeavored to prevent the population of these states; for that purpose obstructing the laws for naturalization of foreigners; refusing to pass others to encourage their migration hither, and raising the conditions of new appropriations of lands.

He has obstructed the administration of justice, by refusing his assent to laws for establishing judiciary powers.

He has made judges dependent on his will alone, for the tenure of their offices, and the amount and payment of their salaries.

He has erected a multitude of new offices, and sent hither swarms of officers to harass our people and eat out their substance.

He has kept among us, in times of peace, standing armies, without the consent of our legislatures.

He has affected to render the military independent of, and superior to, the civil power.

He has combined with others to subject us to a jurisdiction foreign to our constitution, and unacknowledged by our laws, giving his assent to their acts of pretended legislation:

For quartering large bodies of armed troops among us;

For protecting them, by a mock trial, from punishment for any murders which they should commit on the inhabitants of these states;

For cutting off our trade with all parts of the world;

For imposing taxes on us without our consent;

For depriving us, in many cases, of the benefits of trial by jury;

For transporting us beyond seas, to be tried for pretended offenses;

For abolishing the free system of English laws in a neighboring province, establishing therein an arbitrary government, and enlarging its boundaries, so as to render it at once an example and fit instrument for introducing the same absolute rule into these colonies;

For taking away our charters, abolishing our most valuable laws, and altering fundamentally the forms of our governments;

For suspending our own legislatures, and declaring themselves invested with power to legislate for us in all cases whatsoever.

He has abdicated government here, by declaring us out of his protection and waging war against us.

He has plundered our seas, ravaged our coasts, burned our towns, and destroyed the lives of our people.

He is at this time transporting large armies of foreign mercenaries to complete the works of death, desolation, and tyranny already begun with circumstances of cruelty and perfidy scarcely paralleled in the most barbarous ages, and totally unworthy the head of a civilized nation.

He has constrained our fellow-citizens, taken captive on the high seas, to bear arms against their country, to become the executioners of their friends and brethren, or to fall themselves by their hands.

He has excited domestic insurrection among us, and has endeavored to bring on the inhabitants of our frontiers the merciless Indian savages, whose known rule of warfare is an undistinguished destruction of all ages, sexes, and conditions.

In every stage of these oppressions we have petitioned for redress in the most humble terms; our repeated petitions have been answered only by repeated injury. A prince, whose character is thus marked by every act which may define a tyrant, is unfit to be the ruler of a free people.

Nor have we been wanting in our attentions to our British brethren. We have warned them, from time to time, of attempts by their legislature to extend an unwarrantable jurisdiction over us. We have reminded them of the circumstances of our emigration and settlement here. We have appealed to their native justice and magnanimity; and we have conjured them, by the ties of our common kindred, to disavow these usurpations, which would inevitably interrupt our connections and correspondence. They, too, have been deaf to the voice of justice and of consanguinity. We must, therefore, acquiesce in the necessity which denounces our separation, and hold them, as we hold the rest of mankind, enemies in war, in peace friends.

We, therefore, the representatives of the United States of America, in General Congress assembled, appealing to the Supreme Judge of the world for the rectitude of our intentions, do, in the name and by the authority of the good people of these colonies, solemnly publish and declare, that these United Colonies are, and of right ought to be, FREE AND INDEPENDENT STATES; that they are absolved from all allegiance to the British crown, and that all political connection between them and the state of Great Britain is, and ought to be, totally dissolved; and that, as free and independent states, they have full power to levy war, conclude peace, contract alliances, establish commerce, and do all other acts and things which independent states may of right do. And for the support of this declaration, with a firm reliance on the protection of Divine Providence, we mutually pledge to each other our lives, our fortunes, and our sacred honor.

## ARTICLES OF CONFEDERATION

Whereas the Delegates of the United States of America in Congress assembled did on the fifteenth day of November in the Year of our Lord One Thousand Seven Hundred and Seventy seven, and in the Second Year of the Independence of America agree to certain articles of Confederation and perpetual Union between the States of Newhampshire, Massachusetts Bay, Rhode Island and Providence Plantations, Connecticut, New York, New Jersey, Pennsylvania, Delaware, Maryland, Virginia, North Carolina, South Carolina and Georgia in the Words following, viz. "Articles of Confederation and perpetual Union between the states of Newhampshire, Massachusetts Bay, Rhode Island and Providence Plantations, Connecticut, New York, New Jersey, Pennsylvania, Delaware, Maryland, Virginia, North Carolina, South Carolina and Georgia.

*Article I*    The Stile of this confederacy shall be "The United States of America."

*Article II*    Each state retains its sovereignty, freedom and independence, and every Power, Jurisdiction and right, which is not by this confederation expressly delegated to the United States, in Congress assembled.

*Article III*    The said states hereby severally enter into a firm league of friendship with each other, for their common defence, the security of their Liberties, and their mutual and general welfare, binding themselves to assist each other, against all force offered to, or attacks made upon them, or any of them, on account of religion, sovereignty, trade, or any other pretence whatever.

*Article IV*    The better to secure and perpetuate mutual friendship and intercourse among the people of the different states in this union, the free inhabitants of each of these states, paupers, vagabonds and fugitives from Justice excepted, shall be entitled to all privileges and immunities of free citizens in the several states; and the people of each state shall have free ingress and regress to and from any other state, and shall enjoy therein all the privileges of trade and commerce, subject to the same duties, impositions and restrictions as the inhabitants thereof respectively, provided that such restriction shall not extend so far as to prevent the removal of property imported into any state, to any other state of which the Owner is an inhabitant; provided also that no imposition, duties or restriction shall be laid by any state, on the property of the united states, or either of them.

If any Person guilty of, or charged with treason, felony, or other high misdemeanor in any state, shall flee from Justice, and be found in any of the united states, he shall upon demand of the Governor or executive power, of the state from which he fled, be delivered up and removed to the state having jurisdiction of his offence.

Full faith and credit shall be given in each of these states to the records, acts and judicial proceedings of the courts and magistrates of every other state.

*Article V*    For the more convenient management of the general interests of the united states, delegates shall be annually appointed in such manner as the legislature of each state shall direct, to meet in Congress on the first Monday in November, in every year, with a power reserved to each state, to recall its delegates, or any of them, at any time within the year, and to send others in their stead, for the remainder of the Year.

No state shall be represented in Congress by less than two, nor by more than seven Members; and no person shall be capable of being a delegate for more than three years in any term of six years; nor shall any person, being a delegate, be capable of holding any office under the united states, for which he, or another for his benefit receives any salary, fees or emolument of any kind.

Each state shall maintain its own delegates in a meeting of the states, and while they act as members of the committee of the states.

In determining questions in the united states, in Congress assembled, each state shall have one vote.

Freedom of speech and debate in Congress shall not be impeached or questioned in any Court, or place out of Congress, and the members of congress shall be protected in their persons from arrests and imprisonments, during the time of their going to and from, and attendance on congress, except for treason, felony, or breach of the peace.

*Article VI*   No state without the Consent of the united states in congress assembled, shall send any embassy to, or receive any embassy from, or enter into any conference, agreement, or alliance or treaty with any King, prince or state; nor shall any person holding any office of profit or trust under the united states, or any of them, accept of any present, emolument, office or title of any kind whatever from any king, prince or foreign state; nor shall the united states in congress assembled, or any of them, grant any title of nobility.

No two or more states shall enter into any treaty, confederation or alliance whatever between them, without the consent of the united states in congress assembled, specifying accurately the purposes for which the same is to be entered into, and how long it shall continue.

No state shall lay any imposts or duties, which may interfere with any stipulations in treaties, entered into by the united states in congress assembled, with any king, prince or state, in pursuance of any treaties already proposed by congress, to the courts of France and Spain.

No vessels of war shall be kept up in time of peace by any state, except such number only, as shall be deemed necessary by the united states in congress assembled, for the defence of such state, or its trade; nor shall any body of forces be kept up by any state, in time of peace, except such number only, as in the judgment of the united states, in congress assembled, shall be deemed requisite to garrison the forts necessary for the defence of such state; but every state shall always keep up a well regulated and disciplined militia, sufficiently armed and accoutred, and shall provide and constantly have ready for use, in public stores, a due number of field pieces and tents, and a proper quantity of arms, ammunition and camp equipage.

No state shall engage in any war without the consent of the united states in congress assembled, unless such state be actually invaded by enemies, or shall have received certain advice of a resolution being formed by some nation of Indians to invade such state, and the danger is so imminent as not to admit of a delay, till the united states in congress assembled can be consulted: nor shall any state grant commissions to any ships or vessels of war, nor letters of marque or reprisal, except it be after a declaration of war by the united states in congress assembled, and then only against the kingdom or state and the subjects thereof, against which war has been so declared, and under such regulations as shall be established by the united states in congress assembled, unless such state be infested by pirates, in which case vessels of war may be fitted out for that occasion, and kept so long as the danger shall continue, or until the united states in congress assembled shall determine otherwise.

*Article VII*   When land-forces are raised by any state for the common defence, all officers of or under the rank of colonel, shall be appointed by the legislature of each state respectively by whom such forces shall be raised, or in such manner as such state shall direct, and all vacancies shall be filled up by the state which first made the appointment.

*Article VIII*   All charges of war, and all other expences that shall be incurred for the common defence or general welfare, and allowed by the united states in congress assembled, shall be defrayed out of a common treasury, which shall be supplied by the several states, in proportion to the value of all land within each state, granted to or surveyed for any Person, as such land and the buildings and improvements thereon shall be estimated according to such mode as the united states in congress assembled, shall from time to time direct and appoint. The taxes for paying that proportion shall be laid and levied by the authority and direction of the legislatures of the several states within the time agreed upon by the united states in congress assembled.

*Article IX*   The united states in congress assembled, shall have the sole and exclusive right and power of determining on peace and war, except in the cases mentioned in the sixth article—of sending and receiving ambassadors—entering into treaties and alliances, provided that no treaty of commerce shall be made whereby the legislative power of the respective states shall be restrained from imposing such imposts and duties on foreigners, as their own people are subjected to, or from prohibiting the exportation or importation of any species of goods or commodities whatsoever—of establishing rules for deciding in all cases, what captures on land or water shall be legal, and in what manner prizes taken by land or naval forces in the service of the united states shall be divided or appropriated—of granting letters of marque and reprisal in times of peace—appointing courts for the trial of piracies and felonies committed on the high seas and establishing courts for receiving and determining final appeals in all cases of captures, provided that no member of congress shall be appointed a judge of any of the said courts.

The united states in congress assembled shall also be the last resort on appeal in all disputes and differences now subsisting or that hereafter may arise between two or more states concerning boundary, jurisdiction or any other cause whatever; which authority shall always be exercised in the manner following. Whenever the legislative or executive authority or lawful agent of any state in controversy with another shall present a petition to congress, stating the matter in question and praying for a hearing, notice thereof shall be given by order of congress to the legislative or executive authority of the other state in controversy, and a day assigned for the appearance of the parties by their lawful agents, who shall then be directed to appoint by joint consent, commissioners or judges to constitute a court for hearing and determining the matter in question: but if they cannot agree, congress shall name three persons out of each of the united states, and from the list of such persons each party shall alternately strike out one, the petitioners beginning, until the number shall be reduced to thirteen; and from that number not less than seven, nor more than nine names as congress shall direct, shall in the presence of congress be drawn out by lot, and the persons whose names shall be so drawn or any five of them, shall be commissioners or judges, to hear and finally determine the controversy, so always as a major part of the judges who shall hear the cause shall agree in the determination: and if either party shall neglect to attend at the day appointed, without shewing reasons, which congress shall judge sufficient, or being present shall refuse to strike, the congress shall proceed to nominate three persons out of each state, and the secretary of congress shall strike in behalf of such party absent or refusing; and the judgment and sentence of the court to be appointed, in the manner before prescribed, shall be final and conclusive; and if any of the parties shall refuse to submit to the authority of such court, or to appear to defend their claim or cause, the court shall nevertheless proceed to pronounce sentence, or judgment, which shall in like manner be final and decisive, the judgment or sentence and other proceedings being in either case transmitted to congress, and lodged among the acts of congress for the security of the parties concerned: provided that every commissioner, before he sits in judgment, shall take an oath to be administered by one of the judges of the supreme or superior court of the state, where the cause shall be tried, "well and truly to hear and determine the matter in question, according to the best of his judgment, without favour, affection or hope of reward:" provided also that no state shall be deprived of territory for the benefit of the united states.

All controversies concerning the private right of soil claimed under different grants of two or more states, whose jurisdictions as they may respect such lands, and the states which passed such grants are adjusted, the said grants or either of them being at the same time claimed to have originated antecedent to such settlement of jurisdiction, shall on the petition of either party to the congress of the united states, be finally determined as near as may be in the same manner as is before prescribed for deciding disputes respecting territorial jurisdiction between different states.

The united states in congress assembled shall also have the sole and exclusive right and power of regulating the alloy and value of coin struck by their own authority, or by that of the respective states—fixing the standard of weights and measures throughout the united states—regulating the trade and managing all affairs with the Indians, not members of any of the states, provided that the legislative right of any state within its own limits be not infringed or violated—establishing and regulating post-offices from one state to another, throughout all the united states, and exacting such postage on the papers passing thro' the same as may be requisite to defray the expences of the said office—appointing all officers of the land forces, in the service of the united states, excepting regimental officers—appointing all the officers of the naval forces, and commissioning all officers whatever in the service of the united states—making rules for the government and regulation of the said land and naval forces, and directing their operations.

The united states in congress assembled shall have authority to appoint a committee, to sit in the recess of congress, to be denominated "A Committee of the States," and to consist of one delegate from each state; and to appoint such other committees and civil officers as may be necessary for managing the general affairs of the united states under their direction—to appoint one of their number to preside, provided that no person be allowed to serve in the office of president more than one year in any term of three years; to ascertain the necessary sums of Money to be raised for the service of the united states, and to appropriate and apply the same for defraying the public expences—to borrow money, or emit bills on the credit of the united states, transmitting every half year to the respective states an account of the sums of money so borrowed or emitted—to build and equip a navy—to agree upon the number of land forces, and to make requisitions from each state for its quota, in proportion to the number of white inhabitants in such state; which requisition shall be binding, and thereupon the legislature of each state shall appoint the regimental officers, raise the men and cloath, arm and equip them in a soldier like manner, at the expence of the united states, and the officers and men so cloathed, armed and equipped shall march to the place appointed, and within the time agreed on by the united states in congress assembled: But if the united states in congress assembled shall, on consideration of circumstances judge proper that any state should not raise men, or should raise a smaller number than its quota, and that any other state should raise a greater number of men than the quota thereof, such extra number shall be raised, officered, cloathed, armed and equipped in the same manner as the quota of such state, unless the legislature of such state shall judge that such extra number cannot be safely spared out of the same, in which case they shall raise, officer, cloath, arm and equip as many of such extra number as they judge can be safely spared. And the officers and men so cloathed, armed and equipped, shall march to the place appointed, and within the time agreed on by the united states in congress assembled.

The united states in congress assembled shall never engage in a war, nor grant letters of marque and reprisal in time of peace, nor enter into any treaties or alliances, nor coin money, nor regulate the value thereof, nor ascertain the sums and expences necessary for the defence and welfare of the united states, or any of them, nor emit bills, nor borrow money on the credit of the united states, nor appropriate money, nor agree upon the number of vessels of war, to be built or purchased, or the number of land or sea forces to be raised, nor appoint a commander in chief of the army or navy, unless nine states assent to the same: nor shall a question on any other point, except for adjourning from day to day be determined, unless by the votes of a majority of the united states in congress assembled.

The congress of the united states shall have power to adjourn to any time within the year, and to any place within the united states, so that no period of adjournment be for a longer duration than the space of six Months, and shall publish the Journal of their proceedings monthly, except such parts thereof relating to treaties, alliances or military operations as in their judgment require secresy; and the yeas and nays of the delegates of each state on any question shall be entered on the Journal, when it is desired by any delegate; and the delegates of a state, or any of them, as his or their request shall be furnished with a transcript of the said Journal, except such parts as are above excepted, to lay before the legislatures of the several states.

*Article X*    The committee of the states, or any nine of them, shall be authorised to execute, in the recess of congress, such of the powers of congress as the united states in congress assembled, by the consent of nine states, shall from time to time think expedient to vest them with; provided that no power be delegated to the said committee, for the exercise of which, by the articles of confederation, the voice of nine states in the congress of the united states assembled is requisite.

*Article XI*    Canada acceding to this confederation, and joining in the measures of the united states, shall be admitted into, and entitled to all the advantages of this union: but no other colony shall be admitted into the same, unless such admission be agreed to by nine states.

*Article XII*    All bills of credit emitted, monies borrowed and debts contracted by, or under the authority of congress, before the assembling of the united states, in pursuance of the present confederation, shall be deemed and considered as a charge against the united states, for payment and satisfaction whereof the said united states, and the public faith are hereby solemnly pledged.

*Article XIII*    Every state shall abide by the determinations of the united states in congress assembled, on all questions which by this confederation are submitted to them. And the Articles of this confederation shall be inviolably observed by every state, and the union shall be perpetual; nor shall any alteration at any time hereafter be made in any of them; unless such alteration be agreed to in a congress of the united states, and be afterwards confirmed by the legislatures of every state.

AND WHEREAS it hath pleased the Great Governor of the World to incline the hearts of the legislatures we respectively represent in congress, to approve of, and to authorize us to ratify the said articles of confederation and perpetual union. Know Ye that we the under-signed delegates, by virtue of the power and authority to us given for that purpose, do by these presents, in the name and in behalf of our respective constituents, fully and entirely ratify and confirm each and every of the said articles of confederation and perpetual union, and all and singular the matters and things therein contained: And we do further solemnly plight and engage the faith of our respective constituents, that they shall abide by the determinations of the united states in congress assembled, on all questions, which by the said confederation are submitted to them. And that the articles thereof shall be inviolably observed by the states we respectively represent, and that the union shall be perpetual. In Witness whereof we have hereunto set our hands in Congress. Done at Philadelphia in the state of Pennsylvania the ninth Day of July in the Year of our Lord one Thousand seven Hundred and Seventy-eight, and in the third year of the independence of America.

# CONSTITUTION OF THE UNITED STATES OF AMERICA AND AMENDMENTS*

## Preamble

We the people of the United States, in order to form a more perfect union, establish justice, insure domestic tranquillity, provide for the common defense, promote the general welfare, and secure the blessings of liberty to ourselves and our posterity, do ordain and establish this Constitution for the United States of America.

## Article I

*Section 1*    All legislative powers herein granted shall be vested in a Congress of the United States, which shall consist of a Senate and a House of Representatives.

*Section 2*    The House of Representatives shall be composed of members chosen every second year by the people of the several States, and the electors in each State shall have the qualifications requisite for electors of the most numerous branch of the State Legislature.

No person shall be a Representative who shall not have attained to the age of twenty-five years, and been seven years a citizen of the United States, and who shall not, when elected, be an inhabitant of that State in which he shall be chosen.

Representatives and direct taxes shall be apportioned among the several States which may be included within this Union, according to their respective numbers, *which shall be determined by adding to the whole number of free persons, including those bound to service for a term of years and excluding Indians not taxed, three-fifths of all other persons.* The actual enumeration shall be made within three years after the first meeting of the Congress of the United States, and within every subsequent term of ten years, in such manner as they shall by law direct. The number of Representatives shall not exceed one for every thirty thousand, but each State shall have at least one Representative; *and until such enumeration shall be made, the State of New Hampshire shall be entitled to choose three, Massachusetts eight, Rhode Island and Providence Plantations one, Connecticut five, New York six, New Jersey four, Pennsylvania eight, Delaware one, Maryland six, Virginia ten, North Carolina five, South Carolina five, and Georgia three.*

When vacancies happen in the representation from any State, the Executive authority thereof shall issue writs of election to fill such vacancies.

The House of Representatives shall choose their Speaker and other officers; and shall have the sole power of impeachment.

*Section 3*    The Senate of the United States shall be composed of two Senators from each State, *chosen by the legislature thereof,* for six years; and each Senator shall have one vote.

*Immediately after they shall be assembled in consequence of the first election, they shall be divided as equally as may be* *into three classes. The seats of the Senators of the first class shall be vacated at the expiration of the second year, of the second class at the expiration of the fourth year, and of the third class at the expiration of the sixth year,* so that one-third may be chosen every second year; *and if vacancies happen by resignation or otherwise, during the recess of the legislature of any State, the Executive thereof may make temporary appointments until the next meeting of the legislature, which shall then fill such vacancies.*

No person shall be a Senator who shall not have attained to the age of thirty years, and been nine years a citizen of the United States, and who shall not, when elected, be an inhabitant of that State for which he shall be chosen.

The Vice-President of the United States shall be President of the Senate, but shall have no vote, unless they be equally divided.

The Senate shall choose their other officers, and also a President *pro tempore,* in the absence of the Vice-President, or when he shall exercise the office of President of the United States.

The Senate shall have the sole power to try all impeachments. When sitting for that purpose, they shall be on oath or affirmation. When the President of the United States is tried, the Chief Justice shall preside: and no person shall be convicted without the concurrence of two-thirds of the members present.

Judgment in cases of impeachment shall not extend further than to removal from the office, and disqualification to hold and enjoy any office of honor, trust or profit under the United States: but the party convicted shall nevertheless be liable and subject to indictment, trial, judgment and punishment, according to law.

*Section 4*    The times, places and manner of holding elections for Senators and Representatives shall be prescribed in each State by the legislature thereof; but the Congress may at any time by law make or alter such regulations, except as to the places of choosing Senators.

The Congress shall assemble at least once in every year, and such meeting *shall be on the first Monday in December, unless they shall by law appoint a different day.*

*Section 5*    Each house shall be the judge of the elections, returns and qualifications of its own members, and a majority of each shall constitute a quorum to do business; but a smaller number may adjourn from day to day, and may be authorized to compel the attendance of absent members, in such manner, and under such penalties, as each house may provide.

Each house may determine the rules of its proceedings, punish its members for disorderly behavior, and with the concurrence of two-thirds, expel a member.

Each house shall keep a journal of its proceedings, and from time to time publish the same, excepting such parts as may in their judgment require secrecy; and the yeas and nays of the members of either house on any question shall, at the desire of one-fifth of those present, be entered on the journal.

*Passages no longer in effect are printed in italic type.

Neither house, during the session of Congress, shall, without the consent of the other, adjourn for more than three days, nor to any other place than that in which the two houses shall be sitting.

**Section 6**  The Senators and Representatives shall receive a compensation for their services, to be ascertained by law and paid out of the treasury of the United States. They shall in all cases except treason, felony and breach of the peace, be privileged from arrest during their attendance at the session of their respective houses, and in going to and returning from the same; and for any speech or debate in either house, they shall not be questioned in any other place.

No Senator or Representative shall, during the time for which he was elected, be appointed to any civil office under the authority of the United States, which shall have been created, or the emoluments whereof shall have been increased, during such time; and no person holding any office under the United States shall be a member of either house during his continuance in office.

**Section 7**  All bills for raising revenue shall originate in the House of Representatives; but the Senate may propose or concur with amendments as on other bills.

Every bill which shall have passed the House of Representatives and the Senate, shall, before it become a law, be presented to the President of the United States; if he approve he shall sign it, but if not he shall return it with objections to that house in which it originated, who shall enter the objections at large on their journal, and proceed to reconsider it. If after such reconsideration two-thirds of that house shall agree to pass the bill, it shall be sent, together with the objections, to the other house, by which it shall likewise be reconsidered, and, if approved by two-thirds of that house, it shall become a law. But in all such cases the votes of both houses shall be determined by yeas and nays, and the names of the persons voting for and against the bill shall be entered on the journal of each house respectively. If any bill shall not be returned by the President within ten days (Sundays excepted) after it shall have been presented to him, the same shall be a law, in like manner as if he had signed it, unless the Congress by their adjournment prevent its return, in which case it shall not be a law.

Every order, resolution, or vote to which the concurrence of the Senate and House of Representatives may be necessary (except on a question of adjournment) shall be presented to the President of the United States; and before the same shall take effect, shall be approved by him, or being disapproved by him, shall be repassed by two-thirds of the Senate and House of Representatives, according to the rules and limitations prescribed in the case of a bill.

**Section 8**  The Congress shall have power

To lay and collect taxes, duties, imposts, and excises, to pay the debts and provide for the common defense and general welfare of the United States; but all duties, imposts and excises shall be uniform throughout the United States;

To borrow money on the credit of the United States;

To regulate commerce with foreign nations, and among the several States, and with the Indian tribes;

To establish an uniform rule of naturalization, and uniform laws on the subject of bankruptcies throughout the United States;

To coin money, regulate the value thereof, and of foreign coin, and fix the standard of weights and measures;

To provide for the punishment of counterfeiting the securities and current coin of the United States;

To establish post offices and post roads;

To promote the progress of science and useful arts by securing for limited times to authors and inventors the exclusive right to their respective writings and discoveries;

To constitute tribunals inferior to the Supreme Court;

To define and punish piracies and felonies committed on the high seas and offenses against the law of nations;

To declare war, grant letters of marque and reprisal, and make rules concerning captures on land and water;

To raise and support armies, but no appropriation of money to that use shall be for a longer term than two years;

To provide and maintain a navy;

To make rules for the government and regulation of the land and naval forces;

To provide for calling forth the militia to execute the laws of the Union, suppress insurrections, and repel invasions;

To provide for organizing, arming, and disciplining the militia, and for governing such part of them as may be employed in the service of the United States, reserving to the States respectively the appointment of the officers, and the authority of training the militia according to the discipline prescribed by Congress;

To exercise exclusive legislation in all cases whatsoever, over such district (not exceeding ten miles square) as may, by cession of particular States, and the acceptance of Congress, become the seat of government of the United States, and to exercise like authority over all places purchased by the consent of the legislature of the State, in which the same shall be, for erection of forts, magazines, arsenals, dockyards, and other needful buildings; —and

To make all laws which shall be necessary and proper for carrying into execution the foregoing powers, and all other powers vested by this Constitution in the government of the United States, or in any department or officer thereof.

**Section 9**  *The migration or importation of such persons as any of the States now existing shall think proper to admit shall not be prohibited by the Congress prior to the year 1808; but a tax or duty may be imposed on such importation, not exceeding $10 for each person.*

The privilege of the writ of habeas corpus shall not be suspended, unless when in cases of rebellion or invasion the public safety may require it.

No bill of attainder or ex post facto law shall be passed.

No capitation, or other direct, tax shall be laid, unless in proportion to the census or enumeration herein before directed to be taken.

No tax or duty shall be laid on articles exported from any State.

No preference shall be given by any regulation of commerce or revenue to the ports of one State over those of another; nor shall vessels bound to, or from, one State, be obliged to enter, clear, or pay duties in another.

No money shall be drawn from the treasury, but in consequence of appropriations made by law; and a regular statement and account of the receipts and expenditures of all public money shall be published from time to time.

No title of nobility shall be granted by the United States: and no person holding any office of profit or trust under them, shall, without the consent of the Congress, accept of any present, emolument, office, or title, of any kind whatever, from any king, prince, or foreign state.

*Section 10*  No State shall enter into any treaty, alliance, or confederation; grant letters of marque and reprisal; coin money; emit bills of credit; make anything but gold and silver coin a tender in payment of debts; pass any bill of attainder, ex post facto law, or law impairing the obligation of contracts, or grant any title of nobility.

No State shall, without the consent of Congress, lay any imposts or duties on imports or exports, except what may be absolutely necessary for executing its inspection laws: and the net produce of all duties and imposts, laid by any State on imports or exports, shall be for the use of the treasury of the United States; and all such laws shall be subject to the revision and control of the Congress.

No State shall, without the consent of Congress, lay any duty of tonnage, keep troops or ships of war in time of peace, enter into any agreement or compact with another State, or with a foreign power, or engage in war, unless actually invaded, or in such imminent danger as will not admit of delay.

## Article II

*Section 1*  The executive power shall be vested in a President of the United States of America. He shall hold his office during the term of four years, and, together with the Vice-President, chosen for the same term, be elected as follows:

Each State shall appoint, in such manner as the legislature thereof may direct, a number of electors, equal to the whole number of Senators and Representatives to which the State may be entitled in the Congress; but no Senator or Representative, or person holding an office of trust or profit under the United States, shall be appointed an elector.

*The electors shall meet in their respective States, and vote by ballot for two persons, of whom one at least shall not be an inhabitant of the same State with themselves. And they shall make a list of all the persons voted for, and of the number of votes for each; which list they shall sign and certify, and transmit sealed to the seat of government of the United States, directed to the President of the Senate. The President of the Senate shall,*

*in the presence of the Senate and House of Representatives, open all the certificates, and the votes shall then be counted. The person having the greatest number of votes shall be the President, if such number be a majority of the whole number of electors appointed; and if there be more than one who have such majority, and have an equal number of votes, then the House of Representatives shall immediately choose by ballot one of them for President; and if no person have a majority, then from the five highest on the list said house shall in like manner choose the President. But in choosing the President the votes shall be taken by States, the representation from each State having one vote; a quorum for this purpose shall consist of a member or members from two-thirds of the States, and a majority of all the States shall be necessary to a choice. In every case, after the choice of the President, the person having the greatest number of votes of the electors shall be the Vice-President. But if there should remain two or more who have equal votes, the Senate shall choose from them by ballot the Vice-President.*

The Congress may determine the time of choosing the electors and the day on which they shall give their votes; which day shall be the same throughout the United States.

No person except a natural-born citizen, *or a citizen of the United States at the time of the adoption of this Constitution,* shall be eligible to the office of President; neither shall any person be eligible to that office who shall not have attained to the age of thirty-five years, and been fourteen years a resident within the United States.

In cases of the removal of the President from office or of his death, resignation, or inability to discharge the powers and duties of the said office, the same shall devolve on the Vice-President, and the Congress may by law provide for the case of removal, death, resignation, or inability, both of the President and Vice-President, declaring what officer shall then act as President, and such officer shall act accordingly, until the disability be removed, or a President shall be elected.

The President shall, at stated times, receive for his services a compensation, which shall neither be increased nor diminished during the period for which he shall have been elected, and he shall not receive within that period any other emolument from the United States, or any of them.

Before he enter on the execution of his office, he shall take the following oath or affirmation:—"I do solemnly swear (or affirm) that I will faithfully execute the office of the President of the United States, and will to the best of my ability preserve, protect and defend the Constitution of the United States."

*Section 2*  The President shall be commander in chief of the army and navy of the United States, and of the militia of the several States, when called into the actual service of the United States; he may require the opinion, in writing, of the principal officer in each of the executive departments, upon any subject relating to the duties of their respective offices, and he shall have power to grant reprieves and pardons for offenses against the United States, except in cases of impeachment.

He shall have power, by and with the advice and consent of the Senate, to make treaties, provided two-thirds of the Senators present concur; and he shall nominate, and by and with the advice and consent of the Senate, shall appoint ambassadors, other public ministers and consuls, judges of the Supreme Court, and all other officers of the United States, whose appointments are not herein otherwise provided for, and which shall be established by law: but Congress may by law vest the appointment of such inferior officers, as they think proper, in the President alone, in the courts of law, or in the heads of departments.

The President shall have power to fill up all vacancies that may happen during the recess of the Senate, by granting commissions which shall expire at the end of their next session.

**Section 3** He shall from time to time give to the Congress information of the state of the Union, and recommend to their consideration such measures as he shall judge necessary and expedient; he may, on extraordinary occasions, convene both houses, or either of them, and in case of disagreement between them, with respect to the time of adjournment, he may adjourn them to such time as he shall think proper; he shall receive ambassadors and other public ministers; he shall take care that the laws be faithfully executed, and shall commission all the officers of the United States.

**Section 4** The President, Vice-President and all civil officers of the United States shall be removed from office on impeachment for, and on conviction of, treason, bribery, or other high crimes and misdemeanors.

## Article III

**Section 1** The judicial power of the United States shall be vested in one Supreme Court, and in such inferior courts as the Congress may from time to time ordain and establish. The judges, both of the Supreme and inferior courts, shall hold their offices during good behavior, and shall, at stated times, receive for their services a compensation which shall not be diminished during their continuance in office.

**Section 2** The judicial power shall extend to all cases, in law and equity, arising under this Constitution, the laws of the United States, and treaties made, or which shall be made, under their authority;—to all cases affecting ambassadors, other public ministers and consuls;—to all cases of admiralty and maritime jurisdiction;—to controversies to which the United States shall be a party;—to controversies between two or more States;—*between a State and citizens of another State;*—between citizens of different States;—between citizens of the same State claiming lands under grants of different States, and between a State, or the citizens thereof, and foreign states, citizens or subjects.

In all cases affecting ambassadors, other public ministers and consuls, and those in which a State shall be party, the Supreme Court shall have original jurisdiction. In all the other cases before mentioned, the Supreme Court shall have appellate jurisdiction, both as to law and fact, with such exceptions, and under such regulations, as the Congress shall make.

The trial of all crimes, except in cases of impeachment, shall be by jury; and such trial shall be held in the State where said crimes shall have been committed; but when not committed within any State, the trial shall be at such place or places as the Congress may by law have directed.

**Section 3** Treason against the United States shall consist only in levying war against them, or in adhering to their enemies, giving them aid and comfort. No person shall be convicted of treason unless on the testimony of two witnesses to the same overt act, or on confession in open court.

The Congress shall have power to declare the punishment of treason, but no attainder of treason shall work corruption of blood, or forfeiture except during the life of the person attainted.

## Article IV

**Section 1** Full faith and credit shall be given in each State to the public acts, records, and judicial proceedings of every other State. And the Congress may by general laws prescribe the manner in which such acts, records, and proceedings shall be proved, and the effect thereof.

**Section 2** The citizens of each State shall be entitled to all privileges and immunities of citizens in the several States.

A person charged in any State with treason, felony, or other crime, who shall flee from justice, and be found in another State, shall on demand of the executive authority of the State from which he fled, be delivered up, to be removed to the State having jurisdiction of the crime.

*No person held to service or labor in one State, under the laws thereof, escaping into another, shall, in consequence of any law or regulation therein, be discharged from such service or labor, but shall be delivered up on claim of the party to whom such service or labor may be due.*

**Section 3** New States may be admitted by the Congress into this Union; but no new State shall be formed or erected within the jurisdiction of any other State; nor any State be formed by the junction of two or more States, or parts of States, without the consent of the legislatures of the States concerned as well as of the Congress.

The Congress shall have power to dispose of and make all needful rules and regulations respecting the territory or other property belonging to the United States; and nothing in this Constitution shall be so construed as to prejudice any claims of the United States, or of any particular State.

**Section 4** The United States shall guarantee to every State in this Union a republican form of government, and shall protect each of them against invasion; and on application of the legislature, or of the executive (when the legislature cannot be convened), against domestic violence.

## Article V

The Congress, whenever two-thirds of both houses shall deem it necessary, shall propose amendments to this Constitution, or, on the application of the legislatures of two-thirds of the several States, shall call a convention for proposing amendments, which, in either case, shall be valid to all intents and purposes, as part of this Constitution, when ratified by the legislatures of three-fourths of the several States, or by conventions in three-fourths thereof, as the one or the other mode of ratification may be proposed by the Congress; provided *that no amendments which may be made prior to the year one thousand eight hundred and eight shall in any manner affect the first and fourth clauses in the ninth section of the first article;* and that no State, without its consent, shall be deprived of its equal suffrage in the Senate.

## Article VI

All debts contracted and engagements entered into, before the adoption of this Constitution, shall be as valid against the United States under this Constitution, as under the Confederation.

This Constitution, and the laws of the United States which shall be made in pursuance thereof; and all treaties made, or which shall be made, under the authority of the United States, shall be the supreme law of the land; and the judges in every State shall be bound thereby, anything in the Constitution or laws of any State to the contrary notwithstanding.

The Senators and Representatives before mentioned, and the members of the several State legislatures, and all executive and judicial officers, both of the United States and of the several States, shall be bound by oath or affirmation to support this Constitution; but no religious test shall ever be required as a qualification to any office or public trust under the United States.

## Article VII

The ratification of the conventions of nine States shall be sufficient for the establishment of this Constitution between the States so ratifying the same.

Done in Convention by the unanimous consent of the States present, the seventeenth day of September in the year of our Lord one thousand seven hundred and eighty-seven and of the Independence of the United States of America the twelfth. In witness whereof we have hereunto subscribed our names.

# Amendments to the Constitution*

## Amendment I

Congress shall make no law respecting an establishment of religion, or prohibiting the free exercise thereof; or abridging the freedom of speech, or of the press; or the right of the people peaceably to assemble, and to petition the government for a redress of grievances.

*The first ten Amendments (the Bill of Rights) were adopted in 1791.

## Amendment II

A well-regulated militia being necessary to the security of a free State, the right of the people to keep and bear arms shall not be infringed.

## Amendment III

No soldier shall, in time of peace, be quartered in any house without the consent of the owner, nor in time of war, but in a manner to be prescribed by law.

## Amendment IV

The right of the people to be secure in their persons, houses, papers, and effects, against unreasonable searches and seizures, shall not be violated, and no warrants shall issue but upon probable cause, supported by oath or affirmation, and particularly describing the place to be searched, and the persons or things to be seized.

## Amendment V

No person shall be held to answer for a capital, or otherwise infamous crime, unless on a presentment or indictment of a grand jury, except in cases arising in the land or naval forces, or in the militia, when in actual service in time of war or public danger; nor shall any person be subject for the same offense to be twice put in jeopardy of life or limb; nor shall be compelled in any criminal case to be a witness against himself, nor be deprived of life, liberty, or property, without due process of law; nor shall private property be taken for public use without just compensation.

## Amendment VI

In all criminal prosecutions, the accused shall enjoy the right to a speedy and public trial, by an impartial jury of the State and district wherein the crime shall have been committed, which district shall have been previously ascertained by law, and to be informed of the nature and cause of the accusation; to be confronted with the witnesses against him; to have compulsory process for obtaining witnesses in his favor, and to have the assistance of counsel for his defense.

## Amendment VII

In suits at common law, where the value in controversy shall exceed twenty dollars, the right of trial by jury shall be preserved, and no fact tried by a jury shall be otherwise reexamined in any court of the United States, than according to the rules of the common law.

## Amendment VIII

Excessive bail shall not be required, nor excessive fines imposed, nor cruel and unusual punishments inflicted.

## Amendment IX

The enumeration in the Constitution, of certain rights, shall not be construed to deny or disparage others retained by the people.

## Amendment X

The powers not delegated to the United States by the Constitution, nor prohibited by it to the States, are reserved to the States respectively, or to the people.

## Amendment XI

[Adopted 1798]

The judicial power of the United States shall not be construed to extend to any suit in law or equity, commenced or prosecuted against one of the United States by citizens of another State, or by citizens or subjects of any foreign state.

## Amendment XII

[Adopted 1804]

The electors shall meet in their respective States, and vote by ballot for President and Vice-President, one of whom, at least, shall not be an inhabitant of the same State with themselves; they shall name in their ballots the person voted for as President, and in distinct ballots the person voted for as Vice-President, and they shall make distinct lists of all persons voted for as President, and of all persons voted for as Vice-President, and of the number of votes for each, which lists they shall sign and certify, and transmit sealed to the seat of government of the United States, directed to the President of the Senate;—the President of the Senate shall, in the presence of the Senate and House of Representatives, open all the certificates and the votes shall then be counted;—the person having the greatest number of votes for President shall be the President, if such number be a majority of the whole number of electors appointed; and if no person have such majority, then from the persons having the highest numbers not exceeding three on the list of those voted for as President, the House of Representatives shall choose immediately, by ballot, the President. But in choosing the President, the votes shall be taken by States, the representation from each State having one vote; a quorum for this purpose shall consist of a member or members from two-thirds of the States, and a majority of all the States shall be necessary to a choice. And if the House of Representatives shall not choose a President whenever the right of choice shall devolve upon them, before *the fourth day of March* next following, then the Vice-President shall act as President, as in the case of the death or other constitutional disability of the President.

The person having the greatest number of votes as Vice-President shall be the Vice-President, if such number be a majority of the whole number of electors appointed; and if no person have a majority, then from the two highest numbers on the list the Senate shall choose the Vice-President; a quorum for the purpose shall consist of two-thirds of the whole number of Senators, and a majority of the whole number shall be necessary to a choice. But no person constitutionally ineligible to the office of President shall be eligible to that of Vice-President of the United States.

## Amendment XIII

[Adopted 1865]

*Section 1*   Neither slavery nor involuntary servitude, except as a punishment for crime whereof the party shall have been duly convicted, shall exist within the United States, or any place subject to their jurisdiction.

*Section 2*   Congress shall have power to enforce this article by appropriate legislation.

## Amendment XIV

[Adopted 1868]

*Section 1*   All persons born or naturalized in the United States, and subject to the jurisdiction thereof, are citizens of the United States and of the State wherein they reside. No State shall make or enforce any law which shall abridge the privileges or immunities of citizens of the United States; nor shall any State deprive any person of life, liberty, or property, without due process of law; nor deny to any person within its jurisdiction the equal protection of the laws.

*Section 2*   Representatives shall be apportioned among the several States according to their respective numbers, counting the whole number of persons in each State, excluding Indians not taxed. But when the right to vote at any election for the choice of Electors for President and Vice-President of the United States, Representatives in Congress, the executive and judicial officers of a State, or the members of the legislature thereof, is denied to any of the male inhabitants of such State, being twenty-one years of age and citizens of the United States, or in any way abridged, except for participation in rebellion, or other crime, the basis of representation therein shall be reduced in the proportion which the number of such male citizens shall bear to the whole number of male citizens twenty-one years of age in such State.

*Section 3*   No person shall be a Senator or Representative in Congress, or Elector of President and Vice-President, or hold any office, civil or military, under the United States, or under any State, who, having previously taken an oath, as a member of Congress, or as an officer of the United States, or as a member of any State legislature, or as an executive or judicial officer of any State, to support the Constitution of the United States, shall have engaged in insurrection or rebellion against the same, or given aid or comfort to the enemies thereof. Congress may, by a vote of two-thirds of each house, remove such disability.

*Section 4*   The validity of the public debt of the United States, authorized by law, including debts incurred for payment of pensions and bounties for services in suppressing insurrection or rebellion, shall not be questioned. But neither the United States nor any State shall assume or pay any debt or obligation incurred in aid of insurrection or rebellion against the United States, or any claim for the loss of emancipation of any slave; but all such debts, obligations, and claims shall be held illegal and void.

*Section 5*   The Congress shall have power to enforce, by appropriate legislation, the provisions of this article.

## Amendment XV

[Adopted 1870]

*Section 1*   The right of citizens of the United States to vote shall not be denied or abridged by the United States or by any State on account of race, color, or previous condition of servitude.

*Section 2*   The Congress shall have power to enforce this article by appropriate legislation.

## Amendment XVI

[Adopted 1913]

The Congress shall have power to lay and collect taxes on incomes, from whatever source derived, without apportionment among the several States, and without regard to any census or enumeration.

## Amendment XVII

[Adopted 1913]

*Section 1*   The Senate of the United States shall be composed of two Senators from each State, elected by the people thereof, for six years; and each Senator shall have one vote. The electors in each State shall have the qualifications requisite for electors of [voters for] the most numerous branch of the State legislatures.

*Section 2*   When vacancies happen in the representation of any State in the Senate, the executive authority of such State shall issue writs of election to fill such vacancies: Provided, that the Legislature of any State may empower the executive thereof to make temporary appointments until the people fill the vacancies by election as the Legislature may direct.

*Section 3*   This amendment shall not be so construed as to affect the election or term of any Senator chosen before it becomes valid as part of the Constitution.

## Amendment XVIII

[Adopted 1919; Repealed 1933]

*Section 1*   After one year from the ratification of this article the manufacture, sale, or transportation of intoxicating liquors within, the importation thereof into, or the exportation thereof from the United States and all territory subject to the jurisdiction thereof, for beverage purposes, is hereby prohibited.

*Section 2*   The Congress and the several States shall have concurrent power to enforce this article by appropriate legislation.

*Section 3*   This article shall be inoperative unless it shall have been ratified as an amendment to the Constitution by the legislatures of the several States, as provided by the Constitution, within seven years from the date of the submission thereof to the States by the Congress.

## Amendment XIX

[Adopted 1920]

*Section 1*   The right of citizens of the United States to vote shall not be denied or abridged by the United States or by any State on account of sex.

*Section 2*   The Congress shall have power to enforce this article by appropriate legislation.

## Amendment XX

[Adopted 1933]

*Section 1*   The terms of the President and Vice-President shall end at noon on the 20th day of January, and the terms of Senators and Representatives at noon on the 3rd day of January, of the years in which such terms would have ended if this article had not been ratified; and the terms of their successors shall then begin.

*Section 2*   The Congress shall assemble at least once in every year, and such meeting shall begin at noon on the 3d day of January, unless they shall by law appoint a different day.

*Section 3*   If, at the time fixed for the beginning of the term of the President, the President-elect shall have died, the Vice-President–elect shall become President. If a President shall not have been chosen before the time fixed for the beginning of his term, or if the President-elect shall have failed to qualify, then the Vice-President–elect shall act as President until a President shall have qualified; and the Congress may by law provide for the case wherein neither a President-elect nor a Vice-President–elect shall have qualified, declaring who shall then act as President, or the manner in which one who is to act shall be selected, and such persons shall act accordingly until a President or Vice-President shall have qualified.

*Section 4*   The Congress may by law provide for the case of the death of any of the persons from whom the House of Representatives may choose a President whenever the right of choice shall have devolved upon them, and for the case of the death of any of the persons from whom the Senate may choose a Vice-President whenever the right of choice shall have devolved upon them.

*Section 5*   Sections 1 and 2 shall take effect on the 15th day of October following the ratification of this article.

*Section 6*   This article shall be inoperative unless it shall have been ratified as an amendment to the Constitution by the Legislatures of three-fourths of the several States within seven years from the date of its submission.

## Amendment XXI

[Adopted 1933]

*Section 1*   The eighteenth article of amendment to the Constitution of the United States is hereby repealed.

*Section 2*   The transportation or importation into any State, Territory, or Possession of the United States for delivery or use therein of intoxicating liquors, in violation of the laws thereof, is hereby prohibited.

*Section 3*   This article shall be inoperative unless it shall have been ratified as an amendment to the Constitution by conventions in the several States, as provided in the Constitution, within seven years from the date of submission thereof to the States by the Congress.

## Amendment XXII

[Adopted 1951]

*Section 1*   No person shall be elected to the office of President more than twice, and no person who has held the office of President, or acted as President, for more than two years of a term to which some other person was elected President shall be elected to the office of President more than once. But this article shall not apply to any person holding the office of President when this article was proposed by the Congress, and shall not prevent any person who may be holding the office of President, or acting as President, during the term within which this article becomes operative from holding the office of President or acting as President during the remainder of such term.

*Section 2*   This article shall be inoperative unless it shall have been ratified as an amendment to the Constitution by the legislatures of three-fourths of the several States within seven years from the date of its submission to the States by the Congress.

## Amendment XXIII

[Adopted 1961]

*Section 1*   The District constituting the seat of Government of the United States shall appoint in such manner as the Congress may direct:

A number of electors of President and Vice-President equal to the whole number of Senators and Representatives in Congress to which the District would be entitled if it were a State, but in no event more than the least populous State; they shall be in addition to those appointed by the States, but they shall be considered for the purposes of the election of President and Vice-President, to be electors appointed by a State; and they shall meet in the District and perform such duties as provided by the twelfth article of amendment.

*Section 2*   The Congress shall have the power to enforce this article by appropriate legislation.

## Amendment XXIV

[Adopted 1964]

*Section 1*   The right of citizens of the United States to vote in any primary or other election for President or Vice-President, for electors for President or Vice-President, or for Senator or Representative in Congress, shall not be denied or abridged by the United States or any State by reason of failure to pay any poll tax or other tax.

*Section 2*   The Congress shall have the power to enforce this article by appropriate legislation.

## Amendment XXV

[Adopted 1967]

*Section 1*   In case of the removal of the President from office or of his death or resignation, the Vice-President shall become President.

*Section 2*   Whenever there is a vacancy in the office of the Vice-President, the President shall nominate a Vice-President who shall take office upon confirmation by a majority vote of both Houses of Congress.

*Section 3*   Whenever the President transmits to the President pro tempore of the Senate and the Speaker of the House of Representatives his written declaration that he is unable to discharge the powers and duties of his office, and until he transmits to them a written declaration to the contrary, such powers and duties shall be discharged by the Vice-President as Acting President.

*Section 4*   Whenever the Vice-President and a majority of either the principal officers of the executive departments or of such other body as Congress may by law provide, transmit to the President pro tempore of the Senate and the Speaker of the House of Representatives their written declaration that the President is unable to discharge the powers and duties of his office, the Vice-President shall immediately assume the powers and duties of the office as Acting President.

Thereafter, when the President transmits to the President pro tempore of the Senate and the Speaker of the House of Representatives his written declaration that no inability exists, he shall resume the powers and duties of his office unless the Vice-President and a majority of either the principal officers of the executive department[s] or of such other body as Congress may by law provide, transmit within four days to the President pro tempore of the Senate and the Speaker of the House of Representatives their written declaration that the President is unable to discharge the powers and duties of his office. Thereupon Congress shall decide the issue, assembling within forty-eight hours for that purpose if not in session. If the Congress, within twenty-one days after receipt of the latter written declaration, or, if Congress is not in session, within twenty-one days after Congress is required to assemble, determines by two-thirds vote of both Houses that the President is unable to discharge the powers and duties of his office, the Vice-President shall continue to discharge the same as Acting President; otherwise, the President shall resume the powers and duties of his office.

## Amendment XXVI

[Adopted 1971]

*Section 1*  The right of citizens of the United States, who are eighteen years of age or older, to vote shall not be denied or abridged by the United States or by any State on account of age.

*Section 2*  The Congress shall have power to enforce this article by appropriate legislation.

## Amendment XXVII

[Adopted 1992]

No law, varying the compensation for the services of the Senators and Representatives, shall take effect, until an election of Representatives shall have intervened.

| | | | |
|---|---|---|---|
| **1.** *President* | George Washington | 1789–1797 | |
| *Vice President* | John Adams | 1789–1797 | |
| **2.** *President* | John Adams | 1797–1801 | |
| *Vice President* | Thomas Jefferson | 1797–1801 | |
| **3.** *President* | Thomas Jefferson | 1801–1809 | |
| *Vice President* | Aaron Burr | 1801–1805 | |
| *Vice President* | George Clinton | 1805–1809 | |
| **4.** *President* | James Madison | 1809–1817 | |
| *Vice President* | George Clinton | 1809–1813 | |
| *Vice President* | Elbridge Gerry | 1813–1817 | |
| **5.** *President* | James Monroe | 1817–1825 | |
| *Vice President* | Daniel Tompkins | 1817–1825 | |
| **6.** *President* | John Quincy Adams | 1825–1829 | |
| *Vice President* | John C. Calhoun | 1825–1829 | |
| **7.** *President* | Andrew Jackson | 1829–1837 | |
| *Vice President* | John C. Calhoun | 1829–1833 | |
| *Vice President* | Martin Van Buren | 1833–1837 | |
| **8.** *President* | Martin Van Buren | 1837–1841 | |
| *Vice President* | Richard M. Johnson | 1837–1841 | |
| **9.** *President* | William H. Harrison | 1841 | |
| *Vice President* | John Tyler | 1841 | |
| **10.** *President* | John Tyler | 1841–1845 | |
| *Vice President* | None | | |
| **11.** *President* | James K. Polk | 1845–1849 | |
| *Vice President* | George M. Dallas | 1845–1849 | |
| **12.** *President* | Zachary Taylor | 1849–1850 | |
| *Vice President* | Millard Fillmore | 1849–1850 | |
| **13.** *President* | Millard Fillmore | 1850–1853 | |
| *Vice President* | None | | |
| **14.** *President* | Franklin Pierce | 1853–1857 | |
| *Vice President* | William R. King | 1853–1857 | |
| **15.** *President* | James Buchanan | 1857–1861 | |
| *Vice President* | John C. Breckinridge | 1857–1861 | |
| **16.** *President* | Abraham Lincoln | 1861–1865 | |
| *Vice President* | Hannibal Hamlin | 1861–1865 | |
| *Vice President* | Andrew Johnson | 1865 | |
| **17.** *President* | Andrew Johnson | 1865–1869 | |
| *Vice President* | None | | |

| | | | |
|---|---|---|---|
| **18.** *President* | Ulysses S. Grant | 1869–1877 | |
| *Vice President* | Schuyler Colfax | 1869–1873 | |
| *Vice President* | Henry Wilson | 1873–1877 | |
| **19.** *President* | Rutherford B. Hayes | 1877–1881 | |
| *Vice President* | William A. Wheeler | 1877–1881 | |
| **20.** *President* | James A. Garfield | 1881 | |
| *Vice President* | Chester A. Arthur | 1881 | |
| **21.** *President* | Chester A. Arthur | 1881–1885 | |
| *Vice President* | None | | |
| **22.** *President* | Grover Cleveland | 1885–1889 | |
| *Vice President* | Thomas A. Hendricks | 1885–1889 | |
| **23.** *President* | Benjamin Harrison | 1889–1893 | |
| *Vice President* | Levi P. Morton | 1889–1893 | |
| **24.** *President* | Grover Cleveland | 1893–1897 | |
| *Vice President* | Adlai E. Stevenson | 1893–1897 | |
| **25.** *President* | William McKinley | 1897–1901 | |
| *Vice President* | Garret A. Hobart | 1897–1901 | |
| *Vice President* | Theodore Roosevelt | 1901 | |
| **26.** *President* | Theodore Roosevelt | 1901–1909 | |
| *Vice President* | Charles Fairbanks | 1905–1909 | |
| **27.** *President* | William H. Taft | 1909–1913 | |
| *Vice President* | James S. Sherman | 1909–1913 | |
| **28.** *President* | Woodrow Wilson | 1913–1921 | |
| *Vice President* | Thomas R. Marshall | 1913–1921 | |
| **29.** *President* | Warren G. Harding | 1921–1923 | |
| *Vice President* | Calvin Coolidge | 1921–1923 | |
| **30.** *President* | Calvin Coolidge | 1923–1929 | |
| *Vice President* | Charles G. Dawes | 1925–1929 | |
| **31.** *President* | Herbert C. Hoover | 1929–1933 | |
| *Vice President* | Charles Curtis | 1929–1933 | |
| **32.** *President* | Franklin D. Roosevelt | 1933–1945 | |
| *Vice President* | John N. Garner | 1933–1941 | |
| *Vice President* | Henry A. Wallace | 1941–1945 | |
| *Vice President* | Harry S Truman | 1945 | |
| **33.** *President* | Harry S Truman | 1945–1953 | |
| *Vice President* | Alben W. Barkley | 1949–1953 | |
| **34.** *President* | Dwight D. Eisenhower | 1953–1961 | |
| *Vice President* | Richard M. Nixon | 1953–1961 | |

**35.** *President*    John F. Kennedy    1961–1963
   *Vice President*    Lyndon B. Johnson    1961–1963

**36.** *President*    Lyndon B. Johnson    1963–1969
   *Vice President*    Hubert H. Humphrey    1965–1969

**37.** *President*    Richard M. Nixon    1969–1974
   *Vice President*    Spiro T. Agnew    1969–1973
   *Vice President*    Gerald R. Ford    1973–1974

**38.** *President*    Gerald R. Ford    1974–1977
   *Vice President*    Nelson A. Rockefeller    1974–1977

**39.** *President*    James E. Carter    1977–1981
   *Vice President*    Walter F. Mondale    1977–1981

**40.** *President*    Ronald W. Reagan    1981–1989
   *Vice President*    George H. W. Bush    1981–1989

**41.** *President*    George H. W. Bush    1989–1993
   *Vice President*    J. Danforth Quayle    1989–1993

**42.** *President*    William J. Clinton    1993–2001
   *Vice President*    Albert Gore    1993–2001

**43.** *President*    George W. Bush    2001–
   *Vice President*    Richard B. Cheney    2001–

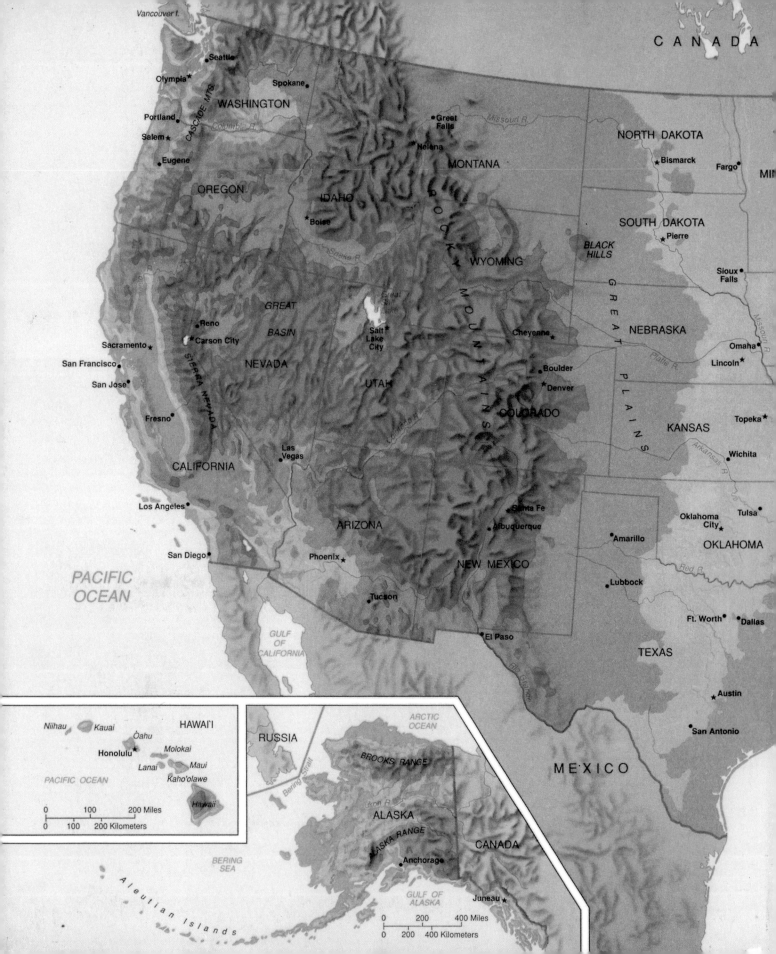